Organization and Management in the Criminal Justice System

SAGE Text/Reader Series in Criminology and Criminal Justice

Craig Hemmens, Series Editor

1. *Corrections: A Text/Reader*, 2nd edition, by Mary Stohr, Anthony Walsh, and Craig Hemmens
2. *Courts: A Text/Reader*, 2nd edition, by Cassia Spohn and Craig Hemmens
3. *Policing: A Text/Reader*, by Carol Archbold
4. *Community-Based Corrections: A Text/Reader*, by Shannon Barton-Bellessa and Robert Hanser
5. *Race and Crime: A Text/Reader*, by Helen Greene and Shaun Gabbidon
6. *Criminological Theory: A Text/Reader*, by Stephen Tibbetts and Craig Hemmens
7. *Victimology: A Text/Reader*, by Leah Daigle
8. *Women and Crime: A Text/Reader*, by Stacy Mallicoat
9. *White Collar Crime: A Text/Reader*, by Brian Payne
10. *Juvenile Justice: A Text/Reader*, by Richard Lawrence and Craig Hemmens
11. *Introduction to Criminology: A Text/Reader*, by Anthony Walsh and Craig T. Hemmens
12. *Organization and Management in the Criminal Justice System: A Text/Reader*, by Matthew Giblin

Other Titles of Related Interest

Administration and Management in Criminal Justice: A Service Quality Approach, Jennifer M. Allen and Rajeev Sawhney
Introduction to Criminology, 8th edition, by Frank Hagan
Criminology: The Essentials, by Anthony Walsh
Criminological Theory, 5th edition, by J. Robert Lilly, Frank Cullen, and Richard Ball
Criminological Theory: The Essentials, by Stephen Tibbetts
Key Ideas in Criminology and Criminal Justice, by Travis Pratt, Jacinta Gau, and Travis Franklin
Crime and Everyday Life, 4th edition, by Marcus Felson and Rachel Boba
Criminal and Behavioral Profiling, by Curt and Anne Bartol
Criminal Justice Ethics, 3rd edition, by Cyndi Banks
Introduction to Policing, 2nd edition, by Steven Cox, William McCamey, and Gene Scaramella
Introduction to Corrections, by Robert Hanseriii
Corrections: The Essentials, by Mary Stohr and Anthony Walsh
Community Corrections, 2nd edition, by Robert Hanser
Correctional Theory, by Frank Cullen and Cheryl Lero Jonson
Violence, 2nd edition, by Alex Alvarez and Ronet Bachman
Race and Crime, 3rd edition, by Shaun Gabbidon and Helen Greene
Women and Crime: The Essentials, by Stacy Mallicoat and Connie Ireland
Juvenile Justice, 8th edition, by Steven Cox, Jennifer Allen, Robert Hanser, and John Conrad
Juvenile Justice: The Essentials, by Richard Lawrence and Mario Hesse
Victimology: The Essentials, by Leah Daigle
Victims of Crime, 4th edition, by Robert Davis, Arthur Lorigio, and Susan Herman
Responding to Domestic Violence, 4th edition, by Eve Buzawa, Carl Buzawa, and Evan Stark
White Collar Crime: The Essentials, by Brian Payne
Deviance and Social Control, by Michelle Inderbitzen, Kristin Bates, and Randy Gainey
Understanding Terrorism, 4th edition, by Gus Martin
Terrorism: The Essentials, by Gus Martin
Gangs in America's Communities, by James Howell
Criminal Courts, 2nd edition, by Craig Hemmens, David Brody, and Cassia Spohn
Criminal Procedure, 2nd edition, by Matthew Lippman
Contemporary Criminal Law, 3rd edition, by Matthew Lippman
Crime Analysis with Crime Mapping, 3rd edition, by Rachel Boba Santos
The Practice of Research in Criminology and Criminal Justice, 5th edition, by Ronet Bachman, Russell Schutt
Fundamentals of Research in Criminology and Criminal Justice, 2nd edition, by Ronet Bachman and Russell Schutt
Statistics for Criminal Justice, by Jacinta Gau
The Mismeasure of Crime, 2nd edition, by Clay Mosher, Terence Miethe, and Timothy Hart

Organization and Management in the Criminal Justice System

A Text/Reader

Matthew J. Giblin

Southern Illinois University Carbondale

Los Angeles | London | New Delhi
Singapore | Washington DC

Los Angeles | London | New Delhi
Singapore | Washington DC

FOR INFORMATION:

SAGE Publications, Inc.
2455 Teller Road
Thousand Oaks, California 91320
E-mail: order@sagepub.com

SAGE Publications Ltd.
1 Oliver's Yard
55 City Road
London EC1Y 1SP
United Kingdom

SAGE Publications India Pvt. Ltd.
B 1/I 1 Mohan Cooperative Industrial Area
Mathura Road, New Delhi 110 044
India

SAGE Publications Asia-Pacific Pte. Ltd.
3 Church Street
#10-04 Samsung Hub
Singapore 049483

Publisher: Jerry Westby
Publishing Associate: MaryAnn Vail
Production Editor: Olivia Weber-Stenis
Copy Editor: Megan Granger
Typesetter: C&M Digitals (P) Ltd.
Proofreader: Sally Jaskold
Indexer: Molly Hall
Cover Designer: Edgar Abarca
Marketing Manager: Terra Schultz
Permissions Editor: Jennifer Barron

Copyright © 2014 by SAGE Publications, Inc.

All rights reserved. No part of this book may be reproduced or utilized in any form or by any means, electronic or mechanical, including photocopying, recording, or by any information storage and retrieval system, without permission in writing from the publisher.

Printed in the United States of America

Library of Congress Cataloging-in-Publication Data

Organization and management in the criminal justice system: a text/reader / [edited by] Matthew J. Giblin.

pages cm

Includes bibliographical references and index.

ISBN 978-1-4522-1992-9 (alk. paper)

1. Criminal justice, Administration of. 2. Police administration. I. Giblin, Matthew J.

HV7419.O74 2014

364.068—dc23   2013017904

This book is printed on acid-free paper.

18 19 20 10 9 8 7 6 5 4 3

Brief Contents

Foreword	xv
Preface	xvii
Section I. Introduction: Why Should We Study Criminal Justice Organizations?	1
Section II. Organizational Structure: How Do We Build Organizations?	15
Section III. Organizational Theory: How Do We Explain What Organizations Look Like?	81
Section IV. Organizational Deviance and Termination: What Explains Failure in Criminal Justice Agencies?	129
Section V. Interagency Collaboration: Are Two or More Organizations (Combined) Better Than One?	174
Section VI. Unions and Collective Bargaining: United We Stand?	224
Section VII. Organizational Socialization: How Does a Person Learn to Behave in an Organization?	274
Section VIII. Motivation and Job Design: How Do We Light a Fire Under Employees?	317
Section IX. Occupational Stress and Burnout: Is This Job Killing Me?	378
Section X. Leadership: Are You a Leader or a Follower?	429
Section XI. Power in Organizations: How Are Subordinates, Suspects, Inmates, and Clients Controlled?	480
Section XII. Organizational Change: What Causes Organizations to Transform?	534
Glossary	584
References	591
Index	611
About the Author	648

Detailed Contents

Foreword   xv
Preface   xvii
    Acknowledgments   xxi

Section I. Introduction: Why Should We Study Criminal Justice Organizations?   1
    The Importance of Studying Organizations   1
    Defining Organization   5
        People   6
        Purpose   8
        Structure   10
        Durability   11
    Public vs. Private Organizations   11
    Key Terms   13
    Discussion Questions   13
    Web Resources   14

Section II. Organizational Structure: How Do We Build Organizations?   15
    Organizational Complexity   17
        Vertical Complexity   17
        Horizontal Complexity   20
        Spatial Complexity   23
    Organizational Control   25
        Formalization   25
        Centralization   27
        Span of Control   28
    Organizational Structure and Criminal Organizations   30
    Key Terms   32
    Discussion Questions   32
    Web Resources   32

How to Read a Research Article   33

Readings   35

    1. The Impact of Centralization and Formalization on Correctional Staff Job Satisfaction and Organizational Commitment   35

Eric G. Lambert, Eugene A. Paoline III, and Nancy Lynne Hogan

In this study of 272 correctional staff members, the authors found that two organizational control mechanisms—centralization and formalization—generally had an adverse effect on employee attitudes.

2. Factors to Consider for Optimal Span of Control in Community Supervision Evidence-Based Practice Environments — 50
Gaylene S. Armstrong

Armstrong's study demonstrates that probation supervisor responsibilities expand considerably when organizations adopt evidence-based practices; the increased need to interact with subordinates leads to recommendations for a narrower span of control.

3. The Organizational Structure of International Drug Smuggling — 64
Jana S. Benson and Scott H. Decker

Drug-trafficking networks are shown to adopt structures (less specialization, less formalization) that ensure continued operation in the event of law enforcement activities.

Section III. Organizational Theory: How Do We Explain What Organizations Look Like? — 81

- Classical Theories — 82
  - Scientific Management — 83
  - Bureaucracy — 85
  - Administrative Management — 87
- Human Relations Theory — 89
- Open Systems Theories — 92
  - Contingency Theory — 92
  - Resource Dependence Theory — 94
  - Institutional Theory — 96
- Key Terms — 98
- Discussion Questions — 98
- Web Resources — 98

Readings — 99

4. "McJustice": On the McDonaldization of Criminal Justice — 99
Robert M. Bohm

The criminal justice system is concerned with efficiency, calculability, predictability, and control. Bohm shows how this focus is part of a larger trend in society to adopt principles exemplified by the fast-food restaurant chain McDonald's, sometimes with unintended consequences.

5. Maintaining the Myth of Individualized Justice: Probation Presentence Reports — 114
John Rosecrance

In this study, Rosecrance finds that probation officers still gather background and social history information on convicted offenders, even though sentences are largely based on seriousness and prior record.

Section IV. Organizational Deviance and Termination: What Explains Failure in Criminal Justice Agencies? — 129

- Defining and Explaining Organizational Deviance — 131
  - Administrative Breakdown — 132
  - Structural Secrecy and Knowledge Conflict — 133
  - Normal Accidents — 135
  - Crisis (Mis)Management — 137
- Preventing Organizational Deviance — 138
- Organizational Termination — 140
  - Organizational Termination Defined — 140
  - The Resilience and Decline of Public Organizations — 141
  - Replacement of Services Lost — 143
- Key Terms — 144
- Discussion Questions — 144
- Web Resources — 144

Readings — 145

6. Bureaucracy, Managerial Disorganization, and Administrative Breakdown in Criminal Justice Agencies — 145
   Clarissa Freitas Dias and Michael S. Vaughn

   Using a variety of examples, the authors contend that organizational deviance is a function of poor administration, specifically a breakdown of Fayol's (classical school) administrative management principles.

7. Social Theory and the Street Cop: The Case of Deadly Force — 161
   David Klinger

   Normal accidents theory is used as a framework for understanding both avoidable and unavoidable shootings. Improper tactics lead to the conditions that increase the likelihood of normal accidents.

Section V. Interagency Collaboration: Are Two or More Organizations (Combined) Better Than One? — 174

- Interorganizational Collaborations — 175
- Impediments to Collaboration — 177
- Criminal Justice Collaborations — 179
  - Law Enforcement Task Forces — 179
  - Police–Corrections Partnerships — 182
  - Pulling Levers and Focused Deterrence Partnerships — 185
- Key Terms — 189
- Discussion Questions — 189
- Web Resources — 189

Readings — 190

8. The Intelligence Fusion Process for State, Local, and Tribal Law Enforcement — 190
   David L. Carter and Jeremy G. Carter

   The authors describe the development of fusion centers, collaborations designed to facilitate the integration and sharing of information across agencies.

9. A Specialized Domestic Violence Court in South Carolina: An Example of
   Procedural Justice for Victims and Defendants   205
   Angela R. Gover, Eve M. Brank, and John M. MacDonald

   South Carolina's domestic violence court, a specialized problem-solving court similar to drug courts, brought together a range of criminal justice and mental health professionals to improve outcomes for victims and offenders. This study examines individual perceptions of the court's efficacy and fairness.

Section VI. Unions and Collective Bargaining: United We Stand?   224
- History of Unionism in Criminal Justice   225
- Collective Bargaining in Justice Agencies   227
  - Content of Agreements   227
  - Coverage of Agreements   228
  - Economic Benefits of Collective Bargaining   229
  - Potential Negative Effects   231
  - Bargaining Impasses   232
- Labor Disputes and Employee Job Actions   233
  - Strike Generation   234
  - Perpetuation   234
  - Resolution   236
  - Other Job Actions   237
- Improving Labor Relations   238
- Key Terms   239
- Discussion Questions   239
- Web Resources   239

Readings   240

10. Police Employee Organizations   240
    Colleen Kadleck

    Kadleck's descriptive study, based on a survey of police employee organization leaders, offers insight into the characteristics of these organizations. The research also details leaders' views on management and the role of employees in management decision making.

11. Prison Officer Unions and the Perpetuation of the Penal Status Quo   247
    Joshua Page

    Page documents the power of correctional officer unions in places such as California and New York, including their role in the criminal justice policymaking process.

Section VII. Organizational Socialization: How Does a Person Learn to Behave in an Organization?   274
- Overview of Organizational Socialization   275
  - Boundaries   275
  - Uncertainty Reduction   276
- Content of Socialization   277
- Anticipatory Socialization   279
- Socialization Strategies   280
- Key Terms   285

Discussion Questions — 286
Web Resources — 286

Readings — 287

12. Saying One Thing, Meaning Another: The Role of Parables in Police Training — 287
Robert E. Ford

    The vast majority of the 89 police officers Ford interviewed reported being affected by war stories told during police academy training. The author organizes the recounted stories around common themes.

13. An Officer and a Lady: Organizational Barriers to Women Working as Correctional Officers in Men's Prisons — 302
Nancy C. Jurik

    According to Jurik, female correctional officers face a variety of constraints in their work due to stereotypes held by others (e.g., females lack physical strength).

Section VIII. Motivation and Job Design: How Do We Light a Fire Under Employees? — 317

Conceptual Issues — 318
Content Theories — 319
    Need Theory — 319
    Motivator–Hygiene Theory — 321
    Achievement, Affiliation, and Power Motives — 323
Process Theories — 325
    Equity Theory and Organizational Justice — 325
    Expectancy Theory — 329
Job Design — 333
Key Terms — 337
Discussion Questions — 337
Web Resources — 337

Readings — 338

14. Motivation as a Predictor of Therapeutic Engagement in Mandated Residential Substance Abuse Treatment — 338
Matthew L. Hiller, Kevin Knight, Carl Leukefeld, and D. Dwayne Simpson

    The study illustrates that issues of motivation for criminal justice employees extend beyond the superior–subordinate relationship. Motivational theory can help us understand why offenders and clients, including felony drug offenders, seek treatment in a diversion-type program.

15. Organizational Justice and Police Misconduct — 347
Scott E. Wolfe and Alex R. Piquero

    The study, based on a sample of nearly 500 Philadelphia police officers, identified a link between organizational (distributive, procedural, and interactional) justice and misconduct, including citizen complaints, internal affairs investigations, and disciplinary violations.

16. Job Design, Community Policing, and Higher Education: A Tale of Two Cities — 365
Charles W. Sherwood

Sherwood examined the motivating potential of the work in two departments, one more advanced in its implementation of community policing than the other. As the results suggest, community policing may be able to increase motivation among police personnel.

Section IX. Occupational Stress and Burnout: Is This Job Killing Me?   378

   Defining Occupational Stress   379
   Major Stressors Affecting Criminal Justice Workers   381
      Factors Inherent in the Task   381
      Individual's Role in the Organization   383
      Relationships at Work   384
      Career Issues   385
      Organizational Factors   385
      Home–Work Interface   385
   Burnout   386
      The Measurement of and Interrelationships Between Burnout Components   387
      Correlates of Burnout   389
   Outcomes of Stress and Burnout   392
   Addressing Stress and Burnout   392
   Key Terms   394
   Discussion Questions   394
   Web Resources   394

Readings   395

   17. A Qualitative Assessment of Stress Perceptions Among Members of a Homicide Unit   395
   Dean A. Dabney, Heith Copes, Richard Tewksbury, and Shila R. Hawk-Tourtelot

   The authors find that major stressors for homicide investigators include the priority given to homicide cases, uncertainty in the workplace and home activities as a result of the work, and scrutiny from supervisors, peers, and others.

   18. The Nature of Occupational Stress Among Public Defenders   413
   David R. Lynch

   Lynch distinguishes between stressors that are frequently occurring and those that intensely affect public defenders. Some are both frequent and intense (e.g., lack of options in mounting a defense) and should be targeted to reduce workplace stress.

   19. Factors Contributing to Levels of Burnout Among Sex Offender Treatment Providers   422
   Rebecca A. Shelby, Rebecca M. Stoddart, and Kathryn L. Taylor

   The authors compare burnout levels among sex-offender treatment providers with other mental health and social service workers. They report that individuals who work in inpatient and prison settings may be more susceptible to burnout than others.

Section X. Leadership: Are You a Leader or a Follower?   429

   Definition of Leadership   430
   Theories of Leadership   431
      Trait Theory   431
      Behavioral Theories   433

   Contingency Theories   435
   Transformational Leadership   443
  Leadership Development   446
  Key Terms   447
  Discussion Questions   447
  Web Resources   448

Readings   449

 20. The Ineffective Police Leader: Acts of Commission and Omission   449
   Joseph A. Schafer

   Rather than studying traits associated with effective leadership, Schafer's research involving a sample of police managers at the FBI National Academy identifies qualities of ineffective leaders.

 21. Leadership and Correctional Reform   468
   James B. Jacobs and Elana Olitsky

   The authors argue that the job of leading a modern correctional organization is challenging and requires a wide range of skills and abilities. They outline a series of recommendations for developing future correctional leaders.

Section XI. Power in Organizations: How Are Subordinates, Suspects, Inmates, and Clients Controlled?   480

  Power Defined   481
  Power, Authority, and Leadership   483
  The Bases of Power   484
   Criminal Justice Applications   485
  Influence Behavior   487
  Effectiveness of Power   489
   Street-Level Bureaucrats   489
   Effective Power Bases   490
  Key Terms   491
  Discussion Questions   492
  Web Resources   492

Readings   493

 22. The Defects of Power   493
   Gresham M. Sykes

   In this excerpt from his classic book, Sykes argues that correctional officers resort to exchange relationships to maintain prison order when other bases of power (e.g., rewards and punishments) are weaker.

 23. The Limits of Individual Control? Perceived Officer Power and Probationer Compliance   505
   Hayden P. Smith, Brandon K. Applegate, Alicia H. Sitren, and Nicolette Fariello Springer

   In this study, probationers were surveyed about their perceptions of power among probation officers. Interestingly, however, officer power was largely unrelated to probationer compliance.

24. Gender, Power, and Reciprocity in the Correctional Setting 518
Denise L. Jenne and Robert C. Kersting

The authors examined whether male and female correctional officers would respond similarly to troublesome inmate behavior (e.g., gambling, smoking in a nonsmoking area).

Section XII. Organizational Change: What Causes Organizations to Transform? 534

Overview of Organizational Change 535
Organizational Change Motors 537
    Planned Change 537
    Conflictive Change 540
    Life Cycle Change 543
    Evolution 545
    Implications of Motors 546
Impediments to Organizational Change 547
Key Terms 548
Discussion Questions 549
Web Resources 549

Readings 550

25. Lessons From the Battle Over D.A.R.E.: The Complicated Relationship Between Research and Practice 550
Greg Berman and Aubrey Fox

Berman and Fox examine how unfavorable research about D.A.R.E. program outcomes influenced implementation at the local level. They found that research competes with a variety of other factors for the attention of decision makers.

26. Improving Criminal Justice Through Better Decision Making: Lessons From the Medical System 559
Daniel P. Mears and Sarah Bacon

The authors discuss decision-making errors, drawing parallels between those made by criminal justice actors and those made by physicians.

Glossary 584

References 591

Index 611

About the Author 648

Foreword

You hold in your hands a book that we think is something new. It is billed as a "text/reader." What that means is we have taken the two most commonly used types of books, the textbook and the reader, and blended them in a way that we anticipate will appeal to both students and faculty.

Our experience as teachers and scholars has been that textbooks for the core classes in criminal justice (or any other social science discipline) leave many students and professors cold. The textbooks are huge, crammed with photographs, charts, highlighted material, and all sorts of pedagogical devices intended to increase student interest. Too often, though, these books end up creating a sort of sensory overload for students and suffer from a focus on "bells and whistles," such as fancy graphics, at the expense of coverage of the most current research on the subject matter.

Readers, on the other hand, are typically composed of recent and classic research articles on the subject. They generally suffer, however, from an absence of meaningful explanatory material. Articles are simply lined up and presented to the students, with little or no context or explanation. Students, particularly undergraduate students, are often confused and overwhelmed.

This text/reader represents our attempt to take the best of both the textbook and reader approaches. It is intended to serve either as a supplement to a core textbook or as a stand-alone text. The book includes a combination of previously published articles and textual material introducing these articles and providing some structure and context for the selected readings. The book is divided into a number of sections. The sections of the book track the typical content and structure of a textbook on the subject. Each section of the book has an introduction that serves to introduce, explain, and provide context for the readings that follow. The readings are a selection of the best recent research that has appeared in academic journals, as well as some classic readings. The articles are edited as necessary to make them accessible to students. This variety of research and perspectives will provide the student with a grasp of the development of research as well as an understanding of the current status of research in the subject area. This approach gives the student the opportunity to learn the basics (in the textbook-like introductory portion of each section) and to read some of the most interesting research on the subject.

There is also an introductory chapter explaining the organization and content of the book and providing context for the articles that follow. This introductory chapter provides a framework for the text and articles that follow and introduces relevant themes, issues, and concepts. This will assist the student in understanding the articles.

Each section includes a summary of the material covered and discussion questions following the introductions and each reading. These summaries and discussion questions should facilitate student thought and class discussion of the material.

It is our belief that this method of presenting the material will be more interesting for both students and faculty. We acknowledge that this approach may be viewed by some as more challenging than the traditional textbook. To that we say, "Yes! It is!" But we believe that if we raise the bar, our students will rise to the challenge. Research shows that students and faculty often find textbooks boring to read. It is our belief that many criminology instructors would welcome the opportunity to teach without having to rely on a "standard" textbook that covers only the most basic information and that lacks both depth of coverage and an attention to current research. This book provides an alternative for instructors who want to get more out of the basic criminology courses and curriculum than one can get from a typical textbook that is aimed at the lowest common denominator and filled with flashy but often useless features that merely serve to drive up its cost. This book is intended for instructors who want to go beyond the ordinary, standard coverage provided in textbooks.

We also believe students will find this approach more interesting. They are given the opportunity to read current, cutting-edge research on the subject, while also being provided with background and context for this research.

We hope that this unconventional approach will be more interesting, and thus make learning and teaching more fun, and hopefully more useful as well. Students need not only content knowledge but also an understanding of the academic skills specific to their discipline. Criminal Justice is a fascinating subject, and the topic deserves to be presented in an interesting manner. We hope you will agree.

Craig Hemmens, JD, PhD
Department of Criminal Justice
Boise State University

Preface

This textbook is not the first to provide a survey of organization and management principles, nor is it the first to address these issues as they apply to the criminal justice system. Indeed, some quality textbooks in the general management and criminal justice literatures tackle these topics. This volume is unique, however, offering features that in combination distinguish it from other similar texts in the criminal justice field. First, the integration of a text and reader into a single volume is a perfect option for students who are increasingly expected to comprehend and analyze original primary source material and, ultimately, synthesize it into a uniform body of knowledge. These are challenging but critical endeavors. The disadvantage of readers is that students are left to struggle through the material on their own, with little assistance in navigating the difficult terrain of original scholarly writing that would help build their confidence and develop their understanding of the requisite knowledge. Moreover, the selection of readings, illustrative of course concepts as they may be, is never quite enough to fully capture the breadth of course material. By coupling a comprehensive review of the field in the form of a traditional text with primary source material (26 readings), this text/reader is designed to facilitate greater student understanding of and appreciation for the study of organizations.

Second, this text/reader, like many other texts, devotes significant attention to classical or foundational approaches to the study of organizations. It is undoubtedly important to understand the roots of organizational theory and behavior and the evolution of management thought. This book extends these discussions by paying close attention to many of the current debates in criminal justice management. For example, while it is not uncommon to see discussions of the open systems approach to the study of organizations—a view that emerged in the 1960s—the modern application of the approach (contingency, institutional, and resource dependence theories) is often ignored. Without reviewing more contemporary theories, we risk ignoring the major contributions made by criminal justice scholars over the past two decades. This text covers key contemporary organizational theories that have made their way into the criminal justice discipline.

Finally, this text/reader takes a broad view of criminal justice and incorporates a large volume of source material from the criminal justice and management fields to illustrate course concepts. It is common for texts to cover the major areas of the criminal justice system: police, the court system (judges, prosecutors, and defense attorneys), and institutional and community corrections. In fact, some texts are divided up into chapters by component after an initial review of the management literature. This text takes a different approach. Examples are drawn from all areas of the criminal justice system and not just from the major agencies. Throughout this text, you will see organizational theory and behavior principles also applied to the study of criminal organizations and populations (e.g., drug traffickers, substance abusers, terrorists), counselors (e.g., sex offender treatment providers), federal law enforcement officials (e.g., the FBI, Transportation Security Administration), and other organizations that, for one reason or another, have a criminal justice nexus (e.g., a school district dealing with school violence or implementing the D.A.R.E. program). Topical variety and the literature cited throughout the text are designed to show the widespread applicability of organizational theory and behavior. Whether you are a supervisor, entry-level worker, or citizen in contact with an agency, organizations matter.

One of the most challenging tasks was sorting through the immense volume of literature in criminal justice to select 26 works that appropriately represent the field. The journal articles, research publications, and book excerpts chosen all illustrate the *application* of core principles of organizational theory and behavior to the study of criminal justice organizations. Most readings reflect contemporary research, published within the past 15 years—though some earlier works, due to their status as classics in the criminal justice literature or their valuable illustrations of organization concepts, are also included. Deliberate choices were also made, as noted earlier, to enhance the variety and balance in topical coverage. The readings were also selected based on their perceived interest and accessibility to students. Articles were edited, where necessary, to reduce heavy statistical language and focus on the content relevant to the topic covered in the section. It is my hope that the material is reader-friendly for all students, regardless of their methodological or statistical skill set, and that the original authors' main ideas remain intact.

This book is designed for use in both undergraduate and graduate courses in criminal justice organizations, administration, and management. For undergraduate courses, this book can serve as the primary text; the coverage within each section provides a comprehensive review of the major elements of organizational theory and behavior, and the readings expose students to valuable primary source material. For graduate courses, the text provides an important introduction to the field, highlighting issues related to the research and measurement of core concepts and summarizing empirical studies addressing organizational topics. The articles represent a useful starting point for more detailed inquiry.

Structure of the Book

The text/reader comprises 12 sections that address many of the core topics in the general management literature. The text opens with a discussion of the importance of taking an organizational approach to the study of the criminal justice system. The next 10 sections (Sections II through XI) are clustered into two broad categories: organizational theory and organizational behavior. Organizational theory topics focus on the organization as a whole (a unit) and as part of a broader group of relationships with other organizations. Sections II through VI—organizational structure, organizational theory, organizational deviance and termination, interagency collaboration, and unions and collective bargaining—take this macro-level approach to the study of organizations. Sections VII through XI emphasize organizational behavior, a micro-level focus on the individuals or groups within organizations. Here the goal is to examine how the organizational context affects individual attitudes and behaviors. Topics include organizational socialization, motivation and job design, occupational stress and burnout, leadership, and power. The text concludes with a final section on organizational change, a topic that brings together elements of both theory and behavior. A brief summary of each of the 12 sections follows.

Preface   xix

Section I. Introduction: Why Should We Study Criminal Justice Organizations?

This section provides a foundation for the study of organizations. The fields of organization and behavior are introduced, and an extended definition of the term *organization* is offered. The section concludes with an overview of the various methods used to classify organizations, including the simple public–private dichotomy.

Section II. Organizational Structure: How Do We Build Organizations?

This section examines the importance of structure for the effective and efficient operation of organizations but recognizes that variation exists across organizations. The two primary components of structure—organizational complexity and organizational control—are introduced and the various dimensions of structure illustrated. Throughout the section, particular attention is paid to highlighting the advantages and disadvantages of specific structural arrangements. At the end of the section, structure-related concepts are applied to the study of criminal organizations.

Section III. Organizational Theory: How Do We Explain What Organizations Look Like?

In this section, the major schools and theories of management thought are presented. The section begins with coverage of the major theories of the classical school (e.g., scientific management, Weber's bureaucracy, and administrative management) and human relations school of management. Significant attention is also given to the major contemporary theories of organization commonly used in criminal justice research today—contingency theory, resource dependence theory, and institutional theory. These theories help us understand why organizations take certain forms.

Section IV. Organizational Deviance and Termination: What Explains Failure in Criminal Justice Agencies?

Some organizations do not always operate as intended and are capable of producing significantly undesirable outcomes (e.g., prison riot, wrongful conviction). Using the concept of organizational deviance as a foundation, this section presents four major explanations for disasters, accidents, and failures within criminal justice organizations. The characteristics of high-reliability organizations—those that are able to avoid organizational deviance—are also discussed. The section concludes with a discussion of organizational termination. Specifically, it explains the process and consequences of the disbanding of criminal justice organizations.

Section V. Interagency Collaboration: Are Two or More Organizations [Combined] Better Than One?

This section describes the problems associated with single organizations handling enduring problems alone and the advantages and disadvantages that result from collaborative action. Three examples of criminal justice collaborations—law enforcement task forces, police–corrections partnerships, and violence reduction partnerships—are described and empirical outcomes addressed.

Section VI. Unions and Collective Bargaining: United We Stand?

Unions are a potent environmental influence on criminal justice organizations. This section provides a brief history of unionism in the field and a discussion of collective bargaining in justice agencies. Attention is paid to the types of matters subject to negotiation and the effects, both positive and negative, of the collective-bargaining process for workers, organizational leaders, and citizens, more generally. The section concludes with a discussion of job actions (e.g., strikes, slowdowns) taken by criminal justice workers past and present.

Section VII. Organizational Socialization: How Does a Person Learn to Behave in an Organization?

This section, the first dealing with an organizational behavior-related topic, discusses how workers learn the necessary skills, values, and behaviors of a new job. As the section illustrates, learning about a job, including the selection of an occupation, begins early in life and continues well into an individual's career. Organizations also use a variety of different strategies to socialize new recruits, as well as those moving to new positions. These strategies, and their implications for employee behavior, are thoroughly detailed throughout this section.

Section VIII. Motivation and Job Design: How Do We Light a Fire Under Employees?

This section examines major theories of motivation, including both content theories (need theory; motivator–hygiene theory; and achievement, affiliation, and power motives) and process theories (equity theory and organizational justice, expectancy theory). The second part of this section describes job design, an approach to structuring the work to maximize motivation.

Section IX. Occupational Stress and Burnout: Is This Job Killing Me?

This section offers clarification on the definitions of both occupational stress and burnout. Key stressors are identified, including factors inherent in the task, role problems, work relationships, career problems, the organization's structure, and the interface between work and home. Both stress and burnout can produce psychological, physical, and behavioral consequences for the individual and adverse outcomes for the organization. Consequently, attention is devoted to a discussion of intervention strategies for preventing and mitigating the negative effects of stress and burnout.

Section X. Leadership: Are You a Leader or a Follower?

This section traces the development of leadership theory, beginning with early trait theories that linked effective leadership to particular personality factors, skills, or physical characteristics. The discussion then shifts to a focus on behavioral theories and the specific actions leaders take, before covering three contingency theories of leadership (Fielder's contingency theory, situational leadership theory, and path–goal theory). The section concludes with a presentation of transformational leadership theory.

Section XI. Power in Organizations: How Are Subordinates, Suspects, Inmates, and Clients Controlled?

As this section shows, all relationships are characterized by unilateral or bilateral power flows. Understanding power helps us understand how goals, rules, and structures are established, compliance ensured, and influence exerted. This section covers the major individual sources of power and influence within an organization. It then addresses how supervisor power is weakened by the very nature of the work in the criminal justice system.

Section XII. Organizational Change: What Causes Organizations to Transform?

The concluding section brings together elements of both organizational theory and organizational behavior. Organizational change can affect multiple levels of an organization—individuals, groups, the entire organization—or even the outside environment. Four mechanisms or motors are presented, each positing a different source of organizational change: planned change, conflict, life cycle, and evolution. Regardless of the mechanisms driving change, any transformation is likely to face some resistance (restraining forces) that must be overcome for the change to take hold. This section addresses these major impediments to change.

Acknowledgments

I would like to thank executive editor Jerry Westby. Jerry's support and constant encouragement were key ingredients in making this project—initially a rough working idea reflecting my interests in organizations—transition into final book form. His knowledge and enthusiasm of the criminal justice field and his trust in authors cannot be overstated. Thanks also go to Erim Sarbuland, Laura Cheung, and MaryAnn Vail, developmental assistants, who answered my many questions over the past two years and otherwise ensured that the book would reach the publication stage much improved and in a timely manner. Thank you to Megan Granger, copy editor, for meticulously reviewing the text and offering suggestions that most certainly improved the final product, and to Olivia Weber-Stenis, production editor, for pulling everything together so seamlessly into final book form. I appreciate Erin Conley for providing her guide for students, "How to Read a Research Article" in Section II; the book's text/reader format was enhanced by this valuable addition.

I consider myself incredibly fortunate to be working during a period of substantial interest in the characteristics of criminal justice organizations. I draw tremendous inspiration and insight from those scholars generating brilliant research in this area. While there are too many names to mention, you will no doubt see them reappear throughout this text, a testament to the influence of their work on my thinking about organizations. Three people, in particular, deserve mention for helping shape my professional career and research interests in significant ways. Steve Chermak provided an intensive introduction to the study of criminal justice systems and organizations in one of my first graduate school courses. His expertise and the extensive literature covered in his class remain with me 15 years later; names such as Lipsky, Prottas, Eisenstein, Jacob, Sykes, and countless others appear throughout this text to illustrate key organizational concepts. Steve also supported my developing interest in organizational theory, ultimately chairing my dissertation committee. Steve Herbert similarly introduced literature (DiMaggio, Powell, Meyer, Rowan) during his graduate policing seminar that formed the basis for much of my scholarly work. Indeed, his course subsequently led me to a dissertation topic using an institutional theory framework and ongoing research focused on the measurement and testing of the theory's core concepts. Finally, I was fortunate to spend more than two years working under Bob Langworthy at the University of Alaska Anchorage. I recently attended a roundtable of police organizational scholars and heard Bob addressed as the "godfather" of this line of inquiry in policing. The experience working with, talking to, and learning from Bob was immensely satisfying and intellectually stimulating. As each of these three individuals contributed to my understanding of criminal justice organizations, I owe tremendous thanks to each of them.

I am truly thankful to the reviewers who devoted their time and energy to provide feedback on the initial proposal and draft sections of the text. These organizational theory experts—in their research and in their teaching of a complex subject—provided constructive commentary that surely improved the overall quality of the final product. I express my sincere gratitude to the following scholars: Joe M. Brown, Fayetteville State University; Dennis Catlin, Northern Arizona University; Michael J. Gilbert, University of Texas at San Antonio; Michael Gizzi, Illinois State University; George E. Higgins, University of Louisville; Tom Jordan, Texas A&M University–Texarkana; William E. Kelly, Auburn University; Jason Lee, University of Wyoming; Eric Metchik, Salem State University; Hal Nees, Metropolitan State University of Denver; Marianne Nielsen, Northern Arizona University; Willard Oliver, Sam Houston State University; Deborah Rhyne, University of Central Florida; Ken Ryan, California State University, Fresno; and Robert M. Worley, Texas A&M University–Central Texas. I also extend my appreciation to Melissa Haynes and Everette Ford, both graduate students in the Department of Criminology and Criminal Justice at Southern Illinois University, for providing additional assistance at various points in the book development process.

Finally, I would like to thank the three most important people in my life: my wife, Melissa, and my two boys, Connor and Ryan. Melissa joined me on a journey that began nearly two decades ago, and we have never looked back. She has celebrated with me all my personal and professional highs and encouraged me through the lows. Connor and Ryan patiently endured my extra time at the office on nights and weekends, recognizing that their Dad was writing a book, even if they did not realize the precise reasons why.

*I dedicate this book to my wife, Melissa, and
to the next generation of scholars, Connor and Ryan. Thank you and I love you.*

SECTION

Introduction

Why Should We Study Criminal Justice Organizations?

Section Highlights

- The Importance of Studying Organizations
- Defining Organization
  - *People*
  - *Purpose*
- *Structure*
- *Durability*
- Public vs. Private Organizations

 The Importance of Studying Organizations

The criminal justice system in the United States is immense: 1,464 adult correctional facilities, 3,061 juvenile residential facilities, 17,985 law enforcement agencies, 2,341 state prosecutors' offices, 93 U.S. attorneys' offices, 94 U.S. judicial districts, and countless other federal, state, and local organizations handle the needs of offenders, victims, clients, witnesses, and the larger society in the interests of crime control (DeFrances, 2002; Maguire, 2013). Stated another way, the system comprises a large number of diverse *organizations*—in purpose, budget, geographic location, and number of workers—employing well over a million workers. At this point in your studies, you may have taken courses centered exclusively on one or more of the primary components of the criminal justice system, leading you rightfully to ask why a course dealing with organizations and their management and administration is necessary.

To illustrate the importance of a course about criminal justice organizations, first consider the general influence of the 9/11 terrorist attacks on the criminal justice system. According to a review conducted by the National Research Council,

> The terrorist attacks of September 11, 2001, may have altered police structure, behavior, and policing style in the United States. . . . Now there are calls for police to respond to suspicious situations, uncover terrorist networks, and work with other agencies and jurisdictions in an unprecedented way. In the event of an attack, police would find themselves as first-line emergency responders, perhaps faced with biological or radiological hazards. (Skogan & Frydl, 2004, p. 209)

Other components are not immune to these additional demands. Terrorism suspects are often detained, sometimes indefinitely, in federal, state, and local correctional facilities (see Chen, 2004). Similarly, many prosecutors participate as part of antiterrorism task forces and prosecute terrorism-related offenses, including "'precursor crimes' (e.g., offenses that may be precursors to terrorist offenses such as identity theft, money laundering, counterfeit identification, etc.)" (Nugent, Johnson, Bartholomew, & Bromirski, 2005, p. v). Clearly, homeland security is a significant responsibility of the criminal justice system and, indeed, an important part of academic inquiry in criminology and criminal justice (see, for example, Lum, Kennedy, & Sherley, 2006; Rosenfeld, 2002).[1] These increasing responsibilities generate challenges, highlighting the importance of examining organizations as a distinct field of study. Consider three examples related to homeland security:

- *Intelligence industry:* After the 9/11 terrorist attacks, efforts were directed at reforming the intelligence community, the agencies responsible for gathering and synthesizing information for national security purposes, to overcome information-sharing barriers (National Commission, 2004; Zegart, 2007). At the same time, the importance of intelligence overall in protecting the homeland was increasingly apparent, as evident in the dramatic expansion of the industry. As a 2010 *Washington Post* investigation revealed, more than 3,000 separate organizations (1,271 government and 1,931 private) "work on programs related to counterterrorism, homeland security and intelligence in about 10,000 locations across the United States" (Priest & Arkin, 2010). These organizations employed about 854,000 people holding top-secret security clearances and produced 50,000 intelligence reports annually. The overall volume of reports was so large that key decision makers, out of necessity, were forced to rely on staffers or other mechanisms to substantially distill important information into more usable formats.

- *Airport security:* Anyone who has traveled by airplane over the past decade has undoubtedly witnessed or experienced the many security procedures designed to thwart terrorist activities. Travelers are asked, among other requirements, to provide photo identification, remove footwear and outerwear for screening, place containers of liquid (3 ounces maximum) in a single 1-quart plastic bag, store prohibited items in checked rather than carry-on luggage, submit to an electronic body scan or pat-down, and remove laptop computers from all but Transportation Security Administration (TSA)–approved cases. Jeffrey Goldberg (2008), a writer for *The Atlantic Monthly,* suggested that the "TSA's security

---

[1]Scholars have distinguished between the study of criminology or criminological theory and criminal justice theory. The former involves the study of crime with the goal of explaining criminal behavior, while the latter not only seeks to describe reactions to criminal behavior but "how and why a particular response is employed" (Duffee & Allan, 2007, p. 8). This book focuses on criminal justice organizations—an area of inquiry where the reactions to criminal conduct are discussed more frequently than the conduct itself.

regimen seems to be mainly thing-based—most of its 44,500 airport officers are assigned to truffle through carry-on bags for things like guns, bombs, three-ounce tubes of anthrax, Crest toothpaste, nail clippers, Snapple, and so on" (pp. 100–101). Goldberg, having written articles on homeland security and terrorism in the past, decided to put these security procedures to the test periodically by attempting to carry banned items (e.g., box cutters) through airport security checkpoints at a number of major and secondary U.S. airports. He also routinely carried items that, while technically not considered contraband, might have aroused the suspicion of security personnel: Islamic Jihad and Hezbollah flags, T-shirts favorably depicting Osama bin Laden, and other similar items. Rarely did he cause much concern, although, on a few occasions, items such as nail clippers were confiscated. Finally, Goldberg attempted to pass through a security checkpoint at the Reagan National Airport in Washington, D.C., with a fake boarding pass (albeit, one with his real name printed on it) produced on a home computer and printer; although the boarding pass was scrutinized by the TSA agent, he was allowed to continue on through the screening process.

- *Job satisfaction in the Department of Homeland Security (DHS):* The DHS is a relatively new cabinet-level department formed after the 9/11 terrorist attacks. Although its history is brief, the department is massive, comprising 22 agencies and more than 200,000 employees previously scattered across other departments within the federal government (e.g., the Secret Service was formerly part of the Treasury Department; Brzezinski, 2004; Perrow, 2007). The agencies folded into the new DHS faced an expanded and sometimes altogether new role—homeland security—to go along with existing roles. Mission reprioritization had important consequences for organizations such as the U.S. Coast Guard; "the Coast Guard's effort in drug interdiction declined 60 percent after 9/11, and time invested in preventing an encroachment on American fishing territories and enforcing fishing rules shrank 38 percent" (Perrow, 2007, p. 97). Since the department's creation, surveys of its employees have consistently shown lower levels of job satisfaction compared with federal government workers more generally (Maurer, 2012). The difference between DHS workers and federal government workers has been as wide as 12 percentage points in 2004 (56% of DHS workers satisfied vs. 68% of federal workers satisfied) to 4 percentage points in 2011 (64% vs. 68%). As shown in Table 1.1, the disparity is especially great for workers in the Transportation Security Administration and the Undersecretary for Intelligence and Analysis, the latter organization being responsible for intelligence gathering for homeland security. Dissatisfaction was linked, in part, to employee beliefs that their talents were not being used and they were not given opportunities to improve their skills within the organization (Maurer, 2012).

The preceding examples represent the types of issues studied by those interested in organizations. Why is organizational inquiry necessary? Scott and Davis (2007) offer several compelling reasons. First, organizations are everywhere. More than 3,000 agencies exist to address the single function of homeland security/intelligence. The DHS employs more than 200,000 workers across its 22 agencies. Moving beyond the thousands of other criminal justice organizations, millions of other establishments exist within the United States (Scott & Davis, 2007; U.S. Census Bureau, 2012). From this perspective, organizations are important to study because they provide critical services to society (e.g., public safety, education, finance), are encountered frequently, and serve as the source of employment for most individuals during their lifetimes.[2] Second, organizations are more than just a collection of individuals; the

---

[2]Even sole proprietors or other individuals in modern society who seek to be self-sufficient likely encounter organizations serving as suppliers, transporters, resource providers, or some other role.

Table 1.1 DHS Component Job Satisfaction Scores, 2011

DHS component	Job satisfaction score (percentage)	Difference from government-wide average (percentage points)
Federal Law Enforcement Training Center	72	4
Office of the Inspector General	71	3
U.S. Coast Guard	70	2
U.S. Secret Service	69	1
U.S. Customs and Border Protection	69	1
U.S. Citizenship and Immigration Services	67	−1
Management Directorate	66	−2
Office of the Secretary	63	−5
Federal Emergency Management Administration	63	−5
National Protection and Programs Directorate	62	−6
Immigration and Customs Enforcement	61	−7
Undersecretary for Science and Technology	60	−8
Undersecretary for Intelligence and Analysis	58	−10
Transportation Security Administration	57	−11
Governmentwide (average score)	**68**	**0**
DHS (average score)	**64**	**−4**

Source: Maurer (2012); Government Accountability Office.

larger organization assumes a life of its own, capable of influencing individual behavior (Hall, 1999; Scott & Davis, 2007). The fact that DHS personnel tended to exhibit lower levels of job satisfaction is a persistent pattern throughout the department's existence. Even as the Secretary of Homeland Security (the individual in charge of the DHS) changed, job satisfaction remained a problem. Evidence points to enduring structural problems as a source of diminished satisfaction. Improving motivation and performance may depend on altering the work itself. Similarly, the coordination challenges within the intelligence community are larger than the Director of National Intelligence. The law that created that position gave the occupant only limited authority over intelligence community members. If removing and replacing personnel has not resolved the issue, characteristics of the organization as a whole might be to blame. Third, studying organizations allows us to move beyond simple description

(Scott & Davis, 2007). Rather than focus on the level of stress within a police department or the practices of a probation office, for example, we can develop theoretical explanations for the *development* of stress or the *adoption* of practices. In other words, an important goal is to produce theories to explain, rather than just describe, why we are observing certain phenomena.

The fields of organizational theory and organizational behavior provide lenses through which we can examine these issues. Organizational theory is the "study of the structure, processes, and outcomes of the organization per se" (Cummings, 1978, p. 92). The focus is on the organization as a unit or, in some cases, the organization as part of a larger group of relationships with other organizations. Two examples above address matters related to organizational theory, or what Scott and Davis (2007) termed the macro-level approach to studying organizations. The first illustrates the interrelationships among intelligence agencies and the consequences of the connections for successful task performance (e.g., redundancies, conflict). The second deals with matters of structure, specifically the adoption of certain policies and procedures. Theory helps us understand why organizations look the way they do and why we observe similarity and variation across a particular industry. Organizational theory topics are addressed in the first half of this volume: structure, theory, organizational deviance, partnerships, and unions. In contrast, organizational behavior emphasizes the individual or groups within the organization (Cummings, 1978). Attention shifts from the macro level to the micro level; the larger organization still matters but as context that potentially influences worker or group attitudes and behavior (Scott & Davis, 2007). Job satisfaction within the DHS is a topic related to organizational behavior. What is contributing to the less-than-favorable attitudes? Is the job designed poorly, or is leadership deficient? Are workers ill trained to complete the work? The second half of the text tackles organizational behavior-related topics, including socialization, motivation, stress, leadership, and power.

▲ **Photo 1.1** Surveys of government workers show that Department of Homeland Security workers, including TSA personnel (shown above), tend to have lower levels of job satisfaction than government workers more generally. (Source: Department of Homeland Security)

Defining Organization

The term organization appears frequently above, and its use perhaps generated little confusion. After all, it is a commonly used word with at least some shared meaning across individuals. Organizational scholars, however, are not content with assuming shared understanding, choosing instead to devote considerable energy to conceptualize precisely what constitutes an organization. Three definitions illustrate outcomes of these efforts:

> Organizations are social units (or human groupings) deliberately constructed and reconstructed to seek specific goals. (Etzioni, 1964, p. 3)

An organization is a collectivity with a relatively identifiable boundary, a normative order (rules), ranks of authority (hierarchy), communications systems, and membership coordinating systems (procedures); this collectivity exits on a relatively continuous basis, in an environment, and engages in activities that are usually related to a set of goals; the activities have outcomes for organizational members, for the organization itself, and for society. (Hall, 1999, p. 30)

Organizations [are] social structures created by individuals to support the collaborative pursuit of specified goals. (Scott & Davis, 2007, p. 11)

In spite of some variation in the precise language used, these definitions overlap to a considerable extent. In fact, Porter, Lawler, and Hackman (1975), after reviewing 10 classic definitions from the 1930s through the early 1970s, identified four common components of formal organizations: people, purpose, structures, and durability.[3] Their definition, based on a synthesis of earlier conceptualizations, views organizations as comprising individuals or groups (people) seeking to realize collective goals (purpose) by dividing up and coordinating the work (structure), and operating over time (durability) (p. 69).

People

The definitions above make clear that organizations are formed by people, either individually or in groups, who have come together for a specific purpose. If organizations are made of people, they must have boundaries that separate organizational members from nonmembers (Hall, 1999). That is, some individuals and groups are part of the organization, while others are external to it. In practice, demarcating the boundaries between insiders and outsiders—members and nonmembers—is no simple task and relates, in some respects, to the interests of those studying organizations. For example, who are the members of a police department? There is probably little dispute in including sworn officers or paid staff members. What about unpaid auxiliary police officers or members of the city government that funds the department (e.g., mayor or council)? What about offenders, victims, bystanders, witnesses, and citizens at large?

Answering these questions has important implications for our understanding of organizations. If an organization has "a relatively identifiable boundary," we are left to address what to do with everything on the outside (Hall, 1999, p. 30). Porter et al. (1975) developed a classification schema, shown in Figure 1.1, to illustrate units of ever-increasing size related to organizations. Following this schema, we can apply a simple example. Police officers (individuals) make up a specialized gang unit (group). This group, combined with others (e.g., detective squad, patrol unit, etc.), represents a single police department. The larger public safety institution comprises police departments, prosecutors' offices, departments of corrections, and other criminal justice organizations. A wide variety of institutions (e.g., education, economic, and public safety) are part of the larger society.

Figure 1.1 also depicts the organization's **environment**, the elements external to the organization that both influence and support it (Katz & Kahn, 1966; Scott & Davis, 2007). Concentrating on

---

[3] Roy Roberg (1979) used this approach—who, why, how, and when—in his classic volume on police organizations.

Figure 1.1 Classification System of Units Related to Organizations

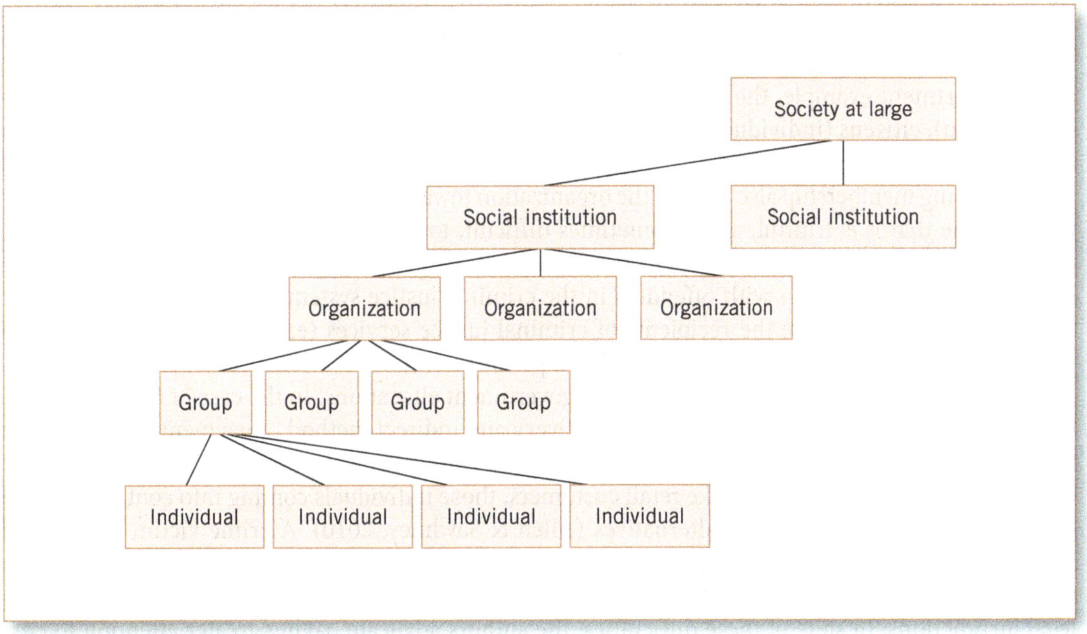

Source: Porter et al. (1975).

one single organization and its group and individual members, we can visually determine what constitutes the larger environment—society at large, social institutions, other organizations, and individuals and groups from other organizations. A police department's environment includes other police departments, criminal justice and non-criminal justice organizations, larger social institutions such as economic and educational systems, and individuals and groups from other organizations. Why does this matter?

Some scholars choose to analyze organizations using a **closed systems** approach, where organizations are largely protected from outside influences. For example, some might view the U.S. Supreme Court as a closed system. Justices are seemingly insulated from political pressures due to a number of constitutional provisions, including lifetime appointments. Consequently, it may be less important to pay attention to relationships between the court and its environment.[4] In contrast, **open systems** approaches recognize the importance of the external environment. Research, for example, shows that economic conditions and crime rates—both factors external to police organizations—influence recruiting. Higher crime rates arguably appeal to those who have an interest in the variety and adventurous nature of police work (Wilson, Rostker, & Fan, 2010). Improved marketing and pay (the internal factors)

---

[4]This is, of course, a simplistic argument. The court must undoubtedly transact with its environment and consider broader societal changes.

may prove insufficient in generating additional applicants due to the constraints posed by the larger economy, crime rates, and competition from other organizations. Scholars and practitioners sometimes find it useful to treat organizations as closed to limit the number of relevant explanatory factors that must be considered, but organizations are rarely closed in actual practice. As a result, specifying the elements of an organization's environment is a useful, if not critical, exercise. Returning to the police department example, the mayor (government organization), crime-watch groups (voluntary organization), citizens (individuals), and others are external to and therefore potential influences on an organization's operations.

Specifying membership also orients the organization toward a customer focus. Allen and Sawhney (2010) argue that it is fruitful, albeit sometimes difficult, to view offenders, victims, and the larger society as customers of the criminal justice system. They suggest that people often are unable to reconcile images of a customer with offenders in the criminal justice system. Part of the problem, they note, is that individuals are the recipients of criminal justice services (e.g., when police respond to calls for service, when an offender is housed in a prison) but those services are not paid for directly. Instead, payment is diffused through taxes and government allocations. In the case of a motor vehicle violator, "this disconnection between service delivery and indirect method of payment may obscure a law enforcement officer's ability to recognize the speed violator as a customer" (p. 85). Another part of the problem is the fact that, unlike retail customers, those individuals coming into contact with the criminal justice system have few alternatives (Allen & Sawhney, 2010). A crime victim has limited recourse beyond turning to the formal criminal or civil justice system for a response. Even then, the victim does not choose the police department, court, or prosecutor; these are matters determined by legal jurisdictions. In spite of these difficulties, the authors advocate paying greater attention to customers, those nonmembers who receive criminal justice services. After all, "if this individual/group/organization did not exist, would it adversely impact the business [operations of the criminal justice organization]?" (p. 91).

Purpose

The three definitions of *organization* offered earlier clearly specify the reason *why* individuals organize: to achieve common goals. Collectively organized individuals are able to accomplish more than any one person or group could accomplish alone; "as the popular expression 'the whole is greater than the sum of its parts' suggests . . . the relations between units add new elements to the situation" (Blau & Scott, 1962/2003, p. 3). The formation of the London Metropolitan Police in 1829, for example, was part of a dramatic historical evolution in policing from informal, avocational ("part time, often unpaid, amateur activity") methods to a formal organizational form (Klockars, 1985, p. 20). While communities were historically protected by some combination of loosely organized, but nevertheless obligated, community members (e.g., frankpledge system, constable and watch model), the weaknesses of earlier models became apparent as cities such as London experienced civil disorder, rising crime (or at least the perception of rising crime), and widespread public drunkenness (Lundman, 1980). In response, the first modern police force was organized in London to more systematically tackle public safety concerns (Critchley, 1967; Lundman, 1980). Of course, the individual officers in London and the employees in many organizations are likely participating in the organization for reasons other than or in addition to the larger organization's goals (Porter et al., 1975).

Officers may join police forces to fight crime and disorder and may derive considerable satisfaction from accomplishing these goals (see Section VIII). Others become part of organizations for reasons apart from larger goals, including pay, benefits, adventure, or camaraderie. In this case, working toward the larger organization's goals is functional to the degree that it helps satisfy individual goals (Porter et al., 1975).

The oft-discussed courtroom workgroup—the judge, prosecutor, and defense attorney—fits within the definitions above. These individuals most certainly are members of their own home or sponsoring organizations (e.g., the defense attorney's law firm) but together compose a completely new organization (Clynch & Neubauer, 1981). If the judicial process is envisioned as an adversarial system, what common goals bring workgroup members together into a single, but less formal, organization (Goodpaster, 1987)? Eisenstein and Jacob (1991) argue that members share the goals of efficiently closing cases, reducing uncertainty, doing justice, and maintaining group cohesion:

- *Efficiently closing cases:* Closing cases quickly allows workgroup members to demonstrate that they are working hard and that justice is served in a timely manner. Moreover, efficiency is necessary to prevent case backlogs given resource constraints. For a prosecutor, protracted cases weaken evidence; witnesses relocate, evidence is lost, and individuals forget facts pertinent to the state's case (Eisenstein & Jacob, 1991). A private defense attorney is also motivated to close cases rapidly to collect fees and move on to the next case, since most clients are unable to pay fees for extended periods (Blumberg, 1967).

- *Reduce uncertainty:* Criminal cases bring uncertainty to all parties (Eisenstein & Jacob, 1991). Defense attorneys and prosecutors risk losing in court, an outcome that could jeopardize reputations and long-term career prospects. A trial also produces uncertainty for judges. They frequently must rule on matters of law that ultimately open the door for appeals. A decision overturned by an appellate court potentially indicates an error on the part of the judge.

- *Doing justice:* "All the principal participants are attorneys, and are bound to that goal by their professional training" (Eisenstein & Jacob, 1991, p. 26). In some cases, a just outcome for a particular offense is embodied in the notion of the normal crime or going rate (Sudnow, 1965). The members of the workgroup develop common punishments for particular crimes that reflect their views of appropriate sanctions given the circumstances.

- *Maintaining cohesion:* To accomplish the first three goals, workgroup members must minimize intragroup conflict (Eisenstein & Jacob, 1991).

Knowing the goals pursued by the workgroup, it is easier to understand the widespread use of plea bargaining as a case disposition method. Trials take time to complete due to the extensive pretrial process, and their outcomes are uncertain. Consequently, an offender may receive a significant penalty or no penalty at all, leading to questions of justice. The adversarial nature of the process is also enough to disrupt group cohesion. If members want to satisfy the aforementioned goals, plea bargaining is the most viable option, since cases are handled more expeditiously and all parties gain something valued. Prosecutors secure a conviction, defense attorneys generally receive some consideration for their clients, and judges are more insulated from appeals. The plea itself can be shaped to ensure justice is served, and the bargaining facilitates continued group cohesion.

The workgroup example demonstrates how organizations are often pursuing multiple goals simultaneously. More problematic, however, is when those goals conflict with one another. For example, Logan (1993) identified eight performance measures for prisons based, in part, on what society expects prisons to accomplish. In addition to security ("keep them in"), safety ("keep them safe"), and order ("keep them in line"), prisons are expected to fairly and efficiently keep inmates healthy and busy (e.g., recreation, therapy, training) while minimizing suffering (pp. 27–31). In some situations, attempts to rehabilitate or provide activity for inmates may be perceived as conflicting with the goals of security, safety, and order. In such cases, security, safety, and order become paramount (Craig, 2004). Victim-witness programs suffer from similar conflicts. Jerin, Moriarity, and Gibson (1995) found that programs provide a range of services to foster victim healing (e.g., referrals, assistance with insurance claims, victim compensation, and counseling) and assist in navigating the court process (e.g., transportation, impact statements, notifications). They concluded after their review of North Carolina victim-witness programming, however, that most adopt a witness orientation emphasizing the importance of the victim in pursuing a case against the accused. Organizations must reconcile conflicting goals, particularly when external evaluation and support is contingent on their achievement.

Structure

Organizations accomplish their goals through the use of a formal structure. To illustrate the concept of structure, famous organizational scholar Henry Mintzberg (1979) opened his classic book, *The Structuring of Organizations,* with a simple example of a successful pottery maker. When the pottery maker worked on her own, she determined how she would accomplish her work and the tasks to be completed. In this case, "coordination [of the work] takes place simply, in one brain" (p. 7). When the pottery maker hired an assistant, she decided how job responsibilities were assigned and ensured that they were completed; "coordination must be achieved across brains" (p. 7). The same decisions are made in criminal justice organizations. This is the essence of organizational structure. As the volume and complexity of tasks increase beyond the capabilities of any single individual, organizations must differentiate or separate the work into distinct tasks to be performed by multiple workers (Porter et al., 1975).

Dimensions of structure, discussed in greater depth in Section II of this text, are often depicted in organizational charts. Figure 1.2 illustrates the structure of the Philadelphia Police Department's Special Investigations Bureau, one part of the overall organization. Even within this single bureau, the work is subdivided into six major areas by task or crime type: homicide, criminal intelligence, special victims, major crimes, citywide vice, and gun permits. The level of complexity of an organization—that is, the degree to which tasks are subdivided—will vary from one organization to the next. However, regardless of the level of complexity, efforts must be made to coordinate or control the work. As Porter et al. (1975) note,

> "Rational coordination" refers to the putting together of the activities or effort of individuals in such a way that it makes sense—seems logical. . . . In any organization at any time, coordination may fall apart due to unexpected events in the environment or poor planning or other factors, yet what is *attempted* in organizations is a conscious effort to put together activities in a meaningful way. (p. 93)

Figure 1.2 Philadelphia Police Department Special Investigations Bureau Organizational Chart

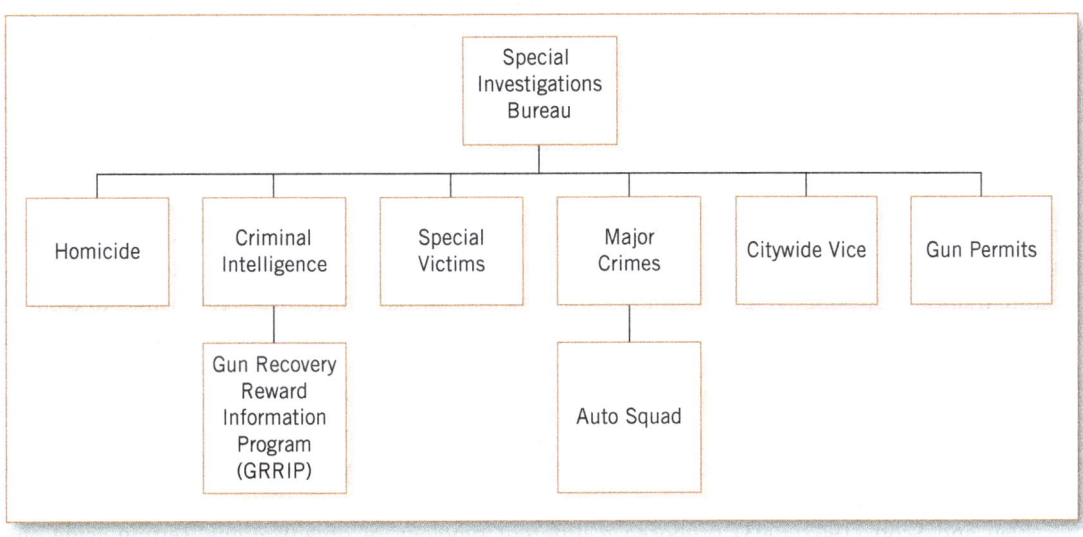

Source: Philadelphia Police Department.

Activities may be guided by rules, varying levels of oversight, and centralized decision making (see Section II). These represent dimensions of an organization's formal structure. In most cases, an informal, non-organizationally prescribed structure operates alongside the formal one. Sections III and VII address issues related to the organization's informal structure.

Durability

Finally, formal organizations are defined, in part, by some degree of continuity of operations. Must organizations last forever once established? Obviously, some organizations experience death, and such termination is not limited to for-profit companies going out of business either; criminal justice organizations have suffered similar fates (see Section IV). The point of noting that formal organizations are characterized by some degree of permanency is to suggest that any one organization exists even with turnover in membership (Porter et al., 1975). Moreover, workers expect organizations to continue functioning. The London Metropolitan Police Department, discussed earlier, has survived for nearly 200 years in spite of regular turnover in membership and leadership. Most criminal justice organizations have similarly experienced regular ongoing operations.

Public vs. Private Organizations

The definition of an organization introduced important concepts that will reappear throughout the text: structure, goals, and durability. Organizational scholars have questioned whether these concepts, and organizational theory and behavior more generally, are equally applicable to all types of organizations.

Of particular interest is whether the distinction between public and private organizations is necessary for studying criminal justice organizations. Early attempts to classify organizations as either public or private rested on funding sources; public organizations were primarily funded by governments (typically with taxpayer resources) and private organizations received funding through donations or the marketplace (i.e., sold, provided, or exchanged goods and services; Rainey, 1983). This distinction is not always useful, given the realities of the criminal justice system. Public organizations sometimes adopt private-like qualities. Bayley and Shearing (2001) pointed out that when police departments permit officers to moonlight in security positions during off-duty hours, they are allowing officers to obtain benefits from nongovernment sources due, in part, to their taxpayer-funded training and uniforms. Similarly, departments may charge contractors for a police presence at construction sites or private businesses if they respond to excessive burglar alarm calls. At other times, private organizations assume traditionally public responsibilities. Governments contract with private companies to confine state-sentenced defendants in privately run facilities across the United States; prisons operated by for-profit companies house roughly 7% of the U.S. adult prison population and, in some states, one in three inmates (Makarios & Maahs, 2012). In still other cases, one organizational type might supplant the other altogether. In 2001, formerly private-sector airline security workers were federalized as part of the Aviation and Transportation Security Act, making airport security the responsibility of the federal government (Selzer, 2003).

Blau and Scott (1962/2003) proposed a different typology of organizations, setting aside one based on ownership (public vs. private) and replacing it with an alternative based on primary beneficiaries. In other words, they asked, "Who benefits" from the existence of the organization? **Mutual benefit organizations** serve the membership at large. Professional associations such as the International Association of Chiefs of Police or unions such as the California Correctional Peace Officers Association advocate for organizational members. **Business organizations** operate to further the interests of ownership. The Corrections Corporation of America, for example, houses both state and federal prisons in its facilities but is geared toward producing a profit for its ownership/investors.[5] **Service organizations** cater to specific clients; examples include drug treatment facilities, public defender organizations, hospitals, and other similar organizations. The clients of these organizations—drug addict, defendant, or patient—are primary beneficiaries (Blau & Scott, 1962/2003). Finally, **commonwealth organizations** benefit the larger society or the "public-at-large" (p. 54). While a police officer might directly arrest an offender observed victimizing a citizen, the officer's actions, and indeed the organization, exist to serve the general public. Perhaps this is most evident in the courts. A prosecutor is the state's (society's) attorney, not the individual victim's attorney. Overall, the value in this typology is in reminding us why organizations exist. When viewing the decisions of the Corrections Corporation of America, it makes more sense to consider it as a business organization with the interests of the commonwealth as a secondary goal. Likewise, a victim viewing a prosecutor's office as a service organization representing his interests may be outraged at the plea disposition in a particular case. If the prosecutor's office is viewed as a commonwealth organization, however, the plea practices may represent the best mechanisms for ensuring justice for the larger society.

Bozeman (1987) argues that "publicness" is a matter of degree, not just a matter of ownership (public or private). Organizations, both public and private, are constrained to varying degrees when it comes to raising and controlling their own resources, establishing organizational goals, planning

---

[5]Corrections Corporation of America is a publicly traded company on the New York Stock Exchange.

operations, and communicating with external agencies (Bozeman & Bretschneider, 1994). A private corrections corporation would be classified, according to definitions presented earlier, as a private or business organization. The company is certainly motivated by profits, but such a simple classification ignores its connection to the larger political system (government). States provide critical resources to private prison contractors (financial, inmates) and establish regulations for housing offenders, thereby setting certain minimum standards for operations. Thus, in spite of the profit motive of a private prison company, it finds itself, in practice, located toward the public end of the continuum. In contrast, a private security firm is less dependent on government resources, relying instead on clients (e.g., housing developments, corporations) to fund operations. Even in these situations, the state may promulgate training standards for security officers. By recognizing this distinction between organizational types—a refined public/private classification—the constraints placed on criminal justice organizations become increasingly apparent (Rainey, 1983). Organizations further along the public continuum face greater challenges in altering structures, determining goals, assessing effectiveness, and motivating and controlling employees (Rainey, Backoff, & Levine, 1976). Subsequent sections in the text illustrate these constraints.

This introductory section outlined the importance of organizational theory and behavior and presented several key concepts—organization, environment, and public and private—that serve as a starting point for the discussion to come. The rest of the text proceeds first with a review of organizational theory-related topics and then shifts to organizational behavior. It concludes with a section on organizational effectiveness and change, drawing on both organizational theory and behavior.

KEY TERMS

business organizations
closed systems
commonwealth organizations
environment

mutual benefit organizations
open systems
organization
organizational behavior

organizational theory
service organizations

DISCUSSION QUESTIONS

1. Goldberg (2008) described airport security as "theater," since it improved the appearance of safety even if it did not necessary improve actual safety (p. 100). Do you agree with his assessment? Assuming his argument is accurate, is making people feel safer or reducing fear an important goal of criminal justice agencies apart from actually reducing risk? In other words, is it a worthwhile investment of resources to reduce fear of crime/terrorism even if the likelihood of becoming a victim of crime/terrorism remains unchanged?

2. Apply the four elements of Porter et al.'s (1975) definition of an organization—people, purpose, structure, durability—to street gangs. Do street gangs fit their definition? Explain.

3. Compare and contrast a private prison operated by a company such as the Corrections Corporation of America with a public prison operated by a state department of corrections. Are private prisons subject to the same environmental constraints as government-run prisons?

WEB RESOURCES

Sourcebook of Criminal Justice Statistics:
http://www.albany.edu/sourcebook/

Washington Post's Top Secret America investigation:
http://projects.washingtonpost.com/top-secret-america/

History of the London Metropolitan Police Department:
http://www.met.police.uk/history/

SECTION

II

Organizational Structure
How Do We Build Organizations?

Section Highlights

- Organizational Complexity
  - *Vertical Complexity*
  - *Horizontal Complexity*
  - *Spatial Complexity*
- Organizational Control
- *Formalization*
- *Centralization*
- *Span of Control*
- Organizational Structure and Criminal Organizations

The Federal Bureau of Investigation (FBI), while headquartered in Washington, D.C., operates 56 field offices throughout the United States. Each field office, headed by either a special agent in charge or assistant director in charge, covers a geographic territory ranging from multiple counties in a single state to several states in their entirety (Masse & Krouse, 2003). This structure affords field office leaders the discretion to make key operation decisions affecting their parts of the overall organization. Zegart (2007) described the FBI as "a system of fifty-six affiliated agencies, each of which set its own priorities, assigned its own personnel, ran its own cases, followed its own orders, and guarded its own information" (p. 123). Although they were held accountable for producing results by agency executives in Washington, D.C., field office executives were free to target local problems with local solutions. The benefits of this arrangement are clear; the field offices were in tune with area problems and arguably more responsive to local needs.

At the same time, the field office structure is arguably dysfunctional in certain respects. The authors of *The 9/11 Commission Report* pinpointed the problem by stating that field offices, prior to the 9/11 attacks, did not generally focus on issues such as homeland security and terrorism that affect the nation as a whole (National Commission, 2004). Moreover, when terrorism and homeland security investigations did occur, the field office structure stifled information sharing. Zegart (2007) demonstrated this problem by recounting the activities of three field offices during July and August 2001, just before the September 11 attacks.[1] On July 10, an agent in the Phoenix field office sent a memorandum to FBI headquarters noting concern about individuals with terrorist ties being trained in U.S. flight schools. In mid-August, agents in the Minneapolis field office investigated and apprehended Zacarias Moussaoui—who would later be referred to as the 20th hijacker—after receiving a tip from a suspicious flight-school instructor. On August 29, the New York field office opened an investigation attempting to locate two terrorism suspects, one of whom was followed but lost by the CIA in 2000 after a meeting with terrorist operatives overseas. Neither individual was located before the attacks, and both were aboard the flight that crashed into the Pentagon. The field office structure ensured that these individual investigations occurred in isolation from one another. The combined knowledge from three investigations would have potentially raised significantly more red flags than a single investigation, but this knowledge did not coalesce until after the 9/11 attacks.

The example above shows the importance of studying **organizational structure**—how organizations divide up their work and coordinate these parts (Gulick, 1937; Maguire, 2003). The purpose of organizational structures, according to Hall (1999), is threefold. First, structure provides the framework in which the work of the organization is completed. When organizations are appropriately structured, it is more likely that they will effectively and efficiently attain organizational goals. When the structure is dysfunctional, as the FBI example above suggests, the organization's performance suffers. Second, organizational structures produce consistency (Hall, 1999). In a supermax prison, for example, prison rules may require correctional officers to handcuff inmates prior to moving them throughout the facility. These rules are designed to ensure the safety and security of both officers and inmates and to reduce the likelihood of workers transporting inmates carelessly. Finally, structure affects other organizational characteristics such as power, interorganizational communication, motivation, and decision making (Roberg & Kuykendall, 1990).

Organizational structures vary from the simple to the complex along multiple dimensions. As Hall (1999) indicated, examining structure is critical to understand a broad range of organizational issues and, importantly, organizational effectiveness. Considerations of structure also extend beyond criminal justice organizations to the criminal organizations (e.g., gangs, terrorist groups) they target. Understanding the structure of illicit organizations may guide enforcement strategies. The remainder of this section identifies the key elements of organizational structure and the advantages and disadvantages of different structural arrangements.

▲ Photo 2.1 Although the FBI headquarters building is located in Washington, D.C., investigations generally operate out of one of the agency's 56 field offices. (Source: FBI)

---

[1]Zegart's analysis addresses many opportunities missed by the CIA (Central Intelligence Agency) and FBI. Three are chosen here for illustrative purposes.

Organizational Complexity

The first broad component of an organization's structure is complexity.[2] The job tasks of an organization—law enforcement, jail operations, and courtroom security in a sheriff's department, for example—are typically divided, or differentiated, among an organization's many parts and workers. "The number of separate 'parts' of the organization as reflected by the division of labor, number of hierarchical levels, and the spatial dispersion of the organization" represent the organization's structure (Hall, Johnson, & Haas, 1967, p. 906; see also Blau, 1970). Tasks are assigned to specific departments, units, or specialists; levels in the chain of command (e.g., officers, sergeants, and lieutenants); and/or geographic areas (e.g., beats, judicial districts, prisons) corresponding to the three types of divisions of work—horizontal, vertical, and spatial (see Figure 2.1). Criminal justice organizations vary along these dimensions, indicating that complexity is a matter of degree; advantages and disadvantages are linked to differing levels of complexity.

Vertical Complexity

Vertical complexity characterizes the hierarchical dimension of an organization's structure. Most often, discussions of vertical complexity in criminal justice organizations address the related concepts of rank structure and the chain of command. According to King (2005), as individuals ascend the organizational hierarchy, they acquire greater power over those lower in the hierarchy. Vertical complexity delineates a chain of command, "an unbroken line of authority that extends from the top of the organization to its lowest echelon and clarifies who reports to whom" (Robbins & Judge, 2008, p. 233; referred to as the "scalar chain" by Fayol, 1949). Job titles or labels are typically used to indicate a worker's location within the hierarchy; in many criminal justice organizations including police, sheriffs', and correctional departments, military ranks designate these positions of authority.

Vertical complexity is assessed by examining the segmentation in and concentration of an organization's hierarchy. These properties are indicative of an organization's vertical structure and are commonly represented by a pyramidal shape (Kaufmann & Seidman, 1970; Langworthy, 1986). Segmentation is indicated by the number of layers in the chain of command or hierarchy from the top of the organization to the bottom. Segmentation, according to Evan (1963), answers the question, "How many levels of authority are engaged in making, interpreting, or implementing various decisions?" (p. 471). Depending on the degree of segmentation, organizations may be described as tall or flat; visually, this is represented by the height of the pyramid (Dalton, Todor, Spendolini, Fielding, & Porter, 1980; Maguire, 2003). In the prosecutor's office shown in Figure 2.1, three supervisory levels are evident—the district attorney, deputy district attorney, and section chief—before reaching the rank-and-file prosecutor. The level of segmentation in organizations can also be compared. In Figure 2.2, for example, the Los Angeles Police Department's sworn ranks range from the police officer at the bottom to the chief at the organization's top, with five intermediate ranks (seven total levels). The Wichita Kansas Police Department is less complex, with a chain of command containing only six levels. In both departments, the chief possesses the greatest amount of formal authority, while the police officer possesses the least. Among all large police departments (100 or more full-time sworn officers), a survey conducted in 1996 revealed that agencies had between four and twelve command levels with a mean and median of six levels (Maguire, 2003).

---

[2] The terms *division of labor*, *complexity*, and *differentiation* are generally used interchangeably when referring to an organization's structure (Maguire, 2003).

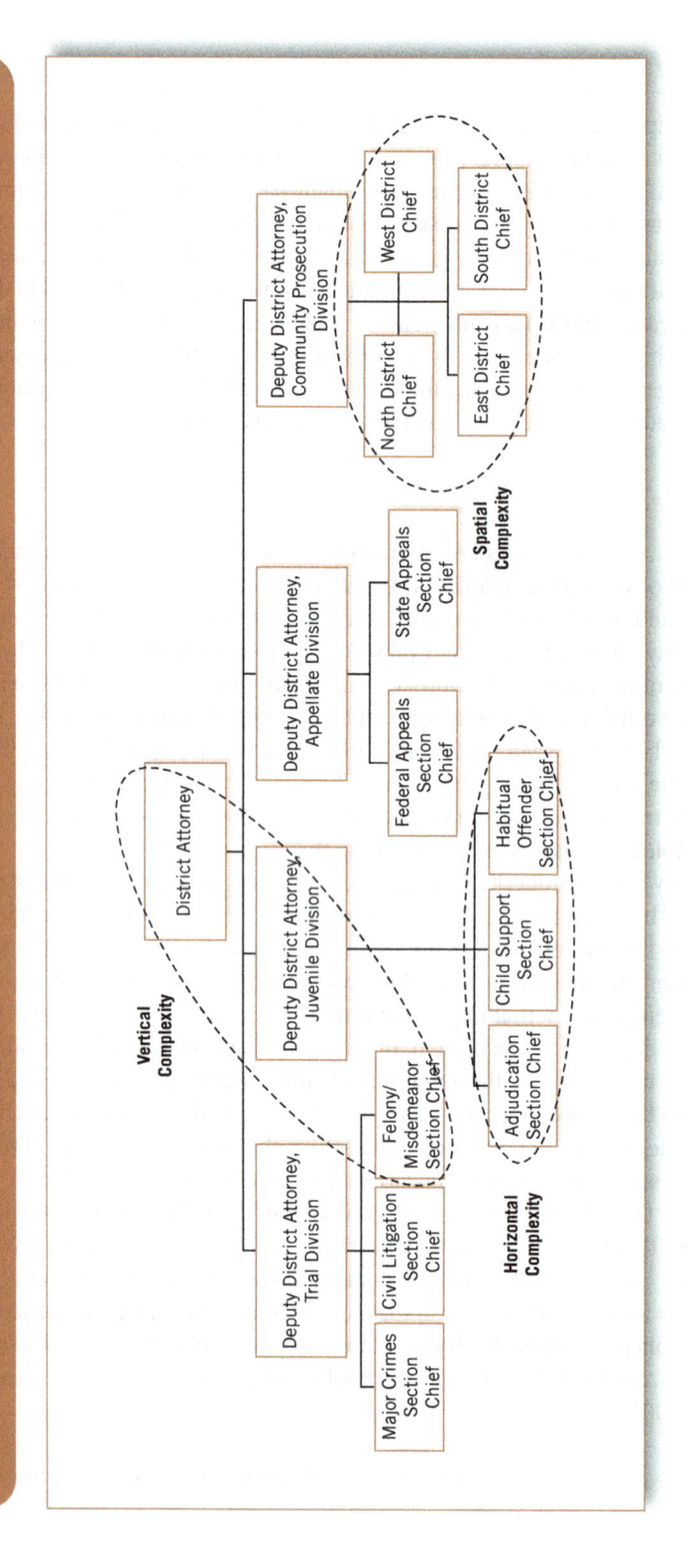

Figure 2.1 Simplified Organizational Chart of a Prosecutor's Office, Illustrating Three Dimensions of Organizational Complexity (Rank-and-File Prosecutors Omitted)

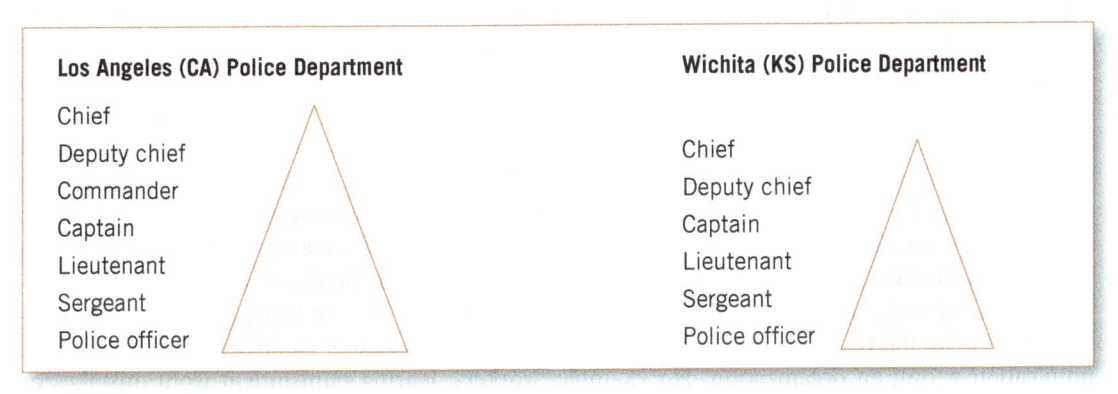

Figure 2.2 Vertical Complexity in Two Large U.S. Police Departments[1,2]

Los Angeles (CA) Police Department
Chief
Deputy chief
Commander
Captain
Lieutenant
Sergeant
Police officer

Wichita (KS) Police Department
Chief
Deputy chief
Captain
Lieutenant
Sergeant
Police officer

Source: Adapted from lapdonline.org and wichita.gov.

[1] Detectives are omitted; in most cases, it is a specialization rather than a hierarchical rank (Maguire, 2003).

[2] The shape of the hierarchy is simply for illustrative purposes and does not necessarily reflect the number of individuals at each rank level.

Beyond the complexity of the organization's chain of command, the shape of the pyramid—referred to as concentration—is employed to illustrate the number of employees at each vertical level within the organization (Kaufmann & Seidman, 1970; Langworthy, 1986; Maguire, 2003).[3] Some organizations have wide bases and narrow considerably toward the apex. These organizations devote most of their resources to direct service delivery rather than supervision and administration. In contrast, others are wider toward the middle and/or top of the pyramid with comparatively fewer employees at the base. In criticizing the vertical structure of some police departments, Kelling and Bratton (1993) argued, "Mid-management ranks are bloated in many departments; some have many captains and lieutenants without commands but serving as aides, often doing relatively menial work" (p. 2). Members of the New York correctional officers union, attempting to block prison closures, identified this same problem within the corrections department. They encouraged the elimination of management jobs (the upper portion of the pyramid) to preserve the jobs for the organization's base (Page, 2011a).

Vertical structures separate policy formation and supervisory responsibilities from the direct provision of the organization's services (e.g., law enforcement, custody, parole supervision, drug treatment; Nealey & Fiedler, 1968). The rank and file—the police, probation, or parole officer on the street; prosecutor in the courtroom; or correctional officer in an institutional setting—carry out the work under the direction of first-line supervisors. This supervision from above is the primary advantage of vertical complexity; "officers at the lowest rank receive their orders from (and report to) the next layer of the hierarchy (composed of sergeants, for example) and this second layer receives its orders from the next layer (e.g., lieutenants)" (King, 2003, p. 209). As shown in the example district attorney's office in Figure 2.1, the intermediate rank of deputy district attorney provides an added

[3] Some scholars use the width of the pyramid to represent the horizontal complexity of organizations, where a wider pyramid base indicates a greater level of functional differentiation within the organization (see Blau & Schoenherr, 1971). When focusing exclusively on the vertical dimension, the pyramid's shape represents the relative size of each level (Kaufmann & Seidman, 1970; Maguire, 2003).

layer of supervision between the section leaders and the elected district attorney. In the absence of this layer—if the organizational chart depicted two rather than three rank levels—the district attorney would be faced with the daunting task of supervising the work of 12 sections while also interacting with external constituents, including citizens, judges, bar members, and others. The introduction of the deputy district attorney level reduces the number of subordinates under the direction of the district attorney and enhances overall supervision.[4] As this example illustrates, the need for additional layers becomes more pronounced as the organization adds additional units or divisions and grows in size (Blau & Schoenherr, 1971). These vertical divisions generate a secondary benefit for the worker as well. In taller, more complex organizations, significant opportunities are available for advancement (see, for example, Dalton et al., 1980; Jacobs & Olitsky, 2004). Individual motivation may increase as workers seek organizational rewards such as pay, benefits, or status (King, 2003).

In spite of these benefits, tall structures may not always be more advantageous than flat structures. One potential issue is the negative influence of a lengthy chain of command on internal communication within an organization. For example, workers, fearing punishment from mistakes or wrongdoing, or reluctant to humiliate a superior by offering input, might refrain from informing supervisors of important matters (Hage, Aiken, & Marrett, 1971; Perrow, 1986). Communication distortion might also occur to benefit certain organizational members. Such was the case with team policing, a 1970s effort to simultaneously reduce crime and connect police with the communities they serve (Walker, 1993). More authority was granted to lower level workers, effectively limiting the power of employees at the middle of the organizational pyramid. Concerned about their loss of authority, middle managers spoke negatively about the reform and expressed their resistance to agency executives (Walker, 1993). Their efforts contributed to the eventual demise of team policing by the end of the decade.

Tall organizations may also adversely affect worker satisfaction and motivation. Perrow (1986) warned, "Subordinates are under constant surveillance from superiors; thus they often give up trying to exercise initiative or imagination" (p. 29). If this occurs, the worker suffers and the organization remains stuck in its current state with limited prospects for innovation. Finally, vertical complexity may reduce resource and staffing levels at the lowest levels of the organization, potentially disrupting service delivery (King, 2003). All else being equal (e.g., similar organizational size), taller organizations tend to employ fewer rank-and-file workers than flatter organizations. Vertically complex organizations, while comprising the same number of workers, locate a greater proportion of them in supervisory positions, resulting in fewer at the street level. Moreover, supervisory employees cost an organization more money than do the rank and file on a per-worker basis. Elaborate rank structures result in significant overhead costs, potentially siphoning away resources from the rank and file.

Horizontal Complexity

Horizontal complexity, indicated more precisely by the related concepts of occupational differentiation and functional differentiation, describes the extent to which the nonsupervisory tasks of the organization are subdivided into specific jobs and separate divisions. **Occupational differentiation**, or role specialization, occurs when the work is broken down into smaller parts and individuals are assigned to

---

[4]Vertical complexity is related to an organizational control strategy, span of control. This is discussed later in the section.

handle only their parts; the organization is making greater use of specialists who focus solely on their contribution to the whole (Child, 1972; Damanpour, 1996). When employees are responsible for completing all tasks rather than just a part of the whole, they are considered generalists rather than specialists, and the organization is less occupationally differentiated. Consider the adoption of community policing in municipal police agencies. If police leadership wanted to encourage police–community collaborations to improve neighborhood quality of life, it could structure the work in two ways. First, occupational differentiation could remain minimal. All police officers (a single discrete position or job title) would be instructed to engage in community policing–related activities. The officers, in this instance, are generalists who are responsible for the range of police activities, including both responding to 911 calls for service and engaging in community policing. The department could also create specialists and become more occupationally differentiated, as evident in both the Indianapolis and St. Petersburg police departments in the 1990s (Parks, Mastrofski, Dejong, & Gray, 1999). Another position—community police officer—would be created to address community policing responsibilities only. Community police officers are specialists in their assigned area, and the regular police officers are more specialized in their work as a result of having been absolved of community policing responsibilities. Falcone and Wells (1995) point out that the organization's size may shape the level of occupational differentiation. Sheriffs' departments serve law enforcement and corrections functions. In larger sheriffs' departments, separate workers perform the tasks; occupational differentiation is less pronounced in the smallest departments, where officers serve as generalists responsible for both functions.

In organizational research, occupational differentiation is measured in a number of different ways. Ideally, researchers would have at their disposal a count of the number of formal job titles (not the count of number of employees) as an indicator of specialization, with more job titles indicating a greater degree of differentiation/specialization. Blau and Schoenherr (1971), for example, obtained job title information from the state civil service commission. As an alternative, police scholars have routinely used civilianization, the percentage of the organization's employees that are nonsworn, as a measure of occupational differentiation (Maguire, 2003). Langworthy (1986) writes, "Meter maids are hired, relieving patrolmen of parking meter duties; clerks and dispatchers are hired, replacing sworn officers in records and communication sections; and finally, research, budget analysis, and other such staff functions are performed by specialists" (p. 65). Officers' responsibilities are narrowed and become more specialized as these new specialized positions are introduced.

These specialized workers are often functionally differentiated, grouped into identifiable units, departments, or divisions within the organization (Child, 1972; Damanpour, 1996; Robbins & Judge, 2008). Once specialists are grouped into separate divisions or departments, they operate under different chains of command. For example, rank-and-file workers in a prison or jail are not generalists, since the work of the facility is divided into security and treatment functions. Some employees may be specialists in the former, while others are specialists in the latter—an indication of occupational differentiation. The structure of the organization, however, might place treatment personnel in a separate department distinct from security personnel and under the supervision of a different deputy warden. The grouping of workers into units or departments represents *functional differentiation*—divisions based on job function (Langworthy, 1986; Maguire, 2003). Functional differentiation is visible on several levels in the example prosecutor's office depicted in Figure 2.1. The organization is split into four major divisions—trial, juvenile, appellate, and community prosecution—and, within each division, further subdivided into two or more sections.

The organization is supposed to benefit from the specialization resulting from functional and occupational differentiation. Employees are assigned to specific tasks and develop an expertise or proficiency by repeatedly handling only that task and developing a deep knowledge foundation on a narrow range of subjects. Some prosecutor's offices are organized horizontally, where attorneys handle only a part of a case (preliminary hearings only, trials only, appeals only) rather than the full case from beginning to end (Neubauer & Fradella, 2011). The individual prosecutor becomes adept at his or her specific function. From an organizational perspective, training in specialized areas is more efficient than training workers to become generalists (Robbins & Judge, 2008). Training each worker in every task is simply not necessary. Specialization is also related to organizational innovation, as the in-depth knowledge stimulates innovative ideas; occupational differentiation "provides a more diversified knowledge base and increases cross-fertilization of ideas, both of which result in more innovation" (Damanpour, 1996, p. 695).

Significant challenges emerge, however, when work is specialized at the individual or unit level. One concern is that these divisions, even if they are on the same level of the organization (see "Vertical Complexity" above), generate animosity, either by creating worker elites or by forming targets of contempt (Perrow, 1986). Workers may aspire to belong to certain special units (e.g., gang or drug enforcement group) or divisions (e.g., detectives/investigations) even though membership brings no additional authority in the organization. Nevertheless, a certain level of prestige is attached to these units. Other functional or occupational divisions produce the opposite effect; workers resist entering those units and frown on their members and/or work. Many police departments attempted to adopt community policing by establishing a special community policing unit. Although this structural arrangement might lead to the creation of elites, a typical finding was that community policing officers were the subject of ridicule by regular patrol officers who were unfamiliar with the reform. Community policing officers were referred to as social workers or "empty holster guys" who did not do real police work (Skogan & Hartnett, 1997).

Conflicts or turf battles are also possibilities as the organization becomes more horizontally complex. Divisions, units, and departments have different goals, different time orientations (long-term vs. short-term targets), and separate chains of command, all of which pose difficulties (Lawrence & Lorsch, 1967). For example, patrol officers, facing public outcry, may arrest a street dealer only to discover that the suspect was critical to a long-term investigation under way in the detective unit. The officers' more immediate, street-level goals did not match the detective unit's long-term focus on the drug network's leadership. Organizations must be aware of these divisions to assuage tensions and coordinate unit activities so goals are well understood.

Specialized organizations have also been criticized for being inflexible in the face of rapid changes. If personnel are so focused on their own isolated area, they may be unable to shift in times of need. The organization as a whole is, consequently, unable to adapt quickly. For example, the CIA would have had difficulty examining terrorist activities in Afghanistan in the late 1990s because, according to a former agent, it did not employ a case officer capable of speaking one of the major languages of the country (Zegart, 2007). This was true even after the bombings of two U.S. embassies in Africa in 1998 were tied to al Qaeda and Osama bin Laden. In spite of internal expertise in some areas, the agency simply could not shift experts to other areas rapidly. A similar situation could emerge in prosecutors' offices if attorneys were asked to see cases through from initial appearance to appeal. They may not be as proficient in some areas of prosecution as they are in their specialty. Generalists, in contrast, are much easier to shift because of their breadth of knowledge on a wider variety of organizational issues.

Spatial Complexity

The final dimension of complexity, spatial complexity, describes how an organization's parts are distributed geographically. Just as banks have branches and colleges and universities have satellite campuses, departments of corrections run separate facilities; police departments have districts, precincts, and beats; and probation and parole departments have field offices. Although "most researchers measure spatial complexity by counting the number of separate operating sites, subsidiary organizations, branch offices, or franchises," complexity is also indicated by the average distance from central headquarters/office to the operating sites and the proportion of employees working away from the central headquarters (Maguire, 2003, p. 16; see also Hall et al., 1967; Hendrick, 1997). Spatial divisions allow organizations to focus on local issues and concerns while increasing accessibility, but they also exacerbate communication and coordination challenges.

The FBI example that opened this section illustrated spatial complexity in a single federal law enforcement agency. Domestically, the FBI comprises 56 field offices beyond the central Washington, D.C., headquarters and, within these areas, operates several hundred resident offices in small cities and towns. Other federal law enforcement agencies have adopted similar field office/division structures, including the Bureau of Alcohol, Tobacco, Firearms, and Explosives (25 field divisions), U.S. Marshals Service (94 districts), and the Drug Enforcement Administration (21 divisions further subdivided into more than 200 district offices, resident offices, and duty posts). These boundaries guide matters related to the initiation of criminal investigations and the general area of focus but are malleable enough to allow for resource sharing or investigative efforts involving more than one office or division. In contrast, the spatial divisions in the federal judiciary are significant and less flexible, dictating the court's jurisdiction to hear particular cases. The Unites States is divided into 94 districts, and each state has one or more U.S. District Courts (federal trial courts). The courts are permitted to hear cases arising in their geographic area only. At the appellate level, the U.S. Courts of Appeals are organized into 12 geographic circuits—each a collection of federal districts—and hear appeals arising from district court cases.[5]

Spatial complexity is also clearly apparent at the state and local level. State corrections departments send inmates to facilities across their respective states. For example, Indiana's 2005 state prison population of 23,205 was distributed across 29 state facilities. Oklahoma, with a similar prison population of 25,149, exhibited a greater degree of spatial complexity, operating 53 correctional facilities across the state. South Dakota, with only 3,451 inmates in six facilities, operated the fewest institutions of any state (Stephan, 2008). A number of different spatial divisions characterize municipal policing, including the number of station houses/precincts and, within these larger areas, the number of patrol beats (Langworthy, 1986; Maguire, 2003). The New York City Police Department (NYPD) is divided into 76 police precincts located in the city's five boroughs. The Chicago Police Department, an organization about one third the size of the NYPD, is organized into 25 districts. At an even smaller geographic level, there is a tremendous amount of variation in the number of beats to which individual officers are assigned during their shifts. In his study of large police departments, Maguire (2003) reported that the average number of beats per department was 28, but the number ranged from 3 to 1,013.

Distributing the work of any organization, particularly criminal justice organizations, across geographic space increases the likelihood that the organization will address local concerns and respond with location-specific strategies. The increasingly geographic complexity in local prosecutors' offices over the past ten to fifteen years exemplifies the effort to deal with neighborhood problems. Historically,

---

[5] A 13th circuit exists but is not geographically based. The Court of Appeals hears cases with specific subject matter.

the prosecutor's office in most counties was centrally located in the county seat, within or in close proximity to the courthouse. This arrangement is still evident today, but with the development of community prosecution over the past two decades, the same offices became more geographically dispersed throughout a city and/or county (Coles, 2000). Community prosecutors direct their efforts toward solving community problems by developing partnerships with police departments, citizens, and other service providers, and employing a wide range of tools to improve neighborhood quality of life (Rainville & Nugent, 2002). Understanding problems and challenges and formulating solutions is critical, and one mechanism for accomplishing these goals is to spread prosecutors throughout the communities they serve by locating them in police district stations or neighborhood-based offices (Coles, 2000). In a pilot program in Washington, D.C., two prosecutors were placed within the Washington Metropolitan Police Department's Fifth District, where they "attended community meetings, responded to citizen quality-of-life complaints, facilitated cooperative efforts with city agencies, and provided onsite advice to Fifth District police officers" (Boland, 2001, p. 5). Overall, prosecutors' offices are less spatially differentiated compared with local police departments when the proportion of employees outside of headquarters is used as an indicator. Yet increasing spatial complexity is a considerable structural change for prosecutors' offices, organizations that have traditionally been centrally located.

Spatial complexity also facilitates access to an organization's services. Federal district courts, as noted earlier, are organized into 94 judicial districts of varying sizes. A citizen called to serve as a juror in federal district court in Oregon, for example, would potentially have to travel hundreds of miles if the only court were in the state's most populous city, Portland. Instead, the U.S. District Court for the District of Oregon spatially divides the work into four courthouses: Eugene, Medford, Portland, and Pendleton (the first three are along the state's more populous western border, while Pendleton is further inland). Police departments also attempt to create more accessible organizations by opening substations or storefront offices. Brown and Wycoff (1987) described a famous Houston Police Department fear-reduction effort involving, among other strategies, opening an office staffed by police officers in a local neighborhood. Residents were encouraged to stop in to pick up information or file reports; "the storefront was intended to enhance residents' sense of community and to give them the sense of being physically closer to their police" (p. 77). The substation was associated with reductions in citizen fear and perceptions of neighborhood crime. It should be noted, however, that the spatial complexity of criminal justice organizations has been used, at times, as leverage for crime control. In the late 1990s, officials in Richmond, Virginia, coordinated their activities to target firearms violators (Richman, 2001). Specifically, offenders were going to be prosecuted in federal court on federal charges to take advantage of tougher sentencing guidelines. Moreover, offenders would be sentenced to a facility in the Federal Bureau of Prisons, meaning that their sentence could be served at any Bureau of Prisons facility in the country. Stated differently, offenders were going to be exiled for long periods of time, potentially far away from families and home communities. In this instance, the spatial complexity in the federal prison system and the inaccessibility of many prisons contributed to the overall deterrence message.

The challenge, of course, with increasing spatial complexity is communicating and coordinating across geographic divisions. Precincts, field offices, divisions, substations, and other spatial divisions may promote their own interests while ignoring the needs of others or of the whole organization. Zegart's (2007) description of three FBI investigations in the months leading up to the 9/11 attacks illustrates this tendency; officials in each field office were concerned about their own investigations but neglected to communicate with other offices or see the larger picture. Similar information-sharing problems can emerge in other criminal justice organizations as well. Crime-related intelligence might not find its way across district boundaries within a police department or different facilities in a department of corrections.

Without this communication, coordinating organizational activities becomes difficult, if not impossible. The al Qaeda suspects sought by the New York field office immediately before the attacks were tracked by the CIA in 2000 after a meeting in Malaysia (a third tracked suspect, as Zegart notes, participated in the planning of the U.S.S. Cole bombing). The CIA's organizational structure relied on geographically located field offices, a structure that resulted in coordination difficulties:

> The Kuala Lumpur field office ran surveillance while the terrorists stayed in Malaysia. Bangkok ran the operation once it realized the terrorists had arrived in Thailand. Nobody, however, was responsible for managing the transition between these two offices or picking up the trail once it had been lost. (p. 103)

The problem is clear. The field offices were giving primacy to activities in their own countries but lost sight of the larger goal: tracking the suspects (Zegart, 2007, p. 103). These examples illustrate the significance of coordinating work once it is differentiated. Coordination and control are the focus of the next section.

Organizational Control

Complexity poses challenges for organizations. Ensuring that the separate parts, whether vertical, horizontal, or spatial, are working toward the achievement of organizational goals is critical. Steps must be taken to coordinate the organization members and the work they perform to avoid duplication of effort, communication difficulties, interdepartmental conflict, reduced employee motivation, substandard performance, and other problems. To address the difficulties created by increasing complexity, organizations institute a variety of control mechanisms (Hsu, Marsh, & Mannari, 1983; Maguire, 2003). Three structural dimensions influence the level of control in organizations—formalization, centralization, and the span of control.

Formalization

Formalization refers to the degree to which an organization and its members are guided by written rules and procedures intended to produce organizationally prescribed behavior (Dalton et al., 1980; Maguire, 2003). These rules and regulations address matters related to job descriptions and roles, authority relationships, communication channels, penalties for organizational misconduct, decision making, training, and a wide range of other topics (Hall et al., 1967). Formalized organizations are rule bound, where the presence of rules is designed to ensure uniformity in the work; if all workers comply with rules and procedures, the same outcomes will occur (Scott & Davis, 2007). Police officer responses to intimate partner violence, for example, can be standardized by enacting mandatory arrest policies. Consequently, the means by which officers resolve such situations will be determined by departmental rules and not the beliefs, attitudes, or experiences of the responding officer. Formalization is exemplified by written job descriptions, standard operating procedure manuals, and paperwork.

Formal job descriptions convey responsibilities and the boundaries of a position to employees. The standardization of roles provides "role definition and qualifications for [the position], role-performance measurement, titles for [the position] and symbols of role status, and rewards for role performance" (Pugh et al., 1963, p. 303). For example, a job announcement for a jailer in a county sheriff's department likely describes responsibilities such as maintaining security, enforcing jail regulations, conducting searches, meeting the daily needs of prisoners, booking new inmates, transporting inmates to and from court, and other jail-related responsibilities. The description defines the role of the jailer clearly. By excluding reference to tasks such as responding to 911 calls for service or making arrests, the jailer role is clearly distinguished from the law enforcement role of deputies. Each employee understands the responsibilities of his or her position, and duplication of work is avoided. Dalton and colleagues (1980) caution, however, that "although this written statement describes a certain behavior expected of persons in the classification, it does not in any way limit or prescribe procedures by which [employees] should fulfill this responsibility" (p. 58).

Organizations typically develop policies and procedures to direct workers on the actions they are required to, permitted to, or barred from taking in specific situations. Fyfe (1988) found that many police departments had adopted policies limiting police use of deadly force to situations involving defense of life, even before the Supreme Court formally limited police shootings of fleeing felons in 1985. The policies elsewhere removed what he termed "license," the ability of officers to use their own discretion in fleeing-felon situations, and created greater uniformity in officer behavior (Fyfe, 1987, p. 85). Not all organizations are equally formalized. A commonly used method for assessing formalization is to count the number of written policies pertaining to major topics within an organization. Police scholars have relied on results from the periodic Law Enforcement Management and Administrative Statistics survey to gauge formalization across departments. Law enforcement agency leaders answer questions about the existence of written policies in areas including deadly force, handling the mentally ill, off-duty employment, citizen complaints, and handling domestic disturbances (Maguire, 2003). Variation in the degree of formalization in police agencies can be seen in police pursuit policies. Some departments are more restrictive than others, limiting pursuits to specific offenses and/or weather and traffic conditions. Policies may also cap pursuit speeds or require the termination of pursuits in certain circumstances (e.g., after driver is identified) (Kenney & Alpert, 1997). When departments have fewer or less restrictive policies, they are less formalized and rely on the judgment of officers to engage in or terminate a pursuit as needed. These are just several examples of the many rules that guide organizations. Maguire (2003) cited an example of a state police agency with an inches-thick standard operating procedure manual; the range of policies in criminal justice organizations cover matters from the critical to the mundane.

Control is also achieved through the use of paperwork. In the parole office studied by McCleary (1992), officers were required to contact each parolee once per month. The officer's job description specified his or her supervision role, but formal departmental regulations dictated how to execute these duties. Compliance was ensured by requiring parole officers to submit monthly reports documenting visitation with parolees. Police officers are also required to fill out paperwork after use-of-force incidents to facilitate oversight. Alpert and MacDonald (2001) found that, in departments where a supervisor or someone other than the officer involved completed the use-of-force paperwork, use-of-force rates were lower than in departments where the officer involved completed the paperwork. The inclusion of supervisors or others in the process added a layer of accountability absent in departments where officers complete the forms on their own. Annual performance reviews also serve the purpose of motivating employees and encouraging desired behaviors.

Codifying appropriate behaviors, particularly successful ones, prevents the organization from having to proverbially "reinvent the wheel" each time a similar situation is encountered. Excessive formalization, however, is prohibitive and perhaps undesirable. Crafting rules to cover all situations is impossible, and attempts to formalize may reduce the organization's flexibility. The grounding of aircraft in the hours after the 9/11 terrorist attacks illustrates the need to retain some degree of flexibility. Air traffic controllers were given the unprecedented responsibility of directing thousands of airplanes out of the sky as government officials tried to grasp the extent of the terrorist plot. In a matter of hours, controllers were able to land all aircraft at airports throughout the United States and in neighboring countries. There was no rulebook to guide controllers since there had never been a need to ground all aircraft. A review of air traffic controllers afterward led to the conclusion that the controllers' judgment, not rules, led to the safe landing of all aircraft; rules might have served only as obstructions, and formalizing procedures in the event of a similar situation in the future is inadvisable (Fine & Marabella, 2005). Rules may be valuable for limiting discretionary decision making, but most criminal justice employees work in dynamic, unpredictable environments where behavior cannot be reduced to rules.

Excessive formalization is predicated on the assumption that rules are superior to employee judgment and discretion. This is a questionable assumption. Fogelson (1977) equated policing to other professions; "like doctors, lawyers, teachers, and engineers, policemen were expected to meet high admission standards, undergo extensive training, serve their clients, devote themselves to the public interest, subscribe to a code of ethics, and possess a wide range of extraordinary skills" (p. 155). To the extent that many criminal justice occupations—prosecutors, defense attorneys, probation and parole officers, corrections officers—fit this description, there appears to be a tension between professional judgment and rules. Well-trained, well-educated, ethical employees should make appropriate decisions even without the threat of sanctions associated with rule breaking. Consequently, formalization potentially has severe repercussions for employee motivation and commitment to the workplace. Ultimately, a balance must be struck between defining roles and also maintaining worker well-being (Dalton et al., 1980).

Centralization

The structural dimension of **centralization** deals with the location in the organization where important decisions are made. Key decisions relate to matters such as personnel/staffing, money and other resources, equipment, policy formation, work assignments, employee evaluation and discipline, and other significant matters (Pugh et al., 1963). A maximum degree of centralization is evident in organizations where a single individual, usually at the top of the organizational chart (see "Vertical Complexity" above), makes all important decisions with little input from subordinates. Centralization produces uniformity, as decisions made at the top are applicable to the entire organization. Accountability is also established since the decisions are the product of only one or a small number of individuals (Carlson, 1999). In contrast, "the minimum degree of centralization (decentralization) would exist in an organization if decision-making authority were exercised equally by every member of the organization" (Dalton et al., 1980, p. 59). In practice, the level of centralization falls somewhere along a continuum and varies according to the nature of the decision. A department of corrections director, for example, might retain decision-making authority over matters related to prison expansion or construction, but day-to-day operations of individual facilities are pushed down the chain of command to the warden level. The degree of centralization is often measured by asking organization respondents where in an organization (at what level) certain decisions are made (Maguire, 2003).

The NYPD's Compstat strategy provides a useful illustration of the concept of centralization. Compstat and similar performance systems in other cities linked police data and police tactics in an effort to reduce crime (Behn, 2008; Walsh, 2001). At the same time, operational leaders—precinct commanders in New York City—were held accountable for the problems in their areas. It was their responsibility to address crime and disorder. Recall from the earlier discussion that the existence of precincts indicated greater spatial differentiation in the NYPD. This is not the same as saying the leaders of those precincts were in control; upper-level command staff could have retained decision-making authority over precinct activities. Instead, the NYPD decentralized authority to these district commanders to give them the freedom to implement effective strategies (Willis, Mastrofski, & Weisburd, 2007). For example, leaders were given authority to call on and employ special units (e.g., gang units) as necessary, a change from the prior situation where units operated independently of district commanders. By giving precinct commanders operational authority, they are able to make rapid decisions without having to move up the chain of command. They are also better situated to understand the needs of their area than more distant top management.

The decentralization of decision-making authority under the Compstat model appears, however, to be more a conceptual element than an operational reality. Weisburd, Mastrofski, McNally, Greenspan, and Willis (2003) surveyed more than 400 large police departments in an effort to understand the diffusion of Compstat throughout the law enforcement industry. They found that operational commanders (e.g., a precinct or district commander) were granted authority to identify strategies to address area problems. Yet the level of decentralization did not generally permit commanders to determine shift-staffing levels or redraw beat boundaries. Authority to make these decisions was left to top management. There were clearly limits to the power granted from upper administration to mid-level managers. Department executives were less likely to relinquish control of operations they historically retained.

As with other dimensions of structure, centralization also has implications for the individual worker. When authority is dispersed to lower levels of the organizational hierarchy (decentralized), workers tend to be more motivated, to be satisfied with their work, to take a greater ownership stake in their efforts, and to communicate more frequently (Carlson, 1999; Cummings & Berger, 1976; Porter & Lawler, 1965). At the same time, decentralization may result in inconsistent decision making and increased training costs (Carlson, 1999).

Span of Control

A third method to control the work is to increase the potency of supervision. This is accomplished by altering the organization's **span of control**, the number of subordinates working under the direction of each supervisor. However, an organization rarely maintains the same ratio of supervisors to subordinates throughout the organization:

> Span of control refers to the ratio of supervisors (at one level) to the number of workers (at the next lower level). This indicator differs from one rank layer to the next and the ratio is usually smaller near the top of the rank structure hierarchy than at the bottom. (King, 2005, p. 102)

As the number of subordinates per supervisor increases, the span of control widens; as the number decreases, the span of control narrows. Span of control is inextricably linked to vertical complexity. Holding constant the number of rank-and-file employees, narrowing the span of control increases the number of levels in the hierarchy (see Figure 2.3).[6] A central issue in organizational studies is the appropriate span of control for accomplishing organizational tasks (Bohte & Meier, 2001; Dias & Vaughn, 2006).

---

[6]If the number of employees is held constant, vertical complexity will also increase by taking away workers from the rank-and-file bottom level.

Figure 2.3 Contrasting Spans of Control

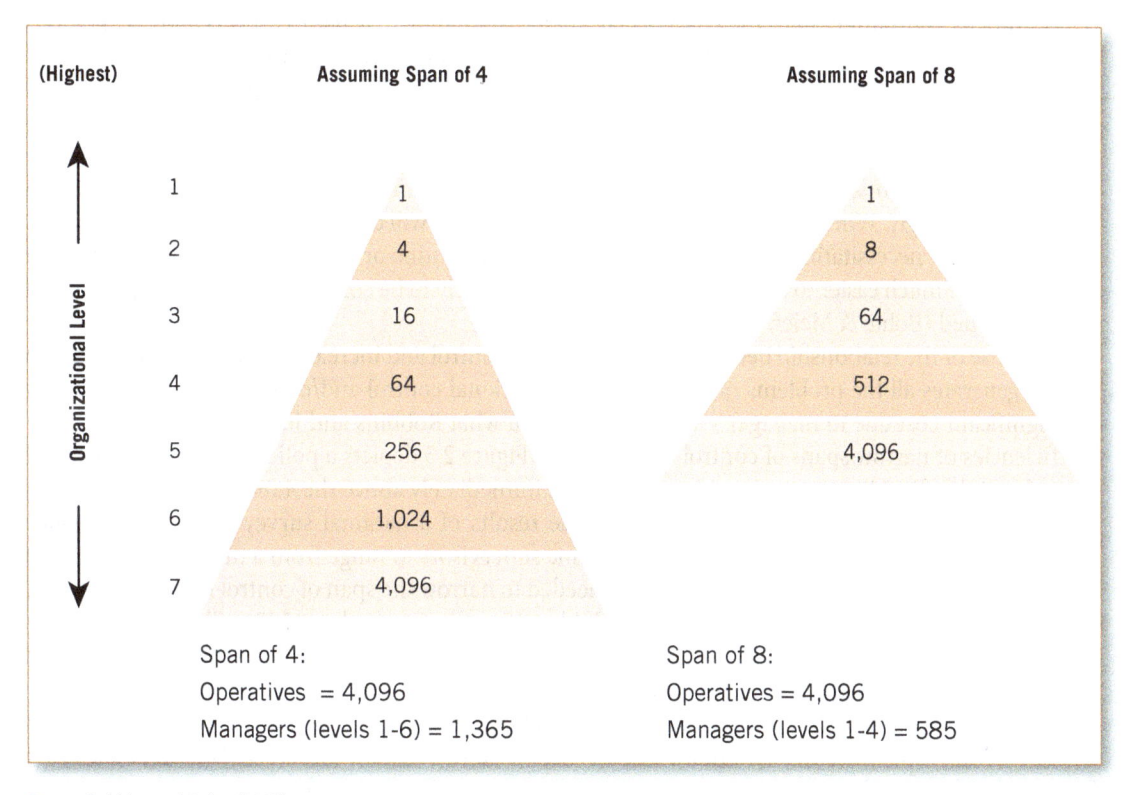

Organizational Level (Highest →)	Assuming Span of 4	Assuming Span of 8
1	1	1
2	4	8
3	16	64
4	64	512
5	256	4,096
6	1,024	
7	4,096	

Span of 4:
Operatives = 4,096
Managers (levels 1–6) = 1,365

Span of 8:
Operatives = 4,096
Managers (levels 1–4) = 585

Source: Robbins and Judge (2008).

A narrow span of control is geared toward more intensive supervision and control. The Federal Bureau of Prisons designates correctional institutions according to security level (minimum, low, medium, and high), where the staff-to-inmate ratio increases (span of control decreases) as the security level increases (Federal Bureau of Prisons, n.d.). In the more than 50 supermax prisons in the United States, single inmates, housed in the facility due to serious-offense convictions or for administrative punishments, are transported by teams of correctional officers (Briggs, Sundt, & Castellano, 2003; Mears & Watson, 2006). Probation officer caseloads, often exceeding 100 probationers per officer, are also narrowed periodically when departments implement intensive supervision programs; the extra control afforded by the narrower span of control has been linked to reduced recidivism and lower community crime rates more generally (Worrall, Schram, Hays, & Newman, 2004). Among organization employees, a narrow span of control also provides direction and ensures compliance with organizational directives. The supervisor's influence is greater over a smaller pool of subordinates (Dias & Vaughn, 2006).

Evidence suggests that a narrow span of control is necessary when the work is complex and unpredictable (Bell, 1967). In supermax prisons, maintaining security of the facility is more complex given the level of dangerousness of many of the inmates and the prevalence of mental illness (Mears & Watson, 2006). What might be considered simple tasks (e.g., transporting prisoners) are fraught with risk. The complexity of the work requires significantly more control in the form of a lower staff-to-inmate ratio.

In contrast, the work in minimum security facilities is more routine and predictable. Offenders are less prone to violence, and the activities of the prison allow for a higher ratio. Langworthy (1986) describes police work as nonroutine, since the types of calls for service handled by patrol officers and the methods officers employ to restore order are not standardized or predictable. Officers must exercise discretion and use their own judgment to address problems of crime and disorder. The narrowing of the span of control may have less to do with increasing control of lower level employees and more to do with increasing communication in the organization's hierarchy (Meyer, 1968). That is, plans of action developed by police officers (or prosecutors, probation or parole officers, or others) can be discussed with supervisors and adjusted accordingly. When situations are complex, subordinates will draw on the counsel of supervisors more frequently, necessitating a narrower span of control. In routine or predictable situations, rules and procedures are much easier to develop, supervisors are less likely to be consulted, and the span of control can be widened (Bohte & Meier, 2001).

Because of the relationship between narrow spans of control and increasing vertical complexity, the former generates all the problems of the latter. The additional control and/or advisory capacity comes at a significant cost due to manager salaries, resulting in what Robbins and Judge (2008) regard as the inefficiencies of narrow spans of control. Suppose that Figure 2.3 depicts a police organization's span of control and that first-line supervisors (sergeants) are immediately above the 4,096 rank-and-file workers in both pyramids. Reaves (2010), reporting the results of a national survey of municipal police leaders, found typical or average salaries for first-line supervisors to range from a minimum of $46,000 to a maximum of $53,500. If 512 sergeants were needed to narrow the span of control from eight to four, the change would produce an additional financial burden of between about $23 million and $27 million. Of course, this figure excludes supervisors at the middle- and top-management ranks, which would produce additional resource demands.

In addition to the financial costs of narrow spans of control, the extra supervision potentially stifles the individual initiative and morale of workers used to constant direction (Dalton et al., 1980; Porter & Lawler, 1965). Both community and problem-oriented policing, for example, advocate measured risk taking by officers in developing innovative solutions to neighborhood problems (Williams, 2003; Zhao, Thurman, & Lovrich, 1995). Excessive control and fear of discipline might discourage such risk taking, leading officers to resort to traditional and typical law enforcement responses (e.g., arrest). It is here, where creativity and innovation are called for, that the supervisor's role as counselor and advisor might be most important (Williams, 2003). While some suggest that spans of control of between four and six subordinates are ideal (Porter & Lawler, 1965; Robbins & Judge, 2008), a perfect number likely depends on a multitude of factors (e.g., the routineness of the task). The real challenge is striking a sufficient balance between effective supervision and organizational efficiency/worker initiative.

Organizational Structure and Criminal Organizations

So far, the focus has been on the organizational structures of criminal justice organizations; examples from policing, courts, and corrections were used to illustrate six key structural dimensions. The same concepts can be applied to illegal organizations. Understanding the structure of illegal organizations such as terrorist groups, gangs, or drug distribution networks may lead to more effective enforcement strategies.

For example, researchers have noted the tendency of criminal organizations to operate according to a set of rules. Decker, Katz, and Webb (2008) found that roughly half of the gang members they surveyed indicated that their gang had a set of rules. Moreover, most reported that punishments were meted out if those rules were violated. Rules were also evident in illegal gambling (numbers games) organizations, particularly in how bets were made and transactions processed (Southerland & Potter, 1993). Unlike lawful criminal justice organizations, however, these illegal organizations did not rely on a *written* set of rules. Instead, conformity to the organization's rules emerged through socialization and indoctrination of new members (Southerland & Potter, 1993).[7] Organization structure concepts also extend into the area of white-collar crime. Structural arrangements present challenges for law enforcement officials investigating wrongdoing. McKendall and Wagner (1997) hypothesize that decentralized organizations are at a greater risk for corporate crime because many people are given decision-making power, leading to "the abdication of personal responsibility" (p. 627). Similarly, when organizations are horizontally complex, many individuals or units are tasked with creating the final product or service (Dugan & Gibbs, 2009). Consequently, law enforcement officials will have a tough time determining the specific person or persons responsible for illegal conduct (Dugan & Gibbs, 2009).

Knowledge of organizational structure is also important in the study of terrorist organizations. Scholar Marc Sageman argued that the most significant present-day threat of terrorism emerges not from a centralized group of al Qaeda members operating in places such as Afghanistan and Pakistan but, rather, from groups of disconnected terrorist groups operating within target countries such as the United States (Sageman & Hoffman, 2008). His work met opposition from Bruce Hoffman, another scholar, who believes that al Qaeda leadership (and leadership of all other terrorist groups for that matter) coordinates terrorist activities (Hoffman, 2008; Picarelli, 2009; Sciolino & Schmitt, 2008). The centralized terrorist leadership, according to Hoffman, initiates attack plans, provides support, and issues directives to other groups (Picarelli, 2009). Much of the Sageman-Hoffman debate addresses the issue of organizational structure. Hoffman's argument illustrates centralized coordination mechanisms, where key leaders devise plans and make important operational decisions. The command hierarchy is evident, with individuals such as Osama bin Laden (before his death in 2011) and Ayman al Zawahiri controlling other al Qaeda members. In Sageman's argument, small terrorist groups make their own decisions independent of the centralized al Qaeda leadership. The organization is neither centralized nor hierarchically structured. As Dugan and Gibbs (2009) pointed out, "Decentralized structures make the organization more flexible, adaptive, and resilient since each unit acts on its own behalf being only loosely connected to the others" (p. 118).

This debate has significant consequences for enforcement and counterterrorism efforts. If, for example, Hoffman's position is correct, antiterrorism efforts will focus on activities such as terrorist training occurring overseas. Removing the centralized leadership might be sufficient to destroy the overall organization (Dugan & Gibbs, 2009). If Sageman's position is accurate, law enforcement must direct their efforts domestically, preventing the independent groups from forming in the first place and ensuring that they do not succeed in carrying out their attacks (Picarelli, 2009).

This section has described the major structural features of organizations, both legal and illegal. It should be clear, at this point, that organizational structures vary across different agencies, even within the same industry. Some organizations may be tall, specialized, and geographically dispersed, while others may be flat, less specialized, and centrally located. The question is, given the advantages and disadvantages of various structural arrangements, how is this variation explained? This is the focus of the next section.

---

[7]The same type of socialization occurs in criminal justice agencies (see Section VII).

KEY TERMS

centralization	functional differentiation	segmentation
complexity	horizontal complexity	span of control
concentration	occupational differentiation	spatial complexity
formalization	organizational structure	vertical complexity

DISCUSSION QUESTIONS

1. In his history of 20th-century policing, Fogelson (1977) writes, "Like doctors, lawyers, teachers, and engineers, policemen were expected to meet high admission standards, undergo extensive training, serve their clients, devote themselves to the public interest, subscribe to a code of ethics, and possess a wide range of extraordinary skills" (p. 155). Yet police organizations (and other criminal justice organizations) tend to be formalized. Is it possible to consider police officers as professionals like lawyers or doctors even though they are in highly rule-bound organizations such as police departments?

2. In many organizations—manufacturing plants, retail establishments, and other private-sector organizations—supervisors are located where the organization's work is performed. In criminal justice organizations such as police departments and probation and parole agencies, the work is performed away from and out of view of immediate supervisors. Given that direct supervision becomes more difficult, is increasing vertical complexity and narrowing the span of control likely to influence the level of supervision appreciably? Explain.

3. In your opinion, should probation officers be specialists, assigned caseloads comprising similar offenders (e.g., only domestic violence offenders, only property offenders), or generalists, assigned caseloads with a mix of offender types? Explain.

WEB RESOURCES

Intelligence Community site (with agency descriptions and career information):
http://www.intelligence.gov

U.S. Department of Homeland Security Organizational Chart (with descriptions of and links to agency websites):
http://www.dhs.gov/xabout/structure/editorial_0644.shtm

Chicago Police Department map of areas, districts, and beats (spatial complexity):
http://gis.chicagopolice.org/pdfs/district_beat.pdf

How to Read a Research Article

"The Impact of Centralization and Formalization on Correctional Staff Job Satisfaction and Organizational Commitment" (Lambert, Paoline, & Hogan, 2006)

1. What is the thesis or main idea in this article?

The thesis of the article is evident in the first paragraph when the authors state, "Centralization and formalization are two major forms of organizational structure found in most organizations, and they both impact job satisfaction and commitment. These, in turn, impact not only the employee, but also the employing organization" (p. 24). In other words, these features of an organization's structure have a significant bearing on the workplace by influencing the attitudes of the individual worker.

2. What is the hypothesis?

The central thesis suggests only that centralization and formalization influence worker attitudes. The hypothesis establishes a specific prediction about the expected relationships between the structural factors (centralization and formalization) and worker outcomes (job satisfaction and organizational commitment). A clear hypothesis is evident in the second paragraph of the "Research Questions" section: "It was predicted that both high level forms of centralization (i.e., low level of input into decision-making and job autonomy) would have negative effects on correctional officer job satisfaction and organizational commitment" (p. 30). No hypothesis was offered related to formalization, likely due to the fact that no prior research exists examining its effects on correctional staff attitudes.

3. Is there any prior literature related to the hypothesis?

Lambert, Paoline, and Hogan provide a literature review section, addressing centralization and formalization in separate subsections within the article. The review provides conceptual definitions, reviews the effects of structure on noncorrectional workers, and concludes by discussing its effects on correctional workers. The review moves from the general (definitions) to the specific (application to the correctional worker).

4. What methods are used to support the hypothesis?

The authors addressed their research question by surveying employees at a Midwestern maximum-security prison for adult males. They received surveys from 272 respondents, roughly 60% to 68% of the employees within the facility. Survey items addressed issues related to the worker's background (e.g., demographic characteristics), perceptions of the organization's structure (e.g., amount of input into decision making), job satisfaction, and organizational commitment.

5. Is this a qualitative study or a quantitative study?

You can determine the type of study by examining both the research methods and results section. In the present study, the authors employed a survey to gather data (see "Methods" section). This alone does not tell us whether the study is qualitative or quantitative. Correctional employees could be instructed to provide narrative responses to survey items and those items presented in narrative form within the article (qualitative). Alternatively, they could be instructed to mark items that are converted to numerical scores and later analyzed using statistical techniques (quantitative). The results section makes it clear that this was a quantitative study. The authors present statistics describing the number of respondents providing each answer and statistically assess the relationship between key variables.

6. What are the results, and how does the author present the results?

The results are presented in both tabular and narrative forms within the "Results" section, and the findings are restated at the beginning of the "Discussion and Conclusion" section. As the authors note, three main findings from their study are as follows: Increased centralization led to a decrease in job satisfaction and organizational commitment; increased formalization led to a decrease in organizational commitment and, in one model, job satisfaction; and individual characteristics (e.g., age, education) play little role in shaping job satisfaction and organizational commitment.

7. Do you believe that the authors provided a persuasive argument? Why or why not?

The reader must determine whether the evidence provided is persuasive enough to be convincing. The findings are consistent with expectations derived from those found in settings outside of corrections. If the authors had uncovered unusual or widely divergent findings that contradicted much of the existing body of literature, the reader would be wise to raise additional questions. The authors also do not overstate their findings. The "Discussion and Conclusion" section clearly frames the findings within a set of limitations (e.g., a single prison was studied; a limited measure of formalization was used). Thus, the findings are useful as a foundation for future research and as part of a larger body of scholarship.

8. Who is the intended audience of this article?

As the authors were writing this article, whom do you suppose they had in mind as their target reader? In some cases, scholarly journals such as *Criminal Justice Studies,* the original outlet of this article, are used to communicate research findings among scholars, researchers, and practitioners. That said, we might more specifically say that organization administrators could benefit from the findings presented in the article.

9. What does the article add to your knowledge of the subject?

The reader will have to determine how the article contributes to his or her own knowledge base. Clearly, the authors saw a gap within the existing organizational theory/corrections literature. Few scholars had examined the influence of centralization and formalization on job satisfaction and organizational commitment among correctional officers. They sought to fill this void.

10. What are the implications for criminal justice policy that can be derived from this article?

Authors are most likely to describe the implications of their findings in a discussion or conclusion section. It is here that they convey the substantive importance of the research, moving beyond just knowing for the sake of knowing. The findings point to changes in organizational structure for the benefit of the employee and the overall organization: "Correctional administrators should share power with employees, especially input into decision-making, including formalization issues and procedures" (p. 40).

READING

Reading 1

Centralization and formalization are two dimensions of organizational structure intended to control the work of employees. As this section suggests, the control may come at a price for the individual worker. Eric G. Lambert, Eugene A. Paoline III, and Nancy Lynne Hogan empirically examine the effects of both centralization and formalization on two employee-related attitudes—job satisfaction and organizational commitment.

Satisfaction addresses the degree to which people like the work they do, while commitment measures a worker's attachment to the organization itself. After studying 272 correctional staff members (e.g., officers, medical staff, and food-service workers) from a single Midwestern maximum-security facility, the authors concluded that correctional employee satisfaction and job commitment suffer when the organization is overly centralized and formalized. When the organizations exert more control via centralization and formalization, workers are not afforded input into key decisions, lack control over their own work, and are governed by written rules and procedures. The effects of centralization on satisfaction and commitment were similar for a subsample of only correctional officers. However, formalization influenced only job commitment and exerted no significant or consistent effect on job satisfaction. The authors argue that formalization might adversely affect job satisfaction for some officers but lead to greater satisfaction for others, as their role is clarified through formalization.

THE IMPACT OF CENTRALIZATION AND FORMALIZATION ON CORRECTIONAL STAFF JOB SATISFACTION AND ORGANIZATIONAL COMMITMENT

An Exploratory Study

Eric G. Lambert, Eugene A. Paoline III, and Nancy Lynne Hogan

Prisons are complex, public organizations, and, thus, there are many different ways to structure, organize, and run them. Nevertheless, the vast majority of prisons in the USA are run as paramilitary, bureaucratic organizations. Centralization, rules, and chains of command are often enforced with a passion. Most prisons try to structure the work environment in order to control the behaviors of employees, especially negative behaviors. Many wardens speak of an employee that will "fit" into their organization. Few discuss how the organization impacts the occupational functioning of the employee, and fewer seriously consider how to improve the work environment. Based upon a nationwide survey of prison wardens, McShane and Williams (1993) concluded that most wardens "believed in participatory management styles yet preferred to keep decisions and authority close at hand while keeping line officers removed from the policy process" (p. 52). Like most complex organizations, for prisons to run smoothly, it helps to have satisfied, committed staff. How a prison is structured can impact the job satisfaction and organizational commitment of employees (Agarwal, 1993). Centralization and formalization are two major forms of organizational structure found in most large

Source: Lambert, E. G., Paoline, E. A., & Hogan, N. L. (2006). The impact of centralization and formalization on correctional staff job satisfaction and organizational commitment: An exploratory study. *Criminal Justice Studies* 19(1), 23–44.

organizations, and they both impact job satisfaction and organizational commitment. These, in turn, impact not only the employee, but also the employing organization.

Job satisfaction is an affective/emotional response by an employee concerning his or her particular job (Cranny, Smith, & Stone, 1992). Basically, it is "the extent to which people like their jobs" (Spector, 1996, p. 214). In the correctional literature, job satisfaction has been linked to positive work outcomes, such as greater support for rehabilitation (Kerce, Magnusson, & Rudolph, 1994) and compliance with organizational rules and goals (Fox, 1982). Conversely, low levels of job satisfaction have been linked to negative work behaviors and intentions among correctional staff, such as burnout, absenteeism, turnover intent, and turnover (Jurik & Winn, 1987; Lambert, 1999; Whitehead & Lindquist, 1986; Wright, 1993). As such, administrators should be concerned about job satisfaction, because its consequences are significant.

Organizational commitment is generally defined as having the core elements of loyalty to the organization, identification with the organization (i.e., pride in the organization and internalization of organizational goals), and involvement in the organization (i.e., personal effort made for the sake of the organization) (Mowday, Porter, & Steers, 1982). "Organizational commitment is a bond to the whole organization, and not to the job, work group, or belief in the importance of work itself" (Lambert, Barton, & Hogan, 1999, p. 100). Organizational commitment has been linked to positive correctional staff behaviors, such as higher levels of job performance (Culliver, Sigler, & McNeely, 1991), and inversely linked with negative correctional staff behaviors, such as absenteeism and turnover (Camp, 1994; Lambert, 1999; Stohr, Self, & Lovrich, 1992).

Because both job satisfaction and organizational commitment are important in terms of the occupational well being of employees, the current study examines factors that shape both. More specifically, this research focuses on the impact of two structural components of organizations (i.e., centralization and formalization) on correctional staff job satisfaction and organizational commitment.

Classical and Behavioral Schools: Two Competing Thoughts of Organizations

Max Weber probably had the greatest impact on the classical viewpoint (Heffron, 1989). Weber wrote about the concept of modern bureaucracy as a structured, highly efficient organization. Weber pointed out that bureaucracies generally have the following four general characteristics: (1) Routinization—do things according to a master plan so valuable resources will not be wasted when the same issue appears again and again. (2) Written rules or formalization—rules and procedures are spelled out beforehand in writing. (3) Division of labor and expertise—to be broken down by function and specialization. Staff are very limited in their areas of expertise. (4) Hierarchy of authority—the need to control people to ensure the work is done properly.

The Behavioral (i.e., Human Relations) school was developed, in part, to counter the perceived coldness and indifference to employees that many observed in the Classical approach. The Behavioral school postulated that the social and psychological needs of employees have to be met for the organization to be healthy and productive, and the best way to do this is to structure the employing organization in an open, supportive, nonrestrictive way. Specifically, the organization should be decentralized in which employees have more say over their jobs and decision-making in the organization. "The Classical authors demanded centralization in the name of control and coordination. The Behavioral authors insisted on decentralization to give more members a greater sense of control over their destinies" (Fry, 1989, p. 5). Thus, the human relations school advocated a more decentralized structure with fewer rules and restrictions.

It is interesting to note that elements of each of these schools of thought are reflected within prison organizations today. The Classical approach is still alive and well within many prisons. Many prisons are run as paramilitary, bureaucratic organizations. However, not all wardens take the Classical approach. The administrators of some prison organizations value and discuss job satisfaction and organizational commitment of staff as well as the effects of the work environment on staff. These wardens are more aligned with the Behavioral school. In both the correctional literature and in the corrections field, there is an ongoing debate about how to best structure correctional organizations. Thus, there is certainly a need for more research in this area.

Literature Review

According to Lincoln and Kalleberg (1990), every organization uses several dimensions of structure to control and influence employee bonds to the organization such as centralization, formalization, specialization, financial rewards, integration, legitimacy (i.e., fairness in terms of workload, rewards, and punishment), promotion, and so forth. Although it is acknowledged that many structural components comprise organizations, two of the more widely cited concepts outside the field of corrections, centralization and formalization, were examined in this study.

Centralization

Centralization is how power is distributed within an organization (Andrews & Kacmar, 2001). As Tobin (2001, p. 95) notes, "Centralization refers to power and the location, division, and amount of decision-making power throughout an organization." There are two levels of centralization (Dewar, Whetten, & Boje, 1980; Wright, Salyor, Gilman, & Camp, 1997). The first is the degree of input that is permitted among employees in shaping and guiding the future of the organization. This type of centralization is frequently referred to in the literature as the degree of input into decision-making. The second type of centralization is the degree that an employee has control and input over the tasks and order of his/her job. In the literature this form of centralization is frequently referred to as the degree of job autonomy. High levels of both represent a decentralized organization, while low levels of both represent a highly centralized organization.

The Classical school argues that an organization should be a structured hierarchy (Fry, 1989), emphasizing executive decision-making responsibilities, with little, if any, power given to staff. It is argued by some that prisons perform such a critical mission to society that tight controls are needed to ensure success. In order to do this, employee discretion must be minimized by tight organizational control (DiIulio, 1987; Wright et al., 1997).

On the other hand, the Behavioral school argues for power to be vested throughout the organization, including line staff (Fry, 1989). This view is also supported in the correctional literature. Jurik and Musheno (1986) point out that in order to increase the professionalization of correctional staff, not only should more educated and trained staff be recruited, but also that the staff be allowed to have more power within the organizational structure through participation in decision-making. "Professionalization requires a management style that promotes far greater participation of line personnel in decision-making, particularly decisions related to the fundamentals of client relations and services" (Jurik & Musheno, 1986, p. 477). The Behavioral school further argues that highly centralized and formalized structures cause employees to become dissatisfied and uncommitted (Organ & Greene, 1982). "It is assumed by proponents of this [human relations] school that employees who are not hindered by strict control and who are allowed to participate in management decisions will be satisfied workers who will be committed to the organization" (Berkson & Hays, 1977, p. 83). There is some support for this postulation in the non-criminal justice literature as well as the correctional literature.

It appears among non-correctional employees, levels of input into decision-making are positively linked to levels of job satisfaction. More specifically, low levels of decision-making input are associated with low levels of job satisfaction, and conversely high levels of input into decision-making are associated with high levels of job satisfaction (Jermier & Berkes, 1979; Kakabadse & Worrall, 1978). Locke and Schweiger (1979) concluded, from a review of the literature, that there is strong evidence that employee participation in decision-making (i.e., decentralization) increases job satisfaction.

Based upon the non-correctional literature, there also appears to be a significant relationship between lack of job autonomy and job satisfaction (Finlay, Martin, Roman, & Blum, 1995; Wycoff & Skogan, 1994). Poulin (1994) concluded, 'Workers who have influence over decisions affecting their jobs and who are given flexibility in carrying out their job tasks tend to have higher levels of job satisfaction than those with less professional autonomy' (p. 35). While a few studies have found no significant relationship between lack of decision-making input and lack of job autonomy (i.e., centralization) and job satisfaction (Curry, Wakefield, Price, & Mueller, 1986; Mueller, Boyer, Price, & Iverson, 1994), the bulk of non-correctional studies suggests that there is a negative relationship for centralization (i.e., low levels of input into decision-making and job autonomy) and job satisfaction.

In the correctional literature, decentralization has also received attention in terms of staff job satisfaction. Using data from Arizona correctional staff, Hepburn and Knepper (1993) found that intrinsic job rewards/aspects (e.g., job autonomy and an opportunity to use one's skills) were positively related to job satisfaction. In a study of employees in the Kentucky Department of Corrections, Dennis (1998) reported that empowerment had a positive effect on job satisfaction. Hepburn (1987) found among correctional officers in prisons across four states that the perception of the ability to influence the prison structure was positively related to job satisfaction. Whitehead and Lindquist (1986) reported that lack of participation in decision-making had a negative impact on job satisfaction among Alabama correctional officers. In addition, Stohr, Lovrich, Monke, and Zupan (1994) reported that employees in participatory management jails had higher levels of job satisfaction than did employees in control-oriented jails. In his study of correctional officers at the Auburn, New York prison facility, Lombardo (1981) found that the lack of input into decisions and responsibility were major sources of job dissatisfaction. However, looking at data from a sample of federal correctional staff aggregated to the institutional level, Wright et al. (1997) found that while job authority positively impacted job satisfaction, participation in decision-making had no significant effect on job satisfaction. DiIulio (1987), from his observational study of three prison systems, argued that prisons with higher control environments were safer, less stressful and, as such, staff were or should be more satisfied. Nevertheless, the vast majority of the correctional empirical findings indicate that high levels of centralization (i.e., lack of input into decision-making and job autonomy) is linked to low job satisfaction and low levels of centralization (i.e., greater input into decision-making and job autonomy) are linked to high job satisfaction.

While there is a large quantity of research that has examined the impact of the degree of centralization on job satisfaction, far less research has been conducted on the impact of centralization on organizational commitment. Moreover, among such studies, the findings tend to be mixed. In several non-criminal justice studies, it was observed that participation in decision-making (i.e., decentralization) had a significant positive relationship with organizational commitment (Morris & Steers, 1980; Rhodes & Steers, 1981). Overall, while there is some support that the degree of centralization has a significant effect on organizational commitment, other studies suggest that there is no relationship (Curry et al., 1986; Mueller et al., 1994).

Only two correctional studies could be located which examined the relationship between the degree of centralization and organizational commitment, and the findings of these two studies tend to mirror the results of general organizational research. More specifically, in a study of five jails, Stohr et al. (1994) found that those institutions that had higher levels of participatory management had higher levels of organizational identification (i.e., a measure that incorporates both organizational commitment and attachment to the organization). Using data aggregated at the facility level, Wright et al. (1997) found that a single measure for participation in decision-making had a positive impact on institution commitment, while a single measure of job autonomy had no effect on institution commitment among federal correctional staff. The results suggest that correctional staff tend to value decentralization over centralization.

Formalization

According to Taggart and Mays (1987), formalization is "the use of well-defined rules and regulations to govern the behavior of individuals so that actions within the organization become standardized" (p. 1986). Therefore, formalization is the degree that rules, regulations, standards of behavior, activities, and so forth are in written form within an organization (Price & Mueller, 1986), and includes things such as employee handbooks and standard operating procedure manuals (Pandey & Scott, 2002). Formalization is comprised of both codification and observation (Pandey & Scott, 2002). Codification is the placement of rules, procedures, and regulations in writing. Observation is the degree that employees are informed of the codification, and the degree that they are expected to follow the rules and regulations.

The Classical school contends that complex organizations need to have a high degree of formalization. Formalization is part of organizational control since its ultimate goal is to channel the productive behavior of workers and to limit harmful, arbitrary behaviors of both employees and supervisors (Marsden, Cook, & Kalleberg, 1994). Adler and Borys (1996) contend that formalization helps employees become more efficient which increases their motivation, which ultimately leads to increased job satisfaction and organizational commitment. Well-delineated, clear rules also allow employees to carry out their tasks with confidence. According to Deming (1986), formalization allows employees to engage in quality work, which raises their self-esteem.

The Behavioral school, on the other hand, argues that high degrees of formalization are unnecessary. Instead, organizations should have a minimal number of written policies, procedures, and rules so as to allow sufficient latitude for the expression of self-initiative and self-control on the part of the worker (Fry, 1989). It is argued that highly formalized organizational structures cause employees to become dissatisfied and uncommitted (Organ & Greene, 1982). Walton (1985) argued that formalization undermines worker commitment since employees feel constrained and hampered by the formalization control mechanisms.

Formalization and bureaucratic red tape are often confused (Pandey & Scott, 2002); however, Bozeman, Reed, and Scott (1992) made it clear that formalization and bureaucratic red tape are two distinct concepts. They argued that bureaucratic red tape is the negative result of irrational and irritating rules resulting from excessive formalization and stagnation within an organization. Rainey, Pandey, and Bozeman (1995) offered a similar definition of bureaucratic red tape, in that it is the result of the creation of rules and procedures without ensuring the efficacy of the rules and procedures for meeting organizational goals, objectives, and tasks. Thus, bureaucratic red tape is the result of excessive formalization with little rational forethought in the formalization of rules, procedures, forms, and regulations (Bozeman & Scott, 1996). Nevertheless, formalization and bureaucratic red tape are generally seen as similar phenomena which hurt not only the employee but also the organization.

Although recognized as different forms of organizational control, centralization and formalization have not received the same amount of empirical attention. The amount of research on formalization is far less than that on centralization. In addition, the overall impact of formalization on both employee job satisfaction and organizational commitment is not as clear as that of centralization. Most importantly, formalization has been ignored among correctional researchers.

Like centralization, there has been research on the effects of varying degrees of formalization among non-criminal justice organizational members. For example, among boarding school workers (Schmid & Bar-Nir, 2001) and among health and service workers (Zeitz, 1984), high levels of formalization have been positively linked to job satisfaction. On the other hand, in a study of nine social service departments, it was found that high levels of formalization had negative effects on job satisfaction (Kakabadse & Worrall, 1978). Finlay et al. (1995) found a negative association between high levels of formalization and job satisfaction among Employee Assistance Program (EAP) administrators. In a study of workers at an electronics firm and radio station, Rousseau (1978) observed that high levels of formalization were inversely related to job satisfaction. As such, it appears that the relationship between formalization and job satisfaction is mixed and may depend upon the occupational group or organization that was studied.

With respect to organizational commitment, Podsakoff, Williams, and Tudor (1986) found that high levels of formalization were a positive influence among a sample of hospital, government, and mental health professionals. Likewise, Jermier (1982) found that high levels of formalization were positively associated with organizational commitment among police officers in an urban Midwestern police department, even after controlling for the dangerousness and unpredictability of their assignment. However, in their study of restaurant managers, DeCotiis and Summers (1987) found no significant relationship between formalization and organizational commitment. Among salespeople, high levels of formalization were found to have no direct effect on organizational commitment (Michaels, Cron, Dubinsky, & Joachimsthaler, 1988). Like that of centralization, among the handful of studies that have been conducted on organizational commitment, the effect of high levels of formalization appears to be rather mixed. As previously noted, no published studies could be located which examined the impact of formalization on correctional staff.

Research Questions

The aim of this study is to add to the existing correctional literature by examining the role of both centralization and formalization on employee job satisfaction and organizational commitment. There has been a fair amount of research that has examined the impact of varying degrees of centralization on correctional staff job satisfaction; however, only one study has included both forms of centralization (i.e., degree of input into decision-making and degree of job autonomy). Wright et al. (1997) examined the impact of both types of centralization on correctional staff job satisfaction of federal correctional staff at the aggregate level (i.e., prison level). There have been no studies that have examined the impact of the two forms of centralization at an individual level. In addition, there has been little empirical research on the impact of the two types of centralization on the organizational commitment of correctional workers. Finally, as previously noted, no published studies could be located that examined the impact of formalization on either correctional staff job satisfaction or organizational commitment.

It was predicted that both high level forms of centralization (i.e., low level of input into decision-making and job autonomy) would have negative effects on correctional officer job satisfaction and organizational commitment. The less power given to an employee in making decisions about his or her work environment, the more likely the employee will be dissatisfied with his or her job and with the organization as a whole. Most adults like to have a degree of input in what they do and how they accomplish a given task (Bruce & Blackburn, 1992). In other words, the greater degree of control a person has over the job, the more that individual will be satisfied with the job, since the work reflects (in part) his or her decisions (Kouzes & Posner, 1995). Many individuals do not appreciate highly centralized environments that significantly restrict their actions and responses. People generally want an active part in the decisions that affect them. Bruce and Blackburn (1992) wrote, "People accept what they help to create" (p. 167).

Therefore, a low level of input into decision-making (i.e., high degree of centralization) should have a negative impact on correctional staff job satisfaction.

According to Covey (1989), "Without involvement, there is no commitment" (p. 143). People identify and extend effort towards those organizations that give them greater degree of control. Therefore, employees are less likely to be attached or committed to an organization with a highly centralized structure with little or no input into decision-making or job autonomy.

Methods

In the fall of 2000, a questionnaire was administered to the staff at a Midwestern correctional institution. The facility was a state run maximum security institution that mainly housed medium to maximum adult male inmates under the age of 26. At full compliment, there were 450 employees who were responsible for the supervision of approximately 1,300 prisoners. Due to sick leave, temporary reassignment, annual vacation leave, etc., it was estimated that only 400–420 employees were available at the time of the survey. The staff were informed that participation was voluntary and that their responses would be anonymous. A cash raffle was used to increase participation. In addition, one follow-up survey was conducted. A total of 272 useable surveys were returned representing a response rate of 60–68%, depending on the actual size of the base population. Respondents represented all areas of the correctional facility, such as correctional officers, case managers, medical staff, industry staff, food service workers, etc. The respondents also represented various administrative levels of the correctional facility, from line staff to supervisors and managers.[1]

Measures

Control Variables

Personal characteristics (e.g., age, tenure, education level, etc.) have sometimes been observed to have significant effects on correctional staff job satisfaction and/or organizational commitment (Britton, 1997; Jurik & Winn, 1987; Rogers, 1991). As such, the following six characteristics were used as control variables in this study: age, highest educational level, gender, work position, race, and tenure at the correctional facility.

Centralization

A total of four items were used to measure the lack of decision-making participation index. The four items utilized a five-point Likert-type response scale ranging from strongly disagree to strongly agree. The four items are presented in Table 1, along with the percentage responses for each item. The four items were summed to form an index of lack of decision-making participation.

Three items were used to measure hierarchy of authority about tasks index (i.e., lack of job autonomy). The three items utilized a five-point Likert-type response scale ranging from strongly disagree to strongly agree. The three items are presented in Table 1, along with the percentage responses for each item. The three items were summed to form an index of lack of job autonomy which ranged from 4 to 11.

Formalization

Six items were used to measure formalization. The six items also utilized a five-point Likert-type response scale ranging from strongly disagree to strongly agree. The six items are presented in Table 1, along with the percentage responses for each item. The six items were summed to form an index of formalization which ranged from 14 to 30.

Job Satisfaction

Job satisfaction was one of the two dependent variables of interest. A global, rather than facet (i.e., specific sub-dimensions, such as pay, co-workers, etc.), measure of job satisfaction was used in this study (Cranny et al., 1992). A total of five items were used to construct the global job satisfaction scale, and are reported in Table 1, along with the

SECTION II ORGANIZATIONAL STRUCTURE

Table 1 Percentage Results for Items Measuring Centralization, Formalization, Job Satisfaction, and Organizational Commitment ($N = 272$)

Item	SD%	D%	U%	A%	SA%
Lack of input into decision-making (DMPI)					
I am frequently asked my input into changes on important institutional matters or procedures (reverse coded).	35	34	13	16	2
I am frequently asked my input on the adoption of new programs at this prison (reverse coded).	31	47	12	9	1
I am frequently asked to participate in the decision of which post I will be assigned to at this prison (reverse coded).	26	47	15	10	2
In ?DOC, staff are frequently asked their input on the adoption of new policies (reverse coded).	25	48	18	7	1
Lack of job autonomy (HAI)					
I have to ask my supervisor before I can do almost anything at this prison.	25	53	7	11	4
At this prison, little action can be taken without a supervisor's permission.	3	47	14	32	4
Even small matters have to be referred to someone higher up for a final answer.	5	39	17	32	7
Formalization					
A "rules and procedures" manual is readily available for my position.	1	10	4	63	22
This prison has a very large number of written rules and policies.	0	5	9	61	25
At this prison, written rules and procedures are highly emphasized.	2	11	15	62	10
There is a complete written job description for most posts at this prison.	1	4	12	68	15
There is a formal orientation program for new staff at this prison.	4	10	20	58	8
Whatever situation arises, we have procedures at this prison to follow in dealing with it.	1	7	15	70	7
Job satisfaction					
I like my job better than the average worker does.	3	15	23	48	11
Most days I am enthusiastic about my job.	3	20	14	52	11
I definitely dislike my job (reverse coded).	33	44	11	8	4
I find real enjoyment in my job.	8	25	23	40	4
I am fairly well satisfied with my job.	4	16	14	59	8
Organizational commitment					
I am willing to put forth a great deal of effort beyond what is normally expected in order to help ensure that the prison is successful.	1	10	16	57	16

Item	SD%	D%	U%	A%	SA%
I tell my friends that this is a great organization to work for.	11	28	26	29	6
I feel little loyalty to this prison (reverse coded).	22	39	16	17	7
I find that my values and the prison's values are very similar.	12	35	30	20	3
I am proud to tell people that I work at this prison.	7	16	23	42	12
This prison really inspires the best in me in the way of job performance.	11	28	30	27	4
I really care about the fate of this prison.	6	7	20	57	11
Deciding to work for this prison was a definite mistake on my part (reverse coded).	32	49	8	7	3
Often, I disagree with the prison agency's policies on important matters (reverse coded).	2	40	26	24	8

Note: SD = strongly disagree; D = disagree; U = uncertain; A = agree; SA = strongly agree. Percentage totals may not equal 100% due to rounding. The question mark in ?DOC in the fourth item under *Lack of input into decision-making (DMPI)* represents the initial of the state which is not reported for confidentiality reasons, and DOC stands for the Department of Corrections.

percentage responses for each item. The five items were also answered by a five-point Likert-type response scale ranging from strongly disagree to strongly agree. The five items were summed to form a global job satisfaction index which ranged from 5 to 25.

Organizational Commitment

Organizational commitment is the second dependent variable for the current study. In the organizational literature, the most common method of measuring organizational commitment is the Organizational Commitment Questionnaire (OCQ) developed by Mowday et al. (1982). This index is designed to assess the degree of commitment that an individual has to the employing organization as a whole, and is generally viewed as an accurate measure for the attitudinal dimension of organizational commitment (Mathieu & Zajac, 1990). Nine items from the OCQ were included in the questionnaire. The nine indicators are reported in Table 1, along with the percentage responses for each item. The nine indicators were summed to form an organizational commitment index which ranged from 9 to 45.

Results

Both measures of centralization had statistically significant negative correlations with the job satisfaction and organizational commitment variables. The formalization index, on the other hand, had a significant positive correlation with correctional staff job satisfaction and organizational commitment. Of the three, the index for lack of input into decision-making had the largest correlation with job satisfaction, while the lack of job autonomy and formalization indices had similar sized correlations. The same findings were observed with correctional staff organizational commitment. Finally, it was interesting to note that formalization had statistically significant negative correlations with the two centralization indices.

On average, women reported higher satisfaction in their jobs than did men. The measures for age, education, position, race, and tenure had insignificant effects on correctional staff job satisfaction. Both centralization indices had statistically significant inverse effects on job satisfaction, while formalization had a significant positive impact. That is, employees who felt that they had little input in decision-making and little job autonomy were less satisfied with their jobs. Conversely, the greater the perception of standardized written rules, the more likely employees liked their jobs. Of all the variables, lack of input into decision-making had the greatest effect on the job satisfaction. Of the remaining variables, lack of job autonomy had the second largest effect, followed closely by formalization. The smallest significant effect on job satisfaction was employee gender.

Turning to the second regression model, organizational commitment.... None of the control variables had a statistically significant impact. Both measures of centralization had statistically significant effects on correctional staff organizational commitment. Formalization was found to have a significant positive relationship with correctional staff organizational commitment. Lack of input into decision-making had the greatest impact on organizational commitment.

The second set of analyses examined the predictors of job satisfaction and organizational commitment for correctional officers. The control variables and the indices for centralization and formalization were entered as independent variables.

For the job satisfaction model for correctional officers, both centralization measures had significant negative effects. Of the two, the lack of input into decision-making had a larger effect than lack of job autonomy. Formalization, while close to reaching the generally accepted statistical level of significance, had an insignificant positive impact. Among correctional officers, gender no longer had a significant effect on job satisfaction. For organizational commitment, the same results found for the full sample of correctional staff were observed for the subsample of correctional officers. Both forms of centralization had statistically significant negative effects, while formalization had a positive impact. As with the full sample, the measure for lack of input into decision-making had the largest effect, followed by the measures for lack of job autonomy and formalization, which had similarly sized effects. Finally, none of the personal characteristics had significant effects.

Discussion and Conclusion

Based on the analyses reported here, there are three main findings. First, personal characteristics have little impact on correctional staff job satisfaction and organizational commitment. Of the six personal characteristics, only gender had a statistically significant impact on job satisfaction for the full sample. Men were less satisfied with their jobs than were women. The relationship, however, disappeared in the analysis that concentrated on correctional officers only. None of the six personal characteristics had a significant effect on organizational commitment. It appears that the work environment is far more important than personal characteristics in shaping correctional staff job satisfaction and organizational commitment.

The second finding was centralization, regardless of its form, had a negative impact on both correctional staff job satisfaction and organizational commitment. This finding applied to the analysis of the full sample and the subsample of correctional officers. Of the two forms of centralization measured, lack of input into decision-making had a greater impact on both job satisfaction and organizational commitment among correctional staff as compared to lack of job autonomy. That is, lack of input into decision-making appears to be more important in shaping correctional staff and correctional officer job satisfaction and organizational commitment than lack of job autonomy. In addition, lack of input into decision-making had a larger negative effect on organizational commitment than it did for job satisfaction. It seems that correctional staff do not desire highly centralized power structures, but instead, want some of the power vested with them. Additionally, they want some say in how they perform their job tasks. These findings are clearly more in line with the Behavioral school rather than the Classical school.

The third main finding is that formalization had a significant impact on organizational commitment for both analyses. Formalization appears to help shape correctional staff organizational commitment.

While formalization had a significant effect on both organizational commitment models, it was only statistically significant for the full sample job satisfaction model. Stevens, Diederiks, and Philipsen (1992) argue that "Bureaucracy has the effect of reducing role ambiguity by delineating clear rules and procedures for work and by enlarging the possibilities for realizing professional and organizational goals" (p. 296). In other non-criminal justice organizations, formalization has been linked to reduced levels of role ambiguity and role conflict (Jackson & Schuler, 1985; Johnson, La France, Meyer, Speyer, & Cox, 1998). Thus, clear, written rules (i.e., formalization) may reduce role ambiguity and role conflict which has been found to be negatively associated with job satisfaction of correctional staff (Hepburn & Albonetti, 1980). In addition, formalization may help improve the communication process within large, bureaucratic organizations (Johnson et al., 1998). Finally, Marsden et al. (1994) argued that formalization "permits specialized departments to work with one another in predictable ways" (p. 914). Since most prisons are complex organizations with many different departments, formalization may allow for an improved work environment which in turn increases staff job satisfaction and organizational commitment.

For correctional officers, there was no effect of formalization on job satisfaction. A plausible explanation for this is the potential offsetting impact of formalization on correctional officer job satisfaction. Given that the daily job of the correctional officer is an unpredictable assignment, formalized rules and procedures might be regarded as constraining for some while needed for others. The correctional environment has been noted to be laden with hostility and danger, both of which come with little or no notice. Specific rules and regulations may be perceived as obstructing correctional officers' ability to deal with the unpredictable and unexpected aspects of their jobs. On the other hand, some line officers might perceive attempts made by the organization to reduce the uncertainty and anxiety of a dangerous and hostile work environment as a positive outcome.

In general, the results suggest that correctional workers want to share in organizational power. That being said, they also are not opposed to written policies, procedures, rules, or regulations. It appears as if, based on the current study, that correctional personnel only want input into the creation of formalization in the organization.

While usually competing concepts, it is possible to have decentralization with formalization (Marsden et al., 1994). Draft (1986) contended that "rules define boundaries so that decisions can be made at a lower level without a loss of control" (p. 179). Marsden et al. (1994) further argued that "formalization through the creation of routines and standard operating procedures serves to channel and limit actions of subordinates, thus reducing the need for direct supervision" (p. 897). Hage and Aiken (1970) reported that centralization and formalization were negatively correlated. On the other hand, other research suggests that centralization and formalization are positively correlated (Pugh, 1968). In this study, both forms of centralization were negatively correlated with formalization. This suggests that employees want a decentralized work environment with formalization. It is however recognized that more research on the subject is needed.

The current exploratory study has illuminated a few important insights, though it is not without some limitations. First, this was only one study of 272 staff at one Midwestern prison. Staff at a multitude of facilities need to be studied to allow for greater generalization of the results found here. Moreover, this study used four to nine survey questions to measure the two forms of centralization, formalization, job satisfaction, and organization commitment. Future research needs to use more refined and more expansive measures, especially for the different forms of centralization and formalization. There are other methods for measuring centralization and formalization besides using questionnaires that could be used. It is clear that more research is needed before firm conclusions can be reached on the relationship between centralization and formalization to correctional staff job satisfaction and organizational commitment, though the first step has been made with the current study. It is hoped that this study will spark this research.

This study only looked at the impact of a general measure of formalization. As previously indicated, there are positive and negative forms of formalization. Future research should also examine the different types of formalization and see how positive and negative forms of it impact correctional staff. Formalization must be rational and help employees complete their tasks in an effective and efficient manner. Irrational formalization and/or too much formalization may lead to the inability of workers to complete their jobs, leading to frustration and decreased motivation. Adler and Borys (1996) call these opposing forms of formalization, enabling and coercive types of formalization. In this study, bureaucratic red tape and its impact on correctional staff was not examined. Irrational formalization can ultimately lead to red tape. As Bozeman and Scott (1996) argue, excessive formalization is the physiology that can lead to the pathology of red tape. Pandey and Scott (2002) point out that "red tape, as pathology, becomes manifest when rules become ends in and of themselves without necessarily serving superordinate organizational or social goals" (p. 564).

Based upon past research and the current findings, there is strong evidence to support the conclusion that both forms of centralization negatively shape correctional staff job satisfaction and organizational commitment. This suggests that correctional administrators should share power with employees, especially input into decision-making, including formalization issues and procedures. This recommendation is, of course, based upon the assumption that the ultimate goal is to increase correctional staff job satisfaction and organizational commitment. It is unclear how decentralization will impact other employee attitudes and behaviors. It must be noted that this study, and most other studies, have not examined the impact of centralization and formalization on other areas, such on productivity, institutional safety, and so forth. These areas clearly need to be studied, and thus should be the targets of future research agendas.

In conclusion, employees are critical elements of a correctional organization. The work environment in a correctional organization has substantial effects on the staff. According to Poole and Pogrebin (1991), "We should be asking what the organization means to the worker instead of what the worker means to the organization" (p. 170). The knowledge of and ability to understand the antecedents of correctional employee attitudes and behaviors is critical for all parties involved, including correctional administrators, correctional employees, inmates, academicians, and society in general. In an era of increasing inmate populations, rising costs, shrinking budgets, and personnel shortages, it is particularly important to keep staff satisfied and committed. In this study, it was found that centralization had negative effects on correctional staff job satisfaction and commitment, while formalization had positive effects. Finally, it is hoped that this paper will spur more research and greater insights into the impact of different bureaucratic organizational structures on correctional staff.

Note

1. The survey was 16 pages in length, and there were 221 questions, covering a wide array of work environment dimensions and issues. The data from this survey have been used in several different papers that have looked at the impact of work–family conflict, organizational justice, fairness, promotional opportunities, feedback, and job characteristics on correctional staff. Therefore, there may be some familiarity in the methods section in the discussion of the data source and the measures of job satisfaction and organizational commitment. Nonetheless, none of the aforementioned studies examined the impact of centralization and formalization.

References

Adler, P. S., & Borys, B. (1996). Two types of bureaucracy: Enabling and coercive. *Administrative Science Quarterly, 41,* 61–89.

Agarwal, S. (1993). Influence of formalization on role stress, organizational commitment, and work alienation of salespersons: A cross-national comparative study. *Journal of International Business Studies, 24,* 715–739.

Andrews, M. C., & Kacmar, K. M. (2001). Discriminating among organizational politics, justice, and support. *Journal of Organizational Behavior, 22,* 347–366.

Berkson, L., & Hays, S. (1977). Applying organization and management theory to the selection of lower court personnel. *Criminal Justice Review, 2,* 81–91.

Bozeman, B., Reed, P., & Scott, P. (1992). Red tape and task delays in public and private organizations. *Administration and Society, 24,* 290–322.

Bozeman, B., & Scott, P. (1996). Bureaucratic red tape and formalization: Untangling conceptual knots. *American Review of Public Administration, 26,* 1–17.

Britton, D. (1997). Perceptions of the work environment among correctional officers: Do race and sex matter? *Criminology, 35,* 85–105.

Bruce, W., & Blackburn, J. (1992). *Balancing job satisfaction and performance: A guide for the human resource professional.* Westport, CT: Quorum Books.

Camp, S. (1994). Assessing the effects of organizational commitment and job satisfaction on turnover: An event history approach. *The Prison Journal, 74,* 279–305.

Covey, S. (1989). *The 7 habits of highly effective people: Powerful lessons in personal change.* New York: Simon and Schuster.

Cranny, C., Smith, P., & Stone, E. (1992). *Job satisfaction: How people feel about their jobs and how it affects their performance.* New York: Lexington Books.

Culliver, C., Sigler, R., & McNeely, B. (1991). Examining prosocial organizational behavior among correctional officers. *International Journal of Comparative and Applied Criminal Justice, 15,* 277–284.

Curry, J., Wakefield, D., Price, J., & Mueller, C. (1986). On the causal ordering of job satisfaction and organizational commitment. *Academy of Management Journal, 29,* 847–858.

DeCotiis, T., & Summers, T. (1987). A path analysis of a model of the antecedents and consequences of organizational commitment. *Human Relations, 40,* 445–470.

Deming, W. E. (1986). *Out of the crisis.* Cambridge, MA: MIT Center for Advanced Engineering Study.

Dennis, G. (1998). Here today, gone tomorrow: How management style affects job satisfaction and, in turn, employee turnover. *Corrections Today, 60*(3), 96–102.

Dewar, R., Whetten, D., & Boje, D. (1980). An examination of reliability and validity of the Aiken and Hage scales of centralization, formalization, and task routineness. *Administrative Science Quarterly, 25,* 120–128.

DiIulio, J. J. (1987). *Governing prisons: A comparative study of correctional management.* New York: Free Press.

Draft, R. L. (1986). *Organization theory and design* (2nd ed.). New York: New York Est.

Finlay, W., Martin, J., Roman, P., & Blum, T. (1995). Organizational structure and job satisfaction: Do bureaucratic organizations produce more satisfied employees? *Administration and Society, 27,* 427–450.

Fox, J. (1982). *Organizational and racial conflict in maximum-security prisons.* Lexington, MA: Lexington Books.

Fry, B. (1989). *Mastering public administration: From Max Weber to Dwight Waldo.* Chatham, NJ: Chatham House.

Gorsuch, R. (1983). *Factor analysis* (2nd ed.). Hillsdale, NJ: Lawrence Erlbaum Associates.

Hage, J., & Aiken, M. (1970). *Social change in complex organizations.* New York: Random House.

Heffron, F. (1989). *Organizational theory and public organizations: The political connection.* Englewood Cliffs, NJ: Prentice Hall.

Hepburn, J. (1987). The prison control structure and its effects on work attitudes: The perceptions and attitudes of prison guards. *Journal of Criminal Justice, 15,* 49–64.

Hepburn, J., & Albonetti, C. (1980). Role conflict in correctional institutions: An empirical examination of the treatment–custody dilemma among correctional staff. *Criminology, 17,* 445–459.

Hepburn, J., & Knepper, P. (1993). Correctional officers as human service workers: The effect of job satisfaction. *Justice Quarterly, 10,* 315–335.

Jackson, S. E., & Schuler, R. S. (1985). A meta-analysis and conceptual critique of research on role ambiguity and role conflict in work settings. *Organizational Behavior and Human Decision Processes, 36,* 17–78.

Jermier, J. (1982). Ecological hazards and organizational behavior: A study of dangerous urban space-time zones. *Human Organizations, 41,* 198–207.

Jermier, J., & Berkes, L. (1979). Leader behavior in police command bureaucracy: A closer look at the quasi-military model. *Administrative Science Quarterly, 24,* 1–23.

Johnson, I. D., La France, B. H., Meyer, M., Speyer, J. B., & Cox, D. (1998). The impact of formalization, role conflict, role ambiguity, and communication quality on perceived organizational innovativeness in the Cancer Information Service. *Evaluation and Health Professions, 21,* 27–51.

Jurik, N. C., & Musheno, M. C. (1986). The internal crisis of corrections: Professionalization and the work environment. *Justice Quarterly, 3,* 457–480.

Jurik, N., & Winn, R. (1987). Describing correctional security dropouts and rejects: An individual or organizational profile? *Criminal Justice and Behavior, 24,* 5–25.

Kakabadse, A., & Worrall, R. (1978). Job satisfaction and organizational structure: Nine social service departments. *British Journal of Social Work, 8,* 51–70.

Kerce, E., Magnusson, P., & Rudolph, A. (1994). *The attitudes of Navy corrections staff members: What they think about confinees and their jobs.* San Diego: Navy Personnel Research and Development Center.

Kouzes, J., & Posner, B. (1995). *The leadership challenge.* San Francisco: Jossey-Bass.

Lambert, E. (1999). *A path analysis of the antecedents and consequences of job satisfaction and organizational commitment among correctional staff (turnover and absenteeism).* Unpublished doctoral dissertation, State University of New York at Albany.

Lambert, E., Barton, S., & Hogan, N. (1999). The missing link between job satisfaction and correctional staff behavior: The issue of organizational commitment. *American Journal of Criminal Justice, 24,* 95–116.

Lincoln, J., & Kalleberg, A. (1990). *Culture, control and commitment: A study of work organization and work attitudes in the United States and Japan.* Cambridge: Cambridge University Press.

Locke, E., & Schweiger, D. (1979). Participation in decision making: One more look. In B. Staw & L. Cummings (Eds.), *Research in organizational behavior* (pp. 265–339). Greenwich, CT: JAI Press.

Lombardo, L. (1981). *Guards imprisoned: Correctional officers at work.* New York: Elsevier.

Marsden, P. V., Cook, C. R., & Kalleberg, A. L. (1994). Organizational structure: Coordination and control. *American Behavioral Scientist, 37,* 911–929.

Mathieu, J., & Zajac, D. (1990). A review and meta-analysis of the antecedents, correlates, and consequences of organizational commitment. *Psychological Bulletin, 108,* 171–194.

McShane, M. D., & Williams, F. P. (1993). *The management of correctional institutions.* New York: Garland.

Michaels, R. E., Cron, W. L., Dubinsky, A. J., & Joachimsthaler, E. A. (1988). Influences of formalization on organizational commitment and work alienation of salespeople and industrial buyers. *Journal of Marketing Research, 25,* 376–383.

Morris, J., & Steers, R. (1980). Structural influences on organizational commitment. *Journal of Vocational Behavior, 17,* 50–57.

Mowday, R., Porter, L., & Steers, R. (1982). *Employee–organization linkages: The psychology of commitment, absenteeism and turnover.* New York: Academic Press.

Mueller, C., Boyer, E., Price, J., & Iverson, R. (1994). Employee attachment and noncoercive conditions of work. *Work and Occupations, 21,* 179–212.

Organ, D., & Greene, C. N. (1982). The effects of formalization on professional involvement: A compensatory process approach. *Administrative Science Quarterly, 26,* 237–252.

Pandey, S. K., & Scott, P. G. (2002). Red tape: A review and assessment of concepts and measures. *Journal of Public Administration Research and Theory, 12,* 553–580.

Podsakoff, P. M., Williams, L. J., & Tudor, W. D. (1986). Effects of organizational formalization on alienation among professionals and nonprofessionals. *Academy of Management Journal, 4,* 820–831.

Poole, E., & Pogrebin, M. (1991). Changing jail organization and management: Toward improved employee utilization. In J. Thompson & G. Mayo (Eds.), *American jails: Public policy issues* (pp. 163–179). Chicago: Nelson-Hall.

Poulin, J. (1994). Job task and organizational predictors of social worker job satisfaction change: A panel study. *Administration in Social Work, 18,* 21–38.

Price, J., & Mueller, C. (1986). *Handbook of organizational measurement.* Marshfield, MA: Pitman.

Pugh, D. S. (1968). Dimensions of organizational structures. *Administrative Science Quarterly, 13,* 65–106.

Rainey, H., Pandey, S., & Bozeman, B. (1995). Research note: Public and private managers' perceptions of red tape. *Public Administrative Review, 55,* 567–574.

Rhodes, S., & Steers, R. (1981). Conventional vs. worker-owned organizations. *Human Relations, 34,* 1013–1035.

Rogers, R. (1991). The effect of educational level on correctional officer job satisfaction. *Journal of Criminal Justice, 19,* 123–137.

Rousseau, D. M. (1978). Characteristics of departments, positions, and individuals: Contexts for attitudes and behavior. *Administrative Science Quarterly, 23,* 521–540.

Schmid, H., & Bar-Nir, D. (2001). The relationship between organizational properties and service effectiveness in residential boarding schools. *Children and Youth Services Review, 23,* 243–271.

Schumacker, R., & Lomax, R. (1996). *A beginner's guide to structural equation modeling.* Mahwah, NJ: Lawrence Erlbaum Associates.

Spector, P. (1996). *Industrial and organizational psychology: Research and practice.* New York: John Wiley.

Stevens, F., Diederiks, J., & Philipsen, H. (1992). Physician satisfaction, professional characteristics, and behavior formalization in hospitals. *Social Science and Medicine, 35,* 295–303.

Stohr, M., Lovrich, N., Monke, B., & Zupan, L. (1994). Staff management in correctional institutions: Comparing DiIulio's "control model" and "employee investment model" outcomes in five jails. *Justice Quarterly, 11,* 471–497.

Stohr, M., Self, R., & Lovrich, N. (1992). Staff turnover in new generation jails: An investigation of its causes and preventions. *Journal of Criminal Justice, 20,* 455–478.

Taggart, W. A., & Mays, G. L. (1987). Organizational centralization in court administration: An empirical assessment. *American Journal of Criminal Justice, 11,* 180–198.

Tobin, T. J. (2001). Organizational determinants of violence in the workplace. *Aggression and Violent Behavior, 6,* 91–102.

Walton, R. E. (1985). Toward a strategy of eliciting employee commitment based upon policies of mutuality. In R. E. Walton & P. R. Lawrence (Eds.), *HRM trends and challenges* (pp. 119–218). Boston: Harvard Business School Press.

Whitehead, J., & Lindquist, C. (1986). Correctional officer burnout: A path model. *Journal of Research in Crime and Delinquency, 23,* 23–42.

Wright, K. N., Salyor, W. G., Gilman, E., & Camp, S. (1997). Job control and occupational outcomes among prison workers. *Justice Quarterly, 14,* 525–546.

Wright, T. (1993). Correctional employee turnover: A longitudinal study. *Journal of Criminal Justice, 21,* 131–142.

Wycoff, M., & Skogan, W. (1994). The effect of a community policing management style on officers' attitudes. *Crime and Delinquency, 40,* 371–383.

Zeitz, G. (1984). Bureaucratic role characteristics and member affective response in organizations. *Sociological Quarterly, 25,* 301–318.

DISCUSSION QUESTIONS

1. Are organizational leaders supposed to deal with employee needs, including their satisfaction and commitment, or are they supposed to focus entirely on the achievement of organizational goals? Are both important?

2. What is role ambiguity, and how is it related to job satisfaction? Is formalization a mechanism for reducing ambiguity? Explain?

3. The researchers examined a number of individual factors (age, education level, sex, race, and years of experience) that potentially relate to job satisfaction and commitment. Are these factors important (significant) predictors? Are individual factors more or less important than organizational characteristics (centralization and formalization) in explaining satisfaction and commitment?

READING

Reading 2

The research article by Gaylene S. Armstrong points to the growing importance of evidence-based practice (EBP) in community corrections agencies. Under an EBP paradigm, probation and parole officers move beyond a limited focus on supervising offenders and ensuring compliance and toward reliance on empirically supported practices that improve the quality of community corrections and produce more positive outcomes (e.g., reduced recidivism). In lean budgetary times, however, when governments are looking to increase the efficiency of criminal justice organizations, spans of control may be widened in an effort to cut supervisory staff and/or increase the number of rank-and-file employees. As a result, control mechanisms are weakened. Armstrong's purpose was to examine how the demands of EBP may determine the ideal span of control in probation and parole agencies. She gathered data through a focus group methodology; 62 community corrections personnel participated, with most coming from two jurisdictions in Iowa and the remainder coming from other jurisdictions throughout the United States. Both supervisors and officers noted an increase in responsibilities as a result of EBP. Supervisors, for example, are required to, among other duties, mentor subordinates, model appropriate EBP actions, encourage and motivate personnel, and research best practices. All these responsibilities place extra time demands on the supervisor and require a greater level of supervisor–officer interaction than was necessary prior to EBP. Results suggest that EBP requires a narrow span of control, a structural characteristic at odds with calls to widen the span of control for cost-saving purposes.

Factors to Consider for Optimal Span of Control in Community Supervision Evidence-Based Practice Environments

Gaylene S. Armstrong

Despite the fiscal constraints of the economic climate, community supervision agencies across the country are forging ahead in their efforts to improve public safety and offender accountability by implementing evidence-based policies and practices (EBP) within their organizations. Led by the efforts of the National Institute of Corrections, the American Probation and Parole Association (APPA), and others, current probation and parole practices have evolved from their former ineffectual emphasis on deterrence strategies in offender supervision (McGuire, 2002) toward increasingly empirically supported offender supervision practices. Officers are progressively using supervision tactics such as motivational interviewing, advanced risk/needs offender assessments, and graduated sanctions (Andrews & Bonta, 2003; Bundy, 2004; Clark, Walters, Gingerich, & Meltzer, 2006; Hartzler & Espinosa, 2011; Madson, Loignon, & Lane, 2009; Miller & Rollnick, 1991; National Institute of Corrections, 2007). Moreover, agencies are focusing on improving the quantity and quality of service linkages with community agencies.

Concurrent with the growth in new and more effective practices is the rising need for budgetary cutbacks; yet there is a lack of research to guide decision makers in factors to consider when balancing human resource decisions, organizational growth in effective practices, and fiscal conservation. Recently, the Iowa Community Based Correctional System (the state's probation and parole agency) was faced with responding to legislative discussions that focused on reduced funding for supervisory staff within their organization. The proposed reduction aimed to decrease the probation supervisor-probation officer span of control ratio from its current ratio of 7:1 to upward of 14:1, while maintaining their implementation of EBP. Based on the experience of this jurisdiction and other community correction experts, this study aimed to identify a series of factors deemed important for consideration in proposed modifications to span of control. To date, there is a shortage of both theoretical speculation and empirical research on the importance of span of control for community corrections in general and more specifically for agencies that have implemented an EBP approach or other significant organizational changes.

Some limited theoretical discussion of span of control exists within the policing literature as well as areas in the management literature; however, there has been no research to our knowledge that has focused on the span of control within the dynamic environment of community supervision agencies. This is an especially important area of knowledge that requires study, given the increased use of EBP in community corrections, as it has led administrators to question numerous organizational aspects of their agency including staffing patterns. This study begins to fill this significant void in the literature using a case study approach and in-depth interviews with stakeholders in the state of Iowa and a convenience sample of national stakeholders to gain insight into span of control determinants. Specifically, this article begins by presenting a brief review of the limited theoretical literature on the span of control concept that helped form the basis of the proposed determinants. These

Source: Armstrong, G. S., (2012). Factors to consider for optimal span of control in community supervision evidence-based practice environments. *Criminal Justice Policy Review, 23*(4), 427–446.

determinants should be considered in selecting an appropriate span of control ratio for community corrections agencies that are involved in significant organizational change or growth. This review is followed by a methodological description of the study and results from interviews with national and state of Iowa stakeholders. Results are framed by theoretical factors presented in the existing literature as they apply to community supervision agencies. Finally, we contextualize our findings by discussing the potential consequences associated with increasing the span of control ratio in EBP community supervision environments as a response to fiscal constraints.

Background

Defining Span of Control

The origin of the span of control terminology is attributed to British General Sir Ian Standish Monteith Hamilton (1853-1947) when he used it in reference to military application (Hamilton, 1921). Since that time, the term *span of control* has become a relatively common term used to describe the number of individuals, or resources, that a person can effectively supervise within a structured organizational, business, or military setting (Eastman & Eastman, 1971; Hanna & Gentel, 1971). Within a critical incident scenario, the Federal Emergency Management Agency (FEMA) has applied the span of control terminology more specifically to indicate the number of individuals that a supervisor can effectively manage in a crisis or emergency situation (Lane, 2006). Regardless of the setting, the underlying principle aims to maximize administrative efficiency (Souryal, 1977), while retaining effectiveness within the organization.

As the terminology has become accepted nomenclature, the ongoing challenge has been the identification of the appropriate span of control within various organizations. In 1937, Graicunas attempted to identify the mathematical complexities associated with the span of control concept by representing it with a statistical formula. He argued that with an increasing number of subordinates, a geometric increase in the number of other relationships that need to be managed also occurs—it is not a direct one-to-one increase. Specifically, Graicunas argued that not only do supervisors manage their direct subordinates but they also oversee the relationships among the individual subordinates. For example, when a supervisor has four subordinates, 11 relationships exist (one direct/single relationship, three cross relationships, and seven direct groups). Thus, with each additional subordinate added, an exponential number of new relationships that may require supervisor response also develops. Accordingly, span of control is a complex issue that must be carefully considered before any modifications are implemented so that a span of control ratio does not reach a level of complexity that is too difficult for a supervisor to control (Bianchi, 2010).

Existing Span of Control Ratios in U.S. Probation Jurisdictions

With the implementation of EBP, it has become essential that agencies work carefully to determine the necessary and appropriate staffing patterns, which includes identifying an appropriate span of control to efficiently fulfill their EBP mission with fidelity. Unfortunately, information-based policy or evidence-based knowledge related to appropriate levels of span of control is limited. To our knowledge, only two studies have considered staffing levels within community supervision agencies and none have linked these ratios to the tasks involved with supervisory roles. The most comprehensive assessment of span of control was completed by Cunniff and Shilton (1991) who ascertained the supervisor to probation officer ratio in 25 jurisdictions across the United States. The ratios were calculated in a straightforward manner dividing the total number of probation officers in the agency by the total number of supervisors in the agency. Unfortunately, this method overlooked variation in specialized versus general caseloads and other factors that could directly affect true span of control ratios; however, the results do provide a crude snapshot of span of control as it existed circa 1991 in a select number of agencies in the United States. As indicated in Table 1, the ratio ranged from a low of 5:1 in Dallas, Denver, and Nassau Counties and New York City to a high of 14:1 in Jefferson County (Kentucky). The average ratio across the 25 jurisdictions was 7:1.

Although informative, this study occurred prior to the bulk of the EBP movement. Interestingly, an updated but informal data collection on the same topic by the APPA occurred in 2006 and demonstrated findings similar to the Cunniff and Shilton study.

Once again, an examination of the tabular data, as presented in Table 2, does not provide significant guidance, given the absence of significant discussion of supervisory roles and responsibilities. The challenges with making generalizations between jurisdictions are highlighted by Cushman and Sechrest (1992) who found a prevailing assumption existed when conducting interviews such that probation agencies, people on probation, and the agency programs were all assumed to be "pretty much the same." Despite these overall assumptions, Cushman and Sechrest noted that their results indicated that "nothing could be further from the truth. There are truly important differences on all three of these dimensions" (p. 27). The question that remains for community supervisors, as it relates to span of control ratios, is the identification of appropriate variants both between and within jurisdictions that should be used in determining appropriate span of control ratios.

Theoretical Factors Directing the Determination of Appropriate Span of Control

Extant literature within the span of control area for police organizations as well as other industries has existed for decades; however, literature specifically addressing span of control within correctional organizations remains wanting. Consequently, this lack of evidence creates difficulty for developing or adapting information-based public policy. Decision makers must therefore rely on the theoretical conjecture regarding span of control in general to guide their policies. Across fields, the term *span of control* has been applied in a variety of ways depending on theoretical interpretation of the concept. It has been used to identify work group size, reporting structure, closeness of contact, employee support, and scope of a role (Meyer, 2008). In community corrections and policing organizations, span of control has traditionally referred to the organizational reporting structure between first-line officers and their immediate supervisors. Within these parameters, the theoretical literature suggests that, in terms of the reporting structure Graiciunas proposed, span of control should be limited to 4–5 individuals if the supervisor is to maintain control. While Graiciunas left the concept of "control" open to interpretation, Bianchi (2010) recently argued that, in addition to what is meant by control, a second concept underlies Graiciunas's argument. Bianchi argued that the nature of the supervisory relationship is also important.

The nature of the supervisory relationship, in turn, could be defined in a variety of ways. Here, we argue that a concrete manner of viewing supervisory relationships are by assessing the responsibilities of supervisors as well as their subordinates. As a general guideline, Hattrup and Kleiner (1993, p. 2) suggested that "if workers are involved in work of a trivial or routine nature, the supervisor will tend to require less application of control than if they perform work of greater significance or complexity" (see also Meyer, 2008). Hattrup and Kleiner also suggested that a supervisor's control could more effectively be implemented over a broader span of subordinates in a stable work environment as compared with one that is experiencing change or exists under dynamic conditions. Other theorists agreed that task complexity should influence span of control ratios. As Bianchi (2010, p. 22) noted in reference to complexity, "We are really speaking about the capability of a manager to face different levels of diversity and in studies on jobs, there is a negative relationship between the number of subordinates and the complexity of the job."

In various other labor fields, when span of control is viewed as a reporting structure, the classical perspectives initially offered by Fayol on span of

Reading 2 Factors to Consider for Optimal Span of Control in Community Supervision

Table 1 Ratios of Probation Officers to Supervisors

	Actual ratio
Baltimore City, MD	8:1
Baltimore County, MD	8:1
Bexar County, MD	7:1
Cook County, IL	7:1
Dade County, FL	10:1
Dallas County, TX	5:1
Denver, CO	5:1
Erie County, NY	7:1
Franklin County, OH	5:1
Harris County, TX	9:1
Hennepin County, MN	9:1
Honolulu, HI	6:1
Jefferson County, KY	14:1
King County, WA	10:1
Los Angeles County, CA	7:1
Maricopa County, AZ	9:1
Milwaukee County, WI	7:1
Monroe County, NY	8:1
Nassau County, NY	5:1
New York City, NY	5:1
Oklahoma County, OK	10:1
Orange County, CA	6:1
Philadelphia, PA	7:1
San Bernardino County, CA	9:1
San Diego County, CA	6:1
San Francisco, CA	9:1
Santa Clara County, CA	6:1
St. Louis, MO	6:1
Suffolk County, NY	8:1
Ventura County, CA	6:1

Source: Adapted from Cunniff and Shilton (1991).

control point to a finite number of factors to consider in making a determination of appropriate ratios. Many of these same factors remain relevant in the contemporary workforce as noted by numerous authors, including process complexity, such as the nature of the task, the nature of instructions provided, the time involved, and the amount of authority delegated; workforce skill level, including the ability of the subordinates and the ability of the supervisor; and work environment, including the geographical area involved and the harmony of the subordinates (see Hanna & Gentel, 1971; Lane, 2006; McManus, 2007; Schroeder, Lombardo, & Strollo, 1995).

Using bounded rationality guided by prior theoretical discussions of span of control, this study aims to fill a knowledge gap in determining whether these same factors are applicable within community supervision agencies. Specifically focusing on correctional agencies that have applied EBP concepts within their organization, we aimed to test whether the theoretical concepts discussed in related areas of literature apply to community corrections and therefore should be considered by policy makers and administrators in determining an appropriate span of control in community supervision agencies. By engaging in multiple focus groups both within the state of Iowa and a national convenience sample of selected administrators and other staff members from community supervision agencies, this study used a conceptual framework based on existing literature in related fields to guide group discussion on staffing patterns and span of control issues in EBP environments.

Method

Participants

Participants were composed of 62 community supervision personnel ranging in rank between chief probation officers and probation/parole officers. Forty-six of the participants were employed within the state of Iowa, whereas the balance of the participants represented a range of other community supervision jurisdictions across the country.

Table 2 Ratio of Supervisor to Line Staff, as Reported to American Probation and Parole Association in January 2006

		Officer to supervisor ratio
Arizona	Maricopa County	10-12:1
	Tucson	5-6:1
Arkansas		10:1, as per ACA standard
California	Alameda County	12:1
	San Diego County	10-12:1
	San Bernardino County	5-6:1
	Santa Clara County	7-10:1
	Trinity County	10:1
Georgia	DeKalb County Probation	11:1
	DeKalb County Parole	7:1
Hawaii	Hawaii Paroling Authority, Oahu	12:1
Idaho		14:1, with parole officers assisting
Illinois		13-16:1
Kansas		8-9:1, with senior parole officers
Minnesota	Hennepin County	7.5-17:1 (average 13:1)
	Washington County	12-14:1
Missouri		9:1
New York	Albany County	7:1
	Chautauqua County	8:1
Ohio	Painesville	5:1
North Carolina		10:1
	Medina County	8:1
Oregon	Washington County	6:1 + 35 caseload
Tennessee		10:1
Texas	Brazoria County	5-7:1
Pennsylvania	Erie County	10:1
Wisconsin		11-12:1
Canada	Federal-Ontario Region	4-7:1

ACA = American Correctional Association

Procedure

Data were collected through a series of focus groups with all available employees during a 4-day site visit to two judicial districts in Iowa. The focus groups were organized by position (e.g., first-line supervisors, probation officers, administrators, and upper-level management). Subsequently, a convenience sample of participants from multiple jurisdictions across the United States formed a second series of focus groups.

Participants in this latter group were selected to participate if they (a) registered and planned to attend the 2010 APPA Winter conference and (b) were from jurisdictions that were known to be in the process of establishing, or already had established, EBP guidelines in their agencies. Focus group questions were aimed at gathering data on similarities and differences across jurisdictions that were related to the theoretical concepts of span of control defined as reporting structure. Reporting structure was operationalized through an examination of the duties of staff. Specifically, prompts were given during focus groups to discuss how the role and duties of supervisors has evolved with the implementation of EBP and the extent and type of interactions that typically occurs between supervisors and their staff.

Results

Based on data gathered through focus groups with 62 community corrections supervisors and line staff, this study found that many of the factors that have been suggested to be theoretically linked to effective span of control decisions in other labor fields were applicable within community supervision environments as well. This section of the article will describe the typical role and responsibilities of supervisors within EBP community supervision environments and contrast that role and associated responsibilities with the theoretical concepts that were noted earlier as key components in span of control decision-making processes.

The Role of the Probation Supervisor Within an EBP Environment

Although jurisdictions varied on EBP implemented in their organization and their stage of change toward an active EBP organization, it was evident that the role of staffing within correctional supervision organizations was perceived to be critical aside from EBP, given the state of fiscal conservation across the country. Participants noted that the roles of both probation officers and their supervisors have significantly evolved with the implementation of EBP, with a general sense that supervisors' duties had significantly increased. Duties of front-line probation officers were also perceived as having increased in responsibilities. Probation officers were now required to be more engaged with clients, necessitating a higher level of direct interaction to implement supervision techniques. Some of the techniques noted include relationship building, motivational interviewing, and adhering to risk, needs, and responsivity principles of treatment. Consistently, participants viewed this shift in the role of probation officers aligned with added oversight by the probation officer supervisory staff to ensure fidelity of these new practices. Thus, the role of supervisors was critical as it pertained to training and guiding their unit staff on a daily basis.

One director adamantly claimed that the success of the jurisdiction's probation department was *dependent* on their first-line supervisors. In efforts to reorganize probation in this particular urban county, the director invested large amounts of resources toward leadership development of their mid-managers (first-line supervisors). These supervisors were responsible for not only traditional supervision responsibilities of the probation officers within their "team" but also the different committees that focused on performance evaluation processes, probation officer training, offender assessment processes, and so on. The first-line supervisors chaired different agency committees, formed committee membership, and were responsible for some implementation activities.

Within these EBP organizations, it was also determined that supervisors were actively involved in leadership activities including strategic planning, data evaluation, making decisions from a "big picture" perspective as well as enhanced supervision activities to include coaching and staffing cases with their probation officers (i.e., case discussion and decision making through a team process). Strong, developed leadership was perceived by participants to provide much of the critical infrastructure from which EBP can become a part of the organization. A number of participants commented that training, organizational processes, and decision making using data (evidence-based decision making) should be the more critical focus of staffing in EBP organizations, as compared with a specific number of supervisory ratios.

As one participant noted, organizations in the public, private, and not-for-profit sectors are becoming more and more concerned with producing *quality* outcomes, whether to enhance competitiveness and profit, to reduce error and harm, or to accomplish good and added value for consumers of their "product." To do this, a great deal of attention must be paid to the role of front-line supervisors. Prior literature noted earlier in this study supported participant comments that supervisors "play a pivotal role in any organization's attempt to improve efficiency and effectiveness" through the application of evidence-based knowledge to the process of work.

According to multiple participants, to be successful in their role, supervisors must master a set of skills that even 10 years ago were not considered a part of their competences. These skills include, among others, transformational leadership, strategic thinking, change management, communication, collaboration, coaching and mentoring, motivating staff, and relationship building. Each of these skills takes time to master and to apply. As one participant noted, "Supervision is no longer just telling people what to do and then monitoring whether they do it; it has become the art and science of human and behavioral encouragement, support, and feedback."

Application of Theoretical Span of Control Factors to an EBP Probation and Parole Environment

Although data gathered from focus group interviews determined that the nature of the supervisory positions has evolved to include new approaches and a deeper level of supervisor interaction with their unit, the very nature of the probation and parole environment itself was perceived by focus group participants to be extremely complex and dynamic. To facilitate presentation of findings, this study next applies the specific theoretical concepts discussed earlier in this article to the data collected herein. In review of extensive notes taken by the researchers, four themes stemming from the theoretical literature on span of control also appeared to dominate discussion by focus group participants: time investment, task complexity, workforce skill level, and contributing work environment.[1]

Time investment. The topic that was most passionately discussed by focus groups (both supervisory and nonsupervisory rank) was the perception that supervisors had an insufficient amount of time to get the "job done right" despite their efforts and/or desires. This fact was recognized as increasingly apparent as their organizations have implemented various new methods, policies, and practices associated with EBP ideals. In fact, the most common phase used by supervisors to describe their daily routine was that they were always busy "putting out fires." Moreover, it was apparent that participants perceived significant collaboration to exist between line staff and others outside of the supervisor's direct span of control, as it would be theoretically defined by Graiciunas and others. Supervisory and nonsupervisory staff indicated examples of required collaborations that included meetings with community partners and stakeholders, both internal and external to the organization. These required collaborations were perceived to consume a significant amount of time. Consequently, participants suggested the extent of collaborations are especially relevant and should be considered as a primary factor in determining an appropriate span of control or reporting structure.

Internally, more recent expectations of front-line probation and parole officers are that they develop much more in-depth relationships with clients/offenders as compared with the past, which requires more training and more supervisor interaction in discussing case management options. As a result, the role of the supervisor is becoming increasingly time-consuming and complex. Administratively, EBP models that were currently being implemented at the participant's various agencies placed a tremendous focus and need on data entry and analysis. Agencies viewed data entry and analysis as a critical component for effective assessment of front-line probation and parole officers. Data and related performance assessments used by the agencies took many forms including quality assurance and direct observation of officer-client interactions. Specifically, the recent EBP model of supervision placed an emphasis on strong report writing directly related to effective offender case management as well as on individual probation officer case reviews. Iowa supervisors, for example, were responsible for completing monthly reports on data/performance measurements. Each of these assessment tasks were perceived to require significant time investment.

The manner in which the theoretical concepts of time investments as, pertinent for span of control, applied to community corrections environments can be illustrated by a final example—the individual perspectives of the supervisor roles as portrayed by themselves. Data from this subset of participants indicated that supervisors consistently cited their desire to provide more individual attention to their line staff team members, especially on coaching and mentoring. Unfortunately, supervisors expressed they were consumed with tasks that were primarily administrative in nature. As a result of limited individualized contact, some supervisors felt relatively unable to hold their staff accountable for quality EBP and follow through with some of the practices and principals that they themselves should be practicing. Moreover, they felt that they did not have enough time to handle critical human resource issues with their staff, such as grievances and investigations, and that the nature of the organizational shift work and extended hours increased supervisors' sense of responsibility, leaving them feeling as if they were always on duty. Thus, data demonstrated that stakeholders viewed the current role of community corrections supervisors within EBP environments as requiring significant time investments with the staff they supervise. This finding suggests that time investment is an appropriate theoretical factor to consider in span of control decisions, and specifically among the participants in this study who were involved in the implementation stage of EBP, a relatively low span of control was a perceived need.

Task Complexity

When questioned about the supervisor responsibilities, participants cited examples of how supervisors in community corrections agencies have experienced a shift in their responsibilities with the ongoing changes in their agencies primarily due to implementation of EBP ideals. Participants specifically noted that the position now has added significant roles, tasks, and expectations to the supervisor workload, significantly increasing the complexity of tasks required. As noted earlier, front-line staff are expected to develop a much more in-depth relationship with clients/offenders, which requires more training and more supervisor interaction with the officers discussing case-management options. Beyond this aspect, audits and staff evaluations were two other specific functions that were highlighted as new complexities to the supervisor position. As a result of EBP implementation at the organizational level, the usage of personnel evaluations were significantly expanded. Several supervisors noted that the evaluations increased the need for providing ongoing feedback about the evaluation process and results as well as the need for coaching and mentoring in the areas of the officer's weakness. Due to the increased frequency of evaluation and required feedback cycle, supervisors felt a heightened level of "responsivity" to their staff than prior to EBP implementation. Furthermore, participants perceived that even simple tasks (i.e., basic supervisor-staff interactions) have increased in complexity because supervisors must model EBP, including motivation interviewing (MI), in all interactions with their staff. These factors were perceived to have added to the task complexity of the supervisors with their direct supervision staff members.

Some participants expressed that their jurisdictions were implementing a greater number of new programs with the onset of EBP, creating a higher workload for supervisors and staff and a higher need for coaching and mentoring as these programs come on line. Furthermore, the Iowa focus group participants pointed out that their supervisors are responsible for supervising both probation and parole officers. Such an organizational structure adds an additional level of complexity, given that probation and parole have different rules, laws, and processes governing each offender and potentially a different focus from a case-management perspective. One participant, for example, indicated that with an active focus on least restrictive sanctions, especially within probation, each unit deals with a different level of offender, which is very different from past years, thereby involving a higher level of knowledge and skills and much more training for both officers and supervisors.

Atypical supervisor positions such as managing probation and parole or even extending to specialized caseloads have some similarities, but varying supervisor responsibilities should be recognized across organizations. Varying responsibilities will likely depend on the unit structures, number of offenders under supervision, specialized units (e.g., sex offender units), specialized programs (e.g., drug court involved), and other factors. Some participants expressed that their supervisors have difficulty to keep up with the activities with which the officers are engaged because their units were so broad. This varying range of activities carries with it an expectation that the supervisors must be proficient experts in many different areas, making their job significantly complex. The varying caseload types and associated complexity of supervision roles is a point to consider in an organization that is inherently a learning organization. Thus, as a probation officer's role grows in complexity (knowledge and skills), there is a direct correlation to the capability of the supervisor and their competence in providing the appropriate and necessary level of guidance, direction, and oversight. Participants clearly demonstrated that the theoretical concept of task complexity applied in consideration of factors for span of control. Participants viewed the role and responsibility of supervisors to be increasingly complex with the implementation of EBP and, consequently, any shift in span of control ratios should consider the complexities of specific staff members prior to that change.

Workforce Skill Level and Capabilities of Staff

As evident from the description of the staff roles earlier in the results discussed herein and the time intensive, complex issues for which supervisors are responsible, the work environment within probation and parole appeared to be dynamic as well. Distinct from a work environment in which an employee knows what to expect each day, supervisors stated that much of their day-to-day focus is driven by crisis management and suggested that "no day is ever the same." The complexity of the process, or more specifically the complexity of the "task" assigned to probation and parole officers and their supervisors, is perceived to have increased with the implementation of EBP approaches. At the same time as task complexity increased, it was perceived that the resulting workload was also dependent on the skill of the officers that were under their supervision. Officers agreed that as they gained the initial skills required, especially in a new area of supervision or tasks, their involvement with their supervisor declined over time. This finding suggests that perhaps as stability in a probation or parole department increased, including agencies that were oriented as learning organizations, the demands on the supervisors decreased. It remained true, however, that with the improved quality-control mechanisms in place with EBP at the organizational level, despite high skill levels of officers, the critical nature of ongoing feedback was still recognized as important. The support system integrity, to this end, is directly related to the span of control or span of support as alluded to in an earlier section.

Organizational transition was noted as difficult in the most supportive environment, even with highly skilled staff willing to implement change. The dynamics of entering into an EBP model within probation and parole may mean that a complete shift in a staff member's approach to their job must be employed. Participants noted that during earlier decades, the consensus of staff attitudes tended toward "trail 'em, nail 'em, and jail 'em," in which client supervision and monitoring were emphasized in their work environment. Many current staff members were hired with this perspective in mind, which may have instilled these values in them or aligned with their own personal values. With a paradigmatic shift in thinking and behavioral expectations toward EBP, probation and parole supervision has become much more than mere "supervision" of offenders. As a result, focus group participants who were in managerial roles emphasized that the role of a supervisor begins with a responsibility in working with staff to develop and insure staff buy-in with EBP ideals. Subgroups of staff exist in which some members refuse to align with an ideological shift in primary position functions, whereas other staff embrace new approaches. Within those staff who buy in to EBP, there is a significant range of officer ability to effectively perform within an EBP environment, resulting in some staff who are now ill suited for their positions. The varying perspectives on the role of probation/parole officers with clients that is possessed by staff, which may not be aligned with current EBP ideals, results in discord in the workplace and thus added challenges for supervisors. Given that many supervisors are still dealing with EBP buy-in and capability issues, the need for retaining a relatively low span of control ratios is underscored during implementation phases of organizational change.

In addition to buy-in, the implications for staff capabilities with the shift toward EBP are numerous. Participants noted that a key change in job functioning of probation/parole offices in an EBP environment is an expansion in the required versatility of an officer to an unprecedented level. Officers must now have both the knowledge and skill set to serve in multiple capacities, including a law enforcement officer, a social worker, and an educator. They must possess critical in-depth knowledge of mental health and substance abuse treatment issues as well as understand and be able to address workforce development issues and housing needs of their clients. In turn, a supervisor's role is additionally affected by these staffing complexities both in their own skills and their supervisory responsibilities. Within their own skill set, the supervisor must possess an even higher level of competency in all the areas noted above than their officers. One of the fundamental responsibilities as a supervisor is to guide and mentor staff. To supervise effectively, a supervisor must possess the knowledge and skills that they want their officers to demonstrate.

Certainly, the new expectations of officers are supported by some level of training. Focus group participants noted that the amount of training has substantially increased for both the supervisor and the probation officer. Moreover, the expectation that the supervisor will be actively involved in training, coaching, and mentoring their staff is significant. Some supervisors emphasized that new probation officers only received a week of formal training and that most training occurred on the job and as such much of the training responsibility rested on supervisors. It is critical to recognize that as organizational changes in practice occur, much of the critical components in developing a skilled workforce is affected by supervisory capabilities. It follows that supervisors themselves have to continually go through training to develop their EBP knowledge and skills, so that they can be effective in modeling, teaching, and leading their staff.

Workforce development is not a static process. Unfortunately, as administrators are all too well aware, turnover can and does happen. This added dynamic influence on the existing function of the supervisory positions should not be undervalued or underestimated. As change does occur, supervisors also need to have time to effectively learn their probation officer personalities, strengths, and weaknesses. It was in this regard that some supervisors noted the importance of being able to "walk the halls" and "work the desk."

Supervisors highlighted that they spend a significant amount of time with staff mentoring, building relationships, and reviewing reports to assist with case management (lots of report reviews) to promote consistency among staff and efficacy of EBP, yet more time is still needed. As a probation officer's role grows in complexity (knowledge and skills), there is a direct correlation to the capability of the supervisor and their competence in providing the appropriate and necessary level of guidance, direction, and oversight. At the same time, as indicated earlier, both supervisors and staff do not perceive the time spent in this component of the job as insufficient, given existing span of control across agencies.

Work Environment—The Dynamic Role of Probation Officers and Supervisors

Existing organizational literature points to the nature of the work as a prime factor to consider when assessing appropriate span of control, specifically, the dynamic versus static nature of the job that is being performed as well as the job that is being supervised. Supervisors within work environments that are relatively static, such as factory or assembly line production, are typically able to handle a broader span of control with fidelity, whereas supervisors within dynamic work environments should have a lesser span of control due to the lack of consistency in daily activities and unanticipated events that may occur. Some examples in the existing literature of such dynamic environments include medicine (i.e., head nurse to nurses), military settings (i.e., rule of three), and policing.

The full dynamics in a probation and parole environment has not been explored in this manner to date. Based on interviews with staff, it became evident very quickly that probation and parole departments are a very dynamic environment. Specifically, many supervisors described their district as a "very dynamic organization that is seemingly in constant change." As a result, the role of supervisors especially in an EBP environment is also a very dynamic position as is the organization which should perhaps be viewed as a "learning organization" in which dynamism is the norm. In addition to an increase in the breadth of responsibility, supervisors are also required to have a significantly greater depth of involvement as discussed in the previous section.

As noted in the primary functions of a supervisor discussed above, a number of responsibilities have remained consistent from earlier decades when EBP was not in place. Consistent with earlier eras, administrative tasks such as maintaining current knowledge on changes occurring in laws and policies is important. Certainly, with the growth of EBP, knowledge of empirically supported practices has become critical. Although administrative responsibilities have not subsided, supervisors have experienced notable increases in administrative tasks more directly related to EBP. The majority of the time consumed with administrative tasks was perceived to be related to activities that focused on ensuring that quality EBP is in place and improving line staff skills sets as it relates to the officer-level responsibilities through the provision of feedback. Specifically, EBP places an emphasis on quality report writing directly related to effective offender case management as well as a strong focus on individual probation officer case reviews. Despite the time consumed by quality assurance-related tasks, supervisors agreed that quality assurance auditing was a critical function.

Another aspect of the supervisory role that cannot be underestimated is the dynamic aspect of the day-to-day roles of supervisors. The message was consistently expressed by supervisors who highlighted "no day is the same" and that they were constantly "putting out fires." Staff discussed that they felt they were dealing with moving targets with respect to case staffing issues, working with officers on intcm1ediate sanctions, and emergencies, while simultaneously assisting with case plan reviews, auditing files (checklist audit), and in-depth audits—a comprehensive review to insure that the officer is targeting the right needs of their clients, making appropriate referrals, using motivational interviewing techniques, and so forth. What became very evident throughout these discussions was that supervisors, due to their existing workload, spend much of their day in a reactive mode. Although supervisors are relatively successful in this role, it does not allow for a significant level of proactive activities associated with effective implementation and sustainment of an EBP model.

Discussion

Based on discussions with a wide range of community supervision stakeholders that ranged from upper-level administrators through line staff, focus group interviews were used to examine the relevancy of applying theoretical concepts discussed in the span of control literature to a community supervision environment. These concepts were examined through the discussion of current roles and responsibilities of officers and supervisors in community corrections agencies that implement an EBP organizational approach. Consistently across the focus groups conducted, regardless of geographical origin of the participant or their rank within their agency, responses indicated that many of the factors presented as relevant in other labor fields when deciding on extensiveness of spans of control are also applicable in community corrections. Specifically, participants emphasized the importance of considering the high level of time commitment and dynamic, complex tasks that are relegated to supervisory staff within an EBP environment. The ever changing nature of challenges that are presented in community corrections environments underscored the need for highly trained, highly skilled, adaptable staff at this level.

Participants noted that significant evolution of the supervisory role has occurred since the onset of EBP implementation and staffing patterns must account for these changes as well as the added duties, which are most prominent during the implementation phase of a paradigm shift. It was evident that the majority of stakeholders interviewed, including those lower in rank than supervisory staff, perceived that an increase in the span of control beyond current levels (in both Iowa and the other jurisdictions represented) would likely initially result in lower fidelity of EBP principles and poorer quality/limited supervision. This lack of fidelity would be due to the newness of the concepts to staff which requires significant supervisor–officer interaction, ongoing training, feedback as well as quality assurance to master these skills.

When considering the above discussion of the increased complexity of the supervisor position and seemingly negative connotation associated with the increased workload, we would be remiss to neglect to share the overall perceptions of EBP held by focus group participants. An important perspective of many participants including line officers was that "EBP has made us more professional." The majority of participants felt that an EBP model of supervision was in line with what the focus of their efforts should be, and many of the staff were able to convey anecdotal evidence of its effectiveness with clients or coworkers. In addition to client and workplace benefits, some staff noted that EBP has caused supervisors to become much more active within the community as indicated by comments such as "EBP has drawn us out of the office" and "we have become much more collaborative and connected to neighborhoods." Also, because an EBP model expects staff to develop a much more in-depth relationship with clients/offenders, which requires more training and more supervisor interaction with officers including discussing case-management options, staff perceived supervisory relationships and the organization as a whole to be less "top down." Moreover, the EBP approach causes staff to think and employ the knowledge in discretionary decisions and engage in a more balanced approach between enforcement and treatment.

Although appreciative of the many positive aspects of EBP, it is equally important to convey that supervisors especially felt that with all the organizational change and added job functions beyond primary job functions associated with EBP, they were maximized in their job responsibilities. Overwhelmingly, supervisors felt that at current span of control ratios (varying across jurisdiction), they already have workload issues with current responsibilities and workload driven by administrative and human resource issues (e.g., employee disciplinary, grievances, investigations). They voiced a passionate belief that a larger span of control would absolutely have negative ramifications because of less supervisory support, oversight, and accountability. At the same time, however, it would be anticipated that after allowing for some organizational growth followed by stability, the demands in terms of training of staff should decrease and officer capabilities/skill sets should increase.

Lack of Existing Policy Guiding Staffing in EBP Environments

Whereas some probation and parole organizations do have specific recommended policy related to the span of control, in other jurisdictions such a policy is absent or is meant only as a guideline. One example of such a policy in the state of Texas suggests that "a full-time supervisor should not supervise more than 10 community supervision officers" (http://www.tdcj.state.tx.us/publications/cjad/PAC_Guidelines_2003.pdf). The intent of the limit is to ensure effective management ensues; however, it does allow some flexibility based on the experience of the field officer and other duties of the supervisor. To reiterate from an earlier point made by Cunniff and Shilton (1991), however, policy from one jurisdiction is not necessarily a good model for application to another jurisdictions, given the potential for between-agency variation. Evidence that documents the roles and responsibility of the supervising officers as well as the supervisory structure that may explain some of the variation in span of control ratios is absent in contextualizing these numbers. As Cushman and Sechrest (1992) explained that if the variation between agencies is not fully understood, replication of policy despite a lack of contextual knowledge is problematic, especially if solely viewed from a budgetary standpoint.

When considering jurisdictions that are engaged in EBP and are composed of specialized units, some generalities might apply. As noted by a chief probation officer of an urban jurisdiction who stated in reference to determining an appropriate span of control in an EBP environment,

> Ultimately, how many probationers would your supervisor be responsible for—with medium and high caseloads, it should have a workable supervisory ratio. I would be very concern[ed] for any specialized caseloads especially sex offenders, serious mentally ill, domestic violence, or problem solving courts with a 1:16 ratio.

Conclusions

When an adequate number of supervision staff is lacking, the danger is that programs and practices that are initially well implemented may erode in quality over time. As one director we spoke with stated, "... EBP takes active supervision and some accountability or it slips." McManus (2007) also discussed a number of other global issues that may result when span of control is inadequate including skill erosion, customer confidence erosion, and morale erosion or bad morale if employees are not supported with effective and adequate levels of supervision. Moreover, probation organizations are in a unique position in that individual officers may also be subject to civil liability suits against them as well as their organizations. One expert we communicated with, for example, conveyed that they were aware of two cases "where the probation officer was sued for being negligent. In both cases, the attorneys hired an expert witness ... and they wanted to know whether they knew or should have known what the evidence says they should have done." This concern was reiterated by a chief probation officer who commented in reference to determining appropriate span of control that "perhaps another way of looking at this is liability that your jurisdiction may incur—failure to train, direct, supervise, entrust, discipline, and assignment to name but a few."

If agencies expect to achieve significant modifications of criminal behavior and to reduce recidivism, they must ensure an adequate span of control exists between supervisors and the officers in their units. Agencies must be confident that their supervisors are able to devote the majority of their work day to collaborating with their staff in the actual conduct of their daily business in line with the organization's desired goals, whether its quality EBP or otherwise. Participants emphasized that supervisors must be able to tutor their staff in the skills of case planning, building meaningful relationships with the offender, engaging offenders in accomplishing treatment plans, using rewards and sanctions, and reducing risk by addressing criminogenic needs. Working with human beings, especially offenders, to change their behavior is always a time-consuming process. Supervisors who cannot model such techniques with their staff because they are "stretched too thin" cannot in turn expect their officers to model such behavior with their correctional clients. Through this study, we have confirmed the concordant application of factors suggested to be important for consideration in span of control decision making between other labor fields and community corrections environments.

Note

1. Although specific quantitative measures were not collected, the various points made throughout an overwhelming, if not complete, majority agreed with comments made. Any limited deviation or disagreement from statements made was noted in the sections that follow.

References

Andrews, D., & Bonta, J. (2003). *The psychology of criminal conduct.* Cincinnati, OH: Anderson.

Bianchi, M. (2010). Perspectives for the extension of Graiciunas' span of control to the process of enterprise creation. *Bridges, 53,* 15-33.

Bundy, C. (2004). Changing behaviour: Using motivational interviewing techniques. *Journal of the Royal Society of Medicine, 97*(44), 43-47.

Clark, M. D., Walters, S., Gingerich, R., & Meltzer, M. (2006). Motivational interviewing for probation officers: Tipping the balance toward change. *Federal Probation, 70*(1), 38-44.

Cunniff M. A., & Shilton, M. K. (1991, March). Variations on felony probation: Persons under supervision in 32 urban and suburban counties. Washington, DC: National Association of Criminal Justice Planners.

Cushman, R. C., & Sechrest, D. (1992). Variations in the administration of probation supervision. *Federal Probation, 56*(3), 19-30.

Eastman, G.D., & Eastman, E. C. (1971). *Municipal police administration.* Washington, DC: International City Management Association.

Hamilton, I. (1921). *The soul and body of an army.* London: E. Arnold.

Hanna, D. G., & Gentel, W. D. (1971). *A guide to primary police management concepts.* Springfield, IL: Charles C. Thomas.

Hartzler, B., & Espinosa, E. (2011). Moving criminal justice organizations toward adoption of evidence based practice via advanced workshop training in motivational interviewing: A research note. *Criminal Justice Policy Review, 22,* 235-253. doi: 10.1177/0887403410371372.

Hattrup, G. P., & Kleiner, B. H. (1993, November 1). *How to establish the proper span of control for managers.* Retrieved from http://findarticles.com/p/articlcs/mi_hb308l/is_n6_v35/ain286325l8/

Lane, T. (2006, November). Span of control for law enforcement agencies. *Police Chief* Retrieved from http://www.policechiefmagazine.org/magazine/index.cfm?fuseactiondisplay_arch& article id 1022&issue id 102006

Madson, M. B., Loignon, A. C., & Lane, C. (2009). Training in motivational interviewing: A systematic review. *Journal of Substance Abuse Treatment, 36,* 101-109.

McGuire, J. (2002). Integrating findings from research reviews. In J. McGuire (Ed.), *Offender rehabilitation and treatment: Effective programmes and policies to reduce re-offending* (pp. 3-38). New York, NY: John Wiley.

McManus, K. (2007, September). Losing our span of control. *Industrial Engineer, 39*(9), 22

Meyer, R. M. (2008). Span of management: Concept analysis. *Journal of Advanced Nursing, 63,* 104-112.

Miller, W. R., & Rollnick, S. (1991). *Motivational interviewing: Preparing people to change addictive behavior.* New York, NY: Guilford.

Miller, W. (2003). *Pros and cons: Reflections on motivational interviewing in correctional settings.* Retrieved from http://www.motivationalinterview.org

National Institute of Corrections. (2007). *A guide for probation and parole: Motivating offenders to change* (NIC Accession Number 022253). Washington, DC: U.S. Government Printing Office.

Schroeder, D. J., Lombardo, F., & Strollo, J. (1995). *Management and supervision of law enforcement personnel.* Binghamton, NY: JBL.

Souryal, S.S. (1977). *Police administration and management.* St. Paul, MN: West Publishing.

The Probation Experiment. (2009). *County Magazine.* Retrieved from http://www.county.org/resources/library/county_mag/county/213/toc.html

DISCUSSION QUESTIONS

1. The article establishes the conflict between supervisory costs on one side and organizational effectiveness via EBP on the other. How would you convince a government body (e.g., state or county government) to increase funding for additional supervisors when resources are already limited?

2. The study suggests that EBP requires a narrow span of control due to the increased responsibilities of probation/parole officers and the increased demands placed on supervisors. Is it possible that higher education—requiring graduate degrees for employment as a probation or parole officer, for example—can mitigate the need to narrow the span of control?

3. Is there a relationship between the span of control of probation officers and the span of control of probation supervisors? For example, if EBP increases the complexity of the probation officer's job, must the supervisor's span of control (oversight of officers) change at the same time? Why or why not?

READING

Reading 3

Jana S. Benson and Scott H. Decker's study, unlike the research presented in Readings 1 and 2, examined the organizational structure of an illegal organization. Data were collected from a sample of 34 individuals held in U.S. federal prisons from 1992 to 1998 for drug-trafficking convictions. The respondents, chosen in part due to their high level of drug-smuggling activity, served various roles in their respective organizations. Researchers interviewed each of the convicted traffickers for about two hours—covering, among other issues, the drug-smuggling organization's hierarchy of authority (vertical complexity), formalization, and task specialization.

Findings demonstrated that these illegal organizations are connected horizontally across functional parts (e.g., supplier, transporter, distributor) rather than tightly connected under a central hierarchy of authority. Formal written rules about payments and delivery schedules were also lacking, suggesting a low degree of formalization in drug-smuggling organizations. With respect to task specialization (in this section, referred to as "occupational differentiation"), individual smugglers did not tend to engage in only one activity; they involved themselves in other parts of the operation and in nontrafficking activities. These structures ensure that the overall operation can avoid law enforcement interdiction. For example, when the risk of apprehension increases, the low degree of formalization means that delivery schedules can be quickly altered, and the limited task specialization increases the likelihood that the work will be accomplished even if members are apprehended.

THE ORGANIZATIONAL STRUCTURE OF INTERNATIONAL DRUG SMUGGLING

Jana S. Benson and Scott H. Decker

Introduction

How well are offenders organized? What are the characteristics of the group in offenses where multiple offenders are involved in committing a crime? The criminological literature is replete with discussions of group offending (McCord & Conway, 2002; Reiss, 1988; Warr, 2002). While rates of co-offending are higher

Source: Benson, J. S., & Decker, S. H. (2010). The organizational structure of international drug smuggling. *Journal of Criminal Justice, 38*(2), 130–138.

among juveniles (Klein, 1995; McCord & Conway, 2002; Warr, 2002), co-offending among adults is also substantial (Reiss, 1988; Warr, 2002). What is missing in the existing understanding of the group context of offending is how well organized groups of offenders are, the characteristics of those groups, and the influence of organization on offending patterns.

Several characteristics of the offending process must be accounted for if criminologists are to promote a broader understanding of crime. The motivation to offend typically receives the most attention, while other important aspects of offending receive scant attention, particularly the degree to which groups of offenders are organized, the characteristics of those organizations, and the impact of organizational structure on behavior. A better understanding of how criminal groups are organized would have implications for theory development as well as policy responses to crime. It is not enough to know that a group of individuals were present at a crime scene or participated in concert with each other. The structure of their interactions is a central feature to this process that must be understood. Specifically, organizational features of group offending such as the adaptability of the group, specialization, hierarchy, roles, and communication are key aspects that must be accounted for.

This article examines the question of how well organized groups of offenders are and builds on the previous literature on the organization of drug smugglers by focusing exclusively on high level offenders who have personal experience smuggling drugs into the United States. The analysis begins by examining the literature on organizational structure of offending to establish a context for the current study of the organizational structure of high level international drug smugglers. Following a discussion of the sample included in this study, six key characteristics of organizational structure are reviewed for their presence in both complex and less formally organized groups. Using thirty-four offender interviews, the organization of international drug smuggling groups is illustrated. Finally, conclusions are drawn and directions for future research are discussed.

Crime, Criminals, and Groups

One of the long-standing "major facts" in criminology (Klein, 1967) is the group context of most offending. Group offending is especially pronounced among youthful offenders, with most estimates that 80 percent (or more) of delinquency occurs in a group context (Shaw & McKay, 1931; Warr, 1996). Group offending is particularly pronounced in offenses that generate revenue, such as burglary, larceny, drug sales, and auto theft, but less common in violent offenses, particularly serious assault. Co-offending may have a larger impact, net of the number of individuals involved, than solo offending. Felson (2003) noted that such offending is more likely to generate additional offenses and generate more harm to victims and offenders. Accordingly, criminologists must pay careful attention to the characteristics of co-offending.

Offending groups tend to be relatively small, between two and four individuals (Warr, 2002), but these groups of offenders are typically nested in larger groups of associates, many of whom are also involved in crime or delinquency. Warr (2002, p. 36) identified the former as offending groups and the latter as accomplice networks. He noted that there was little clarity with regard to roles in offending and that most offenders moved between group and individual offending with relative ease, thus addressing the issue of specialization of roles. Offending groups, particularly delinquent offending groups, have a short life span and display little evidence of the kind of rational planning or calculation often thought to characterize group behavior. Reiss (1988) noted that little is known about co-offending patterns among adults. He described adult offending groups as transitory in nature with individuals drifting in—and out—of the groups on a frequent basis.

There is considerable variation in offending groups and to treat them as all the same would be to mischaracterize the nature of such groups. Reiss (1988) suggested that distinctions among gangs, groups, and networks would be a useful starting point in attempting to understand the nature of offender organizations and their impact on offending. Cressey (1972) used the core concept of rationality to characterize the extent and nature of organization within offending groups. Role specialization, hierarchy, and coordination are all key concepts by which he described variation among offending groups from organized crime to street criminals. For this reason, these characteristics were also employed in the present study to distinguish between varying degrees of organization of drug smuggling groups. Waring (2002) argued that the organization of co-offenders rarely follows a market-driven approach or corresponds to the structure of formal organizations, even among organized crime groups. Her key focus was on behavior within offending networks, not elements of the structure, as a means to avoid a strict focus on hierarchy or structure. This approach was consistent with that championed by Burt (1992), who argued that all social structures are built on relationships between individuals.

There have been several attempts to describe more fully the characteristics of co-offending groups, networks, and criminal organizations. Best and Luckenbill (1994, p. 5) created a descriptive typology of co-offending groups using the nature of the association among individuals involved in offenses together. While they concentrated on explaining deviance rather than serious offending, they contended that deviance is generally not well organized. In addition, relationships among offenders were not formal, had short temporal spans, and were specific to individual offenses. Central to their description of these relationships was the idea that the most prominent features of organizations of co-offenders are not part of group structure, but rather in the interactions and transactions. To examine the nature of the interactions between group members in drug smuggling organizations, the present article examines communication within and between these groups.

Many researchers have concluded that offenders do not organize themselves effectively. These studies included ethnographic work done with burglars (Cromwell, Olson, & Avary, 1994; Shover, 1996; Wright & Decker, 1990); robbers (Einstadter, 1969; Wright & Decker, 1997); carjackers (Jacobs, Topali, & Wright, 2003); and gang members (Decker, Bynum, & Weisel, 1998; Decker, Katz, & Webb, 2007). In this context, Donald and Wilson (2000) differentiated between teams and co-acting. Teams, they argued, display a considerable level of interdependence among actors and produce outputs greater than the simple sum of individuals. Co-acting was characterized by low levels of interdependence among offenders who create little additional output beyond what the sum of the individuals would produce. Ram raiders, individuals who engaged in a pattern of smash, grab, and flee at jewelry stores, rarely exhibited permanence in their relationships, specialization, or high levels of long-term interdependence. They observed that offenders were connected in ways that allowed them to assemble teams, identify targets, commit crimes together, and dispose of the proceeds. These relationships were the consequence of generalized offending roles, weak ties and fluid relationships, not a formal, rational structure. The current study examined interdependence as a characteristic of highly organized groups by investigating the coordination of activities within and among the smuggling organizations.

Gangs merit additional discussion in this context because they are a common example of organization among offenders. Many portrayals of gangs by law enforcement and the media depict youth gangs as instrumental-rational organizations. From this perspective, gangs are described as formal organizations that advance their self-interest in rational ways. Researchers have suggested that drug sales in gangs reflect a high degree of organization that is also visible in their use of violence, neighborhood intimidation, and property offenses (Mieczkowski, 1986; Padilla, 1992; Sanchez-Jankowski, 1991; Skolnick, Correl, Navarro, & Robb, 1988). They asserted that gangs embrace common goals, engage in common enterprise, regulate the revenue generating activities of their members, and thus have a formal structure. This view emphasized the formal, rational, and instrumental aspects of the organization. This research also highlighted the vertical nature of the gang and the role of internal controls on gang member behavior in pursuing common goals. It thus recognized the vertical hierarchy of authority as a central feature of highly organized groups.

A competing view described gangs as somewhat disorganized groups, recognizing that although gangs are united by several common features, they are best characterized as having a diffuse organizational structure. Much research has provided support for this contention (Decker & Van Winkle, 1996; Fagan, 1989; Hagedorn, 1988; Klein, Maxson, & Cunningham, 1991). Findings from this research emphasized the lack of a corporate use for the money generated by drug sales, robbery, and property crime among gang members, noting that most profits from such activities are used for individual purposes. This is evidence of a somewhat disorganized, unstructured gang organization.

The focus of this study was on the organizational structure of international drug smuggling. Burt (1992) and Williams (1998) noted that formal organizations can be composed of a number of smaller cells and co-offending groups that engage in drug smuggling, money laundering, human trafficking, or terrorism may have access to information and technology that allows them to operate independently of a larger organizational structure. Indeed, Williams (1998) argued that the key to understanding such groups is to view them as networks; a series of loosely connected nodes (individuals, organizations, firms, and information sharing tools) that are linked across and within organizations. In fact, descriptions of human trafficking and smuggling (Zhang, 2007, 2008); terrorist groups (Kean & Hamilton, 2004; Sageman, 2008); international trafficking in stolen vehicles (Clarke & Brown, 2003); and international drug smuggling (Decker & Chapman, 2008; Morselli, 2001; Williams, 1998) have depicted such groups as small networks of individuals who lack much in the way of a formal structure.

Zaitch (2002) studied drug importation from Colombia to the Netherlands and found little evidence of vertical hierarchies in drug smuggling. The structure of drug distribution was flexible, horizontal, and relied on ethnic and kinship ties to facilitate relationships among smugglers. These characteristics can hardly be described as inductive of a formal organization. Accordingly, the current study examined the recruitment and promotion procedures used in the organization to gain a better understanding of the nature of the bonds that draw people into drug smuggling organizations.

Zaitch (2002) also depicted drug smuggling operations as flexible networks comprised of dynamic, insulated groups that could quickly change tactics and were relatively separate from those earlier or later in the smuggling transaction chain. Organizational adaptability was addressed in the current article through the subjects' descriptions of the how flexibly their group dealt with a variety of changes. Similarly, Schiray (2001) described the organizational structure of drug distribution markets in Sao Paulo as *ad hoc*, unstable, and not long-term operations. Where specialization is found in international drug trade, it can be quite episodic, and smugglers are often absorbed into other forms of crime. The *ad hoc* or unplanned quality of drug smuggling organizations was inspected here through the subjects' descriptions of the statement of rules and objectives prior to a trip being made. These findings were consistent with exploratory research on high-level drug smugglers (Reuter, 1983; Reuter & Haaga, 1989) as well as research on street-level dealers (Adler, 1985).

While research on group offending and drug smuggling in particular has contrasted criminal organizations to formally organized hierarchies, recent research has moved away from the hierarchy-decentralization dispute and examined organized crime within the social network framework (McIllwain, 1999; Morselli, 2005, 2008; Raab & Milward, 2003). Instead of viewing group offenders as either hierarchical or decentralized, this perspective emphasized the dynamic interactions between individuals in these groups and the utility of pooling their resources. Using the social network framework and the case-study approach, Morselli (2008), a salient author in this field of research, examined the organizational structure of various criminal networks, including street gangs, drug distribution networks, and other forms of organized crime. He concluded that these criminal networks were less centralized and structured than previously believed and created a "flexible order" thesis, which suggested that despite some degree of hierarchy and levels of authority among these groups, they maintain some adaptability that benefited the group in terms of managing resources and detecting law enforcement. The current study examined similar aspects of organizational structure, specifically in high-level drug smuggling groups.

A Review of the Organizational Literature

To better understand the organizational structure of international drug smuggling groups, the authors reviewed commonly recognized characteristics of complex organizations. By establishing the qualities that typify complex organizations, it was possible to examine the organizational context of international drug smugglers. The following six characteristics were addressed: (1) hierarchy, (2) statement of rules, (3) communication, (4) adaptability, (5) specialization/coordination, and (6) recruitment/promotion procedures.

In his discussion of the structure of offending organizations, Cressey (1972) noted that the degree of organization is directly related to the rationality of that group. Following the description of formal or complex organizations, as those most rationally arranged in pursuit of its goals it is logical that many of the structural characteristics discussed below are attempts at maximizing rationality and efficiency. Other researchers have suggested, however, that networks are sometimes forced to sacrifice efficiency for other concerns such as security, depending on such traits as the time-to-task and degree of centrality of the organization (Morselli, 2008; Morselli, Giguère, & Petit, 2007). When considering the following characteristics of formally organized networks, it is important to keep in mind that they are not composed of distinct categories. Rather, as previous researchers have observed (e.g., Cressey, 1972; Morselli, 2008), their differences in organization are a matter of degree.

Hierarchy of Authority

One of the most prominent and readily identifiable characteristics of a complex organization is the existence of a formal hierarchy. Formal hierarchies have ranked levels of authority that clearly delineate super- and subordinates, where those in superordinate positions are responsible for overseeing those in lower offices (Weber, 1946). This organization is based on the rationale that having the most qualified person in each position will place an organization in a position to be most effective. The organizational structures of these groups tend to be pyramidal in nature and have a definite vertical quality due to the ranked nature of positions.

Complex or formally organized groups can also have a structure that is horizontally organized. These organizations do not have such graded positions as in a vertical hierarchy and resemble a line connecting various functions rather than a centralized source of control. It is important to note that these rationally organized groups still have a formal designation of responsibilities, but the span of control no longer functions vertically. Decision-making powers flow across various units rather than coming down from a chain of command that originated from a single, ultimate authority.

In contrast to vertical hierarchies or horizontal structures, some groups are organized in a less formal or rational manner. Williams (1998) suggested that some drug smuggling organizations are more accurately described as networks of connected nodes. There is no definite vertical or horizontal chain of command, as individual units are more independent from the larger organization. Decision-making authority, therefore, does not move freely or continuously between nodes, leaving stages of the drug smuggling process isolated from the others to some degree. Such groups exhibit less coordination among their components.

Statement of Rules

In addition to hierarchical structures, another common feature of complex organizations is the formal or written statement of rules, responsibilities, and operating procedures. The structure of organizations is rooted in the rational pursuit of efficiency; therefore, it is necessary to state the group's objectives clearly and the means to reach those goals. Positions are created based on what is found to be the "best" technique or approach, and individuals in those positions are expected to follow rules accordingly.

Less complex organizations or networks typically do not provide members with such explicit expectations. Instead of written rules, objectives and responsibilities are communicated orally or sometimes simply implied. Since individuals are not placed in such organizations because of rational considerations of the fit between their skills and the needs of the organization, there may not be a formal set of rules to communicate to members of the organization.

Communication

Stemming from the hierarchy of authority and formal expression of rules and objectives, complex organizations are typically characterized by indirect communication between members. Communication in these groups is indirect in two senses. First, because of the vertical ranking of positions and formal directives for member's actions, communication with anyone except one's immediate supervisor is rare. Messages and information must flow through the appropriate channels in the chain of command before they reach their target audience. Communication is also indirect in the sense that little personal interaction occurs in these groups. Instead, information tends to be exchanged through more formal channels, where correspondence is more easily documented. Krebs' (2001) examination of terrorist networks demonstrated that groups characterized by distance between members tended to have lower levels of communication, which in turn resulted in increased security for the networks' activities.

Whereas complex organizations are plagued by slow, indirect passing of information from one party or level to another, the opposite is true for groups with a less complex organizational structure. Messages move more directly between members of different units because the units tend not to be separated by various levels of authority. The absence of formal regulations leaves open the possibility to transmit information through personal contacts instead of written communication. In addition, because units tend to be independent within these networks, it is unlikely that a message would successfully reach its target when it is transmitted by any means other than a direct contact with that individual.

Adaptability

The rational model on which most complex organizations are established leaves these groups in a position where they are unable to adapt quickly to changes. Research has noted that that organizations characterized by hierarchy and formal rules are typically unsuited to be flexible in their norms and regulations (Heimer, 1992). Rational goal directed behavior is based on contingencies that exist in a given space and time. Organizational components are then selected and positioned for their contribution to that goal and formal rules for actions are established. While these written regulations ensure success under certain conditions, most organizations cannot control the environment and market in which they operate. These groups are therefore unable to change methods of operation or procedures quickly when necessary. This is particularly difficult to accomplish in dynamic environments, where change is more common than stability. Watts (2003) noted that highly centralized, formal networks are "vulnerable to cascade failures," but also have the benefit of structural resources that support recovery.

On the other hand, less complex organizations typically enjoy high levels of adaptability. Due to their lack of established procedures for maximizing efficiency and direct communication between units, less complex organizations are better able to change in response to a dynamic environment. These adaptations can be stimulated by changes in market conditions or specific to offending groups, improvements in law enforcement technologies, or changes in law enforcement tactics (Bouchard, 2007; Degenhardt, Reuter, Collins, & Hall, 2005). Consistent with the social network perspective, Morselli (2008) noted that more flexible networks are not the result of a predefined form. Instead, they emerge from a process of interactions among the individuals in the group. Zaitch (2002) observed that segments of drug smuggling groups were quickly able to change their modus operandi without disturbing the entire operation because the subunits were relatively isolated from other steps in the process due to their non-hierarchical nature.

Specialization and Coordination of Activities

Along with the presence of a formal hierarchy, specialization (or division of labor) is a commonly cited indicator of a complex organization. Division of labor is a product of the rational search for maximum efficiency and contributes to that goal in two ways. First, specialization guarantees that multiple people are not performing the same task. Every member or unit focuses his or her attention on one element of the larger organizational function, in effect becoming an expert at it. Second, by assigning only one task to a position, the organization is able to seek the most qualified person for that role and place them accordingly. This division of labor recognizes that members vary in their skills and abilities and uses individuals' specializations to benefit the larger organization.

Specialization alone, however, is not sufficient for maximum rationality. Complex organizations must also coordinate the activities of each unit to ensure that the ultimate objective is reached. These groups, therefore, are characterized by high levels of interdependence between subunits. For the organization as a whole to be successful, it is imperative that each individual task be performed in the most efficient manner.

Coordinating activities in complex organizations is illustrated in the hierarchical distribution of authority discussed previously. With regard to producing and transporting drugs, research has demonstrated the level of specialization required to produce specific substances influences not only individual members' activities, but also the complexity of the overall organizational structure (Reuter & Greenfield, 2001).

Networks that are not as complex or rational rely less on specialization and coordination than do their counterparts. While these groups might have some division of labor, they are unlikely to place the most "specialized" individual in any given position because clearly delineated objectives and rules to establish the best means for fulfilling that role do not exist. Placement in the group could be based on other criteria other than specialization, such as convenience, cost, or patrimony. In addition, because these groups are best described structurally as a series of connected nodes, coordinating activities across the entire organization is highly unlikely. Instead, the success of the entire operation depends *less* on the efficiency of individual tasks, as is the case with complex organizations. Lack of coordinating activities can also be understood to contribute to the high adaptability of these networks.

Recruitment and Promotions

High levels of specialization and rationality are also associated with merit-based recruitment and promotional systems. Selecting and placing members in the group based on their skills and formal qualifications increases the odds that an organization is operating in the most efficient means possible. Promotions in complex organizations are typically merit based, adding an element of competition to motivate members to be efficient. As individuals who have accomplished the most for the organization are promoted up the chain of command, a direct link between member productivity and advancement is established.

In contrast to complex organizations, less rationally organized networks rely less on merit or qualifications. This could be attributed to their lack of clearly enumerated role expectations, which makes developing criteria specific to a position more difficult. The absence of a vertical hierarchy for members to "climb" makes promotions less likely in these groups of connected, but isolated nodes. Recruitment and placement could be based on prior working relationships, kinship, ethnicity, or in more short-term assignments, the nature of the task, as opposed to competency (Donald & Wilson, 2000; Schiray, 2001; Zaitch, 2002). The role of patrimony, kinship, and social capital in recruitment and promotion in organized crime has been documented in the empirical literature (e.g., Block, 2006; Morselli, 2003).

The Drug Smuggler Study

The following analysis was based on interviews conducted with thirty-four individuals held in federal prisons in the United States. The interviews were conducted as part of a larger investigation into the effects of various law enforcement and interdiction techniques on high-level drug smuggling. While the organizational structure of these groups was not a central focus of the original study, information about the way drug smugglers organized themselves was unavoidable in the discussion. A semi-structured, open-ended questionnaire, which was used to elicit information during in-depth interviews, was created from information obtained from interviews with U.S. Customs, U.S. Coast Guard, and prior literature on drug smuggling. The interviews lasted approximately two hours and were conducted in the federal facility where the individual was currently serving time. To acquire the most useful information from the convicted smugglers, a Spanish translator was used when necessary, and all interviews were recorded and transcribed for later analysis.

To focus on high-level drug smuggling, the sample for the current study was selected from individuals serving time for federal drug trafficking convictions from 1992 to 1998. Individuals were selected based on their pre-sentencing investigations and the severity of their score according to the federal sentencing guidelines. Of the 135 "high-level" drug smugglers located in federal prisons, 73 were asked to participate. This produced a sample of 35 individuals that were heavily involved in drug smuggling.

To better understand the characteristics of the interviewed individuals, it is useful to describe them in broad terms. Table 1 presents descriptive characteristics for individuals included in the sample. While the majority of subjects indicated the United States as their country of origin, such nations as Colombia, Cuba, Venezuela, and the Bahamas were also reported. Smuggling activity was described in various locations in the Caribbean and South America, including Colombia, the Bahamas, Panama, Cuba, the Dominican Republic, Mexico, Haiti, Peru, Puerto Rico, and Venezuela.

It should be noted that the sampling procedure employed in the current study had its limitations. While the purpose of this study was to gain a better understanding of *all* aspects of drug smuggling organizations, the sample only included interviews with individuals who were arrested and convicted for that offense. It was possible that some characteristic of these convicted individuals differentiated them from others who had not been caught; for example, the degree of organization of their smuggling group. This concern brought into question the representativeness of the sample and the generalizability of the findings.

The information obtained from this sample was adequately representative of drug smuggling organizations working in the Caribbean during the period of time these offenders were active. First, most of the subjects interviewed were smuggling drugs internationally for many years prior to their arrest and had been involved in multiple trips to various locations. Due to the high-involvement in and experience with international drug smuggling, the experiences the subjects reported were believed to be similar to those of other active high-level offenders. In addition, the results of the study were consistent with most of the findings from earlier work on drug smuggling specifically and that of other types of offenders more generally.

SECTION II ORGANIZATIONAL STRUCTURE

Table 1 Summary of Subject Characteristics

Country of origin	Role	Smuggling region	Age range	Weight of drugs
Bahamas	Recruiter	Colombia/Bahamas	40-49	480 kilos
Colombia	Organizer	Colombia	40-49	1,500 kilos
Colombia	Manager	Colombia	40-49	630 kilos
Colombia	Supervisor	Colombia	40-49	165 kilos
Colombia	Organizer	Colombia	40-49	1,500 kilos
Colombia	Organizer	Bahamas	40-49	3,345.5 kilos
Colombia	Leader	Colombia	60-69	500 kilos
Cuba	Recruiter	Colombia	50-59	40 kilos
Cuba	Broker	Panama	30-39	59 kilos
Cuba	Leader	Cuba/Dom. Republic	30-39	515 kilos
Cuba	Leader	Cuba	40-49	2,350.5 kilos
Cuba	Organizer	Colombia	30-39	728 kilos
Cuba	Transporter	Mexico	40-49	5,000 kilos
Cuba	Captain	Colombia/Haiti	30-39	150+kilos
Cuba	Off-loader	Colombia	40-49	500 kilos
Venezuela	Organizer	Peru	50-59	500 kilos
Venezuela	Leader	Bahamas/Cuba	40-49	50 kilos
U.S.	Manager	Venezuela	30-39	605.5 kilos
U.S.	Leader	Bahamas	50-59	414 kilos
U.S.	Recruiter	Colombia	50-59	15-50 kilos
U.S.	Leader	Caribbean	50-59	1,450 kilos
U.S.	Manager	Haiti	40-49	2,200 kilos
U.S.	Captain/investor	Bahamas	70-79	776.3 kilos
U.S.	Organizer	Panama	30-39	800-1,000 kilos
U.S.	Organizer	Bahamas	50-59	488 kilos
U.S.	Broker	Colombia	30-39	4,500 kilos and 14,000 lbs
U.S.	Organizer	Puerto Rico/Dom. Republic	40-49	480 kilos

Country of origin	Role	Smuggling region	Age range	Weight of drugs
U.S.	Leader	Colombia	20-29	500-600 kilos
U.S.	Leader	Hong Kong/Puerto Rico	60-69	86 kilos and 39 lbs
U.S.	Leader	Colombia/Puerto Rico	60-69	1,000 kilos and 1,000 lbs
U.S.	Manager	Bahamas	60-69	600 kilos
U.S.	Leader	Caribbean	30-39	15-50 kilos
U.S.	Manager	Caribbean	50-59	5,543.8 kilos
U.S.	Owner/financier	Bahamas	30-39	757 kilos

Analyzing the Organizational Structure of International Drug Smuggling

Hierarchy of Authority

When considering all distribution groups as part of a larger organization of drug smugglers, one finds an example of this formal hierarchy in the former Colombian trafficking groups of the Medellin and Cali cartels. During this era, drug smuggling operations had clear leadership positions in charge of various functions in addition to a clearly defined area of control over which they ruled (Filippone, 1994). Consistent with traditional conceptions of highly organized cartels, subjects who had longtime involvement in drug smuggling described the drug trade during the 1970s as follows:

RESPONDENT 26: Those were the people that we met during that time, and they had an organization, a big organization. They were organized. They paid on time. Once it comes in, they've got the cars. They've got everything.

RESPONDENT 24: Well, it's kind of like a company where you have a person in charge, which would be your chairman of the board, CEO, whatever. And he delegates his other officer of his vice presidents, which would be lieutenants... Then from there you had different workers for him that did different jobs.

When asked about the organization of drug trafficking more recently, it became clear that a formal, complex structure had given way to a less organized network of connected units, as was described by Williams (1998):

RESPONDENT 8: Well, it's different—it's smaller groups now. Like before, it was all cartels. It was a group of gentlemen, it was like a board. We make decisions together and stuff. Not it's all broken up... all of those brokers became chiefs, became bosses... they know all of the connections. They have their own networking, they have clients. [Now they are]... smaller groups, unknown small groups like two, three guys, that have people that say, you know, make a batch of 1,000 keys, and they will distribute it differently.

RESPONDENT 20: There is no such thing as the Cali cartel; there are Cali groups, but not a Cali Cartel... Right now that is destroyed. Right now there are thousands of small groups called small offices... So there is not such a thing as a cartel, but a bunch of people together.

This finding is consistent with Morselli's (2001) in-depth examination of high-level marijuana smugglers. Morselli observed that the high status achieved by an individual within the organization was not attributable to his ability to control others and excessive use of force, as is typical in mafia and cartel-linked networks. Rather, the high-ranking position of the individual was a result of his ability to serve as a "network vector" (p. 228), mobilizing the drug trade by connecting key actors.

By exploring the relationship between the groups that are responsible for moving drugs from the supplier to transporter to distributor, one can better understand the nature of the connections between individuals in the organization. Interviews with the thirty-four smugglers revealed that these groups were not well connected between different functions and the units tended to operate independently of the larger organization. Many times, individuals were only aware of their portion of the operation and had very limited knowledge about the other stages and workers:

RESPONDENT 4: I only knew one guy—two guys in this enterprise, and there were about thirteen or fourteen people in the deal, involved there.

RESPONDENT 2: Transportation is one thing, okay. That office in Colombia is supposed to get the people in Miami to do the smuggling, right? And I was the head, you know, my own group. Got twenty people working for me doing the smuggling, ten people, whatever, and it was my responsibility. They got nothing to do with that. They just pay me for me to do the job.

Further evidence of the independent nature of the smuggling networks was found in the description of how loads of drugs are assembled and the autonomy of individuals involved in various stages of the smuggling process. First, subjects reported that many times loads of drugs to be transported to the Unites States were not assembled by a single organization, but rather they were financed by contributions from multiple offices and individuals. Second, the lack of a formal authority structure or chain of command was illustrated by a boat captain who demonstrated independence in decision making about his stage of the process:

RESPONDENT 30: A bunch of people will invest in the load. It's like selling shares of stock. This person will put up this amount of money. Another person will put up another amount of money, and they in effect maybe own 2 or 3 keys. Then the collector, or whoever, whatever you want to call him, puts all this together, and this joint venture goes on a plane.

RESPONDENT 14: I'm the transport. I'm the one that tells them this is how we're going to play the game. We're going to do it this way. We're not going to use this. We're going to do this because I'm in charge, and I'm aware of surveillance. I know how the Government is running things, how things are happening. So I keep constant contact with the office. All the broker does is pick up the drugs and give me the money for my services.

With regard to formal rules, this study found that expectations and objectives were rarely codified. Agreements about payments for loads were made informally and some aspects of the smuggling operations lacked established procedures. This resulted in a variety of methods being employed, some of which were more successful than others. There were aspects of the transaction that were uncertain and highly variable within and between trips:

RESPONDENT 1: I think [payment] would have happened after they took the merchandise, after they sold it. There wasn't any date . . . we never talked about it . . . we don't sign no contract. All we do, we shake hands on it because my word is my vow, and I have to keep it.

RESPONDENT 21: The pickups were usually about the middle of the night... Now I have done it during the day. I pull right up to the seawall, and they'd offload right out of the house. One of them was a boat transfer, but others they just offload right off the seawall right into the boat.

RESPONDENT 1: I would get everybody in a room, the guys that was supposed to be involved in it, and in the planning of the project, how we're going to do it... I always figure that if all of them would come to the same conclusion that *this* is the best way to do it, then the police and the DEA, too, would think this was the best way to do it. So to me, the best way was to go all different [techniques].

The rational organization of these international drug smuggling organizations is also challenged by the indirect and informal nature of their communications. Consistent with prior literature on communication in smuggling networks (Morselli et al., 2007), information obtained during the interviews described communication in international drug smuggling groups as commonly involving face-to-face contact, even between bosses and distant workers. Communication between groups was frequent and quick, relying on such means as phones or radios, and less on written exchanges.

RESPONDENT 20: A group of two or three Colombians owned the load. I started [doing business] with intermediaries, but then went to Barranquilla and went straight to an owner. At that time we were thinking about using ships, commercial cargoes, to transport the cocaine. That was the reason why I went from the island to Barranquilla, to talk about how we were going to do it in the future.

RESPONDENT 8: It's just a matter of a phone call. I say, "I have this package for you. Would you take care of it?" And [the broker] says "Okay, I'll take care of it."

RESPONDENT 29: I would be notified that the drugs had moved from Colombia to the Bahamas... Communicating with the boat crew? I saw them and talked to them almost every day.

RESPONDENT 23: We were in the house, waiting for [the boats] to come and unload. We knew when they were coming because we got a call from the one that I told you it was, the chief, the boss.

Regarding the flexibility of the organizational networks, this sample of offenders suggested that high-level drug smuggling organizations were adaptable to a variety of stimuli. Such stimuli included law enforcement activity, a country's market for the drug, or removing an individual from a position. In addition, the subjects related that changes to the plan of action occurred frequently, often on very short notice. The interviews provided many instances that illustrate rapid change in both the techniques of smuggling and the organizations that smuggle drugs:

RESPONDENT 14: When I met him, we started running things a whole different – since that boat got caught and that whole operation, that whole route got caught, we changed everything. I met this Colombian gentleman and we started working in the Bahamas. We started air-dropping marijuana... Then after the plane crash, I stopped moving through the Bahamas and moved from cigarette boats to lobster boats. Cigarette boats were already obsolete. They were, like we say, hot. Too suspicious.

RESPONDENT 1: Right now the United States is a very—the market is lucrative. But the profit, it isn't there like it used to be. Now, if you do your research and you look at all the countries, Australia, a kilo of coke goes for $8,000. Japan, it goes for $100,000... I had that set up, but like I said... you got to look for different places to go. You got to move on.

RESPONDENT 16: When organizing a group of captains and people who could sell these drugs, they were still able to do it once I was caught. They do it with somebody else. They find somebody, they find somebody. To stop drug smuggling, they [the government] keep on [using] prison, putting people in jail. It stopped me, but 20 more come in.

RESPONDENT 3: That's why people are going from heroin—from marijuana—to coke... You're bringing 80,000 pounds of marijuana. You need 50, 60, 70 [people]. To bring 500 kilos of cocaine, you need only four people. The money is there.

RESPONDENT 5 : We would constantly change the routes... through the Caribbean. You go around through the Peninsula to the west or you go to the east around the Caribbean Basin.

The convicted smugglers described the levels of specialization and coordination in their groups to be relatively low. Many of the subjects did not specialize in drug smuggling, as they reported also being involved in a range of other legitimate and illegitimate endeavors. In addition, instead of employing the *best* person doing a particular task, there were often many people doing the same job, even with some redundancy.

RESPONDENT 34: I am an accountant. I wanted more money, and I saw the money from the drugs... I also had legal businesses... I had a paint franchise... a company for remodeling and interior design... an import-export company for clothes, bicycles, toys and those types of things.

RESPONDENT 5: [In response to "What was your favorite offense?"]: Money laundering... drugs ... robbing the bank... frauds... there's no such thing as a favorite offense. I don't like being caught.

RESPONDENT 14: We don't own certain routes. I mean, there's multiple people working. Doing exactly the same thing I am.

Coordination was also absent or minimal in the drug smuggling process. Interviews suggested that a lack of integration commonly occurred between the transportation and pick-up stages. As expected with less formally organized groups, inconsistencies during important activities *did not* cause the entire operation to fail.

RESPONDENT 21: The[y] just give me Loran coordinates. I've got the maps. And they give me a time. Sometimes I'd go [from Miami to the Bahamas] and nothing would ever happen. And then I would come back empty.

RESPONDENT 17: I had a freighter, I knew the owner of the land strip in Guajira. Sometimes they had the loads waiting there for two or three weeks and no one would show up to pick it up. So this guy would call me to ask if I pick it up, I said yes, and the other people would call me.

In the experiences of the men interviewed, recruitment and promotions in drug smuggling organizations were not based on merit. In fact, many interviewed recounted that at the time of their initial involvement in drug smuggling they were at a low point in their lives, experiencing marital, financial, or drug-related problems. Actual placement into a position in the group was based on shared ethnicity or previous interactions, often based on family connections. In either case, the subjects made clear that establishing trust was the key aspect of recruiting new members.

RESPONDENT 24: When we got divorced, I just really didn't care about anything... So when I was getting a pair of pants done, some guys comes and talks to me, and he said "Listen, how's it going? I see you're from Miami." He asked me if I wanted to make some money, and I said sure, that's cool.

RESPONDENT 30: I met Jorge in prison... We became friends. We kept in contact after we got out. That's where I met him.

RESPONDENT 6: I arrived [in Colombia]. I used to live there, fishing. I meet a girl. Then she die, and I get so damn crazy. That's when I start using [cocaine]. Then I meet people that

I knew—I knew them before. They was lobster fishermen, poor people. I find out they are all rich. Then they give me work smuggling drugs ... they were Cubans, all the time Cubans. There is a bond between Cubans ... you trust another Cuban more than a Colombian or Haitian.

The interviews also revealed that promotions within drug smuggling organizations were not based on productivity, time in the network, or merit. Instead, individuals moved into more autonomous positions once they had amassed enough money and connections to do so, typically resulting in them having their own operation.

RESPONDENT 1: I was a bodyguard for the off-loader ... One day, one of the guys was sick. He could not drive the boat, and I said I can drive the boat.. So I got in the boat and I was the driver then. [The first trip] was a forty mile trip, and I spent three days looking for the place because I could not find it. I didn't know how to navigate.

RESPONDENT 29: The fellow whose deal it was ran short on money, and he started offering back seven to one to anyone who wanted to invest. So I had a little bit of money. Because of a shortage of trustworthy people ... I ended up being on one of these two boats going out to meet a coastal freighter coming up from Colombia ... The fellow whose deal it was, was a cokehead ... so, finally we said the hell with it. We'd buy out own boat. We went down and bought an old fishing boat, and we started in the marijuana-smuggling business. We had people with the connections through him.

Conclusion

This study examined the commonly held features of formal organizations, and contrasted them with descriptions of drug smuggling organizations provided by a sample of high-level international drug smugglers. The six organizational features examined here included hierarchy, statement of rules, communication, adaptability, specialization/coordination, and recruitment/promotion procedures. These attributes are commonly taken to be attributes of formal organizations.

Little evidence was found to support the view that drug smugglers work in groups that are organized in a manner consistent with such organizations. Rather than being characterized as efficient or rational, drug smugglers work in groups that are horizontal rather than vertical. That is, orders or commands seldom come from a centralized authority communicated down an organizational structure. Instead, drug smugglers work in loosely connected nodes where communication is informal. Such groups of drug smugglers described their groups as having few rules, and seldom relied on a meritocracy for selecting, recruiting, or promoting members in the group. Rather, informal associations—personal knowledge, kinship ties, or common experiences—characterized how most decisions were made in this regard. These groups were highly adaptable to their environment. The environment could include threats posed by new law enforcement tactics or technologies, inclement weather, dynamic supply or demand for the drug, or other factors. Rather than working to the detriment of the goal of making profit through drug smuggling, these organizational characteristics seemed to provide a rational means to success. This description of international drug smuggling groups itself must be regarded as dynamic and evolutionary. The horizontal, informal, and loosely connected nodes succeeded the more tightly organized cartels that preceded them. This work has illustrated the adaptability of groups of offenders to their environment.

It should be noted that the generalizability of these findings was limited. The qualitative nature of this study, however, was selected to produce more descriptive findings, specifically about how high-level smugglers move drugs into the United States. A concern that this research failed to incorporate information from *active* drug smugglers is minimized when one considers the research on organization of groups of other *active* offenders (see e.g., Decker et al., 2007; Jacobs et al., 2003; Shover, 1996; Wright & Decker, 1997). Qualitative research on active burglars, armed robbers, carjackers, and gang members had concluded that these offenders are not well organized either. This suggested that the finding that drug smuggling groups were not well organized could not be attributed to the fact that only individuals who were arrested and convicted were interviewed. Future research in this area should attempt to tap into information from active drug smugglers—difficult as this may be—to evaluate whether their organization is, indeed, as disorganized as those offenders included in the present sample.

As previously suggested, to gain a more complete understanding of how groups operate, it is essential to examine not only their structure, but the interactions and transactions that occur between individuals (see e.g., Best & Luckenbill, 1994; Burt, 1992; Waring, 2002). While this article certainly addresses the structure of drug smuggling groups, it only briefly touches on the way members behave and interact with each other. Future research should focus on this aspect of the organization to better understand how these interactions influence the group's offending patterns.

Cressey (1972) noted that the foundation of formal organization is based in a rational search for efficiency and maximized profits. Similarly, Warr (2002) suggested that a low degree of specialization and an absence of clearly stated rules indicated a group is not rationally organized. The findings in this study revealed that was not the case with international drug smuggling groups. Although they failed to demonstrate many of the characteristics of a formally organized group, the interviews suggested that minimizing risk is an essential *rationale* within these operations and might account for the high adaptability of these groups. For example, research has suggested that drug supply chains without a centralized power source are more vulnerable to interdiction because they lack the organized network support and resources associated with a more formal, centralized chain (Reuter, 1983; Tremblay, Cusson, & Morselli, 1998). Research on social systems and networks supports the idea that networks can be organized around a variety of rationalities beyond profit-maximization, depending on their particular organizational norms (Machado & Burns, 1998).

While some might suggest loosely connected individuals would make these smuggling operations less successful than more formally organized drug cartels, this is not necessarily the case. Although it appears that these groups are not highly structured organizations, they still exhibit elements of rationality in their attempts to reduce risk of detection. It is possible, therefore, that instead of being organized around efficiency, which results in the formal structure discussed above, these groups ensure their success by arranging their activities around minimizing risk. For example, Morselli et al. (2007) suggested that the quick, informal communication between central actors in drug trafficking networks actually serves to increase security of the network by creating a periphery that insulates participants at the core. In addition, Reuter (1985) suggested that centrally organized illegal networks are more vulnerable to detection because of their increased visibility. If this is true, then it might be the case that drug smuggling groups are not disorganized, but instead merely organized around an alternative rationale.

Future research should therefore consider how the pursuit of minimized detection risk affects smuggling operations and consequently its organizational structure. For example, while it was shown here that these organizations rely more on trust or association-based recruitment procedures to reduce risk of detection, research has yet to examine the impact of this practice on the offending of the group. In addition, future research should consider the size of the production source when exploring the rationale of minimized risk. Bouchard (2007) found that risk of detection in marijuana distribution networks depended both on the number of cultivators as well as the size of the sites they operate, two variables not examined in the preceding analysis.

Undoubtedly, the current research was more descriptive than causal in nature. It described the structure of drug smuggling organizations, with little emphasis on the impact of organizational structure on operational processes. How does a less structured organization drug smuggling group influence that group's offending patterns? What effect, if any, does a rational organization based on minimizing risk versus maximizing profit have on the activities and life span of an organization? Future research should consider these questions and others to move toward better understanding the organization of international drug smuggling groups and offending groups in general.

References

Adler, P. A. (1985). *Wheeling and dealing: An ethnography of an upper-level drug dealing and smuggling community*. New York: Columbia University Press.

Best, J., & Luckenbill, D. (1994). *Organizing deviance*. Englewood Cliffs, NJ: Prentice Hall.

Block, A. A. (2006). The snowman cometh: Coke in the progressive New York. *Criminology, 17*, 75–99.

Bouchard, M. (2007). A capture-recapture model to estimate the size of criminal populations and the risks of detection in a marijuana cultivation industry. *Journal of Quantitative Criminology, 23*, 221–241.

Burt, R. S. (1992). *Structural holes*. Cambridge, MA: Harvard University Press.

Clarke, R. V., & Brown, R. (2003). International trafficking in stolen vehicles. In M. Tonry (Ed.), *Crime and justice: A review of research* (Vol. 30, pp. 197-228). Chicago: University of Chicago Press.

Cressey, D. (1972). *Criminal organization: Its elementary forms*. New York: Harper and Row.

Cromwell, P., Olson, J., & Avary, D. W. (1994). *Breaking and entering*. Thousand Oaks, CA: Sage.

Decker, S. H., Bynum, T. S., & Weisel, D. L. (1998). A tale of two cities: Gang organization. *Justice Quarterly, 15*, 395–425.

Decker, S. H., & Chapman, M. T. (2008). *Drug smugglers on drug smuggling: Lessons from the inside*. Philadelphia: Temple University Press.

Decker, S. H., Katz, C., & Webb, V. (2007). Understanding the black box of gang organization: Implications for involvement in violent crime, drug sales and violent victimization. *Crime and Delinquency, 54*, 153–172.

Decker, S. H., & Van Winkle, B. (1996). *Life in the gang: Family friends and violence*. New York: Cambridge.

Degenhardt, L., Reuter, P. H., Collins, L., & Hall, W. (2005). Evaluating explanations of the Australian 'heroin shortage.' *Addiction, 100*, 459–469.

Donald, I., & Wilson, A. (2000). Ram raiding: Criminals working in groups. In D. Canter & L. Allison (Eds.), *The social psychology of crime* (pp. 191–246). Burlington, VT: Ashgate.

Einstadter, W. (1969). The social organization of robbery. *Social Problems, 17*, 64–83.

Fagan, J. (1989). The social organization of drug use and drug dealing among urban gangs. *Criminology, 27*, 633–669.

Felson, M. (2003). The process of co-offending. *Crime Prevention Studies, 16*, 149–167.

Filippone, R. (1994). The Medellin Cartel: Why we can't win the drug war. *Studies in Conflict and Terrorism, 17*, 323–344.

Government Printing Office. Klein, M. W. (1967). Criminological theories as seen by criminologists: An evaluative review of approaches to the causation of crime and delinquency. Albany, NY: Governor's Special Committee on the Criminal Offender.

Hagedorn, J. (1988). *People and folks: Gangs, crime, and the underclass in a rustbelt city*. Chicago: Lakeview Press.

Heimer, C. A. (1992). Doing your job and helping your friends: Universalistic norms about obligations to help particular others in networks. In N. Nohria & R. G. Eccles (Eds.), *Networks and organizations: Structure, form and action* (pp. 143–164). Boston: Harvard Business School Press.

Jacobs, B., Topali, V., & Wright, R. (2003). Carjacking, streetlife and offender motivation. *British Journal of Criminology, 43*, 673–688.

Kean, T. H., & Hamilton, L. (2004). The 9/11 Commission report: Final report of the National Commission on Terrorist Attacks upon the United States. Washington, DC: U.S.

Klein, M. W. (1995). *The American street gang*. New York: Oxford University Press.

Klein, M. W., Maxson, C. L., & Cunningham, L. C. (1991). "Crack," street gangs, and violence. *Criminology, 29*, 623–650.

Krebs, V. E. (2001). The network paradigm applied to criminal organizations. *Connections, 24*, 53–65.

Machado, N., & Burns, T. R. (1998). Complex social organization: Multiple organizing modes, structural incongruence, and mechanisms of integration. *Public Administration, 76*, 355–386.

McCord, J., & Conway, K. P. (2002). Patterns of juvenile delinquency and co offending. In E. Waring & D. Weisburd (Eds.), *Crime and social organization* (pp. 15–30). New York: Transaction.

McIllwain, J. S. (1999). Organized crime: A social network approach. *Crime, Law, and Social Change, 32*, 301–324.

Mieczkowski, T. (1986). Geeking up and throwing down: Heroin street life in Detroit. *Criminology, 24*, 645–666.

Morselli, C. (2001). Structuring Mr. Nice: Entrepreneurial opportunities and brokerage positioning in the cannabis trade. *Crime, Law, and Social Change, 35*, 203–244.

Morselli, C. (2003). Career opportunities and network-based privileges in the Costa Nostra. *Crime, Law, and Social Change, 39*, 383–418.

Morselli, C. (2005). *Contacts, opportunities and criminal enterprise*. Toronto, Ontario, Canada: University of Toronto Press.

Morselli, C. (2008). *Inside criminal networks*. New York: Springer.

Morselli, C., Giguère, C., & Petit, K. (2007). The efficiency/security trade-off in criminal networks. *Social Networks, 29,* 143–153.

Padilla, F. M. (1992). *The gangas an American enterprise.* New Brunswick, NJ: Rutgers University Press.

Raab, J., & Milward, H. B. (2003). Dark networks as problems. *Journal of Administration Research and Theory, 13,* 413–439.

Reiss, A. J., Jr. (1988). Co-offending and criminal careers. In N. Morris & M. Tonry (Eds.), *Crime and justice* (Vol. 10, pp. 117–170). Chicago: University of Chicago Press.

Reuter, P. H. (1983). *Disorganized crime: The economics of the visible hand.* Cambridge, MA: MIT Press.

Reuter, P. H. (1985). *Organization of illegal markets: An economic analysis.* Washington, DC: National Institute of Justice.

Reuter, P. H., & Greenfield, V. (2001). Measuring global drug markets. *World Economics, 2,* 159–173.

Reuter, P. H., & Haaga, J. (1989). *The organization of high-level drug markets: An exploratory study.* Santa Monica, CA: Rand.

Sageman, M. (2008). *Leaderless Jihad: Terror networks in the twenty-first century.* Philadelphia: University of Pennsylvania Press.

Sanchez-Jankowski, M. (1991). *Islands in the street: Gangs and American urban society.* Berkeley: University of California Press.

Schiray, M. (2001). Introduction: Drug trafficking, organised crime, and public policy for drug control. *International Social Science Journal, 53,* 351–358.

Shaw, C., & McKay, H. (1931). *Report on the causes of crime: No. 13.* Washington, DC: National Commission on Law Observance and the Administration of Justice.

Shover, N. (1996). *Great pretenders: Pursuits and careers of persistent thieves.* Boulder, CO: Westview Press.

Skolnick, J., Correl, T., Navarro, E., & Robb, R. (1988). *The social structure of street drug dealing.* Report to the Office of the Attorney General of the State of California. Berkeley: University of California.

Tremblay, P., Cusson, M., & Morselli, C. (1998). Market offenses and limits to growth. *Crime, Law, and Social Change, 29,* 31–330.

Waring, E. (2002). Co-offending as a network form of social organization. In E. Waring & D. Weisburd (Eds.), *Crime and social organization* (pp. 31–48). New Brunswick, NJ: Transaction.

Warr, M. (1996). Organization and instigation in delinquent groups. *Criminology, 34,* 11–37.

Warr, M. (2002). *Companions in crime: The social aspects of criminal conduct.* New York: Cambridge University Press.

Watts, D.J. (2003). *Six degrees: The science of a connected age.* New York: W.W. Norton.

Weber, M. (1946). Bureaucracy. In H. H. Gerth & C. W. Mills (Eds.), *Max Weber: Essays in sociology* (pp. 196–244). New York: Oxford University Press.

Williams, P. (1998). The nature of drug-trafficking networks. *Current History, 97,* 154–159.

Wright, R., & Decker, S. H. (1990). *Burglars on the job; Streetlife and residential burglary.* Boston: Northeastern University Press.

Wright, R., & Decker, S. H. (1997). *Armed robbers in action: Stickups and street culture.* Boston: Northeastern University Press.

Zaitch, D. (2002). *Trafficking cocaine: Colombian drug entrepreneurs in the Netherlands.* The Hague, Netherlands: Kluwer.

Zhang, S. X. (2007). *Smuggling and trafficking in human beings: All roads lead to America.* Westport, CT: Praeger.

Zhang, S. X. (2008). *Chinese human smuggling organizations.* Stanford, CA: Stanford University Press.

DISCUSSION QUESTIONS

1. If agreements between the various parts of the drug-trafficking network are not formally written down, how can members of the organization be confident that they will receive shipments and/or payment?

2. Some organizations are characterized by rigid structures, while flexibility describes the drug-trafficking organizations studied. Why is flexibility so important among criminal organizations?

3. Benson and Decker (2010) note, "Many times, individuals were only aware of their portion of the operation and had very limited knowledge about the other stages and workers" (p. 135). Why is this lack of knowledge a virtue in the organizations studied?

SECTION III

Organizational Theory

How Do We Explain What Organizations Look Like?

Section Highlights

Classical Theories
    Scientific Management
    Bureaucracy
    Administrative Management
Human Relations Theory

Open Systems Theories
    Contingency Theory
    Resource Dependence Theory
    Institutional Theory

In 1988, the Junction City Police Department, a pseudonym for a Midwestern police agency studied by Charles Katz (2001), created a specialized gang unit. The formation of the unit, an example of functional differentiation, was a response to concerns about a growing gang problem in Junction City and a belief that many crimes were gang related. Interestingly, Katz's review of records and interviews with departmental personnel revealed that Junction City's gang problem in 1988 was relatively small. In fact, only about 5% of narcotics arrests and less than 5% of robbery, misdemeanor assault, and felony assault incidents could be attributed to gangs. In other words, the creation of the unit was not a response to an *actual* gang problem as much as a response to a *perceived* gang problem. Gangs were receiving significant attention in the national media, and that attention was permeating local communities. In Junction City, community leaders, the local Chamber of Commerce, and members of the police department saw gangs as a problem and a detriment to the city's overall quality of life. The chief was under tremendous pressure to do something about the gang problem and responded by forming a gang unit.

Section II detailed the dimensions of organizational structure but was largely silent on why organizations vary in these same structures. In other words, how are differences across organizations explained? For example, why do police departments such as that in Junction City assign functions to specialized units while other departments remain less differentiated? Organizational theories offer potential explanations for the patterns observed in organizations. Organizational theory, as discussed in Section I, is concerned with the organization as a whole. Some theories, particularly those from the classical and human relations schools, prescribe a single best structural arrangement for achieving organizational goals. Others suggest that there is no single best way to organize since the most effective structure depends on a variety of factors; contingency theorists take this position. Still others contend that organizational structures are largely unrelated to concerns about efficiency and effectiveness and instead reflect the desire to obtain much-needed resources (e.g., money) or conform to what is widely believed to be the best approach to organization. The Junction City Police Department arguably fits this latter description, succumbing to external pressures rather than adapting to any real gang problem.

Why does theory matter? Organizational theory offers a number of important contributions to both organizational personnel and those who interface with organizations. First, theories offer guides for managers interested in improving the efficiency and effectiveness of their organizations. A probation department chief might not fully adopt a bureaucratic form, but she may become more aware of the strengths and limitations of bureaucracy as a result of theory. Second, theories provide insight into improving the workplace for and enhancing productivity of an organization's employees (see Daft, 2010b). Structural choices, as described in theories of organization, work to enhance or stifle individual initiative, motivation, and job satisfaction. Third, the successes or failures of organizational strategies can be reviewed and understood within an organizational theory framework. If, for example, a corrections department adopts an innovative treatment program not to improve service delivery to inmates but to obtain the additional personnel and financial resources that accompany the initiative, the program's implementation may be purely symbolic. The success (or failure) of the program then is related to the motives for adoption. Fourth, theory can also help researchers, policymakers, and others understand how to spread innovative ideas throughout a population of organizations. The fact that funding availability stimulated the corrections department to adopt the treatment program is an important consideration in diffusing the program to other departments. Finally, the evolution of organizational theories affords a historical perspective on thinking about workplaces and organizations over a more than 100-year period (Daft, 2010a). The remainder of this section describes the major theoretical perspectives on organizations, both historical and contemporary.

Classical Theories

The earliest theories of organization and management are collectively referred to as classical theories. Scholars writing in the classical tradition share similar views about the purpose of organizations—they are "organized in such a way as to lead to predetermined goals with maximum efficiency" (Scott & Davis, 2007, p. 35). From this perspective, organizations are rationally oriented toward goal achievement (Scott & Davis, 2007). The challenge for managers is determining and implementing the most effective means for reaching organizational goals, referred to as **instrumental rationality** (Gortner, Nichols, & Ball, 2007). Classical theories are **prescriptive** in their orientation, offering principles or propositions detailing the ideal structure (Rainey, 2009). Three perspectives form the classical school—scientific management, bureaucracy, and administrative management.

Scientific Management

The earliest classical school theory, scientific management, can be traced back to the writings of Frederick Taylor around the turn of the 20th century (Scott, 1961). Taylor's primary concern was lost profits (he examined industrial organizations) due to work inefficiencies and deliberate and unintentional decreases in worker output. In his influential work *The Principles of Scientific Management*, Taylor (1913) espoused the importance of scientifically informed organizations that would generate "maximum prosperity" for both the organization in the form of profits and the individual worker in the form of increased pay (p. 9). "Maximum prosperity can only exist as the result of maximum productivity," however; so he proposed methods for enhancing organizational output (p. 12).

Taylor claimed that increasing productivity and prosperity could be accomplished by overcoming the inertia of poor work habits and ineffective techniques. How are these habitual behaviors displaced? Each work task was to be scientifically studied to determine the best way to perform the work.

Taylor (1913) illustrated the importance of science and time-motion studies—so named for their interest in the duration of and physical movements related to tasks—in the Bethlehem Steel Company. Results of time-motion studies were used in task setting, "the process of defining what a worker is expected to do and how long it should take to do it" (Tompkins, 2005, p. 73). At Bethlehem Steel, workers brought their own shovels to work and were required to move different materials from one location to another. The problem was that the weight of the materials varied, so a shovel load was sometimes very light and other times quite heavy; in both cases, the worker was less productive than if the correct weight were loaded. Scientific study of the task revealed not only the best movements for shoveling (e.g., to reduce fatigue) but also the ideal load on each shovel—21 pounds. Workers were trained on proper physical motions, and shovels of different sizes were provided for each material so that, regardless of the substance being moved, a shovel load always approximated 21 pounds; the result was maximum productivity (21 pounds per load) with maximum efficiency (less fatigue and strain). Returning to the dimensions of organizational structure from Section II, job requirements were formalized so that employees always adhered to the scientifically determined procedures. In the absence of rules or formalization, the workers and the organization are less productive. Taylor also saw the benefits of horizontal complexity or specialization, dividing the work into narrow tasks (Tompkins, 2005). Having the individual both shovel and repair equipment would be inefficient, as it would take time to switch tasks and get oriented to the new task. Specialization generates expertise and efficiencies (Pugh & Hickson, 2007).

The Principles of Scientific Management also identified and circumscribed management's role. Managers are responsible for selecting individuals capable of completing the task, training them according to the scientifically derived principles, and monitoring them to ensure compliance. Like rank-and-file workers, managers must be proficient in the performance of their tasks and specialized accordingly; they are incapable of hiring, training, and supervising an employee if they are unable to perform the tasks themselves (Allen & Sawhney, 2010; Scott & Davis, 2007).[1] Scientific principles also delimited managerial actions and prevented supervisors from making capricious demands of employees. Directives from supervisors must also be governed by science (and, consequently, rules) (Pugh &

---

[1] Taylor supported functional management wherein multiple supervisors, each experts in a particular part of an employee's work (e.g., quality assurance, training, discipline, etc.), lead subordinates (see Taylor, 1913, p. 123). Other classical theorists rejected this view in favor of the unity of command principle—only one direct supervisor per subordinate. Nevertheless, the notion that supervisors must also be experts in their assigned area was an important component of scientific management.

Hickson, 2007; Taylor, 1913). If scientific management principles are followed throughout the organization, then prosperity emerges. The organization sees increased profits and the worker receives financial rewards (Taylor, 1913).

In an article that appeared in the *Harvard Law Review*, famous criminologists Sheldon and Eleanor Glueck (1929) advocated "a scientific management of the problem of crime by courts and administrative agencies" (p. 329). By developing prediction instruments based on studies of actual offenders, researchers can guide judges and other criminal justice officials in their decision making. Science would be used to increase the likelihood of positive, successful parole outcomes. Their work, emerging on the heels of Taylor's book, foreshadowed development of bail schedules in the 1960s and sentencing guidelines in the 1980s.

Elements of Taylor's scientific management are also visible today, both outside and within the criminal justice system, even if not framed explicitly in scientific management terms. Several years ago, United Parcel Service (UPS) utilized a software program to draw driver delivery routes that would minimize vehicle idling time. Routes were constructed to maximize the number of right turns and minimize left turns, the source of considerable idling as trucks wait to execute turns across traffic. In one year, the effort saved three million gallons of gas and reduced vehicle travel by 28.5 million miles (Lovell, 2007). Elsewhere, researchers study the relationship between workplace productivity and interruptions to work flow (Thompson, 2005). For example, larger computer monitors are associated with more efficient task completion, suggesting avenues for increasing productivity in office environments.

In policing, job analyses have been used to construct task-based physical agility tests (for initial screening or academy training) where individuals perform activities similar to those they would be expected to perform on the job (e.g., sprints, climbing walls, dragging dead weights). This procedure contrasts with physical fitness tests where an individual's general fitness level is assessed through exercises such as running, sit-ups, pull-ups, and push-ups (Gaines, Falkenberg, & Gambino, 1993). Science has also been used to standardize criminal justice practices, particularly those supported by (or believed to be supported by) empirical research. The results of the Minneapolis Domestic Violence Experiment, a study assessing different police responses to misdemeanor domestic violence using a randomized research design, pointed to the effectiveness of arrest; apprehending the perpetrator seemed to reduce the likelihood of subsequent violence (Sherman, 1992; Sherman & Berk, 1984). By the mid-1980s, just a few years after the study's results were published, police agencies across the country had implemented mandatory arrest policies (Schmidt & Sherman, 1993). Science had identified the most appropriate response, and departments formalized this behavior via arrest policies. Replication studies failed to reproduce the Minneapolis findings exactly, but the formalized policies were largely retained anyway (see Dunford, Huizinga, & Elliott, 1990; Hirschel, Hutchinson, & Dean, 1992). More recently, the relationship between science and organizational attributes can be seen in calls for "evidence-based" policies in policing and corrections (MacKenzie, 2000; Sherman, 1998). Practices that are demonstrably effective in the research literature are adopted by organizations and structure the work and guide employees.

Taylor's ideas generated criticisms in spite of the appeal of finding the best way to perform a job. Many of the criticisms were directed at the implicit and explicit views of the worker within scientific management theory. For workers, initiative, judgment, and discretion were considered inferior to empirically derived evidence (Guillén, 1994). They were "cogs in the industrial machine," offering little more to the organization than their labor and the occasional suggestion of a topic worthy of scientific study (Tompkins, 2005, p. 81). Employees are instructed to perform the task according to predetermined procedures and to do so at maximum performance levels (Scott & Davis, 2007). Moreover, the incentive system outlined by Taylor was considered exploitive; worker pay might increase by 100% even though scientific principles contributed to a 400% increase in workplace profits. What seemed like benevolence was just a means of controlling workers while maximizing financial gain. Managers, too, failed to embrace scientific management. Their own competence was usurped by researchers and scientific studies (Scott & Davis, 2007). Others argue that research in the public sector is never so conclusive as to be the sole determinant of organizational structures and that such research may lead to a limited menu of inflexible strategies (Sparrow, 2011).

Bureaucracy

Max Weber's writings on **bureaucracy**, a term today equated with inefficiency and red tape, detailed an ideal organizational structure, one that would efficiently accomplish organizational goals (Pugh & Hickson, 2007; Weber, 1946). Unlike Taylor, Weber concentrated on the larger organization, rather than the individual worker or isolated task (Allen & Sawhney, 2010). Weber's work amounted to a historical analysis examining why people acquiesce to the demands of superiors, concluding that, in modern times, such compliance was based on rational–legal principles evident in bureaucratic organizations. Pugh and Hickson (2007) explain, "The system is called rational because the means are expressly designed to achieve certain specific goals" and "legal because authority is exercised by means of a system of rules and procedures" (p. 6). Bureaucratic organizations exhibit certain characteristics that, in combination, produce rationality and goal attainment (Blau & Scott, 1962/2003).

1. Division of labor: Weber (1946) argued, "There is a principle of fixed and official jurisdictional areas . . . the regular activities required [are] distributed in a fixed way as official duties" (p. 196). Each worker is assigned a specific task (their duties) that becomes their area of specialization or jurisdiction. As noted previously, specialization breeds expertise; workers develop maximum proficiency in a narrow area rather than less-than-maximum proficiency in a larger number of areas. A prosecutor with a caseload comprising solely murder and manslaughter cases will arguably be more adept in securing convictions than if he or she were required to retain complete knowledge on a range of offense types.

2. Hierarchy/vertical complexity: Weber's (1946) vision of bureaucracy required a system of "supervision of the lower offices by the higher ones" (p. 197). Recall, horizontal complexity (the division of labor) leads to coordination problems. Organizations must make an effort to coordinate the disparate parts into a cohesive whole; the supervision afforded by the hierarchy provides this control, ensuring that all organization members are working toward goal achievement. Subordinates are obligated to comply with directives from above.

3. Formalization: Not unlike scientific management, activities must be governed by rules and regulations detailing appropriate practices. Rules and procedures ensure that everyone is performing tasks according to the ideal methods, and they also help coordinate work (Blau & Scott, 1962/2003). Decisions are recorded in written form for the purposes of subsequent decision making (Scott & Davis, 2007; Weber, 1946). The rules and records "provide for continuity in operations regardless of changes of personnel" (Blau & Scott, 1962/2003, p. 32). Consequently, the success of the organization is not tied to any one or more specific individuals.

4. Selection/advancement is based on merit, and employment is a career: Workers should be hired for specific positions and be promoted into supervisory positions based on their technical qualifications (i.e., education, job-related knowledge and skills, experience). Adherence to this principle results in an organization staffed by the most qualified personnel. Moreover, if the work is viewed as a career, workers invest in the workplace, free of fear of arbitrary firing, and become more committed to the job (Perrow, 1986; Scott & Davis, 2007).

5. Impersonal relations: Finally, the organization is supposed to be governed impersonally. Organization personnel are "expected to disregard all personal considerations and to maintain complete emotional detachment" to make appropriate decisions guided by rules and in the best interest of organizational goal achievement (Blau & Scott, 1962/2003, p. 33). For example, a supervisor must avoid letting friendships interfere with employee discipline; to do otherwise would allow the organization to function below optimum level.

The principles, if taken together, are intended to produce a well-run, smoothly functioning organization—"a well-designed machine with a certain function to perform, and every part of the machine contributes to the attainment of maximum performance of that function" (Pugh & Hickson, 2007, p. 6). A bureaucracy, according to Weber, organizes a collection of experts with superior qualifications to produce an object or deliver a service according to a system of rules detailing the best ways to perform a task (though not necessarily scientifically derived). The behavior of workers is guaranteed through close supervision and discipline if rules are violated. The work of the organization becomes predictable, with any uncertainty reduced due to bureaucratic principles (Gajduschek, 2003). Such is the case when the courtroom becomes bureaucratized; sentencing decisions are made according to guidelines with considerations for offense seriousness and prior record. Arbitrariness is supposed to diminish as sentence outcomes become more predictable (Dixon, 1995).

The many theoretical advantages of Weber's bureaucracy are clarified by examining late 19th and early 20th century policing, a period prior to reforms that would bureaucratize many law enforcement agencies. Fogelson (1977) described police officers during this political era as ill trained and ill equipped but in search of the good pay of government jobs. Politicians distributed jobs to supporters, or to generate support, and expected favors in return (e.g., enforcing the law against the opposition and not against supporters; blocking voters from polling places; Fogelson, 1977). If political leadership changed, officers lost their jobs as the new leader remade the police force in the spirit of "to the victor belong the spoils" (p. 18). Policing was clearly not a career occupation characterized by merit selection; connections were paramount, and officers were far from experts in law enforcement. Nor was police work governed by a system of rules. In theory, police officers were to enforce the criminal law, but as Fogelson notes, that assumed that officers did their work as assigned (instead of, say, visiting taverns during work hours, as some officers did) and had little opportunity to exercise discretion. Both assumptions were false, leading to differential policing. Supervision from above did not help regain control, as police chiefs and other supervisors also owed their allegiance to politicians. Stated differently, the quality and quantity of policing within a city was unpredictable, determined in large part by the characteristics of the officer addressing the problem. The reforms that emerged in the subsequent professional era of policing were, in many ways, consistent with Weber's bureaucracy: civil service testing was used to separate officer selection and promotion from political spheres, the specific functions of policing (crime control) were defined, a strong hierarchy developed to enhance employee control, and specialized areas (e.g., investigations) emerged.

How did the very organizational structure Weber saw as the most rational, most efficient form come to be associated with dysfunction and inefficiency? As Perrow (1986) argued, the idea of bureaucracy is consistent with the closed-system view of organizations. If the organization is structured according to bureaucratic principles, nothing else outside of the organization should matter in its functioning. This is a tenuous assumption given that workers have lives outside of the organization. The hierarchy, discussed in Section II, encourages employees to deflect responsibility and hide wrongdoing from superiors out of fear of punishment (Blau & Scott, 1962/2003; Perrow, 1986). Bureaucracies also have a tremendously difficult time adapting to external changes due to their rigid structures (Morgan, 2006). Prosecutors' offices, for example, interested in adopting community prosecution, were confronted with the structural inertia of years of felony prosecutions as the primary emphasis (Coles, 2000). They experienced challenges in adapting to the new role of addressing community quality-of-life concerns. Bureaucracies may also encourage an emphasis on means over ends or, returning to the machine analogy, how a product is produced rather than the quality of the product itself. Herman Goldstein (1979) saw this problem in his call for problem-oriented policing: "All bureaucracies risk becoming so preoccupied with running their organizations and getting so involved in their methods of operating that they lose sight of the primary purposes for which they were created" (pp. 236–237). In policing, a preoccupation with means is commonplace, as departments highlight response times, number of officers on the street, clearance rates, number of arrests, and other strategies and methods presumed to be linked to some desirable outcome. The outcome itself—crime reduction, improved neighborhood quality of life, reduced fear—is supplanted. Finally, bureaucracy largely ignores the worker except to say that he or she is a piece of the machinery, potentially leading to dissatisfaction and lack of motivation. In spite of these dysfunctions, most organizations exhibit some degree of bureaucratization (Morgan, 2006). Reading 4 (Bohm, 2006) offers additional examples and concerns of modern bureaucratization in criminal justice.

Administrative Management

The third major strand of classical theory is associated with the works of Luther Gulick (1937) and Henri Fayol (1949). Frederick Taylor's scientific management concentrated on the lower levels of the organization, specifically the individual worker and his or her immediate supervisor, while upper levels of the hierarchy were virtually ignored (Pearson, 1945). This omission was noteworthy, and Gulick and Fayol sought to address this oversight. Fayol, a French mining engineer and manager credited with developing administrative management theory, argued that management above the level of direct supervisors "required an art of formulating plans and, through proper organization of effort, of getting [many] people to work together toward achievement of the planned objectives" (Pearson, 1945, p. 73; see also Fayol, 1949; Pugh & Hickson, 2007). The functions of management included planning, organizing, commanding, coordinating, and controlling; Fayol (1949) proposed a set of 14 principles of **administrative management** to assist in the fulfillment of these functions.

1. Division of work: Work should be divided—horizontal complexity—to facilitate specialization and the development of expertise. An addictions counselor specializing in opiate addictions has arguably more knowledge than one who counsels on a range of drug and alcohol addictions.

2. Authority: Managers must have the right to make demands of subordinates, because of both their superordinate position in the hierarchy and their personal characteristics, and the ability to punish those who fail to comply.

3. Discipline: "Obedience" and "outward marks of respect" must characterize relationships between managers and other employees if the organization is to function properly (p. 22).

4. Unity of command: Each subordinate should receive orders from one supervisor only. If, for example, a police officer receives contradictory directives on matters related to preliminary investigations from his or her immediate sergeant as well as from the leader of the investigations unit, the principles of authority and discipline are disrupted. The officer may not be able to comply with the dual directives.

5. Unity of direction: Similar to unity of command, unity of direction suggests that activities related to the same goal should be led by a single individual. In other words, patrol work should ultimately be coordinated by one supervisor and investigations, a separate activity with distinct goals, coordinated by a different supervisor.

6. Subordination of individual interests to the general interest: The functioning and goals of the overall organization are more important than the personal goals of individual members. Organizational members work toward organization objectives first, followed by individual objectives.

7. Remuneration: Employee pay should be fair and generate satisfaction. Overall, very little attention in classical theory is paid toward worker motivation beyond the idea that monetary rewards are the primary motivator.

8. Centralization: Consistent with the principles of unity of command and direction, orders generally emerge from a central source. However, Fayol argued that the right balance between centralization and decentralization must be determined.

9. Scalar chain: The scalar chain is the hierarchy of authority from the lowest level of the organization to its peak. Fayol believed that the chain should be unbroken from top to bottom.

10. Order: Fayol summed up the principle for both objects and people by stating, "A place for everything/everyone and everything/everyone in its place" (p. 36).

11. Equity: Workers must be treated with fairness and kindness, particularly if they are to be retained (Tompkins, 2005).

12. Stability of tenure of personnel: Just as Weber discussed a career orientation, Fayol stated that stability was essential for developing expertise and ensuring the functioning of the organization.

13. Initiative: Fayol's principles had provisions for employee input and discretion in how the work is accomplished. Of course, the input and discretion were constrained by other principles, including authority, discipline, and the scalar chain.

14. Esprit de corps: According to Fayol, workplace harmony, where employees work together largely conflict free, is an essential element of a successful organization.

Most of Fayol's (1949) principles are aligned with prescriptions found in the works of Taylor and Weber and are apparent in modern criminal justice organizations. Scott and Davis (2007) suggest that they can be grouped into the two dimensions of organizational structure—coordination/control (e.g., authority, discipline, unity of command, unity of direction, scalar chain) and complexity (division of labor), the main components of organization structure discussed in Section II. Dias and Vaughn (2006) illustrated the ramifications of failing to adhere to these principles. In one example, officials in the Texas prison system were sued for failing to prevent the repeated sexual abuse of a homosexual inmate over a nearly two-year period. Officers were accused of lacking the necessary training to properly classify inmates, particularly vulnerable inmates, to protect them from harm (a breakdown in specialization). In a second example, Dias and Vaughn described the situation during the early period of the Los Angeles riots following the Rodney King verdict in 1992. The unity-of-command principle was missing, as no single supervisor was providing instructions to officers on the street. Administrative breakdown is discussed further in Section IV.

Although Fayol's prescriptions were accompanied by the important qualification that they were flexible, they were subjected to intense criticism, most notably from Herbert Simon (1946). Simon asserted that the principles are at times contradictory and lacking in specificity. For example, calls for specialization were imprecise. A police department could divide work by place, assigning detectives to geographic areas, or by offense type. According to Simon, the principles maintain only that a division of labor is necessary, failing to identify the proper way to specialize to maximize efficiency. Simon also believed that the unity-of-command principle conflicts with specialization. Police officers are responsible for conducting preliminary investigations at most crime scenes—taking initial statements, securing the scene, and taking other necessary steps to preserve evidence. The officer operates under the direct supervision of a patrol sergeant. A detective or detective supervisor, an individual with more knowledge about criminal investigations than officers on patrol, would be prohibited from making demands of officers due to the unity-of-command principle. In such a case, unity of command and the scalar principle supersede the expertise resulting from specialization, leading to inefficiency or ineffectiveness. These internal conflicts lead to questions about how rigid classical school prescriptions really are. As we will see, there are other ways to organize and, perhaps, no single best way to organize. Criticisms notwithstanding, "the historical contribution of [administrative management] is undeniable; the table of contents of many contemporary management texts reflect the influence of these theorists' early efforts to conceive the role of management and administration" (Rainey, 2009, pp. 31–32).

Human Relations Theory

Classical theory dominated early 20th century thinking about organizations but was joined by an alternative approach to organization by mid-century. Human relations theorists addressed one of the central shortcomings of classical organizational theory, the neglect of the worker, by stepping away from an immediate focus on formal organizational structure and replacing it with a concern for worker behavior and informal structures (e.g., peer relationships). Interestingly, the research that solidified human relations thinking initially commenced as a series of scientific management-oriented studies at the Hawthorne plant of the Western Electric Company, a manufacturer of communications equipment for the telephone industry (Roethlisberger & Dickson, 1949). The Hawthorne studies, as the research is known, established the human relations school of organizations. Unlike scientific management, bureaucracy, or administrative management theory, the human relations school of management paid greater attention to the needs of the individual worker, viewing each worker as more than just a piece in a larger machine (Scott & Davis, 2007). The recognition of worker needs and behavior resulted in prescriptions for fundamentally different types of organizational structures.

The Hawthorne studies began in 1924 with the goal of identifying proper lighting and workplace incentives, among other issues, to encourage productivity (Roethlisberger & Dickson, 1949). The first set of experiments addressed illumination. Two groups of workers were assigned the same task to be completed. The lighting intensity in one group (the experimental group) varied, while in the other the level was held constant (control group). The findings were unexpected, as levels of lighting did not seem to matter except when the lighting was so dark the task could not be completed. Productivity increased for both groups at relatively equal rates. Researchers attributed the results to what became known as the **Hawthorne effect**; worker productivity increased not because of the variation in lighting but because of the special treatment and attention workers were given for their participation in the study. Perrow (1986) summarized the findings succinctly, stating, "The attention apparently raised morale, and morale raised productivity . . . it was a happy thought" (p. 80).

A second experiment in the Hawthorne plant tested a piecework pay system. Workers completed their tasks together, and the productivity of the entire unit was used to compensate employees; the greater the level of productivity for the unit, the greater the earnings for each worker (Roethlisberger & Dickson, 1949). The study revealed, however, that the pay system did not work as intended. Employees did not work at their optimum level, falling below the ideal levels established by management, in spite of the fact that they were capable of producing more (Blau & Scott, 1962/2003). They did have their own beliefs about what constituted a "day's work" and were not going to let the incentive system dictate output (Roethlisberger & Dickson, 1949, p. 414). Instead, the group of employees developed an informal standard that was reinforced within the group. Individuals who exceeded the informal standard, deemed "rate busters," were subjected to informal sanctions such as ridicule or minor hitting. Individuals perceived as not pulling their weight were similarly admonished by the group. The consequences of violating group standards were enough to suppress individual efforts to over- or underperform. The informal organization operates along with the practices set forth via formalization, centralization, and other formal structural dimensions. Morgan (2006) summarized the Hawthorne studies by stating, "They showed quite clearly that work activities are influenced as much by the nature of human beings as by formal design and that organization theorists must pay close attention to this human side of organization" (p. 35).

The contrast between classical and human relations theories, particularly their views about human nature and human behavior, was demonstrated by Douglas McGregor (1960) in *The Human Side of Enterprise*. The classical theorist view, a position termed **Theory X** by McGregor, assumed that individuals were uninterested in work and would avoid it if possible; they lacked ambition and preferred not to exercise personal initiative. He continued, "Most people must be coerced, controlled, directed, threatened with punishment to get them to put forth adequate effort toward the achievement of organizational

▲ Photo 3.1 Workers participated in a variety of tasks during the Hawthorne experiments, beginning in the 1920s. The results led to a significant shift in thinking about workers and organizational structure. (Source: http://www.library.hbs.edu/hc/hawthorne/big/wehe_131.html, President and Fellows of Harvard College)

objectives" (p. 34). Why then do people continue to work? They want and need the financial security that comes from it. If this is the correct view of workers, then the prescriptions of the classical school make sense. Rules, hierarchical control, centralization, and specialization (small tasks) are necessary since workers cannot be counted on to complete the work absent such controls. In contrast, McGregor's **Theory Y** presupposes that individuals can reap tremendous satisfaction from their work. Control is not necessary when workers are committed to the organization and its goals and motivation is generated from the gratification resulting from task accomplishment. Workers want to use their skills, both physical and mental; "the capacity to exercise a relatively high degree of imagination, ingenuity, and creativity in the solution of organizational problems is widely, not narrowly, distributed in the population" (p. 48). This view, consistent with human relations principles, supports a radically different organizational structure. Professional judgment may be substituted for formalization and lower level decision making for centralization. A lesser degree of horizontal complexity is preferable, allowing workers to utilize a range of skills and break the monotony of performing a single task repetitively.

The effects of human relations theory on the workplace are significant. In criminal justice settings, knowledge gleaned from these studies is critical for understanding the behavior of criminal justice actors. In policing, the occupational peer group exerts significant influence over officer behavior on the street. Mastrofski, Ritti, and Snipes (1994) found that officers in 19 Pennsylvania police departments typically made five or fewer driving under the influence (DUI) arrests in the previous year; about 15% of officers exceeded this number, and only 3.7% made more than 25 DUI arrest. The authors reported that the rate busters, those with the highest numbers of arrests, were alienated from the department and faced pressure from other officers. Moskos (2008) noted a similar phenomenon in Baltimore. Officers responsible for a high volume of all arrests reduced their effort when the morale of the group suffered due to what were considered unfair management practices. In corrections, Marquart (1986) documented the influence of informal structures in the prison environment when he noted the widespread support of the use of physical force. Various degrees of force, termed tune-ups, ass-whippings, and beatings, worked to maintain prisoner control but also gained the officer acceptance among peers. Perhaps nowhere is the formal organizational structure supplanted by informal arrangements more than in the courthouse. Implicit and explicit negotiations between attorneys and judges result in plea bargains guided by formal rules and procedures but not dictated by them (Emmelman, 1996; Heumann, 1977). "The law in action" is different from the "law on the books," as plea bargaining enables the members of the courtroom workgroup to satisfy their collective goals through nontrial dispositions (Leo, 1996, p. 269; see also Eisenstein & Jacob, 1991). As these examples illustrate, informal organizational structures exist apart from the formal structural dimensions discussed in Section II. Human relations theory brought attention to the simultaneous influence of these forces on worker behavior.

Structural implications also arise from human relations theory. If Douglas McGregor's (1960) Theory Y is accurate, less bureaucratic structures are required. Tom Murton (1971), for example, described a novel approach to prison operations that occurred in an Arkansas prison in the late 1960s. A representative council formed of prison inmates (organized by housing unit) was established to share governance over matters related to living conditions, prison work, inmate privileges, and other issues affecting prisoners. They even offered suggestions pertaining to prison security following a series of escapes. Murton, the superintendent of the prison at the time, argued that the council helped in "gaining control" and "revolutionizing" the prison (p. 101). Researchers have also found positive outcomes, including lower absenteeism, increased job commitment and satisfaction, and lower job turnover rates, among criminal justice workers when organizations decentralize, allow individuals to exercise judgment, and reduce the level of control over the work (Lambert & Paoline, 2008; Stohr, Lovrich, Menke, & Zupan, 1994). Human relations theory, like classical theories, was prescriptive in that it supported a nonbureaucratic, decentralized, flat, less formalized, and less specialized organization. Moreover, it affirmed the importance of interpersonal issues such as motivation, leadership, and power (organizational behavior topics to be discussed in later sections).

Two significant criticisms were levied against the human relations school. First, the argument appeared to be simplistic, leading some to call human relations theory "cow sociology" (see Scott and Davis, 2007, p. 69). The metaphor of a happy cow producing a lot of milk was used to illustrate the belief that satisfied and committed workers would be more productive. The goal, then, for organizations was to increase the happiness of workers. As admirable as this may seem, it actually represents a second significant criticism of human relations theory. Satisfying employee needs and well-being were not the most important concerns of the organization. As Scott and Davis (2007) suggest, "Humanizing the workplace was viewed not as an end in itself, but primarily as a means to increasing productivity" (p. 69). In some respects, the criticism of exploitation directed at scientific management was equally applicable to human relations theory. Management's attempt to change the organizational structure is merely an attempt, according to critics, to manipulate the workforce (Landsberger, 1958).

Open Systems Theories

Classical and human relations theories were consistent with the closed-system view of organizations (Silverman, 1968): Organizations need not be concerned with the external environment. The prescriptions offered by each theory were stable, detailing the best approach to organization, and were unaffected by external environmental factors. The principles themselves were universal, with the disagreement only in which set, classical or human relations, was correct. The closed-system perspective persisted until the 1960s, when scholars began recognizing the importance of the environment in shaping the structures and activities of organizations (Burns & Stalker, 1961; Katz & Kahn, 1966; Lawrence & Lorsch, 1967). In fact, the popular depiction of criminal justice agencies as a system emerged during this period. Other agencies of the criminal justice system, the larger crime problem, and citizen reporting behavior—all features of the external environment of any one criminal justice organization—nevertheless exert tremendous pressure on it. This section presents three contemporary ways of viewing the importance of the environment. While contingency, resource dependence, and institutional theories are not the only open systems theories of organization, they are the three most commonly applied to the study of criminal justice organizations.

Contingency Theory

In the 1960s, scholars began to question the "one best way" prescriptions of classical and human relations theories. In their minds, **contingency theory** offered the best explanation for organizational structures and practices, suggesting that the ideal arrangement depends on—or is contingent on—environmental characteristics, organizational size, and other determinants (Burns & Stalker, 1961; Lawrence & Lorsch, 1967). These factors, termed contingencies, affect an organization's performance, and leaders try to steer their organizations toward the successful accomplishment of their goals. Lex Donaldson (1995, 2001), a proponent of contingency theory, connects the three parts of the theory—performance, contingencies, and organizational structure and practices—in what he termed the structural-adaptation-to-regain-fit (SARFIT) model:

Because the fit of organizational characteristics to contingencies leads to high performance, organizations seek to attain fit. For this reason, organizations are motivated to avoid misfit that results after contingency change, and do so by adopting new organizational characteristics that fit the new levels of the contingencies. Therefore, the organization becomes shaped by the contingencies, because it needs to fit them to avoid loss of performance. (Donaldson, 2001, p. 2)

A fast-food restaurant, for example, may offer a menu consisting of only high-fat, high-cholesterol items. If, however, the dietary habits of the population change (the contingency, in this case) and individuals become more health conscious, the restaurant's performance will suffer. Profits will decline as customers flock to other more healthy alternatives. In Donaldson's language, performance is suffering because of the misfit between the organization's practices (menu) and its contingencies (customers' dietary needs). To regain fit and improve or stabilize performance levels, the restaurant must change and offer more low-fat, low-cholesterol options, including salads. The organization must fit the contingencies to be successful.

Among the contemporary open systems theories, contingency theory has garnered the most interest within the criminal justice discipline. Reisig (1998) examined rates of disorder in control, responsibility, and consensual prisons. Facilities labeled control oriented are rule-bound, regimented, and vest authority in prison officials. The other two models allow for greater inmate self-determination (Craig, 2004). In a sample of prisons, control facilities had higher rates of disorder than the other two in spite of the top-heavy control. Reisig (1998) noted, however, that the success of consensual and responsibility models may be due to certain contingencies. Consensual- and responsibility-model facilities tended to be located in smaller, more homogenous states. Given the importance of prisoner input and/or governance in these models, they may be inappropriate in large or more diverse populations where agreements would be more difficult to reach. In policing, Mullen (1996) found that understaffed departments, measured by the police–citizen ratio, were more likely to adopt computer technology. He argued that the misfit created by the unfavorable ratio (the contingency) was rectified by technologies that saved time and allowed officers to return to the streets more quickly. More recently, researchers found that law enforcement agencies adapted to the (perceived) risks of a terrorist attack by taking more preparedness actions, including training personnel, conducting a threat assessment, and adopting an emergency response plan (Burruss, Giblin, & Schafer, 2010).

The Central Intelligence Agency (CIA) was faced with a changing environment (the contingencies) in the early 1990s and, as some have argued, did not adequately adapt to emerging conditions (Zegart, 2007). When the primary adversaries of the United States during the Cold War were nations such as the Soviet Union, CIA officers would attempt to gather intelligence by recruiting foreign officials at diplomatic events (Zegart, 2007). As the Cold War ended and the threat of international terrorism emerged, the enemy was no longer a country but, rather, transnational organizations such as al Qaeda. The CIA was unable to send officers posing as diplomats to recruit spies. The organization did not readily adapt to the new enemy, meaning valuable intelligence was never gathered on al Qaeda or other groups. Adaptation, or the lack thereof, affected performance (Zegart, 2007).

Contingency theory has tremendous intuitive appeal; organizations and their leaders are supposed to rationally construct successful organizations and change them as needed. The theory has been criticized, however, for a seemingly endless list of possible contingencies. The studies reviewed above indicated the importance of dietary habits, population heterogeneity, police officer–citizen ratio, risk of a terrorist attack, and political considerations. These are just a few of the many possible factors affecting organizational performance. More important is the question of whether organizations can rationally adapt to contingencies. Many organizations are plagued by the inability to link their structures and activities to any type of performance outcomes (Salancik, 1981). Although they may make valiant attempts, do police leaders know how to reduce crime or mitigate risks associated with terrorism? Do prison and jail wardens know how to successfully rehabilitate offenders? Do probation and parole officers know how to prevent recidivism? This knowledge is simply not well developed. It is difficult for a police chief to know whether a particular strategy is effective or not since crime is influenced by so many other factors. Lipsky (1980) writes that this is a problem that plagues many public organizations. They are often unable to clearly demonstrate the value of their practices. Moreover, in situations where evidence points to the ineffectiveness of a structure or practice, contingency theory is unable to account for its persistence. The Drug Abuse Resistance Education (D.A.R.E.) program operates throughout the country in spite of evidence that it does not appreciably affect drug use (Berman & Fox, 2009; Rosenbaum, 2007). Contingency theory would argue that the program's ineffectiveness should lead to its abandonment. The fact that it continues suggests that it has value beyond its ability to reduce drug use.

Resource Dependence Theory

Developed in the 1970s, **resource dependence theory** posits that organizations are not always capable of making choices based on the lone consideration of improving organization performance. Organizations, instead, are constrained because of their reliance on the external environment for certain resources critical to the organization's work and, ultimately, its survival (Pfeffer & Salancik, 1978). Organizations are not self-sufficient; they are dependent, in whole or in part, on their environments to provide key resources, often physical capital or monetary resources, needed for continued operation (Aldrich & Pfeffer, 1976; Pfeffer & Salancik, 1978). This is particularly true in public organizations such as criminal justice agencies that rely on support from their sponsoring local, county, state, or federal government. Pfeffer and Salancik (1978) refer to this condition as interdependence, arguing that it "exists whenever one actor does not entirely control all of the conditions necessary for the achievement of an action or for obtaining the outcome desired from the action" (p. 40). Interdependence is not necessarily a problem, however, unless resources are scarce and/or critical (Jaffee, 2001; Pfeffer & Salancik, 1978). It is in these situations when asymmetrical power relationships emerge and the individual, government, or organization distributing the much-needed resources obtains power over the organization dependent on those resources (Pfeffer & Salancik, 1978; Scott, 1998). If the dependent organization wants to ensure continued resource flow, it must comply with the demands of the external organization.

To illustrate resource dependence, consider the situation faced by state legislatures after passage of federal highway fund legislation in 2000. State legislatures, themselves sovereign organizations, are responsible for the creation of state law, including laws related to drunk-driving prevention. Before the mid-2000s, state statutes varied, with some specifying a blood alcohol concentration (BAC) of .10 as legally intoxicated and others codifying a lower level of .08. The federal government, concerned about the harms associated with drunk driving and interested in standardizing the level at .08 nationwide, faced opposition arguing that such legislation was a state's prerogative rather than a federal issue (Eisenberg, 2003). Rather than federalize drunk-driving laws, the federal government instead passed a law that allowed for the withholding of portions of federal highway funds for states that failed to pass .08 legislation (Eisenberg, 2003; O'Neill, 2004). The lost funds were substantial, increasing gradually from 2% in fiscal year 2004 to 8% in fiscal year 2007 and thereafter. New Jersey, for example, lost $7.2 million for failing to comply by 2004 (O'Neill, 2004). States were eligible to recover the money if they adopted the lower standard by 2007. Returning to resource dependence theory, the state legislature is, as noted above, a sovereign organization capable of making rational decisions in the best interests of the state. Yet reducing the legal BAC level was not solely based on concerns about reducing drunk driving. States are dependent on the federal government for a portion of overall operating dollars. These funds are scarce, critical, and available from few other sources (e.g., from raising taxes). To secure these needed funds, states were required to comply with the demands of the external resource provider—the federal government. As of 2011, all states had adopted the lower standard (Governors Highway Safety Association, 2011). This is the essence of resource dependence theory.

The application of resource dependence theory in criminal justice settings is most notable in studies of policing. Specifically, scholars have assessed the importance of grant funding as a determinant of organizational practices. In 1994, the federal government passed the Violent Crime Control and Law Enforcement Act containing, among other things, provisions to encourage the implementation of community policing in U.S. police departments (Worrall & Zhao, 2003). The law led to the establishment of the Office of Community-Oriented Policing Services, a component of the Department of Justice charged with administering grant programs fostering community policing innovation. Oliver (2000) argued that this is when community policing really took hold; "many of the agencies coming to community policing during the third generation [of the reform] were simply seeking grant funding, and they would hire the officers as community-policing officers" (p. 379). Worrall and Zhao (2003) echoed this statement in their findings. Even after considering a range of possible predictors of community policing implementation, including contingency factors such as the local crime rate, "no single variable was as significantly related to COP [community-oriented policing] as the grants variables" (p. 81). Similarly, in a sample of 285 large law enforcement agencies, Katz, Maguire, and Roncek (2002) found that outside financial assistance for the creation or support of a gang unit was more influential in determining whether or not a department had a specialized gang unit than the violent, property, drug, weapons, or simple assault crime rates.

External control raises a number of important issues. First, Worrall and Zhao (2003) ask, "What happens when the well runs dry?" (p. 81). If organizations, including the police departments described above, are adapting to the constraints they face, will it be necessary to continue with community policing or gang units once the constraints ease, as they have with federal funding for community policing? Will funds just shift to other priorities such as homeland security and encourage greater efforts on that front? Oliver (2006) claims that we may have already moved beyond the community policing era and moved into a homeland security era of policing. Moreover, a variety of policing innovations are currently operating in cities throughout the country, with some demonstrably more effective than community policing (Weisburd & Braga, 2006). As such, it is possible that as funding diminishes, community policing and other strategies may fade away unless they are valuable for other reasons (see the next subsection). A second concern is that conformity to external demands might produce additional costs for the organization. As Giblin (2006) stated when discussing the adoption of crime analysis units, "Since there are costs associated with creating special units, the resources acquired from environmental constituents must be both critical and must exceed the costs associated with the organizational change for structural elaboration to occur" (p. 661). If the costs of compliance are too high, the organization may simply resist the demands of external providers or ignore the funding altogether. Feeley and Sarat (1980) provide support for this position in their description of criminal justice planning agencies created by the Law Enforcement Assistance Administration. The planning agencies attempted to induce change in criminal justice organizations but were limited in their success. The money offered was not critical to law enforcement agencies since it was just a small part of overall operating budgets. Consequently, it simply was not worth it to succumb to external demands.

Institutional Theory

A third contemporary perspective on organizations, **institutional theory**, contends that organizational structures and practices are a product of expectations of what organizations should do, irrespective of efficiency and effectiveness concerns (Meyer & Rowan, 1977). In their classic and widely cited article, Meyer and Rowan argued that certain

> positions, policies, programs, and procedures of modern organizations are enforced by public opinion, by the views of important constituents, by knowledge legitimated through the educational system, by social prestige, by laws, and by definitions of negligence and prudence used by the courts. (p. 343)

If powerful actors (public opinion, other organizations, etc.) outside of the organization believe that certain organizational attributes are appropriate, the organization will be under tremendous pressure to comply to demonstrate its "organizational worth" (Hinings & Greenwood, 1988, p. 53). Returning to the example of D.A.R.E. discussed earlier, why would a police department continue to offer drug education in schools despite the absence of demonstrated success? For institutional theorists, the answer lies in wider expectations about best practices, even if the practices are only "hypothetically associated" with successful outcomes (Lipsky, 1980, p. 51). Powerful constituents believe in the efficacy of D.A.R.E., and it is backed by a national organization and "anecdotal testimony of participants, teachers, parents, and police officers who believe DARE is an effective program" (Frumkin & Reingold, 2004, p. 18). If departments fail to respond to these pressures, they risk legitimacy challenges. That is, departments may face criticisms from the outside about their choices (Hinings & Greenwood, 1988; Meyer & Rowan, 1977). The police department described at the beginning of the section faced this predicament—either establish a gang unit for a largely nonexistent gang problem or face criticism for not responding to what many felt was a significant community threat (Katz, 2001).

D.A.R.E. has become what institutional theorists would call an institutional myth. The widely shared belief—the benefits of drug education for school children—has taken on a fact-like quality even though validity of the myth is inaccurate or unproven (Meyer & Rowan, 1977). Additional examples of institutional myths are common throughout the criminal justice system. In the courts, victims are often afforded the opportunity to provide input in the sentencing process, orally or in writing, via victim impact statements. The problem is, at least with respect to oral impact statements at the time of sentencing, judges have already largely determined the sentence, basing their decisions on legal factors such as seriousness of the offense and prior record (Erez & Tontodonato, 1990). In other words, the procedure is largely symbolic, consistent with beliefs that the victim's voice be heard. Similarly, the appearance of individualization is maintained via probation presentence reports even though they only minimally affect judicial sentencing decisions (Rosecrance, 1988). The public and defendants demand individualized justice. In policing, both random preventive patrol and rapid response to 911 hold myth-like status. Research has questioned the efficacy of both strategies in reducing crime (e.g., Spelman & Brown, 1984), yet the public would likely resist efforts to reduce or eliminate random patrol or replace immediate responses with alternatives such as taking reports over the Internet.

Since institutional myths are, by definition, widely shared understandings of how organizations should operate, similar organizations are going to be under similar pressures to respond. That is, police departments, prisons, jails, and other criminal justice organizations will face the constraints associated with their specific industry. Organizations within the same field will tend to resemble one another—adopting similar structures or practices—since "there are only a limited number of acceptable or appropriate organizational features that are viewed as legitimate" (Burruss et al., 2010, p. 83). The tendency of organizations to resemble one another is referred to as **isomorphism** (DiMaggio & Powell, 1983). Three processes contribute to isomorphism: coercive, mimetic, and normative. Coercive isomorphism is evident when organizations are forced to or seduced into adopting particular structures or strategies through laws or funding inducements. For example, isomorphism might be evident among municipal police departments in a number of states in their racial profiling data collection practices. Each agency may require officers to collect basic information (age, race, sex, etc.) related to each stop. Was the decision to implement data collection procedures based on best practices? Not necessarily, as states are increasingly mandating departments to gather this information (Tillyer, Engel, & Cherkauskas, 2010). Grant requirements (see examples in the "Resource Dependence" subsection) may also encourage adoption. A second source of isomorphism is mimetic pressures. Organizations become similar as a result of copying or modeling other organizations perceived to be successful. The New York City Police Department's Compstat management initiative was a commonly modeled program; "should a department implement a Compstat program that does not closely resemble what Compstat is expected to look like (the NYPD model), it risks forfeiting the innovation's legitimating value" (Willis, Mastrofski, & Weisburd, 2007, p. 160). Finally, normative processes contribute to isomorphism. Normative processes are related to education and training; what is learned in these settings is brought back to home organizations by employees helping diffuse ideas throughout an industry. Harris (1999) indicated that 27,000 police officers attended training offered by the Drug Enforcement Administration, where officers learned how to interdict drugs through the use of pretext stops. The concern, of course, is that the training might have contributed to the spread of racial profiling as these officers returned to their own departments. These pressures toward isomorphism are arguably more salient than concerns about organizational performance in explaining structures and practices.

Institutional theory, at first glance, takes a relatively cynical view of organizations. Organizational leaders are viewed as symbolically complying with the demands of external constituents to maintain their support even if the adopted structures and practices are ineffective. Indeed, organizations may **decouple** the institutionally prescribed practices from their day-to-day operations so as not to disrupt the regular organization work flow. For example, a granting agency may require a police department to adopt community policing. Department leaders can simply relegate community policing to a special unit, the responsibility of a handful of officers, while the vast majority of officers police as usual (Parks, Mastrofski, Dejong, & Gray, 1999). A judge can similarly allow for the presentation of a victim impact statement or the preparation of a probation presentence report to satisfy demands, even though neither will substantially influence sentencing decisions. The day-to-day operations are disconnected or decoupled from the more symbolic actions. Criminal justice organizations should not be viewed as completely neglectful of performance concerns. Organizational leaders might truly desire to improve their organizations when confronting a mismatch with the environment (see contingency theory) but are limited in the possible options for adaptation by what the environment supports (institutional theory) (Giblin, 2006). Interested in enhancing homeland security preparedness, for example, police departments may select only from approaches that are supported in law enforcement circles (Burruss et al., 2010).

The organizational theories presented in this section help us understand what organizations look like (Maguire & Uchida, 2000). The focus is on the structures and practices of organizations rather than the actual behavior of the actors within the criminal justice system. As the discussion shows, theories provide insight into the best organizational forms but also help make sense of, or describe, what we observe. Subsequent sections extend this larger discussion by focusing on environmental influences (unions in Section VI) and structural contributions to organizational failure (Section IV), as well as human relations issues such as socialization (Section VII), motivation (Section VIII), and stress (Section IX).

KEY TERMS

administrative management	Hawthorne studies	prescriptive
bureaucracy	human relations school	resource dependence theory
contingency theory	institutional theory	scientific management
decouple	instrumental rationality	Theory X
Hawthorne effect	isomorphism	Theory Y

DISCUSSION QUESTIONS

1. Chief executives of some criminal justice organizations (prosecutors' offices, sheriffs' departments) are elected by the general public. Would Max Weber support elected leadership over other types of hiring/appointment processes? Why or why not?

2. Weber advocates for objective rather than personal considerations in hiring and promotion. Scholars, including Blau and Scott (1962/2003) and Scott and Davis (2007), questioned whether competence for purposes of hiring and promotion is best gauged by experience (time on the job) or training and education away from the job. Which do you think is more important? Explain.

3. Many people who study contingency theory point to the effects of crime-related factors in shaping criminal justice organizations. When crime increases, for example, organizations must adapt to regain effectiveness. Are there other factors, or contingencies, that also affect criminal justice organizational effectiveness? Explain.

WEB RESOURCES

CIA Museum Online Collection (including interactive timeline):
https://www.cia.gov/about-cia/cia-museum/experience-the-collection/index.html

D.A.R.E. (Drug Abuse Resistance Education) America:
http://www.dare.com

U.S. Department of Justice interactive organizational chart:
http://www.justice.gov/agencies/index-org.html#OAAG

READING

Reading 4

In his essay, author Robert M. Bohm takes the concept of McDonaldization developed by sociologist George Ritzer and applies it to the study of the criminal justice system and criminal justice organizations. McDonaldization has its roots in the classical school work of Max Weber and his notion of bureaucracy; organizations are rationally oriented to the efficient and effective achievement of goals, and this is accomplished through appropriate structures (e.g., complexity and control). Four principles—efficiency, calculability, predictability, and control—are consistent with bureaucratization and exemplified by the fast-food restaurant chain McDonald's; the restaurant serves as a metaphor for illustrating the principles and describing how they are coming to characterize other parts of society, including the criminal justice system.

Criminal justice organizations, like McDonald's, emphasize efficiency; a focus on rapid police response to calls for service and the large number of nontrial court dispositions are just two examples. The system also emphasizes calculability, the tendency to highlight numerical or quantifiable information, or quantity over quality (e.g., lengthy sentences, more police officers, value of drug busts). The system also tries to handle cases uniformly, or in predictable fashion, usually by promulgating rules (formalization). Finally, a variety of mechanisms are used to control criminal justice practitioners, from sentencing guidelines to mandatory arrest policies, to ensure that they behave as instructed. The problem with these four elements is that, while they are intended to produce an effective organization and system, they actually produce unintended consequences. As Bohm notes, attempts at rationality produce irrationality, such as when an innocent individual is convicted due to the sloppy procedures brought about by concerns for efficiency. Bohm concludes his essay by citing possible solutions to McDonaldization in criminal justice.

"McJustice"

On the McDonaldization of Criminal Justice

Robert M. Bohm

The purpose of this essay is to examine the "McDonaldization" of criminal justice. The concept of "McDonaldization" or "McJustice" provides another useful way of understanding the development and operation of criminal justice in the United States.[1] "McDonaldization," as employed by sociologist George Ritzer, refers to "the [bureaucratic] process by which principles of the fast-food restaurant

Source: Bohm, R. M. (2006). "McJustice": On the McDonaldization of criminal justice. *Justice Quarterly, 23*(1), 127–146.

are coming to dominate more and more sectors of American society as well as of the rest of the world" (Ritzer, 2004, p. 1). The theoretical basis for McDonaldization is Max Weber's theory of rationality and bureaucracy (Ritzer, 2004, p. 24; but see Wood, 1998, for a critique of Ritzer's use of Weber). The concept of McDonaldization has been used to depict developments in a variety of different social institutions, including religion (Drane, 2001), education (Hayes & Wynyard, 2002; Parker & Jary, 1995), the media (Prichard, 1987), medicine (Reiser, 1978; Ritzer & Walczak, 1987), and leisure and travel (Rojek, 1993), as well as society itself (Ritzer, 2004). However, to date, the concept of McDonaldization has only rarely been employed in the analysis of criminal justice or issues related to criminal justice (see, for example, Kemmesies, 2002; Robinson, 2002; Shichor, 1997; Umbreit, 1999).

The McDonaldization of various social institutions has succeeded because it provides advantages over other, usually older, methods of doing business (see, for example, Ritzer, 2004, p. 16). It has made McDonaldized social institutions bureaucratic and rational in a Weberian sense and, thus, more efficient, calculable, predictable, and controlling over people (often by nonhuman technologies). In the case of McDonaldized businesses, it has also made them more profitable. The principal problem with McDonaldized institutions, and another characteristic of the process, is irrationality or, as Ritzer (2004, p. 17) calls it, the "irrationality of rationality." For example, McDonaldization does not always benefit all of the participants in the process or society in general. Indeed, McDonaldization has several important costs or dangers associated with it. A primary purpose of this essay is to expose the costs, dangers, or irrationalities of "McJustice."

In the following sections the characteristics of McDonaldized criminal justice or "McJustice"—efficiency, calculability, predictability, control, and irrationality—are described. Because of space limitations, only a few criminal justice examples can be provided (for other examples see Kemmesies, 2002; Robinson, 2002; Shichor, 1997; Umbreit, 1999).

Efficiency: Administering Justice by Plea Bargaining

Efficiency is the choosing of "the optimum means to a given end" (Ritzer, 2004, p. 43). Bureaucracies attempt to increase efficiency by requiring employees (and sometimes customers) to follow steps in a predesigned process governed by organizational rules and regulations and by having managers supervise employees (and customers) to make sure they follow the rules, regulations, and process (Ritzer, 2004, p. 13). Increasing efficiency usually entails "streamlining various processes, simplifying products, and having customers do work formerly done by paid employees" (Ritzer, 2004, p. 44). Despite best efforts, however, the optimum means to a given end are rarely found because of historical constraints, financial difficulties, organizational limitations, and uncooperative human nature (Ritzer, 2004, p. 43). Therefore, most bureaucracies are relatively satisfied with the illusion of efficiency (Ritzer, 2004, p. 137) or an incremental increase in efficiency, knowing that maximization of efficiency is probably an unobtainable goal.

With the huge number of cases handled each year by the agencies of criminal justice, operating efficiency has long been a practical necessity, albeit oftentimes an unrealized goal. One of the first scholars to discuss operating efficiency in criminal justice was Herbert Packer (1968), who wrote about the topic in the context of his well-known crime control model of criminal justice. In Packer's crime control model, which is arguably an apt description of the current operation of criminal justice in the United States, the control of crime is by far the most important function of criminal justice (Packer, 1968, p. 158). (Control is another characteristic of McDonaldized institutions.) Although the means by which crime is controlled are important in this view (illegal means are not advocated), they are less important than the ultimate goal or end of control. To better control crime, advocates of the crime control model want to make the process more efficient—to move cases through the process as quickly as possible and to bring them to a close (Packer, 1968, p. 158). Packer (1968, p. 159) characterizes the crime control model as "assembly-line justice." To achieve "quicker closure" in the processing of cases, a premium is placed on speed and finality (Packer, 1968, p. 159). Speed requires that cases be handled informally and uniformly; finality depends on minimizing occasions for challenge, that is, appeals (Packer, 1968, p. 159).

Packer's assembly-line metaphor also describes the process by which McDonald's sells billions of hamburgers. Consider the McDonald's experience. When people order a Big Mac from McDonald's, they know exactly what they are going to get. All Big Macs are the same, because they are made uniformly. Moreover, a person can get a Big Mac in a matter of seconds most of the time. However, what happens when a person orders something different, or something not already prepared, such as a hamburger with ketchup only? The person's order is taken, and she or he is asked to stand to the side because the special order will take a few minutes. The person's special order has slowed down the assembly line and reduced efficiency. This happens in criminal justice, too! If defendants ask for something special, such as a trial, the assembly line is slowed and efficiency is reduced.

Even when criminal justice is operating at its best, it is a slow process. The time from arrest to final case disposition can typically be measured in weeks or months. If defendants opt for a jury trial, as is their right in most felony cases, the cases are handled formally and are treated as unique; no two cases are the same in their circumstances or in the way they are handled. If defendants are not satisfied with the outcome of their trials then they have the right to appeal. Appeals may delay by years the final resolution of cases.

To increase efficiency—meaning speed and finality—crime control advocates prefer plea bargaining (Packer, 1968, p. 162)—the quintessential bureaucratic and McDonaldized process in criminal justice. Plea bargaining also illustrates the interrelationship of all of the characteristics of McDonaldization. Currently, about 95 percent of all convictions in felony cases are the result of guilty pleas (Durose & Langan, 2003, p. 9, table 10). Plea bargains can be offered and accepted in a relatively short time. Also, cases are handled uniformly because the mechanics of a plea bargain are basically the same; only the substance of the deals differs. Additionally, with successful plea bargains, there is no opportunity for challenge; there are no appeals. In short, plea bargaining allows cases to be disposed of quickly, predictably (another characteristic of McDonaldization), and with little of the adversarial conflict associated with criminal trials. In terms of McDonaldization, plea bargaining streamlines and simplifies the administration of justice and, thus, is the perfect mechanism for achieving efficiency.

Although plea bargaining became a common practice in state courts shortly after the Civil War and, as a result of the tremendous number of liquor law violations, was instituted at the federal level during Prohibition in the 1930s (Alschuler, 1979; Padgett, 1990), it has neither a constitutional nor statutory basis. It did not receive formal recognition until 1970 in the case of *Brady v. United States*, in which the Court upheld the use of plea bargaining because of the "mutuality of advantage" it provided the defendant and the state.

Plea bargaining benefits most of the participants in the criminal justice process (Packer, 1968, p. 222) by, among other things, reducing uncertainty or unpredictability. Uncertainty is a characteristic of all criminal trials because neither the duration of the trial, which may be a matter of minutes or of months, nor the outcome of the trial can ever be predicted with any degree of accuracy. Plea bargaining eliminates those two areas of uncertainty by eliminating the need for a trial. Plea bargaining serves the interests of prosecutors by guaranteeing them high conviction rates, which is an indicator of job performance and a useful tool in the quest for higher political office. It serves the interests of judges by reducing their court caseloads, allowing more time to be spent on more difficult cases. In addition, if a large proportion of the approximately 95 percent of felony cases that are handled each year by plea bargaining were to go to trial instead, the administration of justice in the United States would be even slower than it already is. Plea bargaining serves the interests of criminal defense attorneys by allowing them to spend less time on each case. It also allows them to avoid trials. Trials are relatively expensive events. Because most criminal defendants are poor, they are usually unable to pay a large legal fee. Thus, when criminal defense attorneys go to trial, they are frequently unable to recoup all of their expenses. Plea bargaining provides many criminal defense attorneys with the more profitable option of charging smaller fees for lesser services and handling a larger volume of cases. Even most criminal defendants are served by plea bargaining. A guilty plea generally results in either no prison sentence or a lesser prison sentence than the defendant might receive if found guilty at trial. Plea bargaining also often allows defendants to escape conviction of socially stigmatizing crimes, such as child abuse. By "copping" a plea to assault rather than to statutory rape, for example, a defendant can avoid the embarrassing publicity of a trial and the wrath of fellow inmates or of society in general. In sum, there is no question that plea bargaining has many advantages, including making the administration of justice more efficient.

Calculability: Fiscal Costs of Administering Justice

Calculability refers to the quantitative aspects of McDonaldization (e.g., costs and the amount of time it takes to get the product). Calculability allows McDonaldized institutions "to produce and obtain large amounts of things very rapidly" and "to determine efficiency" (Ritzer, 2004, p. 66). Calculability also makes McDonaldized institutions more predictable and enhances control—two of the other characteristics of McDonaldized institutions (Ritzer, 2004, pp. 66–67).

Although the costs of administering justice in the United States are enormous— $167 billion in 2001 (Bauer & Owens, 2004, p. 1)—compared to other government expenditures, the amount spent on justice is modest. Only about 7 percent of all state and local public expenditures in 2001 were spent on criminal *and* civil justice (Bauer & Owens, 2004, p. 1). State and local governments funded about 85 percent of all direct justice system expenses in 2001 (Bauer & Owens, 2004, p. 1). By contrast, state and local governments spent nearly 4 times as much on education, about twice as much on public welfare, and approximately the same amount on hospitals and healthcare (Bauer & Owens, 2004, p. 1). Of the $167 billion spent in 2001, police protection received 43 percent; judicial and legal services 23 percent; and corrections 34 percent (Bauer & Owens, 2004, p. 4, table 3). Note that from 1982 to 1999, judicial and legal services always received less state, local, and total funding than either police protection or corrections (Sourcebook of Criminal Justice Statistics, 2002a, pp. 3–4, table 1.2), which might also help explain the penchant for plea bargaining described above.

For the past three decades, about two thirds of the American public have believed that the amount spent on administering justice in the United States is a bargain—that too little money is spent on crime control (though in 2002, only 56 percent so believed); very few people think that too much money is spent (Sourcebook of Criminal Justice Statistics, 2002b, p. 135, table 2.40). Thanks to efficiencies such as plea bargaining the administration of justice in the United States is generally considered cost effective.

Predictability: Reducing Sentencing and Parole Discretion

In McDonaldized institutions, predictability means that products and services will be uniform everywhere and at all times; there are no surprises (Ritzer, 2004, p. 14). For consumers, predictability provides peace of mind (Ritzer, 2004, p.86). Employees of the process are also predictable in their actions because of rules and supervision (Ritzer, 2004, p. 14). For workers, predictability makes their jobs easier (Ritzer, 2004, p. 86). "To achieve predictability" McDonaldized institutions stress "discipline, order, systemization, formalization, routine, consistency, and methodical operation" (Ritzer, 2004, p. 86).

Beginning in the mid-1970s, state legislatures began replacing indeterminate sentencing—long the principal form of sentencing in the United States—with determinate sentencing, and some states began abolishing parole (federal parole was abolished in 1987) (Carter, 1996, p. 148). These changes were motivated primarily by an increased public fear of crime, the loss of confidence in rehabilitation as a correctional goal, and the unpredictability of decisions made by judges and parole boards. The public began to believe that judges had become "soft" on crime, rehabilitation of criminal offenders was not possible, and parole boards were releasing from prison many dangerous offenders who had served only a small portion of their sentences. The hope of determinate sentencing was that it would at least get criminals off the streets for longer periods of time. Some people also considered a determinate sentence more humane (and predictable) because prisoners would know exactly when they would be released, something that they did not know with an indeterminate sentence (Griset, 1991, pp. 176–177).

Although the evidence never supported the widely held belief that judges were "soft" on crime (see, for example, Reaves, 2001), under indeterminate sentencing schemes judges did vary widely in the sentences they imposed for similar crimes and offenders. Critics argued that, besides being generally unfair (and irrational in a McDonaldized sense), such judicial disparity in sentencing resulted in discrimination against people of color and the poor (see, for example, Spohn & Holleran, 2000; Tonry, 1996, p. 7). As a result, several states and the federal government developed guidelines for determinate sentencing; other states established sentencing commissions to do so (Tonry, 1993, 1996, p. 10). Sentencing guidelines were another way of restricting judicial sentencing discretion.

Another response to the "soft on crime" allegation, and another way that legislatures restricted judicial sentencing discretion in the 1980s, was by enacting "mandatory minimum" sentencing statutes (Ditton & Wilson, 1999; Tonry, 1996, pp. 6–7). "Mandatory minimum" sentences require that offenders—most frequently offenders who commit certain types of offenses such as drug offenses, offenses committed with weapons, and offenses committed by repeat or habitual offenders—serve a specified amount of prison time. All states and the federal government have one or more mandatory minimum sentencing laws. To reduce the discretion exercised by parole boards (in those states that retained them), states in the 1980s also enacted "truth-in-sentencing" statutes that generally required prisoners to serve a substantial portion of their prison sentence, usually 85 percent of it (Ditton & Wilson, 1999). All of these changes made sentencing more predictable.

Control: Rules, Regulations, Structure, and Technology

Control in McDonaldized institutions involves the ability of the institution to get employees and customers to follow the rules and regulations governing the process (Ritzer, 2004, p. 15). In the case of employees, this is accomplished by training them to do a few things in a precise manner with managers and inspectors providing close supervision (Ritzer, 2004, p. 15).

Criminal justice officials are controlled (at least in theory) by a myriad of rules and regulations. The US Constitution, for example, prohibits police officers from engaging in unreasonable searches and seizures (Fourth Amendment) and correctional officers from employing cruel and unusual punishments (Eighth Amendment)—to name just two constraints. State constitutions provide similar limitations. Decisions by the US Supreme Court and other courts also check the behavior of criminal justice officials. For instance, in *Tennessee v. Garner* (1985), the Supreme Court severely restricted police use of deadly force. The cases of *Morrissey v. Brewer*

(1972) and *Gagnon v. Scarpelli* (1973) prescribe strict guidelines for parole and probation revocation. Statutes are another way of controlling the behavior of criminal justice officials. As described in the last section, statutes providing determinate sentencing, sentencing guidelines, and mandatory minimum sentences control judges' sentencing decisions. Rules of evidence and criminal procedure govern practice and procedure in the various courts. Most criminal justice officials are also controlled by professional codes of conduct and departmental policies and regulations.

The military structures of both police and correctional agencies are intended to promote the control of police officers and correctional officers by those higher in the chain of command. Technology has also aided in their control. The police radio, for example, allows supervisors at the stationhouse to control patrol officers by keeping both parties in constant contact.

A new way that McDonaldization is influencing the control of police officers is through the highly touted Compstat program. Begun in New York City in 1994, Compstat is a strategic problem-solving system that combines "state-of-the art management principles with cutting-edge crime analysis and geographic systems technology" (Willis et al., 2004, p. 464; also see Mabrey, 2002; Weisburd, Mastrofski, McNally, Greenspan, & Willis, 2003). Its explicit purpose is to help police departments fight crime and improve the quality of life in their communities by overcoming traditional bureaucratic irrationalities, such as loss of focus on reducing crime, department fragmentation, and lack of cooperation between units because of "red tape" and turf battles, and lack of timely data on which to base crime control strategies and to evaluate the strategies that are implemented (Weisburd et al., 2003, pp. 425–426; Willis et al., 2004, pp. 464, 470). The information produced by Compstat is also used by the chief of police to judge the performance of precinct commanders and by precinct commanders to hold their officers accountable. Unlike traditional police bureaucracies, Compstat is supposed to make police organizations "more focused, knowledge-based, and agile" (Willis et al., 2004, p. 490).

The Irrationality of Rationality: Other, Often Unanticipated Consequences

According to Ritzer (2004, pp. 17, 134), McDonaldized institutions are rational systems, and rational systems inevitably produce irrationalities "that limit, eventually compromise, and perhaps even undermine their rationality." "At the general level," Ritzer (2004, p. 134) notes, "the *irrationality of rationality* is simply a label for many of the negative aspects of McDonaldization" (emphasis in original). It is important to understand that Ritzer is describing a particular kind of rationality—one that has been pejoratively called "technological rationality" or "instrumental reason" (see, for example, Gouldner, 1976; Horkheimer, 1996; Marcuse, 1966). As applied to McDonaldized businesses, it is "rational" only as a business strategy (Schroyer, 1975, p. 26) that has as its ultimate goal profit maximization. In the case of McJustice, it currently promotes "law and order" as instrumental values over alternative ideals such as justice and freedom (see Schroyer, 1975, p. 20).

McDonaldized institutions produce many irrationalities that undermine their rationality. They can be inefficient because of excess red tape and other problems (Ritzer, 2004, p. 27). They can produce poor quality work and a decline in employee effort because of the emphasis on quantification (the substitution of quantity for quality and the resulting mediocrity of both the process and the product), the often mind-numbing routine, and the absence of meaningful employee job input (Ritzer, 2004, pp. 27, 66, 86). Most employees of McDonaldized institutions "are expected to do a lot of work, very quickly, for low pay" (Ritzer, 2004, p. 14). McDonaldized institutions can be unpredictable because employees, no matter how well trained and supervised, sometimes are confused, unsure about what they are supposed to do, inefficient, and apt to make mistakes. To achieve greater control, McDonaldized institutions increasingly attempt to replace employees with more consistent machines and nonhuman technologies (Ritzer, 2004, p. 15).[2] Ironically, those efforts can be counterproductive and control over employees and clients can be lost because they become angry at the machines and nonhuman technologies that replace the former and frustrate the latter (Ritzer, 2004, pp. 27–28). Reliance on machines and nonhuman technologies can also reduce the skills necessary to do the job, and the opportunity, perhaps even the ability, of people to think for themselves (Ritzer, 2004, p. 133). McDonaldized institutions also can be dehumanizing (Ritzer, 2004, p. 27). Weber especially feared what he called the "iron cage" of rationality in which people get trapped in bureaucracies that deny them their basic humanity (Ritzer, 2004, p. 28), as, for example, when crime victims are ignored or mistreated by criminal justice officials. In the remainder of this section irrationalities of plea bargaining, criminal justice fiscal policies, determinate sentencing, and efforts to control criminal justice officials are described.

Plea Bargaining

As noted in the previous section on efficiency, plea bargaining has become the principal method of administering justice in the United States because it benefits most of the participants in the criminal justice process. However, two types of criminal defendants are not served by the practice of plea bargaining and both illustrate irrationalities of the process. The first are innocent, indigent, highly visible defendants who fear being found guilty of crimes they did not commit and receiving harsh sentences. Such defendants are sometimes pressured by overworked and inexperienced defense attorneys into waiving their constitutional right to trial. The second type is the habitual offender. In this context, a habitual offender is a person who has been convicted under a state's habitual-offender statute (sometimes called a "three strikes and you're out" law). Most such statutes provide that upon conviction of a third felony, a defendant must receive life imprisonment. Although habitual-offender statutes would seem to imprison offenders for life, they actually are used mostly as bargaining chips by prosecutors in plea negotiations and not as they were intended (see, for example, LaFree, 2002, pp. 880–881).

The irrationality of habitual-offender statutes is illustrated by the case of *Bordenkircher v. Hayes* (1978). The defendant, who had previously been convicted of two minor felonies, was arrested and charged with forging an $88 check. The prosecutor in the case told the defendant that if he did not plead guilty to the charge and accept a 5-year prison sentence, which on its face seemed very harsh, then the prosecutor would invoke the state's habitual-offender statute. The statute required the judge to impose a sentence of life imprisonment if the defendant were found guilty at trial. The defendant elected to play "you bet your life" and turned down the prosecutor's plea offer. At trial, the defendant was found guilty of forging the check and was sentenced to life imprisonment. Clearly, the defendant in this case was not served by plea bargaining or, perhaps, was not served by refusing the prosecutor's offer.

Crime victims are another group whose interests are not always served by plea bargaining, and their plight illustrates further the process's irrationality. Long ignored in the adjudication of crimes committed against them, victims often feel "revictimized" by the deals that prosecutors offer offenders and believe they have been denied the full measure of justice they seek and deserve.

Another problem with plea bargaining is that it precludes the possibility of any further judicial examination of earlier stages of the process (Packer, 1968, p. 224). In other words, with the acceptance of a guilty plea, there is no longer any chance that police or prosecutorial errors before trial will be detected.

Criminal Justice Fiscal Policies

The public's belief in the general cost effectiveness of criminal justice has been described in the section on calculability. Criminal justice is not always cost effective, however, and the exceptions expose irrationalities of the process. For example, from the mid-1920s until the mid-1970s the costs of prisons and jails were not a major issue because the incarceration rate in the United States remained relatively stable. That did not change until the mid-1970s and the War on Drugs when the incarceration rate began to increase significantly, with each subsequent year showing a new high. By the 1980s, many states and the federal government were facing serious crowding problems. The immediate response was an ambitious and expensive prison and jail expansion program. (Other strategies included privatization and intermediate sanctions.) Between 1977 and 2001, total state and local costs for building and operating correctional institutions increased about 900 percent.[3] Between 1982 and 2001, the corresponding increase at the federal level was about 700 percent (see footnote 3). By comparison, between 1977 and 2001, states and localities increased expenditures to education by 448 percent, to hospitals and healthcare by 482 percent, and to public welfare by 617 percent (Bauer & Owens, 2004, p. 4). In 1995, for the first time ever, more money was spent building new prisons than new university structures in the United States—$2.5 billion for construction in higher education and $2.6 billion for prison construction. From 1987 to 1995, state prison expenditures rose 30 percent while higher education funding fell 18 percent ("More Spent on Prisons," 1997, p. A-6).

Ironically, by 1995, while expenditures for prison construction and expansion were peaking, the overall growth of the state (but not federal) prison population began slowing (Harrison & Beck, 2003). In 2001, the 1.1 percent growth in the state and federal prison population (entirely attributable to the slower growth in the state prison population) was the lowest annual rate recorded since 1972 (Harrison & Beck, 2003). Legislators, in an effort to appear tough on crime by incarcerating increasing numbers of law violators for longer periods of time, and correctional officials, on whose projections the legislators justified their decisions, had miscalculated the confinement space that was needed. Consequently, by the end of the century, many jurisdictions had new or expanded correctional facilities that sat empty or operated well under capacity (Blomberg & Lucken, 2000, p. 182; Camp & Camp, 2002, p. 85). Many of the new facilities could not be used (even where there was a need) because continuing budget crises precluded the hiring of personnel to operate them (Blomberg & Lucken, 2000, p. 182). Other correctional institutions utilized their excess capacity by contracting with other jurisdictions to house the other jurisdiction's prisoners (Camp & Camp, 2002, p. 93).

The costs of capital punishment illustrate another irrationality of criminal justice. As noted previously, about 95 percent of criminal cases never reach trial, but instead are resolved through the cost-effective process of plea bargaining. Capital cases are an exception; they are rarely plea bargained (Bohm, 2003, p. 137). They are also very expensive. The average cost per execution in the United States (i.e., the entire process) ranges from about $2.5 million to $5 million (in 2000 dollars) (Bohm, 2003, p. 135). Extraordinary cases can cost much more. The state of Florida, for example, reportedly spent $10 million to execute serial murderer Ted Bundy in 1989, and the federal government spent more than $100 million to execute mass murderer Timothy McVeigh in 2001 (Bohm, 2003, p. 135).

The costs of capital trials are forcing local governments to make difficult choices. For example, a recent study in Illinois found that capital trials could increase county spending by as much as 1.8 percent per trial. Such trials are often financed through increased property taxes or funds taken from police and highway appropriations (Governor's Commission, 2002, p. 199). A *Wall Street Journal* article reported that the Texas county where the three men convicted of the 1998 murder of James Byrd were tried was forced to raise property taxes by 6.7 percent for 2 years to cover trial costs (Governor's Commission, 2002, p. 199). Even when a capital trial does not result in a death sentence and execution, the added costs associated with the capital punishment process are incurred anyway without any "return" on the state's investment of resources. In some death-eligible cases, prosecutors forgo capital trials altogether rather than incur the expense. Based on cost effectiveness alone, capital punishment does not seem to be the most rational alternative for the most heinous crimes.

Determinate Sentencing

A number of problems or irrationalities have been identified with determinate sentencing schemes, described in the section on predictability. First, it has been argued that the consequences of determinate sentencing include longer prison sentences and overcrowded prisons (Goodstein & Hepburn, 1985, pp. 37–38; Griset, 1991, p. 184). In recent years, the United States has had one of the highest imprisonment rates in the world (see, for example, International Centre for Prison Studies, 2003). Furthermore, as of 2003, the entire correctional departments of 10 states were under court orders to reduce overcrowding or improve other conditions of confinement; in another 17 states, one or more institutions were under court orders for the same reasons (American Correctional Association, 2004, p. 18).

A related problem of determinate sentencing is that it produces an unusually harsh prison system (but see Goodstein & Hepburn, 1985, for another view). For example, because of prison overcrowding, many states have all but abandoned even the pretense of rehabilitating offenders. Prisons are increasingly becoming places where offenders are simply "warehoused." This trend has been referred to as the "new penology" and "actuarial justice" (Feeley & Simon, 1992, 1994). As noted, this new penology has abandoned rehabilitation in favor of efficiently managing large numbers of prisoners. Success for this new penology is not measured by reductions in recidivism (a standard measure of correctional success used in the past) but rather by how efficiently correctional systems manage prisoners within budgetary constraints. In addition, because of the abolition of good time (the number of days deducted from a sentence by prison authorities for good behavior or for other reasons) and parole under some determinate sentencing schemes, prison authorities are having a more difficult time maintaining discipline and control of their institutions (Griset, 1991, p. 141). Eliminating good time and parole removed two of the most important incentives that prison authorities use to get inmates to behave and to follow prison rules. Also, because of the perceived harshness of some of the determinate sentencing schemes, some judges simply ignore the sentencing guidelines (Griset, 1999, pp. 322–323). Other judges have ignored the sentencing guidelines because they believe they are too lenient. In short, many judges resent sentencing guidelines and refer to their use as "justice by computer."

Third, critics claim that determinate sentencing merely shifts sentencing discretion from judges to legislatures and prosecutors (through plea bargaining) (Clear, Hewitt, & Regoli, 1978; Goodstein & Hepburn, 1985, p. 38; Tonry, 1996, p. 7; Tonry & Frase, 2001, p. 230). Whether this shift in sentencing responsibility is desirable is a matter of debate. On one hand, prosecutors generally exercise their discretion in secret, whereas judges exercise discretion in the open. Also, prosecutors and legislators are generally subject to more political influence than are judges.

Fourth, in those jurisdictions that retain good time, sentencing discretion, at least to some degree, actually shifts from legislators and prosecutors to correctional personnel (Clear et al., 1978; Goodstein & Hepburn, 1985, pp. 38–39; Griset, 1991, pp. 139–141, 1999, pp. 318–319). By charging inmates with prison rule violations, correctional personnel can reduce (if the charges are upheld) the amount of good time earned by inmates and, by doing so, increase an inmate's time served.

Fifth, critics contend that it is virtually impossible in determinate sentencing schemes for legislatures or sentencing commissions to define in advance all of the factors that ought to be considered in determining a criminal sentence (Tonry, 1996).

Controlling Criminal Justice Officials

Despite all the rules, regulations, structures, and technology intended to control the behavior of criminal justice officials, mistakes or miscarriages of justice still occur. Although such "irrationalities" have probably always plagued the administration of justice, only relatively recently, with the advent of sophisticated DNA technology, has the extent of the problem been realized. For example, according to attorney Barry Scheck, co-founder of the Innocence Project at the Cardoza School of Law in New York City, "Of the first eighteen thousand results [of DNA tests] at the FBI and other crime laboratories, at least five thousand prime suspects were excluded *before* their cases were tried" (Scheck, Neufeld, & Dwyer, 2001, p. xx). That is, more than 25 percent of the prime suspects were wrongly accused. In a study of wrongful convictions conducted in the 1980s, researchers conservatively estimated that approximately 0.5 percent of all felony convictions are in error (Huff, Rattner, & Sagarin, 1986). Given the annual number of felony convictions, that means there are probably thousands of people wrongfully convicted of felonies each year.[4] The researchers believe that the frequency of error is probably higher in less serious felony and misdemeanor cases. Since 1973 (as of March 28, 2005), 119 people in 25 states had been released from death row because of evidence of their innocence (Death Penalty Information Center, 2005).

Many mistakes and miscarriages of justice are a result of inadequate investigation by law enforcement officials, who sometimes identify the wrong person as the criminal. When law enforcement officials are unable to solve a crime within a reasonable amount of time, they sometimes cut corners and jump to conclusions (Gross, 1998, p. 133). They (or others who aid them such as medical examiners and crime lab technicians) may even go so far as to lose, destroy, or manufacture evidence against a suspect (Forst, 2004, pp. 90–92; Gross, 1998, p.133). They may also ignore or conceal evidence that does not support their suspect's guilt or withhold exculpatory evidence from prosecutors (Westervelt & Humphrey, 2002, p. 5). By using illegal coercive and manipulative methods, law enforcement officials can get innocent suspects to confess to crimes they did not commit (Forst, 2004, p. 90; Gross, 1996, p. 485; Scheck et al., 2001, p. 116; Westervelt & Humphrey, 2002, p. 5). The wrong person is sometimes identified as the culprit because of poorly administered and biased lineups (Forst, 2004, pp. 88–89; Westervelt & Humphrey, 2002, p. 5). At trial, law enforcement officers (and others such as medical examiners and crime lab technicians) sometimes commit perjury (Harmon, 2001; Radelet, Bedau, & Putnam, 1992; Scheck et al., 2001, pp. 138–162, 222–236). Prosecutors ignore evidence counter to their case, withhold exculpatory evidence from the defense, suborn perjury, misuse informants, and use improper evidence (Liebman, Fagan, & West, 2000; Miller-Potter, 2002; Scheck et al., 2001; Westervelt & Humphrey, 2002, p. 5). Defense attorneys fail to communicate with their clients or communicate in a dismissive, callous or hurried manner; their efforts at discovery are sometimes perfunctory or, in some cases, they make no attempt at all; they fail to investigate allegations or investigate them poorly; they fail to retain needed experts and/or test physical evidence; at times their preparation is minimal, their trial advocacy is weak, and their cross-examination is superficial or tentative (Berry, 2003, p. 489). Defense attorneys have been known to sleep through long portions of a trial and not be declared ineffective (Bright, 2003, pp. 136–137; Mello & Perkins, 2003, pp. 371–372; Scheck et al., 2001, pp. 237–249). In capital and other felony trials, judges make many mistakes, including:

> not permitting the defense to present evidence of an alternative theory of the case; not permitting the defense to present certain mitigating evidence; denying the right of defense experts to offer evidence; failing to order a psychiatric examination prior to trial; prejudging the case; incorrectly finding fact; refusing to give certain jury instructions; failing to admonish the prosecutor for an improper closing argument; allowing a highly prejudicial photograph during the penalty phase; failing to permit withdrawal of a guilty plea; and not having jurisdiction. (Burnett, 2002, p. 103)

The gravest miscarriage of justice is undoubtedly the killing of an innocent person by law enforcement officials (see Forst, 2004, pp. 67–68) or by the state in the case of capital punishment (see Bohm, 2003, chap. 7).

As for Compstat, although proponents claim that it decentralizes decision making, in practice it reinforces the traditional control elements of the military model of policing (Willis et al., 2004, pp. 480, 466–467). A problem or irrationality with Compstat is that by reinforcing the hierarchical military model of policing and its emphasis on accountability and predictability, it tends to impede a police department's ability to achieve other organizational objectives (Weisburd et al., 2003, p. 448; Willis et al., 2004, p. 468). For example, problem-oriented and community policing rely on line officers using their discretion to solve community problems (at least in theory). However, because Compstat is based on the bureaucratic military model of policing with its centralized command and control, line officers frequently lack the flexibility to use their discretion to respond to unanticipated community problems or refuse to address unanticipated problems because they fear being disciplined for mistakes. A consequence is that officers appear (and sometimes are) unresponsive to the people they serve (Willis et al., 2004, p. 470; but see Firman, 2003, for a different view). In sum, the ostensible purpose of Compstat is to improve policing by overcoming traditional bureaucratic irrationalities, but bureaucracies are difficult to change. In practice it appears that Compstat, at least so far, is just another way—albeit one that employs advanced technology and different management principles—for police leadership to control mid-level managers (precinct commanders) and street-level police officers (Moore, 2003, pp. 477–478; Weisburd et al., 2003, pp. 424, 448–449).

Conclusion: What to Do?

Ritzer (2004, pp. 213–215) suggests three possible responses to McDonaldization that could be applied to McJustice. The first is to do nothing. Some people like living in a McDonaldized world or, as Ritzer (2004, p. 213) calls it: a "velvet cage." This is a position most likely held by people who have known no other type of world (Ritzer, 2004, p. 213). Such people crave the efficiency, calculability, predictability, and control of a McDonaldized society. A second possible response to McDonaldization applies to people who live in what Ritzer (2004, p.213) calls a "rubber cage." These people like some aspects of McDonaldization but dislike or deplore other aspects. They realize the costs of McDonaldization and attempt to escape it when they can (Ritzer, 2004, p. 214). A third possible response characterizes people who view McDonaldized society as an "iron cage" (Ritzer, 2004, p. 214). These people dislike, even deplore, McDonaldization but do not believe they can do much, if anything, about it. Some of these people may attempt to escape from its influence from time to time but generally they simply resign themselves to it.

Ritzer is fatalistic about the inexorable spread and domination of McDonaldization and its irrationalities (Parker, 1998, pp. 13–14; Ritzer, 2004, p. 243–244; Taylor, Smith, & Lyon, 1998, p. 106). Ritzer does not believe there are any significant collective alternatives (Jeannot, 1998, p. 141, note 3; Rinehart, 1998, pp. 19–23; Taylor et al., 1998, p. 106). He focuses instead on more modest individualistic alternatives or ameliorations. However, a problem with individualistic alternatives, according to at least one critic, is that McDonaldization and its irrationalities are systemic. To transcend McDonaldization a systemic alternative is required (Jeannot, 1998, p. 132). But a systemic alternative is not an option for Ritzer because, as other critics claim, "Ritzer's version of McDonaldized America is apolitical; there is no contest of viewpoints, no mobilization on behalf of shared interests, no imagination of a future much different than the present and worth working for" (Rinehart, 1998, p. 30; also see Taylor et al., 1998; Wood, 1998). Thus, as yet another critic observes, "people, in using McDonaldized systems, are not merely doing things but they are in practice *affirming* a particular way of doing things and, simultaneously, *negating* alternative ways of doing things" (wa Mwachofi, 1998, p. 151;

emphasis in original). In applying these criticisms to McJustice, accepting McJustice is not only supporting the status quo with all of its irrationalities, it is also rejecting viable, especially systemic, alternatives.

Critics fault Ritzer for failing to acknowledge the partisan and ideological nature of rationality and irrationality (wa Mwachofi, 1998). What is rational or beneficial for one person or group may be irrational or harmful for another person or group, or vice versa. What is considered rational or irrational might also take different forms depending on place, time, and culture (Wynyard, 1998, p. 163). Thus, McJustice, like McDonaldization generally, is a political enterprise in which definitions of rationality and irrationality are contested.

Critics also contend that Ritzer is too negative in his characterization of McDonaldized institutions; that he fails to fully appreciate the positive aspects and potential of bureaucracies and bureaucratic rationality (see, for example, Jeannot, 1998; Miles, 1998; Parker, 1998; Taylor et al., 1998; Wood, 1998). Thus, while it is true that McJustice manifests many irrationalities, it can also be enabling, helping people achieve things they otherwise could not accomplish. For example, it sometimes empowers individuals to protect themselves by way of laws and regulations from people and institutions that would otherwise infringe their rights (see Kellner, 1998, p. x). It also protects people from criminal behavior (when it is operating effectively) in cases where people cannot protect themselves. At the least, it can provide people with a sense of stability in a risky and, contrary to Ritzer's contention, oftentimes unpredictable world (Miles, 1998, p. 53).

The concept of McDonaldization or McJustice to describe criminal justice is imperfect, as is any metaphor. Metaphors can be useful in promoting understanding, but they can also limit "the ways in which we think about a problem" (MacCormac, cited in wa Mwachofi, 1998, p. 152). Although fast food restaurants are ubiquitous, no one is forced to eat at them. Some people eschew fast food; other people eat it infrequently. Many people enjoy fast food on occasion, but most people prefer a home-cooked meal or a finer dining establishment. Criminal justice is ubiquitous, too, but most people are not directly affected by it and have no desire to be involved with it. Still, most US citizens pay taxes to support it and others, for whatever reasons, cannot escape it or have a vested interest in it. Many people would prefer an improved criminal justice process or a viable alternative to McJustice that eliminated or at least significantly reduced its many irrationalities. Most people aspire to something better than McJustice. There is no shortage of alternatives, ranging from liberal reforms to more radical transformations (see, for example, Braithwaite, 1989; Currie, 1985; Governor's Commission on Capital Punishment, 2002; Henry & Milovanovic, 1996; Palmer, 1994; Pepinsky & Quinney, 1991; Scheck et al., 2001; Sherman et al., 1997; Stephens, 1987). Hopefully, conceptualizing criminal justice as McJustice will motivate people to explore, debate, and implement alternatives that will improve justice and the quality of life.

Notes

1. A popular way of understanding criminal justice in the United States is by employing metaphors. The most frequently used metaphor depicts the criminal justice process as a "system"—a "criminal justice system." For additional metaphors of criminal justice see Kraska (2004).

2. People control human technologies (e.g., a screwdriver), while nonhuman technologies (e.g., an order window at a drive-through) control people (Ritzer, 2004, p. 106). Machines and nonhuman technologies are employed in McDonaldized institutions for other reasons besides control, such as increasing productivity, greater quality control, and lowering costs (Ritzer, 2004, p. 107).

3. The costs of "all correctional functions" between 1977 and 2001 increased 1,100 percent (Bauer & Owens, 2004, p. 4). "All correctional functions" include the costs of operation and employment for jails, prisons, probation, parole, pardon, and correctional administration for both adults and juveniles (Bauer & Owens, 2004, p. 4). Because approximately 80 percent of all funds allocated to corrections in the United States are spent to build and run institutions, and only about 20 percent are spent on community corrections (Bonczar & Glaze, 1999, p. 2), the increase in costs of prisons and jails during the period is estimated to be about 900 percent.

4. Although an error rate of 0.5 percent may not seem high, consider that in 2001, a typical year, approximately 14 million people were arrested in the United States (US Department of Justice, 2002, p. 232). Assuming conservatively that 50 percent of

all people arrested are convicted (Huff et al., 1986, p. 523)—about 7 million convictions in 2001—then approximately 35,000 people were probably wrongfully convicted.

References

Alschuler, A. W. (1979). Plea bargaining and its history. *Law & Society Review, 13,* 211–245.

American Correctional Association. (2004). *American Correctional Association 2004 directory: Adult and juvenile correctional departments, institutions, agencies and probation and parole authorities.* Lanham, MD: Author.

Bauer, L., & Owens, S. D. (2004, May). Justice expenditure and employment in the United States, 2001. *Bureau of Justice Statistics Bulletin.* US Department of Justice. Washington, DC: GPO.

Berry, S. M. (2003). Bad lawyering: How defense attorneys help convict the innocent. *Northern Kentucky University Law Review, 30,* 487–503.

Blomberg, T. G., & Lucken, K. (2000). *American penology: A history of control.* New York: Aldine de Gruyter.

Bohm, R. M. (2003). *Deathquest II: An introduction to the theory and practice of capital punishment in the United States* (2nd ed.). Cincinnati: Anderson.

Bonczar, T. P., & Glaze, L. E. (1999, August). Probation and parole in the United States, 1998. *Bureau of Justice Statistics Bulletin.* US Department of Justice. Washington, DC: GPO.

Bordenkircher v. Hayes, 434 U.S. 357 (1978).

Brady v. United States, 397 U.S. 742 (1970).

Braithwaite, J. (1989). *Crime, shame and reintegration.* Cambridge: Cambridge University Press.

Bright, S. B. (2003). The politics of capital punishment: The sacrifice of fairness for executions. In J. R. Acker, R. M. Bohm, & C. S. Lanier (Eds.), *America's experiment with capital punishment* (2nd ed., pp. 127–146). Durham, NC: Carolina Academic Press.

Burnett, C. (2002). *Justice denied: Clemency appeals in death penalty cases.* Boston: Northeastern University Press.

Camp, C. G., & Camp, G. M. (2002). *The corrections yearbook 2001: Adult systems.* Middletown, CT: Criminal Justice Institute.

Carter, R. (1996). Determinate sentences. In M. D. McShane & F. P. Williams III (Eds.), *Encyclopedia of American prisons* (pp. 147–149). New York: Garland.

Clear, T., Hewitt, J., & Regoli, R. (1978). Discretion and the determinate sentence: Its distribution, control, and effect on time served. *Crime & Delinquency, 24,* 428–445.

Currie, E. (1985). *Confronting crime: An American challenge.* New York: Pantheon.

Death Penalty Information Center. (2005). Retrieved March 28, from www.deathpenaltyinfo.org

Ditton, P. M., & Wilson, D. J. (1999). Truth in sentencing in state prisons. *Bureau of Justice Statistics Special Report.* US Department of Justice. Washington, DC: GPO.

Drane, J. (2001). *The McDonaldization of the church.* London: Darton, Longman & Todd.

Durose, M. R., & Langan, P. A. (2003). Felony sentences in state courts, 2000. *Bureau of Justice Statistics Bulletin.* US Department of Justice. Washington, DC: GPO.

Feeley, M. M., & Simon, J. (1992). The new penology: Notes on the emerging strategy of corrections and its implications. *Criminology, 30,* 449–474.

Feeley, M., & Simon, J. (1994). Actuarial justice: The emerging new criminal law. In D. Nelkin (Ed.), *The future of criminology* (pp. 172–201). Thousand Oaks, CA: Sage.

Firman, J. R. (2003). Deconstructing Compstat to clarify its intent. *Criminology & Public Policy, 2,* 457–460.

Forst, B. (2004). *Errors of justice: Nature, sources and remedies.* Cambridge: Cambridge University Press.

Gagnon v. Scarpelli, 411 U.S. 778 (1973).

Goodstein, L., & Hepburn, J. (1985). *Determinate sentencing and imprisonment.* Cincinnati: Anderson.

Gouldner, A. W. (1976). *The dialectic of ideology and technology: The origins, grammar, and future of ideology.* New York: Seabury Press.

Governor's Commission on Capital Punishment. (2002). State of Illinois. Retrieved from www.idoc.state.il.us/ccp/ccp/reports/commission_reports.html

Griset, P. L. (1991). *Determinate sentencing: The promise and the reality of retributive justice.* Albany, NY: State University of New York Press.

Griset, P. L. (1999). Criminal sentencing in Florida: Determinate sentencing's hollow shell. *Crime & Delinquency, 45,* 316–333.

Gross, S. R. (1996). The risks of death: Why erroneous convictions are common in capital cases. *Buffalo Law Review, 44,* 469–500.

Gross, S. R. (1998). Lost lives: Miscarriages of justice in capital cases. *Law and Contemporary Problems, 61,* 125–152.

Harmon, T. R. (2001). Predictors of miscarriages of justice in capital cases. *Justice Quarterly, 18,* 949–968.

Harrison, P. M., & Beck, A. J. (2003, July). Prisoners in 2002. *Bureau of Justice Statistics Bulletin.* US Department of Justice. Washington, DC: GPO.

Hayes, D., & Wynyard, R. (Eds.). (2002). *The McDonaldization of higher education.* Westport, CT: Bergin & Garvey.

Henry, S., & Milovanovic, D. (1996). *Constitutive criminology: Beyond postmodernism.* London: Sage.

Horkheimer, M. (1996). *Critique of instrumental reason.* New York: Continuum.

Huff, C. R., Rattner, A., & Sagarin, E. (1986). Guilty until proven innocent: Wrongful conviction and public policy. *Crime & Delinquency, 32,* 518–544.

International Centre for Prison Studies. (2003). World prison brief—Highest prison population rates. King's College London. Retrieved from www.kcl.ac.uk/depsta/rel/icps/worldbrief/highest_ratesmanual.html

Jeannot, T. M. (1998). The McCommodification of society: Rationalization and critical theory. In M. Alfino, J. S. Caputo, &

R. Wynyard (Eds.), *McDonaldization revisited: Critical essays on consumer culture* (pp. 121–142). Westport, CT: Praeger.

Kellner, D. (1998). Foreword: McDonaldization and its discontents—Ritzer and his critics. In M. Alfino, J. S. Caputo, & R. Wynyard (Eds.), *McDonaldization revisited: Critical essays on consumer culture* (pp. vii–xiv). Westport, CT: Praeger.

Kemmesies, U. E. (2002). What do hamburgers and drug use have in common: Some unorthodox remarks on the McDonaldization and rationality of drug care. *Journal of Drug Issues, 32,* 689–707.

Kraska, P. B. (2004). *Theorizing criminal justice: Eight essential orientations.* Long Grove, IL: Waveland Press.

LaFree, G. (2002). Too much democracy or too much crime? Lessons from California's three-strike law. *Law & Social Inquiry, 27,* 875–902.

Liebman, J. S., Fagan, J., & West, V. (2000). A broken system: Error rates in capital cases, 1973–1995. Retrieved from www.justice.policy.net/jpreport.html

Mabrey, D. (2002). Crime mapping: Tracking the hotspots. *Crime & Justice International, 18,* 31–32.

Marcuse, H. (1966). *One-dimensional man.* Boston: Beacon Press.

Mello, M., & Perkins, P. J. (2003). Closing the circle: The illusion of lawyers for people litigating for their lives at the fin de siecle. In J. R. Acker, R. M. Bohm, & C. S. Lanier (Eds.), *America's experiment with capital punishment* (2nd ed., pp. 347–384). Durham, NC: Carolina Academic Press.

Miles, S. (1998). McDonaldization and the global sports store: Constructing consumer meanings in a rationalized society. In M. Alfino, J. S. Caputo, & R. Wynyard (Eds.), *McDonaldization revisited: Critical essays on consumer culture* (pp. 53–65). Westport, CT: Praeger.

Miller-Potter, K. S. (2002). Death by innocence: Wrongful convictions in capital cases. *The Advocate: A Journal of Criminal Justice Education and Research, 24,* 21–29.

Moore, M. H. (2003). Sizing up Compstat: An important administrative innovation in policing. *Criminology & Public Policy, 2,* 469–494.

More spent on prisons than universities in 1995. (1997, February 25). *The Orlando Sentinel,* p. A-6.

Morrissey v. Brewer, 408 U.S. 471 (1972).

Packer, H. (1968). *The limits of the criminal sanction.* Stanford, CA: Stanford University Press.

Padgett, J. F. (1990). Plea bargaining and Prohibition in the federal courts, 1908–1934. *Law & Society Review, 24,* 413–450.

Palmer, T. (1994). *A profile of correctional effectiveness and new directions for research.* Albany: State University of New York Press.

Parker, M. (1998). Nostalgia and mass culture: McDonaldization and cultural elitism. In M. Alfino, J. S. Caputo, & R. Wynyard (Eds.), *McDonaldization revisited: Critical essays on consumer culture* (pp. 1–18). Westport, CT: Praeger.

Parker, M., & Jary, D. (1995). The McUniversity: Organization, management and academic subjectivity. *Organization, 2,* 319–337.

Pepinsky, H. E., & Quinney, R. (Eds.). (1991). *Criminology as peacemaking.* Bloomington: Indiana University Press.

Prichard, P. (1987). *The making of McPaper: The inside story of USA TODAY.* Kansas City, MO: Andrews, McMeel & Parker.

Radelet, M. J., Bedau, H. A., & Putnam, C. E. (1992). *In spite of innocence: Erroneous convictions in capital cases.* Boston: Northeastern University Press.

Reaves, B. (2001). Felony defendants in large urban counties, 1998. US Department of Justice. *Bureau of Justice Statistics Bulletin.* Washington, DC: GPO.

Reiser, S. J. (1978). *Medicine and the reign of technology.* Cambridge: Cambridge University Press.

Rinehart, J. A. (1998). It may be a polar night of icy darkness, but feminists are building a fire. In M. Alfino, J. S. Caputo, & R. Wynyard (Eds.), *McDonaldization revisited: Critical essays on consumer culture* (pp. 19–38). Westport, CT: Praeger.

Ritzer, G. (2004). *The McDonaldization of society* (Rev. new century ed.). Thousand Oaks, CA: Pine Forge Press.

Ritzer, G., & Walczak, D. (1987). The changing nature of American medicine. *Journal of American Culture, 9,* 43–51.

Robinson, M. B. (2002). McDonaldization of America's police, courts, and corrections. In G. Ritzer (Ed.), *McDonaldization: The reader* (pp. 77–90). Thousand Oaks, CA: Pine Forge Press.

Rojek, C. (1993). *Ways of escape: Modern transformations in leisure and travel.* London: Routledge.

Scheck, B., Neufeld, P., & Dwyer, J. (2001). *Actual innocence: When justice goes wrong and how to make it right.* New York: Signet.

Schroyer, T. (1975). *The critique of domination: The origins and development of critical theory.* Boston: Beacon Press.

Sherman, L. W., Gottfredson, D., MacKenzie, D., Eck, J., Reuter, P., & Bushway, S. (1997). *Preventing crime: What works, what doesn't, what's promising.* Washington, DC: US Department of Justice, Office of Justice Programs.

Shichor, D. (1997). Three strikes as public policy: The convergence of the new penology and the McDonaldization of punishment. *Crime & Delinquency, 43,* 470–492.

Sourcebook of Criminal Justice Statistics. (2002a). *Justice system direct and intergovernmental expenditures.* Retrieved August 9, 2005, from http://www.albany.edu/sourcebook/tost_1.html#1_a.

Sourcebook of Criminal Justice Statistics. (2002b). *Respondents indicating too little is spent on selected problems in this country (halting the rising crime rate).* Retrieved August 9, 2005, from http://www.albany.edu/sourcebook/tost_2.html#2_u.

Spohn, C., & Holleran, D. (2000). The imprisonment penalty paid by young, unemployed black and Hispanic male offenders. *Criminology, 38,* 281–306.

Stephens, G. (1987, January–February). Crime and punishment: Forces shaping the future. *The Futurist,* pp. 18–26.

Taylor, S., Smith, S., & Lyon, P. (1998). McDonaldization and consumer choice in the future: An illusion or the next marketing revolution? In M. Alfino, J. S. Caputo, & R. Wynyard (Eds.), *McDonaldization revisited: Critical essays on consumer culture* (pp.105–119). Westport, CT: Praeger.

Tennessee v. Garner, 471 U.S. 1 (1985).

Tonry, M. (1993). Sentencing commissions and their guidelines. *Crime and Justice, 17,* 137–195.

Tonry, M. (1996). *Sentencing matters.* New York: Oxford University Press.

Tonry, M., & Frase, R. S. (Eds.). (2001). *Sentencing & sanctions in western countries.* New York: Oxford University Press.

US Department of Justice, Federal Bureau of Investigation. (2002). *Crime in the United States, 2001.* Washington, DC: GPO.

Umbreit, M. S. (1999). Avoiding the marginalization and "McDonaldization" of victim–offender mediation: A case study in moving toward the mainstream. In G. Bazemore & L. Walgrave (Eds.), *Restorative juvenile justice: Repairing the harm of youth crime* (pp. 213–234). Monsey, NY: Criminal Justice Press.

wa Mwachofi, N. (1998). Missing the cultural basis of irrationality in the McDonaldization of society. In M. Alfino, J. S. Caputo, & R. Wynyard (Eds.), *McDonaldization revisited: Critical essays on consumer culture* (pp. 143–158). Westport, CT: Praeger.

Weisburd, D., Mastrofski, S. D., McNally, A. M., Greenspan, R., & Willis, J. J. (2003). Reforming to preserve: Compstat and strategic problem solving in American policing. *Criminology & Public Policy, 2,* 421–456.

Westervelt, S. D., & Humphrey, J. A. (Eds.). (2002). *Wrongly convicted: Perspectives on failed justice.* New Brunswick, NJ: Rutgers University Press.

Willis, J. J., Mastrofski, S. D., & Weisburd, D. (2004). Compstat and bureaucracy: A case study of challenges and opportunities for change. *Justice Quarterly, 21,* 463–496.

Wood, R. C. (1998). Old wine in new bottles: Critical limitations of the McDonaldization thesis—the case of hospitality services. In M. Alfino, J. S. Caputo, & R. Wynyard (Eds.), *McDonaldization revisited: Critical essays on consumer culture* (pp. 85–103). Westport, CT: Praeger.

Wynyard, R. (1998). The bunless burger. In M. Alfino, J. S. Caputo, & R. Wynyard (Eds.), *McDonaldization revisited: Critical essays on consumer culture* (pp. 159–174). Westport, CT: Praeger.

DISCUSSION QUESTIONS

1. The idea of McDonaldization emphasizes calculability, the quantifiable aspects of organizations/society, and, specifically, the notion that more is better (e.g., billions and billions served, double quarter pounders, super-sized meals). Does plea bargaining and the desire for expeditious handling of caseloads come at the expense of calculability? Explain.

2. Drug courts do not seem to fit the description of McJustice. Drug offender cases are handled intensively and addressed uniquely, challenging both efficiency and predictability. Are there other recent (in the past two decades) strategies in policing, courts, or corrections that contrast with one or more elements of a McDonaldized society?

3. If rationality is irrational, should strategies such as plea bargaining, determinate sentencing, and Compstat be abandoned to prevent the negative consequences? If not, what can be done to mitigate any harm?

READING

Reading 5

John Rosecrance's research addresses a largely neglected topic—the production of probation presentence reports. Although not written from an institutional theory perspective, his article highlights key themes related to the theory, including myths and legitimacy. Drawing from interviews with 37 presentence investigators in two California counties in the mid-1980s, Rosecrance concluded that presentence reports are produced to satisfy the demands of judges and prosecutors; that is, the recommendations offered in the reports are generally derived from considerations of offense seriousness and prior record, while extralegal variables such as social history are relevant only in exceptional cases. Investigators still gather social history information about offenders, but this information is typically employed to support an already generated recommendation based on legal considerations. Why expend energy collecting information that will not likely be considered? Rosecrance argues that there is a strong belief in individualized justice, especially among offenders, where each case receives due consideration by the courts rather than simply being processed in an assembly-line fashion. In institutional theory terms, this is an institutional myth that the system must comply with or else face challenges. The system can satisfy the demands for individualized justice, however symbolically, by conducting presentence reports, although this only perpetuates the myth. Moreover, presentence reports legitimize probation departments, whose very existence is based on individual treatment.

Maintaining the Myth of Individualized Justice

Probation Presentence Reports

John Rosecrance

The Justice Department estimates that over one million probation presentence reports are submitted annually to criminal courts in the United States (Allen and Simonsen 1986:111). The role of probation officers in the presentence process traditionally has been considered important. After examining criminal courts in the United States, a panel of investigators concluded: "Probation officers are attached to most modern felony courts; presentence reports containing their recommendations are commonly provided and these recommendations are usually followed" (Blumstein, Martin, and Holt 1983). Judges view presentence reports as an integral part of sentencing, calling them "the best guide to intelligent sentencing" (Murrah 1963:67) and "one of the most important developments in criminal law during the 20th century" (Hogarth 1971:246).

Researchers agree that a strong correlation exists between probation recommendations (contained in presentence reports) and judicial sentencing. In a seminal study of judicial decision making, Carter and Wilkins (1967) found 95 percent agreement between probation recommendation and sentence disposition when the officer recommended probation and 88 percent agreement when the officer opposed probation. Hagan (1975), after controlling for related variables, reported a direct correlation of .72 between probation recommendation and sentencing. Walsh (1985) found a similar correlation of .807.

Although there is no controversy about the correlation between probation recommendation and judicial outcome, scholars disagree as to the actual influence of probation officers in the sentencing process. That is, there is no consensus regarding the importance of the presentence investigator in influencing sentencing outcomes. On the one hand, Myers (1979:538) contends that the "important role played by probation officer recommendation argues for greater theoretical and empirical attention to these officers." Walsh (1985:363) concludes that "judges lean heavily on the professional advice of probation." On the other hand, Kingsnorth and Rizzo (1979)

Source: Rosecrance, J. (1988). Maintaining the myth of individualized justice: Probation presentence reports. *Justice Quarterly,* 5(2), 235–256.

report that probation recommendations have been supplanted by plea bargaining and that the probation officer is "largely superfluous." Hagan, Hewitt, and Alwin (1979), after reporting a direct correlation between recommendation and sentence, contend that the "influence of the probation officer in the presentence process is subordinate to that of the prosecutor" and that probation involvement is "often ceremonial."

My research builds on the latter perspective, and suggests that probation presentence reports do not influence judicial sentencing significantly but serve to maintain the myth that criminal courts dispense individualized justice. On the basis of an analysis of probation practices in California, I will demonstrate that the presentence report, long considered an instrument for the promotion of individualized sentencing by the court, actually de-emphasizes individual characteristics and affirms the primacy of instant offense and prior criminal record as sentencing determinants. The present study was concerned with probation in California; whether its findings can be applied to other jurisdictions is not known. California's probation system is the nation's largest, however (Petersilia, Turner, Kahan, and Peterson 1985), and the experiences of that system could prove instructive to other jurisdictions.

In many California counties (as in other jurisdictions throughout the United States) crowded court calendars, determinate sentencing guidelines, and increasingly conservative philosophies have made it difficult for judges to consider individual offenders' characteristics thoroughly. Thus judges, working in tandem with district attorneys, emphasize the legal variables of offense and criminal record at sentencing (see, for example, Forer 1980; Lotz and Hewitt 1977; Tinker, Quiring, and Pimentel 1985). Probation officers function as employees of the court; generally they respond to judicial cues and emphasize similar variables in their presentence investigations. The probation officers' relationship to the court is ancillary; their status in relation to judges and other attorneys is subordinate. This does not mean that probation officers are completely passive; individual styles and personal philosophies influence their reports. Idiosyncratic approaches, however, usually are reserved for a few special cases. The vast majority of "normal" (Sudnow 1965) cases are handled in a manner that follows relatively uniform patterns.

Hughes's (1958) work provides a useful perspective for understanding the relationship between probation officers' status and their presentence duties. According to Hughes, occupational duties within institutions often serve to maintain symbiotic status relationships as those in higher-status positions pass on lesser duties to subordinates. Other researchers (Blumberg 1967; Neubauer 1974; Rosecrance 1985) have demonstrated that although judges may give lip service to the significance of presentence investigations, they remain suspicious of the probation officers' lack of legal training and the hearsay nature of the reports. Walker (1985) maintains that in highly visible cases judges tend to disregard the probation reports entirely. Thus the judiciary, by delegating the collection of routine information to probation officers, reaffirms its authority and legitimacy. In this context, the responsibility for compiling presentence reports can be considered a "dirty work" assignment (Hagan 1975) that is devalued by the judiciary. Judges expect probation officers to submit noncontroversial reports that provide a facade of information, accompanied by bottom-line recommendations that do not deviate significantly from a consideration of offense and prior record. The research findings in this paper will show how probation officers work to achieve this goal.

In view of the large number of presentence reports submitted, it is surprising that so little information about the presentence investigation process is available. The factors used in arriving at a sentencing recommendation, the decision to include certain information, and the methods used in collecting data have not been described. The world of presentence investigators has not been explored by social science researchers. We lack research about the officers who prepare presentence reports, and hardly understand how they think and feel about those reports. The organizational dynamics and the status positions that influence presentence investigators have not been identified prominently (see, for example, Shover 1979). In this article I intend to place probation officers' actions within a framework that will increase the existing knowledge of the presentence process. My research is informed by 15 years of experience as a probation officer, during which time I submitted hundreds of presentence reports.

Although numerous studies of probation practices have been conducted, an ethnographic perspective rarely has been included in this body of research, particularly in regard to research dealing with presentence investigations. Although questionnaire techniques (Katz 1982), survey data (Hagan et al. 1979), and decisionmaking experiments (Carter 1967) have provided some information about presentence reports, qualitative data, which often are available only through an insider's perspective,[1] are notably lacking. The subtle strategies and informal practices used routinely in preparing presentence reports often are hidden from outside researchers.

The research findings emphasize the importance of typing in the compilation of public documents (presentence reports). In this paper "typing" refers to "the process by which one person (the agent) arrives at a private definition of another (the target)" (Prus 1975:81). A related activity, *designating*, occurs when "the typing agent reveals his attributions of the target to others" (Prus and Stratten 1976:48). In the case of presentence investigations, private typings become designations when they are made part of an official court report. I will show that presentence recommendations are developed through a typing process in which individual offenders are subsumed into general dispositional categories. This process is influenced largely by probation officers' perceptions of factors that judicial figures consider appropriate; probation officers are aware that the ultimate purpose of their reports is to please the court. These perceptions are based on prior experience and are reinforced through judicial feedback.

Methods

The major sources of data used in this study were drawn from interviews with probation officers. Prior experience facilitated my ability to interpret the data. Interviews were conducted in two three-week periods during 1984 and 1985 in two medium-sized California counties. Both jurisdictions were governed by state determinate sentencing policies; in each, the district attorney's office remained active during sentencing and generally offered specific recommendations. I did not conduct a random sample but tried instead to interview all those who compiled adult presentence reports. In the two counties in question, officers who compiled presentence reports did not supervise defendants.[2]

Not all presentence writers agreed to talk with me; they cited busy schedules, lack of interest, or fear that I was a spy for the administration. Even so, I was able to interview 37 presentence investigators, approximately 75 percent of the total number of such employees in the two counties.[3]

The respondents generally were supportive of my research, and frequently commented that probation work had never been described adequately. My status as a former probation officer enhanced the interview process greatly. Because I could identify with their experiences, officers were candid, and I was able to collect qualitative data that reflected accurately the participants' perspectives. During the interviews I attempted to discover how probation officers conducted their presentence investigations. I wanted to know when a sentencing recommendation was decided, to ascertain which variables influenced a sentencing recommendation decision, and to learn how probation officers defined their role in the sentencing process.

Although the interviews were informal, I asked each of the probation officers the following questions:

1. What steps do you take in compiling a presentence report?
2. What is the first thing you do upon receiving a referral?
3. What do you learn from interviews with the defendant?
4. Which part of the process (in your opinion) is the most important?
5. Who reads your reports?

6. Which part of the report do the judges feel is most important?
7. How do your reports influence the judge?
8. What feedback do you get from the judge, the district attorney, the defense attorney, the defendant, your supervisor?

In addition to interviewing probation officers, I questioned six probation supervisors and seven judges on their views about how presentence reports were conducted.

Findings

In the great majority of presentence investigations, the variables of present offense and prior criminal record determine the probation officer's final sentencing recommendation. The influence of these variables is so dominant that other considerations have minimal influence on probation recommendations. The chief rationale for this approach is "That's the way the judges want it." There are other styles of investigation; some officers attempt to consider factors in the defendant's social history, to reserve sentencing judgment until their investigation is complete, or to interject personal opinions. Elsewhere (Rosecrance 1987), I have developed a typology of presentence investigators which describes individual styles; these types include self-explanatory categories such as hard-liners, bleeding-heart liberals, and team players as well as mossbacks (those who are merely putting in their time) and mavericks (those who strive continually for independence).

All types of probation officers, however, seek to develop credibility with the court. Such reputation building is similar to that reported by McCleary (1978) in his study of parole officers. In order to develop rapport with the court, probation officers must submit reports that facilitate a smooth work flow. Probation officers assume that in the great majority of cases they can accomplish this goal by emphasizing offense and criminal record. Once the officers have established reputations as "producers," they have "earned" the right to some degree of discretion in their reporting. One investigation officer described this process succinctly: "When you've paid your dues, you're allowed some slack." Such discretion, however, is limited to a minority of cases, and in these "deviant" cases probation officers frequently allow social variables to influence their recommendation. In one report an experienced officer recommended probation for a convicted felon with a long prior record because the defendant's father agreed to pay for an intensive drug treatment program. In another case a probation officer decided that a first-time shoplifter had a "very bad attitude" and therefore recommended a stiff jail sentence rather than probation. Although these variations from normal procedure are interesting and important, they should not detract from our examination of an investigation process that is used in most cases.

On the basis of the research data, I found that the following patterns occur with sufficient regularity to be considered "typical." After considering offense and criminal record, probation officers place defendants into categories that represent the eventual court recommendation. This typing process occurs early in the course of presentence inquiry; the balance of the investigation is used to reaffirm the private typings that later will become official designations. In order to clarify the decision-making processes used by probation officers I will delineate the three stages in a presentence investigation: 1) typing the defendant, 2) gathering further information, and 3) filing the report.

Typing the Defendant

A presentence investigation is initiated when the court orders the probation department to prepare a report on a criminal defendant. Usually the initial court referral contains such information as police reports, charges against the defendant, court proceedings, plea-bargaining agreements (if any), offenses in which the defendant has pleaded or has been found guilty, and the defendant's prior criminal record. Probation officers regard such information as relatively unambiguous[4] and as part of the "official" record. The comment of a presentence investigator reflects the probation officer's perspective on the court referral:

> I consider the information in the court referral hard data. It tells me what I need to know about a case, without a lot of bullshit. I mean the guy has pled guilty to a certain offense—he can't get out of that. He has such and such a prior record—there's no changing that. So much of the stuff we put in these reports is subjective and open to interpretation. It's good to have some solid information.

Armed with information in the court referral, probation officers begin to type the defendants assigned for presentence investigation. Defendants are classified into general types based on possible sentence recommendations; a probation officer's statement indicates that this process begins early in a presentence investigation.

> Bottom line; it's the sentence recommendation that's important. That's what the judges and everybody wants to see. I start thinking about the recommendation as soon as I pick up the court referral. Why wait? The basic facts aren't going to change. Oh, I know some POs will tell you they weigh all the facts before coming up with a recommendation. But that's propaganda—we all start thinking recommendation right from the get-go.

At this stage in the investigation the factors known to probation officers are mainly legally relevant variables. The defendant's unique characteristics and special circumstances generally are unknown at this time. Although probation officers may know the offender's age, sex, and race, the relationship of these variables to the case is not yet apparent.

These initial typings are private definitions (Prus 1975) based on the officer's experience and knowledge of the court system. On occasion, officers discuss the case informally with their colleagues or supervisors when they are not sure of a particular typing. Until the report is complete, their typing remains a private designation. In most cases the probation officers type defendants by considering the known and relatively irrefutable variables of offense and prior record. Probation officers are convinced that judges and district attorneys are most concerned with that part of their reports. I heard the following comment (or versions thereof) on many occasions: "Judges read the offense section, glance at the prior record, and then flip to the back and see what we recommend." Officers indicated that during informal discussions with judges it was made clear that offense and prior record are the determinants of sentencing in most cases. In some instances judges consider extralegal variables, but the officers indicated that this occurs only in "unusual" cases with "special" circumstances. One such case involved a probation grant for a woman who killed her husband after she had been a victim of spouse battering.

Probation investigators are in regular contact with district attorneys, and frequently discuss their investigations with them. In addition, district attorneys seem to have no compunction about calling the probation administration to complain about what they consider an inappropriate recommendation. Investigators agreed unanimously that district attorneys typically dismiss a defendant's social history as "immaterial" and want probation officers to stick to the legal facts.

Using offense and prior record as criteria, probation officers place defendants into dispositional (based on recommendation) types. In describing these types[5] I have retained the terms used by probation officers themselves in the typing process. The following typology is community (rather than researcher) designated (Emerson 1981; Spradley 1970): (1) deal case, (2) diversion case, (3) joint case, (4) probation case with some jail time, (5) straight probation case. Within each of these dispositional types, probation officers designate the severity of punishment by labeling the case either lightweight or heavy-duty.

A designation of "lightweight" means that the defendant will be accorded some measure of leniency because the offense was minor, because the offender had no prior criminal record, or because the criminal activity (regardless of the penal code violation) was relatively innocuous. Heavy-duty cases receive more severe penalties because the offense, the offender, or the circumstances of the offense are deemed particularly serious. Diversion and straight probation types generally are considered lightweight, while the majority of joint cases are considered heavy-duty. Cases involving personal violence invariably are designated as heavy-duty. Most misdemeanor cases in which the defendant has no prior criminal record or a relatively minor record are termed lightweight. If the defendant has an extensive criminal record, however, even misdemeanor cases can call for stiff penalties; therefore such cases are considered heavy-duty. Certain felony cases can be regarded as lightweight if there was no violence, if the victim's loss was minimal, or if the defendant had no prior convictions. On occasion, even an offense like armed robbery can be considered lightweight. The following example (taken from an actual report) is one such instance: a first-time offender with a simulated gun held up a Seven-Eleven store and then returned to the scene, gave back the money, and asked the store employees to call the police.

The typings are general recommendations; specifics such as terms and conditions of probation or diversion and length of incarceration are worked out later in the investigation. The following discussion will clarify some of the criteria for arriving at a typing.

Deal cases involve situations in which a plea bargain exists. In California, many plea bargains specify specific sentencing stipulations; probation officers rarely recommend dispositions contrary to those stipulated in plea-bargaining agreements. Although probation officers allegedly are free to recommend a sentence different from that contained in the plea bargain, they have learned that such an action is unrealistic (and often counter-productive to their own interests) because judges inevitably uphold the primacy of sentence agreements. The following observation represents the probation officers' view of plea-bargaining deals:

It's stupid to try and bust a deal. What's the percentage? Who needs the hassle? The judge always honors the deal—after all, he was part of it. Everyone, including the defendant, has already agreed. It's all nice and neat, all wrapped up. We are supposed to rubber-stamp the package—and we do. Everyone is better off that way.

Diversion cases typically involve relatively minor offenses committed by those with no prior record, and are considered "a snap" by probation officers. In most cases, those referred for diversion have been screened already by the district attorney's office; the probation investigator merely agrees that they are eligible and therefore should be granted diversionary relief (and eventual dismissal of charges). In rare instances when there has been an oversight and the defendant is ineligible (because of prior criminal convictions), the probation officer informs the court, and criminal proceedings are resumed. Either situation involves minimal decision making by probation officers about what disposition to recommend. Presentence investigators approach diversion cases in a perfunctory, almost mechanical manner.

The last three typings generally refer to cases in which the sentencing recommendations are ambiguous and some decision making is required of probation officers. These types represent the major consequences of criminal sentencing: incarceration and/or probation. Those categorized as joint (prison) cases are denied probation; instead the investigator recommends an appropriate prison sentence. In certain instances the nature of the offense (e.g., rape, murder, or arson) renders defendants legally ineligible for probation. In other situations, the defendants' prior record (especially felony convictions) makes it impossible to grant probation (see, e.g., Neubauer 1974:240). In many cases the length of prison sentences has been set by legal statute and can be increased or decreased only marginally (depending on the aggravating or mitigating circumstances of the case).

In California, the majority of defendants sentenced to prison receive a middle term (between minimum and maximum); the length of time varies with the offense. Those cases that fall outside the middle term usually do so for reasons related to the offense (e.g., using a weapon) or to the criminal record (prior felony convictions or, conversely, no prior criminal record). Those typed originally as joint cases are treated differently from other probation applicants: concerns with rehabilitation or with the defendant's life situation are no longer relevant, and proper punishment becomes the focal point of inquiry. This perspective was described as follows by a probation officer respondent: "Once I know so-and-so is a heavy-duty joint case I don't think in terms of rehabilitation or social planning. It becomes a matter of how long to salt the sucker away, and that's covered by the code."

For those who are typed as probation cases, the issue for the investigator becomes whether to recommend some time in jail as a condition of probation. This decision is made with reference to whether the case is lightweight or heavy-duty. Straight probation usually is reserved for those convicted of relatively innocuous offenses or for those without a prior criminal record (first-timers). Some probation officers admitted candidly that all things being equal, middle-class defendants are more likely than other social classes to receive straight probation. The split sentence (probation and jail time) has become popular and is a consideration in most misdemeanor and felony cases, especially when the defendant has a prior criminal record. In addition, there is a feeling that drug offenders should receive a jail sentence as part of probation to deter them from future drug use.

Once a probation officer has decided that "some jail time is in order," the ultimate recommendation includes that condition. Although the actual amount of time frequently is determined late in the case, the probation officer's opinion that a jail sentence should be imposed remains constant. The following comment typifies the sentiments of probation officers whom I have observed and also illustrates the imprecision of recommending a period of time in custody:

It's not hard to figure out who needs some jail. The referral sheet can tell you that. What's hard to know is exactly how much time. Ninety days or six months—who knows what's fair? We put down some number but it is usually an arbitrary figure. No one has come up with a chart that correlates rehabilitation with jail time.

Compiling Further Information

Once an initial typing has been completed, the next investigative stage involves collecting further information about the defendant. During this stage most of the data to be collected consists of extralegal considerations. The defendant is interviewed and his or her social history is delineated. Probation officers frequently contact collateral sources such as school officials, victims, doctors, counselors, and relatives to learn more about the defendant's individual circumstances. This aspect of the presentence investigation involves considerable time and effort on the part of probation officers. Such information is gathered primarily to legitimate earlier probation officer typings or to satisfy judicial requirements; recommendations seldom are changed during this stage. A similar pattern was described by a presentence investigator:

Interviewing these defendants and working up a social history takes time. In most cases it's really unnecessary since I've already decided what I am going to do. We all know that a recommendation is governed by the offense and prior record. All the rest is just stuffing to fill out the court report, to make the judge look like he's got all the facts.

Presentence interviews with defendants (a required part of the investigation) frequently are routine interactions that were described by a probation officer as "anticlimactic." These interviews invariably are conducted in settings familiar to probation officers, such as jail interviewing rooms or probation department offices. Because the participants lack trust in each other, discussions rarely are candid and open. Probation officers are afraid of being conned or manipulated because they assume that defendants "will say anything to save themselves." Defendants are trying to present themselves in a favorable light and are wary of divulging any information that might be used against them.

It is assumed implicitly in the interview process that probation officers act as interrogators and defendants as respondents. Because presentence investigators select the questions, they control the course of the interview and elicit the kind of responses that serve to substantiate their original defendant typings. A probationer described his presentence interview to me as follows:

> I knew that the P.O. wanted me to say. She had me pegged as a nice middle-class kid who had fallen in with a bad crowd. So that's how I came off. I was contrite, a real boy scout who had learned his lesson. What an acting job! I figured if I didn't act up I'd get probation.

A probation officer related how she conducted presentence interviews:

> I'm always in charge during the interviews. I know what questions to ask in order to fill out my report. The defendants respond just about the way I expect them to. They hardly ever surprise me.

On occasion, prospective probationers refuse to go along with structured presentence interviews. Some offenders either attempt to control the interview or are openly hostile to probation officers. Defendants who try to dominate interviews often can be dissuaded by reminders such as "I don't think you really appreciate the seriousness of your situation" or "I'm the one who asks the questions here." Some defendants, however, show blatant disrespect for the court process by flaunting a disregard for possible sanctions.

Most probation officers have interviewed some defendants who simply don't seem to care what happens to them. A defendant once informed an investigation officer: "I don't give a fuck what you motherfuckers try and do to me. I'm going to do what I fuckin' well please. Take your probation and stick it." Another defendant told her probation officer: "I'm going to shoot up every chance I get. I need my fix more than I need probation." Probation officers categorize belligerent defendants and those unwilling to "play the probation game" as dangerous or irrational (see, e.g., McCleary 1978). Frequently in these situations the investigator's initial typing is no longer valid, and probation either will be denied or will be structured stringently. Most interviews, however, proceed in a predictable manner as probation officers collect information that will be included in the section of the report termed "defendant's statement."

Although some defendants submit written comments, most of their statements actually are formulated by the probation officer. In a sociological sense, the defendant's statement can be considered an "account" (Scott and Lyman 1968). While conducting presentence interviews, probation officers typically attempt to shape the defendant's account to fit their own preconceived typing. Many probation officers believe that the defendant's attitude toward the offense and toward the future prospects for leading a law-abiding life are the most important parts of the statement. In most presentence investigations the probation investigator identifies and interprets the defendant's subjective attitudes and then incorporates them into the report. Using this procedure, probation officers look for and can report attitudes that "logically fit" with their final sentencing recommendation (see, for example, Davis 1983).

Defendants who have been typed as prison cases typically are portrayed as holding socially unacceptable attitudes about their criminal actions and unrealistic or negative attitudes about future prospects for living an upright life. Conversely, those who have been typed as probation material are described as having acceptable attitudes, such as contriteness about the present offense and optimism about their ability to lead a crime-free life. The structuring of accounts about defendant attitudes was described by a presentence investigator in the following manner:

> When POs talk about the defendant's attitude we really mean how that attitude relates to the case. Naturally I'm not going to write about what a wonderful attitude the guy has—how sincere he seems—and then recommend sending him to the joint. That wouldn't make sense. The judges want consistency. If a guy has a shitty attitude but is going to get probation anyway, there's no percentage in playing up his attitude problem.

In most cases the presentence interview is the only contact between the investigating officer and the defendant. The brevity of this contact and the lack of post-report interaction foster a legalistic perspective. Investigators are concerned mainly with "getting the case through court" rather than with special problems related to supervising probationers on a long-term basis. One-time-only interviews rarely allow probation officers to become emotionally involved with their cases; the personal and individual aspects of the defendant's personality generally are not manifested during a half-hour presentence interview. For many probation officers the emotional distance from offenders is one of the benefits of working in presentence units. Such an opinion was expressed by an investigation officer: "I really like the one-shot-only part of this job. I don't have time to get caught up with the clients. I can deal with facts and not worry about individual personalities."

The probation officer has wide discretion in the type of collateral information that is collected from sources other than the defendant or the official record. Although a defendant's social history must be sketched in the presentence report, the supplementation of that history is left to individual investigators. There are few established guidelines for the investigating officer to follow, except that the psychiatric or psychological reports should be submitted when there is compelling evidence that the offender is mentally disturbed. Informal guidelines, however, specify that in misdemeanor cases reports should be shorter and more concise than in felony cases. The officers indicated that reports for municipal court (all misdemeanor cases) should range from four to six pages in length, while superior court reports (felony cases) were expected to be six to nine pages long. In controversial cases (to which only the most experienced officers are assigned) presentence reports are expected to be longer and to include considerable social data. Reports in these cases have been as long as 30 pages.

Although probation officers learn what general types of information to include through experience and feedback from judges and supervisors, they are allowed considerable leeway in deciding exactly what to put in their reports (outside of the offense and prior record sections). Because investigators decide what collateral sources are germane to the case, they tend to include information that will reflect favorably on their sentencing recommendation. In this context the observation of one probation officer is understandable: "I pick from the mass of possible sources just which ones to put in the report. Do you think I'm going to pick people who make my recommendation look weak? No way!"

Filing the Report

The final stage in the investigation includes dictating the report, having it approved by a probation supervisor, and appearing in court. All three of these activities serve to reinforce the importance of prior record and offense in sentencing recommendations. At the time of dictation, probation officers determine what to include in the report and how to phrase their remarks. For the first time in the investigation, they receive formal feedback from official sources. Presentence reports are read by three groups important to the probation officers: probation supervisors, district attorneys, and judges. Probation officers recognize that for varying reasons, all these groups emphasize the legally relevant variables of offense and prior criminal record when considering an appropriate sentencing recommendation.[6] Such considerations reaffirm the probation officer's initial private typing.

A probation investigator described this process:

> After I've talked to the defendants I think maybe some of them deserve to get special consideration. But when I remember who's going to look at the reports. My supervisor, the DA, the judge; they don't care about all the personal details. When all is said and done, what's really important to them is the offense and the defendant's prior record. I know that stuff from the start. It makes me wonder why we have to jack ourselves around to do long reports.

Probation officers assume that their credibility as presentence investigators will be enhanced if their sentencing recommendations meet with the approval of probation supervisors, district attorneys, and judges. On the other hand, officers whose recommendations are consistently "out of line" are subject to censure or transfer, or they find themselves engaged in "running battles" (Shover 1974:357) with court officials. During the last stage of the investigation probation officers must consider how to ensure that their reports will go through court without "undue personal hassle." Most investigation officers have learned that presentence recommendations based on a consideration of prior record and offense can achieve that goal.

Although occupational self-interest is an important component in deciding how to conduct a presentence investigation, other factors also are involved. Many probation officers agree with the idea of using legally relevant variables as determinants of recommendations. These officers embrace the retributive value of this concept and see it as an equitable method for framing their investigation. Other officers reported that probation officers' discretion had been "short-circuited" by determinate sentencing guidelines and that they were reduced to "merely going through the motions" in conducting their investigations. Still other officers view the use of legal variables to structure recommendations as an acceptable bureaucratic shortcut to compensate partially for large case assignments. One probation officer stated, "If the department wants us to keep pumping out presentence reports we can't consider social factors—we just don't have time." Although probation officers are influenced by various dynamics, there seems little doubt that in California, the social history which once was considered the "heart and soul" of presentence probation reports (Reckless 1967:673) has been largely devalued.

Summary and Conclusions

In this study I provide a description and an analysis of the processes used by probation investigators in preparing presentence reports. The research findings based on interview data indicate that probation officers tend to de-emphasize individual defendants' characteristics and that their probation recommendations are not influenced directly by factors such as sex, age, race, socioeconomic status, or work record. Instead, probation officers emphasize the variables of instant offense and prior criminal record. The finding that offense and prior record are the main considerations of probation officers with regard to sentence recommendations agrees with a substantial body of research (Bankston 1983; Carter and Wilkens 1967; Dawson 1969; Lotz and Hewitt 1977; Robinson, Carter, and Wahl 1969; Wallace 1974; Walsh 1985).

My particular contribution has been to supply the ethnographic observations and the data that explain this phenomenon. I have identified the process whereby offense and prior record come to occupy the central role in decision making by probation officers. This identification underscores the significance of private typings in determining official designations. An analysis of probation practices suggests that the function of the presentence investigation is more ceremonial then instrumental (Hagan 1985).

I show that early in the investigation probation officers, using offense and prior record as guidelines, classify defendants into types; when the typing process is complete, probation officers essentially have decided on the sentence recommendation that will be recorded later in their official designation. The subsequent course of investigations is determined largely by this initial private typing. Further data collection is influenced by a sentence recommendation that already has been firmly established. This finding answers affirmatively the research question posed by Carter (1967:211):

> Do probation officers, after "deciding" on a recommendation early in the presentence investigation, seek further information which justifies the decision, rather than information which might lead to modification or rejection of that recommendation?

The type of information and observation contained in the final presentence report is generated to support the original recommendation decision. Probation officers do not regard defendant typings as tentative hypotheses to be disproved through inquiry but rather as firm conclusions to be justified in the body of the report.

Although the presentence interview has been considered an important part of the investigation (Spencer 1983), I demonstrate that it does not significantly alter probation officers' perceptions. In most cases probation officers dominate presentence interviews; interaction between the participants is guarded. The nature of interviews between defendants and probation officers is important in itself; further research is needed to identify the dynamics that prevail in these interactions.

Attitudes attributed to defendants often are structured by probation officers to reaffirm the recommendation already formulated. The defendant's social history, long considered an integral part of the presentence report, in reality has little bearing on sentencing considerations. In most cases the presentence is no longer a vehicle for social inquiry but rather a typing process which considers mainly the defendant's prior criminal record and the seriousness of the criminal offense. Private attorneys in growing numbers have become disenchanted with the quality of probation investigations and have commissioned presentence probation reports privately (Rodgers, Gitchoff, and Paur 1984). At present, however, such a practice is generally available only for wealthy defendants.

The presentence process that I have described is used in the great majority of cases; it is the "normal" procedure. Even so, probation officers are not entirely passive actors in this process. On occasion they will give serious consideration to social variables in arriving at a sentencing recommendation. In special circumstances officers will allow individual defendants' characteristics to influence their report. In addition, probation officers who have developed credibility with the court are allowed some discretion in compiling presentence reports. This discretion is not unlimited, however; it is based on a prior record of producing reports that meet the court's approval, and is contingent on continuing to do so. A presentence writer said, "You can only afford to go to bat for defendants in a few select cases; if you try to do it too much, you get a reputation as being 'out of step.'"

This research raises the issue of probation officers' autonomy. Although I depict presentence investigators as having limited autonomy, other researchers (Hagan 1975; Myers 1979; Walsh 1985) contend that probation officers have considerable leeway in recommendation. This contradictory evidence can be explained in large part by the type of sentencing structure, the professionalism of probation workers, and the role of the district attorney at sentencing. Walsh's study (1985), for example, which views probation officers as important actors in the presentence process, was conducted in a jurisdiction with indeterminate sentencing, where the probation officers demonstrated a high degree of professionalism and the prosecutors "rarely made sentencing recommendations." A very different situation existed in the California counties that I studied: determinate sentencing was enforced, probation officers were not organized professionally, and the district attorneys routinely made specific court recommendations. It seems apparent that probation officers' autonomy must be considered with reference to judicial jurisdiction.

In view of the primacy of offense and prior record in sentencing considerations, the efficacy of current presentence investigation practices is doubtful. It seems ineffective and wasteful to continue to collect a mass of social data of uncertain relevance. Yet an analysis of courtroom culture suggests that the presentence investigation helps maintain judicial mythology as well as probation officer legitimacy. Although judges generally do not have the time or the inclination to consider individual variables thoroughly, the performance of a presentence investigation perpetuates the myth of individualized sentences. Including a presentence report in the court file gives the appearance of individualization without influencing sentencing practices significantly.

Even in a state like California, where determinate sentencing allegedly has replaced individualized justice, the judicial system feels obligated to maintain the appearance of individualization. After observing the court system in California for several years I am convinced that a major reason for maintaining such a practice is to make it easier for criminal defendants to accept their sentences. The presentence report allows defendants to feel that their case at least has received a considered decision. One judge admitted candidly that the "real purpose" of the presentence investigation was to convince defendants that they were not getting "the fast shuffle." He observed further that if defendants were sentenced without such investigations, many would complain and would file "endless appeals" over what seems to them a hasty sentencing decision. Even though judges typically consider only offense and prior record in a sentencing decision, they want defendants to believe that their cases are being judged individually. The presentence investigation allows this assumption to be maintained. In addition, some judges use the probation officer's report as an excuse for a particular type of sentence. In some instances they deny responsibility for the sentence, implying that their "hands were tied" by the recommendation. Thus judges are taken "off the hook" for meting out an unpopular sentence. Further research is needed to substantiate the significance of these latent functions of the presentence investigation.

The presentence report is a major component in the legitimacy of the probation movement; several factors support the probation officers' stake in maintaining their role in these investigations. Historically, probation has been wedded to the concept of individualized treatment. In theory, the presentence report is suited ideally to reporting on defendants' individual circumstances. From a historical perspective (Rothman 1980) this ideal has always been more symbolic than substantive, but if the legitimacy of the presentence report is questioned, so then is the entire purpose of probation.

Regardless of its usefulness (or lack of usefulness), it is doubtful that probation officials would consider the diminution or abolition of presentence reports. The number of probation workers assigned to presentence investigations is substantial, and their numbers represent an obvious source of bureaucratic power. Conducting presentence investigations allows probation officers to remain visible with the court and the public. The media often report on controversial probation cases, and presentence writers generally have more contact and more association with judges than do others in the probation department.

As ancillary court workers, probation officers are assigned the dirty work of collecting largely irrelevant data on offenders (Hagan 1975; Hughes 1958). Investigation officers have learned that emphasizing offense and prior record in their reports will enhance relationships with judges and district attorneys, as well as improving their occupational standing within probation departments. Thus the presentence investigation serves to maintain the court's claim of individualized concern while preserving the probation officer's role, although a subordinate role, in the court system.[7]

The myth of individualization serves various functions, but it also raises serious questions. In an era of severe budget restrictions (Schumacher 1985) should scarce resources be allocated to compiling predictable presentence reports of dubious value? If social variables are considered only in a few cases, should courts continue routinely to require presentence reports in all felony matters (as is the practice in California)? In summary, we should address the issue of whether the criminal justice system can afford the ceremony of a probation presentence investigation.

Notes

1. For a full discussion of the insider-outsider perspective in criminal justice see Marquart (1986).

2. In a few jurisdictions, officers who prepare investigations also supervise the defendants after probation has been granted, but, this procedure is becoming less prevalent in contemporary probation (Clear and Cole 1986). It is possible that extralegal variables play a significant role in the supervision process, but this paper is concerned specifically with presentence investigations.

3. There was no exact way to determine whether the 25 percent of the officers I was unable to interview conducted their presentence investigations significantly differently from those I interviewed. Personal observation, however, and the comments of the officers I interviewed (with whom I discussed this issue) indicated that those who refused used similar methods in processing their presentence reports.

4. On occasion police reports are written vaguely and are subject to various interpretations; rap sheets are not always clear, especially when some of the final dispositions have not been recorded.

5. I did not include terminal misdemeanor dispositions, in which probation is denied in favor of fines or jail sentences, in this typology. Such dispositions are comparatively rare and relatively insignificant.

6. Although defense attorneys also read the presentence reports, their reactions generally do not affect the probation officers' occupational standing (McHugh 1973; Rosecrance 1985).

7. I did not discuss the role of presentence reports in the prison system. Traditionally, probation reports were part of an inmate's jacket or file and were used as a basis for classification and treatment. The position of probation officers was legitimated further by the fact that prison officials also used the presentence report. I would suggest, however, that the advent of prison overcrowding and the accompanying security concerns have rendered presentence reports relatively meaningless, This contention needs to be substantiated before presentence reports are abandoned completely.

References

Allen, Harry E. and Clifford E. Simonsen (1986) *Corrections in America.* New York: Macmillan.

Bankston, William B. (1983) "Legal and Extralegal Offender Traits and Decision-Making in the Criminal Justice System." *Sociological Spectrum* 3:1–18.

Blumberg, Abraham (1967) *Criminal Justice.* Chicago: Quadrangle.

Blumstein, Alfred J., S. Martin, and N. Holt (1983) *Research on Sentencing: The Search for Reform.* Washington, DC: National Academy Press.

Carter, Robert M. (1967) "The Presentence Report and The Decision-Making Process." *Journal of Research in Crime and Delinquency* 4:203–11.

Carter, Robert M. and Leslie T. Wilkins (1967) "Some Factors in Sentencing Policy." *Journal of Criminal Law, Criminology, and Police Science* 58:503–14.

Clear, Todd and George Cole (1986) *American Corrections.* Monerey, CA: Brooks/ Cole.

Davis, James R. (1983) "Academic and Practical Aspects of Probation: A Comparison." *Federal Probation* 47:7–10.

Dawson, Robert (1969) *Sentencing.* Boston: Little, Brown.

Emerson, Robert M. (1981) "Ethnography and Understanding Members' Worlds." In Robert M. Emerson (ed.), *Contemporary Field Research.* Boston: Little, Brown, pp. 19–35.

Forer, Lois G. (1980) *Criminals and Victims.* New York: Norton.

Goldsborough, E. and E. Burbank (1968) "The Probation Officer and His Personality." In Charles L. Newman (ed.), *Sourcebook on Probation, Parole, and Pardons.* Springfield, IL: Charles C. Thomas, pp. 104-12.

Hagan, John (1975) "The Social and Legal Construction of Criminal Justice: A Study of the Presentence Process." *Social Problems* 22:620-37.

_____. (1977) "Criminal Justice in Rural and Urban Communities: A Study of the Bureaucratization of Justice." *Social Forces* 55:597-612.

_____. (1985) *Modem Criminology: Crime, Criminal Behavior, and Its Control.* New York: McGraw-Hill.

Hagan, John, John Hewitt, and Duane Alwin (1979) "Ceremonial Justice: Crime and Punishment in a Loosely Coupled System." *Social Forces* 58:506-25.

Hogarth, John (1971) *Sentencing As a Human Process.* Toronto: University of Toronto Press.

Hughes, Everett C. (1958) *Men and Their Work.* New York: Free Press.

Katz, Janet (1982) "The Attitudes and Decisions of Probation Officers." *Criminal Justice and Behavior* 9:455-75.

Kingsnorth, Rodney and Louis Rizzo (1979) "Decision-Making in the Criminal Courts: Continuities and Discontinuities." *Criminology* 17:3-14.

Lotz, Ray and John Hewitt (1977) "The Influence of Legally Irrelevant Factors on Felony Sentencing." *Sociological Inquiry* 47:39-48.

Marquart, James W. (1986) "Outsiders As Insiders: Participant Observation in the Role of a Prison Guard." *Justice Quarterly* 3:15-32.

McCleary, Richard (1978) *Dangerous Men.* Beverly Hills: Sage.

McCleary, Richard, Barbara Nienstadt, and James Erven (1982) "Uniform Crime Reports as Organizational Outcomes: Three Time Series Experiments." *Social Problems* 29:361-73.

McHugh, John J. (1973) "Some Comments on Natural Conflict between Counsel and Probation Officer." *American Journal of Corrections* 3:15-32.

Michalowski, Raymond J. (1985) *Order, Law and Crime.* New York: Random House.

Murrah, A. (1963) "Prison or Probation?" In B. Kay and C. Vedder (eds.), *Probation and Parole.* Springfield, IL: Charles C. Thomas, pp. 63-78.

Myers, Martha A. (1979) "Offended Parties and Official Reactions: Victims and the Sentencing of Criminal Defendants." *Sociological Quarterly* 20:529-46.

Neubauer, David (1974) *Criminal Justice in Middle America.* Morristown, NJ: General Learning.

Petersilia, Joan, Susan Turner, James Kahan, and Joyce Peterson (1985) "Executive Summary of Rand's Study, Granting Felons Probation." *Crime and Delinquency* 31:379-92.

Prus, Robert (1975) "Labeling Theory: A Statement on Typing." *Sociological Focus* 8:79-96.

Prus, Robert and John Stratten (1976) "Factors in the Decision-Making of North Carolina Probation Officers." *Federal Probation* 40:48-53.

Reckless, Walter C. (1967) *The Crime Problem.* New York: Appleton.

Robinson, James, Robert Carter, and A. Wahl (1969) *The San Francisco Project.* Berkeley: University of California School of Criminology.

Rodgers, T.A., G.T. Gitchoff, and I. Paur (1984) "The Privately Commissioned Presentence Report." In Robert M. Carter, Deniel Glaser, and Leslie T. Wilkens (eds.), *Probation, Parole, and Community Corrections.* New York: Wiley, pp. 21-30.

Rosecrance, John (1985) "The Probation Officers' Search for Credibility: Ball Park Recommendations." *Crime and Delinquency* 31:539-54.

_____. (1987) "A Typology of Presentence Probation Investigators." *International Journal of Offender Therapy and Comparative Criminology* 31:163-177.

Rothman, David (1980) *Conscience and Convenience: The Asylum and Its Alternatives in Progressive America.* Boston: Little, Brown.

Schumacher, Michael A. (1985) "Implementation of a Client Classification And Case Management System: A Practitioner's View." *Crime and Delinquency* 31:445-55.

Scott, Marvin and Stanford Lyman (1968) "Accounts." *American Sociological Re-view* 33:46-62.

Shover, Neal (1974) "Experts and Diagnosis in Correctional Agencies." *Crime and Delinquency* 20:347-58.

_____. (1979) *A Sociology of American Corrections.* Homewood, IL: Dorsey.

Spencer, Jack W. (1983) "Accounts, Attitudes and Solutions: Probation Officer-Defendant Negotiations of Subjective Orientations." *Social Problems* 30:570-81.

Spradley, Joseph P. (1970) *You Owe Yourself a Drunk: An Ethnography of Urban Nomads.* Boston: Little, Brown.

Sudnow, David (1965) "Normal Crimes: Sociological Features of the Penal Code." *Social Problems* 12:255-76.

Tinker, John N., John Quiring, and Yvonne Pimentel (1985) "Ethnic Bias in California Courts: A Case Study of Chicano and Anglo Felony Defendants." *Sociological Inquiry* 55:83-96.

Walker, Samuel (1985) *Sense and Nonsense About Crime.* Monterey, CA: Brooks/Cole.

Wallace, John (1974) "Probation Administration." In Daniel Glaser (ed.), *Handbook of Criminology.* Chicago: Rand-McNally, pp. 940-70.

Walsh, Anthony (1985) "The Role of the Probation Officer in the Sentencing Process." *Criminal Justice and Behavior* 12:289-303.

DISCUSSION QUESTIONS

1. Rosecrance argues that the myth of individualized justice is important for defendants, as it discourages post-conviction challenges. Do other individuals within or outside of the criminal justice system, such as the average citizen, subscribe to the myth of individualized justice?

2. The article illustrates a divide between the individualized investigation and the actual sentence. The latter does not take into account much of the information in the report beyond offense severity and prior record. What would happen to the court system if judges truly considered the extralegal background information provided by presentence investigators? Would the process be fairer? More efficient? Explain.

3. What repercussions would a presentence investigator face if he or she prepared a report with a recommendation contrary to the typical sentence delivered by the court? Is the probation department independent of the court?

SECTION IV

Organizational Deviance and Termination

What Explains Failure in Criminal Justice Agencies?

Section Highlights

Defining and Explaining Organizational Deviance
- Administrative Breakdown
- Structural Secrecy and Knowledge Conflict
- Normal Accidents
- Crisis (Mis)Management

Preventing Organizational Deviance
Organizational Termination
- Organizational Termination Defined
- The Resilience and Decline of Public Organizations
- Replacement of Services Lost

On March 12, 2003, Josiah Sutton emerged from the Harris County (TX) jail, four and a half years after he was identified as one of the perpetrators of a rape (Fergus, 2004). Convicted and sentenced to a 25-year prison term, Sutton secured his early release after it was determined he was falsely convicted; though, at the time of his release, he was neither declared innocent nor exonerated altogether (Gross, Jacoby, Matheson, & Montgomery, 2005). During his trial, the prosecutor's case against Sutton was bolstered by both the victim's eyewitness identification and the local crime laboratory's analysis of a DNA sample found on the victim's clothes. The strength of the evidence was enough to secure Sutton's conviction. However, questions about the evidence and its production were raised before, during, and after the trial, ultimately leading to the conclusion after many years that Sutton was wrongly convicted of the crime. For example, the perpetrators were initially described as about 5'7" tall and less than 140 pounds. Sutton was identified as a suspect even though he was more than 6 feet tall and 200 pounds. Moreover, the victim identified Sutton and his companion while both parties sat in separate vehicles 10 feet apart, likely affecting the victim's ability to accurately assess the perpetrators' height and weight. Nevertheless, a positive identification was made (Thompson, 2008). The crime lab provided further confirmatory support for Sutton as the offender, but problems plagued both the testing and reporting of results. Moreover, the DNA analyst knew of Sutton's positive eyewitness identification (Thompson, 2008). As a result, the two identifications—the victim's and the analyst's—reinforced each other, only strengthening their conclusions. The totality of evidence, even if improper, led to Sutton's conviction. Post-conviction DNA testing, media reports of problems with the Houston Police Department Crime Laboratory, and the work of a university criminologist, attorneys, and others eventually led to Sutton's release (Fergus, 2004).

Sutton's conviction demonstrates that multiple organizations failed to operate according to their intended goals. For example, the court system, tasked with vigorously testing evidence to make accurate decisions about guilt, erred in convicting Sutton (see Goodpaster, 1987). The crime laboratory also arrived at an incorrect conclusion, identifying Sutton as a perpetrator even though it was later determined that the DNA sample recovered from the crime scene could not be his (Koppl, 2005; Thompson, 2008). In spite of these organizational failings, there is a tendency to want to cast blame on an individual or small group of people. Doing so is convenient, for it allows continued confidence in the larger institutions (e.g., the police, the court system, the crime laboratory) while offering a quick remedy—replacing problem personnel—to avoid future problems. The failing rests with a few "rotten apples" in an organization rather than with the organization as a whole, or the "rotten barrels" (Ivković, 2009, p. 780; King, 2009a).

Unfortunately, this limited focus ignores organizational explanations for adverse events such as the wrongful conviction of Josiah Sutton. In his case, a contributing factor was the interaction between the crime laboratory and the police department post-eyewitness identification; "two pieces of evidence that appeared to be independent and therefore mutually confirmatory were, in reality, connected in a manner that led to simultaneous and mutually reinforcing errors" (Thompson, 2008, p. 1034). The DNA analysis did not independently corroborate the eyewitness testimony. It was conducted within the constraints created by the initial eyewitness identification. In addition, in spite of the formalization of procedures in the crime lab (e.g., documenting notes, procedures to prevent contamination of samples), rules were not always followed and there were limited mechanisms for ensuring compliance (recall the discussion of control in Section II).

Moving beyond individual blame and examining organization-level factors paints a more complete picture of the causes of these types of negative outcomes and offers insight into methods for preventing future occurrences. That said, although organizations, particularly public criminal justice organizations, are incredibly resilient, some experience failure, as evident in their termination or disbanding (King, in press). Like a local retail establishment going out of business, police departments, prisons, and other criminal justice agencies may, for reasons that will be explored, cease to exist. The remainder of this section addresses the idea of failure in organizations, embodied in the concept of organizational deviance—wrongful convictions, riots, school shootings, and police misconduct. Multiple causes for adverse events, as well as strategies to reduce the likelihood of such events, will be discussed. The section concludes with coverage of the topic of organizational termination, including its causes and the consequences for communities when criminal justice organizations disband.

Defining and Explaining Organizational Deviance

The organizational theory literature is replete with books and articles analyzing the dark side of organizations, organizational failures, disasters, breakdowns, latent errors, accidents, and other organizational problems (Anheier, 1999; Dias & Vaughn, 2006; King, 2009a; O'Hara, 2005; Ramanujam & Goodman, 2003; Starbuck & Farjoun, 2005; Vaughan, 1996, 1999). These terms are used to describe the adverse outcomes produced by organizations (e.g., loss of life, erroneous convictions, traffic accidents) and/or the causes of those outcomes, including the violation of rules and regulations, organizational design problems, and interactions between the organization and its environment (Ramanujam & Goodman, 2003). Organizations—recall from the definition offered in Section I—are structured to satisfy their goals reliably, but in some situations, they fail to do so, producing instead unexpected and negative results (Merton, 1936; Vaughan, 1999). Consider the following examples:

- A school tasked with educating and socializing students fails to recognize and help a student in need of counseling. The school later suffers the tragedy of a violent incident at the hands of the same student (Fox & Harding, 2005).

- A police department, responsible for protecting the public, causes harm as a police van accidently runs into a crowd of parade-goers (O'Hara, 2005).

- Prisons are charged with, among other responsibilities, securely confining inmates. When a faulty prison fence leads to a large volume of false alarms, correctional officers become complacent. They fail to respond during an actual escape, leading to public questions about the safety of the facility (Rison & Wittenberg, 1994).

- An intelligence agency is unable to connect the dots to prevent or mitigate a large terrorist attack before it occurs (Zegart, 2007).

Vaughan (1999) attempted to capture the variety of terms above within a single conceptual label, organizational deviance, addressing both the causes as well as the consequences. Organizational deviance is

> an event, activity, or circumstance, occurring in and/or produced by a formal organization, that deviates from both formal design goals and normative standards or expectations, either in the fact of its occurrence or in its consequences, and produces a suboptimal outcome. (p. 273)

Vaughan stressed that organizational deviance does not imply that any individual employee acted inappropriately or in violation of any organization or legal regulations, although it is a possibility. The deviance label refers to the fact that the situation—a disaster, mistake, accident, or some other incident—does not fit the organization's goals or expectations of performance. Josiah Sutton's case and the four examples above illustrate this departure. A number of different theories are available to help us understand organizational deviance. While individual-level explanations might emphasize the attitudes and motivations of the individual employee, the theories addressed below focus on organizational characteristics that contribute to organizational deviance.

Administrative Breakdown

To explain organizational deviance, some scholars have turned to the principles of administration—most important, those that address the control of an organization's work and its members. Fayol (1949; see Section III) detailed 14 principles as part of administrative management theory, covering topics such as unity of command, obedience to authority, the chain of command, and the need for order. If his principles are combined with organizational control mechanisms such as rules (formalization), centralized decision making, and an appropriate span of control, then the organization should, as the theory argues, run smoothly (Dias & Vaughn, 2006; Fayol, 1949). Of course, adhering to classical school principles is just one approach to effective organization, but, as Dias and Vaughn (2006) argued, most criminal justice organizations are structured along bureaucratic/administrative theory lines, so it makes sense to use these principles as a starting point. Organizational deviance and adverse outcomes result when managers fail to adequately implement or enforce administrative principles, referred to as **administrative breakdown** (Dias & Vaughn, 2006).

Administrative breakdown has frequently been used to explain dysfunction in secure facilities, including prisons and jails. In 1980, for example, inmates at the Penitentiary of New Mexico took 12 correctional officers hostage—some of whom were subsequently physically and/or sexually assaulted—killed 33 inmates, and injured more than 200 others over two days (Colvin, 1982). A full accounting of the causes of the riot is beyond the scope of this text, but several contributors deserve mention. First, the chain of command (scalar chain, in Fayol's terms) was weakened in the period leading up to the riots. A well-respected and powerful former warden of the penitentiary, Felix Rodriguez, served in a position between the actual warden and the head of the Department of Corrections. This only served to weaken the power of those immediately above and below Rodriquez, disrupting the hierarchy of authority during the critical period of the prison's deterioration (Useem & Kimball, 1989). Within the prison, disciplinary policies changed (e.g., greater use of solitary confinement) but were not accepted by inmates (Colvin, 1982; Goldstone & Useem, 1999). The wardens "lost control completely . . . unable to compel their subordinates, captains, or line officers to submit to their discipline—for example, to follow security routines" (Useem & Kimball, 1989, p. 91). Crowding, violence, and escapes only reinforced among inmates the perception that prison officials were losing control of the facility (Useem & Kimball, 1989). The destructive events of the riot followed.

Jacoby (2002) offered explanations consistent with administrative breakdown in his description of the failings in the 1970s of the Farview State Hospital, a maximum-security facility for mentally ill offenders in Pennsylvania. The facility neither provided a safe environment for patients and staff nor offered inmates any true psychiatric treatment program. Among the problems plaguing the facility were a lack of treatment personnel, an issue with the division of labor, and the employment of specialists (see Fayol's first principle in Section III). Security concerns dominated, so guards made up more than 93% of the staff. Staff were also accused of abusing patients, in some cases resulting in deaths under suspicious circumstances; employee behavior was attributed in part to the lack of supervision from managers (hierarchy of authority and span-of-control issues). Vaughn (1996) extended the administrative breakdown argument to the many situations where correctional officials are held civilly liable for failing to protect inmates from assaults perpetrated by other inmates. For example, prison officials may fail to properly classify and locate a vulnerable inmate within the prison or neglect to protect inmates on hit lists. In these situations, breakdown enables the violence and opens the organization to civil liability claims.

Administrative breakdowns also occur in other components of the criminal justice system (Dias & Vaughn, 2006). After the verdicts were delivered in the 1992 trial of the officers accused of beating Rodney King, riots erupted in Los Angeles. The opportunity for police to intervene passed almost immediately as the chain of command was lost:

> No one in the [Los Angeles Police Department] took responsibility for stopping the beginning stages of the riot. No specific authority figure was identified from which officers were to receive orders; no supervisor was identified in the hierarchy to which officers would report. (p. 549)

In sum, administrative breakdown draws attention to both the structural and managerial determinants of organizational deviance. When managers fail to properly implement effective structures, it is more likely that negative outcomes will result.

Structural Secrecy and Knowledge Conflict

Adverse events sometimes result from poor decision making based on incomplete information. Members of a police patrol division may, for example, release a traffic violator with a warning, unaware that the individual is being sought by the department's investigations division for multiple violent crimes. The officers simply do not have enough knowledge to sufficiently understand the magnitude of the situation. Had information been shared by the agency's detectives, officers could have acted differently. While it may be argued that the detective on the investigation was being individually secretive by not sharing information—perhaps seeking recognition for apprehending the suspect on his or her own—an alternative argument is that organizations are not designed to effectively share information among personnel and units (Vaughan, 1996, 1998, 1999). The problem, referred to as **structural secrecy**, inhibits knowledge acquisition and development within organizations:

> Secrecy is built into the very structure of organizations. As organizations grow large, actions are, for the most part, not observable. The division of labor between subunits, hierarchy, and geographic dispersion segregate knowledge about tasks and goals. Distance—both physical and social—interferes with the efforts of those at the top to "know" the behavior of others in the organization—and vice versa. Specialized knowledge further inhibits knowing. People in one department or division lack the expertise to understand the work in another or, for that matter, the work of other specialists in their own unit. The language associated with a different task, even in the same organization, can be wondrously opaque. (Vaughan, 1996, p. 250)

Vaughan's description of structural secrecy refers to the three dimensions of complexity—vertical, horizontal, and spatial—discussed in Section II. The structural features of organizations, it is argued, effectively place silos around information, thereby limiting intraorganization information sharing. Consequently, without information on possible actions, fully rational decision making suffers (Gottfredson & Gottfredson, 1988).

An example of structural secrecy opened Section II. Three Federal Bureau of Investigation (FBI) field offices conducted what, at the time, were three disparate investigations that turned out to be part of the single 9/11 terrorist plot. The spatially differentiated structure of the FBI meant that investigations were conducted within, rather than across, field offices under the direction of the special agent or assistant director in charge (Zegart, 2007). The problem, of course, is that the extent of the plot was unknown. In another example, Fox and Harding (2005) suggested that structural secrecy offered an organizational explanation for multi-victim school shootings, such as the incident in West Paducah, Kentucky. Rather than focus on the motives of the perpetrators, the authors addressed organizational characteristics that made it unlikely that officials would be able to intervene before the violence occurred. Identifying troubled, potentially dangerous students is hampered by the specialization within schools. The division of labor, as Vaughan (1996) argues, means that information within the sphere of responsibility of teachers (instruction), guidance counselors (career planning/social and psychological counseling), and principals (discipline) is unlikely to be shared across specialty areas. Even within a particular specialization (e.g., instruction), concerns about a student may not be widely diffused; "since it is not necessary to know about a student's performance or behavior in physical education to teach the student history, teachers often have few incentives to communicate" (Fox & Harding, 2005, p. 73). Yet this information—a sudden drop in grades, threatening writing, in-school discipline—when taken together, provides more complete knowledge about a student in need of intervention.

If structural secrecy occurs when information is limited within an organization, knowledge conflict occurs when management's understanding of events is incompatible with line-level workers' understanding of the same events. The central premise is that what any one employee knows in an organization and how he or she knows it is determined by the individual's vertical position within the organizational hierarchy (Garrett, 2001, 2004).[1] Managers, far removed from the actual work of police officers, probation officers, engineers, construction workers, and others, think about work in scientific, mathematical terms (Garrett, 2004; Hummel, 2006). Garrett (2004) writes,

> Executives know their work in terms of numbers and ask questions such as how many employees it will take to successfully accomplish the mission or task, how much it will cost, and how many missions can be successfully accomplished in a minimal amount of time. (p. 390)

Writing about the disastrous space shuttle *Challenger* launch in 1986 that resulted in the deaths of seven astronauts, Garrett (2001) described NASA administrators' assessment that the probability of launch failure was 1 in 100,000. Line-level workers, according to the knowledge-conflict argument, do not think in such abstract, quantitative terms. For workers, experience matters most; hunches and intuition are not discounted (Garrett, 2004). NASA engineers expressed concern about launching the space shuttle in cold weather but could not back their experiential knowledge with quantifiable data for NASA management. For a worker, a statistic such as 1 in 100,000 might be completely meaningless and disconnected from reality, especially when the shuttle program had launched only 23 missions prior to the fatal *Challenger* mission. The problem emerges when differing knowledge conflicts, typically leading to managerial knowledge being considered superior to the experiential knowledge of line-level workers (Garrett, 2001; Hummel, 2006). A probation officer's assessment of an offender's

---

[1] Garrett (2001, 2004) refers to the differing knowledge within an organization as the knowledge analytic. For ease of explanation, the term *knowledge conflict* is borrowed from the work of Hummel (2006).

recidivism risk may include hunches that extend the quantitative scores obtained through risk-assessment instruments; if managers focus on the latter but ignore the former, the consequence may be inadequate decision making.

Garrett (2001) further illustrates the knowledge-conflict problem using the failed raid of the Branch Davidian compound in Waco, Texas, in 1993. The members of the religious group, including its leader David Koresh, were under investigation for possession of illegal weapons and explosives. The Bureau of Alcohol, Tobacco, Firearms, and Explosives (ATF) had decided to raid the compound to execute the warrants. An undercover agent had infiltrated the compound and communicated to his superiors that the element of surprise was lost; Koresh knew hours before that a raid was imminent. The experiential, "common-sense judgment" of the agent was supplanted by management knowledge (Garrett, 2001, p. 75). The quantifiable information possessed by leaders—number of guns observed, number of members observed taking up arms, tactical advantage of the ATF, time until the raid, and cost–benefit analysis—led to the conclusion to proceed with the raid. As agents attempted to serve the warrants, a gun battle ensued, and four ATF agents were killed (Garrett, 2001). A prolonged, nearly two-month standoff followed before the compound was raided by the FBI.

To overcome structural secrecy and knowledge conflict, organizations must address the underlying problems. Vaughan (1996) observed that organizations often formalize information-sharing procedures and mandate paperwork to ensure that relevant knowledge is passed among organizational personnel. The problem, as she noted, is that this might result in too much information sharing; in an effort to avoid information overload, a type of prioritization occurs where some information is simply ignored. Therefore, it is imperative to determine both the content and quantity of information to share to facilitate effective decision making. To overcome knowledge conflicts, organizations need to reconcile this diverse knowledge rather than view one as inherently superior to the other. To do otherwise, to ignore experiential knowledge, increases the risk of the types of organizational failures discussed in this section.

Normal Accidents

Others have argued that organizational deviance, while rare, is nevertheless inevitable in some organizations, given their characteristics and the arrangement of their parts (Perrow, 1999). The term **normal accidents** was developed to describe these inevitable problems. "Normal," in this context, is not a statement on the appropriateness or acceptability of the outcomes, only the likelihood of their occurrence (Perrow, 1999). The focal point of normal accidents theory is the system created to accomplish work. Systems are made up of parts, "the smallest component of the system that is likely to be identified in analyzing an accident" (p. 65). In his famous book *Normal Accidents,* Perrow illustrated his theory through descriptions of the near-meltdown of the Three Mile Island nuclear power plant and the explosion of the space shuttle *Challenger*. In the case of the former, system parts included the nuclear power structure itself (valves, turbines, water feeding systems, etc.) and the plant operators. Perrow's concern was with the relationship between the parts of the system, arguing that more complex and more tightly coupled systems are at greater risk of experiencing a normal accident. Significant problems emerge when multiple parts malfunction, leading to system failures.

Perrow (1999) described systems according to the level of **coupling** of their parts and their level of **complexity**. In tightly coupled systems, "what happens in one [part] directly affects what happens in the other" (p. 90). In other words, the parts are highly dependent on one another. Consider driving a car on a highway behind another vehicle. When the distance between the two vehicles is great, the actions of the first vehicle, such as stopping quickly, have only a minimal effect on the trailing vehicle. If, however, the vehicles are tightly coupled, with one vehicle following the other too closely, the likelihood of an accident increases. The slack, or ability to absorb the effects caused by one part of the system, is lost by the trailing car. Returning to the Josiah Sutton case, the parts of the system—particularly the crime laboratory and police officers—were connected rather than independent. As Thompson (2008) illustrated, the DNA test results were inconsistent, but the analyst who examined the samples asserted that they identified Sutton. How were inconsistent results interpreted to implicate Sutton? Thompson suggested that the DNA analyst knew of the eyewitness identification based on conversations with police officers. Thus, the analysis was interpreted according to this knowledge. In other words, "analysts can feel pressured to be 'cops in lab coats'—trying to make the science match the police department's case" (Leung, 2009). Likewise, once DNA evidence pointed to Sutton, the victim only gained confidence in her eyewitness identification (Thompson, 2008). In normal accident terms, the system parts—the lab, the police, and the victim—were not independent. They were, in fact, tightly coupled, where the actions of one part interacted with others in a mutually reinforcing way.

Perrow (1999) further described systems as either linear or complex. In linear systems, the parts work together in expected, predictable ways. An organization with a strong chain of command, for example, will operate in this way (Rison & Wittenberg, 1994). Subordinate members will follow the directions of superiors in a planned sequence (Perrow, 1999). When the system is complex, the parts either serve multiple functions or interact with many other system parts (Clarke & Short, 1993; Rijpma, 1997). A police vehicle pursuit in a rural, sparsely populated area is more consistent with linear interactions. The officer pursues the fleeing suspect but need not pay much attention to other system parts. In an urban environment, however, the system is suddenly more complex. The same pursuit is now complicated by other vehicles, pedestrians, additional physical structures, and other system elements. The officer is interacting with significantly more parts than just the fleeing offender. In this case, the risk of injury, death, or property damage has increased for all parties involved. For Perrow, normal accidents (organizational deviance) are more likely, even inevitable, when the system is both tightly coupled and complex.[2]

The interaction of multiple failures is of special interest to those who examine failures from a normal accident perspective. The sloppy DNA analysis in Josiah Sutton's case was not enough to produce the organizational deviance that was his wrongful conviction. Coupled with the less-than-optimum conditions under which the eyewitness identification occurred, the importance of the analysis becomes clearer. Similarly, a faulty prison fence that generates needless false alarms is perhaps not enough to enable escapes (Rison & Wittenberg, 1994). After all, presumably the alarm would continue to sound and correctional officers would investigate in the event of an attempted breach. If, however, the officers fail to investigate properly, ignoring alarms both real and false, then the parts of the system have interacted to increase the likelihood of an escape. Reducing the likelihood of organizational deviance, according to normal accidents theory, would involve creating greater independence and greater simplicity or linearity in organizational parts. Efforts to enhance the ability of organizations to resist failures will be discussed later. If organizational deviance is, however, inevitable, managing the problem becomes paramount.

---

[2]Loose coupling is evident in the examples of school shootings (Fox & Harding, 2005) and terrorism (Zegart, 2007). As Fox and Harding suggest, such loose coupling may allow problems to "fester unnoticed until a larger problem . . . occurs" (p. 73).

Crisis (Mis)Management

The perspectives already discussed—administrative breakdown, structural secrecy, knowledge conflict, and normal accidents—stress the precursors of organizational deviance. Whether the deviance produces limited costs or escalates into a major disaster depends, in large measure, on how officials respond in the face of crisis (Boin & Van Duin, 1995; Vaughan, 1999). Specifically, **crisis management** involves preparing for, responding to, and addressing the aftermath of organizational deviance (Boin & Van Duin, 1995). While crisis management may not allow an organization to stave off accidents, mistakes, or other types of organizational deviance, proper handling of these incidents can mitigate the harms produced by them.

Much of the crisis management literature in criminal justice has centered on riots, disturbances, and disasters. While many agencies are prepared to address significant crises (see, for example, Giblin, Schafer, & Burruss, 2009; Schafer, Heiple, Giblin, & Burruss, 2010), in other situations their lack of preparedness is readily apparent. During the New Mexico prison riot, "although the New Mexico penitentiary had a riot plan, it could not be found by the administrators (although, ironically, copies of the plan circulated freely among inmates)" (Boin & Van Duin, 1995, p. 366). Rojek and Smith (2007) found that many Mississippi and Louisiana law enforcement agencies lacked formal hurricane disaster plans when Hurricane Katrina devastated the Gulf Coast in 2005. Consequently, they developed "ad hoc" responses to address the problems they faced (p. 594). During the 1999 World Trade Organization (WTO) meeting in Washington State, the so-called "Battle in Seattle" broke out, leading to conflict between police and 40,000 to 50,000 protesters (Herbert, 2007). Events were delayed, a state of emergency was declared, curfews were established, and violence and property damage occurred (Perrine, 2001). The Seattle Police Department, in its own assessment of the response to the WTO protests, acknowledged being ill prepared for the events surrounding the meetings. In fact, police officials "put their faith in historical precedent—the Seattle tradition of peaceful protest—in assessing the needs for policing the WTO event" (Seattle Police Department, 2000, p. 4). While it is impossible to prepare fully for the range of all situations and contingencies an organization may face, organizations can make provisions related to issues such as allocating resources, designating incident commanders, and coordinating with other agencies (Boin & Van Duin, 1995). To do otherwise will waste valuable time during an actual crisis, with plans being developed as the events unfold.

Problems may also emerge with the actual response to crises. In Seattle, the police department faced challenges coordinating personnel during the WTO protests. A special squad of officers was designated to arrest key law violators during the protests but was redeployed, removing the possibility of weakening the protest leadership in the early stages of the demonstrations (Seattle Police Department, 2000). Similar coordination problems hampered responses to prison riots. Police officers were summoned to support the efforts of correctional personnel in regaining control of prisons in New York (Attica) and New Mexico (Penitentiary of New Mexico), but the chains of command for the police and prison organizations differed. As Boin and Van Duin (1995) noted, "This centralization of command in the hands of relative strangers to the site, together with the difficult cooperation between the various agencies involved in such unique events, may have contributed to a number of erroneous decisions" (p. 367). Miller (2001) asserted that the Los Angeles Police Department (LAPD) experienced **crisis paralysis** during the 1992 riots; in spite of the disturbances on the street, the argument goes, the LAPD failed to implement an effective response. In each of these examples, attempts to address or failure to address a crisis as it occurred only worked to deteriorate the situation further. It is up to leaders to accomplish the seemingly impossible task of steering the organization through crises by making sound decisions, effectively communicating goals, and providing appropriate direction (Boin & Hart, 2003).

Finally, crisis management includes the handling of the crisis after it ends. Boin and Van Duin (1995) refer to this period as an attempt at "bringing the system back to normalcy" (p. 367). If underlying conflicts and issues remain, the crisis can emerge once again. After the New Mexico prison riot, for example, prison officials attempted to improve the quality of life for inmates (one source of pre-riot complaints) by alleviating overcrowding and curtailing physical abuse by correctional staff (Useem & Kimball, 1989). In contrast, as the riots ended in the Attica prison in New York in 1971, prison officials neglected to administer timely aid to wounded inmates, only perpetuating the underlying conflict between inmates and staff (Boin & Van Duin, 1995). Law enforcement agencies in the post-Hurricane Katrina period were faced with equipment shortages because many vehicles were damaged or destroyed by the flooding (Rojek & Smith, 2007). It was incumbent on the affected departments to reconstitute their patrol fleets to be prepared for future crises; indeed, Hurricane Rita affected some of the same areas about 1 month after Hurricane Katrina. The Seattle Police Department's report reflecting on its actions during the WTO protests indicates an interest in crisis aftermath and strengthening the organization.

The crisis management approach to understanding organizational deviance is a departure from the other explanations offered earlier. While factors such as administrative breakdown and structural secrecy may cause organizational deviance, effective crisis management can minimize the costs associated with it. The converse is also true. The absence of preparation, adequate response, and attention to crisis aftermath only increases the likelihood of significant consequences: loss of life, property damage, challenges to the legitimacy of the organization, loss of the public's trust, and others. Addressing crisis management issues is part of what makes some organizations resilient or, as they are referred to in the next subsection, high-reliability organizations.

Preventing Organizational Deviance

Over the past three decades, scholars turned attention to organizations that, in spite of risky structures, complex and tightly coupled systems, and other factors that may contribute to organizational deviance, have somehow managed to avoid significant failures. These high-reliability organizations (HROs) "share the goal of avoiding altogether serious operational failure," or at least minimizing the frequency of and harm caused by their occurrence (Roberts, Bea, & Bartles, 2001, p. 70; see also LaPorte & Consolini, 1991). The term *reliability* is used to communicate the fact that HROs operate continuously, even when confronted with unexpected challenges; reliability is ensured because the organization and its members look for and deal with unexpected events (Weick, Sutcliffe, & Obstfeld, 2008).

Weick (2007) identified five characteristics of HROs (see Figure 4.1). First, he argues that HROs are preoccupied with failure. In fact, "worries about failure are what give HROs much of their distinctive quality" (Weick et al., 2008, p. 39). These organizations establish mechanisms for detecting, reporting and recording, and learning from failure (Weick, 2007). Ensuring that everyone in a prison, from the custody staff to the administrative assistants, is concerned with safety and security is indicative of an HRO. If police misconduct is treated as organizational deviance, for example, an organization can establish early warning systems to track complaints against officers to detect wrongdoing before it spirals out of control. As King (2009a) points out, when the organization's culture is such that everyone is concerned with failure, even though it is rare, officers may be more inclined to intervene when peers

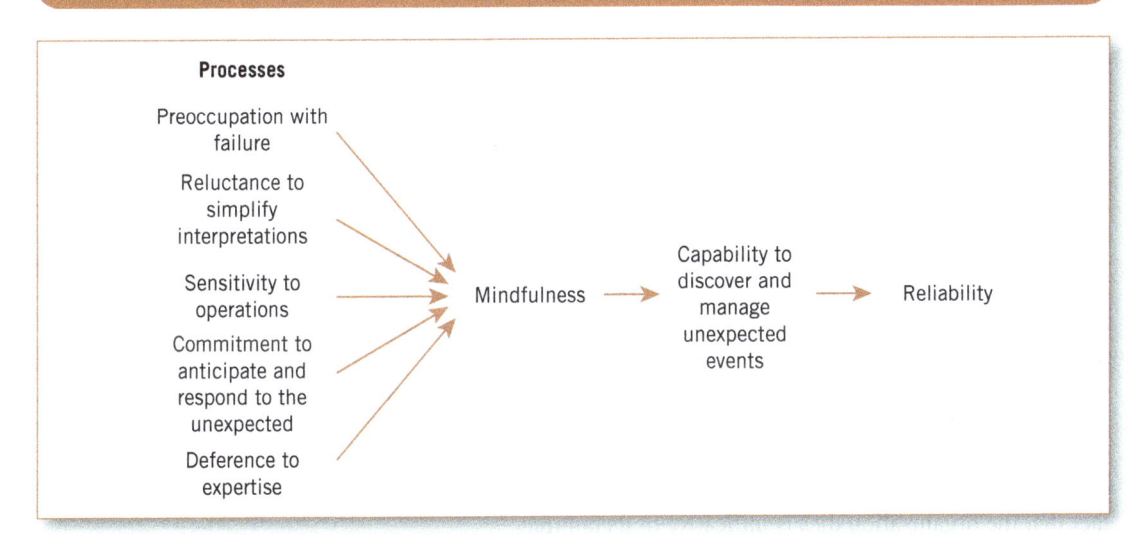

Figure 4.1 Characteristics of High-Reliability Organizations and Their Relationship to Reliability

Processes:
- Preoccupation with failure
- Reluctance to simplify interpretations
- Sensitivity to operations
- Commitment to anticipate and respond to the unexpected
- Deference to expertise

→ Mindfulness → Capability to discover and manage unexpected events → Reliability

Source: Weick et al. (2008).

engage in misconduct. More significant problems are prevented by the individuals in the best position to detect misconduct. In the case of the faulty fence alarm, an organization-wide emphasis on failure should lead individual members to quickly report and fix the fence and address guard complacency.

Second, HROs are reluctant to reduce situations to simple explanations (Weick, 2007). Such narrow views limit the range of possible causes of organizational deviance considered and lead to underestimations of the consequences of that deviance. For example, Thompson (2008) noted that much of the media attention in the Josiah Sutton case centered on the qualifications of the individual analyst who tested the samples. If the lab were to focus solely on this individual as the source of the problem—the finger-pointing fallacy—it would risk oversimplifying the true causes of concern. HROs cast a wide net, considering a range of possible causes of failure. Only then can the organization take appropriate steps to address the multiple precursors of organizational deviance.

Third, HROs are sensitive to the operations of the organization, including "the messy reality inside most systems" (Weick, 2007, p. 59). These organizations pay particular attention not only to the parts of the system but also to the interactions between the parts. Normal accidents theory, for example, illustrated that multiple failures in combination are what produce significant costs.

Two additional characteristics are important if organizational deviance should emerge. They are designed to contain the problem and limit its damage. HROs are committed to anticipating and effectively responding to the unexpected, what has been called resilience (Weick, 2007). For instance, the Federal Bureau of Prisons (BOP) transports tens of thousands of prisoners each year between prisons and to and from medical facilities. Rarely does the BOP experience an escape during the course of transport (Babb & Ammons, 1996). The BOP considers anomalous events, including adverse weather, traffic jams, and other emergencies, and uses redundant systems (additional vehicles) when necessary. By considering what could happen, HROs are ready should such events come to pass. Finally, HROs defer to the expertise within an organization (Weick, 2007). Rather than follow rigid guidelines in the event of an emergency, HROs rely on experts who can guide the organization through crises. King (2009a) extended the notion of HROs to the study of police misconduct, arguing that police officers could be "empowered to correct, coach, and reign in bad officers" (p. 774). Peers can help address officer misconduct in its early stages.

Organizational Termination

Organizational Termination Defined

Agencies experiencing organizational deviance generally recover, managing the crisis and aftermath and restoring normal operations. A second group of agencies may continue to face organizational deviance; Meyer and Zucker (1989) referred to these organizations as permanently failing for their durability in spite of significant shortcomings. Jacoby's (2002) description of the Farview State Hospital (discussed earlier) fits this category. The institution for mentally ill offenders failed to adequately treat, protect, and evaluate patients, yet the facility remained open for 25 years after these problems were first recognized. A third category of agencies, the focus of the remainder of this discussion, are those agencies that experience what has been called organizational termination, death, or disbanding. The very fact that the organization dies is indicative of its failure.

What is **organizational termination** (hereafter, used interchangeably with death and disbanding)? The answer is not straightforward. Organizational death is not determined by name changes. After all, the Phillip Morris Companies, inexorably linked with the tobacco industry, became Altria as part of a rebranding effort, but the change does not represent the termination of the company. Similarly, the Lakewood (CO) Police Department became the Lakewood Department of Public Safety in 1970 (if only temporarily), a name change that did not signify organizational death (Crank & Langworthy, 1992). A change in the functions of the organization, either through addition or deletion, also does not represent agency termination. For example, the Marion County (IN) Sheriff's Department's patrol/law enforcement responsibilities were combined, in 2007, with the Indianapolis Police Department to form the Indianapolis Metropolitan Police Department. Although the responsibilities of the sheriff's department have been scaled back (civil and jail functions, among others, remain), the original organization persists.

Herbert Kaufman (1976), a pioneer in the study of organizational death, concentrated on the boundaries of the organization as indicators of organizational death. He suggested that if the boundaries separating organizational members from those on the outside are "uninterruptedly maintained," then the organization has not experienced termination (p. 28). For Kaufman, boundaries included things such as the organization's jurisdiction and visible symbols, including uniforms. This definition has been criticized for its subjectivity, since it is largely a matter of opinion whether boundaries have been maintained (Adam, Bauer, Knill, & Studinger, 2007). Lewis (2002) expanded on the definition of termination in two ways. First, he asserted that when an organization eliminates certain functions, voluntarily or involuntarily, it continues to exist. If, however, all organizational functions are removed, the organization has no purpose or responsibility and so is effectively terminated. Second, he shared Kaufman's view that the identity of the organization matters. If an organization changes its name, location, *and* function, the original organization no longer exists. As Lewis notes, "The agency has lost its organizational identity, but its personnel and some of its functions persist" (p. 92). Finally, Kuipers and Boin (2005, as cited in Adam et al., 2007) argue that organizational death occurs "when the agency [is] abolished, merged into an organization of a distinctively different signature, or absorbed into a much larger organization, by law or executive order" (p. 227). While all these definitions feature conceptual ambiguities, they capture a range of termination scenarios, including outright disbanding as well as situations when terminated agencies are subsumed by larger organizations.

Within the criminal justice system, there is no doubt that organizations are sometimes terminated: Correctional facilities close, public defenders' officers transfer functions elsewhere, courtrooms go empty, and other agencies cease to exist (Bluestein, 2011). King (in press) found 31 Ohio municipal police agencies that disbanded during the 1990s. The Highland Park (MI) Police Department disbanded in 2001, only to reform years later (see Photo 4.1). In the state of Georgia, county-run public defender organizations were abolished in 2003 in favor of the statewide Georgia Public Defender Standards Council (GPDSC). The individual county organizations were too varied in their capacity to deliver defense services equitably across the state (Rankin, 2010). While this example clearly illustrates terminated organizations (the county offices), others are not so clear. Under the statewide system, the GPDSC planned to close Atlanta's Metro Conflict Defender Office, a group of attorneys "that handle[s] cases in which it would be a conflict of interest for the local public defender's office to represent more than one client charged with the same crime" (Goodman, 2008). Is abolishing this office indicative of agency termination? It is best considered a restructuring of the larger GPDSC. The horizontal complexity of the organization is reduced through the elimination of the defender's office. Similarly, the closure of a single prison, while seemingly an example of organizational death, may also be considered a restructuring effort; the spatial complexity of the department of corrections is reduced through the facility's closure.

The point is that determining organizational death and distinguishing it from larger organizational changes is a challenging endeavor. There is a bit more clarity in establishing the death of police organizations. A municipal organization is locally controlled and not part of a larger organization, and so does not face the same termination/restructuring debate evident elsewhere. King (in press) argued that local police agencies are terminated when they no longer are receiving funding from or are sanctioned by the local government body (e.g., city or township). *Sanctioned* means officially authorized by the government to serve as the police organization for the municipality.

▲ Photo 4.1 The Highland Park (MI) Police Department was dissolved in 2001 due to financial challenges facing the city. The county sheriff's department policed the community until a municipal agency was reformed in 2007. (Source: Dave Hogg http://www.flickr.com/photos/davehogg/222466515/)

The Resilience and Decline of Public Organizations

There is some debate about how resilient public organizations really are. Kaufman (1976) found that, of 175 federal organizations studied in 1923, 85% were still operating 50 years later. Although his research has been criticized for focusing on the beginning and end points and ignoring the creation and death of organizations between those years, the findings do demonstrate what has been referred to as the immortality of organizations (Adam et al., 2007). Other researchers have disagreed, finding evidence of mortality; Lewis (2002) found that more than half the government agencies studied, created since 1946, ceased to exist by 1997.

Regardless of the true termination rate, there is reason to believe that public organizations will survive indefinitely. Kaufman (1976) detailed a number of factors that enhance resilience. First, many organizations are created through some type of legal statute or executive order. The Department of Homeland Security is a prime example. Once the legislation is passed, often after intense debate and concessions, it becomes less likely that legislatures will repeat the process again to repeal the legislation. Moreover, to go back on an earlier decision is, in many respects, an acknowledgement that the original decision was incorrect (Daniels, 1997). Second, Kaufman argues that the budgeting process benefits public organizations. Governments do not draft budgets anew each year but, rather, consider revisions to the previous year's budget. Instead of decisions being made to fund or defund certain agencies, the general decision is usually whether to increase or decrease the organization's budget. This latter decision, critical for the organization's operations, does not generally affect its overall survival. Third, powerful interests resist agency termination. Employees depend on the organization for their livelihoods, and communities rely on public organizations for a range of services. They will challenge attempts to disband an agency.

While these factors might protect public organizations, they do not offer immunity. Multiple factors make public organizations susceptible to termination. Just as supporters want the organization to succeed, opponents want it to fail (Kaufman, 1976; Zegart, 2007). In our political system, it is common for candidates for elected office to emphasize the fact that they opposed laws, wars, and other government initiatives. Agencies thus have a built-in opposition, though it likely becomes more limited as the organization ages and opponents become more distant from the organization's creation. Public organizations, unlike their private counterparts, also have a hard time adapting to improve effectiveness (Zegart, 2007). A business executive has considerable discretion in determining how his or her company operates. A police chief, warden, or other criminal justice executive is subject to the constraints imposed by government officials, public budgets, and other actors. Consequently, public organizations have a harder time remaining competitive (Kaufman, 1976).

Organizations may also be created for symbolic reasons or in response to specific problems. As a consequence, they may no longer be needed as time passes. The Transportation Security Administration (TSA) was created two months after the 9/11 terrorist attacks, assuming the responsibilities formerly reserved to airports and individual airline operators (Krause, 2003). At some point, legislators may decide to return airline security to the private sector, potentially leading to the death of the TSA; various citizen efforts have pushed for its abolition already (Elliott, 2011). Finally, King (in press) points to the importance of crises, both fiscal and nonfiscal, in contributing to the decline of organizations. Combined, these factors are risks or hazards that influence an organization's survival prospects.

Using contemporary organizational theory (see Section III), it is possible to speculate about reasons for organizational termination. Contingency theory was predicated on the idea that organizations must adapt to the changes (contingencies) they face to remain competitive. Organizational death, then, might be explained by their inability to improve performance. In other words, "it is their failure to achieve their goals effectively and their inability to implement changes to lift themselves out of their dysfunctional habit and practices" that result in decline (Maguire & King, 2007, p. 352). King (in press) points to the small size of many disbanded organizations. These organizations may simply be unable to devote enough attention to solving community problems such as drugs, gangs, and violence, thereby forcing the local government to disband the department in favor of other alternatives (Maguire & King, 2007). Institutional theory, in contrast, was less about improving performance than it was about adhering to beliefs regarding how a department should look and operate. A police organization studied by Katz (2001) adopted a gang unit to satisfy external constituents. Smaller agencies, those most susceptible to termination, may simply not be able to make structural changes for symbolic purposes (Maguire & King, 2007). As a result, such an organization risks facing public outcry.

Replacement of Services Lost

When an organization is terminated, the services provided are generally transferred elsewhere (King, in press). In policing, the community continues to receive policing services, usually from a neighboring department, county sheriff's department, or the state police. The municipality, faced with the loss of its own department, may choose to contract for police services from other agencies (Reiss, 1992). This usually requires an agreement on the amount of time the outside agency will patrol the jurisdiction and the cost of providing such services. Alternatively, two or more agencies can merge into a single regional or metropolitan agency. The Indianapolis Metropolitan Police Department represents a merger between the law enforcement division of the Marion County Sheriff's Department and the former Indianapolis Police Department. The new agency is responsible for the entirety of Marion County, save for a few towns that retain their own law enforcement departments.

When an organization fails to the point of termination, does the community experience a significant drop in the quality of services? Some have argued that the community suffers from the loss of a municipal force. Finney (1997), for example, argued that while using alternative forms of police service delivery (contracting, mergers) may save money, it often comes from a reduction in the level of services provided. Moreover, the contracts usually specify the amount of time and personnel the agency dedicates to the jurisdiction without its own police force (Mehay, 1979). Contracts neglect outcomes such as reduced crime or reduced fear of crime. Finally, there is some evidence that the public offers greater support for smaller, independent police departments rather than larger, contracted or regional organizations (Ostrom, Parks, & Whitaker, 1973). This support is translated into effective policing, as the public is more likely to report crimes, contribute to criminal investigations, and assist the police with other matters.

These arguments show how a community may suffer from the loss of its own police department. It is possible, however, that the community may actually be better off. Larger departments can offer a degree of specialization (e.g., special units) and equipment resources (e.g., K-9 units) that are just not feasible in smaller organizations (Pachon & Lovrich, 1977). Costs for policing may actually decline, a particularly important consideration given the influence of fiscal issues on organizational death (King, in press; Mehay, 1979). A consolidated organization may also be able to more effectively tackle crime, especially those offenses that do not observe jurisdictional boundaries.

While organizations are designed to achieve their goals efficiently and effectively, sometimes their operations deviate from intended objectives. The concept of organizational deviance helps us understand when significant mistakes, accidents, disasters, and other organizational crises occur. Organizational deviance is caused by any number of factors, including administrative breakdown, structural secrecy, and crisis mismanagement. Some even argue that organizational deviance is normal or inevitable. Organizational leaders must prepare for these crises by creating high-reliability organizations. If left unaddressed, the consequences of organizational deviance may be disastrous for organizational members, nonmembers, and the organization as a whole (termination).

KEY TERMS

administrative breakdown	crisis management	organizational deviance
complexity (normal accidents)	crisis paralysis	organizational termination
coupling	normal accidents	structural secrecy

DISCUSSION QUESTIONS

1. The purpose of this section was to present organizational explanations for accidents, disasters, and other adverse events. Should we discount entirely the effects of individual actions—the finger-pointing fallacy or idea of rotten apples within the organization? Are there situations, real or hypothetical, when fault lies solely with an individual and the organizational factors discussed in this section do not play a role?

2. Normal accidents theory argues that disasters are inevitable in certain organizations. High-reliability organization theory takes a different view of organizations, positing instead that organizations can limit the possibility of disasters. Are these two theories compatible? Can the principles of high-reliability organizations offset the risks posed by complex and tightly coupled organizations?

3. If a local police department was faced with termination, how would the officers, community citizens, and government officials likely react to the news? Could their reactions be influential enough to reverse the termination decision?

WEB RESOURCES

Attica Prison riot (1971) information, including task force hearing reports, videos, and photos: http://www.talkinghistory.org/attica/

Report of the Independent Commission on the Los Angeles Police Department (Independent Commission investigation of the LAPD in the aftermath of the beating of Rodney King): http://www.parc.info/client_files/Special%20Reports/1%20-%20Chistopher%20Commision.pdf

Seattle Police Department After Action Report (post-WTO protest report): http://www.seattle.gov/police/publications/WTO/WTO_AAR.PDF

READING

Reading 6

Clarissa Freitas Dias and Michael S. Vaughn contend that dysfunction in organizations is the result of poor administration. Using a perspective known as administrative breakdown, they argue that the failure of organizations can be traced back to management's inability to effectively implement principles associated with the classical school of management. Specifically, breakdown results from the inability to clearly delineate organizational goals, the lack of an appropriate division of labor, weaknesses in control and coordination mechanisms (e.g., span of control), limited internal organizational accountability, and poor intraorganizational communication. To illustrate how these factors contribute and are relevant to the concept of administrative breakdown, the authors present a range of examples, including the police response during the 1992 Los Angeles riots, prison abuse in the Abu Ghraib prison during the Iraq War, and civil litigation against the Texas prison system. The authors conclude by stating that, although dysfunction does occur, well-administered organizations are possible. Management plays the critical role in accomplishing this task.

BUREAUCRACY, MANAGERIAL DISORGANIZATION, AND ADMINISTRATIVE BREAKDOWN IN CRIMINAL JUSTICE AGENCIES

Clarissa Freitas Dias and Michael S. Vaughn

Introduction

With the ascendancy of science, Taylor (1911/1947) merged managerial concepts and the application of empirical methods to organizational control of factory workers. Taylor advocated for efficient managers to analyze, predict, and control behavior of employees in complex organizations. Efficacious managers define laws, rules, and principles that incorporate first-class workers within the organizational framework (Freedman, 1992).

Another theorist from the traditional school, Max Weber (1946/1992) argued that bureaucracy was "the core of modern government" (Stillman, 1992, p. 37). From an idealistic organizational perspective, pure bureaucracy relates to Weber's functional, impersonal, and hierarchical system based on legal authority that operates under a system of abstract rules and pursues legitimate organizational goals (Albrow, 1970). Weber saw rationalization of bureaucratic structures as essential to social process and embraced rationality as the central ideal of organizational life (Maier, 1991).

Source: Dias, C. F., & Vaughn, M. S. (2006). Bureaucracy, managerial disorganization, and administrative breakdown in criminal justice agencies. *Journal of Criminal Justice, 34,* 543–555.

Weber's bureaucratic organization follows a structured chain of command, which facilitates accomplishment of organizational objectives (Wren, 1994), with a rigid hierarchy of offices, and formal rules that govern agency action (Stojkovic, Kalinich, & Klofas, 2003). Weberian organizations are characterized as mechanistic and formalistic, with specialized tasks, and division of labor that creates a narrow range of duties. Organization matters because bureaucratic success is related to implementation of efficient and effective organizational systems (Wilson, 1989). In the Weberian tradition, organizational systems are important because they define performance standards, outline a proper chain of command, specify the hierarchy of authority, and establish lines of communication.

Breakdown/disorganization theory was developed from numerous managerial and organizational theories and concepts. Elton Mayo's (1945) human relations school and the contextual approaches of situational leadership (Hersey & Blanchard, 1969) and contingency management (Blake & Mouton, 1964; Fielder, 1998) have made considerable scientific improvements over the basic traditional theories of Taylor and Weber. Absence of these modern theoretical perspectives within modern criminal justice agencies reflects more on the intransigent institutional nature within criminal justice institutions, rather than on the efficaciousness of contingency and situational management. Most criminal justice agencies are rigid, old-fashion, bureaucratic, paramilitaristic organizations that stick to the traditional views of DiIulio, Fayol, Taylor, Weber, and Wilson. For better or worse, criminal justice agencies remain hierarchical organizations, which is the primary focus on this article.

While there is no perfect organizational system, bureaucratic organizations can function appropriately. Fayol (1949), for example, identified several essential elements of organizations that are necessary for operational success. Well-run organizations effectuate these elements, including possession of explicit rules that control the behavior of front-line personnel, a hierarchical system of authority resulting in a chain of command, a system for delegation of authority, coupled with a proper span of control to ensure that procedures are consistently and absolutely followed, maintenance of employee expertise through continual in-service training, and a system of communication that specifies organizational roles and enumerates tasks and duties.

Failure among paramilitaristic criminal justice agencies can be traced to failure to implement human relations and/or contingency management perspectives, failure to follow Fayol's organizational elements, failure to apply the functional aspects of Taylor's scientific management, and failure to adopt Weber's legitimate bureaucratic model. Dysfunction within criminal justice agencies occurs because managers do not adhere to the traditional elements of the organization, resulting in administrative breakdown and managerial disorganization.

Not surprisingly, managers do not consider leadership the major cause of organizational breakdown and disorganization (Kappeler, 2001; Tuchman, 1984). Supervisors routinely underestimate their contribution to organizational failure (Kraska, 2004). Mundane situational factors are often overlooked by management as a cause of organizational collapse as dysfunction becomes systemic and results from years of neglect, routinization, and normalization of deviance within organizational subcultures (D. Vaughn, 1996). Many criminal justice managers reject research that shows the benefits of human relations management and situational leadership in criminal justice organizations, while sticking to the outdated and heavy-handed leadership of tradition.

Too often critics of bureaucracy confuse unworkable, bloated organizational dysfunction and collapse with bureaucracy per se (Mieczkowski, 1991). The real problem resides with poor managers within criminal justice agencies that foster a dysfunctional organizational system that is rigid and reluctant to change (Bayley, 1994), with vague and inconsistent goals, broken lines of communication (DiIulio, 1994a), and a wide span of control with an undefined hierarchy of authority (Wilson, 1989). While an extensive literature on organizational failure and collapse existed (Anheier, 1999), it had not been applied to the criminal justice workplace. Criminal justice had an abundance of case studies, however, from which the dysfunctional organizational literature was applicable (Casamayou, 1993). By analyzing over a dozen case study examples in criminal justice, this article enhances a novel theoretical perspective by combining several traditional theories of administration. What emerges is the perspective of managerial disorganization and administrative breakdown, which molds preexisting organizational perspectives into a new integrative theoretical entity.

Although the word bureaucracy is reviled in the popular culture as representing the epitome of inefficiency, red tape, turf-battles, excessive government entanglement, and waste (Johnston, 1993), properly implemented bureaucratic agencies have theoretical legitimacy (Crouch & Marquart, 1989; DiIulio, 1991; Wilson, 1989) and can function exceedingly well in post-modernistic society (Hassard & Parker, 1993). Despite the negative characteristics of bureaucratic organizations, bureaucracy remains the rule rather than the exception within criminal justice organizations. According to Johnston (1993, p. xvi), "the bureaucratic organizing model is the most common organizing model for private and public sector organizations throughout the world." When properly implemented, bureaucracy provides a positive organizational framework from which to organize criminal justice agencies. Within an open systems perspective, the agency's structure should be centered on Weber's (1994) principles and Fayol's (1949) elements of the organization. In short, bureaucracy plays a functional role, and it is indispensable even in the era of the learning organization (Drucker, 1999).

This article explains managerial collapse in criminal justice agencies from an organizational perspective. Administrative breakdown and managerial disorganization theory is used to explain organizational failure, placing success and failure of criminal justice agencies on the shoulders of criminal justice managers. Mismanagement is analyzed within criminal justice agencies, focusing on the elements of organizational life. Managers are responsible for organizational performance and outcomes, thus, both inside and outside of the agency (Mintzberg, 1989; S. Rosenberg, 1999), managers that treat criminal justice agencies as closed systems, run the risk of administrative breakdown. In organizations experiencing administrative breakdown, there is no crisis management plan in place and no flexible channels of communication have been established, and no procedures have been developed to tap into feedback mechanisms external to the organization, resulting in supervisors being incapable of recognizing the signs of imminent breakdown (M.S. Vaughn, 1996), which leads to organizational chaos and lack of resiliency in times of crises (Sheffi, 2005).

Methodology: Administrative Breakdown and Managerial Disorganization through Weber and Fayol's Elements of the Organization

Mintzberg (1989) argues that management is indispensable in well-functioning organizations; conversely, management is often the direct cause of organizations experiencing paralysis and collapse (DiIulio, 1990a, 1990b; Wilson, 1989). Similarly, administrative breakdown and managerial disorganization theory holds that dysfunctional organizations result from mismanagement. Well-functioning criminal justice bureaucracies incorporate the following: communication along a chain of command, adherence to strict accountability, and reliance on formal written communication. Conflict occurs when unclear goals create unity of direction problems, an ambiguous hierarchy of authority, a malfunctioning unity of command, and an inappropriate delegation of authority.

To understand how managers fail within a bureaucratic organization, this article underlines the extent to which mismanagement of Fayol's (1949) organizational elements can lead to breakdown and disorganization (Wren, 1994). The article uses a series of examples from case studies where criminal justice agencies have failed.

Case study vignettes highlight breakdown from over a dozen criminal justice events, including examples from both law enforcement and corrections.

With respect to law enforcement, the article addresses the New York City Police Department's corruption incident uncovered by the Mollen

Commission (City of New York Commission, 1994), the Rodney King beating within the Los Angeles Police Department (LAPD) that led to the Christopher Commission (Independent Commission, 1991), the collapse of the LAPD during the spring 1992 riots as documented by the Webster Commission (Police Foundation, 1992), the Rampart corruption incident within the LAPD (Parks, 2000), and the FBI's mishandling of the Branch Davidians at Waco, Texas (Garret, 2001). With respect to corrections, the article highlights the Texas (DiIulio, 1987) and Rhode Island (Carroll, 1998) Departments of Corrections running unconstitutional prisons, the Federal Bureau of Prisons (DiIulio, 1990c) violating inmates' constitutional rights, the U.S. military and intelligence personnel committing torture and violating international law at the Abu Ghraib prison in Iraq (Hersh, 2004), the prison riots that spun out of control in New Mexico (Useem & Kimball, 1989), and the failure of staff to protect inmates from violence at the hands of both other prisoners (Johnson v. Johnson, 2004) and abusive staff (Hudson v. McMillian, 1992).

In this article, administrative breakdown and managerial disorganization theory is analyzed through the lenses of six organizational elements that, when lacking, lead to dysfunction and bureaucratic failure: (1) goals and objectives, (2) division of labor, (3) hierarchy of authority, (4) command and control, (5) accountability, and (6) communication. In dysfunctional agencies, the mismanagement of these six elements generates a lack of task specialization and divisionalization, unclear goals that create unity of direction problems, an ambiguous hierarchy of authority, a malfunctioning unity of command, and an inappropriate delegation of authority that shifts accountability for actions taken to no one.

Goals and Objectives

Organizations are created for specific reasons, which are expressed within their mission, goals, and objectives. The broadest orientation of organizational purpose is contained within its mission. Organizational goals are more specific, whereas objectives are still even more precise. The purposes of the organization expressed within its goals and objectives "serve to guide the development of strategies, tactics, programs, tasks, policies, procedures, and rules, all of which in turn guide the behavior of members of the organization." Organizational goals and objectives must be consistent and "contribute to the accomplishment" of the overall mission of the agency (Cordner, Scarborough, & Sheehan, 2004, p. 44). Clear and concise goals minimize the unknown and clarify procedures to enable agency coherence and unity of direction (Gajduschek, 2003). Bureaucratic organizations without managerial disorganization employ unity of direction, serving to control employee behavior by reducing uncertainty, creating stability, and employing unity of purpose (Deflem, 2000).

Managers must guard against dysfunctional bureaucratic tendencies to dehumanize, alienate, and resist change (Paparozzi, 1999). Effective managers militate against the desire to maintain the status quo rather than move into uncharted waters, competing opinions to the organizational mission, and a preference for living a cloistered organizational life (Wilson, 1989). Isolation is particularly a problem within criminal justice agencies where effective managers must harness the power of bureaucratic structures to assure the delivery of relevant criminal justice services. Administrative management, whether public or private, operates in terms of making organizational work and activities match agency mission, goals, and objectives (Stover, 1995).

Managers recruit, select, and train employees to effectively implement the goals and objectives of the organization (Walker, Alpert, & Kenney, 2000). Chubb and Moe (1990) argue that effective managers are democratic leaders with clear goals. Good managers form more cohesive staff with a more developed sense of professional mission. The best leaders in criminal justice work toward congruence between organization goals and objectives (DiIulio, 1989). Effective leaders show subordinates the way and disclose to them the belief that organizational goals are achievable. To have appropriate goals in a complex criminal justice organization, it is necessary to coordinate well-flowing communication through the multiple levels of operations and decision-making authority figures (Comfort, Sungu, Johnson, & Dunn, 2001). Bush (1998) suggests that agencies are more likely to succeed when there is congruity between top managers and subordinates. In other words, when employees perceive authority figures committed to organizational objectives, goals, and procedures, they are more likely to implement those goals and succeed in their tasks.

Decision making and resource allocation are organized by a set of goals that establishes authority, priority, and planning in the organization (Zhou, 1993). Goals are important because they retain organization experience, reduce uncertainty, and channel organizational change. Goals are related to the problems of coordination and efficiency (Zhou, 1993). Weber's (1946/1992) bureaucracy is an efficiency-driven and instrument-oriented organizational form where goals, objectives, and procedures are used to establish authority, accountability, and to manage complex tasks.

During the process of change, the way supervisors manage the organization's new mission has a considerable impact over subordinates' reactions, and how subordinates respond to new goals and objectives (Smith, 1993). The Texas Department of Corrections (TDC) is an example of how change in the organization's hierarchy of authority led to role conflict. During George Beto's administration, he sustained unity of direction through a technique called Management By Walking Around (MBWA), whereas supervision and control were closely monitored by Beto (DiIulio, 1990c). After Beto's retirement, however, the next Director of the TDC was unable to maintain unity of direction, and the control model's building tender system (inmates as guards) collapsed, leading to abuses by inmates, until the federal court intervened and took over the entire Texas prison system (Crouch & Marquart, 1989).

Goal clarity reduces uncertainty (Perrow, 1986), so that subordinates who implement tasks know precisely what is expected and what they are to do. Even though procedures to carry out the goals and objectives are not completely predetermined, the reduction of ambiguity is valued among subordinates. Goal clarity is fundamental to a successful criminal justice work environment (McGregor, 1993). If the relationships between procedures, goals, and objectives are not well understood, subordinates tend to have a higher level of discretion in their decisions, consequently a higher likelihood to not accomplish the goals and objectives of the organization (Simpson, 1985).

The abuses caused by U.S. military and intelligence personnel at Abu Ghraib prison in Iraq are a well-known example of unclear dissemination of procedures, goals, and objectives that can lead subordinates to develop a subculture of deviance different from the organization (Hersh, 2004). At Abu Ghraib prison, soldiers were found committing abuses generated by unclear methods of interrogations; soldiers had conflicting objectives as to the purposes of the investigations and interrogations (Schlesinger, 2004). Despite no field supervisors to clarify goals for subordinates, soldiers were told by the then—White House Counsel and now—Attorney General of the United States, Alberto Gonzales, that prisoners in the war on terror were unlawful enemy combatants, which permitted soldiers to ignore Geneva Convention protocols (Sullivan, 2005). Those unclear goals and procedures left soldiers with a wide level of discretion, which created a culture of deviance generating the abuses against detainees. Thus, the more bureaucratic control managers have over subordinates, the more stable the organization; the more coordinated the tasks, the better the procedures, goals, and objectives are understood by subordinates (Simpson, 1985).

Division of Labor

Organizations possess line, staff, and auxiliary functions (Wren, 1994). Line personnel implement organizational goals and objectives (i.e., police officers, correctional officers, probation officers, juvenile officers). Working behind the scenes, specialized staff supports line personnel by giving advice in such areas as planning, research, and the law (i.e., police staff, attorney, and statisticians). Auxiliary functions provide logistical support for critical operational objectives, including communications, maintenance, record keeping, and human resources (i.e., dispatch–911 operations, evidence room, and prison library). Within complex bureaucratic agencies, tasks are divided on the basis of purpose, process, place, and subject (Souryal, 1995). Employee selection based on competence, education, and merit is positively related to lack of administrative breakdown and managerial disorganization to the extent that these agencies employ officers who are stable, meritorious, and engage in fewer rule violations (Evans & Rauch, 1999). Criminal justice agencies not experiencing administrative breakdown are free from political meddling, allowing independent functioning on the basis of merit, training, specialization, and expertise (Deflem, 2000).

Through job specialization and division of labor, the functional manager trains subordinates and plans tasks that reduce risk to an acceptable level (Bernard, 1938). Even though managers may not be able to prevent crises, specialization and divisionalization of labor can reduce considerably the level or risk associated with organizational disasters. Specialization should bring efficiency in performance, which depends on the quality of education and training. Subordinates in criminal justice organizations should be highly specialized when performing complex, uncertain, and unpredictable tasks (Nass, 1986). This problem in criminal justice exists when police use coercive force against suspects (Bittner, 1970) or when correctional officers use force against prisoners (Hudson v. McMillian, 1992; Whitley v. Albers, 1986). In these situations, the constitutional limits established by the courts are specific and elaborate (Graham v. Conner, 1989; Tennessee v. Garner, 1985). Specialization and divisionalization of labor "focus on understanding the law and mastering some of the technical arts" required to perform the job (Moore, 1994, p. 209).

Training and specialization of labor improve organizational tasks (Houston, 1995). Well-trained subordinates are better able to effectively implement organizational goals. Work specialization promotes skill, and accuracy, which increases output. Specialized and trained subordinates can respond faster to problems involving organizational crisis. Managers should be aware that specialized subordinates are less liable when sued in civil litigation (M.S. Vaughn, Cooper, & del Carmen, 2001). Training and specialization can reduce employees' misbehavior (Walker et al., 2000) on and off-duty (M.S. Vaughn & Coomes, 1995).

An example of administrative breakdown due to untrained and nonspecialized subordinates is Johnson v. Johnson (2004), a case in which an inmate sued Texas prison officials for letting other inmates turn him into a sexual slave. Johnson, a homosexual inmate, was sexually abused over the course of eighteen months, and sold from one inmate gang to another for the purpose of rape. Due to Johnson's sexual orientation, Texas prison classification regulations mandated his placement into the vulnerable inmate category, and dictated that he be housed in protective custody. Despite the regulation, Johnson was placed into the general population, where he was abused. Officers were not trained to identify and protect vulnerable inmates. Training provides officers the ability to recognize inmates who are subject to abuse, or who are potential victims of a sexual assault (M.S. Vaughn, 1996). Trained officers can recommend to superiors which inmates to segregate, punish, or to refer for treatment (Eigenberg, 2000). Training improves officers' skills, enabling them to be aware of the prison environment. Thus, specialized and trained officers may prevent rapes, or at least, make sure that victims get adequate services.

In bureaucratic organizations, each individual subordinate does not perform every agency task. As a result, specialization occurs, tasks are implemented one at a time, and job assignments are divided into logical, homogeneous units so different individuals can specialize (Stover, 1995). Lack of appropriate division of labor coupled with poor training can result in a lack of specialization and an organization suffering administrative breakdown and managerial disorganization.

Hierarchy of Authority

The principle of authority asserts that there is a chain of command that stretches throughout the organization. Weber (1946/1992, p. 40) argues that graded authority means "a firmly ordered system of subordination in which there is a supervision of lower offices by the higher ones." Within Weber's perspective, this type of rational legal authority was necessary to implement organizational rules. The chain of command in militaristic or quasimilitaristic organizations demands exact obedience to orders (Souryal, 1995). Effective control over subordinates' conduct is enhanced by close supervision. Discipline is achieved by fixing accountability and centralizing authority (DiIulio, 1994a). Well-functioning agencies operating with rational legal bureaucratic authority are able to control organizational deviance through the hierarchy of authority (Diggins, 1996).

Authority resides in the position that rests within the hierarchy, but not in the person holding the position. Authority "is a form of domination that provides the superior with unquestioned obedience" (Nass, 1986, p. 62). This is possible when subordinates recognize the legitimacy of superiors' commands. Bernard (1938) referred to this concept as the zone of indifference, where subordinates accept the authority and orders of their supervisors. Bureaucracy reduces discretion when subordinates follow policies, procedures, and orders. Little ambiguity in the chain of command leads to loyalty, the inability to challenge authority, and employment of subordinates who support the legality of the rules (Nass, 1986).

A dysfunctional hierarchy of authority can predict organizational breakdown. Lack of upper-level supervision leads to an inappropriate chain of command within the rank structure, which increases risk of administrative breakdown and managerial disorganization. The Los Angeles Police Department serves as an example of an agency with a dysfunctional hierarchy of authority. According to the Christopher Commission (Independent Commission, 1991), the hierarchical structure of the LAPD practices diffusion of responsibility, which means that no one is accountable for subordinates' behavior. The Christopher Commission said the LAPD's hierarchy failed to control abusive police practices because it lacked centralized authority. In the absence of one chain of command, officers reported to various supervisors, resulting in divergent orders given and conflicting messages on organizational purpose.

According to a follow-up report (Bobb, Epstein, Miller, & Abascal, 1996) that evaluated the LAPD five years after the Christopher Commission, the LAPD still lacked a system of centralized risk management, leading to a fragmented hierarchy of authority with respect to Internal Affairs reports, Use of Force Board reports, and Robbery–Homicide Division officer-involved shootings reports. Risk Management, Legal Affairs, and the Office of Operations and Behavioral Sciences were out of the loop and reported to a different hierarchy. This diverse chain of communication, as noted by the Christopher Commission and the five-year follow-up report, led to inadequate supervision and management of police department problems. An undefined hierarchy of authority lacks appropriate channels of communication, fragments unity of command, and makes specific tasks difficult to delegate. These observations were confirmed in March 2000 "when the LAPD's Board of Inquiry released its report on the Rampart corruption incident, admitting that the Department still ignores civilian complaints about officer misconduct" (Parks, 2000; M.S. Vaughn et al., 2001, p. 20).

To have a consistent hierarchy of authority, trust should be built between managers and workers. "Legitimate 'authority' is the ability to have people anticipate interests and act accordingly without having to rely on explicit communications and the concomitant threat of sanctions" (Feeley, 1973, p. 225). Loyalty, or lack thereof, to the organization before a crisis occurs has profound implications on how the organization will resolve a crisis (Souryal & McKay, 1996). Lack of trust between supervisors and subordinates results in a split between "street cops" and "management cops" (Reuss-Ianni, 1983).

Carroll (1998) discussed a dysfunctional hierarchy of authority in which democratic prison management allowed inmates to participate in policymaking. As a result, Rhode Island inmates were encouraged to participate in decision making, which led them to voice their concerns in unrealistic and abusive ways. Organized crime pervaded the Rhode Island prisoners' union. Completely outside the legitimate hierarchy of authority, prison administrators relied on the organized crime bosses and the prisoners' union to control inmate behavior, which led to a number of abuses and ultimately caused a federal court to take over the prison. Inappropriate delegation of authority by prison administrators led to a nonfunctional chain of command with accountability problems. Carroll (1998) shows that prisons cannot be isolated from community stakeholders, and must respond appropriately to external environments.

Command and Control

The concept of command and control collapses the organizational principles of unity of command and span of control. Unity of command embodies the idea that subordinates report to one supervisor or get their orders from only one boss (Souryal, 1995). Unity of command is closely related to authority structures within the chain of command. The hierarchy of authority is important because it is the superior who transmits the rules that guide subordinates' actions within organizations (Houston, 1995). In other words, clear authority structures result in appropriate delegation of authority, with clear lines of accountability established for actions taken.

The span of control is the "maximum number of subordinates at a given position that a supervisor can supervise effectively" (Souryal, 1995, p. 33). The span of control depends upon the activities of subordinates. The more uncertain and disturbing the situation, the narrower the span of control should be. Managers have difficulty supervising a large number of subordinates during a crisis situation (Ulmer, 2001). To manage crisis situations effectively, managers must rely on the obedience of subordinates. The ultimate task of managers is to provide leadership so that subordinates will implement the goals of the organization, and highlight each person's specific strengths within the agency (S. Rosenberg, 1999). Supervisors must have subordinates that operate within a comfortable zone of indifference, in which orders are accepted without question (Bernard, 1938).

A narrow span of control gives supervisors within the hierarchy of authority more control over crisis situations and faster feedback from subordinates to respond to critical situations. A narrow span of control also provides supervisors with fewer organizational levels, resulting in a more effective channel of communication. Skill levels of employees also influence the amount of control managers must have over subordinates in a crisis situation, where the more specialized the subordinates, the wider the span of control (Souryal, 1995).

The greater the number of subordinates a manager supervises, the less influence he or she will be able to impose to restrict arbitrariness and lawless procedures (N. Rosenberg, 1976). Consequently, subordinates are more difficult to influence in a bureaucracy with a wide span of control. In contrast, a small span of control leads to more influence over subordinates, greater efficiencies, and less tendency for subordinates to create pernicious subcultures (Maguire & Katz, 2002).

Criminal justice subordinates need supervision and discipline to ensure that rules and procedures are followed (Charles, 2000). According to DiIulio (1990a, 1994b), successful implementation of a clear unity of command and a narrow span of control was demonstrated by the Federal Bureau of Prisons (BOP) administrator Norman Carlson. Carlson was aware that to reinforce command and control, he needed to strengthen his control over regional directors by establishing unit management throughout the five regions of the BOP. Under this framework, teams of security staff and counselors were given authority over a specific prison wing and held responsible for the quality of life therein; they reported to the various regional directors, who reported to Washington. Unit managers served as sub-wardens who were responsible for order, service, and amenities, which included arranging sanitation, tracking inmates' activities, and identifying release dates. Carlson's unit management served to narrow the span of control and clarify the unity of command (DiIulio, 1990b). By following Carlson's successful management in the BOP, DiIulio (1990a) stresses that there is no contradiction between strict administrative controls and tight discipline, and the provision of basic amenities and life-enhancing programs to prisoners. In other words, a flexible span of control tailored to the situational contingencies faced by criminal justice managers and a strict unity of command promote discipline, authority, and efficiency (Krygier, 1979).

In contrast, an example of administrative breakdown where subordinates had more than one command was the LAPD during the riots of May 1992 that were sparked after the acquittal of the officers who beat the motorist Rodney King. No one in the LAPD took responsibility for stopping the beginning stages of the riot. No specific authority figure was identified from which officers were to receive orders; no supervisor was identified in the hierarchy to which officers would report (Police Foundation, 1992).

While the span of control and unity of command principles focus on effective supervision, each focuses on lower-level supervision of line personnel. Administrative breakdown and managerial disorganization theory assumes that a lack of effective front-line supervision increases agency dysfunction. Agencies experiencing managerial disorganization routinize inadequate supervision, so that dysfunction becomes the norm. These organizations normalize and systematize dysfunction in response to conditions that threaten organizational stability (Susa, 1997).

Dysfunctional bureaucracy is characterized by rigidity and a waning ability "to adjust, to experiment, and to innovate" (Crozier, 1967, p. 190) because of excessive centralization of command structures (Mieczkowski, 1991). In other words, bureaucracies fail because they close themselves off to external influences, ignore internal disciplinary problems, and are guided mainly by their own agency subcultures that may not conform to the rule of law. According to von Mises (1969), dysfunctional bureaucracy is conservative, deliberately avoiding innovation and improvement, and is averse to reform.

Accountability

Public administration recognizes the principle of correspondence, in which managers are accountable for actions within their organizations (Stover, 1995). Without managers' abdicating their accountability, they delegate tasks down the hierarchy of authority. The subordinate who receives the delegated task is responsible for task implementation. The supervisor who delegated the task remains ultimately accountable to the agency (Geller & Swanger, 1995). Accountability relates to the recognition and adherence to duties. Managers within well-functioning organizations recognize accountability cannot be delegated; however, in agencies experiencing administrative breakdown, supervisors engage in status consciousness, saying "It's not my problem," passing the buck to another organizational entity.

Managers who are not accountable foster an organizational subculture that creates the conditions where subordinates engage in misconduct (Walker et al., 2000). A sheriff who rapes a criminal suspect, for example, creates a subculture of deviance within his agency, leading deputies to engage in traffic stops to meet women, run license plates to get females' addresses, and use the jail to engage in sex. Dysfunction becomes normalized, and violating suspects' rights become normal operating procedure (Eschholz & Vaughn, 2001). Dysfunction and breakdown occur when officers do not recognize and accept their legal responsibilities. Correctional officers, for example, must recognize their duty to protect prisoners from committing suicide (Wever v. Lincoln County, 2004), police officers must recognize their duty not to abandon vulnerable potential crime victims (M.S. Vaughn, 1994), and parole officers should supervise their parolees appropriately (Cromwell, del Carmen, & Alarid, 2002). Failure to accept these duties results in managerial disorganization and administrative breakdown.

Decision making is a fluid concept, and to ensure accountability, criminal justice supervisors must assess environmental factors during the decision-making process. Criminal justice agencies historically have ignored external environments (Walker, 2001), leading to a lack of accountability. Without input from external environments, criminal justice agencies frequently lose touch with the political, economic, social, and legal realities within which they operate. When this occurs, external actors intervene within criminal justice bureaucracies to ensure accountability (Independent Commission, 1991). Stated differently, agencies that do not institute accountability systems to prevent managerial disorganization and administrative breakdown will have accountability forced upon them by external environments (City of New York Commission, 1994), including the courts and civilian review boards.

As mentioned above, managers must recognize that the criminal justice system exists within an open system environment. According to O'Loughlin (1990), organizations can increase accountability when making decisions, by limiting managerial discretion. External environments recognize two types of bureaucratic decision making: discretionary and nondiscretionary. Discretionary decision making is reserved for the criminal justice bureaucrat alone and involves minor decisions. Nondiscretionary decision making involves criminal justice managers receiving input from external forces. The more important a decision made by a manager, the less discretion the manager possesses. To ensure accountability, important decisions must be nondiscretionary, meaning that significant input from external environments limits the discretion of criminal justice supervisors.

Due to lack of competition and the monopoly that criminal justice has on the growing crime industry (Christie, 2000), dysfunctional bureaucratic organizations have flourished in an insular world without regard to influence from courts, legislatures, politicians, or public officials (Johnston, 1993; Rosen, 2005). It is not necessarily market forces that change criminal justice agencies. In fact, because of the closed system view of dysfunctional bureaucracies, criminal justice agencies shut themselves off from the public (they become insular), and this causes them to function with impunity and outside of the rule of law until they are revealed through scandal, judicial intervention, governmental investigation, and/or commission reports (City of New York Commission, 1994; Independent Commission, 1991). Without the pressure of external environments, dysfunctional bureaucratic criminal justice agencies are not concerned with customer service, employee satisfaction, or the rule of law. Successful organizational bureaucracy maintains and enhances the network of outside alliances, building trust, unity of command, specialized staff, and an identifiable hierarchy of authority, all linked in an efficient channel of communication.

Although all organizations possess problems (Perrow, 1997), bureaucratic agencies experiencing managerial disorganization and administrative breakdown have a poor reputation because managers have amassed unilateral power over their subordinates and over centralized power structures, failed to economize on employees' creativity, institutionalized inequities in status and income, and failed to devise effective communication structures (Dahl & Lindblom, 1976). In fact, according to DiIulio (1994a, p. 279), dysfunctional bureaucracies tend to "attract, hire, retain, and promote persons who are highly disposed to shirk, subvert, or steal on the job." DiIulio (1994a, p. 279) argues that some dysfunctional government bureaucracies are prone to "repel people who want meaningful job challenges, not just job security, and who desire extra rewards for extra efforts rather than small but certain pay increases governed by length of service or time in position."

Communication

Communication is the most important organizational element because it is necessary for all other elements to function. Within organizational theory, the principle of definition clearly says that office duties, powers, and responsibilities are written and clearly defined (Stover, 1995). Weber (1946/1992) maintained that office management is based on written documents or files that communicate the essential functions of the job. Effective communication is the key to achieving objectives and goals. Leaders must clearly communicate the goals of the organization so subordinates can accomplish agency objectives and reach agency goals, and know what is valued, expected, and rewarded. This component of successful managerial practice is the supervisors' ability to communicate policies and procedures effectively with line, staff, and auxiliary personnel. Managers must also shape communication strategies continually throughout the organization—both horizontally and vertically (Senese, 1991). Organizational values are developed over time through consistent communicative leadership, which plays an important role in identifying and developing those values that model organizational behavior.

Whether in written or verbal form, organizational communication results in information exchange among line, staff, and management personnel (Stojkovic et al., 2003). The structure of an organization, its management, and the exercise of its leadership are most evident in communication. Understanding the influence of communication from top administrators, to middle supervisors, to the line staff is crucial for assessing organizational success (Geller & Swanger, 1995). Although upper-level administrators are concerned with communicating to subordinates through middle managers, they empower middle management to disseminate directives and successfully implement goals and objectives. Middle managers convey organizational purpose through a consistent unity of direction and opportunity for participatory input. These supervisors provide the communication linkage which fosters organization vision, familiarity with bureaucratic mission, and clarity of purpose.

Senese (1991) contends that jailers are the most visible and active representatives of the criminal justice system within the jail on a daily basis, meaning that jailers have direct impact on how jails operate and serve as communication conduits for line and supervisory personnel. Jailers manage a process of subtle communication, in which line correctional officers serve as liaison between upper jail management and the inmates.

The lynchpin of all activities within bureaucratic organizations is effective communication structures. To effectively reach subordinates and make them follow the rules, managers should communicate clearly and precisely. Although many problems exist in bureaucratic organizations, lack of effective communication appears to be the more severe. Without effective communication organizations cannot properly function. Ineffective communication leads to a series of other problems, such as a lack of command and control, failure to adhere to the hierarchy of authority, failure to implement objectives and goals, and finally breakdown and disorganization of the entire bureaucratic system. An employee's investment in organizational goals determines how communication systems are perceived and implemented within complex bureaucracies (Harlos, 2001).

When managerial disorganization occurs, it is frequently discovered that communication deficiencies that led to administrative breakdown were longstanding, and officers frequently ignored warning signs (Garret, 2001). Dysfunctional organizations do not communicate problems effectively through the organizational hierarchy. For months or years prior to a crisis, problem behaviors and management failures are not appropriately communicated throughout the organizational hierarchy. In dysfunctional agencies, the flow of communication is not clearly identified in written procedures and is not specified in policy manuals, but more importantly, it is not implemented throughout the agency in any meaningful way.

How agencies respond to organizational crises depends more on actions made before the disruption than on the actions taken during the crisis itself. Agencies not experiencing managerial disorganization and administrative breakdown have constructed, precrisis, flexible communications channels that respond in a timely manner to organizational threats (Sheffi, 2005). As an example, take the FBI's handling in 1993 of the Branch Davidian compound at Waco, Texas. Attorney General Janet Reno and FBI Director

William Sessions were not speaking to one another during the Waco incident, the epitome of administrative breakdown and managerial disorganization. The lack of communication between Reno and Sessions highlights the importance of building a solid channel of communication during precrisis management, so that when a crisis erupts a successful crisis plan can be implemented with open and free communication to avoid organizational breakdown and disorganization (Ulmer, 2001). To avoid organizational breakdown and disorganization, managers must plan for the organization's complex communication relationships. In other words, establishing solid command and control, strong communication channels, and positive valued leaders before crises erupt may influence the amount of damage the organization may suffer, and how much time and effort is going to be needed to recover from the crisis (Ulmer, 2001).

In a complex organization such as the FBI, middle managers must be incorporated so upper-level managers are able to reach low-level subordinates. FBI Special Agent in Charge (SAC) Jeff Jamar, the on-scene commander at Waco, served as the middle manager. Jamar's job was to disseminate operational directives from Washington to front-line officers within the Hostage Rescue Team (HRT) and the negotiators (psychologists) on the scene. There was no clarity of purpose or unity of direction and because there were conflicting goals, Jamar gave conflicting orders to line personnel. The Waco incident is a classic example of the failure of management to communicate effectively with lower level subordinates.

Conclusion

This article offers a novel theoretical approach to explain managerial disorganization and administrative breakdown in criminal justice agencies. Explaining organizational failure through breakdown and disorganization theory, which assesses agency success on criminal justice managers, this article joins the call for a return to the study of management as a key variable in criminal justice scholarship

(DiIulio, 1990a, 1990b, 1991, 1994a, 1994b; Wilson, 1989). Successful bureaucratic agencies are exemplified by managers with effective communication skills who implement a functional span of control within the hierarchy of authority, practice strict accountability, rely on a mix of formal written and informal verbal communication, operate with clear goals and objectives, and delegate appropriate tasks to subordinates. While outside the scope of this current article, successful criminal justice agencies may also use elements of Elton Mayo's human relations theory and the contextual approaches of situational and contingency management (for a detailed discussion, see Houston, 1995).

Poor management results in breakdown and disorganization within criminal justice agencies. Managers who ignore warning signs (Boin & Van Duin, 1995)—lack of task specialization and divisionalization, unclear goals, inappropriate delegation of authority that shifts accountability (O'Loughlin, 1990), distorted lines of communication (Garret, 2001), and a malfunctioning unity of command—fail to anticipate risk and demonstrate inability to recover quickly in response to threat (Comfort et al., 2001). Managers fail organizationally when they mismanage Fayol and Weber's elements of the organization, which can lead to breakdown and disorganization of the entire system. Agencies experiencing managerial breakdown and administrative disorganization are frequently plagued with systemic patterns of normalized deviance (Weick, 1993).

Structural dysfunction fosters subordinates' isolation from legitimate authority. Managers construe an environment that can lead subordinates to ignore organizational goals and objectives. Operational dysfunction is the result or absence of supervisors, consequently no one to report to, undefined chain of command, and ambiguous unity of command, which results in no one from which to receive orders (Weick, 1993). Organizations are dysfunctional because managers are not accountable. Dysfunctional agencies lack the structure or operational capacity to deal with problem behavior or organizational collapse, so there is no bureaucratic management structure in place to respond appropriately to a problem (Weick, 1976).

During crisis situations, organizations experiencing breakdown and disorganization are incapable of being managed effectively. Dysfunctional agencies have no unity of command, little hierarchy of authority, a great deal of employee autonomy, enhanced individual employee discretion, little supervision and accountability, planned unresponsiveness to society problems, and operate with a wide span of control. Dysfunctional agencies do not focus on data driven activities; subordinates within dysfunctional agencies do not operate with unity of direction or a set of coherent agency goals (Maguire & Katz, 2002).

The way public organizations are managed has a significant bearing on the quality of system performance (DiIulio, 1989). DiIulio (1987) posits that the quality of prison life depends mainly on the quality of management.

He asserts that prisons managed by a strong and stable team of like-minded executives, structured in a paramilitary, security-driven, bureaucratic fashion, and coordinated proactively in conjunction with the demands of relevant outside actors including legislators, judges, and community leaders had higher levels of order, safety, security, and service than prisons managed in the absence of performance indicators. Similarly, Useem and Kimball's (1989) analysis of prison riots found that breakdown in security procedures contributed to riots, including the absence of routine counting and frisking of inmates, the lack of a system to control contraband, and the failure of guards to routinely search prisoners' cells. Useem and Kimball (1989) concluded that conditions of confinement may lead to prison riots, but administrative breakdown and disorganization makes their frequency and intensity more severe.

Well-functioning organizations exist within bureaucratic structures as long as managers effectively implement Weber and Fayol's organizational principles. Managers of bureaucratic agencies are successful as long as they create specifically defined meaningful work opportunities for their employees, train their subordinates in detail, and establish goals and objectives to clarify the unity of direction. Successful bureaucracies create a welldefined hierarchy of authority, operate a well-functioned unity of command, and appropriately delegate tasks so as to maintain accountability for actions taken.

Future research should focus on the extent to which bureaucratic criminal justice organizations operate within a human relations framework (Miller & Braswell, 1997). Researchers should explore the degree to which an organizations' bureaucratic structure fosters change or serves to be an impediment to change. Conventional wisdom has decried bureaucratic agencies as relics of the past, completely inefficient and useless in today's modern world. Even so, bureaucratic management systems are the norm, not the exception, in criminal justice agencies in the twenty-first century. Given the paramilitaristic nature of most criminal justice agencies, more criminal justice research needs to focus on management as an explanation for organizational failure and dysfunction. This perspective needs to be applied to a variety of criminal justice agencies, including law enforcement, community and institutional corrections, juvenile justice, as well as the criminal and civil courts.

References

Albrow, M. (1970). *Bureaucracy*. London: Pall Mall Press.

Anheier, H. (Ed.). (1999). *When things go wrong: Organizational failures and breakdowns*. Thousand Oaks, CA: Sage.

Bayley, D. H. (1994). *Police for the future*. New York: Oxford University Press.

Bernard, C. I. (1938). *The functions of the executive*. Cambridge, MA: Harvard University Press.

Bittner, E. (1970). *The functions of the police in modern society: A review of background factors, current practices, and possible role models*. Chevy Chase, MD: National Institute of Mental Health.

Blake, R. R., & Mouton, J. S. (1964). *The managerial grid*. Houston, TX: Gulf.

Bobb, M. J., Epstein, M. H., Miller, N. H., & Abascal, M. A. (1996). *Five years later: A report to the Los Angeles Police Commission on the Los Angeles Police Department's implementation of Independent Commission recommendations*. Los Angeles: Los Angeles Police Commission.

Boin, R. A., & Van Duin, M. J. (1995). Prison riots as organizational failures: A managerial perspective. *Prison Journal*, 75, 357–379.

Bush, T. (1998). Attitudes towards management by objectives: An empirical investigation of self-efficacy and goal commitment. *Scandinavian Journal of Management*, 14(3), 289–299.

Carroll, L. (1998). *Lawful order: A case study of correctional crisis and reform*. New York: Garland.

Casamayou, M. H. (1993). *Bureaucracy in crisis: Three Mile Island, the shuttle Challenger, and risk assessment*. Boulder, CO: Westview Press.

Charles, M. T. (2000). Accidental shooting: An analysis. *Journal of Contingencies and Crisis Management*, 8(3), 151–160.

Christie, N. (2000). *Crime control as industry: Towards Gulags Western style* (3rd ed.). London: Routledge.

Chubb, J. E., & Moe, T. M. (1990). *Politics, markets, and America's schools*. Washington, DC: Brookings.

City of New York Commission to Investigate Allegations of Police Corruption and the Anti-Corruption Practices of the Police Department. (1994). *Commission report* [Mollen Commission]. New York: Author.

Comfort, L. K., Sungu, Y., Johnson, D., & Dunn, M. (2001). Complex system in crisis: Anticipation and resilience in dynamic environments. *Journal of Contingencies and Crisis Management*, 9(3), 144–158.

Cordner, G. W., Scarborough, K. E., & Sheehan, R. (2004). *Police administration* (5th ed.). Cincinnati, OH: Anderson.

Cromwell, P. F., del Carmen, R. V., & Alarid, L. F. (2002). *Community-based corrections* (5th ed.). Belmont, CA: Wadsworth.

Crouch, B. M., & Marquart, J. W. (1989). *An appeal to justice: Litigated reform of Texas prisons*. Austin: University of Texas Press.

Crozier, M. (1967). *Bureaucratic phenomenon*. Chicago: University of Chicago Press.

Dahl, R., & Lindblom, C. (1976). *Politics, economics, and welfare: Planning and politico-economic systems resolved into basic social processes*. New York: Harper and Row.

Deflem, M. (2000). Bureaucratization and social control: Historical foundations of international police cooperation. *Law and Society Review*, 34, 739–778.

Diggins, J. P. (1996). America's two visitors: Tocqueville and Weber. *Tocqueville Review*, 17(2), 165–182.

DiIulio, J. J. (1987). *Governing prisons: A comparative study of correctional management*. New York: Free Press.

DiIulio, J. J. (1989). Recovering the public management variable: Lessons from schools, prisons, and armies. *Public Administration Review*, 49(2), 127–133.

DiIulio, J. J. (1990a). Prisons that work: Management is the key. *Federal Prisons Journal*, 1(4), 7–14.

DiIulio, J. J. (1990b). Leadership and social science. *Journal of Policy Analysis and Management*, 9(1), 116–126.

DiIulio, J. J. (1990c). The evolution of executive management in the Federal Bureau of Prisons. In J. W. Roberts (Ed.), *Escaping prison myths: Selected topics in the history of federal corrections* (pp. 159–174). Washington, DC: American University Press.

DiIulio, J. J. (1991). Understanding prisons: The new old penology. *Law and Social Inquiry*, 16, 65–99.

DiIulio, J. J. (1994a). Principled agents: The cultural bases of behavior in a federal government bureaucracy. *Journal of Public Administration Research and Theory*, 4(3), 277–318.

DiIulio, J. J. (1994b). Managing a barbed-wire bureaucracy: The impossible job of corrections commissioner. In E. C. Hargrove & J.C. Glidewell (Eds.), *Impossible jobs in public management* (pp. 49–71). Lawrence: University Press of Kansas.

Drucker, P. F. (1999). *Management challenges for the 21st century*. New York: Harper Business.

Eigenberg, H. M. (2000). Correctional officers and their perception of homosexuality, rape, and prostitution in male prison. *Prison Journal*, 80, 415–433.

Eschholz, S., & Vaughn, M. S. (2001). Police sexual violence and rape myths: Civil liability under section 1983. *Journal of Criminal Justice*, 29, 389–405.

Evans, P., & Rauch, J. E. (1999). Bureaucracy and growth: A crossnational analysis of the effects of Weberian state structures on economic growth. *American Sociological Review*, 64, 748–765.

Fayol, H. (1949). *General and industrial management*. London: Pitman.

Feeley, M. M. (1973). Power, impact, and the Supreme Court. In T. L. Becker & M.M. Feeley (Eds.), *The impact of Supreme Court decisions: Empirical studies* (2nd ed., pp. 218–229). New York: Oxford University Press.

Fielder, F. E. (1998). The leadership situation: A missing factor in selecting and training managers. *Human Resources Management Review*, 8, 335–350.

Freedman, D. H. (1992). Is management still a science? *Harvard Business Review*, 70(6), 26–38.

Gajduschek, G. (2003). Bureaucracy: Is it efficient? Is it not? Is that the question? Uncertainty reduction: An ignored element of bureaucratic rationality. *Administration and Society*, 34, 700–723.

Garret, T. M. (2001). The Waco, Texas, ATF raid, and Challenger launch decision: Management, judgment, and the knowledge analytic. *American Review of Public Administration*, 31(3), 66–86.

Geller, W. A., & Swanger, G. (1995). *Managing innovation in policing: The untapped potential of the middle manager*. Washington, DC: Police Executive Research Forum.

Harlos, K. P. (2001). When organizational voice systems fail: More on the deaf-ear syndrome and frustration effects. *Journal of Applied Behavioral Science*, 37, 324–342.

Hassard, J., & Parker, M. (Eds.). (1993). *Postmodernism and organizations*. London: Sage.

Hersey, P., & Blanchard, K. H. (1969). Life cycle theory of leadership. Training and Development Journal, 23, 26–34.

Hersh, S. M. (2004). *Chain of command: The road from 9/11 to Abu Ghraib*. London: Allen Lane.

Houston, J. (1995). *Correctional management*. Chicago: Nelson Hall.

Independent Commission on the Los Angeles Police Department. (1991). Report [Christopher Commission]. Los Angeles: Author.

Johnston, K. B. (1993). *Busting bureaucracy: How to conquer your organization's worst enemy*. Homewood, IL: Business One Irwin.

Kappeler, V. E. (2001). *Critical issues in police civil liability* (3rd ed.). Prospect Heights, IL: Waveland.

Kraska, P. K. (2004). *Theorizing criminal justice: Eight essential orientations*. Long Grove, IL: Waveland.

Krygier, M. (1979). Weber, Lenin, and the reality of socialism. In E. Kamenka & M. Krygier (Eds.), *Bureaucracy: The career of a concept* (pp. 64–66). London: Edward Arnold.

Maguire, E. R., & Katz, C. M. (2002). Community policing, loose coupling, and sensemaking in American police agencies. *Justice Quarterly*, 19, 503–536.

Maier, M. (1991). We have to make a management decision: Challenger and the dysfunction of corporate masculinity. In P. Prasad, A. J. Mills, M. Elmes, & A. Prasad (Eds.), *Managing the organizational melting pot: Dilemmas of workplace diversity* (pp. 226–254). Thousand Oaks, CA: Sage.

Mayo, E. (1945). *The social problems of an industrial civilization*. Boston: Harvard University, Division of Research, Graduate School of Business Administration.

McGregor, E. B. (1993). Toward a theory of public management success. In B. Bozeman (Ed.), *Public management: The state of the art* (pp. 173–185). San Francisco: Jossey-Bass.

Mieczkowski, B. (1991). *Dysfunctional bureaucracy: A comparative and historical perspective*. Landham, MD: University Press of America.

Miller, L., & Braswell, M. (1997). *Human relations and police work* (4th ed.). Prospect Heights, IL: Waveland.

Mintzberg, H. (1989). *Mintzberg on management: Inside our strange world of organizations*. New York: Free Press.

Moore, M. H. (1994). Policing: Deregulating or redefining accountability? In J. J. DiIulio (Ed.), *Deregulating the public service: Can government be improved?* (pp. 198–235). Washington, DC: Brookings.

Nass, C. I. (1986). Bureaucracy, technical expertise, and professionals: A Weberian approach. *Sociological Theory*, 4(1), 61–70.

O'Loughlin, M. G. (1990). What is bureaucratic accountability and how can we measure it? *Administration and Society*, 22, 275–302.

Paparozzi, M. A. (1999). Leadership: An antidote to bureaucracy and a remedy for public disheartenment. *Corrections Management Quarterly*, 3(1), 36–41.

Parks, B. C. (2000). *Los Angeles Police Department Board of Inquiry into the Rampart area corruption incident: Public report*. Los Angeles: Los Angeles Police Department.

Perrow, C. (1986). *Complex organizations: A critical essay* (3rd ed.). New York: Random House.

Perrow, C. A. (1997). Organizing for environmental destruction. *Organization and Environment*, 10, 66–72.

Police Foundation. (1992). *The city in crisis: A report by the special advisor to the Board of Police Commissioners on the civil disorder in Los Angeles* [Webster Report]. Washington, DC: Author.

Reuss-Ianni, E. (1983). *Two cultures of policing: Street cops and management cops*. New Brunswick, NJ: Transaction.

Rosen, J. (2005, April). Rehnquist the great? *Atlantic Monthly*, 295(3), 79–90.

Rosenberg, N. (1976). Another advantage of the division of labor. *Journal of Political Economy*, 84, 861–868.

Rosenberg, S. (1999, September–October). Management challenges for the 21st century [Review of the book]. *Business Horizons*, 42 (5), 86–87.

Schlesinger, J. (2004, August). *Final report of the Independent Panel to Review DoD Detention Operations*. Washington, DC: Independent Panel to Review DoD Detention Operations.

Senese, J. D. (1991). Communications and inmate management: Interactions among jail employees. *Journal of Criminal Justice*, 19, 151–163.

Sheffi, Y. (2005). *The resilient enterprise: Overcoming vulnerability for competitive advantage*. Cambridge, MA: MIT Press.

Simpson, R. L. (1985). Social control of occupations and work. *Annual Review of Sociology*, 11, 415–436.

Smith, L. G. (1993, Summer). Neutralizing the negative impact of organization change during the transition process. *Large Jail Network Bulletin*, 3–6.

Souryal, S. S. (1995). *Police organization and administration* (2nd ed.). Cincinnati, OH: Anderson.

Souryal, S. S., & McKay, B. W. (1996). Personal loyalty to superiors in public service. *Criminal Justice Ethics*, 15(2), 44–62.

Stillman, R. J. (1992). *Public administration: Concepts and cases* (5th ed.). Boston: Houghton Mifflin.

Stojkovic, S., Kalinich, D., & Klofas, J. (2003). *Criminal justice organizations: Administration and management* (3rd ed.). Belmont, CA: Wadsworth.

Stover, C. P. (1995). The old public administration is the new jurisprudence. *Administration and Society*, 27, 82–106.

Sullivan, A. (2005, January 23). Atrocities in plain sight. *New York Times Book Review*, 8–11.

Susa, O. (1997). Byrokracie, riziko, a diskyse o krizi zivotniho prostredi [Bureaucracy, risk, and environmental crisis discourse]. *Sociologicky Casopis*, 33(2), 157–167.

Taylor, F. W. (1947). *The principles of scientific management*. New York: Norton. (Original work published 1911)

Tuchman, B. W. (1984). *The march of folly: From Troy to Vietnam.* London: Cardinal/Sphere Books.

Ulmer, R. R. (2001). Effective crisis management through established stakeholder relationship. *Management Communication Quarterly,* 14, 590–615.

Useem, B., & Kimball, P. (1989). *Stages of siege,* 1971–1986. New York: Oxford University Press.

Vaughan, D. (1996). *The Challenger launch decision: Risky technology, culture, and deviance at NASA.* Chicago: University of Chicago Press.

Vaughn, M. S. (1994). Police civil liability for abandonment in high crime areas and other high risk situations. *Journal of Criminal Justice,* 22, 407–424.

Vaughn, M. S. (1996). Prison civil liability for inmate-against-inmate assault and breakdown/disorganization theory. *Journal of Criminal Justice,* 24, 139–152.

Vaughn, M. S., & Coomes, L. F. (1995). Police civil liability under section 1983: When do police officers act under color of law? *Journal of Criminal Justice,* 23, 395–415.

Vaughn, M. S., Cooper, T. W., & del Carmen, R. V. (2001). Assessing legal liabilities in law enforcement: Police chiefs' views. *Crime and Delinquency,* 47, 3–27.

von Mises, L. (1969). *Bureaucracy.* New Rochelle, NY: Arlington House.

Walker, S. (2001). *Police accountability: The role of citizen oversight.* Belmont, CA: Wadsworth.

Walker, S., Alpert, G. P., & Kenney, D. J. (2000). Early warning systems for police: Concept, history, and issues. *Police Quarterly,* 3(2), 132–152.

Weber, M. (1992). Bureaucracy. In R. J. Stillman (Ed.), *Public administration: Concepts and cases* (5th ed., pp. 40–49). Boston: Houghton Mifflin. (Original work published 1946)

Weber, M. (1994). *Sociological writings.* New York: Continuum.

Weick, K. E. (1976). Educational organizations as loosely coupled systems. *Administrative Science Quarterly,* 21, 1–19.

Weick, K. E. (1993). The collapse of sensemaking in organizations: The Mann Gulch disaster. *Administrative Science Quarterly,* 38, 628–652.

Wilson, J. Q. (1989). *Bureaucracy: What government agencies do and why they do it.* New York: Basic Books.

Wren, D. A. (1994). *The evolution of management thought* (4th ed.). New York: John Wiley.

Zhou, X. (1993). The dynamics of organizational rules. *American Journal of Sociology,* 98, 1134–1166.

Cases cited

Graham v. Conner, 490 U.S. 386 (1989).
Hudson v. McMillian, 503 U.S. 1 (1992).
Johnson v. Johnson, 385 F.3d 503 (5th Cir. 2004).
Tennessee v. Garner, 471 U.S. 1 (1985).
Wever v. Lincoln County, Lexis 22974 (8th Cir. 2004).
Whitley v. Albers, 475 U.S. 312 (1986).

DISCUSSION QUESTIONS

1. Organizations are notoriously difficult to change, because past decisions place constraints on present leaders. For example, a decision to despecialize a police force in the past assumed the quality of custom, habit, or rule. Is it possible for a single manager at any point in time to make the necessary changes—implement proper administrative principles—to prevent breakdown?

2. Criminal justice agencies are tasked with multiple, sometimes competing, goals. Parole and probation officers are supposed to enforce the law but act as social workers as well. Police must satisfy law enforcement, service, and order maintenance functions. How should managers clarify goals? Is there a way to clearly specify the role of employees?

3. Is specialization or a division of labor necessary to avoid administrative breakdown? Can you think of any situations, real or hypothetical, where the division of labor may produce organizational deviance?

READING

Reading 7

David Klinger examines police shootings within a normal accidents theory framework. Doing so allows Klinger to identify features of police deadly force situations that distinguish between what he refers to as avoidable and unavoidable shootings. The difference between the two comes down to the soundness of the tactics employed by the officers involved. This is where the normal accident theory concepts of complexity and coupling lend insight. Klinger's argument is that sound tactics can minimize the complexity and coupling in police–suspect encounters, thereby reducing the likelihood of deadly force. Officers in deadly force encounters are generally faced with complex environments: multiple officers, different types of equipment (lethal, less-than-lethal), and the built environment. Tactics, however, can be used to make the situation more linear. Determining which officer is the lead officer is one way the complexity of a multiple-officer situation is reduced. Coupling also plays a part in the likelihood of a shooting. When officers leave their cover location and reduce the distance between themselves and suspects, their reaction time diminishes. Keeping slack or reducing coupling (staying behind cover, maintaining distance from the suspect) is a sound tactic. Klinger demonstrates through a number of case studies that proper tactics can reduce the likelihood of an avoidable shooting.

SOCIAL THEORY AND THE STREET COP

The Case of Deadly Force

David Klinger

Social theory can serve many functions in the public policy arena. Two of the most important in the realm of crime and justice are: (1) guiding the actions of criminal justice agencies and personnel; and (2) explaining to members of the public how and why agencies and personnel act the way they do. When members of the criminal justice system have a good understanding of social theory, they can use it as a framework for setting goals, developing procedures to fulfill them, and tailoring training in ways that further them. Similarly, they will find it easier to explain their work to laymen and increase public support for their actions if they grasp the theoretical underpinnings of their operations. This is certainly the case in the world of policing where social theory has guided agencies in a variety of endeavors and helped the public understand both the goals of the police and the methods they use to reach them.

One place where social theory has been lacking, however, is in the critical area of deadly force. No decision that an officer can make is more important than the one to pull the trigger, for doing so is an exercise of the state's supreme power—the ability to end the lives of its citizens. Moreover, the social consequences of exercising this ultimate power can be quite profound, as time and again in our nation's recent history police shootings have led to political upheaval, community outrage, and even full-blown riots (Skolnick and Fyfe 1993).

Most officer-involved shootings do not prompt notable social disruption, but public concern about deadly force is always present. Americans have always been uneasy about being policed by an armed

Source: Klinger, D. (2005). *Social theory and the street cop: The case of deadly force.* Washington, DC: Police Foundation.

constabulary (Chevigny 1996; Klinger 2004), and their queasiness finds its clearest expression among police critics who discover something to complain about nearly every time an officer pulls the trigger. One reason for this state of affairs is that discourse about the use of deadly force has long revolved primarily around competing moral judgments about the police. Critics of law enforcement point, for example, to cases in which officers shoot unarmed citizens and say, "Cops are trigger happy." Meanwhile, police supporters point to officers who are killed or injured in shootouts with criminals and say, "Cops are heroes."

If we are to bridge, or at least narrow, this divide and thereby ease the public's disquiet, I believe we must learn to think about the phenomenon of police shootings from a fresh frame of reference. We must find a standpoint that permits us to move past the passion-laden medium of morality and towards a deeper understanding of the social reality of deadly force in our society. Such a move might well serve to enlighten police critics and other concerned citizens about the nature of police work, the dangers officers face, how this influences their attitudes and actions, and what we can realistically expect police to do when confronted with life-and-death situations. Such enlightenment could, in turn, help the public, critics included, to see that lethal force is sometimes unavoidable; that police officers must sometimes kill people to protect themselves and other innocents from harm. A move away from the moral plane might also help remind police and their supporters that democratic policing requires restraint and forbearance on the part of those who carry a badge and gun. This, in turn, might help officers deal with citizens in ways that minimize the odds that gunfire will erupt, for extensive evidence indicates that how the police structure their interactions with citizens can have a marked effect on the likelihood of violence.

In-depth case studies, practical experience, and empirical research have demonstrated that police will need to use deadly force less frequently if they adhere to a few simple, tactical principles. James Fyfe, for example, has written and spoken extensively during the past quarter century about how officers can use the principles of tactical knowledge and concealment to reduce the likelihood of having to resort to deadly force when handling potentially dangerous situations (Fyfe 2001; Scharf and Binder 1983).

Simply put, the principle of tactical knowledge holds that officers should develop as much information as they can about each potentially violent situation they are called upon to handle before committing themselves to a particular course of action. One critical component of this notion is that officers should keep their distance from potential adversaries, whenever it is possible, so they can limit the threat they face as they seek to understand better what is happening. Concealment refers to officers taking steps to limit the ability of persons who pose a threat to harm them. An important aspect of the concealment principle is the concept of cover—the idea that officers should position themselves behind barriers, such as motor vehicles and telephone poles, when confronting individuals who are a real or potential threat. By maintaining cover, officers limit their exposure to gunfire and other potentially lethal threats. This, in turn, can: (1) dissuade individuals who might otherwise be willing to attack them from doing so; and (2) permit officers to take more time when deciding how to respond to threatening and potentially threatening situations. As a result, officers need not shoot when potential threats fail to materialize, and they may have enough time to decide how to resolve those situations that do involve danger without resorting to gunfire.

Training in the foregoing tactical principles, as well as others that can help prevent shootings, is common in U.S. law enforcement, but officers do not always utilize sound tactics in the field. Moreover, few members of the public at large, and even fewer police critics, seem to know that officers are trained to seek ways to avoid lethal confrontations with citizens.

I believe that one reason for this state of affairs is that the idea of managing interactions with an eye toward avoiding violence is underdeveloped. One consequence of this is that the full implications of the notion have yet to be realized in the law enforcement community. A second is that it has yet to be articulated in a fashion that is readily comprehensible to the general public. This is where social theory comes in, for there exists a body of social scientific theory that can place the work of Fyfe and other commentators on police tactics in a larger intellectual context and therefore shed considerable light on the world of police violence. As a result, both the police and their critics may be able to see things a bit differently and thereby move toward a shared understanding of how to do good police work when lives hang in the balance.

The remainder of this essay articulates just how social theory can help officers to deal better with violent incidents and other potentially threatening situations. It also explains how social theory can help members of the public to understand better what they can realistically expect from those who have sworn to serve and protect them. As an initial step in this process, the next section seeks to establish the value of looking to social theory for guidance in police matters. It will accomplish this by briefly reviewing a few cases where such theory has proven useful in realms of policing that are less dramatic than deadly force.

How Social Theory Has Influenced Police Work and Public Understanding

Our first example of the link between social theory and police operations comes from work that was done in the early 1980s to alter how police dealt with spousal assault. Before this time, police officers frequently did not arrest men who battered their intimate partners. Yielding to calls from battered women and their champions for the police to treat domestic violence more seriously, many state legislatures strengthened their assault laws. The new laws gave officers the legal authority to arrest men who beat their partners, and many police departments developed policies encouraging or mandating that officers make arrests (Klinger 1995; Sherman 1992). A key influence on this shift in law enforcement's approach to domestic violence was a study conducted by Sherman and Berk (1984), which found that men who were arrested when they attacked their female partners were less likely to batter again.

The notion that arrest lowers the odds of subsequent violence, while not always recognized as such, is clearly rooted in the classic theory of deterrence, which holds that punishing offenders leads to lower rates of offending (Beccaria 1764; Gibbs 1975). While subsequent studies of the effect of arrest on domestic violence offenders did not always support Sherman and Berk's finding of a deterrent effect (Sherman 1992), the deterrence doctrine provided a clear, reasonable, and simple message for advocates of legal and policy change. It also provided a clear explanation and justification for officers' actions: arresting batterers will lower rates of domestic violence and protect the vulnerable from aggressors. As a result, the social theory of deterrence has been a crucial guide to the public policy response to the problem of intimate partner violence for more than two decades.

Two other examples of social theory's influence on contemporary police practices come from community- and problem-oriented policing: zero-tolerance policing and the SARA (Scan, Analyze, Respond, and Assess) model. Zero-tolerance policing grew out of Wilson and Kelling's (1982) "broken windows" argument that little offenses lead to big problems if communities aren't vigilant about disorder and minor offenses, a perspective that goes back to the social disorganization tradition of the Chicago school of social ecology (e.g., Shaw and McKay 1942). The core notion of this school of thought is that high levels of crime in communities are due to a decline in the community's capacity to control the behavior of its members. By taking care of small things, the broken windows thesis maintains, people can reassert their right to control the sorts of behavior that go on in their community and thereby short-circuit the dynamic that leads to serious crime problems. Because many of the minor problems that spawn bigger problems are petty crimes and other police concerns, the police play a central role in controlling crime when they address matters that normally fall within their purview. Thus is broken windows policing rooted in a simple yet profound bit of social theory that has been around for decades and gives rise to a dictum that both the police and the public can easily understand: help promote safe communities by taking care of the small stuff.

We can similarly trace the intellectual lineage of the SARA model to the routine activities theory that Cohen and Felson set forth in 1979: crime happens when offenders and victims converge in time and space in the absence of capable guardians. From this is derived the crime- or problem-analysis triangle that officers throughout the nation use in developing strategies and programs to deal with specific problems that give rise to crime. By developing and implementing sound plans to change part of the victim-offender-guardianship dynamic at the time and/or place of incipient problems, officers can nip crime in the bud (Bynum 2001). Again, a profound piece of social theory provides a plan of action that is easily understood by the general public and appreciated by street cops: focus on the problem that gives rise to crime.

With these examples in hand, we can shift gears and move on to a brief discussion of a social science perspective that can help us reach a better understanding of police shootings: the sociology of risk and mistake.

The Sociology of Risk and Mistake

The sociology of risk and mistake is rooted largely in organizational sociology, a subdiscipline that analyzes the structure and operation of formal organizations, such as police departments. Much of the work in the risk/mistake tradition focuses on how individual actors in organizations perceive their environment and how they calculate the likelihood that unwanted, untoward events might occur. A good deal of this work addresses monetary and other economic losses, but is also very concerned with actual and potential human losses (Short and Clarke 1992). As a result, there is a sizable literature that seeks to assess how people's behavior in organizational settings can increase or decrease the threat of injury or death.

A key point in this body of work is the recognition that not all deaths, injuries, and other bad outcomes are avoidable. The notion of prevention is nonetheless central because the risk/mistake tradition focuses attention on attempts to do things better—to design systems better, organize units better, and have individuals behave better. In other words, the sociology of risk and mistake has a high degree of policy relevance, for it seeks to help practitioners identify the odds that something bad will happen and then find ways to reduce, blunt, or avoid these negative outcomes.

A fundamental precept of the sociology-of-risk framework is that mistakes, mishaps, and even disasters are socially organized and systematically produced by social structures, both macro and micro (Vaughn 1996). Therefore, how people are organized and how they operate—not just the traditional villain, operator error—are key to understanding the use of deadly force by police officers. As will be shown below, this line of thinking is vital to understanding the use of deadly force by police officers. Before explaining how the sociology of risk can help us to understand police shootings better, however, some comments about the nature of officer-involved shootings are in order.

Officer-Involved Shootings

Police shootings are quite rare. We don't know exactly how rare because police agencies are not required to report to any national body when their officers fire their weapons, and there is no comprehensive, voluntary data-collection system. The best estimates, however, put the ceiling on the number of officer-involved shootings, including those in which no one is hit by police, at a few thousand per year (Fyfe 2002; Klinger 2004).[1] When one considers that the U.S. has more than 750,000 cops (Hickman and Reaves 2003; Reaves and Hart 2001), who are involved in tens of millions of contacts with citizens each year (Langan et al. 2001), police shootings are clearly what risk scholars call low-frequency events.

A major reason why officer-involved shootings are low-frequency events is that the rules governing firearms use by police permit officers to shoot in just two sorts of circumstances: (1) when they have reasonable belief that their life or the life of another innocent person is in imminent danger; and (2) to effect the arrest of felons fleeing from the scene of violent crimes (Callahan 2001).[2] While millions of violent crimes and other volatile situations take place across our nation each year (FBI 2003), the police are present at just a fraction of them. As a result, cops and crooks don't often find themselves together in time and space under circumstances in which officers *might* theoretically have legal cause to shoot. Furthermore, when officers do find themselves in felonious or other volatile circumstances, the citizens involved usually do not resist to a point that would justify deadly force under either the defense-of-life or fleeing-felon doctrines. It follows that the number of police-citizen encounters in which deadly force is legally permissible is but a fraction of the tens of millions of situations in which police officers interact with citizens each year.

That police infrequently encounter citizens under circumstances in which they have legal cause to use deadly force does not completely explain why shootings are so unusual, however, for research indicates that officers often hold their fire in cases where they could shoot (Scharf and Binder 1983; Klinger 2004). One reason for this would appear to be the simple fact that the vast majority of police officers have no desire to shoot anyone, so they hold their fire out of personal choice (Klinger 2004). A second reason is that officers, as we have seen, are trained to handle encounters in ways that minimize the likelihood that they will have to resort to lethal force. When officers follow their training by deploying behind cover and keeping their distance from armed individuals, for example, they can afford to hold their fire even though shooting would be perfectly permissible.

The use of proper tactics can also prevent volatile situations from escalating to a point at which deadly force would be a legitimate option for police. Few people who might be willing to take on the police will actually do so when officers confront them in ways that place them at a distinct disadvantage. For example, an armed robber is unlikely to try to pull his gun if he is stopped by two police officers who keep their distance and stay behind their patrol cars while aiming their service weapons at him. In sum then, by employing sound tactics, officers can often avoid shootings by both deterring individuals from taking action that would justify gunfire and by providing a margin of safety for themselves in cases in which the use of deadly force would be appropriate.

Unfortunately, the obverse is also true: when officers don't use sound tactics, they can find themselves in shootings that could have been avoided. Take, for example, a hypothetical case in which officers are called to deal with an enraged man armed with a baseball bat who is standing outside his house. The officers walk to within a few feet of him and demand that he surrender his bat. The man refuses and instead strikes one of the officers with the bat. As the stricken officer falls to the ground, his partner draws her weapon and shoots the citizen before he can strike a second, and perhaps fatal, blow. It should be clear by now that the shooting could have been avoided, at least as it played out in this hypothetical scenario, if the officers had simply maintained some distance and kept a barrier, such as their patrol cars, between the man and themselves as they sought to resolve the situation.

The police cannot entirely avoid the use of deadly force, however. Some people, no matter what the police do, will take action that requires officers to fire. Included among such people are those who are more afraid of going back to prison than they are of police bullets, people who believe they will prevail against the police they face, and lost souls who purposely provoke officers to shoot them in an unconventional form of self-destruction known in the business as "suicide-by-cop" (Klinger 2001). Fortunately, the police rarely encounter such individuals. Indeed, the vast majority of people, the vast majority of the time, won't do anything that would justify the use of deadly force, no matter how officers behave. During training sessions on police shootings that I conduct around the nation, I sometimes illustrate this point by noting that officers could take their gun belts off in the vast majority of their interactions with citizens and hand it over to the citizen with no adverse consequences to their safety. In other words, how officers comport themselves tactically in most interactions will not affect the likelihood of a shooting because citizens generally will not take any action that would seriously endanger anyone.

Figure 1

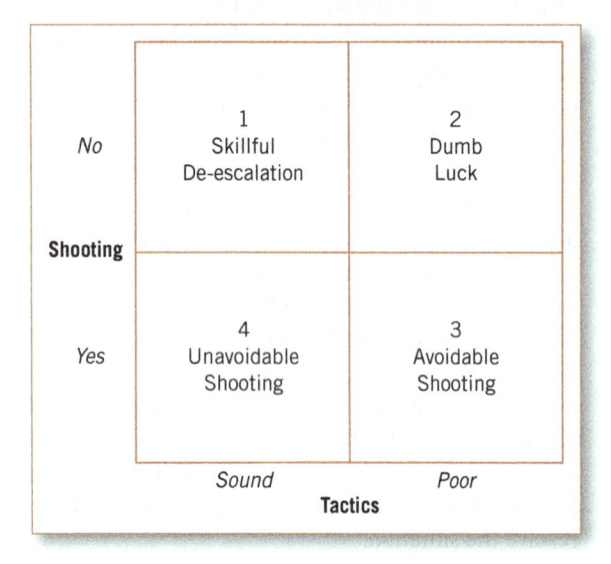

	Sound Tactics	Poor Tactics
Shooting: No	1 Skillful De-escalation	2 Dumb Luck
Shooting: Yes	4 Unavoidable Shooting	3 Avoidable Shooting

One can build on these general ideas about police-citizen interaction to craft a simple, fourfold taxonomy that cross-classifies the quality of officers' tactics against the occurrence of a shooting. As shown in Figure 1, doing so yields a 2x2 table with cells that correspond to cases in which: (1) officers used sound tactics and thus avoided a shooting that might otherwise have occurred; (2) officers used poor tactics and no shooting occurred—because the citizen involved did nothing to threaten the officers; (3) officers used poor tactics and had to shoot their way out of danger; and (4) officers had to fire to protect themselves or others, despite the use of sound tactics. Borrowing heavily from Fyfe (1988), who created a similar taxonomy to address the use of force by officers in general, we can call these four cells:

(1) "skillful de-escalation,"

(2) "dumb luck,"

(3) "avoidable shooting," and

(4) "unavoidable shooting."

Shootings rarely occur, as previously noted, so it is apparent that the vast majority of police-citizen interactions will fall into the first two cells of the table. We should therefore direct our attention to cells 3 and 4 as we try to understand more about how shootings do occur. The next step in this process will be to take a brief tour through normal accident theory (NAT), a theoretical perspective in the sociology of risk and disaster that can help us in our quest for answers.

Normal Accident Theory (NAT) and Deadly Force

The eminent sociologist Charles Perrow developed NAT in the early 1980s to explain how bad things happen in high-tech systems, such as nuclear power plants.[3] NAT asserts that understanding why things sometimes go wrong requires us to pay heed to two key factors: the complexity of systems and the extent to which their elements are coupled, or tied together. As the number of elements in a system grows and the interactions among the elements increase, the system becomes more complex. The more complex the system, the more things can go wrong and the less likely humans are to immediately understand what is happening, which makes it difficult to respond immediately to problems. Where coupling is concerned, as the elements of a system become more tightly bound together, the amount of slack in the system decreases. This, in turn, reduces the capacity of the system to deal with difficulties that might arise before they spin out of control and disaster ensues. Perrow argues that systems are more likely to have problems that lead to negative outcomes as they become more complex and tightly coupled. The term normal accident is thus used to describe his idea that the environments inherent in some types of systems are such that misfortunes are an almost inevitable part of them and hence normal. In sum, it is the core contention of NAT that the likelihood of negative events will increase as systems become more tightly coupled and interactively complex (Perrow 1984).

With this sketch of Perrow's normal accident theory in hand, we can now move on to a discussion of how it applies to police shootings. Our starting point is the recognition that all police-citizen interactions are social systems, which can involve just two people—for example, a single officer and a single citizen at a traffic stop—or encompass hundreds of people who play a variety of social roles—officers, suspects, victims, bystanders, fire-rescue personnel, the media, and so on at a large-scale public disturbance. The next point is to recall the previously mentioned notion that police officers can often structure encounters in ways that reduce the likelihood of a shooting—by keeping some distance and taking cover, for example. If we think about these tactics in the language of NAT, what officers are doing is reducing the degree of coupling between themselves and suspects and thus building slack into the social system in which they find themselves. This slack permits officers to take an extra moment—perhaps just a split second but often much longer—to assess the intentions of citizens before pulling the trigger.

Police-citizen encounters are often quite complex because a good portion of police work involves multiple officers. This is especially true of situations with a higher-than-average chance that gunfire might erupt because it is standard law enforcement practice to send more than one officer to incidents that involve a heightened degree of danger (Klinger 1997). For example, take a situation involving an individual who is wielding a knife and flailing about in a public square, prompting several officers to respond. Well-trained officers respond to such situations by having one officer do all the talking, assigning a small number of officers—usually one or two who are typically called "designated shooters" or "designated cover officers"—to do any shooting that might be necessary if the situation deteriorates, and appointing the remaining officers to other specific roles. Having just one officer talk and/or give commands creates a linear rather than a complex communication process. This, in turn, reduces the likelihood that miscommunication between police and suspect or among the officers themselves might unnecessarily escalate matters. Having designated shooters permits the other officers present to confidently carry out whatever other activities might be useful for resolving the situation short of gunfire—whether they involve deploying less-lethal weapons, such as tasers or beanbag shotguns, or directing citizens away from the area.[4] The decision to draw fewer guns lessens the chance that an accidental discharge could lead to sympathetic gunfire and reduces the number of rounds fired if shooting becomes necessary. This both promotes the odds that the suspect will survive being shot and lessens the chances that stray bullets will hit other officers or innocent bystanders.

The value of the NAT framework can also be seen in the realm of more complicated police activities, such as dealing with barricaded suspects. Standard police doctrine has long held that officers should not rush in and confront armed suspects who barricade themselves inside locations. It advises them, instead, to set up a perimeter to seal the suspect off from others, call for the help of a SWAT team and crisis negotiators, and then try to talk the suspect into leaving his stronghold position and surrendering (Fyfe 1996; Geller and Scott 1992). Staying outside at perimeter positions makes for a relationship between suspect and police that is much less tightly coupled than it would be if officers entered the suspect's location. Calling for SWAT and crisis negotiators rather than simply relying on patrol officers reduces the complexity of the situation because these specialists have unique training and work together as a unit. This means that fewer officers need to be involved, and there is less chance for miscommunication and misunderstanding among the police. Once SWAT and negotiators arrive, a single crisis negotiator will talk with the gunman, which means the communication process will be quite linear, as previously observed. Furthermore, whatever discussions the negotiator has with the suspect will generally be done over the phone, rather than face-to-face, which reduces the physical coupling between police and suspect. The end result of using SWAT and crisis negotiators is to make for less complexity and coupling when dealing with barricaded suspects.

With all of this as background, we now turn our attention to some examples that illustrate both of the shooting cells from Figure 1. We will begin by looking at an unavoidable shooting involving an officer who responds to a robbery call. A well-trained officer, she arrives and deploys outside the location behind the cover offered by the engine block of her car—thereby minimizing the degree of coupling between herself and the suspect—and then waits there for additional units to show up. The suspect spots the officer, realizes that she stands between him and freedom, exits the front door, and runs toward her while raising his gun. In this instance of a very simple, two-person social system, the suspect increased the coupling between himself and the officer, precluding the officer from doing anything but firing her weapon to protect her life and the lives of any innocent bystanders.

Continuing with the armed robber example, we will illustrate a more involved scenario that falls into the unavoidable shooting category. Let us say that the suspect in the previous situation decides to stay put when the first officer arrives while the store clerk and customers flee, creating a classic barricade situation. When the suspect refuses to heed the patrol officers' demands to surrender, patrol calls for SWAT and negotiators. SWAT deploys, and the negotiators then attempt to contact the suspect. Unfortunately, he repeatedly refuses to talk, so the incident commander has the SWAT team employ a series of tactics to get him to peacefully surrender. The suspect still refuses to surrender and ignores additional attempts by the negotiators to open a dialogue. After some time has passed, the incident commander has SWAT fire several rounds of tear gas into the location. The suspect still refuses to negotiate or exit the location. When it becomes clear that the suspect will not come out, the commander decides that SWAT must go into the location to arrest the suspect and resolve the situation. As the officers enter, the suspect fires his weapon and members of the entry team return fire, thereby ending the standoff. In this case, it was the police who took the slack out of the system and increased coupling between themselves and the suspect. They did so, however, only after repeated attempts to use tactics that permit and usually achieve a bloodless resolution from a distance (Klinger and Rojek 2005). Consequently, the police used deadly force only when they had no remaining option to resolve a dangerous situation—in other words, another unavoidable shooting.

With two hypothetical examples of unavoidable shootings in hand, we will use two actual cases to illustrate the notion of preventable shootings. The first is perhaps the most notorious officer-involved shooting in the history of U.S. law enforcement: the killing of West African immigrant Amadou Diallo by four detectives from the NYPD Street Crimes Unit who fired a total of forty-one rounds after Diallo pulled his wallet from his back pocket in the vestibule of a Bronx apartment building early one winter morning in 1999. The details of the incident have been widely reported, but here are the basics.[5] As the four plain-clothes officers were cruising down Wheeler Avenue in the South Bronx in their unmarked vehicle, one of them, Sean Carroll, spotted a slightly built black male acting in what he deemed to be a suspicious fashion at the entrance of an apartment building. Carroll told the driver, Kenneth Boss, to stop so they could investigate. Boss did so, then backed up, and stopped again so that Carroll and

Edward McMellon, the other detective sitting on the car's right side, could get out. Diallo, who was not yet identified, quickly retreated into the vestibule and began "reaching into his right-hand side"[6] with his right hand. Carroll and McMellon, who had drawn their guns in the belief that Diallo might be attempting to pull one himself, charged into the vestibule intending to grab Diallo before he could retrieve the gun for which they believed he was fishing.

As Carroll and McMellon shouted at Diallo to freeze, he quickly pulled a dark object from his right side and began turning his body counterclockwise in their direction. Diallo then started to extend his right hand, which was still clutching the dark object, towards the officers. Believing the object in Diallo's hand to be a firearm, Carroll shouted "Gun!!" and started to shoot. McMellon also commenced firing as both officers scrambled to back out of the small vestibule, which was only about five by seven feet. By this time, Detective Boss and the fourth officer, Richard Murphy, were running to the aid of their partners. As they sprinted to assist, McMellon tripped and fell backwards down the stairs he had just run up. Believing McMellon had just been shot, Boss and Murphy peered into the vestibule, where they saw Diallo standing and pointing a dark object in their direction. They began firing their pistols at him. All four officers ceased firing when Diallo fell down from the cumulative effect of 19 bullets hitting his body.

After reloading his weapon, Carroll went up to check on Diallo and secure what he believed to be the pistol Diallo had pointed at him and his partners. When he grabbed the dark object he saw on the ground near Diallo's right hand, he felt the soft give of leather rather than the hard firmness of steel, realized the object was a wallet, and said, "Where's the fucking gun!" After coming up empty in a quick search of the rest of the vestibule for the gun he had seen, Carroll realized that he and his fellow officers had just shot an unarmed man.

The shooting became a major cause célèbre. The press played up the story of white cops killing an unarmed black man as part of a pattern of oppressive police practices against minorities by NYPD officers.

The race industry and political forces that opposed the administration of former mayor Rudy Giuliani made a huge scene, and the four officers were indicted. All four were acquitted, but many people subscribed and continue to subscribe to the notion of a racially motivated killing. No evidence of racial animus on the part of any of the officers emerged at the trial, however, so the dominant theory of the Amadou Diallo shooting does not offer a sound explanation for what happened early that February morning in 1999.

If we look at the shooting through the lens of Perrow's normal accident theory, however, we can make a good deal of sense about it. Indeed, a review of key points of the incident in light of NAT will disclose that what happened might be viewed as a predictable outcome of a five-person social system in which the behavior of the participants and the nature of the physical space produced a situation that was very tightly coupled and highly complex.

When Carroll and McMellon left the car to investigate, no one was clearly in charge. This meant that the officers were working as independent units instead of a single team, which unnecessarily complicated the social system in place when Carroll and McMellon confronted Diallo. Further difficulty arose when Carroll and McMellon approached Diallo in the vestibule because they greatly reduced the slack in the subsystem involving themselves and Diallo. With just feet between themselves and Diallo, no cover between them, and no place for Diallo to move, the system was very tightly coupled. When Diallo unexpectedly pulled an object from his right hand, the high degree of coupling meant that officers had but a fraction of a second to identify the object before deciding on a course of action.

Once Carroll shouted "Gun," interactions between the people present and the physical environment came into play. As Carroll and McMellon tried to move away from Diallo—and thereby reduce the degree of coupling—an unexpected interaction between McMellon and the stairs emerged when he lost his footing and fell down. The gunshots that were ringing out seemed to indicate to the other officers that one of their team had been shot. Confirming this definition of the situation was additional evidence that resulted from the complex interactions between the participants and the physical environment of the vestibule. The interior door that Diallo was standing in front of had a highly reflective coating of paint, a metal kick plate at the bottom, a small pane of glass in the middle, and additional glass immediately above. As Carroll and McMellon fired their weapons, their muzzle flashes reflected off the door and its surroundings. Meanwhile, some of the officers' shots ricocheted back towards them, making it look as if Diallo was firing at them.

All of this (and other aspects of complexity and coupling that would take more space than would be appropriate here) adds up to a tragic accident in which four officers, one citizen, and their physical surroundings came together in a way that led to the unnecessary death of the citizen. No racial animus, no evil intent, just a group of human beings caught up in a tightly coupled, interactively complex system in which a series of misunderstandings led to disaster. In sum, NAT provides an elegant framework for understanding one of the most controversial applications of deadly force in the history of U.S. policing.

A second and far less well-known example of a normal accident shooting will further demonstrate the value of the NAT perspective for understanding police shootings. In the late evening hours of August 27, 1997, a man named Sap Kray threatened his estranged wife with an assault rifle at her home in Tacoma, Washington. Kray's wife left and went to her job in a neighboring community. Kray then took his rifle and showed up there after a few hours, causing one of his wife's co-workers to notify the local police. When the police arrived, they confronted Kray and saw that he was armed with a rifle. They let him go since he did not seem to have committed any crimes in their jurisdiction. They did, however, advise Kray's wife to tell the Tacoma Police Department about her earlier assault. She left work, drove home, found her husband there, and called Tacoma police. Because the case involved an assault rifle, the Tacoma patrol officers who responded decided to request assistance from their SWAT team.

Soon after the SWAT officers had deployed, a group of them saw Kray exit from the front door and walk towards his vehicle, which was parked in front the residence. Believing him to be unarmed, they demanded that Kray surrender, but he retreated toward the front door. Officer William Lowry and other members of the team gave chase in an attempt to prevent him from reentering the house. Kray nonetheless made it inside the house, while Lowry and some of the other officers who had chased him took cover behind a large tree approximately twenty feet from the door.

The officers tried to convince Kray to surrender, but he refused. At some point, Kray came to the open door, and one of the officers behind the tree shot him twice in the torso with less-lethal munitions from an ARWEN launcher.[7] Kray then fell back inside the residence, and Lowry, followed by three other officers, rushed in after him. As Lowry led the way into the residence, he observed Kray approximately ten feet inside the front door, pointing an assault rifle in his direction. He ordered Kray to drop the weapon, but Kray fired at the officers. Lowry returned three rounds from his weapon, shouted, "I'm hit," and quickly left the house along with the rest of the entry team. Lowry was airlifted to a regional trauma center, where he was pronounced dead.

Several hours after he murdered Lowry, Kray peacefully surrendered to members of the Pierce County SWAT team, who had been called in to relieve Tacoma's team after Lowry's death. Lowry's autopsy showed that a single bullet from Kray's gun had led to his death. This was the only shot that Kray fired, as it turned out, and it went through Lowry's left arm, penetrated his body armor near his left armpit, and exited his torso near his right armpit.[8]

If we look at the tragedy that played out in Tacoma that day through the lens of NAT, we can understand it as a classic example of a normal accident shooting. First off, if we think about the officers' movements from the cover of the tree to the front door in light of normal accident theory, we can quickly see that this move increased the coupling between Kray and the officers.

Had the members of the SWAT team remained behind the tree, they would have maintained slack in the micro social system that had developed that day, which would have kept them from the mortal danger that stood just meters away.

System complexity also played a key role in the Lowry shooting. One of the points that Perrow makes in his discussion of NAT is that the presence of safety devices can create unexpected interactions between system elements, thus increasing the degree of complexity, which in turn increases the degree of danger. Less-lethal launchers— such as the ARWEN used by Tacoma SWAT—are designed to help officers subdue combative or otherwise resistant subjects short of using deadly force while maintaining some distance. In other words, they are safety devices that help police to resolve volatile situations, such as the standoff with Kray, without resorting to gunfire.

In this case, however, it was the presence of the less-lethal ARWEN that set in motion the events that led to Lowry's death. As well-trained officers, Lowry and his partners would not normally leave the safety of a cover point in a confrontation with an armed suspect. In this instance, they left only because the ARWEN rounds had struck Kray. Believing that it was safe to do so, they moved in to take their suspect into custody. By the time they realized that Kray had rearmed himself, the members of the arrest team found themselves in exposed positions staring down the barrel of an assault rifle. With no cover available, Lowry was an easy target for Kray's murderous attack.

The added complexity arising from the presence of the less-lethal ARWEN was therefore a critical determinant of the officers' decision to leave the cover of the tree and increase the coupling between Kray and themselves. Had the system been less complex—had the arrest team not had a purported safety device in the form of the ARWEN— Tacoma SWAT would have used other tactics that would have maintained the relatively loose coupling that linked Kray and police until the arrest team fired the ARWEN rounds.

Concluding Comments

NAT has important implications regarding deadly-force beyond providing insight into specific officer-involved shootings. One of these is that it can help most citizens understand that some shootings are plainly unavoidable. All but the most extreme critics of the police can see that officers must shoot when dangerous suspects force their hand and foil police attempts to avoid gunfire through tactics that make for loose coupling and low complexity. NAT can also help citizens understand shootings that might otherwise seem incomprehensible—or be attributed to evil police designs—for it can make sense of cases such as the Diallo incident. The value of NAT for understanding police shootings is clarified when we reflect on the Diallo shooting in light of Officer Lowry's murder because no reasonable person could argue that the Tacoma SWAT team set out to get Lowry killed. Both tragedies were instances in which well-meaning police officers created tightly coupled, highly complex, social systems that led to disaster. In sum, the perspective provided by NAT can help citizens see that the use of deadly force cannot be eliminated entirely and that shootings that didn't need to happen often involve a large dose of human error rather than evil intent.

NAT can also help the police. Police officers have a good deal of motivation to avoid shootings. In addition to the aforementioned aversion to taking life, officers seek to avoid gunplay because shootings put them in physical danger and can expose them to substantial legal, administrative, and financial liability (Bayley and Garofolo 1989). The desire to avoid these negatives translates into a desire to know how to lower the odds of finding themselves in shootings.

NAT offers an easily understood framework to help officers accomplish this goal: keep things simple and don't get too close, for in its distilled form, that's what NAT is really about as it concerns tactics in police work. Keeping these precepts in mind can help officers on the streets today see the importance of hewing to concepts such as tactical knowledge and concealment. Attention to these precepts, moreover, can also help guide the development of new tactical doctrines that might further reduce the likelihood of shootings in the future.

The underlying simplicity of NAT's message is akin to that of other modern theories that have helped improve policing. The broken windows thesis, which is rooted in the social disorganization framework, can be reduced to "don't let things get out of hand." The routine activities perspective that animates problem-oriented policing can similarly be broken down to "solve the problem that leads to the crime," and the deterrence doctrine behind pro-arrest policies for domestic violence boils down to "arrest the strong to protect the weak." NAT, for its part, offers a simple, elegant idea that can help cops avoid unnecessary shootings and foster public understanding that sometimes police must use deadly force despite their best efforts to avoid it.

In sum, examples from diverse areas of policing show how social theory can serve as a tool to help officers both understand why they are doing what they do and help them to do it better. Because social theory has shown itself to be so valuable, it is my contention that we should search for additional issues in policing—besides those discussed here—on which social theory can shed valuable light. Doing so just might further help street cops as they go about doing the demanding job of protecting and serving the rest of us.

Notes

1. The FBI provides a count of the number of citizens "justifiably killed" by law enforcement each year as part of its UCR program, but these data are incomplete (Fyfe 2002). FBI figures place the number of citizens killed by the police at 338 per year for the five years ending in 2003.

2. These rules reflect basic federal standards, as articulated, for example, in *Tennessee v. Garner* (1985). State law and department policy can, of course, place additional restrictions on when officers may shoot.

3. In fact, Perrow developed the theory of normal accidents during research he conducted on the 1979 accident at the Three Mile Island nuclear power plant outside Harrisburg, PA.

4. This involves actions that make a situation less tightly coupled—by putting more distance between the suspect and potential victims—and complex, since removing others to a distance means there are fewer people directly involved

5. Readers interested in a more finegrained overview of the incident might want to read the sixth chapter of Malcolm Gladwell's *Blink* (2005) or Jim Fyfe's essay, "Reflections on the Diallo Case" (2000), which draws on the work he did as a defense expert in the criminal case against the four officers who shot Diallo.

6. All direct quotes in this discussion of the Diallo case come from Carroll's testimony in the criminal trial that resulted from the shooting.

7. ARWEN stands for Anti-Riot Weapon Enfield. The term "less-lethal munitions" refer to a class of projectiles, such as wooden dowels, plastic batons, rubber bullets, and beanbags that are typically fired from shotguns and 37 or 40mm launching systems, such as the ARWEN (Hubbs and Klinger 2004).

8. For an additional account of the Lowry slaying, see: Jack Hopkins, "Slain Tacoma officer Lowry is hailed as a 'true hero,' final farewell," *Seattle Post-Intelligencer*, 4 September 1997.

References

Bayley, David H., and James Garofalo. 1989. The management of violence by police patrol officers. *Criminology* 27 (1): 1–27.

Beccaria, Cesare. 1764. *On Crimes and Punishment*. Trans. with an introd. by Henry Palucci. Repr., Indianapolis: Bobbs-Merrill, 1963.

Bynum, Timothy. 2001. *Using Analysis for Problem-Solving: A Guidebook for Law Enforcement*. Washington, D.C.: U.S. Department of Justice, http://nicic.org /Misc/URLShell.aspx?SRC=Catalog&REFF=http://nicic.org/Library/018198&ID=018198&TYPE =PDF&URL=http:// www.cops.usdoj.gov/pdf/e08011230.pdf.

Callahan, John M. 2001. *Deadly Force: Constitutional Standards, Federal Policy Guidelines, and Officer Survival*. Flushing, NY: Looseleaf Publications.

Chevigny, Paul. 1996. *Edge of the Knife: Police Violence in the Americas*. New York: New Press.

Cohen, Lawrence, and Marcus Felson. 1979. Social change and crime rate trends: A routine activity approach. *American Sociological Review* 44 (August): 588–608.

Federal Bureau of Investigation. 2003. *Uniform Crime Reports*. Washington, D.C.: U.S. Department of Justice, http://www.fbi.gov/ucr /03cius.htm.

Fyfe, James J. 1988. Metro-Dade Police/Citizen Violence Reduction Project Final Report. Washington, D.C.: Police Foundation.

Fyfe, James J. 1996. Training to reduce police-citizen violence. In *Police Violence: Understanding and Controlling Police Abuse of Force*, ed. William A. Geller and Hans Toch, 151–175. Washington, D.C.: Police Executive Research Forum.

Fyfe, James J. 2000. Reflections on the Diallo case. *Subject to Debate* (April):1–4, http:// www.policeforum.org/PERF Subsite/LL/Who/PI/pblctns.htm.

Fyfe, James J. 2001. The split-second syndrome and other determinants of police violence. In *Critical Issues in Policing:*

Contemporary Readings, ed. Roger G. Dunham and Geoffrey P. Alpert, 583–598. 4th ed. Prospect Heights, Ill: Waveland Press.

Fyfe, James J. 2002. Too many missing cases: Holes in our knowledge about police use of force. *Justice Research and Policy* 4 (Fall): 87–102.

Geller, William A., and Michael S. Scott. 1992. *Deadly Force: What We Know*. Washington, D.C.: Police Executive Research Forum.

Gibbs, Jack P. 1975. *Crime, Punishment, and Deterrence*. New York: Elsevier.

Gladwell, Malcolm. 2005. *Blink: The Power of Thinking Without Thinking*. New York: Little, Brown and Company.

Hickman, Matthew J., and Brian A. Reaves. 2003. *Local Police Departments 2000*. Washington, D.C.: U.S. Department of Justice, http:// www.ojp.usdoj.gov/bjs/pub/pdf/lpd00.pdf.

Hopkins, Jack. 1997. Slain Tacoma officer Lowry is hailed as 'true hero,' final farewell. *Seattle Post Intelligencer*, 4 September 1997.

Hubbs, Ken, and David A. Klinger. 2004. *Impact Munitions Use: Types, Targets, Effects*. Washington, D.C. U.S. Department of Justice, http://www.ncjrs.org/pdffiles1/nij/206089.pdf.

Klinger, David A. 1995. Policing spousal assault. *Journal of Research in Crime and Delinquency* 32 (3): 308–324.

Klinger, David A. 1997. Negotiating order in patrol work: An ecological theory of police response to deviance. *Criminology* 35 (2): 277–306.

Klinger, David A. 2001. Suicidal intent in victim-precipitated homicide: Insights from the study of "suicide-by-cop." *Homicide Studies* 5 (3): 206–226.

Klinger, David A. 2004. *Into the Kill Zone: A Cop's Eye View of Deadly Force*. San Francisco: Jossey-Bass.

Klinger, David A., and Jeff Rojek. 2005. *A Multi-Method Study of Police Special Weapons and Tactics Teams*. Washington, D.C.: National Institute of Justice.

Langan, Patrick A., Lawrence A. Greenfeld, Matthew R. Durose, and David J. Levin. 2001. *Contacts Between Police and the Public: Findings from the 1999 National Survey*. Washington, D.C.: U.S. Department of Justice, http:// www.ojp.usdoj.gov/bjs /pub/pdf/ cpp99.pdf.

Perrow, Charles. 1984. *Normal Accidents: Living with High-Risk Technologies*. New York: Basic Books.

Reaves, Brian A., and Timothy C. Hart. 2001. *Federal Law Enforcement Officers, 2000*. Washington, D.C.: U.S. Department of Justice, http://www.ojp.usdoj.gov/bjs/pub/pdf/fleo00.pdf.

Scharf, Peter, and Arnold Binder. 1983. *The Badge and the Bullet*. New York: Praeger.

Shaw, Clifford R., and Henry D. McKay. 1942. *Juvenile Delinquency and Urban Areas: A Study of Rates of Delinquents in Relation to Differential Characteristics of Local Communities in American Cities*. With chapters by Norman S. Hayner, Paul G. Cressey, Clarence W. Schroeder, and others. Chicago: University of Chicago Press.

Sherman, Lawrence W. 1992. *Policing Domestic Violence: Experiments and Dilemmas*. With Jannell D. Schmidt and Dennis P. Rogan. New York: Free Press.

Sherman, Lawrence W., and Richard A. Berk. 1984. *The Minneapolis Domestic Violence Experiment*. Washington, D.C.: Police Foundation.

Short, James F., Jr., and Lee Clarke, eds. 1992. *Organizations, Uncertainties, and Risk*. Boulder, CO: Westview Press.

Skolnick, Jerome H., and James J. Fyfe. 1993. *Above the Law: Police and the Excessive Use of Force*. New York: Free Press.

Vaughn, Diane. 1996. *The Challenger Launch Decision: Risky Technology, Culture, and Deviance at NASA*. Chicago: University of Chicago Press.

Wilson, James Q., and George L. Kelling. 1982. Broken windows: The police and neighborhood safety. *Atlantic Monthly* (March): 29–38.

DISCUSSION QUESTIONS

1. Organizational deviance is more likely to occur after multiple failures interact with one another. Did multiple failures occur in the shooting of Amadou Diallo? If so, which system parts failed?

2. According to normal accidents theory, how can organizational deviance be prevented? Specifically, how can officers prevent the shooting deaths of fellow officers and unarmed suspects?

3. In Klinger's examples, what types of things make situations more complex? How does specialization (e.g., occupational differentiation) affect complexity?

SECTION V

Interagency Collaboration

Are Two or More Organizations (Combined) Better Than One?

Section Highlights

- Interorganizational Collaborations
- Impediments to Collaboration
- Criminal Justice Collaborations
- *Law Enforcement Task Forces*
- *Police–Corrections Partnerships*
- *Pulling Levers and Focused Deterrence Partnerships*

In her report addressing approaches to campus public safety, Linda Langford (2004) described commonplace thinking about crime and violence on college and university campuses by saying, "Institutions of higher education are often regarded as sanctuaries, protected environments where young people explore great ideas in a collegial atmosphere and make lifelong friendships" (p. 2). While there is some degree of truth to this viewpoint (see, for example, Bromley, 1992; Fox & Hellman, 1985), campuses do experience criminal activity ranging from minor acts to high-profile, mass-casualty events. Two shooting incidents within a 10-month period from April 2007 to February 2008 at Virginia Tech and Northern Illinois Universities were particularly significant, both for the scope of the tragedies and the many commissions that subsequently formed charged with reviewing and updating campus safety policies (e.g., Davies, 2008; Illinois Campus Security Task Force, 2008; Leavitt, Spellings, & Gonzales, 2007).[1] A common recommendation emerging from these commissions included a call for increased collaboration between campus public safety agencies

---

[1] Thirty-two students were killed at Virginia Tech University, and five were killed at Northern Illinois University.

and local law enforcement officials to improve their ability to respond to critical incidents on campus. In this context, collaborations are designed to overcome the challenges created when

> state and municipal police administrators often are not oriented to the needs of university and college campuses and do little to orient their front-line personnel . . . [and provide] little or no training or briefing for officers, deputies, or troopers whose beats include a campus. (*National Summit,* 2004, p. 39)

In the medical field, an event such as the Virginia Tech tragedy would be considered a limited mass-casualty incident; it strains resources for a limited time before operations return to normal (Almgody, Bala, & Rivkind, 2007; Armstrong & Frykberg, 2007; Stein, 2005). How is collaboration advantageous? On April 16, 2007, the morning of the Virginia Tech shooting, the campus police department had about 14 officers on duty (5 in the field and 9 at headquarters), a number that would have been overwhelmed during a critical incident had it not been for a mutual-aid agreement and joint training with the neighboring Blacksburg Police Department; in fact, the two departments had even trained for an active shooter situation (Virginia Tech Review Panel, 2007). Within minutes of the first 911 call, five officers from both the campus and Blacksburg Police Department were on-scene and, as the Virginia Tech Review Panel affirmed, this collaboration proved valuable.

Members of criminal justice organizations routinely interact with one another to share information, provide backup support, and coordinate activities. Weiss (1998), for example, found that 40% of law enforcement planners contact representatives from other agencies at least once per month. At other times, the interactions between organizations extend beyond ad hoc or informal relationships between individuals to more formal coordinated relationships at the organizational level. These relationships have been variously described as joined-up services, coalitions, partnerships, alliances, networks, interorganizational relationships, cooperation, and multiagency or interagency partnerships (Burnett & Appleton, 2004; Himmelman, 2001; Huxham, 2003; Lin & Beyerlein, 2006). Some scholars have argued that the distinctions "are quite tentative, since they are not based on a coherent framework or theory" (Lin & Beyerlein, 2006, p. 65). For the purposes of this section, the generic term *collaboration* will be used to refer to formal organizational connections designed to produce collaborative advantage: when collaboration allows an organization to produce outcomes superior to those possible if it had acted alone (Huxham, 1993, p. 603). This section addresses the origins of criminal justice collaborations and impediments to their successful implementation and continuation. Much of the section is organized around three widely adopted and/or highly regarded collaborations within the criminal justice system: law enforcement task forces, police corrections partnerships, and pulling levers/focused deterrence strategies. Additional examples of collaborations (fusion centers and domestic violence courts) are presented in the reading selections.

Interorganizational Collaborations

Modern society is faced with a host of challenges (e.g., crime, poverty) that have been described in the literature as messes, inherently wicked, and intractable (Williams, 2002, p. 104; see also Gray, 1985). The problems confronted by the criminal justice system—including, but not limited to, crime, disorder, fear, and terrorism—are no exception. Williams argues that these problems share a number of common properties:

- "They bridge and permeate jurisdictional, organizational, functional professional, and generational boundaries" and are interconnected with a range of other problems (p. 104). For example, Chermak and McGarrell (2004) noted the connection between violence—particularly, lethal violence—in Indianapolis and the city's drug markets. Additionally, drug offenders draw the resources of the public health community because of the co-occurrence of drug use and other health problems (e.g., infectious diseases) (Wenzel, Longshore, Turner, & Ridgely, 2001).

- An individual's disciplinary and experiential background influences how a problem is perceived, including its causes and potential solutions. A prosecutor may assert that strict punishments are the answer to a community's drug-market problem, while a treatment coordinator, adopting a public health perspective, may advocate viewing the problem as an issue of addiction.

- They are problems that are not easily addressed, and many require long-term coordinated solutions.

- They are significant problems that are likely unresolvable by any one organization acting alone (Gray, 1985).

Organizations can choose to tackle these challenges on their own without collaboration, but there are considerable risks associated with individual action (Hudson, Hardy, Henwood, & Wistow, 1999; Huxham, 1993; Huxham & Macdonald, 1992). First, organizations face the possibility of **repetition**, where each duplicates the efforts of another. Within a particular city, for example, multiple law enforcement agencies (e.g., city police, county sheriff, university police) might direct resources toward locating and apprehending a wanted offender. Lacking any type of coordination, the agencies could possibly be searching the same areas and interviewing the same citizens for information, thereby wasting limited resources. A second risk of individual action is **omission**. This occurs when certain tasks are ignored "because they have not been identified as important, or because they come into no organization's remit or, ironically, because they are the responsibility of more than one organization so each assumes the other is doing them" (Huxham & Macdonald, 1992, p. 51). A judge may unknowingly assume that a drug offender's treatment needs will be met with a sentence to a state prison even though budget cuts have forced the cancellation of such programs. Again, a lack of coordinated effort would allow the offender's needs to go unaddressed. A third risk is **divergence**, a problem that arises when organizations pursue individual rather than common system goals. Consequently, resources are "diluted" across a range of targets rather than concentrated on a single target (Huxham, 1993, p. 603). If police officers arrest offenders for minor disorder, prosecutors charge only serious offenses, and judges sentence only gun offenders to significant terms of incarceration, each component's resources are directed toward different targets. Coordination across components could enhance resource use by directing energies toward a common problem. A final risk, **counterproduction**, appears when one organization's "activity can result in a kind of cancelling out of the efforts of each organization involved, or worse, may actually negate the efforts of each, leaving both worse off than they were in the first place" (Huxham, 1993, p. 604). If a prosecutor routinely declines to charge offenders arrested by the police because the cases are inconsistent with prosecutorial priorities, public opinion of the police and officer morale might suffer.

Organizations may pursue collaboration to avoid these risks. An organization is motivated, in part, by rational self-interest (Hudson et al., 1999; Van de Ven, 1976). As discussed in Section III, failure to effectively and efficiently achieve goals can raise concerns about an organization's legitimacy, its funding, or even its existence. Alternatively, an organization can be viewed as altruistic in nature, tasked with solving a community's problems independent of its own existence needs (Hudson et al., 1999; Van de Ven, 1976). Wood and Gray (1991) note, "Both the need and the potential for stakeholders [participating organizations] to derive some benefit (individual or collective) are what makes collaboration possible" (p. 161). Collaboration enhances effectiveness, thereby increasing the viability of the organization and addressing difficult societal problems. How is this accomplished? Working together produces collaborative advantage, an ability to accomplish collective and individual organizational goals more effectively than would otherwise be possible. In this regard, the collaboration—an amalgam of separate organizations—is no different from a single organization comprising a collection of individuals (Van de Ven, 1976). Collaboration generates **synergy** (Bardach, 1996; Huxham, 1993; Lasker, Weiss, & Miller, 2001). Each participating organization contributes a combination of expertise; historical knowledge; perspectives; skills; and human, material, and financial resources to the collaboration. The result is "something new and valuable together—a whole that is greater than the sum of its individual parts" (Lasker et al., 2001, p. 184).

Depending on the nature of the collaboration, participating organizations become more or less integrated with one another; these differences are akin, according to Burnett and Appleton (2004) to those between a fruit salad and a fruitcake. As the section opening example illustrates, in spite of a collaboration consisting of a mutual-aid agreement and joint training, the Virginia Tech and Blacksburg police departments maintained their own unique organizational identities. The agencies collaborated but were still distinct units lacking any shared identity (the fruit salad). In contrast, a collaboration "can act as a unit and [have] a unique identity separate from its members" (Van de Ven, 1976, p. 25) and "also [involve] sharing risks, resources, and rewards" (Himmelman, 2001, p. 278). Intelligence fusion centers (see Figure 5.1)—organizations comprising representatives from a diverse range of local, state, and federal law enforcement agencies—draw in and analyze raw information from all sources. Consequently, the analytical products are presumed to be superior, based on more complete information rather than a single agency's, thereby allowing for effective use of law enforcement and homeland security resources (Carter & Carter, 2009). The centers, analogous to the fruitcake, have an identity apart from their constituent agencies.

Impediments to Collaboration

The theoretical benefits of collaboration make joint efforts appealing but, as Weiss (1987) warned, are not always easily achieved. A number of important, though not insurmountable, impediments to successful collaboration have been identified in the literature (additional obstacles are discussed within the context of specific criminal justice examples below). Participating organizations must be cognizant of these issues if successes are to be realized. First, organizations inevitably lose some degree of control and flexibility over operations (Hudson et al., 1999; Huxham, 1993; Van de Ven, 1976; Weiss, 1987). A law enforcement organization participating in a fugitive task force (see below) relinquishes control of the designated human and material resources (e.g., officers, vehicles) to the overall collaboration.[2] An organization's leader is unable to easily divert those resources to other areas as needed. To prevent complete powerlessness, Gray (1985) argues that power within the collaboration must be dispersed among participants so that no organization becomes "dependent on and vulnerable to the actions of others in the network" (p. 926). Second, considerable resources are likely expended simply to plan, establish, and sustain the partnership, often with little guarantee of success (Bardach, 1996; Van de Ven, 1976; Weiss, 1987). Burruss, Schafer, Giblin, and Haynes (2012) found that small law enforcement agencies were better prepared for a homeland security incident when they interacted frequently with large-agency peers. The problem in sustaining these large–small collaborations is that the large agency likely expends a considerable amount of money, directly or indirectly benefiting the small department, but sees little advantage from the collaboration. A system of incentives (e.g., federal grants) can be implemented to make the partnerships mutually beneficial. Third, individual (not organization) participants are likely to assert turf claims as they stand to benefit in terms of power, "prestige, ego gratification, visibility, and hence career opportunities [as well as] the possibilities of a larger number of employees and larger budgets" (Bardach, 1996, p. 177). If organizations are more tightly integrated—the fruitcake analogy above—Bardach advocates addressing this issue by encouraging participants to think in terms of the new collective turf staked via the collaboration. Finally, participants must share in the glories of collaboration's successes and suffer the disappointments of its failures (Bardach, 1996; Huxham, 1993).

---

[2]Wood and Gray (1991) point out that participating organizations retain some degree of autonomy. If all power is granted to another, "a different organization form is created—a merger, perhaps, but not a collaboration" (p. 148).

Figure 5.1 Map of U.S. Intelligence Fusion Centers

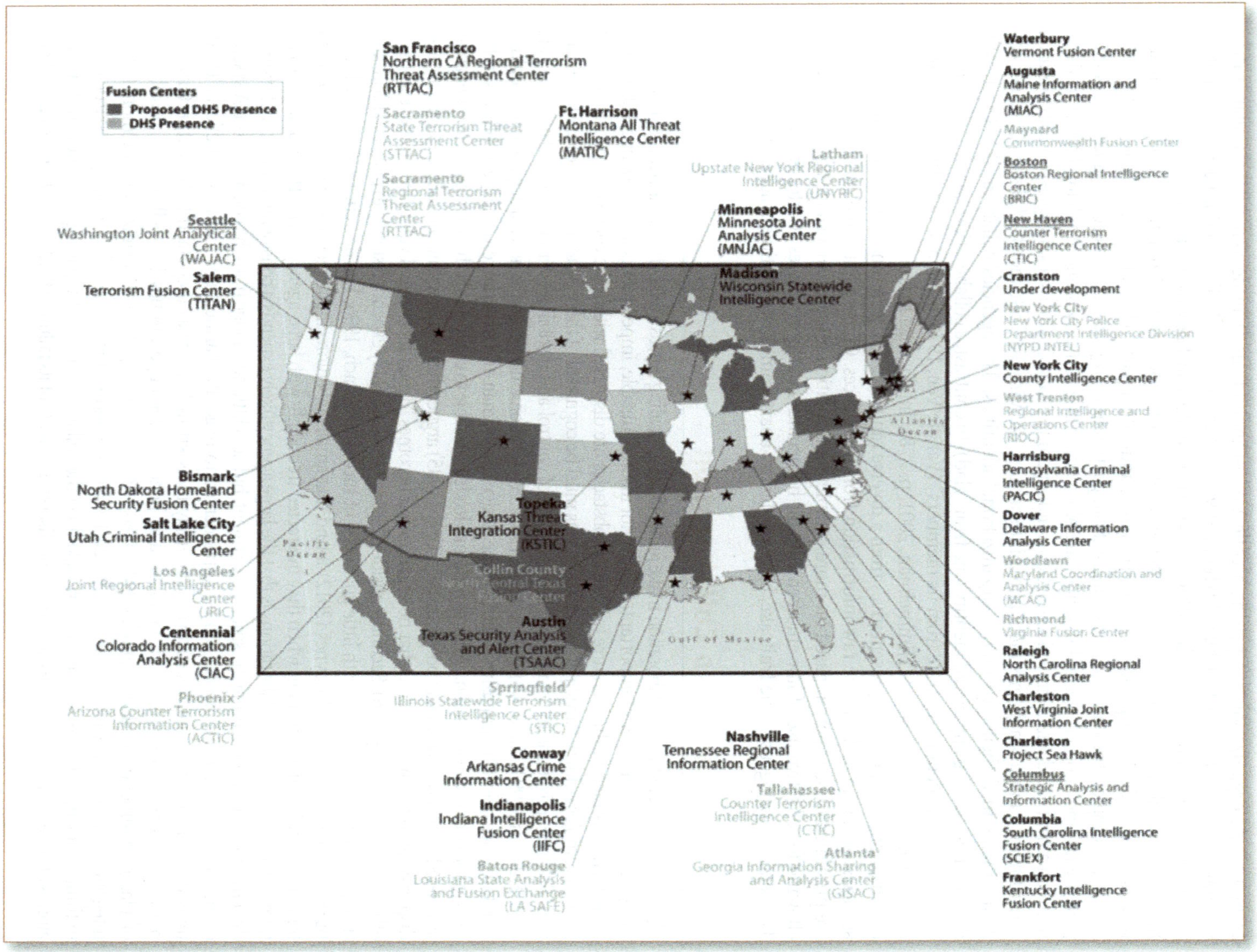
Fusion Centers
Proposed DHS Presence
DHS Presence
San Francisco
Northern CA Regional Terrorism Threat Assessment Center (RTTAC)
Sacramento
State Terrorism Threat Assessment Center (STTAC)
Sacramento
Regional Terrorism Threat Assessment Center (RTTAC)
Ft. Harrison
Montana All Threat Intelligence Center (MATIC)
Latham
Upstate New York Regional Intelligence Center (UNYRIC)
Minneapolis
Minnesota Joint Analysis Center (MNJAC)
Madison
Wisconsin Statewide Intelligence Center
Seattle
Washington Joint Analytical Center (WAJAC)
Salem
Terrorism Fusion Center (TITAN)
Bismark
North Dakota Homeland Security Fusion Center
Salt Lake City
Utah Criminal Intelligence Center
Los Angeles
Joint Regional Intelligence Center (JRIC)
Centennial
Colorado Information Analysis Center (CIAC)
Phoenix
Arizona Counter Terrorism Information Center (ACTIC)
Topeka
Kansas Threat Integration Center (KSTIC)
Collin County
North Central Texas Fusion Center
Austin
Texas Security Analysis and Alert Center (TSAAC)
Springfield
Illinois Statewide Terrorism Intelligence Center (STIC)
Conway
Arkansas Crime Information Center
Indianapolis
Indiana Intelligence Fusion Center (IIFC)
Baton Rouge
Louisiana State Analysis and Fusion Exchange (LA SAFE)
Nashville
Tennessee Regional Information Center
Tallahassee
Counter Terrorism Intelligence Center (CTIC)
Atlanta
Georgia Information Sharing and Analysis Center (GISAC)
Pacific Ocean
Atlantic Ocean
Gulf of Mexico
Waterbury
Vermont Fusion Center
Augusta
Maine Information and Analysis Center (MIAC)
Maynard
Commonwealth Fusion Center
Boston
Boston Regional Intelligence Center (BRIC)
New Haven
Counter Terrorism Intelligence Center (CTIC)
Cranston
Under development
New York City
New York City Police Department Intelligence Division (NYPD INTEL)
New York City
County Intelligence Center
West Trenton
Regional Intelligence and Operations Center (RIOC)
Harrisburg
Pennsylvania Criminal Intelligence Center (PACIC)
Dover
Delaware Information Analysis Center
Woodlawn
Maryland Coordination and Analysis Center (MCAC)
Richmond
Virginia Fusion Center
Raleigh
North Carolina Regional Analysis Center
Charleston
West Virginia Joint Information Center
Charleston
Project Sea Hawk
Columbus
Strategic Analysis and Information Center
Columbia
South Carolina Intelligence Fusion Center (SCIEX)
Frankfort
Kentucky Intelligence Fusion Center

Source: Rollins (2008); Congressional Research Service.

Criminal Justice Collaborations

Within the criminal justice system, collaborations deal with myriad issues, including drugs, fugitives, homeland security, domestic violence, prisoner reentry, and other matters of common interest to multiple agencies. To illustrate the value of and challenges to successful justice system collaboration, three examples are offered spanning criminal justice system components: law enforcement task forces, police–corrections partnerships, and pulling levers/focused deterrence partnerships.

Law Enforcement Task Forces

Multijurisdictional task forces (MJTFs) comprising some combination of local, state, and federal law enforcement organizations are some of the most common types of collaborations within the criminal justice system. Phillips and Orvis (1999) proposed that a

> task force is a special law enforcement organization with multijurisdictional authority created by an agreement among several government bodies to more effectively combat a delineated crime problem [that] use the combined resources, both human and logistical, of several agencies to more efficiently combat the stated problem for the term of the agreement. (p. 442)

Their definition is inclusive in that it avoids specifying criteria related to the number of agencies required to be part of the task force, the number of different levels of government that must be represented, and the types of problems targeted (see U.S. General Accounting Office, 1993, for a discussion). To do otherwise—to delineate arbitrary criteria—creates confusion when it comes to enumerating the number of task forces in existence. Instead, Phillips and Orvis's definition—the one that will guide the discussion below—recognizes variation across task forces. Represented organizations may be drawn from regional or contiguous jurisdictions (horizontal collaborations) and/or different levels of government, including local, county, state, and federal agencies (vertical collaborations) (Hayeslip & Russell-Einhorn, 2002). Size may range from two participants to several hundred. Indeed, according to a 1995 survey of 278 task forces, most had fewer than 10 assigned members but one had as many as 335 (Bureau of Justice Assistance, 1996).[3] Finally, task forces are created for a range of purposes, including drug enforcement, fugitive apprehension, and homeland security.

MJTFs first appeared in the 1960s as U.S. Attorney General Robert Kennedy targeted organized crime, and task forces continued to appear over the next two decades, targeting specific offenses such as financial crimes and serial homicide (Phillips, 1999; Phillips & Orvis, 1999). The number of MJTFs grew exponentially during the 1980s as the War on Drugs led agencies to "the realization that drug sellers did not respect jurisdictional boundaries [and] law enforcement agencies serving contiguous jurisdictions therefore needed to coordinate enforcement activities both to share information and resources and to avoid overlapping investigations" (Jefferis, Frank, Smith, Novak, & Travis, 1998, p. 86; see also Schlegel & McGarrell, 1991). Collaborations were further stimulated by substantial federal investment in task force creation and maintenance (Jefferis et al., 1998; McGarrell & Schlegel, 1993; Phillips & Orvis, 1999; Smith, Novak, Frank, & Travis, 2000). Under the federal Byrne assistance program,

---
[3]Assigned participants are distinct from organizational members. A task force comprising two collaborating organizations may have more than two assigned participants.

the Bureau of Justice Assistance provided more than $700 million in financial support between 1989 and 1994 to criminal justice organizations for the funding of antidrug task forces. Before funding priorities shifted and MJTF growth leveled off, there were an estimated 900 to 1,100 task forces operating across the United States between 1990 and 1993 (Dunworth, Haynes, & Saiger, 1997). Task forces also formed to tackle other problems, including fugitive apprehension and violent crime activity. For example, by the end of the first quarter of 2000, Federal Bureau of Investigation (FBI, 2001) field offices coordinated 55 violent crime, 35 violent crime/fugitive, 43 violent crime/gang, 24 fugitive, and 17 interstate theft/major offender task forces. After the 9/11 attacks, other task forces formed to protect the homeland. As of 2012, joint-terrorism task forces (JTTFs) exist in 103 U.S. cities, combining the resources of more than 600 state and local and 50 federal agencies (FBI, n.d.).

Schlegel and McGarrell (1991) argued more than 20 years ago that, "on its face, the logic behind task forces seems sound" (p. 409). Any single organization—particularly the smaller law enforcement agencies that make up the bulk of the law enforcement industry—lacks the personnel, equipment, expertise, and capacity to handle many intractable crime-related problems (Brewer, Jefferis, Butcher, & Wiles, 2007; Phillips, 1999; Schlegel & McGarrell, 1991; Williams, 2002). Whereas political (e.g., city/township) or administrative (e.g., beat or district) boundaries may be useful from an organizational point of view, criminals do not observe the same divisions. Absent collaborations, multiple organizations would be directing their energies and resources toward the same individuals and problems, a wasteful duplication of effort (Phillips, 1999; Schlegel & McGarrell, 1991). Coordinating activities also facilitates the flow of information, crucial for the development of organization knowledge and expertise or, as described earlier, synergy (Jefferis et al., 1998; Lasker et al., 2001; Phillips, 1999).

Anecdotal accounts and summary data provide preliminary evidence that program logic translates into effectiveness in practice. Jefferis and colleagues (1998) reported that federally funded task forces were making 86,000 drug arrests per year in the late 1980s and seizing $100 million in assets. An account of a Utah fugitive apprehension task force indicated that it was responsible for the arrest of more than 700 individuals within its first year (Buhler, 1999). More recently, JTTFs were credited with thwarting terrorist plots in Portland, Oregon ("Portland Seven"); Buffalo, New York ("Lackawana Six"); and other cities (FBI, n.d.; Stewart, 2011). This evidence provides only an initial indication of the effectiveness of task forces. We do not know how many drug arrests would have been made or whether plots would have been interrupted if task forces had not been in operation.

Several studies attempted to overcome this important limitation. Generally speaking, the research points to improvement in **process goals**, those factors related to the internal operations of the task forces that are presumed to be linked to outcomes. The process goals include factors such as increased collaboration, improved information sharing, clearer understanding of each agency's roles, enhanced case quality, and other internal indicators. In a survey of participants in two multicounty Indiana task forces, as well as organizations in nearby counties not participating in the task forces (the counterfactual), task force participants reported higher levels of communication and cooperation (McGarrell & Schlegel, 1993). Similarly, members of Ohio drug enforcement task forces noted more frequent interagency communication and higher quality drug cases (perceived likelihood of prosecution) than did their non-task-force counterparts (Smith et al., 2000). Interestingly, according to studies in Indiana (Schlegel & McGarrell, 1991) and Ohio (Jefferis et al., 1998; Smith et al., 2000), task forces had little impact on **output goals,** including the number of arrests. In the two Indiana task force regions, only a small percentage of felony drug arrests were actually made by the task force. Even if increases are observed, they may be due to greater resources rather than to the task force itself; arrests may increase without the task force if a single department devotes more personnel and equipment to the problem (Schlegel & McGarrell, 1991). As Smith and colleagues (2000) summarize,

> The traditional production measures of effectiveness did not indicate that membership in a task force was related to success, while members perceived that the task force process positively influenced their exchange of drug-related information and that the task force system was effective in developing higher-quality drug cases. (p. 551)

These process-oriented successes notwithstanding, Guerra (1995) and Herman (2005) both offer a number of cautions related to the power of MJTFs. Guerra addressed vertically organized task forces that included a federal organization representative. Some scholars cite this task force feature as an asset since, if a violation of federal law occurs, the case can be prosecuted in federal court, where "officers generally feel that justice is swifter and more certain...than in most overburdened state criminal courts" (Phillips, 1999, p. 4; see also Brewer et al., 2007). Given that the task force comprises sovereign state and federal governments, each is entitled, with some restrictions, to prosecute offenders in its own courts without violating double jeopardy protections. Court decisions, state law, and U.S. attorney policy manuals provide guidance on when successive prosecutions are unacceptable and permissible (Guerra, 1995). If task forces increase interagency coordination across levels of government, does the likelihood of successive prosecutions increase? Guerra indicated that "successive prosecutions, although still a small fraction of the total volume of criminal cases, have proliferated...even after the first jurisdiction has obtained a conviction and a stiff sentence" (pp. 1207–1208). Absent checks of some sort, the potential for abuse exists, and these successive prosecutions impose substantial hardships on defendants. However, as with the research discussed above, we do not know the extent to which successive prosecutions are directly linked to task force activity or would have occurred in the absence of interagency collaborations.

Herman's (2005) concerns are related to federalism—the relationship between federal and state governments—and the organizational structure of task forces, particularly JTTFs. As the homeland security efforts expanded, the separation of powers between state and federal law enforcement authorities blurred, as evident in task force relationships. For example, "The Tenth Amendment and principles of federalism...prohibit the federal government from 'commandeering' state or local law enforcement officials to assist in implementing federal criminal law" (p. 946). Yet, after the 9/11 attacks in 2001, the FBI asked local law enforcement agencies to assist with interviewing thousands of Arab and Muslim men. The FBI could not compel local law enforcement agencies to perform these duties, but most participated in the wake of the 9/11 attacks; some, however, questioned the legality and appropriateness of the FBI's request. Accountability is also a concern. Local department assignees to JTTFs remain employees and continue to be paid by their home organizations, but they were required "to get the FBI's permission before disclosing information about investigations and their own roles in those investigations" (p. 951). Who controls the officers while they are assigned to the task force, issues related to Fayol's (1949) scalar chain and unity-of-command principles? There is also a concern about funding. If JTTFs comprise a large number of local and state agency personnel, the funding of a federal government function—homeland security—is being distributed across subfederal government units (Herman, 2005). Should the federal government be responsible for providing funding to fulfill its own responsibilities? Organizational leaders will undoubtedly have to weigh these potential concerns when deciding whether to participate in a task force. Do the benefits noted earlier—improved communication and resources—as well as intangible benefits, including the potential for enhanced legitimacy and public opinion, justify the risks/downsides involved?

Police–Corrections Partnerships

The task forces described above are largely made up of law enforcement agencies, although other organizations (e.g., county prosecutors or U.S. attorneys) may participate regularly or on an ad hoc basis. As community policing reforms diffused throughout the law enforcement industry in the late 1980s and 1990s, police departments increasingly established relationships with non-law-enforcement organizations, including community groups and other government entities, to facilitate neighborhood problem solving (Skogan & Frydl, 2004). Parent and Snyder (1999) argue that a concern for public safety, the goal that has driven law enforcement agencies to partner with others, led many correctional agencies, particularly probation and parole, to establish partnerships as well. In fact, during the past two decades, a wide range of police–corrections partnerships emerged, defined as "a formal or informal collaboration between police and correctional agencies that: (1) involves staff from each agency in the joint performance of a line or support function and (2) provides benefits to both agencies" (p. 6).

A five-category classification scheme aids in understanding the various purposes of these partnerships; agencies may come together for one or more of these reasons (Parent & Snyder, 1999):

1. Enhanced supervision: Police and probation/parole officers work together to increase the level of surveillance of offenders under some form of community supervision.

2. Fugitive apprehension: Police and probation/parole officers work to locate fugitive offenders who fled (absconded) from supervision.

3. Information sharing: Law enforcement and correctional organizations share information related to a single offender, groups of offenders, or communities, and/or aggregate data such as revocation or crime rates (see Table 5.1; Jannetta & Lachman, 2011).

4. Specialized enforcement: "Police and correctional agencies, as well as community organizations, collaborate to rid communities of particular problems" such as drugs or gangs (Parent & Snyder, 1999, p. 7; see also Worrall & Gaines, 2006).

5. Interagency problem solving: Agencies representing multiple system components come together to exchange information, discuss mutual concerns, and strengthen interagency relationships.

Some of the partnerships link police and prison officials together to share intelligence (No. 3 above). For example, the Washington State Prison Anti-Gang Program recognized that gang affiliations and tensions were imported into correctional facilities (Parent & Snyder, 1999). If prison officials were able to access the wealth of knowledge possessed by law enforcement officials, particularly officers in gang units, they could use the information to direct operations within correctional facilities. This is precisely what occurred. Additionally, notifications were sent to law enforcement agencies when gang members were released into the community. Other programs, including the Fugitive Apprehension Program in Hennepin County, Minnesota, expanded on the law enforcement-centric fugitive task force (see Brewer et al., 2007) by involving representatives from the Department of Community Corrections to target absconding parolees involved in serious crime (Parent & Snyder, 1999).

Table 5.1 Types of Information and Intelligence

	Purpose	Organization Level	Mechanism	Examples
Routine information	Routine sharing of information fundamental to the partnership	Agency or local office	Data system integration, automated updates	Parolee release dates and addresses, supervising officer, arrest of supervisee
Intelligence	Timely situational/contextual information	Local office and line officer	Joint operations, regular meetings (roll call), special meetings (gang task force)	Sex offender profiling, gang dynamics, information about supervisee sightings in the community
Aggregate data	Problem identification and performance management	Agency or local office	Performance measures, strategic planning sessions	Data on crime problems, revocation rates, recidivism

Source Jannetta and Lachman (2011); U.S. Department of Justice, Office of Community Oriented Policing Services.

The effectiveness of police–corrections partnerships has rarely been studied systematically beyond cursory or anecdotal evaluations. However, a sizeable body of literature has developed describing, assessing, and critiquing collaborations between police and community corrections officials that primarily direct efforts toward enhanced supervision. One of the earliest, most recognized, and most frequently emulated enhanced-supervision partnerships began in Boston in 1992. The program, known as Operation Night Light, paired probation and police officers to undertake visits to criminally active probationers (Corbett, 1998; Parent & Snyder, 1999). Probation officers sought area restrictions and curfews as conditions of probation, and the joint patrols ensured that those conditions were observed (Parent & Snyder, 1999). Visits were made to the homes of probationers, and "it [was] not uncommon for a team to stop at a park or street corner where youth [were] congregating to determine whether any probationers [were] present" (Corbett, 1998, p. 34). Although it is impossible to determine the precise impact of Operation Night Light on crime in Boston, since other anticrime strategies were operating simultaneously, the city did experience a substantial drop in violence, particularly firearm violence, during the mid-1990s (Parent & Snyder, 1999). Similar programs soon emerged elsewhere. For example, San Bernardino, California, organized its own Nightlight (one word, unlike Boston's two) program where teams of probation and police officers would increase the level of supervision of juvenile probationers by making initial home visits to all probationers and return visits to high-risk offenders (Worrall & Gaines, 2006). The teams also enforced curfews and conducted general patrols; "if juvenile probationers were present, they were investigated per probation procedures" (p. 582). An evaluation of the San Bernardino program revealed reductions in juvenile assaults, burglary, and theft but no effect on robbery or motor vehicle theft (Worrall & Gaines, 2006).

Other police–community corrections partnerships operate according to different models. For example, some enhance supervision without actually employing joint patrols. One of the components of the Smart Partners Program (Washington Department of Corrections Regional Community Corrections office and Redmond Police Department) involved assigning a small caseload of offenders to participating police officers who, after receiving training from the Department of Corrections, served as volunteer community corrections officers (CCOs):

> The officers conduct random home visits, usually once or twice a week, to ensure that community custody offenders are complying with their curfews. The police officers cannot enter the offender's residence without permission. If permission is not given, the police officers report the refusal to the offender's CCO. . . . If they are invited to enter, police officers observe the premises to see if there are any violations of conditions of supervision. If the police officer observes evidence of a crime (e.g., cocaine in plain sight), the officer can arrest the offender. If the officer observes a violation of a condition of supervision, he or she notifies the offender's CCO. (Parent & Snyder, 1999, p. 21)

Police officers participating in the Anchorage, Alaska, Coordinated Agency Network (CAN) program were encouraged to make two unannounced contacts per month with one or two assigned juvenile probationers (Giblin, 2002). Information gathered, either directly from the juvenile or indirectly via parents or guardians, was then forwarded to a central CAN coordinator. The program goals were to supplement the monitoring already provided by regular juvenile probation officers and provide positive role models (police officers) to youthful offenders. Results of the program were not surprising, nor were they uncommon for strategies that intensify offender supervision; probationers in the CAN program were more likely to experience a technical violation than juveniles in a control group even though there were no differences in new offending rates.

As these accounts illustrate, one of the main benefits of police–community corrections partnerships is their ability to increase offender supervision beyond levels ordinarily delivered by a probation or parole officer alone (Murphy & Lutze, 2009). It is a matter of the span of control—the number of offenders for every officer (see Section II). In Anchorage, probation officers supervised about 36 probationers each, allowing for roughly one contact per month (Giblin, 2002). Nationwide, some officers have caseloads exceeding 200 probationers (Torbet, 1996). Given these large caseloads and absent the ability to reduce the number of offenders requiring monitoring, two options are available for enhancing surveillance: increase the number of probation/parole officers or supplement probation/parole supervision with outside assistance. The partnerships described above create a more favorable ratio, increasing the number of contacts by drawing on police resources. In theory, police and probation officer efforts should have increased juvenile probationer contact with the criminal justice system by 200% (Giblin, 2002). As information is shared, law enforcement officers also become more informed.

> If police officers know who is on probation and what conditions they are supposed to obey, they may be able to deter violations by increasing the odds that violations will be detected, particularly violations related to curfews and associating with other offenders. (Jones & Sigler, 2002, p. 246)

The partnerships also combine each agency's respective powers in a mutually beneficial way. Police officers provide protection to unarmed probation or parole officers making visits to high-risk offenders at dangerous places or times (Jannetta & Lachman, 2011). Probation/parole officers use their power to search (see below) and quickly remove noncompliant offenders from the streets (Murphy & Lutze, 2009; Parent & Snyder, 1999). Other potential benefits include improved public opinion and greater respect and recognition of each other's roles in the criminal justice system (Parent & Snyder, 1999).

As police–community corrections partnerships evolve, the likelihood of **mission distortion** increases (Corbett, 1998). This occurs as agencies shed their own traditional responsibilities and assume those more consistent with their partnering agency. Although this problem may be less problematic among police officers, it is especially acute within probation and parole agencies (Murphy & Lutze, 2009). Mawby and Worrall (2004) noted that probation officers in the United Kingdom drifted away from their social work and rehabilitative orientations to focus more on policing tasks such as detection and apprehension, essentially merging the two types of officers into a single "polibation officer" role (p. 67). The tensions are evident in the everyday work of CCOs who have "to work with offenders over time versus law enforcement who encounter offenders at only one point in time such as during arrest or during a period of immediate conflict" (Murphy & Lutze, 2009, p. 70). They may face considerable pressure to expeditiously remove offenders from the street for even the slightest of violations even though historically they serve both law enforcement and social service roles (Kim, Gerber, & Beto, 2010).

The primacy of law enforcement is further reinforced in situations where the probation officer's power is used to serve a law enforcement officer's ends, approaching the limits of legality. Probation and parole officers have considerable latitude when it comes to searching offenders and their homes (Jannetta & Lachman, 2011; Kim et al., 2010; Murphy & Lutze, 2009). Individuals supervised within the community do not have the same Fourth Amendment protections as ordinary citizens; some rights are relinquished as conditions of their probation or early release (Colbridge, 2003). In contrast, police officers require probable cause to support a warrant or one of the warrantless exceptions before they are allowed to conduct a search. Research shows, however, "that police officers viewed the probation officer's authority to gain access to offenders' homes as a valuable tool that they can and should share" (Murphy & Lutze, 2009, p. 71). In these cases, the probation or parole officer is said to serve as a **stalking horse** or surrogate for the police; the CCO conducts a search to satisfy a law enforcement request rather than to fulfill his or her own job responsibilities (Colbridge, 2003, p. 29; Murphy & Worrall, 2007). The Supreme Court has said that "so long as the searches themselves are reasonable, it will not inquire into the actual motivations of officers conducting them" (Colbridge, 2003, p. 31). That said, Murphy and Worrall (2007) argue that these types of incidents threaten probation officer–probationer relationships, as offenders come to resent the drift toward and alignment with law enforcement authorities. Clarifying participant responsibilities becomes an essential early stage task for ensuring a successful partnership and warding off concerns about mission distortion and misuse of power.

Pulling Levers and Focused Deterrence Partnerships

Summarizing deterrence theory, Paternoster (1987) stated, "[It] assumes that even if people do not perceive accurately the objective certainty and severity of punishment, at least they are motivated rationally by their perceptions of those risks" (p. 214). In combination with the swiftness (celerity) of punishments, increasing the certainty and severity of sanctions should produce crime reduction effects. In reality, many severe sanctions are applied infrequently and, if used, occur long after the crime is committed (Kennedy, 1996). Kennedy (2006) described the problem succinctly:

It is thus possible for there to be a great deal of enforcement without that enforcement being consistent, predictable, or very meaningful to offenders. A street drug dealer may have been arrested a number of times. But each day, when he considers whether to go work his corner, the chance that he will be arrested *today* will be both small and essentially random. (p. 165; emphasis in original)

As a result, many question the viability of deterrence as they see criminals arrested, released, reoffending, and rearrested, all while seemingly immune to the penalties imposed by the formal criminal justice system (Kennedy, 2006). What if the sanctions imposed on the street drug dealer can be made more certain, severe, and swift? While resource constraints may prevent criminal justice officials from enhancing deterrence for all offenders, the system can focus its efforts on the most chronic and/or violent offenders through collaboration. When a criminal act does occur, all levers can be pulled to quickly and significantly respond to the offender. This is the basic goal of pulling levers or focused deterrence strategies.

The pulling levers strategy originated in Boston in the mid-1990s and expanded to cities such as Peoria (IL), Nashville (TN), Indianapolis (IN), Stockton (CA), Lowell (MA), and Minneapolis (MN). As of 2009, an estimated 75 jurisdictions employed some derivation of a focused deterrence strategy to reduce drug or gang problems (Tillyer, Engel, & Lovins, in press). Kennedy (2006; see also Braga & Weisburd, 2012) suggested that pulling levers/focused deterrence strategies typically follow a framework comprising six elements:

1. *Select a particular crime problem.* Prior to the development of the pulling levers strategy, Boston was plagued by gang violence, although only a small number of gangs/gang members were responsible for the majority of all youth homicides in the city (Braga, Kennedy, Piehl, & Waring, 2000). Other cities tailored the strategy to address specific community needs: Homicide in Indianapolis and Minneapolis (Corsaro & McGarrell, 2009; Kennedy & Braga, 1998), drug markets in Peoria and Rockford (Corsaro, Brunson, Gau, & Oldham, 2011; Corsaro, Brunson, & McGarrell, in press), and gun violence in Chicago (Papachristos, Meares, & Fagan, 2007) are just a few examples.

2. *Coordinate an interagency enforcement group.* For the strategy to be successful, a coordinated effort is required. In Boston, a working group comprising members of the Boston Police Department, probation and parole, district attorney's office, U.S. attorney, juvenile corrections, school police, federal law enforcement, and others came together and decided to focus their attention on the most chronic offenders (Braga et al., 2000). Similarly, 75 representatives from 10 partner agencies converged as part of the Indianapolis Violence Reduction Partnership (Chermak & McGarrell, 2004).

3. *Conduct research to identify key offenders or groups of offenders (e.g., gangs, drug-dealing organizations).* Using crime analysis and officer knowledge, officials in Indianapolis found that about 60% of homicides involved "groups of known, chronic offenders" and that most were connected to the drug trade in some fashion (Chermak & McGarrell, 2004, p. 168). In Peoria, Illinois, analysis revealed a hot spot that produced a disproportionate share of crime (Corsaro et al., 2011). Sixty-one gangs in Boston (comprising only 1% of their age group citywide) were responsible for 60% of youth homicides within the city (Braga et al., 2000). In each case, research helped identify the targets for intervention.

4. *Communicate the deterrence message to offenders.* "Sanctions offenders do not know about cannot deter them, and sanctions offenders do not believe in will not deter them" (Kennedy, 2006, p. 166). Targeted offenders meet with members of the partnership in settings referred to as "call-ins," "notification meetings," or "forums." During these meetings, groups of offenders are called into a central location and confronted by the criminal justice community. They are warned that criminal activity will not be tolerated and informed of the consequences of continued offending, in some cases, by using peers as examples (see Photo 5.1; Kennedy, 2006; Papachristos et al., 2007). They are cautioned that they are now receiving special attention from authorities but are provided instructions on how to avoid trouble (e.g., put the guns down; Kennedy, 2006). Teams of police and probation officers also communicate similar messages to targeted offenders at their homes or in the hospital rooms of victims of violence, warning them against retaliation (Kennedy & Braga, 1998).

5. *Provide services to offenders and communicate the voice of the community.* In Boston, Indianapolis, Chicago, and other cities, the law enforcement message was supplemented with one from a series of community partners. In Chicago, for example, "for the final 30 to 40 minutes [of notification meetings], a series of speakers from various agencies in the community discuss their programs and what offenders need to do to enroll or participate" (Papachristos et al., 2007, p. 232). These programs may include treatment, job training, GED (or other educational), employment, or social services. The goal is to provide offenders, confronted first with the strict deterrence message, with a pathway toward a more law-abiding lifestyle.

▲ Photo 5.1 Public service announcements created for Project Safe Neighborhoods, a federal initiative that utilizes offender notification approaches (Source: Project Safe Neighborhoods, 2013)

6. *Direct a special enforcement operation toward the identified individuals or groups and use "any and all legal tools (or levers) to sanction groups"* (Kennedy, 2006, pp. 156–157). The deterrence message is strong insofar as authorities follow through on it. The collaboration permits a multipronged enforcement strategy. When a targeted crime is committed, the partnership will bring the full brunt of its powers down on the chronic offenders or groups. Participating agencies might step up patrol levels, crack down on drug markets, make unannounced probation and parole visits, push for immediate revocation of probation/parole violators, prosecute offenders in federal court, refrain from offering plea bargains, and seek more severe sentences (Chermak & McGarrell, 2004; Kennedy, 1996). As offenders are warned at notification meetings, "a shooting by one of their number will result in action against all" (Kennedy, 2006, p. 162). By targeting all chronic individuals and groups for the behavior of one or a few, the criminal justice apparatus further communicates the message that criminal activity will not be tolerated. Moreover, it is designed to leverage group dynamics; members of gangs or drug-dealing organizations will discourage one another from engaging in the targeted conduct, knowing that everyone will face the consequences (Kennedy, 2006).

Research evidence points to the successes of pulling levers strategies in cities across the country (Braga & Weisburd, 2012). For example, in Boston, the overall initiative produced a 63%, 32%, and 25% decrease in monthly youth homicides, shots-fired calls, and gun assault incidents citywide, respectively; when compared with other U.S. and New England cities, only Boston experienced a crime drop at the point of the intervention (Braga, Kennedy, Waring, & Piehl, 2001).[4] Sharp declines in homicides were also observed in Minneapolis, Chicago, Stockton, and Indianapolis following the initiation of focused deterrence strategies (Braga, 2008; Corsaro & McGarrell, 2009; Kennedy & Braga, 1998; Papachristos et al., 2007, p. 232). In other cities, the strategy contributed to a drop in gun-related violence (e.g., Braga, McDevitt, & Pierce, 2006).

Cities adopting a pulling levers approach found difficulties in replicating prior successes and sustaining them for a considerable period of time (Braga & Winship, 2006; Chermak & McGarrell, 2004; Tillyer et al., in press). David Kennedy (2007), in testimony before the House Subcommittee on Crime, Terrorism, and Homeland Security, offered a cautionary note that included even the original pulling levers site: "Not all jurisdictions have implemented the strategies properly. Some who have (including Boston, the first and still best-known site) have let effective interventions fall apart, highlighting the need for attention to institutionalization and sustainability" (p. 2). Unlike law enforcement task forces, partnerships such as Boston's working group, the Indianapolis Violence Reduction Partnership, or the Cincinnati Initiative to Reduce Violence comprise organizations from across the criminal justice system and local community, each with their own responsibilities, goals, and resource pools. Bridging these gaps is a daunting task. In Boston, violence started increasing in 2000 at the same time as the pulling levers approach became less intense. The key Boston Police Department task force leader left for another position within the police department, and the new commander did not continue the Operation Ceasefire meetings (Braga, Hureau, & Winship, 2008). Around the same time, the department's staffing levels declined and funding priorities shifted toward homeland security initiatives. Moreover, a coalition of black ministers, a critical ally of the police department since the early 1990s, fractured and devoted significantly less attention to community gang problems than during the 1990s (Braga et al., 2008; Braga & Winship, 2006). The overall pulling levers strategy faltered as a result.

In contrast, participants were able to maintain the Indianapolis Violence Reduction Partnership for years, as they were committed to the same goals (violence reduction), saw the benefits of information sharing, and reaped secondary benefits (e.g., improved public opinion). Also, organizational leaders, in addition to or in lieu of other organizational representatives, often attended the meetings, seeing firsthand the value of the partnership (Chermak & McGarrell, 2004). In other places, the criminal justice and broader community already had a "network of capacity"—strong working relationships—that facilitated the process of developing a pulling levers strategy (Braga & Winship, 2006). Without these preexisting relationships, partnerships are more likely to be fleeting in nature and tied to the interests of specific individuals. In other words, efforts must be made to create a formal structure where the "work would be institutionalized in positions, rather than individuals, to improve the likelihood of continued implementation" (Tillyer et al., in press, p. 7).

Criminal justice collaborations have enjoyed successes over the past 20 years, contributing to reductions in crime, disorder, and drug use, but institutionalizing the partnerships has proven to be more problematic. Some successful collaborations dissolved as funding dried up, key stakeholders departed, or organizational priorities shifted. Considerable energy must be devoted to sustaining these collaborations while ensuring that the collaborative advantage generated (e.g., collective power) is not abused.

---

[4]The pulling levers strategy was coupled with a gun interdiction strategy in Boston as part of an overall strategy known as Operation Ceasefire.

KEY TERMS

collaborative advantage	mission distortion	repetition
counterproduction	omission	stalking horse
divergence	output goals	synergy
horizontal collaborations	process goals	vertical collaborations

DISCUSSION QUESTIONS

1. Available evidence suggests that law enforcement task forces help organizations meet process goals (e.g., improved relationships) rather than output goals (e.g., increased number of arrests). If this is true, are task forces valuable? That is, are improved working relationships and communication worthwhile in their own right even if they do not contribute to outcomes such as more arrests or lower crime rates?

2. Power is greatly enhanced via collaboration, as evident in several of the examples (e.g., law enforcement task forces, police–probation partnerships). Assume you are a public affairs spokesperson for an organization participating in one of these collaborations. How would you convince the public that the collaboration will produce more good (e.g., reduced crime) than harm (e.g., violation of rights, excessive task force power)?

3. In what ways can private-sector organizations participate in and contribute to the partnerships discussed in this section? Explain.

WEB RESOURCES

National Drug Court Institute:
http://www.ndci.org

FBI Joint Terrorism Task Forces (JTTFs):
http://www.justice.gov/jttf/

Report of the Virginia Tech Review Panel:
http://www.governor.virginia.gov/tempcontent/techpanelreport.cfm

Reading 8

David L. Carter and Jeremy G. Carter recount the historical precursors and current issues related to intelligence fusion centers. The organizations draw on the personnel resources (including expertise) of multiple agencies at the federal, state, and local level and, more important, combine and analyze raw data from these disparate sources to produce information useful in preventing and responding to a broad range of hazards (e.g., terrorism, crime, natural disasters). Since 9/11, the federal government has taken an active role in organizing, supporting, and funding the dozens of fusion centers across the United States, guided by the assumption that the ability to successfully address homeland security responsibilities is enhanced when individuals and organizations are more knowledgeable. Such knowledge comes from integrating—fusing—information that previously would have remained within the confines of a single organization. In other words, collaborative capacity, using Huxham's terminology, is strengthened by interorganizational information sharing along the horizontal and vertical levels. Carter and Carter discuss several criteria used to judge the effectiveness of fusion centers, including the flow of information (process), the protection of civil rights, the efficiency of the work, and the ability to identify and prevent terrorist and criminal incidents.

The Intelligence Fusion Process for State, Local, and Tribal Law Enforcement

David L. Carter and Jeremy G. Carter

Over the last several years the U.S. Department of Homeland Security (DHS) has committed millions of dollars to help state and local law enforcement agencies develop intelligence fusion centers (Allen, 2008). Although the funds have been readily accepted, concerns have been expressed about the efficiency of intelligence fusion centers (General Accountability Office, 2007), their effectiveness (Masse & Rollins, 2007), and whether there are adequate protections in place to protect citizens' privacy and civil rights (German & Stanley, 2007).

The fusion process represents a new generation for the intelligence function and a new structure for most state, local, and tribal law enforcement agencies to understand. Contrary to intuition, the fusion process (i.e., analyzing information from diverse resources) and the creation of fusion centers (i.e., the physical plant) are more complex than the mere changing of organizational functions for an existing law enforcement intelligence unit:

- It typically involves either the reengineering of the entire conceptual framework of the intelligence function in an agency or the creation of an entirely new entity.
- It requires engaging an array of people and organizations to be contributors and consumers of the intelligence function.
- It involves changing attitudes and processes of personnel.
- It requires establishing new functional and information-sharing processes among state, county, municipal, tribal, and federal law enforcement partners.

Source: Carter, D. L., & Carter, J. G. (2009). The intelligence fusion process for state, local, and tribal law enforcement. *Criminal Justice and Behavior,* 36(12) 1323–1339.

- It involves the development of new agreements and functional relationships as well as new policies and processes, including the inculcation of the intelligence-led policing[1] philosophy.

As a result, the challenges are multifold, not the least of which is the opening of oneself and one's agency to the challenges of organizational change. Most humans are dogmatic; they resist change. However, if incongruent past practices and erroneous assumptions are not eliminated from the development processes of fusion centers, the likelihood of success is diminished. The following discussion intends to provide insight about the intelligence fusion process by providing a perspective on its role and the challenges posed by the process.

Historical Perspective

Intelligence fusion centers were initially referred to as *regional intelligence centers*. They took different forms throughout the United States with no single model for what the intelligence centers did or how they should be organized. The centers evolved largely on the basis of local initiatives as a response to perceived threats related to crime, drug trafficking, and/or terrorism within a geographic region (Carter, forthcoming). The intent was to marshal the resources and expertise of multiple agencies within the region to deal with cross-jurisdictional crime problems. In some cases, a region was defined as a county (e.g., Rockland County Intelligence Center, New York), as the area surrounding a major city (e.g., Los Angeles Joint Regional Intelligence Center), as a portion of a state (e.g., Northern California Regional Intelligence Center), or as an entire state (e.g., Minnesota Joint Analysis Center).

Most of the earliest regional intelligence centers began in the 1980s as the product of counterdrug initiatives. Indeed, the High Intensity Drug Trafficking Area (HIDTA) intelligence centers[2] served as models for successful structures and initiatives as well as for the identification of systemic issues that needed to be overcome.[3] The HIDTA centers embraced federal, state, and local partnerships and focused on developing the expertise of their analysts to provide intelligence to their operational consumers. Interestingly, the HIDTA centers are organized under the Office of National Drug Control Policy yet have personnel assigned from the Drug Enforcement Administration. Because they are organizationally separate from Drug Enforcement Administration, they provide greater support to local task forces and agencies than that of the broader operational missions of the administration. As time passed, administration operations relied much more heavily on the El Paso Intelligence Center than on the HIDTA intelligence centers, although there was regional variation. As a result of this unique organizational framework and its unitary mission of drug control, the HIDTA intelligence centers, though effective in counterdrug operations, did not evolve into the all-crimes fusion center model.

In the late 1990s, the U.S. Bureau of Alcohol, Tobacco, Firearms and Explosives (2008) developed a number of new programs designed to reduce gun violence. Emerging from these initiatives were the bureau's regional Crime Gun Centers. The centers, in some cases co-located with the HIDTA regional intelligence center, had a number of intelligence-related roles, including the analysis of trace data to identify gun traffickers, disseminate investigative leads, and coordinate with the HIDTA regional intelligence center to identify drug traffickers and their sources of guns. In virtually all cases, both the HIDTA and the bureau intelligence centers had a great deal of interaction with state, local, and tribal law enforcement agencies. The intent was to integrate—that is, fuse—information from diverse sources to better understand and prevent multijurisdictional crime problems. Hence, the foundation was laid for intelligence fusion centers. However, beyond idiosyncratic local crime issues, there was little incentive to expand the centers. Of course, this changed after September 11, 2001.

Because of the regional intelligence centers' demonstrated successes and the information-sharing challenges of counterterrorism, additional state and local entities embraced the concept and began developing their own centers. The federal government (first, the DHS) saw the value of these initiatives and began providing funding support. Fusion centers were about to experience an expanding role.

> Recognizing that state and local fusion centers represent a critical source of local information about potential threats and a mechanism for providing terrorism-related information and intelligence from federal sources, the Program Manager for the [Information Sharing Environment] (PM-ISE), the DHS, and the Department of Justice are taking steps to partner with and leverage fusion centers as part of the overall information sharing environment. (General Accountability Office, 2007, p. 2)

Building on this observation, the General Accountability Office (2007) went on to document a number of federal efforts designed to support fusion centers and address the challenges and obstacles identified by fusion center directors.

The first effort cited by the General Accountability Office (2007) is that the DHS, the Federal Bureau of Investigation (FBI), and the PM-ISE have taken actions to assist fusion centers in gaining access to and so managing multiple federal information systems, including classified systems. This means that state, local, and tribal fusion center personnel have access to information collected by the intelligence community and/or information collected via less stringent legal standards than what is required for law enforcement agencies. Access to these systems is viewed by law enforcement as an important factor in helping to connect the dots about threats, thereby more effectively protecting the community. Conversely, the American Civil Liberties Union is concerned that efforts such as this will turn "local police officers into national domestic intelligence agents" (German & Stanley, 2008, p. 2).

The second effort (General Accountability Office, 2007) is that both the DHS and the FBI have committed to providing security clearances to state, local, and tribal fusion center personnel and reducing the time that it takes for a clearance to be processed. This has been a significant issue for law enforcement executives because they believe that state, local, and tribal law enforcement personnel responsible for counterterrorism cannot be effective if they do not have routine access to classified information that reflects the most comprehensive information about threats. Once again, civil rights advocates have expressed concern that the widespread granting of security clearances to state, local, and tribal law enforcement personnel is evidence that fusion centers and their personnel are becoming federalized. In turn, they argue that this will reduce privacy protections as well as the accountability of the fusion center to state and local governments (Electronic Privacy Information Center, 2008; German & Stanley, 2007, 2008).

The next federal initiative (General Accountability Office, 2007) is that the DHS and the FBI are assisting fusion centers in obtaining and retaining qualified personnel, through assignments of federal employees to state fusion centers and through some DHS funding support. The major concern on this issue relates to sustainability. Federal funding to state and local government is almost always limited to a few years. If the fusion center is relying on federal support to operate, then its sustainability is tenuous. The fusion center guidelines state that although federal funding can be important for fusion center development, the center's operation should rely on standard appropriated funds to help ensure sustainability (Global Intelligence Working Group, 2005a). The other concern on this initiative is that fusion centers will rely on federal employees who will likely be reassigned when another problem or crisis takes precedence over the fusion centers.

The final two federal initiatives identified by the General Accountability Office (2007) are less controversial. The penultimate initiative is that federal funds in support of fusion centers have become more readily available and streamlined in operation to make grant awards faster and easier to obtain. Finally, the Department of Justice and DHS have provided training and technical assistance in support of fusion center development and maturation. On this last point, although the availability of training programs has increased, there are still comparatively limited offerings of these programs largely because of funding limitations. It is a massive task to provide law enforcement training throughout the United States. With comparatively small training staffs, the new intelligence training efforts have significant challenges to overcome.

Although progress has been made in the evolution of fusion centers in a comparatively short amount of time, many observers and fusion center governing officers appear to believe that fusion centers have a long way to go before they will seamlessly fulfill their envisioned role.

Refining the Fusion Center Concept

It was clear after the September 11 terrorist attacks that there had been poor information sharing among and between all levels of law enforcement and the intelligence community (National Commission on Terrorists Attacks Upon the United States, 2004). As more information came out about the terrorists and their minor encounters with state and local law enforcement in the weeks and months before the attacks, it was painfully evident that current information systems and processes were simply inadequate to deal with threats of this nature. It was also evident that if a diverse array of raw information was collected by different agencies, it would be essential to have a mechanism to provide data integration and analysis so that its meaning would be of value to operational law enforcement personnel.

State and local law enforcement leaders increasingly recognized that the experiences of the HIDTAs and regional intelligence centers could be applied to counterterrorism. Because of the need to have two-way information sharing directly with federal law enforcement and indirectly with the intelligence community, the fusion centers, the FBI, and the DHS reached out to one another to develop fusion centers more holistically. Indeed, "federal departments and agencies—including DHS, FBI, and [Department of Defense]—launched efforts to develop strategies to incorporate these fusion centers into their information and intelligence activities" (PM-ISE, 2006, p. 18).

Masse and Rollins (2007) note that fusion centers represent a vital part of the nation's homeland security and so rely on at least four presumptions—the first of which is that intelligence and the intelligence process play a vital role in preventing terrorist attacks. Second, it is essential to fuse a broader range of data, including nontraditional source data, to create a more comprehensive threat picture. Third, state, local, and tribal law enforcement and public sector agencies are in a unique position to make observations and collect information that may be central to the type of threat assessment referenced above. Last, having fusion activities take place at the subfederal level can benefit state and local communities and possibly have national benefits as well (Masse & Rollins, 2007).

The initial focus of many new fusion centers was exclusively on terrorism—indeed, that still remains the case for a few of the centers, such as the Georgia Information Sharing and Analysis Center.[4] However, most centers broadened their focus to embrace all crimes and all threats. The reason was twofold: First, they recognized that most terrorist acts had a nexus with other crimes; hence, by focusing exclusively on terrorism, they may miss some important indicators. Second, because a variety of crime was transjurisdictional and involved in complex criminality (notably, criminal enterprises),[5] they recognized that the fusion process would be of value in dealing with these crimes.

Further evolution of fusion center responsibilities has moved into the arena of an all-hazards focus (in addition to all crimes and all threats). Inclusion of the all-hazards approach has come from two sources: first, the special conditions on some DHS grants that specify "all hazards"; second, mandates from states or fusion center governing boards. Moreover, given the DHS's responsibility to protect the homeland, its reach extends beyond terrorism to include natural disasters, chemical weapons, weapons of mass destruction, and basic law enforcement (Harris, 2008).

Recognizing that fusion centers were increasingly integrating the concepts of established law enforcement intelligence activities with the "all crimes, all threats, all hazards" model of intelligence, the Homeland Security Advisory Council (2005) observed,

> Although the primary emphasis of intelligence/information fusion is to identify, deter, and respond to emerging terrorism-related threats and risks, a collateral benefit to state, tribal and local entities is that it will support ongoing efforts to address non-terrorism related issues by... allowing State and local entities to better identify and forecast emerging crime, public health, and quality-of-life trends... supporting targeted law enforcement and other multidisciplinary, proactive, risk-based and community-focused, problem-solving activities; and... improving the delivery of emergency and nonemergency services. (p. 2)

Structural Issues

There is no single model for a fusion center, namely because of the diverse needs and environmental characteristics that affect the structure, processes, and products of such a center. In states such as Texas and California with their large land mass, large population, and international border, the structure and processes of fusion centers will be significantly different from those of predominantly landlocked rural states, such as Wyoming or Nebraska.

A Congressional Research Service report raised questions regarding the current and potential efficacy of fusion centers. The report notes that in light of the growth of the fusion centers in state and local jurisdictions without a coordinated national plan, "there appears to be no 'one-size-fits-all' structural or operational model for fusion centers" (Masse & Rollins, 2007, p. 18). From a centralized federal perspective—as reflected in the report—the lack of a uniform model is assumed to be a flaw. However, the state and local perspective is somewhat different. Indeed, the ability to build a fusion center around grassroots needs is preferred—this permits state and local agencies to mold the fusion center into a model that best suits the needs and challenges that are idiosyncratic to each jurisdiction. As noted by Johnson and Dorn (2008) in describing the New York State Intelligence Center,

> Creating one center for intelligence and terrorism information—to combine and distribute that information to law enforcement agencies statewide—prevents duplication of effort by multiple agencies. Additionally, one state fusion center serving the entire New York law enforcement community provides a comprehensive picture of criminal and terrorists networks, aids in the fight against future terrorists events and reduces crime. (p. 38)

Within this same line of thought, fusion centers are also structured differently on the basis of legislative and executive mandates. For example, Montana's fusion center—Montana All Threat Intelligence Center—is mandated to focus on all threats; the New Jersey Regional Operations Intelligence Center includes emergency operations as well as fusion; the Massachusetts Commonwealth Fusion Center focuses on all crimes; and the Oregon Terrorism Intelligence Threat Assessment Network limits its focus to terrorism. The variability of fusion centers' structure is broad because of functional necessity and the inherent nature of local control and states' rights perspectives.

Although the structure and operational processes of fusion centers may be different, national professional standards have been articulated that outline good practice in critical administrative areas regardless of the center's mission. That is the intent of the fusion center guidelines.[6]

Despite some criticisms, that fusion centers are structured differently is not a weakness but a strength. It exemplifies that each center is designed to meet local and regional needs as well as become able to best integrate the fusion center with existing organizational components and priorities.

For example, the Michigan State Police have widespread responsibility for traffic and criminal law enforcement throughout the state. As such, the Michigan Intelligence Operations Center is organizationally placed in the state police. However, Florida has two predominant state law enforcement organizations: the Florida Highway Patrol (responsible for traffic law enforcement) and the Florida Department of Law Enforcement (responsible for criminal law enforcement). As a result, the Florida Fusion Center is organized as part of the department's Office of Statewide Intelligence. Hence, each state has structured its fusion center in a manner that best fits existing organizational structures and functional responsibilities.

Note that there are different operational and functional models of law enforcement throughout the United States. Fusion centers are no different, given that they are an element of state or local government and so have the challenge to meet the unique needs of the jurisdiction they serve. As observed in one study,

> fusion centers [must identify] their mission and their customers, at what level of analytic product they will produce, and to whom. Not all fusion centers will need the same amount of strategic analysis or tactical analysis, but, in order to determine what to produce, they will have to understand their customers' needs and ensure they are educated so they understand the difference between the two products. Fusion centers will also need to determine how they will integrate the emergency responder community. (Nenneman, 2008, p. 109)

It is perhaps this last point that will be the most challenging to define, given that all hazards intelligence and meeting the needs of the emergency responder community are not traditional roles for the law enforcement intelligence function. Some guidance to assist fusion centers in this area is being developed through the identification of baseline capabilities.

Baseline Capabilities for Intelligence Fusion Centers

As a result of national plans that seek to increase the efficiency and effectiveness of information-sharing efforts, fusion centers serve as the interlink between state, local, and tribal law enforcement and the federal Information Sharing Environment (ISE) for the exchange of terrorism information. As such, there was a need to define fundamental baseline operational capabilities to be used by fusion centers as well as major urban area intelligence units to meet the information needs of all consumers of the various intelligence centers. In practice, the baseline capabilities serve as performance standards that can measure the effectiveness of the fusion center, the fusion process, and the personnel.

A joint project of the Global Intelligence Working Group, U.S. Department of Justice, DHS, and PM-ISE resulted in a companion document to the fusion center guidelines; this document identifies elements that serve as the foundation for integrating state and major urban area fusion centers into the federal ISE. The project is based on the fusion process capabilities outlined in the 2007 fusion center assessment and the 2007 and 2008 Homeland Security Grant Program—specifically, the supplemental resource entitled the Fusion Capability Planning Tool (DHS, 2007a). In addition to the 2007 assessment, the baseline operational standards outlined in the project were developed using guidance provided in the fusion center guidelines (Global Intelligence Working Group, 2005a), the National Criminal Intelligence Sharing Plan (NCISP; U.S. Department of Justice, 2005), the Information Sharing Environment Implementation Plan (PM-ISE, 2006), and the DHS's National Preparedness Guidelines (DHS, 2007b) and Target Capabilities List (Federal Emergency Management Agency, 2007). Relying on the guidance of these national standards, the baseline capabilities for fusion centers are guided by the requirements of the presidential National Strategy for Information Sharing.

The limitation, however, is that the capabilities are directed only toward terrorism information—which includes terrorism and crimes that have a terrorism nexus—as a result of the ISE's legislative mandate from the Intelligence Reform and Terrorism Prevention Act of 2004. The DHS Intelligence and Analysis Directorate (2008) has completed an appendix to the baseline capabilities document that deals with such capabilities for critical infrastructure and key resources. Additional baseline capabilities are being prepared for fire service and public health as appendices to the baseline capabilities document.

Although determining the structure and processes of baseline capabilities for fusion centers is an important step for increasing efficiency and effectiveness, a significant gap remains. Specifically, most fusion centers will be dealing with all crimes, using intelligence analysis to guide day-to-day law enforcement activities—particularly, those fusion centers expressly supporting law enforcement agencies that have implemented an intelligence-led policing philosophy (Ratcliffe, 2008). However, there is currently no initiative going forward that will define baseline capabilities for the type of information and analysis to which many fusion centers will devote the preponderance of their time: crimes of violence, drug trafficking, organized crime, and other transjurisdictional complex criminality.

The Intelligence Fusion Process

The fusion process is an overarching methodology of managing the flow of information and intelligence across levels and sectors of government to integrate information for analysis (Lessons Learned Information Sharing, 2005). That is, the process relies on the active involvement of state, local, tribal, and federal law enforcement agencies—and sometimes on non–law enforcement agencies (e.g., private sector)—to provide the input of raw information for intelligence analysis.

As the array of diverse information sources increases, there will be more accurate and robust analysis that can be disseminated as intelligence.

Although the phrase *fusion center* has been used widely, there are often misconceptions about the function of the center. Perhaps the most common is that the center is a large room full of work stations where the staff are constantly responding to inquiries from officers, investigators, and agents. This vision is more accurately a watch center or an investigative support center—not an intelligence fusion center. Another common misconception is that the fusion center is minimally staffed until there is some type of crisis wherein representatives from different public safety agencies converge to staff workstations to manage the crisis. This is an emergency operations center, not an intelligence fusion center.

The fusion center is not an operational center but a support center. It is analysis driven. The fusion process proactively seeks to identify threats posed by terrorists or criminal enterprises and to stop them before they occur—prevention is the essence of the intelligence process. The distinction, however, is that the fusion center is typically organized by amalgamating representatives—ideally, intelligence analysts—from different federal, state, local, and tribal law enforcement agencies into one physical location. Each representative is intended to be a conduit of raw information from his or her agency, a representative who can infuse that agency-specific information into the collective body of information for analysis. Conversely, when the fusion center needs intelligence requirements,[7] the representative is the conduit back to the agency to communicate, monitor, and process the new information needs. Similarly, the agency representative ensures that analytic products and threat information are directed back to one's home agency for proper dissemination.

According to the fusion center guidelines, a fusion center is

> defined as a collaborative effort of two or more agencies that provide resources, expertise, and/or information to the center with the goal of maximizing the ability to detect,

prevent, apprehend, and respond to criminal and terrorist activity. The intelligence component of a fusion center focuses on the intelligence process, where information is collected, integrated, evaluated, analyzed, and disseminated. Nontraditional collectors of intelligence, such as public safety entities and private sector organizations, possess important information that can be "fused" with law enforcement data to provide meaningful information and intelligence about threats and criminal activity. (Global Intelligence Working Group, 2005a, p. 8)

Of course, not every law enforcement agency can contribute a person to work in the fusion center. Hence, the fusion center must develop mechanisms for two-way information sharing that captures information from the nontraditional collectors and provides threat-based information back to those who have the need to know. As a result, multiple strategies and technologies need to be developed for diverse two-way information sharing.

For example, electronic two-way information sharing via the various secure electronic information systems—Regional Information Sharing System, Law Enforcement Online, Homeland Security Information Exchange, Anti-Terrorism Information Exchange—can be effective. In the case of Anti-Terrorism Information Exchange, individuals beyond the law enforcement community who have a demonstrated need (including private sector persons) may have access to the system and use it for secure two-way information sharing. Another example is the New York Police Department's Operation Nexus:

> a nationwide network of businesses and enterprises joined in an effort to prevent another terrorist attack against our citizens. Our detectives [visit] firms that have joined us in this mutual effort. Members of Operation Nexus are committed to reporting suspicious business encounters that they believe may have possible links to terrorism. The NYPD believes terrorists may portray themselves as legitimate customers in order to purchase or lease certain materials or equipment, or to undergo certain formalized training to acquire important skills or licenses.... Through Operation Nexus, the NYPD actively encourages business owners, operators and their employees to apply their particular business and industry knowledge and experience against each customer transaction or encounter to discern anything unusual or suspicious and to report such instances to authorities. (NYPD Shield, 2008)

Another model has emerged and is being increasingly adopted throughout the United States. Developed in Los Angeles, the Terrorism Early Warning Group (TEW) has multiple functions, including supporting the intelligence fusion center:

> The Los Angeles TEW includes analysts from local, state and federal agencies to produce a range of intelligence products at all phases of response (pre-, trans-, and post attack) specifically tailored to the user's operational role and requirements. The TEW bridges criminal and operational intelligence to support strategic and tactical users. As part of this process, the TEW seeks to identify emerging threats and provide early warning by integrating inputs and analysis from a multidisciplinary, interagency team. Toward this end, the TEW has developed a local network of Terrorism Liaison Officers at law enforcement, fire, and health agencies, formed partnerships with the private sector to understand threats to critical infrastructure, and has developed and refined processes to analyze and synthesize threat data to support its client agencies. (Sullivan, 2005, p. 1)

Regardless of the method of information sharing, the key factors are as follows: There must be diverse raw input; it must be analyzed; and intelligence output must be shared with appropriate consumers.

Why Fusion Centers?

The heart of good intelligence analysis is to have a diverse array of valid and reliable raw information for analysis (Clark, 2007). The more robust the raw information, the more accurate the analytic output (i.e., the intelligence). If one thinks of information input in terms of bandwidth, the typical law enforcement intelligence unit has a narrow bandwidth; that is, information is gathered from a fairly narrow array of sources, thereby limiting the quality of the analysis and the ability to see the big picture of a criminal enterprise. Quite simply, the more limited the input of raw information, the more limited the quality of intelligence. However, if the number of sources is broadened to include a range of agencies representing much broader geographic and jurisdictional parameters, then the bandwidth is much wider. With wider bandwidth, there is a greater and more diverse information flow. Therefore, with greater information flow, the analysis becomes more accurate and utilitarian. As the quality of analysis increases, the ability to prevent or mitigate the operations of a terrorist or criminal organization increases exponentially.

Recent analyses of law enforcement and national security intelligence operations reinforce these observations in referring to a problem termed the "stovepipe" of information in agencies (Kindsvater, 2003); that is, each agency would develop a large body of information and analytic products that would be retained within the agency and rarely shared with other agencies. Analysis was generally limited to the information that came from internal sources, and its dissemination would be largely internal. As a result, while agencies were developing information, it was simply being stacked like a stovepipe. Current thought recognizes that far more value can be derived from information that is widely shared for analysis: Information from one agency may be a key when integrated with information from another agency in learning about a threat—hence, the need to fuse as much information as possible. The fusion center would not simply duplicate the activities of existing agencies but would enhance and improve their efforts by providing a service that did not yet exist (Dillon, 2002).

A Reorientation from the Current Intelligence Model

Law enforcement intelligence at the state, local, and tribal levels has been organizationally and operationally haphazard at best. Most of America's law enforcement agencies had no intelligence capacity at all. Many that did have an intelligence unit of some form were doing little, if any, analysis. In reality, most were investigative support centers where officers could call and get various types of information about investigations and cases. The personnel staffing the units, although perhaps having the title of *analyst*, were typically clerical people who had been promoted, often with little, if any, training in formal intelligence analysis techniques.

Some agencies had formally trained analysts; however, their analytic products were frequently inconsistent and stovepiped. One reason for the lack of information sharing involved the predominant philosophy of operations security for intelligence reports. Fundamentally, this meant that because information from intelligence reports might be leaked, rigid "right to know" and "need to know" dissemination standards had to be used, which essentially meant that an officer would not see an intelligence report unless he or she was working on the inquiry.

Fusion centers and the NCISP have changed many of these traditional characteristics. Having multiple agencies participate in a center means that there is a less likelihood that the intelligence will be stovepiped and will, conversely, be more widely disseminated. On this last point, the philosophy of intelligence has also changed. Although operations security remains a concern, the predominant approach is to disseminate intelligence to as many law enforcement officers as possible. The rationale is that the more officers who have information about threats, the more likely that threat will be identified and mitigated.

Human Resource Issues

Staffing the fusion centers is a critical responsibility. Because centers take different forms, staffing patterns vary but certain trends have emerged. The lead agency[8] for the fusion center has primary staffing responsibility. It provides the center's management personnel and most operational staffing, and it employs new staff, such as intelligence analysts. Larger agencies within the fusion center's service area are asked to contribute staff, typically on a temporary status, with assignment and duty responsibilities articulated in a memorandum of agreement between the fusion center and the contributing agencies.

Beyond these staff members, the FBI assigns at least one agent (and, sometimes, analysts) to each fusion center. In addition, the Intelligence and Analysis Directorate of the DHS assigns at least one person to most of the primary state fusion centers. In many cases, the National Guard assigns analysts, and various federal agencies assign personnel (e.g., the Drug Enforcement Administration and the Bureau of Alcohol, Tobacco, Firearms and Explosives). Once again, there is no explicit model for assignment; it is usually based on local needs and personal relationships.

In reality, there is a limited supply of professional law enforcement intelligence analysts in the United States, largely because most law enforcement agencies did not want to budget for professional positions. Many analysts were clerical personnel with limited knowledge, skills, abilities, and training in intelligence—an issue compounded by a lack of recognized professional standards for intelligence analysts (Marrin, 2008). Rather, they were reliable employees who were given expended duties. One major reason why this occurred was that many law enforcement executives thought that they could not justify paying high salaries to nonsworn analysts—they would opt to hire sworn officers instead. Some executives, however, saw the value of intelligence analysts and ensured that they had the best and brightest people, whom they could pay competitively.

One example of this is retired Spokane, Washington, police chief Roger Bragdon (personal interview, August 10, 2008). When faced with a multimillion-dollar budget reduction, Chief Bragdon realized that some Spokane police employees would inevitably lose their jobs. When given this difficult decision, the chief elected to furlough a number of sworn officers; however, none of his department's crime analysts or intelligence analysts lost their jobs. His reasoning, as based on his experience, was simple: By using the analysts' reports, Spokane officers worked smarter. It was, in Chief Bragdon's view, the most reasonable alternative. The investment in analysts permitted the department to continue maintaining a safe community by focusing operational activities to crime and threat priorities.

Collateral Issues

Beyond questions related to the efficacy of the intelligence fusion process, a number of issues have emerged about the operations of fusion centers. There are sharply diverse perspectives of these issues between advocates and critics.

Is There a Role for the Private Sector?

The PM-ISE observed that the private sector can be a rich resource of information, which adds a broadened dimension to information collection. Many large corporations have sophisticated security operations that monitor global threats to their facilities, products, and personnel, as posed by organized crime and criminal extremists as well as predatory criminals (National Infrastructure Advisory Council, 2006). This type of information is often different from that collected by law enforcement organizations, and it can add a unique, more insightful component to the body of information being analyzed by the fusion center.

Similarly, the private sector is a legitimate consumer of law enforcement intelligence, meeting the "right to know" and "need to know" information-sharing standards. For example, the private sector owns 85% of the critical infrastructure in the United States (National Preparedness Directorate, 2006). Moreover, the private sector has a large personnel force that, if given the proper information, can significantly increase the eyes and ears on the street to observe individuals and behaviors that pose threats. As noted in one of the best-practices papers produced by the DHS, of jurisdiction's analysis and synthesis entity, such as a fusion center, should establish processes for sharing information with the local private sector (Lessons Learned Information Sharing, 2005). However, critics have expressed the concern that fusion centers have information that private sector personnel should not have access to (German & Stanley, 2007). Furthermore, the inclusion of the private sector represents "the creation of a 'Surveillance–Industrial Complex' in which security agencies and the corporate sector join together in a frenzy of mass information gathering, tracking and routine surveillance" (p. 11).

Of course, some information-sharing issues need to be resolved. For example, certain types of personal information may be inappropriate for law enforcement to release to the private sector. Similarly, many in the private sector are concerned that proprietary information related to corporate products may be inappropriately released. Despite these limitations and concerns, there appears to be a legitimate role for the private sector in fusion centers. Just as in the case of law enforcement partners, memoranda of understanding and nondisclosure agreements need to be in place and so include provisions on information-sharing processes and restrictions.

Resistance to the Fusion Center Concept

Law enforcement agencies have historically been resistant to information sharing, for several reasons. One concern has been that when information is shared, the original agency loses control of future dissemination. This concern is legitimate because of privacy and liability issues—notably, if there is no guarantee that the information will be controlled (Federal Computer Week, 2008). Another reason for poor information sharing involves agency ego—information is power and those who have more information can have more influence (Beare & Murray, 2007). Although this appears to represent a minority of cases, it nonetheless exists. A final reason for poor information sharing is somewhat mundane: It was not convenient because of technological or logistical reasons (Slayton, 2000).

Agencies recognized post–September 11 that the intelligence community needed to become more adept at information sharing and so did the law enforcement community. With policy recommendations established in both the NCISP and the fusion center guidelines, many of the logistical issues were resolved. Similarly, with growing access to secure information systems based on Internet protocols—Regional Information Sharing System, Law Enforcement Online, and Homeland Security Information Exchange—the technology was facilitating widespread information sharing to agencies of all sizes.

Not everyone welcomed this enhanced information sharing. In a statement released by the American Civil Liberties Union (2005), civil libertarians expressed concern that intelligence fusion centers may jeopardize civil rights: "The establishment of a single source intelligence center raises important issues concerning the scope of its operations and need for safeguards to ensure that its operation do not violate civil liberties or intrude on personal privacy" (para. 2). Continuing this theme, the union explicitly stated questions that it wanted answered about fusion center operations: "We need a lot more information about what precisely the fusion center will do, what information it will be collecting, who will have access to the information, and what safeguards will be in place to prevent abuse" (para. 5). Every fusion center commander should be able to answer those questions—if not, the policy and process infrastructure of the center need to be reexamined.

Fusion Centers and Civil Rights Issues

Many privacy advocates share a concern that the growth of fusion centers will increase the jeopardy to civil rights and privacy (Dinh, 2004; Majority Staffs of the Committee on Homeland Security and the Committee on Foreign Affairs, 2008; Rossler, 2003; Sullivan, 2003). As noted in a National Governors Association best-practices paper, "The risks to individuals' privacy begin when personal information of any kind is entered into criminal justice information systems" (MacLellan, 2006, p. 4). Complicating this issue is the fact that many privacy advocates do not understand the concept of the fusion process; that is, they fear that the centers are the next iteration of the centralized surveillance of citizens.

One of the greatest concerns about fusion centers in this regard is participation of federal law enforcement agencies and National Guard personnel whose jurisdictions for information collection and retention are different from those of state, local, and tribal law enforcement agencies. Certainly, when a state, local, or tribal law enforcement agency is the custodian of an intelligence records system, it must take care to exclude information from the fusion center that does not meet the standards of information collection, retention, dissemination, and purging as articulated in 28 CFR Part 23,[9] per the recommendations in the fusion center guidelines and the NCISP.

Fundamentally, the privacy and civil rights issues related to fusion centers are the same as any other aspect of the intelligence process. Those relevant standards of the NCISP apply in the same manner and should be fully adhered to. Furthermore, Guideline 8 of the fusion center guidelines states that the management of the fusion center should "develop, publish, and adhere to a privacy and civil rights policy" (Global Intelligence Working Group, 2005a, p. 49). Commentary on this guideline goes on to note that

> one of the critical issues that could quickly stop intelligence sharing is the real or perceived violation of individuals' privacy and constitutional rights through the use of intelligence sharing systems. In order to balance law enforcement's ability to share information while ensuring that the rights of citizens are upheld, appropriate privacy policies must be in place. (p. 49)

As a consequence, civil rights issues for fusion centers have components related to policy, training, supervision, and public information that must be addressed in the development and implementation stages.

Fusion Centers and the Information Sharing Environment

The Information Sharing Environment Implementation Plan (PM-ISE, 2006) embraced the growth of fusion centers as a critical linchpin to serve as information clearinghouses between federal entities (federal law enforcement and the intelligence community), nonfederal law enforcement, and the private sector.

> Many states and localities emphatically moved to create and invest in fusion centers in the post–September 11 environment. These fusion centers now play a prominent role in collecting, analyzing, and sharing terrorism information. Individually, these centers represent vital assets for collecting terrorism-related information. Collectively, their collaboration with the Federal government, with one another (state-to-state, state-to-locality), and with the private sector represents a tremendous increase in both the nation's overall analytic capacity and the multi-directional flow of information. It is important to note that these centers are not homogenous—considerable variations exist in terms of operations and mission focus (e.g., homeland security, law enforcement, emergency response). To date, more than 40 such centers have been established across

the United States, and significant effort has gone into developing and adopting standards to facilitate easier information access, sharing, and use. (pp. 7-8)

To further this plan, the PM-ISE has established a National Fusion Center Coordination Group, led by the DHS and the Department of Justice, to identify federal resources to support the development of a national integrated network of fusion centers (General Accountability Office, 2007). Moreover, the ISE

recognizes the "all-crimes and all-hazards" nature of state and local sharing, where state, local and tribal organizations may share and fuse together multiple types of information to address a variety of needs including law enforcement, preparedness, and response and recovery. In many instances, this information may not initially be recognized as terrorism information, but may be information that could ultimately prove crucial in preventing, preparing for, or responding to terrorism. The ISE focus on terrorism information will not impede or interrupt these additional fusion center functions. (PM-ISE, 2006, p. 11)

Effectiveness of Fusion Centers

For the most part, fusion centers are so new that there has been no empirical assessment of their effectiveness. There is some anecdotal evidence that suggests success in four ways (Carter, forthcoming). In our experience (we have worked with agencies in all regions of the United States), the fusion centers that are currently operating have dramatically increased the amount of information shared among law enforcement agencies. Most have developed explicit intelligence products and have proactively engaged agencies in their service area to join their networks.

The first measure of success is whether more information is being shared among law enforcement agencies at all levels of government. There is significant evidence to suggest that information sharing has increased (McNamara, 2008); however, factors beyond the creation of fusion centers have contributed to broader information sharing. These include the creation of the Criminal Intelligence Coordinating Council; overt initiatives by the FBI Directorate of Intelligence to create discernable intelligence products that are written for release[10] to state, local, and tribal law enforcement agencies; and the widespread adoption of the NCISP, which inherently enhances information sharing.

The second measure of success deals with the ability to collect, retain, and disseminate information while protecting civil rights and privacy. Once again, our experiences indicate that the fusion centers carefully adhere to policy and legal standards for maintaining their intelligence records systems. None of the centers have been sued for civil rights violations, although several have been the subject of Freedom of Information Act requests to determine the types of information that they are collecting and retaining (Electronic Privacy Information Center, 2008). Moreover, training programs for fusion center commanders and personnel all contain components of civil rights issues.

The third measure of effectiveness is more elusive—whether the information and intelligence disseminated by the fusion centers have resulted in the prevention, mitigation, and control of crime and terrorism. Once again, some anecdotal evidence from different fusion centers suggests some successes (Carter, forthcoming)—largely owing to better communications between agencies—but it is far too early for a definitive conclusion or any type of empirical assessment of success.

The fourth measure is whether a fusion center is cost-effective, which is extremely difficult to measure and so involves some value judgments. The intelligence process is inherently inefficient; however, it appears to be the best methodology to employ for preventing complex multijurisdictional criminality and terrorism. The amalgamation of intelligence resources in a single fusion center would logically help to increase the cost-effectiveness of the process; however, an empirical assessment of these factors will provide better insight after a track record has been established. A final difficult factor to determine in cost-effectiveness is how to balance the monetary investment in a fusion center against the fiscal and emotional costs that are spared from a terrorist attack. The answers will not be easy to achieve.

A joint report prepared by the U.S. House of Representatives (Majority Staffs of the Committee on Homeland Security and the Committee on Foreign Affairs, 2008) views the status of determining the effectiveness of fusion centers rather critically, mentioning that the identification of stakeholders and the quantitative instruments to determine the extent to which their needs are being met has yet to occur. Moreover, this report questions the quality and value of the intelligence produced by fusion centers to provide actionable intelligence to those who need it most. In reality, it is far too early to evaluate the effectiveness of fusion centers; however, these variables provide guidance for important factors to measure in the near future.

Conclusion

The intelligence fusion process holds a great deal of promise for effective intelligence operations. This is particularly true given the multijurisdictional character of terrorists' operations and criminal enterprises. The three greatest challenges are as follows: first, to develop a cooperative and committed relationship among all stakeholders; second, to establish policies and processes that support efficient, effective, and lawful intelligence operations; and, third, for fusion centers to stay on message as an analytic center.

As with any organization or aspect within society, transformation and reform will not occur overnight. Law enforcement intelligence personnel are continually learning and developing best practices to protect the American people from foreign and domestic threats while observing the rights afforded to those who are being protected. Fusion centers are diverse and still evolving and so present a new type of institution in American life (German & Stanley, 2007). The individuals involved and the organization as a whole are responding to meet the needs of law enforcement and, as a result, are learning to perform in a manner consistent with the post–September 11 environment.

Notes

1. See http://www.theiacp.org/LinkClick.aspx?fileticket=0CTTgvc%2fcuc%3d&tabid=36 and http://www.cops.usdoj.gov/default.asp?Item=1395.

2. See http://www.whitehousedrugpolicy.gov/hidta/newyork_newjersey.html.

3. The Counterdrug Intelligence Executive Secretariat (1331 F Street, NW, Suite 700, Washington, DC 20530; telephone: 202-353-1875; fax: 202-353-1901) has an insightful unpublished report entitled *Metropolitan Area Consolidation/Collocation of Drug Intelligence Elements*, which describes the successes of and challenges for regional intelligence centers.

4. See https://www.llis.dhs.gov/channel/channelContentListing.do?channelId=90287&categoryId=5546.

5. *Complex criminality* refers to criminal enterprises that are involved in a range of criminal activities in support of their core enterprise. For example, a drug-trafficking organization may be involved in drug production, drug trafficking, money laundering, smuggling, corruption of public officials, fraud, and other offenses.

6. The fusion center guidelines are often referred to as *federal guidelines* because they are a product of the Global Intelligence Working Group of the Global Justice Information Sharing Initiative, which is funded by and an advisory to the Bureau of Justice Assistance, Office of Justice Programs, U.S. Department of Justice. However, note that the majority of working group members are from state, local, and tribal law enforcement agencies. Similarly, the group of subject matter experts assembled to develop the fusion center guidelines predominantly comprised state, local, and tribal representatives.

7. *Intelligence requirements* refer to information that is needed to help make a comprehensive and accurate analysis of a threat (Global Intelligence Working Group, 2005b).

8. The lead agency is the organization that has primary responsibility for creating and operating the fusion center. On a state level, it is typically either the state police (as in Michigan) or the state office of homeland security (as in Kentucky). In other cases, a city police department may be designated the lead agency (as in Indiana). There is no definitive model beyond the fact that one agency must have primary responsibility.

9. 28 Code of Federal Regulations Part 23 is "a guideline for law enforcement agencies: It contains implementing standards for operating federally grant-funded multijurisdictional criminal intelligence systems. It specifically provides guidance in five primary areas: submission and entry of criminal intelligence information, security, inquiry, dissemination, and the

review-and-purge process" (as quoted from http://www.iir.com/28cfr/Overview.htm).

10. *Writing for release* means that the intelligence products are prepared in a "sensitive but unclassified" form, permitting more widespread distribution among law enforcement.

References

Allen, C. (2008). *Information sharing and the federal state and local levels. Testimony before the Senate Committee on Homeland Security and Governmental Affairs. July 23, 2008.* Washington, DC. Retrieved July 28, 2009, from http://www.dhs.gov/xnews/testimony/testimony_1216992676837.shtm

American Civil Liberties Union. (2005, May 11). ACLU of Massachusetts questions scope of fusion center activities [Press release]. Retrieved July 28, 2009, from http://www.aclu.org/privacy/spying/15315prs20050511.html

Beare, M. E., & Murray, T. (2007). *Police and government relations: Who's calling the shots?* Toronto, Ontario, Canada: University of Toronto Press.

Carter, D. L. (2009). *Law enforcement intelligence: A guide for state, local and tribal law enforcement agencies* (2nd ed.). Washington, DC: Office of Community Oriented Policing Services.

Clark, R. M. (2007). *Intelligence analysis: A target-centric approach* (2nd ed.). Washington, DC: CQ Press.

Dillon, D. R. (2002). *Breaking down intelligence barriers for homeland security* (Backgrounder No. 1536). Washington, DC: Heritage Foundation.

Dinh, V. D. (2004). Freedom and security after September 11. In M. K. B. Darmer, R. M. Baird, & S. E. Rosenbaum (Eds.), *Civil liberties vs. national security: In a post-9/11 world* (pp. 105-113). Amherst, NY: Prometheus Books.

Electronic Privacy Information Center. (2008). *Project on information fusion centers and privacy.* Retrieved July 28, 2009, from http://epic.org/privacy/fusion/

Federal Computer Week. (2008). *A new threat, a new institution: The fusion center.* Retrieved July 28, 2009, from http://www.fcw.com/print/22_4/features/151627-1.html

Federal Emergency Management Agency. (2007). *Target Capabilities List.* Retrieved July 29, 2009, from http://www.fema.gov/pdf/government/training/tcl.pdf

General Accountability Office. (2007). *Homeland security: Federal efforts are helping alleviate some challenges encountered by state and local fusion centers* (No. GAO-08-35). Washington, DC: Author.

German, M., & Stanley, J. (2007). *What's wrong with fusion centers?* New York: American Civil Liberties Union.

German, M., & Stanley, J. (2008). *Fusion center update.* New York: American Civil Liberties Union.

Global Intelligence Working Group. (2005a). *Guidelines for establishing and operating fusion centers at the local, state, tribal and federal level.* Washington, DC: U.S. Department of Homeland Security.

Global Intelligence Working Group. (2005b). *Recommendations for intelligence requirements for state, local and tribal law enforcement agencies.* An unpublished report of the Intelligence Requirements Subcommittee of the Global Intelligence Working Group.

Harris, B. (2008, August). *Fusion centers may strengthen emergency management.* Retrieved July 28, 2009, from http://www.govtech.com/gt/365393?topic=117680

Homeland Security Advisory Council. (2005). *Intelligence and information sharing initiative: Homeland security intelligence and information fusion.* Washington, DC: U.S. Department of Homeland Security.

Johnson, B. R., & Dorn, S. (2008). Fusion centers: New York state intelligence strategy unifies law enforcement. *The Police Chief, 75*(2), 38.

Kindsvater, L. C. (2003). The need to reorganize the intelligence community. *Studies in Intelligence, 47*(1). Retrieved July 28, 2009, from https://www.cia.gov/library/center-for-the-study-of-intelligence/kent-csi/docs/v47i1a03p.htm

Lessons Learned Information Sharing. (2005). *Local anti-terrorism information and intelligence sharing: Information sharing overview.* Washington, DC: U.S. Department of Homeland Security.

MacLellan, T. (2006). *Protecting privacy in integrated justice systems.* Washington, DC: National Governors Association Center for Best Practices.

Majority Staffs of the Committee on Homeland Security and the Committee on Foreign Affairs. (2008). *Wasted lessons of 9/11: How the Bush administration has ignored the law and squandered its opportunities to make our country safer.* Washington, DC: U.S. House of Representatives.

Marrin, S. (2008). *Intelligence analysis: Turning a craft into a profession.* Arlington: University of Virginia. Retrieved July 28, 2009, from https://analysis.mitre.org/proceedings/Final_Papers_Files/97_Camera_Ready_Paper.pdf

Masse, T., & Rollins, J. (2007). *A summary of fusion centers: Core issues and options for Congress.* Washington, DC: Congressional Research Service.

McNamara, T. (2008). *Annual report to the Congress on the Information Sharing Environment.* Washington, DC: Program Manager–Information Sharing Environment.

National Commission on Terrorists Attacks Upon the United States. (2004). *9/11 commission report.* Retrieved from http://govinfo.library.unt.edu/911/report/index.htm

National Infrastructure Advisory Council. (2006). *Public–private sector intelligence coordination.* Washington, DC: Author.

National Preparedness Directorate. (2006). *National infrastructure preparedness plan.* Washington, DC: U.S. Department of Homeland Security.

Nenneman, M. (2008). An examination of state and local fusion centers and data collection methods. Monterey, CA: Naval Postgraduate School.

NYPD Shield. (2008). *Operation Nexus.* Retrieved July 28, 2009, from http://www.nypdshield.org/public/nexus.nypd

Program Manager for the Information Sharing Environment. (2006). *Information Sharing Environment Implementation Plan.* Washington, DC: Office of the Director of National Intelligence.

Ratcliffe, J. (2008). *Intelligence-led policing.* Portland, OR: Willan.

Rossler, T. (2003). New mission and new challenges: Law enforcement and intelligence after the USA Patriot Act. *Journal of the Institute of Justice and International Studies, 3,* 70-79.

Slayton, J. (2000). *Establishing and maintaining interagency information sharing.* Washington, DC: U.S. Department of Justice.

Sullivan, J. P. (2005). *Terrorism early warning and co-production of counterterrorism intelligence.* Paper presented at the Canadian Association of Security and Intelligence Studies, Montreal, Quebec, Canada.

Sullivan, K. (2003). Under the watchful eye: Incursions on personal privacy. In R. Leone & G. Anrig Jr. (Eds.), *The war on our freedoms: Civil liberties in an age of terrorism* (pp. 128-246). New York: Century Foundation.

U.S. Bureau of Alcohol, Tobacco, Firearms and Explosives. (2008). *Crime Gun Center.* Retrieved July 28, 2009, from http://www.atf.gov/field/newyork/rcgc/

U.S. Department of Homeland Security. (2007a). *FY 2007 Homeland Security Grant Program. Supplemental resource: Fusion capability planning tool.* Washington, DC: Author.

U.S. Department of Homeland Security. (2007b). *National Preparedness Guidelines.* Retrieved July 29, 2009, from http://www.dhs.gov/xlibrary/assets/National_Preparedness_Guidelines.pdf

U.S. Department of Homeland Security, Intelligence and Analysis Directorate. (2008, January). *Critical infrastructure and key resources support annex.* Washington, DC: Author.

U.S. Department of Justice (2005, June). *National Criminal Intelligence Sharing Plan.* Retrieved July 29, 2009, from http://www.it.ojp.gov/documents/National_Criminal_Intelligence_Sharing_Plan.pdf

DISCUSSION QUESTIONS

1. The authors argue that fusion centers increase the amount of available information and the range of sources from which that information is drawn. Is more information always better? Could the sheer volume of information lead to difficulties in identifying useful intelligence, what has been described as looking for a red flag in a sea of red flags (Zegart, 2007)?

2. How should fusion centers, largely developed at the state and local levels (see Figure 5.1), balance the dual needs of protecting the nation (a federal function) while addressing local concerns (a state and local function)? Even in state- and locally run centers, is the federal government's interest in homeland security likely to result in power struggles within these organizations?

3. Recall the discussion of resource dependence and contingency theories from Section III. Describe the growth of fusion centers since 9/11 using a contingency theory framework. Repeat the exercise using a resource dependence framework. Which, in your opinion, provides a more viable account for fusion center growth?

READING

Reading 9

Problem-solving courts originated in Florida in 1989, with the opening of a drug court focused exclusively on drug offenders. Since that time, the number of drug courts nationwide has expanded dramatically and new courts have formed to specifically handle other problems, including mental health issues, gun crimes, and—as described in this article by Angela R. Gover, Eve M. Brank, and John M. MacDonald—domestic violence. Berman and Feinblatt (2001) suggest that problem-solving courts leverage the power of the judicial system and interagency collaborations to improve case outcomes for victims, offenders, and the broader community. The Lexington County Criminal Domestic Violence Court brought together judges, criminal investigators, prosecutor, victims' advocate, court administrator, legal advocate, and mental health counselor to protect victims, hold offenders accountable, and provide cognitive therapy programming. Prior evaluation results pointed to the success of the courts. The current study assessed the perceptions of victims, offenders, and organizational participants (e.g., program staff) regarding the court process. Overall, respondents reported satisfaction with the court and indicated that they were treated in a procedurally just fashion.

A Specialized Domestic Violence Court in South Carolina

An Example of Procedural Justice for Victims and Defendants

Angela R. Gover, Eve M. Brank,
and John M. MacDonald

The results from an outcome evaluation of a specialized court in South Carolina indicated that systematic localized court interventions aimed at domestic violence defendants were effective at enhancing enforcement and improving victim safety. Specifically, the results indicated there were significant reductions in rearrests for domestic violence for defendants processed in this court compared to a historical sample of defendants processed in traditional criminal court settings (Gover, MacDonald, & Alpert, 2003).[1] Although the significant reduction in reoffending among domestic violence offenders suggests positive results for the domestic violence court, it is unclear why the court was effective. One possible explanation for the reduction in recidivism was the court's emphasis on procedural justice principles. The current article moves beyond the findings from the outcome evaluation of the court and explores the court's procedures as described in qualitative interviews with victims and defendants and complemented by courtroom observations and interviews with court personnel. The goal of this study is to examine how procedural justice principles fit within the context of a specialized domestic violence court.

Scope of the Problem

During the past decade, empirical data on domestic violence have led to a growing recognition that

Source: Gover, A. R., Brank, E. M., & MacDonald, J. M., (2007). A specialized domestic violence court in South Carolina: An example of procedural justice for victims and defendants. *Violence Against Women, 13*(6), 603–626.

domestic violence is a serious social problem. The data indicate that domestic violence is highly prevalent in the United States. According to the FBI's supplemental homicide reports, domestic violence claimed the lives of roughly 1,800 victims in 1997; nearly 3 out of 4 of the victims were female (U.S. Department of Justice, Bureau of Justice Statistics, 1998). In 2001, the homicide rate among female victims murdered by males (their husbands, common-law husbands, ex-husbands, or boyfriends) in the United States was 1.35 per 100,000 (Violence Policy Center, 2003). For that same year, South Carolina ranked first as the state with the highest intimate partner homicide rate among female victims by male offenders in single victim–single offender incidents. In fact, the state's rate of 3.15 per 100,000 was more than twice the national average (Violence Policy Center, 2003).

Estimates suggest that only one half of domestic violence incidents are reported to law enforcement, which means that official statistics grossly underestimate the prevalence of domestic violence (U.S. Department of Justice, Bureau of Justice Statistics, 1998). As a result, more recent efforts to estimate the prevalence of domestic violence have focused on self-reported data. A survey funded by the National Institute of Justice and the Centers for Disease Control and Prevention, for example, found that approximately 1.5 million women and 834,700 men are raped and/or physically assaulted by their partners annually (Tjaden & Thoennes, 1998). Other estimates suggest that more than 2 million women are severely assaulted annually by their male partners (American Medical Association Council on Scientific Affairs, 1992).

Regardless of the data source, it is clear that domestic violence is a serious social problem. In addition to the increased awareness of domestic violence, and perhaps as a consequence, during the past decade there have been significant changes in the justice system's response to domestic violence (Clark, Burt, Schulte, & Maguire, 1996). Although most attention has been placed on law enforcement responses to domestic violence (Sherman, 1992), criminal courts have experienced an increase in domestic violence cases during the past decade. The majority of the increase in domestic violence cases in court systems can be attributed to the implementation of mandatory arrest policies in law enforcement agencies. Between 1984 and 1997, for example, domestic relations cases in the United States grew by 177% (Ostrom & Kauder, 1997). Today, domestic violence cases represent a large proportion of all cases that are processed within the criminal justice system.

One innovative judiciary response to the increase in domestic violence cases has been the development of specialized domestic violence courts. According to the National Center for State Courts (Keilitz, 2000), there are more than 300 courts nationwide that devote specialized prosecution practices to domestic violence. Conceptually similar to drug courts (Rottmann, 2000), domestic violence courts represent a collaborative and multidisciplinary approach to case processing (Tsai, 2000). The consolidation of all domestic violence cases into one court conserves resources and theoretically enables the members of the court to better understand and address the underlying issues in domestic violence cases. Specialized courts acknowledge that violence between intimates involves unique dynamics that are not common in stranger violence cases (Mazur & Aldrich, 2003).[2]

In essence, domestic violence courts attempt to improve the judiciary's response to this issue by increasing collaborative efforts between criminal justice and social service agencies. In addition, a common goal of these courts is to hold defendants accountable while also properly addressing the needs of victims and the therapeutic needs of defendants.[3] Given these goals, an emphasis is placed on the experiences that victims and defendants have with the court while their cases are being processed. Research suggests that the treatment victims and defendants receive from representatives of the criminal justice system influences their perceptions of the system and perhaps their future behavior (Tyler, 1990). Therefore, the emphasis that domestic violence courts place on victims' and defendants' experiences during the court process makes this specialized court model an ideal setting for a procedural justice inquiry.

An Overview of Procedural Justice

Introduced by Thibault and Walker (1975) in their comparison of the adversarial and inquisitorial systems, procedural justice is defined as examining the processes employed rather than just the outcomes from a dispute. Researchers have consistently found that the manner in which legal decisions are imposed, rather than the outcome of the legal process alone, has a powerful and independent effect on why people obey the law (Tyler, 1988, 1990). In addition, procedural justice research suggests that legal authorities will be viewed as more legitimate and respected by those under their authority if fair procedures are employed (Tyler & Lind, 2001). Proponents of procedural justice support the notion that actors within the legal system can resolve conflicts amicably while also instilling greater faith in the system.

In operationalizing procedural justice, Leventhal (1980) expanded Thibault and Walker's (1975) work by focusing more broadly on the various components of procedural justice. In doing this, he outlined several factors that contribute to one's notions of fairness, such as the opportunity to provide input during the process and being treated with respect. The opportunity to provide input during the process itself has proved to be a well-replicated finding (Fondacaro, Jackson, & Luescher, 2002). This "voice" effect, as it is often referred, is likely to be the most widely supported concept of procedural justice (Lind & Tyler, 1988).

Procedural justice judgments have been examined in a variety of formal and informal settings. For example, procedural justice factors have been examined among citizen experiences with the police and courts (Tyler, 1984, 1988; Tyler & Folger, 1980), employment decisions (Folger & Konovsky, 1989), employee attitudes toward drug testing (Konovsky & Cropanzano, 1991), and organizational change (Korsgaard, Sapienza, & Schweiger, 2002). These inquiries have consistently demonstrated the importance of procedural justice factors. For instance, Tyler and Folger (1980) found that citizens' appraisals of police contact were influenced by the way the police treated them independent of the actual outcome of the case. No matter the outcome, citizens who felt they had been treated fairly by the police were more likely to provide favorable evaluations of the police they encountered and of police in general compared to those who felt they had not been treated fairly. In the business world, Folger and Konovsky (1989) found that although distributive justice factors (e.g., "To what extent did your raise give you the full amount you deserved?") had the most influence on satisfaction with pay raise decisions, procedural justice factors contributed to the level of organizational commitment and trust ratings of supervisors. Similarly, procedural justice principles were predictive of employee job satisfaction, management trust, commitment, turnover intentions, and performance, whereas outcome fairness was not predictive of any of these factors (Konovsky & Cropanzano, 1991). Additionally, in the nonlegal and less formal area of family disputes, Fondacaro et al. (2002) demonstrated that the presence of procedural justice factors, such as personal respect, status recognition, correction (i.e., having an opportunity to have the decision reconsidered), and trust were significantly related in the expected directions to family cohesion and conflict.

Procedural justice practices have also been found to have an important influence on domestic violence cases. Research by Paternoster, Bachman, Brame, and Sherman (1997) suggested that the manner in which sanctions were imposed on domestic violence offenders had a stronger influence on subsequent behavior than the sanction itself. Even when case outcomes were unfavorable for defendants; for example, this study reported that the use of procedurally fair methods by law enforcement during the arrest process resulted in a reduction in subsequent violence. Specifically, domestic violence offenders who were arrested and viewed the process as fair were more likely to comply with sanctions, even after controlling for a number of important predictor variables (Paternoster et al., 1997). Procedural justice attitudes also have been found to be significantly related to perceptions of the court's effectiveness (Richman, 2002). Collectively, the procedural justice literature confirms the need to focus not only on case outcomes but also on information that only those involved in the process can provide.

In addition to the influence that procedurally just processes has been found to have on offender behavior (i.e., compliance), the experiences that victims have with the criminal justice system can have an impact on their future behavior. As suggested by Hickman and Simpson (2003), the criminal justice system is initially mobilized by crime victims in most cases because they are the ones who decide whether to report a crime. Therefore, the treatment that victims receive during their interaction with law enforcement can potentially affect whether they decide to report crime in the future. According to the philosophy of procedural justice, victims who have positive experiences and feel that they were treated fairly by representatives of the criminal justice system will be more inclined to make contact with the criminal justice system in the future.

Davis and Taylor's (1997) randomized experiment of a proactive family violence program in New York City also suggested that positive interactions between victims and representatives of criminal and social service agencies can influence subsequent reporting. According to interviews with victims, there were no differences in reoffending rates between offenders assigned to the treatment condition and those who were assigned to the control condition. However, victims in the treatment group reported a greater number of subsequent violent offenses to the police compared to reports made by victims in the control group. Although speculative, these researchers suggest that a joint social service and law enforcement response to family violence can positively influence victims' perceptions of law enforcement. Moreover, these positive experiences that victims in the treatment group had with the criminal justice system influenced their decision to report subsequent victimizations. Bowman (1992) notes that although it is likely that the treatment victims receive by law enforcement influences whether they decide to contact the criminal justice system in the future, it is important to also examine victim experiences during other stages in the process, such as the prosecutorial stage. The following section describes a court in South Carolina that incorporated and emphasized procedural justice practices throughout many of the stages within a specialized domestic violence court setting.

The Lexington County, South Carolina, Domestic Violence Court

The current study examines the contextual role of procedural justice practices in the Lexington County Criminal Domestic Violence Court (CDVC). The CDVC was established within South Carolina's magistrate court system in 1999 with funding from the Violence Against Women Act.[4] According to the Census Bureau (U.S. Department of Commerce, Bureau of the Census, 2000), the population of Lexington County is approximately 220,000, and 84% of the residents are White. The majority of the county is geographically dispersed in small rural communities. The county is predominately working class and the per capita income is approximately $22,000 a year.

Since the implementation of the CDVC, all magistrate-level nonfelony cases of domestic violence that have occurred in Lexington County have been processed by the specialized court.[5] The specialized court was designed to hold perpetrators of domestic violence more accountable by imposing fines in a majority of the cases and by increasing the amount of time offenders spent in jail pretrial.[6] In addition, the CDVC promoted offender accountability while placing a strong emphasis on mandatory batterer treatment. Offender treatment was emphasized by the court's suspension of jail sentences in lieu of the successful completion of a 26-week group-based cognitive therapy program for domestic violence batterers. Batterers were required to pay for their treatment on a weekly basis. Progress in the treatment program was monitored on a weekly basis, and if defendants failed to comply with treatment conditions, bench warrants would be issued and suspended jail sentences imposed.

The overall goal of the CDVC was to improve the criminal justice system's response to domestic violence in Lexington County. To achieve this goal, the CDVC implemented a multiagency collaborative approach to processing domestic violence cases. For example, Lexington County appointed two full-time investigators and a full-time prosecutor to work as a team on domestic violence cases. A full-time victim advocate was hired to assist domestic violence victims, and a court administrator was hired to handle the administrative tasks involved in running a separate court docket for domestic violence cases. In addition, two magistrate-level judges were assigned to the CDVC. The Lexington County Department of Mental Health dedicated a mental health counselor to diagnose and assign proper treatment plans for offenders, and a legal advocate from a local domestic violence shelter was assigned to the court to make contact with victims and to be present in court.

The repetition of domestic violence cases resulted in the CDVC personnel developing expertise in the issues inherent in domestic violence cases. In addition to the on-the-job training and education the court staff received because of the volume of cases with which they were working, the prosecutor and investigators attended a national domestic violence conference and statewide domestic violence trainings sponsored by the South Carolina Attorney General's Office. The prosecutor also conducted in-house domestic violence trainings for employees of the Sheriff's Department. The appointment of a designated prosecutor, investigators, and judges and the emphasis placed on specialized domestic violence training showed the court's attempt to improve the system's response to domestic violence cases. By increasing resources and encouraging collaboration among representatives of the court, the CDVC implemented a progressive new approach for the investigation and prosecution of domestic violence cases.

Case Processing by the Lexington County Domestic Violence Court

The basic court intervention is displayed in Figure 1. In Lexington County, South Carolina, case processing for criminal domestic violence begins when Sheriff's Department road deputies respond to a 911 call. In all domestic violence cases, responding officers are required to write a report and cases are immediately assigned to one of two criminal domestic violence (CDV) investigators.[7] The majority of arrests are made by officers who initially respond to calls because of Lexington County's mandatory arrest law that was implemented in 1994.

Investigators collect additional information and evidence in cases that involved an initial arrest by responding officers and follow up on further evidence collection in cases that did not result in an initial arrest. For example, investigators determine whether a history of violence exists between the individuals involved in the dispute by reviewing in-house records to see if calls were previously made by the victim. The National Crime Information Center (NCIC) rap sheets are checked to see if the offender has prior convictions or arrests. Investigators also request 911 tapes, which can be particularly useful in cases that involve an uncooperative victim.[8] Investigators make immediate contact with the victim to obtain more details in the case. For example, if witness statements were not obtained or if pictures were not taken by responding officers, investigators attempt to obtain this additional evidence.

In cases that did not result in an arrest when an officer responded to the incident, after further evidence has been collected, investigators may obtain an arrest warrant from a magistrate judge.

After an arrest is made (either initially or later after further evidence collection), a defendant is required to appear in bond court. Judges impose a "no contact" order (NCO) on the offender's bond restriction in about 90% of the cases that are processed in the CDVC. NCO provisions prohibit the offender from making any kind of contact with the

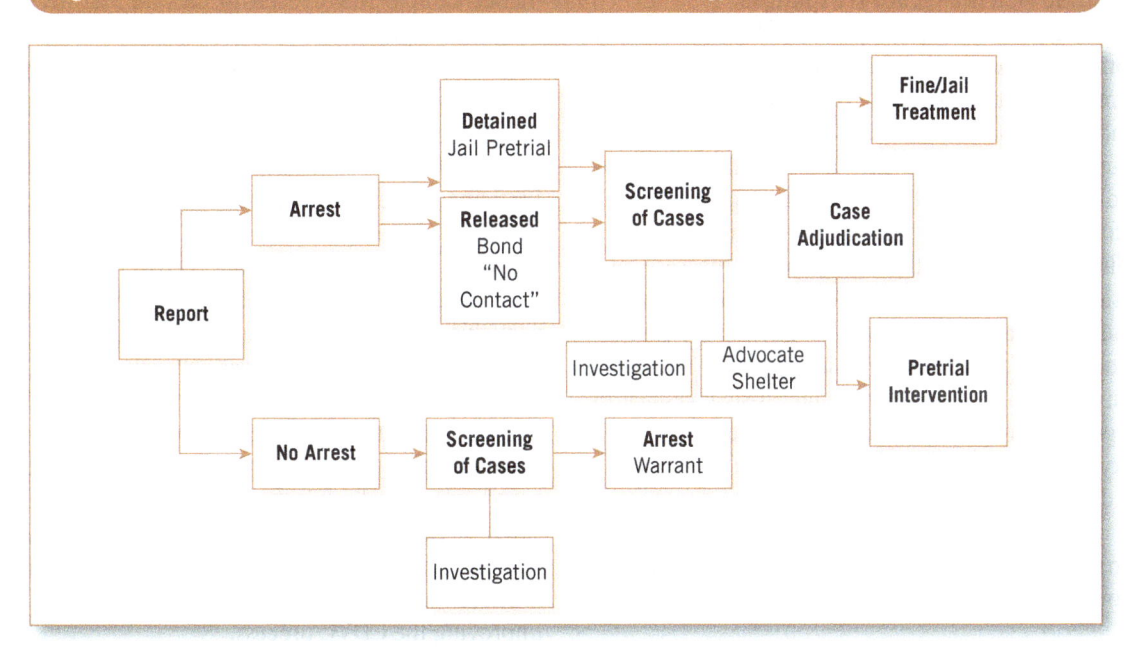

Figure 1 The Criminal Domestic Violence Court Intervention Strategy

victim (e.g., in person, by phone, by leaving messages) during the period between the defendant's arraignment and sentencing (O'Connor, 1999). In relationships in which the victim and offender share a residence, offenders must find alternative living arrangements. These bond restrictions remain intact until the defendant appears in the CDVC and a disposition is made in the case. Defendants appear in the CDVC approximately 30 days after their bond hearing.

During case adjudication, all representatives of the CDVC are present (the victim advocate, investigators, mental health personnel). Court participants watch a video, narrated by the judge, that explains the four options that defendants have: pretrial intervention (PTI), guilty plea, bench trial, or jury trial. After the video, each defendant receives a document that further explains the options available. Each defendant is then individually called up to the front of the courtroom by name. There, one of the aforementioned court players asks the defendant what option he or she will exercise. The defendant is required to indicate his or her choice on the document and sign and date it. After all of the defendants have been processed, the judge enters and the trials begin.

Participation in the PTI program is an option only for defendants who are not currently on probation and have not been previously convicted of a felony or criminal domestic violence. Admission to PTI is governed by South Carolina Codes of Law 17-22-50 and 17-22-60.[9] The CDVC refers approximately 10% of cases to PTI, and approximately 50% of the cases referred are accepted and successfully complete the program. Offenders who are accepted into PTI participate in the 26-week therapy program (mentioned above) in lieu of their jail sentence. Offenders in PTI follow the same treatment program rules as non-PTI offenders participating in the treatment program. A mental health counselor pursues a strict weekly follow-up on defendants' progress in the PTI treatment program, and if a defendant fails to comply with his or her treatment conditions, a bench warrant is issued and his or her suspended jail sentence is imposed. However, if participants successfully complete PTI, their domestic violence record is expunged.

One of the unique aspects of the way criminal domestic violence cases are processed in the CDVC compared to the processing of criminal domestic violence cases in traditional courts is the involvement of the court's dedicated victim advocate. The CDVC advocate provides emergency crisis counseling to victims, informs victims about their rights and procedures to be followed through to the conclusion of the case, and assists victims in preparing to testify in court. The advocate also provides victims with general information about courtroom procedures, accompanies victims to court as requested by victims, and assists investigators in gathering criminal intelligence information as necessary. In sum, the dedicated advocate's role in the specialized court is crucial to the court's success.

The current research takes a step away from the formally defined procedures of the court to examine the process from the perspective of those persons involved.

Procedure

Participants and Observations

During the same time frame as the outcome evaluation (Gover et al., 2003) mentioned above, face-to-face interviews were conducted with a convenience sample of 50 victims and 50 defendants whose cases were processed in the CDVC. Eighty-four percent of the victims interviewed were female, and 88% of the defendants interviewed were male.[10] In addition, research staff observed 30 court sessions and conducted semistructured interviews with seven members of the court staff. Interviews with victims and defendants, courtroom observations, and interviews with court personnel were completed between May 2001 and July 2002.

Instruments and Procedures

Interviews with victims and defendants were conducted in person in the lobby of the courthouse immediately after their case was heard. A convenience sample was chosen to capture victims' and defendants' perceptions immediately following their court experience and to improve the accuracy of responses. Before the interviews were conducted, the purpose of the research was explained to victims and defendants, and full informed consent was obtained. Participants were not compensated for their participation but were assured that their responses to questions would remain confidential. Only four of the 104 individuals (victims and defendants) approached to participate in the survey refused. Therefore, the overall interview response rate was approximately 96%.

Victims and defendants were asked structured questions about their experiences with the court and whether they perceived their court experience as being procedurally fair. Specifically, questions measured victims' and defendants' overall level of satisfaction with the court process, their perceptions of fairness and justice, and recommendations for improving the CDVC process.

During the courtroom observations, trained research staff observers documented the general context in which court cases were processed in the CDVC. The qualitative data gathered through courtroom observations were meant to complement the interview data and describe the general courtroom work group. Based on the emphasis on collaboration in these nontraditional courts (Rottman & Casey, 1999), one focus of the observations was the level of cooperation among the sheriff's investigators, the domestic violence prosecutor, the judge, the mental health personnel, victim advocates, the victim, and the offender. Observations were guided by an open-ended instrument that required research staff to identify the extent to which the court process was collaborative, whether victims and defendants were given an opportunity to voice their concerns to the court, and whether victim and defendant concerns had an impact on the decision-making process.

Interviews were also conducted with the seven professionals who played a key role in the court's operation: two judges, two law enforcement investigators, the court's prosecutor, a mental health counselor, and a legal advocate from a local battered women's shelter. Interviews were conducted at the Lexington County Sheriff's Department in private conference rooms. The interviews lasted between 1 and 2 hours and were tape-recorded with each participant's consent. The interview format consisted of semistructured questions that were followed by probes to pursue topical leads provided by the subjects. This method allowed the participants to elaborate on important aspects of the court development and operation that they perceived to be most critical instead of only responding to structured interview questions. The primary purpose of these interviews was to obtain data on perceptions of how the Lexington County Sheriff's Department's response to domestic violence had changed since the court's inception and how its role as a representative of the court affected the court's operation. To search for general relationships among question responses, the tapes were transcribed for qualitative data analysis. In the next section, information from victim and defendant interviews, courtroom observations, and interviews with court personnel describe the incorporation of procedural justice components within the CDVC process in terms of victim and defendant impressions of the court process, victim and defendant "voice" in the process, and perceptions of fairness, justice, and respect.

Results

General Impressions of the Court Process

Research staff classified 26 of the 30 courtroom observations as collaborative in some way. Although few cases had the involvement of every court player, most of the CDVC personnel were involved in some aspect of case processing. A large majority of these cases did not involve defense counsel because magistrate courts do not require defendants to retain counsel. The most common collaboration occurred before court even began. In nearly every court observation, many of the court players, including the sheriff's investigators, the mental health counselor, the court administrator and staff, and the prosecutor, worked together to process each defendant's case.

Collaboration was further documented by the communication among the court players during case processing. Communication between the judge and the prosecutor was common, with the prosecutor making sentencing recommendations to the judge regarding fines, jail time, and counseling. In one case observed, the prosecutor recommended a reduced sentence for the defendant because he was providing financial support to the victim and their children. In another case, the prosecutor recommended that the judge sentence the defendant to 30 days in jail, suspended, and 26 weeks of counseling and to remove the fine as an incentive to attend counseling. The judge followed the recommendations of the prosecutor in both of these cases.

In general, if cases had lethality indicators, the prosecutor recommended that defendants receive counseling or jail, without the option for a fine. The court offered a scheduled payment plan to defendants who could not pay an ordered fine in full, and the prosecutor viewed this as a way for offenders to pay their way out of a crime. In addition, the prosecutor did not view fines as an adequate deterrent and saw many instances when they further harmed victims and children by creating more financial stress or, if the couple separated, interfered with the payment of child support.

Overall, the judge and prosecutor communicated effectively, and it was rare that the judge did not follow sentence recommendations made by the prosecutor. This was not a unique aspect of the CDVC because most summary and circuit court judges follow prosecutor recommendations. The most common recommendation that was not always followed by a judge was when the prosecutor wanted jail time to be the only option if the defendant failed counseling. Sometimes, despite the prosecutor's recommendation, the judges would offer the fine as an alternative. According to one courtroom observer,

It was apparent that everyone (prosecutor, judge, mental health counselor, sheriff's deputies) there had a specific role to play (i.e., questioning defendants and victims, sentencing, reading incident reports, discussing the treatment program with defendants). There was teamwork that was evident on the prosecutor's behalf: She addressed a victim's concern and a defendant's wife's concerns while the judge was listening to the defendant tell what happened on the night of the incident. There was teamwork by the officers—they had a role to play to give evidence against the defendant, and they carried out their role successfully. The mental health counselor did not come into play until the end of court, when she was instructing all of the PTI defendants about coming to her office.

Another observer noted that the mental health counselor and the legal advocate from the shelter were valuable key players in the courtroom and made substantial contributions to the processing of cases:

> The mental health counselor was present to enroll offenders in treatment programs required as a condition of sentencing. She met with all of the offenders after court let out and explained to them their obligations and consequences if they failed to comply with the order. The legal advocate from the shelter also contributed to the process. After each case was heard, she escorted the victim out of the courtroom. She also provided additional methods of support to victims who needed it.

The collaborative nature of the CDVC personnel resulted in efficient and effective case processing. As stated by one courtroom observer,

> Each member of the team worked together so that the court system was able to process and move through the docket more efficiently and effectively. Each team member worked together in order to resolve cases to the satisfaction of the defendant and victim as well as the justice system. Each member of the court system worked well with each other communicating and assisting each other to help resolve the case so that each party in the case was informed as to the court process and making sure that they were pleased with the court's solution.

The collaborative process documented by observers may have had a positive influence on victims' and defendants' perceptions of their experience. According to interviews with victims and defendants, most had positive feelings about their court experiences. When asked for their overall impression of the way their cases were handled, 74% of victims rated their impressions as either good or excellent. In comparison, when defendants were asked about their overall impression of the way their cases were handled, the most frequent response (34%) was fair. Forty-six percent of defendants rated the overall handling of their case as good or excellent. Only 16% of victims and defendants rated the handling of their case as poor.[11] Overall, victims and defendants had positive perceptions of the quality and professionalism of the CDVC. A majority (74%) of victims rated the overall quality and professionalism of the court as either excellent or good. Sixty-two percent of defendants rated the court as either excellent or good. Only 10% of victims and 14% of defendants rated the quality and professionalism of the court as poor. In addition, the majority of victims and defendants were satisfied with the amount of time they had to wait before their case was heard. Fifty-six percent of victims and 62% of defendants described the waiting time before their case was heard as excellent or good.

The positive experiences victims and defendants had with the court were not surprising given the extent to which the CDVC personnel indicated support for the court's mission. According to one CDVC personnel, the prosecutor,

In Lexington County we have one of the most proactive domestic violence programs in the state, maybe even one of the most proactive programs in the Southeast. It is all based on the personnel because of their dedication to the program. For example, our two investigators get warrants that nobody else would get. They are both very, very aggressive and that is why the program works.

The CDVC personnel expressed a comprehensive understanding of the dynamics involved in domestic violence cases and attributed much of the court's success to the working relationships among the court personnel. One investigator expressed that she obtains job satisfaction from knowing that she is helping people in need. She said,

> Working domestic violence cases can be very rewarding. The thing that I like about it when I deal with the victims, they tell me, "No one has ever listened to me before. No one has ever believed me. No one has ever asked me those questions." Those are the things that make it worth it to me because you know that you are actually helping someone out of a terrible situation. Or even if you can't get them out right then, they know that they can contact you for help.

Although the majority of victims and defendants viewed their court experiences in a positive way, several recommended that the court could improve experiences for future victims and defendants by providing information in advance as to what to expect the court process to be like. For example, the following suggestions were made by victims as ways to improve the court experience: "Better communication with victims. No one sat down with you to explain the process;" "Victims should be told what to expect ahead of time;" and "Someone should have prepared victims prior to coming to court regarding what was going to happen."

Similarly, several defendants suggested that the court should have more communication with them prior to court so that they would have a better understanding of the court process. Defendants made the following suggestions about how the court could improve the process for future defendants: "Provide information to defendants of what to expect in court;" "Spend more time talking with defendants prior to court;" and "Have a pretrial phone call or conversation." These sentiments were confirmed by one judge who thought that many defendants did not understand what was taking place in court and that this lack of understanding had an impact on their decision to plead guilty. According to this judge,

> They don't know what the court is all about. They don't know what they're doing. They don't tend to listen when they're in court because they're scared to death, so most of the victims... The defendants aren't getting treated fairly. They don't know what they're pleading to and that's what I try to explain at my bond courts on a CDV. I'll tell them to make sure they listen to the film that we show because it shows different ways they can be tried, but that doesn't stick in their head either because they're scared. I just try to listen to both sides. I don't prejudge them. I hate for them to stand up there and say "I'm guilty" unless they really, really know that they're guilty of the charge and what the charge is all about.

Victim and Defendant "Voice" in the Court Process

Overall, the majority of court observations indicated that victims were given an opportunity to address the court; however, many victims did not take advantage of this opportunity. In all cases involving a sentence through PTI, the judge first asked the victim if she or he had any objections because victim consent is a condition of the defendant's sentence. Most victims granted consent but did not choose to comment further.

The input from victims who chose to testify or address the court was diverse. Some victims testified against the defendants; however, some strongly defended their abusers. In one observed case, the victim testified against her abuser and was noticeably upset at the brevity of his sentence. In this instance, the defendant was found guilty and sentenced to time served. It was the defendant's second offense, and he had spent slightly more than a week in jail. The victim was clearly upset and confused. As the defendant walked out of the courtroom, the victim asked, "What was he found guilty of?" The victim advocate then led her out of the courtroom, attempting to explain what had happened. Another observed case involved a boyfriend as the defendant and his girlfriend as the victim. The responding officer testified in this case, and photos of the victim's injuries were entered into evidence as well as pictures of a torn, bloody shirt. When the victim was asked if she would like to address the court, she spoke in support of the defendant. She said, "The pictures look a lot worse than it was. I bruise easily. We have been together for 7 years and that is the only time he has hit me." Nonetheless, the judge found the defendant guilty and sentenced him to 30 days or a $1,025 fine, suspended upon the successful completion of a treatment program and payment of a $225 fine.

Courtroom observations indicated that the most common request from a victim who was on friendly terms with the defendant was that the no-contact order be lifted to allow the defendant to contact the victim. Before each court session, the prosecutor addressed the issue of bond restrictions (no-contact orders) in her speech to victims and defendants sitting in the courtroom. She stated that victims and defendants should contact her to request that the no-contact order be lifted, and if appropriate, she would request it from the judge. Although many victims and defendants made statements in court that could potentially have an impact on their case's disposition, the case outcome was not always what they anticipated. For example, in one case the defendant and victim wanted to reconcile and have the bond restrictions lifted; however, the judge did not feel that it would be to anyone's benefit for the couple to live under the same roof at that time. In another case, the victim was pregnant with the defendant's child. The defendant asked the judge to remove the bond restrictions (the no-contact order) so that he could see his child. The victim was asked how she felt about this and she stated that she wanted the bond restrictions to remain until the baby was born. The prosecutor instructed the victim to contact the court after her baby was born, at which time visitation could be resolved.

Although some victims chose not to speak when given the opportunity, when directly questioned they would usually offer helpful insight into the case. According to interviews with victims, 90% of those who addressed the court felt that they were given adequate time to do so, and 72% felt that the judge was concerned with their side of the story. According to one observer, the judge not only asked the victim if she had anything to say but also used a more direct line of questioning. For example, the judge asked the victim, "Does this situation pose a threat to you? Has he been to see you?" These specific questions encouraged the victim to have a voice in the process.

Courtroom observations indicated that many defendants were given an opportunity to voice their concerns to the court. Defendants who enter into pretrial intervention are not afforded an opportunity to address the court, and defendants who enter a guilty plea also give up their right to address the court; however, based on the court observations, many do so at the discretion of the judge. In addition, the prosecutor would sometimes question the defendant about his or her actions and the rationale behind those actions. According to interviews with defendants, of those who had an opportunity to address the court, 68% felt that they were given adequate time to explain their side of the story, and 44% felt that the judge was concerned with their side of the story.

According to several court observations, victims' and defendants' concerns had an impact on the decision-making process. The observed impact, however, varied largely on the credibility of the victims and defendants. Several observations indicated that the outcome of a case would probably have been different if the defendant and victim were not given an opportunity to address the court. In several cases, defendants expressed concern about the need to remain employed because they were the sole supporter of their child/children. Courtroom observations indicated that the judge took family income and dependent children into consideration before sentencing a defendant. One courtroom observer noted,

> Victim's and defendant's concerns had an impact on the decision-making process. If children were part of the relationship between the victim and the defendant, the judge and prosecutor considered the impact that the court's findings would have on the children. The best interest of the child was considered when determining treatment programs or fines, so as not to place an emotional or financial burden on the family of the defendant or victim or on them individually.

In another case, a defendant was charged with assaulting his wife. The victim in this case argued on the defendant's behalf and stated that mental illness was to blame for the incident. The judge ordered the defendant to be evaluated by the Department of Mental Health for treatment but imposed no fine or jail time. In another observed case, the statements made by the defendant appeared to influence the outcome of the case. In this case, the defendant was brought before the judge because he had failed to attend his pretrial intervention appointments. The defendant told the judge that he was unable to attend the appointments because of conflicts with his work schedule, which meant he was at risk of losing his job as a truck driver. In this case, the judge delayed making a decision until the defendant had an opportunity to speak with court representatives about possible treatment alternatives. In general, judges did take into account what was in the best interest of all parties.

Although in many observed cases defendants were given an opportunity to voice their concerns to the court, there were instances when having a voice in the process did not lead to a defendant's desired outcome. For example, when addressing the judge, one defendant stated, "I am not a violent person. I would not have done that." The judge then reviewed the defendant's criminal history and laughed because the judge noted that the defendant had prior convictions for assault and criminal domestic violence.

Overall, the majority of the courtroom observations and interviews with victims and defendants indicated that an attempt was made by the court to give them input in the process; however, two defendants suggested that this is an area the court could improve for future defendants. According to defendants, the court should "give you a chance to explain your side of the story" and "listen a little more and realize that not everyone who comes in here is a bad person." One victim indicated that she was uncomfortable speaking in front of the entire courtroom and suggested that the court, "Put up a wall so that the entire courtroom doesn't hear your story."

Perceptions of Fairness, Justice, and Respect

The CDVC placed an emphasis on therapeutic options for defendants by exploring potential treatment needs of defendants on a case-by-case basis. According to interviews with victims and defendants, courtroom observations, and interviews with the court personnel, the CDVC replaced the traditional way of processing domestic violence offenders with a new problem-solving method that tried to identify and address the underlying cause of the criminal behavior through treatment. According to a courtroom observer,

> There was a great deal of emphasis placed on alternative methods of dispute resolution by the court. In nearly every case where the defendant was found guilty, part of their sentencing was the completion of a

treatment program. The mental health counselor explained that once they are enrolled in the [treatment] program, a specialist decides what treatment would be beneficial to the offender.

Several representatives of the CDVC were very supportive of the court's emphasis on rehabilitation and treatment and specifically for first-time offenders. In fact, one investigator felt that the court's 26-week treatment program was not long enough to accomplish much with a "true" batterer. According to this investigator, "Domestic violence offenders are going to batter regardless of what you do for them, because it is ingrained in them." This investigator suggested that the duration of the counseling program should be increased to influence defendant behavior. The legal advocate from the domestic violence shelter also agreed that long-term therapy is necessary. She believed that continued quality counseling for offenders that focuses on issues of power and control and offender accountability is the only way that counseling is going to change defendants' behavior. One judge emphatically supported the court's emphasis on treatment and viewed offenders as being misguided because they see violence as a way of life. This judge emphasized the importance that treatment plays in addressing the underlying conflicts that lead to violence. As stated by this judge,

> You know, the yelling and arguing is the way they communicate . . . it's a means of communication. They don't understand how to communicate outside of violence or yelling, and again, I don't think the violence comes from a hate or dislike. It comes from a communication barrier they can't seem to get past. Generally, I think the situation that we're addressing is what needs to be addressed. I think that the communication issue and the anger management issue needs to be resolved in order to save some of the relationships and stop the violence in the household.

In terms of perceptions of fairness and justice, victims and defendants were asked if they felt the outcome of their case was fair and just. Seventy-seven percent of victims and 68% of defendants believed the outcomes of their cases were fair and just. Victims and defendants also were asked if they felt they had been treated with respect and dignity by the court. An overwhelming majority (88%) of victims and defendants (86%) felt they were treated with respect and dignity by the court.

It is not surprising that the majority of victims felt that the court treated them with respect and that the court process was fair given the extent to which the court personnel considers the victim's needs and well-being during the entire process. One investigator acknowledged that in the past, the majority of domestic violence victims did not receive a great amount of support from the law enforcement community but that the CDVC approach to case processing involves recognizing that many victims are reaching out for help for the first time. She stated,

> A lot of police officers would tell victims that they are not social workers and not to call them anymore. I cannot do that. Especially if this is somebody that for the first time has reached out and is getting help and is really trying to get out of the situation. If you turn your back on them, they are not going to come back for help. They will just stay in that situation until they end up dead, or whatever may happen. There are so many reasons that women cannot leave. I think it is amazing that any woman ever gets out. Someone has to help them.

Another investigator acknowledged the importance of treating victims with respect by making their interactions with the criminal justice system positive, especially if it is their first time dealing with the system. This investigator said,

> The way I treat the victim the first time may make or break my case, or make or break

her ability to leave, or feel like she can trust the system, or feel like she's got somebody there who is going to be supportive of her. So I've got to treat these victims with respect so that they can have trust in me. They've got to know that I believe them and that I am going to help them.

Much of the attention that victims received was from the legal advocate from the domestic violence shelter. Some of the direct services provided by the legal advocate included attendance at bond hearings, assistance with alternative housing, providing transportation to court, assistance with completing legal forms, assistance with submitting forms for reimbursement of medical expenses from injuries sustained during the incident, assistance with safety precautions (changing locks at her residence, installing outside lights, providing a 911 cell phone), and assistance with preparing for court. According to the legal advocate,

> We actually come to court with them. We help them prepare for presenting in front of the judge . . . staying composed and factual . . . keeping eye contact with the judge . . . . After court we refer them to our follow-up program. During follow-up we might work with them to find a job if they haven't had a job in the past. We also work with them if they have an interest in continuing their education. We've been successful at helping women get scholarships to go back to school and pay for childcare while they are in school. We help them from beginning to end.

CDVC personnel made an attempt to make sure that victims' needs were met, even after court was dismissed. For example, a courtroom observer noted,

> Even after cases were decided, members of the court team would approach the victims and make sure that they understood the verdict and also understood what was required by both the victim and defendant. If the victim needed any assistance with shelter or legal assistance, the team members were there to help obtain it.

Victims and defendants were also asked about the court's overall response to domestic violence. The majority of both victims and defendants thought that the court's response to domestic violence cases was "just right." Two thirds (67%) of victims believed that this court's response was "just right," 23% believed it was "too easy," and only 10% believed the court's response was "too harsh." In contrast, only 2% of defendants thought that the court's response was "too easy," and 40% of defendants thought the court's response was "too harsh." The majority (58%) of defendants thought that the court's response was "just right." Additionally, victims were asked if, on the basis of their experience, they would recommend that other victims seek prosecution. Approximately 90% of victims said they would recommend that other victims seek prosecution.

Discussion and Conclusion

In an attempt to improve the judiciary's response to domestic violence cases, a specialized domestic violence court was established in Lexington County, South Carolina. The court implemented a number of changes to its response to domestic violence, such as an emphasis on collaboration between the judge, prosecutor, victim advocate, mental health counselor, sheriff's investigators, victim, and defendant. Additionally, the court focused on the individual needs and desires of both the victims and the defendants. Case outcome comparisons revealed a significant reduction in rearrests for domestic violence offenders processed in the new court system as compared to a historical sample of offenders processed in the traditional court setting. The current article shifts the focus away from the outcome evaluation data (Gover et al., 2003) and onto the perceptions of the participants in this modified court.

Previous research has demonstrated that implementing procedurally just practices will often have positive effects on the perceptions of those involved (Tyler & Lind, 2001). More important, the process may have a stronger influence on offenders' subsequent behavior than the actual sanction imposed (Paternoster et al., 1999). If defendants feel that they were treated fairly, then they are more likely to abide by court sanctions and reform their behavior. The process may also influence whether a victim will decide to report a future crime (Hickman & Simpson, 2003) or encourage other victims to prosecute.

Overall in the Lexington County CDVC, both victims and defendants suggested a high rate of satisfaction with the court. The majority of victims and defendants, for example, thought that their case was handled in a fair, good, or excellent manner. Additionally, the majority of victims and defendants thought they were treated with respect and dignity by the court. The interviews with court personnel and the court observations confirmed a high level of commitment to a fair and just process for both the victims and the defendants.

The interviews and observations highlight the court's success in providing the victims and defendants with a voice in their case. Similar to findings from more experimental procedural justice research, the "voice effect" appeared to be quite strong in the minds of the CDVC participants. A number of victims, defendants, and court personnel focused on the opportunities for defendants and victims to express their concerns to the court. Both victims and defendants, on average, thought that they had been given adequate time to explain their side of the story.

As a result of the nature of the inquiry, it is impossible to link together the observations, interviews, and outcomes for each of the cases. This aspect is an obvious limitation; however, the results are still instructive as a guide for development and future inquiry of specialized domestic violence courts. Clearly, the rearrest data suggest that the new court reduced recidivism (see Note 1), and the interview data from the current study suggest that the court also was successful in providing a procedurally fair and just system for both victims and defendants.

Together, the results from the qualitative interviews and observations of the CDVC indicate that an effective courtroom work group emerged and that important systemic changes occurred in the manner in which domestic violence cases were processed. Specifically, the court changed the focus of domestic violence prosecution from a traditional, passive approach to an active approach that emphasizes victim safety, offender accountability, and batterer treatment. Victims and defendants generally thought the court staff treated them with respect, felt the judge was concerned with their side of the story, and thought the outcomes of their cases were fair. These results suggest that specialized domestic violence courts that emphasize collaboration between law enforcement officials, prosecutors, judges, and treatment providers can be successfully implemented and can change the intervention process through which domestic violence cases are adjudicated. The contextual examination of procedural justice factors in this domestic violence court suggest that it is possible for the criminal justice system to be more effective in handling domestic violence cases if it focuses efforts on coordinating its response to involve multiple social services entities and at the same time holds domestic violence offenders accountable for their actions.

Notes

1. An interrupted time-series analysis was used to compare Lexington County's monthly arrest rates of criminal domestic violence for 34 months prior to the implementation of the court to monthly arrest rates for 26 months after the implementation of the court. The analysis indicated that on average, arrest rates for criminal domestic violence significantly increased by approximately 6 arrests each month after the court was developed. In addition, domestic violence rearrest rates of a random sample of 189 offenders processed in traditional courts before the implementation of the specialized court were compared to rearrest rates of a random sample of 197 offenders processed by the specialized court. Offenders who were processed by the specialized court had significantly lower rearrest rates (12%) compared to the historical comparison group of offenders (19%). Overall, the results indicated that enforcement of criminal domestic violence increased while recidivism for domestic violence decreased in Lexington County after the inception of the court.

2. Unlike violence between strangers, there are powerful social, emotional, and economic factors that bind victims of domestic violence to their abusers (Fritzler & Simon, 2000).

3. Significantly diverse prosecutorial practices and procedures have been implemented within judicial systems to address violence against women cases. Although no single court has emerged as a model domestic violence court, the fundamental goals of many courts include victim safety and offender accountability (Tsai, 2000).

4. Prior to the establishment of the Criminal Domestic Violence Court (CDVC) in Lexington County, domestic violence cases were assigned to one of eight Lexington County magistrate courts. Magistrate courts in South Carolina process all nonfelony-related cases and can assign a maximum penalty of 30 days in jail or a $1,000 fine. Because of the fact that magistrate courts process all misdemeanor cases, individual domestic violence cases did not get the attention they needed. In other words, because of a lack of resources in magistrate courts, many domestic violence cases were either dismissed or assigned minor fines. When minor fines were imposed on offenders, traditional courts did not hold offenders accountable for fines imposed. It was believed that the lack of resources and attention was allowing a continued trend of domestic violence in Lexington County.

5. According to South Carolina Code of Law Title 16, Section 25-20,

> it is unlawful to: (1) cause physical harm or injury to a person's own household member or (2) offer or attempt to cause physical harm or injury to a person's own household member with apparent present ability under circumstances reasonably creating fear of imminent peril.
>
> The term *household member* refers to current and former spouses, persons who have a child in common, males and females who are currently cohabitating or have formerly cohabitated, and persons related by consanguinity or affinity within the second degree.

6. According to the recidivism analysis from the outcome evaluation, offenders who were processed in the CDVC spent a significantly longer amount of time in jail compared to offenders who were processed in traditional magistrate courts (Gover et al., 2003). Specifically, offenders processed in the CDVC spent an average of 5 days in jail pretrial compared to offenders processed in traditional courts, who spent an average of 4.14 days in jail pretrial.

7. Formal job duties and responsibilities of criminal domestic violence investigators employed by the Lexington County Sheriff's Department include investigating incidents of domestic violence, securing and supervising crime scenes, reviewing evidence and reports, obtaining and serving search warrants, conducting searches, obtaining arrest warrants, apprehending and arresting suspects, interviewing victims and witnesses, questioning suspects, preparing statements, maintaining communication with informants, preparing cases for prosecution in court, providing court testimony as necessary, attending bond hearings, and conducting background investigations of suspects.

8. The decision to prosecute a case in the CDVC is not based on the willingness of a victim to testify in court. The decision to prosecute is based on the strength of the evidence in the case. It is not unusual for victims to contact the prosecutor to recant statements made to the responding officer, and often this is viewed as not cooperating with the prosecution. Many times victims will not attend court because they were intimidated or threatened by the offender. At the beginning of each court session, the prosecutor tells defendants that cases will be heard with or without the victim's testimony. Furthermore, defendants are told that if the CDVC has knowledge that the victim did not attend because of threats or intimidation by an offender, the CDVC can charge them with interfering with a state's witness, a 10-year felony.

9. According to Section 17-22-60, pretrial intervention is appropriate only where (a) there is substantial likelihood that justice will be served if the offender is placed in an intervention program; (b) it is determined that the needs of the offender and the state can better be met outside the traditional criminal justice process; (c) it is apparent that the offender poses no threat to the community; (d) it appears that the offender is unlikely to be involved in further criminal activity; (e) the offender, in those cases where it is required, is likely to respond quickly to rehabilitative treatment; (f) the offender has no significant history of prior delinquency or criminal activity; and (g) the offender has not previously been accepted in a pretrial intervention program.

10. In consideration of the fact that victims and defendants were asked to participate in the survey after their case was heard and while they were leaving the courthouse and to ensure a high rate of participation, researchers attempted to minimize time spent on the interviews from start to finish. Therefore, additional demographic data were not collected from victims and defendants who participated in the interviews. However, according to a random sample of criminal domestic violence offenders processed in the Lexington County court system between January 1997 and December 2000, 12% of offenders were female, the average offender age was 34, 20% of offenders were unemployed, and about 26% were African American (Gover et al., 2003).

11. Because this question was closed-ended, we do not have explanations provided by victims and defendants as to why they thought their cases were handled poorly. However, we can

speculate that the responses obtained at the end of the interview to the open-ended question shed some light on why some victims and defendants thought that the handling of their cases was poor.

References

American Medical Association Council on Scientific Affairs. (1992). Violence against women: Relevance for medical practitioners. *Journal of the American Medical Association, 267,* 2184-2189.

Bowman, C. G. (1992). The arrest experiments: A feminist critique. *Journal of Criminal Law and Criminology, 83,* 201-208.

Clark, S., Burt, M., Schulte, M., & Maguire, K. (1996). *Coordinated community responses to domestic violence in six communities: Beyond the justice system.* Washington, DC: Urban Institute.

Davis, R. C., & Taylor, B. G. (1997). A proactive response to family violence: The results of a randomized experiment. *Criminology, 35,* 307-333.

Folger, R., & Konovsky, M. A. (1989). Effects of procedural and distributive justice on reactions to pay raise decisions. *Academy of Management Journal, 32,* 115-130.

Fondacaro, M. R., Jackson, S. L., & Luescher, J. (2002). Toward the assessment of procedural and distributive justice in resolving family disputes. *Social Justice Research, 15,* 341-371.

Fritzler, R. B., & Simon, L. M. J. (2000). Creating a domestic violence court: Combat in the trenches. *Court Review, 37,* 28.

Gover, A. R., MacDonald, J. M., & Alpert, G. A. (2003). Combating domestic violence in rural America: Findings from an evaluation of a local domestic violence court. *Criminology and Public Policy, 3,* 109-132.

Hickman, L. J., & Simpson, S. S. (2003). Fair treatment or preferred outcome? The impact of police behavior on victim reports of domestic violence incidents. *Law and Society Review, 37,* 607-633.

Keilitz, S. (2000). *Specialization of domestic violence case management in the courts: A national survey.* Williamsburg, VA: National Center for State Courts.

Konovsky, M. A., & Cropanzano, R. (1991). Perceived fairness of employee drug testing as a predictor of employee attitudes and job performance. *Journal of Applied Psychology, 76,* 698-707.

Korsgaard, M. A., Sapienza, H. J., & Schweiger, D. M. (2002). Beaten before begun: The role of procedural justice in planning change. *Journal of Management, 28,* 497-516.

Lind, E. A., & Tyler, T. R. (1988). *The social psychology of procedural justice.* New York: Plenum.

Leventhal, G. S. (1980). What should be done with equity theory: New approaches to the study of fairness in social relationships. In K. Gergen, M. Greenberg, & R. Willis (Eds.), *Social exchange* (pp. 27-55). New York: Plenum.

Mazur, R., & Aldrich, L. (2003). What makes a domestic violence court work? Lessons from New York. *Judges' Journal, 42,* 5-11.

O'Connor, C. (1999). Domestic violence no-contact orders and the autonomy rights of victims. *Boston College Law Review, 40,* 937-967.

Ostrom, B., & Kauder, N. (1997). *Examining the work of state courts, 1997: A national perspective from the Court Statistics Project.* Williamsburg, VA: National Center for State Courts.

Paternoster, R., Bachman, R., Brame, R., & Sherman, L. W. (1997). Do fair procedures matter? The effect of procedural justice on spouse assault. *Law and Society Review, 31,* 163-204.

Richman, K. D. (2002). Women, poverty, and domestic violence: Perceptions of court and legal aid effectiveness. *Sociological Inquiry, 72,* 318-344.

Rottmann, D. (2000). Does effective therapeutic jurisprudence require specialized courts (and do specialized courts imply specialist judges)? *Court Review, 37,* 22-27.

Rottmann, D., & Casey, P. (1999, July). Therapeutic jurisprudence and the emergence of problem-solving courts. *National Institutes of Justice Journal,* 12-19.

Sherman, L. (1992). *Policing domestic violence: Experiments and dilemmas.* New York: Free Press.

Thibault, J., & Walker, L. (1975). *Procedural justice.* Hillsdale, NJ: Lawrence Erlbaum.

Tjaden P., & Thoennes, N. (1998). *Prevalence, incidence, and consequences of violence against women: Findings from the National Violence Against Women Survey.* Washington, DC: U.S. Department of Justice, National Institute of Justice.

Tsai, B. (2000). The trend toward specialized domestic violence courts: Improvements on an effective innovation. *Fordham Law Review, 68,* 1285-1327.

Tyler, T. R. (1984). The role of perceived injustice in defendants' evaluations of their courtroom experience. *Law and Society Review, 18,* 51-74.

Tyler, T. R. (1988). What is procedural justice? Criteria used by citizens to assess the fairness of legal procedures. *Law and Society Review, 22,* 103-135.

Tyler, T. R. (1990). *Why people obey the law.* New Haven: Yale University Press.

Tyler, T. R., & Folger, R. (1980). Distributional and procedural aspects of satisfaction with citizen-police encounters. *Basic and Applied Social Psychology, 1,* 281-283.

Tyler, T. R., & Lind, E. A. (2001). Procedural justice. In J. Sanders & V. Hamilton (Eds.), *Handbook of justice research in law* (pp. 65-92). New York: Kluwer Academic/Plenum Publishers.

U.S. Department of Commerce, Bureau of the Census. (2000). State and county quick facts. Available at http://quickfacts.census.gov/gdf/index.html

U.S. Department of Justice, Bureau of Justice Statistics. (1998). *Violence by intimates: Analysis of data on crimes by current or former spouses, boyfriends, and girlfriends.* Washington, DC: Author.

Violence Policy Center. (2003). *When men murder women: An analysis of 2001 homicide data.* Washington, DC: Author.

DISCUSSION QUESTIONS

1. Compared to other collaborations reviewed in this section (e.g., focused deterrence partnerships), how integrated are the organizational members participating in the Lexington County Criminal Domestic Violence Court? Using the earlier analogy, are they more like fruitcake or fruit salad? In your opinion, is the level of integration critical in determining the outcomes of the collaboration?

2. Although recommendations encourage diffusing power within collaborations, that is often difficult to accomplish. Do you think any members of the domestic violence court had more power than others? If so, which ones? Explain.

3. Defendants are offered the opportunity to participate in the pretrial counseling program in lieu of a trial or guilty plea. Does this create a situation where offenders are coerced into participating, since the alternative (assuming a conviction) is a traditional court sanction?

SECTION

VI

Unions and Collective Bargaining

United We Stand?

Section Highlights

- History of Unionism in Criminal Justice
- Collective Bargaining in Justice Agencies
    - Content of Agreements
    - Coverage of Agreements
    - Economic Benefits of Collective Bargaining
    - Potential Negative Effects
- Bargaining Impasses
- Labor Disputes and Employee Job Actions
    - Strike Generation
    - Perpetuation
    - Resolution
    - Other Job Actions
- Improving Labor Relations

Between April 1994 and December 1998, more than 45,000 offenders entered the California Department of Corrections under the state's 1994 three strikes law targeting habitual offenders (Austin, Clark, Hardyman, & Henry, 2000). The law provided for enhanced penalties for offenders with prior serious offense convictions; a third strike produced a sentence of 25 years to life in prison (Petersilia, 2008). During the same year, California also passed a truth-in-sentencing provision requiring offenders to serve 85% of their sentences before becoming eligible for release, an increase from the 50% that was common for incarcerated offenders (Page, 2011b). The California Correctional Peace Officers Association (CCPOA), a union of more than 33,000 correctional workers, lobbied for and financially supported efforts to pass both laws (Page, 2011b; Petersilia, 2008). More recently, the CCPOA opposed and worked to defeat several pieces of legislation that would weaken existing three strikes laws (Page, 2011b). While these efforts may be legitimate attempts to improve public safety (Kirchhoff, 2010), others point to a greater level of union self-interest: "More prisoners lead to more prisons; more prisons require more guards; more guards means more dues-paying members and fund-raising capability; and fund-raising, of course, translates into political influence" (Petersilia, 2008, p. 224).

Labor unions, described as mutual benefit organizations in Section I (Blau & Scott, 1962/2003), are potentially powerful environmental influences on criminal justice organizations, reaffirming the open-systems view of organizations. As the example above illustrates, these effects are far reaching. Budget development, resource and staffing allocation, management decision making, and agency policy formation are circumscribed by union activities. This impact may extend into larger, extraorganizational policymaking, as the CCPOA example demonstrates. The union, by its very nature, takes an active role in these areas of an organization to protect the interests of its members. Unionization in criminal justice has a lengthy history, but union power increased significantly in the 1960s and beyond, to the point where police, correctional, and probation and parole officers and other unionized employees have a significant voice in criminal justice system operations.

History of Unionism in Criminal Justice

Criminal justice employee organizations, early predecessors to modern unions, emerged in the 1800s as fraternal and support organizations that frequently lobbied for better pay and/or working conditions. Examples include the St. Louis Police Relief Association, formed in 1867 (Bouza, 1985), and the Prison Keeper's Association, operating in the early 1900s (Wynne, 1978b). Both organizations offered a variety of benefits to members, including what would now be considered some form of death, disability, and health insurance (Juris & Feuille, 1973). Governments were not supportive of unionization among public-sector workers, and national labor unions such as the American Federation of Labor (AFL) were opposed to the idea of organized police officers (Slater, 1997). The former saw affiliation with organized labor as a threat to the independence of the police (Fogelson, 1977), while the latter saw the police as a threat to workers since police had worked on behalf of employers to break strikes (Slater, 1997).[1]

The stance of the AFL weakened during the early 1900s. Police officers in many cities complained of low pay, long hours, and horrible working conditions and sought union help in effecting change. The AFL began granting charters to police organizations in 1919, essentially allowing them to affiliate with the national union (Bouza, 1985; Slater, 1997). Boston police officers received a charter from the AFL and continued to push for changes in the department even though department regulations prohibited them from affiliating with any outside organization (Slater, 1997). After several officers—considered union leaders—were suspended by the department's chief, the officer union voted to strike. During the Boston Police Strike in September 1919, more than 1,100 officers walked off the job, and what followed had significant repercussions for criminal justice unions specifically and public-sector unions more generally (Bouza, 1985; Slater, 1997). With the police force depleted and no replacements available, the city succumbed to crime and violence before Massachusetts Governor (and future president) Calvin Coolidge called on the National Guard to deal with the disorder. The officers eventually voted to return to work but were fired for illegally striking; the department dismissed more than 1,100 officers, leading to an almost entirely new police department (Bouza, 1985).

---

[1] Monkkonen (1992) argues that, despite high-profile examples of police conflict with workers, they were not wholly anti-labor.

▲ Photo 6.1 When more than 1,100 officers from the Boston Police Department went on strike, Massachusetts Governor Calvin Coolidge called in the state militia to restore order in the city. (Source: Boston Public Library, Leslie Jones Collection)

As a result of the strike, unionism in criminal justice declined significantly. The AFL no longer granted charters to police unions (Juris & Feuille, 1973). Although labor law was favorable to private-sector workers during the first half of the 20th century, the legacy of the Boston Police Strike did not earn public-sector workers similar privileges (Piskulich, 1992). As wages and other concerns continued to plague public-sector workers in the 1950s and 1960s, fraternal employee organizations again lobbied for improved salaries and against poor working conditions such as arbitrary discipline (Juris & Feuille, 1973). Conditions became more favorable to unions in the 1960s and 1970s as presidential executive orders and state laws began to recognize the right of public-sector workers to unionize and, perhaps more important, to collectively bargain the nature of their work (see below; Horowitz, 1994; Piskulich, 1992). For example, California correctional officers won the right to collectively bargain after the state legalized bargaining for all state employees in 1978, a law upheld by the state's supreme court in 1981 (Page, 2011b).

At the same time as criminal justice employee unions were receiving a boost in the 1960s and 1970s, discussions of prison inmate unions were becoming more commonplace (Comeau, 1971; Huff, 1974). By the late 1970s, more than 11,000 inmates were organized into councils, lobbying groups, and unions (Traub, 1977). Inmates in Ohio, for example, organized—though not formally unionized—in the late 1960s and early 1970s, following several prison riots and what they perceived to be unfair treatment by correctional staff and administration (Huff, 1974). Many of the goals sought by the prisoner union were similar to those sought by other public-sector labor unions—better economic benefits and improved working conditions. Among other things, the prisoner union sought better pay for prison work (perhaps on par with civilian salaries), the establishment of vocational programs, and the reduction of dangerous working conditions. Interestingly, they even advocated for higher correctional officer salaries in hopes of elevating the quality of personnel. The Supreme Court ruled in 1977, however, that the state's interest in providing for prisoner security is enough to curtail a prisoner's right to unionize (Traub, 1977).[2]

Today, unionization in criminal justice is quite common. Page (2011b) found that all but 13 states had a state prison officer union; most are affiliated with the AFL/CIO, a large national labor union, while the remaining unions are independent, unaffiliated organizations such as the CCPOA. In policing, data are available on the prevalence of collective bargaining rather than the number of unions. Nationally, slightly more than one third of departments authorize collective bargaining with officers (Reaves, 2010). Larger departments are more likely than smaller ones to authorize collective bargaining; more than 60% of agencies serving populations of 10,000 or more residents have such authorization.

---

[2] *Jones v. North Carolina Prisoners' Labor Union*, 433 U.S. 119 (1977).

Collective Bargaining in Justice Agencies

Organized labor, as discussed above, has always attempted to exert control over its work through lobbying or other collective actions, but it is arguably the power to engage in **collective bargaining** that is a union's most important responsibility. When unions bargain collectively, they negotiate the terms and conditions of their work with representatives designated by the appropriate unit of government (e.g., state, county, local).[3] The issues subject to negotiation vary but generally include matters related to economic benefits and working conditions (Wilson, Zhao, Ren, & Briggs, 2006). Conflict is inherent in the bargaining process; government designees resist relinquishing control and autonomy over organizational matters, while union representatives seek greater control over matters of interest to employees (Piskulich, 1992). The two sides work toward a contract containing the language of the agreed-on terms. The contract's duration is specified but most often covers multiple years before negotiations restart.

Not all public-sector workers have the right to collectively bargain with units of government, since laws vary across the states. Most states recognize the right for municipal, county, and state employees to collectively bargain, but others either are silent on the matter, authorize but do not require bargaining, allow for the exchange of proposals without any obligations ("meet and confer"), or forbid bargaining altogether (Piskulich, 1992; Shimabukuro & Mayer, 2010). Public agencies in Virginia, for example, are forbidden from recognizing and negotiating with labor unions for collective bargaining purposes. Missouri public employees (state and local police and deputy sheriffs excluded) may unionize and present proposals related to wages and working conditions, but the organization is not compelled to agree to the proposals (Shimabukuro & Mayer, 2010). The Missouri case illustrates how various criminal justice employees within the same state can be treated differently with respect to collective bargaining laws. Until 2003, collective bargaining rights of Florida deputy sheriffs were not uniformly applied across the state, even within the same occupation (Doerner & Doerner, 2010; Pynes & Corley, 2006). The right to bargain was generally forbidden except in the small number of counties where the Florida legislature allowed for a special privilege. Deputies were considered "appointees," rather than "employees," who were deputized by an elected sheriff (Doerner & Doerner, 2010, p. 368). A Florida Supreme Court case in 2003 eliminated this distinction as it applied to deputies and opened the door to collective bargaining.

Content of Agreements

Collective bargaining contracts, although possibly limited by relevant legal statutes, cover a broad range of issues related to economic benefits and working conditions. Economic concerns include wages, retirement benefits/pensions, and health insurance. These issues are often a source of contention as budget-conscious governments deal with the challenges of providing a range of services to citizens. Criminal justice employees' economic demands compete against demands from workers in other areas of government, all of whom must be supported with finite resources. The matter of economic benefits is further complicated by issues related to parity with other organizations, pay increases across different ranks, and minimum, maximum, and intermediate pay levels (Juris & Feuille, 1973). A 1971 New York City police officer wildcat strike, a job action not authorized by the officers' union, resulted from a dispute over pay parity. Officers believed they were entitled to the same $1,200 pay increase given to sergeants two years earlier; to do otherwise would distort the pay differential between ranks (Perlmutter, 1971).

---

[3]Union representatives would negotiate with a private business if the employees worked in the private sector.

Agreements also cover issues related to the policies and operations of the organization (Wynne, 1978a). Historically, these matters were the purview of the organization's leadership—the chief, warden, commissioner, or other executive—but unions have increasingly become involved in these issues, citing their effects on employee working conditions (Walker, 2008). Negotiated areas include job assignments and transfers (including the role of seniority), disciplinary actions and procedures, mechanisms for handling employee grievances, work hours (e.g., 12-hour vs. 8-hour shifts), the employment of non-union or nonsworn personnel, staffing (e.g., one vs. two officer patrols; inmate-to-guard ratios), and other department policies. The Rhode Island correctional officer union assured job security for member officers by preventing "anyone else from doing a job that could be done by a correctional officer" (Mooney, 2000, p. 1A). In California, contracts were reached with the CCPOA in the 1990s and later included post-and-bid language (Page, 2011b). As Page describes the system, the prison advertises (posts) available jobs internally, "officers then bid for job assignments, and management allocates the assignments to the most senior bidders (regardless of factors such as physical fitness, skill level, or dependability)" (p. 163). This system severely restricts management flexibility in making operational/staffing decisions but ensures a largely predictable process for employees.

Contracts may also include provisions specifically related to the union itself (Wynne, 1978a). One example is a **dues check off** agreement, where the employing organization automatically deducts union dues from employee paychecks and forwards the money to the union; this eliminates the need for the union to seek payment individually from each member and "guarantees income" for the union (Kadleck, 2003, p. 343). The contract may also ensure that unions are able to conduct certain business (e.g., communicate with members) at the workplace. For example, a recent agreement between the Missouri Department of Corrections and the correctional officer union states,

> The [union] shall be permitted use of adequate and accessible space on employer's bulletin boards . . . for communications with bargaining unit members in the staff assembly area, staff dining area and one or more areas agreed upon by the facility head and [union]. (*Agreement Between*, 2007–2012, p. 3)

These provisions grant security to unions, allowing them to continue to operate.

Whether contracts favor management over labor or labor over management is unclear. Carter and Sapp (1992) examined 328 police collective bargaining agreements from 1991 and compared their findings with results from a similar study conducted a decade earlier. They found that "almost every difference favorable to management noted between the 1981 and 1991 studies is counterbalanced by a movement that favors the labor side of the equation" (p. 40).

Coverage of Agreements

If the union is permitted to negotiate the terms of one or more of the aforementioned issues with management, a critical question is, "On whose behalf is the union bargaining?" Up until this point, the generic term *employees* has been used to refer to those interested in negotiating the nature of their work. This terminology is too vague. Through the process of **unit determination**, the composition of the bargaining unit is established.[4] This requires that membership be clearly delineated. The resulting body

---

[4] Determining which union will represent the employees is another critical issue, generally occurring when bargaining rights are first secured. Fogelson (1977) documents several cities where multiple groups sought to represent the police; a vote of members determined the victor.

is recognized as the authorized bargaining unit for purposes of collective bargaining negotiations. Wynne (1978a) calls the bargaining unit "a group of employees that the state or local jurisdiction has deemed an appropriate group to be represented by a single employee organization for the purpose of collective bargaining" (p. 94). Ultimately, unit determination dictates who will be bound by any negotiated agreement.

Unit determination is no easy task, especially when work is divided so many different ways (see Section II). Diversity exists across job responsibilities (horizontal complexity), supervisory tasks (vertical complexity), and geographic location (spatial complexity). Should line-level personnel such as correctional officers and police officers be in the same bargaining unit as mid-level managers such as lieutenants? Should treatment staff and custody staff be covered under the same contract? Some states prescribe the boundaries of a bargaining unit within state law, while more freedom may be granted in others. Regardless of the source of bargaining unit guidelines, they typically embody one or more standards of determination (Piskulich, 1992; Wynne, 1978a). For example, membership in a bargaining unit may be determined by "communities of interest" where employees are grouped according to similar skills, working conditions, promotional opportunities, or other similarities. In other cases, the bargaining unit may be established to eliminate fragmentation and promote efficiency. It would simply be unwieldy for an organization to negotiate separately with multiple bargaining units (e.g., officers, supervisors, detectives, and civilians in a police department). It is also important to ensure that members of the bargaining unit are adequately represented, a difficult task when units comprise diverse employees. Wynne (1978a) illustrated this point by noting how probation and parole officers in Washington during the 1970s were able to separate from the larger public assistance bargaining unit by arguing that their interests were not sufficiently represented. There may also be interest in preventing the establishment of a single unit covering both officers and supervisors (Piskulich, 1992). Walker (2008) argued that a conflict of interest could exist if, for example, supervisors face a union grievance for disciplining an officer from the very union that represents both the supervisor and the officer. Evidence suggests considerable variation in the composition of bargaining units in criminal justice (Kadleck, 2003; Wynne, 1978a).

Economic Benefits of Collective Bargaining

The overall value of unionization for the public-sector worker is difficult to quantify, especially when the gains are specific policy provisions (e.g., alterations in disciplinary process). Both the popular media and scholarly articles tend to illustrate key bargaining victories for specific unions. For example, the CCPOA successfully negotiated for the right of its members to carry firearms (Petersilia, 2008). These victories shed light on the benefits in particular cases but do not allow for generalized statements about the value of unions. To make inferences about the advantages of unions and collective bargaining, researchers more commonly examine the economic benefits of unions and collective bargaining by employing a comparative methodology where outcomes for union and non-union workers are assessed. Emphasizing economic outcomes is also warranted given the prevalence of economic concerns among disputed issues.

The Bureau of Labor Statistics (2011) recently reported median weekly salaries for workers in protective service occupations, an encompassing category including, among other positions, corrections officers, police officers, security guards, firefighters, animal control workers, lifeguards, transportation security screeners, and fish and game officers. Union members in the protective service industry earn a median salary of $995 per week, compared with $629 for their non-union counterparts. Other studies have addressed law enforcement officer salaries only. Studying the effects of an important collective bargaining court case affecting Florida sheriff's deputies, Doerner and Doerner (2010) found that unionized sheriff's deputies in the state earned nearly $5,000 more per year than did non-union deputies. Wilson and colleagues (2006) noted smaller yet still significant benefits in their study of officer salaries during the 1990s; collective bargaining netted gains of $941 in the minimum officer salary in sampled departments during the period.

Unionized officers are also more likely than non-union officers to receive **supplemental pay**. Examples of supplemental pay include bonuses for longevity, shift differentials (e.g., working nights or weekends), hazardous duty, merit, and additional education. The distribution of supplemental pay benefits in different law enforcement agencies is presented in Table 6.1. Using data collected in 1990, Zhao and Lovrich (1997) found a relationship between collective bargaining in large police departments and the existence of three different types of supplemental pay: hazardous duty, shift differential, and educational incentives. Collective bargaining, however, did not increase the likelihood that

Table 6.1 Salary and Supplemental Pay by Collective Bargaining Across Three Agency Types[1]

| | Municipal Police | | Sheriffs' Departments | | State Police | |
	Collective Bargaining Authorized/Provided (%)		Collective Bargaining Authorized/Provided (%)		Collective Bargaining Authorized/Provided (%)	
	Yes	No	Yes	No	Yes	No
All agencies	53.5	46.5	32.2	67.8	51.1	48.9
Offer supplemental pay Educational incentive	63.6	37.3	44.7	21.2	47.8	18.2
Hazardous duty	17.2	9.2	19.5	11.9	30.4	27.3
Merit/performance	21.2	39.1	29.3	28.2	26.1	68.2
Shift differential	51.4	16.5	57.5	10.5	69.6	36.4
Special skills	32.0	20.4	29.3	12.5	39.1	31.8
Bilingual ability	17.6	12.4	18.0	5.2	17.4	13.6
Tuition reimbursement	68.9	46.4	51.1	24.1	60.9	54.5
Military service	27.3	17.5	28.9	16.8	43.5	22.7
Residential incentive	3.0	2.4	5.3	0.7	4.3	22.7
Mean starting salary	$42,444	$32,290	$38,178	$31,598	$43,439	$37,033

[1]Based on responses from 1,968 municipal departments, 827 sheriffs' departments, and 45 state police agencies. Responses are unweighted.

Source: Adapted from Bureau of Justice Statistics (2007).

departments would offer financial rewards for exceptional workers. The authors argue that "the first three forms of extra compensation represent the supplemental benefits typically favored by police officers, while merit pay reflects the discretionary use of monetary rewards favored by management" (p. 512). Stated differently, merit requires subjective decision making, essentially granting management a level of power that officers are reluctant to relinquish.[5] Similar patterns have been observed in corrections. Fringe benefits, including supplemental pay, sick leave, holiday/vacation days, uniform allowances, and other perks, were more common in state correctional systems where collective bargaining agreements were in place than in states without collective bargaining agreements (Smith & Sapp, 1985).

In recent years, public-sector worker compensation packages and unions more generally have been the target of criticism by the public and government officials. These criticisms must be considered along with the secondary benefits of such packages. For example, monetary compensation may contribute to worker productivity and motivation (see Section VIII) while also saving money in recruitment and retention costs. California prison workers, with their high wages and excellent benefits, leave their jobs at low rates (3.6%) compared with other states (some with rates as high as 32%) (Petersilia, 2008). Consequently, the state saves considerable resources on recruiting and training new workers. Moreover, the compensation may entice workers who otherwise might have chosen more lucrative jobs in other industries to enter the criminal justice field (Walker, 2008).

Potential Negative Effects

In spite of the benefits of collective bargaining, the content of negotiated agreements may actually be detrimental to management and the communities served by criminal justice organizations. Samuel Walker (2008), writing specifically about police unions, detailed some of these potential impacts, which have applicability beyond law enforcement organizations. Agreements, by their very nature, weaken the ability of organizational leaders to make unilateral decisions, which may restrain efforts to innovate or improve efficiency or effectiveness. For example, Mooney (2000) wrote that, before reaching a new agreement with the Rhode Island correctional officer union in 2000, prison leadership was largely prohibited from moving officers from one position to another because seniority, a common provision in collective bargaining contracts, determined work position, shift, and workdays for officers. In policing, seniority clauses typically result in the least experienced officers working the most crime-ridden areas and shifts (Walker, 2008).[6]

Collective bargaining contracts also affect matters of discipline and accountability. The contracts, or a related Bill of Rights, may specify requirements that must be adhered to during the course of investigations (e.g., location, right to union representation; Walker, 2008). Beyond investigations, Veatch (2008) found that civilian review boards and in-car cameras, both viewed as mechanisms for increasing management oversight of personnel, were less common in police departments where collective bargaining was authorized than in departments where it was not. In other words, agreements may work to inhibit accountability and discipline.

Collective bargaining contracts, as shown above, typically result in higher salaries for represented employees, which influence city, county, or state budgets (Walker, 2008). The services provided by criminal justice employees cannot simply be replaced by nongovernment agencies, but workers can take

---

[5]Doerner and Doerner (2010) argue that the simple bargaining/no-bargaining dichotomy used in many studies may be insufficient to detect the effects of unions. Instead, they note that the benefits of unionization may accrue over time, with salaries being the initial concern and additional benefits coming later.

[6]For a lengthy list of issues resisted and "headaches" caused by unions, see Kadleck and Travis (2008, p. 4).

jobs elsewhere or enter the private sector. Taxpayers, as a consequence, must often pay a premium for government labor (Wellington & Winter, 1988).

Finally, unions are often quite active in the political process. In negotiating contracts, employee unions are working toward agreements with management within a larger political context. That is, governments provide the resources that support public-sector workers. Unions can attempt to influence resource flows by engaging in political activities—supporting candidates who are more supportive of the union's positions and challenging those who are hostile (Farber, 2005). Potential strategies include donating to specific candidates, lobbying legislative bodies, and engaging in publicity campaigns (O'Brien, 1994). In the 1998 California gubernatorial election, the CCPOA spent more than $2 million endorsing the eventual victor, Gray Davis (Page, 2011b). Davis, a Democrat, received the union's support because "he was pro-labor and as tough on crime as most Republicans. . . . As an example of his toughness, [he] vowed that if elected, murderers would not receive parole on his watch" (p. 61). While not always negative, union influence may distort the political process (see below).

Bargaining Impasses

Given the stakes for all parties involved, it is not uncommon for talks to break down for some length of time during contract negotiations. While the threat of job actions always looms, multiple options are available to encourage a negotiated settlement. These intermediate steps—mediation, fact finding, and arbitration—involve third parties and are designed to allow the parties involved to bridge their differences and arrive at a resolution (Horowitz, 1994; Piskulich, 1992).

When parties agree to **mediation**, they have an impartial third person participate in the negotiation. As Piskulich (1992) notes, the mediator's role is to "promote continued talks, to discuss disagreements with each side, to channel messages, and to suggest means for reconciling disputes . . . to facilitate compromise between the parties themselves" (p. 43). In other words, the mediator helps the parties voluntarily resolve their disagreements but does not decide on a settlement. **Fact finding** is a process whereby a neutral party investigates disputed issues to discover the true facts relevant to each claim. For example, contract negotiations may stall over disagreements about appropriate wage increases. Government officials claim that budget crises do not allow for any increase; union representatives argue that the city does have money and that officers are woefully underpaid compared with peer departments. A fact finder can investigate and present the "reality" surrounding these two issues: the extent of the budget crisis and the cross-agency comparisons. These facts are then used as negotiations continue. Finally, the parties might enter an **arbitration** process. An arbitrator makes actual decisions on the appropriate resolution, and unless the arbitration is voluntary or nonbinding, the decision is binding on the parties (Delaney & Feuille, 1977; Horowitz, 1994; Piskulich, 1992). When the arbitration is nonbinding, the parties may agree to, consider, or ignore the arbitrator's ruling.

In some states with collective bargaining legislation for public-sector employees, the particular mechanism for dispute resolution may be codified in law. Michigan provides for compulsory arbitration in its legal code, stating,

> It is the public policy of this state that in public police and fire departments, where the right of employees to strike is by law prohibited, it is requisite to the high morale of such employees and the efficient operation of such departments to afford an alternative, expeditious, effective and binding procedure for the resolution of disputes. (423 MCL 231)

Even with impasse procedures in place, disputes may linger for years. Members of the Rhode Island Brotherhood of Correctional Officers, the state's correctional officer union, worked for more than four years without a pay increase until a 13% pay raise was negotiated as part of a contract settlement in 2000 (Mooney, 2000). The agreement was reached less than two months after correctional officers resorted to a more significant job action—a one-day strike that resulted in the mobilization of the National Guard.

Labor Disputes and Employee Job Actions

For most public-sector criminal justice employees, the right to unionize and to collectively bargain does not necessarily result in the right to strike. State and local government workers are prohibited from striking in all but 10 states; in the remaining states, limited rights are granted to certain categories of workers or after certain procedures (e.g., cooling-off periods) are followed. The exceptions do not typically allow for police or correctional officer strikes or other stoppages that jeopardize public safety (Cimini, 1998). Wohlers (1978) offers several arguments to account for differences between strike options for public- and private-sector workers:

- *Sovereignty:* If strikes are permitted by government workers who are tasked with serving the public welfare, then workers supplant the public good (e.g., public safety) with private interests (e.g., wages, benefits, working conditions). Governor Calvin Coolidge famously stated during the Boston police strike, "There is no right to strike against the public safety—by anybody, anywhere, at any time" (Slater, 1997, p. 26).

- *Rebellion:* Striking government employees disrupt the functioning of a community—trash may not be picked up, fires may burn with no fire department response, criminals may offend without fear of apprehension. A strike, therefore, contributes to disorder (Wohlers, 1978).

- *Protection:* There are certain occupations—arguably, firefighting, policing, and corrections—deemed essential for public safety. To grant members of these professions the power to strike places public safety in jeopardy.

- *Economics:* A significant though not necessarily realized concern is that striking workers wield incredible power and will be able to win large concessions from government officials using taxpayer money, because there are limited alternatives in the event that workers do strike. This results in larger organizational and city expenditures and an increased tax burden (see, for example, Putchinski, 2007).

- *Distortion of the political process:* Government resources are finite, and multiple parties (government agencies, citizens, etc.) compete for limited funds. Allowing government workers to strike provides them with an advantage in terms of resource acquisition. Moreover, citizens, if unhappy with the unions or the absence of service caused by a strike, are able to express their frustrations only by targeting elected officials. This does not necessarily result in dramatic change in anything more than the criminal justice agency's top leadership.

The legal prohibitions and arguments against public-sector strikes notwithstanding, government workers, including police and correctional officers, have walked off the job. The evolution of these job actions is described below using Meyer's (1976) three stages of a strike: generation, perpetuation, and resolution.

Strike Generation

The very same elements that make up a collective bargaining contract—economic benefits and conditions of work—are potential issues of dispute that can generate job actions, including strikes. Meyer (1976) notes that when "employees perceive any existing conditions or policies as undesirable," specific actions become possibilities to facilitate resolution (p. 548). He grouped 26 police strikes that occurred worldwide between 1899 and 1970 by the "disputed issue" to illustrate common generators. In 18 strikes, wages and benefits were the sole issue of contention; in four others, disagreements over policy matters led to the strike. The remaining strikes resulted from either pressure for union recognition (particularly with early strikes) or, as was the case in London in 1918, multiple issues. Another method for examining points of contention during bargaining is to review arbitration decisions in disputes between police officer unions and management. An analysis of more than 300 arbitration awards from 1982 to 1983 indicates that the five most common issues decided on by an arbitrator were police officer maximum salary, police officer minimum salary, longevity pay, annual clothing allowances, and maximum amount of vacation time (Delaney & Feuille, 1988). Non-economic policy concerns (e.g., disciplinary procedures, residency requirements, use-of-force policies) were also relevant but were not among the most contested issues.

Perpetuation

The perpetuation stage represents the actual strike, or as Meyer (1976) describes it, "the second stage begins when the employees leave their assignments and ends when they agree to return to work" (p. 554). The duration of public-sector strikes is generally much shorter than for strikes by private-sector workers. In 1980, for example, work stoppages resulted in the loss of 24.4 days per worker, on average, in all industries. Government workers, in contrast, each lost 10.5 days due to work stoppages (Lewin, Feuille, Kochan, & Delaney, 1988).

When police or correctional officers leave their posts during a strike, regardless of the length of the dispute, organizational leaders must adapt to the circumstances to continue at least some level of service delivery. In some cases, nonstriking personnel attempt to fulfill the duties of striking employees. During a strike of the Klamath Falls, Oregon, Police Department in 1973, nine sergeants and lieutenants who were outside of the bargaining unit were assigned to work 12-hour shifts to cover for the 18 striking officers throughout the 2-week strike (Widenor, 1991). In other situations, the void left by striking workers is filled with the assistance of additional agencies. When police in Memphis engaged in an 8-day strike in 1978, members of the Tennessee Highway Patrol, county sheriffs' departments, and the National Guard helped nonstriking Memphis Police Department supervisory personnel deliver police services (Williams, Smith, Manning, & Fuller, 1978). The role of the National Guard in labor disputes is also evident during prison strikes. In a notable example, more than 12,000 troops operated New York state prisons for the duration of a 17-day correctional officer strike in 1979 (Zimmer & Jacobs, 1981). Arguably, these solutions do not result in equivalent service provision; as Meyer (1976) noted, replacement workers are not as familiar with the jurisdiction/facility, may operate on different radio frequencies, and may be subjected to hostility from striking workers.[7] That said, at least partial service delivery is maintained.

---

[7] Zimmer and Jacobs (1981) write of the 1979 New York prison guard strike, "[The National Guard troops] initially encountered sharp resistance from picketing prison guards: during the first few days of what provided to be a seventeen-day strike, the prison guards threatened and perpetuated a good deal of violence and property damage" (p. 531).

In the absence of full continuity in the level of services provided, a strike potentially increases the risk of community or institutional (jail/prison) crime and disorder, depending on the nature of the strike. Ironically, it is the very possibility of lawlessness that provides unions with leverage when threatening or actually striking.[8] If order were preserved, even in the absence of a police force or prison staff, then the strike would lose potency (Meyer, 1976). The absence of more than 1,100 officers during the 1919 Boston strike resulted in an escalation of crime and violence until order was restored by the National Guard. Concerns about unionization and similar job actions continued for decades as fears about the consequences of strikes remained. Fifty years after the Boston strike, similar outcomes were realized once again in Montreal, Canada, when police officers walked off the job for 16 hours. As *Time* magazine ("City Without Cops," 1969) reported the week following the strike:

> The lesson was costly. Six banks were robbed, more than 100 shops were looted, and there were twelve fires. Property damage came close to $3,000,000; at least 40 carloads of glass will be needed to replace shattered storefronts. Two men were shot dead.

Other research has questioned the inevitability of a crime spike during police job actions. Erdwin Pfuhl (1983) examined crime rates in 11 cities that experienced police strikes during the 1970s. The cities ranged in size from Las Cruces, New Mexico (pop. 46,400) to Memphis, Tennessee (pop. 683,112), and strike durations varied from two days to one month. He found little evidence that the absence of officers due to strikes systematically and detrimentally influenced reported rates of burglary, larceny, and automobile theft.

During the New York prison guard strike of 1979, "the union's only hope of victory was a deterioration of conditions within the [state's] prisons" (Zimmer & Jacobs, 1981, p. 540). The leverage was lost when the National Guard and New York State Police officers (the latter assuming duties requiring the use of firearms) proved able to maintain order throughout the system. Zimmer and Jacobs described the situation by noting that the National Guard presence effectively doubled the ordinary level of staffing in each facility and inmates were initially locked down in their cells all day. As the strike progressed, typical prison operations resumed. Zimmer and Jacobs referred to this as the "honeymoon period," where respect characterized relationships between inmates and new staff (p. 540). The power of the strike diminished as a result. The discrepancy in findings, where crime and disorder develop during strikes in some contexts but not in others, may be explained by the level of protection that remains during the walkout. If a city or correctional facility is left largely unprotected, as was the case in Boston in 1919, crime and disorder may increase. If a city or facility retains some degree of protection through the use of nonstriking (e.g., supervisory) personnel or other agencies (e.g., state police, county sheriff's office, National Guard), crime and disorder levels may be unaffected.[9]

---

[8] Striking workers also attempt to gain leverage by striking at particularly important times. New Orleans Police Department officers struck in 1979 during the city's annual Mardi Gras festivities, leading to the cancellation of many events (Bouza, 1985), and city officials in Boston were concerned that a labor dispute would lead Boston Police Department officers to picket during the 2004 Democratic National Convention (Greenhouse, 2004).

[9] Pfuhl (1983) suggests that the fact that police strikes do not inevitably result in spikes in crime rates is evidence of an overall weak relationship between police presence and crime. For a discussion of the effects of variation in patrol levels, see Sherman and Eck (2002).

Resolution

The short length of most criminal justice strikes is indicative of the general rapid resolution (once the strike commences) of the conflict producing the strike in the first place. For workers and organizations alike, the question becomes, "Was it worth it?" It is presumptuous to assume that striking workers hold power and, as a result, receive more favorable resolution terms after a strike than they would have through a nonstrike resolution. As research evidence suggests, "the more accurate answer to the question of 'Who wins?' in strike situations is 'It depends'" (Lewin et al., 1988, p. 333). Meyer (1976) attempted to capture the variation in strike outcomes by identifying four categories of resolutions: mutual agreement, capitulation, cooptation, and replacement.[10]

First, strikes may be settled by mutual agreement. Meyer (1976) specifically addressed mutually satisfactory solutions that occurred after a strike was threatened but before one actually occurred, but there is no reason to believe that such win–win or lose–lose settlements cannot be reached after a strike begins. Guards at the privately operated South Texas Detention Facility, a holding center for immigration detainees, threatened to strike in 2009 before ultimately agreeing on a contract with the company that runs the facility ("Prison Union Leaders," 2009). Second, employers may capitulate to the demands of the union and striking workers. In these situations, the strike proves beneficial to the employees, while the organization is criticized for allowing the disruption of a strike with outcomes that could have occurred through negotiated settlements. For example, prison workers in a daylong 1971 strike in New York State ended their walkout when government officials offered sufficient pay increases and bonuses (Clarity, 1972). Third, resolution may occur through the cooptation of striking employees by employers, often through the use of threats or legal coercion against striking workers. The realities of significant financial penalties influenced striking prison guards in New York in 1979 (Zimmer & Jacobs, 1981), and threatened fines and loss of union certification played a role in resolving the 17-hour Montreal police strike (Clark, 1969). A fourth resolution mechanism is to permanently replace striking workers, something that was done in early strikes, including that in Boston. Replacing entire police or correctional staffs is impractical given recruitment and training costs (Meyer, 1976), but mass firings on a smaller scale have indeed occurred as a tactic to promote resolution. During Baltimore's 1974 strike, the police commissioner fired 82 striking officers who were still on probation (Franklin, 1974). The four categories are not rigid, and settlement outcomes ultimately reflect multiple types. Striking workers may ease their demands (e.g., compromise on wage increases) when faced with potential sanctions.

Regardless of the type of resolution, it is critical to reiterate that most strikes by public-sector criminal justice employees are illegal, specifically banned by state or federal statutes. As a consequence, penalties may be prescribed for unions and employees engaging in strike actions. Among the penalties that may be imposed on the union itself are a loss of certification (i.e., it is no longer recognized as the bargaining unit by government/administration), fines, and the elimination of dues check off. Individuals potentially face dismissal, demotion, fines, or probation (see, for example, Olson, 1986). A well-known strike deterrent, New York's Taylor Law, stipulates that individuals who illegally strike face fines equivalent to two days' pay for every one day on strike; New York prison guards received these fines as a result of the 1979 strike.[11] In practice, strike resolutions include discussions and/or

---

[10] Meyer's (1976) categorization was developed by examining police strikes, but the categories are equally applicable as outcomes for other public-sector strikes.

[11] According to Zimmer and Jacobs (1981), prison guards were encouraged to manipulate overtime following the strike to compensate for the Taylor Law fines.

agreements about penalties. During the 1978 strike involving officers of the Memphis Police Department, the city's mayor stated that he was going to fire striking employees, but in the end, an agreement was reached that allowed officers to return to their jobs without penalties (Williams et al., 1978). Evidence supporting the deterrent effect of penalties is mixed, with some claiming that they can discourage strikes and others suggesting that they might actually make resolution more challenging as the parties negotiate post-strike penalties (Horowitz, 1994; Lewin et al., 1988; Piskulich, 1992). Needless to say, the nature of the strike's resolution, both in terms of the final contract decisions and penalties imposed, has lasting effects on the level of conflict between employees and administration.

Other Job Actions

Short of striking, criminal justice employees have at their disposal other job actions that allow them to express dissatisfaction with management, air grievances, and secure favorable bargaining outcomes. Mass sickouts and work slowdowns are two options.[12] Interestingly, however, a broad definition of strikes encompassed in the Taft-Hartley Act—a key piece of labor relations legislation from the 1940s—includes the following: "any strike or other concerted stoppage of work by employees (including a stoppage by reason of the expiration of a collective-bargaining agreement) and any concerted slowdown or other concerted interruption of operations by employees" (29 U.S.C. 142). Sickouts and slowdowns, although designed to make a political statement or compel action on the part of management, are typically viewed as "illegal strikes," and those who are absent without legitimate reason are subject to disciplinary action.[13]

Mass sickouts—called the "blue flu" when the action is taken by police personnel—occur when large numbers of employees collectively take sick leave at the same time. This results in the organization having to adapt quickly, shuffle resources, and expend money for overtime to address the sudden staff shortage. Recent examples abound. Wisconsin prison employees, protesting the lack of pay increases and a finalized contract agreement, staged a sickout in 2003 where between 20% and 33% of officers per shift were absent (Richmond, 2003). In New Haven, Connecticut, in 2011, 17 police officers called in sick during an overnight shift, allegedly protesting the layoffs of 16 fellow officers (Harish, 2011). This job action came 20 years after members of the same department did not report for duty across several shifts, leaving the department with only half its normal complement of officers (Johnson, 1991). A union representative at the time indicated that officers were upset over the department's decision to discipline two officers for their involvement in the shooting of a drug suspect.

When employees strike, they fail to perform their assigned duties. When workers engage in a **slowdown**, they only minimally (and some would argue, inadequately) perform their responsibilities. Before striking in 1974, Baltimore police officers expressed their conflict with management by filling out lost property reports for change found on the streets and measuring the distance cars were parked from curbs ("Chaos in Charm City," 1974). The work kept officers tied up for extended periods with paperwork on minor offenses. In another example, the city manager in Galveston, Texas, accused officers of writing fewer traffic tickets, leading to a $400,000 drop in revenue for the city. There was speculation that officers were upset over changes in department policies that prevented them from

---

[12]Organizational members might also issue votes of no confidence against leadership, file grievances, lobby for changes, and file lawsuits (Kadleck & Travis, 2008).

[13]Providing examples of sickouts and work slowdowns is complicated by the fact that unions may not publicly state that such actions are under way. In these cases, examples can be identified based on allegations from organization management.

moonlighting at bars, though officers countered that the decline was due to, among other factors, fewer police officers on duty (Uchida, 2010). As this example shows, slowdowns are potentially powerful when they deprive city officials of much-needed resources.

Improving Labor Relations

Sirene (1985) argued that management's inattention to key areas of the workplace contributes to unionization and labor strife; "rarely does the seed of organized labor sprout in a well-managed organization which has as one of its major objectives the welfare of its employees" (p. 162). Consequently, to prevent sickouts, slowdowns, strikes, or other job actions, managers must focus on several key issues in the workplace, including, but not limited to, salaries, workplace fairness, and the status of employees. Low salaries or declining benefits are a common source of employee discontent.[14] This issue presents a dilemma for managers who must operate with finite resources, particularly in times of budgetary crises, and possible taxpayer resistance to paying more for government services. At the same time, failure to address salary and benefit issues can generate employee dissatisfaction and result in the types of job actions discussed earlier (Herzberg, Mausner, & Snyderman, 1959). Therefore, while managers should not automatically surrender to employee salary demands, the costs associated with higher wages should be assessed in relation to the benefits of avoiding these problems (Ichniowski, Freeman, & Lauer, 1989).

Managers must also ensure that employees have a mechanism for airing grievances and fairly resolving matters of employee discipline (Sirene, 1985). This idea is captured in the concept of organizational justice (see Section VIII for a more detailed discussion). As Wolfe and Piquero (2011) explain, there are three components to organizational justice: distributive, procedural, and interactional. Distributive justice represents a concern for outcomes. For example, a correctional officer may sense injustice if he or she receives a more severe punishment than another officer for the same rule-violating behavior. Procedural justice emphasizes how decisions about outcomes are made. The same correctional officer, even if he or she received the same penalty as the colleague, may view the process as unfair if he or she was not given the opportunity to present evidence or not provided with details of how penalties were going to be determined. In other words, the process itself, not the outcome, was perceived as unjust. Finally, interactional justice is based on the quality of interactions between supervisors and employees during interactions or communications. Perceptions of justice might suffer if these interactions are characterized by hostility, animosity, and/or disrespect. Clear policies and procedures (e.g., the disciplinary hearing process) work to enhance perceptions of organizational justice.[15]

Labor conflict can also be prevented by addressing issues related to the status of employees; specifically, workers want to be recognized for the value of their contributions to the organization (Sirene, 1985). In the years preceding the 1979 New York prison guard strike, officers saw their role diminish in importance as others, including rehabilitation personnel, assumed greater responsibilities in the prison. Correctional officers were increasingly relegated to a disciplinarian role only, and even this responsibility was weakened by the increasing rights afforded to inmates (Zimmer & Jacobs, 1981). Management should work to enhance the status of criminal justice occupations. For example, employees can be given a greater voice in organizational policymaking and be given significant and varying job responsibilities.

---

[14] Perceptions affect definitions of "low wages." Others argue that the market itself is structured to prevent low wages in public-sector jobs (Wellington & Winter, 1988).

[15] In addition to reducing labor conflict, organizational justice may produce additional benefits such as reducing misconduct (see, for example, Wolfe & Piquero, 2011).

As this discussion demonstrates, unions are an important force in the criminal justice system. Criminal justice agency leaders must be cognizant of union forces and must attempt to strike a necessary balance between the needs of the workers and the needs of the organization. Failure to address these issues increases the probability of some type of organizational disruption.

KEY TERMS

arbitration	dues check off	supplemental pay
blue flu	fact finding	unit determination
Boston Police Strike (1919)	mediation	
collective bargaining	slowdown	

DISCUSSION QUESTIONS

1. Are there issues that, in your opinion, should be determined solely by organizational leadership and not subject to collective bargaining negotiations? What issues, and why should control over these issues be retained by management?

2. In light of at least some evidence that suggests criminal justice strikes do not lead to crime and disorder, are the sovereignty, rebellion, and protection arguments against public-sector strikes still valid? Explain.

3. Public-sector unions have at their disposal several options to compel action on the part of management, including mass sickouts and work slowdowns. Aside from the discipline workers may receive from their organizations for engaging in these behaviors, are there other potential consequences for employees, the unions, and the organization as a whole?

WEB RESOURCES

Boston Public Library online collections related to Boston Police Strike of 1919:
http://www.bpl.org/online/govdocs/police_strike_1919.htm

California Correctional Peace Officers Association (CCPOA):
http://www.ccpoa.org

Canadian Broadcasting Corporation (CBC) digital archives of 1969 Montreal police strike:
http://archives.cbc.ca/war_conflict/civil_unrest/clips/12238

READING

Reading 10

Much of the literature on police employee organizations (including unions) addresses the potential or actual effects of these organizations on law enforcement operations; with the exception of several small sample studies, most researchers have failed to describe police employee organizations—their size, union affiliation, bargaining unit, dues collection, and other major organizational attributes. Colleen Kadleck's study offers a descriptive account of these issues based on survey responses from a sample of 648 police employee organization leaders. In addition to the aforementioned topics, the study examined employee organization leaders' perceptions of employee–agency relations.

The findings demonstrated that most police employee organizations formed during or after the 1960s, a period when public-sector unions obtained significant legal recognition. Most of the employee organizations collectively bargained with their agencies/government and were supported by dues check off provisions. Consistent with the view of shared governance, police employee organization leaders believed that their organizations should have a voice in policymaking, even in matters that do not specifically deal with employee issues. The importance of the employee organizations is perhaps best viewed in the mixed responses from employee organization leaders regarding the trustworthiness of management. A majority of the respondents indicated that management was not trusted to make good decisions. Given the possibility for poor decision making (at least as perceived by employee organization leaders), it is no wonder that employee organization leaders want the ability to contribute to decision making on key issues.

Police Employee Organizations

Colleen Kadleck

Problem Statement

Police employee organizations and unions have been described as obstacles to police chiefs and to policy implementation (Walker, 1984). Police employee organizations have been described as opposing many different policies, including:

- professionalization attempts (DeCotiis and Kochan, 1978);
- civilian review boards (Randall, 1978; Bouza, 1985);
- promotion procedures (Randall, 1978);
- organizational change (Goldstein, 1979);
- lateral entry (Guyot, 1979);
- manpower allocation, disciplinary procedures, recruitment and selection procedures (Eltzeroth, 1980);
- one officer cars (Mastrofski, 1990);
- changes in department directives (Carter and Barker, 1994);
- changes in overtime procedures (Bayley and Worden, 1998); and
- the implementation of a fourth shift (Walker, 1999).

Source: Kadleck, C. (2003). Police employee organizations. *Policiing: An International Journal of Police Strategies and Management, 26*(2), 341–351.

In short, the existing literature on police employee organizations describes them primarily as actors or entities that have resisted organizational change, with little attention to their organizational structures or characteristics.

Literature Review

Examination and summary of the literature is complicated by the methods used to study police labor relations. Three characteristics of the existing literature are problematic. First, police employee organizations have been studied by the use of the case study method (see Levi, 1977, for a representative piece of research), or the examination of a small number of large police employee organizations (Juris and Feuille, 1972). Second, the police labor relationships studied tend to be selected because of widely publicized conflicts between the police department and the employee organization (Burpo, 1971; Levi, 1977). Third, many of the examinations of police employee organizations have not included a "union" perspective, in that the research has been conducted largely without surveys of police employee organizations or members (Kelling and Kliesmet, 1995). Many studies outline the "ideal" police labor relationship based on the opinion of the authors, and in some cases, interviews with police chiefs (Aussieker, 1969; Bowers, 1974; Burpo, 1971; Juris and Feuille, 1972; Levi, 1977; Maddox, 1975).

The police labor relations literature is essentially silent on the nature of police employee organizations generally but does provide insight into the types of characteristics that may be important in understanding these organizations. The size of the police employee organization has potential implications for the nature of the relationships between the police department and the police employee organization. More members, particularly dues paying members, can increase the range of activities (e.g. lobbying, lawsuits) that the police employee organization can take advantage of to advance the interests of the membership (Piskulich, 1992).

The date that the police employee organization was founded is important in understanding the nature of the organization. Several researchers suggest that police employee organizations founded before the 1960s tended to be fraternal or benevolent associations rather than labor organizations (Bouza, 1985; Burpo, 1971; Fogelson, 1977; Grimes, 1975; Juris and Feuille, 1972; Maddox, 1975). It was not until the 1960s that collective bargaining by police officers was provided the statutory protections which could allow these organizations to thrive (Bowers, 1974; Eltzeroth, 1980; Fogelson, 1977; Juris and Feuille, 1972). One study of 22 unions revealed that new labor focused organizations were founded in the 1960s and that existing fraternal organizations also took on the characteristics of labor unions at about the same time (Juris and Feuille, 1972). It is important to remember that groups of police officers organized by fraternal organizations still had the ability to engage in some activities which were aggravating to chiefs, whether they had collective bargaining ability or not.

Collective bargaining, however, is thought to change the nature of the relationship between the police department and police employee organization. Observers have noted that collective bargaining reduces the authority of the chief (Hewitt, 1978; Salerno, 1981). Prior to a bargaining relationship, a chief had the ability to change policy without consulting the police employee organization. Some contracts, however, require consultation before policy changes are made (Sylvia, 1994). Collective bargaining should be related to region. Kearney (1995, p. 178) suggests that police "unions are strongest in the Northeast and Midwest, and weakest in the South."

Policing is generally regarded as local in nature (Langworthy and Travis, 1999; Reaves, 1996). Most police agencies are local (Reaves, 1996). Police employee organizations have also been described as primarily locally based organizations (Juris and Feuille, 1972; More, 1992). Several researchers who have studied police employee organizations have indicated that affiliation with other organizations at the state or national level has implications for the behavior of a police employee organization. Carter (1988, p. 124) explains that the impact of the organization should vary by its "affiliation with a regional, state, or national organization." Others have argued that police employee organizations affiliated with national labor are more militant than locally based organizations (Burpo, 1971; Eltzeroth, 1980).

Just as police employee organizations are expected from previous case studies to be local organizations, Juris and Feuille (1972, p. 116) explain that these organizations are led by "locally elected policemen leaders." Levi (1977) also suggests that police employee organization leaders are elected. The leaders of these organizations are not typically described. It seems reasonable to assume that the leaders of these organizations are officers and that police employee organization leaders are elected, but no systematic empirical work has addressed this issue.

Dues check off is "a union security clause whereby employee organization dues are automatically 'checked off' by payroll deduction and remitted to the employee organization by the employer" (Juris and Feuille, 1972). Having a dues check off agreement guarantees income for the police employee organization without requiring the organization to expend as much time and energy collecting dues from members. Dues paying members also are an important resource in determining the range of activities that a police employee organization can engage in (Piskulich, 1992).

Three issues of police employee organization membership have been addressed in the literature:

(1) mandatory membership;

(2) whether membership is restricted to particular groups of employees; and

(3) the nature of those limitations.

Mandatory membership (and mandatory dues) clearly benefit a police employee organization. The likelihood of mandatory membership varies by statutory regulations which are likely to vary by region (Kearney, 1995). Most researchers agree that membership in police employee organizations is restricted or limited to sworn officers, and in larger organizations, to particular ranks, with different organizations for different ranks (Burpo, 1971; Juris and Feuille, 1972; More, 1992). Several researchers have addressed the inclusion of supervisors or sergeants in police employee organizations and the potential problems this may cause because supervisors are in some cases responsible for enforcing the contract provisions, and can therefore be seen as management employees (Aussieker, 1969; Bell, 1981; Bowers, 1974; Burpo, 1971; International Association of Chiefs of Police [IACP], 1977; Maddox,1975).

As stated earlier, the literature on relationships between police departments and police employee organizations has generally dealt with issues important from a police chief perspective. Examination of the literature suggests that there are eight major themes. These themes address the nature and amount of influence that police employee organizations have, union "voice" in departmental decision making, and the perceptions of the legitimacy of the parties involved in these relationships.

Police employee organizations and unions have rarely been accused of having too little influence in appropriate areas. These organizations are generally argued to have too much influence in several respects. First, unions are perceived to interfere with the management of the police department by taking decision-making power away from the police chief (Hewitt, 1978; Salerno, 1981). Second, these organizations are viewed as delving into inappropriate areas of influence (Bouza, 1985), using informal influence, which is usually considered inappropriate as well (Walker, 1984; Juris and Feuille, 1972), and having too much influence in general (Andrews, 1985; Bell, 1981; Bouza, 1985; Kearney, 1995). In addition to actual police employee organization actions, the anticipated (and usually negative) reaction of the police employee organization is also thought to limit the decisions of police chiefs (Juris and Feuille, 1972; Travis, 2000).

Particularly when police employee organizations and unions were beginning to become concerns for police chiefs, the literature contained many discussions of what sorts of decisions these organizations ought to be involved in and which should be solely the decision of the police chief. Maddox (1975) suggests that police employee organizations should only have a voice in "employee issues," meaning hours of work, pay rates, working conditions, and benefits. Some researchers argued that union focus on these issues is related to the idea that it is easier to obtain agreement that a raise is in order than it is to obtain agreement about the departmental use of force policy (DeCotiis and Kochan, 1978; Kelling and Kliesmet, 1995). Several authors have argued that police employee organizations should not have influence in traditional management areas, including most policy decisions directly unrelated to "employee issues" (Burpo, 1971; Maddox, 1975). Kelling and Kliesmet (1995) argue, however, that many policy decisions in policing do in fact impact on working conditions, and therefore, police employee organizations should have a voice in these decisions. They provide the example of two-officer cars and explain that while it is a policy decision, it also affects the perceived safety of working conditions (Kelling and Kliesmet, 1995). While there is some evidence to suggest that unions do have an effect on policy through collective bargaining (Zhao and Lovrich, 1997), empirical work has not addressed the extent to which police employee organization leaders perceive that they are involved in decisions or which kinds of areas they perceive as legitimate areas of influence.

The literature on police labor relationships addresses whether the "players" involved are seen as legitimate. The issue of whether police management is trusted to make decisions has been raised by several authors. Sirene (1985) argues that unions are proof of bad management by police chiefs. Others note that unionization is the result of a failure to effectively respond to the needs of police employees (Bolinger, 1981; IACP, 1977). Some directly question the ability of chiefs to correctly make decisions absent involvement of employees (Bell, 1981; Kliesmet, 1989). The issue of the accountability of police employee organizations, particularly unions, has also been addressed. Several authors argue that these unions are not accountable to the public because these organizations have a hand in making governmental policy (in some cases influencing the budgets of government), but are not elected or appointed by the citizens (IACP, 1977; Kearney, 1995; Levi, 1977). Zeidler (1967) questions whether these organizations can be accountable when the negotiations are held in secret meetings away from the eyes of the public.

The existing literature suggests that several aspects of police employee organizations and police labor relations are important. This study attempts to explore these issues systematically with a relatively large sample of police employee organizations rather than using the traditional method of a case study of one or several police employee organizations.

Data and Methods

The data used for the analyses reported here were taken from a larger study which examined police chief and police union leader perceptions of community policing as well as management rights issues, and perceptions of labor relationships (Travis and Kadleck, 2001). Using the 1993 Law Enforcement Management and Administrative Statistics (Reaves, 1996) sample of municipal agencies as a starting point ($n = 1,779$), surveys were sent first to police chiefs, and later to associated police employee organization leaders identified through the police chief survey and membership information provided by the National Association of Police Organizations and the Fraternal Order of Police. These methods identified 1,117 police employee organizations associated with the police departments in the 1993 LEMAS sample. The surveys were distributed to potential respondents using the Dillman (1978) total design method for self-administered mail surveys. Responses were received from 648 police employee organizations for a response rate of 58 percent.

Findings

The results of the descriptive analysis are presented in Table I. It should be apparent that the measure of size is highly skewed. While there are some very large police employee organizations, the typical police employee organization appears to be relatively small. Most police employee organizations (76.2 percent) in our sample were founded after the 1960s. Just over 70 percent engage in collective bargaining. The typical police employee organization is local, but a somewhat surprising number are affiliated at the state level. The typical police employee organization leader is an elected sworn officer. While most police employee organizations do not have mandatory membership requirements, about 73.2 percent have a dues check off agreement with their employer. Although only about 50 percent report limiting their membership, just about all of the respondents did detail some restrictions. The two most common sets of restrictions are limiting membership to any sworn member (37.2 percent) or to patrol officers and sergeants (25.9 percent).

Collective bargaining is clearly related to region, with collective bargaining relationships being more likely in the Northeast (88.9 percent), West (82.0 percent), Midwest (78.9 percent) than in the South (34.5 percent). Although rates of mandatory membership are higher in the Northeast (39.3 percent), Midwest (27.7 percent), and West (21.9 percent), most police employee organizations do not appear to have these requirements. Mandatory membership is also lowest in the South, with only 1.8 percent of police employee organizations requiring membership.

While much is made in the literature of these organizations seeking to limit the power of management, few (31.8 percent) of the leaders agreed this was the case. Less than 30 police employee organization leaders (4.6 percent) thought that their organizations had too much influence. Nearly all of these leaders believe their organization's reaction should be considered when policy changes are contemplated, and that they should have a voice in employee issues as well as policy issues (91.8 percent, 96.9 percent, and 88.0 percent respectively). Few leaders (12.0 percent) believe their organizations are not accountable to the public. Less than half of the leaders (42.4 percent) agree that management is trusted to make good decisions. Even though most leaders agreed that they should have a voice in policy decisions, only a little more than half (54.0 percent) thought that they actually did.

Discussion and Conclusions

Even though the prior work on police employee organizations relies heavily on the case study of one or several unions, it provides a relatively accurate picture of these organizations. The analyses reported here

Table 1 Characteristics of Police Employee Organizations

	n	%
Size (number of members)		
Mean	230.36	
Median	60.00	
Mode	8.00	
Range	2–11,879	
Decade founded		
Before 1930	34	6.5
1940s	28	5.4
1950s	44	8.4
1960s	74	14.1
1970s	126	24.1
1980s	110	21.0
1990s	89	17.0
Collective bargaining		
Yes	453	70.6
No	189	29.4
Affiliation		
Local	304	52.4
County	22	3.8
State	192	33.1
Federal	62	10.7
Leader is a sworn officer?		
Yes	617	96.0
No	26	4.0
Selection of leader		
General election	579	92.2
Board election	26	4.1
Other methods	23	3.8

Table 1 Characteristics of Police Employee Organizations *(Continued)*

	n	%
Dues check off		
Yes	460	73.2
No	168	26.8
Mandatory membership		
Yes	145	22.9
No	487	77.1
Restricted membership		
Yes	341	54.4
No	286	45.6
Limitations on membership		
Patrol officers only	70	10.9
Patrol and sergeants	161	25.9
Any sworn member	239	37.2
Any police employee	101	15.7
Rank specific	69	10.8
Other	3	0.5

allow us to sketch out the typical police employee organization in terms of several characteristics. The typical police employee organization was founded after 1960, is a relatively small, local organization led by a police officer who was elected by the membership. The organization has both a contract (unless it is in the South) and a dues check off agreement. Most of the members are sworn officers and membership is likely to be voluntary. The leaders of these organizations see their organizations as entitled to an important role in policy development, whether the policies relate to "employee issues" or other issues. The leaders of these organizations clearly do not believe that they have too much influence, or in many cases, even voice decisions regarding policies in their departments. The leaders are unlikely to feel that they can trust police management to make good decisions.

This study adds to the literature by providing a first empirical look at these organizations. However, these findings do have their limitations. While the response rate obtained is acceptable, it is not ideal. In addition, reliance on police chiefs and large national organizations of police employee groups probably does not well represent some of the potential respondents, in particular, the groups without collective bargaining ability. Few organizations with female only membership or groups including only a particular racial or ethnic group were identified with these methods. The nature of these organizations cannot be inferred from these findings.

In addition, because this research was based on existing work on police labor relations, which excluded any examination of the potential positive aspects of labor relations, this work is silent on those issues. This analysis does, however, provide a starting point for future research.

These findings suggest several potential avenues for future research. Certainly, it is important to describe these organizations empirically, and as suggested by other researchers, it also important to examine whether the characteristics of these organizations are linked to their behavior. The behavior of these organizations is well documented in case studies of well-publicized conflicts between employee groups and police departments (Ayres, 1977). The typical behavior of these organizations, what they regularly do, is essentially unknown.

As noted above, research could also examine the employee groups which this study did not. Better yet, future work could develop a national sampling frame of these organizations, which would greatly facilitate future empirical work. If half of the work of a study is simply locating the respondents, it is likely to scare well-meaning researchers to the realm of secondary data analysis. Moving beyond the case study approach to studying these organizations would be an important next step in developing our understanding of them.

Future work could also investigate the benefits of these organizations as well as the characteristics that are related to good labor relations between the police employee organization and the police department.

Much previous work has concentrated on the conflict between these organizations, without any attention to how management and labor can work together. It is important to look at these relationships generally, rather than giving full attention to those relationships that are faulty. Examining only police labor relations with conflict to understand labor relations is similar to drawing a marriage study sample from a divorce attorney's files.

References

Andrews, A.H. (1985), "Structuring the political independence of the police chief", in Geller, W.A. (Ed.), *Police Leadership in America: Crisis and Opportunity*, Praeger, New York, NY.

Aussieker, M.W. (1969), *Police Collective Bargaining*, Public Personnel Association, Chicago, IL.

Ayres, R.M. (1977), "Case studies of police strikes in two cities – Albuquerque and Oklahoma City", *Journal of Police Science & Administration*, Vol. 5 No. 1, pp. 19-31.

Bayley, D.H. and Worden, R.E. (1998), *Police Overtime: An Examination of Key Issues*, National Institute of Justice, Washington, DC.

Bell, D.J. (1981), "Collective bargaining: perspective for the 1980s", *Journal of Police Science & Administration*, Vol. 9 No. 3, pp. 296-305.

Bolinger, H.E. (1981), "Police officers' views on collective bargaining and use of sanctions", in More, A.H. (Ed.), *Critical Issues in Law Enforcement*, Anderson, Cincinnati, OH, pp. 165-74.

Bouza, A.V. (1985), "Police unions: paper tigers or roaring lions?", in Geller, W.A. (Ed.), *Police Leadership in America: Crisis and Opportunity*, Praeger, New York, NY, pp. 241-80.

Bowers, M.H. (1974), *Labor Relations in the Public Safety Services*, International Personnel Management Association, Chicago, IL.

Burpo, J.H. (1971), *The Police Labor Movement: Problems and Perspectives*, Charles C. Thomas, Springfield, IL.

Carter, D.L. (1988), "The police union and departmental drug control policies", in Carter, D.L. and Stephens, D.W. (Eds), *Drug Abuse by Police Officers: An Analysis of Critical Policy Issues*, Charles C. Thomas, Springfield, IL.

Carter, D.L. and Barker, T. (1994), "Administrative guidance and control of police officer behavior: policies, procedures, and rules", in Barker, T. and Carter, D.L. (Eds) *Police Deviance*, 3rd ed., Anderson, Cincinnati, OH.

DeCotiis, T.A. and Kochan, T.A. (1978), "Professionalization and unions in law enforcement", in Cromwell, P.F. and Keefer, G. (Eds), *Police-Community Relations: Selected Readings*, West, New York, NY.

Dillman, D.A. (1978), *Mail and Telephone Surveys: The Total Design Method*, Wiley, New York, NY.

Eltzeroth, R.L. (1980), "Police unions", in Leonard, V.A. (Ed.), *Fundamentals of Law Enforcement: Problems and Issues*, West, New York, NY, pp. 247-69.

Fogelson, R.M. (1977), *Big-City Police*, Harvard University Press, Cambridge, MA.

Fraser, D.M. (1985), "Politics and police leadership: the view from City Hall", in Geller, W.A. (Ed.), *Police Leadership in America: Crisis and Opportunity*, Praeger, New York, NY.

Goldstein, H. (1979), "Improving policing: a problem-oriented approach", *Crime & Delinquency*, Vol. 25, pp. 236-58.

Grimes, J.A. (1975), "The police, the union, and the productivity imperative", in Wolfle, J.L. and Heaphy, J.F. (Eds), *Readings on Productivity in Policing*, Police Foundation, Washington, DC, pp. 47-85.

Guyot, D. (1979), "Bending granite: attempts to change the rank structure of American police departments", *Journal of Police Science & Administration*, Vol. 7 No. 3, pp. 253-84.

Hewitt, W.H. (1978), "Current issues in police collective bargaining", in Cohn, A.W. (Ed.), *The Future of Policing*, Sage, Beverly Hills, CA, pp. 207-23.

International Association of Chiefs of Police (1977), *Critical Issues in Police Labor Relations*, International Association of Chiefs of Police, Washington, DC.

Juris, H. and Feuille, P. (1972), *The Impact of Police Unions*, LEAA, Washington, DC.

Kearney, R.C. (1995), "Unions in government: where do they go from here?", in Hays, S.W. and Kearney, R.C. (Eds), *Public Personnel Administration: Problems and Prospects*, Prentice-Hall, Englewood Cliffs, NJ, pp. 177-90.

Kelling, G.L. and Kliesmet, R.B. (1995), "Police unions, police culture, the Friday Crab Club and police abuse of force", in Geller, W.A. and Toch, H. (Eds), *And Justice for All: Understanding and Controlling Police Abuse of Force*, Police Executive Research Forum, Washington, DC, pp. 187-204.

Kliesmet, R.B. (1989), "Police unions and the rejuvenation of American policing", in Kenney, D.J. (Ed.), *Police and Policing: Contemporary Issues*, Praeger, New York, NY, pp. 241-6.

Langworthy, R. and Travis, L.F. (1999), *Policing in America: A Balance of Forces*, Prentice Hall, Upper Saddle River, NJ.

Levi, M. (1977), *Bureaucratic Insurgency: The Case of Police Unions*, Lexington, Lexington, MA.

Maddox, C. (1975), *Collective Bargaining in Law Enforcement*, Charles C. Thomas, Springfield, IL.

Mastrofski, S.D. (1990), "The prospects of change in police patrol: a decade in review", *American Journal of Police*, Vol. 9 No. 3, pp. 1-79.

More, H.W. (1992), *Special Topics in Policing*, Anderson, Cincinnati, OH.

Piskulich, J.P. (1992), *Collective Bargaining in State and Local Government*, Praeger, New York, NY.

Randall, F. (1978), "Holding on: union resistance to civilian employees in the Boston police department", in Larson, R.C. (Ed.), *Police Accountability: Performance Measures and Unionism*, Lexington, Lexington, MA, pp. 167-82.

Reaves, B.A. (1996), *Local Police Departments, 1993,* Bureau of Justice Statistics, Washington, DC.

Salerno, C.A. (1981), *Police at the Bargaining Table,* Charles C. Thomas, Springfield, IL.

Sirene, W.H. (1985), "Management: labor's most effective organizer", in Fyfe, J.J. (Ed.), *Police Management Today: Issues and Case Studies,* International City Management Association, Washington, DC, pp. 162-70.

Sylvia, R.D. (1994), *Public Personnel Administration,* Wadsworth, Belmont, CA.

Travis, L.F. (2000), *Managerial Freedom and Collective Bargaining in Ohio Municipal Police Agencies: The Current State of the Art,* Law Enforcement Foundation, Dublin, OH.

Travis, L.F. and Kadleck, C. (2001), "Police department and police officer association leader's perceptions of community policing: describing the nature and extent of agreement", University of Cincinnati, Cincinnati, OH.

United States Department of Commerce (1994), *Geographic Areas Reference Manual,* United States Department of Commerce, Washington, DC.

Walker, S. (1984), *Background Paper. The Future of Policing: A Panel Report,* William O. Douglas Institute for the Study of Social Problems, Seattle, WA.

Walker, S. (1999), *The Police in America: An Introduction,* McGraw-Hill, New York, NY.

Zeidler, F.P. (1967), "Impact of collective bargaining on public administration", in Warner, K.O. (Ed.), *Collective Bargaining in the Public Service: Theory and Practice,* Public Personnel Association, Chicago, IL, pp. 151-62.

Zhao, J. and Lovrich, N.P. (1997), "Collective bargaining and the police: the consequences for supplemental compensation policies in large agencies", *Policing,* Vol. 20 No. 3, pp. 508-18.

DISCUSSION QUESTIONS

1. Kadleck's study documents membership restrictions. Employee organizations tend to limit membership by rank or sworn status. Are there advantages and disadvantages to having a more encompassing membership, such as the "any police employee" requirement?

2. Is limiting the power of management a goal of police employee organizations according to their leaders? Is the fact that employee organization leaders believe that their organizations should have a voice in department policymaking consistent with or contrary to responses about limiting the power of management? Explain.

3. Police employee organizations are rarely affiliated with federal/national unions. How does this compare with correctional union affiliations discussed in the section? Why do police employee organizations choose a local or state affiliation instead of a national affiliation? Consider the localized nature of policing.

READING

Reading 11

In 2009, the number of prisoners in state prisons declined by 0.2%, a small but significant number given the more than 30-year trajectory of increasing prison populations (West, Sabol, & Greenman, 2010). Joshua Page argues that the likelihood of a sustained reduction in the overall prison population in the United States is complicated by the fact that correctional officer unions wield tremendous power within the prison. As he notes, these unions were not responsible for the initial push for mass incarceration in the 1970s. The precipitous rise in the number of prisoners only strengthened unions as their membership numbers expanded. The unions then worked to resist measures that would reduce the overall incarcerated population.

Page focuses on the powerful California Correctional Peace Officers Association but provides a comparison to the New York State Correctional Officers and Police Benevolent Association. In California, the union aligned itself with victims' groups in an effort to portray the image that the union existed for more than just mutual benefit of members. The union would later support the passage of three strikes legislation and oppose attempts to weaken the law; both efforts illustrate the union's desire to perpetuate mass imprisonment. In New York, the union has resisted attempts to close prisons, arguing, among other things, that the closures would threaten public safety in the state and local economic interests in cities and towns where prisons are located. Recognizing the power of correctional officer unions, Page concludes his article by offering several suggestions for overcoming union barriers.

Prison Officer Unions and the Perpetuation of the Penal Status Quo

Joshua Page

On March 17, 2010, the nonpartisan, nonprofit Pew Center on the States released a report that began with a triumphant tone—"For the first time in nearly 40 years, the number of state prisoners in the United States has declined" (Pew Center for the States, 2010: 1). It continued optimistically, "the decline in 2009 could be a harbinger of a prolonged pattern" (6). The report reflected (and undoubtedly inspired) cautious optimism that policy makers would implement sentencing and prison reforms capable of substantially reducing penal populations and correctional spending over the long run.

Propitious economic decline and backbreaking budget deficits are the main factors driving lawmakers to reconsider the penal policies, practices, and priorities that undergird "mass imprisonment."[1] Prison systems in many states are dangerously overcrowded, money to build additional facilities is scarce, and voters are reluctant to pass bond measures for prison expansion. Few resources are available for rehabilitation programs, medical and mental health care, and other prison-based services, eroding the already poor quality of life on the inside as well as leaving states vulnerable to court intervention (not to mention prisoner unrest). Moreover, sky-high criminal justice spending decreases resources for other vital, but underfunded, social services such as education (Austin et al., 2007; Jacobson, 2005; Greene and Mauer, 2010; Pew Center for the States, 2009, 2010; Steinhauer, 2009). These signs are not positive, but some believe that, in light of the dire economic environment and long-term drops in crime (particularly murder), policy makers will work to shrink America's enormous penal system (Simon, 2010: 373–374).

Recent analyses suggest that the dip in imprisonment might be a short-lived event rather than the beginning of a long-term process. Marie Gottschalk (2010: 345–348), for example, argued that persistent economic decline might "foster public punitiveness" because politicians tend to scapegoat "others" (e.g., immigrants and the "marauding underclass") in periods of financial free-fall and criminalize social protest of class inequality. Cracking down on crime is one way for the government to demonstrate that it is doing something to increase security and stability for working- and middle-class individuals teetering on

Source: Page, J. (2011). Prison officer unions and the perpetuation of the penal status quo. *Criminology & Public Policy, 10*(3), 735–770.

the edge of financial disaster. That "something" might include hardening penal sanctions (including those targeting immigrants) and/or resisting sentencing reform, prison closures, and cuts to correctional budgets.

A related reason for tempering optimism about the possibilities for upending mass imprisonment is that states have slashed resources for prison- and community-based service programs (Weisberg and Petersilia, 2010: 131). Therefore, considerable risk persists that parolees or individuals diverted from prison to probation or other community programs will return to crime. Without allocating sufficient resources to help ex-offenders obtain work, housing, and other necessities, the system raises the risk of parolees and probationers reoffending or violating the terms of their supervision. In addition, if recidivism rates remain high (or worse, substantially increase), then opponents of alternative penal strategies will argue that trying to undo mass imprisonment is a dangerous fool's errand.

This article encourages a measured view on the prospects for extensive, long-term sentencing and prison reform capable of rolling back mass imprisonment. It argues that, in key states, prison officer unions and their allies have fiercely and effectively resisted—and will likely continue to resist—major efforts to *downsize prisons*. "Downsizing" is more than "decarceration," or the reduction of a penal population.[2] It also includes shedding prisons and related carceral infrastructure, reducing workforces, and slashing spending. I show that the California Correctional Peace Officers Association (CCPOA) grew alongside the prison population, becoming an effective and powerful union. As it gained members, wealth, and political capital, the CCPOA became an influential actor within a coalition of actors that props up mass imprisonment, even as state leaders attempt to decrease the state's penal system.

I focus on the CCPOA because it is the most successful and politically influential prison officer union in the United States, and likely the world. In this regard, it is an extreme case that shows the *potential* effects prison officer unions can have on penal policy, especially on efforts to reform or eliminate the laws and practices that fuel the prison boom (Flyvbjerg, 2006: 229). California is a particularly important case because of its incredibly large, costly prison system. The state has approximately 165,000 people behind prison bars and an annual corrections budget of roughly $10 billion. Unlike other states, which *want* to downsize their prison systems (largely to save money), California *has* to achieve this goal. Federal judges have ordered the state to decrease its prison capacity from 190% to 137.5% within 2 years. Hence, understanding roadblocks to downsizing prisons is essential for scholars and policy makers alike.

To enhance our understanding of how prison officer unions obstruct downsizing-oriented reforms, I examine recent events in New York—another state trying to shrink its penal system in the face of incredible budget deficits. As with California, New York has a large, wealthy prison officer union. However, the CCPOA is far more powerful than its East Coast counterpart. As shown in the subsequent sections, the New York union has not obstructed efforts to reduce the prison population; however, it has effectively frustrated attempts to close state prisons and decrease correctional spending. Examining the New York case, then, helps us to understand how a prison officer union that does not enjoy the CCPOA's political clout affects efforts to downscale prisons.

Although the California and New York unions differ in power and effectiveness, they use similar methods to reach their goals; in conjunction with other actors, they engage in campaigns that drum up fear of changing the penal status quo. They insist that reducing correctional populations, closing prisons, and shedding staff will compromise public safety, destroy local economies (particularly in prison towns), and enhance general insecurity. Moreover, they strike fear in politicians who might support downsizing prisons but do not want to be opposed by law enforcement, crime victim, and related organizations in future elections.[3]

This article unfolds in five sections. The first situates the analysis within research that seeks to understand the varied consequences of the prison boom and obstacles to shrinking the penal system. The next section describes the rise of the CCPOA and the union's pivotal role in a power bloc within the penal field, and the third section presents examples that show how the CCPOA and its allies frustrate efforts to change California's sentencing laws—the bedrock of mass imprisonment in that state (Krisberg, 2008; Little Hoover Commission, 2007; Zimring, Hawkins, and Kamin, 2001). The subsequent section examines the counterfactual case of the New York prison officers union, demonstrating how a union with far less political acumen and power still can obstruct efforts to downscale prisons. Drawing lessons from the case studies, the final section lays out four propositions that might help policy makers who face resistance from prison officer unions as they struggle to reform sentencing laws, release prisoners, close prisons, and cut correctional spending.

Extending the Consequences of Mass Imprisonment

A large body of research investigates the "unintended" (also called "collateral") consequences of mass imprisonment. Studies demonstrate how the prison boom negatively affects prisoners and ex-convicts, families, communities, state priorities, civic participation, and patterns of racial and class inequality (Braman, 2007; Clear, 2007; Comfort, 2008; Manza and Uggen, 2006; Western, 2006; Wildeman, 2009). This scholarship implicitly (and, at times, explicitly) argues that mass imprisonment creates or exacerbates conditions that perpetuate it. For example, Todd Clear (2007: 5) argued that "[c]oncentrated incarceration in . . . impoverished communities has broken families, weakened the social-control capacity of parents, eroded economic strength, soured attitudes toward society, and distorted politics; even, after reaching a certain level, it has increased rather than decreased crime." Persistence of high crime in these impoverished areas, then, justifies policies and practices at the heart of mass imprisonment. A cyclical process exists in which the consequences of mass imprisonment sustain the penal status quo.

Another influential, unintended consequence of America's prison boom is the development of powerful organizations with interests in maintaining existing penal arrangements. This article demonstrates, for example, that prison officer unions did not factor centrally in the prison explosion in the large states of California and New York (both in terms of general and prison populations). These organizations were small and politically weak when the carceral population shot upward (the CCPOA was not even an official union when California began its prison binge). Instead, the unions grew alongside the prison population; increased membership rolls translated into greater financial resources, which the unions could use to gain political capital and influence penal policy. Put simply, the prison boom provided prison officer unions with the essential resources to become major players in the political and penal fields. Mass imprisonment was a necessary but not sufficient condition for the development of powerful interest groups (in this case, prison officer unions) that promote the "tough on crime" penal status quo.

Like earlier research on the consequences of mass imprisonment, this analysis contends that the factors that sustain the prison boom are not necessarily those that caused it.[4] Hence, downsizing prisons requires that we understand both the factors that sparked mass imprisonment and those that continue to breathe life into the phenomenon. Several recent studies recognize that prison officer unions in key states are obstacles to downsizing the penal system; Jacobson (2005: 69) wrote that "correction unions" pose a "formidable obstacle to downsizing-oriented reforms," and Gottschalk (2006: 242) contended that the groups have become a "significant factor" in sustaining the carceral state.[5] This article extends this line of thought by examining *how* these organizations obstruct efforts to downsize prisons. It goes beyond identifying unions as hurdles to delineate a set of propositions that might aid public officials and other actors who must overcome pushback from prison officers unions as they try to reform sentencing policies, implement early release programs, or shutter penal facilities. Through a combination of accommodation and confrontation, it is possible to soften resistance from groups like the CCPOA. However, doing so will take major political will. Policy makers will have to become as committed to downsizing prisons as they once were to building and filling them.

Building a Power Bloc

Prison officer unions in the United States developed as part of the larger public sector labor movement that gained steam in the 1960s (Aronowitz, 1998). As shown in Figure 1, prison officers have formed unions in 38 states. With the exceptions of Missouri and Maine, all states that do not have prison officer unions are "right-to-work" states; workers in these states do not have to join a union or pay dues or an agency fee as a condition of their employment. In general, unions in states with right-to-work laws tend to be weaker than unions in states without the laws (Fantasia and Voss, 2004: 51). Also depicted in Figure 1, most prison officer unions are affiliated with the American Federation of Labor and Congress of Industrial Organizations (AFL-CIO), but a growing number are independent (i.e., not affiliated with the AFL-CIO or Change to Win Coalition). I discuss the significance of independence versus affiliation in a subsequent section.

Prison officers in California did not form their union until 1982. They had a professional organization dating back to 1957; however, the government

Figure 1 Prison Officer Unions in the United States

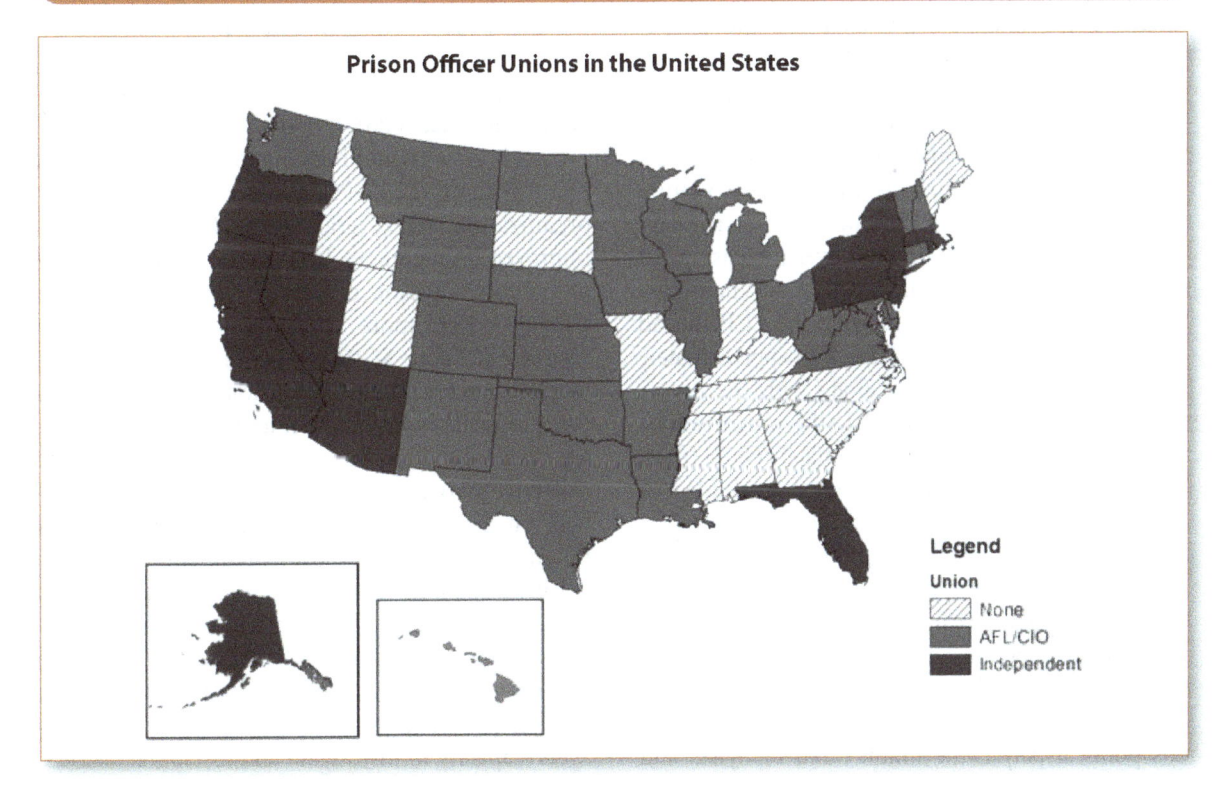

Note. Essam Sater and I collected the data on prison officer unions in the United States, and Sarah Shannon created the map.

did not provide collective bargaining rights to state workers until 1981. One year later, the CCPOA won a fierce battle against The Teamsters and the California State Employees Association to represent prison officers and other correctional employees such as medical technical assistants (hybrid nurses and officers) and parole agents (Page, 2011: Chapter 2). From the start, the CCPOA was atypical. It was a fiercely independent association that defined itself in opposition to the "labor movement"; its leaders and members were prison officers, not union bureaucrats. Unlike other state worker unions, which allied almost solely with Democrats, the CCPOA was nonpartisan, forming strong relationships with both law-and-order Republicans and labor-friendly Democrats (Page, 2011: Chapter 3).

Also from the start, the CCPOA opposed rehabilitation and supported "punitive segregation" (Page, 2011: 125)—an orientation that promotes long sentences in austere prisons as well as extensive and intensive postrelease supervision as the proper responses to crime (Garland, 2000). However, the CCPOA did not spark California's prison boom. When Governor Jerry Brown signed legislation in 1976 to end indeterminate sentencing, the CCPOA was not even a union, and when the legislature passed laws that greatly lengthened prison terms and mandated imprisonment for an ever-increasing list of crimes, the union was in its infancy. When mass imprisonment began in California, the CCPOA had only 5,000 members and a budget of approximately $462,000. The CCPOA grew along with the prison population. From 1982 to 2002, the organization's membership increased by approximately 600% (from 5,000 to 31,000). By 2002, the union had a budget of approximately $19 million (Page, 2011: 48).

The CCPOA used its abundant resources to develop an impressive political apparatus. Its leaders understood early on that public-sector unions are fundamentally political entities. The governor (not a CEO or board of directors) signs the checks, and legislators approve the contracts. To become a serious political player, the union hired lobbyists and developed political action committees, which it used to reward its friends and punish its enemies (Page, 2011: 51). By the 1990s, the CCPOA was one of the state's largest contributors to political candidates. In 1998, the union set a state record by contributing $1.9 million to Democratic and Republican candidates for the state senate and assembly (Warren, 2000). The next year, the CCPOA broke its own record, contributing $2.3 million (Yamamura, 2002).

Along with building its political infrastructure, the CCPOA used its resources to enhance the image of prison officers and the union. It spent millions making the case that prison officers are professional public servants who work "the toughest beat in the state." This contention rested on the presumption that California prisons were incredibly dangerous and that inmates were inherently manipulative, violent, and for the most part, irredeemable (Page, 2011: 72). Only well-trained, professional officers were capable of taming this beat and, ultimately, of protecting public safety. Along with media campaigns, the union advanced legislation to professionalize the occupation. CCPOA-sponsored laws improved officer training and enhanced hiring standards (Page, 2011; Petersilia, 2006).

As it grew in numbers, financial resources, and political clout, the CCPOA worked to strengthen its organization in several ways. First, it greatly improved its members' take-home; the average pay of California prison officers is slightly more than $73,000—58% more than the national average (Bureau of Labor Statistics, 2008). Moreover, these workers have a fantastic pension plan that allows them to retire at age 50 with up to 90% of their salary (Petersilia, 2006: 23). Second, the union used the collective bargaining process to enhance its members' on-the-job autonomy and authority in matters ranging from shift and post assignments to personnel investigations and discipline. As these changes took effect, prison administrators, newspaper editorialists, and even some politicians insisted that the union and its members effectively ran the prisons, and a federal judge argued that, by decreasing managers' capacity to investigate and discipline officers, the CCPOA promoted a "code of silence" that made it nearly impossible to sanction "rogue officers." The union responded that it simply promoted members' due process rights and protected them against vindictive managers (Page, 2011: Chapters 7–8).

Third, the union has worked to gain and maintain support from female officers and officers of color. In its formative years, the CCPOA strongly opposed affirmative action policies designed to hire and promote women and people of color as well as groups that formed within the Department of Corrections to advance the interests of female and minority officers. The union was considered a "good old boy" organization, and its leaders were publicly accused of sexual harassment (MeCoy, 1985: A1; Page, 2011: Chapter 1). In the 1990s, however, CCPOA officials sought to change the association's image and appeal to its increasingly diverse membership (more gender and ethnic–racial diversity is present among prison officers than any other law enforcement workforce in California). They established the Minorities in Law Enforcement political action committee (MILE PAC) and financially supported other ethnic- and gender-based criminal justice organizations, including the Association of Black Correctional Workers, the Chicano Correctional Workers Association, and the Women Peace Officers Association of California. The CCPOA also has come to promote Hispanic and African American officers to its own leadership positions. For example, the CCPOA's current president is Hispanic and its legislative director is African American. Although no female members are present on its executive council, women serve as chapter presidents and committee leaders. By promoting ethnic–racial and gender diversity, the union now seeks to maintain organizational unity and strength, allowing it to focus on winning legislative and contractual battles, rather than on continually putting out fires within its ranks (Page, 2011: 49).

The CCPOA also tapped into its financial windfall to establish and maintain ties with other organizations that could help it achieve its goals. Most notably, the union effectively created the following crime victim rights' groups: Crime Victims United of California (CVUC) and the Doris Tate Crime Victims Bureau (CVB). The CCPOA committed extensive resources to their development, providing the groups with office space, lobbying staff, attorneys, and seed money (78% of CVB's and 84% of CVUC's initial funding) (Shapiro, 1997: 13–14). Harriet Salarno, president of CVUC, is forthright about the importance of CCPOA's financial assistance, "I could not do this without CCPOA, because we didn't have the money to it" (quoted in Page, 2011: 86). Along with material resources, the CCPOA taught the victims' groups how to play the political game. Salarno explains that former CCPOA President Don Novey "steered us in the right direction, opened the door, and taught us what to do. He educated us" (Center for Juvenile and Criminal Justice, 2002: III–13).

The union developed these organizations principally for strategic purposes, which is not to say that CCPOA's leaders do not genuinely care for and want to assist victims and their families—they do. But, the victims' groups also help the CCPOA achieve its goals from *outside of its ranks* in three main ways. First, they validate the CCPOA's claims that prison officers are uniquely skilled professionals who work the "toughest beat in the state." Second, they legitimate the CCPOA's claims that the union serves universal purposes (rather than its individual, pecuniary interests) by supporting crime victims and bolstering public safety. Third, the victims' groups provide political cover for their patron by taking public positions on controversial crime and punishment policies the CCPOA sidesteps, fearing public officials and the media will label the union "self-interested" (Page, 2011: Chapter 4).

Together, the union and victims' groups are a formidable political force. The CCPOA has financial resources, political acumen, and connections, and the victims have the moral authority. To foster their strong alliance, the CCPOA and victims' organizations routinely team up with the California District Attorneys Association and other law enforcement groups such as the California Police Chiefs Association, the California State Sheriffs Association, and the California Coalition of Law Enforcement Associations.

Together, these organizations constitute a power bloc in the penal field (Page, 2011: Chapter 5).

As used here, a bloc is an association of actors with similar interests who work toward shared goals. Blocs are not formal organizations with membership rolls (although they might become formal organizations). Actors in a bloc do not always work together to accomplish particular tasks (such as passing a piece of legislation); however, their collective efforts advance the actors' shared interests and worldviews. As examples in the following section demonstrate, the CCPOA is the anchor of the bloc rather than simply one participant among many. In campaigns against policies that would seriously decrease the prison population, other actors in the bloc expect the CCPOA to play the roles of financier and strategist. The union generally comes through.

Circumscribing Change

Since the early 1990s, interest groups and wealthy individuals have used California's ballot initiative process to go around the legislature to implement "tough on crime" penal measures, including the state's notoriously expansive Three Strikes and You're Out law (Barker, 2009; Zimring et al., 2001). In recent years, others have tried to use that same tool to reform sentencing laws and to reduce prison and parole populations. This section shows that these efforts have faced rigid, effective resistance from the CCPOA and its allies—the power bloc in California's penal field.

In 2004, opponents of the criminal punishment status quo in the Golden State sought major reforms to Three Strikes. Passed in 1994, the law mandates that individuals with a record of one "serious" or "violent" offense who commit any additional felony receive a sentence twice as long as the current offense term. Additionally, these "second strikers" must serve 80% of their prison sentence before they are eligible for release. The third-strike enhancement is reserved for offenders with two prior convictions of "serious" or "violent" crimes and a third conviction for *any* felony. Third strikers receive prison sentences of 25 years to life and are not eligible for parole until they serve 80% of the 25-year term (Zimring et al., 2001: 8).

Three Strikes casts a wide net. As of April 2009, 43,000 of the state's 171,500 prisoners (roughly 25%) were sentenced under the law (California State Auditor, 2009). Of this total, 8,500 are serving 25 years to life (Bazelon, 2010). On average, "striker" inmates serve sentences that are 9 years longer than nonstrikers. The state will pay roughly $19.2 billion in additional costs because of the current striker population's extended sentences. Remarkably, the convictions that triggered the Three Strikes law for more than half of the total striker population were nonserious and nonviolent (California State Auditor, 2009: 23, 27), and approximately 3,700 prisoners are serving 25 years to life for nonserious and nonviolent offenses (Bazelon, 2010).

The fact that people received 25 years to life for nonserious and nonviolent crimes became increasingly known in the early 2000s. The media profiled individuals who received Three Strikes convictions for crimes like stealing pizza from a group of children (Leonard, 2010). Some former supporters of Three Strikes felt duped, arguing that they would not have backed the law had they known that people like the "pizza thief" would receive life sentences. In 2003, two of these former supporters launched a campaign for a ballot initiative that would drastically narrow the scope and reduce the effects of Three Strikes.[6] Specifically, their proposal would require that all strikes be serious or violent and that the state must resentence offenders serving indeterminate life sentences under Three Strikes if their third strike was nonviolent or nonserious. The initiative also would mandate that the state try eligible offenses in separate trials for each offense to be counted as a strike (the original Three Strikes law allowed for a defendant to receive multiple strikes in a single trial).

The reform initiative received the required number of signatures to qualify for the 2004 statewide election. "The Three Strikes and Child Protection Act of 2004" (Proposition 66) provided voters with an opportunity to change Three Strikes and, in doing so, to constrict a source of prison growth and signal a move away from the state's rigid commitment to incapacitation and retribution.[7] For the initiative to become law, however, its proponents would have to win what would prove to be a fierce, expensive battle against a powerful coalition of actors.

The CCPOA organized opposition to the initiative. It hired Nina Salarno-Ashford, daughter of the president of Crime Victims United, Harriet Salarno, to coordinate an alliance of law enforcement and victims' groups ("Californians United for Public Safety" [CUPS]) opposed to Proposition 66 (Page, 2011: 124). CUPS established a political action committee called "Californians United for Public Safety, Independent Expenditure Committee" (CUPS-IEC). CUPS would serve as the organizational base for the anti-66 campaign.

As of mid-October 2004, the CCPOA had spent more than $250,000 on the "No on 66" campaign—$199,000 of which went into CUPS-IEC (California Secretary of State, 2006). With funds from the CCPOA and several other contributors, CUPS conducted a relatively minor public relations campaign against Proposition 66. For example, on September 21, 2004, the coalition launched its "Felon A Day" campaign against Proposition 66 (see Figure 2). The press release for the campaign read as follows:

> "Every day between now and the election, we'll be releasing at least one mug shot and rap sheet of a felon who will be released early by Proposition 66," said campaign spokesperson Cam Sanchez, president of the California Police Chiefs Association. "These are very dangerous people—serial child molesters, rapists, murders [sic] and career criminals with long histories of serious crime," said Sanchez. "They and thousands more like them will be back on the street if Proposition 66 becomes law." (Californians United for Public Safety, 2004a, 1)

CUPS also sent out press releases announcing that major law enforcement officials and organizations opposed Proposition 66.

Even though CUPS's efforts received media attention, they did not change public opinion, which favored reforming Three Strikes. As shown in Table 1, 65% of likely voters supported Proposition 66 on October 13, just over 2 weeks before the election. As it began to appear that the critics of Three Strikes would celebrate on election night, CUPS received a major infusion of cash for a full-scale media campaign. During the last week of October 2004, Henry T. Nicholas III, founder of Broadcom Corp. and Orange County billionaire, contributed $1.9 million to the "No on 66" campaign. Nicholas would chip in an additional $1.6 million to the anti-Proposition 66 efforts for a total of $3.5 million (Garvey, 2004).

Nicholas's family background sheds light on his personal opposition to Proposition 66. In 1983, his sister was murdered by her ex-boyfriend. In response to the murder, Marcella Nicholas Leach (Henry's mother) cofounded Justice for Homicide Victims and later became vice chair of CVUC. Newspaper reports suggested that Nicholas was a rich, bereaved brother who unexpectedly rescued the "No on 66" campaign, rather than a rich, bereaved brother who was related (literally) to CVUC and, by extension, the CCPOA.

Right after Nicholas pledged to help bankroll a media blitz against Proposition 66, former Governor Pete Wilson pulled then Governor Arnold Schwarzenegger headfirst into the initiative fight.

Table 1 Trend of Voter Preference Regarding Proposition 66 (Among Likely Voters)

Dates (2004)	Yes	No	Undecided
May	76%	14	10
June	76%	14	10
August	69%	19	12
October 13	65%	18	17
October 21–27	55%	33	12

Source: The Field Poll (2004a, 2004b).

Figure 2 Felon A Day

Felon A Day

RELEASE REPORT

Proposition 66 removes several crimes from the "serious felony" strike list. Because it's retroactive to 1994, thousands of inmates with long histories of serious and violent crime will have their sentences dramatically reduced and be back on the street. Here's just one example.

Name: Daniel Ozuna Smith

Criminal history: Criminal history began at 19. Convicted of robbery in 1961. Violated parole three times in 1979 and once in 1980 when he forced two 15-year-old males into his car, then sodomized one at knife-point. Convicted of kidnapping in 1980, served one year in jail. In 1981, convicted of raping a pregnant woman at gunpoint, sentenced to 12 years. Two parole violations in 1989, one parole violation in 1990. Convicted of possession of drugs for sale in 1991, sentenced to five years. Released on parole in 1994, arrested within four months for heroin possession. Now serving 25 years to life.

Proposition 66 release date: Under Proposition 66, Mr. Smith's sentence would be reduced to a maximum of six years. Because of time served and "good time" credits, would be eligible for immediate release.

NO on 66
PROTECT PUBLIC SAFETY

To view mug shots and rap sheets of felons released by Prop 66, or for more information, visit www.noprop66.org or call 916-447-8186.

Californians United for Public Safety, NO on Prop. 66 • 1415 L St. Ste. 410, Sacramento, CA 95814

Wilson convinced Schwarzenegger to put money and effort into defeating Proposition 66. The *Los Angeles Times* reported, "On Oct. 22, the day after Wilson's call, Schwarzenegger made 'No on 66' the top priority of his ballot measure campaigning. On Oct. 23, the governor spent the afternoon making TV advertisements opposing the initiative in a Los Angeles studio. He also converted TV time he had bought to fight two gambling measures into time for 'No on 66' ads" (Mathews, 2004: B1).

Schwarzenegger's "California Recovery Team," a fund he developed to pay for ballot initiatives, contributed more than $2 million to the fight against Proposition 66, and the CCPOA added another $500,000 to the cause. The union had paid the public relations firm McNally Temple Associates to develop a couple of anti-Proposition 66 commercials. Now the "No on 66" coalition used its financial windfall to air the ads throughout California.[8]

As in the "Felon a Day" fliers, the anti-66 television and radio commercials warned of impending doom. Using harrowing music and images of reviled criminal types like sex offenders and career criminals, the anti-66 advertisements communicated a simple yet powerful message; the initiative would lead to chaos and destroy communities and families. For example, the television commercial, *He Raped Me*, featured a White middle-aged victim. As eerie music played in the background, the woman said, "He had a knife at my throat and said he was going to kill me. Then he raped me." A mug shot of the rapist, a White man with his head hanging listlessly to the side, appeared on screen as the woman continued, "He killed two women. Now Prop. 66 will set him free." The camera panned over mug shots of convicts (the same mug shots used in the "Felon a Day" campaign) as the narrator intoned, "Proposition 66 creates a loophole that will release 26,000 dangerous felons." The advertisement ended with David Paulson, a member of the California District Attorneys Association, standing in front of what seems to be a courthouse to say, "These aren't petty offenders. They're career criminals with long histories of serious crime." As the advertisement concluded, the collage of mug shots reappeared with a large red "No on 66" stamped across it. The narrator ended simply: "Protect your family. No on 66" (Californians United for Public Safety, 2004b).

Contemporary political tacticians (including those who worked on the campaign against Proposition 66) routinely frame penal policies to stir up voters' fears and anxieties not just about crime but also about an assortment of other issues such as family stability, economic security, access to quality education, availability of health care, demographic diversity, and international developments (e.g., terrorism and the "war on terror") (Garland, 1990: 264–265). If voters feel a penal policy will intensify disorder and insecurity in their lives, then they are apt to oppose it (Frieberg, 2001: 269; Tyler and Boeckmann, 1997: 255–256). The "No on 66" campaign capitalized on this political reality.

The strategy worked. As I noted previously, most of the likely voters favored Proposition 66 until late October 2004, but support for the proposition fell quickly as the public campaign against the measure gained steam. It continued to fall in the final days leading up to the election. The initiative enjoyed an early lead on election night, but that lead dropped propitiously, and Proposition 66 failed 53% to 47%. Voters seemed to support reforming an extremely costly and, according to Proposition 66's proponents, broken law until they were repeatedly told that such reform would cause chaos in a social world marked by rapid, major changes, making their lives dangerous and unmanageable.

Media reports primarily credited Governor Schwarzenegger and Henry Nicolas for Proposition 66's defeat. In doing so, they missed the critical role that CCPOA and its allies had played in "No on 66." As discussed earlier, the union organized "Californians United for Public Safety," the campaign's infrastructure, and it pushed along an ailing anti-66 operation when other opponents (including Governor Schwarzenegger) were missing in action. *Los Angeles Times* reporter Joe Matthews (2004: B1), who closely followed the Proposition 66 fight, said simply, "The anti-66 campaign had been kept alive since the spring by the California District Attorneys Assn. and the state prison guards union, which hired the campaign's political consultants and paid for focus groups." Along with contributing more than $850,000 to defeat the measure, the CCPOA brought together various like-minded groups to oppose Proposition 66 with one voice (California Fair Political Practices Commission, 2010: 42). Finally, the CCPOA, with the assistance of talented public relations professionals, developed images and arguments that attempted to frighten the public into voting against the initiative. The union would play similar roles in defeating another reform initiative in 2008.

Four years after Proposition 66 went down, reformers championed a ballot initiative to change drug-related sentencing laws and parole policies. Proposition 5, The Nonviolent Offender Rehabilitation Act (NORA), was the brainchild of the Drug Policy Alliance, which purports to be the "nation's leading organization promoting policy alternatives to the drug war" (Drug Policy Alliance, 2010). With financial backing of billionaire businessman George Soros, Proposition 5 qualified for the 2008 general election.

The initiative was designed to shrink the prison population primarily by targeting so-called nonviolent, nonserious drug offenders. Individuals without prior records of violent or serious crimes who were convicted of drug possession would be eligible for diversion from prison to treatment. People convicted of nonviolent, nonserious crimes (e.g., theft) while under the influence of drugs also would be eligible for diversion (unless a judge decided that the person was unworthy of diversion). NORA also would have made marijuana possession an "infraction," so marijuana possessors would receive citations rather than incarceration or community sanctions such as probation. Finally, the measure would have allowed for certain drug and nonviolent property offenders to earn additional "good time" credits for participating in programs, thereby reducing their sentences. (The initiative also called for drastic expansion of rehabilitation services, providing prisoners access to programs that would allow them to earn the good time credits: Legislative Analyst's Office, 2008.)

Along with trying to reduce the prison population at the front end (i.e., at the point of sentencing), Proposition 5 sought to shrink it at the back end by reforming parole policies. Specifically, it would have decreased the length of parole for "nonviolent, low-risk parolees" from 3 years to 1 year and diverted parolees who violated the terms of their parole or committed misdemeanor offenses from prison. NORA also would have provided resources to ensure that parolees received services to aid their reentry (Legislative Analyst's Office, 2008). California's nonpartisan Legislative Analyst's Office (2008) concluded that Proposition 5 "would eventually result in savings on state operating costs, potentially exceeding $1 billion annually, due mainly to reductions in prison and parole supervision caseloads. Specifically, this measure could eventually reduce the state prison population by more than 18,000 inmates and reduce the number of parolees under state supervision by more than 22,000."

Shortly after Proposition 5 qualified for the November ballot, district attorneys, law enforcement organizations (e.g., the state police chiefs' association), and crime victims' organizations formed a coalition, "People Against Proposition 5," to oppose the measure. The CCPOA, however, did not immediately take a position on NORA or join the anti-Proposition 5 coalition. The architects of NORA believed that the initiative had a decent chance of passing if the CCPOA stayed on the sidelines; without the CCPOA, the "No on 5" campaign did not have the funds to launch a media onslaught (D. Abrahamson, personal communication, August 1, 2008).

When the CCPOA gathered in Las Vegas for its convention in September 2008, it still had no formal position on Proposition 5. The election was a little less than 2 months away, and the "No on 5" alliance was getting desperate; it still did not have enough money to conduct a widespread media campaign against NORA. Three leaders of the anti-Proposition coalition, Jerry Dyer (president of the California Police Chiefs Association), Jan Skully (district attorney of Sacramento County), and Jeff Denham (Republican state senator), traveled to Las Vegas to plead for CCPOA to join their fight. They made an impassioned presentation to the convention delegates, calling NORA the "Drug Dealers' Bill of Rights" and "the worst anti-public safety measure we have ever seen." The speakers ended by warning that NORA likely would become law (they claimed it was "polling at 60%") if they did not raise enough money to spread their message.[9] After the "No on 5" presenters left the convention, President Jimenez signaled that the union would oppose NORA.[10]

Approximately 3 weeks after the convention, the CCPOA joined the campaign to defeat Proposition 5. According to union official Lance Corcoran, they wanted to "maintain our focus on protecting public safety" (California Correctional Peace Officers Association, 2008). On November 15, 2008, the union contributed $1 million to the "No on 5" political action committee, and 9 days later, it spent another $830,000 to air commercials opposing NORA. No other group contributed nearly as much money to defeat Proposition 5 (California Secretary of State, 2008).

The "No on 5" group produced a commercial (financed primarily by the CCPOA) featuring Democratic U.S. Senator Dianne Feinstein that lambasted the initiative as the "drug dealers' bill of rights" and a "get out of jail free card." With tense music playing in the background, the ad warned that NORA would "shorten parole for meth dealers from 3 years to just 6 months" and would "let drug dealers, drunken drivers, child abusers, burglars, thieves, con artists, embezzlers, and others stay on the streets" (People Against the Proposition 5 Deception, 2008). The initiative, the ad maintained, would fill the streets with convicted felons, sacrificing public safety just so convicted criminals could enjoy their "rights" and freedoms.

The voters rejected Proposition 5, 60% to 40%. The extent to which the CCPOA-backed media campaign contributed to this result is unknowable. However, that campaign was chiefly responsible for framing a sensible penal reform as a scary, potentially life-threatening risk—clearly one that voters were unwilling to take.

The Proposition 66 and Proposition 5 cases exemplify the roles that the CCPOA plays in frustrating large-scale efforts to chip away at mass imprisonment.

It is the central strategist and financer within a larger bloc of individuals and organizations with similar perspectives on crime and punishment. But although the CCPOA brings material, political, and organizational resources to the table, it is not a particularly good messenger for several reasons. First, since the early 2000s, the union has been roundly criticized in the press for its cozy relations with politicians (particularly former Governor Gray Davis) and lucrative contracts (Page and Heise, 2011). Second, Republicans and some Democrats now routinely blame public-sector employees and labor unions for budget shortfalls, underperforming state programs and agencies, runaway pension costs, and political gridlock (Smith and Haberman, 2010). Third, the public image of prison officers has been traditionally negative; movies and other forms of popular entertainment routinely depict these workers as inept, uneducated, and abusive (Keinan and Malach-Pines, 2007: 382). For these reasons, the CCPOA smartly puts actors with moral authority (such as crime victims, police chiefs, and district attorneys) in front of the cameras.

As seen with Propositions 66 and 5, the CCPOA and its allies make it extremely difficult to pass major, long-term sentencing reforms through the ballot initiative process. When faced with a "yes" or "no" question, voters predictably choose what they perceive to be the least risky option (i.e., the option that seems to pose the least risk of making their lives more precarious, unsafe, or disorderly; Tyler and Boeckmann, 1997). The union and related groups make sure that voters view measures like Proposition 66 and Proposition 5 as extremely hazardous and scary.

To be clear, I do not believe the CCPOA was the sole reason why these ballot initiatives failed. Rather, I maintain that policy makers and other actors who seek to take advantage of the current window of opportunity to roll back mass imprisonment in California must develop strategies for overcoming resistance from the CCPOA and its allies. Even though crime rates are down (and have been down for years), these groups and their political allies continue to "govern through crime" (Simon, 2007), stoking fear of a downsized penal system.

New York: A Counterfactual Case

The CCPOA is uniquely influential. Prison officer unions in other states—either alone or with coalition partners—hold far less sway over penal policies and priorities and represent smaller obstacles to rolling back mass imprisonment. Nevertheless, these unions still challenge policy makers seeking to shutter penal facilities and cut corrections budgets. This section turns from California to New York to show how a prison officer union with far less political power than the CCPOA affects efforts to downsize prisons.

New York's prison population shot up near the end of the 20th century from 12,579 in 1970 to 71,446 in 2000 (an increase of more than 550%) (Wagner, 2002). By 2000, the Empire State spent $2.8 billion on annual prison expenditures, ranking second behind California ($4.2 billion) (Stephan, 2004: 2). New York, at that point, could not afford its large, incredibly expensive prison system. With annual state budget deficits of more than $10 billion, New York sought to implement substantial downsizing-oriented reforms (Jacobson, 2005: 35).

Scholars increasingly point to New York as a model case of such downsizing (Gartner, Doob, and Zimring, 2010; Greene, and Mauer, 2010; Jacobson, 2005: 58). In the years between 1999 and 2009, New York decreased its prison population by 20% from 72,899 to 58,456. In that same period, the state's imprisonment rate declined by 23% from 400 per 100,000 to 307 per 100,000 (Greene and Mauer, 2010: 5–6). The following factors contributed to the decline: falling crime rates in New York City, changes in law enforcement policies (e.g., decreases in felony arrests and indictments), diversion of drug offenders from prison to treatment, reforms to the state's notoriously harsh Rockefeller drug sentencing laws, and early release of prisoners convicted of drug and other nonviolent crimes (Greene and Mauer, 2010: 5–25; Jacobson, 2005: Chapter 4). The New York Department of Corrections (2010a: 1) has projected that these factors will keep the prison population on a downward slope.

New York has reduced its prison population, but it has had little success closing prisons and shrinking corrections spending, which is where the prison officer union comes into play. New York's prison officers have been unionized since 1953 (Jacobs and Crotty, 1978: 10), but they did not receive collective bargaining rights for another 14 years (Jacobs and Crotty, 1978: 45). Although prison officers in California formed their own, independent union, their counterparts in New York joined American Federal, State, County, and Municipal Employees (AFSCME), a large union that represents a diverse array of public employees and is part of the AFL-CIO. The officers became part of a unit within AFSCME called "Council 82." Although other public "security" workers were part of the council (e.g., state capitol police and museum caretakers), prison officers dominated it (Jacobs and Crotty, 1978: 20).

As in California, the prison officer labor force grew along with the incarcerated population. From 1978 until 1998, the number of officers grew from 5,500 (Jacobs and Crotty, 1978: 10) to approximately 26,000 (Conover, 2000: 15), an increase of more than 450%. Although large, the New York officers' union did not play a major role in toughening penal policy or promoting mass imprisonment. For the most part, AFSCME Council 82 concentrated on "bread-and-butter" issues (e.g., wages, benefits, job security, and job safety) and professionalization matters (e.g., training and hiring standards) (Conover, 2000; Jacobs and Crotty, 1978). But, although the union was not a central force behind prison expansion, it did alter the prisons' "internal management and organization." Transferring power from administrators to rank-and-file workers, the union "brought the guards more job security, more control over their work assignments, and more say in decision making at all levels" (Jacobs and Crotty, 1978: 41).

In 1998, New York prison officers left AFSCME and formed an independent union in the mold of CCPOA. Long-time CCPOA activists even advised their New York peers in their drive to decertify from AFSCME and establish a new labor organization, The New York State Correctional Officers & Police Benevolent Association (NYSCOPBA) (Page,

2011: 78).[11] The New York officers left AFSCME because they felt that the organization limited their capacity to influence penal and labor policy. They were frustrated that they had little control over how their dues were spent, and there were tensions between officers' political and social views and those of their union. As former NYSCOPBA Vice President Carl Canterbury explained in a 2002 interview,

> Independence is the only way. . . . I can't see sending money someplace else, so somebody else's political agenda can be followed. I mean you look at AFSCME; they're a very liberal organization. Their money goes basically towards Democrats and liberals *all the time*. Okay, correctional officers are a little different, they're law enforcement, many times [they are] Republican and conservative. So you had your dues money going somewhere else, supporting candidates from say Washington or Oregon, and it's like "Why?" "Why you wasting good money?" So people had enough of that umbrella.

NYSCOPBA's leadership needed independence to develop a formidable political action operation—the key to CCPOA's success in California.

The New York union has become more politically aggressive in the last 10 years. NYSCOPBA did not contribute to New York's prison boom (the organization was established just before the state's prison population began its steady decline), but it currently is fighting efforts to downsize the system. More specifically, it is obstructing efforts to close prisons and to decrease the correctional workforce. Former Governor David Paterson's 2010–2011 executive budget called for closing three facilities, shutting down a large section of a fourth, and eliminating 637 positions. Addressing custody staff, the Department of Corrections says it "anticipates offering a fillable vacancy to every affected uniformed employee. . . . Each month, approximately 84 security staff employees leave the payroll statewide to retire or pursue other opportunities. Attrition should create fillable vacancies for the majority of affected staff" (New York Department of Correctional Services, 2010b). The closures and cuts would save an estimated $59 million over 2 years (Matthews, 2010).

NYSCOPBA has fought prison closures by lobbying legislators, organizing protests, and conducting an intensive (and expensive) media campaign. Although information on the exact costs of the media offensive is not publicly available, NYSCOPA President Donn Rowe has claimed his organization would spend several hundred thousand dollars to make its case (Matthews, 2010).[12] The union presents five arguments. First, shutting the prisons "is a direct threat to the public safety of all New Yorkers" (the union does not elucidate how the actions would compromise public safety) (Rowe, n.d.: 1). Second, closing prisons "will jeopardize the safety of the inmates and the brave men and women who serve as New York's correctional officers." This is related to the third argument: The prison system is "overcrowded and understaffed," and therefore, sufficient space or security personnel to maintain order are not available (Rowe, n.d.: 1). Fourth, the state of New York in general and prison towns in particular cannot afford to lose the facilities' jobs and tax revenue. Finally, the state should save money by reducing the "top-heavy bureaucracy within the [prisons] agency." In other words, the newly elected Cuomo Administration should eliminate managers and administrative buildings rather than officers and prisons (Rowe, n.d.: 1).

The union's media push includes television and radio commercials and direct mailings, all of which seek to generate or exacerbate fear. Echoing the central message of the campaign against California's Proposition 66, NYSCOPBA insists that closing the prisons will increase insecurity and disorder. For example, the narrator in the union's professionally made television commercial, "Keeping Us Safe," says the following in a low voice:

> Correction officer. It's a thankless and dangerous job. Working day and night in overcrowded prisons, guarding the most violent offenders, keeping us safe. But Albany politicians want to balance the budget by laying off our hardworking officers instead of

cutting department of corrections bureaucrats. That's a dangerous choice, and it could mean the difference between life and death. Tell Albany to cut management, not correction officers. Our safety depends on it. (New York State Correctional Officers and Police Benevolent Association, 2010a)

When the narrator says "keeping us safe," the screen shows a fearful, young, White girl looking through a staircase banister. At the end of the ad, as the narrator remarks "our safety depends on it," the viewer sees a concerned White woman holding a cute White baby boy with his fingers in his mouth. The woman strokes his head to comfort him (see Figure 3). The message is clear: Closing prisons will allow for New York's prisoners (who primarily come from New York City and surrounding areas and are disproportionately Black and Latino) to be released from prison and harm White suburban and rural women and children.

The union insists in its mailers that prison closures not only threaten people's physical safety, but they also threaten economic security. Bold text reads as follows: "Endangering our families and big job losses are simply not an option" (New York State Correctional Officers and Police Benevolent Association, 2010b). Closing the prisons undoubtedly would eliminate jobs. In some counties, New York's prison system is the main employer (Gramlich, 2009). However, NYSCOPBA discounted the government's claims that it would facilitate the "reuse of the closed facilities . . . by another State or local government or private industry" (New York Department of Correctional Services, 2010a). The union skillfully fused a message of economic insecurity with a message of physical security, making prison closures seem like "life-and-death" choices.

The NYSCOPBA has not been alone in its fight against the prison closures. Local and state politicians have worked with the union. The *New York Times* describes a "powerful alliance of upstate lawmakers and correction officers' unions" that "guard their constituents' and members' state-financed

Figure 3 Keeping Us Safe

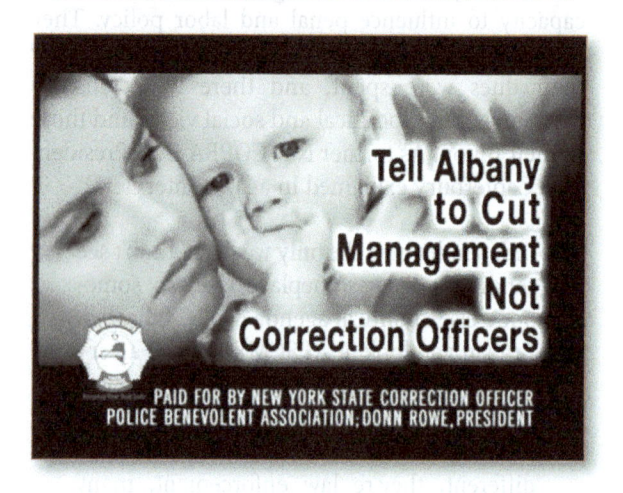

jobs" (Confessore, 2007: B, 4). This alliance's efforts have paid off. In July 2010, the Department of Correctional Services Commissioner Brian Fischer sent a letter to NYSCOPBA's president and local lawmakers; the state would not close two prisons. The last sentence of the letter read, "Any decision regarding the future of Moriah and Ogdensburg Correctional Facilities will be left to the next administration" (Fischer, 2010: 1). Clearly, the Paterson Administration and Department of Correctional Services were no longer up to fighting NYSCOPBA and its allies. Downsizing New York's prison system will be a long, slow process.

Unionized Opposition

When commentators refer to the power of prison officer unions, they typically point to the CCPOA. The CCPOA is unquestionably a formidable organization that heavily influences penal policies and priorities in a state with an incredibly large and costly prison system. However, the CCPOA is exceptional. No other prison officer union is as influential as the California outfit. Two principle differences explain the CCPOA's incredible achievements and political authority. First, it developed a distinctively independent, intensely political model of public-sector labor unionization in the early 1980s. This process included establishing mutually beneficial alliances with like-minded groups, some of which the union effectively created (e.g., the state's two most powerful crime victims' rights organizations). Unlike those affiliated with the AFL-CIO (as the New York union was until the late 1990s), the CCPOA and other independent prison officer unions develop their own agendas (without approval from a parent organization) and can use all of their money to generate influence and advance their goals rather than those of the AFL-CIO or labor more generally. (As shown in Figure 1, more than one third of all prison officer unions in the United States are independent.) Second, California's neopopulist political culture and institutions (e.g., the ballot initiative) allow for interest groups like the CCPOA to shape penal policy directly and indirectly (Barker, 2009). Because of these two factors, the CCPOA could help to entrench mass imprisonment and now helps to obstruct efforts to downsize California's prison system.

New York is an instructive comparative case. NYSCOPBA (and AFSCME Council 82 before it) is far less successful and powerful than the CCPOA. The prison officer union in New York was not an important actor in that state's prison expansion, nor did it stand in the way of reforms that have led to a 20% drop in the state's prison population. NYSCOPBA has been less influential than the CCPOA largely because it did not become an independent, politically savvy organization until 1998, which was about the time New York began downsizing its prison system. Also, New York's political system is insulated and expert-driven, making it more difficult for interest groups to dominate penal policy as they do in California (Barker, 2009).

Although NYSCOPBA does not enjoy the same influence as the CCPOA, it is now an important political player that obstructs efforts to downscale the prison system even more. The two unions simply struggle against downsizing at different points in the process; the CCPOA is working to block major reforms to decrease the prison population over the long term, whereas the NYSCOPBA is fighting against closing facilities and decreasing the workforce. (The CCPOA will undoubtedly resist downsizing California's prison infrastructure if and when the Golden State seriously reduces and keeps down its incarcerated population.) In their efforts, both unions use *fear* to achieve their goals. More specifically, they seek to generate or exacerbate fear of change in the penal status quo. They insist that reforms will add insecurity and disorder in people's lives. In addition, they strike fear in politicians, threatening to brand lawmakers who support reforms as responsible for and insensitive to voters' anxieties about physical, economic, and other harm.

The unions have sufficient resources to carry out their campaigns because of their size (between 20,000 and 30,000 dues-paying members), and the unions are so large because of the prison boom. In this respect, imprisonment provided the raw materials that the organizations use to resist downsizing prisons. A consequence of the prison boom, then, was the empowerment of actors with a material stake in and ideological commitment to the penal status quo. In sum, neither the CCPOA nor NYSCOPBA (or its predecessor) sparked mass imprisonment in their respective states, but the unions are now obstacles to rolling back that phenomenon. Therefore, the factors that started mass imprisonment are not necessarily the same factors that sustain it.

Overcoming the obstacles to downsizing prisons featured in this article will not be easy. In this final section, I delineate four propositions, which encourage both accommodating and confronting prison officer unions, that might help policy makers and other actors as they attempt to implement sentencing and prison reform, shutter penal facilities, streamline workforces, and rein in correctional budgets.

Proposition 1: Maintain Commitments

Corrections unions' resistance to downsizing prisons stems in large part from the officers' fear of losing their jobs. In states like California and New York, these jobs pay well, have solid benefits, and provide excellent retirement packages—all evidence of union success. They are solid middle-class jobs. With the withering of the manufacturing sector, working as a prison officer is one of an increasingly limited number of jobs that provide upward social mobility to people who lack advanced educational credentials. This situation is particularly true in the rural counties where many prisons (particularly in California and New York) are located. Prison officers and their families justifiably fear that downsizing prisons might close one, if not the only, path they have into the middle class.

People who live in prison towns also worry about downsizing the penal system. Since the 1980s, government officials and local leaders have propped up prisons as powerful, sustainable engines of economic development (King, Mauer, and Huling, 2004: 455–456). However, studies indicate that the economic promises of prisons have proven largely illusory. King et al. (2004), for example, demonstrated that placing prisons in rural counties in New York did not significantly reduce unemployment (much of the prison staff, particularly prison officers, lived elsewhere) or decrease poverty. Studies in California (Gilmore, 2007), Missouri (Thies, 1998), and Washington (Carlson, 1992) have reached similar conclusions. Making matters worse, evidence suggests that prison sitings produce environmental harm (Braz and Gilmore, 2006; King et al., 2004: 475–476) and rural prison towns "may be closing themselves off to other options of sustainable development" (King et al., 2004: 477).

Although the economic benefits of prisons to counties might not be real, fears associated with losing prisons likely are. The prisons provide hope for potential economic development. As King et al. (2004: 455) stated, "the existence of the finished product, a hulking institution, gives residents the perception that opportunities are abundant." Residents likely think that once the prisons go, all employment possibilities will vanish, and as shown in New York, politicians and prison officer unions play into these fears.

Actors who seek to downsize prisons, then, must recognize and deal with the anxieties of officers and residents alike. Jacobson (2005: 177) rightly argued that states should decrease correctional workforces through attrition whenever possible. In other words, positions should be shed through retirement or voluntary termination. This is one way to allay fears of layoffs. In New York, Department of Corrections officials maintain that they will not lay off officers but will put them in "fillable vacancies." They must make good on that promise or face even more intense resistance when they try to close additional facilities in the future. Jacobson (2005: 177–178) wrote that officers "will be much more cooperative and might well participate in efforts to retrain and reassign officers if they understand that their ranks are not going to be forcibly reduced by layoffs." Helping to ensure workers remain employed (even if in different occupations) is a way to accommodate officers and the unions that represent them.

The state also might set up retraining programs or pay for officers to take classes that would allow them to find other sources of work within and outside the prison system (e.g., officers could train in drug and alcohol counseling, assuming the treatment field will grow as states divert drug offenders from prison to counseling). If officers could move out of their current positions and into new jobs, then they would create additional vacancies, helping the state to refrain from laying off custody staff.

State governments also will need to invest in communities that would lose prisons. By bringing governmental entities or private business into towns with prisons slated for closure, the states can ease community opposition as well as alleviate fears and possible resistance when they attempt to close more prisons in the future. Again, it is imperative that state governments make good on assurances to help prison officers and others negatively affected by prison closures. If they do not, then they will intensify opposition to downsizing-oriented reforms, and the unions' messages of fear will continue to resonate with community members and their leaders.

Proposition 2: Challenge the Dominant Narrative

Clearly, prison officer unions resist downsizing the penal system for material reasons. A fundamental purpose of unions is to promote job security. Moreover, shrinking the correctional workforce will reduce union membership and dues. That being said, prison officer unions (at least in California and New York) do not oppose downsizing solely for material reasons. Their resistance is also ideological. They believe that "prison works"— particularly for serious and violent offenders. They believe "tough" sentencing laws like Three Strikes decrease crime through deterrence and incapacitation. In addition, although the unions recognize that the prison systems could do more to rehabilitate prisoners, cut wasteful spending, and shed unnecessary bureaucracy, they are committed to the penal strategy of punitive segregation (Page, 2011). Therefore, it is a mistake to think only in economic terms.

The prison officer unions' perspective on crime and punishment fits within a larger narrative that permeates public and political discourse. Fear-based campaigns reflect and reinforce popular representations of offenders and imprisonment, which maintain that prisons are filled with extremely violent, manipulative, rapacious offenders ("career criminals," "sexual predators," "gang bangers," etc.) who will automatically reoffend if set free. Comprehensive efforts to downscale prisons must challenge the dominant narrative of crime and punishment, which undergirds mass imprisonment.

Public officials must play central roles in challenging the dominant narrative. For most of the last 30 years, politicians and Department of Corrections officials have either supported "tough on crime" policies or remained on the sidelines of debates over penal policy (Gilmore, 2007; Miller, 2008; Simon, 2007). This stance is no longer possible. Instead, they can help to reeducate the public by countering popular perceptions that mass imprisonment makes us safer and decreasing prison commitments compromises public safety. They can make the case that mass imprisonment actually makes us less safe because it drains money from prevention, in-prison rehabilitation, and reentry programs. Moreover, it cannibalizes funding for education, job creation, and social services. When policy makers decrease the size of the prison system without jeopardizing public safety, they must tell voters. Bragging about successes is a great way to counter the doomsday scenarios described in the campaigns against Propositions 66 and 5 in California and prison closures in New York.

State executives and Department of Corrections officials need not make their case alone. Some actors with extensive moral authority oppose the penal status quo but, for the most part, have not participated in public campaigns to downsize the penal system. For example, some judges oppose laws that eliminate discretion and force them to impose laws they view as unjust, some district attorneys oppose locking up drug users and other nonviolent offenders for long periods of time, and some crime-victim advocates support restorative justice, believing that punitive laws and the death penalty do not lead to "closure" (but simply cause more suffering).

California's newly elected attorney general, Kamala Harris, is in a particularly good position to challenge the dominant narrative about imprisonment. Harris opposes the death penalty and strongly supports reentry programs, and she is a critic of the Golden State's sentencing policies. In her book, *Smart on Crime*, she states the following:

> For several decades, the passage of tough laws and long sentences has created an illusion in the public's mind that public safety is best served when we treat all offenders pretty much the same way: arrest, convict, imprison, parole.... What the numbers say loud and clear, however, is that most nonviolent offenders are learning the wrong lesson... are becoming better and more hardened criminals during their prison stays. (quoted in *Sacramento Bee*, 2010: 12A)

It is possible that Harris will use her office as a bully pulpit, advocating for policy changes that might roll back mass imprisonment. Her focus, however, is on "nonviolent offenders." Other statements she has made indicate that she supports current punitive sentencing laws targeting "violent" and "serious" offenders (Harris, 2009). Therefore, she might not back (or even might oppose) policy changes that would reduce prison terms for offenders convicted of violent or serious crimes. As Jonathan Simon (2009) asserted, major, long-term reductions in imprisonment will require reducing sentences for all offenders—not just those convicted of "nonviolent" or "nonserious" crimes.

Of course, California's new governor and former attorney general, Jerry Brown, also has an ideal platform to challenge the dominant narrative about imprisonment and institute alternative penal policies. However, he has given no indications that he intends to support actions to make substantial cuts in mass imprisonment. Brown's actions in recent years show he does not support sentencing reforms that seriously would reduce prison terms; he actively campaigned against both Propositions 66 and 5 (Page, 2011). Although it is doubtful that Governor Brown will use the authority of his office to make a case against mass imprisonment, California's incredible budget deficits, pressure from the federal courts, and the lack of resources to make prisons anything other than mere warehouses might move the governor toward sentencing reforms capable of greatly decreasing and maintaining a lowered prison population.

In short, by participating in public relations campaigns, engaging in legislative debates, and taking stands on key policy initiatives, policy makers and other authoritative actors can challenge the "prison works" narrative (or, at least, publicize alternative narratives). In doing so, they might make it more difficult for prison officers and related groups to frighten voters (and voters' representatives) into opposing measures designed to shrink the penal system.

Proposition 3: Make It Personal

Ensuring prison officer jobs and altering the narratives about downsizing prisons likely would not be enough to keep unions like CCPOA and NYSCOPBA from opposing efforts to shrink the penal system. It needs to be in unions' self-interest to not oppose meaningful reforms, prison closures, and so on, no matter how strong their ideological attachment to punitive segregation.

To do so, policy makers will need to use confrontation and *make it personal* (i.e., they need to argue publicly that the unions are stonewalling out of self-interest). As argued earlier, I personally do not believe that unions oppose downsizing efforts simply to save jobs and maintain union power; however, their competitors can make that argument. Students of public-sector unions demonstrate that these organizations bolster their cases by showing how they serve the public interest; after all, they are paid with taxpayer dollars, and their contracts are matters of public policy (Johnston, 1994; Lopez, 2004). Prison officer unions routinely state that they serve the public good, but proponents of downsizing prisons could argue that prison officer unions actually are opposing reforms that are in the public interest. By flipping the discussion, reformers could assert that the unions care more about power and their pecuniary interests than what is good for the taxpayers and are therefore unworthy of solid contracts.

To some extent, actors in California have implemented this tactic. In the last several years, the media (particularly newspaper editorial boards), former Governor Schwarzenegger, and federal judges have branded the CCPOA as a self-interested enemy of reform that promotes lawlessness behind bars, controls politicians and prison administrators, and increases the state's bloated correctional budget. Moreover, the Schwarzenegger Administration refused to grant the CCPOA a new contract, claiming that provisions of previous labor agreements compromised prison management and cost the state too much money (Page, 2011: Chapter 8).

This intense pressure has forced the union to soften its rhetoric and policy positions (Page, 2011: Chapter 8).[13] Whereas CCPOA officials used to celebrate prison expansion and castigate prisoners publicly, the union's current president, Mike Jimenez, has suggested he and his union are committed to rolling back mass imprisonment. For example, in a speech at the 2007 California Democratic convention, Jimenez stated the following:

> To borrow from Martin Luther King, Jr., as well, today I have a dream. I have a dream that the bricks and mortar that were planned to build new prisons will instead be used to build new schools. Today I have a dream that not one of these cells will ever be occupied by the child of a person in this room today. Today I have a dream that an ounce of prevention will be embraced instead of a pound of cure by the California legislature and this administration. (quoted in Page, 2011: 196)

Along with changing its rhetoric, the CCPOA has put out two "blueprints for reform" that advocate for an advisory sentencing commission, improved rehabilitative programming, additional reentry facilities to help decrease recidivism, and shorter periods of parole for some ex-offenders (California Correctional Peace Officers Association, 2010a). It also officially endorsed legislation that would have allowed for juveniles sentenced to life in prison without parole to petition courts for a reduced sentence (the legislation failed). In addition, the CCPOA filed a brief on behalf of the Prison Law Office (a former foe) supporting a federal court ruling to reduce prison overcrowding (California Correctional Peace Officers Association, 2010b) as the result of two class action lawsuits (*Coleman v. Wilson*, 1995; *Plata v.Davis/Schwarzenegger*, 2003). The court ruled that overcrowding made it impossible for the government to provide prisoners with constitutionally adequate mental and medical health care, and it ordered the state to decrease prison overcrowding from 190% design capacity to 137.5% design capacity, which is an overall population reduction of roughly 40,000 prisoners (Three-Judge Court, 2009).

Importantly, the CCPOA has become less isolationist vis-à-vis other state workers' unions. Because of former Governor Schwarzenegger's hostility toward public-sector employees (and the national trend of blaming state workers for government problems), the CCPOA teamed up with the California Teachers Association and other labor unions to oppose measures that would have reduced the influence of the unions (e.g., one proposition would have forced the unions to receive permission from each member to use dues for political purposes) (Matthews, 2006). Moreover, the CCPOA allied with other unions to help Jerry Brown win the 2010 governor's race. The CCPOA's proreform rhetoric at least partly might be a result of the prison officer unions' alliances with fellow state workers' unions. Whether the CCPOA continues to work with these other unions now that Brown, a friend of labor, is in office is an open question.

In recent years, the CCPOA has undoubtedly changed; it has sought common ground with individuals and groups it previously deemed enemies such as academics, prisoner rights' attorneys, and unions affiliated with the AFL-CIO; changed its rhetoric from virulently antiprisoner and proprison growth to proreform; and signaled support for some measures that could make a dent in the state's penal population. However, the union also has taken actions that question the extent of its transformation. For example, after it began to talk about sentencing and prison reform in 2007, the CCPOA bankrolled the opposition to Proposition 5 and fought a proposed sentencing commission that would have had the authority to change the state's sentencing laws (Moore, 2009). In 2008, it backed Proposition 9 ("Marsy's Law"), which, among other things, made it more difficult for prisoners with life sentences to receive parole and forbade the state from using early release to alleviate prison overcrowding (Page, 2011: 202).

Additionally, the CCPOA encouraged its partners (particularly CVUC) to oppose policies that the union itself claimed to support. As mentioned previously, the CCPOA registered support for a bill that would have made it possible for some juveniles serving sentences of life without the possibility of parole to reduce their prison terms. At the union's 2010 membership convention, President Jimenez addressed criticisms, claiming that the CCPOA only supported the measure after union officials knew it had no chance of passing. After Jimenez finished, a representative of CVUC took the podium. She explained that the CCPOA had instructed victims' rights groups like hers to defeat the bill and provided the resources to do so: "They gave us the resources and the ability to defeat that bill."[14] In short, the CCPOA publicly endorsed the bill and privately helped CVUC defeat it.

The CCPOA took a similar approach when it filed the legal brief in favor of the federal court's ruling to decrease overcrowding in the state's prison system. Although the CCPOA expressed support for the federal court's actions, the CVUC was suing the state of California for increasing the amount of "good time" credits "nonviolent" prisoners might earn to reduce their sentences (Lagos, 2010). The organization argued that this policy violates a provision of Marsy's Law that forbids the government from using early release to alleviate overcrowding. The same CVUC representative who spoke at CCPOA's 2010 convention explained to the union's delegates that CCPOA funded the lawsuit. When union members protested that, in filing the legal brief, the CCPOA supported shortening prison sentences, she assured delegates the CCPOA's support of her group's suit was evidence that the union did not really support early release. CCPOA officials did not disagree with her claim.[15] (In fact, the union accurately states in its legal brief that overcrowding can be reduced effectively through prison expansion, sending state prisoners to county jails, and other means that do not decrease the prison population; California Correctional Peace Officers Association, 2010b.) The union's legal brief, then, was an attempt to demonstrate to the federal judges that the union is not an enemy of reform and therefore should have a seat at the table during deliberations over how to decrease overcrowding. It was also an effort to draw attention to the disastrous consequences of overcrowding for prison staff (not just prisoners) and need to hire more officers (California Correctional Peace Officers Association, 2010b).[16] It was not a sign of support for shortening sentences or early release.

Taken together, "making it personal" forced the CCPOA to budge; yet, the union and its allies (particularly CVUC, which is almost solely funded by the CCPOA) continue to fight against major efforts to downsize prisons, particularly those that would lead to early release or shorter prison sentences for many offenders. It is incumbent upon policy makers and other actors seeking to shrink the penal system to confront unions that say one thing and do another. In addition, if unions continue to obstruct downscaling efforts, they must hold the organizations accountable (and keep "making it personal"). By doing so, they can make it in the unions' self-interest to stop fighting efforts (either directly or through proxies) capable of truly shrinking the penal system.

Proposition 4: Don't Scapegoat the Unions

Governors and other policy makers only should confront prison officer unions if they are fully committed to downsizing prisons, not to make prison officer unions scapegoats for their own inability or unwillingness to promote real penal change. After all, as previously noted, politicians now regularly blame state workers and their unions for an array of governmental problems (Smith and Haberman, 2010). Unless politicians are willing to take hard positions to shrink the prison system, they should not blame prison officer unions for the failures to enact serious reforms.

Lawmakers and state officials routinely argue that they cannot make major policy changes because of "special interests." This claim often seems like an excuse for not taking politically unpopular positions. State officials should not use the need for downsizing prisons as justification to weaken unions. "Making it personal" is only a strategy for getting unions not to oppose reforms. Indeed, if unions refrain from opposing sentencing reform and prison closures, then they should be rewarded with good contracts that professionalize prison officer work, provide solid wages and benefits, and offer job security. In other words, incentives should be given for cooperation, not just disincentives for noncooperation. After all, research indicates that, by enhancing training, increasing professionalism, and decreasing turnover, prison officer unions improve the quality of life for staff and inmates alike (Crewe, Liebling, and Hulley, in press).

Conclusion

Policy makers made choices that created mass imprisonment, and they will have to make choices to downscale prisons. Public officials might be tempted to ship state prisoners to private facilities, enact symbolic reforms, blame prison officer unions and other "special interests" for their lack of action, or claim that "the public" does not want different penal policies. However, to create meaningful, lasting policy change capable of keeping crime down without locking up millions of people, lawmakers and other leaders have to insist publicly that such change is necessary, possible, and desirable. Moreover, they need to confront interest groups that generate or exacerbate fear of altering the penal status quo. If they are unwilling to engage in this kind of struggle, then fear-based campaigns organized by prison officer unions and their allies will continue to resonate with the electorate, and the current window of opportunity for implementing substantial, long-term reforms capable of downscaling the penal system will close, further empowering organizations that support and benefit from mass imprisonment.

References

Aronowitz, Stanley. 1998. *From the Ashes of Old: American Labor and America's Future*. New York: Basic Books.

Austin, James, Todd R. Clear, Troy Duster, David F. Greenberg, John Irwin, Candace McCoy, Alan Mobley, Barbara Owen, and Joshua Page. 2007. *Unlocking America: Why and How to Reduce America's Prison Population*. Washington, DC: JFA Institute.

Barker, Vanessa. 2009. *The Politics of Imprisonment: How the Democratic Process Shapes the Way America Punishes Offenders*. New York: Oxford University Press.

Bazelon, Emily. 2010. Arguing three strikes. *New York Times*. May 17. Retrieved May 24, 2010 from nytimes.com/2010/05/23/magazine/23strikes-t.html.

Braman, Donald. 2007. *Doing Time on the Outside: Incarceration and Family Life in Urban America*. Ann Arbor: University of Michigan Press.

Braz, Rose and Craig Gilmore. 2006. Joining forces: Prisons and environmental justice in recent California organizing. *Radical History Review*, 96: 95–111.

Bureau of Labor Statistics. 2008. *Occupational Employment and Wages, May 2008* ("Correctional Officers and Jailers"). Washington, DC: Author. Retrieved June 29, 2009 from http://www.stats.bls.gov/oes/current/oes333012.htm.

California Correctional Peace Officers Association. 2007. *From Sentencing to Incarceration to Release: A Blueprint for Reforming California's Prison System*. Sacramento, CA: Author.

California Correctional Peace Officers Association. 2008. *5150 Hotline from Lance Corcoran, October 21, 2008*. Retrieved January 6, 2009 from ccpoa.org/5150hotline_102108.html.

California Correctional Peace Officers Association. 2010a. *New Directions: A Blueprint for Reforming California's Prison System to Protect the Public, Reduce Costs and Rehabilitate Inmates*. Sacramento, CA: Author.

California Correctional Peace Officers Association. 2010b. Brief for Appellee Intervenor California Correctional Peace Officers' Association, RE: *Ralph Coleman et al. v. Arnold Schwarzenegger et al. and Marcianno Plata, et al. v. Arnold Schwarzenegger et al*. In U.S. Supreme Court on appeal from the U.S. District Courts for the Northern and Eastern Districts of California. October 25.

California Fair Political Practices Commission. 2010. *Big Money Talks*. Sacramento: Author.

California Secretary of State. 2006. *Cal-Access*. Retrieved October 7, 2006 from calaccess.ss.ca.gov/.

California Secretary of State. 2008. *Cal-Access*. Retrieved December 5, 2009 from calaccess.ss.ca.gov/.

California State Auditor. 2009. *California Department of Corrections and Rehabilitation* (Report 2009–107.2). Sacramento, CA: Author.

Californians United for Public Safety. 2004a. *Felon a Day* (flier).

Californians United for Public Safety 2004b. *He Raped Me* (advertisement).

Carlson, Katherine. 1992. Doing good and looking bad: A case study of prison/community relations. *Crime & Delinquency*, 38: 56–69.

Carrasco, Ben. 2006. Assessing the CCPOA's Political Influence and its Impact on Efforts to Reform the California Corrections System. Unpublished manuscript.

Center for Juvenile and Criminal Justice. 2002. *California Prisons*. San Francisco, CA: Author.

Clear, Todd. 2007. *Imprisoning Communities: How Mass Incarceration Makes Disadvantaged Neighborhoods Worse*. New York: Oxford University Press.

Comfort, Megan. 2008. *Doing Time Together. Love and Family in the Shadow of the Prison*. Chicago, IL: Chicago University Press.

Confessore, Nicholas. 2007. Spitzer seeks ways to find state prisons he can close. *New York: Times*. February 5, section B, 4.

Conover, Ted. 2000. *Newjack: Guarding Sing Sing*. New York: Random House.

Corrections USA. 2011. *About Us*. Retrieved December 21, 2010 from cusa.org/aboutus.html.

Crewe, Ben, Alison Liebling, and Susie Hulley. In press. Staff culture, abuse of authority and prisoner quality of life in public and private prisons. *Australian and New Zealand Journal of Criminology*.

Domanick, Joe. 2004. *Cruel Justice: Three Strikes and the Politics of Crime in America's Golden State*. Berkeley: University of California Press.

Drug Policy Alliance. 2010. *About DPA*. Retrieved December 21, 2010 from drugpolicy.org/about/.

Fantasia, Rick and Kim Voss. 2004. *Hard Work: Remaking the American Labor Movement*. Berkeley: University of California Press.

Fischer, Brian. 2010, July 9. *Closure Rescission* (memorandum).

Flyvbjerg, Bent. 2006. Five misunderstandings about case-study research. *Qualitative Inquiry*, 12: 219–245.

Freiberg, Arie. 2001. Affective versus effective justice: Instrumentalism and emotionalism in criminal justice. *Punishment & Society*, 3: 265–278.

Garland, David 1990. *Punishment and Modern Society*. Chicago, IL: University of Chicago Press.

Garland, David. 2000. The culture of high crime societies: Some preconditions of recent "law and order" policies. *British Journal of Criminology*, 40: 347–375.

Garland, David. 2001. *Mass Imprisonment: Social Causes and Consequences*. Thousand Oaks, CA: Sage.

Gartner, Rosemary, Anthony Doob, and Franklin E. Zimring. In press. The past as prologue? Decarceration in California then and now. *Criminology & Public Policy*.

Garvey, Megan. 2004. Big money pours in for 3-strikes ads. *Los Angeles Times*. October 28, section B, 1.

Gilmore, Ruth Wilson. 2007. *Golden Gulag: Prisons, Surplus, Crisis, and Opposition in Globalizing California*. Berkeley: University of California.

Gottschalk, Marie. 2006. *The Prison and the Gallows: The Politics of Mass Incarceration in America*. New York: Cambridge University Press.

Gottschalk, Marie. 2010. The Great Recession and the Great Confinement: The economic crisis and the future of penal reform. In (Richard Rosenfeld, Kenna Quinet, and Crystal Garcia, eds.), *Contemporary Issues in Criminological Theory and Research: Papers from the American SocietyofCriminology2010 Conference*. Belmont, CA: Wadsworth.

Gramlich, John. 2009, June 1. Tracking the recession: Prison economics. *Stateline.org*. Retrieved August 5, 2010 from stateline.org/live/printable/story?contentId=403563.

Greene, Judith and Marc Mauer. 2010. *Downscaling Prisons: Lessons from Four States*. Washington, DC: The Sentencing Project.

Harris, Kamala. 2009, August 14. *Smart on Crime: More Safety at Less Cost*. Retrieved December 16, 2010 from kamalaharris.org/news/489.

Jacobs, James and Norma Meacham Crotty. 1978. *Guard Unions and the Future of the Prisons*. Ithaca, NY: Ithaca Regional Office.

Jacobson, Michael. 2005. *Downsizing Prisons: How to Reduce Crime and End Mass Incarceration*. New York: New York University Press.

Jimenez, Mike. 2007, April 28. *The California Democratic Party 2007 State Convention*, San Diego, CA. Transcribed by author.

Johnston, Paul. 1994. *Success While Others Fail: Social Movement Unionism and the Public Workplace*. Ithaca, NY: Ithaca Regional Office.

Keinan, Giora and Ayala Malach-Pines. 2007. Stress and burnout among prison personnel. *Criminal Justice and Behavior*, 34: 380–389.

King, Ryan, Marc Mauer, and Tracy Huling. An analysis of the economics of prison siting in rural communities. *Criminology & PublicPolicy*, 3: 453–480.

Krisberg, Barry. 2008. *Getting the Genie Back in the Bottle: California's Prison Gulag*. Oakland, CA: National Council on Crime and Delinquency.

Lagos, Marisa. 2010. Advocacy group sues over early-release. *San Francisco Chronicle*. February 18, section C, 2.

Legislative Analysts' Office. 2008. *Proposition5*. Sacramento: Author. Retrieved August 5, 2010 from http://www.lao.ca.gov/ballot/2008/5_11_2008.aspx.

Leonard, Jack. 2010. "Pizza thief" walks the line. *Los Angeles Times*. February 10. Retrieved July 30, 2010 from articles.latimes.com/2010/feb/10/local/la-mepizzathief10–2010feb10.

Little Hoover Commission. 2007. *Solving California's Corrections Crisis: Time Is Running Out*. Sacramento, CA: Author.

Lopez, Steven. 2004. *Reorganizing the Rust Belt*. Berkeley: University of California Press.

Manza, Jeff and Christopher Uggen. 2006. *Locked Out: Felon Disenfranchisement and American Democracy*. New York: Oxford University Press.

Matthews, Cara. 2010. Corrections officers fighting proposed closure of four prisons over two years. *Ithaca Journal*. February 10.

Matthews, Joe. 2004. How prospects for Prop. 66 fell so far, so fast. *Los Angeles Times*. November 7, section B, 1.

Matthews, Joe. 2006. *The People's Machine*. New York: Public Affairs.

McCoy, Laura. 1985. Sex abuse at Folsom Prison, women charge. *Sacramento Bee*. February 21, section A, p. 1.

Miller, Lisa. 2008. *The Perils of Federalism*. New York: Oxford University Press.

Moore, Solomon. 2009. California state assembly approves prison legislation. *New York Times*. August 31. Retrieved December 5, 2010 from nytimes.com/ 2009/09/01/us/01prison.html?_r=1&emc=eta1.

New York Department of Correctional Services. 2010a. DOCS planning for additional closures, consolidation in 2010–11 as inmate population continues to decline. *DOCS Today*, Winter: 1.

New York Department of Correctional Services. 2010b. *DOCS Fact Sheet, 2011 Prison Closures*. Albany, NY: Author. Retrieved April 15, 2010 from http://www.docs.state.ny.us/FactSheets/PrisonClosure2011.html.

New York State Correctional Officers and Police Benevolent Association. 2010a. *Keeping Us Safe*. Albany, NY: Author.

New York State Correctional Officers and Police Benevolent Association. 2010b. *Join the Fight to Keep Camp George town from Closing* (mailer).

Page, Joshua. 2011. The *Toughest Beat: Politics, Punishment, and the Prison Officers Union in California*. New York: Oxford University Press.

Page, Joshua and Kia Heise. 2011. The Modern Octopus: Newspapers Take on the "Powerful Prison Guards Union." Unpublished manuscript.

People Against the Proposition 5 Deception. 2008. *No on 5*. Sacramento: Author (commercial).

Petersilia, Joan. 2006. *Understanding California Corrections*. Berkeley: California Policy Research Center.

Pew Center on the States. 2009. *One in 100: Behind Bars in America 2008*. Washington, DC: Author.

Pew Center on the States. 2010. *Prison Count 2010*. Washington, DC: Author.

Rowe, Donn. n.d. Statement by NYSCOPBA President Donn Rowe on the Executive Budget Proposal to Close State Prisons. Albany, NY: NYSCOPBA.

Sacramento Bee. 2010. Kamala Harris' idea could ease prison crowding. November 20, section A, 12.

Shapiro, Bruce. 1997 (February 10). Victims & vengeance: Why the victims' rights amendment is a bad idea. *The Nation*, 11–19.

Simon, Jonathan. 2007. *Governing Through Crime: How the War on Crime Transformed American Democracy and Created a Culture of Fear*. New York: Oxford University Press.

Simon, Jonathan. 2009. No Rationale for the Law of Homicide: How Governing through Crime Has Devolved the Law of Homicide and Locked in Hyper-Punishment. Presented at the 4th Annual Roger Hood Public Lecture, Centre for Criminology, University of Oxford, Oxford, U.K.

Simon, Jonathan. 2010. Mass incarceration and the Great Recession: A comment on Gottschalk. In (Richard Rosenfeld, Kenna Quinet, and Crystal Garcia, eds.), *Contemporary Issues in Criminological Theory and Research: Papers from the American Society of Criminology 2010 Conference*. Belmont, CA: Wadsworth.

Smith, Ben and Maggie Haberman. 2010. Polls turn on labor unions. *Politico*, June 6. Retrieved December 18, 2010 from politico.com/news/stories/0610/38183.html.

Steinhauer, Jennifer. 2009. To cut costs, states relax prison policies. *New York Times*, March 24. Retrieved December 17, 2010 from nytimes.com/2009/03/25/us/25prisons.html?_r=1&ref=prisonsandprisoners.

Stephan, James J. 2004. *State Prison Expenditures, 2001*. Washington, DC: Bureau of Justice Statistics.

The Field Poll. 2004a. *Large Majority Supports Easing of Three Strikes Law*. San Francisco, CA: Field Research Corporation.

The Field Poll. 2004b. *Late-Breaking Surge of No Votes on Prop. 66*. San Francisco, CA: Field Research Corporation.

Thies, Jeanie. 1998. The Big House in a Small Town: The Economic and Social Impacts of a Correctional Facility on its Host Community. Ph.D. dissertation, University of Missouri, St. Louis.

Three-Judge Court. 2009. Opinion and Order Re: Ralph Coleman, et al. v. Arnold Schwarzenegger al. and Marcianno Plata, et al. v. Arnold Schwarzenegger et al. U.S. District Courts for the Eastern District of California and the Northern District of California. August 4.

Tyler, Tom and Robert Boeckmann. 1997. Three strikes and you're out, but why? The psychology of public support for punishing rule breakers. *Law & Society Review*, 31: 255–256.

Wagner, Peter. 2002. Importing constituents: Prisoners and political clout in New York. *Mass: Prison Policy Initiative*, August 22. Retrieved July 28, 2010 from prisonpolicy.org/importing/importing.html.

Warren, Jenifer. 2000. When he speaks, they listen. *Los Angeles Times*. August 21, section A, 1.

Western, Bruce. 2006. *Punishment and Inequality in America*. New York: Russell Sage Foundation.

Weisberg, Robert and Joan Petersilia. 2010. The dangers of pyrrhic victories against mass incarceration. *Daedalus*, 139: 124–133.

Wildeman, Christopher. 2009. Parental imprisonment, the prison boom, and the concentration of childhood disadvantage. *Demography*, 46: 265–280.

Yamamura, Kevin. 2002. Report links money to key legislation. *Sacramento Bee*. March 19, section A, 3.

Zimring, Franklin E., Gordon J. Hawkins, and Sam Kamin. 2001. *Punishment and Democracy: Three Strikes and You're Out in California*. New York: Oxford University Press.

Court Cases Cited

Coleman v. Wilson, 912 F. Supp. 1282 (1995).
Plata v. Davis/Schwarzenegger, 329 F. 3d 1101 (2003).

Notes

1. As defined by Garland (2001: 1), mass imprisonment has two characteristics. First, it is a "rate of imprisonment and a size of prison population that is markedly above the historical and comparative norm for societies of this type." And, second, it is a "social concentration of imprisonment's effects." The growth and effects of the U.S. prison boom are concentrated within economically disadvantaged groups, particularly African Americans.

2. I borrow the concept "downsizing prisons" from Jacobson (2005). I use the terms "downsizing prisons" and "downscaling prisons" synonymously.

3. The data for the California case are drawn from my larger study on the CCPOA and transformation of criminal punishment in California from the end of World War II to 2009. The study included nearly 100 interviews, direct observation, and archival analysis (for a detailed description of the study, see Page, 2011: Methodological Appendix). To bring the case up-to-date, I gathered additional data from media and government reports, CCPOA documents, informal interviews with CCPOA leaders, and observation of CCPOA events such as the union's 2010 convention. The data for the New York case are from secondary sources, media and government reports, and an in-depth interview I conducted in 2002 with a former president and vice president of the New York State Correctional Officers and Police Benevolent Society.

4. In making this argument, I am drawing on the following analytical insight articulated by Gottschalk (2006: 14): "Identifying the political factors that help us understand the construction of the carceral state beginning in the 1970s is not the same as identifying all the factors that sustain it today."

5. Several studies critique the CCPOA's political action, positions on sentencing legislation, and influence on prison operations and management (Carassco, 2006; Center for Juvenile and Criminal Justice, 2002; Petersilia, 2006). However, they do not specifically analyze efforts by the union and its partners (particularly crime victims' groups the union effectively created) to obstruct policy changes designed to loosen the state's commitment to mass imprisonment.

6. Critics of Three Strikes unsuccessfully tried to reform the law through the legislative process on seven separate occasions between 1996 and 2003 (Page, 2011: 122). As former Assemblywoman Jackie Goldberg, the sponsor of several of those reform bills, attested, the CCPOA and related groups fiercely opposed the legislative attempts. "So what has happened is you have an enormous amount of [political] intimidation. People who are in assembly races know that they're term-limited [to two terms], know that they may want to run in a senate race a few years from now, and know that certain groups like police and prison guard unions, district attorneys, and crime victims' organizations will pay for [or against] campaigns" (quoted in Domanick, 2004: 249). Reformers have turned to the ballot initiative in large part because of the limited success of implementing major penal reforms through the normal legislative process.

7. "Child Protection" was included in the initiative's title because the proposal, along with reforming Three Strikes, would increase prison sentences for offenders convicted of sexual crimes against children under the age of 14 years. The sexual crimes provision was a transparent effort to prevent accusations that the proposition was "soft on crime."

8. CUPS paid McNally Temple Associates at least $1,282,492 for commercials and other expenses (e.g., bumper stickers and "fax bursts") (California Secretary of State, 2006).

9. I did not find polling data on Proposition 5. Therefore, I do not know whether the speakers' claim was accurate or just a tactic to get CCPOA onboard.

10. Unpublished field notes, 2008 CCPOA Convention, Las Vegas, Nevada, September 18, 2008.

11. The CCPOA has influenced prison officer unions throughout the United States. CCPOA activists have helped prison officers in other states form independent unions and establish their political action operations (Page, 2011: 78–80). Also, the CCPOA is a central figure in an organization called Corrections USA, which brings together prison officers and prison officer unions from across the nation to fight prison privatization, improve the image of prison officers, and advocate for laws at both the state and federal levels that benefit rank-and-file prison staff (Corrections USA, 2011).

12. Rowe's estimate should be viewed with caution because interest groups tend to exaggerate their resources and willingness to spend those resources to enhance perceptions of their organization's power and threat to adversaries (see Page, 2011).

13. Change in CCPOA leadership also contributed to the union's slight change in direction. In 2002, Mike Jimenez replaced Don Novey as the union's president. Novey led the organization since its inception. He is strongly committed to punitive segregation and did not engage groups or ideas associated with prisoners' rights. Jimenez is much less ideologically rigid and far more open to meeting with individuals and groups traditionally deemed CCPOA enemies. Therefore, he is amenable to supporting reform as a means of advancing the interests of the CCPOA and its members (Page, 2011, Chapter 8).

14. Unpublished field notes, 2010 CCPOA Convention, Las Vegas, Nevada, November 7, 2010.

15. Unpublished field notes, 2010 CCPOA Convention, Las Vegas, Nevada, November 7, 2010.

16. Unpublished field notes, 2010 CCPOA Convention, Las Vegas, Nevada, November 7, 2010.

DISCUSSION QUESTIONS

1. In your opinion, does the California Correctional Peace Officers Association have too much power, too little power, or an appropriate amount of power within the state? Explain.

2. Page describes some of the wages, benefits, and working conditions secured by correctional officers in California. Should the prison union be criticized for pursuing the best compensation package for its members? In other words, should the union have as its goals both self-interests (employee benefits) and community interests (public safety)?

3. How does Page suggest that state and prison officials overcome union power? Do you think these efforts are likely to be successful? Explain.

SECTION VII

Organizational Socialization

How Does a Person Learn to Behave in an Organization?

Section Highlights

Overview of Organizational Socialization
    Boundaries
    Uncertainty Reduction

Content of Socialization
Anticipatory Socialization
Socialization Strategies

Police officer recruits spend substantial amounts of academy training time learning about self-defense and firearms skills—roughly 51 and 60 hours, respectively (Reaves, 2009). Rookie officers learn through a combination of this training and coursework in constitutional and criminal law that coercive force, including deadly force, is permissible only in certain situations (e.g., defense of life). They are instructed to act in accordance with legal principles and internal departmental regulations, thereby reducing the likelihood of subsequent allegations of excessive force (Hunt, 1985). After 18 months of observing officers in both the police academy and on the street, scholar Jennifer Hunt (1984, 1985) concluded that classifying force as either legal or excessive is overly simplistic. She noted instances where officers administered force in a way that, while technically in violation of legal or departmental regulations, was *defined by officers* as normal rather than excessive. Stated differently, "normal force involves coercive acts that specific 'cops' on specific occasions formulate as necessary, appropriate, reasonable, or understandable" (Hunt, 1985, p. 317). For example, officers may act more aggressively, using force beyond what is legally allowed, against certain offenders (e.g., child perpetrators) or after intense situations such as pursuits. In spite of the formal academy training defining such actions as impermissible, officers were informally taught by peers to exercise authority, demonstrate toughness, avoid hesitation, and protect other officers—qualities likely resulting in incidents of normal force (Hunt, 1985). As the example below illustrates, the reactions of a group of officers sent signals about the appropriateness of coercive force:

> One female officer, for example, learned she was the object of a brutality suit while listening to the news on television. At first, she felt so mortified that she hesitated to go to work and face her peers. In fact, male colleagues greeted her with a standing ovation. . . . In their view, any aggressive police officer regularly using normal force might eventually face a brutality suit or civilian complaint. Such accusations confirm the officer's status as a "street cop" rather than an "inside man" who doesn't engage in "real police work." (p. 319)

The larger group's conduct served to inform the specific officer and others in the department about expected or preferred workplace behaviors, even though they departed from what was taught through formal training channels.

As we transition from broader discussions of the organization as a whole to a more narrow focus on the employee within the organization, it makes sense to begin with an overview of the socialization process. When employees enter an organization for the first time, move to a different special unit or position, or rise up in the rank structure, they bring to their new role their own experiences, attitudes, and values (Jurik, 1985a; Lundman, 1980). While these individual characteristics may continue to influence behavior throughout a career (see, for example, Jurik, 1985a), the general belief is that **organizational socialization**, a process whereby a worker learns the necessary skills, appropriate values, and expected behaviors associated with a given job, works to prepare and mold employees, imparting to them the requisite knowledge to successfully complete tasks (Van Maanen & Schein, 1979). This section addresses the purposes and mechanisms/tactics of organizational socialization.

Overview of Organizational Socialization

Boundaries

The organizational socialization literature rightfully devotes the greatest attention to the socialization of "newcomers" or "rookies" coming into organizations for the first time (e.g., Louis, 1980; Mignerey, Rubin, & Gorden, 1995).[1] After all, this is the point when an individual makes the significant transition from someone outside the organization to someone inside the organization (Ashford & Nurmohamed, 2012; Feldman, 1981; Wanous, 1977). However, socialization is typically considered to be an ongoing process within organizations, though particularly salient at certain points during an individual's career (Van Maanen & Schein, 1979). Not only do individuals, upon entry, cross a boundary separating the organization from its environment, but many will cross boundaries related to the organization's structure (Ashford & Nurmohamed, 2012; Chao, O'Leary-Kelly, Wolf, Klein, & Gardner, 1994; Van Maanen, 1978). As discussed in Section II, the work of an organization is divided along three dimensions: horizontal, vertical, and spatial. As a worker crosses one of these divisions,

---

[1] Except where otherwise noted, the term *newcomer* applies to all individuals new to a role, not just those new to an organization.

additional socialization becomes necessary to acquire the knowledge and skills associated with the new position or role. For example, Van Maanen (1984) described the socialization of police sergeants as "personalized, sudden, disjointed, and difficult to categorize" (p. 162). Since sergeant candidates are arrayed on a promotional list awaiting a vacancy, appointment to the new rank comes quickly, with little notice. Training is limited, and new sergeants are left to learn from experience. Similarly, socialization for new roles will undoubtedly occur as workers move to different special units, departments, or geographic divisions within the organization.

Uncertainty Reduction

Regardless of the boundary crossed, individuals new to a role face a common source of strain: uncertainty. Saks and Ashforth (1997) write, "Newcomers, like any organizational members, are motivated to reduce their uncertainty such that the work environment becomes more predictable, understandable, and ultimately controllable" (p. 236; Falcione & Wilson, 1988; Saks & Gruman, 2012). Employees likely face both evaluative and behavioral uncertainty (Lester, 1987; see also Saks & Gruman, 2012). Evaluative uncertainty reflects the inability to accurately predict how one will perform in a new role. A new probation officer, for example, is perhaps unsure of her overall job performance as she awaits her first formal review. Behavioral uncertainty occurs when newcomers lack the skills or knowledge to perform a task and/or an understanding of the social dynamics of the workplace (Lester, 1987). A new correctional officer in the Texas prison system during the 1980s would not immediately be accepted by the "members of a primary group and social circle [of officers] that had daily face-to-face interaction . . . [and] associated with each other off the job" (Marquart, 1986, p. 361). Over time, the new officer would learn that willingness to use physical punishment within the facility was a prerequisite to group acceptance.

The socialization process, then, becomes a means to reduce uncertainty. Organizations provide newcomers with technical knowledge and information on social dynamics within the workplace that create greater levels of both evaluative and behavioral certainty. Employees also initiate uncertainty reduction efforts on their own (Mignerey et al., 1995; Morrison, 1993). Information seeking potentially mitigates feelings of uncertainty if employees gather feedback on appropriate behaviors and overall performance (the former predictive of the latter). Morrison (1993) outlines two information-seeking strategies: inquiry and monitoring. The act of inquiry involves asking someone—a supervisor, peers (experienced coworkers or fellow newcomers), and organizational outsiders—to aid in filling in gaps in newcomer knowledge. Alternatively, an individual may consult impersonal sources of information such as department procedural manuals, law books, or other written documents (Ostroff & Kozlowski, 1992). Heumann (1977) noted that, in the weeks before taking the bench for the first time, new judges spent time reviewing case law in areas where their knowledge base was weak. Reducing uncertainty via impersonal sources allows the newcomer to better manage his or her image; seeking help from others may be perceived as a sign of incompetence (Kramer, 2010; Morrison, 1993). At the same time, information gathered from written documents often lacks the richness and immediate situational applicability of information acquired from others. Monitoring is a different approach to reducing uncertainty. Newcomers observe the behavior and performance of others or, equally important, how others respond to their own behavior. A new defense attorney who regularly files pretrial motions in court will face repercussions for taking time away from prosecutors and judges; "simple harassing of the defense attorney [by prosecutors] is replaced by an unwillingness to show him any files, by a refusal to plea bargain in any cases, and by a real threat to go to trial in every case" (Heumann, 1977, p. 64). These reactions might be sufficient to weaken the defense attorney's adversarial position. The danger, of course, is that observations may be misinterpreted (e.g., believing that peer reactions represent tacit approval of all types of force in law enforcement and corrections). Nevertheless, socialization, regardless of whether the process is organization driven or individually initiated, is designed to reduce newcomer uncertainty.

Content of Socialization

What do newcomers learn about their new roles? At the most fundamental level, they must learn specific task requirements, what Chao and colleagues (1994) referred to as performance proficiency (see also Feldman, 1981; Haueter, Macan, & Winter, 2003; Ostroff & Kozlowski, 1992). This includes responsibilities and an "understanding [of] task duties, assignments, priorities, how to use equipment, how to handle routine problems and so forth" (Ostroff & Kozlowski, 1992, p. 852). Prison chaplains, for example, were undoubtedly familiar with the spiritual aspects of their work prior to beginning work in correctional facilities but had to learn rules related to institutional security (Hicks, 2008). Issues related to pens and pencils (for underlining religious passages) and the color of rosary beads (possible gang indicators) posed security threats. Elsewhere, police recruits trained through the Phoenix Regional Police Training Academy were exposed to a curriculum that, in the mid-1990s, increasingly integrated the principles of community and problem-oriented policing (Haarr, 2001). Research shows that, without communicating the meaning of and expectations associated with reforms such as community policing, officer support is likely to be lacking (Sadd & Grinc, 1993).

Individuals are also socialized about the organization itself, including its history, mission, overall structure, power/authority relationships, and policies and procedures (Chao et al., 1994; Haueter et al., 2003). Police academy recruits learned the importance of rank even if it meant showing deference to personnel from another agency:

> For example, the academy's class coordinator was a sergeant from a local sheriff's office. Although he was "in charge" of the class, he showed the respect and deference to the rank of the particular instructor of any of the curriculum units no matter the agency affiliation of the instructor. A captain coming from a local municipal police department to teach outranked him, and the sergeant respected that difference. "Captain" would be the noun of address. (Chappell & Lanza-Kaduce, 2010, p. 195)

Organizational level understanding also involves becoming accustomed to the everyday language or jargon used to facilitate communication inside an agency. In human service fields such as criminal justice, understanding a task requires becoming familiar with frequently encountered clientele or citizens (Haueter et al., 2003). Police recruits are told that "there's a bad guy on every call" and come to label offenders as "dirt bags" or "perps" (Chappell & Lanza-Kaduce, 2010, p. 201). Similarly, newcomers learn the meaning of widely used acronyms (e.g., SARA = Scanning, Analysis, Response, Assessment) and become accustomed to communicating in specific ways (e.g., using a phonetic alphabet). Martin (1992) suggested that many of these elements are indicative of an organization's culture, a set of beliefs, values, and behavioral guides shared by an organization's members (see also Denison, 1996; Schein, 2005). That is, culture becomes a "tool kit" used to guide, along with situational factors, individual action (Swidler, 1986, p. 277; see also Schein, 2005). To illustrate, consider local courts. They are often described as communities characterized by their own legal cultures (Church, 1985; Eisenstein, Flemming, & Nardulli, 1988; Ulmer, 1995). In this context, culture provides judges, prosecutors, and defense attorneys with a set of agreed-on values and norms for disposing of criminal cases (Church, 1985; Ulmer, 1995). If workgroup members share a common understanding about the importance of case disposition time, they will be more apt to rely on informal plea arrangements rather than trials to handle caseloads (Church, 1985; Eisenstein & Jacob, 1991).

While some organizations are viewed as having a single unified organizational culture, others comprise many different subcultures operating within different subpopulations (Martin, 1992). As such, newcomers must be socialized into their immediate workgroups (e.g., patrol), learning values, expectations, relationships, and desirable behaviors. Reuss-Ianni (1983) observed distinct subcultural values across patrol and managerial groups within a police department. Separate cultures may also form along demographic lines. Haarr (1997) observed racial and gender segmentation within interactions among police officers in the department; white officers tended to interact with one another on patrol (e.g., during meals, informal conversations) and sat together during roll call. Cultures and subcultures generally develop as individuals collectively cope with the problems they confront on a regular basis (Paoline, 2003; Schein, 2005). Interaction patterns reflect perceptions of intergroup distrust, suspicion, and hostility (Haarr, 1997). Likewise, officers in both law enforcement and correctional environments value the use of coercion and "maintaining the edge" as a way to cope with threats of danger in the workplace (Paoline, 2003, p. 202).

Task, organization, and group-related socialization, including the transmission of culture, is a temporal process, starting before an individual crosses an organizational boundary (e.g., before entering an organization, receiving a promotion, etc.) and proceeding to and beyond the point where he or she fully occupies the new role.[2] Most commonly, socialization is viewed as occurring across discrete but nevertheless connected stages: anticipatory, encounter, and metamorphosis (Falcione & Wilson, 1988; Feldman, 1981; Kramer, 2010; Porter, Lawler, & Hackman, 1975).[3] Organizational socialization starts with **anticipatory socialization**, the learning and preparation that occur prior to assuming a new role in an organization. Labeled the prearrival stage by some (see Porter et al., 1975), the anticipatory socialization stage captures the formation of role expectations and job-related values not only in the period immediately before a boundary crossing but also throughout an individual's life. The **encounter** stage begins once an individual actually enters an organization. Some scholars suggest that the encounter phase is a limited period, perhaps lasting only 10 months or less (see Louis, 1980). Others suggest that the encounter stage may extend for longer periods (Jablin, 2001). The point is that this stage covers the initial socialization experiences that occur when a new role is assumed (see discussion of socialization strategies below). The final stage in the socialization process, referred to as **metamorphosis**, represents the individual's transition to a full-fledged organization member (Kramer, 2010). According to Falcione

---

[2]In some frameworks, the departure or exit from a role is also considered (Jablin, 2001).

[3]Some authors describe socialization as consisting of anticipatory, formal, and informal stages (Bennett, 1984; Stohr & Collins, 2009; Stojkovic, Kalinich, & Klofas, 2012). This framework lacks a temporal dimension. For example, individuals may learn about an organization during the anticipatory period (prior to entering) through both formal mechanisms such as official recruiting pamphlets and recruiter pitches, or through informal channels such as family members and friends. Likewise, at the point of entry, a newcomer receives both formal messages (e.g., classroom courses) and informal messages (e.g., war stories and gossip). As such, the distinction between informal and formal is viewed in this section as related to socialization strategies (see Van Maanen & Schein, 1979) rather than temporal stages in the overall process.

and Wilson (1988), this is the period when the individual "settles in" (p. 154). Haarr (2001), for example, observed that police officers' attitudes toward community and problem-oriented policing did not change significantly from the end of field training to the end of their first year on the job.

Anticipatory Socialization

A tremendous amount of socialization occurs before an individual ever enters an organization or a new role within an organization. Over time, people develop preferences, assumptions, and decisions steering them toward particular career fields, a process referred to as occupational choice (Jablin, 2001). The decision to follow a specific career path evolves over a considerable period of time and is made at a subconscious level; "most individuals cannot pinpoint the day that they decided to pursue a certain occupation" (Kramer, 2010, p. 47; Wanous, 1977). Nevertheless, a variety of forces, including family, friends, educational and prior job experiences, and the media, shape individual occupational choices (Jablin, 2001; Kramer, 2010). Consider childhood experiences. Martin (1980) argued that the anticipatory socialization process for female police officers is different than for male police officers. As children, males are more likely to have played "cops and robbers" and thought of policing as a career; consequently, these early experiences likely affected subsequent occupational choices. In another study of career choice in law enforcement, Kaminski (1993) examined interest in police work among a sample of Albany (NY) high school seniors; respondents were asked to indicate whether they would accept a job from the local police department upon graduation if it were offered. Among the significant predictors of job acceptance was parental support. Students were more likely to indicate accepting the job if they believed that their parents would support such a decision and, conversely, turn down the job if parents would disapprove. In this example, the students are clearly influenced by parental opinions, especially their reservations about the dangers of the job (Kaminski, 1993). The media, both news and popular, affect choices as well. The success of television programs such as *CSI* stimulated interest in the criminal investigation field. From the weekly, hour-long programs, viewers learn that the crime scene technician's job is "glamorous and exciting, never boring" (VanLaerhoven & Anderson, 2009, p. 31). The law enforcement field, more generally, is portrayed favorably in the popular media, with television programs and movies often depicting competent officers and detectives capable of using individual skills and judgment to resolve cases. In contrast, images of correctional officers in the mass media are more often less than favorable. Prison movies and television shows such as the *Shawshank Redemption, Oz,* and *Prison Break* paint officers as brutal, corrupt, or crazy (Gutterman, 2002). As Gutterman points out, "*Cool Hand Luke* symbolizes the central theme encountered in prison movies: the brutality of a penal system that encourages sympathy for the underdog convict" (p. 1550). These images contribute to the development of expectations about specific occupations.

While the occupational choice decision evolves over a considerable period of time, organizational choice moves much more quickly (Wanous, 1977). Individuals are socialized as they locate an organization believed to fit their skill set, training, and interests (Jablin, 2001; Kramer, 2010). A recent college graduate interested in police work may have job options at the municipal, county, state, or federal level. She must choose the agency to enter, presumably using knowledge gleaned about specific organizations. The same sources that influenced occupational choice can affect organizational choice, but organizations play a much more active role in the latter. For example, more than 75% of police agencies reported recruiting through career fairs, the Internet, newspapers, community organizations, or college outreach initiatives (Wilson, Rostker, & Fan, 2010). Even then, advertising matters less than more practical considerations such as compensation and work variables such as crime rates, the latter appealing "to candidates with a 'taste' for police work by providing more adventurous or non-routine work opportunities" (p. xvii).

The anticipatory socialization stage is successful to the extent that it produces a realistic view of the organization and the job itself (Feldman, 1976, 1981). Police and correctional officers attracted by the (perceived) excitement of the work may be disappointed by periods of monotonous activity (Farkas & Manning, 1997; Ford, 2003). Aspiring crime scene investigators might be even more surprised to learn that their fictional counterparts are actually combinations of multiple roles (e.g., detective, forensic scientist) in a single position (VanLaerhoven & Anderson, 2009). Successful anticipatory socialization means understanding reality prior to organizational entry or boundary crossings. If misguided perceptions persist, negative consequences, up to and including early organizational departure, may result. Beyond realistic expectations, anticipatory socialization should also facilitate appropriate occupational and organizational choices. That is, individual skills, needs, and values should match organizational demands, needs, and values. This is, unfortunately, not always the case. Jurik, Halemba, Musheno, and Boyle (1987) found that college-educated correctional officers were less satisfied with their jobs than others, due in part to the controlling work environment. More-educated officers sought autonomy but were afforded few opportunities to influence their work or organizational decisions.

Socialization Strategies

At this point, organizations use a variety of strategies to socialize new members as well as employees crossing organizational boundaries. Saks and Gruman (2012) defined these techniques as "organization-initiated activities, programs, events, and experiences that are specifically designed to facilitate newcomers' learning, adjustment, and socialization into a job, role, work group, and organization so that they can become effective members of the organization" (pp. 28–29). The organizational behavior literature provides useful frameworks for organizing and understanding these socialization efforts. John Van Maanen and Edgar Schein (1979; see also Van Maanen, 1978) situated tactics along six dimensions based on the level of structure offered by the socialization experiences (Saks & Gruman, 2012).

1. *Collective vs. individual socialization.* In the case of **collective socialization**, a group of individuals transitioning together (e.g., entering an organization, moving up the hierarchy, etc.) are socialized in unison. Police and correctional officer recruits train in groups at their respective academies, and future prosecutors, defense attorneys, and judges are socialized within entering law school cohorts. Collective socialization tactics are commonly used with new organizational members but are also evident in the socialization and training of in-service workers. Police officers and supervisors from all across the country routinely attend sessions offered by the FBI National Academy, Northwestern University's Center for Public Safety, and other collective training programs (Baro & Burlingame, 1999). Collective socialization is said to produce an "'in the same boat' consciousness" among members who experience the same highs and deal with the same problems associated with their new role (Van Maanen & Schein, 1979). Median class sizes for law enforcement training academies typically range from 14 to 48 officers (Reaves, 2009). Recruit values tend to become more homogenous during this training but, upon graduation, start to diverge (Bennett, 1984). At this point, **individual socialization** strategies replace collective socialization strategies as graduates link up with field-training officers for

a period of more personalized training. Post-academy, the police department socializes "recruits singly and in isolation from one another through a more or less unique set of experiences" (Van Maanen & Schein, 1979, p. 233). New sergeants are more likely to experience individual rather than collective socialization as well. Even if multiple officers are promoted, Van Maanen (1984) points out that their early experiences are likely to be unique, as they are given different and geographically dispersed job assignments. As a consequence, individual socialization strategies are more likely to generate diverse views and behaviors rather than a uniform or collective set of beliefs.

2. *Formal vs. informal socialization.* **Formal socialization** occurs when individuals new to the organization, position, or rank are socialized apart from those already occupying those roles. Van Maanen and Schein (1979) state that "the newcomer is more or less segregated from regular organizational members while put through a set of experiences tailored explicitly for the newcomer" (p. 236). A police academy trains recruits in operations, weapons and self-defense, the substantive and procedural criminal law, and other topics through classroom and practical exercises, not by performing the same tasks alongside in-service law enforcement officers (Reaves, 2009). The separation between new and existing members is further reinforced by visible differences in clothing (Van Maanen & Schein, 1979). For example, Conti (2009) studied one academy where participants were first required to wear black pants and white shirts; only later were they issued traditional police dress, though, since training was still incomplete, the uniforms lacked badges and patches. The formal training regimen clearly demarcated the boundary between newcomer (i.e., rookie) and officer. Jacobs and Grear (1977) reported how differences in uniform created problems for new correctional officers in the Stateville Correctional Center in Illinois. Due to resource needs, recruits were often asked to serve as regular guards, but given their distinctive uniforms that clearly identified them as "guard fish" (i.e., newcomers), they were afforded less respect by peers and inmates. In contrast, defense attorneys entering the bar or a public defender's office generally lack formal socialization programs or visible identifiers indicative of newcomer status; instead, they learn via **informal socialization**. One defense attorney in Milton Heumann's (1977) volume on the courtroom workgroup and plea bargaining described how he learned to handle criminal cases:

> I didn't, and I found when I first started practice . . . I didn't know how to handle it. I'd go over and watch, or I'd go over and ask some other lawyer and say: "What do you do with this? It's a breach of peace." And you go up and talk to a prosecutor. You didn't know how to handle it, but what I used to do—I had time—I used to go in and sit and watch other lawyers practicing . . . and how they worked it. You'd watch their results. (p. 54)

Unlike police recruits, lawyers learned through experience, performing the same tasks as more seasoned role occupants. While formal socialization tactics might be more effective in providing individuals with organizationally supported knowledge (e.g., proper behaviors and attitudes), many believe that the information is disconnected from the realities of the job (Van Maanen & Schein, 1979). Where correctional officers are trained in an academy prior to entering prisons or jails, individuals learn about rules, procedures, and control techniques. The academy experience, however, is much different from handling actual inmates within an institution (Regoli, Poole, & Schrink, 1979). Likewise, new prosecutors may learn about trial work via a law school's curriculum but are unprepared for the prevalence of plea bargaining within the court system (Heumann, 1977). Individual or on-the-job tactics are presumed to be much more efficient in building the skills necessary for the job.

3. *Sequential vs. random socialization.* When organizations employ **sequential socialization** tactics, individuals must complete predetermined and ordered stages to be considered fully prepared for their new role (Van Maanen, 1978). Deputy sheriffs are often tasked with working in the county jail before assignment to law enforcement duties, even if the latter is the newcomer's primary area of interest (Poole & Pogrebin, 1988). New police officers progress through the academy first, followed by field training with a more experienced officer. Additionally, the typical police officer is required to continue training—completing, on average, 35 hours per year of continuing education (Reaves, 2010). Some correctional agencies follow this model—training precedes placement. In other situations, a correctional officer might actually work in a facility prior to formal academy training (Jurik, 1985b). Ohio's Corrections Training Academy, for example, requires personnel to first undergo 40 hours of "orientation training" on the job before proceeding to classroom and hands-on training (Ohio Department of Rehabilitation and Correction, 2013). Other experiences are classified as **random socialization** due to the fact that there is only a single stage to complete or the sequence of stages is ill defined. Van Maanen's (1984) description of police sergeants provides a useful illustration of the more random, less structured approach. Some sergeants rose directly from lower positions after spending their time exclusively within the patrol division, while others first rotated across different department divisions to garner experience and connections. The latter approach was advantageous in securing promotion, but even then, the organization failed to provide any explicit guidance on divisions to choose or the time to spend in each. The socialization process was random or nonsequential (Van Maanen, 1978). Sequential socialization tactics, unlike random tactics, can work in an iterative fashion, where each stage builds on the last. A police officer first learns material in the classroom and through practical exercises before proceeding to the streets and formal application of academy knowledge. The officer then works under the eyes of a field-training officer before embarking on his or her own. Absent efforts to integrate the stages, however, both sequential and random socialization pose risks if conflict is present across the stages (Van Maanen & Schein, 1979). Police academy graduates, for example, are often told by field-training officers to forget everything taught in the academy (Ford, 2003). As Van Maanen (1973) observed, "During the protracted hours on patrol with his FTO [field-training officer], the recruit is instructed as to the real nature of police work" (p. 412). Clearly, each of the sequential stages led to the inconsistent socialization of new officers.

4. *Fixed vs. variable socialization.* **Fixed socialization** tactics are employed if organizations delineate the amount of time necessary to complete a boundary crossing. On average, a new police officer must complete 613 hours of academy training, 309 hours of field training, and a probationary period before becoming a full-fledged member of a police department (Reaves, 2010; see Table 7.1). Faculty members at universities serve a fixed period prior to tenure, usually five or six years. Law school training lasts three years and a defined number of credit hours. According to Ronald Kessler (2010), special agents in both the Secret Service and, to a lesser extent, the FBI can expect to transfer across geographic divisions (spatial complexity) at relatively fixed intervals during their careers:

> The FBI has taken steps to retain agents, while the Secret Service has not. In contrast to the Secret Service, after three years with the bureau, unless he or she chooses to go into management, an FBI agent can stay in the same city for the rest of his or her career. An agent going into management can remain in the same city for five years. The Secret Service, on the other hand, typically transfers agents three to four times during a twenty-five-year career. An agent who enters management may move five to six times. The rationale is that agents need to acquire experience in different offices. (p. 120)

As the passage indicates, the transfers represent a sequential socialization strategy (see earlier discussion), but the time period in each field office is largely known. Where future job openings are predictable, fixed socialization strategies make sense. It is easier to specify ahead of time a socialization timetable for organizational entry if the number of recruits matches the number of openings. In situations where the number of individuals awaiting a boundary crossing (e.g., promotion) exceeds the number of positions available, organizations may adopt **variable socialization** tactics. In these instances, an individual is generally unaware how long it will take to complete the socialization process or transition. In Van Maanen's (1984) study of police sergeants, officers were required to wait a 3-year period before becoming eligible for promotion, but, on average, 12 years passed before appointment to sergeant. Variable strategies are necessary given limitations in the number of positions but undoubtedly produce anxiety as individuals wait for word of successful boundary crossings (Van Maanen & Schein, 1979). Moreover, those who continually wait for their chance at promotion, appointment to a special unit, or some other opportunity may suffer from low morale (Van Maanen, 1978).

5. *Serial vs. disjunctive socialization.* **Serial socialization** strategies rely on members already in a given role (e.g., within the organization, in a unit, in a management role) to socialize those preparing to make the transition (Van Maanen & Schein, 1979). Police officers learn from police educators and field-training officers who already are part of police organizations. Heumann (1977) reported that, during their first two weeks on the job, new prosecutors shadowed and observed more experienced prosecutors who could "readily explain or justify his actions, and the newcomer can ask any and all relevant questions" (p. 93). Because existing organizational or division members are socializing new

Table 7.1 Training Requirements for New Officer Recruits in Local Police Departments, by Size of Population Served, 2007

	Average Number of Hours Required		
	Total	Academy	Field
All sizes	922	613	309
1,000,000 or more	1,700	1,033	667
500,000 to 999,999	1,783	1,063	720
250,000 to 499,999	1,542	906	636
100,000 to 249,999	1,463	809	654
50,000 to 99,999	1,341	731	610
25,000 to 49,999	1,241	698	543
10,000 to 24,999	1,101	666	434
2,500 to 9,999	979	634	345
Under 2,500	691	538	153

Source: Reaves (2010); U.S. Department of Justice, Bureau of Justice Statistics.

ones, similar outlooks, values, and behaviors are passed from one group to the next; consequently, the organizational practices are perpetuated and difficult to change (Van Maanen, 1978). In these situations, **disjunctive socialization** tactics may be required, where nonmembers contribute to organizational socialization. For example, to facilitate the adoption of community policing, it may be worthwhile to bring in outside consultants to train a department's staff (Stojkovic et al., 2012). Disjunctive socialization also occurs when organizational role models are unavailable (Van Maanen & Schein, 1979). For instance, even though in-service officers socialize new recruits in policing and corrections, female recruits may not find enough experienced female officers to serve as role models in organizations. This problem is especially pronounced in periods where certain groups (e.g., women, minorities) are viewed as tokens within organizations (Jurik, 1985b).

    6. *Investiture vs. divestiture strategies.* **Investiture socialization** strategies recognize the value of what individuals bring to their new roles in organizations. Law school graduates spend three years learning about all realms of law and procedure. Prosecutor and public defender offices are uninterested in removing or replacing this knowledge. Indeed, a law school education is likely the reason why formal socialization strategies (see earlier discussion) are lacking in the legal profession. New members enter with a considerable amount of training intact. **Divestiture socialization** strategies, in contrast, remove ("deny and strip away") certain characteristics of an individual before an organizational boundary is crossed (Van Maanen & Schein, 1979, p. 250; see also Mignerey, Rubin, & Gordon, 1995). Conti's (2009) study of a police academy illustrated some of these tactics. Recruits were forced to perform push-ups if observed demonstrating the "civilian characteristics of weak upper body strength" (p. 421). All trainees were required to stand at attention for all non-recruits, demonstrating their subordinate status while in the academy. They were routinely treated as if they were in boot camp, yelled at for their behavior and appearance. Van Maanen and Schein (1979) argue that any divestiture tactic "serves to commit and bind the person to the organization and is typically premised upon a strong desire on the part of the recruit to become an accepted member of the organization" (p. 251). In some respects, the tactics become a rite of passage for the new recruit to align himself or herself with the new organization (Van Maanen, 1973).

    These six dimensions were offered not only to describe how socialization is accomplished but also to explain how people respond to the process (Van Maanen & Schein, 1979). Depending on the combination of tactics used, individuals may accept and perform their new roles as they have always been performed or they may decide to innovate, changing how work is ordinarily accomplished. As shown in Figure 7.1, Jones (1986) further classified the six socialization dimensions into three broad categories: the context or format in which socialization is delivered, the content of socialization (e.g., how long and in what order material is delivered), and the interpersonal aspects of socialization. Workers are more likely to accept the status quo when the six institutionalized tactics—collective, formal, sequential, fixed, serial, and investiture—are used (Jones, 1986, Saks & Gruman, 2012; see Figure 7.1). The organization is able to officially communicate expectations (formal) and produce standardized ways of completing the work (collective). Knowledge about the role is communicated across stages, each perhaps building on the previous one (sequential). An employee, aware of the timetable for forthcoming boundary crossings, is likely to comply with expectations rather than risk jeopardizing opportunities by rocking the boat (Jones, 1986). Serial tactics ensure that existing operations continue as new members enter and old members exit the organization. Finally, individuals will tend to see their role from a single perspective—their own—since it was supported by the organization; innovation is therefore unlikely (investiture).

Figure 7.1 A Classification of Socialization Tactics

Tactics concerned mainly with:	Institutionalized	Individualized
CONTEXT	Collective	Individual
	Formal	Informal
CONTENT	Sequential	Random
	Fixed	Variable
SOCIAL ASPECTS	Serial	Disjunctive
	Investiture	Divestiture

Source: Jones (1986).

Individualized tactics promote innovation and dissimilarity in how workers handle their roles (Jones, 1986; Van Maanen, 1978). They are socialized individually and through hands-on experience (informal) leading to differential responses. Individuals may also innovate when they lack a clear understanding of how socialization stages fit together (random) or timelines for completion (variable). "In organizations in which newcomers' abilities to deal competently with uncertain situations govern upward mobility," innovative responses might expedite the promotion process (Jones, 1986, p. 265). Socialization by outsiders (disjunctive) further disrupts the status quo, as do divestiture tactics. In the latter case, workers may ultimately question the organization's perspective if it clashes with their own. Regardless of the strategies used, at this stage individuals should more fully understand their roles and responsibilities within the organization, develop the technical skills to complete work, begin integrating into the organization's social structure, and effectively balance work and personal demands (Feldman, 1981).

If successful, socialization enables the newcomer to master the work, successfully balance the demands of the role, and adjust to the organization's culture and social structure (Feldman, 1981). As this discussion illustrates, socialization is of critical importance for organizations and shapes the discussion to follow. Inability to perform tasks negatively affects motivation and requires a different leadership approach. Poor adjustment and role difficulties are sources of organizational stress. In contrast, complete and successful socialization should lead to long-term benefits such as improved job satisfaction, heightened motivation, and greater commitment to the job (Feldman, 1981).

KEY TERMS

anticipatory socialization	disjunctive socialization	fixed socialization
collective socialization	divestiture socialization	formal socialization
culture	encounter	individual socialization

informal socialization
investiture socialization
metamorphosis
organizational socialization
random socialization
sequential socialization
serial socialization
variable socialization

DISCUSSION QUESTIONS

1. How does a college education in criminology or criminal justice fit into the anticipatory socialization process? Does it facilitate the development of more realistic expectations of the criminal justice field, or does it work to heighten unrealistic expectations? Explain.

2. Some new correctional officers are placed inside correctional facilities prior to attending a training academy, while others first receive formal collective training. In your opinion, which is a more beneficial socialization strategy for the individual and the organization?

3. Table 7.1 illustrates a positive relationship between jurisdiction size and training hours required of new recruits. Stated differently, police departments in smaller jurisdictions use formal socialization strategies (academy and field training) that, while fixed, are shorter in duration. Why do you suppose training hours are so dramatically different across agencies serving different population sizes?

WEB RESOURCES

Federal Law Enforcement Training Centers:
http://www.fletc.gov

John Jay College of Criminal Justice Center on Media, Crime, and Justice:
http://www.jjay.cuny.edu/centers/media_crime_justice/2734.htm

Office of Community Oriented Police Services Training:
http://www.cops.usdoj.gov/Default.asp?Item=1974

READING

Reading 12

As this section illustrates, occupational socialization and uncertainty reduction are inextricably related. Telling war stories is one mechanism for reducing uncertainty and an important part of the socialization of police officer recruits. In fact, of the 89 officers interviewed from multiple departments in a single metropolitan county, only two reported being unaffected by the war stories told during their academy training. Altogether, the officers recalled and described 269 separate stories that were subsequently analyzed for content. The majority of the stories described useful skills necessary for officers out on the street (e.g., how to obtain consent to search persons or vehicles). A large proportion of stories also described the dangers or unpredictability of police work. Other topics were mentioned much less frequently. Stories generally supported police subcultural values but were largely neutral when it came to ethics, the overall police organization, and legal restrictions. That said, some storytellers did take positions, either in support of or opposition to these issues. For example, one officer described the importance of treating all citizens equally by recounting how a minority citizen provided the officer with assistance in a time of need (a story in support of ethical values). In contrast, other officers told stories of lying in court (a story in opposition to legal values).

SAYING ONE THING, MEANING ANOTHER

The Role of Parables in Police Training

Robert E. Ford

It has been long held that police officers espouse a set of informal values and attitudes. These informal attitudes and values have been so persistent and so universal that one prominent researcher has labeled them "the working personality of police" (Skolnick, 1993, p. 49). A number of researchers have visited police culture and have reached conclusions similar to Skolnick's (e.g., Crank, 1998; Niederhoffer, 1967; Senna & Siegel, 1987; Westley, 1970; Wilson, 1968).

Researcher interest in police culture has been piqued by the twin realizations that police work is highly discretionary and that discretion deployment is often unrelated to law or formal organizational mandates (see Riksheim & Chermack, 1993; Sherman, 1980). Persistent patterns of police behavior have been chronicled that violate organizational policies, the canons of ethics, and the law (Bahn, 1975). The persistence of questionable behavioral patterns has been linked frequently to police culture (Brooks, 1989).

Informal values within an occupation can arise in two ways. First, those possessing such values bring them to the occupation (Crank & Caldero, 2000). Alternately, these value systems can be learned on the job. Research suggests that values and attitudes defining the working personality of police are learned on the job (Lundman, 1980; Niederhoffer, 1967; Van Maanen, 1973).

Source: Ford, R. E. (2003). Saying one thing, meaning another: The role of parables in police training. *Police Quarterly,* 6(1), 84–110.

Research has failed to identify police recruit characteristics that differ significantly from the general population before hire (Carpenter & Raza, 1987; Kennedy & Homant, 1981; Sayles & Albritton, 1999).[1] The larger proportion of police applicants come to policing from successful working-class families. Their values appear roughly similar to those of their working-class peers (Burbeck & Furnham, 1985).

> Police applicants tend to see police work as an adventure, as a chance to work outdoors without being cooped up in an office, as a chance to do work that is important for the good of society, and not as a chance to be the toughest guy on the block. (Sherman, 1999, p. 302)

Police recruits come to the profession with high ideals and positive ethical standards (McNamara, 1967).

This means that candidates enter the field with positive values, a notion of helping people and making a difference (Bayley & Mendelson, 1969; Carpenter & Raza, 1987; Lefkowitz, 1975). Yet within a short period of exposure to the occupation, attitudes and values undergo significant change and soon differ from general population attitudes (Crank, 1998; Lundman, 1980; Reuss-Ianni, 1984). Recruits enter high-minded and service oriented. They may be at their ethical zenith.

As early as the police academy, subtle shifts in values and attitudes with ethical implications can be identified (Bennett, 1984). A number of authors, particularly Sherman (1980), Van Maanen (1973), Lundman (1980), and McNulty (1994), have suggested that socialization into police culture begins soon after a recruit's initial entry into the police academy. This anticipatory socialization sets the stage for the crucial transfer of values and attitudes that occurs during the rookie year.

Informal socialization continues and intensifies during the practical training regimen and field training (Gaines, Kappler, & Vaughn, 1997). In most agencies, new recruits leaving the academy are placed in a field training officer (FTO) program. This field training typically extends 14 to 16 weeks. By the end of field training, the adoption of a set of values and attitudes distinct from the value set that brought them to the profession is well under way (Gaines et al., 1997).

A number of authors have concluded that by the end of the rookie year, many subcultural attitudes and values have been fixed. What are the mechanisms of transmission? How are these values being transmitted, often even before officers go on the street? This article looks at one possible vehicle of cultural transmission—"war stories."

Researchers (Bahn, 1984; Reuss-Ianni, 1984; Sherman, 1999; Van Maanen, 1973) have spoken of the role of war stories in this socialization process. Authors have mentioned war stories as a vehicle of cultural transmission. Although fewer researchers have addressed or analyzed this socialization mechanism, there is a small but quality literature emerging (see Buerger, 1998; Crank, 1998; McNulty, 1994; Shearing & Ericson, 1991).[2]

War stories are defined as a recounting of idealized events, entertaining humor, or police-related social commentary. They carry a message celebrating police values or techniques. They are aptly named war stories because they often deal with the physical side of policing. War stories deal with the heroic, the extreme, and the cynically humorous. They paint a picture of policing that is often at odds with daily tedium and frequently contradict official ways. War stories, however, provide more than just entertaining fare.

"Like biblical parables and legends police stories provide direction for being a police officer, guidance as to how officers should experience the world if they are to act as police officers within it" (Shearing & Ericson, 1991, p. 491). Shearing and Ericson (1991) suggested that war stories provide for officers a "library of gambits," a "vocabulary of precedents," and "a worldview that provides a way of seeing and experiencing a world" (p. 492). War stories, rather than setting rules or recipes for police street behaviors, provide informative or representative anecdotes that select or highlight reality (p. 489). War stories present a general sense of a range of behaviors appropriate to certain classes of situations.

In much the same vein, McNulty (1994) saw stories as a vehicle to pass on and generate "commonsense knowledge" to the new officer. McNulty described police academy staff as incorporating commonsense assumptions of working police officers into many of their presentations and employing interactive scenarios, jokes, and war stories to reinforce these themes (p. 283). War stories are, for police, a medium to transfer and maintain their commonsense understanding of their world.

This article will further explore the role that war stories play. It also details conditions necessary for war stories to be accepted. Finally, content analysis provides an opportunity to decipher messages in war stories.

Value Shifts

Do the attitude and value shifts rookies experience during academy and field training signal real change, or do they involve simply fine-tuning of previously held propolice values? Changes in crucial attitudes and values—related to topics as cynicism, "testilying," attitudes toward the public, and use of force—suggest that changes involve altering values rather than fine-tuning existing beliefs (Crank, 1998; Lundman, 1980; Reuss-Ianni, 1984).

Altering values is a two-step process. Similar to the process discussed by Matza (1964) of the neutralization of societal values among gang youth and later applied to police by Kappeler, Studer, & Alpert (1994), the existing values must be neutralized before new values are inculcated. War stories may play as much a part in discrediting values rookies bring to policing as they do in socializing the recruit to police subcultural values.

Four factors appear to be involved in this value change. First, procedures at the academy may provide an atmosphere conducive to value neutralization and the adoption of new values (Berg, 1990). The academy, Berg (1990) argued, is structured in such a way as to limit individual initiative, to increase uncertainty and insecurity in the individual recruit, and to open students to peer pressure and group "norming." Van Maanen (1973) argued that the paramilitary nature of the academy leads recruits to understand that they only receive notice when they make a mistake, and thus, they learn to maintain a low profile. The limitation of individual initiative and the paramilitary structure contribute to recruit uncertainty and insecurity. This leaves recruits open to new interpretations.

Second, officers come to the profession with conceptions about the everyday nature of policing. Born of movies and media, these views are romanticized. Gleaned from the epic stories recounted in police lore, media tales take rare events and magnify and describe heroic stories as the everyday grist of police work. As early as the first few weeks of the police academy, recruits sense that what they will be doing is a far cry from the media's promise. Not only are materials studied at odds, the stories told by instructors alert young officers that "real policing is not Hollywood." Rather than heroic sagas, the recruit confronts tales of the mean streets. The recruit hears of danger, betrayal, and anger. The recruit gains a glimpse of an unforgiving bureaucracy. Field officer training further reinforces this perception of the real world (Sherman, 1999).

Third, policing remains a craft, not a profession (Greene & Klockars, 1991). By observing colleagues handle events, police skills are learned. The academy spends a large proportion of its resources in training officers in critical but rarely used skills, for example, firearms or pursuit driving. Essential interaction skills, such as how to approach and convince suspects to comply, receive scant academy treatment.[3]

Topics covering interpersonal relations and communication are treated as filler, taught by academics or social workers. Instructors, aware that officers will leave the academy poorly prepared to confront the highly interactive world that waits, frequently admonish student officers, "You'll have to learn it all over again on the street." Rookies receiving the message that what they are learning in the academy is irrelevant are further disquieted.

Arriving on the street, the just-trained officer's disquiet will intensify. Realizing during the first few interactions on the street how ill prepared they are, new officers remember their instructor's admonition, "Once you get on the street, you will need to forget everything you learned at the academy." With the perception of the irrelevance of formal training, informal training takes over during the first several weeks of field training.

Fourth, those teaching at the police academy are practitioners or retired officers. They bring their profession-born cynicism and hostility to the classroom. The ideals that students bring to the academy are challenged by the cynicism of the instructors. Instructor cynicism also impacts the state-imposed curriculum. Unwilling to directly contradict the curriculum and imperil their job, instructors subtly undermine formal curriculum, often unconsciously, through reminiscences called war stories (Reuss-Ianni, 1984). Buerger (1998) labels war stories that subtly contradict the instructional message "black swans" (p. 43). Experiencing contradictory messages, officers may become cynical and defensive (Crank, 1998; Niederhoffer, 1967).

Method

A metropolitan county of 600,000 in a southeastern state served as the research site. Interviews were conducted with a convenience sample of 89 officers.[4] Respondents were representative of the mix of area agencies: 26% were from small municipal agencies, 23% were from large municipal police departments, 26% were from the sheriff's department, and 18% were state highway patrol officers. The age of officers interviewed ranged from 22 to 57 years, with a median age of 33. Female officers made up 8% of those interviewed.

Respondents attended either the local regional police academy (82%) or the state's highway patrol academy (18%). The regional academy, administered by a community college, is staffed with part-time current officers and retired police officers working full time. The state highway patrol academy, attended by all highway patrol officers, is a centralized residential academy. The regional police academy has a more relaxed and academic character, whereas the state highway patrol academy is more disciplined and militaristic. Analysis of war stories revealed no significant differences between the two academies in content of war stories.[5]

A five-page interview instrument recorded war stories. The interview also identified respondents' reaction to a specific war story; perceptions of war stories; and respondent demographics of age, gender, rank, experience, and academy attended. The interviews identified 269 separate war stories. The number of war stories recounted by individual officers ranged from a 0 to 5. The modal number of stories was 4, with a median of 3. Whereas 3 older interviewees did not remember any war story content from their youth, they did recall war stories being told. All but 2 officers noted that war stories did impact their values and attitudes.

The unit of analysis was set as the individual war story. A war story is a narrative presented to an academy class or during field training that describes a particular incident or circumstance. The war story's purpose is to provide concrete meaning. Each of the 269 war stories was content-analyzed and categorized. War stories were analyzed for manifest and latent content. Content analysis is particularly suited to this research question because a majority of stories carried multiple messages, according to whether the manifest or latent content was coded. For example, the story below tells the activities the officer needs to engage in to stay out of trouble.

> When you get out on the street, check what you need to do. When I was a rookie to stay out of trouble, you had to write reports and check businesses. The Captain was out to make examples. You know that the brass get their jollies busting officers. You had to check every closed business early every morning, making sure you shook each back door knob. One of the Captain's flunkies would put a red slip on the doorknob and if it was there in the morning you were in trouble. The other thing was you had to write at least 3 reports each night or they would check on you. It did not matter much what you wrote, they did not read them, they just counted them. That Captain is still there. Remember just like you catch criminals they catch you. (Instructor, Patrol Techniques, War Story [WS] 203)

This story provides specific instructions as to how many businesses need checking, how many reports need to be written. The surface or manifest content of this story is coded as "providing job instructions." There was also a latent side to this story, an underlying meaning. This story conveyed by comment and innuendo an imagery to the officer of a mean-spirited police organization that was looking for an excuse to degrade and discipline. On a latent level, the story conveyed distrust and disdain for the police organization and its "brass."

Manifest Content Analysis

Content analysis of the war stories revealed 10 distinct categories for war stories (see Table 1). These categories are mutually exclusive and exhaustive. Story analysis included identification of primary and secondary messages. Rare was the war story that recounted only one message. Only 10% of war stories did not contain a second theme.

Table 1 Classifications of War Story Content (in percentages)

Classification	Primary[a]	Secondary[b]
Teaching street skills	58	3
Danger/uncertainty	21	29
Animosity toward citizens	8	7
Pro–police organization	4	9
Anti–police organization	3	10
Racism/sexism/homophobia	2	12
Police solidarity	2	4
Suspiciousness/cynicism	2	3
Use of force	1	7
Citizen positives	1	6

Note: N = 269.

a. Totals equal more than 100% due to rounding.

b. Secondary classifications occurred in 90% of cases; for 10% of cases, there was no secondary classification.

Teaching Street Skills

The topics of war stories are suggestive of their function. Transmission of street/police skills was the most common purpose. Utilizing the concrete modality of a parable, more than half of the war stories (58%) had as their primary focus a description of techniques and strategies physically, socially, or organizationally to control situations. These stories conveyed behavioral rules to address reoccurring and troublesome interactions. The following story, for example, provides a strategy for traffic stops.

> I remember as a young officer, I'd stop a speeder and walk up to the car. The person would ask what they did and I would tell them. Then, when I asked for their license and registration, they would not give it to me, saying they did not do what I said they did. Then one day I had a brainstorm. I walked up to the car and the person said, "What did I do officer?" I said, "License and registration first." They gave me their license and then I told them. I never had a problem after that. (Instructor, Traffic Control, WS 80)

These behavioral rules are what Erikson (1981) termed social recipes. These social recipes for controlling street interactions were classified for this study as teaching street skills. When a war story contained a social recipe for controlling street behavior, it tended to dominate the story. Teaching street skills (social recipes) generally was the primary focus for war stories of this genus. Teaching street skills was a secondary focus in only a few stories (3%). Teaching street skills involved 61% of total stories as either primary or secondary focus. For example, the following stories teach strategies for gaining assent for consent searches.

> As a cop, everybody wants to tell you their side of the story. I remember once at a fight call, the perp ran up to me and wanted to tell me what happened. So, I said to the guy, "I can't talk to you unless you waive your rights." He wanted to explain his side so

much that he waived his rights... and I made the case. (Academy Instructor Law, WS 31)

The sergeant walked up to this car of dirtbags and asked, "Have you any stolen diamonds in the car?" The driver looked real confused and replied, "No, officer." So, then the sergeant said, "If you don't have any diamonds you wouldn't mind if I looked for them?" The driver responded in obvious confusion, "No, I don't mind, go ahead and look, I don't have any diamonds." The instructor went on to tell the class the sergeant really wanted to look for drugs. By getting permission to look for diamonds, he could look into the smallest places and find drugs. The confused drivers would always give permission to look for diamonds. (Academy Instructor, Patrol Technique, WS 217)

The prevalence of skill-teaching stories fits well with the concept of policing as a craft-based enterprise (Greene & Klockars, 1991). These stories provided concrete exampling for craft-technique transfer. These street skills summarized commonsense solutions for frequently encountered problems that other officers had found effective. These techniques were in essence "a cultural tool kit for carrying out everyday activities" (Crank, 1998, p. 19; Swidler, 1986).

I remember one stop one night. I went up to the vehicle and kept the squad's spotlight shining directly on the driver. I stood slightly behind and to the side, so the glare of the light made it difficult for the driver to know exactly where I was, what I was doing. Later he admitted he was planning to attack me but the light disoriented him. (WS 212)

Teaching street skills stories addressing physical threat incidents were most common. These stories discussed handgun retention. They identified when force was appropriate. They cautioned as to whom to watch at domestic scenes. They taught verbal repertoires for incidents getting out of hand. They provided examples of what not to say. They taught how to handle street interactions in a manner that would not have administrative repercussions.

As is common with informal practices, teaching street skills stories addressed items ignored or poorly defined by formal training and policy. Skills taught involved reoccurring and problematic street situations where no formal solutions existed. Whereas the majority addressed officer safety issues, also encapsulated in these stories were suggestions for handling death notifications, for addressing the elderly, and for giving citations without drawing a complaint. Stories suggested when to do paper and what to do when a complaint was coming.

During content analysis, a characteristic of war stories was troubling. Even the stories that were just discussed—teaching street skills—were most often vague and open-ended. It was the infrequent story that provided clear guidelines or precise instructions. Even precise stories conveyed the sense that they were exampling as opposed to providing a definite prescription.

Danger/Uncertainty

Numerically second in primary message were war stories that warned of danger/uncertainty. Such stories related tales of the most innocuous situation going bad. They preached that danger was not only ever present but also likely to appear at the most unexpected and inopportune times.

These stories also spoke of uncertainty, suggesting that events often take the most unexpected turns. Attacks and problems come unexpectedly. The street is unpredictable. Uncertainty tales frequently focused on attacks by citizens on police. The victim attacks the officer. The man in the Brooks Brother suit in an expensive sports car is a hit man armed with a gun with a silencer. The 10-year-old picked up for truancy and put in the back seat of the car without a search possesses a concealed handgun (WS 203). As one academy instructor recounted to the recruit class,

My partner was a trusting guy. I'll never forget the time he was driving down Palmetto, he sees a man beating the hell out of this fancy, red-dressed woman. He got out of the car and ran to the beating. He grabbed the guy and they started wrestling. The next thing he knows is that he is attacked by the woman he was protecting. She hurts him bad by striking him several times on the head with her high-heel shoe. He had to get stitches and was off work a month with blurred vision. (Academy Instructor, Defensive Tactics, WS 41)

There is also an ironic side to uncertainty tales. The few uncertainty tales that do not correlate with danger celebrate the unusual, the provocative, and the tawdry. A drunk reported seeing an elephant. Officers laugh and ask whether it was pink. Ten minutes later, an elephant comes running down the street, a circus escapee (WS 127). Another story tells of checking a young woman in a very expensive and badly dented car simply stopped in the middle of a major thoroughfare. The woman, totally unclothed and extremely intoxicated, berates the officer for stopping her and demands to see a supervisor. The story concludes with the remark, "You never know what you are going to see out there" (WS 43).

Initially, an effort was made to analyze danger and uncertainty separately. In most stories involving uncertainty, danger was a key element. The two themes were highly interrelated. As independent variables, reliability ratings were poor. Due to high intercorrelation and reliability concerns, danger and uncertainty were collapsed into a single variable.

Danger/uncertainty was the primary message in 21% of the war stories analyzed. A larger proportion of secondary messages were devoted to underscoring danger/uncertainty (29%). Danger/uncertainty is a frequent secondary message in technique-transfer stories. In these war stories, danger/uncertainty served as justification for such techniques—particularly those techniques that stretched ethical or legal boundaries. A sizeable proportion of danger/uncertainty stories appear to have the singular purpose of convincing rookies of the dangerousness of the streets. The sizeable proportion of stories devoted to danger and uncertainty suggest that these twin themes have an important role in the early socialization of police officers. Half of war stories (50%) conveyed warnings of danger/uncertainty in either primary or secondary content.

These two story foci of teaching street skills and danger/uncertainty account for 79% of the primary and 32% of the secondary content of the stories analyzed. The remaining stories were distributed among eight categories.

Citizen Tales

A series of stories spoke negatively of citizens, conveying to the rookie officer disrespect for citizenry (primary focus 8%, secondary focus 7%). These stories talked about the perfidy of the citizen-complainant.

Upon arraignment and court appearance my complainant found that she was unable to appear in court because she couldn't find a baby-sitter. After the defendant cursed me and the court officer and took 4 or more punches at us while we were trying to restrain him, the judge hollered, "No brutality in my courtroom." After cursing us and the judge, the judge dropped the charges and dismissed the case because the complainant could not appear on time. (Story told by FTO, WS 40)

Trust was to be found only in the "sworn." Often overlapping stories about the perfidy of citizens were tales of solidarity with brother officers (primary focus 2%, secondary focus 4%).

War stories are not the domain of any one view. There were stories that spoke to the positive nature of citizen/police interactions. These stories told of incidents where residents put themselves at risk to protect officers; they heralded kindness, quality citizenship, and honesty among some members of the populace.

I remember a story from my defensive tactics instructor. The instructor was involved in a physical fight with a man. The instructor stated that he struck the man multiple times with his ASP impact weapon because the man was aggressively resisting his attempt to make an arrest. The man kept attacking despite the blows; they began to wrestle on the ground. The instructor was losing strength. He was exhausted from fighting this man. He still would not give up. A good citizen pulled the man off him and subdued him until other officers arrived. (Academy Instructor, Defensive Tactics, WS 72)

Positive citizen stories were not as frequent as stories that criticized citizens. Whereas 15% of the war stories (primary focus 8%, secondary focus 7%) emphasized animosity toward the citizenry, nearly half that proportion (7% combined: 1% primary focus, 6% secondary focus) reflected favorably on police/citizen encounters. This distribution suggests ambiguity in the police perceptions about those whom they protect.

Police Administrative Stories

There were stories that spoke to the small-mindedness of police administrators, of the insanity of police policies and procedures, of stress and the punishing nature of the police bureaucracy.

During my first year, the desk sergeant only spoke to you when you made an arrest to tell you to take the arrest out of his sight until you got the complaint right. The Captain was never seen. The Lieutenant only appeared or talked to you when he was looking for a reason to write you up on a complaint for disciplinary action for any reason. Production and no complaint from citizens was the only way to get relief from hard and heavy supervision. (Academy Instructor, Patrol Techniques, WS 65)

Accounting for 3% of the primary foci, these war stories cautioned of the threat that the police bureaucracy held for the individual street officer. Yet anti–police organization values were most often a secondary feature of war stories (10%). There also were contradictory stories justifying police organizational goals and speaking to the wisdom of police policies and procedures. These stories told how "the brass" was there when police needed them. They often spoke to the wisdom of following procedures and attention to the law.

One story I remember is that of two officers parked at the end of a road on a quiet night. One car was newer than the other, although the dashboard was faded. So they decided to swap the dash of one with the other because the older car was going to auction. During the nightmare of screws, nuts and bolts, they cracked the windshield of the newer car. The younger officer wanted to cover up and say the windshield broke as a result of the spotlight. The older of the two insisted on the truth. They pulled a case number and wrote a report. No one was disciplined and all turned out well. (FTO, WS 183)

Such stories numerically were as common as warnings of organizational perfidy and policy irrelevance (pro–police organization: primary focus 4%, secondary focus 9%; compared to anti–police organization: 3% primary focus, 10% secondary focus). This dualism in war stories supports an imagery of a police value system conflicted and often diverse in opinions. As seen in the war stories about police/citizen encounters, the basic tenets of police values may be in conflict. Within the force itself, there are significant differences and ambiguity relative to values.

Prejudicial Parables

Other stories subtly reinforced racist/sexist/homophobic beliefs within the primary story line (2%). Primary story lines underestimate the count of stories with sexist, ethnic, or racist content. Racist, sexist, and ethnic comments appeared often as an aside in a story with another focus. Few stories had a singular purpose of conveying a sexist, racist, or ethnic theme. Racist or sexist themes appeared as a secondary focus in 12% of war stories. Most resembles the example below, addressing officer safety but subtly suggesting women are not to be trusted.

> The FTO told me to keep an eye on the female in a domestic violence incident. He told a story of a domestic where the female had a cut on her hand because she had broken into a boat she shared with a man. A disturbance occurred. The man was arrested instead of the female. All the while, the man was saying he was innocent and it was the female. While the man was in jail the woman went to the man's mother's house, stabbed the mother twice, and stole money for drugs. The FTO said he knew the woman was the instigator but arrested the man because of the laceration and the woman had made the call. (FTO Instructing on Domestics, WS 19)

Force/Cynicism/Police Solidarity

These three categorizations of war stories stand out in their lack of appreciable numbers. Rare was the story that glorified physical force. Use of force was a primary theme less than 1% of the time. As with the story below, most tales treated glorification of violence as a secondary theme. At first glance, this story teaches a technique to deal with spitters.

> He told me a story of when a drunk became unruly in his patrol car. He had a real bad attitude with the officer. The unruly drunk was in front, passenger seat, cuffed (the car did not have a cage). When the drunk started spitting, the officer gave him a backhand in the head that shut him up for the remainder of the night. (FTO, WS 107)

Stories touting the virtue of physical force accounted for a 7% of secondary emphasis. Cynicism themes were primary in 2% of the tales and secondary in 3% of war stories. Stories exalting police solidarity appeared far less frequently than originally anticipated. Less than 2% of police stories spoke of police solidarity as a primary focus. As secondary focus, less than 4% of war stories shared this theme.

Latent Content Findings

Analysis of latent messages is often challenging as a researcher tries to catch the hidden message or underlying theme. In coding latent content, the subtly of the message argues for keeping the analysis general. This was the approach utilized in this study (see Table 2). Analysis of war stories' latent content was limited to determining whether the stories supported, questioned, or were neutral toward ethical standards, the law, the police subculture and formal organizational values.

Analysis of latent content of war stories found a significant proportion supporting police subcultural values. In fact, 83% of war stories contained latent messages paralleling the themes Crank (1998) has developed. The police subculture receives solid support from war stories.

The greater percentage of war stories proved ethically neutral (48%). Thirty-eight percent of subcultural stories contained unethical attitudes or

Table 2 Latent Content of War Stories (in percentages)

	Supporting	Neutral	Against
Police subcultural	83	15	2
Ethical values	14	48	38
Organizationally acceptable message	18	57	25
Legal	4	85	11

Note: $N = 269$.

behavioral references. Stories that supported ethical values occurred 15% of the time. Typically, these stories involved values advanced by community policing. Such stories directly confronted values of the police subculture. Although not as common as war stories supporting subcultural values, the stories endorsing an ethical perspective appeared to be more recent and were recounted by younger respondents. These stories stressed that the citizens were not the enemy and, if treated right, would treat the police right. Another theme was that an officer cannot tell a book by the cover; treat everyone the same. Examples from this research were "He didn't look like a judge, but he was; you need to treat everyone you talk to like they were a judge" and "Who came to my aid and saved me from a real beating? It was the black guy, so don't go around thinking that blacks are always out to get you."

Most war stories were legally neutral (85%) regarding their content about the law. Four percent of the stories reinforced the law, whereas 11% contained references that supported illegal behavior. Most support of illegal behavior involved use of force, illegal searches, or "testilying" (i.e., creatively testifying at trial).

Regarding the latent content of war stories for the police organization—support or derogation of the police organization's policies, procedures, leadership, and organization goals and directives—the majority of war stories were classified as neutral. Fifty-seven percent of the war stories were judged neutral with regard to the police organization. Twenty-five percent conveyed negative sentiments about the organization itself, whereas 18% of the war stories favorably spoke of organizational values, directives, or leadership. In the 25% of war stories that negatively treated the police organization, Brueger (1998) would find a number of "black swan" stories or stories with underlying themes counter to the overt message.

The content analysis uncovered a troubling characteristic in the majority of stories. Even stories that taught police skills were often vague and open ended. It was the infrequent story that provided clear guidelines or precise instructions. Even the stories that did appear to provide precise instructions may in fact be applicable to a variety of circumstances. The diamond story is an example. It was not all that clear whether the teller was really proposing to search for diamonds. The diamonds were but an illustration of what officers should indicate to suspects (searching for something small) so they can justify searches into the tightest area that could hide drugs.

Discussion

Study findings have implications for a number of theoretical and practical applications. Cultural theorists have long noted the role of stories and storytelling in culture generation and maintenance. Few have failed to mention police fondness for stories when describing the world of police (Manning, 1978; Reuss-Ianni, 1984). A number of authors have specifically addressed the role of police stories in the socialization of police recruits and that stories are a window into the nature and dynamics of police culture (McNulty, 1994; Shearing & Ericson, 1991; Sherman, 1999). This study suggests that war stories remain a key component in police training and socialization. All officers interviewed noted that war stories were common in both the academy and in their field officer training. Of the 89 officers interviewed, only 2 did not feel that they were impacted in important ways by war stories heard in their academy or during their first year on the street.

Because war stories frequently function as socialization mechanisms, analysis of war stories should provide a semblance of the beliefs held by the subculture.[6] Analysis should also provide a sense of the primacy of such beliefs. Crank's (1998) typology of police culture served this research as the standard for defining war stories as supportive, neutral, or oppositional to police subcultural beliefs. The research plan was to test the fit between Crank's typology and war story content. Such analysis does run the risk of tautology, because the typology to frame the research may indeed force a fit between the study's results and Crank's typology. This did not appear to be the case. There was no need for forcing. Crank's typology fit well with the recounted war stories. The themes that Crank described were present and easily identified. There were no surprises.

Although the typology worked well in differentiating types of stories, the numerical distribution of stories among Crank's (1998) categories was theoretically disquieting. The expectation was that the more crucial the theme to the subculture, the more predominant and frequent its expression in war stories should be. Danger/uncertainty clearly demonstrates such a pattern. Other themes defined by Crank as key elements in the culture do not fare as well. Category counts and primary focus suggest a local police culture differing at least in emphasis from descriptions provided by a number of researchers (Crank, 1998; Reuss-Ianni, 1984).[7]

Police Subculture

The relative absence of stories touting police solidarity is noteworthy (2% primary, 4% secondary). It was expected that this key police belief would be widely proclaimed, particularly with new recruits. It did not receive the attention anticipated. Similarly, antiorganization tales, though present, did not seem as antagonistic or as numerous as a reading of the literature might suggest. In fact, there were as many proadministration messages as antiadministration (antiorganization: 3% primary, 10% secondary; proadministration: 4% primary, 9% secondary). Cynicism has been cited by a number of researchers as a key aspect of police culture (Niederhoffer, 1967). War stories addressing cynicism were surprisingly uncommon in this data set (2% primary, 3% secondary).

The literature discusses the nature of "police subcultural rules." Researchers have taken one of two approaches to conceptualizing subcultural rules. The traditional approach looks to cultural rules as somewhat specific instructions for accomplishing ends (Reuss-Ianni, 1984). However, recent authors have cast subcultural recipes as "general sense-makers that can be used in myriad of settings" (Shearing & Ericson, 1991, p. 489). McNulty (1994) characterized these more general dictums as commonsense knowledge.

The stories analyzed here more closely resemble the general sense makers of Shearing and Ericson (1991) or the commonsense knowledge of McNulty (1994). The stories teaching street skills could be better characterized as teaching street sense. Stories told of those who did not stand away from suspects and the negative consequences. They did not state how far away, which direction, which stance; rather, stories simply suggested, stay out of reach. The stories conveyed to the recruits a general sense of what to watch, whom to watch, and in a most general sense, how to proceed.

Danger

McNulty's (1994) development of the concept of police commonsense knowledge is premised on another characteristic of policing—situational uncertainty. McNulty argued that precisely because the street is so uncertain, commonsense solutions must remain open and broad to address this uncertain nature of police incidents. Uncertainty generally travels police circles with a companion—danger. Danger heightens the primacy of uncertainty. In the context of danger, uncertainty is not merely frustrating or confusing; it is a harbinger of harm. Out of this sense of the unpredictability of the streets, the uncertainty attending citizen response, and the potential for danger, police culture evolves.

This analysis of war stories found danger/uncertainty holding a pivotal position in the police subculture. The theme of uncertainty and danger was present in half the stories recounted. In both the police academy and in the field-training program, officers reported stories warning of the unpredictability and dangerousness of the street. Danger/uncertainty themes frequently accompany racist/sexist stories; Blacks, Hispanics, and women were characterized as unpredictable. Danger/uncertainty had a higher association than most other variables with unethical, illegal, anti–police organization and prosubculture content. Danger/uncertainty may be the bridge that permits the transition to a set of beliefs unacceptable outside of police culture.

In an earlier section, danger/uncertainty was discussed in terms of its conceptual importance to an understanding of police culture. Crank (1998, p. 110) identified danger as a ubiquitous police cultural theme. Other researchers have seen war stories as helping officers "vicariously experience, learn and relearn the potential for danger through war stories" (Kappeler et al., 1994, p. 246). These authors rightfully have seen danger as altering the techniques employed and the attitude of officers and providing a base for officer solidarity (Skolnick, 1993).

This study suggests an additional function for war stories—stressing danger. Young officers come to the profession with the ethics and values of their communities (Carpenter & Raza, 1987; Kennedy & Homant, 1981). In the academy and during their initial year on the street, their values undergo change (Niederhoffer, 1967; Van Maanen, 1973). Is the constant emphasis on the dangerousness of the street linked to rookie value change?

For values to alter, there must be a precipitating factor. The high incidence of danger stories and the correlation of danger and subculture themes suggest that the perception of danger may be the catalyst that triggers value change. With danger ever present, extraordinary measures are warranted. Regular rules no longer apply. Danger unmasks the essential fallacies of civilian values. Danger may be the justification for the unethical and the illegal.

In terms of objective measures of physical injury and death, policing does not particularly stand out in numbers of practitioners injured or killed (Bureau of Labor Statistics, 2000). The majority of injuries to police, particularly serious injuries, occur in car crashes. Yet in terms of verbal and nonverbal threat behavior, danger stimuli are pervasive. Policing is an enterprise where threat is common and the frustration and adrenaline rushes of conflicted conversation are ever present. Being conflicted, threatened, and harassed may be no better than being in actual danger, but it is different and requires alternative strategies and approaches. Would providing a realistic image to recruits of the actual danger of the profession alter officer allegiance to subcultural values?

Should administrators be attentive to reducing employee perceptions of danger? Should the squad room refrain "Be safe out there" heard frequently as officers leave for patrol be replaced with a more accurate "Drive safely and be calm when confronted with threat and aggravation"?

For example, transforming the message of confrontation—teaching that the threat behavior is often necessary for young males to maintain "face" before they comply—suggests a different kind of police response, one counter to subcultural norms. Teaching officers that tensing up or refusal to move on the part of most arrestees is not a prelude to battle but rather the last symbolic protest before surrender provides a different message about citizen compliance. Should new officers be taught when danger is in fact probable and when it is improbable?

Practical Applications

The literature identifies war stories as frequent bearers of subcultural messaging—and they often are. However, war stories as a communication style are value-neutral carriers. The findings clearly show that a number of war stories questioned and contradicted subcultural values—particularly unethical aspects of the subculture. The ethics, legality, and degree of support for organizational policies, expressed in war stories, varied by storyteller.

In a craft-based discipline, more hands-on and more specific and applied training is needed. Police academies, in their attempt to upgrade and become more "academic," have sacrificed trade-type, scenario-based training. The use of stories to clarify and to illustrate abstract concepts is a valuable heuristic tool. It is the stories that convey unethical, illegal, and antiorganization values and instructors and FTOs presenting them that need to be addressed. Academy, field-training program administrators, state certification authorities, and administrators should monitor classroom and field training efforts. Given the deeply ingrained nature of many of these beliefs, such monitoring will not solve the problem but could reduce excesses.

What would be the impact of changing the content of war stories to focus on ethical and citizen-supportive themes? Would the content and message of war stories presented to new officers be altered by a different mix of instructors? If more ethically and community-oriented instructors and field training officers were employed, would the future socialization of officers be altered?

Interaction Gambits

War stories do more than translate abstract concepts into concrete applications. War stories fill gaps in police training. As earlier findings reveal, 58.7% of the stories involved teaching street skills. War stories prove a favored mechanism to introduce officers to techniques and interaction gambits not formally taught or organizationally sanctioned.

Current police training regimens are silent relative to a wide range of situations, many of which are potentially controversial. Experienced officers develop responses to reoccurring troublesome incidents. These evolve into social recipes and the grist for war stories. Whether it is the arrestee in the backseat of the patrol car spitting at the officer driving, or the motorist complaining of a ticket, officers need recipes to address problematic and reoccurring encounters. Blau's (1956) observation rings true so many decades later: When formal solutions do not exist for recurring problems, informal solutions soon arise.

One challenge to social recipe transmission is that there is no quality control for subcultural solutions. Some proposed recipes may be ineffective. Others may work well for the officer but may have negative consequences for the police organization and/or society as a whole. A number of these techniques/recipes, as earlier noted, are ethically offensive, illegal, or policy violations.

In recent years, there have been increasing calls for scenario-based training for police basic recruit classes. This analysis suggests that these calls for more concrete, realistic, and scenario-based training should be heeded. There also is a need for formal social recipes to address reoccurring and problematic social situations. Attention must be paid in the profession to developing research-based interaction strategies (recipes) that are not only effective but also consistent with the long-term goals of the profession.

A number of academy administrators have tried to address the need for proven interaction gambits by inviting psychologists and sociologists into academy classes. Experienced police officers frequently take strong issue with the strategies presented. The psychologists and sociologists making such presentations are most often presenting their opinions. Their presentations are based neither on research nor on street experience. Sorely needed for police training is objective research that identifies those approaches to domestics, traffic stops, interactions with drunks, and a number of other recurring incidents that are most likely to reduce violence and achieve police goals. Police administrators should be seeking a research agenda from federal and state authorities that includes such practical applications.

Conclusion

Several final comments are in order. First, this research was focused on a limited period of an officer's career, the rookie year. Initial socialization may have a focus and concerns different from later stage subcultural communications. The mix of war stories is reflective of this difference. It may be that in early socialization, themes such as teaching street skills and uncertainty/danger predominate. In later stages of the police career, the content mix of squad room stories will differ. The primacy of stories teaching street skills suggest that there may be merit to this contention.

An alternative hypothesis is that police culture across time, agency, and work groups exhibits variation. The literature of police culture tends to present a monolithic vision of police culture. Most commonly, researchers describe patterns of police subcultural values often based on a single site and apply them to all police.

Policing is a remarkably diverse enterprise. Across more than 18,000 American departments, one can find diversity in mission, duties, style, and membership. Subtle differences in police duties, organizational size, community compositions, and other variables may reflect differences in allegiance, focus, and content of police culture. There are common aspects of policing (coercive force, danger/uncertainty), and these ensure some common central themes.

Robert Redfield, the cultural anthropologist, once characterized culture as group problem solving (Redfield, 1941). This more dynamic and diverse image of police culture argues that as problems police confront change, the culture likewise alters. This is an image of police culture in which beliefs and perceptions are renegotiated daily, reflecting changing needs, as the legal, political, and technological landscapes alter. This model for police culture suggests that police "sense making" is located in an ongoing social construction of reality—a reality shaped and defined by problems encountered and shared.

This data set provides some support for this view. Analysis of war story content and focus reveals differences by agency size. Those reporting stories from smaller agencies generally recounted stories that were less antiorganization and less ethically negative. This finding parallels observations from other studies (Mastrofski, Ritti, & Hoffmaster, 1991).

This exploratory research raises a number of provocative questions, then, that have both theoretical and practical significance. The most interesting question awaits an answer: Can the high ideals and positive ethical standards that rookies initially bring to the academy be sustained well into their careers?

Notes

1. The initial explanation for police culture looked to the characteristics of those becoming police officers (Lundman, 1980, p. 73). Research into values and beliefs of new hires has failed to discover significant differences from the values of the general population.

2. Appreciation to an anonymous reviewer bringing this fact to my attention.

3. A number of police trainers have noted this deficiency. In Florida, for example, the state has mandated that all basic police training have scenario-based training.

4. Maxfield and Babbie (2000) defined convenience samples as reliance on available subjects. Interviewers went to police agencies and college classes and interviewed available officers.

5. Differences were found by department size. Variations were found in latent content; respondents from smaller agencies recorded more ethical and pro-organizational stories.

6. This assumes numerical frequency can be taken as signals of cultural focal concerns.

7. Whereas all elements of police culture could be identified in at least a few war stories, story emphases and numbers revealed a different profile. Profiled beliefs such as police solidarity, cynicism, and celebration of force were not present in the numbers anticipated.

References

Bahn, C. (1975). The psychology of police corruption: Socialization of the corrupt. *Police Journal, 48*, 30-36.

Bahn, C. (1984). Police socialization in the eighties: Strains in the forging of an occupational identity. *Journal of Police Science and Administration, 12*(4), 390-394.

Bayley, D. H., & Mendelson, H. (1969). *Minorities and the police.* New York: Free Press.

Bennett, R. (1984). Becoming blue: A longitudinal study of police recruit occupational socialization. *Journal of Police Science and Administration, 12*, 47-58.

Berg, B. L. (1990). First day at the police academy: Stress reaction training as a screening out technique. *Journal of Contemporary Criminal Justice, 6*, 89-105.

Blau, P. (1956). *Bureaucracy in modern society.* New York: Random House.

Brooks, L. (1989). Police discretionary behavior: A study of style. In R. Dunham & G. Alpert (Eds.), *Critical issues in policing: Contemporary readings* (pp. 121-145). Prospect Heights, IL: Waveland.

Buerger, M. E. (1998). Police training as Pentecost: Using tools singularly ill-suited for reform. *Police Quarterly, 1*, 27-63.

Burbeck, E., & Furnham, A. (1985). Police officer selection: A critical review of the literature. *Journal of Police Science and Administration, 13*, 58-69.

Bureau of Labor Statistics. (2000). *National census of fatal occupational injuries, 1999* (U.S. Department of Labor, USDL 00-2360). Washington, DC: Government Printing Office.

Carpenter, B. N., & Raza, S. M. (1987). Personality characteristics of police applicants: Comparisons across subgroups and with other populations. *Journal of Police Science and Administration, 15*, 10-17.

Crank, J. P. (1998). *Understanding police culture.* Cincinnati, OH: Anderson.

Crank, J. P., & Caldero, M. A. (2000). *Police ethics: The corruption of a noble cause.* Cincinnati, OH: Anderson.

Erikson, R. (1981). Rules For police deviance. In C. Shearing (Ed.), *Organizational police deviance.* Toronto, Canada: Butterworths.

Gaines, L., Kappler, J., & Vaughn, J. (1997). *Policing in America* (2nd ed.). Cincinnati, OH: Anderson.

Greene, J., & Klockars, C. (1991). What police do. In C. Klockars & S. Mastrofski (Eds.), *Thinking about police: Contemporary readings* (pp. 273-384). New York: McGraw-Hill.

Kappeler, V., Studer, R., & Alpert, G. (1994). *Forces of deviance: The dark side of policing*. Prospect Heights, IL: Waveland.

Kennedy, D. M., & Homant, R. (1981). Nontraditional role assumptions and the personality of policewoman. *Journal of Police Science and Administration, 9*, 346-355.

Lefkowitz, J. (1975). Psychological attributes of policemen: A review of research and opinion. *Social Issues, 31*(1), 3-26.

Lundman, R. J. (1980). *Police and policing: An introduction*. New York: Holt, Rinehart & Winston.

Manning, P. K. (1978). Lying, secrecy and social control. In P. K. Manning & J. Van Maanen (Eds.), *Policing: A view from the street* (pp. 238-254). Santa Monica, CA: Goodyear Publishing.

Mastrofski, S. D., Ritti, R., & Hoffmaster, D. (1991). Organizational determinants of police discretion: The case of drinking driving. In C. Klockars & S. Mastrofski (Eds.), *Thinking about police: Contemporary readings*. Boston: McGraw-Hill.

Matza, D. (1964). *Delinquency and drift*. New York: John Wiley.

Maxfield, M., & Babbie, E. (2000). *Research methods for criminal justice and criminology*. Belmont, CA: Wadsworth.

McNamara, J. H. (1967). Uncertainties in police work: The relevance of recruit's background and training. In D. Bordua (Ed.), *The police: Six sociological essays*. New York: John Wiley.

McNulty, E. (1994). Generating common sense knowledge among police officers. *Symbolic Interaction, 17*(3), 281-294.

Niederhoffer, A. (1967). *Behind the shield: The police in urban society*. Garden City, NJ: Doubleday.

Redfield, R. (1941). *Folk culture of the Yucatan*. Chicago: University of Chicago Press.

Reuss-Ianni, E. (1984). *Two cultures of policing*. New Brunswick, NJ: Transaction.

Riksheim, E., & Chermack, S. M. (1993). Causes of police behavior revisited. *Journal of Criminal Justice, 21*, 353-382.

Sayles, S., & Albritton, J. (1999). Is there a distinct subculture in American policing? In J. Sewell (Ed.), *Controversial issues in policing* (pp. 154-171). Boston: Allyn & Bacon.

Senna, J., & Siegel, L. (1987). *Introduction to criminal justice* (4th ed.). St. Paul, MN: West.

Shearing, C., & Ericson, R. (1991). Culture as figurative action. *British Journal of Sociology, 42*, 481-506.

Sherman, L. W. (1980). Causes of police behavior: The current state of quantitative research. *Journal of Research in Crime and Delinquency, 17*, 69-100.

Sherman, L. W. (1999). Learning police ethics. In L. K. Gaines & G. W. Cordiner (Eds.), *Policing perspectives: An anthology* (pp. 301-310). Los Angeles: Roxbury.

Skolnick, J. H. (1993). *Justice without trial: Law enforcement in a democratic society* (3rd ed.). New York: Macmillan.

Swidler, A. (1986). Culture in action: Symbols and strategies. *American Sociological Review, 51*, 273-286.

Van Maanen, J. (1973). Observations on the making of policemen. *Human Organization, 32*, 407-418.

Westley, W. A. (1970). *Violence and the police*. Cambridge, MA: MIT Press.

Wilson, J. Q. (1968). *Varieties of police behavior*. Cambridge, MA: Harvard University Press.

DISCUSSION QUESTIONS

1. Robert E. Ford's article notes that a police recruit is presented with a depiction of police work that does not necessarily conform to media images. Are war stories accurate portrayals of police work? Are war stories ever embellished? Does the representativeness or accuracy of war stories matter, or is the general content (e.g., teaching specific skills, alerting recruits to dangers of job, etc.) most important?

2. The research shows that war stories classified as unsupportive of ethical values, the organization, or legal restrictions are relatively uncommon, especially compared with more value-neutral messages. Is an officer recruit likely to disregard the infrequent messages, or are they still potent influences on future behavior (e.g., conducting illegal searches)? Explain.

3. Do you think the socialization process of other criminal justice workers—prosecutors, defense attorneys, treatment counselors, private security officers—also includes the use of war stories? If so, what is their likely content or emphasis?

Reading 13

Nancy C. Jurik's study of the experiences of female correctional officers working in male prisons in a Western state revealed significant barriers affecting their adjustment to their work. In the early 1980s, when she conducted her research, roughly one in eight correctional officers working in the state's male prisons were female. They faced resistance from others based on common stereotypes that carried over into the work environment: they lacked physical strength, were mentally weak, and, potentially, were emotionally involved in their work and with offenders. These qualities were considered liabilities in dangerous prison environments, though, as Jurik alluded to, they may be considered assets in facilities where rehabilitation and service are emphasized. Supervisors considered these factors in making job assignments, keeping female officers out of positions where the potential for coercion was elevated. Consequently, these assignments limited future promotional opportunities.

An Officer and a Lady

Organizational Barriers to Women Working as Correctional Officers in Men's Prisons

Nancy C. Jurik

Despite frequent media accounts of female advancement in the labor market, social scientists continue to document the persistent segregation patterns which limit women to a narrow range of occupations and industries (Bridges, 1982; Hacker, 1979). Since the early 1970s, women have slowly begun to infiltrate a greater variety of occupations in our society. These pioneers have attracted both popular and scholarly attention.

Researchers have taken two major directions in their studies of women in non-traditional occupations. The first and more traditional line of research focuses on individuals. The problems women face in achieving organizational parity have been analyzed in terms of human relations (the difficulties in dealing with resentful co-workers and supervisors) and as consequences of sexual stereotyping.[1] Such discussions are frequently concerned with the abilities of women to survive in their non-traditional work settings. Their survival entails not only learning new skills but also dealing with resentful co-workers and supervisors. Clients, co-workers, and supervisors often demand proof of women's abilities, yet establish interaction patterns which make it almost impossible for women to produce such evidence (Bourne and

Source: Jurik, N. C. (1985). An officer and a lady: Organizational barriers to women working as correctional officers in men's prisons. *Social Problems, 32*(4), 375–388.

Wikler, 1978; Miller et al., 1975). For example, Martin (1980) finds that exclusion from many day-to-day departmental interactions results in policewomen being denied important work-related information, support in relations with management, and patronage for advancement. In addition, Wilson (1982:360) has suggested that a major problem for women entering criminal justice fields is the conflict between the stereotyped attributes associated with the status of women and those associated with the status of criminal justice professionals.

The major shortcoming of these social psychological analyses is that the responsibility for barriers which face women attempting to integrate into male-dominated occupations is placed solely on the behavior of individuals. Organizational structures and policies which may also inhibit the advancement of women are overlooked (Holland et al., 1979; Kissell and Katasampes, 1980).

The second line of research in this area examines the barriers posed by organizational structures to women's performance in non-traditional occupations. Kanter (1976, 1977) argues that the inability of women to succeed in the work-place cannot be sufficiently explained without reference to organizational-level variables. She criticizes individual-level analyses for assuming that workers create their own fate. Instead, she argues that organizational conditions frame the possibilities for the success or failure of individuals in the work-place by shaping work and promotional opportunities. She identifies three organizational variables—the opportunity structure, the power structure, and the sex ratio—which affect occupational role performance.

Although her primary focus is on the manner in which organizational factors determine women's occupational role performance, Kanter also suggests that these same organizational factors shape the biases against women held by others in the work-place. She criticizes models which blame female work-place failures on the "sexist" behavior of male co-workers and supervisors, arguing that these explanations "forget that organizations make their workers (male and female) into who they are" (1977:263). She concludes that whether they place the blame for sex segregation on a lack of assertiveness by female entrants, or on the discriminatory behavior of supervisors and co-workers, social psychological models provide an inadequate understanding of the structural forces which limit female advancement opportunities.

By concentrating on the organizational determinants of work-place behavior, Kanter (1976, 1977) and others (e.g., Hacker, 1979; Izraeli, 1983) counteract the exclusive emphasis on worker attributes and behavior which characterized earlier work in this area. However, it is important to remember that individuals' pre-employment values and attitudes do influence their perceptions of and reactions to specific work environments (Miller, 1980). Therefore, it is critical to develop new analyses which explicate the *interplay* between organizational context and individual characteristics in producing work-place behavior patterns.

Along these lines, this analysis will identify aspects of the organizational environment which reinforce sexist attitudes and practices and thereby limit the advancement opportunities for women employed in a non-traditional occupation. The subject of this analysis is women working as correctional officers in men's prisons. In the research setting, the assignment of female officers to men's prisons was made in conjunction with a variety of other correctional reform efforts. However, a number of problems at the organizational-level made the implementation of these changes, including the acceptance of female officers, extremely difficult.

The focus of this analysis is two-fold. First, it will identify the organizational problems which have frustrated attempts at correctional reform and have encouraged staff suspicions surrounding the competence of female officers. Second, the analysis describes the effect of this organizational context on advancement opportunities for female officers. The organizational problems are manifested in the job training, work assignment allocation, and performance evaluation of these women. An understanding of the organizational milieu of this correctional agency gives us insight into the hostile and suspicious reactions of male co-workers and supervisors to female officers, and shows that such hostility is not simply the result of pre-existing sexist attitudes, but it is also behavior perpetuated by this organizational environment.

This analysis of the experiences of female officers in men's prisons illustrates the interplay between individual characteristics and organizational context in producing and reinforcing workplace attitudes and behavior. In addition, the study identifies some key barriers to organizational reform. Such identification is important because attempts to equalize work opportunities involve organizational change.

Method and Setting

The data for the present study come from a variety of sources within a state department of corrections located in the western United States (hereafter referred to as Western D.O.C.). Currently, this department has the responsibility for administering at the state level all matters relating to the confinement, rehabilitation, and parole functions of adult and youth offenders. As of January, 1984, Western D.O.C. had jurisdictional responsibilities for 7,183 adults and 623 youths.

The primary data for this analysis are in-depth, open-ended interviews. Interview respondents included 22 female and 10 male correctional officers. Interviews were also conducted with four administrators, six supervisors, and six training coordinators.

Respondents were selected through purposive sampling methods (Babbie, 1983:178-179; Glaser and Strauss, 1967). That is, a variety of respondents were selected for purposes of comparison along the lines of gender, race, age, educational level, length of employment, institutional rank, locale, and type of job assignment (including maximum, medium, and minimum security prisons). Respondents were located in three ways: (1) directly by the principal investigator during visits to seven of the ten prisons run by Western D.O.C.; (2) through referrals by prior interview respondents; and (3) through referrals by staff trainers in five of the prisons. When compared with available departmental demographic and employment information, this sample was found to reflect the general population of Western D.O.C. correctional officers at the time.

In addition to the information derived from these in-depth interviews, data were obtained from observations and informal conversations with personnel and inmates at six prison facilities in the Western D.O.C.[2] Relevant demographic information on employees was obtained from department records. Necessary background information was gathered from reviews of policy and procedure manuals and from a review of department-related articles appearing in local newspapers between 1976 and 1982. Finally, this analysis also drew on a survey of 179 line correctional officers (male and female) employed in one medium security prison in the Western D.O.C. This survey addressed the respondents' background characteristics and their attitudes related to work and training. Forty of the respondents in this survey were women.[3]

The Entry of Women Into Corrections

Corrections traditionally has been a male-dominated profession, with women relegated to work in female institutions or to clerical duties in male facilities; but the roles women assume in corrections have changed during the past decade. By 1978, 33 states and many cities began assigning women to work as officers in men's prisons, and they now comprise approximately 12 percent of correctional protective service workers — a significant increase over past years (Chapman et al., 1980; National Institute of Justice, 1978).

Legal pressure is frequently cited as the major impetus for women's expanding role in corrections (Feinman, 1980; Wilson, 1982). However, in addition to legal pressures, conditions at the national level and within the western state have prompted organizational changes in corrections that have advanced female employment opportunities.

Within the Western D.O.C., a confluence of factors produced a change in orientation; these factors were prison violence, class action suits alleging overcrowding and abuse by guards, and federal court orders to reduce overcrowding and improve prison living conditions. Under threat of a federal court seizing control of its prison system, the state legislature increased Western D.O.C. budgetary allocations and hired a new director of corrections. The new director was given a mandate to professionalize and reform the state correctional system.

This mandate was to reflect a shift in correctional philosophy and management. The traditional informal and arbitrary prison management systems were to be replaced with more formal and bureaucratic structures.[4] This reorientation included the requirement that hiring and promotion be based on objective qualifications rather than on informal alliances with superiors (Perrow, 1979:8). Furthermore, physical coercion and intimidation as methods of inmate control were to be de-emphasized. Rehabilitative programs and other inmates services—such as education, counseling, vocational training, and recreational activities—were added to existing prison custodial responsibilities. The change in correctional philosophy placed greater emphasis on the service rather than coercive responsibilities of security officers. This change in orientation was reflected by a change in job description and title (to Correctional Service Officer from Correctional Security Officer) for the line security position.

These changes facilitated the entry of women into the Western D.O.C. Six percent of the correctional officers employed by Western D.O.C. in 1978 were women, all of whom were employed in the women's prisons. By 1983, 13 percent of the officers working in the men's prisons and 15 percent of *all* Western D.O.C. officers were women.

The assignment of female officers to positions in men's prisons was encouraged directly by the new administrative emphasis on equal employment practices. It was encouraged indirectly by the change in philosophy that placed greater value on an officer's service capabilities (for instance, communication and counseling skills) which, in our society, are more frequently perceived as "feminine" talents. The case for hiring women was frequently advanced by administrators who cited the contribution which "typically feminine" qualities could make in a more service-oriented prison setting.

Organizational Barriers to Female Correctional Officers

Despite these improved opportunities, female officers experienced great difficulties surviving and advancing in the Western D.O.C. While as a group correctional officers faced many common problems, female officers faced additional barriers not confronted by their male counterparts. These women overwhelmingly attributed the resistance they experienced at work to the biased attitudes and behavior of individual male officers and supervisors:

> The major problem for women officers is male staff. We expect it from the inmates ... but the male officers make demeaning remarks! If you say something, they pout in a corner (female officer).

And, in fact, several male officers and supervisors did acknowledge some prejudice regarding women employed in men's prisons.

Both male and female officers expressed concern about women's reliability in violent situations. These fears appeared to be rooted in three popular beliefs about women. One objection centered on the "greater physical weaknesses" of women. Although there were no height and weight requirements for male or female security officers in the Western D.O.C., it was still commonly believed that women were not capable of functioning in dangerous situations.

They are just not strong enough to struggle with a six-foot inmate. Then I get hurt trying to make sure they aren't beaten to death (male officer).

Another objection focused on the "mental weaknesses" of women.

This place works on your mind after a while. Women just can't take that kind of strain. Most of them will crack (male officer).

A final set of concerns focused on the sexual identity and behavior of female officers. There was considerable fear that women might become emotionally involved with inmates.

The first thing I always ask about an officer is "Who owns him?—Me or the inmate?" Women sometimes go soft on the inmates. We had one who got involved. She started bringing stuff in to him. She got dirty (i.e., smuggled contraband to inmates) (male supervisor).

At first glance, the suspicions surrounding female officers appeared to be a manifestation of the biased attitudes held by *individual* male staff and supervisors. Researchers frequently attribute these sentiments to childhood and adult gender-role socialization (see Wilson, 1982). However, further analysis of my data revealed that this explanation was only part of the story. Barriers to female correctional officers also include those set up by the organizational structure of the Western D.O.C. Such barriers include tokenism, conflicting organizational goals, external environmental conditions, informal organizational structures, and inadequate strategies for institutionalizing correctional reforms.

Tokenism

The suspicion surrounding female officers stemmed in part from the relatively small numbers of women who occupied security positions in men's prisons. Kanter (1977:206-42) defines "tokens" as members whose social type constitutes a minority within the organization. She observes three perceptual phenomena associated with the presence of "tokens," each of which has consequences for their organizational positions: (1) they are highly visible and so capture a disproportionate share of others' awareness; (2) their presence polarizes the differences between tokens and dominants; and (3) their attributes become distorted to fit the dominants' sterotypes about tokens.

At the time of this study, the percentage of female officers assigned to men's prison facilities in Western D.O.C. ranged from zero to 26 percent. In the two newer male prison facilities, approximately 26 percent of the correctional officers were women; in the older facilities approximately seven percent were women. In one facility, there were no women at all. In interviews, it was readily apparent that female officers perceived their heightened visibility in men's prisons:

We need only the most qualified women. There are so few women that every incompetent one hurts all the others who come after her (female supervisor).

If a women falls short, she's censored, ostracized, talked about, whereas ten incompetent men are not noticed (female officer).

In addition to the barriers posed by tokenism, the following organizational-level problems *indirectly* limited the integration and advancement of female officers in Western D.O.C. by thwarting the implementation of the new service orientation and blocking accompanying reforms in personnel hiring and promotional practices.

Service and Security as Conflicting Organizational Goals

As noted frequently in the prison literature, correctional security workers must continually confront a variety of conflicting and ambiguous organizational directives (Cressey, 1966; Fox, 1982). Simultaneous efforts to achieve the goals of social control and inmate service or rehabilitation often collide. Within the Western D.O.C., the service philosophy was never intended by the administration to replace or compromise the security function of the correctional system. It was hoped that, in the long run, the two would complement each other (i.e., more active and satisfied inmates would be less likely to cause altercations). However, in practice, these expectations had little chance of succeeding. On one hand, rational management of security matters required that officers treat all inmates alike and enforce rules in a consistent manner. On the other hand, inmate service and program responsibilities required that officers pay attention to individual needs and tailor inmate activities accordingly. In addition, inmate involvement in programs sometimes required a loosening of certain institutional security constraints. For example, increased inmate movement within and outside of the prison was necessary to allow participation in educational programs. Such movement posed additional security problems for prison facilities which were already understaffed and overcrowded. When such conflicts arose, security concerns frequently predominated.

> I agree with the administration's idea of combining security and treatment responsibilities. But it fell through. I do not see any difference today. Now they are trying to keep officers in the same units every day to do both counseling and security. It's a good idea, but officers get burned out so fast. They can't do both jobs. Security winds up being all most can handle (female supervisor).

While stereotypic feminine qualities were seen as an asset in the more service-oriented prison environment, these same attributes were a liability in the more security-oriented environment.

> The male officers and even the supervisors tend to think that brute strength is all they can count on. In a pinch, women will be relegated to a worthless role (female officer).

> One night, my sergeant said there were only three officers on the yard and he didn't know what they would do if there was trouble. He said that he wasn't counting me because I was a female (female officer).

In the long-run, inmate programs and services might have lessened the danger in Western D.O.C. facilities thereby complementing security functions. However, in the short run the staff perceived these different goals as conflicting. When security concerns predominated to the exclusion of the service dimension—as was frequently the case in Western D.O.C.—the role of women in the male correctional environment was viewed more negatively. Co-workers and supervisors suspected that women were too weak physically and emotionally to handle potentially explosive situations.

Extra-Organizational Conditions

A number of external factors greatly exacerbated prison over-crowding and staff shortages which, in turn, increased the level of danger in the facilities. During 1982 and 1983, serious financial constraints were placed by the state on the hiring of new program staff. Further, determinant sentencing laws and other efforts by the state to "crack down" on crime resulted in larger-than-expected increases in the prison population. Although a new institution was added in 1981, the expanding inmate population quickly filled that facility as well as others in the system. By the end of 1982, many of the facilities were operating significantly above capacity levels. Simultaneously, the turnover rate among correctional officers was so high (40 percent per year) that many shifts were understaffed. In a dangerous, crowded environment, new service-oriented programs were not implemented effectively. Given these tensions, officers' security responsibilities preempted their program-related functions.

> At first, the department was trying to develop rehabilitation programs. Now with all the overcrowding we face, it's mostly a

matter of caretaking. We just don't have the resources to hire programs staff (male trainer).

These problems combined to reduce the number of programs available to inmates and diminish the *security* staff-to-inmate ratio to levels which all personnel described as dangerous. This level of danger bolstered suspicions regarding female officers' competence:

> The male officers don't trust us as back-ups. The supervisors and administrators don't think that women can maintain order in the prisons now because they're crowded and dangerous. They are afraid women would be the first hostages (female officer).

Informal Organizational Structure

A third barrier to the implementation of the correctional reforms was posed by the informal organizational structure of the Western D.O.C. The obstacles which informal work structures pose to women entering non-traditional occupations are frequently noted in the literature (Martin, 1980; O'Farrell and Harlan, 1980). The conflict between security and service functions—and the dangerous, overcrowded conditions in these facilities—intensified hostile reactions. While most of the newer staff supported the change in philosophy, there was a significant amount of resistance on the part of many of the "old-guard" (pre-1978) supervisors and line staff—most of whom were men.

> This emphasis on the *service* functions of officers makes it seem like we're maids or something. We have less power than the inmates now. The change in our job title underlines that... *service officers!* That's a joke! (male officer).

Resistance to the service philosophy reinforced suspicions surrounding the ability of women to perform adequately as correctional officers in men's prisons. These opponents expressed resentment regarding the interference of the central office in hiring, evaluation, and promotional decisions.

> To meet their quotas, they've hired a lot of female officers who just aren't qualified. They've got women working in places they just shouldn't be.... They should not be in the yard or in housing. They are much more likely than a man to get hurt (male officer).

In addition, the combination of these old-guard hostilities with the informal rules governing advancement further limited the opportunities available to female officers in two ways. First, in the absence of adequate formal opportunities for power and advancement, informal connections and favors became increasingly important to department staff. Women and other minorities are generally disadvantaged by these informal advancement structures (see Kanter, 1977:264).

> Advancement is contingent on several factors. One of the most important is still the superior's hidden selection criteria. Certain people are primed for promotion by giving them special assignments and increasing their educational opportunities. That depends on your connections and relationships with those higher up.... It's who you know. Women don't usually fare too well. The higher ups are men, of course (female administrator, formerly a line officer).

Second, major changes in departmental philosophy and the entry of a new group of workers encountered great hostility from old-time employees who felt that they had benefited from the informal occupational culture of the status quo.

> A lot of male officers see us as a threat. They think if we do the job well, then somehow it takes away from their abilities. So, they try

to burn women out or to "backstab" (female officer).

Therefore, the perceived threat was not caused solely by a fear of outsiders disrupting the subculture's solidarity (as argued by Martin, 1980:138-57). It was also due to a perceived threat to promotional advancement in an organization where such opportunities were scarce.

Inadequate Implementation Strategies

The failure of Western D.O.C. departmental administrators to be aware of and plan for the resistance of the informal subculture severely hampered their ability to implement new reform-oriented policies effectively. Strategies helpful in facilitating acceptance of organizational change have been frequently discussed in the policy implementation literature (see Aronson et al., 1984:453-86; Jurie, 1984). Yet, in Western D.O.C., there was no program designed to facilitate implementation. No plans existed to counteract resistance. There were, for example, no training seminars for mid-management. There were no specific incentives for cooperation or careful communication of changes to the various management levels. Staff had no input on proposed changes, nor were the personal benefits of the changes made apparent to them. Similarly, there was no systematic plan of negative sanctions for failure to conform to new policies.

> Nobody asked us how we felt about any of these changes. Half the time we don't even know why things are changed. We just have to pass the rules down to the line staff. Sometimes, we know a policy won't work. Those making the policy may have never even worked with inmates (male supervisor).

> Administrative policies should reflect more communication from the bottom to the top. There should be more accountability of the line staff to insure and encourage more consistent performance. Policy implementation depends too much upon who is in the chain of command, whether that individual likes the policy or not (female officer).

Because of these inadequacies, both the institutionalization of the new service philosophy and the integration of new female recruits were thwarted.

> The whole issue of women working in housing areas has not been dealt with at the administrative level. Little was done to prepare for the entry of women officers into male prisons. Administrators need to be aware of these issues. They should support those new female staff and not just throw them in there (female supervisor).

Without plans to counteract informal resistance to its new policies, Western D.O.C. placed itself in the position of dictating rather than negotiating reform. The discretion held by mid-management and line-staff made the institutionalization of administrative reform policies quite difficult (see Lipsky, 1980). Intimidation, aggressiveness, and informal opportunity arrangements continued to permeate the organizational structure of the Western D.O.C. and to reinforce the skepticism surrounding female officers. As a result, the relatively few female officers bore the burden of "proving themselves" in the face of suspicious staff:

> It's an aggressive environment. You have to act macho to make it. If you don't do that, it's hard to make them believe you're competent, and you'll never get anywhere in the job. But even then, they say that you're "hard" (female officer).

Impact of Organizational Barriers on Female Officer Advancement

The inadequate institutionalization of departmental reform policies affected the career progress of female officers at several crucial points—in training, work assignments, and performance evaluation. These organizational problems limited the availability and coherence of *training* programs offered to correctional officers. Officers were forced to rely on informal instruction by colleagues on the job. These problems also reinforced the importance of supervisor discretion in allocating *work assignments* and conducting officer *performance evaluations*. At each of these three points in the officer's career path, the suspect status of female officers, combined with the predominance of traditional security functions and informal opportunity structures, limited the integration and advancement opportunities available to female officers.

Pre-employment Experience and Training

As a group, women entered correctional employment with less "anticipatory socialization" than male recruits. For example, among those officers surveyed, only 38 percent of the female officers compared to 68 percent of the males reported any previous employment in either corrections or a related occupation. None of the women had served in the military. In contrast, 46 percent of the men reported military service records.

On-the-job training should have provided recruits with the requisite skills for their work. Such training was especially crucial for recruits who had no previous employment experience in that *field*. As we have seen, women were much more likely to fall into this inexperienced group. In the Western D.O.C., training had the additional important function of disseminating and institutionalizing the new service-oriented correctional philosophy adopted by the administration. As explained earlier, the adoption of a service-oriented philosophy established an area in which it was perceived that women could make a major contribution. However, the organizational problems discussed in the preceding section limited the effectiveness of training programs in three ways.

First, because of a rapidly growing inmate population and consequent staff shortages, many officers did not receive formal training prior to their first day of work. Attending in-service training courses became a problem for similar reasons. These difficulties occured despite departmental policies which specified that each officer had to complete a minimum of 80 training hours per year.

> At the main facility, they don't go to work without first attending the academy. Here, we've been understaffed since we opened and a lot of our officers haven't ever been to the academy (male training coordinator).

In the survey, 33 percent of the officers reported that they had never attended any entry-level training program offered by the department. In addition, 21 percent stated that they had received less than ten hours of in-service training during the year preceding the survey.

Second, it was difficult to develop a coherent and relevant training program because officer performance standards were inadequately specified, another result of the ambivalent incorporation of the new correctional philosophy. The ambiguity and conflict surrounding the necessary duties of correctional officers resulted in diverse, and sometimes inconsistent, themes in department training programs. Some classes emphasized physical abilities while others focused primarily on management and communication skills.

> Our training makes them tough. We let them know what it is like to have urine thrown in their face. They can't be shocked on their first day of work. We prepare them (training officer).

> The important thing for them to learn is that they are people managers. They must

be able to communicate. We no longer have the manpower to force the inmates to do what we want. We have to know how to manage them (training coordinator).

Finally, the manner in which training was conducted frequently prevented officers and supervisors from taking it seriously. Training was provided outside the prison work units. As a consequence, trainers had little direct authority over the correctional officers and virtually no influence over supervisors in the units.

If they (captains) don't want to let the guys off for training, there's not much I can do about it. Going through channels and complaining, well, that takes a long time (trainer).

Moreover, much of the training neglected the social control-oriented reality of the officer's work day.

What the trainers say is so different from what my supervisor tells me to do on the unit. It sounds good in the class, but I am not allowed to use it at work. A lot of it wouldn't work anyway (male officer).

Because, as a group, they came to the department with less related experience, inadequate training forced female officers to become more dependent on the informal training offered to them by veteran officers. These veterans were most likely to be male officers. Lacking adequate training, female recruits initially reaffirmed male co-workers expectations that women were less capable officers.

Everybody goes out there and they are scared. They will make mistakes. But when you're a woman, they remember. You represent other women who will come after you. You're a woman making a mistake . . . not just another new officer (female officer).

Without adequate training in management techniques, communication skills and crisis intervention strategies, line officers were not able to implement alternatives to more traditional tactics of intimidation as a form of inmate control. Physical strength and mental aggressiveness persisted as valued abilities for line security staff. Given stereotypes about women held by the majority of male staff, women remained less valued officers when such skills were deemed important.

Work Assignments

The duties assigned to officers had a tremendous impact on their occupational role learning. Although the majority of correctional officers had the same rank, the activities they performed varied greatly. Officers' assignments affected their attitudes toward work, the department and themselves. More importantly, however, assignments frequently determined later chances for advancement, because type and variety of experience gained by line officers at work heavily influenced their future evaluations for promotion. Interview and survey data indicated that in most men's prisons within the Western D.O.C. the range of work assignments allocated to female officers was more limited than those of their male counterparts. In the absence of specific regulations assuring equal assignment allocation, some supervisors used their discretion to restrict the tasks performed by female officers.

Although it was departmental policy to extend equal work opportunities to women, there were no formal policies regulating the placement of female officers in particular work areas. Duties were assigned primarily through supervisor preferences. The frequency with which they were changed and the criteria for determining who received which assignment were determined by the supervisor of each unit.

Some superintendents and supervisors opposed the assignment of women to duties in cellblocks, housing units, and yards. Objections to such assignments centered on perceived physical weaknesses of female officers. However, inmate rights to privacy were also utilized as a justification for restricting women's work assignments. There was considerable disagreement as to the validity of this explanation. A training coordinator comments facetiously:

> There is no problem with women in the yard, in living quarters, if they are not correctional officers. I can come and go as I please with no questions asked. That uniform does something. They are not supposed to see the men nude then (female trainer).

As a result of such limitations, female officer assignments were concentrated in control room, visitation, and clerical areas.

> My captain once said—he was serious—"Women in corrections are great. Every control room should have some" (female officer).

In the survey responses, the work assignment checked by the largest percentage of male officers as "consuming most of my time" was yard duty (51 percent). In contrast, the modal work assignment for female officers was control room duty (39 percent).[5]

The interpretation of work assignment policy varied both over time within the same prison, and across different institutions.

> When I first worked here, female officers worked every area that men did. Our current administrator won't allow women in the housing area—he says it's a violation of inmate privacy. Now women are pretty much confined to control booths, visitation, property or central communications units (female officer).

Restrictions in routine work assignments were significant because they ultimately limited the promotional possibilities for female officers. Without experience working in the yard and in housing, women found it difficult, if not impossible, to be promoted either to higher security levels or into the counseling officer track.

> The one thing an officer does not want to do is work the control room and work it extremely well. Their supervisor will never want to let them move anywhere else, . . . they'll go nowhere in the department, nowhere up, that is (male supervisor).

There were job assignments which were viewed by some supervisors as "appropriate" duty positions for women such as clerical work or duty in the control room or mail room. This information was communicated to female officers.

> Some sergeants don't make any bones about telling you that women don't belong in security positions with the residents (male inmates). . . . Or after you're there for a while, you see what positions they let women in (female officer).

These allocation patterns served to encourage "intrasex" competition for the valued assignments:

> One of the most powerful positions a female officer can hold is in central communications. Another good place is in transportation. The women know that and they compete with each other for what they can get. The men don't mind that. . . . I mean we can't compete with them. Women wind up telling on each other . . . (by) passing incidents to the sergeant (female officer).

Ironically, in addition to their effect on promotional decisions, restrictions in female work assignments fueled the resentment of male officers for the "special treatment" given to women.

I work here typing all day. I hate it. Then the guys come in, the other officers, and they say, "How do you rate being in here out of the hot sun, in this nice air-conditioned room!" They are irritated that I make the same wages they do and get the "cush" jobs! (female officer).

In absence of specific guidelines for greater integration of female officers, an informal network of opportunity took over. Their duty assignments were dependent on the attitudes of their supervisors:

I guess I should be grateful in one sense. My captain said, "Hey, I'm gonna get you out of here and in the yard!" At that time, women did not work the yard in that unit. I went out. I had a very liberal lieutenant and sergeant and I *worked the yard!* I was there during the food riot. I found out I could do the job. Now my major says, "I wouldn't put you in the yard unless you had a man next to you." So now I work in his office . . . answer his phone (female officer).

This informal opportunity network most often worked to the disadvantage of women working in men's prisons. The suspect status of female officers, combined with the discretionary nature of duty assignment, prevented them from obtaining the experience and recognition which were vital to promotion. Without the opportunity for such experience, their abilities were never fully demonstrated; their suspect status was merely reaffirmed.

Performance Evaluations

The annual performance evaluations of correctional officers became part of their permanent work records within the department. These evaluations were conducted by supervisors according to broad departmental guidelines. Later, these evaluations were scrutinized carefully when officers applied for promotions. Despite formal attempts to substitute universalistic for particularistic criteria in these reviews, the ambiguous and discretionary nature of the guidelines lead to inconsistent evaluations of officers.

Recognition? It depends on who your lieutenant and captain are, especially for women. It's how "in" you are . . . . You can work your bippy off and get passed over for someone you know isn't worth table salt (female officer).

In the absence of clear directives, supervisors' ratings were more easily influenced by their stereotyped views of women as seductive or weak.

My first time on yard duty, a resident came up and asked me a question and I was written up. On my performance evaluation, it said: "Over-familiar with residents." (female officer).

The subjectivity inherent in the officer review process was, in part, a side-effect of both the inadequate institutionalization of the service philosophy and the conflicting nature of correctional work. A content analysis of the departmental performance evaluation form for correctional service officers revealed the continued emphasis on security to the exclusion of service responsibilities. Out of the 18 categories of responsibilities evaluated, only one dealt with any service function performed by officers for inmates—that of administering first aid in an emergency situation. Communication skills, conflict diffusion or other service-related functions were not addressed. Eight categories related to line officers' responsibilities to follow orders and show respect for superiors. The remaining categories dealt with such issues as report writing, care of state property, control and direction of inmates, and proficiency in the use of firearms. The continued prevalence of para-military custodial and security functions supported traditional stereotypes of prison guards and indirectly accentuated the perceived weaknesses of female officers.

Even if performance ratings were based on universal standards, most officers felt that their use in promotions and other decisions was permeated by favoritism. Such perceptions reinforced beliefs that evaluations and promotions of women were based either on physical appearance or on the promise of sexual favors. Male officers resented this alleged favoritism. Female officers, in turn, feared retaliation if they responded negatively to sexual harassment from supervisors.

> When this male investigator tried to kiss me at work, I didn't tell anyone. It's not good to make waves that way. Your supervisors think you're just trying to cause trouble (female officer).

When women were promoted, they often felt a need to prove their qualifications and disprove the innuendos of "sexual" favoritism.

> Our captain was known for hiring and promoting women officers. When he moved me into administrative duties, a lot of the guys there said, "She's just another one of the captain's harem." After a few months, I was able to prove that I was competent *and* that I was not screwing the boss (female officer).

Without clear and uniform standards for officer evaluations, female officers were again dependent on the goodwill of individual supervisors. If gender stereotypes entered their performance evaluations, they had little formal recourse. Grievance procedures required employees to file with their immediate supervisors. If the superior was the subject of the grievance, this requirement presented a serious obstacle to the grievance process. Given the subjectivity of the review process, it was extremely difficult to document the degree to which the evaluations of particular employees were biased. Finally, the subjectivity of the process also ignited male co-worker hostilities because they believed that positive evaluations and promotions of female officers were often "sexually motivated."

Conclusion

This analysis has illustrated the manner in which a specific organizational milieu reinforced biases against women working in a non-traditional occupation. The findings suggest that an exclusive focus on the psychological traits and attitudes of supervisors, colleagues, clients, and workers themselves presents an incomplete explanation of the barriers confronting women in this field. The "token" position of women in corrections, the conflicting nature of the work, extra-organizational conditions, informal organizational resistance, and the absence of adequate administrative implementation strategies also posed important barriers to the full integration of female officers. These conditions frustrated administrative attempts at organizational reform, reinforced the biased attitudes held by correctional personnel, and permitted individual sentiments to play an important role in the advancement of women within the organization. In other words, the seemingly "sexist" attitudes of these individuals were not *solely* the result of prior gender-role socialization, but were also a response to working conditions within a given organizational context.

These findings demonstrate the relevance of both organizational dynamics *and* individual attitudes in developing more complete explanations of the difficulties that women experience in non-traditional occupations. Although not suggesting that an understanding of individual attitudes is unimportant, this investigation emphasizes the necessity of examining the organizational context of individual work behavior which, at first glance, may appear to emanate exclusively from stereotypes and personal biases. Further research is clearly needed on the interplay of organizational and individual factors on women's advancement in non-traditional careers—especially in light of limitations in the sample and generalizability of the present study.

Another important point revealed in this analysis is that research on problems encountered by women in non-traditional occupations requires a broad understanding of general problems affecting *both* men and women in the workplace. As Kanter (1977:264) has argued, we must "turn attention away from inter-group competition and toward the real problem: the ways systems of work are organized and how these systems themselves can be modified."

Notes

1. See McIlwee (1981) for a more in-depth discussion of "human relations" models.

2. A total of three weeks of observation was conducted by this investigator and three graduate students at one medium security prison. Two other facilities were visited twice, while the remaining facilities were visited once.

3. The survey was conducted in a medium security prison facility in the western D.O.C. At the time of the survey, this prison employed approximately 230 correctional service officers. Data were collected from self-administered questionnaires distributed and collected by the investigator and graduate research assistants. We obtained completed surveys from 179 officers—40 women and 139 men. These numbers represent an 85 percent response rate for officers working day and swing shifts, and a 50 percent response rate for those officers assigned to graveyard duty (the latter group did not receive time off to complete the survey). See Jurik and Halemba (1984) for a more detailed description of the survey items.

4. See Jacobs (1983) for a discussion of these changes as a national trend.

5. Control rooms were the communication centers and walkways into and out of each unit or group of cells. Duty in these rooms consisted of opening and closing electronic doors, transferring phone calls and transmitting orders to staff who carried mobile communication devices.

References

Aronson, D. C., Dienes, T., & Musheno, M. C. (1984). *Public policy and police discretion*. New York: Clark Boardman.
Babbie, Earl. (1983). *The practice of social research* (3rd edition). Belmont, CA: Wadsworth.
Bourne, P. G., & Wikler, N. J. (1978). Commitment and cultural mandate: Women in medicine. *Social Problems, 25,* 430–440.
Bridges, W. P. (1982). The sexual segregation of occupations: Theories of labor stratification in industry. *American Journal of Sociology, 88,* 270–295.
Chapman, J. R., Minor, E. K., Rieker, P., Mills, T. L., & Bottum, M. (1980). Women employed in corrections. Washington, DC: Report from the Center for Women Policy Studies.
Cressey, D. (1966.) Contradictory directives in complex organizations: the case of the prison. In Hazelrigg, H., *Prison within society* (pp. 349–373). New York: Doubleday.
Feinman, C. (1980.) *Women in the criminal justice system*. New York: Praeger.
Fox, J. (1982). *Organizational and racial conflict in maximum security prisons*. New York: D.C. Heath.
Glaser, B., & Strauss, A. (1967.) *The discovery of grounded theory*. New York: Aldine.
Hacker, S. (1979.) Sex stratification, technology and organizational change: A longitudinal case study of AT&T. *Social Problems, 26,* 539–557.
Holland, T. R., Levi, M., Beckett, G. E., & Holt, N. (1979.) Preferences of prison inmates for male versus female institutional personnel. *Journal of Applied Psychology, 64,* 564–568.
Izraeli, D. N. (1983.) Sex effects or structural effects? An empirical test of Kanter's theory of proportions. *Social Forces, 62,* 153–165.
Jacobs, J. (1983.) *New perspectives on prisons and imprisonment*. New York: Cornell University Press.
Jurie, J. D. (1984.) *Policy implementation*. Unpublished doctoral examination. Arizona State University, Tempe.
Jurik, N. C., & Halemba, G. J. (1984.) Gender, working conditions and the job satisfaction of women in a non-traditional occupation: Female correctional officers in men's prisons. *Sociological Quarterly, 25,* 551–566.
Kanter, R. M. (1976.) The impact of hierarchical structures on the work behavior of women and men. *Social Problems, 23,* 415–430.
Kanter, R. M. (1977.) *Men and women of the corporation*. New York: Harper & Row.
Kissell, P., & Katasampes, P. (1980.) The impact of women corrections officers on the functioning of institutions housing male inmates. *Journal of Offender Counseling Services and Rehabilitation, 4,* 213–231.
Lipsky, M. (1980.) *Street-level bureaucracy: Dilemmas of the individual in public services*. New York: Russell Sage Foundation.
Martin, S. E. (1980.) *Breaking and entering: Policewomen on patrol*. Berkeley: University of California Press.
McIlwee, J. S. (1981.) Organizational theory and the entry of women into non-traditional occupations. *Western Sociological Review, 12,* 33–52.
Miller, J. (1980.) Individual and occupational determinants of job satisfaction. *Sociology of Work and Occupations, 7,* 337–366.
Miller, J., Labovitz, S., & Fry, L. (1975.) Inequities in the organizational experiences of women and men. *Social Forces, 54,* 365–81.
National Institute of Justice. (1978.) *The national manpower survey of the criminal justice system: Corrections*. Washington, DC: U.S. Government Printing Office.
O'Farrell, B., & Harlan, S. (1982.) Craftworkers and clerks: The effect of male coworker hostility on women's satisfaction with non-traditional jobs. *Social Problems, 29,* 252–263.
Perrow, C. (1979.) *Complex organizations* (2nd edition). Glenview, IL: Scott Foresman.
Wilson, N. K. (1982.) Women in the criminal justice professions: An analysis of status conflict. In Rafter, N. H., & Stanko, E. A. (eds.), *Judge lawyer victim thief* (pp. 359–374). Boston: Northeastern University Press.

DISCUSSION QUESTIONS

1. In the state prison system Jurik studied, only 15% of correctional officers were women. Are the barriers noted likely to diminish if female officers, over time, make up an increasing proportion of prison staff? Why or why not?

2. Perceived concerns about a female correctional officer's physical abilities served as barriers for women working in male prison environments, particularly when perceived danger increased (e.g., when overcrowding occurred). Whose responsibility is it to address this apprehension and allow for greater integration of the officer force? Female officers? Male officers? Organization managers? Explain.

3. As Jurik explained, circumstances required the use of informal and individualized socialization tactics. Would barriers diminish if training were more formalized and collective (both males and females)?

SECTION VIII

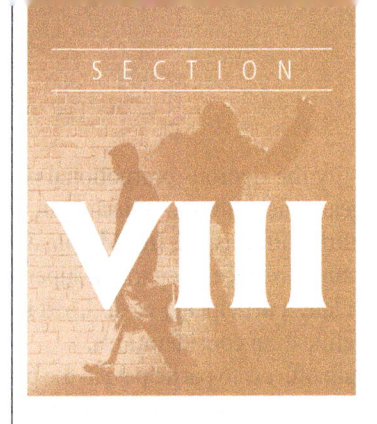

Motivation and Job Design
How Do We Light a Fire Under Employees?

Section Highlights

Conceptual Issues
Content Theories
   Need Theory
   Motivator–Hygiene Theory
   Achievement, Affiliation, and Power Motives

Process Theories
   Equity Theory and Organizational Justice
   Expectancy Theory
Job Design

Climbing the organizational ladder potentially generates a host of rewards for the individual ascending the ranks: increased pay, greater prestige, a sense of accomplishment, new roles and responsibilities, and expanded opportunities (Gaines, Van Tubergen, & Paiva, 1984; Whetstone, 2001). Given these benefits, it may seem surprising that studies from the past two decades found that only 1 in 5 sworn police officers eligible for promotion to sergeant actually participated in the promotional process (Scarborough, Van Tubergen, Gaines, & Whitlow, 1999; Whetstone, 2001). While some officers may decline to participate due to actual or perceived lack of qualifications, "a shortage of aspirants may well be a cause for organizational alarm" if those who continue with the process are *less* qualified than those who decline (Whetstone, 2001, p. 147; see also Scarborough et al., 1999). If the latter is true, a possible long-term consequence is weakened front-line supervision and leadership. Why do officers decline participation in the promotional process? Research suggests that promotion is simply not important in satisfying needs; the rewards are not worth the effort or are not perceived as rewards at all.

For example, the extra pay, if it is even a pay increase, may not justify the rigorous promotional process (Scarborough et al., 1999). Whetstone (2001) discovered that sergeants actually saw a decline in pay in spite of the promotional bump as overtime and court time opportunities diminished. In addition, officers who valued the social element of police work actually devalued promotion since it separated supervisors from line-level personnel/peers (Gaines et al., 1984). Clearly, candidates participated or declined to participate in the promotional process for reasons other than pure qualification considerations.

The example above illustrates the lack of motivation among certain officers to participate in the process or, conversely, their motivation or decision to remain at the lower rank. Vroom (1964) argued that motivation is what energizes and provides direction for behavior. An individual's behavior in the workplace (and elsewhere)—whether to apply for promotion, make an arrest, arrive at work that day, report a probationer for a technical violation, strike an inmate, resign from a position, or any other activity—can be linked back to that person's level of motivation to engage in that behavior.[1] His or her very performance in an organization and success in activities are a combination of both motivation and ability or skill set (Maier, 1955). Those studying motivation are therefore interested, as Weiner (1992) summarized, in a variety of topics:

> Motivational psychologists . . . observe and measure what the individual is doing, or choice behavior; how long it takes before the individual initiates the activity when given the opportunity, or the latency of behavior; how hard the individual is working at that activity, or the intensity of behavior; what length of time the individual will remain at that activity, or the persistence of behavior; and what the individual is feeling before, during, or after the behavioral episode, or emotional reactions. (p. 2)

Motivation thus occupies a central position in understanding both what people do and how well they do it. This section addresses motivation within the criminal justice system, focusing on an overview of the concept, key motivators, and significant theories of motivation and their application to justice agencies. It concludes with a discussion of job design, how the work of criminal justice organizations can be altered to facilitate higher levels of motivation.

Conceptual Issues

Theories of motivation are typically grouped into two broad categories according to their primary focal point. **Content theories** identify needs linked to motivation (Steers, Mowday, & Shapiro, 2004; Tosi, Rizzo, & Carroll, 1986). As the three theories (need theory, motivator–hygiene theory, and achievement/power/affiliation theory) discussed below illustrate, scholars attempted to catalogue either exhaustive lists of human needs or the most salient human needs driving behavior. In contrast, the goal of **process theories** is to "understand the thought processes that people go through in determining how to behave in the workplace" (Steers et al., 2004, p. 381). In many cases, the particular motives are less important than the process by which those needs are translated into actual behavior in the workplace. Rather than assume that unfulfilled needs will automatically lead to action, process theories (e.g., equity theory and expectancy theory) consider factors such as the value associated with rewards and fairness in the workplace as additional determinants of workplace behavior.

The types of rewards (or needs) that serve as motivators are varied, ranging from pay to internal feelings of self-worth. Scholars have categorized these rewards under two broad headings: extrinsic and

---

[1] Vroom (1964) argues that any behavior, as long as it is "under central or voluntary control," must be motivated (p. 8).

intrinsic motivators (Lawler & Porter, 1967). Extrinsic rewards include those controlled and allocated by the organization (Lawler, 1969). An individual engages in the work to receive some reward upon its completion, what Amabile (1993) considered a "means to some external end" (p. 189). Examples include pay, health benefits, nearby parking spots, status indicators such as job titles (e.g., Patrol Officer II) or private offices, or other benefits externally bestowed on the worker by others. In contrast, intrinsic motivators are those that "stem directly from the performance itself . . . the individual rewards himself" (Lawler, 1969, p. 428). The work itself is gratifying and the individual engaging in that work experiences the awards directly. Rather than rely on some external agent to provide the rewards, the employee's feelings about the work serve as a self-reward. When intrinsic motivation exists, the work is inherently rewarding. Examples of intrinsic rewards include feelings of accomplishment, achievement, importance, self-esteem, and challenge. The theories of motivation, particularly the content theories discussed in the next section, further illustrate the importance of these categories of motivators. Table 8.1 illustrates the relationship between intrinsic and extrinsic motivators and concepts found in the three major content theories discussed below.

Table 8.1 Relationship Between General Motivation Concepts and Content Theory Elements[1]

Motivator Type (Lawler & Porter, 1967)	Level of Needs (Wahba & Bridwell, 1976)	Need Theory (Maslow, 1943)	Motivator-Hygiene Theory (Herzberg, Mausner, & Snyderman, 1959)	Achievement/ Power/Affiliation Theory (McClelland, 1961, 1965, 1985)
Intrinsic	Higher order (growth needs)	Self-actualization Esteem[2]	Motivators	Achievement/power
Extrinsic	Basic (deficiency needs)	Belonging Security/safety Physiological	Hygiene factors	Affiliation

[1]The table depicts approximate rather than precise correspondence between concepts.

[2]Technically, esteem needs are intrinsic if related to self-esteem or extrinsic if related to recognition externally bestowed.

Content Theories

Need Theory

Content theories slowly emerged beginning in the 1940s and were the focus of much research by the 1950s (Steers et al., 2004). Arguably the most well-known theory in this area was Abraham Maslow's **need theory**, proposed in a 1943 article titled "A Theory of Human Motivation" and more fully developed in a subsequent book (1954). He organized human needs into five classifications:

- *Physiological needs:* Of critical importance is satisfying basic survival needs, including the need for food, water, and shelter. Within a workplace setting, workers trade their efforts for a salary that enables them to satisfy these basic needs.

- *Safety needs:* Individuals want to live and work free from harm or feelings of fear. In addition to physical safety, people want predictability in their work (Maslow, 1943). They do not want to have to worry how bills will be paid in the event of a catastrophic illness or loss of employment.

- *Belonging:* Maslow argued that people "hunger for affectionate relations with people in general" (p. 381). Individual friendships and social relationships are important needs for many individuals.

- *Esteem:* Esteem needs can be subdivided. On one hand, people seek the recognition of others. They want attention, appreciation, respect, and to be valued. On the other hand, self-esteem is an important need. Maslow referred to feelings of confidence, achievement, and adequacy as needs that many individuals long to fulfill.

- *Self-actualization:* Maslow described self-actualization vaguely: "to become everything that one is capable of becoming" (p. 382). While everyone wants to reach their potential, what self-actualization represents is a variable concept. Each person's self-actualization need is going to be different.

Understanding that humans possess these needs, we can begin to understand human motivation as an attempt to satisfy needs. Maslow's theory was more complex, however, than just a listing of important motives. The needs were fashioned into a hierarchy, with physiological needs at the bottom and self-actualization needs at the top. The bottom three categories—physiological, safety, and belonging—are generally referred to as basic or deficiency needs (see Table 8.1) because motivation is designed to fill gaps in these areas (Steers et al., 2004; Wahba & Bridwell, 1976). An unemployed worker lacks the ability to satisfy some basic human needs (a deficit), so aggressively pursues a variety of job opportunities. A new correctional officer struggling to fit into the correctional officer subculture may resort to using coercive force against inmates to garner peer acceptance and fill a belonging void (see, for example, Marquart, 1986). The upper categories—esteem and self-actualization—are higher-order or growth needs. They help fulfill personal needs and "sustain our interest without our being driven by feelings of deprivation" (Neher, 1991, p. 91; see also Steers et al., 2004).[2]

Maslow argued that the importance of any category of needs is related to the degree to which the need is satisfied or, in his language, gratified. Individuals are first motivated by the desire to satisfy physiological needs. They cannot possibly be driven by the desire to affiliate with others in the workplace if they are unable to feed their families. In this context, the need driving behavior is the lowest unfulfilled need in the hierarchy (physiological). As the need is satisfied, it "allows the next higher set of needs in the hierarchy to emerge, dominate, and organize the personality" (Wahba & Bridwell, 1976, p. 214). As a worker satisfies physiological needs, preserving his or her job (safety/security) becomes a primary motivator. Again, other needs such as belonging, esteem, and self-actualization are not relevant at this point. The process continues until the individual fulfills self-actualization needs, but this occurs only after all four other sets of needs are satisfied.

In spite of the intuitive appeal of Maslow's theory, it has been subjected to a number of general and criminal justice–specific criticisms. For example, Wahba and Bridwell's (1976) review of the literature

---

[2]The literature points to disagreement regarding the demarcation between deficiency and growth needs. Neher (1991) includes only self-actualization in the growth needs category, while Steers et al. (2004) include both esteem and self-actualization. In Table 8.1, two levels are included, with the note that esteem is likely a growth need to the extent that the focus is on self-esteem rather than external recognition.

revealed only limited support for the central tenants of Maslow's theory. For example, researchers have not found conclusive evidence in support of a five-level hierarchy; at best, two factors (growth and deficiency needs) may be in operation. Others have questioned whether self-actualization (human potential) is a legitimate need or an ideal imposed on society. In other words, we should ask whether all people share this need or whether pursuing self-actualization needs is just a positive yet unrealistic view of human behavior. Another criticism relates to the universality of the theory. Maslow (1943) argued that the needs and the hierarchy itself were fixed for most people, although he did note several exceptions. Neher (1991) disagreed, noting that the lower-order needs (physiological and safety/security) are likely fixed but that the potency of higher-order needs undoubtedly varies across individuals. Conser (1979) found difficulty applying Maslow's theory to police organizations because, he asserted, the theory did not account for individual differences among officers. Some officers may be more motivated by external recognition (esteem needs) than by peer groups (belonging), while others may desire the reverse. Maslow's theory does not generally account for the uniqueness of individuals and individual situations. As further evidence of the flexibility in the hierarchy, Herbert (1998) indicated that adventure/machismo (aggressiveness, courage) is an important part of the officer subculture. Conforming to cultural norms and maintaining peer group connections (belonging) may, at times, increase the likelihood of danger for the officer. Based on his extensive observations of the Los Angeles Police Department, Herbert noted, "Officers must demonstrate their courage and bravery by willingly placing themselves in potentially dangerous or otherwise uncomfortable situations" (p. 356). Overall, the value of Maslow's theory may be in explicating a series of needs, not the hierarchy of those needs. Indeed, subsequent theories abandoned the hierarchical component.

Motivator–Hygiene Theory

Frederick Herzberg and colleagues (Herzberg, Mausner, & Snyderman, 1959) further studied motivation in the workplace and, in doing so, challenged the inherent sequence of Maslow's needs hierarchy. Their **motivator–hygiene theory** was based on a sample of more than 200 engineers and accountants in the Pittsburgh metropolitan area. Interviews with participants largely revolved around a single question:

> Think of a time in the past when you felt especially good or bad about your job. It may have been on this job or any other job. Can you think of such a high or low point in your feelings about your job? Please tell me about it. (p. 20)

After reviewing the responses, Herzberg and colleagues uncovered a clear pattern where factors that created "highs" in the workplace were independent of the factors that generated "lows."

Among the most commonly reported items related to positive work attitudes were successful task accomplishment (achievement); recognition for quality job performance; opportunities to engage in creative, challenging, and varied work tasks; increased responsibilities; and advancement within the organization. These factors are intrinsically rewarding; they lead to self-reward, a sense of personal growth, and, in some cases, self-actualization. Even recognition and advancement, factors that would appear to be extrinsic in nature, generated positive feelings due to their relationship to both growth and self-actualization. Herzberg and colleagues (1959) also noted that many of these factors tended to produce lasting effects that positively contributed to job performance. Specifically, "the factors of work itself [creative, challenging, etc.], responsibility, and advancement are almost always associated with long-term changes in job attitudes" (p. 64). Achievement and recognition, in contrast, are usually specific to a situation and are more fleeting in nature. When workers were asked to pinpoint low points in their work, they noted factors such as company policy, relationships with supervisors, quality of supervision (e.g., fairness, abilities), and working conditions (e.g., quality of the work environment, amount of work; Herzberg et al., 1959).

The two sets of factors—those contributing to highs and lows—operated largely independent of each other. Those identified as producing positive feelings—achievement, recognition, the work itself, responsibility, and advancement—were less commonly mentioned in low situations. Similarly, policies, relationships with supervisors, and working conditions rarely emerged as explanations of highs. Herzberg and colleagues concluded that "there were certain factors that would operate only to increase job satisfaction and that there would be other factors with the power only to decrease job satisfaction" (Herzberg et al., 1959, p. 80). Intrinsic factors, including achievement, growth, and the task itself, were associated with positive work outcomes such as increasing productivity, reducing the likelihood of job turnover, improving attitudes toward the organization, and generating other positive outcomes. These are true motivators, the factors that stimulate performance. The factors associated with supervision, working conditions, and policies rarely serve as motivators. The authors, using a medical analogy, referred to them as hygiene factors. If they are not addressed, dissatisfaction will likely occur and, indeed, motivation will become more difficult. If working conditions, policies, and supervision are dealt with, however, enhanced motivation is not an automatic result, since opportunities must be available to intrinsically reward employees.

Focus-group interviews with a small sample of officers in a metropolitan police department revealed findings consistent with motivator–hygiene theory (Monk-Turner, O'Leary, & Sumter, 2010). In describing the positive aspects of their work, officers concentrated on the control they maintained over their work, their ability to help others, and the interesting and challenging aspects of the job. As expected given Herzberg's findings, extrinsic factors dominated the list of dissatisfiers. Officers reported problems with equipment and personnel availability. Two other factors—supervisory relationships and opportunities—were alternatively viewed as both satisfiers and dissatisfiers. For some, "supervisors who allow officers the possibility of achievement, recognition, and responsibility at work are building environments that encourage job satisfaction and retention" (Monk-Turner et al., 2010, p. 177). For others, supervisors are a source of discontent (e.g., by criticizing officers), an element of the work environment that generates dissatisfaction. Similarly, promotional opportunities are symbols of recognition or advancement but may also produce frustration if they are limited or distributed inequitably.

Motivator–hygiene theory represented an advance in the study of employee motivation. Maslow's (1943) needs hierarchy suggested that lower-order needs (physiological, security, and affiliation) are, in order, the most important motivators until satisfied. Motivator–hygiene theory challenges this argument. Extrinsic needs explained only negative reactions (dissatisfaction) but not positive reactions (satisfaction). A different set of factors was necessary for motivation, job satisfaction, and other positive outcomes to occur. The dual or two-factor nature of motivator–hygiene theory has significant implications for organizational life (Conser, 1979). An organization may have more control over intrinsic elements of the work even when restrictions are placed on extrinsic reward opportunities (e.g., by union contracts) and may be able to promote motivation even in the face of some mild employee dissatisfaction. Overall, however, the best approach to motivation, given the central elements of theory, is "ensuring adequate pay and creating a work environment that offers challenges and opportunities for achievement" (Monk-Turner et al., 2010, p. 165).

Achievement, Affiliation, and Power Motives

Rather than create an exhaustive list, David McClelland (1961, 1962, 1965, 1985) focused much of his attention on three key needs: achievement, affiliation, and power. Symbolized as *n* achievement, *n* affiliation, and *n* power, these needs are said to be of varying salience to individuals. These needs, consistent with the upper parts of Maslow's hierarchy, advanced the earlier work by specifically identifying important motives rather than relying on more general or vague terminology such as self-actualization (Steers et al., 2004). Individuals with a strong achievement motive desire to be successful. As McClelland (1985) writes, "What should be involved in the achievement motive is doing something better for its own sake, for the intrinsic satisfaction of doing something better" (p. 228). For example, detectives want to clear open cases, police officers seek to apprehend big-time offenders, prosecutors look to win in court, and probation officers hope to steer offenders to law-abiding lifestyles. To the extent that individual behavior is guided by the desire to be successful in these pursuits, the achievement motive is salient. As these examples illustrate, it is the job itself that provides satisfaction; motivation is not based on external rewards such as pay increases or other extrinsic benefits.

Certain tasks are particularly suitable for high *n* achievement individuals (McClelland, 1962, 1985). First, they like to work independently and take personal responsibility for their performance. A hobbyist who assembles a computer from scratch without instructions may take more satisfaction in the work than one who relies on a kit. In the latter situation, the developer's instructions, not personal know-how, led to the successful completion of the task. Similarly, a prosecutor who sees a case through from initiation to conviction can take greater pride in the outcome than a prosecutor who handled only the closing arguments of the case. Second, they appreciate moderately challenging tasks over simplistic or extremely difficult ones. Writing traffic tickets is not a motivating task, as all officers are capable of doing so successfully, but requiring officers to reduce crime in their beats to zero is likely an unrealistic target; officers with high achievement needs will confront failure. In contrast, requiring officers to select and attempt to solve a particular problem in their beat is a more realistic yet challenging goal. It is one that could provide a significant level of pride for those who can craft successful solutions. Finally, high *n* achievement individuals require feedback. Without it, they are unaware of their successes (or failures). As will be shown later in this section (see "Job Design"), tasks can be structured to accommodate high *n* achievement workers.

A second common motive, the affiliation motive, is predicated on the belief that individuals value interpersonal relationships (McClelland, 1962). In a review of research on the affiliation motive, McClelland (1985) noted that high *n* achievement is linked to the desire to avoid conflict and criticism. The result, according to this line of thinking, is poor leadership (McClelland, 1985; McClelland & Burnham, 1976). Consider the following example. A corrections supervisor with a high *n* affiliation confronts a subordinate who inadvertently left an inmate alone in an unsecure area of the prison. The supervisor, wishing to avoid conflict, calmly reminds the offending officer of the policy violation even though the repercussions of such an oversight are significant. As McClelland and Burnham (1976) argue, "if [the managers] make exceptions for the particular needs of individuals, the whole system will break down" (p. 103). Nevertheless, the discussion of the human relations school in Section III demonstrated the importance of informal relationships and social connections in the workplace. These needs are clearly important for a significant portion of criminal justice agency employees. In the example that opened this section, promotion could be looked at from multiple perspectives. For the high n achievement individual, participating and successfully completing the promotional process may be the type of challenging activity these individuals demand. In contrast, officers who have a high n affiliation would be less intrigued by the prospects of promotion. Leaving the officer ranks for a field supervisor position will sever ties that are important for satisfying affiliation needs (Gaines et al., 1984). In these cases, it may be worth it to decline participation in the promotional process.

The third of McClelland's three key motives, the **power motive** (n power) was based simply on the idea that individuals "desire to have impact, to be strong and influential" (McClelland & Burnham, 1976, p. 103). The power motive may manifest in a variety of ways within the workplace (McClelland, 1985). There is some evidence that the need for power is linked to aggressiveness, though this may be moderated by other factors, including an individual's personal values. To satisfy this need, people may look for symbols of status or prestige (e.g., titles, ranks, upgraded equipment), seek positions of influence (e.g., managerial fields), and/or enter into more prestigious occupations such as medicine. As McClelland and Burnham (1976) caution, those with the need for power should not be considered dictatorial. However, some individuals work to accumulate as much power, prestige, and status as possible for no other purpose than to demonstrate superiority over others (Kirkpatrick & Locke, 1991; Tosi et al., 1986). Kirkpatrick and Locke (1991) argue that "individuals with a **personalized power motive** [seek] power as an end in itself" (p. 53). In contrast, individuals may satisfy their power needs and use that power to benefit the organization as a whole. The **socialized power motive** balances an individual's need for power with self-control or inhibition (McClelland & Burnham, 1976). In other words, the manifestation of personalized power is restrained, and "they use their power to build up their organization and make it successful" (Kirkpatrick & Locke, 1991, p. 53). Power is used for the benefit of others within and/or outside the organization.

Compared to the achievement need, power motives have not been studied as frequently (McClelland, 1985). Nevertheless, an examination of occupational choice in policing illustrates the utility of the theory in understanding aspects of the criminal justice system. Are recruits drawn to police work by factors such as power, prestige, and control? Above all, police work is defined by the officer's legitimate right and capacity to use coercive force where necessary, a significant manifestation of power (Bittner, 1990). Studies conducted during the mid-20th century questioned the prestige of policing as a profession, particularly given the frequent negative conflicts between police officers and the community (McNamara, 1967). Officers were entering police work due to practical considerations; it was a secure, steady job with decent pay (Westley, 1970). In more recent studies, power-related motives continued to be less important than other factors. For example, when New York City police officers who entered the academy in 2001 were asked why they entered police work, power and authority were cited as the least important reason among the 16 identified (White, Cooper, Saunders, & Raganella, 2010). Again, practical considerations—job security, job benefits, early retirement, and opportunities for advancement—were deemed most relevant. Officers also cited a desire to help members of the community and the excitement of the work. A majority of the 234 San Diego Police Department recruits surveyed in a different study noted the desire to help the community and stable employment as important factors leading them to pursue a career in law enforcement (Ridgeway et al., 2008). Interestingly, 46% of recruits cited "status/pride in being a police officer" as one of their three most important reasons. Among New York City officers, prestige ranked ninth among 16 items (White et al., 2010). These results suggest that prestige matters to some but that wielding power directly is of limited importance. Power and influence are discussed in greater detail in Section XI.

Process Theories

Equity Theory and Organizational Justice

Each of the preceding theories of motivation presupposes an exchange between individuals where their inputs—what they bring to the exchange—is reciprocated with some type of reward (e.g., pay, fringe benefits, recognition, job titles) or punishment (e.g., demotions, criticism, reassignment, termination; Adams, 1963; Walster, Walster, & Berscheid, 1978). These inputs include valuable things such as "education, intelligence, experience, training, skill, seniority, age, ethnic background, social status, and very importantly, the effort he expends on the job" (Adams, 1963, p. 422). These characteristics, in many respects, are viewed as assets warranting positive rewards, but other characteristics (e.g., irresponsibility) may produce negative outcomes (Walster et al., 1978). Equity theory argues that employee motivation and other work-related behaviors and attitudes are determined by the perceived fairness of this exchange. Although the importance individuals attach to inputs and outcomes is purely subjective, the perceived ratio of inputs to outputs is used to determine whether the exchange was fair in individual minds. Unfortunately, judgments about fairness are difficult to make in isolation; instead, they are made through a comparison process where an individual's ratio is gauged relative to other individuals, groups, or even one's self in another position or time (Adams, 1963). If inequity in treatment is perceived, deleterious outcomes such as diminished work effort or negative job attitudes may result.

Perceptions of inequity occur when an individual is either under-rewarded/underpaid or over-rewarded/overpaid (Adams, 1963).[3] For example, two correctional officers bring the same level of experience, training, and work effort to the job, but Correctional Officer B receives overtime opportunities. In such a case, Correctional Officer A might feel under-rewarded, since equal effort is met with unequal rewards. Correctional Officer A may feel similarly under-rewarded if she receives the same number of overtime opportunities as Correctional Officer B in spite of putting in extra effort on the job. Her surplus work is essentially unreciprocated. In contrast, overpayment occurs when Correctional Officer A receives the same benefit (overtime opportunities) as Correctional Officer B for expending less effort or receives extra benefits for the same level of effort. In both cases, negative reactions may occur; "overpaid workers would feel guilty and . . . underpaid workers would feel angry" (Greenberg, 1987, p. 11; see also Kidd & Utne, 1978; Walster et al., 1978). Clearly, merit plays a central role in this version of equity theory. People will make the investment of their inputs (e.g., a prolonged graduate education, extra hours of case preparation) only if they can be assured some reward. Likewise, from an organizational perspective, it only makes sense to facilitate the achievement of organizational goals by rewarding significant contributions (Deutsch, 1975). Inequity results when the merit principle is violated (Leventhal, 1980).

It is important to reiterate that inequity is in the eye of the beholder (Kidd & Utne, 1978). If the outcomes—overtime opportunities, in the examples above—are not valued, they will not figure into an

---

[3] Recognizing that the exchange can result in both rewards and punishments, Walster et al. (1978) argue that outcomes are the rewards minus the costs/punishments.

individual's calculation of the input/output ratio. Similarly, individuals have different views on important inputs or contributions to an exchange. For example, within a sample of Canadian regional police officers, significant differences emerged about important factors to consider in promotional decisions (Buckley, McGinnis, & Petrunik, 1992). Officers with a university degree were more likely than officers with no degree or some university credits to believe that university education should be a determinant of promotion decisions. In contrast, officers without college degrees emphasized the relevance of factors such as loyalty, hard work, and experience. The officers clearly differed in the importance they attached to various inputs. In correctional settings, perceived inequity may occur as male correctional officers receive promotions ahead of female correctional officers in spite of similar qualifications. Female officers, faced with incidents of sexual harassment in male-dominated correctional environments, believed that reporting such behavior would affect their chances of promotion even though this should be an irrelevant consideration (Matthews, Monk-Turner, & Sumter, 2010; see also Griffin, Armstrong, & Hepburn, 2005).

Distress may occur in the individual who perceives inequity, resulting in changes in work behavior and attitudes (Cohen-Charash & Spector, 2001). Typically, these changes follow attempts to restore equity in relationships (Adams, 1963). For example, if the two correctional officers discussed earlier are receiving different outcomes for the same inputs, the "underpaid" correctional officer may attempt to restore balance to the relationship by giving less effort (thereby matching inputs with outcomes) or maintaining inputs but taking unauthorized benefits (e.g., leaving work 15 minutes early each day). If they receive the same benefits but one correctional officer is working harder (again, is underpaid relative to effort), she may reduce her performance level to match her comparison peer's. In each case, individuals attempt to achieve equity in relationships. They may also attempt to restore equity psychologically. As Walster et al. (1978) suggest, the correctional officer could diminish the importance of the rewards to rationalize the inequity; the correctional officer might say that the overtime would have interfered with family time anyway (p. 19). As these examples illustrate, failing to maintain equitable relations within an organization may produce harmful results. At the most extreme, the organization may experience turnover as disgruntled employees leave for other opportunities (Adams, 1963).

So far, the discussion has centered on the fairness of outcomes in relation to contributions. **Distributive justice** addresses perceived inequity in outcomes but takes a broader view of fairness and how outcomes are distributed (Cohen-Charash & Spector, 2001; Leventhal, 1980). Instead of determining fairness solely on merit or contributions, perceived fairness may also be based "on a needs rule which dictates that persons with greater need should receive higher outcomes, or an equality rule which dictates that everyone should receive similar outcomes regardless of needs or contributions" (Leventhal, 1980, p. 29). Kenneth Feinberg, an attorney responsible for the unenviable task of disbursing 9/11 compensation fund monies, was required to place value on the lives of victims (Grimes, 2005). As award decisions were made, undoubtedly some families of victims judged awards according to need standards. Indeed, it would be difficult to "[tell] the wife of a fireman, for example, that her husband was worth less than a stockbroker," especially if the former perceived her need for financial assistance to be greater (Grimes, 2005). Feinberg subsequently handled funds for victims of the Virginia Tech shooting and the Gulf Coast oil spill. In still other cases, fairness in outcomes is based on principles of equality rather than proportional to contributions or need. Recall the discussion of supplemental pay for union members in Section VI. Police departments operating under collective bargaining agreements were less likely to include provisions for merit pay, the types of systems that may contribute to feelings of inequity, as managers define meritorious behavior (Zhao & Lovrich, 1997). Instead, fairness is best achieved by distributing raises based on some clear criteria (e.g., educational credits). Unions also tend to support across-the-board pay increases, where all members reap the benefits equally. These pay systems, based on equality, should promote cordial within-union relationships, but individual members, relying on need or contribution-based judgments, may feel that their performance is undervalued by the organization (Deutsch, 1975). All three allocation types—contributions, need, and equality—can be seen in judicial sentencing decisions. A person may view two sentences as fair to the extent that they are proportional to the inputs (e.g., prior record, demographic characteristics). This is consistent with the original version of equity theory. Alternatively, a sentence is fair only if it considers offender needs; all else being equal, a defendant with a family to care for should, in some people's minds, receive a lighter sentence (Daly, 1987). Last, ideas of justice could be based on equality, where individuals convicted of the same crime receive the same punishment regardless of other characteristics (Izzett, 1981). Distributive justice recognizes the multiple ways of making justice determinations. Of course, this places decision makers in interesting predicaments; they can try to produce just results by allocating rewards and punishments according to any of these principles, but because justice is subjective, any one individual may disagree with the fairness of those decisions.

Limiting the study of justice in organizations to only outcomes, or distributive justice, has been criticized for neglecting all the steps that "precede the distribution of reward, and the evaluation of those events" (Leventhal, 1980, p. 35). **Organizational justice** represents a more complete view of fairness within organizations. It includes three parts: distributive justice (discussed earlier), procedural justice, and interactional justice. **Procedural justice** is process based, focused on the perceived fairness of the procedures used to make decisions about rewards, punishments, and dispute resolution (Cohen-Charash & Spector, 2001; Colquitt, Conlon, Wesson, Porter, & Ng, 2001; Greenberg, 1987; Henderson, Wells, Maguire, & Gray, 2010; Leventhal, 1980). Greenberg (1987) refers to procedural justice as a reactive theory, because the primary focus is how people respond to the decision-making process. A tremendous amount of decision making occurs in organizations, leading to the allocation of rewards and punishments—hiring, discipline, raises and promotions, terminations, and job assignments being just a few examples (Lind & Tyler, 1988). Individuals are concerned with both the fairness of the decision outcomes, such as whether their raise was equitable, and how those raise decisions were reached. If those procedures are viewed as unfair, an individual's motivation, job satisfaction, and attitudes toward the organization may suffer.

What factors are used to judge the fairness of procedures? Leventhal (1980) proposed six procedure-related justice rules that guide individual perceptions. First, procedures must be consistent. Regardless of the outcomes they receive, procedures should be consistently applied across individuals and over time. A police officer punished for accepting free coffee from a restaurant may view the department's process as unfair if the rule prohibiting such behavior had previously gone unenforced. Second, decisions are judged according to the level of representation afforded to affected parties. Front-line workers desire a voice during disciplinary proceedings, want input in organizational changes, and desire some control over the decision-making process (e.g., a vote; see Tyler, 1988). When they are effectively sealed off from any decision making, the process is more likely to be viewed as unfair. Third, decision procedures should be impartial and bias free. If individuals sense favoritism, they are likely to view the decision process as unjust. Fourth, the decision must be based on accurate and complete information. That is, decision makers must be informed. Police resistance to civilian oversight can be partially attributed to this fact. As Alpert, Dunham, and Stroshine (2006) argue, "[Police] claim that police behavior and operations cannot be fairly evaluated if one has never been involved personally in crime control" (p. 130). The process, some officers allege, would be inherently unfair if judgments were made by lay individuals with no experience in police work. Fifth, decision-making procedures should afford some opportunity for appeal or, using Leventhal's (1980) terminology, correctability. This acknowledges that errors can be made but erroneous decisions are open to modification. Last, judgments of procedural fairness are often made based on some moral or ethical standard (e.g., do unto others . . .) subscribed to by the person making the judgment. If the procedures do not conform to these standards, perceptions of injustice emerge.

A considerable volume of research has demonstrated the importance of procedural justice in determining stress, job satisfaction, and other job-related outcomes. In many cases, perceptions of procedural justice (the fairness of the process) are more important than perceptions of distributive justice (the fairness of actual outcomes; Lind & Tyler, 1988). For example, among a sample of 272 correctional officers in a state prison, both distributive and procedural justice were positively related to the level of job satisfaction, but only procedural justice was related to an officer's level of commitment to the organization (Lambert, 2003). The procedural justice concept can also be used to understand relationships between front-line personnel and clients. Paternoster, Brame, Bachman, and Sherman (1997) found that police officer treatment of domestic abusers (procedural justice as perceived by offenders) affected future criminal activity. When offenders saw their treatment as fair, they were less likely to reoffend in the future. Procedural fairness is important in relations between organizational members and between members and clients/customers.

Interactional justice, the third and final component of organizational justice, addresses the interpersonal conduct of the individuals who make decisions (Bies & Moag, 1986; Brockner & Wiesenfeld, 1996). Individual judgments about fairness, in other words, are based on their actual treatment by or interactions with others, independent of their assessments of fairness of procedures or outcomes (Bies, 2001; Bies & Moag, 1986). Interactional justice generally takes two forms: interpersonal justice and informational justice (Colquitt et al., 2001). In the case of the former, individuals want respectful and polite treatment from others in the organization, which makes decisions about rewards, discipline, or other important personnel matters (Cohen-Charash & Spector, 2001; Colquitt et al., 2001). Informational justice refers to the desire to be offered adequate explanations for decisions made (Greenberg, 1990). In a recent study examining undercover-officer selection procedures, interactional justice was measured by asking respondents their level of agreement with statements such as "assessors treat the applicant with respect" and "applicants receive honest feedback about their performance in the (undercover officer) selection system" (Farmer, Beehr, & Love, 2003, p. 380). The first item captured interpersonal justice, while the second indicated informational justice. Including interactional justice as an element of organizational justice helps us understand the importance of communication in organizations. For example, Greenberg (1990) found that internal theft rates increased in three manufacturing plants following the imposition of pay cuts as employees sought to restore equity, but "pay cuts that were explained in an honest and caring manner were not seen by employees as being as unfair as pay cuts that were not explained carefully" (p. 566). Interactional justice moderated the negative effects of the pay cuts to the point of curtailing employee theft rates. Even if procedures and outcomes are fair, people may feel injustice if they sense interpersonal mistreatment.

Overall, organizational managers and front-line personnel must work to ensure organizational justice—a combination of distributive, procedural, and interactional justice. Research consistently indicates that a variety of outcomes (satisfaction, motivation, etc.) are influenced by perceptions of fairness and justice in the workplace and on the streets. Individuals must work to operate according to fair procedures, distribute rewards according to some definition of equity, and treat others with respect and dignity.

Expectancy Theory

Expectancy theory, closely associated with the work of Victor Vroom, was initially developed to explain a wide range of behaviors but became synonymous with workplace motivation (Latham, 2007; Vroom, 2005). Lawler (1973) succinctly described expectancy theory as follows: "People will be motivated to be highly productive if they feel they can be highly productive and if they see a number of positive outcomes associated with being a high producer" (p. 27). Unlike the theories discussed so far, expectancy theory does not attempt to catalogue important needs or outcomes (e.g., achievement, power, self-esteem, self-actualization, or fairness) as Maslow, Herzberg, McClelland, or others did. Instead, it simply assumes that workers have diverse needs and goals and make decisions about their behavior relevant to the satisfaction of those needs/goals (Nadler & Lawler, 1977). Expectancy theory is, however, similar to equity theory in its incorporation of individual perceptions as a central component of the overall model (Latham, 2007). In the case of expectancy theory, the perceptions are assessments of the probabilities of outcomes actually occurring rather than perceptions of fairness.

Vroom's (1964) classic book, *Work and Motivation*, detailed the core elements of expectancy theory. The original presentation of the theory relied on mathematical formulae, a strategy Vroom (2005) later attributed to the culture of his place of employment (University of Pennsylvania). Although it is not necessary to understand expectancy theory quantitatively, the three major components discussed below will be discussed in both qualitative and mathematical terms.

1. *Valence (V)*. Expectancy theory assumes that actions produce outcomes. A student may study five hours the night before an examination, leading to a B grade (outcome), or a police officer may position himself at a four-way intersection and cite three drivers in 60 minutes for failing to stop (outcome). *Valence* refers to the importance of a particular outcome to any one person (Vroom, 1964). For example, students may disagree about the importance of a B grade on an exam. For some, passing is an equally acceptable result. If police officers are polled as to the "value, worth, [or] attractiveness" of traffic enforcement, differing opinions are likely to emerge (Nadler & Lawler, 1977 p. 28).

These examples are overly simplistic since actions rarely produce only a single outcome or consequence. If we mathematically represent the valence of every outcome considered by the individual as a positive or negative number (or zero if the individual is indifferent), we start to see the decision-making process emerge. When an outcome is preferred, valued, or sought after, it is said to have a positive valence. In contrast, when the outcome is undesirable or something to be avoided, it has a negative valence (Vroom, 1964). Assume then that a valence can range from –1.0 to +1.0. Issuing three citations provided the officer with a sense of achievement (a hypothetical valence of +0.8), but waiting for violations resulted in boredom (valence of –0.5) and caused the officer to miss a more significant call for service (valence of –0.2). The total outcome valence associated with the act of enforcing the traffic law is +0.1 (the sum of the three values), an indication that the activity was only weakly attractive to the officer. What if the officer used his time to patrol for drug offenders instead? A drug arrest provides a greater sense of achievement (+0.9), greater recognition from peers and superiors (+0.9), but a tremendous amount of paperwork (–0.5) and greater risk to safety (–0.5). In this case, the associated valence is +0.8. On the basis of outcomes alone, the officer would seem to prefer drug enforcement to traffic enforcement.

2. *Performance–outcome expectancy (P→O)*. The decision to behave in one way or another does not rest solely on the outcomes. Individuals gauge the likelihood that certain outcomes will follow their performance (**performance–outcome expectancy**; Lawler, 1973; Vroom, 1964). Additionally, outcomes may be instrumental in obtaining other outcomes (referred to as second-level outcomes). The student's B grade may allow her to enter an honor society, and the citations may bring the officer informal recognition. Even though these outcomes are valued or, in expectancy theory terms, have positive valences, a person must believe that a certain level of performance will lead to the valued outcome (Nadler & Lawler, 1977). Vroom (1964) referred to this perception as instrumentality, the expectation that performance (or one outcome) is instrumental in securing other positive outcomes. If the student values admission to the honor society, she will work toward earning a B on the exam only if she believes that the grade is instrumental in securing entrance. If the two are unrelated or believed to be unrelated, studying will likely be avoided. Similarly, an officer will issue citations only if doing so is linked to outcomes with positive valences, such as recognition from supervisors.

Returning to the mathematical formula, each of the individual outcome valences must first be multiplied by the perceived probability of their occurrence given a certain level of performance. For example, the valence for recognition for a drug arrest above was +0.9, indicating a valued outcome. If peers and supervisors rarely bestow the recognition (say, in only 10% of cases), the valence must be multiplied by the probability of recognition occurring (0.10 x +0.9).[4] The result is an adjusted valence for the outcome of +0.09. The remaining outcomes are computed similarly and summed to arrive at a total valence given the performance–outcome expectancy (Lawler, 1973). If an individual believes that the outcomes are never going to occur regardless of the level of performance (probability of 0), then the valence assigned to the outcome is irrelevant (Lawler, 1973). An officer could strongly desire the most sought-after position in the department (a high positive valence), but if the outcome is disconnected from job performance and has no chance of occurring, there is no reason to perform well.

3. *Effort–performance expectancy (E→P)*. The first two elements of the expectancy theory model address the value a person places on outcomes and whether those outcomes are likely to result if a worker performs at a given level (**effort–performance expectancy**). The final component of the model addresses whether a person believes he or she can perform at a given level; "people have expectancies about the likelihood that an action (effort) on their part will lead to the intended behavior or performance" (Lawler, 1973, p. 49). A student earning an A in a course (performance) may be assured admission into an honor society, a valued outcome. If, however, the student pessimistically assumes that, no matter how much effort she puts forth, she will not earn an A for the course, motivation will suffer. Even though performance is linked to a valued outcome, the student does not believe that she can perform at the necessary level.

The three components of expectancy theory combine to form the motivational forces on an individual (Nadler & Lawler, 1977; Vroom, 1964). Mathematically, the expectancy theory formula is depicted as follows (Lawler, 1973):

$$(E \rightarrow P) \times [(P \rightarrow O)(V)]$$

While the model looks complex, it is rather simple. The right side of the model has already been addressed: The importance of any outcome (its valence, V) is adjusted to take into account the likelihood

---

[4] $[(P \rightarrow O)(V)]$

of it occurring given a certain level of performance (P→O). In the example above, the adjusted valence of a drug arrest, after taking into consideration the unlikeliness of peer and supervisor recognition, was +0.09. The left side (E→P) of the formula asks whether the officer, if he puts forth the effort, will be able to perform at the level necessary to secure the rewards he seeks. Will he be able to make a drug arrest? Suppose the officer works the morning shift, where the opportunities to make drug arrests are more limited, and so he believes the likelihood of making an arrest is about 1 in 20 (E→P = 0.05). If the effort–performance probability is multiplied by the adjusted valence (+0.09), we arrive at a motivational force value of just +0.005. Recall, values of 0 indicate indifference, negative values represent a preference against the activity, and positive values show a preference for the activity. In this case, the officer is not likely to put forth the effort given that both the likelihood of making a drug arrest and receiving a reward are low. When will effort be made? Nadler and Lawler (1977) explain:

> Motivation to attempt to behave in a certain way is greatest when: a) the individual believes that the behavior will lead to outcomes (performance–outcome expectancy); b) the individual believes that these outcomes have positive value for him or her (valence); c) the individual believes that he or she is able to perform at the desired level (effort–performance expectancy). (p. 28)

It is important to remember that these assessments are not actual probabilities of successful performance or rewards. They are an individual's perceptions of the likelihood of success and the likelihood of receiving rewards.

Expectancy theory has been used to explain a range of criminal justice employee behaviors—most prominently, police activities (DeJong, Mastrofski, & Parks, 2001; Johnson, 2009, 2010; Mastrofski, Ritti, & Snipes, 1994). Mastrofski et al. (1994) used the theory to explain the number of driving under the influence (DUI) arrests made by 954 officers in 19 Pennsylvania police departments over a 12-month period. Variation in enforcement activity existed across officers, where a small proportion of all officers made a large proportion of all arrests. Why do some officers act with more vigor—"the degree to which officers extend their formal legal authority"—when it comes to DUI enforcement (Klinger, 1997, p. 279)? The three components of the expectancy model provide insight. Officers must believe that their efforts will lead to a certain level of performance (effort–performance expectancy). Efforts, however great, will never result in a large number of arrests if officers lack the capabilities or opportunities to make DUI arrests. Mastrofski and colleagues considered factors such as training and years of experience, as well as working a midnight shift (more chances for enforcement), as indicators of the effort–performance expectancy. The model also states that performance must lead to rewards (performance–outcome expectancy). Officers were asked, among other things, whether supervisors made DUI enforcement a priority, whether overtime was available for DUI details, and whether enforcement helped with departmental advancement. If rewards follow strong performance, an officer's motivational force should be greater. Finally, officers were asked about the valence attached to the rewards or outcomes of DUI enforcement. This is a difficult area to study because, as noted earlier, there are so many possible outcomes it would be necessary to have officers assign weights to all those considered. Mastrofski et al. examined officer perceptions on a range of possible outcomes: Do they consider DUI enforcement a priority? Is DUI enforcement time-consuming? Will colleagues resent excessive enforcement? These items were designed to capture both the benefits and costs associated with DUI enforcement. In general, DUI enforcement behavior was found to be predicted by capability and opportunity and, to a lesser extent, by the valence assigned to outcomes. Interestingly, whether rewards followed performance—the performance–outcome expectancy—did not play a significant role in shaping officer behavior.

Johnson (2009, 2010) used a similar set of measures to examine drug and domestic violence arrest behavior within a sample of 401 officers in 23 Cincinnati metro-area police departments. Like Mastrofski, Ritti, and Snipes, Johnson included measures of capability and opportunity, including specialized training, night shift, time, and the availability of equipment (drug arrests only). The performance–outcome expectancy addressed perceptions of management priorities but also included the presence of a mandatory arrest policy (domestic violence only). In neither case did Johnson include indicators of the valence assigned to rewards. Once again, general support was found for the expectancy theory model, even measures associated with the performance–outcome expectancy. The discrepancy between Johnson's studies and the earlier DUI study may be due, in part, to the exclusion of any measures gauging the importance of the organizational rewards that resulted from successful performance.

Expectancy theory is not limited to explaining enforcement activity only. Indeed, it is capable of explaining a wide variety of workplace and nonworkplace behaviors (Latham, 2007). Smith, Themessl-Huber, Akbar, Richards, and Freeman (2011), for example, examined the occupational choice of a sample of 10 Scottish dentists. In particular, they were interested in learning why they chose to work in Scottish prisons rather than other environments. Interviews revealed motivational patterns consistent with the core components of expectancy theory. Dentists clearly had the training and skills to adequately treat inmate patients, but the prison setting often interfered with their performance (the effort–performance expectancy). One dentist noted, "They won't give out floss . . . makes quite a good garrotte [strangulation instrument]. You can also use it to throw needles from window to window" (p. 3). In other cases, their work was halted due to disturbances in the facility and tightened security procedures. Nevertheless, the dentists did claim to have a good deal of control over their work, especially as relationships developed with prison officials. They also saw rewards associated with their performance (performance–outcome expectancy). The authors confirmed, "The dentists consequently felt that they had been given an opportunity to make a real difference to the lives of their prison-patients" (p. 4). Finally, the rewards, both financial and intrinsic, were incredibly valuable to the dentists (valence). Taken together, these factors pushed the dentists toward the prison as a professional setting.

The theory also provides a useful framework for understanding interactions with community members or other clients. In a study of early community policing implementation in the 1990s, Grinc (1994) found only limited familiarity with the goals of the innovation among community members. Even community leaders did not fully understand how community policing was premised on police–community partnerships to address neighborhood problems. Others associated community policing with large neighborhood block parties, again overlooking the partnerships for crime reduction. When police wonder why performance suffers—when residents fail to work to improve their own neighborhoods or participate in crime prevention/community improvement activities—they need only look at elements of the expectancy theory model (Powers & Thompson, 1994). It may be true that reporting drug dealing (performance) will result in a desirable outcome (reduced crime), but if a resident is uncertain of his or her role or incapable of reporting out of fear, motivation breaks down (Grinc, 1994).

Expectancy theory represents a considerable advance in our understanding of motivation. It is a broad theory with wide-ranging application. It shows that people make rational decisions based on the information available to them at the time. Manipulating rewards is, by itself, insufficient without considering the value placed on those rewards, the likelihood of their occurrence, and the skills, abilities, and opportunities available to workers.

Job Design

It is clear that a diverse range of factors motivate employees within and outside the criminal justice system. Individuals neither share the same needs nor make decisions based on the exact same criteria, but each person is motivated by some factor or another. For managers to extract successful performance from each worker, it becomes necessary to encourage behavior by remaining cognizant of the important motivators. Ideally, an organization should be able to satisfy the needs of workers and, simultaneously (or as a result), achieve its own goals. Job design matches workers to tasks and manipulates the nature of the work to facilitate motivation. Daft (2010a) defines job design as the "application of motivational theories to the structure of work for improving productivity and satisfaction" (p. 454). Although there are several approaches to redesigning job tasks, Hackman and Oldham's (1980) job characteristics model provides a useful framework for organizing the discussion.

The content theories discussed earlier in this section illustrated the importance of both intrinsic and extrinsic motivators. Generally speaking, intrinsic motivators were more powerful determinants of worker behavior; they were represented in the upper levels of the hierarchy of needs, as motivators in the two-factor theory, and as the most salient needs in the achievement/power/affiliation approach. Hackman and Oldham (1980) similarly argue that it is these intrinsic factors—what they call internal motivation—that initiate and sustain activity. They argue, "When people are well matched with their jobs, it rarely is necessary to force, coerce, bribe, or trick them into working hard and trying to perform the job well . . . good performance is an occasion for self-reward" (pp. 71–72). Individuals are gratified by feelings of achievement, responsibility, accomplishment, and other internal rewards, and will continue to do well to experience those feelings further. This motivation should occur even in the absence of extrinsic motivators such as elevated pay, pats on the back, or desirable benefits.

The job characteristics model (see Figure 8.1) proposes that internal motivation is likely to occur only when the individual experiences three conditions (termed *psychological states*)—experienced meaningfulness, experienced responsibility, and knowledge of results (Hackman & Oldham, 1980; Hackman, Oldham, Janson, & Purdy, 1975). First, a worker must view his or her job task as important. If the worker is counting out advertising materials for shipments to retail outlets, he or she may not consider the work worthwhile. In contrast, a police officer stopping a robbery in progress is likely to view that activity as incredibly important. It should be noted, however, that what is important or meaningful is subjective; what matters is whether the person performing the task views the work as meaningful. Second, experiencing responsibility is a necessary condition for internal motivation. Hackman and Oldham (1980) write, "The person must experience responsibility for the results of the work, believe that he or she is personally accountable for the work outcomes" (p. 72). A correctional officer who, upon direction from a sergeant, detains an escaping inmate may not experience responsibility. Preventing an escape is an achievement and potentially a source of internal motivation, but the detection of and instructions for apprehension came from a superior. The officer is not directly responsible for preventing the escape. If the officer noticed the security breach on his or her own, internal motivation would likely be present. Finally, workers require knowledge of the results. If internal motivation is linked to feelings of achievement and accomplishment, then those feelings can occur only if a person is aware of his or her successes and failures. To illustrate the critical psychological states, Hackman et al. (1975) describe the game of golf. Golf enthusiasts find the game meaningful, which is why they play. They are responsible for the quality of their play (in spite of protestations about wind and faulty equipment!). When the golfer strikes the ball, his or her successes are the product of personal efforts alone. Finally, golf provides feedback in the form of a score and a visible indicator of success (proximity to the hole).

Having determined the factors that lead to internal motivation, it is possible to determine the characteristics of job tasks themselves that encourage the critical psychological states. Hackman and Oldham (1980) identified five core job characteristics linked to meaningfulness, responsibility, and knowledge of results. Three job characteristics are related to feelings of meaningfulness—skill variety, task identity, and task significance. When the job involves a number of different activities requiring diverse employee skills and abilities, it is said to involve considerable **skill variety**. **Task identity** is the extent to which a job involves the completion of an entire task from beginning to end, rather than just a piece of a task. An artist's work is high in task identity, while a worker on an assembly line experiences weaker task identity. **Task significance** is based on the degree of impact the job has on the lives of others. A police officer's work has a tremendous effect on many lives (victims, witnesses, offenders,

Figure 8.1 Hackman and Oldham (1980) Job Characteristics Model

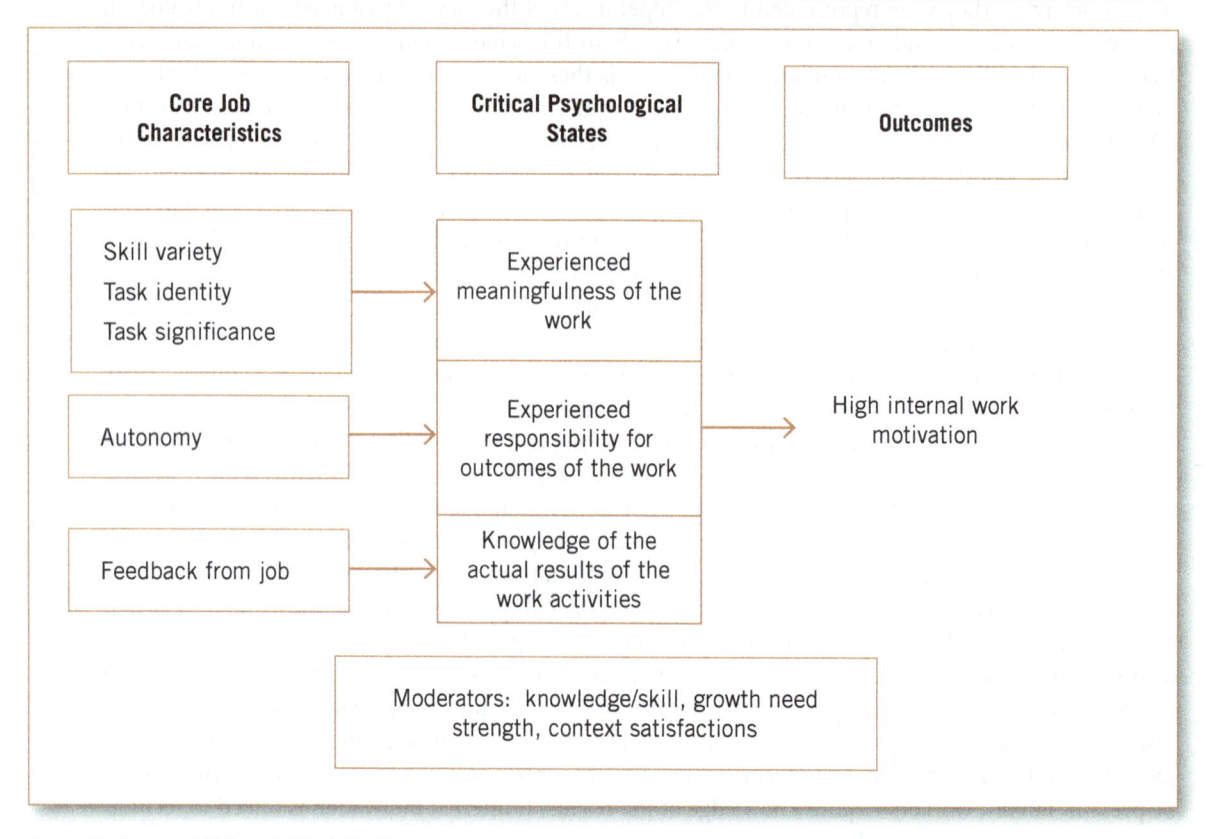

Source: Hackman and Oldham (1980, p. 83).

general population), while a store cashier's work is much more circumscribed in its effect on others. According to the job characteristics model, when at least one of the three core job dimensions leading to experiencing meaningfulness is high, internal motivation is more likely to follow. **Autonomy** is the sole core job dimension linked with experiencing responsibility. Job tasks that afford workers the freedom to make decisions and work independently are considered autonomous. These are the types of jobs that allow employees to feel responsible for successes and failures. Finally, Hackman and Oldham argue that workers need **feedback** from the job itself to have knowledge of results. They argue that a commendation from a supervisor is not as valuable as seeing the results of the work firsthand. For example, a correctional officer may see the life of an inmate change due to her efforts, or a police officer might notice improvements in crime and disorder on his beat.

What are some specific actions that might facilitate internal motivation? If skill variety is an essential job characteristic, it does not make sense to specialize at the level advocated by classical school theorists (see Section III). While specialization generates efficiencies and expertise, it contributes to demotivation. Not only are workers restricted in the range of skills used on a regular basis (skill variety), they are less likely to see whole tasks through from beginning to end (task identity). Instead, creating more generalist positions by combining tasks (referred to as job enlargement) is a more appropriate solution to motivational problems (Hackman et al., 1975). In the courts, horizontal prosecution arrangements place different prosecutors in control of different phases (e.g., charging, arraignment, trial) of the process. Both task identity and skill variety are likely to be low; a prosecutor will handle only his or her small part of the case and exercise a limited amount of professional knowledge applicable to that assigned stage in the process. Replacing horizontal arrangements with vertical ones may encourage internal motivation by allowing prosecutors to handle cases from arraignment through sentencing. The case outcome will be the responsibility of one prosecutor rather than a group.

Another approach is to vertically load job tasks. If combining tasks is related to horizontal complexity in the workplace, vertical loading (sometimes referred to as job enrichment) is related to vertical complexity. Workers can be assigned additional responsibilities normally reserved for supervisors, such as planning and directing (Hackman et al., 1975). John Angell (1971) proposed a radically different police organizational structure in which officers would operate as generalists without direct supervisors. As part of a team, officers would determine how particular areas of the community would be policed and would be responsible for calling on and directing specialists, including criminal investigators. His proposal was based, in part, on the significant problems he noticed with police organizations. Patrol officers, the largest group of employees within police organizations, were undervalued and their skills ignored. His redesigned department would place a heavier emphasis on patrol officer knowledge and abilities. Vertical loading would give employees more freedom (autonomy) and allow them to exercise a completely new set of skills (skill variety).

The value of the job characteristics model is evident in modern prison and jail architecture and structures (see Photo 8.1 for depictions). Traditionally, prisons and jails were built with long corridors of individual cells; security was maintained through surveillance from a centralized control room and by segmenting the facility into secure areas (Wener, 2006). By the late 1970s, new facilities (sometimes referred to as new generation facilities) were being built with direct supervision in mind. Prisons and jails are instead organized into housing pods (also referred to as modules or mods) wherein a correctional officer directly supervises inmate behavior. The pods may be designed as a certain number of cells surrounding a common area. The officer is typically located within this common area. Stohr, Lovrich, Menke, and Zupan (1994) describe the more expansive responsibilities of correctional staff in podular direct supervision facilities:

> The correctional officer in the module is trained not only to use supervisory rule enforcement skills, but also to employ proactive interpersonal skills in his or her relations with inmates.... The officer in many "new generation" jails is urged to develop more of a guidance role, in which "personalization of supervision" and "leadership skills" are exercised. (p. 478)

The new facilities have been associated with improved inmate and staff safety, reduced tension, minimal disorder, and fewer suicides (Wener, 2006). Related to the issue of motivation, there is some evidence pointing to increased job satisfaction, organizational commitment, and motivation (Stohr et al., 1994; Wener, 2006). Applying the job characteristics model, a direct supervision facility affords correctional officers the opportunities to use a variety of skills. Not only do they have to address custody-related issues, but they serve as arbitrators of disputes, activity planners, social workers, and supervisors, among other roles (Stohr et al., 1994). They serve autonomously, so disturbances within the pod are their responsibility, just as disruption-free work shifts are the results of their own efforts. The setting also provides immediate feedback. An officer can see from the conduct of inmates whether his or her performance is acceptable.

It is important to note that the applicability of the job characteristics model depends on a number of factors, including an individual's growth needs. If workers do not aspire to higher-order needs (recall Maslow) such as achievement, esteem, or self-actualization, combining tasks and adding supervisory-type responsibilities will actually have a detrimental rather than beneficial effect on the employees (Hackman et al., 1975; Wener, 2006). In fact, enlarging or enriching the job may only produce resistance on the part of the worker. In these cases, shrinking the tasks by making them less complex is a better solution. Alternatively, the manager may try to stimulate interests in higher-level needs by increasing their perceived valence.

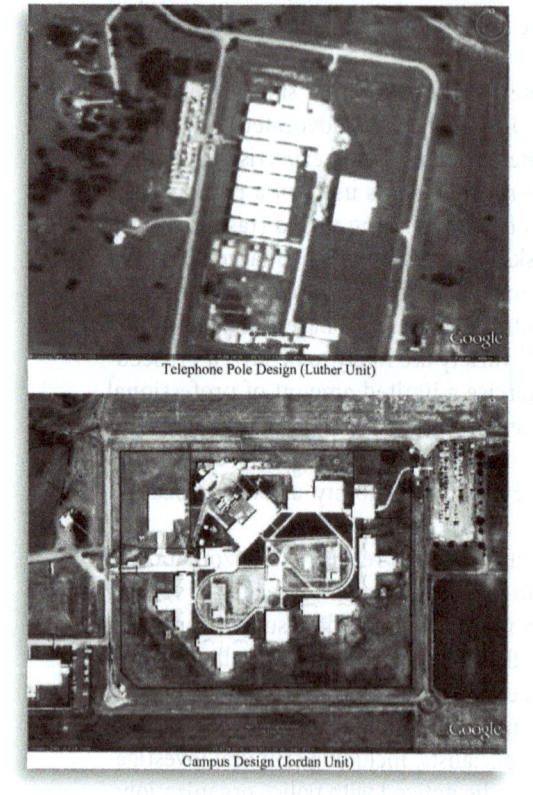

▲ **Photo 8.1** Satellite images of two Texas correctional facilities, illustrating the layout of linear, corridor-type facilities (referred to above as telephone pole design) and new generation, podular designs (referred to above as campus designs) (Source: Morris & Worrall, in press)

This section discussed the importance of a variety of motivators. Contrary to classical school principles, administering pay is not sufficient to ensure continued motivation. As many studies suggest, self-reward or intrinsic motivation also drives individuals. From a management perspective, this knowledge is critical. Union contracts (see Section VI) often limit the extrinsic rewards that managers can mete out to exceptional employees. When rewards are few, managers can continue to motivate employees by emphasizing the intrinsic rewards of the work and fairness in the workplace. Moreover, the work itself can be structured consistent with the job characteristics model to facilitate intrinsic motivation.

KEY TERMS

achievement motive	interactional justice	power motive
affiliation motive	job characteristics model	procedural justice
autonomy	job design	process theories
content theories	motivator–hygiene theory	skill variety
distributive justice	need theory	socialized power motive
effort–performance expectancy	organizational justice	task identity
equity theory	performance–outcome expectancy	task significance
expectancy theory	personalized power motive	valence
feedback		

DISCUSSION QUESTIONS

1. Maslow places salary and job security at or near the bottom of his hierarchy. According to his theory, these must be satisfied before other needs are met. If this is true, why would some police and/or correctional officers engage in conduct—excessive force, abuse of authority, corruption—that threatens these basic needs?

2. Some individuals believe, in spite of research to the contrary, that police officers are drawn to police work because of the opportunities to wield power—make arrests, carry firearms, and exercise authority. The research suggests that other reasons, particularly practical benefits, are more basic; so it is important to ask, where do these beliefs originate? Why do some link officers with the power motive instead of other needs such as affiliation, achievement, or even more basic human needs?

3. Suppose you work in a large prosecutor's office. The lead prosecutor is searching for someone to work as "second chair" on a large case, a position that is likely to bring a significant amount of prestige and experience to the holder. In determining the distributive justice (fairness in outcomes) of her decision, would you rely on principles of equity (contributions), need, or equality? Explain.

WEB RESOURCES

Discover Policing:
http://discoverpolicing.org/

National Institute of Corrections, resources on direct supervision jails:
http://nicic.gov/DirectSupervisionJails

Office of Community Oriented Policing Services:
http://www.cops.usdoj.gov/

Reading 14

Given the prevalence of drug offenders in the nation's prisons and jails, it is no surprise that a variety of residential treatment alternatives to long-term incarceration have emerged. Offenders who enter these diversion-type programs (such as the Dallas County Judicial Treatment Center [DCJTC] discussed in this article) bring with them varying levels of motivation to engage in treatment. As Matthew L. Hiller, Kevin Knight, Carl Leukefeld, and D. Dwayne Simpson suggest, an offender may complete treatment while maintaining active involvement in all facets of the program, may simply attend sessions without any engagement, or may drop out altogether. Understanding the link between motivation and engagement in treatment is therefore essential for understanding its success. The authors do not use any one of the motivation frameworks discussed in this section, but they do address the "choice" and "persistence" components of motivation noted in the section's introduction. Why do certain offenders become more engaged than others? This question was addressed using a sample of 419 felony offenders entering the DCJTC in 1998. The measures of motivation used included recognition of a problem (e.g., it is causing problems with the law), a desire for help (e.g., your life has gone out of control), and treatment readiness (e.g., treatment may be your last chance to solve drug problems). Engagement represented the offender's own perceptions of involvement, personal progress in treatment, and psychological safety. In general, desire for help and treatment readiness were related to measures of engagement in substance abuse treatment. In other words, the authors conclude that even where offenders are forced into drug treatment, their own personal levels of motivation are important predictors of how strongly they will engage in programming.

Motivation as a Predictor of Therapeutic Engagement in Mandated Residential Substance Abuse Treatment

Matthew L. Hiller, Kevin Knight, Carl Leukefeld, and D. Dwayne Simpson

Motivation predicts both retention and engagement in community-based treatment for substance abuse (De Leon & Jainchill, 1986; De Leon, Melnick, & Hawke, 2000; Simpson & Joe, 1993). This is a consistent pattern shown across the major treatment modalities,

Source: Hiller, M. L., Knight, K., Leukefeld, C., & Simpson, D. D. (2002). Motivation as a predictor of therapeutic engagement in mandated residential substance abuse treatment. *Criminal Justice and Behavior, 29*(1), 56–75.

including outpatient methadone, outpatient drug free, and long-term residential programs (Joe, Simpson, & Broome, 1998, 1999). More specifically, several motivation models have been described to explain how individuals change their addictive behaviors. In a well-known example—the transtheoretical model (Prochaska & DiClemente, 1986; Prochaska, DiClemente, & Norcross, 1992)—substance users can be classified into one of several cognitive stages of change. Precontemplation represents the first motivational stage, and it is characterized by unawareness that the addictive behavior is causing problems and by resistance to change. The four stages of the model (i.e., contemplation, preparation, action, and maintenance) show how an individual might progress toward recovery by realizing that their drug use is a problem, by preparing to take and then taking specific actions to quit their drug use, and by using a variety of cognitive strategies to ensure that positive change is maintained.

Readiness for treatment models represent a conceptual shift from the more broadly defined behavioral change models (Battjes, Onken, & Delany, 1999) because they attempt to explain why people enter treatment for their drug abuse problems. The Texas Christian University (TCU) motivation model (Simpson & Joe, 1993), for example, suggests that three motivational stages—comprising problem recognition, desire for help, and treatment readiness—preface seeking treatment. Problem recognition is characterized by the realization that one's substance use is resulting in severe personal difficulties that might stop if one quits using drugs. Desire for help represents the next cognitive step that is taken when an individual recognizes that he or she needs help to resolve one's drug problem. Finally, treatment readiness requires a mental shift from just wanting some form of help to personally committing oneself to actively participating in a treatment program. Because those who are unwilling to commit to a long-term treatment program are likely to drop out prematurely, determination of therapeutic readiness is essential for maximizing treatment efficiency and effectiveness (De Leon, Melnick, & Kressel, 1997; Joe et al., 1998; Melnick, De Leon, Hawke, Jainchill, & Kressel, 1997).

Length of treatment stay, however, is only a rough behavioral proxy for the extent to which an individual becomes engaged in his or her own recovery. Obviously, a drug user may remain in a treatment program but be psychologically detached from it and refuse to participate by skipping sessions or by not becoming cognitively committed to the therapeutic process—and research shows that level of treatment motivation is key to becoming actively engaged. For example, Simpson, Joe, Rowan-Szal, and Greener (1995) showed that higher motivation was predictive of higher rates of session attendance during the first 90 days of treatment. Session attendance represents a refinement beyond length of stay as an engagement measure, but the assumption that the individual is truly involved in treatment because they are physically present remains problematic. Furthermore, recent studies also have examined cognitive indicators of treatment engagement by focusing on the client's expressions of their commitment to and progress during the treatment episode (Broome, Knight, Hiller, & Simpson, 1996). A series of papers from the Drug Abuse Treatment Outcome Studies (DATOS) (the third in a succession of national studies of community substance abuse treatment) (Simpson & Curry, 1997), for example, showed that treatment motivation is associated with psychological measures of therapeutic engagement (Broome, Simpson, & Joe, 1999; Joe et al., 1998, 1999). Specifically, higher motivation was found to be associated with improved perceptions of personal progress and with stronger intentions to remain in treatment.

However, it is unclear how well findings from community settings that treatment readiness predicts higher client retention rates and better engagement generalize to corrections-based programs or even if this type of internal motivation is relevant in coercive criminal justice environments. Recent studies of treatment motivation among inmates in prison-based therapeutic community programs have begun to focus on this issue by examining the link between motivation and postrelease outcomes (De Leon, Melnick, Thomas, Kressel, & Wexler, 2000; Wexler, Melnick, Lowe, & Peters, 1999). Findings indicate that higher treatment readiness is related to a significantly greater likelihood of entering aftercare and thus has an indirect relationship with recidivism and relapse (Melnick, De Leon, Thomas, Kressel, & Wexler, in press). Relatively few studies, however, have looked specifically at the influence of motivation on therapeutic engagement in correctional treatment settings. One notable exception showed that offenders in a therapeutic community who had greater recognition of their drug-use-related problems formed stronger therapeutic relationships with their counselors (Broome, Knight, Knight, Hiller, & Simpson, 1997). Therefore, examining how motivation influences treatment engagement in correctional settings therefore warrants further consideration.

The overall goal of this study is to extend findings from community-based treatment settings by exploring the relationships between motivation and engagement in a corrections-based therapeutic community. Specifically, we begin by examining the simple relationships between scores on the TCU Treatment Motivation Assessment (Joe, Knezek, Watson, & Simpson, 1991; Simpson & Joe, 1993) and measures of engagement obtained approximately 30 days after treatment entry. Then, we assess the influence of motivation on engagement in a multivariate framework, statistically controlling other factors found to be associated with both constructs. It is expected that offenders entering treatment with higher levels of motivation will exhibit significantly better therapeutic engagement.

Method

Program Description

The Dallas County Judicial Treatment Center (DCJTC), located in Wilmer, Texas, was founded in 1991 by a council of 15 county and district judges as a response to Texas House Bill 2335, which authorized the development of residential correctional treatment centers for the diversion of drug-involved felony offenders from long-term incarceration. Essentially, this program represents the final and most restrictive sanction these judges use before imposing state jail or prison terms. Similar to many corrections-based treatment programs (Knight, Simpson, Chatham, & Camacho, 1997; Wexler, 1995), the DCJTC is modeled after traditional community-based therapeutic communities (TCs), with three major phases, including orientation, main treatment, and reentry. Treatment methods include group and individual counseling, behavior modification, peer-to-peer therapy, life skills training, vocational and educational instruction, and regular meetings with on-site probation officers while emphasizing 12-step recovery, criminal thinking patterns, and relapse prevention. Other traditional TC techniques also are used, including confrontation groups, "pull-ups," and morning and evening meetings (Barthwell et al., 1995). Offenders advance through a hierarchical treatment sequence whereby they receive progressively more responsibilities and privileges as they become more senior members of their community.

Sample

A total of 419 felony probationers were mandated to the DCJTC between January and December 1998 as part of a project called *Process Assessment of Correctional Treatment*, which was funded by the National Institute of Justice. Ten others were admitted during this time but were dropped from the sample because they had incomplete intake data for analysis. The sample was predominantly male (70%), African American (48%) or Caucasian (39%), and had never been married (43%). Most (60%) were between the ages of 17 and 34 (the median age was 32).

Measures

Demographic and social history. Sociodemographic information was collected during the Initial Assessment and Intake Interview, including gender, ethnicity, marital status, age, education level, and employment history. These variables were selected as statistical controls in the prediction models reported later in this article because several studies have shown them to be associated with retention and engagement in community-based TCs (Broome et al., 1999; De Leon, 1991; De Leon & Schwartz, 1984; Hiller, Knight, Broome, & Simpson, 1998; Joe et al., 1998, 1999) and with posttreatment outcomes from prison-based TCs (Martin, Butzin, Saum, & Inciardi, 1999; Wexler et al., 1999).

Classification of drug problems. Four independent sections in the Initial Assessment interview were used to assess *Diagnostic and Statistical Manual of Mental Disorders* (*DSM-IV*) (American Psychiatric Association, 1994) dependence criteria for alcohol, cannabis, cocaine, and opioids. Wording of these items closely followed those established in the *DSM-IV*, and scoring was identical (i.e., three or more met criteria needed to assign a classification of dependence). More than half (56%) of the probationers scored dependent for alcohol, 70% for cocaine, 36% for cannabis, and 16% for opioids.

Criminality and criminal history. Criminal involvement was gauged using self-reports in the Intake Interview about previous arrests and incarcerations. The majority of offenders had been arrested and incarcerated at least six times (54% and 52%, respectively), and many (42%) had been arrested as adolescents. Prior research has shown that individuals with severe criminal histories are significantly more likely to leave correctional substance abuse treatment or aftercare early (Hiller, Knight, & Simpson, 1999a, 1999b), so these indicators were included in later analyses as statistical control variables.

Motivation for treatment. The TCU Treatment Motivation Assessment (Joe et al., 1991; Knight, Holcom, & Simpson, 1994; Simpson & Joe, 1993) was administered as part of the Self-Rating Form at treatment intake. Scales representing the motivational readiness stages of problem recognition, desire for help, and treatment readiness were assessed. The Problem Recognition Scale included items that examined the extent to which the probationers recognized that many of their problems were caused by their substance abuse. The scale contained items such as "Your drug use is a problem for you" and "Your drug use is making your life become worse and worse" and used a Likert-type scale that ranged from 1 (*strongly disagree*) to 7 (*strongly agree*). The Desire for Help Scale asked probationers to rate their endorsements of statements such as "You need help in dealing with your drug use" and "It is urgent that you find help immediately for your drug use." Finally, the Treatment Readiness Scale included questions such as "This treatment program can really help you" and "This treatment program seems too demanding for you" (reverse coded). As also reported in Simpson and Joe (1993), scale intercorrelations showed stronger associations between theoretically contiguous stages (i.e., problem recognition and desire for help, and desire for help and treatment readiness) than for nonadjacent stages (i.e., problem recognition and treatment readiness), suggesting the possibility of a linear progression between motivational stages.

Therapeutic engagement. Three scales taken from the REST completed at the end of the orientation phase (i.e., about 30 days into treatment) were used as the criterion variables for this study. These measures were adapted from scales developed by De Leon (1997) for assessing treatment process in community-based TCs and included scales for measuring personal involvement, personal progress, and psychological safety. Collectively, these constructs provided psychological indicators of therapeutic engagement, reflecting cognitive appraisals of commitment to the treatment episode and recovery. Items for the Personal Involvement Scale assessed the probationers' perceptions of their participation in the therapeutic community using a

Likert-type scale that ranged from 1 (*strongly disagree*) to 7 (*strongly agree*). It included statements such as "You are willing to talk about your feelings in group" and "You say things to give support and understanding to others in the group." Personal progress reflected the probationers' satisfaction with self-improvements made during treatment and about how they handled issues surrounding their drug abuse and emotional problems. They rated their agreement with statements such as "You have made progress in your drug/alcohol problems" and "You have made progress toward your treatment goals." Finally, psychological safety referred to the perceived level of trust the probationers had for their peers and for program staff members. Scale intercorrelations were relatively large, with the strongest association between the Personal Involvement and Personal Progress scores and the weakest correlation between the Psychological Safety and Personal Progress scales. Psychological Safety and Personal Involvement scales also were strongly related.

Results

Bivariate Analyses

Examination of the simple relationships between the Treatment Motivation and Engagement scales showed that problem recognition was not related to any indicators of involvement in the therapeutic process. A small but not statistically significant association was observed between problem recognition and personal progress. Stronger relationships were found between the Desire for Help and Treatment Readiness scales with the indicators of therapeutic engagement. The Desire for Help Scale had modest but statistically significant associations with all three of the engagement measures, as did the Treatment Readiness Scale. The strongest association was observed between the Treatment Readiness and Psychological Safety scales.

Multivariate Analyses

Motivation and engagement in treatment, of course, have multiple determinants. Therefore, it was important to control for factors that could have acted as confounds in the following multivariate models. A series of linear regression models was constructed using background factors as covariates (i.e., gender, ethnicity, marital status, age, employment history, drug use problems, and arrest histories—selected because they were found to be associated significantly with either motivation or engagement). Along with these characteristics, the Motivation scales (i.e., Problem Recognition, Desire for Help, and Treatment Readiness) also were used to predict the scores on the three Engagement scales (i.e., Personal Involvement, Personal Progress, and Psychological Safety).

Three variables emerged as significant predictors of personal involvement in the first model. Specifically, higher levels of both desire for help and treatment readiness were related to higher levels of personal involvement in the treatment program. Being clinically dependent on opioids, however, was associated with lower involvement. Findings from the second regression model showed that higher Desire for Help scores were related to improved feelings of personal progress in treatment. Older probationers also reported more progress, but offenders who were dependent on cocaine or opioids and those that had been divorced, separated, or widowed reported significantly less progress during their treatment episode. Finally, higher ratings of psychological safety were related to higher levels of desire for help, treatment readiness, and age. Women reported that they felt more trust in treatment staff and group members than did men.

Discussion

As expected, motivation for treatment was associated with psychological indicators of engagement in a corrections-based therapeutic community even after statistically controlling for additional factors that could have been confounded with these relationships. Higher levels of motivation were generally associated with higher levels of personal commitment to the treatment episode. More specifically, desire for help and treatment readiness were positively associated with higher degrees of personal involvement, better ratings of personal progress, and stronger feelings of being psychologically safe in the program.

These findings underscore the importance of examining the influences of motivation on treatment process and outcomes for offenders mandated into substance abuse programs. Although some researchers contend that coerced treatment cannot be effective because the offender is not motivated to participate in his or her own recovery (Hartford, Ungerer, & Kinsella, 1976), others suggest that the relationships between intrinsic and external sources of motivation are complex (De Leon, 1988; Farabee, Prendergast, & Anglin, 1998). For example, both legal pressure and readiness for treatment were shown to exert independent but significant influences on the likelihood that clients would remain at least 90 days in the long-term residential substance abuse treatment programs that participated in the DATOS evaluation (Knight, Hiller, Broome, & Simpson, 2000).

Treatment motivation among probationers in the current study showed a high degree of variability. Some offenders appeared to be self-motivated to begin the recovery process by becoming engaged in the treatment program, but others were not. For those not yet ready for treatment, practitioners might want to use a specialized readiness and induction intervention to increase early engagement and involvement (see Farabee, Simpson, Dansereau, & Knight, 1995). It is important to note that a set of treatment readiness and induction interventions has been designed by researchers at Texas Christian University to enhance early therapeutic engagement in corrections-based substance abuse programs. These materials give offenders unique opportunities to define their roles in treatment and to discover their positive personal strengths and hidden cognitive potentials. They help boost offender confidence in treatment by emphasizing the idea that treatment can help them and that they can be successful in their recovery (Blankenship, Dansereau, & Simpson, 1999; Czuchry & Dansereau, 2000; Newbern, Dansereau, & Pitre, 1999; Sia, Dansereau, & Czuchry, 2000). A different approach designed for specific application in community-based therapeutic communities also may be appropriate for use in correctional programs. The senior professor model (see De Leon, Hawke, Jainchill, & Melnick, 2000) uses a program counselor or a senior peer group member to conduct initial treatment induction sessions to help motivate offenders to become involved in and to finish the program.

The putative mechanism for how pretreatment motivation can exert an influence on posttreatment outcomes is shown in Figure 1. The TCU treatment process model was developed during research in community settings (see Simpson, 2001; Simpson, Joe, Greener, & Rowan-Szal, 2000; Simpson, Joe, Rowan-Szal, & Greener, 1995, 1997) and has recently been adapted for correctional substance abuse treatment (Hiller, Knight, Rao, & Simpson, in press; Simpson & Knight, in press). This framework presents treatment as a series of distinct phases (i.e., intake/baseline, early engagement, early recovery, and transition to the community), and it is similar to other stage models for substance abuse treatment (De Leon, 1996, 2000; Simpson, 1997). It is implicit in these staged or sequential views of treatment that performance at any point in the model is determined in part by the elements that precede it (Judd & Kinney, 1981). Treatment, therefore, can be conceptualized as an interrelated chain of events both external and internal to the individual.

Motivation represents one characteristic that the individual presents with at treatment intake. Because it is the first element in the model, it can be hypothesized to influence the entire treatment episode as well as posttreatment outcomes. It might do

Figure 1 Texas Christian University Treatment Process Model

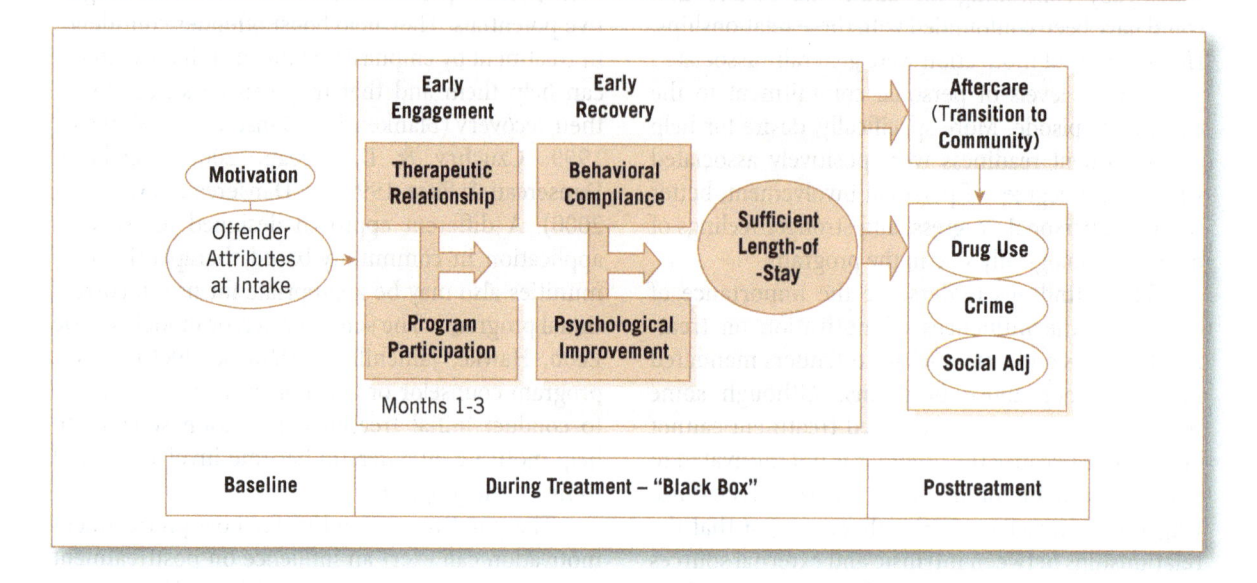

this by affecting the early engagement phase (shown in the central box of the model presented in Figure 1) by helping to determine in part how one perceives one's peers, program staff members, and their own willingness to become involved in and committed to their recovery during the first few months of the treatment episode. Findings from the current study support the linkage between pretreatment motivation and the early engagement treatment phase, but additional work is needed to determine to what extent higher motivation and greater levels of early engagement are related to long-term outcomes in this sample. Also, as was noted previously, pretreatment levels of motivation have been shown to play an important role in the development of therapeutic relationships with counselors and to indirectly determine the likelihood of rearrest following treatment in a 4-month modified TC for probationers, which is similar in structure to the program examined in the current study (Broome et al., 1996, 1997). Therapeutic activities and feelings of personal progress made during the early engagement phase also can impact early recovery when the client is making critical behavioral and psychosocial changes that will facilitate long-term recovery upon return to the community. Collectively, pretreatment characteristics (e.g., motivation), early engagement, and early recovery help determine postrelease outcomes. Future studies should focus on generalizing these findings and on determining the relative effect of stronger motivation and better engagement on the likelihood of reoffending and return to drug use after treatment (see De Leon, Melnick, Thomas, et al., 2000).

In conclusion, this study contributes to the growing body of knowledge on coerced substance abuse treatment by helping extend findings from community-based studies to evaluations of corrections-based settings. Results show that motivation is an important influence on psychological indicators of therapeutic engagement, and contrary to what some believe, many offenders enter coerced treatment with a desire to begin their recovery. Recommendations for correctional treatment practitioners are twofold. First, motivational readiness for treatment can and should be measured using empirically validated instruments such as the TCU Treatment Motivation Assessment. Second, motivational readiness and treatment engagement can be therapeutically enhanced through targeted induction interventions easily implemented within extant treatment protocols. Focusing additional resources on offenders with low motivation will likely improve treatment efficiency and effectiveness within correctional settings.

References

American Psychiatric Association. (1994). *Diagnostic and statistical manual of mental disorders* (4th ed.). Washington, DC: Author.

Barthwell, A. G., Bokos, P., Bailey, J., Haser, N., Nisenbaum, M., Devereux, J., et al. (1995). Interventions/Wilmer: A continuum of care for substance abusers in the criminal justice system. *Journal of Psychoactive Drugs, 27*, 39-47.

Battjes, R. J., Onken, L. S., & Delany, P. J. (1999). Drug abuse treatment entry and engagement: Report of a meeting on treatment readiness. *Journal of Clinical Psychology, 55*, 643-657.

Blankenship, J., Dansereau, D. F., & Simpson, D. D. (1999). Cognitive enhancements of readiness for corrections-based treatment for drug abuse. *The Prison Journal, 79*, 431-445.

Broome, K. M., Knight, K., Hiller, M. L., & Simpson, D. D. (1996). Drug treatment process indicators for probationers and prediction of recidivism. *Journal of Substance Abuse Treatment, 13*, 487-491.

Broome, K. M., Knight, D. K., Knight, K., Hiller, M. L., & Simpson, D. D. (1997). Peer, family, and motivational influences on drug treatment process and recidivism for probationers. *Journal of Clinical Psychology, 53*, 387-397.

Broome, K. M., Simpson, D. D., & Joe, G. W. (1999). Patient and program attributes related to treatment process indicators in DATOS. *Drug and Alcohol Dependence, 57*, 127-135.

Czuchry, M., & Dansereau, D. F. (2000). Drug abuse treatment in criminal justice settings: Enhancing community engagement and helpfulness. *American Journal of Drug and Alcohol Abuse, 26*, 537-552.

De Leon, G. (1988). Legal pressure in therapeutic communities. *Journal of Drug Issues, 18*, 625-640.

De Leon, G. (1991). Retention in drug-free therapeutic communities. In R. W. Pickens, C. G. Leukefeld, & C. R. Schuster (Eds.), *Improving drug abuse treatment* (NIDA Research Monograph 106, DHHS Publication No. ADM 91-1754, pp. 218-244). Rockville, MD: National Institute on Drug Abuse.

De Leon, G. (1996). Integrative recovery: A stage paradigm. *Substance Abuse, 17*, 51-63.

De Leon, G. (1997). *Client self-rated progress checklist*. New York: Center for Therapeutic Community Research at the National Development Research Institute.

De Leon, G. (2000). *The therapeutic community: Theory, model, and method*. New York: Springer.

De Leon, G., Hawke, J., Jainchill, N., & Melnick, G. (2000). Therapeutic communities: Enhancing retention in treatment using "Senior Professor" staff. *Journal of Substance Abuse Treatment, 19*, 375-382.

De Leon, G., & Jainchill, N. (1986). Circumstance, motivation, readiness and suitability as correlates of treatment tenure. *Journal of Psychoactive Drugs, 18*, 203-208.

De Leon, G., Melnick, G., & Hawke, J. (2000). The motivation-readiness factor in drug treatment: Implications for research and policy. *Advances in Medical Sociology, 7*, 103-129.

De Leon, G., Melnick, G., & Kressel, D. (1997). Motivation and readiness for therapeutic community treatment among cocaine and other drug users. *American Journal of Drug and Alcohol Abuse, 23*, 169-189.

De Leon, G., Melnick, G., Thomas, G., Kressel, D., & Wexler, H. K. (2000). Motivation for treatment in a prison-based therapeutic community. *American Journal of Drug and Alcohol Abuse, 26*, 33-46.

De Leon, G., & Schwartz, S. (1984). Therapeutic communities: What are the retention rates? *American Journal of Drug and Alcohol Abuse, 10*, 267-284.

Farabee, D., Prendergast, M., & Anglin, M. D. (1998). The effectiveness of coerced treatment for drug-abusing offenders. *Federal Probation, 62*, 3-10.

Farabee, D. J., Simpson, D. D., Dansereau, D. F., & Knight, K. (1995). Cognitive inductions into treatment among drug users on probation. *Journal of Drug Issues, 25*, 669-682.

Hartford, R. J., Ungerer, J. C., & Kinsella, J. K. (1976). Effects of legal pressure on prognosis for treatment of drug dependence. *American Journal of Psychiatry, 133*, 1399-1404.

Hiller, M. L., Knight, K., Broome, K. M., & Simpson, D. D. (1998). Legal pressure and treatment retention in a national sample of long-term residential programs. *Criminal Justice and Behavior, 25*, 463-481.

Hiller, M. L., Knight, K., Rao, S. R., & Simpson, D. D. (in press). Assessing and evaluating mandated correctional substance abuse treatment. In C. G. Leukefeld, F. M. Tims, & D. Farabee (Eds.), *Clinical and policy responses to drug offenders*. New York: Springer.

Hiller, M. L., Knight, K., & Simpson, D. D. (1999a). Prison-based substance abuse treatment, residential aftercare, and recidivism. *Addiction, 94*, 833-842.

Hiller, M. L., Knight, K., & Simpson, D. D. (1999b). Risk factors that predict dropout from corrections-based treatment for drug abuse. *The Prison Journal, 79*, 411-430.

Joe, G. W., Knezek, L. D., Watson, D. D., & Simpson, D. D. (1991). Depression and decision-making among intravenous drug users. *Psychological Reports, 68*, 339-347.

Joe, G. W., Simpson, D. D., & Broome, K. M. (1998). Effects of readiness for drug abuse treatment on client retention and assessment of process. *Addiction, 93*, 1177-1190.

Joe, G. W., Simpson, D. D., & Broome, K. M. (1999). Retention and patient engagement models for different treatment modalities in DATOS. *Drug and Alcohol Dependence, 57*, 113-125.

Judd, C. M., & Kinney, D. A. (1981). Process analysis: Estimating mediation in treatment evaluations. *Evaluation Review, 5,* 602-619.

Knight, K., Hiller, M. L., Broome, K. M., & Simpson, D. D. (2000). Legal pressure, treatment readiness, and engagement in long-term residential programs. *Journal of Offender Rehabilitation, 31,* 101-115.

Knight, K., Holcom, M., & Simpson, D. D. (1994). *TCU psychosocial functioning and motivation scales: Manual on psychometric properties.* Fort Worth: Texas Christian University, Institute of Behavioral Research.

Knight, K., Simpson, D. D., Chatham, L. R., & Camacho, L. M. (1997). An assessment of prison-based drug treatment: Texas' in-prison therapeutic community program. *Journal of Offender Rehabilitation, 24,* 75-100.

Martin, S. S., Butzin, C. A., Saum, C. A., & Inciardi, J. A. (1999). Three-year outcomes of therapeutic community treatment for drug-involved offenders in Delaware: From prison to work-release to aftercare. *The Prison Journal, 79,* 294-320.

Melnick, G., De Leon, G., Hawke, J., Jainchill, N., & Kressel, D. (1997). Motivation and readiness for therapeutic community treatment among adolescent and adult substance abusers. *American Journal of Drug and Alcohol Abuse, 23,* 485-506.

Melnick, G., De Leon, G., Thomas, G., Kressel, D., & Wexler, H. K. (in press). Treatment process in prison therapeutic communities: Motivation, participation, and outcome. *American Journal of Drug and Alcohol Abuse.*

Newbern, D., Dansereau, D. F., & Pitre, U. (1999). Positive effects on life skills motivation and self-efficacy: Node-link maps in a modified therapeutic community. *American Journal of Drug and Alcohol Abuse, 25,* 407-423.

Prochaska, J. O., & DiClemente, C. C. (1986). Toward a comprehensive model of change. In W. R. Miller & N. Heather (Eds.), *Treating addictive behaviors: Process of change* (pp.3-27). New York: Plenum.

Prochaska, J. O., DiClemente, C. C., & Norcross, J. C. (1992). In search of how people change: Applications to addictive behaviors. *American Psychologist, 47,* 1102-1114.

Sia, T. L., Dansereau, D. F., & Czuchry, M. (2000). Treatment readiness training and probationers' evaluations of substance abuse treatment in a criminal justice setting. *Journal of Substance Abuse Treatment, 19,* 459-467.

Simpson, D. D. (1997). Effectiveness of drug abuse treatment: A review of research from field settings. In J. A. Egertson, D. M. Fox, & A. I. Leshner (Eds.), *Treating drug abusers effectively* (pp. 41-77). Cambridge, MA: Blackwell.

Simpson, D. D. (2001). Modeling treatment process and outcomes. *Addiction, 96,* 207-211.

Simpson, D. D., Chatham, L. R., & Joe, G. W. (1993). Cognitive enhancements to treatment in DATAR: Drug abuse treatment for AIDS risks reduction. In J. Inciardi, F. Tims, & B. Fletcher (Eds.), *Innovative approaches to the treatment of drug abuse: Program models and strategies* (pp. 161-177). Westport, CT: Greenwood.

Simpson, D. D., & Curry, S. J. (Eds.). (1997). Drug Abuse Treatment Outcome Study (DATOS) [Special issue]. *Psychology of Addictive Behaviors, 11*(4).

Simpson, D. D., Dansereau, D. F., & Joe, G. W. (1997). The DATAR project: Cognitive and behavioral enhancements to community-based treatments. In F. M. Tims, J. A. Inciardi, B. W. Fletcher, & A. M. Horton, Jr. (Eds.), *The effectiveness of innovative approaches in the treatment of drug abuse* (pp. 182-203). Westport, CT: Greenwood.

Simpson, D. D., & Joe, G. W. (1993). Motivation as a predictor of early dropout from drug abuse treatment. *Psychotherapy, 30,* 357-368.

Simpson, D. D., Joe, G. W., Greener, J. M., & Rowan-Szal, G. A. (2000). Modeling Year 1 outcomes with treatment process and posttreatment social influences. *Substance Use and Misuse, 35,* 1911-1930.

Simpson, D. D., Joe, G. W., Rowan-Szal, G., & Greener, J. (1995). Client engagement and change during drug abuse treatment. *Journal of Substance Abuse, 7,* 117-134.

Simpson, D. D., Joe, G. W., Rowan-Szal, G. A., & Greener, J. M. (1997). Drug abuse treatment process components that improve retention. *Journal of Substance Abuse Treatment, 14,* 565-572.

Simpson, D. D., & Knight, K. (in press). TCU model of treatment process and outcomes in correctional settings. In A. Fins (Ed.), *State of corrections.* Lanham, MD: American Correctional Association.

Wexler, H. K. (1995). The success of therapeutic communities for substance abusers in American prisons. *Journal of Psychoactive Drugs, 27,* 57-66.

Wexler, H. K., Melnick, G., Lowe, L., & Peters, J. (1999). Three-year reincarceration outcomes for Amity in-prison therapeutic community and aftercare in California. *The Prison Journal, 79,* 321-336.

DISCUSSION QUESTIONS

1. Although expectancy theory was not used as a framework in this study, it is potentially useful. Consider the three main components of expectancy theory: valence, effort–performance expectancy, and performance–outcome expectancy. How might each of these components help us understand why offenders *fail to complete* substance abuse treatment?

2. The study examined the motivation level of offenders. As a worker in an organization (e.g., a drug treatment counselor, a prison worker, a probation officer), what can you do to increase the level of motivation of drug offenders to engage in substance abuse treatment? In other words, how can you help them recognize the need for help and become treatment ready, the two factors most strongly linked to engagement?

3. The authors addressed the personal motivation of offenders (problem recognition, desire for help, treatment readiness). At the same time, offenders may be sentenced to jail or prison if they fail to complete treatment programming. In your opinion, which is a more potent source of motivation for the offender—internal motivation or external coercion? Explain.

READING

Reading 15

The organizational justice perspective of motivation and behavior asserts that employees respond negatively to perceived injustices in the distribution of rewards (distributive justice), the procedures related to how rewards are distributed (procedural justice), and the relationships between managers and subordinates (interactional justice). Scott E. Wolfe and Alex R. Piquero draw on the organizational justice perspective as a framework for explaining police misconduct (i.e., number of citizen complaints, internal affairs investigations, or disciplinary violations). The authors speculate that officers who repeatedly see managers violate standards of organizational justice will violate rules themselves, as they see misconduct as acceptable. The organizational justice–misconduct link was examined in a sample of 499 Philadelphia Police Department sworn personnel (rank of office through lieutenant). Even after considering factors such as deviant peers, demographic characteristics, the presence of a code of silence, and beliefs about noble cause corruption, perceived organizational justice was related to less frequent officer misconduct. The results suggest that managers, through their internal dealings with employees, can take steps that enhance perceptions of fairness and generate beneficial effects on officer behavior.

ORGANIZATIONAL JUSTICE AND POLICE MISCONDUCT

Scott E. Wolfe and Alex R. Piquero

Police officers—as the gatekeepers of formal social control—are not only responsible for enforcing laws and protecting the public but also are entrusted to represent order and justice in society. Why, then, do some subset of officers with such a high level of social responsibility abuse their power, become corrupt, and engage in misconduct? Beginning with some of the classic police behavior studies (Reiss, 1971; Sherman, 1975), a large body of research has established numerous community-, individual-, and organizational-level correlates of police misconduct (Ivković, 2005; King, 2009). Although the literature has provided results that have helped guide policy, there are still large gaps in our understanding of police misconduct—one of which concerns the largely atheoretical nature of this line of work (Chappell & Piquero, 2004; Hickman, Piquero, Lawton, & Greene, 2001; Kane, 2002; Kane & White, 2009; Lawton, 2007; Pogarsky & Piquero, 2003).

Parallel to research on corporate crime (Simpson, Paternoster, & Piquero, 1998), the literature often neglects examinations of organizational theory despite the fact that it is difficult to separate individual officer misconduct from the organizational context in which it takes place. A number of organizational-level factors, such as recruitment, training, and agency policy, have emerged as significant predictors of officer misconduct (Ivković, 2005; Skolnick & Fyfe, 1993); however, this line of research has largely ignored the role of organizational injustice (e.g., perceived unfair policies and managerial practices) in perpetuating the behavior. Scholars have suggested that responsibility for officer misconduct ultimately resides at the organizational level (Ivković, 2005, 2009; King, 2009), but research has not investigated the organizational mechanisms that may contribute to police misconduct or attitudes favorable to such behavior. Research in organizational theory, however, has suggested that organizations perceived as unjust and unfair by their employees are more likely to experience employee deviance (Greenberg, 1993). Thus, organizational justice may offer a useful framework from which to build a theoretical understanding of individual-level police misconduct, given its focus on the social psychological relationship between organizations and human behavior (Lind & Tyler, 1988). Not only should perceptions of organizational injustice be associated with police misconduct, but it may also help explain other correlates of the behavior, such as the "code of silence" and "noble-cause corruption," to be defined below.

Using survey data from a random sample of 483 officers from the Philadelphia Police Department, this study examines whether organizational justice explains adherence to the code of silence and noble-cause corruption beliefs and then assesses the effect of perceptions of organizational justice on several forms of police misconduct while controlling for code-of-silence attitudes and noble-cause beliefs. The study concludes with a discussion of how organizational justice can serve as a useful theoretical model for understanding police misconduct. In so doing, the study moves beyond blaming police agency administrators for individual officer deviance (Manning, 2009) and instead focuses on understanding the organizational mechanisms that may relate to police misconduct, which will allow administrators to improve agency operation and policy to assist in proactively reducing this deviance.

Police Misconduct Research

Officer misconduct has been an oft-studied topic despite the fact that a consistent theoretical understanding of the phenomenon has remained elusive. The inability to test theories is not the fault of the scholarly community but rather the consequence of the lack of access to sufficient data and the ambiguity that is attached to the term *police misconduct* (Ivković, 2005; Kane, 2002; Kane & White, 2009), a term whose meaning has been frequently debated (Ivković, 2005; Kane & White, 2009; Sherman, 1978). For the purposes of this study, behavior considered to be misconduct refers to actions that resulted in the filing of a formal complaint, an internal affairs investigation, or departmental disciplinary charges against the officer (Chappell & Piquero, 2004; Greene, Piquero, Hickman, & Lawton, 2004;

Source: Wolfe, S. E., & Piquero, A. R. (2011). Organizational justice and police misconduct. *Criminal Justice and Behavior, 38*(4), 332–353.

Hickman et al., 2001; Hickman, Piquero, & Greene, 2000; Hickman, Piquero, & Piquero, 2004).

Extant research has ascertained a great many explanatory variables related to police misconduct. For example, Ivković (2005) demonstrated that the predictors of misconduct can be classified as community, individual, or organizational characteristics. With respect to the community correlates, Kane (2002) used a social ecological approach to demonstrate that neighborhoods characterized by structural disadvantage and population mobility were more likely to experience police misconduct. Terrill and Reisig (2003) showed similar neighborhood characteristics to be associated with a greater likelihood of elevated officer use of force. The influence of neighborhood context on police misconduct seems to be a promising avenue for future research; however, relatively few data permit testing this hypothesis.

For this reason, research has mainly focused on the link between individual-level correlates, such as age (Greene et al., 2004; McElvain & Kposowa, 2004), gender (Greene et al., 2004; Grennan, 1987; Hickman et al., 2000; McElvain & Kposowa, 2004; Sherman, 1975), race (Greene et al., 2004; Hickman et al., 2004; Kane & White, 2009; Rojek & Decker, 2009), education (Kane & White, 2009; Truxillo, Bennett, & Collins, 1998), length of service (Hickman et al., 2004; McElvain & Kposowa, 2004; Micucci & Gomme, 2005), rank (Hickman et al., 2004), prior employment problems (Greene et al., 2004; Kane & White, 2009), and criminal history (Greene et al., 2004; Kane & White, 2009; Mollen Commission, 1994), with various forms of misconduct. Although many of these factors can be used to guide agency policy, the discussion of each has rarely been explained in a theoretically meaningful manner (see Kane & White, 2009, for an exception). Understanding the reasons behind the role of significant predictors of misconduct allows for more informed strategies to reduce the behavior. Absent theory, police administrators are left to blindly apply policies that target a "significant" correlate of misconduct with no idea *why* the variable has an impact or, perhaps more importantly, whether the variable even has a logical causal relationship with misconduct.

It has only been recently that researchers have started to study police misconduct with a rigorous theoretical lens. For example, control balance theory (Hickman et al., 2001), social disorganization theory (Kane, 2002; Terrill & Reisig, 2003), deterrence theory (Pogarsky & Piquero, 2003), and the racial threat hypothesis (Lawton, 2007) have been used to explain police misconduct. A recent analysis by Chappell and Piquero (2004) using social learning theory as a theoretical guide found that deviant peers had a significant effect on whether officers had citizen complaints filed against them. According to these scholars, officers' susceptibility to organizational subcultures makes differential peer associations important, as they "may facilitate deviant behavior by transmitting the beliefs, values, definitions, and manners of expression that depart from acceptable behavior" (Chappell & Piquero, 2004, p. 93).

Two additional individual-level explanations of police misconduct, code-of-silence attitudes and noble-cause beliefs, also warrant attention. The code of silence has been discussed at length and has been shown to be present in agencies throughout the United States and internationally (Brereton & Ede, 1996; Chin & Wells, 1997; Knapp Commission, 1972; Micuccui & Gomme, 2005; Mollen Commission, 1994; Rothwell & Baldwin, 2007a, 2007b; Skolnick, 2002, 2005). Research has shown that officers who adhere to the code of silence are less likely to report fellow officer excessive use of force or corruption (Knapp Commission, 1972; Micuccui & Gomme, 2005; Mollen Commission, 1994; Skolnick, 2005) and more likely to commit perjury during a trial (Chin & Wells, 1997). Policing is characterized by a close-knit subculture because the "unique demands that are placed on police officers, such as the threat of danger as well as scrutiny by the public, generate a tightly woven environment conducive to the development of feelings of loyalty" (Skolnick, 2005,

p. 302). The code of silence, therefore, develops into a subcultural attitude on how one must behave to be perceived as a "good" officer by peers. Although Skolnick (2005) contended that the code of silence and corruption are intertwined, he stated that the code "cannot, strictly speaking, be considered *the* cause of police corruption . . . partly because understanding [corruption] . . . is a complex causal undertaking" (p. 302). Thus, a goal of research should be to determine the factors that are associated with officer adherence to the code of silence and to better assess whether and to what extent adherence to the code of silence is related to actual involvement in police misconduct.

Along similar lines, noble-cause police corruption has also been an important concept in police deviance research (Caldero & Crank, 2004; Crank, Flaherty, & Giacomazzi, 2007). Although noble cause is normally discussed in negative terms (e.g., in connection with corruption), it is technically defined as "a moral commitment to make the world a safer place to live . . . . Put simply, it is getting bad guys off the street" (Caldero & Crank, 2004, p. 29). Klockars (1983) was one of the first to give attention to corruption of the noble cause with his discussion of the "Dirty Harry" problem. His discussion and subsequent research led to the definition of noble-cause corruption as "the achievement of a good greater than the harm caused by any illegal behavior of the police" (Crank et al., 2007, p. 105). The corruption of noble cause is, therefore, a utilitarian action (Crank et al., 2007) where officers feel justified in committing what would normally be conceived as misconduct to achieve the noble cause of public safety and justice. Similar to code-of-silence research, studies that examine whether beliefs supportive of corruption for a noble cause are associated with actual police misconduct and the determination of the factors associated with such beliefs are currently lacking.

The above-cited research indicates that several important individual-level correlates of police misconduct warrant further investigation. Specifically, research needs to determine the factors associated with code-of-silence attitudes and noble-cause corruption beliefs and the relationship these concepts have with police misconduct. In turn, these issues bring forward a third broad category of misconduct predictors. As Ivković (2005) highlighted, organizational factors, such as managerial ambivalence to misconduct, ambiguous policies about misconduct, and poor recruitment and training practices, are associated with officer deviance. However, little research has examined how the organizational behavior of a police agency can lead to and/or produce a context that fosters or permits misconduct. One potentially useful framework, organizational justice, may offer an opportunity to build our understanding of the behavior.

Organizational Justice

The study of fairness in organizations has a long history in social psychology. Two recent meta-analyses on the effects of justice in organizations showed that the various components of organizational justice have implications for how employees react when faced with different managing approaches (Cohen-Charash & Spector, 2001; Colquitt, Conlon, Wesson, Porter, & Hg, 2001). Although some disagreement exists, scholars of organizational justice tend to agree that there are three main components to organizational justice— distributive, procedural, and interactional—that if followed by supervisors will be associated with positive outcomes for the given organization (Cohen-Charash & Spector, 2001).

Adam's (1963) research on equity theory stressing the value of distributive justice was largely responsible for the study of justice within organizations. The concept of distributive justice concerns the perceived fairness of outcomes and, thus, has implications in the organizational context. Employees who perceive their superiors to distribute outcomes (e.g., pay and promotion decisions) fairly to all subordinates of equal status have been shown to increase both the quantity and quality of their work production (Cohen-Charash & Spector, 2001;

Colquitt et al., 2001). As Cohen-Charash and Spector (2001, p. 280) discussed, outcomes that are perceived by employees to be unfair will affect their emotions, cognitions, and ultimately, their behavior in negative ways.

Scholars shifted their attention from distributive to procedural justice as a result of the "inability of equity theory and other distributive justice models to completely explain and predict peoples' reactions to perceived injustice" (Cohen-Charash & Spector, 2001, p. 279). Rather than focusing on the outcome, the procedural-justice perspective emphasizes the perceived fairness of the process by which the outcome was determined. Procedural-justice research took root with the work of Lind and Tyler (1988) that showed that the fairness of the process by which an outcome is reached is often more important than the distributional fairness of the outcome. Thus, even in the face of undesirable outcomes (e.g., pay reduction, disciplinary action), employees may remain committed to the organization if they perceive the process that allocated the outcome to be fair (Lind & Tyler, 1988; Tyler, 2006). Supervisors of organizations can attain positive procedural-justice perceptions by interacting with subordinates in respectful, nonthreatening, and unbiased ways; clearly explaining the purpose and reasons for their actions; and allowing the subordinates to have a voice and express their opinions (Cohen-Charash & Spector, 2001; Colquitt et al., 2001; Lind & Tyler, 1988; Tyler, 2006; Tyler & Huo, 2002).

Around the same time that the procedural-justice perspective was gaining popularity, a third form of justice, interactional justice, drew attention (Bies & Moag, 1986). Similar to the previous concepts, interactional justice emphasizes the role of supervisor politeness, honesty, and respect during the interpersonal communication with and treatment of employees (Cohen-Charash & Spector, 2001). When taken together, the concepts of distributive, procedural, and interactional justice form organizational justice (Aquino, Lewis, & Bradfield, 1999; Cohen-Charash & Spector, 2001; Colquitt et al., 2001). Scholars tend to agree that adherence to all three concepts is essential for an organization to truly be perceived by its employees as just and fair. Thus, it is important for research that focuses on organizational justice to incorporate aspects of all three concepts. Research has revealed that organizational justice is related to increased work performance, organizational commitment, and organizational citizenship behavior, whereas organizational injustice is associated with counterproductive work behavior (Cohen-Charash & Mueller, 2007; Cohen-Charash & Spector, 2001; Colquitt et al., 2001). Employees who experience some form of injustice from the organization sometimes restore feelings of justice by reducing the quality or quantity of their production (Cohen-Charash & Spector, 2001).

Organizational Injustice and Employee Deviance

Overall, research has consistently shown that organizations that are perceived as unjust by their employees produce situations conducive to employee deviance (Aquino et al., 1999; Cohen-Charash & Spector, 2001; Greenberg, 1990, 1993). As Cohen-Charash and Spector (2001) observe,

> To the extent employees perceive their organization to be unfair because it uses unfair procedures for resource allocations, employees will develop negative attitudes toward the organization (e.g., lower trust and commitment and greater anger). Negative attitudes and emotions lead to employees not having incentives to work in favor of the organization. Moreover, they might lead employees to act against the organization. (p. 288)

Early research in the area of organizational justice and workplace deviance demonstrated that perceptions of distributive injustice were associated with employee theft from the organization (Greenberg, 1990, 1993). More recent research has incorporated all aspects of organizational justice and demonstrated that perceptions of injustice predicted retaliatory behavior toward the organization (Skarlicki & Folger, 1997) and deviance directed at the organization and its employees (Aquino et al., 1999). It has been argued that "when employees are dissatisfied with fairness of procedures, they are more likely to violate organizational norms and commit acts of deviance" (Aquino et al., 1999, p. 1076).

Organizational Injustice and Police Misconduct

In the context of policing, organizational-injustice perceptions may be associated with retaliatory behavior toward the agency but may also yield perceptions of managerial illegitimacy (French & Raven, 1959; Lind & Tyler, 1988; Tyler, 2006). Lack of legitimacy is likely to be related to disobedience of organizational rules and regulations (French & Raven, 1959; Lind & Tyler, 1988; Tyler, 2006). Accordingly, police officers who perceive their organization to engage in unfair managing procedures, inequitable distribution of resources, or disrespectful interpersonal treatment may be more inclined to violate agency norms and regulations by committing acts of misconduct. And while procedural and distributive justice has been examined, most notably in the context of law obedience (Reisig, Bratton, & Gertz, 2007; Tyler, 2006; Tyler & Huo, 2002), satisfaction with the police (Reisig & Parks, 2000) and courts (Higgins, Wolfe, & Walters, 2009), and its relation to criminal activity (Fagan & Piquero, 2007; Piquero, Fagan, Mulvey, Steinberg, & Odgers, 2005), no research has explored the role of organizational justice in explaining police misconduct.

Some critics have argued that examining organizational correlates of police misconduct wrongly places blame on police supervisors when, in reality, individual officers must *choose* to engage in the behavior regardless of other circumstances (Manning, 2009). Although plausible, this criticism does not negate the fact that police officers and their behavior are enmeshed within the organization that employs them. One cannot separate individual officer behavior from the social context in which it takes place (Smith, 1986). More importantly, identifying the organizational correlates of misconduct does not relinquish responsibility from the officer but instead emphasizes ways in which agencies can improve their operation and policy to subvert situations that are conducive to individuals' choosing to engage in misconduct. Armacost (2003), for instance, argued that officers "are embedded in an organization that makes them more likely to frame their judgments in terms of role-based obligations and expectations than according to a simple cost-benefit analysis of their potential actions" and that placing blame for misconduct solely at the feet of individual officers (e.g., using the "rotten apple" explanation) is simply "a search for scapegoats" (p. 493).

Recent research has shown that organizational justice constructs are related to correctional officer job stress, organizational commitment, and job satisfaction (Lambert, Hogan, & Griffin, 2007; Taxman & Gordon, 2009). Perceptions of procedural and distributive justice by officers given undercover assignments were also shown to be related to job satisfaction, organizational commitment, and work performance (Farmer, Beehr, & Love, 2003). Furthermore, investigations of complaints against officers that were perceived to be carried out in a procedurally fair manner were associated with officers' satisfaction with the process regardless of the outcome (De Angelis & Kupchik, 2007). Although research has separately examined organizational justice and employee deviance, there has yet to be a study that connects the two ideas in an attempt to explain police misconduct.

As such, research is needed to examine whether perceptions of organizational injustice are associated with this behavior. The interpersonal communications and relations that occur between police administrators and subordinate officers are complex social-psychological processes. Organizational justice is a theoretical construct that can be used to understand how officers view the fairness of their supervisors' managerial practices and policies and to determine whether these perceptions are related to individual officer misconduct. Not only may this offer a more theoretically informed understanding of the organizational mechanisms associated with misconduct, it could also help inform police administrators on ways to proactively combat the problem by demonstrating interpersonal managerial techniques that are likely to produce perceptions of organizational justice from subordinates.

Organizational Justice and Correlates of Police Misconduct

Organizational injustice should be related to misconduct, but it should also help explain other variables related to police deviance. Schein (1993, p. 361) has noted that "organizational cultures are created in part by leaders, and one of the most decisive functions of leadership is the creation, the management, and sometimes even the destruction of culture." Superiors who use fair and just managing techniques are perceived as legitimate authority figures whose cultural norms and rules should be followed (French & Raven, 1959; Schein, 1993). Conversely, police administrators who consistently violate organizational justice may legitimize deviant activity or delegitimize their authority to enforce rules and create situations conducive to adherence to the code of silence and noble-cause corruption beliefs.

Organizational culture is viewed as a mechanism of social control that can be used to manipulate subordinates into perceiving, thinking, and feeling in certain ways (Schein, 1993). Because of this fact, the consequences of illegitimate use of managerial power can be devastating to an organization. Tosi, Mero, and Rizzo (2000) argued that when legitimate use of power fails, individual goals become paramount to organizational goals. Ultimately, subordinates who perceive managerial practices as lacking organizational fairness are more likely to pursue individual interests (French & Raven, 1959; Tyler, 2006). This pursuit may manifest itself in one of two ways. For one, organizational injustice may lead some officers to engage in noble-cause corruption out of the belief that unfair organizational policies and managerial practices prevent the true pursuit of justice. Thus, engaging in "street justice" is seen as the only means to achieve public protection and justice (Caldero & Crank, 2004).[1] Second, and similarly, those who feel that their agency has unfair investigatory procedures of police misconduct may be more likely to adhere to the code of silence out of fear that regardless of the circumstances of a particular incident, an officer accused of misconduct will never receive a fair hearing. Rothwell and Baldwin (2007b) provided evidence supporting this assertion by showing that policies perceived as procedurally just were more likely to result in officer willingness to report misconduct. In short, organizational injustice is likely to result in the individual goals of code-of-silence attitudes and noble-cause corruption beliefs that override the organizational goals of honesty, public protection, and due process.

Current Study

This study offers and applies the organizational-justice framework as a potentially useful explanatory mechanism for police misconduct. Specifically, the study examines two issues. First, the role of organizational justice in explaining adherence to the code of silence and beliefs in noble-cause corruption is explored. It is expected that officers who perceive their organization to be more just and fair will have weaker adherence to the code of silence and be less likely to believe that corruption of the noble cause is justified. The second purpose is to assess whether perceptions of organizational justice relate to police misconduct. Officers perceiving their agency to engage in fair managing practices are expected to have engaged in less misconduct. To remove as many potential spurious relationships as possible, these hypotheses are tested while controlling for individual characteristics (i.e., officer age, gender, race ethnicity, rank, years of service, and deviant peers) that research has shown to be associated with misconduct.

Method

Participants

This study uses data originally collected by Greene and Piquero (2000) in a study of police integrity in

Philadelphia funded by the National Institute of Justice. A simple random sample of 504 police officers was drawn from all 3,810 Philadelphia Police Department (PPD) officers of rank patrol officer, sergeant, or lieutenant as of January 2000 (see Chappell & Piquero, 2004; Greene et al., 2004; Hickman et al., 2000, 2001, 2004; Lawton, 2007). A total of 499 officer surveys were returned for a response rate of 99%. The high response rate is likely attributable to the fact that surveys were administered after the respondents' roll call and directly before going out on the street for duty. Therefore, all selected officers were easily contacted to participate. Similar response pattern imputation (SRPI) was used to replace missing values, which is available in PRELIS Version 2.30 (Scientific Software International, Chicago, IL). SRPI replaces missing values on a specific case with values from a "donor case" that has a similar response pattern across a set of matching variables. Gmel (2001) showed SRPI to be an effective and reliable procedure for imputing missing values. After imputation, complete information for 483 officer respondents was available for analysis.

Dependent Variables

Three dependent variables were examined in this study, each capturing varying degrees of police misconduct that the officers were responsible for during their time with the PPD: how many times they had been (1) subject to a formal citizen complaint, (2) investigated by the department's internal affairs division (IAD), or (3) charged with a violation of the department's disciplinary code. These measures have been previously used to capture a wide range of officer misconduct (Chappell & Piquero, 2004; Greene et al., 2004; Hickman et al., 2000, 2001, 2004; Lawton, 2007). Officers with higher frequencies of each of these variables have engaged in more misconduct, as their actions have more readily come to the attention of the public or the PPD's IAD or have violated a formal departmental disciplinary code.[2] Officers' frequency of each measure of misconduct was coded trichotomously (i.e., zero times, one time, or two or more times). Although the three dependent variables may appear to be steps in a process that emerge from a single event, this does not necessarily have to be the case, as these data contain the officers' history with respect to these specific outcomes during the course of their careers in the PPD. Accordingly, the analyses treat these variables as separate measures that represent simple counts and are not reflective of a single event that produced multiple outcomes.

Independent Variables

Organizational justice. Six items were used to capture the three aspects of organizational justice (i.e., distributive, procedural, and interactional), and all were measured on the same 5-point Likert-type scale (1 = *strongly disagree*, 2 = *disagree*, 3 = *neutral*, 4 = *agree*, 5 = *strongly agree*). Distributive justice was measured by asking officers their level of agreement with the following questions: "Disciplinary action is a result of pressure on supervisors from command staff to give out discipline," and "Getting special assignments in the police department depends on who [sic] you know, not on merit." Procedural justice was measured with two items: "When a police officer appears before the Police Board of Inquiry, the officer will probably be found guilty even when he/she has a good defense," and "The rules and regulations dealing with officer conduct are fair and sensible." Last, interactional justice was captured by asking officers two questions: "When you get to know the department from the inside, you begin to think that it is a wonder that it does one-half as well as it does," and "Police supervisors are very interested in their subordinates." The items are consistent with those used in previous organizational justice research (Aquino et al., 1999; Cohen-Charash & Spector, 2001; Colquitt et al., 2001).

All of the questions were coded so higher scores indicated higher perceptions of justice.

Code-of-silence attitudes and noble-cause beliefs. To assess the role of the code of silence in police misconduct and to determine the factors associated with higher beliefs in "the code," three questions were asked in the survey. Officers were asked to respond on a 5-point Likert-type scale (1 = *strongly disagree*, 2 = *disagree*, 3 = *neutral*, 4 = *agree*, 5 = *strongly agree*) to the following questions: "Unless it is an extremely serious matter, officers should protect each other when misconduct is alleged"; "Professional courtesy (excusing a fellow officer for minor violations of the law) is generally OK"; and "Most officers would take action if they knew of misconduct, even if it was a friend" (reverse coded).

To measure noble-cause beliefs, the officers were asked to respond to eight questions on a 5-point Likert-type scale (1 = *strongly disagree*, 2 = *disagree*, 3 = *neutral*, 4 = *agree*, 5 = *strongly agree*): "Sometimes, an officer has to use methods prohibited by directives to enforce the law or make an arrest"; "An officer cannot be consistently productive unless he/she bends or breaks the rules from time to time"; "Sometimes officers use methods prohibited by directives to achieve arrest of a criminal, if it's the only way that it can be done"; "It is sometimes necessary to be verbally disrespectful or abusive to a person because that is the only way they will understand or comply"; "Most supervisors agree that rules must be broken or bent to get the job done, but wouldn't admit it"; "Sometimes officers have to exaggerate probable cause to get a crook off the street"; "An officer occasionally has to bend the facts a little in court or in a report in order to get a criminal convicted"; and "Some people should get street justice after hurting a police officer because that is the only real punishment they will get."

All of the code of silence and noble-cause items were analyzed to determine whether two distinct constructs are observable or whether they simply represent an overall factor of ethics. Consistent with expectations, the items loaded onto their hypothesized constructs. The code-of-silence attitude items and the noble-cause belief items were combined into additive scales, both of which demonstrated reasonable to strong internal consistency.

Control variables. To isolate the direct effect of our key independent variables on the misconduct measures, several potential intervening variables were controlled for in the analysis. As several demographic variables have been shown to be relevant correlates of police misconduct, the analyses control for officer age, gender (1 = male, 0 = female), race-ethnicity (1 = racial-ethnic minority, 0 = White), rank (1 = patrol officer, 0 = supervisor), and years of service.[3]

Additionally, we controlled for deviant police officer peer associations. As Chappell and Piquero (2004) showed, association with officer peers who adhere to deviant norms and beliefs regarding police misconduct increases a respondent officer's chances of engaging in his or her own deviance. Specifically, a set of six hypothetical vignettes (Klockars, Ivković, Harver, & Haberfield, 2000) was used in the survey to measure officers' perceptions of deviant peer associations within the PPD (see appendix). This procedure is commonly used and is believed to be an appropriate method for measuring differential association (Akers, 2009; Chappell & Piquero, 2004; Holtfreter, Reisig, Piquero, & Piquero, 2010; Piquero & Bouffard, 2007). Two of the vignettes involved an officer accepting free meals and gifts, one involved an officer not reporting a fellow officer for drunk driving (i.e., professional courtesy), one involved street justice of a fleeing suspect, and two involved officer theft. After reading each of the vignettes, the officers were asked to respond on a 5-point Likert-type scale (1 = *not at all serious*, 5 = *very serious*) to the following question: "How serious do most police officers in the Philadelphia Police Department consider this behavior to be?" The dimensionality of the items was assessed using PCA with varimax rotation. The six questions were first reverse coded so higher scores indicated peer associations favorable to misconduct. PCA demonstrated two distinct differential association components. The first included the free gifts or meals, street justice, and drunk driving vignette questions. These items were combined into an additive scale labeled Minor Deviant Peers (i.e., differential peer associations favorable to lesser forms of police misconduct). The second component included the two theft vignette questions and was labeled Serious Deviant Peers (i.e., differential peer associations favorable to serious forms of police misconduct). Higher scores on each of the scales indicated peer associations favorable to police misconduct. Controlling for the above variables allows one to be confident that the effect of organizational justice, code-of-silence attitudes, and noble-cause beliefs on the misconduct outcomes is unbiased and not simply a spurious result of officer demographics, rank, years of service, or the influence of associating with deviant peers.

Analysis

The analysis proceeded in two steps. First, the relationships between organizational justice, code-of-silence attitudes, and noble-cause beliefs were analyzed. These analyses were designed to shed light on the organizational factors linked to adherence to the code of silence and belief in corruption of the noble cause, controlling for the potential confounding influence of officer demographic characteristics, rank, years of service, or deviant peers. The second step examined the relationship between organizational justice, code-of-silence attitudes, noble-cause beliefs, and the control variables and the outcome measures of police misconduct.

Results

Predicting Code-of-Silence Attitudes and Noble-Cause Corruption Beliefs

Association with peers who favor minor forms of police misconduct is associated with significant increases in code-of-silence attitudes. Association with peers who favor serious misconduct did not significantly influence attitudes about the code of silence. Importantly, organizational justice significantly predicted code-of-silence attitudes. Racial- or ethnic-minority officers had weaker adherence to the code of silence than Whites. In all, it seems that associating with peers who favor minor forms of police misconduct may increase individuals' adherence to the code of silence, whereas increased perceptions of organizational justice are linked with weaker adherence to the code of silence.

The second model examines beliefs in noble-cause corruption. Organizational justice and minor deviant peers significantly predicted beliefs in noble-cause corruption. Officers who perceived more of their peers to favor minor forms of police misconduct held stronger beliefs in noble-cause corruption, whereas those who viewed the agency as engaging in fair managing practices held fewer beliefs favorable to noble-cause corruption.

Citizen Complaints

Deviant peers, code-of-silence attitudes, and noble-cause beliefs failed to significantly predict citizen complaints. However, for every 1-year increase in age, officers were approximately 6% more likely to have zero versus two or more complaints, whereas for every 1-year increase in years of service, officers were approximately 13% less likely to have zero complaints compared to two or more. Accordingly, older officers were less likely to have complaints filed against them, but more years on the job placed officers at greater risk to have complaints filed against them. Interestingly, these effects were not significant in the one-versus two-or-more-complaint contrast, but racial-ethnic-minority officers were approximately 93% more likely to have only one versus two or more complaints filed against them compared to their White colleagues. Most importantly, with all other variables held constant, organizational justice had a significant effect on the likelihood of being in the lower-frequency-of-complaints groups. Specifically, every unit increase in organizational justice was associated with an 18% greater likelihood of having zero citizen complaints versus two or more and a 12% greater likelihood of having only one complaint versus two or more. These are rather large effects, given that the Organizational Justice scale has a range of 24. Officers who perceived the PPD to be just and fair were less likely to have citizen complaints filed against them.

IAD Investigations

The second model presents the results predicting frequency of IAD investigations that have been conducted against the officer. Once again, deviant peer associations do not seem to play a role in predicting police misconduct in the presence of the other variables. Age and years of service had a significant effect on both contrasts. One-year increases in age were associated with a 6% greater likelihood of having zero versus two or more IAD investigations and a 12% greater likelihood of having been investigated only once versus two or more times. Conversely, 1-year increases in years of service was associated with officers being 11% less likely to have zero versus two or more and one versus two or more complaints. Organizational justice significantly predicted whether an officer would have zero investigations against him or her versus two or more. Accordingly, a one-unit increase in perceived organizational justice corresponded to a 14% greater likelihood of having zero IAD investigations against the officer compared to having two or more. Interestingly, officers who more strongly adhere to the code of silence are more likely to have fewer IAD investigation against them. That is, one-unit increases in code-of-silence attitudes provided officers with a 23% greater likelihood of having only one investigation versus two or more. This relationship, which will be discussed in more detail later, suggests that the code of silence shields officers from IAD investigations.

Departmental Disciplinary Charges

The final model predicts the frequency of disciplinary charges filed against the officer. Organizational justice had a significant effect on disciplinary charges across the two contrasts. One-unit increases in organizational justice resulted in a 25% greater likelihood of having zero charges filed against an officer versus having two or more and an 18% greater likelihood of having only one charge versus two or more. Thus, officers are less likely to have departmental charges filed against them if they perceive organizational justice in the department. None of the other variables had a significant effect on frequency of disciplinary charges.

Discussion

Police misconduct is a topic of great interest to police administrators who are responsible for enacting policies and strategies to control the behavior. Numerous studies have been conducted on the subject, and several commissions have famously investigated allegations of corruption and misconduct within police agencies (e.g., Knapp Commission, 1972; Mollen Commission, 1994). Although many variables have been found to be associated with police misconduct, ultimate responsibility for such behavior is often levied against the police agency (Ivković, 2005). Still, a theoretical explanation of the organizational mechanisms that are associated with the incidence of individual officer misconduct has remained elusive. The current study addressed this gap in the literature by examining the role of organizational justice in predicting police misconduct. The application of this organizational theory to police misconduct in a large police department provided four theoretical and policy-relevant implications that should be considered by future researchers and police administrators.

The first, and perhaps most important, finding was that organizational justice was associated with several forms of police misconduct. Officers who viewed the PPD as distributing decisions fairly, engaging in procedurally just managerial actions, and interacting in a polite and courteous manner toward subordinates were more likely to have been involved in few incidents of police misconduct. Specifically, perceptions of organizational justice were associated with lower likelihoods of officers having citizen complaints filed, IAD investigations instigated, or disciplinary charges brought against them. As this is the first empirical linkage between officers' perceptions of organizational justice and their misconduct, this finding suggests that from a policy perspective, agencies that engage in organizational justice may reduce the chances of their officers engaging in these forms of misconduct. Police supervisors need to pay particular attention to developing agency policies that are procedurally fair, communicating with subordinate officers about specific policies and why they are in place, and allowing officers to voice concerns about such policies. This suggestion applies to policies concerning departmental rules, disciplinary processes, hiring and firing practices, and promotional procedures, to name a few. In sum, police administrators can learn much from the principles of organizational justice when designing policies, which in turn will make police agencies more successful organizations.

At the same time, however, an alternative relationship between organizational justice and police misconduct is possible. Although our focus was on how perceptions of organizational injustice increase the likelihood that officers will engage in misconduct, it is possible that officers who have been the subject of (especially erroneous) complaints, investigations, or discipline are more likely to react with feelings of unfairness (i.e., within the context of general strain theory), which may generate feelings that the organization is unjust. Agnew (1992) argued that feelings of injustice may morph into anger and ultimately produce deviance. Thus, future research is needed to determine not only whether experiencing negative outcomes from a department produces perceptions of injustice but also whether, in turn, these emotions increase officers' chances of resorting to misconduct or deviance as a way to cope with the experienced strain. Given the cross-sectional nature of our data, we cannot speak to these relationships, but future scholars are poised to answer such questions when appropriate data become available.

Second, organizational justice and deviant peers (favoring less serious forms of police misconduct) significantly predicted code-of-silence attitudes and noble-cause corruption beliefs. Not only are deviant peer associations important in predicting police misconduct (Chappell & Piquero, 2004), it seems that they may also be an important precursor to adherence to the code of silence and belief that noble-cause corruption is justified. These findings suggest that officers who associate with deviant peers are more likely to subscribe to the police subcultural belief that an officer should protect his or her colleagues regardless of allegations of misconduct. Furthermore, association with deviant officer peers places officers at increased risk to believe that violating suspect constitutional rights is required if one is to achieve justice and protect the public from harm. Conversely, officers adhere to the code of silence less strictly and have fewer beliefs that justify noble-cause corruption if they view their agency to behave in organizationally just ways. That is, as officers' perceptions of organizational justice increase, their level of attitudes favorable to the code of silence and noble-cause corruption is likely to decrease. From a policy perspective, police administrators who make an honest effort to ensure that departmental discipline is disseminated in a fair manner (i.e., not arbitrarily or as a result of external pressure), disciplinary proceedings are procedurally fair (i.e., represent fair rules and regulations), promotions are distributed on the basis of legitimate factors (i.e., not simply on "who you know"), and communication between subordinates is polite and sincere are likely to have lower levels of adherence to the code of silence within their departments and fewer officers under their control who feel that noble-cause corruption is necessary in the pursuit of justice. Once again, future research should attempt to further examine the causal structure underlying this relationship, as our cross-sectional data are unable to establish perfect time-order of the independent and dependent variables.

Third, aside from organizational justice, several other variables were associated with police misconduct. Increases in officer age were shown to correspond with lower frequencies of citizen complaints and IAD investigations. This finding may be attributable to several factors. First, it may be that supervisors view an officer as more trustworthy with every year he or she ages and is not investigated by IAD. This increased trust may result in less IAD suspicion. Alternatively, citizens may be more likely to complain against younger officers. However, it seems most logical that older officers would engage in less misconduct because they occupy different positions in the department or possess more stakes in conformity (e.g., promotion potential, pension) that could be jeopardized by deviant involvement. If this is the case, it is interesting to note that quite paradoxically increases in years of service were related to citizen complaints and IAD investigations in the opposite direction. That is, the longer an officer served on the department, the more likely he or she was to have more citizen complaints and IAD investigations filed against him or her.

In analyses not shown, we attempted to explain this peculiar finding by conducting several ancillary investigations of the issue. For example, although varying slightly in magnitude, both age and years of service were positively correlated with the dependent variables. We also examined cross-tabulations and scatter plots of age and years of service on each of the dependent variables to determine whether several officers were driving the effects. The results of both analyses suggested that there were no influential cases. Last, we reestimated the models while excluding age and years of service. Importantly, the effect of the key independent variables on the misconduct measures remained substantively unchanged. Potentially, although aging may protect officers from misconduct through a bonding mechanism, more years on duty may inevitably place an officer at greater risk to have a complaint or IAD investigation against him or her. This finding raises several interesting questions that await further data collection and analysis.

Despite theoretical expectations, noble-cause corruption beliefs were not significantly related to any forms of misconduct, and code-of-silence attitudes were related only with IAD investigations. However, the direction of this relationship was somewhat counterintuitive at first inspection. Results showed that officers who had stronger attitudes favorable to the code of silence were more likely to have only one IAD investigation against them versus two or more. It seems that stronger adherence to the code of silence protects officers who have been investigated by IAD once from being subject to a second investigation. This result is interesting because it presents a compelling policy issue. A number of questions are yet to be answered. For example, are officers who are strong adherents to the code of silence so quiet about their own and others' behavior that IAD investigations are difficult to conduct? Are these officers more apt at avoiding detection? Do officers who were investigated once feel that it is necessary to subscribe more strongly to the code of silence to avoid future investigations? Or is the actual IAD investigation process flawed in that it gives officers the perception of organizational injustice and, in turn, produces more attitudes favorable to the code? These questions notwithstanding, the results show that police departments that manage and supervise officers in ways consistent with organizational justice may have weaker adherence to the code of silence and fewer officers engaging in misconduct that necessitates IAD investigations.

Last, the organizational-justice framework has offered a theoretically useful explanation of the interpersonal organizational-justice (distributive, procedural, interactional) mechanisms and potential correlates associated with police misconduct. That is to say, police agencies that adhere to these constructs are using the mechanisms that are associated with less officer misconduct, and they may create organizational environments that control against the proliferation of behavior guided by the code of silence and beliefs that justify the use of noble-cause corruption. The organizational-justice theoretical model has moved the study of police misconduct forward by demonstrating the organizational behavioral mechanisms that are associated with such behavior. Thus, scholars can move beyond attributing police misconduct to police agencies and instead offer suggestions to administrators on how they can behave toward subordinates in ways that are likely to reduce misconduct. Although data agreement restrictions precluded a cross-check analysis of officer self-reported misconduct and official departmental misconduct records, some research has reported a moderate correspondence between self-report and official police discipline data (Hickman, 2007). Still, future research should examine this issue in greater detail so as to afford an investigation into whether officers who have a greater link to the agency and express a sense of organizational justice are more likely to answer in a socially desirable way (i.e., not report their misconduct when, in fact, they have committed deviance).

The results of this study provide five broad actions that police administrators can take to reduce individual officer misconduct: (a) Fairly allocate promotions and special assignments and ensure that officers understand why such decisions are made; (b) fairly distribute disciplinary actions and clearly explain the reasons for such actions; (c) engage in investigations of officers that are procedurally fair and ensure that officers perceive the procedures as such; (d) ensure that agency policies, rules, and regulations allow the goals of justice to be accomplished while simultaneously being fair and sensible to individual officers; and (e) honestly show subordinate officers that the agency cares for their well-being and that their opinions are taken seriously.

In this regard, Acker (1992) discussed how organizational efforts to gender-norm the work environment can backfire on managers, as employees sometimes develop feelings of unfairness. Thus, simple organizational policies, such as gender-neutral physical fitness standards, in police departments may result in subordinate perceptions that managers engage in illegitimate hiring practices. It is imperative for police managers to realize such nuances in the development of justice perceptions, especially because their reach may extend beyond reducing misconduct. Officers who perceived the department to be organizationally just were likely to have fewer citizen complaints filed against them. Therefore, police agencies that implement managerial practices shaped by organizational justice are not only likely to reduce officer misconduct, but they may also enhance implementation of community policing initiatives.

In the end, organizational justice offers an important theoretical perspective of police misconduct, yet further analysis is required. Specifically, research is needed to better understand the relationship that appears to exist between organizational justice, deviant peer associations, the code of silence, and noble-cause corruption beliefs. Although it is plausible to assume that organizational factors contribute to the proliferation of the code of silence and noble-cause beliefs, it may also be that such variables have reciprocal relationships with organizational justice. For example, officers who are punished for violating agency policy may be more likely in the future to adhere to the code of silence, which may in turn influence their perceptions of agency organizational justice. Such questions cannot be adequately addressed until longitudinal data are collected that assess changes in officers' perceptions, peer associations, attitudes, and beliefs over time. Future study should investigate whether our findings generalize to other agencies. Because this study focused on one large, eastern, inner-city police department, the results may not generalize to smaller, rural, or western agencies. For now, however, it seems that organizational justice holds promise in the pursuit of explaining police officer misconduct and should be considered as part of criminologists' understanding of this behavior.

Appendix

Police Misconduct Vignettes Used to Measure Deviant Peer Associations

1. A police officer routinely accepts free meals, cigarettes, and other items of small value from merchants on his beat. The officer does not solicit these gifts and is careful not to abuse the generosity of those who gave the gifts to him.

2. A police officer is widely liked in the community, and on holidays, local merchants and restaurant and bar owners show their appreciation for the officer's attention by giving the officer gifts of food and liquor.

3. At 2 a.m., a police officer who is on duty is driving his patrol car on a deserted road. The

officer sees a vehicle that has been driven off the road and is stuck in a ditch. The officer approaches the vehicle and observes that the driver is not hurt but is obviously intoxicated. The officer also finds that the driver is a police officer. Instead of reporting this accident and offense, the officer transports the driver to his home.

4. A police officer on foot patrol surprises a man who is attempting to break into an automobile. The man flees. The officer chases him for about two blocks before apprehending him by tackling him and wrestling him to the ground. After the offender is under control, the officer punches him a couple of times in the stomach as punishment for fleeing.

5. A police officer discovers a burglary of a jewelry shop. The display cases are smashed and it is obvious that many items have been taken. While searching the shop, the officer takes a watch, worth about two days' pay for that officer. The officer reports the watch had been stolen during the burglary.

6. While on duty, a police officer finds a wallet in a parking lot. It contains the amount of money equivalent to a full day's pay for that officer. The officer reports the wallet as lost property but keeps the money.

Note: To measure deviant peer associations, the officers were asked the following question after reading each vignette: "How serious do most police officers in the Philadelphia Police Department consider this behavior to be?"

Notes

1. Although pursuing the utilitarian motive of public safety (i.e., the noble cause) may not seem to be acting in self-interest at first, it is the fixation on the noble cause that propels officers to accomplish the goal despite having to violate laws and departmental regulations (i.e., individual interests taking supremacy over the dual departmental goals of public safety and protection of individual rights). As a reviewer astutely observed, the experience of organizational injustice may also weaken an officer's ties to his or her department, thereby opening the door for the officer to align with influential social pressures (e.g., peers) that also see the department's policies as a hindrance to the pursuit of the noble cause and, in turn, lead to noble cause corruption beliefs.

2. The data do not distinguish between complaints or investigations that resulted from officer conduct while on or off duty. Importantly, however, all complaints, investigations, and disciplinary charges were handled within the police agency. Thus, all three dependent variables represent acts that are deemed unacceptable by the public or the agency itself.

3. The supervisor category included corporals, sergeants, detectives, and lieutenants. Because of the low frequency of each of these groups, they were collapsed into a single supervisor category.

4. This category was chosen as the reference as additional analyses revealed no substantively relevant differences between those officers who had committed zero versus one of each of the misconduct measures. Thus, the most meaningful differences of each misconduct measure were observed between those with zero or one event and those who had engaged in two or more acts of misconduct. This fact highlights the importance of using multinomial logistic regression as opposed to collapsing the one and two-or-more response groups into a single category to allow the use of binary logistic regression.

5. Multicollinearity is not a concern in these data because principal component analysis showed the code-of-silence and noble-cause items to load on their respective components, all of the variance inflation factors were below 3, and condition indices fell below 30 (Tabachnick & Fidell, 2007).

References

Acker, J. (1992). Gendering organizational theory. In J. M. Shafritz, J. S. Ott, & Y. S. Jang (Eds.), *Classics of organization theory* (pp. 450-459). Florence, KY: Wadsworth.

Adams, J. S. (1963). Toward an understanding of inequity. *Journal of Abnormal and Social Psychology, 67*, 422-436.

Agnew, R. (1992). Foundation for a general strain theory of crime and delinquency. *Criminology, 30*, 47-87.

Akers, R. L. (2009). *Social learning and social structure: A general theory of crime and deviance.* New Brunswick, NJ: Transaction.

Aquino, K., Lewis, M. U., & Bradfield, M. (1999). Justice constructs, negative affectivity, and employee deviance: A proposed model and empirical test. *Journal of Organizational Behavior, 20*, 1073-1091.

Armacost, B. E. (2003). Organizational culture and police misconduct. *George Washington Law Review, 72*, 453-545.

Bies, R. J., & Moag, J. F. (1986). Interactional justice: Communication criteria of fairness. In R. J. Lewicki, B. H. Sheppard, & M. H. Bazerman (Eds.), *Research on negotiations in organizations* (pp. 43-55). Greenwich, CT: JAI Press.

Brereton, D., & Ede, A. (1996). The police code of silence in Queensland: The impact of the Fitzgerald Inquiry Reform. *Current Issues in Criminal Justice, 8*, 107-129.

Caldero, M. A., & Crank, J. P. (2004). *Police ethics: The corruption of noble cause.* Cincinnati, OH: Anderson.

Chappell, A. T., & Piquero, A. R. (2004). Applying social learning theory to police misconduct. *Deviant Behavior, 25*, 85-108.

Chin, G. J., & Wells, S. C. (1997). The "blue wall of silence" as evidence of bias and motive to lie: A new approach to police perjury. *University of Pittsburgh Law Review, 59*, 233-258.

Cohen-Charash, Y., & Mueller, J. S. (2007). Does perceived unfairness exacerbate or mitigate interpersonal counterproductive work behaviors related to envy? *Journal of Applied Psychology, 92*, 666-680.

Cohen-Charash, Y., & Spector, P. E. (2001). The role of justice in organizations: A meta-analysis. *Organizational Behavior and Human Decision Processes, 86*, 278-321.

Colquitt, J. A., Conlon, D. E., Wesson, M. J., Porter, C. & Hg, K. Y. (2001). Justice in the millennium: A meta-analytic review of 25 years of organizational justice research. *Journal of Applied Psychology, 86*, 425-445.

Crank, J., Flaherty, D., & Giacomazzi, A. (2007). The noble cause: An empirical assessment. *Journal of Criminal Justice, 35*, 103-116.

De Angelis, J., & Kupchik, A. (2007). Citizen oversight, procedural justice, and officer perceptions of the complaint investigation process. *Policing: An International Journal of Police Strategies and Management, 30*, 651-671.

Fagan, J., & Piquero, A. R. (2007). Rational choice and developmental influences on recidivism among adolescent felony offenders. *Journal of Empirical Legal Studies, 4*, 715-748.

Farmer, S. J., Beehr, T. A., & Love, K. G. (2003). Becoming an undercover police officer: A not on fairness perceptions, behavior, and attitudes. *Journal of Organizational Behavior, 24*, 373-387.

French J. R. P., & Raven, B. (1959). The bases of social power. In D. Cartwright (Ed.), *Studies in social power* (pp. 150-167). Ann Arbor: University of Michigan, Institute for Social Research.

Gmel, G. (2001). Imputation of missing values in the case of multiple item instrument measuring alcohol consumption. *Statistics in Medicine, 20*, 2369-2381.

Greenberg, J. (1990). Employee theft as a reaction to underpayment inequity: The hidden cost of pay cuts. *Journal of Applied Psychology, 75*, 561-568.

Greenberg, J. (1993). Stealing in the name of justice: Informational and interpersonal moderators of theft reactions to underpayment inequity. *Organizational Behavior and Human Decision Processes, 54*, 81-103.

Greene, J. R., & Piquero, A. R. (2000). *Supporting police integrity in Philadelphia [Pennsylvania] Police Department, 1991-1998 and 2000* [Computer file]. ICPSR version. Boston, MA: Northeastern University (producer), 2002. Ann Arbor, MI: Inter-university Consortium for Political and Social Research (distributor), 2004. doi:10.3886/ICPSR03977

Greene, J. R., Piquero, A. R., Hickman, M. J., & Lawton, B. A. (2004). *Police integrity and accountability in Philadelphia: Predicting and assessing police misconduct.* Washington, DC: National Institute of Justice.

Grennan, S. A. (1987). Findings on the role of officer gender in violent encounters with citizens. *Journal of Police Science and Administration, 15*, 78-85.

Hickman, M. J. (2007). Validity of officer self-reported citizen complaints: A research note. *Police Quarterly, 10*, 332-341.

Hickman, M. J., Piquero, A. R. & Greene, J. R. (2000). Discretion and gender disproportionality in police disciplinary systems. *Policing: An International Journal of Police Strategies and Management, 23*, 105-116.

Hickman, M. J., Piquero, A. R., Lawton, B. A., & Greene, J. R. (2001). Applying Tittle's control balance theory to police deviance. *Policing: An International Journal of Police Strategies and Management, 24*, 497-519.

Hickman, M. J., Piquero, N. L., & Piquero, A. R. (2004). The validity of Niederhoffer's Cynicism scale. *Journal of Criminal Justice, 32*, 1-13.

Higgins, G., Wolfe, S. E., & Walters, N. (2009). Sex and experience: Modeling the public's perceptions of justice, satisfaction, and attitude toward the courts. *American Journal of Criminal Justice, 34*, 116-130.

Holtfreter, K., Reisig, M. D., Piquero, N. L., & Piquero, A. R. (2010). Low self-control and fraud: Offending, victimization, and their overlap. *Criminal Justice and Behavior, 37*, 188-203.

Ivković, S. K. (2005). *Fallen blue knights: Controlling police corruption.* Oxford, UK: Oxford University Press.

Ivković, S. K. (2009). Rotten apples, rotten branches, and rotten orchards. *Criminology and Public Policy, 8*, 777-785.

Kane, R. J. (2002). The social ecology of police misconduct. *Criminology, 40*, 867-896.

Kane, R. J., & White, M. D. (2009). Bad cops: A study of career-ending misconduct among New York City police officers. *Criminology and Public Policy, 8*, 735-767.

King, W. R. (2009). Police officer misconduct as normal accidents: An organizational perspective. *Criminology and Public Policy, 8*, 771-776.

Klockars, C. B. (1983). The Dirty Harry problem. In C. Klockars (Ed.), *Thinking about police: Contemporary readings* (pp. 238-438). New York, NY: McGraw-Hill.

Klockars, C. B., Ivković, S. K., Harver, W. E., & Haberfield, M. R. (2000). The measurement of police integrity. *National Institute of Justice Research in Brief*, 1–11.

Knapp Commission. (1972). Report of the New York City Commission to Investigate Allegations of Police Corruption and the City's Anti-Corruption Procedures. New York, NY: Bar Press.

Lambert, E. G., Hogan, N. L., & Griffin, M. L. (2007). The impact of distributive and procedural justice on correctional staff job stress, job satisfaction, and organizational commitment. *Journal of Criminal Justice*, 35, 644-656.

Lawton, B. A. (2007). Levels of nonlethal force: An examination of individual, situational, and contextual factors. *Journal of Research in Crime and Delinquency*, 44, 163-184.

Lind, E. A., & Tyler, T. R. (1988). *The social psychology of procedural justice*. New York, NY: Plenum Press.

Manning, P. K. (2009). Bad cops. *Criminology and Public Policy*, 8, 787-794.

McElvain, J. P., & Kposowa, A. J. (2004). Police officer characteristics and internal affairs investigations for use of force allegations. *Journal of Criminal Justice*, 32, 265-279.

Micucci, A. J., & Gomme, I. M. (2005). American police and subcultural support for the use of excessive force. *Journal of Criminal Justice*, 33, 487-500.

Mollen Commission. (1994). *Anatomy of failure, a path for success: The report of the Commission to Investigate Allegations of Police Corruption and the Anti-Corruption Procedures of the New York City Police Department*. New York, NY: City of New York.

Piquero, A. R., & Bouffard, J. A. (2007). Something old, something new: A preliminary investigation of Hirschi's redefined self-control. *Justice Quarterly*, 24, 1-27.

Piquero, A. R., Fagan, J., Mulvey, E., Steinberg, L., & Odgers, C. (2005). Developmental trajectories of legal socialization among serious adolescent offenders. *Journal of Criminal Law and Criminology*, 96, 267-298.

Pogarsky, G., & Piquero, A. R. (2003). Studying the reach of deterrence: Can deterrence theory help explain police misconduct? *Journal of Criminal Justice*, 32, 371-386.

Reisig, M. D., Bratton, J., & Gertz. M. (2007). The construct validity and refinement of process-based policing measures. *Criminal Justice and Behavior*, 34, 1005-1028.

Reisig, M. D., & Parks, R. (2000). Experience, quality of life, and neighborhood context: A hierarchical analysis of satisfaction with police. *Justice Quarterly*, 17, 607-630.

Reiss, A. J. (1971). *The police and the public*. New Haven, CT: Yale University Press.

Rojek, J., & Decker, S. H. (2009). Examining racial disparity in the police discipline process. *Police Quarterly*, 12, 388-407.

Rothwell, G. R., & Baldwin, J. N. (2007a). Ethical climate theory, whistle-blowing, and the code of silence in police agencies in the state of Georgia. *Journal of Business Ethics*, 70, 341-361.

Rothwell, G. R., & Baldwin, J. N. (2007b). Whistle-blowing and the code of silence in police agencies. *Crime & Delinquency*, 53, 605-632.

Schein, E. H. (1993). Defining organizational culture. In J. M. Shafritz, J. S. Ott, & Y. S. Jang (Eds.), *Classics of organization theory* (pp. 360-367). Belmont, CA: Wadsworth.

Sherman, L. (1975). An evaluation of policewomen on patrol in a suburban police department. *Journal of Police Science and Administration*, 3, 434-438.

Sherman, L. (1978). *Scandal and reform: Controlling police corruption*. Berkeley: University of California Press.

Simpson, S., Paternoster, R., & Piquero, N. L. (1998). Exploring the micro-macro link in corporate crime research. In P. Bamberger & W. J. Sonnenstuhl (Eds.), *Research in the sociology of organizations: Special volume on deviance in and of organizations*. Greenwich, CT: JAI Press.

Skarlicki, D. P., & Folger, R. (1997). Retaliation in the workplace: The roles of distributive, procedural, and interactional justice. *Journal of Applied Psychology*, 82, 434-443.

Skolnick, J. H. (2002). Corruption and the blue code of silence. *Police Practice and Research*, 3, 7-19.

Skolnick, J. H. (2005). Corruption and the blue code of silence. In R. Sarre, D. K. Das, & H. J. Albrecht (Eds.), *Police corruption: An international perspective* (pp. 301-316). Oxford, UK: Lexington Books.

Skolnick, J. H., & Fyfe, J. J. (1993). *Above the law: Police and the excessive use of force*. New York, NY: Free Press.

Smith, D. A. (1986). The neighborhood context of police behavior. In A. J. Reiss Jr. & M. Tonry (Eds.), *Crime and justice: Vol. 8. Communities and crime*. Chicago, IL: University of Chicago Press.

Tabachnick, B. G., Fidell, L. S. (2007). *Using multivariate statistics*. Boston, MA: Allyn and Bacon.

Taxman, F. S., & Gordon, J. A. (2009). Do fairness and equity matter? An examination of organizational justice among correctional officers in adult prisons. *Criminal Justice and Behavior*, 36, 695-711.

Terrill, W., & Reisig, M. D. (2003). Neighborhood context and police use of force. *Journal of Research in Crime and Delinquency*, 40, 291-321.

Tosi, H. L., Mero, N. P., & Rizzo, J. R. (2000). *Managing organizational behavior*. Cambridge, MA: Blackwell.

Truxillo, D. M., Bennett, S. R., & Collins, M. L. (1998). College education and police job performance: A ten-year study. *Public Personnel Management*, 27, 269-280.

Tyler, T. R. (2006). *Why people obey the law*. Princeton, NJ: Princeton University Press.

Tyler, T. R., & Huo, Y. J. (2002). *Trust in the law: Encouraging public cooperation with the police and courts*. New York, NY: Russell Sage.

DISCUSSION QUESTIONS

1. The findings indicate that perceptions of organizational justice predict officer misconduct. The authors acknowledge, however, that the time ordering or sequence of their variables may be incorrect. How might officer misconduct be related to perceptions of organizational justice (misconduct preceding rather than following perceptions)?

2. The research studied organizational justice as a single concept. Do you think that any one component—distributive, procedural, or interactive—is more important than any other in shaping officer behavior, specifically as it relates to misconduct? Explain.

3. In your opinion, are perceptions of organizational justice difficult to change, or are they easily moved? In other words, are opinions developed over time, are they changed over time, or can one single event (e.g., a meeting with a superior) be enough to dramatically and quickly change perceptions? Explain.

READING

Reading 16

Charles W. Sherwood examined the motivating potential of police work using the job characteristics (job design) model developed by Hackman and Oldham (1980). A survey was distributed to members of two police departments, one more advanced in its implementation of community policing than the other, asking respondents about core job dimensions—skill variety, task significance, task identity, autonomy, and feedback. The author hypothesized that core job dimension scores would be higher in the advanced community policing department, where officers were provided with training in a variety of areas and given opportunities to see problems to their resolution through permanent beat assignments. Moreover, the author speculated that these practices would have a positive effect on officers possessing college degrees, who value the greater freedom and flexibility that comes with community policing. Findings only partially supported these hypotheses. The motivating potential score was higher in the community policing department, but, with only one exception, level of education played no significant role in shaping perceptions of the core job dimensions. In other words, community policing reforms may increase worker motivation but do not seem to interact with employee education level.

JOB DESIGN, COMMUNITY POLICING, AND HIGHER EDUCATION

A Tale of Two Cities

Charles W. Sherwood

An important part of a manager's job is to be able to work with people toward the achievement of organizational objectives. Managers must seek to identify those factors that support motivation of the persons in the organization and that contribute to desired performance.

Job design is one strategy that managers can use to support the motivation of organizational members. This approach involves defining job tasks and the work arrangements necessary to accomplish these tasks (Schermerhorn, Hunt, & Osborn, 1997). Optimally, job design will meet the requirements of the organization, create a good match with the individual's needs and skills, and provide a setting in which the individual will be satisfied (Schermerhorn et al., 1997).

Of the approaches to job design, job enrichment appears particularly promising. Based on the hygiene motivation theory (Herzberg, Mausner, & Snyderman, 1959), enrichment attempts to build intrinsic motivating factors into a job in an effort to support a person's motivation to do better work. Job enrichment differs from its precursors, job enlargement and job rotation, in that those actions seek to increase the number and variety of tasks involved in a job, but maintain the task's degree of challenge. Job enrichment is aimed at increasing the depth of the job by giving workers more managerial duties such as planning, organizing, and assessing the level of success. Thus, job enrichment creates more opportunities for intrinsic work rewards while simultaneously moving the job away from task specialization (Schermerhorn et al., 1997). These rewards include satisfying the needs for esteem and self-actualization (Maslow, 1970).

Despite its intuitive appeal, job enrichment may not apply to all work situations. To assist in identifying those organizational settings in which job enrichment may be appropriate, the job characteristics model was developed (Hackman & Oldham, 1980). This model provides a means for managers and organizational consultants to diagnose a job setting and evaluate its potential to be enriched successfully.

The job characteristics model would seem to be well suited to the study of the effect of community policing on police personnel (Lurigio & Rosenbaum, 1994). The purpose of this article is to present the findings of a study that applied the job characteristics model to two urban police departments in the Northeast to examine the enrichment of the police job as it relates to community policing and higher education.

Review of the Literature

Job Enrichment and Job Characteristics

Management researchers have long been studying job design to unlock the secrets of increasing employee performance and satisfaction. Early efforts focused on the application of science to make people more efficient and find the "one best way" of performing a task (Taylor, 1947). It soon became clear, however, that scientific management did not appropriately consider human variables. The Hawthorne studies (Roethlisberger & Dickson, 1956) introduced a new approach to management aimed at increasing performance by gaining a better understanding of the needs

Source: Sherwood, C. W. (2000). Job design, community policing, and higher education: a tale of two cities. *Police Quarterly, 3*(2), 191–212.

of individuals. Subsequent research by McGregor (1960) and Maslow (1970) provided further information about individuals and their desire for more autonomy, responsibility, and challenge in their work.

The study of how variables in human behavior affect work performance continued with the development of the hygiene motivation theory (Herzberg et al., 1959). Hygiene factors include policies and procedures, compensation, relationships with other workers, and overall working conditions. Although the presence of positive hygiene factors will not necessarily cause the individual to be satisfied at work, they will help to lower feelings of dissatisfaction. Conversely, the presence of motivator factors, such as achievement, recognition, responsibility, and advancement, will help to increase job satisfaction for the worker. Jobs whose content is high in these factors are said to be enriched.

Managers should be aware that job enrichment does not apply to all persons in all job settings. The job characteristics model developed by Hackman and Oldham (1980) seeks to address this void by providing a diagnostic tool for determining the enrichment potential of a job and increasing the likelihood that work redesign can be sustained. Hackman and Oldham (1980, pp. 78-80) identified five core characteristics of a job that contribute to positive psychological states and positive organizational outcomes: skill variety, task identity, task significance, autonomy, and feedback from the job itself. In the model, skill variety, task identity, and task significance contribute to the meaningfulness of the work, autonomy contributes to the responsibility for work outcomes, and feedback contributes to knowledge of work results. The three psychological states contribute to desired outcomes including internal work motivation and job satisfaction. Internal work motivation is that condition in people where they feel rewarded when they do their work well. The rewards then become incentives for additional quality performance. Later research supports the existence of a link between improving job core characteristics and increasing job satisfaction (Gerhart, 1987; Kelly, 1992; Loher, Noe, Moeller, & Fitzgerald, 1985).

Hackman and Oldham (1980, pp. 80-82) developed the motivating potential score (MPS) as a method to measure the combined effect of the core characteristics in creating motivating potential for the job. The score reveals the overall potential of the job to support internal work motivation. The MPS is calculated using the formula displayed in the box below.

According to Hackman and Oldham, jobs high in motivating potential provide reinforcing conditions so that those persons who perform well will experience positive outcomes, including job satisfaction. Such jobs fortify the inner state in individuals that results in them exhibiting positive work behaviors. Jobs with low MPS provide little support even if the internal motivation exists in the person. The calculation of the scores for the five core characteristics also provides information about specific aspects of the job that the workers found to be most wanting. It is on these characteristics that managers should focus in trying to improve the motivating potential of the job.

Hackman and Oldham (1980, pp. 82-88) provided an important caveat to the job characteristics model. A positive response to a job high in motivating potential is related to the attributes of the person. Three areas of particular concern are the knowledge and skill of the person, the person's growth need strength, and the person's satisfaction with contextual aspects of the job. It is important to attempt to match persons likely to possess these attributes with those jobs found to be high in motivating potential.

Hackman and Oldham (1980) also presented principles for implementing work redesign. Combining existing tasks into new modules of work allows one person to do a complete piece of work, thereby increasing both skill variety and task identity.

$$MPS = \left[\frac{\text{Skill Variety} + \text{Task Identity} + \text{Task Significance}}{3}\right] \times \text{Autonomy} \times \text{Feedback}$$

Furthermore, the formation of natural work units, such as geographical units or customer groups, increases task identity and task significance. When natural work units are formed, it is often possible to establish direct contact with specific client groups and develop a relationship with them. For community policing, this relationship would be similar to the partnership that citizens and police form in a patrol sector.

Yet another principle of work redesign implementation is vertically loading the job. Through this process, responsibility and authority are pushed down to the lower levels of the organization, resulting in higher levels of autonomy. Employees are urged to do independent problem solving rather than having supervisors develop solutions to problems.

Job Enrichment and Community Policing

Recent studies that have examined the prospect of job redesign in policing have done so in conjunction with the emergence of community policing. Greene (1989) examined a sample of officers from the Philadelphia Police Department, who participated in a community education and policing project, with respect to job satisfaction and job redesign. The results indicated that job redesign, based on the tenets of community policing, affects officers differently. For those who value growth on the job, increased responsibility, and more decision making, such job redesign is welcomed. However, for officers who view community policing as merely more work to be done or who need a more structured work environment, this type of job redesign may not be viewed favorably.

In their evaluation of quality policing and participatory management in the Madison (Wisconsin) Police Department, Wycoff and Skogan (1994) investigated changes in officers' attitudes as they related to participating in the quality policing project. Three of the items investigated were taken from the job characteristics model: task significance, task identity, and autonomy. Although the entire department was trained in the quality-productivity management philosophy (Q-P), an experimental police district (EPD), representing about one sixth of the organization, was given greatest emphasis in the Q-P implementation. Measurements of officer attitudes were taken before Q-P implementation and 20 months after the process was begun. A comparison of the three job characteristics for both EPD and non-EPD officers showed statistically significant increases in task significance for non-EPD officers and in task identity for EPD officers.

Rosenbaum, Yeh, and Wilkinson (1994) examined the impact on police personnel of a community policing project in Joliet, Illinois. Among the measures used by the researchers were the five core dimensions of the job characteristics model. When compared with the scores reported by the members of the Joliet Police Department who did not participate in the project, there were no significant differences for any of the five dimensions. When compared with the Evanston (Illinois) Police Department, which was used as a control group in the study, there were significant differences for skill variety and job autonomy. Thus, although Joliet officers participating in the project reported higher scores for the core dimensions, no statistically significant differences were found with the intradepartmental control group and only two were found with the interdepartmental control group. It is the belief of Rosenbaum et al. that these findings result from the ongoing implementation of the project and that additional research in the future will provide a better assessment of the project's true effects.

Effect of Higher Education

Since the issuance of the report of the President's Commission on Law Enforcement and the Administration of Justice (1967), researchers on policing have spent a large amount of time investigating the effects of higher education in law enforcement. The commission found that there was a need for advanced education in the police service and referred to the nature of the police task as a main reason to elevate educational requirements (p. 126).

In the ensuing 30 years, many people have attended college and then pursued careers in the police service. According to Carter, Sapp, and Stephens (1989), the average educational level among law enforcement officers increased from 12.4 years to 13.6 years from 1967 to 1989. This increase was perceived as a qualitatively significant social change by the authors, given the large number of officers involved. In subsequent research, Carter and Sapp (1992) concluded that higher education facilitates innovative practices by the police and that the need for higher education in policing will continue in the future.

One of the important questions with regard to police higher education has been the relationship between education, job satisfaction, and job characteristics. Early work in this area suggested that officers with a college education would be more frustrated because of unmet expectations for promotion (Neiderhoffer, 1967). Griffin, Dunbar, and McGill (1978) found that as education increases, sources of satisfaction may be more related to internal factors, such as control. These researchers recommended that structural changes be implemented in police departments to allow for more control for lower-level officers.

Mottaz (1983) examined levels of work alienation among police officers. He defined alienation, or self-estrangement, as a lack of intrinsic fulfillment in work and hypothesized that the lack of intrinsic fulfillment was brought about by officers' feelings of powerlessness and meaninglessness with regard to their job. To attain self-fulfillment, officers must experience some degree of autonomy and purpose in the performance of tasks. Mottaz found that educated officers will place a greater importance on self-fulfillment and that jobs with higher levels of autonomy, skill usage, and achievement are more likely to be self-fulfilling.

In a survey of police officers in three metropolitan areas, Worden (1990) examined the effect of higher education on attitudes among the police. Although education was not found to be a strong determinant, college-educated officers did display a greater preference for autonomy.

These findings suggest that police jobs that are designed around increased levels of autonomy, control, skill usage, and achievement may be more fulfilling and satisfying for police officers. This effect may be stronger for those with more education.

Methodology

Population of the Study

Police officers of all ranks from departments in two cities composed the population of the study. One of the cities is located in Connecticut and the other is in New York state. The cities had populations between 100,000 and 200,000. Urban departments were chosen because many of the critical issues facing the police today are occurring in the cities. A second reason is that there may be a greater likelihood of obtaining a broader cross section of participants such as racial minority groups, women, and persons with varied educational backgrounds. The smaller department will be referred to as Department 1, and the larger department will be referred to as Department 2.

Characteristics of Department 1

Department 1 adopted the community policing philosophy several years before this data collection. It had taken a number of steps to develop a partnership with the community. Several neighborhood substations had been established that served not only as the base for police operations in that neighborhood but also as sites for community meetings and gatherings of local leaders. Police officers had been assigned to specific neighborhoods with minimum rotation so that they would have the time to work with local citizens, to learn their concerns, and to assist them with problem solving.

The department management structure was also revised. Layers of upper management were reduced as the department implemented a more decentralized structure. The neighborhood policing efforts were now generally headed by lieutenants and sergeants who were known to the public as district managers.

To help inculcate the skills needed for police officers engaged in community policing, the training academy underwent significant changes. Greater emphasis was placed on reading and writing skills, communication skills, and being able to identify and solve problems. The training academy took on an atmosphere more similar to an academic university than a paramilitary academy. Inclusion, respect, and anti-discrimination policies were stressed. A number of workshops on quality-of-life issues were used to augment other training mandates, and role-playing was frequently employed to make the classes more interactive. To help maximize community input into the police training process, the department drew on university and professional resources to design and deliver specialized training.

The department continues to emphasize target populations in need. It has established a young adult board of police commissioners to discuss issues important to community youth; it interacts regularly with senior citizens to help prevent elderly abuse; and it is active in community efforts addressed at violence against special groups, such as women, children, and AIDS victims. Included in these efforts is affiliation with a local university to help children in crisis.

Characteristics of Department 2

Department 2 serves a larger city, has a greater number of officers, and has expressed support for community policing concepts. The department had established a system in which officers could work the same shifts in the same neighborhoods. It also had had more officers reassigned to field duties from support functions.

The department had taken several initiatives to reach out to the community. Department command staff met regularly with the leadership of many ethnic organizations in the city. At these meetings, numerous issues were discussed, and the perceptions and positions of each group were made known.

A number of prevention programs had also been initiated, programs that target at-risk populations within the community. Most of these were spearheaded by the Community Affairs Division. These programs included Drug Abuse Resistance Education for young people in schools, Police Athletic League functions in the municipal housing complexes, and programs using citizen volunteers to help patrol neighborhoods.

However, no information was obtained about whether Department 2 had changed its organizational structure to help advance community policing in the department. Furthermore, nothing was learned that would indicate that the department had made significant changes in its training program or other management systems. Although some effort had been made by the department to become more proactive in its service to citizens, it does not appear that it had taken substantial actions to mobilize community resources to partake in the policing of the city.

Hypotheses

Based on the information gleaned about both departments, Department 1 will be considered for this research to be more advanced in the implementation of community policing. This department had made more significant organizational changes, taken additional steps to reinforce the community policing philosophy with its personnel, and been more successful in mobilizing community resources to support its policing efforts. Although Department 2 had been involved in some community policing efforts, the actions taken were not as organizationally integrated as were the actions taken by Department 1. For the purposes of this study, Department 1 will be viewed as the experimental group and Department 2 will be viewed as the comparison group.

Three research hypotheses were tested in this study:

Hypothesis 1: For each job core characteristic, there is a positive difference in feelings toward the job between officers who work in a department that has substantially implemented a community policing system and officers who work in a more traditional department.

Hypothesis 2: For each job core characteristic in a department that has not substantially implemented community policing, feelings toward the job will be negatively affected by level of education.

Hypothesis 3: For each job core characteristic in a department that has substantially implemented community policing, feelings toward the job will be positively affected by level of education.

Data Collection and Procedure

The data collection instrument included questions from the Job Diagnostic Survey short form (Hackman & Oldham, 1980), an instrument that has been widely used in social science research to assess the appropriateness of job redesign. The survey questions were used to obtain information on the core characteristics of the job. Measures of skill variety, task identity, task significance, autonomy, and feedback from the job itself provided information on how the police officers felt about the characteristics of their job.

The response rate from Department 1 was 171 (42.4%) survey forms, whereas Department 2 respondents numbered 243 (47.7%). The total response rate is similar to previous studies on work attitudes that used survey instruments with criminal justice personnel (Griffin et al., 1978; Hepburn & Knepper, 1993; Winfree, Guiterman, & Mays, 1997).

Findings

Tests of Research Hypotheses

Table 1 provides a comparison of the core characteristic scores for this population. The data also provide

Table 1 Comparison of Respondents at or Below Sergeant for Job Core Characteristics

Core Characteristic	Professional Norm	Department	Mean	Standard Deviation
Skill variety	5.4	1	5.00	1.48
		2	4.65	1.30
Task identity	5.1	1	4.58	1.45
		2	4.23	1.51
Task significance	5.6	1	5.72	1.19
		2	5.34	1.27
Autonomy	5.4	1	5.15	1.30
		2	4.77	1.20
Feedback	5.1	1	4.48	1.49
		2	4.20	1.46
Motivating potential score	154	1	118	
		2	95	

norm scores for professionals, which was the job family I chose for comparison with the police. The norm scores for professionals are taken from a large national data set of Job Diagnostic Survey scores collected from workers in a wide variety of job families (Hackman & Oldham, 1980, p. 316). Hackman and Oldham posited that core characteristic scores for a target job that are within one standard deviation unit of the scores for the norm group do not show a significant difference.

The table reveals that no core characteristic score for this population is significantly lower than core characteristic score for the norm group. It also shows, however, that the MPS for each department was substantially lower than the norm group MPS of 154. As stated earlier, the MPS was developed by Hackman and Oldham (1980) to measure the overall potential of a job to support internal work motivation. Thus, although no single job characteristic is significantly lower than the norm, the overall motivating potential for the police job appears to be low.

The findings reveal a statistically significant positive difference for skill variety, task identity, task significance, and autonomy for the officers from Department 1. These results provide substantial support for the first research hypothesis. However, a significant difference was not found for feedback from the job.

To explore how different jobs within the police department may affect these findings, analysis of variance was performed using rank as the independent variable (see Table 2). For Department 1, the results show a statistically significant difference for skill variety, task identity, and feedback from the job itself. Further analysis revealed a significant difference between patrol officers and detectives and patrol officers and sergeants for skill variety, and a significant difference between detectives and patrol officers and detectives and sergeants for both task identity and feedback from the job itself. In Department 2, statistically significant differences were found for task identity and autonomy. For both characteristics, the significant differences were between patrol officers and detectives and patrol officers and sergeants. Detectives consistently recorded higher scores than patrol officers and, in several cases, supervisors. This pattern was found in both departments.

The data suggest that level of education made no difference in how the police officers viewed their jobs. The only core characteristic that showed a statistically significant difference was task significance in Department 2. Furthermore, only two statistically significant differences were identified through a more stringent multiple comparison procedure. Overall, the data did not support the second and third research hypotheses.

Discussion

Job Characteristics

This article reports the findings of research that applied the Hackman and Oldham (1980) job characteristics model to two urban police departments in the Northeast. The article also examines the effect of community policing and higher education on the potential for the police job to be enriched.

Respondents reported the highest scores for task significance, suggesting that officers were most satisfied with the concept that their work is significant and contributes to the social welfare. The overall motivating potential of the job, however, was found to be low. Although no single characteristic was significantly lower than the norm, the combined effect of all scores as measured by the MPS was considerably below the norm group.

These findings suggest that police managers should be attentive to multiple characteristics of the police job for enrichment opportunities. In particular, attention should be focused on improving task identity and feedback where the lowest scores were reported. In a small number of follow-up interviews that were conducted to help interpret the statistical results, the consensus of the officers interviewed was that they wished they could pursue tasks on the job to a more clear result. Officers felt especially frustrated by their inability to follow through on

Table 2 Core Characteristics by Rank at or Below Sergeant

Core Characteristic	Department	Rank	Mean	Standard Deviation
Skill variety	1	Patrol	4.66	1.50
		Detective	5.47	1.31
		Sergeant	5.47	1.36
	2	Patrol	4.57	1.30
		Detective	5.17	1.12
		Sergeant	4.60	1.38
Task identity	1	Patrol	4.26	1.43
		Detective	5.49	1.08
		Sergeant	4.36	1.46
	2	Patrol	3.82	1.39
		Detective	5.46	1.56
		Sergeant	4.89	1.47
Task significance	1	Patrol	5.54	1.17
		Detective	6.02	1.09
		Sergeant	5.91	1.31
	2	Patrol	5.29	1.25
		Detective	5.37	1.52
		Sergeant	5.52	1.18
Autonomy	1	Patrol	5.03	1.28
		Detective	5.57	1.13
		Sergeant	4.95	1.50
	2	Patrol	4.57	1.18
		Detective	5.21	1.06
		Sergeant	5.21	1.17
Feedback	1	Patrol	4.10	1.48
		Detective	5.21	1.20
		Sergeant	4.74	1.50
	2	Patrol	4.06	1.43
		Detective	4.82	1.38
		Sergeant	4.21	1.55

Note: Department 1: patrol *(n = 93)*, detective *(n = 39)*, sergeant *(n =27)*. Department2: patrol *(n = 134)*, detective *(n = 26)*, sergeant *(n =34)*.

investigations and having to pass the investigation onto another unit in the department or onto another agency.

According to Hackman and Oldham (1980, p. 135), forming natural work units is useful in addressing task identity shortcomings. If police officers are regularly assigned to the same patrol area, they will have the opportunity to establish relationships with the people in that area, work with them on matters of concern, identify problems, and develop and implement courses of action. Equally important, officers remaining in the same patrol area will be able to evaluate their ideas for effectiveness and make corrections as needed. This can become a particularly valuable learning environment for those officers with high growth needs and is likely to increase their intrinsic motivation and satisfaction.

Another step that can be taken is additional training in problem analysis and problem resolution. This type of training equips officers with the requisite skills to follow through on cases to a conclusion, not just report them for referral. Training that police managers should consider includes identifying the actual problem, not just its symptoms; analyzing the problem to determine why it is occurring; being able to realistically assess the likelihood of success of alternative resolutions; identifying criteria to be used for evaluating the implemented alternative; group dynamics; and interpersonal and written communication.

Hackman and Oldham (1980) also recommended combining tasks to alleviate low feelings of task identity. This would mean that patrol officers would be given additional responsibility for follow-through of incidents. In this way, the patrol task would not just be the preliminary processing of the incident, but would also comprise such duties as evidence collection, interviews, and preparation of arrest warrant applications.

Respondents also reported lower scores for job feedback. It is important to note that the feedback being measured is that derived directly from the job, such as when an auto mechanic works on a car that will not run and, after the work is complete, the car runs well.

The nature of the social problems that police officers are asked to solve often makes it difficult to gain this type of feedback. Situations are frequently complex, resolution takes time, and improvements are not easily measured. The actions outlined above for task identity may also help to improve feelings of job feedback. By being able to see a job from beginning to end and being able to witness an outcome, officers will be better able to have direct information about their level of effectiveness. When they are asked only to take preliminary reports or are frequently moved from patrol sector to patrol sector, they are more likely to deal only with a fragment of the problem and to experience limited feedback from the job.

Another action would be increased computer applications especially through mobile terminals. Access to this level of technology can bring crime analysis data to the officer in the field more efficiently and provide the officer with additional information on police effectiveness.

The skill variety and autonomy job characteristics should also receive the consideration of police managers. The skill variety scores were somewhat surprising given that the police officer's job is often described as requiring a multitude of skills to fulfill the myriad of roles that are expected. Furthermore, in postsurvey interviews several officers expressed satisfaction with the variety of skills that they use on the job. One explanation may be that officers with different skill sets may report widely varying scores with respect to how their individual talents are being used on the job. Persons who possess a number of different skills and who enjoy using those skills may be more dissatisfied with a highly structured job than persons who are content with work that is more limited and repetitive. This explanation would tend to support earlier research on the work effects of community policing (Greene, 1989). Interestingly, the data do not provide evidence that this disparity is a function of educational level.

According to Hackman and Oldham (1980), autonomy is the degree to which the job provides independence and discretion to the individual in scheduling the work and in determining how it will be carried out. When autonomy is present in a job the individual is more likely to view job outcomes as being the result of his or her own effort and ability rather than the result of environmental factors. Again, officers who work well independently and who enjoy making decisions about their work will benefit from a job that permits independent decision making. It appears from this data set that making jobs more autonomous is another facet of work that police managers should examine.

The study found significant differences between patrol, detective, and supervisory personnel across both departments and for all job characteristics except task significance. For most of the characteristics, the highest scores were recorded by detectives. The findings indicate that detectives are more satisfied with the range of skills that they use on the job. The findings suggest further that detectives view their jobs as encompassing a broader and more identifiable unit of work, one that they can follow through to a logical conclusion. The detectives are also satisfied with their ability to exercise independent judgment on the job and to determine how the job is done. Thus, they are more likely to feel a sense of personal responsibility for successes and failures. Finally, detectives have a greater feeling for how effective their performance has been.

These findings are instructive for police managers. The detective position is well known to most police managers, with many having served in the position in an earlier career stage. The results of this study suggest that the characteristics of the detective's position may be useful in determining how to redesign a patrol officer's job. It would be challenging for a police manager to incorporate elements of the detective's position into the patrol position especially with the ongoing pressure of other calls waiting. It would also require additional training for the members of the patrol division. On balance, however, managers should consider integrating aspects of detectives' work into patrol work.

Effect of Community Policing

The data do suggest that departments that make changes in their structure and function toward a more community-based system of policing are better positioned to bring about job enrichment. Although assessing the degree to which a department has adopted community policing is a formidable undertaking, it does appear that Department 1 has taken more actions to implement community policing than has Department 2. If this observation is true, it is worthwhile to note that for all core characteristics except feedback, the officers from Department 1 reported significantly higher mean scores compared with the officers from Department 2.

Based on these data, community policing may hold some promise for improving officers' feelings with regard to the core characteristics of the job. Community policing is a strategy that helps to personalize police service, allows officers to work with people in neighborhoods, and allows officers to take a proactive approach to solving problems for citizens (Goldstein, 1990; Trojanowicz & Bucqueroux, 1994). These aspects of community policing seem to fit well with the work redesign strategies of Hackman and Oldham (1980). Allowing officers to work regularly with neighborhood residents creates a natural work unit that will increase skill variety and task identity. Furthermore, by granting police officers the increased responsibility and authority to engage in proactive problem solving, managers enhance the vertical loading of the job and increase autonomy. Combining tasks into a more identifiable and complete piece of work to be performed by the officer also strengthens skill variety and task identity.

Effect of Higher Education

Higher education appears to have no effect on officers' feelings about job core characteristics in this population. The only statistically significant differences found among levels of education were for task significance and autonomy in Department 2. Furthermore, no linear relationships were suggested.

These data provide evidence that level of education is unrelated to police officers' feelings about the core characteristics of their jobs. This finding held true irrespective of the degree to which the department has implemented community policing. One explanation may be that although job enrichment is important, it is important for persons of all educational levels. Formal higher education may not be as strongly associated with the knowledge and growth need moderators as may have been suspected. It would seem that other life experiences and personality characteristics may also be important in preparing individuals for an enriched job in the police service.

Management Implications

Police managers must be cognizant of the need to design jobs that support the motivation and satisfaction of the members of their organizations. This is important not only for organizational productivity but also for officer retention because prior studies have provided substantial evidence to indicate that job satisfaction is related to employee turnover (Klenke-Ramel & Mathieu, 1990; Porter & Steers, 1973; Vroom, 1964).

Traditionally, police managers have tended to design police work to minimize errors by instituting rules and procedures and by strong oversight of officers' actions. These steps may actually run counter to officers doing highquality work. Supporting internal work motivation and creating job satisfaction may be more reliant on designing tasks that are nontraditional.

This research provides some clues for how this can be done. Use of a variety of skills, the ability to follow the task through to a conclusion, freedom to make decisions, and knowledge of the effectiveness of one's efforts are aspects of the patrol officer's job to which attention should be paid. The data suggest that incorporating more elements of the detective's position into patrol work may be helpful.

The study further suggests that departments that are more advanced in instituting community policing may hold some advantage over more traditional departments. According to Hackman and Oldham (1980, p. 8), more people now desire jobs that are not monotonous or controlling or that do not underuse one's abilities. Less mechanistic organizations would seem to be a better setting for these types of jobs.

It has been reported in previous research that college-trained candidates are more likely to have better communication skills, have better problem-solving ability, and tend to be more responsive to changing social conditions (Carter et al., 1989; Carter & Sapp, 1992). It appears, however, that enrichment may be important for officers with no college as well. Based on the present findings, there is not a clear relationship between higher education and the knowledge and skill and growth need moderators identified by Hackman and Oldham (1980). Police managers should use measures such as comprehensive psychological testing and an extensive background review to look for other indicators of these moderating factors in the candidate.

The managers of police organizations should also select persons who have a good understanding of what the day-to-day police job entails. In the course of interviewing prospective candidates for the police position, a clear picture of the actual job should be provided. Heneman, Schwab, Fossum, and Dyer (1986) called this technique a realistic job preview and stated that it is important in increasing worker retention. This action will increase the likelihood of a stronger job-employee fit and help to preserve the police department's human resources.

References

Carter, D. L., & Sapp, A. D. (1992). College education and policing: Coming of age. *FBI Law Enforcement Bulletin, 1,* 8-14.

Carter, D. L., Sapp, A. D., & Stephens, D. W. (1989). *The state of police education: Policy direction for the 21st century.* Washington, DC: Police Executive Research Forum.

Dillman, D. A. (1978). *Mail and telephone surveys-The total design method.* New York: John Wiley.

Gerhart, B. (1987). How important are dispositional factors as determinants of job satisfaction? Implications for job design and other personnel programs. *Journal of Applied Psychology, 72,* 366-373.

Goldstein, H. (1990). *Problem-oriented policing.* New York: McGraw-Hill.

Greene, J. R. (1989). Police officer job satisfaction and community perceptions: Implications for community-oriented policing. *Journal of Research in Crime and Delinquency, 26,* 168-185.

Griffin, G. R., Dunbar, R.L.M., & McGill, M. E. (1978). Factors associated with job satisfaction among police personnel. *Journal of Police Science and Administration, 6*(1), 77-85.

Hackman, J. R., & Oldham, G. R. (1980). *Work redesign.* Reading, MA: Addison-Wesley.

Heneman, H., Schwab, D., Fossum, J., & Dyer, L. (1986). *Personnel/human resource management.* Homewood, IL: Irwin.

Hepburn, J. R., & Knepper, P. E. (1993). Correctional officers as human services workers: The effect on job satisfaction. *Justice Quarterly, 10,* 315-337.

Herzberg, F., Mausner, B., & Snyderman, B. B. (1959). *The motivation to work.* New York: John Wiley.

Kelly, J. (1992). Does job redesign theory explain job redesign outcomes? *Human Relations, 45,* 753-774.

Klenke-Hamel, K. E., & Mathieu, J. (1990). Role strains, tension and job satisfaction influences on employees' propensity to leave: A multi-sample replication and extension. *Human Relations, 43,* 791-807.

Loher, B. T., Noe, R. A., Moeller, N. L., & Fitzgerald, M.P. (1985). A meta-analysis of the relationship of job characteristics to job satisfaction. *Journal of Applied Psychology, 70,* 280-289.

Lurigio, A. J., & Rosenbaum, D.P. (1994). The impact of community policing on police personnel. In D. P. Rosenbaum (Ed.), *The challenge of community policing: Testing the promises* (pp. 147-163). Thousand Oaks, CA: Sage.

Maslow, A. (1970). *Motivation and personality* (2nd ed.). New York: Harper & Row.

McGregor, D. (1960). *The human side of enterprise.* New York: McGraw-Hill.

Mottaz, C. (1983). Alienation among police officers. *Journal of Police Science and Administration, 11*(1), 23-30.

Neiderhoffer, A. (1967). *Behind the shield: The police in urban society.* Garden City, NY: Doubleday.

Porter, L. W., & Steers, R. M. (1973). Organizational, work and personal factors in employee turnover and absenteeism. *Psychological Bulletin, 80,* 151-176.

President's Commission on Law Enforcement and the Administration of Justice. (1967). *Taskforce report: The police.* Washington, DC: Government Printing Office.

Roethlisberger, F. J., & Dickson, W. J. (1956). *Management and the worker* (2nd ed.). Cambridge, MA: Harvard University Press.

Rosenbaum, D. P., Yeh, S., & Wilkinson, D. L. (1994). Impact of community policing on police personnel: A quasi-experimental test. *Crime & Delinquency, 40,* 331-353.

Schermerhorn, J., Jr., Hunt, J. G., & Osborn, R. N. (1997). *Organizational behavior:* New York: John Wiley.

Taylor, F. W. (1947). *The principles of scientific management.* New York: Harper & Bros.

Trojanowicz, R. C., & Bucqueroux, B. (1994). *Community policing: How to get started.* Cincinnati, OH: Anderson.

Vroom, V. H. (1964). *Work and motivation.* New York: John Wiley.

Winfree, L. T., Jr., Guiterman, D., & Mays, G. L. (1997). Work assignments and police work: Exploring the work world of sworn officers in four New Mexico police departments. *Policing: An International Journal of Police Strategies & Management, 20,* 419-441.

Worden, R. E. (1990). A badge and a baccalaureate: Policies, hypotheses and further evidence. *Justice Quarterly, 7,* 565-592.

Wycoff, M. A., & Skogan, W. G. (1994). The effect of a community policing management style on officers' attitudes. *Crime & Delinquency, 40,* 371-383.

DISCUSSION QUESTIONS

1. In many cases (see skill variety, task identity, autonomy, and feedback), detectives scored higher on specific job dimensions than did patrol officers. What is it about the detective function that would lead to higher scores on these dimensions?

2. The authors found that, with one exception, college education plays only a limited role in shaping perceptions of the motivating potential of the work. What are the implications of this finding, if any, for efforts to require college degrees for police officers? Explain.

3. The officers studied scored particularly low on the measures of task identity and feedback. What can the police organization do to improve these dimensions so that the overall motivating potential of the job increases?

SECTION IX

Occupational Stress and Burnout

Is This Job Killing Me?

Section Highlights

- Defining Occupational Stress
- Major Stressors Affecting Criminal Justice Workers
  - Factors Inherent in the Task
  - Individual's Role in the Organization
  - Relationships at Work
  - Career Issues
  - Organizational Factors
  - Home–Work Interface
- Burnout
  - The Measurement of and Interrelationships Between Burnout Components
  - Correlates of Burnout
- Outcomes of Stress and Burnout
- Addressing Stress and Burnout

Alaska, in spite of having the fourth smallest population among U.S. states, is the nation's largest state by land area, covering a territory more than twice the size of Texas. Much of Alaska comprises rural areas not connected to populous cities such as Anchorage or Fairbanks by any road networks. Consequently, the work of the Alaska State Troopers, the organization with primary responsibility for law enforcement in rural areas, is "often hampered by delayed [crime] notification, long response distance, and the uncertainties of weather and transportation" (Department of Public Safety,

Alaska State Troopers, 2013). The state, beginning in 1981, supplemented the efforts of state troopers in rural communities with the creation of the Village Public Safety Officers (VPSOs) program (Wood, 2002). VPSOs receive about one quarter of the training hours of Alaska State Troopers but are first responders (the VPSO motto is "first responders—last frontier") responsible for law enforcement, firefighting, search and rescue, water safety, and emergency medical services within their assigned villages (*Alaska Intertribal Council v. State of Alaska*, 2005; Wood, 2000). Although they may be permitted to investigate minor crimes, they are expected to report serious crimes to their oversight trooper within the Alaska State Troopers organization (Wood, 2002). VPSOs rarely remained with the program for long periods of time; annual turnover rates approached 55% between 1983 and 1997, and the typical VPSO spent roughly a year in the program before departing (Wood, 2001). Why was the program characterized by such high turnover rates? What differentiated VPSOs who departed from those who remained? Officers were less likely to leave the program if they were married, connected to Alaska Native culture (e.g., from a Native village), worked in their home villages, and worked with other police officers or VPSOs within the same village (Wood, 2000, 2001). These personal and job characteristics provide the VPSO with support in the face of geographic isolation, low pay and benefits, and other job-related stressors. Wood (2001), writing about the benefits of working with others, stated that

> [having a co-stationed peer] will help officers feel that they are part of something bigger than their little corner of the world and will give them someone with whom they can share the ups and downs of the police occupation. (p. 23)

Individuals working within other criminal justice organizations similarly experience a range of stressful job demands. Many justice occupations involve some degree of danger, while others, including victim counseling positions, subject workers to what has been described as "compassion fatigue" or vicarious trauma as a result of working with crime victims (Baird & Jenkins, 2003, p. 71). Some positions require long and/or rotating work shifts, demanding caseloads, inflexible organizational practices, and other stressors. If left unaddressed, these factors may adversely affect the individual's psychological, physical, and behavioral well-being, and the organization as a whole. Outcomes such as turnover, absenteeism, and employee conflicts increase as a result of stress, potentially affecting overall organizational performance. Wood (2002), for example, noted that it costs about $6,200 to hire, train, and equip each new VPSO. As officers leave the program, they take with them the organization's financial investment as well as their own institutional knowledge about the community they serve. Therefore, it is critical to understand the role that occupational or workplace stress plays in an organization. Specifically, this section examines common stressors within criminal justice organizations and their consequences, and offers descriptions of strategies for addressing occupational stress and burnout.

Defining Occupational Stress

At first glance, *stress* appears to be a word everyone knows. Whether a person declares, "My job is stressing me out" or "My chest hurts because I am stressed," we generally can understand his or her plight and communicate effectively without wrestling over definitions. However, these statements reveal conceptual ambiguities in the use of the term, a problem that scholars working in the area of occupational stress have struggled to address. The first statement ("My job is stressing me out") centers on the causes of stress. Definitions of this nature, referred to as stimulus-based definitions, "[treat] stress as an independent variable that elicits some response from the person" (Cooper, Dewe, & O'Driscoll, 2001, p. 8). The second statement ("My chest hurts because I am stressed") addresses the responses to rather than the causes of stress, a common focus in the medical field, where symptoms such as disease and increased heart rate are indicators of stressful states (Lazarus & Folkman, 1984). The problem with these limited definitions is that they are circular. A factor is a stressor if it produces a response, but responses must be considered by referencing their causes (Lazarus & Folkman, 1984).

Cummings and Cooper (1979) offered a process model to better understand the connections between stimuli and responses. In doing so, they separated occupational stress into its constituent parts, providing some measure of conceptual clarification. Most individuals, according to the model, desire to operate within some steady state—what some describe as homeostasis or constancy. They possess goals for where they would like to be at any given time (e.g., emotionally, professionally, etc.), and they seek to maintain that steady state of affairs (Cartwright & Cooper, 1997). For each of these goal states, individuals possess a "specific range of stability" (Cummings & Cooper, 1979, p. 397). In other words, people are able to tolerate minor deviations from their desired states but may suffer from more dramatic departures. For example, during the recent recession, many criminal justice employees in diverse organizations were asked to take furlough days—unpaid leave—to help governments preserve limited resources. A worker may be able to absorb a single furlough day without much strain, but multiple days extend beyond the individual's range of stability. If the deviations are great, strain will occur and the worker will try to restore a sense of stability (Cummings & Cooper, 1979). Stated differently, the worker will attempt to cope with the problems that are generating strain.

The Cummings and Cooper (1979) model is useful for the discussion to follow in a number of important respects. First, it clarifies some important terminology. Although it refers to the external demands that actually produce the deviation from the steady state as stresses, it is more useful to draw on language from other models and call them **stressors** (Cooper et al., 2001; Kahn & Byosiere, 1992). These are the factors that are viewed, in the words of Lazarus and Folkman (1984), "as taxing or exceeding [an individual's] resources and endangering his or her well-being" (p. 19).[1] While specific stressors will be described below, it is enough here to say that some are considered **routine occupational stressors** (e.g., compensation, work relationships, role conflict), encountered fairly regularly, and others are considered **traumatic stressors** (e.g., shootings, notifying families of deaths), critical incidents encountered relatively rarely. Even though traumatic stressors are related to danger and critical incident exposure, routine stressors related to management, relationships, and other more common aspects of the job also predict worker strain (Liberman et al., 2002).[2] In the stress model, **strains** represent the individual's reactions—psychological, physical, and behavioral—to actual or threatened stressors (Cooper et al., 2001; Cummings & Cooper, 1979; Kahn & Byosiere, 1992). Manifestations of strain include sleeplessness, hypertension, and irritability. Strain has the potential to produce long-term costs for both the individual (e.g., heart disease, suicide, divorce) and the organization (e.g., turnover, diminished performance). Cooper and colleagues (2001) reserve the use of **stress** to describe the overall process, rather than just the stimulus or response. The more generic term includes the causes, outcomes, and processes through which the former affects the latter (Lazarus & Folkman, 1984).

---

[1]Most stressors are viewed as harmful or distressful. It is worth pointing out, however, that stressors (stimuli) may also be beneficial, or eustress (Kahn & Byosiere, 1992). For example, external demands may produce the motivation or biological responses (e.g., adrenaline) that enhance performance. This section, however, focuses on the damaging effects of stressors.

[2]This finding was derived from a study of policing. It is likely that, based on prior research, the findings would apply to other criminal justice occupations as well.

A second strength of the Cummings and Cooper (1979) model is its introduction of coping into the discussion of occupational stress. A shortcoming of many occupational stress definitions is the absence of any discussion of factors that mediate the relationship between stressors and strain (Newton, 1989). A dangerous job confronting criminal offenders may prove stressful for only some workers; others are better able to successfully adjust or cope with the job's demands and reduce the amount of strain experienced (or, as described above, the deviations from steady states; Cummings & Cooper, 1979). A third strength of the model is its ability to incorporate individual perceptions. The overall stress process involves a worker's evaluation of stressors and whether any deviations are beyond the individual's preferred range of stability, thereby indicating strain (Cummings & Cooper, 1979). Scholars have referred to this as the *primary appraisal* process (Dewe, 1991). If strain is present, workers will perform a *secondary appraisal* to assess the availability of coping mechanisms. As Dewe states, during this period, people ask, "What can I do?" (p. 333). Understanding occupational stress requires us to think about each of these elements: the stressors, the strains, coping strategies, and how individuals perceive each during specific situations.

Major Stressors Affecting Criminal Justice Workers

The number of specific stressors is immense, precluding any attempt to provide an exhaustive list. Cartwright and Cooper (1997), however, offer a useful framework for organizing key stressors for discussion purposes. Each of the six categories, shown in Figure 9.1, will be addressed in turn.

Factors Inherent in the Task

Many stressors are attributable to the job itself, including the presence of danger, long or irregular work hours, and general workload (Cartwright & Cooper, 1997; Cooper et al., 2001). Dangerousness, to the extent that workers are regularly exposed to actual or threatened physical harm, is widely believed to be a significant stressor across most criminal justice organizations. Correctional officers, for example, typically work in overcrowded facilities, exacerbating challenges related to inmate management. Officers in three Alabama prisons reported that crowding contributed to their own strain, jeopardized their safety, and increased within-facility violence (Martin, Lichtenstein, Jenkot, & Forde, 2012). The significance of danger was also evident in two studies of police officers that measured the influence of various stressors on officer heart rates (an indicator of strain or the body's response to stressors). Anderson, Litzenberger, and Plecas (2002) fitted a sample of Canadian officers with heart rate monitors and recorded their activities (sometimes as many as nine per minute) during 121 ride-alongs. Not surprisingly, they observed elevated heart rates when officers engaged in physically strenuous activities. Officers also showed signs of strain (higher heart rates) in risky but not necessarily physically demanding situations. Elevated heart rates were observed when officers placed their hands on their firearms, and heart rates were even faster when officers opened the snap to the firearm holster and when a suspect was present. Similar patterns emerged as the severity of the dispatch code (Code 1 vs. Code 3) increased. The authors argued that the findings are "clearly demonstrating the anticipatory stress response or anxiety" officers face rather than physical exertion (p. 413). Hickman, Fricas, Strom, and Pope (2011) also used a heart rate monitor, this time equipping only a single officer with the device to track place-based stressors. By linking the data from the monitor to data from a global positioning system (GPS) receiver, researchers demonstrated that officer stress was tied to particular locations, or hot spots, within the city. While this was likely due to the nature and/or quantity of the calls for service

Figure 9.1 Relationship Between Occupational Stressors and Individual and Organizational Outcomes

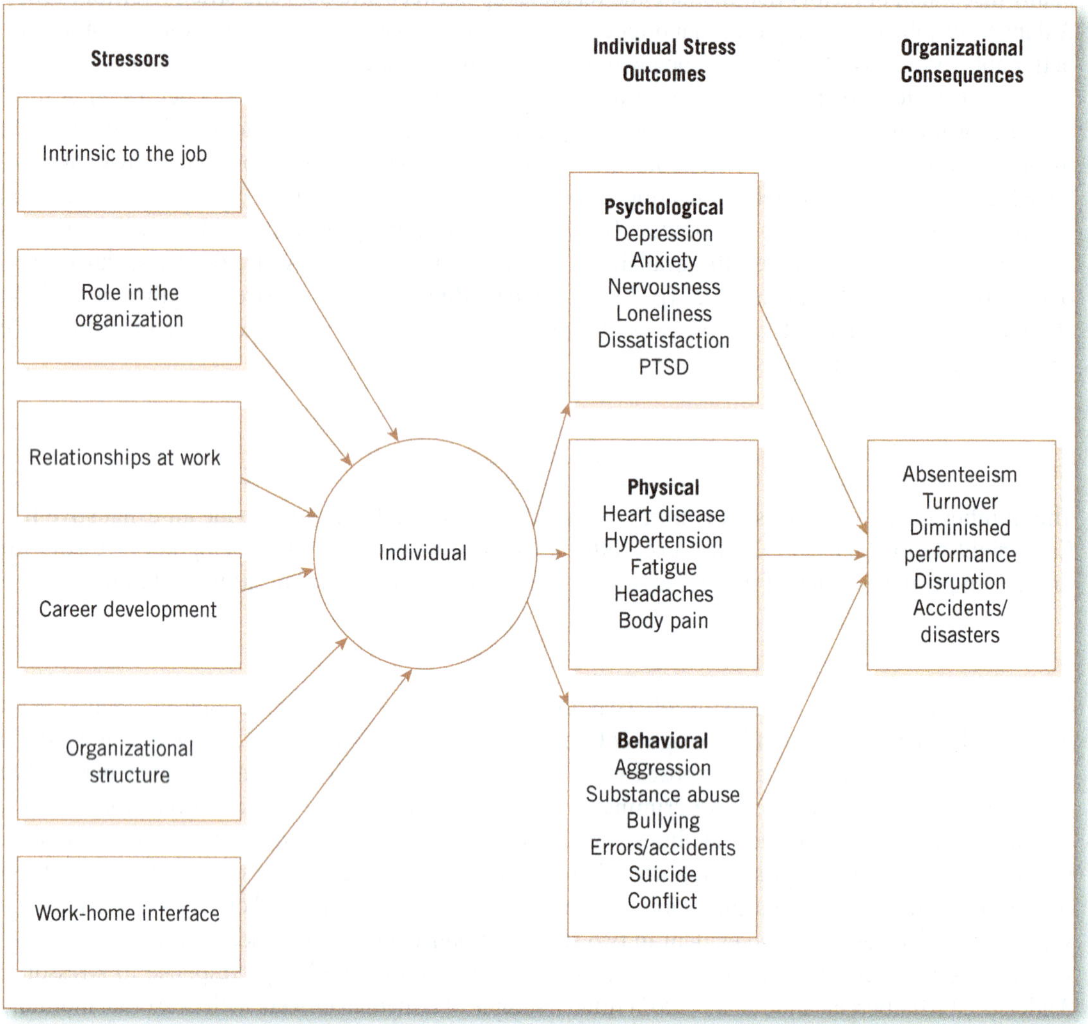

Stressors	Individual Stress Outcomes	Organizational Consequences
Intrinsic to the job	**Psychological** Depression, Anxiety, Nervousness, Loneliness, Dissatisfaction, PTSD	Absenteeism, Turnover, Diminished performance, Disruption, Accidents/disasters
Role in the organization	**Physical** Heart disease, Hypertension, Fatigue, Headaches, Body pain	
Relationships at work	**Behavioral** Aggression, Substance abuse, Bullying, Errors/accidents, Suicide, Conflict	
Career development		
Organizational structure		
Work-home interface		

Source: Adapted from Cartwright and Cooper (1997).

generated from particular areas of the city, the findings clearly suggest that rotating officers out of stressful beats may prevent significant individual strain. Although other studies also point to more general concerns about safety, it is worth noting that danger is not always reported as a potent stressor (e.g., Finn & Kuck, 2003).

The scheduling of work also poses difficulties for workers (Cooper et al., 2001). Amendola, Weisburd, Hamilton, Jones, and Slipka (2011) recently studied the effects of different police shift arrangements on a number of officer-level outcomes. The typical 8-hour shift/5-day workweek, they reported, was increasingly being supplanted within organizations by alternatives, including 10-hour shift/4-day workweeks or 12-hour shift/3-day workweeks. To measure the effects of shift on officer outcomes, participating officers in three cities were randomly assigned to one of the three shift schedules (8-, 10-, or 12-hour shifts) for a 6-month period. When compared with officers on other shift arrangements, those working the 10-hour/4-day shifts slept more per night during off-duty hours, worked fewer overtime hours, and reported a higher quality of life. A longer work day—the 12-hour shift—proved detrimental, however, as officers acknowledged sleepiness and lower levels of alertness. Among a sample of New Zealand correctional officers, task pressures (including work scheduling) were second only to work relationships as significant sources of stress (Long, Shouksmith, Voges, & Roache, 1986). These schedule-related stressors included irregular hours, longer periods without days off, lack of breaks during work shifts, and difficulties arranging leave.

The workload or, more precisely, work overload, may also produce strain (Cartwright & Cooper, 1997). Probation and parole officers manage large numbers of offenders, prosecutors and defense attorneys oversee significant caseloads, police officers handle high call volumes, and counselors interact with many clients. Writing about probation and parole officers, Finn and Kuck (2003) note that "high caseloads, excessive paperwork, and deadlines, while distinct sources of stress, typically combine to have a widespread frustrating result: individually and, especially, cumulatively *they make it difficult for many officers to find the time to supervise their caseloads properly*" (p. 20; emphasis in original). If time is limited, workers must resort to working late (usually unpaid) or taking their work home, common behaviors reported by public defenders to meet their caseload demands (Lynch, 1997). These are stressful actions in and of themselves but also lead to disruptions in home lives (see below). These examples illustrate **quantitative overload**, an indication that the workplace demands exceed the time available to complete the work. Stressors might also appear in the form of **qualitative overload**, a situation that occurs when an individual lacks the skills or knowledge to perform a given task.

Individual's Role in the Organization

An individual may experience strain if his or her work role lacks clear definition or definite expectations (**role ambiguity**) or involves two or more competing demands (**role conflict**) (Cartwright & Cooper, 1997; Cooper et al., 2001). A police officer tasked with fulfilling a community policing function without understanding what such a role requires faces role ambiguity. He is unable to fulfill his responsibilities absent direction on the appropriate role. In contrast, role conflict occurs when two demands are present but are in opposition with each other; fulfilling one role typically means sacrificing the other role. Within the literature on probation, the common law enforcer and social worker dichotomy appears. Are officers supposed to enforce the conditions of probation or rehabilitate offenders or both? Can both goals be accomplished simultaneously? Role ambiguity and conflict are significant sources of stress. A sample of more than 200 New Jersey correctional officers indicated that the "lack of clear guidelines for job performance" was the most stressful aspect of working in the correctional field, more stressful than crisis conditions, pay, or 106 other possible stressors (Cheek & Miller, 1983, p. 115). Similarly, research on more than 5,000 correctional officer and prison treatment personnel from 10 Southwest prisons demonstrated that role problems were the single greatest sources of workplace stress (Armstrong & Griffin, 2004). The study's authors measured role ambiguity and role conflict with statements such as, "Often times, one rule will tell us to do one thing, but another rule tells us to do something else" and "One of the problems here is that it is never very clear as to who is responsible for doing different jobs" (p. 584).

Relationships at Work

Negative relationships with organizational supervisors, subordinates, and peers may also cause strain, while positive or supportive relationships may moderate the influence of stressors (Cartwright & Cooper, 1997; Cooper et al., 2001). Illinois police officers from eight departments identified superiors as a common stressor within their organizations (Crank & Caldero, 1991). One officer, for example, resented what was referred to as oversupervision:

> They [supervisors] arrive at minor scenes and quickly make a mountain out of a mole hill, issue various orders (to hear themselves and sound important), and then vanish into thin air leaving the beat officer to straighten out the mess they made. (p. 344)

Worker concerns about supervision are not unique to policing. A survey of nearly 200 Florida probation officers revealed considerable dissatisfaction with supervisors. Nearly three quarters (72%) of responding probation officers said that they received inadequate support from their supervisor and/or organization, and the overwhelming majority (87%) indicated that they disliked their supervisor (Simmons, Cochran, & Blount, 1997).

Peer relationships are equally important predictors of workplace stress. He, Zhao, and Archbold (2002), for example, noted that camaraderie among male police officers (cooperation between units, trust with work partner) was significantly and negatively related to physical and psychological strains. The authors, reaffirming the importance of exposure to stressful job-related incidents, nevertheless argued that positive work relationships "could counteract its negative impact on the well-being of male police officers" (p. 699).[3] Similarly, coworker support, including helpful, respectful, and competent peers, reduces the likelihood of job stress (e.g., pressure, tension) and health complications among treatment and security personnel in multiple prisons (Armstrong & Griffin, 2004).

Negative relationships might also take the form of a bullying relationship. Indeed, **workplace bullying** is increasingly recognized as a significant problem in modern organizations (Cowie, Naylor, Rivers, Smith, & Pereira, 2002). On school playgrounds, bullying is often associated with some sort of physical abuse. In the workplace, bullying can involve a range of behaviors. Cowie and colleagues (2002) define bullying as repeated aggression directed at a victim who, because of some power difference, faces challenges in addressing such aggression (see also Samnani & Singh, 2012). These power imbalances may result from differences in rank, experience, prestige, or some other factor associated with real or perceived power differentials (see Section XI for a further discussion of power). Workplace bullying behavior typically falls into one or more of the following five categories (Rayner & Hoel, 1997):

> Threat to professional status (e.g., belittling opinion, public professional humiliation, accusation regarding lack of effort); threat to personal standing (e.g., name-calling, insults, intimidation, devaluating with reference to age); isolation (e.g., preventing access to opportunities, physical or social isolation, withholding of information); overwork (e.g., undue pressure, impossible deadlines, unnecessary disruptions); and destabilization (e.g., failure to give credit when due, meaningless tasks, removal of responsibility, repeated reminders of blunders, setting up to fail). (p. 183)

Workers who are repeatedly subjected to bullying may experience considerable strain, leading to a range of individual and organizational consequences.

---

[3]Individual or personal characteristics such as race, gender, or personality characteristics are related to strain but are not stressors. Instead, these factors are said to affect how individuals experience strain (Cooper et al., 2001) and are beyond the scope of this section.

Career Issues

Cartwright and Cooper (1997) argue, "A host of issues can act as potential stressors throughout one's working life. Lack of job security; fear of job loss, obsolescence, or retirement, and numerous performance appraisals—all can create pressure and strain" (p. 19). Even if criminal justice personnel are unhappy with career-related aspects of their job, evidence suggests that such concerns are secondary to other more important factors. Whitehead (1986) found that only 36% of probation managers were satisfied with their pay and a much smaller percentage (9%) were satisfied with available promotional opportunities; at the line level, some officers work multiple jobs to offset low wages (Finn & Kuck, 2003). In a study of correctional officers, lack of adequate pay was ranked 17th out of 109 possible stressors (Cheek & Miller, 1983). Elsewhere, promotion-related issues in corrections were ranked behind task pressures and relationships with staff and inmates in importance (Long et al., 1986).

Organizational Factors

The organization's structure, as discussed in earlier sections, provides a framework for accomplishing work but may also generate individual strain. A frequent criticism, for example, is that decision making within organizations is too centralized and rules too constraining; lower-level workers lack input over key decisions that will affect the quantity and quality of their work and autonomy to perform the work as deemed necessary. Zhao, He, and Lovrich (2002), for example, found that reduced autonomy and bureaucracy (e.g., red tape, rules) increased the likelihood of stress outcomes, including depression, obsessive/compulsive behavior, and anger and hostility. Overall, workers may experience strain when they are unable to control their own work lives (Owen, 2006).

Home–Work Interface

Cooper and colleagues (2001) argue that many of the work-related stressors affect an individual's life outside of work; "another danger . . . is the effect that work pressures—fear of job loss, thwarted ambition, work overload, and so on—have on the families of employees" (Cartwright & Cooper, 1997, p. 21). In her classic 1980 volume on female police officers, Susan Martin (1980) described these stressors:

> The conflicts between work and family demands are even greater for policewomen than for policemen because the domestic responsibilities associated with the roles of wife and mother are greater than those of husband and father. . . . While none of the women [officers studied] mentioned difficulties maintaining the house or fulfilling housekeeping responsibilities, several acknowledged that their husband or boyfriend became jealous at the prospect of their working all night with another man, or being continuously in the company of many men. (p. 200)

Strain also results from a type of "spillover" effect where workers (police officers, in this example) return home after a work shift too exhausted to handle household problems, treat family members like suspects, and fail to separate the police officer and family member roles (He et al., 2002). Even irregular work schedules take their toll on family life; homicide investigators spoke of missing special occasions as they waited to "catch a case" (Dabney, Copes, Tewksbury, & Hawk-Tourtelot, 2011).

Burnout

By the late 1960s and early 1970s, a new term—*burnout*—appeared within the popular and scholarly literature, embodying the outcomes some individuals were experiencing as a result of chronic stressors.[4] Bradley (1969), for example, describing an intensive treatment program for youthful offenders that afforded treatment staff the opportunity to take a leave after working for a period of four to six months, argued that the break from job demands would presumably allow the worker to return to the job with "renewed vigor" and avoid the "'burn out' phenomenon" (p. 366). The early work on the subject and, indeed, the term *burnout* itself reflected its "grass-roots" and "nonacademic origins" (Maslach, Schaufeli, & Leiter, 2001, p. 398). Freudenberger (1974, 1975), referred to as the "founding father of the burnout syndrome" (see Schaufeli & Buunk, 2004, p. 383), noted that his interest in the subject was stimulated, in part, by his own feelings of burnout and conversations with others working in a free clinic. Clearly, the term was used in everyday language and among workers even if not yet studied scientifically. That would change beginning in the mid-1970s as researchers began to specifically define, measure, and explain burnout.

Since its introduction into the academic and professional lexicon, burnout has garnered tremendous interest. Schaufeli and Buunk (2004) reported that there were more than 6,000 publications on the topic by the year 2000. Some of this research specifically addressed burnout among criminal justice employees. For example, roughly 3% of all burnout articles appearing before 1996 examined burnout among police officers (Schaufeli & Buunk, 2004). What is **burnout**? Although diverse definitions exist, most include, among other dimensions, the component of emotional exhaustion (Maslach, 1998; Maslach et al., 2001). Exhaustion has been described as "depletion" (Schaufeli & Buunk, 2004, p. 386), where "workers feel they are no longer able to give of themselves at a psychological level" (Maslach & Jackson, 1981, p. 99). To exhaust emotional resources, scholars allege that workers must first operate at a high level of arousal (Jackson, Schwab, & Schuler, 1986; Maslach, 1998; Pines, 1993). Stated differently, "you cannot burn out [experience exhaustion] unless you were 'on fire' initially" (Pines, 1993, pp. 386–387). Exhaustion, however, is viewed as a necessary rather than sufficient condition of burnout (Maslach et al., 2001).

Limiting the definition solely to emotional exhaustion does little to distinguish burnout from general occupational stress. Consequently, others have added additional dimensions to the overall definition. For example, some scholars believe that burnout is a combination of emotional, physical (e.g., fatigue, low energy), and mental (e.g., low sense of self-worth, disillusionment) exhaustion (Etzion, 1984; Pines, 1993). Schaufeli and Enzmann (1998) offered a more extensive definition:

> Burnout is a persistent, negative, work-related state of mind in "normal" individuals that is primarily characterized by exhaustion, which is accompanied by distress, a sense of reduced effectiveness, decreased motivation, and the development of dysfunctional attitudes and behaviours at work. (p. 36)

This definition captures the fact that burnout also leads individuals to view themselves as less efficacious in their work, feeling as though they are not accomplishing their own or their organization's goals. Moreover, it suggests that burned out workers become increasingly detached and cynical toward others in the workplace, particularly clients (depersonalization), and distance themselves from the work altogether (Maslach et al., 2001). Depersonalization may manifest itself during interactions with clients, who may be

---

[4]The early literature on burnout reflects the lack of standardization in its usage (*burn out, burnout, burn-out*). Contemporary literature has generally settled on the single-word version.

labeled (e.g., "inmate," "con," or "crackhead") or treated as objects rather than as people (Jackson et al., 1986). All this leads to the most commonly employed definition of burnout within the literature and the one that will guide the remainder of this section: a syndrome or condition involving a combination of emotional exhaustion, depersonalization, and a diminished sense of personal accomplishment that most commonly affects workers in human service fields (e.g., law enforcement, corrections, nursing, education, social work) requiring regular interpersonal interactions with clients (Jackson et al., 1986; Maslach & Jackson, 1981; Schaufeli & Buunk, 2004). Burnout has been described as "the erosion of engagement with the job" (Maslach et al., 2001, p. 416); indeed, burnout and engagement are considered opposite ends of one continuum (Maslach, 1998). An engaged worker exhibits high energy, involvement, and feelings of efficacy rather than exhaustion, depersonalization, and diminished feelings of accomplishment.

Some have questioned whether burnout is truly distinct from general occupational stress, given the similarities in the concepts. Maslach and Schaufeli (1993) acknowledge that the two concepts are related but offer two key distinguishing qualities. First, they define burnout by explicitly incorporating a temporal dimension; burnout is "prolonged job stress" (p. 9). Second, burnout occurs over time as individuals experience stress and are unable to adequately adapt to the stressors they confront (Maslach & Schaufeli, 1993; Schaufeli & Buunk, 2004). In this sense, Maslach and Schaufeli (1993) argue that "the relative distinction with respect to time between (job) stress and burnout implies that both concepts can only be discriminated retrospectively when the adaptation has been successfully performed (job stress) or when a breakdown in adaptation has occurred (burnout)" (p. 10). Other scholars have offered additional ways to separate the two concepts. Pines (1993) suggests that stress can be experienced by anyone but that only highly involved workers (e.g., motivated, dedicated) are susceptible to burning out. Those lacking motivation, dedication, or other evidence of high arousal will not experience the same type of emotional exhaustion, depersonalization, or diminished sense of accomplishment. Finally, unlike job stress, burnout is generally accompanied by "negative attitudes and behaviours towards recipients [clients], the job and the organization" (Schaufeli & Buunk, 2004, p. 389).

The Measurement of and Interrelationships Between Burnout Components

Acceptance of the definition of burnout comprising emotional exhaustion, depersonalization, and diminished sense of accomplishment is related, in large measure, to the widespread use of the Maslach Burnout Inventory (MBI), a tool for measuring burnout among individuals (Cooper et al., 2001; Maslach, 1998). The original MBI, introduced in Maslach and Jackson (1981), included 22 items measuring each of the three dimensions of burnout. Survey respondents were to answer how frequently ("a few times a year" to "every day") and how intensely ("very mild/barely noticeable" to "very strong/major") they experienced each of the attitudes or feelings contained within the survey items. Emotional exhaustion was captured with statements such as, "I feel emotionally drained from my work," "I feel I'm working too hard on my job," and "I feel like I'm at the end of my rope." Example personal accomplishment items included, "I feel exhilarated after working closely with my recipients" and "I have accomplished many worthwhile things in this job." Finally, depersonalization was measured by presenting respondents with statements such as, "I worry that the job is hardening me emotionally" and "I've become more callous toward people since I took this job" (pp. 102–103). Subsequent research determined that the frequency and intensity of attitudes and feelings were so highly correlated (related) that the intensity question is often excluded from studies employing the MBI (Schaufeli, Enzmann, & Girault, 1993). Two additional versions of the MBI were later created to address burnout in other nonclient settings. One version focuses on teachers and includes minor wording modifications (*student* replaces *recipient*; Schaufeli & Buunk, 2004).

Another version is designed for non-human-service occupations and reworks the depersonalization dimension, a component largely related to client contact, to address more general attitudes toward the job (Maslach, 1998; Schaufeli & Buunk, 2004).

Once a tool was readily available to measure burnout, researchers directed attention to the interrelationships between its three components and the overall development of the burnout syndrome in individuals. In a series of works, Golembiewski and colleagues proposed a phase model of burnout wherein the three components are both "progressive" and "differentially virulent" (Golembiewski, Scherb, & Boudreau, 1993, p. 230; see also Golembiewski, Munzenrider, & Carter, 1983). Golembiewski et al. (1983) theorize that depersonalization occurs early in the development of burnout. Many human-service workers develop a type of detachment from their clients as a way to cope with the demands of the job. For example, probation officers may avoid becoming emotionally involved with offenders' struggles with drug addiction, knowing that, at some point, their work may require enforcement of the conditions of community supervision. Likewise, police officers might consciously work to separate themselves from clients so as not to bring the emotional demands of the workplace into their homes. Dabney and colleagues (2011) reported that homicide detectives considered victims' bodies evidence rather than people; the grisly crime scenes were a necessary component of the job of solving crimes. Sometimes, however, the detachment turns to depersonalization: Clients are referred to in derogatory terms or as objects. As depersonalization occurs, the actual quality of services provided to clients suffers and workers start to view their own work negatively (Golembiewski et al., 1983). They develop a diminished sense of accomplishment. Together, these factors contribute to emotional exhaustion, the most important component of burnout in the phase model (Burke, 1989).

This progression of burnout from depersonalization to diminished sense of accomplishment to emotional exhaustion occurs across eight phases (see Table 9.1). On each of the burnout dimensions, individuals are characterized as scoring either high or low on the MBI (note, however, that a low score on personal accomplishment indicates a high sense of accomplishment and vice versa for the purposes of the phase model). The phases represent each of the possible combinations of high and low across the three dimensions, with Phase I (all three dimensions are low) representing the early phase of burnout and Phase VIII representing extreme burnout. Individuals need not proceed through each level, nor do they need to start at Phase I (Golembiewski et al., 1993). While some workers may experience **chronic burnout** and progress through many of the model's phases as stressors worsen, others experience **acute onset**. In the latter case, "some sudden, traumatic stimulus" generates a level of burnout at one of the higher levels (Golembiewski et al., 1993, p. 230). For example, a police officer who loses a partner or a correctional officer who works through a riot may jump immediately to Phase V or beyond. Research indicates that as burnout progresses into higher phases, workers experience increasingly negative consequences such as greater dissatisfaction, decreasing self-esteem, and declining work performance (Golembiewski et al., 1983).

Several authors have applied the phase model to the study of law enforcement organizations, lending insight into the distribution of officer burnout across the eight phases. Burke and Deszca (1986) surveyed police employees attending classes at the Ontario Police College. As shown in Table 9.1, nearly half of all individuals surveyed fell into either the most burned out phase (VIII) or least burned out phase (I). The remaining officers fell into the middle phases, indicating that burnout is far from an either/or proposition. Rather, experienced burnout represents a continuum. Their findings also revealed that progression from early to latter stages of burnout was linked to negative outcomes, including turnover intentions (desire to leave the job), nonwork conflict (e.g., with a spouse), psychosomatic symptoms (e.g., headaches, chest pains), and negative feeling states (e.g., depression, insomnia). Other studies have confirmed the concentration of burnout at the extremes. Golembiewski and Kim (1990) reported similar findings

Table 9.1 Phase Model of Burnout and Distribution Across Public Sector and Policing Fields

MBI Subscale	I	II	III	IV	V	VI	VII	VIII
Depersonalization	Low	High	Low	High	Low	High	Low	High
Personal accomplishment (reversed)	Low	Low	High	High	Low	Low	High	High
Emotional exhaustion	Low	Low	Low	Low	High	High	High	High
Distribution of officers (%)								
Golembiewski et al. (1998) 13 U.S. public-sector sites	24.0	6.5	9.1	5.1	11.3	14.7	7.4	22.0
Burke & Deszca (1986) Canadian police officers	23.3	7.1	14.5	4.9	7.3	11.9	7.9	23.0

Source: Adapted from Burke and Deszca (1986); Golembiewski, Boudreau, Sun, and Luo (1998); and Golembiewski et al. (1983).

in a sample of state police officers, and as shown in Table 9.1, the pattern emerged in a sample of more than 6,000 public-sector workers from 13 U.S. worksites, including probation offices, schools, hospitals, and military bases (Golembiewski et al., 1998).

More recently, scholars proposed an alternative model positing a development sequence beginning with emotional exhaustion and ending with diminished personal accomplishment. In this model, depersonalization is both a product of emotional exhaustion and a cause of diminished personal accomplishment (Leiter & Maslach, 1988; Schaufeli & Buunk, 2004).

Emotional exhaustion >>>> Depersonalization >>>> Diminished personal accomplishment

The demands of the work, particularly the stressors associated with people work, generate exhaustion. Searching for a way to cope, the exhausted worker becomes more cynical and depersonalizes clients (Lee & Ashforth, 1990; Leiter & Maslach, 1988). The distance between individuals (the worker and the clients) increases, leading to feelings of reduced efficacy or accomplishment. Adjustments were later made to the model to acknowledge that feelings of diminished effectiveness may result from both exhaustion and/or depersonalization; "It is difficult to gain a sense of accomplishment when feeling exhausted or when helping people toward whom one is hostile" (Maslach, 1998, p. 78).

Correlates of Burnout

Although burnout affects individuals, much of the scholarly attention on the topic has addressed the work itself and the organizational context in which it is performed as primary correlates of the burnout syndrome (Lee & Ashforth, 1996; Maslach et al., 2001). Cordes and Dougherty (1993) used a three-category classification scheme to group the commonly studied antecedents of burnout: job and role characteristics, organizational characteristics, and personal characteristics. The first category includes factors such as client demands, workload, the characteristics of the job, and role conflict/ambiguity.

Since burnout was originally viewed as an issue for human-service workers, scholars believed that frequent client contact would only exacerbate the problem (Maslach, 1998). Dowler (2005) reported that officers within the Baltimore City Police Department having frequent and/or physical contact with suspects were more likely to "feel burnt out" than other officers. However, the detrimental effects of client contact have not generally appeared in correctional settings (Holgate & Clegg, 1991; Morgan, Van Haveren, & Pearson, 2002; Whitehead & Lindquist, 1986). One possibility is that the probation or parole officer is capable of determining both the frequency and nature of his or her contacts with offenders, thereby minimizing the demands that confront social service workers or even police officers (Holgate & Clegg, 1991). In institutional settings, many inmates try to avoid contact with correctional officers. Whitehead and Lindquist (1986) speculated that "outside of a correctional institution, contact with clients causes concern because it is intensely emotional; within an institution, contact is often superficial and is problematic only in certain circumstances, such as those suggestive of physical harm to the officer" (p. 37). This may explain why physical contact and other threats (possibility of physical violence, illegal threats, and harassment) were potent predictors of burnout among samples of police officers; contact with suspects is intertwined with these stressors (Dowler, 2005; Vuorensyrjä & Mälkiä, 2011). Other scholars suggest that the absence of core job characteristics consistent with the model described in Section VIII contribute to burnout. For example, lower levels of burnout were reported by correctional personnel in a Midwestern prison who exercised autonomy on the job and received feedback from their work (Lambert, Hogan, Dial, Jiang, & Khondaker, 2012). Similarly, both job autonomy and job variety were negatively related to all three components of burnout among staff at a private correctional facility (Griffin, Hogan, & Lambert, 2012).

Burnout may also result from the policies and practices of the organization as a whole (Cordes & Dougherty, 1993). In a study of Finnish police officers, for example, researchers found that defective leadership increased the likelihood of subordinate burnout (Vuorensyrjä & Mälkiä, 2011). This form of poor leadership included undesirable qualities such as lack of openness, incompetence, unfair conduct, and poor relationships with subordinates. The organization may also contribute to burnout by failing to provide a supportive environment, particularly support from supervisors (Cooper et al., 2001; Etzion, 1984; Lee & Ashforth, 1996; Schaufeli & Buunk, 2004). Adequate support enables individuals to cope with the demands of the job, lessening strain and reducing the likelihood of burnout. Neveu (2007), discussing support within a prison environment, argues that "in work settings such as prisons, interpersonal bonds are therefore expected to act as a powerful resource against danger and aggression while securing performance through team cohesion" (p. 30). Whitehead and Lindquist's (1986) correctional officer sample suffered from a lack of social support: "Having someone to share problems with may be a positive coping strategy for the individual officer" (p. 38).

Finally, individual characteristics such as gender, age, and personality may moderate the effects of job and organizational stressors on burnout. For example, Morgan and colleagues (2002) found that older and more educated correctional officers possessed a greater sense of efficacy (engagement, or the opposite of burnout), though neither age nor education influenced emotional exhaustion and depersonalization. Similarly, older correctional officers were less likely to report symptoms of burnout, perhaps due to their ability to cope with stressors (Whitehead & Lindquist, 1986). These other individual characteristics are routinely included in criminal justice stress and burnout research but are rarely the focus of those studies. In the general burnout literature, evidence is mixed for many demographic variables (see, for example, Cooper et al., 2001; Cordes & Dougherty, 1993).

These studies reveal an extensive list of correlates of the burnout syndrome but lack a theoretical framework. Leiter and Maslach (1999) proposed a theory emphasizing the mismatch between the individual worker and his or her job; the central feature is the "relationship [between the worker and the workplace] rather than the needs or objectives of the organization or for the individual" (p. 473). As long as there is a match or fit in each of the six areas of work life, the likelihood of burnout is minimized. As the strains increase due to a mismatch, burnout becomes more likely (Maslach et al., 2001; Schaufeli & Buunk, 2004). These six areas are as follows:

1. *Workload:* Excessive or demanding workloads generate exhaustion, a key component of burnout. A match occurs to the extent that an individual is able to handle or balance job demands. If the worker lacks the time, energy, motivation, skills, or knowledge to perform, detrimental outcomes may follow. A public defender may burn out due to the large client caseloads and a finite amount of time available to prepare for court. Similarly, probation officers may suffer from the need to curtail the criminal activity of an extremely large number of probationers.

2. *Control:* As noted in Section VIII, employees desire autonomy to exercise control over their jobs. When that control is removed or retained by superiors, workers are unable to exercise discretion in ways deemed necessary, thereby resulting in strain. For example, police managers in departments adopting a Compstat management strategy were held accountable for crime reduction in their areas but were not given control over police resources (Weisburd, Mastrofski, McNally, Greenspan, & Willis, 2003).

3. *Reward:* Burnout may also be the product of the failure to receive intrinsic and/or extrinsic rewards for effective job performance (see motivation in Section VIII). Employees require positive feedback to avoid the diminished sense of personal accomplishment that is part of burnout.

4. *Community:* Criminal justice organizations, particularly police and correctional agencies, are widely viewed as settings where subcultures form among workers. The social support that comes from the job provides a source of satisfaction and camaraderie. If the workplace lacks "a sense of positive connection with others" or is rife with conflict, then the possibility of burnout increases (Maslach et al., 2001, p. 415).

5. *Fairness:* Theories of procedural justice (Section VIII) demonstrate that individuals value fairness and respect in how they are treated and how decisions are made within the organization. If decisions about promotions, grievances, and other matters (some related to earlier areas of work life) are perceived as unfair, workers become disconnected with their employers. In other words, depersonalization within the organization occurs. An aggrieved probation officer passed over for a promotion may separate from peers as well as from management decision makers, contributing to the burnout.

6. *Values:* Finally, workers may experience value conflict that contributes to burnout. For example, a variety of studies have addressed whether an individual's orientation toward aggressive law enforcement shapes his or her participation in community and/or problem-oriented police activities (see, for example, Dejong, Mastrofski, & Parks, 2001). If managerial philosophies conflict with an individual's internal value system, strain may result. Workers may be similarly conflicted when faced with pressures from peer groups or others to engage in actions, legal or illegal, that contradict their own values.

These six areas incorporate many of the individual predictors discussed earlier into a single theoretical framework. This allows individuals and managers to think broadly about the causes of burnout.

Outcomes of Stress and Burnout

The individual consequences of stress and burnout are far-reaching, potentially affecting an individual's psychological, physical (or physiological), and behavioral well-being (Gershon, Barocas, Canton, Li, & Vlahov, 2009).

1. *Psychological:* Commonly reported psychological consequences of stress include depression, anxiety, posttraumatic stress, nervousness, loneliness, work dissatisfaction, and loss of self-confidence (Cheek & Miller, 1983; Gershon et al., 2009; Kahn & Byosiere, 1992). In a sample of Baltimore Police Department officers falling into a low-stress category (e.g., stress was below the median for the department), signs of depression, anxiety, and posttraumatic stress were common, reported by roughly one third of officers. Among those in the high-stress category, these outcomes were twice as prevalent (Gershon et al., 2009).

2. *Physical:* Symptoms of strain include body aches and pains, high blood pressure, heart disease, headaches, ulcers, and fatigue (Cooper et al., 2001; Kahn & Byosiere, 1992). For example, 17% of correctional officers reported high blood pressure within the previous six months, and 8% acknowledged that they experienced migraines or other severe headaches (Cheek & Miller, 1983).

3. *Behavioral:* In addition to harm to the individual, overt job behaviors are potentially the most destructive to the organization's operation, visible in actions such as drinking and drug use, intimate partner violence, interpersonal conflict within the workplace, bullying, carelessness and accidents, and other harmful or counterproductive behaviors (Cooper et al., 2001; Kahn & Byosiere, 1992; Waters & Ussery, 2007).

The consequences of stress and burnout for the organization are great. Strained or burned-out workers are frequently absent, lack commitment to the work, suffer diminished performance, disrupt operations, and/or leave the workplace altogether (turnover) (Kahn & Byosiere, 1992). For example, Holgate and Clegg (1991) discovered that probation officers suffering from burnout interacted with clients less frequently, suggesting that the quality and quantity of offender supervision suffers as a result of chronic stress. It is therefore critical for organizations to formulate strategies to successfully address the sources of strain and aid individuals in coping with stressors.

Addressing Stress and Burnout

Organizational attempts to deal with occupational stress are useful but largely misdirected. They focus more on individual coping or the effects of stress rather than on the actual stressors that are producing strain (Kahn & Byosiere, 1992). Stress is treated as an "individual disorder" instead of "organizational dysfunction," the real problem (Stinchcomb, 2004, p. 268). Overall, scholars have generally classified stress and burnout interventions into three categories—primary, secondary, and tertiary—depending on where the intervention occurs.

Primary interventions are designed to somehow reduce or modify the intensity of stressors within the organization (Cooper et al., 2001; Quick, Quick, & Nelson, 1998). While such interventions are relatively rare, those that do exist are directed at the broad categories of stressors described earlier (e.g., those inherent in the task, work–home interface). Many of the interventions are related to concepts discussed throughout this text—structure, motivation, job design, leadership, and power.

Stinchcomb (2004), for example, prescribes a number of viable strategies for reducing organization-based stressors: decentralizing decision making and empowering employees, allowing input into management-level policymaking, promoting team building and conflict resolution, improving interorganizational communication, and providing greater clarity in and justification for management commands. Coupled with improvements in management's ability to recognize the stress-inducing implications of its decisions, these actions are designed to promote positive relationships, clarify roles, and eliminate chronic organizational stressors. As noted, primary interventions targeting the sources of stress are less common than those tackling individual reactions to stressors or symptoms of stress.

Secondary interventions largely ignore the stressors themselves and instead address the ways individuals respond to them. That is, they address what was referred to earlier as the primary appraisal process, the ways workers assess the significance of stressors in their own lives. Some evidence suggests that criminal justice employees respond to stressors by denying their importance or through dissociative strategies. Cheek and Miller (1983), for example, found that correctional officers were unlikely to report their own job-related strain, yet routinely acknowledged it among their coworkers. Aaron (2000) noted that some police officers responded to stressors through dissociation—"splitting off from awareness thoughts, feeling, or memories of a painful or distressing event" (p. 439). The problem is that these strategies, while potentially viable in the short-term, actually produce long-term harmful effects. Consequently, a variety of secondary prevention strategies are available to assist individuals in coping with stressors. Church and Robertson (1999) surveyed state police organizations and found that many administered wellness-oriented programs designed to support the overall health (physical, mental, emotional) of employees. Specifically, 55% had physical fitness programming, 78% offered stress-management support, 61% provided nutrition and dietary services, and 71% assisted those with alcohol or chemical dependency issues. Some of these offerings (e.g., physical fitness) provide a distraction to workers and may actually build resilience to stressors (Anshel, 2000; Colvin & Taylor, 2012). Others (e.g., stress management) provide tools allowing workers to better control stress-inducing situations or appraise the situation differently (Anshel, 2000).

Tertiary interventions are designed to provide aid when negative strain outcomes—health consequences, aggression, absenteeism, psychological difficulties, and others—appear. Programs generally take the form of counseling, therapy, substance-abuse treatment, medical care, or some other intervention geared toward addressing the symptoms of strain. One such program was the COP-2-COP hotline, a service started in New Jersey in 2000. As described by Waters and Ussery (2007), COP-2-COP is "the first confidential hotline for police officers and their families.... It utilizes retired police officers trained in assessment and in crisis intervention techniques to answer the phones" (p. 171). Through 2007, the hotline fielded more than 18,000 calls. A recurring challenge, however, is encouraging officers to seek help absent some department referral or order. The Cleveland Police Department sought to incentivize help seeking by providing officers experiencing strain with military-style dog tags for either looking for help on their own or helping a partner in need (Chapin, Brannen, Singer, & Walker, 2008). It is essential to provide services for those who have manifest signs of strain, but it is also critical to ensure that services are utilized by those who need them most.

All three intervention types are necessary to create a resilient workforce—one that has "the ability to rebound after adversity" (Colvin & Taylor, 2012). The benefits of these interventions are potentially great, especially when their modest costs are considered. Finn (2000) described a number of corrections-based stress programs (e.g., counseling, peer support, critical incident debriefing, referrals, and training) offered in seven systems, documenting annual costs of operation from $27,000 to $87,000. These programs were generally secondary or tertiary interventions. Overall success will require greater attention to primary interventions, efforts that have generally lagged behind other intervention techniques. Beehr and O'Hara (1987) stated,

> Stress management programs attempt to teach the employee how to cope with the stressors present.... This is essentially an inoculation approach, which does not address the issue of changing the work environment to make it inherently less stressful. (p. 81)

KEY TERMS

acute onset	quantitative overload	stress
burnout	role ambiguity	stressors
chronic burnout	role conflict	tertiary interventions
engagement	routine occupational stressors	traumatic stressors
primary appraisal	secondary appraisal	workplace bullying
primary interventions	secondary interventions	
qualitative overload	strains	

DISCUSSION QUESTIONS

1. The literature on stress and burnout distinguishes between routine and traumatic stressors and chronic and acute onset of burnout. What are some traumatic stressors or critical incidents that may generate stress or acute onset burnout in policing? What about in corrections? Victim counseling?

2. Researchers generally agree that organizations have failed to address the larger sources of stress, choosing instead to intervene at the individual level. What factors might explain organizational reluctance to address the true causes of stress?

3. Assume you are the warden in a state prison. What strategies might you employ to address stressors related to the interface between staff members' home and work lives?

WEB RESOURCES

Coping with workplace stress (Mayo Clinic):
http://www.mayoclinic.com/health/coping-with-stress/SR00030

Philadelphia Area Law Enforcement Peer Support Network:
http://www.lepsn.org/

Stanford Prison Experiment:
http://www.prisonexp.org/

READING

Reading 17

While extant research in law enforcement typically treats police employees as a singular group uniformly affected by similar stressors, Dean A. Dabney, Heith Copes, Richard Tewksbury, and Shila R. Hawk-Tourtelot assert that such stressors may be a product of the employee's position or assignment within the organization. Consequently, they studied occupational stress among the 26 members of a homicide unit within a large metropolitan city. Their findings, based on interviews, observations, and ride-alongs with unit members, suggest that stressors are related to the priority given to homicide cases, the uncertainty associated with homicide investigations, and scrutiny by supervisors, peers, the media, prosecutors, and others. For example, investigators are required to be on-call when it is their turn in the case assignment rotation; this creates uncertainty in workplace and personal activities, as they can be called away at any time. Investigators are also repeatedly questioned by supervisors and members of the media about the status of investigations, thereby increasing the pressures they experience.

A QUALITATIVE ASSESSMENT OF STRESS PERCEPTIONS AMONG MEMBERS OF A HOMICIDE UNIT

Dean A. Dabney, Heith Copes, Richard Tewksbury, and Shila R. Hawk-Tourtelot

Over the past several decades scholars from various disciplines have produced an abundance of literature on how "first responders" experience and respond to stress (Malasch, 1982; Patterson, 1992). Prominently featured in this literature is research that focuses on stress and coping among law enforcement personnel. Scholars generally agree that members of the policing profession are subject to a multitude of stressors, that these stressors are correlated with negative events on and off the job, and that individuals employ a host of coping strategies to mitigate these negative conditions and outcomes (Abdollahi, 2002; Stevens, 2008; Terry, 1981; Waters & Ussery, 2007). Reviews of the police stress literature suggest that the scholarship is replete with multiple avenues of measurement, data collection, and empirical interpretation, which makes it difficult for researchers and practitioners alike to flesh out the complex nature and dynamics of stress in policing. As such, there exists considerable disagreement as to the dimensions of stress experienced by police officers, how to most effectively measure said dimensions, and how the kind and level of stressors vary across demographics and by department size and location (Lord, Gray, & Pond, 1991; Malloy & Mays, 1984; Terry, 1981; Waters & Ussery, 2007).

We contend that much of the disagreement and confusion can be traced to the fact that scholars have rarely imposed an inductive frame on the topic. In a rush to yield generalizable and theoretically informed findings, researchers have borrowed or extended conceptual frameworks and/or stress-related indices from other social science disciplines and applied them to large samples using a deductive approach. This approach rests on the assumption that stress can be operationalized generically across one or more police departments and that there exists a one-size-fits-all

Source: Dabney, D. A., Copes, H., Tewksbury, R., & Hawk-Tourtelot, S. R. (2011, November 21). A qualitative assessment of stress perceptions among members of a homicide unit. *Justice Quarterly.* doi:10.1080/07418825.2011.633542

conceptual model that can account for the nature and dynamics of stress within law enforcement. A more reasonable approach assumes that the source and form of the stressors are influenced significantly by the nature of the police work in question and the organizational context within which the work occurs.

The present study uses inductive ethnographic methods to shed light on manifestations of stress among officers tasked with the investigation of homicide.[1] We chose this group for several reasons. First, there are unique characteristics associated with the occupational context of doing homicide work. The caseload in homicide is generally lighter than other units but investigators work in an "on call" status and thus may be called to a crime scene without warning. Also, for homicide investigators acute stress levels are high, as "mundane" calls do not exist; someone will always have just had their life cut short and the resultant crime scene is likely to be populated with emotional onlookers (e.g. distraught friends and family of the victim) and scrutinizing members of the media. Additionally, homicide work is mentally demanding, as investigators have to endure long hours, reconstruct events in chaotic crime scenes, comprehend a breadth of forensic science, and work with uncooperative witnesses and suspects. Sustained focus and coordination are also critical for homicide investigators. Unlike cases in other units, the lead detective usually maintains primary responsibility for the case file from response to the crime scene through final disposition; regardless of how long it takes or how involved the tasks become. Scholars suggest that these forms of chronic stress may have more deleterious effects on officers than the acute stress experienced while fielding calls (Hickman, Fricas, Strom, & Pope, 2011).

A second reason we focus on homicide investigators regards unique aspects related to the organizational context of homicide work. Homicides are relatively rare events, even for a metropolitan police force. Yet, homicides are designated as the highest priority crimes and investigators are expected to bring them to a prompt and just resolution. Unit and departmental command staff routinely inquire about specific cases and expect immediate results. Moreover, homicide cases are subject to heightened scrutiny by outsiders, including the media, prosecutors, elected officials, and the public. While other areas of police work yield external scrutiny, homicide is generally considered to be well above average in this regard (Innes, 2003).

Collectively, these organizational and occupational characteristics produce qualitatively, and perhaps quantitatively, different stress manifestations for homicide investigators relative to other police personnel. These factors make understanding stress related to homicide investigators particularly important. By examining how stressors emanate from the way that the work is organized and operationalized, we hope to better inform the ongoing conceptual and methodological discussion of stress within law enforcement.

Stress and Policing

Studies from a variety of disciplines have sought to document the nature, extent, and consequences of stress among police officers. This literature is often contradictory and inconclusive, a likely by-product of the interdisciplinary nature of the research (Abdollahi, 2002). What most do agree on is that there are numerous sources of stress for police officers and this stress has psychological and physical consequences.

It is generally agreed that the sources of stress stem from two broad areas. The first involves occupational stressors, which emerge from the tasks and inherent dangers of police work roles. For example, police typically rank being in shoot-outs and high speed chases as the most stressful aspects of their jobs. Although contentions about the dangers of police work may be exaggerated (Zhao, He, & Lovrich, 2002), there is always the potential for an officer to either use or become the victim of lethal force and this often leads to them rating such situations as highly stressful (Patterson, 1992; Violanti & Aron, 1994, 1995).

The second broad category of stress includes organizational stressors. Day-to-day aspects of the job structure, such as strict hierarchies and chains of command, size of the department, overbearing rules and regulations, rotating shift work, and institutional pressures to reduce crime, have all been shown to be major sources of stress (Brooks & Piquero, 1998; Brown & Campbell, 1990; Violanti & Aron, 1994, 1995). It is important to note that organizational stressors may emanate both from structural issues within the law enforcement agency and other agencies with which law enforcement works closely, including the courts and other public officials (Ayres & Flanagan, 1994; Kroes, 1985). Such organizational issues are usually seen to be more influential and important for law enforcement officers' experiences than are occupational or task-based stressors (Gershon, Barocas, Canton, Li, & Vlahov, 2009; Kop, Euwema, & Schaufeli, 1999; Lord, 1996; Shane, 2010; Storch & Panzarella, 1996). For example, Amaranto, Steinberg, Castellano, and Mitchell (2003) found that organizational stressors were over six times more influential on officers' experiences than were task-based stressors. Scholars have also sought to discern individual variations in the sources and consequences of stress for police officers. Race shows a strong association with stress levels; non-white officers tend to report higher levels of stress than white officers (Dowler, 2005; Garcia, Nesbary, & Gu, 2004; Morash & Haarr, 1995). For women, the issue of a perceived "token status" appears to be related to increased stress (He, Zhao, & Ren, 2005; Morash, Haarr, & Kwak, 2006). It is further observed that organizational sources of stress may have differential impacts on male and female police officers, especially as stressors impact officers emotionally and in their performance of personal/family obligations (He, Zhao, & Archbold, 2002). Additionally, factors related to an officer's career trajectory appear to be related to the experience of stress among police officers. It is during the middle part of officers' careers that stress levels are most acute (Violanti & Aron, 1995). In a similar vein, research shows that one's position in the agency's hierarchy is related to experienced levels of stress. Specifically, lower ranking officers, such as patrol officers and sergeants (as front line supervisors), report higher levels of stress than others (Brown & Campbell, 1990; Violanti & Aron, 1995).

Interestingly though, what remains largely missing in the literature on police stress are assessments of experiences by officers of various specialty units and functions. In addition to neglecting the experiences of officers carrying out specialized law enforcement tasks, there are two other primary limitations in the previous research. First, previous studies tend to over-rely on quantitative measures of stress, coping, and consequences (for notable exceptions see Kroes, Margolis, & Hurrell, 1974; Toch, 2002). The majority of research that investigates stress among police relies on general stress scales (e.g. Des-champs, Paganon-Badinier, Marchand, & Merle, 2003; Lord et al., 1991; McCarty, Zhao, & Garland, 2007; Van Patten & Burke, 2001). At times, these scales are adapted for policing, but not always. The use of in-depth interviews and inductive data analyses stand to provide greater insight into the nature of police stress than general stress surveys. The subjective nature of stress suggests that it is necessary to assess how people recognize, interpret, and make sense of potential stressors. By using an inductive approach, it is possible to develop scales and diagnostics that are more refined and specific to the population being studied.

A second limitation of the existing literature is that the majority of police stress research relies on sampling that aggregates officers at the departmental level (Hickman et al., 2011). Doing so assumes the variety of factors that have stress-producing effect on both task-oriented and organizational pressures, operate uniformly for most officers. This clearly is not the case. Officers in other units are not only exposed to different types of stressors but the routinization and bureaucratization of their jobs leads to particular interpretations and experiences of the stressors (Kroes, 1985). While homicide detectives experience many of the same stressors faced by other law enforcement officers, the actual tasks and expectations associated with homicide investigations likely yield unique stressors. In spite of this, the current research detailing the sources of stress for homicide detectives and the consequences of stress is sparse and underdeveloped.

Stress and Homicide Work

The limited research on stress among homicide investigators focuses either on highly specific types of homicide investigations (e.g. child homicide) or on providing a general overview of job-related stressors (Sewell, 1994; Van Patten & Burke, 2001). For example, Van Patten and Burke (2001) demonstrate that detectives who are involved in investigating child homicides have especially high levels of stress. The emotional difficulty of investigating offenses against children is well known and it is not surprising that detectives in such cases experience high levels of stress (also see Krause, 2009). Alternatively, Sewell (1994) provides a conceptual framework for understanding the sources of stress that are unique to homicide investigators as a class. Drawing explicitly on his own experiences and anecdotes from other investigators, Sewell outlines a variety of potential stressors for homicide investigators. The stressors he identifies can be grouped into three general categories: pressures to do their work effectively and efficiently, encountered barriers to success generated by structural issues both within and outside the police agency, and investigators' personal reactions and experienced consequences of attempting to but not succeeding fully in their goals.

Within the category of pressures to do the work effectively and efficiently is recognition that homicide investigators carry the "awesome burden" of being responsible for investigating and solving the most important crime (Sewell, 1994, p. 566). This burden can weigh heavy on investigators, as they place great demands on themselves to manage and solve the case. When coupled with time pressures (e.g. a large caseload and the call for a prompt resolution of each), many investigators become consumed with the task or occupational aspects of their investigations.

Sewell (1994) identifies a perceived lack of support from the judicial system, recognition of the failure of social support services in the community that could both assist those affected by homicide and prevent homicides, and interagency rivalries, competition, and lack of cooperation in investigations as examples of structural issues that yield stress among homicide investigators. He describes the necessity to deal with the significant others of homicide victims as another specific organizational pressure facing homicide detectives. When investigating an offense, detectives have to deal with highly emotional, demanding, distraught, and disoriented friends and family members. These emotions are often heightened when one or more friend or family member becomes a suspect in the investigation.

Finally, Sewell (1994) contends that there exist reciprocating forms of frustration, anger, and fatigue that manifest themselves as personal forms of stressors with which homicide investigators must contend. These largely psychological and emotional reactions evolve out of constant exposure to violence and its consequences, and may lead investigators to "feelings that society is lawless beyond control, communities are too insensitive to sights of violence, and little effective rehabilitation or punishment exists" (Sewell, 1994, p. 571). While not fitting neatly under either the organizational or occupational rubric of stressors, this third category of stressors may be especially important in that "the very emotion resulting from stress can simmer and cause further stress," which in turn "often materializes in anger and hostility directed against superiors, suspects, the system, and even the uninvolved" (Sewell, 1994, p. 572). This leads to the suggestion that individual level perceptions shape how investigators experience and respond to job stress.

While Sewell's framework for the stress experiences of homicide investigators is clear and logical, it is nonetheless anecdotal. Referring to the paucity of research on homicide stress, Henry (1995, p. 95) noted, "To date, no attempt has been made to explore systematically the impact of exposure to death upon police officers or their subculture." Unfortunately, this claim remains true today. The present study seeks to fill this gap through an investigation of the experiences of members of one large metropolitan police department homicide unit. Specifically, we rely on semi-structured interviews coupled with extensive fieldwork to inductively identify the aspects of their jobs that homicide investigators find the most stressful. Doing so will provide an empirical validity check of Sewell's proposed framework. More importantly, systematic observations about the nature and dynamics of stress within specialty units, such as homicide, will serve as a viable point from which to develop a middle range theory of police stress. Such a theory shall incorporate inductive observations relevant to specialty units, and deductive points of logic that have been shown to apply to policing in general. Armed with such a conceptual tool, scholars can then begin to propose and pursue future research directions that operationalize and test the tenets of a middle range theory. Presumably, more effective interventions and policy initiatives could then follow.

Methods

This study relies on ethnographic data collected from homicide investigators employed by a single metropolitan police department. The department in question has an authorized force of just under 2,000 officers, who are responsible for a jurisdiction of a little less than 150 square miles.[2] This jurisdiction faces considerable levels of property and violent crime. The homicide unit is a centralized entity that is tasked exclusively with investigating homicides, kidnappings, officer involved shootings, and all suspicious non-vehicular deaths. At the time of the study, the unit was comprised of 26 sworn officers and a handful of support staff who handled an annual caseload of roughly 100 homicides. Late in 2008, the lead author was granted access to all members of the homicide unit, including officers and administrators. The unit commander introduced the researcher at a unit-staff meeting, and the researcher briefed all sworn officers in the unit about the purpose and scope of the project. The researcher was assigned a ride-along time with interested participants. Before the ride-along sessions, the detailed study aims and procedures were provided to prospective participants with an informed consent document. All 26 sworn members of the unit consented to participate.

Roughly 300 hours of field work was conducted over the course of a nine-month data collection effort (2009-2010). These activities included ride-along sessions with 19 investigators, five line supervisors holding the rank of sergeant, and two lieutenants with unit command responsibilities. Each ride along lasted at least the duration of an 8-hour shift with additional time spent in the squad room and in social settings interacting with unit members in a collective format. Significant rapport was developed with the investigators during this time. During moments of down time and immediately after leaving the research setting, the lead author used a digital recording device to take notes of key observations. These recordings were later transcribed verbatim.

In addition to this fieldwork, face-to-face, semi-structured interviews were conducted with all 26 sworn members of the unit. A major advantage of the semi-structured interview is that it allows respondents to answer questions in their own words with minimal direction from the interviewer, with the flow of the discussion determined in part by the officer. This leads to a more natural description of events by the respondent. The main disadvantage of this approach is that the responses can sometimes be wide-ranging and not every respondent may cover all issues. The interviews lasted between 90 and 150 minutes and were designed to take on a conversational format driven by an interview guide. The goal was to stimulate discussion around a predetermined set of topics. An interview guide built around a dozen core topics was designed prompt discussion about one's work history, perceptions of the homicide investigator's role, and to probe the perceived nature of various forms of occupational, organizational, and personal stressors potentially affecting homicide work. While there was no expectation that the topics would be covered in order or during one sitting, the research plan called for each officer to be engaged on all the topics during the course of the interview. Interviews were audio-recorded and transcribed verbatim. The data were subject to thematic content analysis using the NVivo software program and the following series of theoretical observations were generated inductively.

Event or Occupational Stressors

The nature of homicide work produces a number of unique circumstances that act as potential stressors on homicide investigation unit members. These circumstances appear to be relatively routinized within investigators' daily work experiences and generally mirror those detailed in Sewell's (1994) conceptual framework. More precisely, these task-related issues include that the nature of homicide work involves repeated exposure to homicide crime scenes, time pressures, staffing rotations that dictate when officers are assigned lead investigator roles, paperwork demands, and long-term ownership over individual case files (i.e. from crime scene to final verdict). Our interview data reveal that each of these occupational or event characteristics yield perceived stress in unit members.

Working Crime Scenes

Crime scenes present a host of potential stressors for members of a homicide unit. Many of these factors are simply unwavering realities of the job (i.e. location or condition of the dead bodies), while others are the deliberate outcome of human action or error. Interviews revealed that homicide officers downplay the significance of the former and highlight the latter.

In the eyes of a homicide investigator, dead bodies are part of the job. They learn to dehumanize them and treat them as evidence rather than as someone's sons or daughters. Thus, investigators claimed that the presence of dead bodies did not cause them undue stress. When asked directly if gruesome crime scenes are stressful, a veteran sergeant in the unit replied:

> I have seen it [the gore] a million times, from maggots coming out of the body to decapitation. You become desensitized to it. . . . You don't look at it like, "poor guy;" you look at it like evidence. Let's get to work, you know? I mean I have sat next to a guy that has been in the woods with maggots crawling out of his eye sockets and ate a double stack from Wendy's. This intern she was like, "How in the world can you eat with that smell?" And I am like, "What smell?"

Referring to the repeated exposure to death and gore, an investigator with almost two years on the unit said:

> It's part of a job and I'm not trying to take any dignity or humanity away from someone, but you know I have to do this every day. . . . You have to learn how to control your emotions and not let your emotions control you. And I control mine, you know? I don't allow it to bother me. I don't think about it . . . I've been on some stinky crime scenes and you just go, "Well, whatever." You know, it's just part of the job and I think that's part of what it is; we accept that this is our job, so we have to do this.

Perhaps because death is such a routine part of the job the investigators did not perceive this aspect of the crime scene as being too stressful. Alternatively, failing to "get it right" at the crime scene was consistently mentioned as a major source of acute stress for these investigators. As one investigator said bluntly, "if someone is still alive and they're in pain there's things that I can do to help them. The only thing that I can do to help this dead person is make sure I get this right." Regardless of the complexity of the task before them, the wealth or dearth of physical evidence, and the skills or lack thereof of other law enforcement representatives, the homicide team cannot return to a crime scene the next day to gather new evidence.[3] As one five-year veteran investigator in the unit said:

If an interview doesn't go right or if a statement doesn't go right, you can call that person back in, you can re-interview them. ... You only got one shot at a crime scene. So, if that's screwed up or evidence is contaminated or lost or whatever, that's the only chance you ever get at that. So, I mean that's the beginning of the investigation and often times the most crucial.

Echoing this sentiment about the crime scene, an investigator who had been on the unit for roughly two years said, "You don't want to miss it because you will never have that scene again and to me that's the stressful part. I got to make sure I get enough right there that's gonna assist me in my investigation and then the prosecution will put this guy away. If I don't get it, I blew, I blew it." Time and again, officers noted how the pressure of gathering the right information weighed heavily on the members of the homicide unit.

Per standard operating procedure in the department under study, the lead homicide investigator has primary authority over the crime scene and all agency staff who are present. This means that they must make sure all support staff are going about their designated tasks, that uniformed officers have cordoned off an appropriate size area and made a crime scene log of all persons present, and that other homicide unit members are securing witnesses, taking measurements of the crime scene, drafting a crime scene sketch, and canvassing the area. This can be an enormous endeavor, yielding significant occupational stress for the lead investigator. This is reflected in the following account from a three-year veteran of the unit:

> I had a case at that nightclub. ... When I got on the scene, there were still probably 150 people there. My crime scene log was five pages long. You gotta kind of sift through the people, get the information, pull out the key people that you're gonna interview that night. You know, try to determine who didn't see shit and was just in the other side of the building and get them out, but still record their information.... It's crazy and chaotic even when you get there 20, 30, 45 minutes later, it's still crazy and chaotic. Then you have family coming up and you're trying to secure witnesses and you don't have enough people on the scene. Your crime scene's not big enough. ... It's just everything.

Lead detectives consistently maintained that they do not stress much about what goes on outside of the crime scene tape, as that is the responsibility of uniformed officers. Conversely, interactions with persons present inside the crime scene tape were repeatedly noted as a potential or likely source of stress. Uniform personnel often engage in behavior that compromises the integrity of the investigation. Given that these are sworn law enforcement officers who "should know better," their transgressions are described as stress inducing. As one veteran investigator said:

> [Uniformed officers] don't want to go the extra mile. They want to cop attitudes, cut corners. We have a lot of problems with them responding to scenes and taking information from a witness and letting the witness go and then it takes that much more time to go find the witness or just basic common sense things.

Another commented, "I'd say the biggest thing that's stressful about a crime scene is getting there and officers aren't doing what they're supposed to do, they've messed things up. ... That's like the number one rule, don't contaminate the crime scene."

Homicide investigators also frequently cited crime scene unit personnel as a major source of stress on the murder scene. In the department in question, these are civilian personnel trained and tasked with visually documenting the crime scene and collecting physical evidence. In more egregious cases, investigators noted that the actions of the crime scene technician can compromise the integrity of the entire case due to errors or oversights.

This was seen as particularly stressful to the homicide investigator who knows that he/she is the individual who holds primary responsibility for the overall investigation and will likely be expected to testify in court about any errors or issues attributed to poor follow through on the crime scene. This is evident in the following quote from an investigator with four years in the unit:

> Our crime scene unit is stressful to me, because they're missing a lot and it's not anything you could do. You're just not getting it done from them and you can't go back out [to the crime scene]. I always get the feeling like they don't want to be there . . . I've never gotten the feeling like they're actually trying to help you. They're just trying to get through it.

The interviews uniformly demonstrate that homicide investigators go about their work in a very methodical, non-emotional manner. The routine exposure to dead bodies is mitigated by a sterile approach to blood, human loss, and the like as such conditions are deemed beyond their control. Conversely, trying to direct, supervise and manage crime scene personnel and rely upon these people to competently preserve and gather all relevant evidence is a clear source of acute stress. Summarizing the occupational stressors emanating from crime scenes, one investigator said, "I've got the family to worry about, I've got the victim, I got the ME's [Medical Examiner's] Office, I got witnesses, I've got a whole big crime scene, I got to worry about patrol, I've got to worry about my crime scene tech missing something or I got to worry about my Crime Scene Tech not doing a walk through." Noticeably absent from this list is the presence of dead bodies.

Time Pressures

In most homicide units, case assignments are made on a rotational basis; lead investigators or investigation teams are placed in an order so that members know who will receive lead responsibility on the next case. The rotation order is often depicted on a white board so that all unit members or teams are aware of the number of murders that must occur before they assume primary responsibility for a case. Investigators use the term "being up" to refer to their time at or near the top of the rotation. They are in an on call status when they are "up"; when the next "body drops," regardless of whether they are on duty or not, they must report immediately to the crime scene. This places serious stress on investigators, as they cannot plan personal and family functions and must limit the location of social events. The indecision and stress is illustrated well in the following quote from a three-year veteran of the unit:

> Well the first thing, at least with me, is like, "Fuck, I'm almost up again." Especially when you get to like two or three [on the list] . . . "Is it gonna be on my off days? Is it gonna be in the middle of the night?" . . . It's always a guessing game; you just don't know where it's gonna fall. I guess the not knowing is the biggest thing. "Do I have another beer? Do I plan something with my family or whatever?" So you'll start thinking about it. But what if you're that number one person for five, six, seven weeks? Now you start guessing on where's this thing gonna fall. It's just a guessing game. You feel that relief once I get the call the first question I ask is, "Are they dead yet? Just tell me they're dead." Because the worst thing is getting called in on somebody that may or may not die. . . . And then you could be out of the rotation for a couple of days and then you could be back up. It's a roller coaster.

Echoing this sentiment an investigator with just over one year in the unit said:

> You know you're gonna get that call. You could be in the middle of celebrating someone's birthday or your daughter's dance recital or a nice dinner out with your girl or wife or

whoever and you gonna have to put that down and come in to do your job and they might not see you for 12, 16, 24, 48 hours. . . . You got to call home; you have childcare issues, so that is immediately stressful.

Homicide investigators are subject to a new set of time pressures once called to a crime scene. While the homicide team tries to be deliberate and methodical in its crime scene work, there is a palpable sense that they need to make progress on the investigation. Unit members press to reconstruct the events leading up to the murder, interview key individuals, identify a solid suspect, and notify family members of the loss (all while also being in command of the crime scene and other personnel present). In the hours immediately following the death, these tasks are accomplished in a team format, with multiple members of the homicide unit descending on the crime scene along with medical examiners, crime scene technicians, and uniform officers. As time passes, those with long-term responsibility over the case must forge ahead. Investigators go from being overwhelmed by a mass of support staff to trying to achieve significant results on their own or in a small group. Investigators routinely spend long hours on the crime scene, only to follow these up immediately with a barrage of interviews with potential suspects and witnesses, track down family members, contact credit card or cell phone providers for pertinent records, and/or pull criminal records and assemble photo line-ups, making fatigue an important occupational stressor. As a nine-year veteran investigator noted, "It's like a dog, you're gonna hunt. And if you have to take a nap, take a nap, because nobody's gonna work it as hard as you. This last homicide I had, I was so tired, I needed two hours so badly it ain't funny." Another commented, "there's some cases that you know you need to put in the time. You need to put in the time. You need to manage your time. Sometimes you have to do that 48 hours straight. You don't want to do it, you got to do it."

Having multiple open cases at once poses another time-related occupational stressor. Time sensitive leads often present themselves simultaneously for multiple cases. The investigator must prioritize this work and find ways to progress his/her entire caseload in an effective and efficient manner. As one 14-year veteran investigator noted, "When you're bombarded with a lot of cases, you prioritize and you move the cases you can solve quicker. And then sometimes you continuously get bombarded with one case after the other and then years go by before you could ever go back to something." Having unsolved cases that one believes can be advanced was repeatedly cited as a point of tension for investigators. As a 10-year veteran detective noted, "You always have those open cases that you go back and ask, 'Did I do everything?' And they bother you."

Once a case is cleared by arrest, a new set of time demands are encountered. Courts will set "non-negotiable" hearing dates. The prosecutor will often call the investigator to testify or follow up on evidentiary issues according to his/her own scheduling constraints with little concern for the investigator's time. To this point, a veteran sergeant explained:

> Court is a bear. . . . Probably the second biggest frustration is the court–house. . . . We're on call for cases for a month at a time. You know, they can call you at any time to go. You sit down there for eight, nine hours and they don't get called on the stand.

As one investigator put it, "Oh, they don't give a shit if it's your off day, or you work morning watch. That is a huge pain in the ass. 'Cause they'll say, 'Oh no, you gotta come in.'"

Paperwork Demands

The typical robbery or burglary case file is relatively thin, including a small stack of reports and evidentiary documents assembled by the lead investigator and support personnel. To a large degree, the robbery, or burglary investigator assembles his/her own case file and passes it along to prosecutors. However, with a homicide case file, there is routinely several inches of materials, including a host of evidentiary documents and supplemental reports provided by every individual who was party to the investigation. This includes the first officer on the scene, the medical examiner's office, crime lab personnel, crime scene technicians who processed evidence, and the numerous members of the homicide unit who assisted in the investigation by interviewing witnesses, canvassing the community, drawing crime scene diagrams, and the like. All witness and suspect interviews must be included in written or video form. In short, the files can be quite large, complex, and unwieldy. This is a critical part of the work role and the investigators know it; as the unit commander said bluntly, "Your files are looked at. I mean your files have to be in order. You have to be able to do paperwork. This job just requires you to put a good file together." Not surprisingly then, investigators almost always reported that collecting and compiling case file materials is a significant source of stress, one that is unique in scope and complexity to the homicide investigator. Referring to the factors that shape how to best construct a case file, an investigator who was a four-year veteran of the unit commented:

> Write a story. Document everything. Everything! Because you know when it goes to trial, everything hinges on you. ... A lot of guys are fearful of the documentation because you know when it goes to trial everything hinges on you. The spotlight is on you. And then you know that defense attorney has a year or two years to look over through your file and figure out what I need to do to make him look incompetent. And that's one of the most stressful things when you come in you know you got one person gonna make you look good. You got that one person try his best to destroy your credibility.

Adjudication Demands

Once the case file is assembled and a copy is passed along to the prosecutor, the homicide investigator will most likely be subject to a spate of court hearings to justify the legitimacy of his/her decisions and conclusions. This process is far more intense and prolonged for the homicide investigator than it is for other detectives. If all goes well, the case proceeds to trial. If it does not and the case is dismissed on a legal "technicality," the homicide investigator experiences frustration watching his/her hard work disintegrate. In the metropolitan jurisdiction under study, a full year will usually pass between the arrest and the scheduled trial dates. During this time, the investigator will likely be responsible for an additional 5-10 cases, each with its own unique circumstances and problems. Once the trial date arrives, the lead investigator and all members of the homicide unit who played a role in evidence collection can expect to be called to the witness stand. This necessitates one becoming reacquainted with the case, and disentangling its details from all the other cases that he/she has been a part of in the interim. This process was consistently described as stress inducing. As one investigator reflected, "Did I put the best file together? Am I gonna get hammered in court? Am I gonna look like a fucking idiot when I get up on the stand? ... You don't want to look like an idiot when you go to court." Another detective, this one a nine-year veteran on the unit, spoke of the gamesmanship of court testimony and how it is stressful:

> They'll keep me up there for three or four hours and then me and him [defense attorney] will go at it. This is my chance to shine. This is your all-star game. ... There's loopholes in everything and those little fucking rat finks [defense attorneys] over there they know the loop holes and they try to get everything out of you they can.

Organizational Stressors

A significant amount of the interview content sought to explore the form and content of organizational stressors experienced by homicide investigators. It was found that structural issues from both within and outside the police agency generate stress for the investigator. Perceived internal sources include managing the pressures that come from the high priority status of homicide cases, navigating the bureaucratic processes associated with case assignment and case processing, and wrestling with the tight knit nature of the homicide unit culture. Organizational stressors that originate from outside the police department include pressures from the media, actors within the adjudication process, community stakeholders, and members of the public.

Administrative Pressure

Within the department under study, it was standard practice for at least one homicide sergeant and the lieutenant (unit commander) to be present at every crime scene. Usually joining these unit level superiors were the major who oversees the Major Crimes Section and at least one patrol lieutenant or major. If the crime is high profile, one could expect the presence of an upper level superior, perhaps even the Chief of Police, and one or more members of the district attorney's (DA) office. Beyond the justice system personnel present, a homicide crime scene was sure to attract multiple-media outlets, onlookers, and frequently key stakeholders from the community (politicians, neighborhood activists, or faith leaders). Homicide investigators cannot help but be aware of these various spectators of their work. As one sergeant who had worked homicide for nearly 10 years said:

> Some of these [young investigators] get overwhelmed with the pressure of the media. I mean if there's a bigger media story this year I don't know what it is. The media, the supervisors, the fact that he's still catching [additional homicide] cases. This isn't just the one case that he's working on [as lead detective]. He's working this and he's working other things and I think that we do a huge disservice to some of the young detectives, that come over here that we just don't give them the training on how to juggle pressures, cases, and prioritize what you have and what you need. You know, it's like I guess a MASH Unit.

Once the crime scene is cleared and the homicide investigator embarks on the investigation, he/she can expect follow-up inquiries from police superiors both within and outside the homicide unit. Within the unit, sergeants and lieutenants will query progress, inject theories about case details, and/or possible directions to explore. This comes in addition to the formal case reviews noted above and often engenders resentment and stress due to the lack of investigative experience in most supervisors. As one seasoned investigator noted, "I don't think if you took anybody from our command staff and said, 'show me how to work a murder,' I don't think they would have the foggiest clue." Referring more pragmatically to the unit commander, an investigator with three years in the unit noted, "He [the lieutenant] wants them [offenders] locked up as fast as freaking possible. So, he was riding my ass about locking up the guys."

Beyond the unit, the investigator can expect a homicide case to remain on the radar of upper administrators. Not only are the majors and chiefs keenly aware of year-to-date clearance rates, they routinely expect briefings on individual cases. Speaking about the heightened attention to homicide cases, one investigator noted, "The whole chain of command staff is a little more involved, from the lieutenant on up. And passing the information becomes a number one priority. I got to explain to the uppers why this [arrest] hasn't happened yet. I think their pressure becomes my pressure." The department under study functioned using a Compstat model. This accountability driven management system calls for weekly crime analysis briefings in which a room full of 50-100 mid and upper level administrators consider crime events and crime patterns from the previous week and expect commanding officers to detail plans to address the work load before them. In this regard, the centrality of open homicide cases and corresponding patterns was described by many as further adding to the stress on the unit.

Unit Culture

There are unique characteristics about the organizational culture of a homicide unit that produce pressures on homicide investigators as they go about their work. For one, all unit members tend to work in contiguous space and spend significant time together. They eat meals together, discuss case details with one another, and often socialize outside of work. Everyone knows everyone else's personal and professional business, which frequently produces stressful interactions. It is not that these cultural pressures do not exist in other units, but rather that they are more intense and palpable in a homicide unit. This is reflected well in the following quote:

> [There's] definitely a lot of inter shift competition. . . . Every once in a while you hear a guy say, "Oh, you got a bone [easy case]. You can finally closed one, huh?" So yeah, there's some of that. . . . I don't want to hear it because it's already on my mind and it bothers me.

There are other structural aspects of a homicide unit that add to the organizational stress. For one, there is a decidedly social nature to the workload and productivity. Front and center in every homicide unit is a "homicide board" that details all the case assignments for each investigator and documents for all to see his/her open and closed cases for the current and previous year. This generates competition, ridicule, and bravado from unit members. Referring to the homicide board, one fledgling investigator said:

> A lot of people could tell you probably better about my cases than I could. . . . You really don't want to leave a board full of open cases. It's just not cool. It's not good for business. It's not good for the public. You just, if you're leaving them open every year it's no coincidence, there's something wrong with you. . . . I think everybody knows when you got to get it done. If you are not going to get it done, they will find somebody else who will. We are known to be the best of the best here. We work the hardest cases here. If you can't handle it they will find somebody that can.

At every turn, from the constant ribbing that senior members dispense upon fellow investigators to the prominently featured homicide board to the localized rituals,[4] the organizational culture of the homicide unit serves to push unit members to achieve the highest standards. While at times a source of reinforcement for the successful unit members, these traditions also serve as stressors when expectations are not met.

External Demands

Members of a homicide unit face additional structural pressures originating from entities outside of the police organization. These include demands imposed by other justice system officials, the media, and public stakeholders that resonate in the mind of homicide unit members. Chief among the stress inducing interactions are those with members of the judiciary and the DA's office. As an investigation unfolds, detectives must abide by due process afforded all criminal suspects. In the days and weeks following an arrest, investigators are mandated to secure search and arrest warrants and appear before a judge for requisite hearings (e.g. first appearance, evidentiary hearings, and arraignment). However, judges are not always accessible at the odd hours of a homicide investigation and do not consult homicide detectives when setting court hearings. These obstacles weigh upon homicide investigators as they seek to preserve evidence, advance investigations, and go about their multitude of time sensitive work responsibilities. While all police officers must respect and work within the same due process stipulations, the fact that a homicide investigator assumes sole responsibility for a case file from crime scene to verdict means that they encounter these organizational prerogatives more frequently and more intensely than their fellow officers. Moreover, they are well aware that the consequences of losing a homicide case on a technicality are far more troubling than losing a property crime case on similar grounds.

As the homicide investigator draws in on his/her prime suspect, he/she is inclined to consult with members of the DA's office to seek advice about whether probable cause exists to make an arrest. If the DA's office is not invested in a case, the arrest charges are likely to be dismissed. There exists a subtle but important disconnect between the goals of the homicide investigator and those of the prosecutor. The former is focused on meeting evidentiary standards to affect a lawful arrest and get a killer off the street. The latter shares these concerns but also factors in the likelihood of securing a conviction based on the facts of the case. This perceived disconnect often yields tension between the two justice entities. A 10-year veteran investigator captured this point well:

> You got some DAs that are not too helpful on the investigative side of it. They want all these elements in the case and it's like we're not gonna get that. This is the best we're gonna do. So they don't want to try the case. Then you got some of the younger DAs that want the case handed to them with a bow and a nice little string to it. Then sometimes they don't make a big enough argument. They'll dead docket a case or have a case dismissed because they feel as though that person goes out and kills somebody and the first thing they say is, "The police didn't do this or the police didn't do that."

Once all the pre-trial hearings have been resolved and a murder case is set for trial, the homicide investigator returns to his/her caseload to advance open investigations and await the next one in the rotation. To the detective, he/she no longer has primary responsibility over the case; the prosecutor's office takes over in this regard. That said, organizational stressors remain. As the trial date approaches, investigators are often subject to demands from the DA's office to further develop case materials. Court appearances are often not well coordinated by the DA's office and homicide investigators are made to "waste" a day sitting in the courthouse for their turn on the witness stand. Similarly, prosecutors often cut plea agreements or dismiss a case without fully articulating their logic or satisfying the investigator of the veracity of their decision. This produces additional strains on the homicide investigator that are seemingly more significant than those faced by other police officers. For one, the homicide investigator invests far more time in the average case. Second, and more importantly, the suspect is an alleged murderer and the public safety threats associated with setting the accused free are more severe. As one investigator with five years on the unit noted:

> Our agenda a lot of times is different than their agenda. Our agenda is to identify and build up enough PC [probable cause] to arrest the person and their agenda is to convict this case. "We aren't gonna try it if we don't think we can get a conviction." And that leads to a lot of frustration to the [homicide] guys, because there is enough to go to trial.

Members of the media exert additional demands on homicide unit personnel. This begins at the crime scene where multiple media outlets routinely scramble to get a sound bite from someone in the unit about what happened and where the initial investigation stands. Few other forms of crime scenes produce this level of media attention. As a homicide investigation progresses, especially if it takes on a high profile status, members of the media inquire further into the details of the case. At times, their reporting efforts are seen by investigators as compromising the integrity of the case. In the department under study, the unit or section commander handles crime scene media inquiries but investigators are afforded no protection from the follow-up reporting of the media. Here, the big concern is the control of information so as to not compromise the case outcome. As one rookie investigator noted, "The media can go against you when they put too much information out there for you. It may be some information that we could have used later. So that's gonna hurt you if they put it out there. So sometimes they help you and sometimes they hurt you. I just don't think you need give them too much. Let them [superiors] just give them [the media] enough to keep the interest going."

Stakeholders within the community pose yet another source of organizational stress upon members of a homicide unit. These include grief stricken families and friends of the victim, faith leaders, politicians, community activists, and even curious or persistent residents (Stretesky, Shelley, Hogan, & Unnithan, 2010). While their level of intervention varies widely across murder investigations, members of the homicide unit frequently encounter demands for more information or added investigative efforts. Regardless, due to the enormity of the crime, outside forces tend to expect immediate positive results. Speaking about the perspective of victim's family, a rookie investigator noted:

> They don't care about the other cases. You know, you might be having your twelfth homicide of the year. You might have had two in a month and then you get this one. But no one wants to hear [excuses]. They want to know how come six months in and my baby's case is still open. You know they are wearing your phone out [calling constantly]. You got some family that will flat just wear you out, and that's stressful. I know it's got to be stressful to them because it, sometimes it is to me.

For the homicide investigator, these demands come without the context of external entities knowing the full details or directions of the investigation and/or without sensitivity for the rest of the investigator's caseload. In short, politicians and other community entities want answers irrespective of whether these added insights will help or hinder the work of the detective.

Discussion

The ethnographic data from this study suggest that homicide investigators experience high and unique sources of job related stress, including pressures to succeed effectively and efficiently, barriers to success arising from both internal and external to the agency structural issues, and personal reactions and experiential consequences of not fully succeeding in their efforts. The present study provides important, initial evidence and documentation of the stressors experienced by police officers involved in investigations of homicides. In particular, interview and observational data identify various occupational and organizational factors that generate stress among members of the homicide unit.

Compared to other police detectives or patrol officers, what may be unique about the stress experiences of homicide investigators identified herein is in the intensity of the stress and the specific sources from which these identified stressors arise. For police performing general investigation and/or patrol duties, performance pressures, structural barriers to success, and personal reactions to crime scenes, suspects, witnesses, victims' loved ones, and other agency personnel may be significantly less frequent than those experienced by homicide investigators. While there is a need for additional research to solidify this assertion, it raises the possibility that homicide investigators should be expected to experience greater levels and more intense stress than others within the department.

The event characteristics that give rise to stress for homicide investigators may be unique to their specific niche in law enforcement. However, in contrast, many of the occupational stressors are similar to those reported by patrol officers (the typically studied members of law enforcement). Indeed, bureaucratic elements of law enforcement may have important, negative impacts on police performance (Dowler, 2005; Morash et al., 2006; Zhao et al., 2002). Sewell (1994) astutely notes that homicide investigators are not immune to these standard bureaucratic pressures. As such, homicide investigators experience the "regular" acute stresses of policing in addition to the chronic stressors that are often highly emotional, time-pressured, and necessitate well-documented tasks specifically associated with homicide investigations.

We found that many of the characteristics of the job that one would expect to be very stressful (i.e. death and gruesome crime scenes) are in fact viewed as manageable. Repeated exposure to dead bodies was described as a necessary condition of the job. Organizational and occupational stressors are not. Thus, it was common for investigators to lay blame for stress onto outsiders. Homicide investigators appear to be more troubled with the factors that they deem to be controllable. Incompetent and/or apathetic crime scene investigators, micro-managing superior officers, meddling media, frustrated families, and judicial practitioners driven by goals that conflict with those of the homicide investigator were the primary sources of stress. It is likely that this ability to externalize the sources of stress is what makes homicide investigators resilient. If they were to internalize the many problems that can and do go wrong with investigations, detectives would likely be overwhelmed by pressure and self-doubt. Blaming others may free them to focus on the important and necessary demands of the job and overlook the frequent brushes with the worst of humanity.

Developing Middle Range Theory on Police Stress

The previous findings suggest the utility of a broader theory of stress for homicide investigators, perhaps even police in general. By moving up a level of analysis, we can look for more general stressors than the nuanced ones just presented. Doing so allows for more generalizable data and broader understanding of the causes of stress. A closer examination of the results suggests that the "awesome burden of homicide" brings with it unique stressors. Sewell (1994, p. 566) observes that "citizens and detectives alike have ranked murder as the most important crime." To this point, a detective from Simon's (1991) ethnographically inspired investigation of the Baltimore homicide unit said, "Homicide is the major leagues, the center ring, the show. It always has been" (p. 17). This burden of being tasked with the highest priority job in the department is at the root of the general and chronic stressors common to homicide investigators. While outsiders may think that working with dead bodies, grieving families, and outraged, frightened or otherwise impaired communities are major sources of acute stress, we did not find this to be the case. Instead, the stressors can be grouped into three categories: (1) responsibility for high priority cases; (2) uncertainty throughout cases; and (3) potential scrutiny from others.

For obvious reasons, solving homicide cases takes high priority within police departments. With high priorities comes a heightened sense of responsibility. In most police departments, those assigned to a particular homicide case are given full responsibility for handling it from outset to conclusion. This involves collecting relevant information at the crime scene, following leads, interviewing witnesses and suspects, keeping up with paper work, and eventually presenting enough information to prosecutors to clear the case. Being responsible means that investigators have little leeway for error or uncertainty. They must be comprehensive, in command, and without error. They also must take responsibility for crime scene operations, be in command of staff who may be uninterested or untrained, and supervise the scene and others' activities. As lead detective, they must deal with inquiries, uncertainties and requests from victims' families, uniformed officers, superiors, media, community members, and all who enter the crime scene. On top of all of these responsibilities, the homicide investigator must respond to and manage time demands. They know that the chances of solving the case decrease as time passes and they know the community and agency superiors are impatient about homicide case outcomes. There exist high profile responsibilities within all police assignment and it stands to reason that the unique aspects of homicide work will be stress inducing for unit members.

Stress that comes from job aspects not directly emerging from activities at crime scenes includes uncertainty. Uncertainty for a homicide investigator arises from not knowing when they will catch a case, whether they are effectively managing follow up investigations, when they will be called to court, and if their case files are sufficiently thorough. They must cope with ambiguities in information and processes, insecurities about how each case is progressing, and the reactions of other constituencies. These pressures begin before a case is even assigned to an investigator, through its final disposition by the criminal justice system. As with task prioritization, uncertainty is a core part of all police work and should be expected to be stress inducing.

The high priority of the job also means that homicide investigators are under constant scrutiny from inside and outside the department. Scrutiny is assumed for homicide detectives, and is likely to come from both within the law enforcement agency, and from interested and invested constituencies in the community. This scrutiny begins when they first appear at the crime scene. Inevitably, the crime scene is populated by onlookers who are watchful and critical of any potential missteps the investigators make. Much of this scrutiny is driven by assumptions and misunderstandings about what investigators can and should do to work a crime scene. The scrutiny continues throughout the course of the case, and may be intensified when their case files are examined by prosecutors and others in the judicial system. Prosecutors need proper documentation to either convince the defense to accept a plea or win the trial. The defense team is looking for mistakes to weaken the prosecution's case. In short, both sides are examining the files and procedures with a careful eye. Any mistakes fall on the shoulder of the lead homicide investigator. Given the top-down bureaucratic structure of police organizations, stress researchers should more carefully consider these conditions as they manifest themselves in the police samples under study.

Stress is an inevitable component of all occupations, especially policing. In developing this broader theory of homicide investigator stress, we do not mean to imply that police departments should seek ways to eliminate the occupational and organizational demands that contribute to stress, rather we are suggesting that they should be aware that various stress manifestations exist. For instance, investigators acknowledged that pressure from above and within the unit to solve cases weighed heavy on them. The homicide board, with its graphic depiction of solved and unsolved cases, was a frequently cited source of stress. However, decades of stress research suggests that not all stress is negative. In fact, some stress, commonly referred to as eustress, can lead to enhanced performance. It is possible that being responsible for cases and being scrutinized pushed them to be better investigators. Thus, before administrators rush to remove such visible components of homicide investigator culture, more needs to be known about how stress affects investigators.

The practical implications of these results are clear in that homicide investigators in urban police departments have significant demands on their time, energies, emotions, and managerial skills. Homicide investigation is a job that is distinctly different from other law enforcement roles in structure, process, and experiences of stress. Therefore, it should be recognized and treated as such. Support services for homicide investigation unit members need to address the unique task-oriented stresses that are common for such officers, as well as the organizational stressors that are similar to those experienced by all officers.

Study Limitations

This study, while providing data-based documentation of the unique task and occupational stressors experienced by police homicide investigators, is not without limitations. First, the sample is drawn from a single municipal police department, one with a fairly heavy overall caseload. The fact that the officers interviewed in this research work in such an environment may well be important in the construction of their identification and experience of job related stressors. Second, while documenting the presence and experiential consequences of these stressors, we are unable to identify specific and precise ways in which these stressors are experienced by officers of differing demographics, professional experience, and personalities, all of which likely affect experiences of stress. Such tasks remain to be addressed, and future researchers are urged to engage such questions. A third limitation is that stressors arising from organizational or occupational sources may well vary across agencies of differing cultures, degree of urbanization in communities being policed, and bureaucratic idiosyncrasies of specific agencies. The present study is based on data from a single metropolitan police department with a unique organizational culture; this may significantly limit generalizability.

Future Research Directions

While the present study provides significant advances in understanding and theorizing stress experienced by homicide investigators, this study also points to the need for continued research on the issue. In concluding his overview, Sewell (1994, p. 580) acknowledges the need to evaluate his model and suggests that "the first item in a research agenda would be to assess quantitatively the impact of stress-causing and stress-reducing practices." While such an approach is most certainly of value, we argue that it is more important to first document the presence of these stressors by drawing on systematically collected data, which was the goal of the present study. Now is the time that it is appropriate to employ a quantitative methodology to examining the severity, impacts, and responses to such stressors, knowing that they in fact are present. Such a study may now be more clearly outlined, drawing on the findings of the present analysis. Moreover, such studies would allow scholars to test and refine the broader theory of police stress that we proposed. Specifically, large samples of police officers could be used to determine the effects of responsibility, scrutiny, and uncertainty on police officers of all types, especially homicide investigators.

It is also important to continue a qualitative line of inquiry focusing on how the findings of this study may generalize to other jurisdictions, and to other specialized dimensions of law enforcement work. Based on the findings of the present study, it may now be feasible to develop practical methods and instruments for both assessing and monitoring stress experiences of homicide investigators. Such an endeavor is critical for maintaining high quality investigations—if investigators are identified as experiencing high levels of stress they may be less likely to function effectively and efficiently (Vuorensyrja & Malkia, 2011). Such a situation would not only inhibit effective investigations in the short-term, but would likely also contribute to ongoing stress and increases in frustration and physical, psychological, and emotional consequences (including burnout) for investigators. Therefore, the development of easily implementable instruments for monitoring the key components and contributors of homicide investigator stress may directly contribute to more effective (and efficient) investigations. Such instrument construction should draw upon inductive efforts, such as this one, but must be expanded to include additional qualitative inquiries that seek to identify and theorize contextually specific stressors in policing. Armed with these results, instrument development and validation can then be undertaken that combines the inductive observations from studies such as this one with the deductive materials present in existing measurement protocols. It is only then that we will begin to gain an informed and effective means of measuring and then combating stress within policing.

In the end, this study makes clear that members of police homicide investigation units experience significant degrees of job stress. The occupational and organizational stressors that they experience appear to be bound to the nature of the work assignment. Conceptually, the stresses experienced by homicide investigators can be reduced to the issues of responsibility, uncertainty, and scrutiny. While many of the specific stress inducing aspects of their jobs that give rise to heightened responsibilities, uncertainties, and scrutiny are similar to those also experienced by their police peers not engaged in homicide investigations, for homicide investigators more frequent and intense stress experiences emanate from the unique aspects of taking on the "awesome burden" of homicide investigation.

Notes

1. In the present study, we focus solely on manifestations of stress. Issues pertaining to negative psychological or physiological outcomes of stress or the manner in which officers manage or cope with stress are beyond the scope of this inquiry.

2. The descriptions of the agency under study are intentionally vague in an effort to respect confidentiality assurances that were extended at the outset of the research project.

3. Such a course of action raises contamination and legitimacy issues that can undercut the case in court.

4. After clearing their first case members of the unit are ceremoniously given a Fedora style hat, which he/she then wears while on the job.

References

Abdollahi, M. K. (2002). Understanding police stress research. *Journal of Forensic Psychology Practice, 2*, 1-24.

Amaranto, E., Steinberg, J., Castellano, C., & Mitchell, R. (2003). Police stress interventions. *Brief Treatment and Crisis Intervention, 3*, 47-53.

Ayres, R., & Flanagan, G. (1994). *Preventing law enforcement stress: The organization's role*. Washington, DC: US Department of Justice.

Brooks, L., & Piquero, N. (1998). Police stress: Does department size matter? *Policing: An International Journal of Police Strategies and Management, 21*, 600-617.

Brown, J. M., & Campbell, E. A. (1990). Sources of occupational stress in the police. *Work and Stress, 4*, 305-318.

Deschamps, F., Paganon-Badinier, I., Marchand, A., & Merle, C. (2003). Sources and assessment of occupational stress in police. *Journal of Occupational Health, 45*, 358-364.

Dowler, K. (2005). Job satisfaction, burnout, and perception of unfair treatment: The relationship between race and police work. *Police Quarterly, 8*, 476-489.

Garcia, L., Nesbary, D. K., & Gu, J. (2004). Perceptual variation of stressors among police officers during an era of decreasing crime. *Journal of Contemporary Criminal Justice, 20*, 33-50.

Gershon, R. M., Barocas, B., Canton, A. N., Li, X., & Vlahov, D. (2009). Mental, physical, and behavioral outcomes associated with perceived work stress in police officers. *Criminal Justice and Behavior, 36*, 275-289.

He, N., Zhao, J., & Archbold, C. (2002). Gender and police stress: The convergent and divergent impact of work environment, work-family conflict and stress coping mechanisms of female and male police officers. *Policing: An International Journal of Police Strategies and Management, 25*, 687-708.

He, N., Zhao, J., & Ren, L. (2005). Do race and gender matter in police stress? A preliminary assessment of the interactive effects. *Journal of Criminal Justice, 33*, 535-547.

Henry, V. E. (1995). The police officer as survivor: Death confrontations and the police subculture. *Behavioral Science and the Law, 13*, 93-112.

Hickman, M. J., Fricas, J., Strom, K. J., & Pope, M. W. (2011). Mapping police stress. *Police Quarterly, 14*, 227-250.

Innes, M. (2003). *Investigating murder: Detective work and the police response to criminal homicide*. Oxford: Oxford University Press.

Kop, N., Euwema, M., & Schaufeli, W. (1999). Burnout, job stress and violent behavior among Dutch police. *Work and Stress, 13*, 326-340.

Krause, M. (2009). Identifying and managing stress in child pornography and child exploitation investigators. *Journal of Police and Criminal Psychology, 24*, 22-29.

Kroes, W. H. (1985). *Society's victim: The police officer*. Springfield, IL: Charles C. Thomas.

Kroes, W. H., Margolis, B. I., & Hurrell, J. J. (1974). Job stress in policemen. *Journal of Police Science and Administration, 2*, 145-155.

Lord, V. (1996). An impact of community policing: Reported stressors, social support and strain among police officers in a changing policing department. *Journal of Criminal Justice, 24*, 503-522.

Lord, V. B., Gray, D. O., & Pond, S. B. (1991). The police stress inventory: Does it measure stress? *Journal of Criminal Justice, 19*, 139-149.

Malasch, C. (1982). *Burnout: The cost of caring*. New York, NY: Prentice-Hall.

Malloy, T. Y, & Mays, G. L. (1984). The police stress hypothesis: A critical evaluation. *Criminal Justice and Behavior, 11*, 197-224.

McCarty, W. P., Zhao, J., & Garland, B. E. (2007). Occupational stress and burnout between male and female police officers: Are there gender differences? *Policing: An International Journal of Police Strategies and Management, 30*, 672-691.

Morash, M., & Haarr, R. (1995). Gender, workplace problems, and stress in policing. *Justice Quarterly, 12*, 113-140.

Morash, M., Haarr, R., & Kwak, D. (2006). Multilevel influences on police stress. *Journal of Contemporary Criminal Justice, 22*, 26-43.

Patterson, B. L. (1992). Job experience and perceived job stress among police, correctional, and probation/parole officers. *Criminal Justice and Behavior, 19*, 260-285.

Sewell, J. D. (1994). The stress of homicide investigations. *Death Studies, 18*, 565-582.

Shane, J. M. (2010). Organizational stressors and police performance. *Journal of Criminal Justice, 38*, 807-818.

Simon, D. (1991). *Homicide: A year on the killing streets*. New York: Owl Books.

Stevens, D. J. (2008). *Police officer stress: Sources and solutions*. Upper Saddle River, NJ: Prentice-Hall.

Storch, J. E., & Panzarella, R. (1996). Police stress: State-trait anxiety in relation to occupational and personal stressors. *Journal of Criminal Justice, 24*, 99-107.

Stretesky, P. B., Shelley, T., Hogan, M. J., & Unnithan, N. P. (2010). Sense-making and secondary victimization among unsolved homicide co-victims. *Journal of Criminal Justice, 38*, 880-888.

Terry, W. C. (1981). Police stress: The empirical evidence. *Journal of Police Science and Administration, 9*, 61-75.

Toch, H. (2002). *Stress in policing*. Washington, DC: American Psychological Association.

Van Patten, I. T., & Burke, T. W. (2001). Critical incident stress and the child homicide investigator. *Homicide Studies, 5*, 131-152.

Violanti, J. M., & Aron, F. (1994). Ranking police stressors. *Psychological Reports, 75*, 824-826.

Violanti, J. M., & Aron, F. (1995). Police stressors: Variations in perceptions among police personnel. *Journal of Criminal Justice, 23*, 287-294.

Vuorensyrja, M., & Malkia, M. (2011). Nonlinearity of the effects of police stressors on police burnout. *Policing, 34*, 382-402.

Waters, J., & Ussery, W. (2007). Police stress: History, contributing factors, symptoms, and interventions. *Policing: An International Journal of Police Strategies and Management, 30*, 169-188.

Zhao, J., He, N., & Lovrich, N. (2002). Predicting five dimensions of police officer stress: Looking more deeply into organizational settings for sources of police stress. *Police Quarterly, 5*, 43-62.

DISCUSSION QUESTIONS

1. The depersonalization dimension of burnout has been described as "a negative, callous, or excessively detached response to various aspects of the job" (Maslach et al., 2001, p. 399). When homicide investigators view encounters with deceased individuals and gruesome crime scenes as routine but necessary parts of the job and "as evidence rather than as someone's sons or daughters," are detectives displaying signs of burnout? Alternatively, are these necessary responses for coping with the stresses of the job?

2. In Section II, differentiation—both occupational and functional—was said to contribute to the development of subject-matter expertise. In the present case, assigning specific detectives the responsibility of investigating homicides illustrates specialization. At the same time, specialization, including the occupational and organizational demands associated with handling homicides, produces stress for members of the department. Is despecialization—allowing detectives to handle a variety of case types—a way to reduce the stress described in the article, or is the development of expertise reason for maintaining specialization?

3. In your opinion, does the way homicide investigators are depicted in the popular media (e.g., television shows such as *CSI* and *Law and Order*) contribute to occupational stress among actual investigators? Explain.

READING

Reading 18

Public defenders, like all criminal defense attorneys, are tasked with preserving the rights of the accused in the justice system. Their work is complicated by the fact that they must handle large caseloads comprising a high proportion of factually guilty defendants. David R. Lynch further notes that the work is performed under less-than-favorable conditions of low pay and low status. Not surprisingly, he argues that personnel turnover or "revolving doors" characterize many public defender offices. In his study, Lynch examined the primary stressors among a sample of more than 200 New York State public defenders. He found that while some potential stressors were frequently encountered by public defenders (e.g., conducting legal research, representing serious offenders, advocating positions not believed in), they did not intensely affect attorneys. In contrast, other stressors such as conducting trials and lacking skills necessary to perform were "taxing" on public defenders but infrequent. Of more significant concern for both the public defender and his or her client are stressors that are both frequent and intense. Two stressors appeared among the top five items in each list—lacking options to mount a defense in the event of a trial and lacking trial options due to trial penalties. Lynch offers some recommendations for reducing these stressors, such as raising judicial awareness of how actions (e.g., imposing trial penalties, departing from neutral arbiter role) affect public defenders.

The Nature of Occupational Stress Among Public Defenders

David R. Lynch

People who represent those charged with crimes who are too poor to hire private attorneys are supposed to be under a lot of stress. One hears tales of excessive caseloads, distrustful clients, unreasonable prosecutors, and overbearing judges. Then, of course, there is the work itself: representing the guilty, performing before juries, and doing complex legal research. Public defenders are supposed to endure all of these hardships for notoriously low pay and undeserved low status. Given all of this, the image of public defenders' offices as "revolving doors" in terms of personnel turnover should not come as a big surprise.

But precisely what are the stressors that most bother public defenders? Are some stressors more powerful than others? Which are the strongest of all? Because reform usually comes piecemeal, it would be very helpful to know which stressors should be dealt with first.

These are very important questions given the overwhelming importance of public defenders in American criminal courts. Excessive occupational stress damages not only public defenders themselves but also the system that relies so heavily upon them. Nearly two out of every three Americans accused of a felony require a free lawyer (Wice, 1985). Though assigned counsel programs serve most counties, the 1,144 counties that use public defenders represent more than 70 percent of the nation's population (U.S. Dept. of Justice, 1988). Nevertheless, the number of public defenders is relatively small. Of the 600,000 or so practicing American attorneys, only 10,000 to 20,000 regularly accept criminal clients, and of these, only about 5,000 are public defenders (Cole, 1992). What deeply affects these 5,000 people deeply affects the American criminal court system.

Fortunately, some studies have been done on occupational stress among public defenders. However, almost without exception they have been based entirely on interviews or observations (i.e., qualitative methods). Those based on numbers (i.e., quantitative

Source: Lynch, D. R. (1997). The nature of occupational stress among public defenders. *Justice System Journal, 19*(1), 17–35.

methods) are virtually unheard of. Though qualitative studies are useful, they do have weaknesses. For example, they typically examine occupational stress among public defenders piecemeal, focusing on some potential stressors while ignoring others. Thus, comparisons that consider the whole spectrum of potential stressors simultaneously are apparently nonexistent. Furthermore, some potential stressors (e.g., not knowing when a case might be called suddenly into trial or judges being partial) have barely been examined. Additionally, the various qualitative studies usually rely heavily upon the subjective impressions of the interviewer or observer, and this poses its own problems when it comes to deciding which stressors are greater than others.

To address the stress problem confronting public defenders, therefore, we first need to accurately measure and define it. This study used statistical methods to identify with far more precision than has ever been done those stressors that most bother public defenders. Despite conflicts in the literature, some stressors, like advocating causes one does not believe in, were not found in this study to be very bothersome to attorneys. Others, like "too much work to do," confirmed common belief by proving to be among the highest stressors. Yet, still others, such as stresses caused by judicial attitudes and practices, surprisingly seemed to be most taxing of all. Before considering all of the results of this study, however, let us first consider what has been written on this important subject and the precise methods employed in this study.

Stress Defined

As a pioneer of general stress theory, Hans Selye (1936:32) conceptualized stress as a "general adaptation syndrome," in which stress was simply a "nonspecific response of the body to any demand." Although Selye's discipline was medicine, his concept of stress as a nonspecific response has been widely embraced by others, including those in the behavioral and social sciences (Marshall and Cooper, 1979). In simple terms, stress is the general physiological and psychological response one makes to a perceived threat to one's well-being (Klarreich, 1990). Often this is perceived as the "fight or flight" syndrome, in which one's mind and body gear up for action after one perceives a threatening or novel situation (Yates, 1989).

When one becomes overstressed for extended periods, stress becomes harmful. One's system is never able to fully return to a healthy, "normal baseline of activity" (Yates, 1979:22). This situation can lead to high blood pressure, absenteeism, burnout, or low performance (Zaccaro and Riley, 1987). In addition, excessive stress can lead to headaches, heart disease, backaches, and ulcers (Yates, 1979). In fact, some estimate that about 50 percent of all health problems have some relation to stress (Klarreich, 1990).

Different work settings result in different stressors. Most professionals do not have to suffer from cold, heat, dampness, or noise, but they nevertheless can be subject to intense stress. Principal among such sources of stress are quantitative role overload—too much work; qualitative role overload—work that is too difficult; role insufficiency—work that is unchallenging; subjective role conflict—duties that violate one's personal values; and objective role conflict—work that involves contradictory demands from different factions (see, e.g., French and Caplan, 1972; Warshaw, 1979; Osipow and Spokane, 1987; Matteson and Ivancevich, 1987). It is not difficult to see how the above concepts might manifest themselves in public defense work. In fact, though it rarely uses such classifications, the qualitative literature on public defenders has spoken to many of these.

Previous Qualitative Studies

Ogletree (1993), a former public defender turned Harvard law professor, cites beliefs held by many court observers that public defenders see excessive caseloads (i.e., quantitative role overload) as the single worst burden they must bear. Wice (1985:47) observed public defenders in courtrooms who were frequently saddled with "mound[s] of case folders." Uphoff (1992:445), writing as a former public defender, states that "heavy case loads create time pressure and stress that can overwhelm even the best-intentioned, most competent defense lawyer." Giant caseloads and resultant lack of client contact have also been thought to lead to client distrust and hostility (Bartollas, Miller, and Wice, 1983; Flemming, 1986).

Qualitative role overload, or work that is "too difficult," was suggested by Heumann (1978), who noted that new defense attorneys come to the arena not knowing how to go about their tasks—nor are they ever taught how to perform them. Rather, they must learn how to perform their roles through an adaptation process over time. McIntyre (1987) found that public defenders received very little supervision, and though they often enjoyed their independence, many seemed ambivalent. They mentioned that they would create more structure and support were they in charge. Cherniss (1980:21), who studied burnout by interviewing professionals (including lawyers), found that "the one theme that most strongly shaped and colored the experience of new professionals was a deep concern with personal competence."

The theme of role insufficiency (boredom with one's duties) has been touched upon by students of the criminal courts only fleetingly and indirectly. Criminal lawyer turned sociologist Abraham Blumberg (1967:106) noted in his frequently cited study that his fellow criminal lawyers often complained that they "rarely had a genuine opportunity to exercise their professional skills." Instead, they spent their time fixing plea bargains. Kunen (1983:153), writing after having served two-and-a-half years as a public defender in Washington, D.C., commented, "I'm thinking what a way to spend my energy, my substance, my life ... on this deadbeat who's guilty anyway." Yet, Kittel (1990) found that a majority of those public and private criminal lawyers surveyed did not desire to change careers. The effect of role insufficiency therefore is still ambiguous.

The literature suggests that subjective role conflict (doing things that violate one's values) also occurs. Scholars have noted that although public defenders represent clients, they also must work with prosecutors and judges toward shared goals of disposing of cases, maintaining work group cohesion, and lowering feelings of stress and uncertainty (see, e.g., Eisenstein and Jacob, 1977; Bartollas, Miller, and Wice, 1983). There is still a lack of information as to the degree that painful effects from this potential conflict haunt the individual attorney. Are public defenders coldhearted con artists who trick their clients into pleading guilty in order to quickly turn around a case, as Blumberg (1972) suggested? Or are they "beleaguered dealers," themselves the pained victims of a system beyond their control (Uphoff, 1992)?

Subjective role conflict also can result when one must defend serious violators whom one believes to be guilty. McIntyre (1987) observed that when asked how they could defend people who commit crimes, most public defenders responded that they were supporting a constitutional right. But she also observed some who could not so justify their actions. Ogletree (1993:1242) argues from personal experience that to avoid becoming burned out, public defenders need a "sufficiently compelling motivation—an impetus to do the work, rather than a theory [like upholding constitutional rights] that merely argues that it is *defensible, excusable,* or *laudable* for someone to do the work" (emphasis in original). It is therefore unclear whether most public defenders really find sufficient comfort in defending the guilty by thinking in abstract terms, or whether Ogletree's implication that such rationales are generally insufficient is more accurate.

Objective role conflict (getting caught between contradictory demands from different factions) was noted by Neubauer (1974:67), who stated that "the lawyer's task is not easy, because he must mediate between the demands of his client, the dictates of the law, and the working realities of the prosecutor and the rest of the court community." Fighting and confrontations with clients, prosecutors, and judges are consequences for defense attorneys as they go about this mediation process. On the one hand, the attorney is legally bound to represent the client's best interests. Yet, on the other hand, as French and Bell (1990:45) claim, "one of the most psychologically relevant references for most people is the work group.... What goes on in the work team has great significance for feelings of satisfaction and competence." One suspects that the contradiction of having to get along both with one's client and one's courtroom work group would lead to problems. But the precise degree to which public defenders are bothered by contending with prosecutors, judges, and even clients is still relatively unknown.

Previous Quantitative Studies

Although few published quantitative studies have been done on occupational stress among attorneys, even fewer have focused on public defenders. Kobasa (1982) used correlations and similar procedures to analyze data obtained from 157 lawyers (mostly general practitioners), but could find no correlation between lawyers' stressful life events and reports of diagnosable illnesses. Krakowski (1984) compared the occupational stress of lawyers in one New York county with that of physicians. He found that fewer lawyers than physicians experienced "marked compulsivity" (28 percent vs. 80 percent); fewer lawyers than physicians suffered from compulsive personality disorder (12 percent vs. 20 percent); and that lawyers suffered only one-third the level of depression experienced by physicians. Cherniss (1992), researching burnout among lawyers (coming from diverse practices), teachers, and nurses, found support for the counterintuitive idea that those who suffer burnout early in their careers were better able to adapt later on than those who suffer it later. Members of the early burnout group were also less likely to ultimately change careers. Benjamin, Darling, and Sales (1990), using a random sample of 10 percent of the Washington State Bar, found that 33 percent of respondents suffered from depression, alcohol abuse, or cocaine abuse.

No quantitative study has been discovered that attempts to answer these two questions: Which of all the potential stressors confronting public defenders do public defenders say occur the most frequently? And which are most intensely felt whenever they do occur? McPeak's (1987) unpublished dissertation, which researched stress among general members of the Florida Bar, comes closest to addressing these issues. However, he did not specifically consider criminal lawyers in his analysis and therefore did not ask questions that would be of vital interest regarding them. Because one cannot begin to find solutions to a problem until one can define it, answers to questions of specific relevance to public defenders would be important to have.

Method

Questionnaire Development

This project used self-reporting as the means for assessing occupational stress among public defenders. A standardized, self-administered, mailed questionnaire was used to gather the data, which were collected in the summer and fall of 1994.

As noted earlier, the general literature on occupational stress suggests quantitative role overload, qualitative role overload, subjective role conflict, objective role conflict, and role insufficiency as common "white-collar" stressors.

Scale Development

Rather than using a single questionnaire item to represent a potential stressor (e.g., "too much work" used to represent quantitative role overload), multiple forms of a question were asked (e.g., "too much work," "working overtime," "being too busy for breaks," etc.). Separate scales were then constructed for "frequency" (e.g., how often did a respondent experience quantitative role overload) and for "intensity" (e.g., how taxing did a respondent feel quantitative role overload to be whenever it did occur). Each "frequency scale" was constructed by computing the mean "frequency" score for all multiple forms of a particular question. Similarly, each "intensity scale" was constructed by computing the mean "intensity" score for all multiple forms of a question.

A total of seventeen different stress concepts were ultimately produced from the sixty relevant questionnaire items using the tools of factor analysis and reliability analysis. Part of this process also included comparisons between a frequency factor and its intensity factor counterpart to assure that items in one also appeared in the other. Items that did not appear in both were not used. In other words, the frequency scale for a particular stress concept and the intensity scale of that same concept always included identical questionnaire items.

Characteristics of the Subjects

All public defenders and assistant public defenders in the state of New York, exclusive of New York City, were surveyed. New York City was excluded because of its extraordinary size (with eight million people it would constitute a study in and of itself) and unique status as a world-class city. Counties that used assigned counsel in lieu of public defenders were excluded as well. This procedure yielded a wide variety of counties, ranging from tiny agricultural counties to major urban centers like Buffalo.

No random sample was necessary because the entire universe of subjects was surveyed. The study was limited to public defense attorneys for two reasons. First, public lawyers are easier to identify and locate. Second, all public defenders clearly devote themselves to the intensive practice of criminal law, whereas some private "criminal" attorneys may take criminal cases, but only as a minor supplement to their civil practices.

Response Rates

Every public defender office in the state was contacted by phone, letter, or both to learn the identities of current staff. The questionnaires were sent out with a cover letter and a handwritten note addressed to each individual attorney asking for his or her support. A follow-up mailing was done to help improve the response rate.

A total of 389 questionnaires were mailed. Fourteen of these questionnaires were not suitable for inclusion in the study because they were addressed to attorneys who, though nominally public defenders, were assigned exclusively to child custody matters in civil court or who otherwise had no active criminal caseload of any kind. Excluding them from the study resulted in 375 questionnaires, of which 217 were returned, producing a final response rate of 58 percent.

Results

Each concept can then be placed into a cell representing a combined frequency-intensity score of either "low-low," "low-high," "high-low," or "high-high." Because a 0 to 5 point scale was used to separately measure both frequency and intensity, 2.5 (the midpoint) will be used as the cutoff point between the cells. Hence, stressors falling in the "high-high" category on average would occur more frequently than "sometimes" and would, on average, be at least "fairly taxing" whenever they did occur.

It would appear that seven stressors happen more often than "sometimes" and are at least "fairly taxing" whenever they do occur (see Table 1):

1. Quantitative role overload (too much work)
2. Qualitative role overload from the unpredictability of trial occurrences
3. Qualitative role overload from possible trials in which there would be no defense
4. Objective role conflict in general (having to satisfy parties making contradictory demands)
5. Objective role conflict from having to deal with upset and angry clients and their family members
6. Objective role conflict from arguing with prosecutors
7. Objective role conflict from having no realistic trial options because of judicial policies of punishing defendants who exercise their trial rights with overly harsh sentences

Although there were seven concepts in the "high-high" category (see Table 1), it would be valuable to separately note which potential stressors occur most frequently and which are most taxing whenever they do occur. This information is listed below:

Table 1 Combined Frequency-Intensity Cells

	INTENSITY	
	Low (less than 2.5)	**High (greater than 2.5)**
FREQUENCY High (greater than 2.5)	• Doing legal research • Routine duties, paperwork • Lack of chance to get more trial experience • Representing serious offenders • Advocating positions not believed in	• Too much work to do • Unpredictability of trial occurrences • No defense if trial • Having to satisfy conflicting parties • Upset and angry clients and family • Arguing with prosecutors • No trial options because of harsh sentences
Low (less than 2.5)	(No entries)	• Lack of skills, training to do assignment • Actually doing trials • Courtroom work group pressures to avoid assertiveness • judicial interference • Lack of judicial impartiality

The 5 Concepts of Highest "Frequency" (descending order)	The 5 Concepts of Highest "Intensity" (descending order)
1. Routine duties, paperwork	1. Lack of judicial impartiality
2. Representing serious offenders	2. Actually doing trials
3. Too much work to do	3. No trial option because of punishing those who go to trial
4. No trial option because of punishing those who go to trial	4. Dealing with angry and suspicious clients and their families
5. No defense if a case were to go to trial	5. No defense if a case were to go to trial

It is interesting to note that the above two lists share two concepts that might warrant particular concern among those concerned with occupational stress among public defenders:

1. Objective role conflict resulting from having no realistic trial option due to judicial policies of excessively punishing those who exercise their right to trial.
2. Qualitative role overload resulting from cases that are potentially going to trial but for which there would be no defense.

Finally, in addition to questions regarding the frequency and intensity of potential stressor items, the public defenders surveyed were also asked questions of general interest regarding personal and professional factors in their lives.

Discussion and Implications

This study reveals that though many things bother public defenders, some things stand out as particularly troublesome. The quantitative data suggest that public defense attorneys are particularly stressed by having too much work to do, fighting with clients and prosecutors, not being able to know when cases might be suddenly called into trial, having trial-bound cases that seem hopelessly indefensible, and having no real trial options due to punishingly harsh sentences. Though public defenders very frequently represent serious offenders and advocate positions they do not personally believe in, they are not particularly bothered by doing either. Nor do they feel taxed by their frequent legal research duties or because they have few opportunities to get more trial experience in a system based largely on plea bargaining.

Of the five stress concepts of highest "frequency" and the five stress concepts of highest "intensity," the two concepts that appeared on both lists involved stress not from abusive clients or from having too much work to do, but rather from judges: 1) having no realistic trial options due to judicial policies of excessively punishing those who exercise their trial rights and 2) having cases that are potentially going to trial but for which there would be no defense. (Interviews conducted with attorneys in aid of questionnaire construction suggest that the link to judges of the latter involves the displeasure attorneys feel from judges who resent having their time "wasted" on allegedly frivolous trials that the attorneys are expected to somehow always prevent.) Another interesting point is that the single stress concept with the highest "intensity" score (though of low frequency) also involves judges: having to argue before judges who lack judicial impartiality.

The apparent remedy, therefore, for reducing some of the major stressors affecting public defenders involves the judiciary. If they can be convinced to change their attitudes, much of the stress associated with public defending would be mitigated.

Judges therefore need to be made aware (or perhaps reminded) of the tremendous effect they have on the professional lives of the public defenders working with them. Judges have a lot of authority and status. With this authority and status comes an obligation to avoid creating unnecessary or excessive stress in the lives of those working with them.

For example, the fact that lawyers find the perceived presence of judicial favoritism to be the most intensely taxing of all stressors underlines the high standards that judges must maintain. Judges must take great care to avoid even the appearance of lack of neutrality. Fortunately, though lawyers found lack of neutrality to be the most intense stressor whenever it did occur, they reported that it did not occur all that frequently.

However, other stressors involving judges occurred not only with high intensity but with very high frequency as well. For example, judges need to avoid punishing or appearing to punish defendants who exercise their trial rights. Apparently, many public defenders believe that judges are routinely violating the Sixth Amendment by excessively punishing their clients who elect to have trials. If judges are punishing people merely for going to trial, they need to stop. If they only appear to be doing so in the eyes of public defenders, they should do more to correct this damaging but widely held perception.

Judges also need to remember that some defendants will insist on trials no matter how strong the case is against them and no matter how skillfully an attorney tries to convince them to accept a plea bargain. Lawyers need permission to sometimes "fail" at getting clients to accept plea bargains, even in supposed "dead bang loser" cases.

Caseload is another area that needs to be reformed. Preparing trials in elevators on the way to court is hardly conducive to effective representation. Legislatures are unlikely to care about public defender caseloads. Perhaps someday appellate courts, concerned about Sixth Amendment right to effective assistance of legal counsel, might be convinced to exercise their power to mandate reform. In the meantime, efforts might be made to flatten out any peaks and valleys of workload that may exist due to the way criminal court sessions are being calendared.

A reduction in caseload almost certainly would lead to a reduction in public defenders' fighting with clients and prosecutors. Attorneys would be less prone to fight with clients if they could afford to invest more time with them toward gaining their trust. (Of course, attorneys might need to be exhorted to actually spend the extra time with their clients should it become available.) Attorneys would also be less likely to snap at prosecutors were they not so weighed down by mounds of files and time pressures.

Chief public defenders could also do things on their own to reduce stress among their attorneys. For example, trial stress might be reduced by providing opportunities for seasoned trial attorneys to mentor inexperienced members of the office. Paralegals and investigators might be employed (or better trained if they are employed) to take some of the caseload pressure off of attorneys.

Finally, docket reform could go far toward minimizing the stress associated with not knowing exactly when any particular case might suddenly be called up for trial (another major stressor of public defenders). At a minimum, professionally trained and neutral court administrators should be hired to handle the docket. Allowing inexperienced assistant district attorneys with professional agendas to decide when and which cases will be called for trial (as is the case in many counties) is inappropriate.

Public defenders are indeed under stress. Though a fair amount of stress undoubtedly goes with the job, much of it is unnecessary and could be mitigated through enlightened policy changes. These policy changes are important to reduce unnecessary harm to those citizens charged with crimes, to those public servants asked by society to represent them, and to the Sixth Amendment right to adequate and effective representation. Many ordinary citizens are charged with a crime during their lifetimes and many of these will be represented by public defenders. A system that is unnecessarily abusive to these civil servants and those they represent is a threat to the legitimacy and efficacy of the entire criminal adjudication process.

References

Bartollas, C., S. Miller, and P. Wice (1983). *Participants in American Criminal Justice: The Promise and the Performance.* Englewood Cliffs, NJ: Prentice-Hall.

Benjamin, G. A., E. Darling, and B. Sales (1990). "The Prevalence of Depression, Alcohol Abuse, and Cocaine Abuse Among United States Lawyers," 18 *International Journal of Law and Psychiatry* 233.

Blumberg, A. S. (1972). "The Practice of Law as a Confidence Game: Organizational Cooptation of a Profession," in G. Cole (ed.), *Criminal Justice: Law and Politics.* North Scituate, MA: Duxberry Press.

——(1967). *Criminal Justice.* Chicago: Quadrangle Books.

Carmines, E. G., and R. A. Zeller (1979). *Reliability and Validity Assessment.* Newbury Park, CA: Sage Publications.

Cherniss, C. (1980). *Professional Burnout in Human Service Organizations.* New York: Praeger Publishers.

Cole, G. F. (1992). *The American System of Criminal Justice,* 6th ed. Belmont, CA: Brooks/Cole.

Eisenstein, J., and H. Jacob (1977). *Felony Justice: An Organizational Analysis of Criminal Courts.* Boston: Little, Brown.

Flemming, R. B. (1986). "Client Games: Defense Attorney Perspectives on Their Relations with Criminal Clients," *American Bar Foundation Research Journal* 253.

French, W., and C. Bell (1990). *Organization Development.* Englewood Cliffs, NJ: Prentice-Hall.

French, J., and R. Caplan (1972). "Organizational Stress and Individual Strain," in A. Marrow (ed.), *The Failure of Success.* New York: AMACON.

Heumann, M. (1978). *Plea Bargaining: The Experiences of Prosecutors, Judges, and Defense Attorneys.* Chicago: University of Chicago Press.

Kittel, N. G. (1990). "Criminal Defense Attorneys: Bottom of the Legal Profession's Class System?" in F. Schmalleger (ed.), *Ethics in Criminal Justice.* Bristol, IN: Wyndham Hall Press.

Klarreich, S. (1990). *Work Without Stress.* New York: Brunner/Mazel.

Kobasa, S. (1982). "Commitment and Coping in Stress Resistance Among Lawyers," 42 *Journal of Personality and Social Psychology* 707.

Krakowski, A. (1984). "Stress and the Practice of Medicine: Physicians Compared with Lawyers," 42 *Psychotherapy and Psychosomatics* 143.

Kunen, J. (1983). *"How Can You Defend Those People?": The Making of a Criminal Lawyer.* New York: Random House.

Lazarus, R. S. (1966). *Psychological Stress and the Coping Process.* New York: McGraw-Hill.

Lazarus, R. S., and S. Folkman (1984). *Stress, Appraisal, and Coping.* New York: Springer Publishing Company.

Marshall, J., and C. Cooper (1979). *Executives Under Pressure.* New York: Praeger.

Matteson, M. T., and J. M. Ivancevich (1987). *Controlling Work Stress: Effective Human Resource and Management Strategies.* San Francisco: Jossey-Bass.

McIntyre, L. J. (1987). *The Public Defender: The Practice of Law in the Shadows of Repute.* Chicago: University of Chicago Press.

McPeak, A. (1987). "Lawyer Occupational Stress." Ph.D. dissertation, Florida State University, Tallahassee.

Neubauer, D. W. (1974). *Criminal Justice in Middle America.* Morristown, NJ: General Learning Corporation.

Ogletree, C. (1993). "Beyond Justifications: Seeking Motivations to Sustain Public Defenders," 106 *Harvard Law Review* 1239.

Osipow, S., and A. Spokane (1987). *Occupational Stress Inventory: Manual, Research Version.* Odessa, FL: Psychological Assessment Resources.

Selye, H. (1936). "A Syndrome Produced by Diverse Nocuous Agents," 138 *Nature* 32.

Uphoff, R. J. (1992) "The Criminal Defense Lawyer: Zealous Advocate, Double Agent, or Beleaguered Dealer?" 28 *Criminal Law Bulletin* 419.

U.S. Department of Justice (1988). "Criminal Defense for the Poor, 1986," *Bureau of Justice Statistics Bulletin,* September.

Warshaw, L. (1979). *Managing Stress.* Reading, MA: Addison-Wesley.

Wice, P. B. (1985). *Chaos in the Courthouse: The Inner Workings of the Urban Criminal Court.* New York: Praeger.

Yates, J. (1979). *Managing Stress.* New York: AMACOM.

Zaccaro, S. J., and A. W. Riley (1987). "Stress, Coping and Organizational Effectiveness," in A. W. Riley and S. J. Zaccaro (eds.), *Occupational Stress and Organizational Effectiveness.* New York: Praeger.

DISCUSSION QUESTIONS

1. In a 1987 book about public defenders, author Lisa McIntyre asked in one of the chapter titles, "How can you sleep nights?" Basic to this question is how (whether) an attorney can manage the occupational stresses associated with representing criminal defendants, many of whom are factually guilty. If you were a criminal defense attorney, particularly a public defender, how would you describe your role in society in such a way that allows you, drawing on the chapter title, to sleep at night?

2. The sources of stress included in Lynch's survey address work-related factors. Not included are other factors that may interact with the work of a public defender to increase stress (e.g., student loan debt from law school, family). What additional factors beyond those included in the study might generate stress for defense attorneys?

3. Consider the five highest "frequency" items and five highest "intensity" items. Do you suppose that prosecutors face similar stressors in their everyday work, or are these factors unique to criminal defense work? Explain.

READING

Reading 19

Rebecca A. Shelby, Rebecca M. Stoddart, and Kathryn L. Taylor investigated burnout among sex-offender treatment providers using the Maslach Burnout Inventory (MBI) instrument discussed within this section. Mental health providers, they hypothesize, may experience burnout as a result of difficult clients, personal safety risks, and other pressures stemming from the provider–client relationship or the organization itself (e.g., large caseloads). Burnout, in turn, may contribute to employee turnover, absenteeism, or substandard treatment provision. To examine burnout, researchers distributed surveys to a sample of inpatient and outpatient treatment providers across the country. Compared with other mental health and social service workers, sex-offender treatment providers exhibited greater levels of personal accomplishment. The authors speculated that they may "feel more effective in their work, even though their clients may be more difficult" (p. 1212). Additionally, they were more likely to experience emotional exhaustion compared with mental health workers. The authors attempted to explain the levels of emotional exhaustion, depersonalization, and personal accomplishment among sex offender treatment providers using a variety of predictors (e.g., gender, number of years of practice), and few patterns emerged. In fact, the only consistent predictor across the three dimensions of burnout was facility type. Individuals who provided treatment in inpatient or prison settings had higher levels of emotional exhaustion and depersonalization and lower levels of personal accomplishment. The authors speculate that prison settings, particularly the more difficult clients, increase the likelihood of burnout and make it difficult for providers to feel as though they are providing effective services.

FACTORS CONTRIBUTING TO LEVELS OF BURNOUT AMONG SEX OFFENDER TREATMENT PROVIDERS

Rebecca A. Shelby, Rebecca M. Stoddart, and Kathryn L. Taylor

There has been a recent trend in the judicial system to sentence sex offenders to treatment as a condition of probation or prison. This practice has resulted in increasing numbers of sex offenders requiring treatment services. In a report from the Bureau of Justice Statistics, Greenfield (1997) reported that about 234,000 sex offenders are under the care, custody, or control of corrections agencies on any given day. Nearly 60% of these offenders are under conditional supervision in the community. Furthermore, many sex offenders receive shorter prison sentences if they agree to participate in treatment. A substantial amount of research regarding the assessment and treatment of sex offenders exists, but few studies have focused on the personal and professional impact of treating sex offenders on the providers who do so. Despite the importance of this work and its difficult nature, little is known about the levels of burnout experienced by treatment providers and the factors that contribute to burnout. To maintain an effective workforce and to provide therapy to a growing number of sex offenders requiring treatment, the factors that contribute to burnout must be identified so that staff training to reduce burnout can be developed (Abel, 1983).

Four studies have documented the impact of working with sex offenders on providers (Edmunds, 1997, Ellerby, 1997; Farrenkopf, 1992; Jackson, Holzman, & Barnard, 1997). In a study examining the effects of treating sex offenders on therapists, Farrenkopf (1992) reported that 54% of therapists felt they had become discouraged about client change and had lower expectations when working with sex offenders. Almost half of the therapists

Source: Shelby, R. A., Stoddart, R. M., & Taylor, K. L. (2001). Factors contributing to levels of burnout among sex offender treatment providers. *Journal of Interpersonal Violence, 16*(11), 1205–1217.

surveyed reported experiencing emotional hardening, rising anger, declining tolerance, and increasing confrontational behavior. In a descriptive study examining the impact of working with sex offenders, Edmunds (1997) found that 29% of respondents experienced an overall increase in emotional, psychological, and physical symptoms associated with burnout. More than half of respondents reported increased fatigue and frustration, and one third reported increased cynicism, sleep disturbances, and irritability.

Farrenkopf (1992) reported that 29% of surveyed therapists, particularly females, experienced increased suspiciousness, vulnerability, and vigilance in their daily lives. Ellerby (1997) reported that after treating sex offenders, providers had become more cautious in personal relationships and more concerned about family safety and generally felt unsafe, whereas Jackson et al. (1997) found that participants felt more anxious about their children's safety and were more vigilant around strangers. Providers also reported experiencing threats to personal safety by clients, with 84% of female therapists reporting that sex offender clients had violated their personal boundaries (Ellerby, 1997). Jackson et al. (1997) found that 51% of providers had been verbally or physically assaulted by clients, and 27% believed that security in their workplace was inadequate. Farrenkopf (1992) hypothesized that client characteristics contribute to levels of burnout. Sex offenders present therapists with characteristics identified as the most stressful for clinicians, which include being unmotivated, hostile, deceptive, and manipulative; posing a threat to the safety of others; and entering treatment involuntarily (Ellerby, 1997). In addition to working with difficult clients, sex offender treatment providers must also contend with obstacles created by the correctional system. For example, sex offenders in a prison setting are often reluctant to participate in treatment and overcome denial of responsibility for their offense because such behavior may pose a threat to their safety within the prison. Farrenkopf (1992) reported that 38% of surveyed therapists were disillusioned with the justice system and frustrated by the lack of support for services within the correctional system. Of therapists surveyed by Jackson et al. (1997), 62% reported viewing the criminal justice system as less effective than they had viewed it prior to working with sex offenders.

Sex offender treatment providers may be more susceptible to burnout compared to other therapists due to the large number of difficult clients in their caseload, the severity of client problems, the risk of client recidivism, and threats to providers' personal safety (Abel, 1983; Ellerby, 1997; Farrenkopf, 1992). Recognizing and treating burnout is extremely important due to its impact on the quality of life of treatment providers, their health, and their effectiveness as clinicians (Browner et al., 1987; Corrigan, Kevartarini, & Pranana, 1992; Donovan, 1987; Hamburg, Elliott, & Parron, 1982). Maslach has defined burnout as a syndrome characterized by three components: (a) emotional exhaustion, which is characterized by tension, anxiety, physical fatigue, and insomnia; (b) depersonalization of others, which is used as a defense mechanism to reduce the amount of emotional energy needed to work with people; and (c) feelings of reduced accomplishment, which are a result of low self-esteem and efficacy (Browner et al., 1987; Kahill, 1988; Lee & Asforth, 1990; Maslach, 1982; Perlman & Hartman, 1982). Burnout manifests itself in attitudes about work, absenteeism, turnover rates, and reduced performance (Maslach, Jackson, & Leiter, 1996). Furthermore, Corrigan et al. (1992) asserted that staff members experiencing burnout may offer less effective treatment because they perceive greater barriers to implementing treatment innovations and experience higher levels of self-doubt.

To maintain treatment effectiveness and improve the working conditions of treatment providers, the factors that contribute to high levels of burnout must be identified. Previous studies have provided descriptive information regarding the impact of working with sex offenders, but little is known about the factors that contribute to burnout.

The purpose of the present study was to assess levels of burnout among sex offender treatment providers and identify factors that contribute to increased levels of burnout.

Method

Subjects and Procedure

In May 1997, informational questionnaires and Maslach Burnout Inventories (MBIs) were mailed to 150 randomly selected licensed mental health providers who treat sex offenders. For this pilot study, only 150 questionnaires were mailed to determine the feasibility of conducting research using mailed questionnaires with this population. Of the 150 providers who were mailed questionnaires, 50% *(n = 75)* worked in inpatient facilities or prisons, and the remaining 50% *(n = 75)* worked in outpatient facilities. All providers were randomly selected from mailing lists provided by the Safer Society Foundation's treatment referral service (a nonprofit organization that provides referrals for sex offender treatment). It is important to note that the mailing list used for selection of inpatient/prison providers was nationwide, whereas the mailing list for outpatient providers only included addresses from Ohio, Indiana, Illinois, Michigan, and Wisconsin. A nationwide mailing list was needed for inpatient providers due to the small number of inpatient facilities in operation across the country. Due to the large number of outpatient facilities in operation across the country, addresses from the above five states were used to obtain a sample size equivalent to the nationwide sample of inpatient facilities.

Of the 150 people who were mailed questionnaires, 86 completed and returned the questionnaires (response rate = 57.3%). Among the 86 completed questionnaires, 43% *(n = 37)* were returned by providers who worked in inpatient facilities or prisons, 51 % *(n = 44)* were returned by providers who worked in outpatient facilities, and 6% *(n = 5)* were returned by providers who worked in both inpatient and outpatient facilities.

Measures

The MBI was used to assess the levels of burnout experienced by treatment providers (Maslach et al., 1996). The MBI includes 22 items intended to measure the psychological or affective dimensions of burnout (Arthur, 1990). Items include statements such as "I feel depressed at work." Respondents are asked to rate each statement, using a fully anchored Likert-type scale (0 = *never,* 6 = *every day*). The inventory contains three separate subscales that measure emotional exhaustion (EE), depersonalization (DP), and personal accomplishment (PA). Subscale scores are computed as the sum of responses for each item in a subscale, and high levels of burnout are indicated by high scores on the EE and DP subscales (> 27 and > 13, respectively) and a low score on the PA subscale (< 31).

In addition to the MBI, respondents were asked to complete an informational questionnaire that assessed gender, number of years working with sex offenders, type of facility (inpatient versus outpatient), percentage of clients who are sex offenders, type of therapy provided (group versus individual therapy), employment status (full- versus part-time), and treatment methods used (e.g., cognitive restructuring, relapse prevention, masturbatory reconditioning). Participant age, ethnicity, and education level were not collected.

Results

Comparison to MBI Subscale Norms

To provide some information regarding differences in levels of burnout between sex offender treatment providers and other mental health workers, we compared this sample's MBI subscale scores with MBI subscale norms. It is important to note that the comparisons between this sample's subscale scores and MBI subscale norms must be interpreted with caution due to large differences in sample sizes, differences in methods of questionnaire administration (i.e., mailed questionnaire versus in person), and an inability to determine whether demographic differences exist between this sample and the sample used to create the subscale norms. Because a comparison sample of general mental health providers was not included in this study, these comparisons are presented in an effort to place the levels of burnout among sex offender treatment providers into a larger context.

We conducted t tests between our sample and the MBI subscale norms for mental health workers (e.g., psychologists, mental hospital staff). Sex offender treatment providers reported higher levels of EE. Sex offender treatment provider scores were also compared with MBI subscale norms for social service workers (e.g., child protective workers, social workers) to obtain a comparison with providers working with resistant clients who may threaten the safety of others. Relative to social service workers, sex offender treatment providers reported higher levels of PA, but similar levels of EE and DP. Sex offender treatment providers working in inpatient or prison settings reported higher levels of DP, relative to social service workers' subscale norms.

Bivariate Analyses Between Provider Characteristics and MBI Subscale Scores

Contrary to previous findings (Farrenkopf, 1992), there were no differences in levels of burnout by gender. Furthermore, there were no differences by percentage of clients who were sex offenders, by whether providers worked in an individual or group therapy setting, or by the type of intervention techniques used. Relative to providers working in outpatient facilities, those in inpatient or prison facilities reported marginally higher levels of EE, significantly higher levels of DP, and lower levels of PA.

Regression Analyses

We sought to further explore the relationship between the MBI subscales and type of facility in which providers were practicing. In addition to its association with the MBI subscales, the type of facility was significantly related to four other predictor variables, including number of years treating sex offenders, percentage of clients who were sex offenders, type of therapy (group versus individual therapy), and the type of intervention techniques employed. Providers who worked in inpatient/prison or outpatient facilities ($n = 81$) were included in the analyses, whereas those who worked in both inpatient and outpatient facilities ($n = 5$) were excluded. In all three equations, facility (inpatient or prison versus outpatient) was the only predictor variable that significantly contributed to burnout.

Discussion

The present article examined the association between levels of burnout and sex offender treatment provider characteristics. Compared with MBI subscale norms for mental health workers (e.g., psychologists, mental hospital staff), scores of sex offender treatment providers showed higher levels of EE and DP. Despite the elevated levels of EE and DP, sex offender treatment providers reported higher levels of PA relative to mental health workers. This indicates that sex offender treatment providers feel more effective in their work, even though their clients may be more difficult. To obtain a comparison with providers working with resistant clients, sex offender treatment providers were also compared with social service workers (e.g., child protective workers, social workers). Sex offender treatment providers reported levels of EE and DP similar to scores of social service workers, suggesting that client characteristics are contributing to levels of burnout. Both social service workers and sex offender treatment providers work with clients who are resistant, have been court-ordered to enter treatment, and may threaten the safety of others. These client characteristics may contribute to high levels of burnout (Ellerby, 1997). However, whereas levels of EE and DP were similar, sex offender treatment providers reported higher levels of PA relative to social service workers. As found in the comparison with mental health workers, this suggests that sex offender treatment providers feel effective despite the difficult characteristics of their clients.

Contrary to previous findings (Farrenkopf, 1992), there was no association between gender and level of burnout. The lack of association between gender and burnout levels may be due to the low response rate, as those who are experiencing the highest levels of burnout may be least likely to complete questionnaires. However, gender differences were previously reported in studies using unstandardized measures, and it is possible that gender differences were not found in this study because we measured burnout with a different, standardized measure. Further research is needed regarding the assessment of burnout with standardized measures among sex offender treatment providers. Also, contrary to previous findings (Farrenkopf, 1992), there was no association between the number of years working with sex offenders and levels of EE and DP. However, marginally higher levels of PA were found among longer term providers, suggesting that those who choose to continue working with sex offenders for many years may believe their work is worthwhile and effective.

The results of this study indicate that providers working with the most difficult sex offenders, those sentenced to prison or inpatient treatment, experience higher levels of burnout relative to outpatient providers. Compared to outpatient providers, those working in inpatient or prison facilities reported higher levels of EE and DP and lower levels of PA. This suggests that those working in inpatient or prison facilities experience more difficulty without the feelings of effectiveness that may work to reduce the negative impact of working with difficult clients. Inpatient or prison providers work with the most difficult clients, have a high percentage of clients who are sex offenders, and use intrusive behavioral techniques such as masturbatory reconditioning. Furthermore, inpatient or prison providers work in an environment that may pose a greater threat to their safety compared with providers working in outpatient settings. Jackson et al. (1997) reported that more than half of surveyed sex offender treatment providers feared for their own safety, and about one quarter attributed their safety concerns to inadequate security in their workplace.

Although this study is limited by a low response rate and a lack of information regarding providers' level of education, ethnicity, and age, it has added new information by examining the association between provider characteristics and burnout. Previous studies (Edmunds, 1997; Ellerby, 1997; Farrenkopf, 1992; Jackson et al., 1997) have provided descriptive information about sex offender treatment providers' characteristics and levels of burnout but have not examined the relationship between provider characteristics and burnout. By examining the factors that contribute to high levels of burnout, those providers most in need of additional support and training can be identified.

Ellerby (1997) reported that sex offender treatment providers often receive little or no support from the community, correctional system, and mental health professionals who do not treat sex offenders. Only 47% of surveyed sex offender treatment providers reported receiving positive reactions to their work whereas 90% reported receiving negative responses, 71% felt they needed to justify their work, and 68% reported discomfort with telling others they work with sex offenders (Ellerby, 1997). Because sex offender treatment providers work with extremely difficult clients and may not receive needed support, identification of the factors contributing to burnout and development of training programs designed to help providers prevent and cope with burnout must be a priority.

Further investigation of factors contributing to high levels of burnout is necessary to develop staff training and support that will help maintain the provider workforce, reduce the negative impact of treating sex offenders, and increase treatment quality. If future studies also find an association between levels of burnout and inpatient or prison facilities, sex offender treatment providers may consider adopting caseloads that include both inpatient and outpatient clients to reduce levels of burnout. In addition to examining levels of burnout, future studies should focus on the relationship between burnout and providers' training, frustration with the correctional system, feelings of safety, coping strategies, and client characteristics. Because many sex offenders remain in the community or receive early release into the community based on treatment participation, maintaining a high quality of treatment is critical. To help our communities, we must ensure that treatment providers working with the most challenging sex offenders receive the support they need to continue this work effectively.

References

Abel, G. (1983). Preventing men from becoming rapists. In G. W. Albee, S. Gordon, & H. Leitenberg (Eds.), *Promoting sexual responsibility and preventing sexual problems* (pp. 238-250). Hanover, NH: University Press of New England.

Arthur, N. M. (1990). The assessment of burnout: A review of three inventories useful for research and counseling. *Journal of Counseling and Development, 69,* 186-189.

Browner, C. H., Ellis, K. A., Ford, T., Silsby, J., Tampoya, J., & Yee, C. (1987). Stress, social support, and health of psychiatric technicians in a state facility. *Mental Retardation, 25,* 31 -37.

Corrigan, P. W., Kevartarini, W. Y., & Pranana, W. (1992). Staff perception of barriers to behavior therapy at a psychiatric hospital. *Behavior Modification, 16,* 132-144.

Donovan, R. (1987). Stress in the workplace: A framework for research and practice. *Social Casework, 68(5),* 259-266.

Edmunds, S. B. (1997). The personal impact of working with sex offenders. In S. B. Edmunds (Ed.), *Impact: Working with sexual abusers* (pp. 11 -29). Brandon, VT: Safer Society Press.

Ellerby, L. (1997). Impact on clinicians: Stressors and providers of sex offender treatment. In S. B. Edmunds (Ed.), *Impact: Working with sexual abusers* (pp. 51-60). Brandon, VT: Safer Society Press.

Farrenkopf, T. (1992). What happens to therapists who work with sex offenders. *Journal of Offender Rehabilitation, 18(3/4),* 217-223.

Greenfield, L. A. (1997). *Sex offenses and offenders: An analysis of data on rape and sexual assault* (Bureau of Justice Statistics, NCJ-163392). Washington, DC: U.S. Department of Justice.

Hamburg, D. A., Elliott, G. R., & Parron, D. L. (1982). *Health and behavior: Frontiers of research in the biobehavioral sciences.* Washington, DC: National Academy Press.

Jackson, K. E., Holzman, C., & Barnard, T. (1997). Working with sex offenders: The impact on practitioners. In S. B. Edmunds (Ed.), *Impact: Working with sexual abusers* (pp. 61-73). Brandon, VT: Safer Society Press.

Kahill, S. (1988). Symptoms of professional burnout: A review of empirical evidence. *Canadian Psychology, 29,* 284-297.

Lee, R. T. & Asforth, B. A. (1990). On the meaning of Maslach's three dimensions of burnout. *Journal of Applied Psychology, 75(6),* 743-747.

Maslach, C. (1982). Understanding burnout: Definitional issues in analyzing a complex phenomenon. In W. S. Paine (Ed.), *Job stress and burnout: Research, theory, and intervention perspectives* (pp. 29-40). Beverly Hills, CA: Sage.

Maslach, C., Jackson, S. E., & Leiter, M. P. (1996). *Maslach burnout inventory manual* (3rd ed.). Palo Alto, CA: Consulting Psychologists Press.

Perlman, B., & Hartman, E. A. (1982). Burnout: Summary and future research. *Human Relations, 33,* 238-305.

DISCUSSION QUESTIONS

1. Difficult involuntary clients, especially those who are sentenced to prison, pose particular problems for treatment providers. Do you suppose the voluntary–involuntary client dichotomy would be relevant to the study of burnout in other areas of the criminal justice system (e.g., drug treatment)? That is, would treatment providers who work with clients who are court mandated to attend treatment report different levels on the MBI than those who work with voluntary clients? Explain.

2. What steps can the organization take to enhance feelings of personal accomplishment among sex-offender treatment providers, particularly among providers who work within institutional settings?

3. Some would suggest that burnout is a product of time as well as other factors. The research reported here showed that increasing years of experience significantly affected neither emotional exhaustion nor depersonalization. How come treatment providers, operating under difficult conditions, were unaffected by prolonged contact with clients as measured by years of experience treating sex offenders?

SECTION X

Leadership

Are You a Leader or a Follower?

Section Highlights

Definition of Leadership
Theories of Leadership
   Trait Theory
   Behavioral Theories

Contingency Theories
Transformational Leadership
Leadership Development

New York City began the 1990s with a single-year total of 2,245 murders, which, after taking into consideration the city's more than seven million residents, represented a rate of nearly 31 murders per 100,000 people (Bureau of Justice Statistics, 2010). The 1990 peak was called the "bloodiest year in the City's history" and "foretold of a nightmarish future, and many longtime residents proclaimed their intention of escaping from an unlivable and unworkable metropolis that had deteriorated into an urban battleground" (Karmen, 2000, p. 1). By 1993, murder and violent crime rates had declined from their 1990 peak but remained 2.5 to 3 times higher than national rates. As the city confronted its crime problem, the New York City Police Department (NYPD) was simultaneously plagued by funding constraints, a corruption scandal, low officer morale, and difficulties implementing community policing reforms (Kim & Mauborgne, 2003; Silverman, 1999). In early 1994, New York's mayor Rudolph Giuliani appointed William Bratton to lead the police force and "turnaround" the city's crime problem.[1] Bratton established a vision for the department and stimulated significant organizational change. He firmly believed that "leading, inspiring, and directing middle-management was the key to

---

[1] Bratton would later cowrite a book titled *Turnaround: How America's Top Cop Reversed the Crime Epidemic* (Bratton & Knobler, 1998).

improving police organizations," so many of his efforts were directed at captains and lieutenants (Kelling & Bratton, 1998, p. 1226; see also Kelling & Bratton, 1993). As Karmen (2000) explained:

> A new philosophy replaced the former bureaucratic mind-set: manage the NYPD like a corporation. Hold local precincts responsible for meeting performance standards. Imbue commanding officers with the entrepreneurial spirit and encourage them to take initiatives to reject the old organizational culture in which supervisors responded with caution and resisted change. (p. 94)

Bratton decentralized authority to each of the department's precinct commanders (generally a captain or deputy inspector), affording them the opportunity to craft effective crime reduction strategies consistent with area needs. The commanders were held accountable for results, as Bratton and his leadership team placed heavy emphasis on monitoring crime statistics as a means for understanding departmental operations and performance (Karmen, 2000; Silverman, 1999). Officers were freed from the restrictions that promoted timidity and caution on the streets and directed to enact a "virtual zero tolerance campaign" against those who disrupt community quality of life: aggressive panhandlers, subway turnstile jumpers, drug dealers, and others (Karmen, 2000, p. 94; see also Gladwell, 2000). Personnel buy-in to Bratton's transformation attempts was accomplished, in part, by encouraging departmental employees to see problems firsthand; for example, officer meetings with citizens revealed community concern about less serious disorder rather than more serious crime (Kim & Mauborgne, 2003). At the end of 1996, the year Bratton resigned his leadership position, the murder rate in New York City was 50% lower than the 1993 pre-Bratton rate and overall crime rates had declined substantially. Supporters contend that Bratton's leadership efforts led to fundamental changes within the police department, contributing to more effective use of resources and enhanced internal accountability (Kelling & Bratton, 1998; Kim & Mauborgne, 2003). Others argue that crime reductions were independent of or only partially due to policing efforts and that policing strategies may have actually produced harmful effects (e.g., Fagan & Davies, 2000; Greene, 1999; Harcourt & Ludwig, 2006).

What strategies do leaders like Bratton use to promote change within their organizations and accomplish their (sometimes lofty) objectives? This section introduces the subject of leadership. Much of the discussion centers on how scholars have defined and theorized effective leadership over time. Are leaders born to lead? Do they act in certain ways on the job that breed success? These and other questions will be answered by reviewing the four major strands of leadership theory—trait, behavioral, contingency, and transformational. Their application to criminal justice organizations will be illustrated using relevant literature.

Definition of Leadership

Leadership is a difficult term to define, resulting in a wide variety of conceptualizations within the literature (Bass, 1990a). Definitions typically recognize its social nature, referring to the relationship between individuals and, more precisely, the influence of one individual over another or a group (Yukl, 1994). Hemphill and Coons (1957) wrote half a century ago, "Leadership, as tentatively defined, is the behavior of an individual when he is directing the activities of a group toward a shared goal" (p. 7). In an overview of the leadership literature, Northouse (2007) adopts a similar definition: "Leadership is a process whereby an individual influences a group of individuals to achieve a common goal" (p. 3). To lead, an individual needs to be able to understand the situation, adapt his or her behavior to meet its requirements, and secure acceptance from followers (Hersey, Blanchard, & Johnson, 1996). An effective leader satisfies individual and organizational goals, improves group performance, and achieves a range of other outcomes (Yukl, 1994).

Even though leadership and management both involve interpersonal relationships between members of a group, most writers view the two concepts as conceptually distinct (see Bass, 1990a). Kotter (1990a, 1990b) argued that management functions are geared toward a much more limited time frame of up to a few years: budgeting, organizing and scheduling workers, overseeing operations and ensuring compliance, and, most important, producing predictability (Kotter, 1990a). In contrast, leaders provide direction and inspire workers to promote significant long-term changes within the organization. They communicate "the new direction to those who can create coalitions that understand the vision and are committed to its achievement" (Kotter, 1990b, p. 104). Of course, managers often, by necessity, exhibit leadership qualities and vice versa, distinguishing them from the routine manager (Bass, 1990a; Gardner, 2000). For example, the chief of the Lowell, Massachusetts, Police Department committed, upon taking the position in 1994, to make the city the safest of its size in the United States (Willis, Mastrofski, & Weisburd, 2004). Operational decisions (e.g., adoption of Compstat) were needed to turn the leader's vision into a reality.

Theories of Leadership

Studies of leadership have evolved over the past century, each falling into one of four broad theoretical frameworks (Bryman, 1999). Some scholars searched for inherent leadership traits (trait theories), while others sought to identify ideal leader actions (behavioral/style theories). In both cases, the broad approaches were considered universal—the traits or behaviors isolated through research were considered appropriate in all situations. By the 1960s, theory and research shifted to more contingent propositions; proper behaviors were dependent on situational characteristics (Bryman, 1999; Jago, 1982). Finally, a new approach—transformational leadership—emerged in the 1980s, arguing that leaders elevate followers to high performance (Bryman, 1999).

Trait Theory

Until the 1940s, **trait theory** dominated studies of leadership. This theory was characterized by a search for a set of individual traits and characteristics that distinguished leaders from nonleaders and effective leaders from ineffective leaders (Bryman, 1999; Jago, 1982).[2] Stimulated, in part, by the desire to identify the qualities associated with strong historical leaders (e.g., Abraham Lincoln, Napoleon), the theory "treated [leadership] as a second-level trait construct composed of, or highly related to, more fundamental first-level trait constructs that included physical and constitutional factors, skills and abilities, personality characteristics and social characteristics" (Jago, 1982, p. 317; see also Northouse, 2007). The specification of leadership traits typically involved studying leader biographies, surveying individuals about effective leadership qualities, or observing the characteristics of those in leadership positions or recognized by others as leaders (Bass, 1990a). Across hundreds of studies conducted over a seven-decade period, a diverse and lengthy set of significant leadership traits emerged (see Table 10.1). In recent years, attention has turned to the linkages between traits and

---
[2]House and Podsakoff (1994) argue that most trait studies neglected the effective/ineffective leadership comparison.

Table 10.1 Leadership Traits

Physical and Constitutional Factors	Personality Characteristics	Social Characteristics
Activity, energy	Achievement drive, ambition	Cooperativeness
Appearance, grooming	Adaptability	Interpersonal skills, sensitivity
Height	Adjustment, normality	Popularity, prestige
Weight	Aggressiveness	Sociability
	Alertness	Socioeconomic position
Skill and Ability	Anti-authoritarianism	Talkativeness
Administrative ability	Dominance	Tact
Intelligence	Emotional balance, control	
Judgment	Enthusiasm	
Knowledge	Extraversion	
Technical competence	Independence, nonconformity	
Verbal fluency	Initiative	
	Insightfulness	
	Integrity	
	Objectivity	
	Originality	
	Persistence	
	Responsibility	
	Self-confidence	
	Sense of humor	
	Tolerance of stress	

Source: Jago (1982).

perceptions of leadership (Allen & Sawhney, 2010; House & Podsakoff, 1994; Lord, De Vader, & Alliger, 1986). For example, Schafer (2010a) found that police supervisors perceived honesty and integrity, caring for employee needs, strong communication skills, a strong work ethic, and approachability as traits associated with effective police leadership. If these and other traits are accurate indicators of effective leadership (or perceptions of effective leadership), an organization need only select leaders from among those possessing the desirable characteristics. Applicants for leadership roles could complete some type of personality inventory or skills assessment to help executives more systematically select strong candidates (Jago, 1982; Northouse, 2007). Leadership training and development, discussed later, would prove inconsequential. Leaders either possess the traits or they do not; they are born, not made (Bryman, 1999).

While the utility of trait theory might be high, reviews conducted in the 1940s and later questioned its empirical support, "[sounding] the seeming death-knell of a pure traits approach to the study of leadership" (Bass, 1990a, p. 78). Evidence supporting any given trait tended to remain inconclusive (Bryman, 1999). The focus on perceptions of leadership may prove more fruitful (Lord et al., 1986), but this area of research is still open to criticism. The trait approach ignores what leaders actually do to lead. For example, Schafer's (2010a) list of important police leadership traits includes elements (e.g., caring for employee needs) that move beyond personal characteristics toward on-the-job behaviors. Respondents are identifying important behaviors in addition to important traits; behaviors, unlike inherent traits, can be taught to potential leaders. Trait theory also generally disregards the fact that situational determinants matter; a trait that proves useful in one setting might be detrimental in another (Northouse, 2007; Stogdill, 1948).

Behavioral Theories

Upon recognizing the limitations of the trait approach, researchers at Ohio State University commenced a research program in the 1940s examining observable leader behavior (Shartle, 1957). This work, along with similar work conducted at the University of Michigan, ushered in an era of **behavioral or style theories of leadership** that would dominate scholarship for a quarter century (Bryman, 1999). The members of the Ohio State team first generated nearly 1,800 survey questions addressing behaviors consistent with their own conceptualization of leadership (e.g., distributing rewards, changing group activities, emphasizing the work; Hemphill & Coons, 1957). From this initial list, 150 items were chosen to form the Leader Behavior Description Questionnaire (LBDQ); respondents were asked to indicate how often leaders exhibited the behaviors contained within each statement (Bass, 1990a; Hemphill & Coons, 1957).[3] Analyses of responses revealed two primary dimensions of leadership behavior: **initiating structure** and **consideration**.[4] Leaders who initiate structure provide followers with direction on accomplishing the work. As Bass (1990a) explained, "The initiation of structure includes such behavior as insisting on maintaining standards and meeting deadlines and deciding in detail what will be done and how it should be done" (p. 512). The leader's focus is on the task itself. In contrast, a considerate leader directs energies toward followers, paying attention to their needs and "building camaraderie, respect, trust, and liking between leaders and followers" (Northouse, 2007, p. 71). The two dimensions of leader behavior were independent, meaning that an individual could engage in actions consistent with a single style, both, or neither (Jago, 1982). As researchers tried to link these behaviors to effectiveness or performance, they encountered inconsistent findings, with studies at times finding value of one style over the other (Bryman, 1999). Later, a combination of initiating structure and consideration was deemed preferable; the successful leader both provided direction and supported followers (Jago, 1982).

---

[3] The LBDQ would ultimately be reduced to 40 items (Bass, 1990a).

[4] At the University of Michigan, these dimensions were referred to as employee orientation and production orientation (Northouse, 2007).

Subsequent research by Blake and Mouton (1964, 1978) reaffirmed the importance of both types of behaviors. In their *Managerial Grid,* initiating structure and consideration were renamed concern for production and concern for people, respectively. Leader behavior varied along each dimension on a scale ranging from 1 to 9 (higher scores indicating greater concern). They delineated five major leadership styles, depending on where a leader's scores intersected on the grid (Blake & Mouton, 1978). A leader using the *authority–obedience* style (high concern for production, low concern for people) would emphasize task accomplishment above all, wielding power to complete the work with little concern for followers. In contrast, *country club management* (low concern for production, high concern for people) places all attention on the employees to create "a comfortable friendly organization atmosphere and work tempo" (Blake & Mouton, 1978, p. 11). The *impoverished management* style (low concern for both people and production) involves very little actual leadership. In fact, the individual does only what is required to keep his or her job. The *middle-of-the-road* style (moderate concern for people and production) achieves "adequate performance" by accomplishing work and maintaining morale (Northouse, 2007, p. 74). Finally, Blake and Mouton prescribed the *team management* style (high concern for people and production) as the most effective. By demonstrating concern for both dimensions, tasks are accomplished by motivated and satisfied employees. All this research led to a profound change in leadership selection. It was no longer necessary to simply select preordained leaders possessing desirable traits. Instead, training programs, such as the ones developed by Blake and Mouton, could produce effective leaders concerned with both the work and employees.

The two dimensions of leader behavior, regardless of the precise term used to describe them, are widely used in general leader scholarship and found their way into many studies of criminal justice leadership. For example, Kuykendall (1977) described a sample of police leaders using Blake and Mouton's (1978) *Managerial Grid* labels. He administered a survey instrument to upper-level managers in an urban police department to determine their primary and secondary leadership styles. Most (65%) of the 20 supervisors surveyed were classified as employing the *team management* style, while another 30% relied primarily on the *authority–obedience* style. The *impoverished management* style emerged as neither a primary nor backup approach to leadership. In contrast, Roberg and Krichhoff (1985) found that supervisors in a small police organization and a sheriff's department showed little consideration or initiating structure behavior as measured by the Ohio State University–developed LBDQ, a situation analogous to impoverished management (Southerland & Reuss-Ianni, 1992). Engel (2000, 2002) more recently used measures of relationship and task-oriented behavior, along with other dimensions of leadership (e.g., expectations for aggressive enforcement), to produce four descriptive labels for police leaders: traditional (task oriented, expect enforcement), innovative (considerate/relations oriented, expect community policing), supportive (considerate/relations oriented, reward and inspire subordinates), and active (engage in supervisory and street officer behavior). She moved beyond simple description by examining the effects of leadership style on follower behavior in the field. Interestingly, she found that leadership style did not affect subordinate arrest decisions in traffic and nontraffic cases (Engel, 2000). However, officers with active supervisors were more likely to use force in nontraffic situations, perhaps due to the fact that "these supervisors create an atmosphere where aggressive tactics by their subordinates are tolerated (and perhaps expected)" (p. 283).

Others have applied behavioral dimensions to courtroom leadership. For example, appellate court judges, as they interact with their colleagues, may adopt leadership behaviors described as either task and/or social oriented (e.g., Haynie, 1992; Ostberg, Wetstein, & Ducat, 2004). Justices adopting a task style are described as able to get others to acquiesce to their views, even if conflict results (Ostberg et al., 2004). Social leadership approaches are designed to minimize conflict and encourage collaborative efforts to accomplish job tasks. According to this line of inquiry, a leader with a strong task orientation may be able to produce consensus when rendering legal decisions. Excessive task-oriented leadership, however, can have important repercussions. An autocratic leader, one who retains all decision-making power and directs others, "stifles initiative, reduces responsibility, and leads to feelings of [follower] anonymity, powerlessness, and alienation" (Wright, 1994, p. 11; see also Tannenbaum & Schmidt, 1973). Kevin Wright (1994), in *Effective Prison Leadership,* advocates sharing decision-making authority as a way of building organizational commitment.

Regardless of the labels used to describe the central elements of behavioral theories of leadership (e.g., initiative structure, concern for production, task-oriented behavior), the underlying concepts are still widely used in contemporary leadership theories (see below). In spite of this legacy, behavioral theories fell out of favor by the late 1960s for failing to consider the leader's situation. Although the best behavior might be both initiating structure and consideration, that combination might not be appropriate in all situations (Northouse, 2007). Should a first responder be concerned about employee needs and morale during an emergency situation or should he or she be concentrating on managing the critical events? By the 1960s, scholars were paying more attention to these situational concerns, or contingencies.

Contingency Theories

Contingency theorists avoid the universalistic position evident in earlier theories (Jago, 1982). There is no single best way to lead. Simply stated, the most effective leadership style depends. What it depends on has been the subject of considerable debate, leading to multiple theories, each describing its own determinants or contingencies. Three widely studied contingency theories—Fiedler's contingency theory, situational leadership theory, and path–goal theory—are described below.[5]

Fiedler's Contingency Theory

In a 1965 article, scholar Fred Fiedler challenged commonplace assumptions that effective leadership was simply a matter of recruiting, selecting, and training individuals for the job. Fiedler, along with others, worked to identify the key situational factors that shaped leadership effectiveness (Hersey et al., 1996). While trait and behavioral theorists viewed the key to leadership success as selecting leaders displaying certain characteristics or training leaders to behave in desirable ways, Fiedler argued that the most effective style of leadership was *contingent* on characteristics of the situation. Fiedler's contingency theory of leadership included two different leadership styles—task-oriented leadership and relationship-oriented leadership (Fiedler, 1965). Although these labels were largely consistent with initiating structure and considerate behavior, Fiedler's leadership styles fell along a single dimension (Jago, 1982).

Fiedler's early work led to the development of a series of survey items that together produced a least preferred coworker score, purportedly measuring an individual's leadership style. Survey respondents are asked to think about a past or present coworker "with whom [they] can work least well... [and] had the most difficulty in getting a job done" (Fiedler, 1967, p. 41). They were then

---

[5]Other contingency theories exist but were omitted due to the limited number of studies applying their propositions to criminal justice leadership.

Figure 10.1 Example Questions From the Least Preferred Coworker Measure

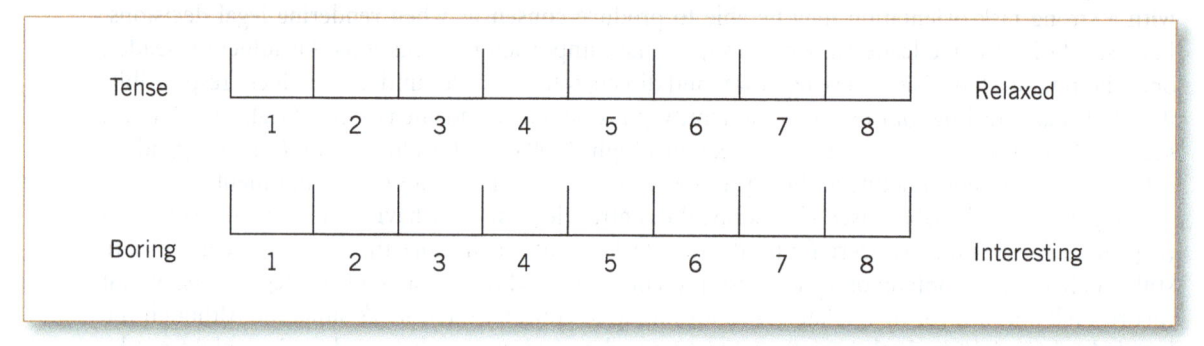

| Tense | 1 2 3 4 5 6 7 8 | Relaxed |
| Boring | 1 2 3 4 5 6 7 8 | Interesting |

Source: Fiedler (1967, p. 41).

presented with a series of 16 favorable–unfavorable labels presented at the extremes of an 8-point scale and asked to describe their least preferred coworker (two examples are shown in Figure 10.1).

Scores for each of the 16 items are summed into a least preferred coworker (LPC) score. Individuals who describe their least preferred coworker more favorably (high LPC scores) exhibit behaviors consistent with the relationship-oriented style: "permissive, human relations-oriented, and considerate of the feelings of his men" (Fiedler, 1965, p. 116). Leaders who describe their coworker in less flattering terms (low LPC scores) are more task oriented in their leadership style. Considerable research has been undertaken examining the LPC score. Does it really measure leadership style? Jago (1982), summarizing the underlying assumptions of the LPC measure, wrote:

> Interpreting your LPC score hinges on the assumption that your descriptions of your co-worker says more about *you* than about the person you have described. In essence, it is assumed that everyone's least preferred co-worker is about equally "unpleasant" and that differences in descriptions of these co-workers actually reflect differences in an underlying personality trait among the people doing the describing. (p. 322)

In spite of alternative interpretations of the LPC score, studies have supported the validity of the measure in distinguishing between task and relationship styles of leadership (Bass, 1990a; Rice, 1978).

Fiedler (1965, 1967) spent nearly a decade studying the relationship between leadership style and performance within a variety of groups, including sports teams, military bomber crews, survey teams, and others. Across the various groups, the different leadership styles had diverse effects on performance levels. In some situations, task-oriented leadership was most effective, while in others relationship-oriented behavior proved desirable. In other words, the situation mattered. Fiedler indicated that the effectiveness of a particular leadership style was contingent on three factors. First and foremost among the factors were the personal relationships between leaders and followers (Bass, 1990a; Fiedler, 1967). Was the leader trusted, accepted, and liked (Fiedler, 1965, 1967)? Second, the task's structure was an important consideration. Northouse (2007) defined a task as structured when

(a) the requirements of the task are clearly stated and known by the people required to perform them, (b) the path to accomplishing the task has few alternatives, (c) completion of the task can be clearly demonstrated, and (d) only a limited number of correct solutions to the task exist. (p. 114)

Finally, the leader's position power was relevant but, among the three contingencies, of least importance. Position power allows a leader to accomplish tasks because he or she has legitimate authority (rank) over followers and the ability to reward and punish (Fiedler, 1967; see Section XI).

These contingencies combine to describe the favorability of any situation leaders may encounter (Bass, 1990a). When leader–member relations are good, when the task is clear and structured, and when position power is available, situational favorability is high. When relations are poor, the task ambiguous, and power lacking, situational favorability is low. Fiedler made sense of the mixed style–performance research by introducing these contingencies into the analysis. What he found was that task-oriented behavior was most effective when situational favorability was either extremely favorable or extremely unfavorable (see Figure 10.2). As Fiedler (1965) indicated, "Where the situation is very favorable, the group expects and wants the leader to give directions" (p. 119). Likewise, when the leader confronts a poor situation, directive, task-oriented behavior is warranted to accomplish the work. Relationship-oriented behavior is reserved for situations of intermediate favorability where conditions are mixed. A leader confronted with poor leader–member relationships, for example, should adopt a relationship-oriented style. It is worth pointing out that the effects of these contingencies on the leader style–performance relationship, at the time, lacked any type of theoretical explanation (Jago, 1982), but Chemers (1997) has since offered a possible explanation for the observed relationships. Favorable situations allow a leader to simply establish goals for followers and work to ensure that those goals are met. When favorability is low, the task style "can provide at least a minimal amount of organization to the situation to get the group moving along" (p. 38). In intermediate situations, a relationship orientation

Figure 10.2 Relationship Between Contingencies and Leadership Style as Indicated by LPC Score

Leader–Member Relations	Good				Poor			
Task Structure	High structure		Low structure		High structure		Low structure	
Position Power	Strong power	Weak power	Strong power	Weak power	Strong power	Weak power	Strong power	Weak power
	1	2	3	4	5	6	7	8
Preferred Leadership Style	Low LPCs/middle LPCs				High LPCs			Low LPCs

Source: Northouse (2007).

can help the group clarify the task together or build morale, depending on the circumstances. Thus, rather than focus solely on training leaders and placing them in situations that fit their leadership styles, the situation can be manipulated to match the leader's style by altering the amount of leader power, clarifying job tasks, and improving group relations (Fiedler, 1965).

Wrightsman (1999), in one of the few attempts to apply Fiedler's theory in a criminal justice setting, examined leadership among the nine justices of the U.S. Supreme Court. He first addressed the theory's three contingencies. He regarded the position power of the chief justice (the formally designated leader) as rather limited. Justices are granted lifetime appointments, and the chief justice cannot remove any individual justice for wrongdoing. In legal decision making—either deciding to hear a case or handing down a legal opinion—the chief justice's vote is weighted the same as other members' votes. Wrightsman acknowledged, "About the only discernable example of the leader's position power is the chief justice's prerogative in assigning authorship of opinions when he is in the majority" (p. 98). Task structure, by contrast, is more favorable to the leader. The only real question in the work of the court is knowing whether its decision is the correct one or not. Given these two characteristics of the court, leader–member relations are the determining factor in whether the overall situational favorability is high or intermediate according to Fiedler's theory. Some chief justices (e.g., Earl Warren) are highly regarded by colleagues, while others lack such esteem. For example, Warren Burger was considered by some justices to be "an intellectual lightweight" (p. 96). According to Fiedler's theory, chief justices faced with strong relationships and clear tasks should, even in the absence of position power, assume a task-oriented, low-LPC leadership style (LPC score of 2 in Figure 10.2). Where relations are poor, a high-LPC, relationship-oriented approach is warranted. Chief Justice Morrison Waite (1874–1888) serves as an exemplar of a justice entering the court lacking strong relationships (Wrightsman, 1999). He assumed the chief justice position as President Grant's seventh choice for the position; also, several justices on the court had sought the position only to be passed over for Waite, an individual perceived as less qualified. Clearly, the relationship between Waite and the other justices was less than favorable. To overcome these challenges, Waite "worked hard, he assigned opinions fairly and sensibly, and he wrote more than his share of opinions" (p. 101). In other words, he used relationship behavior in leading the court. Chief Justice Burger (1969–1986), in contrast, used task-oriented behavior even though he lacked strong relationships with the court's members.

Critics allege that many studies of Fiedler's theory are incapable of establishing the time ordering of relevant concepts (Bass, 1990a). For example, the theory suggests that the contingencies indicate appropriate leadership styles and that, if there is congruence, performance should be positively influenced. The problem, of course, is that factors such as leader–member relations may follow, rather than cause, leadership behavior. Wrightsman (1999) noted that Burger was not well regarded by other members of the court. It is possible that the poor relations were due to his leadership style; "he took over the judicial conference room as his own office, he changed the structure of the courtroom table from rectangular to boomerang-shaped, and he even tried to standardize the justices' chairs" (p. 102). His behavior may have explained relations, rather than the reverse. Similarly, poor group performance might lead to low LPC scores rather than leadership style affecting performance (Bass, 1990a). Notwithstanding these criticisms, Fiedler's legacy cannot be ignored. He introduced situational determinants to the study of leadership and paved the way for alternative contingency theories (Jago, 1982).

Situational Leadership Theory

Hersey and Blanchard (1969, 1974), like Fiedler, believed that the most effective style of leadership was dependent on certain factors, but they disagreed about the precise contingencies. They developed and refined *situational leadership theory*, originally known as life cycle theory, to introduce the key contingency of follower maturity. That is, the best style of leadership was linked to the readiness and willingness of followers to handle the task at hand. For Hersey and Blanchard, leadership behavior included the now familiar dimensions of task and relationship orientations (consistent with initiating structure and consideration):

> Task behavior is defined as the extent to which the leader engages in spelling out the duties and responsibilities of an individual or group. Those behaviors include telling people what to do, how to do it, when to do it, and who is to do it. . . . Relationship behavior is defined as the extent to which the leader engages in two-way or multiway communication. The behaviors include listening, facilitating, and supportive behaviors. (Hersey et al., 1996, p. 191)

In practice, leaders could exhibit any combination of task and relationship behavior, and recurring patterns were considered a leader's style, descriptively labeled as either *telling, selling, participating,* or *delegating* (see Table 10.2). The telling style (high task, low relationship behavior) is characterized by directive behavior, one-way communication, oversight, and positive and negative reinforcement in the form of rewards and punishments (Hersey et al., 1996; Northouse, 2007). The selling style (high task, high relationship behavior) introduces two-way communication and persuasion. Northouse (2007) indicates that "the leader [makes] the final decision on the what and how of goal accomplishment" but "[involves] himself or herself with subordinates by giving encouragement and soliciting subordinate input" (p. 93). When the participating style is used (low task, high relationship behavior), decision making is a "shared responsibility" of both the leader and follower (Hersey et al., 1996, p. 2004). In other words, followers may be granted authority to make a variety of decisions, although the leader is available for guidance, support, and input where needed. Finally, the delegating style (low task, low relationship behavior) involves granting considerable freedom to followers to perform the work as they see fit

Table 10.2 Connections Between Leader Behavior and Follower Maturity in Situational Leadership Theory

Subordinate's Level of Maturity	Leader's Behavior Should Be Oriented Toward — Relations	Leader's Behavior Should Be Oriented Toward — Task	Prescribed Leadership Behavior
1. Unable–unwilling	Low	High	Telling
2. Unable–willing	High	High	Selling
3. Able–unwilling	High	Low	Participating
4. Able–willing	Low	Low	Delegating

Source: Bass (1990a).

(Northouse, 2007). Delegation should not be confused with the impoverished management style noted earlier as part of the *Managerial Grid*. While there are circumstances where delegation may prove disastrous, as we will see, delegation can be an effective leadership style.

According to the theory, an individual's dominant leadership style could be determined through the use of the Leadership Adaptability and Style Inventory (LASI; Hersey & Blanchard, 1974), an instrument that would later be renamed the Leader Effectiveness and Adaptability Description (LEAD; Hersey et al., 1996).[6] The survey included 12 brief scenarios, each accompanied by choices for possible courses of action indicative of the four leadership styles. For example, the first situation in the 1974 LASI (Hersey & Blanchard, 1974, p. 23) read:

> Your subordinates are not responding lately to your friendly conversation and obvious concern for their welfare. Their performance is in a tailspin.
>
> A. Emphasize the use of uniform procedures and the necessity for task accomplishment.
>
> B. Make yourself available for discussion but don't push.
>
> C. Task for subordinates and then set goals.
>
> D. Intentionally do not intervene.

Responses to the brief scenario include options consistent with the telling (A), selling (C), participating (B), and delegating (D) styles. For the purposes of identifying dominant leadership styles, there are no "correct" answers. A dominant style emerges if respondents routinely resort to the same style when choosing courses of action.

Hersey and Blanchard were not solely interested in identifying leadership styles, something that had been accomplished in prior research. They argued that "the more leaders can adapt their behaviors to the situation, the more effective their attempts to influence will be" (Hersey et al., 1996, p. 192). They acknowledged the importance of a wide range of contingencies but strongly believed that the characteristics of the follower were critical. The key contingency is follower **readiness** (previously termed *maturity*), both job readiness and psychological readiness (Bass, 1990a; Hersey & Blanchard, 1974; Hersey et al., 1996). Job readiness refers to an individual's ability to perform a task, including his or her experience, background, training, and education, while psychological readiness addresses follower motivation and willingness to perform a task (Bass, 1990a). As workers develop, their overall readiness level presumably increases; though, as will be discussed below, there is nothing to preclude reversion to lower levels of readiness. Situational leadership theory matches leadership styles to follower readiness levels (see Table 10.2; Bass, 1990a; Hersey et al., 1996). When followers know little about a task and are unwilling to perform either due to lack of motivation or confidence, a leader should adopt a telling style to provide necessary direction and reinforcement. As confidence and willingness increase, the leader can establish two-way communications through a selling style. Nevertheless, he or she will need to continue with high task behavior given the followers' low task readiness. When followers know how to perform a task but lack confidence or seem unwilling, the leader can participate, providing supportive

---

[6] Students can determine their own leadership style using the original LASI survey. The scenarios and scoring procedures are available in Hersey and Blanchard's 1974 article.

mechanisms to boost confidence. Finally, if followers are both able and willing, leaders can delegate authority and largely step aside. The LASI and LEAD instruments, in addition to identifying dominant leadership styles, indicate the ability of respondents to adapt styles to the followers' readiness level. In the LASI scenario provided earlier, the followers appear unable (performance in decline) and unwilling (not responding to suggestions) to correct the situation. As a leader, a directive telling approach would be most appropriate until readiness improves. The worst option would be delegation (choice D) as this would only allow the problem to continue unabated.

Kuykendall and Unsinger (1982) administered the LEAD instrument to 155 police managers in managerial training programs in both Arizona and California between 1978 and 1980. About half (51%) of leaders exhibited selling as their dominant style, and another 45% had no single dominant style; even in these no-dominant-style situations, selling was used frequently, along with either participating or telling. Interestingly, the delegating style was rarely chosen in response to any of the 12 scenarios, due in part to its reputation as a "risky style" (p. 318). Moreover, the authors argued that accountability concerns may compel leaders to retain some degree of input into follower decisions through the use of one of the nondelegating styles. Six years later, Kuykendall, along with Roy Roberg (1988), focused on the follower typology inherent in situational leadership theory. In addition to job and psychological readiness, Kuykendall and Roberg added work-related attitudes as an important contingency. Using labels such as rookie, star, and retiree (see Table 10.3) to describe employee behavior, they specified effective leadership behavior. For example, rookies, new to the organization and eager to perform, are psychologically ready but lack the necessary skills to be considered job ready. As such,

Table 10.3 Police Employee Characteristics and Leadership Style

	Employee Characteristics				
Employee Type	Motivation	Positive Work-Related Attitudes	Competency	Maturity	Managerial Style[1]
Rookie	High	High	Low	Low	Telling, selling
Worker	Moderate-high	High	Moderate-high	Moderate	Participating, selling
Star	High	Moderate-high	High	High	Delegating, none
Cynic	Low-high	Low-high	Moderate-high	Low-high	Selling, telling, participating
Retiree	Low	Low-moderate	Moderate-high	Low	Telling, selling
Depleted	Low	Low	Low	Low	Referral for professional assistance

Source: Kuykendall and Roberg (1988).

[1] The first style listed is considered the most appropriate style. The remaining are considered secondary.

a telling or selling style is appropriate until technical knowledge is developed. Kuykendall and Roberg also showed that follower development does not occur in a linear fashion with age or experience. Retirees, older workers nearing their exit from the organization, suffer from declining motivation, indicating that readiness levels both progress and regress over time.

Situational leadership theory has intuitive appeal. Through workshops and online tools, it is widely deployed within the business community and used for teaching effective leadership (Northouse, 2007). In spite of its popularity, it is not immune to critique. For example, Northouse argued that the "approach underscores that subordinates have unique needs and deserve our help in trying to become better at doing their work" (p. 97). However, this flexibility opens the door for follower accusations of leadership inconsistency and inflexibility (Bass, 1990a). Fairness and consistency are essential elements of organizational justice (see Section VIII), and employee motivation may suffer if leaders routinely treat followers differently (e.g., directing/telling vs. delegating). The theory has also been criticized for its definition of readiness, including the continuum from least to most ready (Northouse, 2007). Is a correctional officer who is strongly motivated to perform but lacks the appropriate skill set (unable–willing in Table 10.2) less motivated than an officer who is able but lacks motivation (able–unwilling)? Graeff (1983) asserts that, according to the theory, "a motivated person without ability is less mature than an unmotivated person with ability" (p. 287). In reality, this may be an inaccurate assumption, as motivation may be enough to allow a person to obtain the needed technical skills; moreover, helping others overcome a lack of technical skills may be less challenging than resolving motivational problems. Other criticisms are directed at the validity and reliability of the LASI and LEAD instruments, potentially shedding light on the finding by Kuykendall and Unsinger (1982) that police leaders rarely delegate. The LASI and LEAD instruments use descriptions such as "intentionally do not intervene" and "take no definite action" (see Hersey & Blanchard, 1974) to express the delegation option. These choices "reflect extreme delegation if not abdication of the leadership role, or no leadership at all, instead of an adequate description of the low task–low relationship behaviors" (Graeff, 1983, p. 288). Police leaders may have shied away from delegation, even with capable followers, because the response options described a lack of leadership. The descriptions would be more appropriate if they described a minimal rather than nonexistent leadership role (Graeff, 1983). Nevertheless, in spite of these criticisms, situational leadership theory is valuable for its "recognition of the subordinate as the most important situational determinant of appropriate leader behavior . . . a perspective that seems justified and highly appropriate if leadership is defined conceptually as usually is the case" (p. 290).

Path–Goal Theory

Shortly after situational leadership theory emerged in 1969, a third contingency theory of leadership, **path–goal theory**, was formally explicated by House in a 1971 article. The theory draws heavily on the expectancy theory of motivation (see Section VIII); workers consider both the importance of intrinsic and extrinsic rewards and the probabilities of goal attainment when making decisions about how to behave in the workplace. The leader's role then becomes "increasing personal pay-offs to subordinates for work-goal attainment, and making the path to these pay-offs easier to travel by clarifying it, reducing road blocks and pitfalls, and increasing the opportunities for personal satisfaction en route" (p. 324). In other words, the leader must help satisfy the motivational needs of followers (Northouse, 2007). This is generally accomplished by adopting one of four leadership styles (House, 1996). *Directive* behavior is analogous to initiating structure or telling where the leader establishes expectations, and clarifies follower behaviors (Northouse, 2007). *Supportive* behavior involves satisfying followers by "displaying concern for subordinates' welfare and creating a friendly and psychologically supportive work environment" (House, 1996, p. 326). Shared decision making and open channels of communication characterize *participative* behavior. Finally, leaders engage in *achievement-oriented* behavior when they challenge followers to accomplish significant goals (Northouse, 2007). As a contingency theory, House (1971, 1996) argued that leaders should engage in leadership behavior most appropriate to the task (e.g., routine/clear vs. nonroutine/ambiguous) and the characteristics of followers themselves (e.g., skills, desire for control) (see also Northouse, 2007; Tosi, Rizzo, & Carroll, 1986). Path–goal theory is complex, comprising a large number of propositions (26 in House's 1996 formulation) that link leadership style, contingencies, and outcomes of performance and job satisfaction. For example, when the task being performed is nonroutine or ambiguous, directive behavior provides the clarity necessary to facilitate employee goal accomplishment (House, 1971). If employees are responsible for stressful or dangerous work, as they are in many criminal justice settings (see Section IX), then a supportive approach is more appropriate. Yukl (1994) also notes that supportive behavior can be used to reduce the boredom of menial work. Participative leadership is useful when followers desire autonomy; subordinates are offered an opportunity to contribute to decision making that will affect their work (Northouse, 2007). In situations where followers view their work as unchallenging, an achievement-oriented style could be employed, where high goals are established and challenge restored (Hersey et al., 1996).

Studies of path–goal theory, both within and outside of the criminal justice literature, have typically been narrow in scope. Most have examined directive and supportive leadership behaviors to the neglect of other styles and task structure rather than subordinate characteristics as the primary contingency (Evans, 1996).[7] In spite of the appeal of its motivational components, path–goal theory has seldom been tested within criminal justice organizations. In a sample of 800 police employees in a Midwestern agency, Jermier and Berkes (1979) found support for several key propositions of path–goal theory. For example, employees desired role clarification from a leader when they viewed their tasks as unpredictable. When tasks were considered routine, a more supportive leadership style was preferred. A directive leader becomes unnecessary under these conditions. Subsequent research questioned the importance of role clarification in shaping officer outcomes (e.g., satisfaction; Brief, Aldag, Russell, & Rude, 1981).

Research in the general organizational theory literature has also produced mixed results, perhaps due to the difficulties in testing the complex theory (Bass, 1990a; Robbins & Judge, 2008; Tosi et al., 1986). The theory has also been subject to modification over the course of its four-decade existence (House, 1996). These two factors led scholars to focus on certain parts of the theory without testing the overall framework. The specific propositions aside, the theory does illustrate that leaders can alter employee calculations that are part of expectancy theory by establishing and clarifying workplace goals (Tosi et al., 1986).

Transformational Leadership

By the 1980s, a new leadership approach—transformational leadership—became firmly entrenched within the general organizational theory and, over the decades to follow, appeared within criminal

---

[7]Directive and supportive leadership were the only two styles in House's (1971) original version of the theory (Yukl, 1994).

justice scholarship. James MacGregor Burns is largely credited with establishing the roots of transformational leadership theory in his 1978 volume on political leadership. He depicted leadership as falling along a single continuum ranging from transactional to transformational leadership (Judge & Piccolo, 2004). The first, referred to as **transactional leadership**, occurs through a process of exchange, or a transaction (for more on exchange relationships, see Section XI). This is most evident in the exchange inherent when politicians trade campaign promises for citizen votes but may include exchanges for less tangible rewards such as trust and respect (Kuhnert & Lewis, 1987). Within an organization, a manager would provide followers with expectations, directions, and the rewards that would result from goal achievement. These exchanges satisfy the immediate self-interests of the parties involved and may prove effective in some situations, but, as Burns (1978) warned, "the bargainers have no enduring purpose that holds them together. . . . A leadership act took place, but it was not one that binds leader and follower together in a mutual and continuing pursuit of a higher purpose" (p. 20). In contrast, **transformational leadership** inspires followers to move beyond immediate self-interests to think about broader issues such as "achievement, self-actualization, and the well-being of others, the organization, and society" (Bass, 1999, p. 11). Leaders accomplish this by creating a singular purpose for the leader, follower, and organization as a whole (Bass & Riggio, 2006). If leaders are successful, the organization might see substantial improvements in performance, sharp shifts in follower attitudes and values, and the introduction of innovative ideas (Bass, 1985b).

Since the publication of Burns's work, scholars have elaborated on and further refined transformational leadership theory. Two of the more significant advances are in the areas of conceptualization and measurement. Both transactional and transformational leadership are now viewed as multidimensional concepts; each dimension is indicative of behavioral styles (or personality traits; see discussion of criticisms below) consistent with the types of leaders. Transactional leadership includes *contingent reward* and *management by exception* (active and passive) behaviors. The former is a type of positive reinforcement. Leaders work to recognize and acknowledge follower achievements to promote goal accomplishment (Bass, 1990a, 1990b). King (2008) illustrated transactional behavior among judges working in drug and other problem-solving courts. Judges reward offenders who abstain from drug use with additional privileges and less onerous monitoring requirements. The leader (judge) secures desirable behavior from followers (offenders) through the exchange process. Leaders use management-by-exception behaviors when they point out and correct rule violations and other deviations from desirable behavior. Some leaders regularly monitor for deviations (active management by exception), while others step in only when something goes awry (passive management by exception). Conditions might prevent a parole officer, for example, from actively monitoring a client, but the officer will step in to address wrongdoing if he becomes aware of violations.

Transformational leadership is made up of four dimensions: charisma/idealized influence, inspirational leadership, individualized consideration, and intellectual stimulation (Bass, 1985a). An individual exhibits *charisma or idealized influence* when he or she generates enthusiasm and loyalty and engenders follower trust (Bass, 1990b; Northouse, 2007). Charismatic leaders are "emotionally arousing, animating, enlivening, and even exalting to followers and their efforts," serving as models for followers to emulate (Bass, 1985a, p. 62; Bass & Riggio, 2006). *Inspirational motivation* involves establishing high expectations and follower belief in the goals of the group and organization (Bass, 1985a, 1990b; Bass & Riggio, 2006). *Individualized consideration* behavior recognizes the importance of treating followers as unique and deserving of individual attention (Bass, 1985, 1990a). Leaders become aware of follower needs, offer support, and work to fulfill those needs; they serve as coaches and mentors (Bass & Riggio; 2006). Finally, transformational leaders provide *intellectual stimulation*. To promote change, the leader promotes creative and innovative thinking among followers and works to solve the problems associated with organizational change (Bass, 1985b). Bass and Riggio (2006) wrote, "Transformational leaders stimulate their followers' efforts to be innovative and creative by questioning assumptions, reframing problems, and approaching old situations in new ways" (p. 7). King (2008) suggests that judges in problem-solving courts ideally exhibit the characteristics of a transformational leader. They model desirable qualities (e.g., fairness, consistency, compassion) that are intended to produce respect for the court process and the officer (charisma/idealized influence). Judges encourage commitment to the goals of the court—desistance from drug use in the case of drug courts—by allowing offenders to participate in the establishment of individual goals (inspirational motivation). Due to the frequency in which they encounter offenders in problem-solving court, judges are in a position to develop greater knowledge of and relationships with those who come before them. This should enable them to tailor problem-solving approaches to meet offender needs (individualized consideration). Offenders may also be asked to formulate strategies to accomplish goals and to think about strategies to prevent deviation from program plans (intellectual stimulation).

Unlike Burns (1978), who saw transactional and transformational leadership as a single continuum, others now suggest that the most effective leaders demonstrate both approaches (Bass & Riggio, 2006; Judge & Piccolo, 2004). The most ineffective leaders are those who adopt neither transactional nor transformational approaches. This nonleadership style has been termed *laissez-faire leadership* (Judge & Piccolo, 2004). Given the knowledge of transformational leadership that has accrued since 1978, it is no surprise that the theory found its way into the criminal justice literature (e.g., Deluga & Souza, 1991; Murphy, 2008; Murphy & Drodge, 2004; Won-Jae, Koenigsberg, Davidson, & Beto, 2010). Densten (1999) compared the survey results from more than 400 senior (sergeant or above) officers in an Australian police force with norms established in business and industry. He found that officers were significantly less likely to use any of the four transformational and contingent reward behaviors than were respondents in other industries but were more likely to use management by exception or lead using a laissez-faire approach. As Densten explained, the officers were "after-the-fact supervisors," taking action only when something went wrong (p. 49). Punishment of wrongdoing was more important than rewarding successes or inspiring followers. The lack of transformational behaviors is troubling given that, within the policing literature and elsewhere, evidence points to their preference among leaders and their benefits either alone or in combination with various transactional behaviors (Andreescu & Vito, 2010; Campbell & Kodz, 2011; Trottier, Van Wart, & Wang, 2008). For example, within a sample of officers in an Israeli police department, transformational leadership behavior contributed to greater follower compliance regardless of the level of transactional leadership (Schwarzwald, Koslowsky, & Agassi, 2001). Furthermore, survey results from 126 police leaders from 23 states indicated a leader preference for the transformational style over both transactional and laissez faire (Andreescu & Vito, 2010). Evidence also suggests that female police leaders are more likely to use and to prefer transformational leadership styles than are male leaders (Andreescu & Vito, 2010; Silvestri, 2007). Less is known about transformational leadership in corrections. Taxman, Cropsey, Melnick, and Perdoni (2008) examined service provision to offenders with co-occurring disorders (e.g., mental health problems). Even though community corrections organizations and jails are considered innovative or cutting edge if they offer such services, organizational leadership played no significant role in determining whether services were provided. Leaders might prefer but be precluded from enacting a transformational style due to larger demands posed by the criminal justice system's environment.

Leaders work to ensure compliance with rules, accreditation guidelines, and court orders before significant change can occur. DiIulio (1990) summarizes this dilemma by stating, "Sometimes [a leader] is forced to choose between being held in contempt of court and being held in contempt by his or her subordinates" (p. 60).

Transformational leadership theory has been criticized for its lack of clarity (Northouse, 2007). Just as Jacobs and Olitsky (2004) catalogue a lengthy list of qualities and traits of effective correctional system leaders, transformational leaders are also expected to embody an array of qualities and behave in diverse ways. Is it realistic to expect leaders to be responsible for all tasks, including "creating a vision, motivating, being a change agent, building trust, giving nurturance, and acting as a social architect, to name a few" (Northouse, 2007, p. 192)? In some respects, the characteristics of transformational leadership move theory back to elements of earlier perspectives. For example, charisma/idealized influence is largely a trait characteristic (Northouse, 2007). Scholars (e.g., Trottier et al., 2008) have used measures indicating honesty, integrity, and fairness to capture the concept. Is the research measuring a trait or a behavior? If a trait, then leadership theory has returned to the point where leadership cannot be taught. Putting aside these criticisms, transformational leadership theory has become one of the dominant themes in present-day leadership theory.

Leadership Development

Preparing the next wave of leaders is an acute problem in criminal justice circles where executive tenure is typically short. Gilmore and McCann (1982) found, for example, that leadership in state departments of corrections changed, on average, every two to three years during the second half of the 1970s. Ten states experienced three or more leadership changes between 1974 and 1980. Police chiefs, operating without any type of contract, generally serve about three to five years, depending on the size of the city (Rainguet & Dodge, 2001). Each of the leaders enters the organization with his or her own initiatives and seeking to establish "a predictable work climate and tone for the department, particularly about behaviors that are rewarded or expected" (Gilmore & McCann, 1982, p. 256). To the extent that turnover makes this a relatively recurring process, leadership development becomes essential, especially when the current state of training and mentoring is viewed as inadequate by some (Hogan, Bennell, & Taylor, 2011).

Identifying and selecting leaders should be based, in large measure, on individual performance (Howard, 2007). Of course, predicting how a person is likely to perform in a leadership position is different from describing how he or she performs in the present position. Schafer (2010b), describing the well-known "Peter principle," stated, "The limits of a supervisor's skills and abilities were only discovered once that supervisor had been placed in a position that exceeded their capacities, at which time it was often too late to correct the matter" (pp. 738–739). McCall and Hollenback (2007) argue that it is important to gauge the qualities associated with performance by moving beyond a simple list of desirable qualities (traits) to a concrete listing of relevant experiences. According to the authors,

> Certain kinds of assignments (start-ups, turnarounds, increases in scope and scale, various projects, and the like), exposure to exceptional people (usually superiors, both good and bad), overcoming hardships and difficult times, and even some training and educational programs, are what drive development.... On the job experience, supplemented by strategic interventions, is where the greatest leverage is. (p. 93)

Federal Bureau of Prisons officials, for example, make conscious decisions to transfer individuals across the federal prison system as they move up the organization's hierarchy, preventing them from learning the ways of a single facility (Boin, 2001).

Leadership development programs can support those formally selected to occupy supervisory positions and others within the organization. Day (2001) defined leadership development as "expanding the collective capacity of organizational members to engage effectively in leadership roles and processes" (p. 582). Providing intraorganizational mentoring, coaching, opportunities to expand skills, and feedback is essential to the development process. For example, the Minnesota Department of Corrections offers an Advanced Leadership Development Program, involving a 200-hour commitment (Cornelius & Dively, 2008). Among other tasks, participants attend workshops, receive mentoring from senior department management, discuss key books and articles, and work on departmental problem-solving projects. One exercise involved a mock legislative hearing. Through the program, participants acquire skills and experiences useful for their jobs within correctional facilities. Similar programs could be developed in-house or in conjunction with colleges and universities to address leadership in other system components.

This section presented the many perspectives on and evolution of leadership theory over the past century. Criminal justice scholars have applied many of these frameworks in studying leadership within police, court, and correctional organizations. Although the behavior of an individual leader does not change rapidly, the frequent turnover of criminal justice executives confirms the importance of selecting leaders who can maximize organizational performance and capably manage the image of the organization (Hersey et al., 1996; Mastrofski, 2001).

KEY TERMS

behavioral or style theories of leadership

consideration

Fiedler's contingency theory of leadership

initiating structure

least preferred coworker score

path–goal theory

readiness

situational leadership theory

trait theory

transactional leadership

transformational leadership

DISCUSSION QUESTIONS

1. Most studies of leadership in criminal justice are descriptive in nature, describing the styles or traits of organizational leaders within system agencies. Fewer actually study the effects of this behavior on follower behavior (see Engel, 2000, for an exception). In your opinion, does leadership matter within the criminal justice system? In other words, does the organization have more to do with the leader's behavior, follower's behavior and motivation, or a combination of both? Explain.

2. Transformational leadership theory is commonly discussed in the organizational theory and criminal justice literatures. In your opinion, are the elements of transformational theory (e.g., inspirational motivation, charisma/idealized influence) teachable, or are they inherent personality traits?

3. Many studies point to the importance of what has been referred to as consideration, relationship-oriented behaviors, or concern for people. Are police chiefs or correctional wardens hired from within more or less likely to exhibit these behaviors than one hired from outside the organization? Alternatively, are there likely to be no differences? Explain.

WEB RESOURCES

FBI National Academy:
http://www.fbi.gov/about-us/training/national-academy

National Institute of Corrections:
http://nicic.gov

National Parole Resource Center:
http://nationalparoleresourcecenter.org/

READING

Reading 20

The vast majority of literature addressing organizational leadership, including the content of this section, focuses on the behaviors of effective leaders. Joseph A. Schafer's study takes an alternative approach, identifying characteristics associated with ineffective leadership in policing. The characteristics were identified by surveying 304 police managers participating in the FBI's National Academy program. Most respondents had observed instances of ineffective leadership within their respective agencies, even if only sporadically. Schafer ultimately grouped the traits identified into two broad categories: acts of commission (actions by the leader viewed as ineffective) and acts of omission (actions the leader should have taken but did not). In the former category, respondents reported leadership behaviors such as self-interest, arrogance, failure to consider the views of others (closed-mindedness), micromanagement, and arbitrary decision making (capricious behavior). In the latter category were poor work ethic, failing to act, ineffective communication, poor communication skills, and lack of integrity. Some of these challenges can be overcome (e.g., ineffective communication) by restructuring the organization or removing barriers, while others are more deeply fixed personality traits that are difficult to resolve (e.g., lack of integrity).

THE INEFFECTIVE POLICE LEADER

Acts of Commission and Omission

Joseph A. Schafer

Introduction

Across a variety of occupational and professional contexts, studies of effective leaders overwhelmingly focused on leadership as a positive, benevolent process (Bennis & Nanus, 1997; Burns, 1978; Conger & Benjamin, 1999; Kotter, 1990; Peters & Waterman, 1982). Theoretical developments in leadership scholarship advanced appreciably from the mid-20th Century, providing a robust understanding of the traits and habits of leaders regarded as effective. Leadership scholars and authors provided extensive articulations of how leaders were able to achieve their desired outcomes through a range of strategies and tactics (see generally Northouse, 2007; Yukl, 2002). Empirical inquiry provided a robust body of research testing various theories and perspectives linking behaviors with actual outcomes (see generally Bass, 1990). A large body of academic and professional publications articulated these insights, often gearing the message toward corporate audiences.

Extant literature tended to cast persons in positions of power who abuse their authority, commit acts of corruption, engage in untoward conduct, or who fail to shoulder the mantle of their responsibilities are not considered to be actual leaders despite holding a leadership position. Leadership is considered a set of positive traits; those lacking the requisite

Source: Schafer, J. A. (2010b). The ineffective police leader: Acts of commission and omission. *Journal of Criminal Justice, 38*(4), 737–746.

skills are not true leaders. The proclivity to ignore the "darkside" of leadership is an ironic omission. Despite a half-century of research, the publication of more than 15,000 books and journal articles, and annual "leadership development" expenditures in excess of $50 billion, many organizations are considered to lack effective leadership (Burke, 2006). This situation led some (e.g., Burke, 2006; Kellerman, 2004a, 2004b) to contend the tendency to overlook ineffective leadership in scholarship, training, and education is a key factor contributing to the perceived shortage. By limiting or omitting the attention given to ineffective leaders or leadership traits, lessons for prospective leaders are artificially constrained.

In critiquing the tendency to frame leadership as positive behavior Barbara Kellerman challenged the idea that "to be a leader is, by definition, to be benevolent" (2004b, p. 44; see also Clements & Washbush, 1999; Einarsen, Aasland, & Skogstad, 2007; Gardner, 1990; Kellerman, 2000, 2004a; Kets de Vries, 1993). She saw the tendency to focus research and writing on skilled and successful leaders as an extension of humankind's passion for compelling stories with happy endings. Paraphrasing political philosopher Leo Strauss, Kellerman observed that "[c]apricious, murderous, high-handed, corrupt, and evil leaders are effective and everywhere—except in the literature of business leadership" (2004b, p. 43). Kellerman argued that constricting the definition of leadership (and, therefore, the focus of most leadership scholarship) to only those who lead properly and effectively ignored the reality that leaders can be bad, ineffective, and failures, either in part or in whole. The "leadership-is-a-positive-action" orientation overlooked the reality that even effective and well-regarded leaders are not perfect; they had short-comings, sometimes used less-than-ideal means in pursuing desired ends (Bailey, 1988), and may have achieved their goals nonetheless. Leaders who might generally be viewed in a favorable manner can still display poor choices and counter-productive behaviors; those appointed or anointed to leadership positions can fail to live up to the responsibility they are given.

Since the late 1980s a growing body of leadership scholarship considered leadership as more than just a positive process and outcome. A modest but increasing number of scholars considered ineffective leadership practices and results, often framed as examinations of leadership failures, bad leadership, power failures, derailed leadership, or the dark side of leadership. These volumes focused on the leadership and personal shortcomings of leaders in the corporate sector (Burke, 2006; Einarsen et al., 2007; Finkelstein 2003; Kellerman, 2004a, 2004b; McCall & Lombardo, 1983; McCauley, 2004; Schackleton, 1995; Swartz & Watkins, 2003) and, to a lesser extent, in government executive offices (Barras, 1998; Stanton, 2003). Largely absent from this small but growing body of scholarship was consideration of poor leadership within policing contexts. The moderate level of direct supervision given to most police employees and the geographically diffuse nature of police work environments, coupled with the centrality of concerns of ethics and integrity, it is reasonable to question whether prevailing theories and models derived primarily the corporate sector have applicability for policing. Using data derived from surveys of police supervisors, this study offers insights into the traits and habits of ineffective police leaders. The data and analysis focus on those leaders deemed to be ineffective by the respondents.[1] Consensus data are used to provide a better understanding of the ways in which police leaders fail to achieve positive and benevolent outcomes.

Literature Review

Scholars employed a range of conceptual and operational definitions in studying both effective (see McCauley, 2004) and ineffective (see Burke, 2006) leadership practices. As the definition of "leadership" varied widely across scholars and studies (Bass, 1990), so did the conception and definition of what it meant for a leader to be "effective" (Brewer, Wilson, & Beck, 1994). Effective leaders were often characterized as having strong interpersonal skills, an ability to articulate a vision, a capacity to motivate others to follow that vision, and an ability to effectively involve others in decision making processes (Bass, 1990; Bennis, 2003; Burns, 2003; Gardner, 1990; Kouzes & Posner, 2002; Yukl, 2002). Less evident in scholarship written for corporate settings, but very important in policing contexts, was the role of leader integrity in shaping effective outcomes (Anderson, Gisborne, & Holliday, 2006; Meese & Ortmeier, 2004). Taken as a whole, these traits and habits were viewed as enabling leaders to achieve a variety of desired outcomes, including achieving desired change (Kotter, 1996).

Dominant perspectives suggested that an ineffective or poor leader would be the inverse of a well-regarded leader (Kellerman, 2004b). More contemporary perspectives framed the quality and outcomes of a given leader in a broader fashion. In the latter framework, leaders were viewed as working to balance traits and habits that both enhanced and diminished their efficacy (Bailey, 1988; Clements & Washbush, 1999; Dotlich & Cairo, 2003; Kets de Vries, 1993). More effective leaders were those who maximized their assets and minimized their liabilities, or who had a mixture of assets and liabilities that was well-suited for a particular contextual or situational environment (McCall & Lombardo, 1983; Schackleton, 1995). This conceptualization allowed for variation in the specific acts of commission or omission that would relegate an individual to be classified as an ineffective leader. For example, an ineffective leader might have had poor interpersonal skills, failed to delegate, or been indecisive (Einarsen et al., 2007; Kelloway, Sivanathan, Francis, & Barling, 2005; Kets de Vries, 1993).

The Significance of Ineffective Leadership in Policing

Ample research existed to demonstrate the favorable outcomes leaders and supervisors can achieve within the workplace.[2] Empirical inquiry assessing supervisory influence generally considered the capacity of supervisors to shape traditional policing outcomes (such as enforcement decisions and the use of force). Studies offered at least tentative evidence supervisors can reduce incidents of misconduct and abuse of authority (Huberts, Kaptein, & Lasthuizen, 2007; Weisburd, Greenspan, Hamilton, Williams, & Bryant, 2000) and influence patrol officer conduct and decision making in desired manners (Engel, 2000, 2001, 2002; Engel & Worden, 2003; National Research Council, 2004), at least in the aggregate. Leaders who were open, followed rules, and led by example were thought to achieve more favorable performance from subordinate personnel (e.g., followers), including greater organizational commitment (Brewer, et al, 1994; Huberts et al., 2007; Jermier & Berkes, 1979). Prevailing evidence endorsed the contention effective leadership practices equated with desired outcomes in police organizations.

Yet leadership, regardless of how well-intended, was not always wielded in a benign manner (Clements & Washbush, 1999). Poor leadership was linked with a variety of mental health issues among employees, including stress, retaliation, helplessness, alienation, anxiety, depression, and general distress (Buzawa, 1984; House & Podsakoff, 1994; Kelloway et al., 2005). Poor leadership and supervision practices, including bullying, abusive, and destructive behaviors, were associated with decreased job satisfaction, organizational commitment, and professional motivation (Einarsen et al., 2007; Kelloway et al., 2005). For example, five to ten percent of corporate workers reported being the target of workplace bullying; among those reporting such experiences, eighty percent indicated the offender was their supervisor (Einarsen et al., 2007). Ineffective leadership, particularly the failure to act or respond to known problems, was identified as a recurrent factor in organizational failures (Dias & Vaughn, 2006; Garrett, 2004; Hall, 1980; McCabe, 2005; O'Hara, 2005). In policing, such organizational failures might have extended into matters that generated adversarial relationships with employees and/or the community, increased unionism, litigation, turn-over, or outside involvement in local police operations (Jermier & Berkes, 1979; Krimmel & Lindenmuth, 2001; O'Hara, 2005).

The Emergence of Ineffective Leaders and Leadership

Existing leadership and policing scholarship offered a variety of explanations for why ineffective leadership and leaders might have emerged within an agency. Police departments, like many other organizations, too often failed to identify those with a strong potential to be effective leaders. Given the multiple and competing definitions and measurements of leadership, too often agencies defaulted toward "safe" methods of assessing those seeking promotion. The tendency to base promotion assignments on performance on exams measuring mastery of bureaucratic rules and protocols (i.e., "book smarts" and "bean counting"), as well as the interfering influence of departmental politics and personalities (Hall, 1980), contributed to the gap often observed between "street cops" and their supervisors (Manning, 1997; Mastrofski, 2002; Reuss-Ianni, 1983; Van Maanen, 1984; Wilson, 1968). In other words, ineffective leadership outcomes were a partial product of an individual's personality, traits, habits, and actions (Dotlich & Cairo, 2003), however those individual factors were conditioned and constrained by aspects of the prevailing institutional environments and practices observed in police organizations.

Furthermore, popular vernacular included the idea of the "Peter principle"—that employees rose to their highest level of incompetence (Peter & Hull, 1969). The limits of a supervisor's skills and abilities were only discovered once that supervisor had been placed in a position that exceeded their capacities, at which time it was often too late to correct the matter. The supervisor's career might stall at that level, but the net effect was the individual was not competent to perform the duties of his/her assignment. In studying corporate executives who "derailed" in their careers, McCall & Lombardo (1983; see also Leslie & Van Velsor, 1996; Schackleton, 1995) found a common reason for the interruption of a seemingly promising career occurred when leaders were placed in situations where their skill set no longer provided effective outcomes. This might have occurred in a situation where promotion decisions were made based upon observed efficacy at a prior level of responsibility, rather than predicted success at future levels of responsibility. A good police officer did not always make a good sergeant; the behaviors and actions associated with being an effective officer may have differed from those associated with being an effective first-line supervisor. Leaders were unwilling or unable to adapt their style and techniques to meet the new context; in some cases, the traits and habits that had brought them prior success ultimately became a liability contributing to their downfall (Kets de Vries, 1993; Maccoby, 2000; Panzarella, 2003).

Consideration of ineffective leaders and leadership was rare in policing literature. When leadership has been considered, it was often used as a variable predicting other policing outcomes such as the exercise of discretionary behavior (Engel, 2000, 2002) or planned organizational initiatives. Most considerations of the influence of leadership did not directly incorporated leadership as a variable. Jermier and Berkes (1979) offered one of the most significant early studies of leadership in their exploration of the outcomes of leader behavior. Their focus, and the focus of most subsequent police leadership scholarship, was on "what works" in creating leadership efficacy or how effective or favorable leadership relates with other organizational outcomes (e.g., Adlam & Villiers, 2003; Anderson, Gisborne, & Holliday, 2006; Geller, 1985) though a few notable exceptions were evident (see Haberfeld, 2006; Mastrofski, 2002; Reese, 2005). The present study sought to contribute to the modest body of scholarship considering ineffective leaders and leadership.

Research Objective

Within the complexity of organizational environments it becomes difficult to sort out competing factors that might contribute to organizational failures and inefficiencies. How do we differentiate a leader who fails due to their traits, habits, actions, or decisions, from a leader who fails due to a structural dysfunction endemic to their agency and its bureaucracy? From an empirical perspective, the lack of consistent and valid metrics that assess the efficacy of a leader is problematic. One approach to overcome the latter weakness is to consider leadership (in)efficacy through a consensus model, such as asking personnel to reflect on (in)effective leaders. Though employee perceptions of leadership efficacy (in general or in the context of a specific supervisor) may not always be valid, in the aggregate such an approach is thought to yield valid outcomes. For example, within the corporate world it is popular to subject leaders to "360 evaluations" in which the leader, their supervisors, their peers, and their subordinates all provide input and feedback on the individual's performance. While such subjective assessments may individually be separate from a leader's objective successes or failures, the presumption is that on the whole a reasonably robust picture of the leader will be developed.

The objective of this research was to develop a better understanding of the traits and habits ineffective police leaders are perceived to display. Specifically, using a consensus approach this study sought to identify what leaders rated as ineffective did or failed to do in order to contribute to the perception of inefficacy. Two primary questions were addressed. First, what were the undesirable actions these leaders exhibited; what traits and habits did they demonstrate that worked against their ability to be effective leaders? Second, what were the desirable actions ineffective leaders failed to demonstrate; what acts of omission undercut the perception they were effective leaders? These insights provide a framework for future efforts seeking to measure actual behaviors and leadership, or lack thereof. Though perceptions may not equate with actual performance, a leader who is perceived as ineffective might be reasonably presumed to achieve lesser outcomes by virtue of that stigmatizing label.

Data and Methods

Findings were based upon open-ended surveys completed by police supervisors attending the Federal Bureau of Investigation National Academy (NA) in Quantico, VA. The NA was intended to be a mid-career developmental experience for police supervisors from a cross section of American and international agencies. The program was structured as a ten-week session comprised of 250-300 officers. They resided at the FBI Academy and completed the equivalent of one quarter of university-level education. The NA allowed officers to earn credit through the University of Virginia for the courses they completed. The faculty were comprised of FBI agents and support personnel. Attendees selected from a catalog of courses to fill their academic schedule. The duration and residential aspect of the program were intended to help attendees step away from the day to day "noise" and distractions within their agency. Participants were encouraged to think critically and creatively about how they could improve both their agency's performance and their own professional development, while networking with peers from around the world.

Individual law enforcement agencies nominated their supervisory personnel to attend the program. A small number of international participants were included in each session, comprising around ten percent of attendees. Domestic participants represented all forms and levels of American policing. Seats in NA sessions were assigned to agencies, which selected the specific supervisor who would fill the available slot. Those responsible for operating the NA made an effort to distribute seats to agencies in such a way that attendees represent diverse experiences, mandates, and regions, though such intents were not based on rigorous statistical sampling. Given these circumstances, supervisors sent to the NA were generally among the "best and brightest" within their agency, though departmental politics, favoritism, and nepotism sometimes dictated who agencies select to attend the program. While a purposive sample, NA participants represented a highly diverse mix of agencies (e.g., agency size, location, context, and jurisdiction) and they could answer key research questions based on extensive knowledge and familiarity with supervision, management, and leadership. The sample provided insights from a collection of police professionals and was well-suited to support inductive inquiry into aspects of police supervision and leadership.

Participants in NA Sessions 227-229 (October 2006 – April 2007) were asked to complete an open-ended survey instrument addressing a range of leadership and leadership development topics. During this timeframe 835 supervisors participated in the NA.[3] Of the 418 asked to describe ineffective leaders, 304 (72.7 percent) chose to participate in the research project and respond to this question.

The resulting narrative responses were subjected to several rounds of analysis to facilitate the identification and classification of primary patterns and themes within the answers (see Lee, 1999; Strauss, 1987). The survey question's open-ended format produced individual responses that ranged in length from a few words to a long paragraph. Some participants included or utilized bulleted lists of phrases, abbreviations, or short-hand in lieu of complete sentences, a situation that at times made problematic the determination of the author's exact intent and meaning. Consequently, the analysis focused on latent patterns and themes, such as identifying common traits and habits that emerged across the responses (Berg, 2001). The vague and ambiguous nature of some responses precluded precise categorization in all instances; therefore the following findings report the approximate prevalence of individual themes. The proportions reported in this study should be viewed as representing each theme's general pervasiveness rather than its exact prevalence. In addition, response themes were not mutually exclusive; a given reply could have reflected multiple themes.

Findings

Respondents did not reveal their identity or specific agency affiliation, however they were asked to report their years of service, years as a supervisor, military experience, level of education, agency size,[4] agency type,[5] current job title, and whether they were American or an international officer. Quotes provided in this section are attributed to individuals based on their title, agency size, and agency type in order to provide a contextual framework; unless otherwise noted, respondents were American. On average, respondents had just less than twenty years of policing experience (range six to thirty-seven years) and just over ten years of supervisory experience (range zero to thirty-six years[6]); 91 percent were American. Approximately one-quarter (seventy-four respondents) indicated prior military service with an average duration of just over eight years (range less than one to thirty years). Table 1 provides additional contextual information on respondent education, agency size, and agency type. Nearly all participants had some level of college education, with one-third reporting the completion of post-baccalaureate coursework. Participants in the NA tend to be from medium and large agencies relative to the actual distribution of agencies by size in the United States (see Hickman & Reaves, 2006). Smaller agencies likely have more trouble finding the resources to release personnel for a ten-week program.

Respondents were first asked to estimate how often they observed effective leadership practices within their agency. Responses to this open-ended comment were quite diverse. Approximately one-third of respondents indicated they observed effective leadership practices never, rarely/seldom, or not often enough. Approximately one-quarter reported they often or frequently observed effective practices. The remaining respondents indicated they observed effective leadership practices very often, always, or all the time. Interestingly, within the latter group there was a modest proportion of respondents that also indicated seeing ineffective practices with the same regularity. These findings are not intended to provide precise measurement of the frequency of effective leadership practices in policing. Rather, they illustrate that most respondents had regular exposure to ineffective leadership. Indeed, a respondent reporting daily exposure to effective leadership might have also had daily exposure to ineffective practices. Thus, it is reasonable to presume the respondents had sufficient exposure and context to describe the traits and habits of ineffective police leaders.

Table 1 Respondent Education, Agency Type, and Agency Size

		Frequency	Percent
Respondents' highest level of education	High School/GED	9	3.0
	Some college	51	17.0
	Associates degree	35	11.7
	Bachelors degree	99	33.0
	Some graduate/law work	31	10.3
	Graduate/law degree	75	25.0
Respondents' agency type	Municipal/city	164	54.7
	County	64	21.3
	State	38	12.7
	National	21	7.0
	Other	13	4.3
Respondents' agency size	0-50	82	27.3
	51-100	48	16.0
	101-250	48	16.0
	251-1000	67	22.3
	1001 +	55	18.3

Note: Data were available for 300 of the 304 respondents; percents may not sum to 100.0 due to rounding.

Characterizing the Ineffective Leader

Though subsequent sections elaborate on specific common elements of ineffective leadership practices, some responses provide rich insight into the overall characteristics of the ineffective police leader. A captain from a mid-size municipal agency described ineffective leaders as:

> ... quick temper, judgmental, lazy, inability to follow through, lack of focus, poor communication/interpersonal skills, moody, negative thinkers, lack of ability to delegate, lack of confidence in others, micromanagers.

These are all things that make people poor leaders. Most of these, they would like to overcome, but are either unable, or don't know how.

The experiences of a captain from a small municipal agency demonstrated that ineffective leaders displayed (emphasis provided in the original response):

> Dishonesty, lack of candor, lack of empathy, selfishness. They fail to inspire, fail to lead by example, and fail to <u>work hard</u> to solve long-term problems, and fail to empower

subordinates to solve the short term problems. Failure to recognize good, hard work.

A captain from a mid-size municipal agency noted that

> Among the traits I have witnessed in those described: selfishness, unwillingness to make tough decisions, failure to delegate responsibilities, making decisions while angry/upset, failure to trust others. Most of those I am describing failed to use to resources around them, namely the experiences and minds of those around them.

A lieutenant from a large county agency described ineffective leaders as "usually inconsistent and do not possess the characteristics or self discipline needed to become and effective leader. Where many fail is by not taking a balanced approach to their role; either too authoritarian or fail to transition into the role and try to remain 'one of the guys.'" Similar themes emerged in the response from a commander in a small state agency, who noted ineffective leaders are "self-centered, only interested in making him/herself look good, lack of confidence and trust in subordinates, micro-managing, knee jerk reactions to situations, and over-reacting to simple matters."

These global responses illustrated a key theme emerging from the responses. The traits and habits associated with ineffective leaders could be divided into two categories: actions/behaviors and actions/behaviors that *should have* been taken, but were not. The former (acts of commission) served to erode leaders' efficacy because they presumably embodied behaviors that were deleterious to a leader's objectives and ability to secure followers. The latter (acts of omission) undermined efficacy presumably by representing situations where leaders failed to embody their label—they failed to lead. The following sections detail five acts of commission (focus on self over others, ego/arrogance, closed mindedness, micromanagement, and capriciousness) and five acts of omission (poor work ethic, failure to act, ineffective communication, lack of interpersonal skills, and lack of integrity) that emerged as dominant themes in the survey responses.

Focus on Self Over Others

Some larger law enforcement organizations used the term "careerism" to refer to employees who were focused on their own professional interests and aspirations above the concerns of others, the organization, and the community. One-third of the respondents characterized ineffective police leaders as displaying this type of "self-first" focus, a proclivity that appeared to generate additional problems. Leaders seeking continued career advance were likely to focus on what was necessary to secure their next promotion, rather than doing what was needed to achieve goals in their present position. "It's all about them and doing whatever is needed to climb the promotional ladder" (sergeant major municipal agency). They may have failed to be mindful of their current duties, what was in the long-term best interests of the office they currently hold, and the human needs of the personnel they supervised. "The largest failure occurs when leaders forget their own responsibilities to the position they hold and to the people under them" (investigation supervisor small state agency). As such, they may "look at the position as a job and not a career" (captain major county agency); this could be particularly problematic if the leader's aspirations were outside of the agency (i.e., obtaining employment with an alternative agency or within another industry).

Any number of examples of this conduct could be seen in the various corporate scandals that plagued the financial industry in the 1990s and 2000s (McLean & Elkind, 2003). At times the "self-first" problem was exacerbated because organizational structures created incentives to take a selfish focus, such as performance bonuses that pushed executives to pursue a payout rather than doing what was best for the corporation's health and stability. This situation has parallels in policing, where leaders may have opted to do what would help them secure continued career advancement (which might actually have involved inaction or indecision) rather than what was best for the agency and/or community. "They fail because they are not concerned about others and more focused on themselves and their progress, instead of the agency being successful and the community being a safer place — self above service" (commander major state agency). The low tolerance for failure found in many police organizations might have resulted in leaders who avoided actions and judgments likely to invoke negative outcomes. As stated by a major from a medium municipal agency, "we promote those who do not self-destruct." All-too-often, avoiding self-destruction meant placing self-first and averting actions that might have repercussions, even when a decision needed to be made.

Ego/Arrogance

Ego and arrogance represented a fine line for leaders to tread. On the one hand, it might have been quite desirable for a leader to have a measure of confidence in themselves and their abilities (Lipman-Blumen, 2005; Maccoby, 2000). In order to secure followers, a leader needed to convey to others that their objectives and methods were appropriate; followers needed confidence that their leader was working to achieve a proper goal using a sound plan. However, taken too far, a leader's behavior might have been deemed "selfish, stubborn, self-righteous, [and] egotistical" (district commander major state agency). One-third of the respondents identified ego and arrogance as characteristics displayed by ineffective leaders. These characteristics had presumably gone beyond the normal realms of confidence and self-assurance that might be healthy and productive. "They have an inflated sense of self-importance and display it" (lieutenant medium municipal agency).

Ego or arrogance might not have generated problems in and of themselves. Rather, it is possible problems arose from the positions and actions ineffective leaders took because of their ego or arrogance. For example, ineffective leaders might have tended to adopt the attitude that it is "my way or the highway" and demonstrated "unyielding personalities, [and] lack of self confidence" (commander large municipal agency). Their near-absolute belief in their own opinions and judgments could have been their undoing. "What keeps them from being effective is they cannot see their own faults an accept responsibility for those faults" (lieutenant small municipal agency). This situation introduced a degree of subjectivity into the process of evaluating a given leader's efficacy and behavior; what one person saw as self-confidence and drive, another may have perceived as an arrogant refusal to listen to others. It may be difficult or impossible for the average leader to be judged as appropriately confident and humble by all those around them.

Closed Minded

Related with arrogance and ego is the tendency for ineffective leaders to be closed minded to the suggestions of others, a trait discussed by around fifteen percent of respondents. For various reasons, these leaders seemed unable or unwilling to listen to other perspectives, opinions, and voices. As stated above, this represented a fine line leaders needed to navigate. They required self-confidence and a capacity to be decisive, yet they must had to recognize the value of other voices and the need to take time, when possible, in making decisions to consider alternatives and ramifications. A captain from a large municipal agency described ineffective leaders as "inflexible, uncompromising, and don't foster a participatory style of leadership." Though police supervisors had to bear a tremendous responsibility for the choices they made, management and leadership experimentation yielded evidence supporting the effectiveness of participatory models of leader-follower interactions and organizational decision making (Steinheider & Wuestewald, 2008).

Being closed minded was also characterized to include not adapting, innovating, or changing when such actions were needed within an organization. Ineffective leaders "fail to examine issues from all sides. They fail to consider unintended consequences.

They don't educate themselves on the big picture, so when circumstances change (as they always do) ineffective leaders fail to adapt" (deputy chief large municipal agency). This stood in contrast to the very concept of leadership, which implied a capacity to move a group to an alternative position. Being closed minded to the need for change—for leadership to guide a group or organization toward an alternative state—may have been a reflection of a leader who was out of touch, was too stubborn to listen to others, or feared change might result in failure. Policing has not, however, excelled in cultivating visionary leaders. A tendency to produce leaders who were closed-minded to alternative structures and approaches was not surprising from a highly bureaucratic and entrenched profession (Mastrofski, 1998; Sklansky, 2007).

Micromanagement

Leadership scholars, trainers, and consultants have gone to great length to differentiate between leadership and management (Northouse, 2007; Yukl, 2002). Leadership has been defined in countless ways, but was generally conceived as a capacity to move a group and/or organization through a process of change. Management, on the other hand, represented technical proficiency at a more finite set of tasks. Truly effective leaders were likely to need proficiency in both leadership and management (Stamper, 1992); they required an ability to motivate and develop personnel, while also attending the nuances of budgets, law, and contracts. The efficacy of a leader may have been partially predicated on their ability to delegate responsibilities and trust that subordinates would exercise appropriate discretion and due diligence in fulfilling assigned tasks. Police leaders, as leaders in many other sectors, may have struggled to embody this ideal. American police agencies tended to do a poor job developing leadership skills among supervisory personnel (Van Maanen, 1984). The litigious nature of American society also created avenues by which liability for an officer's conduct could be attached to supervisory personnel (e.g., Ross, 2000). Consequently, newly promoted personnel struggling to delegate and demonstrate leadership may have defaulted to bureaucratic management tactics (Krimmel & Lindenmuth, 2001) or preferred a focused style of supervision in order to mitigate liability risk.

Approximately fifteen percent of respondents indicated that a tendency to manage or, worse yet, to micromanage was common among ineffective leaders. A sergeant from a small municipal agency noted most ineffective leaders were "far too autocratic and fail to delegate when appropriate." Requiring that subordinates secure excessive permission, approval, and review, particularly for routine choices, slowed the pace of organizational action and output, while sending the message to subordinates that their judgment was not trusted. Such a heavy focus on controlling subordinate and routine actions could have actually prevented desired outcomes because ineffective leaders "fail to delegate authority [to subordinates] that is necessary for the success of desired results" (chief of detectives mid-size municipal agency). Though a proclivity toward management may have emerged when supervisors lack comfort with other forms of personnel management and/or fear liability, it could also arise when supervisors feared that subordinates would outshine the leader's own accomplishments if they were empowered. In the case of the latter, ineffective leaders may "lack self-confidence. They make up for it by micromanaging people" (lieutenant medium municipal agency).

Capricious/Political

Though leaders made decisions within the context of a given situation and timeframe (Brewer et al., 1994), respondents indicated they desired a sense of continuity in how decisions were derived. A follower who has a history with a given leader should have been able to generally assess the likely choice that leader would make. Ten percent of respondents characterized ineffective leaders as being arbitrary and capricious in how they made decisions. A commander in a large state agency noted such leaders were "inconsistent and [they] don't adhere to a systematic approach." Having a general sense of a leader's likely response to a situation was of importance because peers and followers wanted to make decisions and take actions in support of the leader. If they did not understand the base from which the leader operated it became difficult for followers to know how to exercise their own discretionary authority. Followers wanted to function in a manner that supported the leader and her/his objectives, while knowing how to avoid the leader's wrath and criticism. Followers wanted to understand "what matters" within the agency and to the leader in furthering the standing of the agency and, in some cases, advancing their own career objectives.

Capriciousness also extended into how leaders made personnel decisions. Organizational politics had the potential to become significant sources of stress when leaders demonstrated "[i]nconsistent, arbitrary discipline. Cronyism, nepotism" (sergeant mid-sized municipal agency). Ineffective leaders were described as tending to put personal relationships ahead of what was right, just, and consistent with past practices. Followers wanted to know that all rules, criteria, and standards applied equally to all personnel; that friends and relatives of police leaders did not enjoy special privilege in how they were treated. Likewise, officers may have sensed that leaders were not likely to support them if their actions were appropriate, but generated public outcry (i.e., the use of force or the handling of major cases). Ineffective leaders tended to engender the feeling that "officers often do not know where he [sic] stands, they cannot count on him in controversy" (chief small municipal agency). It was well-established that officers prefer to have the sense peers and leaders "had their back" (Manning, 1997; Rubenstein, 1973). The absence of that perception may have generated distrust, hostility, and strain in the leader-follower relationship (Reuss-Ianni, 1983).

Poor Work Ethic

The concept of "leadership by example" suggested leaders ought not to ask followers to perform any task or exhibit a work ethic they were not prepared to demonstrate themselves. Almost two-thirds of respondents indicated ineffective leaders lacked a proper work ethic. Respondents cast ineffective leaders as being lazy, doing the minimal amount of work, and failing to "give 100 percent" to the job and their responsibilities. Some of these leaders were labeled with conventional policing terms for this act of omission, such as "ROD" (retired on duty) or "RIP" (retired in place) (see Barker, 1999). Ineffective leaders who displayed a poor ethic were frequently framed as being late in their careers; there were noted as having lost their enthusiasm for, and commitment to, the job. These ineffective leaders were consumed by "[l]aziness, negativity . . . They fail to have passion for the work" (captain major municipal agency). "They are lazy, don't provide guidance, never jump in and do their fair share, always have excuses" for why they fail to be productive workers (lieutenant medium state agency).

This situation represented a fine line for a leader. To avoid being characterized as a micromanager a leader must have sought to empower subordinates and delegate responsibility, while not being seen as shirking too many tasks. A reasonable rejoinder to the "poor work ethic" critique would be to ask whether these types of leaders should be criticized for not "giving 110 percent" or whether they deserved praise for having a more healthy and evenhanded approach to balancing their career and personal life. Variation on this issue was, of course, expected across a sample of leaders. By not displaying an honest work ethic and by not demonstrating the proper way to police a given community, ineffective leaders failed to show the dedication and standard of performance they presumably expected from others. Quite simply, they "fail to lead by example" (captain small municipal agency). This inability or refusal to show commitment to the organization and its objectives undermined the leader's credibility and/or implied to followers that a committed, diligent work ethic was not expected.

Failure to Act

Leaders were expected to live up to their label—to lead. Though leaders might have been expected to engage in appropriate contemplation and consult with relevant parties, ultimately leadership required decisiveness and action. One-third of respondents described ineffective leaders as failing to act in a variety of circumstances. "Leaders must be able to make decisions" (sergeant small municipal agency). Lacking sufficient self-confidence, a leader might have struggled to trust his/her own judgment enough to select from a range of options when confronted with a choice. "Ineffective leaders often refuse to make a decision" (captain major county agency; emphasis in response). A leader might have avoided taking critical or unpopular actions as a means to preserve their career trajectory. A preferred strategy would have been to put an issue on the proverbial "back burner," leaving it up to a successor to be the "bad guy." Alternatively, a leader may have feared that action later deemed poor or inappropriate could harm the leader's career aspirations, generate liability, or, in extreme cases, result in injury, loss of life, or property damage. Though police officers were routinely confronted with situations in which they must make a decision and act, a leader may have struggled to do so when a poor choice could have resulted in harm to subordinates. More simply, they may have a "fear of looking bad or not knowing what to do" (sergeant small county agency).

In chronicling fifty years of executive leadership in the Los Angeles Police Department, Reese (2005) contrasted leaders who acted in the best interests of the agency with those who acted in the best interests of police officers, particularly front-line patrol personnel. For some ineffective leaders this failure to act could have reflected concern over personal popularity with subordinate personnel and/or an aversion to situations likely to generate conflict. "They are afraid to be disliked by their subordinates and refuse to discipline them" (sergeant medium municipal agency). Ineffective leaders may have had a "fear of confrontation, fear of hurting feelings" (sergeant small county agency) and might have been "more concerned with upsetting their subordinates rather than doing their jobs" (captain mid-size municipal agency). They had an "inability or unwillingness ... to make unpopular decisions that are in the best interest of the organization" (supervisor major county agency). A failure to act might have also reflected divergent perceptions as to whether or not change or decision was actually warranted; a leader who was quite comfortable with the prevailing *status quo* in a system could disagree with followers who viewed this situation as ripe for change, enhancement, elimination, or modification.

Ineffective Communication

One-third of respondents characterized ineffective leaders as having trouble with communication. This situation was not simply a matter of weak written or verbal expression skills. Rather, it encapsulated a number of fundamental communication omissions, including an inability or unwillingness to participate in two-way dialog, a refusal to explain key decisions and actions, and a failure to accept input and criticism. Ineffective leaders were described as being unwilling to give a "chance to the team to participate in making the decision" (captain major international federal agency). This circumstance served to constrain the input and outflow of communication through a leader's office or position. Ineffective leaders exhibiting this trait felt little need to seek out or listen to the suggestions of others and would see little reason to articulate their rationale for decisions. Subordinates and co-workers found this situation frustrating and it was not uncommon to see this appearing in conjunction with comments alluding to a leader being closed-minded or arrogant.

Ineffective leaders were typified by "not [being] willing to explain the reason why a decision needs to be made" (captain from a medium municipal agency). They "fail to effectively communicate change in an organization or the reason for change or decisions made" (sergeant small municipal agency). Whether this act of omission was due to arrogance (e.g., the belief the leader did not have to rationalize or justify her/his actions) or indifference (e.g., not being concerned that followers might desire more information) varied within the data. Respondents also expressed a desire to see leaders who were open to the possibility that there might be ways to improve aspects of an agency or unit's operations. Ineffective leaders were resistant to this type of constructive input from those internal and/or external to the agency. They did not want to "listen to other ideas or admit there is a better way" (captain mid-size municipal agency).

Lack of Interpersonal Skills

One quarter of respondents described ineffective leaders as lacking appropriate interpersonal skills, such as the inability to understand the human needs and motivations of those they sought to influence. This act of omission was distinct from poor communication in that the former related more with the informal and "human" aspects of the workplace. Interpersonal skills were not simply a matter of communicating and explaining policy changes; they were a matter of developing and maintaining positive relations with peers, supervisors, subordinates, and constituents. Strong interpersonal skills were often characterized as a hallmark of effective leadership, as in the case of the "charismatic leader" (Conger, 1989). Ineffective leaders struggled in trying to "know their officers and tend to their welfare" (executive officer major military service), "They lack of basic human personal skills. They fail to realize that they are leading people" (investigations supervisor small state agency). Such relationships were important because they could engender a sense of trust between a leader and her/his followers. "Sometimes you have to care from the heart, then the mind will follow" (commander large state agency).

Interpersonal relationships mattered because they helped to develop trust and allegiance between leaders and followers. The failure to "develop some level of relationship with the employees and to gain their respect" (special agent in charge mid-size state agency) could erode a leader's efficacy and impact. Interpersonal relationships should not have mattered when organizations were viewed as Weberian bureaucracies, however since the 1950s organizational research suggested that outcomes were often predicated on the bonds, allegiance, trust, and respect that interpersonal relations engendered. While charisma may not have been sufficient to ensure leadership efficacy, the data strongly suggested it was a necessary, or at least important, trait for leaders to express. Ineffective leaders either did not recognize the importance of relationships or struggled to establish and maintain these connections. Because subordinates and followers saw the leader as distant, detached, and disinterested in getting to know them as a person, the follower's starting orientation was to not trust or act upon the leader's call to action. This created an interesting challenge for leaders in larger agencies, where developing that level of connection and interaction may have been difficult or impossible.

Lack of Integrity

Honesty and integrity had long-been considered virtuous within policing. The belief in policing by consent that served as one of the anchors of British policing was predicated in part on the idea the police were only effective so long as they maintained the public's trust. Actions that abrogate that trust acted as a corrosive force on the capacity of the police to achieve desired outcomes. Parallels were seen with the importance of integrity and trust in the relationship between leaders and followers (Villiers, 2003). A leader's ability to establish effective relationships with followers was partially predicated on being viewed as trustworthy, honest, and ethical.

Problems associated with an absence of integrity were mentioned by one-fifth of respondents in characterizing ineffective leaders. Ineffective leaders were characterized as lacking the requisite level of integrity to maintain the trustful following of subordinates and others. These leaders were described as being "immoral, unethical" (captain major municipal agency) and having "no core values" (commander large municipal agency). Poor integrity was also similar to the underlying behaviors related to a poor work ethic; leaders were framed as being less effective when they performed their duties in a manner that lacked professionalism, diligence, and dedication. Such a situation might often have been a subjective determination for individual followers. For example, a leader who allegedly engaged in marital infidelity or poor integrity in an off-duty business transaction might have been vilified by some followers, while generating indifference among others. Poor integrity (or the perception thereof) had a lingering effect. Ineffective leaders often had "done something in their past to lose the trust and respect of the employees" (commander large state agency). That trust and respect, once lost, was difficult to recapture.

Discussion

Ineffective leadership is not simply a product of a leader's actions or inactions. To the extent that efficacy is based on the assessments of those a leader seeks to influence, the leaders traits and habits are interpreted and filtered through the expectations of would-be followers. The relationship between leaders and followers (at times referred to as leader-member exchange) has been the focus of more scholarly inquiry in recent decades (Engle & Lord, 1997; Martin, Thomas, Charles, Epitropaki, & McNamara, 2005; Shamir, Pillai, Bligh, & Uhl-Bien, 2007). Within a discussion of the traits and habits of leaders it is necessary to recognize that followers/members will evaluate leadership through the lens of their individual expectations. This is a relevant issue given the nature of the data in this study. The perceptions and experiences NA participants have with ineffective leaders are partially a function of their own beliefs about effective leadership. It is possible that based on other outcome metrics (evaluations by peers or superiors, citizen perceptions, achievement of performance objectives, etc.) the ineffective leaders characterized in the data might have received a different evaluation. Given the centrality of followers/members in helping leaders achieve outcomes perceptions of the former remain salient despite the filtered interpretation of efficacy.

Leaders were characterized as ineffective for exhibiting behaviors that undermined and eroded follower's senses of trust, legitimacy, and confidence. Leaders were also characterized as ineffective when they failed to exhibit the key actions that might be associated with actual leadership. These traits and habits represent ways in which leaders worked against their own interests and/or failed to live up to their label or position. Trait-based research seeking to predict leadership efficacy in corporate settings has not been found to be highly predictive of specific outcomes, though this is partially due to methodological issues (Lord, De Vader, & Alliger, 1986), as well as the tendency of this approach to ignore situational variables (Brewer et al., 1994). The intent of these findings is not to test causal connections between leadership (in)actions and specific policing outcomes. Rather, the research sought to provide a better understanding of the traits and habits police supervisors perceived within less effective leaders they had observed. To an extent the findings mirror what would be expected based on corporate leadership literature, but this is an important confirmation largely absent from studies specific to policing contexts.

Beyond the action/inaction dichotomy, the ten emerging traits and habits can be loosely grouped into three categories of problematic behaviors: individual problems, occupational problems, and leadership problems. Individual problems were actions, inactions, traits and behaviors that would more generally reflect the character and personality of the ineffective leader, including ego, poor integrity, a poor work ethic, and placing one's self before others. Certainly these characteristics have a strong subjective element; one observer's egomaniac is another's self-confident and decisive leader. In the context of leadership development or enhancement, these individual problems might be the most difficult to overcome. The nature of the problems could suggest leaders would resist seeing a need for personal development or improvement within these or any other behavioral domains. Because they are partially a reflection of the leader's character and personality, it might be difficult for a leader to recognize and acknowledge that he/she is engaging in these behaviors. Even in situations where these traits are recognized it may be difficult for a leader to learn how to overcome and correct such entrenched behaviors.

Occupational problems are, relatively speaking, more susceptible to improvements and enhancements. Issues with communication, micromanagement, and being closed-minded can certainly reflect upon the character and personality of an individual leader, but they also can emerge within bureaucratic and litigious organizations. Given the latter, organizations can take measures to overcome these problems by instituting protocols and practices that, for example, routinize employee input into decision-making loops (see Steinheider & Wuestewald, 2008). These problems also represent behaviors more susceptible to correction through leadership development processes. Though a leader might be predisposed to micromanage for a variety of reasons, a common factor might be a lack of familiarity and/or comfort with alternative methods of leadership and supervision. Absent an awareness of, and comfort with, leadership styles emphasizing delegation and empowerment, a leader may default to micromanagement (Krimmel & Lindenmuth, 2001). Introducing leaders to alternative styles and approaches would seem to hold strong potential for overcoming occupational problems, particularly when coupled with structures that encourage or even mandate a leader's style.

Finally, leadership problems most centrally relate with the failure of leaders to personify their label and actually lead. As detailed above, the failure to take action can be caused by a variety of organizational, environmental, situation, and personal circumstances. Leaders can fail to act in order to avoid unpopular choices that may halt their professional advancement. Alternatively, leaders can fail to act because they lack confidence in their own judgment. The diverse origins of a failure to actually lead make overcoming this inaction a challenge because it suggests the need for multiple potential corrective measures. The problem is not merely a function of individuals, but is also a reflection of the prevailing culture of police organizations and leadership selection practices.

Consideration of ineffective leaders and leadership must also take into account the dominant elements found in police organizations and culture. To an extent, ineffective leaders might be products of their own environment. As a profession policing has not placed a high primacy on the development of prospective and current leaders (Anderson et al., 2006; Van Maanen, 1984). In the absence of education and mentoring on how to lead in a more effective manner, it is perhaps not surprising that subsequent problems and tensions can be observed in the supervisor-subordinate relationship (Reese, 2005; Reuss-Ianni, 1983). Those who are or desire to be a leader bear some responsibility for educating themselves on various theories, styles, and perspectives, yet organizations also contribute to this situation. In effect, leadership is lacking in policing because there is a lack of leadership; as a profession current police leaders have been late in realizing their collective responsibility to develop those who will someday assume leadership roles. Resource constraints, personnel limitations, and lack of suitable training and education opportunities contribute to this divide, but so do ego, culture, tradition, and indifference. In the end the responsibility for advancing the quality of police leadership might lie with the profession itself.

Perhaps one of the most striking concerns associated with the tendency of literature to focus on leadership as ever virtuous and a leader as nearly infallible is the risk of distorting the realities of both leaders and leadership. Immanuel Kant noted that "... from such warped wood as is man made, nothing straight can be fashioned" (trans., 1983). Joanne Ciulla extended Kant's idea to the realm of organizational leadership, suggesting leaders are "morally fallible humans who are put in positions where they are expected to fail less than most people" (2001, p. 313). Ciulla's contention is often lost in the writings and scholarship that dominate the discourse on leaders and leadership. This situation extends into policing literature, which has succumbed all-too-often to the "romance" of police leadership (Mastrofski, 2002). This study adds to the limited literature considering the "dark side" of leadership in policing by describing the common traits and habits displayed by those leaders deemed to be ineffective by others. Much of what has been written about leadership failures appears in media sources, rather than academic and professional literatures. The result may be the perpetuation of myths or over-simplifications describing why leaders fail to achieve desired outcomes (Finkelstein, 2003).

Consideration of these ten acts of commission and omission is not meant to imply that all ineffective leaders display all of these behaviors; indeed, it is quite possible that even leaders regarded as effective might demonstrate one or more of these acts periodically or even on a recurring basis. As Ciulla's observation implies, it is not that strong leaders are perfect; rather, strong leaders may find ways to avoid personal and professional errors more often than those who surround them. Leaders are periodically called upon to make difficult choices that will displease at least a segment of their followers or constituents. It has been argued that in some instances the most expedient way to accomplish individual or organizational objectives is through manipulative and deceitful actions (Bailey, 1988; Kets de Vries, 1993). Those in leadership and supervisory positions are not immune from the allure of "blue lies" and "police placebos" (Klockars, 1984). Consequently, "no leader can survive as a leader without deceiving others (followers know less than opponents) and without deliberately doing to others what he would prefer not to have done to himself" (Bailey, 1988, p. ix).

The line separating effective and ineffective leaders remains unclear. Framing effective leaders as occasionally using improper, ineffective, destructive or deceitful methods only exacerbates that uncertainty. Though a consensus model might be used to generate a general agreement on the line between efficacy and inefficacy, subjective individual assessments will mean some leaders are disparaged by many, yet followed by a few. The data in this study do not provide direct clarification of that situation. The complexity of leadership and leader tactics makes strong empirical assessment of key concepts quite challenging. Even where efforts are made to quantify leadership outcomes, it has been suggested that its effect size is more modest than conventional thinking implies and that "... it is easier to believe in leadership than to prove it" (Meindl, 1990, p. 161).

Though it might be unexpected to see an ineffective leader as a highly placed and/or long-standing supervisor, such circumstances do arise. Ineffective leaders might have a long track record of problematic and sub-standard performance, as observed by a Precinct Commander in a large county agency.

> In most cases they were ineffective officers to begin with but somehow get promoted. They do not pay attention to what goes on around them, they do not set the example, they lack interest, motivation & dedication. They fail to recognize when something is wrong and correct the problem. They don't lead.

This gives raise to vital questions about how ineffective leaders manage to obtain a supervisory position. Given the low tolerance for failure in many American law enforcement agencies such undesirable outcomes may be far too common. In addressing this situation, a major from a small municipal agency remarked that agencies have an unfortunate tendency to "promote and continue to promote those officers who avoid self-destructing" over the course of their career.

Future studies might build upon this descriptive foundation by seeking ways to more systematically study the prevalence of these behaviors and to determine whether they can be empirically linked with undesirable policing outcomes. Do leaders judged to display a large number of these traits and habits receive lower evaluations, exert less influence over employees, "derail" in their rise to higher ranks, or receive less favorable assessments from followers? For now, these empirical questions remain open. Making such assessments is complicated if, in fact, leaders are accurately framed as being "warped wood" prone to error or fault. Those working to develop police leadership and leaders might incorporate consideration of the "dark-side" of leadership into curricula. Those seeking to study policing and police outcomes might be well-served by considering both effective and ineffective police leaders and leadership. A better understanding of ineffective leaders and leadership practices might not only enhance understanding of this problematic circumstance, but might also offer a more realistic and robust understanding of the type of leadership that is effective and desired in modern police organizations.

Acknowledgements

The author thanks the officers who participated in FBI National Academy sessions 227-229 for their cooperation and candor. Additional thanks to Dr. John Jarvis (FBI Behavioral Science Unit), Supervisory Special Agent Dr. Carl Jensen (FBI retired), Mr. Harry Kern (retired Unit Chief of the FBI Behavioral Science Unit), and the staffs of the FBI National Academy Unit and Behavioral Science Unit for their support of this project.

Notes

1. The present focus did not overlook the fact that generally effective leaders could make poor choices and/or demonstrate weaknesses and failings. As the prior paragraphs suggest, this situation was largely overlooked in extant research literature. Due to space and resource limitations, this study was only able to focus on leaders generally regarded as ineffective, though even the latter likely had redeeming traits and periodic success.

2. The focus in this literature review and study is on traits and outcomes that are widely regarded as effective or ineffective. Followers and other key constituents did not always respond in a uniform fashion to a given leader and her/his leadership approach and personal traits/habits (Jermier & Berkes, 1979; Krimmel & Lindenmuth, 2001). This study concerned itself with those behaviors that facilitated or inhibited effective outcomes in the aggregate, recognizing that even effective leaders were held in low-regard by some and even ineffective leaders likely had at least a few champions.

3. The total number of participating officers was based on first day counts provided by the FBI Academy.

4. Respondents reported sworn agency size using fixed categories. For the purpose of this analysis agency size was categorized as small (0-50), medium (51-100), midsize (101-250), large (251-1000), and major (1001 or more).

5. Respondents selected from the following classifications: municipal/city, county, state, nation, or other.

6. Though the NA was intended for those with supervisory experience, in rare cases agencies were allowed to send non-supervisory personnel. This generally occurred in small special jurisdiction agencies with compressed hierarchies.

References

Adlam, R., & Villiers, P. (Eds.). (2003). *Police leadership in the twenty-first century: Philosophy, doctrine and developments.* Winchester, UK: Waterside Press.

Anderson, T. D., Gisborne, K., & Holliday, P. (2006). *Every officer is a leader* (2nd ed.). Victoria, BC: Trafford Publishing.

Bailey, F. G. (1988). *Humbuggery and manipulation: The art of leadership.* Ithaca, NY: Cornell University Press.

Barker, J. C. (1999). *Danger, duty, & disillusion: The worldview of Los Angeles police officers.* Prospect Heights, IL: Waveland.

Barras, J. R. (1998). *The last of the Black emperors: The hollow comeback of Marion Barry in the new age of Black leaders.* Baltimore, MD: Bancroft Press.

Bass, B. M. (1990). *Bass & Stogdill's handbook of leadership: Theory, research, & managerial applications* (3rd ed.). New York: The Free Press.

Berg, B. L. (2001). *Qualitative research methods for the social sciences.* Boston: Allyn & Bacon.

Bennis, W. (2003). *On becoming a leader.* New York: Basic Books.

Bennis, W., & Nanus, B. (1997). *Leaders: Strategies for taking charge.* New York: Harper Business.

Brewer, N., Wilson, C., & Beck, K. (1994). Supervisory behavior and team performance among police patrol sergeants. *Journal of Occupational and Organizational Psychology, 67,* 69–78.

Burke, R. J. (2006). Why leaders fail: Exploring the dark side. In R. J. Burke & C. L. Cooper (Eds.), *Inspiring leaders* (pp. 237–246). London: Routledge.

Burns, J. M. (1978). *Leadership.* New York: Harper & Row.

Burns, J. M. (2003). *Transforming leadership: A new pursuit of happiness.* New York: Atlantic Monthly Press.

Buzawa, E. (1984). Determining patrol officer job satisfaction: The role of selected demographic and job-specific attitudes. *Criminology, 22,* 61–84.

Ciulla, J. B. (2001). Carving leaders from the warped wood of humanity. *Canadian journal of Administrative Science, 18,* 313–319.

Clements, C., & Washbush, J. B. (1999). The two faces of leadership: Considering the dark side of leader-follower dynamics. *Journal of Workplace Learning, 11*(5), 170–175.

Conger, J. A. (1989). *The charismatic leader: Behind the mystique of exceptional leadership.* San Francisco: Jossey-Bass.

Conger, J. A., & Benjamin, B. (1999). *Building leaders: How successful companies develop the next generation.* San Francisco: Jossey-Bass.

Dias, C. F., & Vaughn, M. S. (2006). Bureaucracy, managerial disorganization, and administrative breakdown in criminal justice agencies. *Journal of Criminal Justice, 24,* 543–555.

Dotlich, D. L., & Cairo, P. C. (2003). *Why CEOs fail: The 11 behaviors that can derail your climb to the top—and how to manage them.* San Francisco: Jossey-Bass.

Einarsen, S., Aasland, M. S., & Skogstad, A. (2007). Destructive leadership behavior: A definition and conceptual model. *The Leadership Quarterly, 18,* 207–216.

Engel, R. S. (2000). The effects of supervisory styles on patrol officer behavior. *Police Quarterly, 3,* 262–293.

Engel, R. S. (2001). Supervisory styles of patrol sergeants and lieutenants. *Journal of Criminal Justice, 29,* 341–355.

Engel, R. S. (2002). Patrol officer supervision in the community policing era. *Journal of Criminal Justice, 30,* 51–64.

Engel, R. S., & Worden, R. E. (2003). Police officers' attitudes, behavior, and supervisory influences: An analysis of problem solving. *Criminology, 4,* 131–166.

Engle, E. M., & Lord, R. G. (1997). Implicit theories, self-schemas, and leader-member exchange. *Academy of Management Journal, 40,* 988–1010.

Finkelstein, S. (2003). *Why smart executives fail: And what you can learn from their mistakes.* New York: Penguin Group.

Gardner, J. W. (1990). *On leadership.* New York: The Free Press.

Garrett, T. M. (2004). Whither Challenger, wither Columbia. *American Review of Public Administration, 34,* 389–402.

Geller, W. A. (Ed.) (1985). *Police leadership in America: Crisis and opportunity.* New York: Praeger.

Haberfeld, M. R. (2006). *Police leadership.* Upper Saddle River, NJ: Pearson Prentice Hall.

Hall, P. (1980). *Great planning disasters.* London: Weidenfeld and Nicolson.

Hickman, M. J., & Reaves, B. A. (2006). *Local police departments, 2003.* Washington, DC: Bureau of Justice Statistics.

House, R. J., & Podsakoff, P. M. (1994). Leadership effectiveness: Past perspectives and future directions for research. In J. Greenberg (Ed.), *Organizational behavior: The state of the science* (pp. 45–82). Hillsdale, NJ: Lawrence Erlbaum.

Huberts, L. W. J. C., Kaptein, M., & Lasthuizen, K. (2007). A study of the impact of three leadership styles on integrity violations committed by police officers. *Policing: An International Journal of Police Strategies & Management, 30,* 587–607.

Jermier, J. M., & Berkes, L. J. (1979). Leader behavior in a police command bureaucracy: A closer look at the quasi-military model. *Administrative Science Quarterly, 24,* 1–23.

Kant, I. (1983). The idea for a universal history with a cosmopolitan intent. In T. Humphry (Ed. & Trans.), *Perpetual peace and other essays.* Indianapolis, IN: Hackett.

Kellerman, B. (2000). Hitler's ghost: A manifesto. In B. Kellerman & L. R. Matusak (Eds.), *Cutting edge leadership 2000* (pp. 65–68). College Park, MD: Center for the Advanced Study of Leadership.

Kellerman, B. (2004a). *Bad leadership: What it is, how it happens, why it matters.* Boston: Harvard Business School Press.

Kellerman, B. (2004b). Leadership: Warts and all. *Harvard Business Review, 82*(1), 40–45.

Kelloway, E. K., Sivanathan, N., Francis, L., & Barling, J. (2005). Poor leadership. In J. Barling, E. K. Kelloway, & M. R. Frone (Eds.), *Handbook of work stress* (pp. 89–112). Thousand Oaks, CA: Sage.

Kets de Vries, M. F. R. (1993). *Leaders, fools and imposters: Essays on the psychology of leadership.* San Francisco: Jossey-Bass.

Klockars, C B. (1984). Blue lies and police placebos: The moralities of police lying. *American Behavioral Scientist, 27,* 529–544.

Kotter, J. P. (1990). *Force for change: How leadership differs from management.* New York: Free Press.

Kotter, J. P. (1996). *Leading change.* Boston: Harvard Business School Press. Kouzes, J. M., & Posner, B. Z. (2002). *The leadership challenge* (3rd ed.). San Francisco: Jossey-Bass.

Krimmel, J. T., & Lindenmuth, P. (2001). Police chief performance and leadership styles. *Police Quarterly, 4,* 469–483.

Lee, T. W. (1999). *Using qualitative methods in organizational research.* Thousand Oaks, CA: Sage.

Leslie, J. B., & Van Velsor, E. (1996). *A look at derailment today: North America and Europe.* Greensboro, NC: Center for Creative Leadership.

Lipman-Blumen, J. (2005). *The allure of toxic leaders: Why we follow destructive bosses and corrupt politicians—and how we can survive them.* New York: Oxford University Press.

Lord, R. G., De Vader, C. L., & Alliger, G. M. (1986). A meta-analysis of the relation between personality traits and leadership: An application of validity generalization procedures. *Journal of Applied Psychology, 71,* 402–410.

Maccoby, M. (2000, January/February). Narcissistic leaders: The incredible pros, the inevitable cons. *Harvard Business Review, 78*(1), 68–77.

Manning, P. K. (1997). *Police work* (2nd ed.). Prospect Heights, IL: Waveland.

Martin, R., Thomas, G., Charles, K., Epitropaki, O., & McNamara, R. (2005). The role of leader-member exchanges in mediating the relationship between locus of control and work reactions. *Journal of Occupational and Organizational Psychology, 78,* 141–147.

Mastrofski, S. D. (1998). Community policing and police organizational structure. In J. Brodeur (Ed.), *How to recognize good policing: Problems and issues* (pp. 161–189). Thousand Oaks, CA: Sage.

Mastrofski, S. D. (2002). The romance of police leadership. In E. Warin & D. Weisburd (Eds.), *Advances in criminological theory, volume 10: Crime & social organization* (pp. 153–195). New Brunswick, NJ: Transaction Publishers.

McCabe, B. (2005, April/May). The disabling shadow of leadership. *British Journal of Administrative Management, 46,* 16–17.

McCall, M. W., Jr., & Lombardo, M. M. (1983). *Off the track: Why and how successful executives get derailed.* Greensboro, NC: Center for Creative Leadership.

McCauley, C. D. (2004). Successful and unsuccessful leadership. In J. Antonakis, A. T. Cianciolo, & R. J. Sternberg (Eds.), *The nature of leadership* (pp. 199–221). Thousand Oaks, CA: Sage.

McLean, B., & Elkind, P. (2003). *The smartest guys in the room: The amazing rise and scandalous fall of Enron.* New York: Portfolio.

Meindl, J. R. (1990). On leadership: An alternative to the conventional wisdom. *Research in Organizational Behavior, 12,* 159–203.

Meese, E., & Ortmeier, P.J. (2004). *Leadership, ethics, and policing: Challenges for the 21st Century.* Upper Saddle River, NJ: Pearson.

National Research Council. (2004). *Fairness and effectiveness in policing: The evidence* (Committee to Review Research on Police Policy and Practices, W. Skogan & K. Frydl, Eds.). Washington, DC: The National Academies Press.

Northouse, P. G. (2007). *Leadership: Theory and practice* (4th ed.). Thousand Oaks, CA: Sage.

O'Hara, P. (2005). *Why law enforcement organizations fail.* Durham, NC: Carolina Academic Press.

Panzarella, R. (2003). Leadership myths and realities. In R. Adlam & P. Villiers (Eds.), *Police leadership in the twenty-first century: Philosophy, doctrine and developments* (pp. 119–133). UK, Waterside Press: Winchester.

Peter, L. J., & Hull, R. (1969). *The Peter principle.* New York: William Morrow.

Peters, T. J., & Waterman, R. H. (1982). *In search of excellence: Lessons from America's best run companies.* New York: Harper & Row.

Reese, R. (2005). *Leadership in the LAPD: Walking the tightrope.* Durham, NC: Carolina Academic Press.

Reuss-Ianni, E. (1983). *Two cultures of policing: Street cops and management cops.* New York: Transaction Books.

Ross, D. L. (2000). Emerging trends in police failure to train liability. *Policing, 23,* 169–193.

Rubenstein, J. (1973). *City police.* New York: Farrar, Straus & Giroux.

Schackleton, W. (1995). *Business Leadership.* London: Routledge.

Shamir, B., Pillai, R., Bligh, M. C., & Uhl-Bien, M. (2007). *Follower-centered perspectives on leadership: A tribute to the memory of James R. Meindl.* Charlotte, NC: Information Age Publishing.

Sklansky, D. (2007). Seeing blue: Police reform, occupational culture, and cognitive burn-in. In M. O'Neil, M. Marks, & M. A. Singh (Eds.), *Police occupational culture: New debates and directions* (pp. 19–46). Oxford: Elsevier Science.

Stamper, N. H. (1992). *Removing managerial barriers to effective police leadership.* Washington, DC: Police Executive Research Forum.

Stanton, M. (2003). *The prince of Providence: The life and times of Buddy Cianci, America's most notorious mayor, some wiseguys, and the feds.* New York: Random House.

Steinheider, B., & Wuestewald, T. (2008). From the bottom-up: Sharing leadership in a police agency. *Police Practice and Research, 9,* 145–163.

Strauss, A. L. (1987). *Qualitative analysis for social scientists.* New York: Cambridge University Press.

Swartz, M., & Watkins, S. (2003). *Power failure: The inside story of the collapse of ENRON.* New York: Doubleday.

Van Maanen, J. (1984). Making rank: Becoming an American police sergeant. *Urban Life, 13,* 155–176.

Villiers, P. (2003). Leadership by consent. In R. Adlam & P. Villiers (Eds.), *Police leadership in the twenty-first century: Philosophy, doctrine and developments* (pp. 223–236). Winchester, UK: Waterside Press.

Weisburd, D., Greenspan, R., Hamilton, E. E., Williams, H., & Bryant, K. A. (2000). *Police attitudes toward abuse of authority: Findings from a national study.* Washington, DC: National Institute of Justice.

Wilson, J. Q., (1968). *Varieties of police behavior.* Cambridge, MA: Harvard University Press.

Yukl, G. (2002). *Leadership in organizations* (5th ed.). Upper Saddle River, NJ: Prentice Hall.

DISCUSSION QUESTIONS

1. Situational leadership theory (discussed in this section) comprises two leadership styles—telling and selling—that require a leader to provide considerable direction about a task. How should a leader offer these directions in a way that avoids misconceptions that they are driven by ego or arrogance or that the leader is micromanaging? Can follower ego, arrogance, or overconfidence contribute to perceptions of leader ineffectiveness? Explain.

2. Many of the characteristics of ineffective leaders identified by the National Academy respondents are connected to the principles of organizational justice discussed in Section XIII. When a leader acts in a closed-minded, capricious, and micromanaging way, how might perceptions of organizational justice be affected?

3. Schafer asserts that individual problems—ego, poor integrity, poor work ethic, and placing one's self above others—are more difficult to overcome than occupational problems. As such, these behaviors are more likely to persist. Is it possible to identify individuals who exhibit these behaviors prior to placing them in leadership positions? If so, how?

READING

Reading 21

James B. Jacobs and Elana Olitsky duly note that leading a correctional organization is a challenging endeavor. These leaders must simultaneously balance the problems associated with an underpaid and outnumbered correctional workforce characterized by low morale, the conflicts and health needs of a large inmate population, and the demands of courts, legislators, and other external constituents. The authors argue that, given these demands and constraints, correctional leaders must be well versed in a wide variety of areas, including, but not limited to, public administration, criminology, psychology, minority studies, law, public relations, and accounting. Arguing that the current correctional system is not suitable for developing a large pool of effective leaders, the authors offer a series of recommendations for investing in leadership development: education, including correctional colleges; better pay; service corps for recent college graduates; and strategies for identifying prospective leaders early in their careers.

LEADERSHIP AND CORRECTIONAL REFORM

James B. Jacobs and Elana Olitsky

I. The Crucial Importance of Correctional Leadership

It should be obvious to anyone familiar with the last quarter century struggle to improve prison conditions that professional correctional leadership is *the key* to establishing and maintaining humane prisons. Well-run prisons are not brought into being by good philosophy, good laws, or good lawsuits, although, to be sure, these are very important.[1]

Without intelligent, competent and even inspiring prison leadership, there is little chance of creating decent, much less constructive prison environments and operations.[2] Even unconstitutional conditions of confinement lawsuits that result in sweeping remedial orders can only succeed if there are professional prison personnel willing and able to carry out court-mandated reforms.[3] The most skillful prison leaders are able to utilize court interventions as opportunities to improve the prison's physical plant

Source: Jacobs, J. B., & Olitsky, E. (2004). Leadership and correctional reform. *Pace Law Review, 24,* 477–496.

and administration. Contrariwise, if prison officials are hostile, recalcitrant or incompetent, reform cannot be accomplished. It *matters* who leads our prison systems and individual prisons.[4] Prison history is full of examples of exceptional leaders who have made a difference, at least for a time,[5] as well as with examples of leaders whose failures in vision, values and capacity have led to squalor, chaos and human suffering.

Leadership is crucial to all organizations, e.g., educational, military, and commercial. Many private organizations, and the U.S. armed forces, invest heavily in recruiting and developing leaders who can define, refine and achieve goals, solve problems effectively, creatively and efficiently and elicit their subordinates' best efforts. There is a vast academic and popular literature on leadership.[6] Given the socio-political importance of the vast jail and prison system in our society, defining the ideal qualities and characteristics of prison and jail leaders should generate a substantial corpus of professional and academic writing. Unfortunately, literature on correctional leadership scholarship is very thin,[7] making it all the more important that now (at this late date) we make the topic a top priority.

At a minimum, we need prison and jail leaders who are highly motivated, energetic, humanistic, mature, reflective and innovative. They should be capable of relating well with, and bringing out the best in, their subordinates and inmates.[8] They must have very strong organizational management skills, based on expertise in human resources, personnel management, labor relations and public administration. They also need to be conversant and comfortable with public accounting and budgeting, prison law, maintenance and operation of the physical and mechanical penal infrastructure, public relations and legislative politics. Moreover, they should be well educated in penology, criminology, correctional law, sociology of organizations, sociology of poverty, African-American studies, Latino studies and psychology. Finally, these correctional leaders ought to have a solid grounding in the scholarly and popular literature on leadership.[9]

This is quite a list of qualities and capacities. Can we be serious? Yes, indeed—very serious. One can hardly imagine a more difficult job than running a prison or large jail. The assignment is to keep order, discipline and a modicum of good morale among troubled, anti-social and dangerous inmates,[10] who live under conditions of extreme deprivation including idleness, lack of privacy, sexual frustration and inter-personal and inter-group conflict;[11] add to that overcrowded facilities,[12] deteriorating physical plants, dwindling budgets, demanding litigation and public health problems like AIDS, tuberculosis and hepatitis.[13] Managing a penal institution so that its inmates will conform to reasonable rules, achieve and maintain good mental and physical health, not victimize one another, the staff and the facility and even have a positive outlook is a mind-numbing challenge, but that is not all. The correctional leaders have to manage a workforce that is massively outnumbered by the inmates, often poorly educated, poorly trained, poorly paid, feeling chronically unappreciated[14] and laced with interpersonal and inter-group frictions and gang conflicts. In addition, in many prisons and jails, there is the union to contend with. It constitutes a powerful stakeholder that limits (or can potentially limit) the managers' ability to effectuate policy choices. Finally, correctional managers have to deal with a complicated external environment of legislators, interest groups, volunteer groups, laws, lawyers, courts and media.[15] For institutional-level leaders, the correctional department's central office is a powerful "external" player that impacts all operations and decisions.

It must be emphasized that prison cannot be effectively managed by a single person, no matter how able and energetic; good administration requires more than just a charismatic state director of corrections or city jail director, or a heroic prison or jail warden. Leadership may start at the top, but it needs reinforcement and amplification all the way down and across the organization.[16] One of the most important qualities of an effective leader is the ability to recruit and inspire subordinates. Leaders need to have a breadth of vision so they can challenge their subordinates to think and operate in new ways. Prisons can no longer be run as authoritarian command-and-control organizations.[17] Top officials must empower their subordinates to make appropriate decisions and encourage them to communicate information, ideas, and visions to the wardens.

Although the importance of running safe, orderly and constructive prisons and jails should not be minimized, our focus on leadership should aspire to do much more. Ideally, correctional leaders should rethink the potential and limits of American corrections. It is hardly controversial to suggest that there must be a better way to respond to crime than to lock people up in expensive jails and prisons where their personal problems are aggravated, they become further confirmed in their deviancy and to which a majority return after committing another crime. The current system does not successfully serve convicted criminals, taxpayers or society in general. It is imperative that we encourage a new generation of correctional leaders to rethink the whole mission and scope and organization of "corrections." These leaders can work in concert with leaders from other societal sectors to invent and implement new responses to crime that will move us beyond the expensive and dysfunctional jails and prisons that we have been supporting and tinkering with for more than two centuries.

The human infrastructure requirements of American corrections are daunting. There are at least 3,376 local jails,[18] 1,320 state prisons, 84 federal prisons, and 264 privately run penal facilities.[19] Each state prison system needs outstanding leadership at the departmental level—director and assistant directors in charge of adult facilities, juvenile facilities, financial operations, community relations and legal counsel. Each prison and jail needs a warden, assistant wardens, top security officer, program heads, physical plant manager, chief of budget, recreation director and disciplinary officers. Even filling all those positions with competent leaders, while a great accomplishment, will not be sufficient. It is important to have good leadership at the middle management levels, e.g., in each cell house, especially in administrative and disciplinary segregation units, in the workshops and in the school. If the fifty state and/or federal prison systems each require ten leaders at the central office, and if each jail requires five leaders, and if each prison requires ten, the nation needs roughly 32,000 leaders at any given time.[20] This leadership pool must be constantly replenished due to retirements, resignations and proliferation of institutions.[21]

Recruiting, developing, promoting and supporting this professional correctional corps ought to be considered a national responsibility and challenge. Yet, to date there has been no such national commitment. Indeed, there seems to be little recognition that we have a national problem. To the contrary, the nation, including politicians and correction officials themselves often act as though correctional leadership is in abundant supply, as though no special strategies are needed to recruit and nurture it and as though the leadership and potential leadership that we do have can be squandered with impunity.[22]

II. Recruiting, Developing, and Retaining Correctional Leaders

We cannot address the strategies necessary for improving the correctional system's human infrastructure without first recognizing the impediments to recruiting, developing, and retaining potential jail and prison leaders. The first challenge is to **recruit** potential leaders into corrections. Some potential leaders may be recruited into corrections as young men and women who will develop personally and professionally in the system. Other potential leaders will be laterally recruited from other organizations. Thus, the leadership pool from which we can draw depends upon the extent to which we are free to recruit people directly into middle and upper management. Lateral recruitment has major advantages, allowing prisons and jails to benefit from the training and experience that other private and public organizations provide.[23]

Whether recruitment is vertical or lateral, prison work is a hard sell. Neither remuneration[24] nor prestige is high.[25] Working conditions (in prisons) are harsh.[26] The majority of the human contacts for many prison staff, especially those at the lower level, is with prisoners who are loaded with psychological and social problems that are exacerbated by the deprivations of imprisonment.[27] They routinely vent their frustrations on the staff, and rarely acknowledge a job well done. At best, prisoners are not likely to be successful in their interpersonal relations and therefore to be good daily "company" for members of the staff. There is physical danger in prison work. Stress is high and morale low. Prison employees feel chronically under-appreciated, perceiving that there is more societal concern for the well-being of prisoners than for prison staff. Even among the best-intentioned and most mentally healthy employees, stress and burnout constantly undermine job satisfaction.

The second challenge is for prisons and jails is to stimulate and encourage personal and leadership development. Most prison regimes are paramilitary and hierarchical. Young officers and other employees are subject to strict, sometimes arbitrary rules and discipline. Many young men and women do not respond well to that style of management.[28] A certain kind of leader who would be very valuable to corrections will be immediately "turned off."[29] Moreover, in many states, collective bargaining agreements mean that assignments and promotions are dictated by seniority.[30] Prison and jail bureaucracies are often muscle bound and overly regulated, discouraging (or even punishing) initiative. Over the past generation, decision making increasingly has been concentrated at ever-higher administrative levels.[31] Ideas from the rank and file, even from middle and upper management, are often neither solicited nor welcome.[32] Turnover among prison staff is often very high, reinforcing negative morale.[33] The most ambitious and talented young officers are the most likely to leave for other job opportunities.

The rapid prison expansion of the past two decades has generated unusual opportunities for rapid promotion, but that too presents problems.[34] Prisons and jails present many occasions for failure and few for success. Because of rapid prison expansion, prison personnel have been promoted without adequate training. They have thus been vulnerable to errors and mistakes leading to demotion and dismissal.[35] It would be illuminating to see what percent of potential leaders is more or less driven out of corrections by an inflexible discipline and management.[36]

This leads to the third challenge—retaining talented middle and upper level personnel. Responsibility is great, hours long, working conditions poor. To retain personnel with strong leadership potential will require making their working lives satisfactory and stimulating. Salaries need to keep pace at least with other law enforcement agencies, and the qualities of facilities (exercise rooms, showers, cafeteria) should make officers feel valued and appreciated.

A fourth challenge, actually an impediment to correctional leadership development, is the revolving door that characterizes the tenure of state directors of correction. These top officials average just three years on the job.[37] They move on with a change in the gubernatorial administration, or on account of some crisis or scandal or simply to take advantage of another job opportunity. It is true that some of them, like baseball managers, move from one state prison system to another and are therefore not inexperienced when they assume the job. Nevertheless, one must seriously ask how much leadership can be developed and exerted over the course of such a short term tenure. The staffs expectation that the head of the system will soon be gone is by itself is a recipe for organizational stagnation or worse. It is no coincidence that the Federal Bureau of Prisons, whose directors have enjoyed much longer security than their state counterparts, is generally regarded as the best-run prison system in the nation.

Leadership may, to some extent, be innate, linked to basic intelligence and personality. But a complex organization cannot rely on a few individuals' instincts and personalities. Thus, the fifth challenge for corrections is to systematically nurture and develop leadership. Unfortunately, in most states leadership training is rudimentary; in some states it hardly exists at all.[38] Most prisons and jails treat *any* training beyond entry level as a luxury. There are not enough resources and often not enough officers to allow many employees to be released for training, at least not often and not for long. The content of the training that does exist tends to be practical nuts and bolts skills, focusing on survival, rather than on imbuing personnel with strategies for becoming effective leaders. There is no "in-house" expertise to deliver the kind of high-power leadership training that we have in mind, and such training has not been available to more than a few individuals via outside providers.[39] It requires magical thinking to believe that somehow the human infrastructure of American prisons and jails will just will itself to the next level of expertise.

III. Investing in Correctional Leadership

Improving corrections' human infrastructure requires imagination and resources. There are many reasons to be pessimistic. But things will not get better unless we generate some positive goals to strive toward. Therefore, the rest of this essay sets out some ideas for improving leadership in corrections, no matter how politically impractical they may seem at the present time.

Our view is that the human infrastructure of corrections ought to be seen as a national resource and its improvement a national priority. Could an individual state or a combination of states do this themselves? Our federalism creates a disincentive for any single prison system (or several systems within a region) to invest heavily in training and leadership development. If any one state were to make such an investment, other states and counties (and private prison companies) would simply hire its expensively trained leaders away. Eventually the high-spending states would cut back on staff development. The states also lack the resources and economies of scale to mount sophisticated prison leadership programs.[40] This makes it clear that we need a federal initiative that looks to improving the nation's overall human correctional infrastructure.

The National Institute of Corrections (NIC) has, in fact, pioneered in leadership training for state and local jail personnel. Some of its programs have been and are excellent. The problem is that NIC has not been funded or even imagined at anything like the level and size that is necessary.[41]

Given the extent of our investment in imprisonment, the United States should have the best national prison and jail college in the world. American corrections needs a major correctional college running five or six days a week, all year long.[42] It should be a college with a permanent staff of correctional professionals and a "civilian" faculty perhaps recruited for one or two year stints from prestigious departments of criminology, liberal arts, management and law. There ought to be both long and short courses and everything in between. This college ought to be a place where all levels of prison personnel can learn the latest ideas about leadership. The college should promote an environment where up-and-coming correctional personnel from all over the country can meet, formally and informally with one another, with senior correctional officials, leading scholars and teachers. It is vital that this college be broadly integrated into higher education. Corrections needs more support from and integration with the larger society. The very existence of a college like this would increase the profession's prestige, expand its recruitment base, broaden its perspective and energize its ranks.

We would prefer the kind of prison and jail college sketched above, but the federal government could make its investment in corrections' human infrastructure through grants to "civilian" colleges and universities for offering different kinds of leadership training: one university might pioneer a course on human relations, while another might develop a course on the history, sociology and management of rehabilitation.

The state prison systems should concentrate on entry-level training and on doing as much as possible to identify potential leaders. Here it would probably make sense for more than one state to jointly operate or fund an entry-level training academy. A cooperative venture might offer economies of scale that would enable a training academy to be in use throughout the year, thereby allowing for better staff salaries, and a larger and richer curriculum.

The state prisons and the county jails need programs to identify potential leaders and to develop their full potential at every step of the organizational ladder. It is necessary to focus on finding, rewarding and encouraging the best performing personnel. Rewards need not only be monetary, but monetary rewards ought not to be overlooked. Prisons and jails require salary scales that encourage employees to seek promotion and to remain in the organization.

Ideally, prisons and jails would provide a transitional leadership course to every person slated for promotion.[43] Before assuming their new post, the just-promoted employee could be sent to the prison and jail college for a management course. In addition, or alternatively, he or she could be sent on a week-long visit to a "model" (or at least highly regarded) prison or jail outside the state, thereby broadening the individual's base of experience; hopefully the employee would return to the home institution with new ideas and perspectives. Why couldn't the National Institute of Corrections invest in several "model prisons" which could serve this kind of national training function by hosting visiting personnel from all over the country? Another idea would be simply to identify and persuade (perhaps with financial rewards) the dozen best managed correctional facilities to play this role. Perhaps the host institutions could be paid to play this role. Such a strategy might generate healthy competition for recognition as a prison or jail in the top group. For those personnel selected to visit, the trip itself would be a reward, a vote of confidence and an investment in the individual's career development.

Another possibility would be to send newly promoted prison personnel to a university-based course for middle or upper level managers. Perhaps there should be a dozen such college or university based courses in the country focusing on leadership, management generally, criminology and penology. Quite possibly, successful completion of such courses would become a positive, even necessary, marker on the correctional curriculum vitae. Instructors might keep tabs on "students" who stand out as most promising.

More could and should be done to build cooperative programs between corrections, philanthropic foundations, academia and the private sector. University-prison partnerships will benefit both the prisons and the university. To date, there has almost certainly been more academic attention to educating prisoners than prison personnel. Indeed, this is a source of resentment among correctional staff. One model is to bring correctional personnel to the college; another model is to take a college program to the prison. Yet a third model is for the prison organization to recruit faculty to the institution for long or short stints. Why couldn't every prison aim to recruit a scholar in residence for a few weeks or longer each year? Perhaps a foundation would sponsor such a program? Private businesses could lend executives or leadership trainers to prisons for short periods of time.

Prison systems could provide promising mid and upper-level administrators with sabbaticals. This would represent a big investment in those few individuals' human and intellectual capital, adding to their breadth of knowledge and depth of expertise. If the host organization could be assured that this individual would contribute to the organization for a significant period of time, such an investment might pay off. But this is a big if. What would prevent another state from poaching those individuals who have just completed their sabbaticals?[44] This problem could be avoided if the federal government or a private philanthropic foundation sponsored the sabbatical program.

The more other societal sectors, institutions and groups that support prison and jail leadership, the better. Several hundred criminal justice programs flourish in our colleges and universities. Some of the thousands of correctional personnel who have obtained degrees in such programs now hold top correctional leadership positions in jails and prisons. More could be done. The courses could be made more accessible and more relevant. The professors could play a larger role in mentoring and supporting the best-performing students.

IV. Correctional Service Corps

Another idea with real potential to improve correctional leadership is a "Correctional Service Corps." The time is ripe for state-level or national correctional service corps that would expand the recruitment base for correctional leaders by attracting idealistic college graduates for a year or two of public service in corrections.[45] These young people would be a breath of fresh air for penal facilities that all too easily become highly insulated from the larger society. The Correctional Service Corps could follow the model of the Corporation for National and Community Service (Americorps) programs, which expose young people to various fields of public service.[46] Some participants in the Correctional Service Corps would be attracted to the field as a career, thus contributing to the pool of potential future leaders. Some of those who don't sign on with corrections will become part of a broader constituency for humane and constructive prison conditions and operations. Finally, the very presence of one or two dozen Correctional Service Corps participants in each prison would help to break down parochialism and insularity. They will provide "outside eyes" on the regime's operations.[47]

V. Conclusion

We have fifty-one state and federal prison systems and several thousand county jails, all separately funded, administered and monitored. Our history is replete with instances of penal institutions degenerating into squalor and violence.[48] For more than a generation, prisoners' rights litigation has played a crucial role in exposing unconstitutional conditions. Federal courts (and the parties themselves) have responded with hundreds of orders and consent decrees mandating improved conditions and operations.[49] While conditions and operations have improved, there is still a *long way* to go. While litigation is effective in exposing and remediating truly deplorable conditions and abuses, it is less effective in creating decent conditions and operations and ineffective in bringing about excellent conditions and operations. Those goals require the commitment and skills of correctional managers who can creatively solve (or at least manage) the incredibly difficult problems that prisons and jails face.

Effective administration of prisons and jails demands outstanding leadership at the central office and institutional levels. We need good policy and the ability to implement it. We need leaders who can translate good intentions into good works, inspire their staffs to work hard and humanely in the face of difficult conditions and challenges, recognize and deal with legitimate inmate complaints and concerns, lobby effectively with the legislature and communicate constructively with the community and the courts. Such leadership is not abundant. Its existence is problematic. Its creation should be regarded as a challenge and responsibility for everybody who cares about civilized prisons and jails.

In this article we argue for recognizing the importance of investing in the leadership cadre of American prisons and jails. We point out the obstacles to recruitment, development, promotion and retention of leaders for this field. We sketch out some proposals for moving in that direction. We recognize that such proposals need to be fleshed out, that they will not be easy to implement and that that they will not (in most cases) be cheap. At this point, however, we think it is important simply to generate and call attention to goals for leadership development that might attract governmental, foundational and academic interest and support. Working towards these goals would be a major contribution to addressing a major national problem. The human infrastructure of corrections must be considered a national resource; nurturing and improving it must become a national goal.

Notes

1. Prison litigation has spawned a number of new roles in prison, such as law librarians, substance abuse counselors, nutritionists, and compliance personnel. See James B. Jacobs, *The Prisoners' Rights Movement and Its Impacts 1960-80*, 2 CRIME & JUST. 429, 429 (1980) for a history and analysis of prison reform and its impacts.

2. *See* James B. Jacobs, Stateville: The Penitentiary in Mass Society (1977); *see also* John J. DiIulio, Jr., Governing Prisons: A Comparative Study of Correctional Management (1987).

3. See the protracted and unsuccessful effort to reform Puerto Rico's system through litigation, now ten years in the courts. The history is told in the following opinions: *In re Justices of Supreme Court of P.R.*, 695 F.2d 17 (1st Cir. 1982); Schneider v. Colegio de Abogados de Puerto Rico, 565 F. Supp. 963 (D.P.R. 1983), *vacated by*, 742 F.2d 32 (1st Cir. 1984); Schneider v. Colegio de Abogados de Puerto Rico, 572 F. Supp 957, 957-58 (D.P.R. 1983); Schneider v. Colegio de Abogados de Puerto Rico, 670 F. Supp 1098 (D.P.R. 1987); Schneider v. Colegio de Abogados de Puerto Rico, 682 F.Sup.674 (D.P.R. 1988), *rev'd in part by*, 917 F.2d 620 (1st Cir. 1990); Schneider v. Colegio de Abogados de Puerto Rico, 947 F. Supp 34 (D.P.R. 1996); and Schneider v. Colegio de Abogados de Puerto Rico No., 187 F.3d 30 (1st Cir. 1999).

4. "Looking back over time . . . it would appear that the reformist periods were more the results of charismatic reformers, individuals and groups, who were able to sway decision makers, than of any dramatic shifts in public opinion." Allen Breed, The State of Corrections Today: A Triumph of Pluralistic Ignorance 3 (1986).

5. *See* Thomas O. Murton & Joe Hyams, Accomplices To The Crime: The Arkansas Prison Scandal (1969). A less radical example is Norman Carlson, who during his eighteen-year tenure as director of the Federal Bureau of Prisons was able to effect safe, civilized, humane prisons, carefully controlled and run by a professional staff. Kevin N. Wright, Effective Prison Leadership 5-6 (1994).

6. For example, Joseph Jaworski's book has attracted enormous attention in the business world and in schools and programs of management. Joseph Jaworski, Synchronicity: The Inner Path of Leadership (1996). In this highly experiential account Jaworski contends that leadership is about personal transformation as a leader rather than about getting subordinates to comply with orders. *See id.; see also* Robert K. Greenleaf et al., Servant Leadership: A Journey Into the Nature of Legitimate Power and Greatness (Larry C. Spears ed., 25th Anniv. ed. 2002) (an eastern-philosophy-influenced book that has had tremendous influence in the field of organizational leadership).

7. *But see* Wright, *supra* note 5; Stan Stojkovic & Mary Ann Farkas, Correctional Leadership: A Cultural Perspective (2002); Peter M. Carlson & Judith Simon Garrett, Prison and Jail Administration: Practice and Theory (1999); Richard P. Seiter, Correctional Administration: Integrating Theory and Practice (2001); *see also* Dan Richard Beto & Melvin Brown, Jr., *Effective Correctional Leadership for the 21st Century*, 3 Corrections Mgmt. Q., 47 (1999).

8. There is a massive and rich literature on leadership that is widely used in business schools and private sector organizations. See, *e.g.*, JAWORSKI, *supra* note 6; Greenleaf, *supra* note 6: Peter M. Senge, The Fifth Discipline: The Art and Practice of the Learning Organization (1990); Margaret J. Wheatley, Leadership and the New Science: Learning About Organization From an Orderly Universe (1992); John W. Gardner, On Leadership (1989); James M. Kouzes & Barry Z. Posner, The Leadership Challenge: How to Get Extraordinary Things Done in Organizations (1987); TOM Gilmore, Making a Leadership Change (1989). Arguably, all middle and upper level prison officials should have the opportunity (probably more than once) to take a leadership seminar based around books like these. In top business schools and schools of management, courses on leadership are common. See, *e.g.*, the Wharton School's Center for Leadership and Change Management, *at* http://leadership.wharton.upenn.edu/ welcome/ index.shtml.

9. "Effective prison leaders balance the need for continuity with the need for change, and the need for standardization with the need for self-expression and creativity[They] view their staff as mutually interdependent, and they constantly work to ensure a sense of community among them." Wright, *supra* note 5, at 11.

10. Nationally, the number of inmate-on-inmate assaults in correctional facilities rose from 25,948 to 34,355 from 1995 to 2000, and assaults on staff rose from 14,165 to 17,952. Bureau of Justice Statistics, U.S. Dep't of Justice, Bull. No. NCJ 198272, Census of State and Federal Correctional Facilities 2000 10 (2003), *available at* http://www.ojp.usdoj.gov/bjs/pub/pdf/ csfcf00.pdf [hereinafter Correctional Facilities].

11. There are countless examples, but for a recent one, see Dwight F. Blint, *Gang Worries Prison Workers*, Hartford Courant, Oct. 13, 2003, at A1. See *generally* Mark S. Fleisher & Scott H. Decker, *An Overview of the Challenge of Prison Gangs* 5 Corrections. Mgmt. Q., 1 (2001).

12. Overcrowding and understaffing is one of the biggest problems prisons face. Forty-five state prison systems are operating at or above intended capacity. Twenty-two states are operating under court-ordered population caps. Eric Schlosser, *The Prison Industrial Complex*, Atlantic Monthly, Dec. 1998, at 51.

13. Prison healthcare and disease is a major issue. In 1997, a study of Bureau of Justice Statistics data showed that released

inmates accounted for 20 to 26% of the HIV/AIDS cases in the United States, 12 to 16% of hepatitis B infections, 29 to 32% of hepatitis C infections, and 39% of tuberculosis cases. Thomas M. Hammett et al., *The Burden of Infectious Diseases Among Inmates and Releases From US Correctional Facilities, 1997*, 92 Am. J. Pub. Health 1789, 1792 (2002).

14. For a description of the media's negative image of prisons and its influence on prison staff, see Robert M. Freeman, *Here There Be Monsters: Public Perception of Corrections*, 63 Corrections Today 108 (2001); Tim Kneist, *Old Habits Die Hard: Corrections Professionals Constantly Struggle Against Negative Stereotypes*, 60 Corrections Today 46, 46-48 (1998).

15. Add to these factors the effect of privatization on the prison system. Between 1995 and 2000, the number of private facilities rose from 110 to 264. These facilities are highly controversial and have been opposed by many prison reform organizations. In 2000, thirty-three of them were under court order or consent decree, up from fifteen in 1995. Correctional Facilities, *supra* note 10, at 9. They also tend to have higher staff turnover (probably due to lower pay) and higher inmate escape rates. See Scott D. Camp & Gerald G. Gaes, *Growth and Quality of U.S. Private Prisons: Evidence from a National Survey*, 1 CRIMINOLOGY & PUB. POL'Y 427 (2002).

16. Kevin Wright makes a similar point: "The ability of the senior executive to surround himself or herself with a knowledgeable interdisciplinary team to support efforts to respond appropriately to the myriad of tasks will determine success." Kevin N. Wright, *The Evolution of Decisionmaking Among Prison Executives, in* 3 Criminal Justice 2000: Policies, Processes, Decisions of the Criminal Justice System, 177, 200 (Nat'l Inst, of Justice ed., 2000), *available at* http://www.ncjrs.org/criminaljustice2000/vol_3/03e.pdf.

17. *See* Jacobs, *supra* note 2.

18. Bureau of Justice Statistics, U.S. Dep't of Justice, Sourcebook of Criminal Justice Statistics, 2002 90 tbl.1.94 (Kathleen Maguire & Anne L. Pastore eds., 2002).

19. *Id.* at 94 tbl.1.98.

20. In 2000, there were a total of 430,033 employees in correctional facilities under state or federal authority, a 23.8% increase from 1995. Correctional Facilities, *supra* note 10, at vi.

21. In 1992, the number of retirements per department of corrections was sixty-three, up from fifty-nine the previous year; the number of resignations was 271. Half of all staff departures in 1992 were resignations. Nat'l Inst, of Corrs., U.S. Dep't of Justice, Managing Staff: Corrections' Most Valuable Resource 17 fig.7 (1996) (study conducted by George Camp on methods of effectively managing corrections staff), *available at* http://www.nicic.org/pubs/1996/013216. pdf [hereinafter Managing Staff].

22. State directors of correction serve about three years. According to Bob Brown at the National Institute of Corrections, thirty-four directors of corrections are up for appointment this year. Some "new" directors have just left similar jobs in other states, so their knowledge and skills are not lost. Telephone Interview with Bob Brown, National Institute of Corrections, Academy Division (Oct. 20, 2003). Still, this revolving door of state directors of corrections may place a huge constraint on the capacity of prison systems to improve significantly.

23. Ironically, perhaps, the directors of state prison systems are often lateral recruits.

24. In January 2001, the national average annual starting salary for correctional officers was approximately $24,000; the average maximum salary was $38,000. The average minimum salary for wardens was $54,250, while the average maximum salary was $86,275. James B. Jacobs, *Prison Reform in the 21st Century, in* The Future of Imprisonment (Michael Tonry ed. 2004).

Some salary figures from Texas: based on the salaries of individuals listed, correctional administrators earn about $88,000, and wardens earn about $100,000. *25 Years: 2002 Public Employee Salary Survey,* The Reporter, Dec. 16, 2001, *at* http://63.192.157.117/Specials/salary/2OO2AistO2.html (last visited Apr. 22, 2004). In 2001, the starting salaries for majors was $36,864; captains, $34,380; lieutenants, $33,240; sergeants, $32,000. Correctional officers started at $20,592. *See* Texas Dep't of Criminal Justice, *TDCJ Corrections as a Career, at* http://web. archive.org/web/20030210165555/http://www.tdcj .state.tx.us/vacancy/COinfo/ca-reer.htm (last updated Aug. 9, 2002).

Salary is often cited as a reason for high correctional turnover. A 1987 study found that 50% of those working in corrections chose the field because of economic necessity, and only 22% chose the field as their first choice of careers. Seiter, *supra* note 7, at 320 (citing M.J. Shannon, *Officer Training: Is Enough Being Done?*, 49 Corrections Today 172 (1987)).

25. Jane Sachs describes how correctional staff internalize the negative media images. She points out that although correctional work should be categorized as white-collar, it is typically thought of as blue-collar work. Jane Sachs, *Professional Development for Correctional Staff,* 61 Corrections Today 90, 92 (1999). Allen Breed has also spoken on the need to change the public image of corrections. Breed, *supra* note 4, at 6-7.

26. See Jacobs *supra* note 2.

27. In his article Secretary of Washington State Department of Corrections, Joseph D. Lehman says, "Historically, corrections has been a closed and isolated culture. We, in fact, were created to be out of sight, out of mind. We have operated on the premise that our job was primarily one of keeping the bad offender separated from the good, law-abiding citizen." He goes on to say, "The

public will not tolerate the isolationism that has become our armor against a seemingly hostile environment." Joseph D. Lehman, *The Leadership Challenge: Back to the Future*, 3 Corrections Mgmt. Q. 19, 20 (1999). He and Wright both argue that corrections leaders must adopt a more contextual view of their role, and enter into a dialogue with the larger community. *See id.* ; *see also* Wright, *supra* note 16.

28. Clear and Cole's introductory textbook says prison administration "is dominated by uncreative thinking, ungrounded and idiosyncratic conceptualization, and an unwarranted commitment to traditionalism." TODD R. CLEAR & GEORGE F. COLE, AMERICAN CORRECTIONS 151 (2d ed., 1990).

29. It is interesting to note that in the British Prison Service, there is tension between the senior-level managers who want innovation and change, and the entry-level personnel who are suspicious and doubtful of changes. *See* Alison Liebling, Prisons and their Moral Performance 344 (forthcoming July 2004). For a discussion of manager qualities and organizational dynamics in British prisons, as well as the importance of creative, clear and communicative leaders in creating a positive prison atmosphere see *id.* at 339-90.

30. See James B. Jacobs & Norma Crotty, Guard Unions and the Future of the Prisons (1978).

31. For information about the historical evolution of prison administrative decisions see JACOBS, *supra* note 2, at 73; WRIGHT, *supra* note 5.

32. Because of the attention paid to corrections by the public and by elected officials, managers and administrators who become too visible or step too far outside the box can find their job security in jeopardy. *See* Richard P. Seiter, *The Leadership and Empowerment Triangle*, 3 Corrections Mgmt. Q. iv (1999),

33. In George Camp's 1996 study, he found that while the growth in prison populations was rising, a trend that continues today, the growth of staff populations was shrinking. Turnover rates could be as high as 50% in some institutions, though not in entire systems. See Managing Staff, *supra* note 21, at 19-20.

34. It is possible now to be promoted to warden within ten years, something unheard of in the past. Brown, *supra* note 22.

35. One study found that turnover rates among correctional officers are 15.4% in publicly run prisons, 40.9% in privately run prisons. Tracy Huling, *Building a Prison Economy in Rural America*, *in* Invisible Punishment: The Collateral Consequences of Mass Imprisonment 202 (Marc Mauer & Meda Chesney-Lind, eds. 2002). This statistic does not distinguish those who are dismissed from those who leave voluntarily. Turnover rates vary widely by state, and by number of years of employment. Many correctional officers leave for jobs with other local law enforcement agencies. Am. Corr. Ass'n, *Staff Hiring and Retention*, 26 Corrections Compendium 6 (2001) [hereinafter *Staff Hiring and Retention*].

36. For an insightful view of how organizational attributes create stress and turnover, see Ojmarrh Mitchell et al., *The Impact of Individual, Organizational, and Environmental Attributes on Voluntary Turnover among Juvenile Correctional Staff Members*, 17 Justice Quarterly 333 (2000).

37. *See supra* note 22.

38. Entry-level training includes instruction on such topics as: constitutional law and cultural awareness, inmate behavior, contraband control, custody and security procedures, fire and safety, inmate legal rights, written and oral communication, use-of-force, first aid, and physical fitness training. Training is conducted on-site. Jess Maghan, *Correctional Officers in a Changing Environment: 21st Century—USA* 4 (2002), *at* http://www.jmfcc.com/CorrOfficersChangingEnvirnmnt.pdf.

State entry-level training programs have been cut in recent years. Illinois, for example, has closed its statewide correctional academy for budgetary reasons. Among the forty-two state and federal correctional agencies included in a recent survey, introductory or basic training can range from 40 to 400 hours of introductory training, which includes both classroom and on-the-job training. Seiter, *supra* note 7, at 324.

The National Institute of Corrections' distance learning program is utilized at many prisons as a way of training new wardens and supervisors. Several state systems use educational reimbursement as an incentive to retain staff. Arizona provides 100% reimbursement for department-requested courses and 80% for approved employee requested courses. See Ariz. Rev. Stat. § 41-1664 (1984); *see also* Arizona Dep't of Corrections, ADC Department Order Manual (2003) (department order 509.11), *available at* http://www.adc.state.az.us/Policies/509.htm#509.05. California provides a monthly incentive of $100 toward educational pursuits, and Colorado reimburses half the cost of tuition when an associate degree is obtained. *See generally* California Department of Corrections, Benefits Information, *at* http://www.corr.ca.gov/SelectionsStandards/SelectionAndStandardsPages/AdditionalBenefitsInfo.asp (last visited Apr. 22, 2004); *see also* Press Release, Colorado Department of Corrections, Colorado Department of Corrections Hosts Higher Education Fair (Nov. 28, 2001), *available at* http://www.doc.state.co.us/releases/2001_releases/2001-November-28.htm. Missouri varies its reimbursements according to grades. Nebraska requires officers to remain employed by the correctional system for twelve months following any reimbursed course. Idaho provides some management and supervision courses. *Staff Hiring and Retention, supra* note 35, at 6-12.

The American Correctional Association (ACA), the largest and most important professional correctional organization in the U.S., is a valuable source of information regarding policy, procedure and professional standards for corrections. SEITER, *supra* note 7, at 312. The ACA also provides some educational materials, on-site training and access to self-instructional courses. See American Correctional Association, *at* http://www.aca.org.

39. Ninety percent of new wardens surveyed said they received no special training or orientation in their new job responsibilities prior to, or just after they assumed their assignment. About half reported that no formal mentoring program was made available to them. Susan W. McCampbell et al., Resource Guide for Newly Appointed Wardens (2002). It should be noted that the very existence of this publication, aimed to serve as an orientation for wardens to their new position, indicates the lack of formal training they receive before assuming their new position. Another excellent manual that serves a similar purpose is N. Am. Ass'n of Wardens and Superintendents, A View From the Trenches: A Manual for Wardens by Wardens (Sharon Johnson Rion ed. 1999).

40. Many state correctional systems do have their own leadership programs. *See, e.g.*, Nebraska Commission on Law Enforcement and Criminal Justice, *at* http://www.nol.org/home/crimecom/; Oklahoma Department of Corrections Training Administration, *at* http://www.doc.state.ok.us/Training/index.htm; Florida Criminal Justice Executive Institute, *at* http://www.fdle.state.fl.us/fcjei/. However they are limited in scope by financial constraints, and many are not more than a couple of days long. The Oregon Department of Corrections has offered both two-week and sixteen-hour long formal leadership training courses in preparation for supervisory positions. Gregory Morton, *Step-by-Step Program Offers Comprehensive Training*, 4 CORRECTIONS PROF. 9 (1999). It is modeled after the NIC courses. *Id.* South Carolina's Department of Corrections sends fifty employees to six two-day sessions throughout the year; they deal with such issues as leadership, environment and the economy, education, governance, total quality management, and health. William Gengler & Connie Riley, *Two States' Training Programs Lead the Way Into the 21st Century*, 57 CORRECTIONS TODAY, 104 (1995). It involves field visits and meetings with community and business leaders. *Id* at 104-6. One example that has stood out above the rest is the Leadership Institute in California, a six-week intensive program run by California State University. It has been temporarily suspended due to budget cuts.

41. The NIC provides information services, technical assistance and training programs for correctional practitioners in its Academy, Prisons, Jails, and Community Corrections divisions. Most of these trainings occur at its Longmont, Colorado site, and there are trainings from manager to senior executive levels. The executive trainings in particular are learner-centered and occur over a period of ten months. The manager programs use Kouzes and Posner's leadership challenge model and focus on managerial styles and teamwork. *See generally* National Institute of Corrections, *Training Services for Corrections Professional, at* http://nicic.org/Services/TrainingServices.aspx (last visited Apr. 22, 2004).

There is an eighteen-month program for administrators interested in becoming senior level leaders, which occurs in three phases and involves making organizational changes during that time and completing an academic paper around a problem of interest. The courses are treated similarly to graduate level courses. Unlike the authoritarian structure of the prisons themselves, the courses are designed to be participatory and to encourage thinking outside the box. There is also a special course for women and minorities, designed toward helping them advance in the leadership system. This is a less intensive training program and focuses more on personal growth and on individual managerial style. The course looks at racism and sexism in our society, and at ways to use informal power and networking to both become an effective manager and to move up in the ranks. There is also an advanced course that promising students can take. *See id.*

These programs are by application and are competitive to get into. Most of them consist of only thirty-six or seventy hours. Prison administrators and managers apply on their own initiative, and their supervisors must sign off on the applications. The NIC offers distance learning options, and partners with other agencies for additional trainings (although it will not pay for partnered trainings). The NIC also has a Technical Assistance program that provides onsite support for correctional facilities to help improve their program. *See* National Institute of Corrections, *NIC On-Site Technical Assistance, at* http://nicic.org/Services/OnSiteSer-vices.aspx (last visited Apr. 22, 2004). In addition, there are several distance learning options. In recent years, these have been used increasingly, as they are easier and less costly to implement. *See* National Institute of Corrections, *NIC Correctional e-Learning Center, at* http://nicic.org/Services/eLearning.aspx (last visited Apr. 22, 2004). However, they do not provide the same level of training and individualized attention. The extent of the NIC program seems to be around enriching and improving the capabilities of administrative and managerial staff, rather than providing a basic level of training for everyone. About 1000–1200 prison staff members come to the Academy for training, while another 4000–6000 are educated by the NIC staff at their facilities. Another 12,000–20,000 are educated via distance learning. Brown, *supra* note 22. Telephone Interview with John Eggers, National Institute of Corrections, Academy Division (Sept. 29, 2003); Telephone Interview with Nancy Shoemaker, National Institute of Corrections, Academy Division (Oct 6, 2003).

42. There are some European examples that we might look to. The Bavarian Prison Staff Training School, for example, provides leadership and management courses in the framework of further training for staff members who are either already or expect to be in leadership positions. This is a four-week program

with both classroom time and project time, and a practical focus with some theoretical grounding. Email from Bernhard Wydra, Director, Bavarian Prison Training School, to James B. Jacobs, Professor of Law, New York University School of Law (Oct. 26, 2003) (on file with author).

43. The California Department of Corrections' Leadership Institute might serve as a model. This highly competitive program trains management staff from captain up, from prisons around California. Over its nine years of existence it has come to be considered a necessary step to the top positions. Jointly sponsored by the California State University at Chico, the Leadership Institute provides an intensive training for one week per month for six months. The curriculum exposes its students to organizational leadership literature, ethics, character development and strategic planning. Each student must complete a project, some of which have turned into policy changes. The program serves not only to train promising leaders but also to foster connections between people in different positions within prisons and in different prisons throughout the state. It graduated 350 students, before being suspended because of state financial troubles. Telephone Interview with Stan Stojkovic, Academic Director, Leadership Institute (Nov. 5, 2003). For more information on this program, see Stan Stojkovic et al., *Correctional Leadership Education Into the 21st Century: The California Leadership Institute* 61 Fed. Probation 50 (1997).

44. Of course, university sabbatical programs face the same problem. Some universities require the sabbatical taker to return to the host institution for one year or pay back the sabbatical salary. See, *e.g.,* Univ. of Mass. Med. Sch., University Sabbatical Leave Procedure 3 (2000), *at* http://www.umassmed.edu/facultyadmin/pdfs/sabbatical.pdf; Kan. State Univ., *Sabbatical Leave Guidelines*, *at* http://www.k-state.edu/academicservices/depthead/sabbat/sabblv.html (last updated Apr. 5, 2004).

45. *See* James B., Jacobs, New Perspectives on Prisons and Imprisonment (1983).

46. *See* www.americorps.org; *see also* www.teachforamerica.org.

47. Several states use interns to fill many of their entry-level positions. In Montgomery County Corrections, in Maryland, student interns are recruited and hired part-time at minimum wage, and also get college credit for working there. The facility can then hire them full time when they graduate. A significant percentage of their current staff came in as interns. E-mail from Jane Sachs, Manager, Montgomery County Pre-release Services to James B. Jacobs, Professor of Law, New York University School of Law (Oct. 27, 2003).

48. Jacobs, *supra* note 1.

49. *See* Correctional Facilities, *supra* note 10. In 2000, 357 prison facilities were operating under consent decree or court order, the most common reason being overcrowding. Perhaps because of the Prison Litigation Prison Litigation Reform Act, Pub. L. No. 104-134, 110 Stat. 1321 (1996) (codified at 11 U.S.C. § 523; 18 U.S.C. §§ 3624, 3626; 28 U.S.C. §§ 1346, 1915, 1915A; 42 U.S.C. §§ 1997-1997h), the number of prisons under court order for staffing, counseling, library services or food services decreased dramatically since 1995. CORRECTIONAL FACILITIES, *supra* at 9.

DISCUSSION QUESTIONS

1. Jacobs and Olitsky outline a lengthy list of qualities and capacities necessary for effective correctional leadership. Are there other qualities and capacities that should be included in the list? Explain. In your opinion, is it realistic to expect correctional leaders to be proficient in all these areas?

2. Consider your own criminal justice, criminology, or related program (or look up a nearby program on the Internet). Are the course offerings—elective and required—sufficiently balanced, exposing students to the major areas of the criminal justice system, or does one get more attention? What do you think the experience would be like attending a school devoted to corrections only?

3. Jacobs and Olitsky argue that correctional leaders should make significant changes within prisons and jails. How easy is this to accomplish given public opinion, legislatures, the courts, and other external factors?

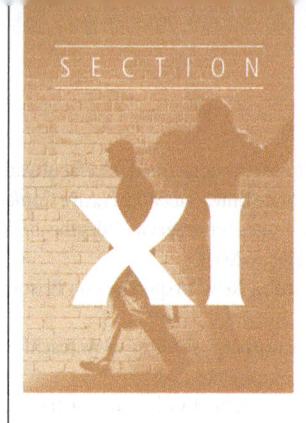

Power in Organizations

How Are Subordinates, Suspects, Inmates, and Clients Controlled?

Section Highlights

Power Defined
Power, Authority, and Leadership
The Bases of Power
    Criminal Justice Applications

Influence Behavior
Effectiveness of Power
    Street-Level Bureaucrats
    Effective Power Bases

As a supplement to their own means of ensuring control and securing compliance from inmates, Texas prison guards established and maintained a hierarchy of elite prisoners that acted as an extension of the guard force (Crouch & Marquart, 1989). Building tenders (BTs), as these inmates were known, emerged in the late 1800s and persisted until the system's court-ordered dissolution in the early 1980s (Crouch & Marquart, 1989; Marquart & Crouch, 1985). They were tasked with serving as representatives of cell blocks, conducting hourly block counts, reporting inmate misbehavior, enforcing prison regulations, and protecting correctional officers. On what basis did the ordinary inmate comply with the demands of BTs? Although also inmates, BTs possessed a privileged status that distinguished them from other inmates within the prison hierarchy. Their superordinate position afforded them some degree of power over others, akin to the power of a correctional sergeant over a correctional officer. Moreover, they served at the whim but acted with the support of correctional officers. Consequently, they were seen by other inmates as arms of the prison's staff. Finally, their ability to secure compliance was buttressed by their willingness to use force. As Crouch and Marquart (1989) noted,

With the tacit approval of the guards, BTs possessed such weapons as pipes, clubs, knives, and blackjacks in their cells. . . . The regular inmates knew that the BTs had an arsenal of weapons and feared the BTs because of this. (p. 105)

These factors were enough to produce widespread compliance and order among inmates.

As the example illustrates, a power structure emerged, separating inmates from one another on the basis of their capacity to influence others. All relationships—between organizations, departments, groups, and individuals—are characterized by unilateral or bilateral power flows. From an organizational theory and behavior standpoint, power is a critically important concept, helping us understand how organizational goals, rules, and structures are established, subordinates are directed, compliance is ensured, and influenced is exerted. For example, the U.S. Department of Justice is permitted, under the provisions of federal law, to file lawsuits against local police agencies accused of a "pattern or practice" of depriving citizens of constitutional rights (e.g., systematic discrimination in use of force; Ross & Parke, 2009). In many circumstances, agreements (e.g., consent decrees) are reached between the Department of Justice and local departments specifying necessary organizational changes. The Department of Justice, using the threat of a lawsuit, compels substantial changes within the affected departments, thereby removing the ability of police agencies to make autonomous decisions. Yet power is used in more benign ways every day (Lucas & Baxter, 2012). Police officers restore order in many situations without relying on arrests, but their decisions are backed by their ability to take citizens into custody. Supervisors complete performance appraisals for employees as a means of inducing organizationally prescribed behavior in employees. Power is wielded throughout the criminal justice system, in relations among organizational members and between members and clients. This section addresses the interconnected issues of power and influence, focusing on individual rather than organizational or other group-level power. (Resource dependence power, discussed in Section III, provides an example of interorganizational power.) Of particular importance is how it is developed or acquired and how it is effectively exercised.

Power Defined

Power is an essential feature of organizational life, a tool for controlling and obtaining compliance from others. In criminal justice organizations, power is even more critical given the dual need to control the actions of individuals/employees within the organization and secure obedience from typically uncooperative clients (e.g., inmates, offenders). Definitions of power abound, and, in combination, they offer clarity about this important organizational concept. Five definitions are presented below:

- "Potential influence" (Raven, 1993, p. 232).
- "The capacity to effect (or affect) organizational outcomes" (Mintzberg, 1983, p. 4).
- "A has power over B to the extent that he can get B to do something that B would not otherwise do" (Dahl, 1957, pp. 202–203).
- "Any force that results in behavior that would not have occurred if the force had not been present" (Mechanic, 1962, p. 351).
- "The power of actor A over actor B is the amount of resistance on the part of B which can be potentially overcome by A" (Emerson, 1962, p. 32).

If these definitions are taken together, several key themes emerge. First, power is an inherently social phenomenon impossible to study without understanding the dynamics between those who possess power (power holder) and those who experience it (power recipient; Scott & Davis, 2007). We might argue, for example, that a police officer possesses a tremendous amount of power, because "the policeman, and the policeman alone, is equipped, entitled, and required to deal with every exigency in which force may have to be used, to meet it" (Bittner, 1990, p. 256). Declaring the officer's unilateral power is meaningless, however, without considering the recipient of that power and the relations between the two parties. William Ker Muir's (1977) classic volume *Police: Streetcorner Politicians* exemplifies the need to treat power as a relational and situational concept (Scott & Davis, 2007). Muir described what he referred to as the paradox of dispossession, the idea that the less one has, the less one has to lose. Applying this idea to police use of force situations, the seemingly powerful police officer would be unable to use threats of deadly force to wrest compliance from an armed suspect. If the offender does not value his life or other important possessions, the officer cannot use those possessions as a means of coercion. In other situations, similar threats may be incredibly powerful. The point is that both the power holder and recipient must be discussed when addressing the issue of power.

Raven's (1993) and Mintzberg's (1983) definitions highlight a second theme: Power is a capacity or ability, something to be energized, mobilized, or exercised. Once power is exercised, it becomes influence or, as French and Raven (1959) describe it, "kinetic power" (p. 152).[1] Figure 11.1 illustrates this relationship between power, influence, and compliance. Power is derived from certain sources or bases. But having power, the ability or capacity, is not sufficient to get others to acquiesce to, or comply with, the power holder's demands. The power holder must have the "will and skill" to use the power he or she possesses (Mintzberg, 1983, p. 25). A parole officer has the power to punish offenders, potentially returning them to prison for technical violations or new offenses. If the officer chooses to overlook these behaviors, the power is never exercised. That said, the potential exists for the exercise of power; a parolee may abide by regulations in recognition of the officer's capacity to punish even if the officer takes no overt steps to coerce compliance (Brass & Burkhardt, 1993).

The third theme addresses what this capacity or ability (power) allows the power holder to do. The definitions crafted by Dahl (1957), Mechanic (1962), and Emerson (1962) establish power as the capacity or ability to get others (power recipients) to comply or conform to the demands of the power holder, even in the face of physical, verbal, or other forms of resistance. In the Baltimore Police Department, for example, command staff attempted to wield power over officers by establishing minimum performance standards pertaining to arrests (Moskos, 2008). Officers were instructed to produce at least one arrest (later two) per four-week period. Those who failed to meet the performance standards were required to complete a memo, referred to as a "95," detailing the reasons for this lack of performance. Department officials were using punishments—in this case, paperwork, an official record, and the possibility of subpar employee evaluations—as mechanisms for compelling officers to meet established standards.

Finally, power relations can exhibit reciprocal characteristics (Scott & Davis, 2007). In the Baltimore example, the officers were not completely powerless. Due to low morale and anger over the department's standards, some officers stopped making arrests altogether; these actions potentially

---

[1] As Mintzberg (1983) notes, part of the reason for the many terms stems from the fact that power cannot be translated into a verb (e.g., the correctional officer *powered* the inmate). Consequently, power must be translated into influence or some other term that can be used as a verb. Others have struggled with the conceptualization of both power and influence (Zimmerling, 2005).

Figure 11.1 The Relationship Between Power, Influence, and Compliance

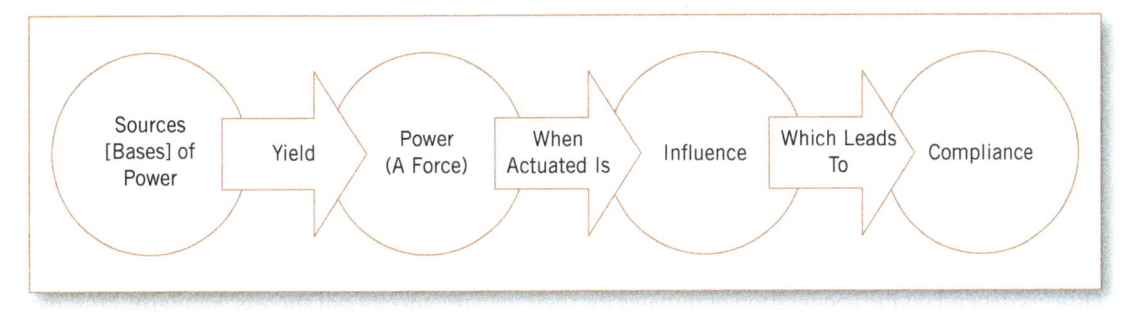

Sources [Bases] of Power → Yield → Power (A Force) → When Actuated Is → Influence → Which Leads To → Compliance

Source: Tosi, Rizzo, and Carroll (1986).

punish superiors who are evaluated according to arrest totals. Additionally, Peter Moskos, an officer and academic who was soon to be leaving the force, tried to alter the department's practices by using the undesirable term *quota*, instead of *minimum performance standards*, when writing memos to command staff. Departments are reluctant to establish or acknowledge the existence of arrest quotas, so Moskos tried to use this pointed language as leverage, although its effects were minimal. While the department exercised power over officers, the officers did the same in return. Yukl (1994) contends that it is perhaps more useful to examine net power, "the extent to which the [power holder] has more influence over the [power recipient] than the [power recipient] has over the [power holder]" (p. 195).

Power, Authority, and Leadership

In casual conversations, *power* is often used interchangeably with other related terms, including *authority* and *leadership*. In contrast to power, authority represents the right to make demands of others, what some have called "legitimate power" (French & Raven, 1959; Scott & Davis, 2007). In most organizations, this right is closely associated with one's position (i.e., rank) within the organization's hierarchy (Tosi et al., 1986). Subordinates have an organizationally prescribed duty to conform to the demands of superiors, and if true authority exists, compliance will be based solely on the differences in rank, irrespective of possible punishments or rewards. Young children are expected to obey parents' wishes because of the authority relationship that exists between parent and child. The same is true of a supervisor–subordinate relationship. Power may exist in place of or in conjunction with authority. Armed robbers have no authority; they have no legal right to demand a victim's money, nor does the victim have any obligation to obey. The presence of the firearm and the robber's threatening behavior does, however, potentially give the robber power to secure compliance from a victim. Within an organization, an administrative assistant—a staff position on an organizational chart—may lack authority over others but may accumulate power over time via the ability to access important departmental records. Even a supervisor, bestowed with authority by virtue of an elevated rank, may use power against those who fail to recognize that authority.

Leaders use both power and authority to facilitate the achievement of organizational or group goals, but power should not be confused with leadership. Instead of using the terms synonymously, Robbins and Judge (2008) argue that three key differences must be recognized. First, leadership requires some degree of goal compatibility between the leader and followers, while power holders and power recipients need not agree on the purpose of their actions. A resisting suspect and a pursuing officer seek diverse goals—escape and apprehension, respectively. The officer has power (i.e., the ability to use coercive force) and may exercise it to secure the suspect, but unlike leadership, goal compatibility is unimportant. As the definitions of power discussed earlier illustrate, the very possibility of goal incompatibility—getting individuals to do things they would not otherwise do—is the essence of power. Second, leadership emphasizes influence that moves from leader to follower. However, individuals may possess power without necessarily occupying leadership roles within an organization. Studying power allows for an examination of influence irrespective of rank, leadership titles, status, and other hierarchical structures. If, for example, performance evaluations of correctional officers are based, in part, on how orderly cell blocks appear, inmates obtain some measure of power over officers. Officers depend on the cooperation of inmates for their own organizational success. Similarly, Moskos's letter to police management was an attempt to influence superiors. Finally, studies of leadership tend to address the most effective styles or behaviors. Studies of power deal with the methods of securing compliance from subordinates, clients, or others. Returning to the example that opened this section, rather than focus on whether BTs were task or relationship centered, studies of power would address the specific strategies—a combination of coercive force and hierarchical authority—BTs used to obtain cooperation from other inmates.

The Bases of Power

What gives an individual power over another? Bertram Raven, one of the coauthors of the famous power typology, and his colleagues answered the question by stating, "Social power can be conceived as the resources one person has available so that he or she can influence another person to do what that person would not have done otherwise" (Raven, Schwarzwald, & Koslowsky, 1998, p. 307). In other words, individuals must have a base of power, something that backs power holder requests. One of the most widely cited power classification schemes or typologies was developed by French and Raven in 1959. They proposed five bases or sources of power that can be identified by examining the relationship between two individuals. First, an individual has the capacity for **coercive power** when he or she can punish, or at least is believed to be able to punish, those who fail to comply with directives. If an individual does not control at least some punishments, his or her coercive power is likely weak. Coercive power can be seen in interactions among police officers. The strong police officer subculture can lead officers to ostracize others who fail to conform to group attitudes or behaviors. Compliance allows the power recipient to avoid any punishments (e.g., returning to prison for recidivism, disciplinary report for failing to complete paperwork, etc.). Second, others acquire **reward power** through their ability to distribute intrinsic and extrinsic rewards. In response to compliant behavior, supervisors may offer pay raises to subordinates, judges can relax restrictions on drug court participants, and correctional officers may extend television viewing time for inmates. Where rewards are limited, so, too, is reward power. Third, **legitimate power** represents French and Raven's decision to include authority in their typology. Legitimate power is based on the power recipient's belief that the power holder has the right, usually derived from his or her position or rank, to make demands and secure compliance. In other words, position is a resource and a source of power. Fourth, **referent power** is based on one party's identification with another. The power recipient admires, respects, or seeks to associate with the power holder. A well-respected police field-training officer likely has considerable power over the probationary officer for a number of reasons, including the field-training officer's likeability and the probation officer's desire to please. Finally, some individuals acquire *expert power* for their extensive knowledge in a specific field. For example, if a mechanic tells you that you need to spend $1,000 for repairs on your car, you might comply given the skills of the mechanic even though you would not ordinarily part with that amount of money. Similarly, jurors may give tremendous weight to the testimony of expert witnesses, deferring to their proficiency in the subject matter.

French and Raven (1959) acknowledged that there were "undoubtedly many possible bases of power which may be distinguished," but they focused their attention on the five identified above (p. 155). Since the publication of their original typology, the number of power bases has expanded in recognition of additional power sources (Yukl, 1994; Yukl & Falbe, 1991). *Information power* is possessed by individuals who control information flows within an organization or who have access to information sought by others.[2] Consider a police informant. Even though the individual has been arrested and faces criminal charges, she nevertheless has some power over criminal justice officials to the extent that she has access to information others need. *Resource power* is wielded by those who control or who can secure much-needed resources for the organization or others. Section III addressed resource dependence theory. The central argument of the theory is that external organizations that control resources are able to compel dependent organizations to change. Within criminal justice organizations, central figures, including those who can acquire grant funding or lobby government officials for appropriations, acquire considerable power. An inmate with access to contraband (e.g., tobacco) also acquires resource power (Stojkovic, 1984). Finally, the importance of *charismatic power* as a base was also recognized. A charismatic individual is able to inspire enthusiasm and has the capacity to influence via "extraordinary ability and strong personal magnetism" (Yukl, 1994, p. 207). The five original and three new bases of power together have been classified into two categories: *position power* and *personal power* (Yukl, 1994). Position power bases—legitimate, resource, reward, coercive, and information—are derived from one's position in the organization. An individual's ability to control resources, rewards, and punishments, as well as access information, is largely dependent on that person's location in the organizational hierarchy. In contrast, personal power bases—expert, referent, and charismatic—are independent of position; consequently, these types of power can be possessed by anyone, regardless of position.

Criminal Justice Applications

A number of scholars have applied the bases of power to the study of criminal justice organizations, particularly correctional organizations. These works offer additional examples that both clarify the bases of power and afford insight into the means of achieving control in justice settings. Tifft (1978), for example, conducted an observational study of power bases in a large police department, contending that the source of power was contingent on the individual's position, the nature of his or her work, and contact with subordinates. How were officers controlled, if at all? Patrol sergeants generally had weakly developed reward power bases; benefits such as salaries, job assignments, and shifts were often determined by collective bargaining agreements rather than supervisor prerogative. Expert power was

---

[2] Multiple definitions have been applied to information power. Others have described information power in terms of persuasion; an individual has information power to the extent that he or she has information that can be used to convince others to change their positions (Raven, 1993; Yukl, 1994). In this section, information power is defined by access to information, which is how it is commonly described in criminal justice research.

similarly limited, as first-responding officers were more knowledgeable about the specific circumstances generating calls for service than was a late-arriving sergeant. In the department observed, officers rotated across both time (shifts) and space (beats), constantly working under different supervisors. As a result, they rarely identified with any one particular sergeant (weak referent power). Sergeants did retain some ability to punish (coercive power) officers via disciplinary infractions and performance appraisals, and legitimate power was still evident by virtue of the sergeant's position. Tifft contrasts the patrol sergeant with a tactical (e.g., SWAT) team leader. Again, the position affords the leader a certain degree of legitimate power, but unlike for the patrol sergeant, the constant team training leads to the development of referent power. The leader's expertise in planning tactical maneuvers is an additional source of compliance. Although Tifft recognized that coercive and reward power were unlikely to be relevant during a tactical situation (e.g., raid, hostage situation, etc.), they were relevant during non-call-out periods. After all, the leader makes team assignments and can dismiss members as needed.

Others have studied power within institutional settings. Among prison administrators, coercive, reward, and information power were critical (Stojkovic, 1986). Recalcitrant inmates were transferred to other facilities or placed in administrative segregation or detention as punishment. Inmates seeking to avoid these additional pains of imprisonment would have to comply with staff requests. Cooperative inmates were rewarded for their compliance and desirable behavior with jobs or other privileges. Stojkovic also referenced the importance of information. Typically, information power is generated when an individual possesses information sought by others. Administrators within the prison develop a network of snitches providing useful information about drugs, violence, and other activities that may potentially disrupt prison operations. In this way, it is the inmate, not the prison administrator, who possesses information power. Prison officials extract this information through an exchange process, trading rewards for information useful for controlling the facility. Interestingly, correctional officers themselves contended that their power was based on sources other than rewards and punishments. In a survey of 360 correctional officers in five facilities across four states, John Hepburn (1985) found that correctional officers' power was commonly derived from their position (legitimate power) and their competence as good officers (expert power). Less common sources included referent, reward, and coercive power. Why the discrepancy between administrators and correctional officers? As will be discussed below, there are significant problems with relying on coercion as the primary means of compliance. Officers work with inmates every day and must be cognizant of the potential for retaliation if threats and force are regularly applied. For administrators, identifying the utility of punishments when the pattern of strict regimentation breaks down clearly conveys an image of who is in control of the prison. Moreover, administrators tend to note officially supported rewards such as job assignments. In reality, correctional officers may more readily offer inmates nonsanctioned benefits in exchange for compliance. A correctional officer may overlook minor offenses in exchange for information or support during administrative inspections. Therefore, rewards may be used by officers, if not officially recognized rewards.

Recognizing that power is a social phenomenon and compliance is a product not only of the power holder's base of power but also of how it is interpreted by the recipient, more recent researchers altered the methods for studying organizational power (Podsakoff & Schrieschiem, 1985; Yukl & Falbe, 1991). Instead of relying on a respondent's self-identified power bases or a researchers interpretation of power sources, subordinates or, in some cases, peers are asked to describe the power bases of superiors. After all, the power bases are salient only if perceived by the subordinate. Male inmates in an Ohio high-security facility only partially confirmed Hepburn's (1985) earlier findings suggesting that correctional officers relied on legitimate and expert power bases (Stichman, 2002). About half of the 396 inmates surveyed indicated that guards have the right to be obeyed, have the right to control inmates, and compliance occurs simply because so ordered by guards (all indicative of legitimate power). Unlike Hepburn, Stichman found little evidence of correctional officer expert power. Referent power, however, was more fully developed; a majority of inmates reported respecting correctional officers and cooperating with some officers because of their fairness. Few inmates recognized the reward power of correctional officers, and although they indicated that correctional officers used threats, most inmates stated that such coercion was unrelated to their own compliance with guard demands. Using a similar approach, Smith, Applegate, Sitren, and Springer (2009) surveyed nearly 376 probationers in a Southeastern city to examine their perceptions of probation officer power. Their findings are suggestive of versatility. With the exception of reward power, all bases of power were at the disposal of community corrections personnel. At this point, it is worth noting that respondents may be reluctant to acknowledge a superior's power base due to a social desirability bias (Podsakoff & Schriesheim, 1985; Yukl, 1994; Yukl & Falbe, 1991). As Stichman writes, "The inmates might not want to appear that officers are able to control them through these threats [coercive power] as that might undercut their 'being a man'" (p. 123). Further discussion of the effectiveness of the bases of power appears later in this section.

Influence Behavior

The bases of power bestow the power holder with the capacity to influence, but he or she may resort to a variety of techniques to get others to accomplish goals. A police officer, although permitted to use coercive force in certain situations (coercive power), may extract compliance using alternative approaches (e.g., simply asking for cooperation). As clarified by Hellriegel and Slocum (2004), "having the capacity (power) to influence the behaviors of others and effectively using this capacity (power) aren't the same thing" (p. 277). Power holders generally have one or more influence objectives in mind—assigning work, changing behavior, obtaining assistance, acquiring support, or securing personal benefit—and they use a variety of influence tactics to satisfy these objectives (Yukl, Guinan, & Soitolano, 1995). Nine common tactics, techniques, and strategies are identified in Table 11.1.[3] Among the influence tactics, the last three—legitimating, pressure, and coalition—are referred to as forcing styles due to their focus on "blocking non-compliance behavior, or making that kind of behavior too unattractive to be performed" (Emans, Munduate, Klaver, & Van de Vliert, 2003, p. 37). Pressure involves punishing or threatening to punish those who fail to comply, legitimating strategies involve assertions of authority, and coalition techniques draw strength from numbers. The remaining techniques are so-called nonforcing because they all afford targets a greater degree of choice in whether or not to comply. Individuals attempting to influence others use techniques that lead to voluntary rather than forced or dutiful compliance.

In criminal justice settings, exchange tactics are particularly important for two reasons. First, recall that rarely is a power recipient completely powerless. Often they possess some degree of power, leading to reciprocal power relationships where both parties attempt to influence the other. In situations where both parties possess power and attempt to influence others, power bases may be ineffectual. Second, Cohen and Bradford (1989) argue for the existence of a law of reciprocity—"that people should be paid back for what they do, that one good (or bad) deed deserves another" (p. 7). The solution, commonly observed in criminal justice organizations, is to address reciprocal power relationships through a process of exchange.

---

[3]Others have offered similar categories of influence tactics with slightly different labels (see, for example, Kipnis, Schmidt, & Wilkinson, 1980).

Table 11.1 Definitions of Influence Tactics

Rational persuasion

You use logical arguments and factual evidence to persuade the person that a proposal or request is practical and likely to result in the attainment of task objectives.

Consultation

You seek the person's participation in planning a strategy, activity, or change for which you desire his or her support and assistance, or you are willing to modify a request or proposal to deal with the person's concerns and suggestions.

Inspirational appeals

You make a request or proposal that arouses enthusiasm by appealing to the person's values, ideals, and aspirations, or by increasing the person's confidence that he or she would be able to carry out the request successfully.

Personal appeals

You appeal to the person's feelings of loyalty and friendship toward you when you ask him or her to do something.

Ingratiation

You seek to get the person in a good mood or to think favorably of you before making a request or proposal (e.g., compliment the person, act very friendly).

Exchange

You offer an exchange of favors, indicate willingness to reciprocate a favor at a later time, or promise the person a share of the benefits if he or she helps you accomplish a task.

Legitimate request/legitimating tactics

You seek to establish the legitimacy of a request by claiming the authority or right to make it, or by verifying that it is consistent with organizational policies, rules, practices, or traditions.

Pressure

You use demands, threats, frequent checking, or persistent reminders to influence the person to do what you want.

Coalition tactics

You seek the aid of others to persuade the target to do something, or use the support of others as a reason for the target person to agree to your request.

Source: Yukl et al. (1995).

Michael Brown (1988) illustrated exchange between police field supervisors (sergeants) and patrol officers by noting that sergeants have legitimate power by virtue of their rank and expert power given their years of experience. They are able to discipline and evaluate officers, thereby offering rewards and punishments. Officers may also identify with sergeants since most are drawn from the patrol ranks. This combination should give sergeants a significant measure of power over officers. In reality, the power is weakened and officers are able to develop some of their own sources of power. Supervisors are incapable of directly observing most officer–citizen encounters and so rely on information from other officers for an understanding of what is happening on the streets. This gives officers information power over sergeants. Officers are also able to "punish" superiors by pointing out mistakes to upper-level managers or by embarrassing sergeants during roll call. To resolve this reciprocal power relationship, both parties relinquish some degree of power, complying with the demands of the other. Sergeants refrain from over-enforcing discipline (e.g., wearing a hat, arriving to work on time) to keep information channels open. In return, officers avoid making trouble for their supervisors. As Brown explains, "The outcome is a pattern of mutual accommodation in which field supervisors reassert the semblance of discipline and behave as bureaucrats in the station house, while confronting patrolmen as colleagues on the street" (p. 110). Within the courts, defense attorneys can create havoc for prosecutors who are evaluated in terms of victories. Trials create uncertainties by increasing the likelihood of a loss. At the same time, a defense attorney's client also faces risks in the form of more severe punishments (the so-called trial penalty). This, in turn, affects the defense attorney's reputation as an effective advocate. Plea bargaining represents an exchange where all parties—judge, prosecutor, defendant, and defense attorney—win but relinquish something (e.g., full prosecution) in return (Eisenstein & Jacob, 1991). Exchange is a mechanism for creating symbiotic relationships when both parties assert their power.

Effectiveness of Power

The discussion has so far proceeded under the assumption that power holders are generally effective at producing compliance from power recipients. Such an assumption may be unwarranted. Within criminal justice and other public service organizations, subordinates are often able to neutralize the power of supervisors due to their considerable discretion and lack of direct oversight. Michael Lipsky (1980) described them as street-level bureaucrats, and because of this role, supervisory power is limited. Additionally, research has shown that the bases of power are not equally effective in exacting compliance from subordinates or clients. In fact, relying on some forms of power may actually have detrimental effects on power recipients and the overall organization. Both topics—street-level bureaucrats and the effectiveness of individual bases of power—are addressed in turn.

Street-Level Bureaucrats

In theory, a supervisor has the right to make demands of and ensure compliance from street-level, line-level, or frontline employees within the organizational hierarchy (Vinzant & Crothers, 1998). These employees, referred to as street-level bureaucrats, occupy positions that, in practice, complicate supervision. Lipsky (1980) applied the term **street-level bureaucrats** to those public-sector workers who "actually constitute the services delivered by government" (p. 3). It does not matter whether the law states that a given person is eligible for welfare benefits, that the speed limit is 65 miles per hour, or that religion must be taught in a high school history class. What matters is how the frontline worker—the social worker, the police officer, or the teacher—exercises the considerable discretion at his or her disposal. If, for example, officers never cite drivers for going 70 mph in a 65 mph zone, then the speed limit, for all intents and purposes, is no longer the 65 mph established by the legislature. The actual limit is determined via the officer's enforcement decisions. Street-level bureaucrats make decisions that affect the lives of others but do so with limited resources (i.e., there are only so many police officers) and with limited supervision (Lipsky, 1980; Vinzant & Crothers, 1998).

The nature of the street-level bureaucrat's work weakens managerial power in three ways (Prottas, 1978). First, most criminal justice employees are characterized by what Prottas referred to as low "**compliance observability**" (p. 298). It is simply difficult to know whether or not they comply with supervisory, organizational, and/or legal directives because they work independently with little supervision. For example, a police chief could instruct all officers to confront truants and transport them back to school. Because the desired action—addressing truant behavior—occurs on the street beyond the view of supervisors, officers face little pressure to conform. This is not to suggest that officers will knowingly and willfully disregard orders; partial or full compliance is possible and likely. Managerial power is nevertheless weakened because of the inherent difficulties in ascertaining whether employees actually comply with orders.

Prottas's (1978) second factor extends this argument. The demands that originate from upper levels of the organization (or legal mandates) are intended to specify appropriate employee behavior, but such behavior is contingent on the client, offender, or situation. Consider three rules and regulations that appear in some criminal justice organizations: The offender must be arrested in misdemeanor domestic violence situations (police); two years must be added to the sentence of any offender convicted of a felony if a firearm was used (courts); and inmates with evidence of mental illness must be placed within a specific facility (corrections). In each of these examples, desirable behavior can be framed in the form of an *if–then* statement (e.g., *if* an offender commits a misdemeanor infraction, *then* the officer must arrest the offender). The result is that "the hierarchy can judge street-level bureaucrat behavior only on a contingent basis, i.e., only in relation to the way a client has been slotted, but it is dependent on the street-level bureaucrat to first slot the client" (p. 297). Supervisory orders to arrest misdemeanor domestic violence offenders can be enforced only if the officer has first defined the situation as a misdemeanor offense. The officer need only redefine the situation to avoid the arrest mandate and counteract supervisory power. Because of low compliance observability, the supervisor's power to enforce compliance with desired behavior (the *then* part of the statement) is limited by the employee's description of that situation (the *if* part of the statement). A judge can avoid demands to increase penalties for crimes committed with firearms by classifying the offense as a non-firearm crime. Likewise, an intake specialist can decide to place an offender with no evidence of mental illness in a special facility by first classifying the offender as having a mental illness. As these examples illustrate, although adherence to rules and regulations might be demanded by superiors, it is the street-level bureaucrat who controls the decisions on which desired behavior is based.

The final factor limiting supervisor power, according to Prottas (1978), is a weak incentive system that is ineffective at producing compliance. Even if the organization has significant rewards and punishments at its disposal, the low compliance observability of street-level bureaucrats means that positive or negative behavior will generally go unnoticed. In reality, incentives such as raises or benefits are limited by collective bargaining contracts and civil service regulations.

Effective Power Bases

Few scholars have moved beyond describing the bases of power of criminal justice employees to an examination of the effectiveness of these bases across a variety of domains, including securing compliance, job satisfaction, and others (for exceptions, see Schwarzwald, Koslowsky, & Agassi, 2001; Smith et al., 2009). In spite of the absence of evidence from within criminal justice circles, significant insight can be obtained from the large number of empirical studies available within the general organizational theory literature regarding the effectiveness of various bases of power. Yukl and Falbe (1991) found among a sample of workers in three companies that perceptions of managerial effectiveness were more closely linked to the manager's perceived personal power (e.g., expert or referent) than to his or her position power (e.g., legitimate or reward). Similarly, in their review of studies addressing the relationship between power and performance, satisfaction with supervision, and overall job satisfaction, Podsakoff and Schriesheim (1985) concluded that personal power, particularly expert and referent bases, was superior. Recall from the earlier discussion that personal power bases, coupled with legitimate power, were commonly reported by or attributed to criminal justice personnel.

Why is personal power more effective than position power within organizations? Several explanations have been offered. Two position power bases, coercive and reward power, rely on **surveillance** to ensure successful compliance (Raven, 1993). The promise of rewards and threat of punishments are ineffective unless the power holder is able to monitor power recipient behavior. Consider a teacher who, while administering an in-class examination, decides to leave the classroom. She admonishes students to keep their eyes on their own papers or risk failing the exam. The teacher's power is linked to her ability to detect cheating. If students believe that they will be unmonitored for a certain period of time—lacking surveillance—then the threat may not carry much weight. Similarly, power holders have difficulty distributing rewards if they cannot witness compliance. This brings us back to the issue of low compliance observability. Personal power bases, including referent, expert, and charismatic power, are surveillance independent. If you have ever taken medicine prescribed by a doctor, you have likely experienced this phenomenon. You deferred to the doctor's medical expertise and complied with his or her orders; you took the medicine even though the doctor was not monitoring your behavior. The doctor's expertise produced compliance. These examples suggest that in occupations where monitoring is difficult, it is not surprising that power holders must place greater emphasis on personal rather than position power.

Coercive and reward power, if used with legitimate power, may produce compliance, but they also may generate detrimental outcomes for the organization (Tosi et al., 1986). When punishments and incentives are used, subordinates may offer resistance if the demands are perceived as unreasonable. Section VI documented examples of work slowdowns and other job actions in response to what were perceived as unreasonable organizational demands. More substantial, according to Tosi and colleagues, is the possibility that subordinates will "develop a counterforce" (p. 542)—in other words, that coercive behavior will be reciprocated. Gresham Sykes (1958), for example, found that prison guards were reluctant to use coercive force due to concerns of retaliation. Strategies that rely on exchange produce more superior outcomes than those that rely on coercion. Finally, both coercive and reward power may lead to learned helplessness, a situation where the subordinate loses autonomy (see Section VIII for the importance of autonomy in job design) and experiences depression and diminished morale. The exercise of personal power does not generate these same deleterious effects.

As this discussion demonstrates, power is an essential concept for understanding compliance within the criminal justice system. However, it should now be clear that the exercise of power by criminal justice officials does not always mean the use of coercion. In fact, evidence suggests that coercion is ineffective, and, indeed, frontline personnel rely on other bases of power to gain compliance from clients. Exchange relationships become an important tool for dealing with reciprocal power situations.

KEY TERMS

charismatic power

coercive power

compliance observability

expert power

influence tactics

information power

legitimate power	power	reward power
personal power	referent power	street-level bureaucrats
position power	resource power	surveillance

DISCUSSION QUESTIONS

1. You are tasked with investigating a riot within a large state prison. Do you think it is more important to understand power and compliance from the perspective of the correctional staff or inmates, or are both equally important? Explain.

2. Criminal justice employees often encounter situations in which they are outnumbered, sometimes substantially. Correctional officers are surrounded by hundreds of inmates, as are police officers by people on the scene of a large-scale demonstration. In your opinion, how do these officials secure compliance from such a large number of individuals? What is their power based on?

3. Is it possible to train employees to rely on different bases of power? For example, could officers be taught to develop a referent or expert power base to gain compliance instead of relying on more coercive strategies?

WEB RESOURCES

Tennessee v. Garner, 471 U.S. 1 (1985) (Supreme Court case regarding police use of deadly force):
http://caselaw.lp.findlaw.com/scripts/getcase.pl?court=US&vol=471&invol=1

National Legal Aid and Defender Association:
http://www.nlada.org

Review of Stanley Milgram's experiments on obedience and authority (including slide show):
http://www.nytimes.com/2008/07/01/health/research/01mind.html

READING

Reading 22

Gresham M. Sykes's classic work, *The Society of Captives*, details the realities of correctional officer power within correctional facilities. Conventional wisdom suggests that correctional officers possess total power over inmates, but Sykes's research within the New Jersey State Prison led him to conclude that this view was purely fictional. Their position as keepers would seemingly afford them considerable amounts of legitimate power, but as Sykes notes, inmates have no duty to comply with correctional officer demands. Moreover, the punishments and rewards available to correctional officers (coercive and reward power) are neither effective nor salient in ensuring compliance. If prison personnel are unable to secure compliance via legitimate power, carrots, or sticks, how then is control achieved? Sykes argues that control can be achieved only by allowing the power of the correctional staff to be weakened. Correctional officers enter into exchange relationships with inmates wherein minor infractions are overlooked, thereby creating more tolerable prison conditions in exchange for more general cooperation at other times. Although Sykes refers to these relationships as a "sort of moral blackmail," they essentially represent instances of reciprocal power where influence flows in both directions.

The Defects of Total Power

Gresham M. Sykes

"For the needs of mass administration today," said Max Weber, "bureaucratic administration is completely indispensable. The choice is between bureaucracy and dilettantism in the field of administration."[1] To the officials of the New Jersey State Prison the choice is clear, as it is clear to the custodians of all maximum security prisons in the United States today. They are organized into a bureaucratic administrative staff—characterized by limited and specific rules, well-defined areas of competence and responsibility, impersonal standards of performance and promotion, and so on—which is similar in many respects to that of any modern, large-scale enterprise; and it is this staff which must see to the effective execution of the prison's routine procedures.

Of the approximately 300 employees of the New Jersey State Prison, more than two-thirds are directly concerned with the supervision and control of the inmate population. These form the so-called custodian force which is broken into three eight-hour shifts, each shift being arranged in a typical pyramid of authority. The day shift, however—on duty from 6:20 A.M. to 2:20 P.M.—is by far the largest. As in many organizations, the rhythm of life in the prison quickens with daybreak and trails off in the afternoon, and the period of greatest activity requires the largest number of administrative personnel.

In the bottom ranks are the Wing guards, the Tower guards, the guards assigned to the shops, and those with a miscellany of duties such as the guardianship of the receiving gate or the garage. Immediately above these men are a number of sergeants and lieutenants and these in turn are responsible to the Warden and his assistants.

Source: Sykes, G. M. (1958). *The society of captives: A study of a maximum security prison.* Princeton, NJ: Princeton University Press.

The most striking fact about this bureaucracy of custodians is its unparalleled position of power—in formal terms, at least—vis-à-vis the body of men which it rules and from which it is supposed to extract compliance. The officials, after all, possess a monopoly on the legitimate means of coercion (or, as one prisoner has phrased it succinctly, "They have the guns and we don't"); and the officials can call on the armed might of the police and the National Guard in case of an overwhelming emergency. The 24-hour surveillance of the custodians represents the ultimate watchfulness and, presumably, noncompliance on the part of the inmates need not go long unchecked. The rulers of this society of captives nominally hold in their hands the sole right of granting rewards and inflicting punishments and it would seem that no prisoner could afford to ignore their demands for conformity. Centers of opposition in the inmate population—in the form of men recognized as leaders by fellow prisoners—can be neutralized through the use of solitary confinement or exile to other State institutions.[2] The custodians have the right not only to issue and administer the orders and regulations which are to guide the life of the prisoner, but also the right to detain, try, and punish any individual accused of disobedience—a merging of legislative, executive, and judicial functions which has long been regarded as the earmark of complete domination. The officials of the prison, in short, appear to be the possessors of almost infinite power within their realm; and, at least on the surface, the bureaucratic staff should experience no great difficulty in converting their rules and regulations—their blueprint for behavior—into a reality.

It is true, of course, that the power position of the custodial bureaucracy is not truly infinite. The objectives which the officials pursue are not completely of their own choosing and the means which they can use to achieve their objectives are far from limitless. The custodians are not total despots, able to exercise power at whim, and thus they lack the essential mark of infinite power, the unchallenged right of being capricious in their rule. It is this last which distinguishes terror from government, infinite power from almost infinite power, and the distinction is an important one. Neither by right nor by intention are the officials of the New Jersey State Prison free from a system of norms and laws which curb their actions. But within these limitations the bureaucracy of the prison is organized around a grant of power which is without an equal in American society; and if the rulers of any social system could secure compliance with their rules and regulations—however sullen or unwilling—it might be expected that the officials of the maximum security prison would be able to do so.

When we examine the New Jersey State Prison, however, we find that this expectation is not borne out in actuality. Indeed, the glaring conclusion is that despite the guns and the surveillance, the searches and the precautions of the custodians, the actual behavior of the inmate population differs markedly from that which is called for by official commands and decrees. Violence, fraud, theft, aberrant sexual behavior—all are common-place occurrences in the daily round of institutional existence in spite of the fact that the maximum security prison is conceived of by society as the ultimate weapon for the control of the criminal and his deviant actions. Far from being omnipotent rulers who have crushed all signs of rebellion against their regime, the custodians are engaged in a continuous struggle to maintain order—and it is a struggle in which the custodians frequently fail. Offenses committed by one inmate against another occur often, as do offenses committed by inmates against the officials and their rules. And the number of undetected offenses is, by universal agreement of both officials and inmates, far larger than the number of offenses which are discovered.

Some hint of the custodial bureaucracy's skirmishes with the population of prisoners is provided by the records of the disciplinary court which has the task of adjudicating charges brought by guards against their captives for offenses taking place within the walls. The following table shows a typical listing for a one-week period.

	Charge		Disposition
1)	Insolence and swearing while being interrogated	1)	Continue in segregation
2)	Threatening an inmate	2)	Drop from job
3)	Attempting to smuggle roll of tape into institution	3)	1 day in segregation with restricted diet
4)	Possession of contraband	4)	30 days loss of privileges
5)	Possession of pair of dice	5)	2 days in segregation with restricted diet
6)	Insolence	6)	Reprimand
7)	Out of place	7)	Drop from job. Refer to classification committee for reclassification
8)	Possession of home-made knife, metal, and emery paper	8)	5 days in segregation with restricted diet
9)	Suspicion of gambling or receiving bets	9)	Drop from job and change Wing assignment
10)	Out of place	10)	15 days loss of privileges
11)	Possession of contraband	11)	Reprimand
12)	Creating disturbance in Wing	12)	Continue in segregation
13)	Swearing at an officer	13)	Reprimand
14)	Out of place	14)	15 days loss of privileges
15)	Out of place	15)	15 days loss of privileges

Even more revealing, however, than this brief and somewhat enigmatic record are the so-called charge slips in which the guard is supposed to write out the derelictions of the prisoner in some detail. In the New Jersey State Prison, Charge Slips form an administrative residue of past conflicts between captors and captives and the following accounts are a fair sample:

This inmate threatened an officer's life. When I informed this inmate he was to stay in to see the Chief Deputy on his charge he told me if he did not go to the yard I would get a shiv in my back.

Signed: Officer A_____

Inmate X cursing an officer. In mess hall inmate refused to put excess bread back on tray. Then he threw the tray on the floor. In the Center, inmate cursed both Officer Y and myself.

Signed: Officer B_____

This inmate has been condemning everyone about him for going to work. The Center gave orders for him to go to work this A.M. which he refused to do. While searching his cell I found drawings of picks and locks.

Signed: Officer C_____

Fighting. As this inmate came to 1 Wing entrance to go to yard this A.M. he struck inmate G in the face.

Signed: Officer D_____

Having fermented beverage in his cell. Found while inmate was in yard.

Signed: Officer E_____

Attempting to instigate wing disturbance. When I asked him why he discarded [sic] my order to quiet down he said he was going to talk any time he wanted to and _____ me and do whatever I wanted in regards to it.

Signed: Officer F_____

Possession of home-made shiv sharpened to razor edge on his person and possession of 2 more shivs in cell. When inmate was sent to 4 Wing officer H found 3" steel blade in pocket. I ordered Officer M to search his cell and he found 2 more shivs in process of being sharpened.

Signed: Officer G_____

Insolence. Inmate objected to my looking at papers he was carrying in pockets while going to the yard. He snatched them violently from my hand and gave me some very abusive talk. This man told me to _____ myself, and raised his hands as if to strike me. I grabbed him by the shirt and took him to the Center.

Signed: Officer H_____

Assault with knife on inmate K. During Idle Men's mess at approximately 11:10 A.M. this man assaulted Inmate K with a homemade knife. Inmate K was receiving his rations at the counter when Inmate B rushed up to him and plunged a knife in his chest, arm, and back. I grappled with him and with the assistance of Officers S and V, we disarmed the inmate and took him to the Center. Inmate K was immediately taken to the hospital.

Signed: Officer I_____

Sodomy. Found inmate W in cell with no clothing on and inmate Z on top of him with no clothing. Inmate W told me he was going to lie like a _____ to get out of it.

Signed: Officer J._____

Attempted escape on night of 4/15/53. This inmate along with inmates L and T succeeded in getting on roof of 6 Wing and having home-made bombs in their possession.

Signed: Officer K_____

Fighting and possession of home-made shiv. Struck first blow to Inmate P. He struck blow with a roll of black rubber rolled up in his fist. He then produced a knife made out of wire tied to a tooth brush.

Signed: Officer L_____

Refusing medication prescribed by Doctor W. Said "What do you think I am, a damn fool, taking that _____ for a headache, give it to the doctor."

Signed: Officer M_____

Inmate loitering on tier. There is a clique of several men who lock on top tier, who ignore rule of returning directly to their cells and attempt to hang out on the tier in a group.

Signed: Officer N_____

It is hardly surprising that when the guards at the New Jersey State Prison were asked what topics should be of first importance in a proposed in-service training program, 98 percent picked "what to do in event of trouble." The critical issue for the moment, however, is that the dominant position of the custodial staff is more fiction than reality, if we think of domination as something more than the outward forms and symbols of power. If power is viewed as the probability that orders and regulations will be obeyed by a given group of individuals, as Max Weber has suggested,[3] the New Jersey State Prison is perhaps more notable for the doubtfulness of obedience than its certainty. The weekly records of the disciplinary court and Charge Slips provide an admittedly poor index of offenses or acts of noncompliance committed within the walls, for these form only a small, visible segment of an iceberg whose greatest bulk lies beneath the surface of official recognition. The public is periodically made aware of the officials' battle to enforce their regime within the prison, commonly in the form of allegations in the newspapers concerning homosexuality, illegal use of drugs, assaults, and so on. But the ebb and flow of public attention given to these matters does not match the constancy of these problems for the prison officials who are all too well aware that "Incidents"—the very thing they try to minimize—are not isolated or rare events but are instead a commonplace. The number of "incidents" in the New Jersey State Prison is probably no greater than that to be found in most maximum security institutions in the United States and may, indeed, be smaller, although it is difficult to make comparisons. In any event, it seems clear that the custodians are bound to their captives in a relationship of conflict rather than compelled acquiescence, despite the custodians' theoretical supremacy, and we now need to see why this should be so.

II

In our examination of the forces which undermine the power position of the New Jersey State Prison's custodial bureaucracy, the most important fact is, perhaps, that the power of the custodians is not based on authority.

Now power based on authority is actually a complex social relationship in which an individual or a group of individuals is recognized as possessing a right to issue commands or regulations and those who receive these commands or regulations feel compelled to obey by a sense of duty. In its pure form, then, or as an ideal type, power based on authority has two essential elements: a rightful or legitimate effort to exercise control on the one hand and an inner, moral compulsion to obey, by those who are to be controlled, on the other. In reality, of course, the recognition of the legitimacy of efforts to exercise control may be qualified or partial and the sense of duty, as a motive for compliance, may be mixed with motives of fear or self-interest. But it is possible for theoretical purposes to think of power based on authority in its pure form and to use this as a baseline in describing the empirical case.[4]

It is the second element of authority—the sense of duty as a motive for compliance—which supplies the secret strength of most social organizations. Orders and rules can be issued with the expectation that they will be obeyed without the necessity of demonstrating in each case that compliance will advance the subordinate's interests. Obedience or conformity springs from an internalized morality which transcends the personal feelings of the individual; the fact that an order or a rule is an order or a rule becomes the basis for modifying one's behavior, rather than a rational calculation of the advantages which might be gained.

In the prison, however, it is precisely this sense of duty which is lacking in the general inmate population. The regime of the custodians is expressed as a mass of commands and regulations passing down a hierarchy of power. In general, these efforts at control are regarded as legitimate by individuals in the hierarchy, and individuals tend to respond because they feel they "should," down to the level of the guard in the cellblock, the industrial shop, or the recreation yard.[5] But now these commands and regulations must jump a gap which separates the captors from the captives. And it is at this point that a sense of duty tends to disappear and with it goes that easily-won obedience which many organizations take for granted in the naïveté of their unrecognized strength. In the prison power must be based on something other than internalized morality and the custodians find themselves confronting men who must be forced, bribed, or cajoled into compliance. This is not to say that inmates feel that the efforts of prison officials to exercise control are wrongful or illegitimate; in general, prisoners do not feel that the prison officials have usurped positions of power which are not rightfully theirs, nor do prisoners feel that the orders and regulations which descend upon them from above represent an illegal extension of their rulers' grant of government. Rather, the noteworthy fact about the social system of the New Jersey State Prison is that the bond between recognition of the legitimacy of control and the sense of duty has been torn apart. In these terms the social system of the prison is very similar to a *Gebietsver-band*, a territorial group living under a regime imposed by a ruling few.[6] Like a province which has been conquered by force of arms, the community of prisoners has come to accept the validity of the regime constructed by their rulers but the subjugation is not complete. Whether he sees himself as caught by his own stupidity, the workings "of chance, his inability to "fix" the case, or the superior skill of the police, the criminal in prison seldom denies the legitimacy of confinement.[7] At the same time, the recognition of the legitimacy of society's surrogates and their body of rules is not accompanied by an internalized obligation to obey and the prisoner thus accepts the fact of his captivity at one level and rejects it at another. If for no other reason, then, the custodial institution is valuable for a theory of human behavior because it makes us realize that men need not be motivated to conform to a regime which they define as rightful. It is in this apparent contradiction that we can see the first flaw in the custodial bureaucracy's assumed supremacy.

III

Since the Officials of prison possess a monopoly on the means of coercion, as we have pointed out earlier, it might be thought that the inmate population could simply be forced into conformity and that the lack of an inner moral compulsion to obey on the part of the inmates could be ignored. Yet the combination of a bureaucratic staff—that most modern, rational form of mobilizing effort to exercise control—and the use of physical violence—that most ancient device to channel man's conduct—must strike us as an anomaly and with good reason. The use of force is actually grossly inefficient as a means for securing obedience, particularly when those who are to be controlled are called on to perform a task of any complexity. A blow with a club may check an immediate revolt, it is true, but it cannot assure effective performance on a punch-press. A "come-along," a straitjacket or a pair of handcuffs may serve to curb one rebellious prisoner in a crisis, but they will be of little aid in moving more than 1200 inmates through the messhall in a routine and orderly fashion. Furthermore, the custodians are well aware that violence once unleashed is not easily brought to heel and it is this awareness that lies behind the standing order that no guard should ever strike an inmate with his hand—he should always use a night stick. This rule is not an open invitation to brutality but an attempt to set a high threshold on the use of force in order to eliminate the casual cuffing which might explode into extensive and violent retaliation. Similarly, guards are under orders to throw their night sticks over the wall if they are on duty in the recreation yard when a riot develops. A guard without weapons, it is argued, is safer than a guard who tries to hold on to his symbol of office, for a mass of rebellious inmates may find a single night stick a goad rather than a restraint and the guard may find himself beaten to death with his own means of compelling order.

In short, the ability of the officials to physically coerce their captives into the paths of compliance is something of an illusion as far as the day-to-day activities of the prison are concerned and may be of doubtful value in moments of crisis. Intrinsically inefficient as a method of making men carry out a complex task, diminished in effectiveness by the realities of the guard-inmate ratio,[8] and always accompanied by the danger of touching off further violence, the use of physical force by the custodians has many limitations as a basis on which to found the routine operation of the prison. Coercive tactics may have some utility in checking blatant disobedience — if only a few men disobey. But if the great mass of criminals in prison are to be brought into the habit of conformity, it must be on other grounds. Unable to count on a sense of duty to motivate their captives to obey and unable to depend on the direct and immediate use of violence to insure a step-by-step submission to the rules, the custodians must fall back on a system of rewards and punishments.

Now if men are to be controlled by the use of rewards and punishments—by promises and threats—at least one point is patent: The rewards and punishments dangled in front of the individual must indeed be rewards and punishments from the point of view of the individual who is to be controlled. It is precisely on this point, however, that the custodians' system of rewards and punishments founders. In our discussion of the problems encountered in securing conscientious performance at work, we suggested that both the penalties and the incentives available to the officials were inadequate. This is also largely true, at a more general level, with regard to rewards and punishments for securing compliance with the wishes of the custodians in all areas of prison life.

In the first place, the punishments which the officials can inflict—for theft, assaults, escape attempts, gambling, insolence, homosexuality, and all the other deviations from the pattern of behavior called for by the regime of the custodians—do not represent a profound difference from the prisoner's usual status. It may be that when men are chronically deprived of liberty, material goods and services, recreational opportunities and so on, the few pleasures that are granted take on a new importance and the threat of their withdrawal is a more powerful motive for conformity than those of us in the free community can realize. To be locked up in the solitary confinement wing, that prison within a prison; to move from the monotonous, often badly prepared meals in the messhall to a diet of bread and water;[9] to be dropped from a dull, unsatisfying job and forced to remain in idleness—all, perhaps, may mean the difference between an existence which can be borne, painful though it may be, and one which cannot. But the officials of the New Jersey State Prison are dangerously close to the point where the stock of legitimate punishments has been exhausted and it would appear that for many prisoners the few punishments which are left have lost their potency. To this we must couple the important fact that such punishments as the custodians can inflict may lead to an increased prestige for the punished inmate in the eyes of his fellow prisoners. He may become a hero, a martyr, a man who has confronted his captors and dared them to do their worst. In the dialectics of the inmate population, punishments and rewards have, then, been reversed and the control measures of the officials may support disobedience rather than decrease it.

In the second place, the system of rewards and punishments in the prison is defective because the reward side of the picture has been largely stripped away. Mail and visiting privileges, recreational privileges, the supply of personal possessions—all are given to the inmate at the time of his arrival in one fixed sum. Even the so-called Good Time—the portion of the prisoner's sentence deducted for good behavior—is automatically subtracted from the prisoner's sentence when he begins his period of imprisonment.[10] Thus the officials have placed themselves in the peculiar position of granting the prisoner all available benefits or rewards at the time of his entrance into the system. The prisoner, then, finds himself unable to win any significant gains by means of compliance, for there are no gains left to be won.

From the viewpoint of the officials, of course, the privileges of the prison social system are regarded as rewards, as something to be achieved. That is to say, the custodians hold that recreation, access to the inmate store, Good Time, or visits from individuals in the free community are conditional upon conformity or good behavior. But the evidence suggests that from the viewpoint of the inmates the variety of benefits granted by the custodians is not defined as something to be earned but as an inalienable right—as the just due of the inmate which should not turn on the question of obedience or disobedience within the walls. After all, the inmate population claims, these benefits have belonged to the prisoner from the time when he first came to the institution.

In short, the New Jersey State Prison makes an initial grant of all its rewards and then threatens to withdraw them if the prisoner does not conform. It does not start the prisoner from scratch and promise to grant its available rewards one by one as the prisoner proves himself through continued submission to the institutional regulations. As a result a subtle alchemy is set in motion whereby the inmates cease to see the rewards of the system as rewards, that is, as benefits contingent upon performance; instead, rewards are apt to be defined as obligations. Whatever justification might be offered for such a policy, it would appear to have a number of drawbacks as a method of motivating prisoners to fall into the posture of obedience. In effect, rewards and punishments of the officials have been collapsed into one and the prisoner moves in a world where there is no hope of progress but only the possibility of further punishments. Since the prisoner is already suffering from most of the punishments permitted by society, the threat of imposing those few remaining is all too likely to be a gesture of futility.

IV

Unable to depend on that inner moral compulsion or sense of duty which eases the problem of control in most social organizations, acutely aware that brute force is inadequate, and lacking an effective system of legitimate rewards and punishments which might induce prisoners to conform to in-stitutional regulations on the grounds of self interest, the custodians of the New Jersey State Prison are considerably weakened in their attempts to impose their regime on their captive population. The result, in fact, is, as we have already indicated, a good deal of deviant behavior or noncompliance in a social system where the rulers at first glance seem to possess almost infinite power.

Yet systems of power may be defective for reasons other than the fact that those who are ruled do not feel the need to obey the orders and regulations descending on them from above. Systems of power may also fail because those who are supposed to rule are unwilling to do so. The unissued order, the deliberately ignored disobedience, the duty left unperformed—these are cracks in the monolith just as surely as are acts of defiance in the subject population. The "corruption" of the rulers may be far less dramatic than the insurrection of the ruled, for power unexercised is seldom as visible as power which is challenged, but the system of power still falters.[11]

Now the official in the lowest ranks of the custodial bureaucracy—the guard in the cellblock, the industrial shop, or the recreation yard—is the pivotal figure on which the custodial bureaucracy turns. It is he who must supervise and control the inmate population in concrete and detailed terms. It is he who must see to the translation of the custodial regime from blueprint to reality and engage in the specific battles for conformity. Counting prisoners, periodically reporting to the center of communications, signing passes, checking groups of inmates as they come and go, searching for contraband or signs of attempts to escape—these make up the minutiae of his eight-hour shift. In addition, he is supposed to be alert for violations of the prison rules which fall outside his routine sphere of surveillance. Not only must he detect and report deviant behavior after it occurs; he must curb deviant behavior before it arises as well as when he is called on to prevent a minor quarrel among prisoners from flaring into a more dangerous situation. And he must make sure that the inmates in his charge perform their assigned tasks with a reasonable degree of efficiency.

The expected role of the guard, then, is a complicated compound of policeman and foreman, of cadi, counsellor, and boss all rolled into one. But as the guard goes about his duties, piling one day on top of another (and the guard too, in a certain sense, is serving time in confinement), we find that the system of power in the prison is defective not only because the means of motivating the inmates to conform are largely lacking but also because the guard is frequently reluctant to enforce the full range of the institution's regulations. The guard frequently fails to report infractions of the rules which have occurred before his eyes. The guard often transmits forbidden information to inmates, such as plans for searching particular cells in a surprise raid for contraband. The guard often neglects elementary security requirements and on numerous occasions he will be found joining his prisoners in outspoken criticisms of the Warden and his assistants. In short, the guard frequently shows evidence of having been "corrupted" by the captive criminals over whom he stands in theoretical dominance. This failure within the ranks of the rulers is seldom to be attributed to outright bribery—bribery, indeed, is usually unnecessary, for far more effective influences are at work to bridge the gap supposedly separating captors and captives.

In the first place, the guard is in close and intimate association with his prisoners throughout the course of the working day. He can remain aloof only with great difficulty, for he possesses few of those devices which normally serve to maintain social distance between the rulers and the ruled. He cannot withdraw physically in symbolic affirmation of his superior position; he has no intermediaries to bear the brunt of resentment springing from orders which are disliked; and he cannot fall back on a dignity adhering to his office—he is a *hack* or a *screw* in the eyes of those he controls and an unwelcome display of officiousness evokes that great destroyer of unquestioned power, the ribald humor of the dispossessed.

There are many pressures in American culture to "be nice," to be a "good Joe," and the guard in the maximum security prison is not immune. The guard is constantly exposed to a sort of moral blackmail in which the first signs of condemnation, estrangement, or rigid adherence to the rules is countered by the inmates with the threat of ridicule or hostility. And in this complex interplay, the guard does not always start from a position of determined opposition to "being friendly." He holds an intermediate post in a bureaucratic structure between top prison officials—his captains, lieutenants, and sergeants—and the prisoners in his charge. Like many such figures, the guard is caught in a conflict of loyalties. He often has reason to resent the actions of his superior officers— the reprimands, the lack of ready appreciation, the incomprehensible order—and in the inmates he finds willing sympathizers: They too claim to suffer from the unreasonable irritants of power. Furthermore, the guard in many cases is marked by a basic ambivalence toward the criminals under his supervision and control. It is true that the inmates of the prison have been condemned by society through the agency of the courts, but some of these prisoners must be viewed as a success in terms of a worldly system of the values which accords high prestige to wealth and influence even though they may have been won by devious means; and the poorly paid guard may be gratified to associate with a famous racketeer. Moreover, this ambivalence in the guard's attitudes toward the criminals nominally under his thumb may be based on something more than a *sub rosa* respect for the notorious. There may also be a discrepancy between the judgments of society and the guard's own opinions as far as the "criminality" of the prisoner is concerned. It is difficult to define the man convicted of deserting his wife, gambling, or embezzlement as a desperate criminal to be suppressed at all costs and the crimes of even the most serious offenders lose their significance with the passage of time. In the eyes of the custodian, the in-mate tends to become a man in prison rather than a criminal in prison and the relationship between captor and captive is subtly transformed in the process.

In the second place, the guard's position as a strict enforcer of the rules is undermined by the fact that he finds it almost impossible to avoid the claims of reciprocity. To a large extent the guard is dependent on inmates for the satisfactory performance of his duties; and like many individuals in positions of power, the guard is evaluated in terms of the conduct of the men he controls. A troublesome, noisy, dirty cellblock reflects on the guard's ability to "handle" prisoners and this ability forms an important component of the merit rating which is used as the basis for pay raises and promotions. As we have pointed out above, a guard cannot rely on the direct application of force to achieve compliance nor can he easily depend on threats of punishment. And if the guard does insist on constantly using the last few negative sanctions available to the institution—if the guard turns in Charge Slip after Charge Slip for every violation of the rules which he encounters—he becomes burdensome to the top officials of the prison bureaucratic staff who realize only too well that their apparent dominance rests on some degree of co-operation. A system of power which can enforce its rules only by bringing its formal machinery of accusation, trial, and punishment into play at every turn will soon be lost in a haze of pettifogging detail.

The guard, then, is under pressure to achieve a smoothly running tour of duty not with the stick but with the carrot, but here again his legitimate stock is limited. Facing demands from above that he achieve compliance and stalemated from below, he finds that one of the most meaningful rewards he can offer is to ignore certain offenses or make sure that he never places himself in a position where he will discover them. Thus the guard—backed by all the power of the State, close to armed men who will run to his aid, and aware that any prisoner who disobeys him can be punished if he presses charges against him—often discovers that his best path of action is to make "deals" or "trades" with the captives in his power. In effect, the guard buys compliance or obedience in certain areas at the cost of tolerating disobedience elsewhere.

Aside from winning compliance "where it counts" in the course of the normal day, the guard has another favor to be secured from the inmates which makes him willing to forego strict enforcement of all prison regulations. Many custodial institutions have experienced a riot in which the tables are turned momentarily and the captives hold sway over their quondam captors; and the rebellions of 1952 loom large in the memories of the officials of the New Jersey State Prison. The guard knows that he may some day be a hostage and that his life may turn on a settling of old accounts. A fund of good will becomes a valuable form of insurance and this fund is almost sure to be lacking if he has continually played the part of a martinet. In the folklore of the prison there are enough tales about strict guards who have had the misfortune of being captured and savagely beaten during a riot to raise doubts about the wisdom of demanding complete conformity.

In the third place, the theoretical dominance of the guard is undermined in actuality by the innocuous encroachment of the prisoner on the guard's duties. Making out reports, checking cells at the periodic count, locking and unlocking doors—in short, all the minor chores which the guard is called on to perform—may gradually be transferred into the hands of inmates whom the guard has come to trust. The cellblock runner, formally assigned the tasks of delivering mail, housekeeping duties, and so on, is of particular importance in this respect. Inmates in this position function in a manner analogous to that of the company clerk in the Armed Forces and like such figures they may wield power and influence far beyond the nominal definition of their role. For reasons of indifference, laziness, or naïveté, the guard may find that much of the power which he is supposed to exercise has slipped from his grasp.

Now power, like a woman's virtue, once lost is hard to regain. The measures to rectify an established pattern of abdication need to be much more severe than those required to stop the first steps in the transfer of control from the guard to his prisoner. A guard assigned to a cellblock in which a large portion of power has been shifted in the past from the officials to the inmates is faced with the weight of precedent; it requires a good deal of moral courage on his part to withstand the aggressive tactics of prisoners who fiercely defend the patterns of corruption established by custom. And if the guard himself has allowed his control to be subverted, he may find that any attempts to undo his error are checked by a threat from the inmate to send a *snitch-kite*—an anonymous note—to the guard's superior officers explaining his past derelictions in detail. This simple form of blackmail may be quite sufficient to maintain the relationships established by friendship, reciprocity, or encroachment.

It is apparent, then, that the power of the custodians is defective, not simply in the sense that the ruled are rebellious, but also in the sense that the rulers are reluctant. We must attach a new meaning to Lord Acton's aphorism that power tends to corrupt and absolute power corrupts absolutely. The custodians of the New Jersey State Prison, far from being converted into brutal tyrants, are under strong pressure to compromise with their captives, for it is a paradox that they can insure their dominance only by allowing it to be corrupted. Only by tolerating violations of "minor" rules and regulations can the guard secure compliance in the "major" areas of the custodial regime. Ill-equipped to maintain the social distance which in theory separates the world of the officials and the world of the inmates, their suspicions eroded by long familiarity, the custodians are led into a modus vivendi with their captives which bears little resemblance to the stereotypical picture of guards and their prisoners.

V

The fact that the officials of the prison experience serious difficulties in imposing their regime on the society of prisoners is sometimes attributed to inadequacies of the custodial staff's personnel. These inadequacies, it is claimed, are in turn due to the fact that more than 50 percent of the guards are temporary employees who have not passed a Civil Service examination. In 1952, for example, a month and a half before the disturbances which dramatically underlined some of the problems of the officials, the Deputy Commissoner of the Department of Institutions and Agencies made the following points in a report concerning the temporary officer of the New Jersey State Prison's custodial force:

1. Because they are not interested in the prison service as a career, the temporary officers tend to have a high turnover as they are quick to resign to accept more remunerative employment.

2. Because they are inexperienced, they are not able to foresee or forestall disciplinary infractions, the on-coming symptoms of which the more experienced officer would detect and take appropriate preventive measures.

3. Because they are not trained as are the regular officers, they do not have the self-confidence that comes with the physical training and defensive measures which are part of the regular officers' pre-service and in-service training and, therefore, it is not uncommon for them to be somewhat timid and inclined to permit the prisoner to take advantage of them.

4. Because many of them are beyond the age limit or cannot meet the physical requirements for regular appointment as established by Civil Service, they cannot look forward to a permanent career and are therefore less interested in the welfare of the institution than their brother officers.

5. Finally, because of the short period of employment, they do not recognize the individual prisoners who are most likely to incite trouble or commit serious infractions, and they are at a disadvantage in dealing with the large groups which congregate in the cellblocks, the messhall, the auditorium, and the yard.[12]

Now the guard at the New Jersey State Prison receives a salary of $3,240 per year when he is hired and he can reach a maximum of $3,840 per year; and there is little doubt that the low salary scale accounts for much of the prison's high turnover rate. The fact that the job of the guard is often depressing, dangerous, and possesses relatively low prestige adds further difficulties. There is also little doubt that the high turnover rate carries numerous evils in its train, as the comments of the Deputy Commissioner have indicated. Yet even if higher salaries could counterbalance the many dissatisfying features of the guard's job—to a point where the custodial force consisted of men with long service rather than a group of transients—there remains a question of whether or not the problems of administration in the New Jersey State Prison would be eased to a significant extent. This, of course, is heresy from the viewpoint of those who trace the failure of social organizations to the personal failings of the individuals who man the organizational structure. Perhaps, indeed, there is some comfort in the idea that if the budget of the prison were larger, if higher salaries could be paid to entice "better" personnel within the walls, if guards could be persuaded to remain for longer periods, then the many difficulties of the prison bureaucracy would disappear. From this point of view, the problems of the custodial institution are rooted in the niggardliness of the free community and the consequent inadequacies of the institution's personnel rather than flaws in the social system of the prison itself. But to suppose that higher salaries are an answer to the plight of the custodians is to suppose, first, that there are men who by reason of their particular skills and personal characteristics are better qualified to serve as guards if they could be recruited; and second, that experience and training within the institution itself will better prepare the guard for his role, if greater financial rewards could convince him to make a career of his prison employment. Both of these suppositions, however, are open to some doubt. There are few jobs in the free community which are comparable to that of the guard in the maximum security prison and which, presumably, could equip the guard-to-be with the needed skills. If the job requirements of the guard's position are not technical skills but turn on matters of character such as courage, honesty, and so on, there is no assurance that men with these traits will flock to the prison if the salary of the guard is increased. And while higher salaries may decrease the turnover rate—thus making an in-service training program feasible and providing a custodial force with greater experience—it is not certain if such a change can lead to marked improvement. A brief period of schooling can familiarize the new guard with the routines of the institution, but to prepare the guard for the realities of his assigned role with lectures and discussions is quite another matter. And it seems entirely possible that prolonged experience in the prison may enmesh the guard deeper and deeper in patterns of compromise and misplaced trust rather than sharpening his drive toward a rigorous enforcement of institutional regulations.

We are not arguing, of course, that the quality of the personnel in the prison is irrelevant to the successful performance of the bureaucracy's tasks nor are we arguing that it would be impossible to improve the quality of the personnel by increasing salaries. We are arguing, however, that the problems of the custodians far transcend the size of the guard's pay check or the length of his employment and that better personnel is at best a palliative rather than a final cure. It is true, of course, that it is difficult to unravel the characteristics of a social organization from the characteristics of the individuals who are its members; but there seems to be little reason to believe that a different crop of guards in the New Jersey State Prison would exhibit an outstanding increase in efficiency in trying to impose the regime of the custodians on the population of prisoners. *The lack of a sense of duty among those who are held captive, the obvious fallacies of coercion, the pathetic collection of rewards and punishments to induce compliance, the strong pressures toward the corruption of the guard in the form of friendship, reciprocity, and the transfer of duties into the hands of trusted inmates—all are structural defects in the prison's system of poiver rather than individual inadequacies.*[13]

The question of whether these defects are inevitable in the custodial institution—or in any system of total power—must be deferred to a later chapter. For the moment it is enough to point out that in the New Jersey State Prison the custodians are unable or unwilling to prevent their captives from committing numerous violations of the rules which make up the theoretical blueprint for behavior and this failure is not a temporary, personal aberration but a built-in feature of the prison social system. It is only by understanding this fact that we can understand the world of the prisoners, since so many significant aspects of inmate behavior—such as coercion of fellow prisoners, fraud, gambling, homosexuality, sharing stolen supplies, and so on—are in clear contravention to institutional regulations. It is the nature of this world which must now claim our attention.

Notes

1. Max Weber, *The Theory of Social and Economic Organization*, edited by Talcott Parsons, New York: Oxford University Press, 194.7, p. 337.

2. Just as the Deep South served as a dumping-ground for particularly troublesome slaves before the Civil War, so too can the county jail or mental hospital serve as a dumping-ground for the maximum security prison. Other institutions, however, are apt to regard the Trenton Prison in somewhat the same way, as the report of the Governor's committee to investigate the prison has indicated. *Supra* page 22.

3. *Ibid.*, p. 324.

4. *Ibid.*, Introduction.

5. Failures in this process within the custodial staff itself will be discussed in the latter portion of this chapter.

6. *Ibid.*, p. 149.

7. This statement requires two qualifications. First, a number of inmates steadfastly maintain that they are innocent of the crime with which they are charged. It is the illegitimacy of their particular case, however, rather than the illegitimacy of confinement in general, which moves them to protest. Second, some of the more sophisticated prisoners argue that the conditions of imprisonment are wrong, although perhaps not illegitimate or illegal, on the grounds that reformation should be the major aim of imprisonment and the officials are not working hard enough in this direction.

8. Since each shift is reduced in size by vacations, regular days off, sickness, etc., even the day shift—the largest of the three—can usually muster no more than 90 guards to confront the population of more than 1200 prisoners. The fact that they are so heavily out-numbered is not lost on the officials.

9. The usual inmate fare is both balanced and sufficient in quantity, but it has been pointed out that the meals are not apt to be particularly appetizing since prisoners must eat them with nothing but a spoon. CF. Report of the Governor's Committee to Examine the Prison and Parole System of New Jersey, November 21, 19S2, pp. 74-79.

10. See footnote 9, page 28.

11. Portions of the following discussion concerning the corruption of the guards' authority are to be found in Gresham M. Sykes, *Crime and Society,* New York: Random House, 1956.

12. See New Jersey Committee to Examine and Investigate the Prison and Parole Systems of New Jersey, *Report,* November 21, 1952.

13. Those who are familiar with prison systems such as those of the Federal government or the State of California might argue that I have underestimated the possibilities of improvement which can be won with well-trained, well-paid, well-led guards. They might be right, but I think it is important to stress the serious, "built-in" weaknesses of the prison as a social system.

DISCUSSION QUESTIONS

1. Sykes's work illustrates that full enforcement of rules and regulations is replaced with partial enforcement; the latter, he argues, is more likely to result in control and conformity within the prison. In your opinion, is it acceptable for criminal justice personnel (correctional officers, probation/parole officers, police officers, etc.) to overlook infractions to secure cooperation in other areas or at other times?

2. *The Society of Captives* was originally published in 1958. Since that time, the correctional system in the United States has undergone a tremendous transformation. Changes include increasing size, an influx of gangs within facilities, and more court interventions into prison conditions. Given these changes, are the conditions that Sykes observed in the 1950s likely to be observed today? Do you suspect that correctional officer power—particularly legitimate, reward, and coercive power—is still as limited today as it was more than half a century ago?

3. Is it possible to ensure compliance in other ways (e.g., referent, information, resource, expert power) without having correctional staff power corrupted by inmates? If so, how? What particular strategies should correctional officers employ?

READING

Reading 23

Studies of the bases of power within criminal justice settings have been hampered by two important limitations. First, with few exceptions (see the discussion of Stichman's 2002 study in this section), researchers have tended to address power holder perceptions of the bases of power even though the perceptions of the power recipient are most critical for understanding reasons for compliance. Second, even though researchers have addressed power bases that are believed to lead to compliance with power holder demands, they have neglected to examine whether actual compliance follows. Hayden P. Smith, Brandon K. Applegate, Alicia H. Sitren, and Nicolette Fariello Springer tackle both of these problems in their study of 376 probationers in a Southeastern metropolitan area. Probationers were surveyed about the power bases of their probation officer. Probationers tended to rank expert power and legitimate power the highest, followed closely by coercive and referent power. Given that probation officers had few rewards to hand out, probationers viewed reward power as weak. Researchers had expected power and probationer compliance (e.g., complying with drug requirements, probation success) to be positively related; that is, as the perceived power of probation officers increases, so, too, should the likelihood of probation success or compliance. Contrary to expectation, perceptions of power and probationer compliance were largely unrelated to demographic (e.g., sex) and employment characteristics more predictive of success. The authors suggest that probation officers are either ineffectual in supervising clients or are not adequately exercising the power they do possess.

The Limits of Individual Control?

Perceived Officer Power and Probationer Compliance

Hayden P. Smith, Brandon K. Applegate, Alicia H. Sitren, and Nicolette Fariello Springer

Introduction

The issues surrounding the use of power and power-relations become highly salient when one examines criminal justice organizations. Indeed, one of the central functions of the criminal justice system involves controlling defendants and offenders (Packer, 1968). Among other activities, police detain and arrest suspects, judges impose sentences, and correctional agencies exercise their power to control and sometimes confine convicted offenders. In the context of probation, officers use a variety of techniques to constrain the behavior of probationers in order to promote compliance with the conditions of their sentence. Still, relatively little is known about the use of power in correctional settings. In fact, to date only four studies had differentiated the bases of power used by correctional personnel, and all four addressed this issue in the context of prisons (Hepburn, 1985; Stichman, 2002; Stojkovic, 1984, 1986). No study had yet examined the role of power in probation supervision.

The prison power studies could only suggest what one might expect from the officer-client relationship in probation. Serving a sentence within an institution can alter the way in which inmates interact with others (Sykes, 1958; Toch, 1992). Moreover, those who are in prison may be supervised by several different officers,

Source: Smith, H. P., Applegate, B. K., Sitren, A. H., & Springer, N. F. (2009). The limits of individual control? Perceived officer power and probationer compliance. *Journal of Criminal Justice*, 37(3), 241–247.

in different contexts, and at different times. In contrast, people serving probation sentences are typically supervised by a single officer, serve their sentence in the community, and have committed crimes that are much less serious than those committed by those who go to prison. The community context and more personal nature of supervision on probation, therefore, may result in different power relationships. The present study began to address this neglected area of research by determining what sources of power probationers believe their supervising officers possess and to what extent these bases of power are related to probationers' misbehavior. As a prelude to the current study, the nature of power, how it relates to correctional supervision, the approaches that have been used previously to assess the bases of power in corrections, and what is currently known about this issue are discussed below.

Literature Review

Power and the Coercive Institution

Issues of power are inextricably linked to the criminal justice system, with expressions of power in criminal justice institutions primarily demonstrated through coercive organizational goals. Here, criminal justice agencies are deemed successful when they maximize offender compliance with a set of requirements. Comparative studies of prisons and jails, for example, have used low inmate infraction rates as indicators of superior institutions (see, for example, Dilulio, 1987; Keller & Wang, 2005; Senese, 1997). Officers are given specific authority to limit the offender's freedom and choices, and as such, power in this sense reflects the ability to coerce and abrogate prima facie rights (Airaksinen, 1988). The offender faces the classic utilitarian decision: balancing a need to maximize potential pleasures while minimizing potential pains. In short, it is the coercive criminal justice institution and its agents that deliver power directives towards the offender, and the offender from whom compliance is expected.

To sociologists like Etzioni (1961), criminal justice institutions are predominately coercive, exhibiting power through physical or symbolic expressions of violence, reduced freedoms, and restricted movement. Etzioni asserted that coercion was particularly salient in the prison setting, where low power-holders (prisoners) lacked commitment towards organizational goals. Sykes (1958) also recognized the coercive nature of prisons, though he argued that directives and force were largely ineffective against strong inmate cohesion. Sykes (1958) stated that in prison, "power must be based on something other than internalized morality and the custodians find themselves confronting men who must be forced, bribed, or cajoled into compliance" (p. 47).

While criminal justice institutions demonstrate power in the formal sense, a host of informal power directives are used by criminal justice agents. For example, Cloward (1968) suggested that it was in fact the inmate "elite" who largely controlled the social equilibrium within prison. As such, formal restrictions from the institution were viewed as having a minimal effect on inmates. Cloward observed that prison guards were forced to rely on a complex process of ignoring certain rules, manipulating information, and generally propagating an informal system in which inmates were used to control each other. More recently, Marquart (1986) revealed that prison guards used physical coercion to control inmates and that willingness and ability to exert such power was intricately entwined in informal relationships among officers.

These formal and informal power relations expressed in the prison setting may shed light on the coerciveness of probation supervision. Like the prison setting, the institution of probation is responsible for controlling and coercing offenders. As such, the punitive power entrusted to probation officers to enforce compliance is both necessary and viable for the criminal justice system. Yet at the same time, probation officers are required to provide rehabilitation and reintegration within a traditional law enforcement setting. In probation, the role ambiguity between control and rehabilitative orientations is further compounded by inconsistent mission goals at the department level (Lindner, 1994). As a result of this ambiguity, little is known about the manner in which probation agents administer power directives.

Currently, there are over four million American adults under federal, state, or local probation jurisdiction (Glaze & Bonczar, 2007). Restated, this means that at the end of 2006, the equivalent of one in every fifty-three American adults was under probation supervision. In terms of power relations, the potential benefits of understanding how probation officers monitor and direct probationers become apparent. In light of the economic and social benefits of having fewer probationers occupying jail or prison space due to revoked probation, and the importance of identifying "what works" in probation, the practical aspects of understanding probation officer power are paramount.

The existing literature contends that criminal justice institutions may be viewed as predominately coercive out of necessity, with the demonstration of power being both formal and informal. While this conclusion is supported by previous research on power relations in the prison setting, it not yet clear whether the same can be said of power relations within probation supervision. Like prison, probation is responsible for coercing and controlling offenders. Unlike most prison guards, however, probation officers are also required to provide rehabilitation and reintegration (Steiner, Wada, Hemmens, & Burton, 2005). Probation holds a distinctive niche in the criminal justice system. It has a unique clientele, and it is guided by conflicting mission goals and strategies that are designed to encourage probationer reform as well as compliance. With this in mind, the concept of power is revealed to be complex and dynamic, and rarely has it been studied in criminal justice.

Bases of Power

Power is regularly defined as "the probability that one actor within a social relationship will be in a position to carry out his own will despite resistance, regardless of the basis on which this probability rests" (Weber, 1968, p. 53). Thus, the concept of power includes the assumption that social actors frequently possess different goals. Power becomes salient when an "inferior" actor yields to the will of a "superior" actor, and is forced to relinquish personal status, goods, or goals. In fact, Lukes (1974) stated that power could only exist in the presence of some form of resistance.

Starting from this definition, French and Raven (1959) developed a classic typology of the social bases of power. French and Raven divided the bases of social power into five types: reward power, coercive power, legitimate power, referent power, and expert power. Briefly, reward power is the perception of the "inferior" that the "superior" can issue rewards for desired behavior. Coercive power is the perception that the "superior" can inflict punishment on the "inferior" for undesired behavior. Legitimate power refers to perceptions that the "superior" possesses inherent rights to direct actions, while referent power finds its efficacy in the level of personal identification that the "inferior" feels towards the "superior." Under expert power, the basis of control is the "inferior's" perception that the "superior" holds knowledge or skill in a given area.

Theoretically, all of these bases of power may be exercised in probation supervision. Although the opportunities appear slim, probation officers may offer rewards—requests for the judge to reduce supervision, requests for early sentence termination, free transportation coupons—that may be used to encourage probationer compliance. Initiating the process of loosening probation restrictions may be among the most valuable rewards at an officer's disposal. In light of their structural position, officers also hold legitimate power. Exercise of legitimate power, however, rests on acceptance of the structural hierarchy of authority imposed by the probation system. Officers may display expert power through superior knowledge about probation, legal processes, the vagaries of particular judges or the local probation office, the effectiveness of treatment, or other areas salient to probationers. Frequently, knowledge is demonstrated by instructing probationers and through familiarity with the nomenclature of probation. Officers obtain referent power in direct proportion to the level of respect and admiration they receive from offenders on their case loads. Finally, coercive power seems to undergird the entire probation experience. Noncompliance can result in a host of sanctions, including informal and formal reprimands, increased surveillance, and initiation of revocation proceedings resulting in incarceration. Probation officers may use the threat of such consequences to motivate desirable behavior among probationers.

Previous Studies of Power Bases in Corrections

To date, only four studies had been conducted that examined power relations within correctional settings. In two of the earliest studies, Stojkovic employed a qualitative methodology in a maximum security prison. First, Stojkovic (1984) formally interviewed forty male inmates in order to ascertain their use of power on other prison inmates. Second, Stojkovic (1986) identified the bases of power used by twenty prison officers and eleven prison administrators on prison inmates. During this time period, Hepburn (1985) also studied prison guards' perceptions of power, but used a quantitative methodology. Here, Hepburn (1985) distributed self-administered questionnaires to 360 guards employed at five different prisons, asking for their views on why inmates did what officers wanted. Building on this study, Stichman (2002) surveyed nearly 400 male inmates housed in an Ohio high-close security facility in order to ascertain inmates' perceptions of the bases of power used by prison guards.

Examination of these four power studies revealed a modest degree of concurrence. In the qualitative studies, Stojkovic (1984) found that inmates primarily used referent and coercive powers to control other inmates. Supplemental bases of power were largely dependent upon circumstance and opportunity. For example, legitimate power was used by older respected inmates, expert power was used by inmate-lawyers, and reward power was virtually nonexistent. In the case of prison administrators and guards, Stojkovic (1986) found that coercive and reward were key bases of power, while administrators and officers considered referent, legitimate, and expert forms of power ineffectual. Use of reward power, however, was restricted to more reliable inmates who supported institutional goals, operating under the risk of a backlash due to competition for coveted positions. Thus, coercive power was a favored approach among prison inmates and administrators alike as a method of control.

The two relevant quantitative studies also showed some consistency, with legitimate and referent bases of power being the most important, and coercive and reward being the weakest bases of power (Hepburn, 1985; Stichman, 2002). Specifically, Hepburn (1985) discovered that legitimate and expert power ranked highest among the guards' perceptions of why "inmates do what you want them to do" (p. 151). This result was largely stable across all five correctional institutions. Stichman's (2002) survey of inmates also found a high ranking for legitimate power ("respect for the position") and referent power ("respect for the person"). Similar to Hepburn, reward power was viewed as largely ineffectual. In contrast to Hepburn, however, inmates believed that their officers could exercise power through the manipulation of possible punishments (coercive power). Inmates also tended to reject the idea that guards have any particular expertise and asserted that the officers' skill level had no effect on their compliance with prison directives.

Stichman (2002) has been the only researcher to assess the extent to which inmates believe officers have certain bases of power at their disposal. The perspective of offenders is particularly critical because it is their behavior that is targeted for control through the exercise of power. As Stichman (2002) observed, "power is effective only when the person being controlled perceives it" (p. 7; also see French & Raven, 1959). Stichman's (2002) study, however, did not fully disentangle inmates' perceptions that their officers held certain attributes from how those perceptions related to inmates' behavior. An inmate may perceive expertise among officers—"corrections officers have an ability to resolve conflicts between inmates" (Stichman, 2002, p. 89)—but this perception may have no bearing on his or her behavior. The perception in this case creates the possibility of power (what may be termed "perceived power")—but it does not necessarily result in real manifestations of power (what may be distinguished as "manifest power"). Stichman (2002) addressed this issue to some extent by including the idea of control in some of her survey items. For example, inmates who agreed that they "cooperate with some officers because they are fair" (p. 89) attributed their good behavior to a referent power base. Still, self-evaluations of the reasons for behavior are bound to be problematic in correctional populations. There is evidence that even among the general population, people have considerable difficulty accurately specifying the causes of their actions. Frequently, people attribute their behavior to plausible explanations rather than accurate ones, and they seldom develop multivariate or generalizable models (Bishop, 2004). As such, Stichman's study omitted valid and reliable measures of manifest power, thus limiting the understanding of the association between the dynamics of power in a real-world context and the associated rates of offender compliance.

The Current Study

The current study aimed to develop knowledge in several important areas that were lacking in the existing literature on bases of power. Prior academic studies on the bases of power used by correctional agents had been restricted to the prison setting. For at least three reasons, the power dynamic between prison guards and prisoners may be dissimilar to what occurs in the relationship between probation officers and probationers.

First, power relations are assumed to be overt in prisons, with control of inmates a key concern for an outnumbered officer staff. Inmates in a correctional facility are highly alienated from society and are required to display a degree of reverence and subordination to guards (Marquart, 1986). They are in the community, thus, probationers are far less alienated from society, and they may feel much less obliged to demonstrate subordination. Thus, the line between probation officer and probationer is less bold than that between prison guard and inmate. Second, prisons are more likely to contain inmates convicted of violent and predatory felonies compared to probation departments where half of all probationers are convicted solely of a misdemeanor (Glaze & Bonczar, 2007). Third, communication within the prison setting frequently occurs within earshot of other inmates. The bases of power used on a specific individual, therefore, quickly resonate to other inmates. Where a strong inmate network is present, demonstrations of power by correctional officers find a wide audience. Comparatively, probation tends to include one-on-one meetings where power relations take place "behind closed doors." Moreover, there is no evidence of a strong "probationer-culture" where officer actions would be discussed in the broader probation population. As Gibbons and Rosecrance (2005) have pointed out, probation supervision is "played out over long periods of time in small offices far from the spotlight, often with ambiguous guidelines" (p. 131).

This research also addressed the theoretical weakness inherent in the previous four power studies. All but one of these studies had been based on perceptions of one's own expressions of power—the self-perceptions of inmates in influencing other inmates (Stojkovic, 1984), the self-perceptions of administrators and guards in influencing inmates (Stojkovic, 1986), or the self-perceptions of the guards in influencing inmates (Hepburn, 1985). Only one study specifically examined inmates' perceptions of the bases of power afforded to guards (Stichman, 2002). As discussed, Stichman's (2002) study suffered from another weakness, as it conflated self-perceptions of the bases of power used by guards with self-perceptions of what base of power facilitates compliance. Due to the fact that no data on inmate compliance were collected in any of these studies, one is only provided with assumptions about what base of power could *potentially* influence inmate behaviors ("perceived" power), devoid of any objective measure of what *actually* does influence inmate behaviors ("manifest" power). Several researchers have argued that in order to "test" power, one must first identify the "manifest" variable (Debnam, 1984; Lukes, 1974). By failing to document offender compliance, prior studies revealed only self-reported perceptions of how power is used within corrections, and thus have failed to investigate the outcomes associated with power directives.

The current study addressed a significant gap in the power literature, as no previous studies had examined the bases of power within the probation setting. This study also furthered the existing literature research on bases of power by assessing perceived power and determining empirically whether each base of power is manifest in encouraging probationer compliance with supervision. These tests were based on self-reported behavior, as well as official measures drawn from case file reviews.

Methods

Sampling and Data Collection

Participants were drawn from a misdemeanor probation department in a large southeastern metropolitan area. This probation department served all community corrections offenders in the county and all face-to-face meetings with probation officers were conducted at this single location. In an effort to encourage candid responses, the researchers informed each respondent that their answers would be kept completely confidential and would not be shared with their supervising officers. The research team also made a concerted effort to appear separate from the probation department administration and staff. During data collection visits, researchers refrained from interacting with the probation officers as much as possible, and each researcher wore a prominent name badge bearing the logo of the University of Central Florida. The questionnaire itself also clearly identified the study as being conducted by the university.

Between May and September 2006, data were collected by surveying probationers at the county office before they met with their supervising officers. In all, 376 probationers provided usable survey responses. Due to item missing data, some of the analyses were based on fewer cases. In addition to the surveys, data were collected by reviewing probationers' files. Unfortunately, eighty-eight of the survey responses could not be matched to individual probationers. As a result, official data obtained from file reviews were available for fewer cases.

Random selection of research participants from the department's client roles was not possible. The researchers, therefore, attempted to obtain a sample that was as representative as possible in two ways. First, data collection occurred on a rotating basis in order to access individuals meeting with their probation officers across all days of the week and at different times throughout each day. Second, every person who arrived at the probation department during each data collection visit was approached and invited to participate in the study. As such, only probationers who could not speak and read English, lacked reading skills, and those supervised via the telephone were excluded from the study. There was no clear reason to expect that including these probationers would have produced different results, but it was possible.

Operationalization of Dependent Variable

Probationer compliance was operationalized three ways. The first measure assessed *self-reported compliance* and was based on survey responses to three distinct questions. Participants were asked, "How often do you follow your probation officer's directions?"; "When your probation officer says you cannot do something, how often do you do it anyway?"; and "Regardless of whether your probation officer knows or not, how many times would you say you have violated some condition of your probation?" When respondents replied to all three items indicating perfect compliance, they were coded as compliant (1). Otherwise, they were coded as self-reporting noncompliance (0). The second and third measures were based on official data from files maintained by the probation department. Here, it was determined whether each probationer had ever tested positive for drug use (0) versus remaining drug free (1)—*drug use compliance*—and whether each probationer ultimately completed his or her sentence successfully (1) or had his or her probation revoked (0)—probation *success*. *Drug use compliance* was examined only for those who had been tested at least once (n = 210), and *probation success* was assessed only for those who were no longer under supervision at the time of data collection (n = 227).

Operationalization of Independent Variables

The main independent variables were the bases of power outlined above. Operationalization followed the theoretical meaning of each base and was similar to the approaches used in previous quantitative studies of power. Each base was measured by asking the probationers to indicate their level of agreement or disagreement with statements about their probation officer. Two or three items in the survey pertained to each of the bases of power: reward, coercive, legitimate, referent, or expert. For each statement, respondents could select from one of four points on a Likert scale: strongly agree, agree, disagree, and strongly disagree. The wording of these items is shown in Table 1.

Also important to understanding the relationship between perceived power and probationer compliance is the inclusion of correlates of probationers' propensity for success or failure while on probation. Morgan (1994) identified nine factors associated with probation compliance: gender, age, marital status, education level, race, employment, prior criminal history, offense type, and sentence length. Data on age, race, educational attainment, marital status, and whether probationers' were employed were gathered from survey data. Probationers' files provided data on gender and probation risk, which encompassed issues of current offense and criminal history. In December of 2005, the probation department adopted a new risk-assessment instrument. Thus, three-quarters of the sample had been assessed using the old instrument, while the remaining participants were scored on the new one. The metrics of the two tools were not equivalent, so to produce comparable values for all members of the sample, all risk scores were converted to standard scores.

Findings

Table 1 presents descriptive statistics for the individual base of power items and cumulative indexes. Index means show clearly that probationers perceived the existence of expert (3.28), legitimate (3.25), coercive (3.10), and referent (3.04) bases of power most strongly. Thus, more than nine out of ten probationers believed that their officers knew their job, occupied an official position to tell them what to do, and could get them punished for misbehavior. Nearly as many supported the notion that probation officers have the right to tell them what to do and have the necessary knowledge and skills to be probation officers. Conversely, reward power ranked last with little consensus on whether a probation officer could reward good behavior (agree categories = 56.3 percent; disagree categories = 43.7 percent) and whether a probation officer could provide special benefits (agree categories = 46.1 percent; disagree categories = 53.9 percent).

With regard to probationer compliance, 68 percent of probationers self-reported zero violations while on probation, compared to 32 percent of probationers who self-reported at least one violation. The two measures drawn from official records—*drug use compliance* and *probation success*—yielded highly consistent aggregate estimates of success. Compliance with the requirement to remain free of illegal drugs occurred for 69 percent of probationers, compared to failed drug testing in 31 percent of cases. Successful probation completion occurred in 66 percent of cases, whereas 34 percent of probationers had their probation revoked.

Only two bases of power related to the measures of compliance. *Self-reported compliance* was significantly related to referent power and expert power. As such, the perception held by probationers that their officers possessed referent and expert bases of power correlated with higher chances of reporting compliance with probation. Perceived expert power also predicted a greater chance of remaining drug-free and of completing probation supervision successfully. Only three other variables were significantly related to probationer compliance. Females and married respondents were significantly more likely to self-report compliance with probation conditions. Risk score predicted outcomes on drug testing and completion of supervision in the expected directions, where higher risk scores were associated with testing positive for drugs and failing to complete probation successfully.

Probationers' perceptions of their officers' bases of power were almost entirely independent of demographic characteristics. Only race, gender, and education produced significant correlations, and these variables were each related to only one power base at a statistically significant level. Here, coercive power was positively correlated with being female, referent

Table 1 Descriptive Statistics for Bases of Power

Base of power	Strongly agree (%)	Agree (%)	Disagree (%)	Strongly disagree (%)	Index mean
Expert power					3.28
My probation officer does not have the skills or experience to be a good probation officer [a]	5.8	5.8	51.3	37.1	
My probation officer knows his/her job	42.3	54.4	2.5	0.8	
Legitimate power					3.25
My probation officer has the right to tell me what to do	34.6	53.1	10.3	2.0	
My probation officer is in a position to tell me what to do	38.7	53.9	6.4	1.1	
Coercive power					3.10
My probation officer can make life difficult for me	23.9	45.2	23.1	7.8	
My probation officer can make sure I get punished if I don't do the right things	42.6	52.8	4.0	.6	
My probation officer can get my probation revoked	32.0	42.2	18.3	7.6	
Referent power					3.04
My probation officer is fair	38.7	56.2	3.4	1.7	
I respect my probation officer	47.0	49.3	2.3	1.4	
My probation officer is also my friend	11.6	32.7	40.3	15.3	
Reward power					2.57
My probation officer can reward me for my good behavior	15.8	40.5	36.4	7.3	
My probation officer can give me special benefits that will make my life easier	11.6	34.5	43.8	10.1	

[a] Item's coding is reversed for computation of the index.

power was negatively correlated with employment status, and reward power was negatively correlated with being White. Second, the indexes for the five bases of power were related, but these correlations were, at best, moderate. Only one correlation—expert [x] referent—exceeded .5 and seven of the ten correlations range between 0.23 and 0.45. These results suggested that probationers perceived these bases of power as at least somewhat distinct among their supervising officers.

The logistic regression analyses produced weak models that could account for only 13 to 15 percent of the variation in probationer compliance. Moreover, the expected relationship between bases of power and measures of compliance failed to be substantiated. The only exception was a statistically significant relationship between expert power and self-reported compliance. Thus, probationers who rated expert power higher were more likely to report that they complied with all probation conditions. A one-unit increase in the four-point expert power index raised the odds of self-reported compliance by 87 percent. None of the bases of power, including expert, were related to *drug use compliance* or *probation success*. Probationers' perceptions of their officers' expertise, ability to punish, to reward, or to gain respect and be a friend, and perceptions that their officers were in a hierarchically structured position of authority had no impact on the official measures of probationer compliance.

More predictive of probationer compliance were the control variables gender, employment, and standardized risk score. Females were significantly more likely to self-report compliance and to complete probation successfully. The predicted odds of *self-reported compliance* for a female were 174 percent higher than the predicted odds for a male. The odds differential by gender was almost as great for successful completion of probation. Females were not significantly more likely to abstain from drug use. Being employed was significantly associated with probationer compliance on all three measures. Specifically, the predicted odds of self-reporting compliance for employed probationers were twice those for unemployed respondents, and the odds ratio was somewhat greater for *drug use compliance* and *probation success*. Lastly, probationer risk scores were negatively related to *drug use compliance* and *probation success* at a statistically significant level. In both cases, a one-unit increase in standardized probation risk score decreased the predicted odds of success by approximately one-third.

Discussion and Conclusion

Stichman (2002) had observed that the "maintenance of order among [prison] inmates is essential for the prevention of prison riots, the reduction of inmate victimization, and the success of treatment programs" (p. 3). In the context of probation, the stakes may be lower, as misbehavior is likely to be individual rather than collective. Still, the vicious media and political attacks on the criminal justice system that ensue when an offender commits a heinous crime while under community supervision (Surette, 2006) highlight the important role of probation in public safety. How officers achieve compliance from their charges, then, is a critical concern. The current study sought to go beyond the existing literature on bases of power in corrections by examining probationers' views and their behavior. The four previous studies on the bases of power focused only on "perceived power"; that is, they examined inmate perceptions of correctional officer bases of power without determining whether those perceptions were related to any inmate behavior. This study assessed what power correctional clients believed their supervising officers held, but also examined whether this power was manifest—did perceived power affect actual outcomes on self-reported compliance, drug use, and successful completion of probation?

Before discussing the findings, three limitations of the current study should be mentioned. First, the current study drew on a nonrandom sample of participants from a single probation department. Unique characteristics of the participants and the agency to which they reported may have affected the results. Future studies should determine to what extent the results reported here generalize to other contexts. This is particularly salient in the modern-day context whereby the majority of probation officers are also responsible for the supervision of parolees. Second, the current study included only probationers who could speak and read English. To assess the possibility that Spanish-speaking clients are affected differently by the aforementioned bases of power, a study could be conducted with enhanced ability to examine language and cultural differences. Third, the present study relied on survey data to assess probationers' subjective perceptions of their officers' bases of power. Perceptions figure prominently in theoretical discussions of power (see Bacharach & Lawler, 1975) and individual behavior (e.g., Paternoster, 1987). As discussed below, however, it would be useful to also know about probation officers' actual inclinations, attributes, and activities. Such data could advance understanding of power relationships and probation compliance in a more holistic manner.

Regarding perceptions of officers, this study revealed similarities to prior work. Stichman's (2002) was the only prior study to examine perceived power from the perspective of correctional clients. Her results (based on prison inmates) and the current ones (drawn from probationers) showed that the relative ranking of bases of power was quite similar for two very different populations. Both groups of subjects tended to report the highest levels of agreement that their officers' power was based on the legitimacy of their position, their fairness and respectfulness, and their ability to impose punishments for inappropriate behavior. These results appeared to be in harmony with the nature of probation. Probation clients tended to embrace the legitimacy of their inferior structural position. To them, it was right for their officer to tell them what to do and not to do. Had they rejected this notion, they would be questioning the very mandate of probation supervision. The respondents also largely believed that their officers' directives were backed by real consequences for misbehavior. Knowing that noncompliance may result in sanctions, and ultimately, revocation from probation is a potential motivator. Finally, probationers' acknowledgment of a referent base of power suggests that personal relationships are being formed. From the probationers' perspective, perhaps probation can be more than "superficial cooperation" between officers and clients (Gibbons & Rosecrance, 2005, p. 277).

The current study also echoed previous findings in that the probationers were less inclined to embrace notions about reward power. Hepburn (1985) has suggested that the relatively low perception of reward power may reflect actual conditions in prison where officers have few tangible incentives under their control. Stojkovic's (1986) administrators and guards also reported limited use of reward power, employing it only with particular inmates. Anecdotal comments from the probation officers in the current study reinforced the interpretation that low perceptions of reward power are based on the reality of meager available rewards. The officers contended that they had few meaningful rewards at their disposal.

In contrast to Stichman's (2002) inmates, the probationers in the present study perceived their officers to hold considerable power through expertise. Whereas the prison inmates in Stichman's (2002) study rejected notions that their officers had good conflict resolution skills and that they listened to their officers because of their expertise, this study's respondents believed their officers knew their job and rejected the idea that their officers were not skilled. Many possible explanations for the difference in results exist, including the composition of the offender groups, the context of prison versus probation, and possible unique aspects of the agency and institution included. Typical prisoners would likely have committed more serious offenses and have more serious criminal histories than individuals on misdemeanor probation roles. As others have observed, the prison experience can also engender a host of negative reactions from inmates and guards alike, degrading interpersonal relationships (see e.g., Haney, 2003; Johnson, 1996; Lombardo, 1981).

The present study moved well beyond the prior literature on the bases of power by examining not only perceived power, but also manifest power. In this regard, it tested the extent to which the five bases of power could predict probationers' compliance with their sentence. The results suggest little actual power among probation officers. While risk scores and two demographic variables predicted success, nearly all possible relationships between perceived bases of power and probation compliance were statistically insignificant. Thus, relatively high perceived power did not result in manifest power. The mean score for four of the five base of power indexes was approximately 3 or greater, translating to "agreeing" that officers possessed the potential for expert, legitimate, coercive, and referent power. These perceptions, however, did not predict compliance with probation requirements.

These null findings point to two possibilities. First, it may be that officers are not capitalizing on the potential power they hold. Based on the univariate results, it appears they could realize the greatest pay-off in terms of affecting probationer behavior by playing on perceptions that they are knowledgeable, and that have the right to direct probationers and the ability to punish noncompliance. As noted earlier, direct evidence on probation officers and how they interacted with their clients would be useful. Without such data, it is not possible to know to what extent probation officers are already trying to wield the power that probationers believe they hold. This raises a second possible explanation for the current finding that perceived power was unrelated to compliance. Rather than failing to mobilize their potential power, and despite their best efforts, officers may hold little actual sway over probationers' compliance with the conditions of their supervision. It would be ignorant to suggest probation is wholly ineffectual. Indeed, there is compelling evidence that community corrections programs that adhere to theoretically and empirically derived principles of intervention foster law-abiding behavior (Gendreau, 1996; Lowenkamp, Latessa, & Smith, 2006; Lowenkamp, Pealer, Smith, & Latessa, 2006). True power, however, may not rest at the individual level, instead being vested with probation *organizations*. In this way, probabilities of probationer misbehavior would be unrelated to variations in the perceived power among individual officers—as they are in this study—but would respond to broader structural arrangements of probation supervision.

In his classic work, *Dangerous Men*, McCleary (1978) reached a similar conclusion regarding parole supervision. He argued that power was a concept best explored in the organizational or group context, not the individual. In practical terms, McCleary found that the heterogeneity between parole officers and parolees was so pronounced that power issues rarely surfaced at the individual level. According to McCleary, individual parole officers might have enjoyed significant discretionary power, however, "they exercise this power only to benefit a few *special* clients" (p. 103, italics in original).

Conversely, McCleary found that parole officers were fighting, resisting, and manipulating, the organizational directives of "superiors" on a regular basis. This suggests that criminal justice agencies with high degrees of homogeneity between work groups may produce a competitive environment in which power relations are more prominent. Adding to this argument, McCleary (1978) stated:

> It is clear that parole officers enjoy substantial discretionary power. What is not immediately clear is that, if individual parole officers routinely exercised their powers, the bureaucratic dynamic described in the last chapter would collapse. The branch offices (and the people who work in them: POs and supervisors) and the central authority (DC officials) co-exist in a status quo that serves the interests of both. (p. 81)

The emphasis on bases of power at the organizational level should direct future research. McCleary (1978) simply observed that within parole, "power was enjoyed by groups or classes, not by individuals," an insight that "contradicts the conventional wisdom of criminology, which tries to explain parole outcomes at least in part as a function of PO discretion" (p. 79).

Testing the proposition that manifest power resides at the organizational level in probation was not possible with this data. Future research should consider approaching studies of power using multilevel models that could examine the place that individuals occupy within institutions. The concept of power is fundamental to criminal justice and it merits continued efforts to further understand how it functions.

References

Airaksinen, T. (1988)., *Ethics of coercion and authority: A philosophical study of social life*. Pittsburgh, PA: University of Pittsburgh Press.

Bacharach, S. B., & Lawler, E. J. (1975). The perception of power. *Social Forces, 55*, 123–134.

Bishop, G. F. (2004). *The illusion of public opinion: Fact and artifact in American public opinion polls*. Lanham, MD: Rowman and Littlefield.

Cloward, R. A. (1968). Social control in the prison. In L E. Hazelrigg (Ed.), *Prisons within society: A reader in penology* (pp. 78–112). Garden City, NY: Doubleday.

Debnam, G. (1984). *The analysis of power: Core elements and structure*. New York: St. Martin's Press.

Dilulio, J. (1987). *Governing prisons*. New York: Free Press.

Etzioni, A. (1961). *A comparative analysis of complex organizations*. New York: Free Press.

French, J., & Raven, B. (1959). The bases of social power. In D. Cartwright (Ed.), *Studies in social power* (pp. 259–269). Ann Arbor: University of Michigan Press.

Gendreau, P. (1996). The principles of effective intervention with offenders. In A. T. Harland (Ed.), *Choosing correctional options that work: Defining demand and evaluating the supply* (pp. 117–130). Thousand Oaks, CA: Sage.

Gibbons, S. G., & Rosecrance, J. D. (2005). *Probation, parole, and community corrections in the United States*. New York: Pearson.

Glaze, L. E., & Bonczar, T. P. (2007). *Probation and parole in the United States, 2006*. Washington, DC: U.S. Department of Justice.

Haney, C. (2003). The psychological impact of incarceration: Implications for postprison adjustment. In J. Travis & M. Waul (Eds.), *Prisoners once removed* (pp. 33–66). Washington, DC: Urban Institute Press.

Hepburn, J. R. (1985). The exercise of power in coercive organizations: A study of prison guards. *Criminology, 23*, 145–164.

Johnson, R. (1996). *Hard time: Understanding and reforming the prison*. New York: Wadsworth.

Keller, M., & Wang, H. (2005). Inmate assaults in Texas county jails. *The Prison Journal, 85*, 515–534.

Lindner, C. (1994). The police contribution to the development of probation: A historical account. *Journal of Offender Rehabilitation, 20*, 61–84.

Lombardo, L. X. (1981). *Guards imprisoned: Correctional officers at work*. New York: Elsevier.

Lowenkamp, C. T., Latessa, E. J., & Smith, P. (2006). Does correctional program quality really matter? The impact of adhering to the principles of effective intervention. *Criminology and Public Policy, 5*, 575–594.

Lowenkamp, C. T., Pealer, J., Smith, P., & Latessa, E. J. (2006). Adhering to the risk and need principles: Does it matter for supervision-based programs? *Federal Probation, 70*, 3–8.

Lukes, S. (1974). Power: *A radical view*. New York: Macmillan.

Marquart, J. W. (1986). Prison guards and the use of physical coercion as a mechanism of prisoner control. *Criminology, 24*, 347–366.

McCleary, R. (1978). *Dangerous men*. Beverly Hills, CA: Sage.

Morgan, K. D. (1994). Factors associated with probation outcome. *Journal of Criminal Justice, 22*, 341–353.

Packer, H. L. (1968). The *limits of the criminal sanction*. Stanford, CA: Stanford University Press.

Paternoster, R. (1987). Deterrent effect of the perceived certainty and severity of punishment: A review of the evidence and issues. *Justice Quarterly, A*, 173–217.

Senese, J. D. (1997). Evaluating jail reform: A comparative analysis of podular/direct and linear jail inmate infractions. *Journal of Criminal Justice, 25*, 61–73,

Steiner, B., Wada, J., Hemmens, C., & Burton, V. S., Jr. (2005). The correctional orientation of community corrections: Legislative changes in the legally prescribed functions of community corrections 1992-2002. *American Journal of Criminal Justice, 29*, 141–159.

Stichman, A. J. (2002). *The sources and impact of inmate perceptions of correctional officers' bases of power*. Unpublished doctoral dissertation, University of Cincinnati, Cincinnati, OH.

Stojkovic, S. (1984). Social bases of power and control mechanisms among prisoners in a prison organization. *Justice Quarterly, 1*, 511–528.

Stojkovic, S. (1986). Social bases of power and control mechanisms among correctional administrators in a prison organization. *Journal of Criminal Justice, 14*, 157–166.

Surette, R. (2006). *Media, crime, and criminal Justice: Images and realities* (3rd ed.). Belmont, CA: Wadsworth.

Sykes, G. (1958). *The society of captives: A study of a maximum-security prison*. Princeton, NJ: Princeton University Press.

Toch, H. (1992). *Living in prison: The ecology of survival*. Washington, DC: American Psychological Association.

Weber, M. (1968). *Economy and society*. New York: Bedminster Press.

DISCUSSION QUESTIONS

1. According to probationers, probation officers possess only limited reward power. Presently, judges determine the length of probation, albeit with possible input in the form of a presentence report. Do you think it would be possible to empower probation officers, allowing them to change the terms and length of probation to reward compliant offenders?

2. Suppose an offender is sentenced to one year of probation. During that period, what actions could a probation officer take to enhance his or her expert and referent power bases?

3. Coercive power was ranked third among the five bases of power. Why, if failure to comply may result in prison/jail time, was coercive power not ranked higher?

READING

Reading 24

Recognizing that coercive force is rarely used within correctional facilities, Denise L. Jenne and Robert C. Kersting examine how control is actually accomplished (exchange). Using a sample of male and female correctional officers working in six male correctional institutions in a single state, the researchers address the issue of reciprocity. Specifically, do male and female officers differ in their likelihood of overlooking minor infractions to gain compliance with more significant matters? Recall that Sykes (1958) argued that these types of exchange relationships develop because of the inherent weaknesses in correctional officer power. The question is whether female officers act differently than their male counterparts. Given four scenarios—a recalcitrant inmate, another dumping his tray, gambling in the housing unit, and smoking within a nonsmoking area—most correctional officers, regardless of gender, indicated that they would take some action, and both male and female officers were virtually identical in their tendency to take the most aggressive action possible. Follow-up interviews with 10 correctional officers reaffirmed the general tendency to enforce violations when they are observed. Yet officers acknowledged that overlooking behaviors was sometimes necessary but largely situational. Selective enforcement allows correctional officers to secure subsequent compliance from certain inmates, at certain times, and/or in certain locations.

Gender, Power, and Reciprocity in the Correctional Setting

Denise L. Jenne and Robert C. Kersting

All correction officers (COs) must develop strategies for gaining routine inmate compliance or risk forfeiture of their authority. The primary alternatives officially available to them are physical force, persuasion, and threats of punishment.

Existing evidence reveals that COs rarely use physical force to maintain order. Instead, they must establish personal authority, which is demonstrated by the way they carry out routine duties. Control is achieved through "skillful interpersonal relations" that rely on negotiation, accommodation, and manipulation (Jacobs, 1981, p. 62). Developing a personal style using these skills appears to be essential to occupational success.

For the female CO in male prisons, her choice of style will affect her ability to handle the prisoners, their response to her, and her safety on the job. The daily tasks she faces "do not call for physical strength, yet they do require [a woman] to be close to inmates, to touch them, and even to see them dressing, in a

---

Source: Jenne, D. L., & Kersting, R. C. (1998). Gender, power, and reciprocity in the correctional setting. *Prison Journal, 78*(2), 166–185.

shower, or using a toilet" (Crouch, 1985, p. 537). They also require her to violate traditional power relationships by having control over adult men. The inmates are thus provided the opportunity to use their sex status to redefine the authority relationship.

Regardless of how rarely force is actually used on a routine basis, the strategy is always available to the staff. That reality underlies all that COs do. In most situations where they use other methods to gain compliance, both officers and inmates recognize that coercion is an option the custodians can choose. Yet, it is generally assumed that women are even less able or less willing to use physical coercion and thus will rely more heavily on reciprocity than their male colleagues. This assumption then raises the dilemmas posed by reduced social distance between the women and their charges and the corollary corruption of authority.

Little empirical research has been conducted that addresses these concerns and examines the methods or effects of crossed-sex guarding. Yet, this deployment practice offers the unique opportunity to explore the role of gender as a master status and the effect of putting women in the nontraditional position of power and control.

Literature Review

Most of what is known about the styles of women COs in male prisons is taken from data on women working in other nontraditional occupations. Existing typologies describe polar extremes on a continuum ranging from those who most closely adhere to traditional stereotypes to those who attempt to overcome these assumptions through professionalism. For example, Martin (1980, pp. 185-199; see also Zimmer, 1986, pp. 108-109) found that policewomen are forced to choose between the extremes of "defeminization" and "deprofessionalization," stressing either occupational role obligations or female sex-role norms, respectively.

Similarly, Pollock (1995, pp. 97-116; see also Simpson, 1989, pp. 620–621) assumes that COs fall on a continuum of supervising styles that range from traditional, impersonal, and regimented to nontraditional, nurturing, and individualized. Women are more likely to approach the job with a "caring ethic" that reflects the latter style.

Some scholars assert that these depictions represent an androcentric analysis in which men's experiences are "taken as the norm and generalized to the population." According to Daly and Chesney-Lind (1988, pp. 499-500, 511), the liberal feminist perspective "assumes that when women become less feminine in outlook or enter roles occupied previously by men, they will begin to think and act like men." By contrast, radical or socialist feminists view gender as constructed by power relations, not simply roles. Research has borne out that women's choices are limited by such structural and organizational constraints as the formal and informal policies and practices regarding female officers (Pogrebin & Poole, 1997, pp. 45-47; Pollock, 1995, p. 109; Zimmer, 1986, p. 137).

When women COs were first deployed in male prisons, there was a spurt of research on the topic. Most of it focused on attitudes then, and most still does (see, e.g., Alpert & Crouch, 1991; Feinman, 1984; Holland et al., 1979; Potter, 1980; Szockyj, 1989). To date, Zimmer (1986) has provided the most substantial research on the actual styles women COs use in crossed-sex institutions. Through an ethnographic study using observation and interviews within two state Departments of Corrections (DOCs), she found the two polar extremes identified by her predecessors: Some women adopt the "institutional role," downplaying any gender differences by adhering to all of the prison rules. Others, who she tagged modified women, believe they are not able to perform the job as well as men, as evidenced by fear and avoidance of the inmates. According to Zimmer, both roles can leave the women trapped in a "cycle of failure."

However, Zimmer (1986, p. 142) found a third style: This "inventive role" is composed of women officers who find their female status a "distinct advantage." These women compensate for their perceived physical weakness by integrating counseling services into the job. Making use of their intuition, communication skills, and ability to win the inmates' respect, they work in direct contact posts with little fear. As with any CO who relies on reciprocity, the exchange relationships they develop can reduce the amount of social distance between the woman and the prisoners (Sykes, 1958, pp. 61-62). Yet, Zimmer contends that inventive women are often successful in prisons for men because they hone techniques that rely on the use of men's assumptions about and their stereotypical responses to women: "In general, inmates do not interact with female guards on a sex-neutral basis, and women's female status and how they use it remain important factors in their ultimate adjustment to the job" (p. 104). Furthermore, officers who use the inventive style are actually using a style adapted from that of successful male COs, only supplemented with the "female touch."

However, Zimmer's (1986) findings are speculative and unsupported. According to Zupan (1992, p. 337), they are not congruent with previous research. Although Zimmer argues that the styles she identified are unique to women officers, she fails to provide conclusive evidence of any gender differences. These styles could represent the stereotyped assumptions of either the respondents or the researcher, or both. In addition, her findings may not be generalizable and as yet are unsubstantiated by further research. One study comparing male and female COs on their rule violation practices found no significant differences in the number or type of infractions reported (Simon & Simon, 1988, p. 134).

Indeed, the differences between the inventive style and reciprocity as used by most veteran male officers may not be as sharp as they first appear. There is no evidence of any substantial gender differences regarding the use of reciprocity. Although it is possible women ignore more infractions than their peers, it is also feasible that they are no more nurturing, supportive, and empathetic than most men who have learned to rely on their intuition, communication skills, and ability to win the inmates' respect. If such distinctions exist, they may be more a matter of degree than true differences. As Carlen (1990) noted regarding female criminality, "One of the major problems of writing specifically about women... is that such gender specification can imply that women-as-a-biological-grouping have essentially different reasons than do men for [their behavior]" (p. 109).

Preliminary research supports divergent styles of supervising inmates based on gender. However, most of this research has been done on COs in same-sex institutions and is subsequently of limited usefulness. The styles used by female COs working with female prisoners may provide no insight into whether women in crossed-sex facilities employ different strategies than their male colleagues. As Pollock (1986) suggests, it is unknown whether women officers are more empathetic because they deal with women inmates, or if female inmates are more open "because they have a sympathetic ear with female officers" (p. 95).

Although contributing to our knowledge in the area, existing research on the use of women's strategies in male prisons provides insufficient data to formulate answers. These studies are frequently limited by the small number of women in these facilities and/or direct contact posts. In addition, they have been confined to ethnographies. As such, they provide a basis for more quantitative research that can offer more refined operationalizations and definitive descriptions (Babbie, 1995, p. 273). Pollock (1995) recently stated,

> Before one can dismiss the anecdotal evidence and widely held beliefs of practitioners and inmates that men and women supervise in ditierent ways, there needs to be a more direct objective measurement.... Only in this way would one have a true sense of any supervision differences between men and women. Unfortunately, no one, as yet, has conducted such a study. (pp. 107-108)

The research methodology that follows addresses this need. It explores the following questions: Are the strategies employed by women in crossed-sex guarding significantly different than those used by male officers? Does gender determine the amount of reciprocity in which officers engage? And, when put in the nontraditional position of power and control, do women rely on their sex status to manipulate the situation?

Methodology and Sample

As part of a larger study, from November 1991 through June 1992, mail questionnaires were sent to individual officers of both genders working in six male penitentiaries within a Northeastern state DOC. The questionnaire partially replicated an earlier study of COs by Crouch and Alpert (1982). Its three parts were composed of demographics; the Critical Incidents Scale (CIS), which was developed by Kercher and Martin (1975) and used by Crouch and Alpert (1982); and an 11-item Likert-type scale created by the latter. The scale operationalized COs' attitudes toward inmates and control issues. It allowed respondents to place themselves on a continuum presenting opposite statements about inmates and their jobs. To augment the questionnaire and provide data it would not likely tap, a sample of the women respondents participated in a brief follow-up telephone interview (for a more complete description of the methodology, sampling, and questionnaire used, see Jenne, 1995, pp. 52-68, 150-159).

The CIS was designed to measure aggressiveness in inmate encounters through a series of hypothetical but realistic prison confrontational situations. Each incident allows for five responses ranging from passive (e.g., taking no action) to aggressive (e.g., physically restraining the inmate). Intermediate responses provide for varying degrees of assertiveness. The instrument was constructed with the aid of veteran COs and has been shown to have good content validity (Crouch & Alpert, 1982, pp. 159-160).

The original CIS was changed to provide for a wider range of responses. This process was aided by experienced COs of both sexes in both same-sex and crossed-sex guarding and drew on one of the writer's knowledge as a jail liaison worker, supporting its face validity.

Comparisons of male and female responses to the four critical incidents that addressed minor rule violations were used to test the hypothesis that women COs overlook minor rule infractions more frequently than their male coworkers:

1. You are given responsibility for awakening inmates for early duty. You awaken inmate "X," whereupon he repeatedly tells you to "go fuck yourself."

7. You are assigned to the dining hall during noon feeding. An inmate deliberately dumps his tray on the floor.

9. You are working a housing unit where you find several inmates gambling.

12. While en route to your assigned post, you see an inmate smoking a cigarette in a "no smoking" area.

Comparisons were also conducted on the second part of each item, which asked, "What would you write on the incident?" and allowed for the responses "nothing," "an informational report," or "a disciplinary charge."

The female return rate was 34.9% of the original 229 contacted, providing a final number of 80 women COs. The return rate for male officers was 40.7% of the original 162, providing a final number of 66 men. The total number for both male and female COs is 146, or 37.3% of 391. For the follow-up interviews, a random sample of the 23 who agreed was contacted, resulting in 10 interviews, with at least one respondent from each facility.

Although there is no agreed-upon standard for a minimum acceptable response rate (Maxfield &

Babbie, 1995, p. 226), the current response rate of 37.3% is low. Nonresponse analysis revealed only one relevant difference between both the sample women and the population of female COs working within these institutions and between the male and female subsamples: That difference related to the length of time they had been COs. As suggested by Table 1, female respondents had a mean length of service greater than the population's, whereas men have much more time on the job than either the population or sample of women (for a more detailed account of the nomespouse analysis, see Jenne & Kersting, 1996, pp. 446-447). The importance of this variable might be to reduce any gender differences, especially if length of time on the job affects the style used by an officer. Because the sample women more closely resemble the male officers in terms of experience, they might do the job more like the men than other women COs, downplaying any differences.

Caution must be exercised with regard to generalizing from these data. The possibility of response bias cannot be eliminated. Also, the need to limit the study to one state DOC means it would be erroneous to attempt to generalize from these findings to the total population of female COs. There is no reason to believe that this is a representative state, nor are the experiences of its correctional staff similar to those elsewhere. Thus, this study is useful as an initial attempt to provide an objective measure of gender differences in guarding and for generating hypotheses for future research.

Quantitative Results

Analysis of COs' responses to the four minor incidents found no gender differences. In general, neither men nor women overlooked the minor rule infractions presented.

The situation where the CO is given the responsibility for awakening an inmate and is told to "go fuck yourself" elicited strikingly similar responses, with 94% of women and 95% of men choosing to "put the inmate on report" as their immediate response.

As seen in Table 2, the incident where an inmate dumps his food tray had a broad range of responses, but the majority of both men and women selected "order the inmate to clean it up" as their response (76% and 60%, respectively). Gender differences here were not statistically significant.

In the incident involving inmates caught gambling, the majority of COs responded that they would confiscate the paraphernalia (66% for women and 76% for men), and the remainder said they would order the inmates to stop. The differences between women and men on this item were not statistically significant.

In the final minor incident, regarding smoking, a majority of both men and women would order the inmate to extinguish the cigarette (78% and 71%, respectively), with the remaining responding that they would "ask the inmate to stop." Again, gender differences were not significant.

To further explore the responses of women and men to minor incidents, an aggressive response to minor incidents index was developed. This index was a count of the frequency that officers selected the most aggressive response available in the four incidents. The mean for women and men was almost identical (1.35 and 1.30, respectively). This difference was not statistically significant.

Clearly, these data suggest that women and men see themselves neither as responding differently to the provided minor incidents nor as overlooking these infractions when they occur. However, it remains possible that they might follow up on such incidents differently. Overlooking an incident might be exhibited in whether COs write a report on the infractions. Thus, respondents were asked how they would follow up on each incident-that is, whether they would write a disciplinary charge, an informational report, or no report.

No differences were found between men and women regarding whether they would write a report or the type of report, as shown in Table 3. For the first incident (awakening an inmate), the majority of officers indicated they would write a disciplinary charge (84% of women and 81% of men). For the dumped tray incident, again a majority of men and women would write a disciplinary charge (68% of each). The gambling incident had the highest percentages of women and men writing a disciplinary charge (92% and 91%, respectively). Finally, the smoking incident was the only one likely to result in no report by a majority of both men and women (63% and 74%, respectively).

The final question to be explored statistically was whether other variables affected or camouflaged the effect that gender might have on report-writing

Table 1 Descriptive Statistics

	Females	Males	Population Females
Gender			
%	54.8	45.2	100
n	80	66	229
Age (in years)			
M	36.2	36.7	34.6
SD	7.9	9.2	8.1
Time in corrections (in months)			
M	66.4	100.5	55.8
SD	45.5	66.7	40.7
Time at current facility (in months)			
M	52.9	78.8	
SD	35.5	54.3	
Time at current post (in months)			
M	23.5	35.9	
SD	19.6	28.7	
Current rank Officer			
%	92.4	83.3	95.2
n	73	55	218
Supervisor (sergeant or lieutenant)			
%	7.6	16.7	4.8
n	6	11	11

practices. Specifically, time as a CO, the facility in which the officer worked, and the CO's attitude about inmates and the need for control were examined.

To test this question, an analysis of variance was estimated, with the dependent measure being the number of disciplinary charges the officer would have written. Gender remains a nonsignificant predictor of a CO's response, as is time on the job. What is not surprising from a commonsense perspective is that a CO's attitude about control does predict whether he or she would write a disciplinary charge. Even more interesting, though, is that there is something about the facility where the officer works that predicts the writing of a disciplinary charge.

In summary, this analysis has found no support for the hypothesis that women COs overlook minor rule infractions more frequently than their male coworkers. This conclusion is supported by the evidence regarding both their immediate response to the incidents presented and the likelihood and type of written follow-up action.

Qualitative Interviews and Discussion

Exchange relationships. There is little doubt among scholars and practitioners that, although coercive power is the officially recognized strategy for gaining inmate compliance, it is not the dominant method used by COs. The deficiencies inherent in coercive strategies result in the use of exchange relationships inside prison walls (see, e.g., Clear & Cole, 1997, pp. 26-27). This trade enables COs to maintain order.

COs gain inmate compliance in the areas that "count" (i.e., the ones on which they will be judged

Table 2 Responses to Incident 7: Dumps Tray

You are assigned to the dining hall during noon feeding. An inmate deliberately dumps his tray on the floor.

	No Action	Order Clean Up	Ask What Happened	Ask to Clean Up	Send for Supervisor	Total
Male						
n	2	38	6	8	9	63
%	3	60	9	13	14	45.3
Female						
n		58	1	9	7	76
%		76	1	12	9	54.7
Total						
N	3	96	7	17	16	139
%	2.2	69.1	5.0	12.2	11.5	100.0

Note: Missing cases= 7.

in terms of inmate behavior) in exchange for overlooking minor rule violations, the "most meaningful reward" they can offer because it enables inmates to establish an economic and social system. The staff's tacit approval of minor infractions is facilitated, not by corruption or bribery but by the claims of reciprocity necessitated by the defects of total power and by the close contact between the two groups, which tends to reduce social distance and to produce, at least to some degree, feelings of mutual empathy (Sykes, 1958, pp. 54-56).

The current hypothesis predicted that women COs would make more use of exchange relationships than their male counterparts, as operationalized by the response to minor rule infractions. Contrary to this hypothesis and previous research, the findings suggest that few officers, regardless of gender, attest to overlooking minor infractions by taking no action, and the majority follow up their actions with a written report.

One possible explanation for this inconsistency is that the use of questionnaires, and interviews is not an adequate means of measuring the prevalence of this practice. For example, because overlooking rule infractions is contrary to official procedures, officers might be reluctant to admit engaging in the behavior, even in an anonymous questionnaire.

Table 3 Responses to Type of Report by Gender

	No Report n (%)	Informational n (%)	Disciplinary Charge n (%)
Incident 1: Awaken inmate ($\chi^2 = 0.40$, $df = 2$, $p = .82$)			
Women	5 (6)	7 (9)	67 (84)
Men	6 (9)	6 (9)	54 (81)
Incident 7: Dumped tray ($\chi^2 = 0.66$, $dt = 2$, $p = .72$)			
Women	15 (19)	10 (13)	54 (68)
Men	15 (23)	6 (9)	44 (68)
Incident 9: Gambling 2 ($\chi^2 = 0.12$, $df = 2$, $p = .94$)			
Women	4 (5)	2 (2)	73 (92)
Men	4 (6)	2 (3)	59 (91)
Incident 12: No smoking ($\chi^2 = 2.26$, $dt = 2$, $p = .32$)			
Women	59 (74)	5 (6)	16 (20)
Men	40 (63)	7 (11)	17 (26)

When respondents were asked in interviews to explain the discrepancy, many presented the official position.

> CO#1: Well . . . you know we have set rules that we have to go by . . . so they are just going by the procedure.
>
> Interviewer (1): Do you think most officers do go by the procedures most of the time?
>
> CO#1: Yes.
>
> CO#2: You get paid to correct behavior, it's called the Department of Corrections, we get paid to correct behavior. . . . Almost like your children, you always have to do something. It might not always be the top of the list. . . but you always have to do something. You always have to do something when an inmate does anything.
>
> I: Okay, and you don't think minor rule infractions are overlooked?
>
> CO#2: No.
>
> CO#3: There are rules and regulations basically for all state institutions that the inmates have to go by. And if they don't go by them, they go on disciplinary action brought against them.

Similarly, they explained the need for full enforcement of the prison's many rules.

> CO#4: Yes . . . that's necessary, because they have to know when they step over the line. And it's really necessary to let him know where to draw the line-what you expect out of him, because if you don't tell the inmate what you expect out of him, and you don't give him some type of reprimand, if it's nothing but verbal, he thinks he's got you in his pocket. And the inmates once they think they can manipulate you . . . because we've had of ticers that have been manipulated by inmates. So you always have to let inmates know that you have the upper hand, that you are in control.
>
> CO#5: Control of the institution, you have to, you have to enforce even the smallest things, [because] they can, can lead to . . . [it's] incredible what it can lead to inside an institution. You know, you are forced to, not only for your own safety, but for the running of the institution, to keep, you know, an eye on any little thing.
>
> CO#6: Because that in itself would create a big problem. There might be a circumstance, at some given point in time, that will make it necessary, at that time, to overlook. But, as a rule, you don't. Because minor things cause big things. And, what's minor can be major later on. So, you don't overlook minor as a rule, and as a habit.
>
> CO#3: As far as the inmate swearing, if they let an inmate swear at them, they are going to get it. If you stop it in the beginning, you don't have that problem. That's a matter of respect, that's something you have to demand. . . . I don't use . . . let them disrespect me, no matter whatever.
>
> CO#7: Everything is straight on the line. I don't play with the inmates, I don'tjoke with them. They are not my friends, and the minute you get a little lax, then one thing's going to lead to another. And, they are going to look at a female, like she's weak and I can overcome her.

One interviewee attributed the similarities between COs to the training they receive.

> CO#8: Ah, I think that's because we've all had the same training, we all been, ah, told to handle a situation the same way. The only time it would differ is when you bring your own personality into a situation. So we have all received the same training, you know? . . . Basically, we would try to handle situations the same way. Unless your personality comes into it.

I: And, what do you think happens more often? Do you think people respond the way they were trained to? Or, do you think their personality comes into it?

CO#8: I, I think we try to handle it the way we were trained to . . . as much as possible, because that's what we go by. Ah, we are safer with what you know.

However, in the course of discussing other aspects of their work, the same women provided evidence of exchange relationships. For example, when the officer just cited was asked, "When do you think the situation arises when you don't rely on how you were trained?" she responded as follows:

CO#8: Well, just when you have to use your own judgment. I mean, a lot of times, ah, you are trained . . . sometimes you just have to use your own judgment in a situation. You can't always go by the book. . . . That depends on the situation, you know. Um, every case is different. . . . Um. . . if an inmate refuses an order, tell him to do something, and he just ignores you. . . . It just depends on the situation. You know whether or not he's going to do it, or if he's definitely not going to do it, and then you have to do something about it.

Others also made references to the practice. Some attributed it to individual differences in officers.

CO#3: So it depends on the officer also. Some officers are very lenient, others aren't, some are very firm, others aren't. I myself, I am [in] between, it depends on what it is.

CO#1: Okay. Well, I handle aggression head on. Whereas other females, they seem to let it go by . . . you know, just . . . you know, kind of ignore it.

Others saw it as a matter of gender.

CO#4: Someone wasn't being quite honest with their answers. Or people didn't understand the questions. . . . Oh, you know, as far as the reaction of the men. Ah, I don't know, men have a different attitude about how things work. Sometimes they look the other way. They try to act like it's no big deal.

CO#7: If you are a little bit late for work, the female may let them off a little bit more. And just maybe yell at them and say don't do it no more. Whereas the male officer will have a little more to say. They'll have a verbal thing and write them a charge.

This last interviewee further predicted our finding that the specific prison would influence behavior.

CO#7: Ah, this prison compared to [another prison] is day and night. Up there, there is more control over inmates because there are cells. You can control them more. Here they are dormitory-style wings, and they have to be given a little more privilege in order to maintain control of the jail.

Regardless of the explanation offered, the pragmatics of reciprocity were recognized.

CO#6: And whether you should overlook something minute, in order to cover something major you know. . . . Sometimes it comes to a place where you cannot. . . pick on everything all the time. Sometimes you can, but sometimes you have to live and let live. If you overlook something minor doesn't mean you overlook the situation—you may overlook some minor thing, in order to catch something major—or uncover something major.

CO#9: A . . . minor rule infraction is not something to . . . you know, you have to be able to win sometimes you know. . . . You don't want to constantly be a heavy because ... it's ... we can't whip them all, we have to learn how to bend a little bit.... Um, I can only give you something like this. If a minor incident is basically not going to [be] a ... harm to security. If it's a minor incident like a radio or something, that's a minor incident, okay? Walk down, the radio is on, right? I didn't do anything. Because to me everybody has to cut loose once in a while.... And even a prisoner has to cut loose once in a while. That's a minor, minor infraction with a radio.... That's about the only minor infraction I can tell you that I would go with.... But I ... we have to deal that way, we have to do it that way. You know, because we are outnumbered about 10 to 1.... But we have to tell [them], when to eat, when to get up–and certain incidents we have to overlook.... We have to do it that way.

This respondent also suggested that, rather than an act of leniency or incompetence, the practice of overlooking infractions by not writing a report is a demonstration of control or the officer's ability to handle the situation.

CO#9: I am aggressive in my ways. I am a wing officer. But, I have always been that way.... Because being that way... being real soft is not going to get you anywhere in corrections. They are going to take your kindness for the most biggest weakness of all. I am aggressive, but I am very kind.... And, I let them know that just because I am kind, that gives me my strength. ... They know, if I put it on the blue sheet—they have lost it. I am not one of those people that use a blue sheet to control anything. A blue sheet to me is ... ifI have to write [up] an inmate ... is a person who has lost control. Every time I write a blue sheet I have lost control. So, I write very few blue sheets. So, I have more control. I feel I have more control because of the way I present myself, the way I carry myself. Because the guys think I am talked out, you know, they can't believe that I am the way I am.

Unlike the survey items, the interviews support previous research by suggesting that COs do overlook minor infractions as a control strategy.

Selective enforcement. One reason the CIS might not have tapped this information is that, although exchange relationships are not recognized as a general practice, they are entered into selectively. In other words, an officer, who will ordinarily enforce all rules, will overlook some rule infractions when committed by specific inmates. "Different guards have different rule enforcement standards, but most guards are willing to ignore some minor rule infractions by those inmates who voluntarily comply with the more critical rules and regulations" (Zimmer, 1986, p. 21).

Such selective enforcement would not be reflected in answers to the questionnaire items, as officers would be likely to consider only the specific infraction when the identity of the rule violator is unknown. However, support for this possibility is provided by handwritten comments that some respondents added to particular questionnaire items, such as the following: "depends on the situation," "if he picks it up," "charge only written if necessary," "if I/M [inmate] refuses," "if he ... continues with his mouth," "if I/M doesn't get smart," and "depends on where he was at."

The interpretation was also recognized by several interview respondents who referred to the salience of the individual inmate's behavior.

CO#10: It's possible ... [COs] are ... more apt to accelerate the degrees of punishment. So, probably with the minor rule infractions they will give them a verbal warning.... Tell them once, and if the individual chooses to do it again, they already know they are not supposed to. So, it's the responsibility of the individual.... I'm dealing personally, now I tell an individual they have violated a minor rule infraction I say, "you are not permitted to do it, this is what you are required to do." The individual on a second infraction chose to ignore my verbal correction and committed a minor rule infraction, then the responsibility is on the inmate.... And, then he will be corrected... written up, whatever.

CO#3: A lot of times if an inmate decides he's going to do something stupid, and instead of me writing him a charge, and he has a life sentence, it doesn't make any sense. I'll get on the intercom and... embarrass him in front of his boys, and he won't do that again.... Because basically it's the only way we have to deal with them. The older guys don't pull it as much as the younger guys that just come in, that have long to go.

Further support was provided by those who discussed the importance of the CO's familiarity with the setting or the inmate himself.

CO#8: If you had a detail and one of the guys cussed at you or whatever, this is a guy you have all the time, you deal with it. If it's a guy that you don't... that you never have, that you don't know... do you know what I mean?

CO#6: Well, the only thing I can say in regards to that, when you are caught up in a situation, you as an officer, if that's your regular place, or assignment, you as an officer have to rely on how well you know your area, how familiar you are with the people you are working with.

CO#1: Ah... I think a lot of them are [overlooked]. I have overlooked some that are minor. You know, one that's not life threatening, or a breach in security, I overlook a lot of things. It depends on the inmate too.... If he's a pretty decent inmate and he doesn't give you a lot of backlash and hard time or anything, I might overlook something minor. But if he [is] constantly a... pest to someone, always doing what he's not supposed to do, even a little minor infraction I would write it up.

CO#9: I have to... I have to read the situation I am in. You can't get aggressive until you know the type of situation. If it is not a situation that can erupt in your... your face, and it's just sitting around BS-ing it's... you can act like a little bit more aggressive. If you... if you are familiar with that inmate. But you are not going to do that with an inmate you are not familiar with.

Selective enforcement would also be consistent with previous research. For example, officers have reported that, at the start of their careers, they relied on rules to maintain order, but as they became more seasoned and learned what they "can and can't expect of inmates" and themselves, the rules were used only "in extreme cases or to set an example" (Lombardo, 1981, pp. 74-78, 98-108).

Although the current quantitative analysis did not find a correlation between length of service and the practice of overlooking minor infractions, the interviews suggest otherwise by reference to skills that are acquired through experience—such as the role of knowing one's post and how to read both situations and inmate behavior.

Previous research has shown that most rule infraction reports that are written come from the parts of the prison where personal relationships are "least likely to legitimize authority." Because once a relationship of authority exists, the officer can word his or her orders as mere suggestions that generally will be readily followed, averting the need for routine sanctions. In other words, the tendency of officers to report infractions is closely related to the opportunities provided by their posts to interact with and get to know individual inmates and to establish authority relationships (Lombardo, 1981, pp. 98-108; see also Crouch & Alpert, 1982, pp. 160-161; Marquart, 1983, pp. 99-101; Pollock, 1986, p. 3).

Although this study was unable to test the relationship between an officer's post and the tendency to overlook minor infractions, the interviews support the possibility:

CO#8: Some of us haven't had as much one-to-one contact as the males. We haven't had the same details. Where we have six or eight inmates every day assigned to us I think it's just not having as much experience, really. Because those jobs, those details, things like that, they are . . . they only go to the officers with the most seniority I don't know. I have 10 years—but, that's not considered that much. I really couldn't say about other females. I don't think that too many have a whole lot more. But I'm sure there's a few, but on average, I don't think they have too much more than that.

Selective enforcement would be consistent with both organization theory (see, e.g., Lipsky, 1980, pp. 14-15) and existing research in corrections. Most officers believe that full enforcement of the hundreds of prison rules is an unrealistic goal. The enforcement decision is situationally defined, with the determinative factor being the officer's perception of the actual or potential impact the offending behavior has on himself or herself and all officers, inmates, or the "atmosphere" of the institution (Lombardo, 1981, pp. 55, 82-92).

Gender and authority. COs tend to believe that most prisoners (at least tacitly) acknowledge the need for rules (Zimmer, 1986, p. 164). As suggested by the clarifications written on the questionnaires and some of the interviews, most officers rely on warning or telling offenders to alter their behavior as the primary intervention strategy. They have at their disposal any number of "informal punishments" they can use if deemed necessary or appropriate (Lombardo, 1981, pp. 78-87). For example, one interviewee said,

CO#3: I've never had a problem, I've never had to touch an inmate. I've never came in contact with an inmate that ever touched me, that ever hit me, that ever threatened me. Inmates joke around with you, and you joke back around with him. And they may say their body feels nice up next to you. And I may say, "It ain't going nowhere." Or, I may say, "Did I hear physical threat, that sound like physical threat, I think I hear 90 days in the hole." And, they like chill out and say "Oh, miss it wasn't like that." But I've never had a problem. . . . I've had tendencies where men . . . male inmates have a tendency [to] want to stand there and masturbate. . . . And it's no wonder, and I'll start up the hall real easy, and while they are standing there, I'll get on the intercom and say, "Is there something you want to show everyone in the unit?" And that will solve the whole thing. He will be embarrassed and sit right back down, and they will say, "I'm sorry, I shouldn't have done that." And I'll say, "That's right you shouldn't have did it." Because if I let that get to court line, I know I will lose that. Because they will tell me point blank, you are at an all-male institution, you're going to expect that. You should expect that from them because they don't have physical contact with a woman.

To many officers, these informal strategies are seen as "alternative formal methods" because they achieve the ultimate goal of compliance. However, some inmates see the rules as a personal challenge and, when their actions exceed acceptable limits, finding some rule to fit the situation is never impossible (Lombardo, 1981, pp. 80-87).

Researchers have found that each situation is approached individually, and the most important variable determining the CO's response is the interaction between the officer and the inmate. When an encounter threatens to diminish the officer's authority or respect and thus his or her ability to do the job, official action is likely (see, e.g., Marquart, 1983, pp. 100-101). The inmate's attitude is the cue to this threat and may be viewed as either heightening the apparent severity of a violation or as a separate, additional offense: 43% of the 541 written reports analyzed in one study were for refusing an order, threatening an officer, or showing disrespect to an officer as current questionnaire respondents suggested the salience of refusing a request, continuing "with his mouth," or getting "smart."

Officers feel justified in ignoring some rule infractions but intervene formally when an inmate displays an "inappropriate" attitude (Lombardo, 1981, pp. 75, 85, 92-97; see also Simon & Simon, 1988, p. 134).

Whenever rules are enforced on a selective basis, a pathway to corruption is opened. Whether most COs are engaged in an exercise of discretion or an exercise in corruption (Lombardo, 1981, p. 161), exchange relationships do raise the possibility that the behavior of some, if not many, will be outside tolerable limits. As Sykes (1958) wrote, "The custodians . . . are under strong pressure to compromise with their captives, for it is a paradox that they can insure their dominance only by allowing it to be corrupted" (pp. 57-58). Clearly, they are, in effect, "buy[ing] compliance in certain areas at the cost of tolerating disobedience elsewhere"—a situation ripe for corruption whether the result of greed, indifference, blackmail, or the "innocuous encroachment" of the officers' duties.

Whether women officers present more of an opportunity for corruption through reciprocity than their male colleagues is not directly addressed by the findings. However, it would seem safe to speculate that they pose no more risk than the men. As noted, neither male nor female COs indicated frequent use of this strategy, although it is feasible that the instruments used would not be sensitive to its selective use. In addition, it must be remembered that the current sample was skewed in terms of length of time on the job, which could serve to reduce gender differences (i.e., the sample women tended to have more experience than the population of female COs but significantly less than the sample of men). Because engaging in exchange relationships seems to be a preferred style of more experienced officers, the possibility is raised that, as they gain more experience, the women would increase their use of this strategy and surpass their male colleagues. Thus, it remains conceivable that women do overlook minor rule infractions and thus risk corruption of their authority more than male officers. However, the evidence suggests that this is unlikely. The prediction that women are more vulnerable to corruption is based on what appears to be two faulty assumptions: (a) Women COs make greater use of reciprocity than men, and (b) they do not rely on force as readily as the men (Jenne & Kersting, 1996).

Conclusions and Implications

Although the study found little quantitative evidence of exchange relationships behind bars, qualitative interviews were suggestive of the practice. However, neither supported the hypothesis that women COs use the strategy more frequently than their male counterparts. Rather, the evidence indicates that the facility in which officers work is a more salient factor than gender. In conclusion, it would seem that women in crossed-sex guarding generally face many of the same exigencies as their male coworkers and, for the most part, do the job in ways similar to the men.

However, questions remain regarding gender as a master status (Pogrebin & Poole, 1997, p. 53). This study does not address whether women are learning to act like the men who have defined the CO's role (i.e., the liberal feminist perspective) or the occupational socialization they receive, and the demands of the job counter any gender differences that might otherwise exist (the radical feminist perspective).

Furthermore, the study is limited by a number of factors, and caution must be exercised in generalizing from its findings. Future research must examine the dynamics of exchange relationships—the interactional, situational, and organizational factors that influence the decision-making process. In doing so, it can define the role played by the facility in this process. Also, research must explore the relationship between length of service and use of reciprocity, especially as women gain experience in male prisons that is on par with the men. And through more sensitive measures and longitudinal studies, further tests of gender differences in reciprocity will clarify the impact of crossed-sex guarding and further refine theories of gender and power.

References

Alpert, G. P., & Crouch, B. M. (1991). Cross-gender supervision, personal privacy, and institutional security. *Criminal Justice & Behavior, 18,* 304.

Babbie, E. R. (1995). *The practice of social research* (7th ed.). New York: Wadsworth.

Carlen, P. (1990). Women, crime, feminism and realism. *Social Justice, 17*(4), 106-123.

Clear, T. R., & Cole, G. F. (1997). Exchange. In *American corrections* (4th ed., pp. 26-27). New York: Wadsworth.

Crouch, B. M. (1985). Pandora's box: Women guards in men's prisons. *Journal of Criminal Justice, 13,* 535-548.

Crouch, B. M., & Alpert, G. P. (1982). Sex and occupational socialization among prison guards: A longitudinal study. *Criminal Justice Bulletin, 9,* 159-177.

Daly, K., & Chesney-Lind, M. (1988). Feminism and criminology. *Justice Quarterly, 5*(4), 497-538.

Feinman, C. (1984). Modesty or muscle: Conflicting views of the role of women working in the penal system. In S. Hatty (Ed.), *Women in the prison system* (pp. 69-83). Australian Institute of Criminology.

Holland, T., Levi, M., Beckett, G., & Holt, N. (1979). Preferences of prison inmates for male or female institutional personnel. *Journal of Applied Psychology, 64,* 564-568.

Jacobs, J. B. (1981). The sexual integration of the prison guard force: A few comments on *Dothard v. Rawlinson*. In B. H. Olsson (Ed.), *Women in corrections* (pp. 57-85). College Park, MD: American Correctional Association.

Jenne, D. L. (1995). *Methods used by women correction officers to handle male inmates.* Doctoral dissertation, Rutgers University. *Dissertation Abstracts International, 56*(10A), 41-55. (University Microfilms 9603548)

Jenne, D. L., & Kersting, R. C. (1996). Aggression and women correctional officers in male prisons. *The Prison Journal, 76*(4), 442-460.

Kercher, G., & Martin, S. (1975). *Severity of correctional behavior in the prison environment.* Paper presented before the Texas Academy of Sciences, Huntsville, TX.

Lipsky, M. (1980). *Street-level bureaucracy: Dilemmas of the individual in public services.* New York: Russell Sage.

Lombardo, L. X. (1981). *Guards imprisoned: Correctional officers at work.* New York: Elsevier.

Marquart, J. W. (1983). Cooptation of the kept: Maintaining control in a Southern penitentiary. *Dissertation Abstracts International, 45*(IA), 307. (University Microfilms AAC 8408457)

Martin, S. E. (1980). *Breaking and entering: Policewomen on patrol.* Berkeley: University of California Press.

Maxfield, M.G., & Babble, E. (1995). Asking questions: Survey research. In *Research methods for criminal justice and criminology* (pp. 211-241). New York: Wadsworth.

Pogrebin, M. R., & Poole, E. D. (1997). The sexualized work environment: A look at women jail officers. *The Prison Journal, 77*(1), 41-57.

Pollock, J. M. (1986). *Sex and supervision: Guarding male and female inmates.* New York: Greenwood.

Pollock, J. M. (1995). Women in corrections: Custody or the "caring ethic." In A. V. Merlo & J. M. Pollock (Eds.), *Women, law and social control* (pp. 97-116). Needham Heights, MA: Allyn & Bacon.

Potter, J. (1980). Should women guards work in prisons for men? *Corrections Magazine, 6,* 30-38.

Simon, R. J., & Simon, J. D. (1988). Female COs: Legitimate authority. *Corrections Today, 50*(5), 132-134.

Simpson, S. S. (1989). Feminist theory, crime and justice. *Criminology, 27*(4), 605-632.

Sykes, G. M. (1958). *Society of captives.* Princeton, NJ: Princeton University Press.

Szockyj, E. (1989). Working in a man's world: Women correctional officers in an institution for men. *Canadian Journal of Criminology, 31*(3), 319-328.

Zimmer, L. E. (1986). *Women guarding men.* Chicago: University of Chicago Press.

Zupan, L. L. (1992). The progress of women correctional officers in all-male prisons. In I. L. Moyer (Ed.), *The changing roles of women in the criminal justice system* (2nd ed., pp. 323–343). Prospect Heights, IL: Waveland.

DISCUSSION QUESTIONS

1. Jenne and Kersting note that a correctional officer's assignment or post is related to the development of referent power. Additionally, referent power reduces the need to discipline (i.e., "write up") inmates for minor rule infractions. How does referent power emerge? Why does referent power reduce the likelihood of formal disciplinary violations?

2. Both the quantitative analysis and qualitative responses suggest some location effect. The facility in which the respondent/interviewee was located influenced his or her responses to questions. Unfortunately, Jenne and Kersting do not give much attention to this finding. Why do you think some facilities are more likely than others to be staffed by correctional officers who overlook minor infractions? Stated differently, what is it about certain prison types that might contribute to this reciprocal behavior?

3. Researchers have devoted considerable energy to studying criminal justice employee behavior, particularly differences between male and female police, correctional, probation, and parole officers. Jenne and Kersting's research finds that differences are minimal or nonexistent. Why do individuals expect to observe differences in behavior between male and female employees? Why do you suppose those differences failed to emerge?

SECTION XII

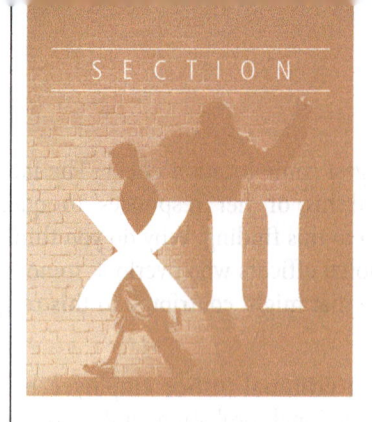

Organizational Change
What Causes Organizations to Transform?

Section Highlights

Overview of Organizational Change
Organizational Change Motors
   Planned Change
   Conflictive Change
Life Cycle Change
Evolution
Implications of Motors
Impediments to Organizational Change

In 1997, the U.S. Department of Justice (DOJ) announced a consent decree—a type of legal agreement, discussed below—with the Pittsburgh Bureau of Police designed to reform the department and end an alleged "pattern or practice" of depriving citizens of constitutional rights or protections afforded under federal law (Davis, Henderson, & Ortiz, 2005). The DOJ specifically noted patterns of excessive force, violations of citizens' Fourth Amendment rights, and false arrests (Livingston, 1999). Under provisions of the 1994 Violent Crime Control and Law Enforcement Act, the DOJ used its authority to file a formal complaint against the Bureau of Police in federal district court. Rather than target individual officers responsible for the alleged conduct, the DOJ's filing represented an attempt to address the organizational conditions that allowed the actions to occur in the first place. The city signed a consent decree, requiring substantial organizational change enforced by the power of the court (Davis et al., 2005). The consent decree stipulated, among other reforms, improved officer training, the establishment of an early intervention system to track officers across a number of different indicators (e.g., use-of-force incidents, citizen complaints), revisions to the bureau's use-of-force policy, and data collection efforts designed to assess for disparity in officer behavior (Davis et al., 2005; Livingston, 1999; Walker, 2003). A court-appointed monitor assured compliance with the decree's mandates (Walker, 2003).

Evidence suggests that, by the last year of the agreement in 2002, the Pittsburgh Bureau of Police had successfully implemented the major changes required by the decree even though some officers expressed reservations about the reforms and their impact on street-level behavior (Davis et al., 2005). The DOJ has used consent decrees to reform departments in other cities, including, as recently as summer 2012, the New Orleans, Louisiana, Police Department (Ross & Parke, 2009; Schwartz, 2012; Walker, 2003). While Pittsburgh's former chief Robert McNeilly indicated that he intended "to ease in over five years other major changes [after his 1996 hire]," the consent decree with the DOJ hastened the organizational change process intended to improve the functioning of the organization and eliminate constitutional violations (Fuoco, 2006). The city's department became more formalized in its policies and procedures, added additional layers of oversight, and further developed the skill set of officers via training.

The Pittsburgh example illustrates Lewin's (1951) well-known and widely cited model of organizational change: unfreeze-move-freeze. Generally some catalyst is needed to alter the status quo within organizations. As Mills, Dye, and Mills (2009) explain, "It must be made clear why the 'old way' of doing things is no longer acceptable" (p. 47). The DOJ investigation, initiated after a series of citizen complaints, provided the opportunity to unfreeze the organization. The consent decree monitored oversight, and Chief McNeilly's leadership enabled the department to move toward substantial organizational change over the course of five years. The problem, however, with any change is that "permanency of the new level, or permanency for a desired period, should be included in the objective [of change]" (Lewin, 1951, p. 228). If resistance to change is not addressed or if the organization is not serious about reform, it will simply revert to its previous state; it is essential to freeze the organization after the change. The general depiction of organizational change embodied in Lewin's model provides the outline for the discussion to follow. Topics addressed below include an assessment of organizational performance, the causes of organizational change, and challenges to freezing organizations post-change.

Overview of Organizational Change

Organizational change has been defined simply as "a transformation of an organization between two points in time" (Barnett & Carroll, 1995, p. 219). Recall that an organization comprises both individuals and groups and that the organization itself is situated within a larger environmental context (see Figure 1.1 in Section I). Any one of these levels—individual, group, organization, or environment—is a target for organizational change (Burke, 2002; Greene, 1998). In his study of community policing as planned change, Greene (1998) demonstrated how community policing reforms are designed, in theory, to alter each of these four levels of an organization (see also Cordner, 2000).[1] At the environmental level, organizational change is focused on "organizations, groups, and other sources of influence that help define the sources of input for community policing, as well as being the ultimate consumers and evaluators of goods and services produced" (Greene, 1998, p. 151). Among other changes, the police department redefines its relationship with citizens and businesses within the jurisdiction. They become more than just "eyes and ears" told to report crimes observed; instead, citizens serve as coproducers of public safety (Bayley, 1994). The organization itself changes to redefine outcomes to include fear reduction, improved quality of life, and other indicators beyond just crime reduction. Moreover, it alters structures (e.g., adding community policing units) and strategies (e.g., foot patrols, neighborhood substations) to improve community relationships and public safety (Cordner, 2000; Maguire, Shin, Zhao, & Hassell, 2003).

---

[1]These changes are consistent with the literature on community policing. Many were not actually implemented in practice.

Under a community policing philosophy, groups within and outside of the police department are encouraged to collaborate to solve community problems requiring greater information sharing and trust across the units. Finally, individual officers are encouraged to become invested in the communities they serve and adopt a broad view of the police role that places greater emphasis on service and order maintenance responsibilities (Greene, 1998).

Organizational changes have been further characterized by the depth or suddenness of the change (Burke, 2002). Generally speaking, these changes take one of two forms:

1. *Evolutionary change* (Burke, 2002): Also referred to as incremental (Mills et al., 2009; Nadler & Tushman, 1995), continuous (Weick & Quinn, 1999), or first-order (Levy & Merry, 1986) change, evolutionary change is characterized by more subtle or gradual modifications within an organization. Such changes have also been described as "minor improvements and adjustments that do not change the system's core" (Levy & Merry, 1986, p. 5) and as change that "attempts to build on the work that has already been accomplished . . . in relatively small increments" (Nadler & Tushman, 1995, p. 22). The changes are more likely to affect parts of the organization than the whole and to modify rather than replace existing arrangements. For example, adding a dedicated gang unit within a police department increases the horizontal complexity of the organization but does not replace existing structural arrangements with new ones (Katz, 2001). The new unit becomes an additional appendage of the organization (Maguire et al., 2003). Similarly, some police departments require officers to document the characteristics of citizens contacted during traffic stops in an effort to monitor for and/or address disparity in police activity (Schultz & Withrow, 2004). The change—instituting the requirement—is incremental to the extent that it does not alter the underlying core (e.g., the mission) of the organization (Hannan & Freeman, 1984). Burke (2002) argues that more than 95% of all organizational changes are evolutionary in nature.

2. *Revolutionary change* (Burke, 2002): Similar to episodic (Weick & Quinn, 1999), discontinuous (Nadler & Tushman, 1995), or second-order (Levy & Merry, 1986) change, revolutionary change occurs infrequently but abruptly, and dramatically transforms the core of the organization or replaces many of its elements (Nadler & Tushman, 1995). For example, problem-solving courts incorporate the notion of therapeutic jurisprudence by using the court's resources to address issues such as drug addiction, domestic violence, and mental illness (King, 2008). The court process changes dramatically. Judges take a more active role in ensuring compliance with court orders, the court collaborates with other service providers (e.g., drug treatment specialists), and adversarial process is supplanted by coordinated efforts to help victims, offenders, and communities (Berman & Feinblatt, 2001). Community policing has similarly been called a paradigmatic shift in policing, leading to an entirely new era in the history of law enforcement (Pelfrey, 2000). These types of substantial changes are relatively infrequent but typically occur more suddenly. Nadler and Tushman note that they tend to be "more traumatic, painful, and demanding on the organization [and] by its very nature, discontinuous change means that a certain degree of shock will be administered to the organization" (p. 23).

Sometimes changes, both evolutionary and revolutionary, emerge as a reaction to certain conditions (e.g., loss of performance, a court decision), while in other cases they are anticipatory in nature (e.g., planning ahead; Nadler & Tushman, 1995). As will be discussed below, certain changes are more likely to occur given the right conditions.

Organizational Change Motors

How and why do organizations change? Do leaders sense opportunities to improve performance and alter structures, purpose, or other organizational attributes? Are organizations coerced into some degree of transformation? Explaining the process of organizational change is an enduring challenge within the organizational theory field (Van de Ven & Poole, 1995; Van de Ven & Sun, 2011). Although multiple frameworks exist, Van de Ven and Poole (1995) synthesized the diverse literature, ultimately arriving at a typology comprising four theories, or *motors*, that describe the mechanisms through which organizational changes are produced. These motors, alone or in combination, provide leaders with a clearer understanding of the processes of change, common impediments, and viable solutions for successfully promoting change efforts (Poole & Van de Ven, 2004, p. 382; Van de Ven & Sun, 2011). Each of the four motors—planned change, conflictive change, life cycle, and evolution—are discussed in turn.

Planned Change

If organizations are designed to achieve goals, they might undertake planned change, as opposed to reacting to unplanned crises or events, to accomplish these ends. Van de Ven and Poole (1995) described the *planned change motor* "as a repetitive sequence of goal formulation, implementation, evaluation, and modification of goals based on what was learned or intended by the entity" (p. 516). As organizations establish new goals—eliminating triple celling of inmates, reducing crime by 10% per year, increasing prosecutions of domestic batterers—other areas of the organization must change as well to facilitate goal achievement. Returning to Lewin's (1951) unfreeze-move-refreeze model, it is clearly not enough to move the organization in the direction of its goals. Planned change requires consideration of all three components: recognizing the need for change and overcoming resistance, implementing the change, and solidifying the new state as the norm (Burnes, 2004). More recently, Bullock and Batten (1985) proposed a four-part planned change model based on a review of 30 such models in the organizational development literature. Their model starts with an *exploration* stage that represents some need or problem requiring change to achieve organizational goals. Members of the organization may look for resources, both internal and external, to help with the change. At this point, *planning* begins and organizational members design the specific change strategy and make important decisions about the actions to be taken. The *action* stage represents the actual implementation of the change, but "its effects are being evaluated through progress reviews, data feedback, and continued testing" (p. 407). Finally, analogous to Lewin's refreezing state, the change must be *integrated* so that the organization does not return to its previous form.

The planned change process can be illustrated by studying the adoption of community policing in the Philadelphia Police Department in the late 1980s as described by Greene, Bergman, and McLaughlin (1994). Public confidence in the police department plummeted in the mid-1980s as a result of a corruption scandal and the bombing of a row house during a police standoff that led to the destruction of a city block. The department was roundly criticized for its structures, management practices, and culture. The need for change was clearly present (*exploration stage*). The department commissioned a task force to provide an assessment and offer recommendations for reforming the department. The task force produced 92 recommendations for the department, essentially providing a plan of action (*planning stage*). The Philadelphia Police Department responded by making widespread changes, including, but not limited to, the establishment of a community policing policy and the restructuring of the organization. To enhance contact between police and citizens and foster collaborative partnerships—core features of community policing—the department shuffled officers from specialized positions to patrol and opened substations within the community to enhance citizen access to police resources (*action stage*). The changes became *integrated* and formalized in a number of ways. A test of a decentralized management approach that began in 1986 in one policing district was expanded citywide six years later. Bullock and Batten (1985) refer to this process as diffusing successful changes throughout the entire system. Similarly, management-training programs were formed to encourage acceptance of community policing; to the extent that managers understood the reforms and the key dimensions, they were less likely to resist implementation (Greene et al., 1994).

Planned change models, at first glance, seemingly point to the rationality of decision makers, implying that they "choose among alternatives by considering their consequences and selecting the alternative with the largest expected return" (March, 1994, p. 18). As Philadelphia residents lost confidence in the police department and officers experienced conflict with citizens on the street, managers turned to community policing as the appropriate course of action for the department. Was adopting community policing the optimum change for the organization? Planned change models are able to incorporate organizational theories from the mid-20th century that view the rationality assumption as tenable. Scholars James March and Herbert Simon (1958; see also March, 1994) asserted that managers (and others, for that matter), when faced with decision choices, are simply incapable of acting in a fully rational way. Specifically, they noted that the rational model is based on three erroneous assumptions (see March & Simon, 1958, p. 138):

1. Decision makers have available all possible alternatives (choices) when making a decision.
2. Decision makers know the consequences or outcome of each choice should it be selected.
3. Decision makers are capable of rank ordering the choices according to a calculation of and preferences for certain outcomes.

If these assumptions are met, decision makers will choose the best paths. Unfortunately, March and Simon (1958) point out that individuals rarely consider all choices, seldom truly can predict the full consequences of their actions, and do not have the capacity to analyze the value of all choices. Consequently, a substantial number of all decisions made in organizations can be classified as failed decisions (Nutt, 1999). Why? March and Simon stated, "Most human-decision making, whether individual or organizational, is concerned with the discovery and selection of satisfactory alternatives; only in exceptional cases is it concerned with the discovery and selection of optimal alternatives" (pp. 140–141). This process has been referred to as **satisficing** (combining satisfactory and sufficient) rather than optimizing outcomes (March, 1981, 1994). In no way does this suggest that decision makers are acting irrationally. Instead, the planned change process points to **limited or bounded rationality**, the fact that they operate within the constraints of the organization and their own cognitive limits (March, 1994).

Even though the success of planned changes is circumscribed by the limits of truly rational decision making, the planned change motor expressly includes elements of evaluation and modification of decision choices (Van de Ven & Poole, 1995). As such, any agency has the potential to become a **learning organization** capable of adjusting goals and structures as new knowledge becomes available. Specifically, Huber (1991) argued, "an organization learns if any of its units [e.g., divisions, precincts] acquires knowledge that it recognizes as potentially useful to the organization" (p. 89). In recent years, organizations have been encouraged to learn from scientific research studies as part of the evidence-based movement in criminal justice and beyond (Lum, Koper, & Telep, 2011; MacKenzie, 2000; Sherman, 1998; Sparrow, 2011). The primary thrust of this movement is that scientific research can inform organizations, shaping practices based on evidence of what works (Weisburd & Neyroud, 2011). It is necessary, however, for the organization to take steps so that learning is more than just the aggregate of individual-level learning (Lipshitz, Freidman, & Popper, 2007). Stated differently, learning organizations establish mechanisms that allow them to acquire and interpret knowledge, disseminate information throughout the organization, and establish an organizational memory (Crank & Giacomazzi, 2009; Geller, 1997; Huber, 1991; Lipshitz et al., 2007). Consider the description of Maryland's Proactive Community Supervision (PCS) program:

> Supervisors . . . learned about research findings in corrections and about how to apply them to their organization, as well as how to provide a business process for each office that was supportive of PCS and also suitable to their own sociolegal culture. Additionally, the agency used book clubs as well as the reading of journal articles and other literature to encourage staff members to broaden their perspective and to take the challenge of being a change agent seriously. (Taxman, 2008, pp. 287–288)

Walsh (2001) similarly described the New York Police Department's Compstat process as indicative of organizational learning. By gathering and disseminating timely intelligence on crime trends and patterns (e.g., weekly instead of annually), precinct commanders and the organization as a whole become more effective, because they develop the capability to modify strategies quickly as conditions warrant (see also Silverman, 1999). Others have recommended that organizations create their own in-house research and development units to assess operational strategies (Geller, 1997). In each case, organizational components facilitated learning; they provided the settings in which knowledge was examined and disseminated. Additionally, an organizational memory develops as members recall what worked from past efforts.

Of course, the organizational learning perspective assumes that research is used *instrumentally* to guide decision making. Unfortunately, rarely does research play such a prominent role in the rational (but bounded) decision-making process. As Weiss, Murphy-Graham, and Birkeland (2005) noted,

> Decision makers pay attention to many things other than the evaluation of program effectiveness [including] the desires of program participants and staff, the support of constituents, the claims of powerful people, the costs of change, the availability of staff with necessary capabilities, and so on. (p. 13)

In a study of 27 correctional administrators and research personnel, Lovell (1988) identified only three examples of instrumental research use over a two-year period. In most situations, research is used to support decisions already reached (*political/symbolic use*) or to enlighten (*conceptual use*) (Lovell, 1988; Weiss et al., 2005). For example, he found that correctional officials used research to justify budgets or support policy recommendations. This use was largely symbolic, however, in that budget and policy decisions were formulated prior to consulting the research. In conceptual use situations, "decision makers considered research and evaluation studies useful, even when they didn't act on them in direct and immediate ways" (Weiss et al., 2005, p. 14). Research may also be ignored altogether for a variety of reasons, hampering the capacity of the organization to learn (Moore, 2006; Sparrow, 2011). Research findings take time to generate, often too long given the more immediate demands faced by criminal justice organizations. Moreover, social science research often produces subtle, inconclusive, or contradictory findings that may have only limited utility for justice organizations. Finally, there are questions whether the gaps between researchers and practitioners (e.g., language, understanding of problems at hand, etc.) can be bridged to promote the adoption of evidence-based strategies. In spite of these challenges, considerable attention has been directed at fostering organizational learning via greater investments in research, partnerships between researchers and criminal justice organizations, and other approaches (Weisburd & Neyroud, 2011).

Conflictive Change

The **conflictive change motor** is predicated on the idea that the organizational structures, goals, and operations are seldom permanent (Benson, 1977). Individuals and groups within and outside of an organization have different ideas about key elements, producing what Benson referred to as contradictions (see also Van de Ven & Poole, 1995). While not ordinarily problematic, "change occurs when these opposing values, forces, or events gain sufficient power to confront and engage the status quo" (Van de Ven & Poole, 1995, p. 517). Police organizations, operating under a professional model of policing that emphasized crime control via three dominant strategies (random patrol, rapid response, and criminal investigation), faced challenges beginning in the 1960s as rioting, rising crime, national commissions, and scholarly research challenged the dominant paradigm (Pelfrey, 2000; President's Commission, 1968). Section III opened with the discussion of organization change in the Junction City Police Department, specifically the adoption of a police gang unit (Katz, 2001). The local community's notion of gang activity in the city compelled the police department to add a special unit to address the perceived problem. Organizational change is also related to internal conflicts. Walker and Bumphus (1992) pointed out that police unions led to the abolition of several civilian review boards (groups of community members responsible for reviewing complaints against the police) during the 1960s but that, over the next several decades, the boards reemerged in many big cities as support overpowered union resistance.

Conflict is also evident when courts intervene in the affairs of organizations following litigation. Judicial intervention is perhaps most notable in the area of corrections. Inmates file a significant number of mostly unsuccessful lawsuits against correctional authorities, alleging staff violence, improper medical care, unfair disciplinary processes, poor living conditions within correctional facilities, or other issues (Schlanger, 2003). Inmates have easy access to the court system, and the costs of filings are minimal; in addition, they often lack an attorney to provide guidance about the prospects for success. As such, inmates "had little disincentive to file cases in which the expected values were low" (p. 1608). In the event that courts side with inmates, the consequences for organizations are potentially substantial. Courts, using "rules from existing correctional literature, sociology, and their [the judges'] own perceptions of political morality," have imposed comprehensive and far-reaching (revolutionary) reforms on correctional facilities in what some have described as acts of policymaking (Feeley & Rubin, 1998, p. 14). In the 1980 case *Ruiz v. Estelle*, a federal judge dramatically altered traditional mechanisms of prisoner control (e.g., building tenders) and reached into other areas of the prison organization (Marquart & Crouch, 1985). In a 1981 case related to the Santa Clara County jails, an inmate petitioned the court alleging significant overcrowding and other inadequate conditions (Feeley & Rubin, 1998). While a judge initially ordered the sheriff to reduce overcrowding, the order was later expanded, demanding the improvement of other conditions as well (repairing plumbing, replacing sheets, etc.). In these cases, the courts assumed a significant role in correcting deficiencies observed within the operations of the jails.

Although courts may impose organizational reform following litigation in cases like *Ruiz v. Estelle*, the parties to the dispute may also negotiate settlements in the form of **consent decrees** requiring changes to organizational structures or practices. Consent decrees are intended to remedy the conditions that give rise to disputes and, as Schwarzschild (1984) notes, are quite unique:

> [A consent decree] has characteristics both of a contract and of a court order. It is contractual in the obvious sense that it is drafted and agreed upon by the parties; it is their bargain, it represents the terms on which they are prepared to settle. But a consent decree is not just a private contract. Unlike a contract, or a private out-of-court settlement, a consent decree can be enforced by citation for contempt of court; it has the authority of a judicial decree. (pp. 894–895)

Settling via consent decrees provides an obvious benefit to the defendant in the case, the organization alleged to have violated individual rights: It avoids the potential costs of extended litigation, and in most cases (see Prisoner Litigation Reform Act below), there is no requirement to acknowledge any wrongdoing (Decker, 1997). While most agreements are reached before a judge is able to render a decision in the case, some are produced even before a complaint is filed with the court (Schwarzschild, 1984). In the latter situation, the complaint and consent decree are entered together and approved by a judge.

Consent decrees have been widely used both within and outside of the criminal justice system for decades, providing remedies in matters related to equal employment opportunity, prison conditions, and police practices (Livingston, 1999; Schwarzschild, 1984). For example, minority correctional officers in New York in the early 1980s contended that the promotional examination process was discriminatory and resulted in a disproportionately low number of minorities elevated into higher-ranking positions. As part of a consent decree, the Department of Correctional Services agreed to modify procedures by temporarily promoting a sufficient number of minority candidates proportional to their representation on the promotional eligibility list and altering testing procedures in the future to eliminate adverse effects (Schwarzschild, 1984). In another case, inmates at a Federal Bureau of Corrections facility in the U.S. Virgin Islands filed a lawsuit alleging horrendous conditions and extreme overcrowding; the facility held 202 inmates, nearly four times its capacity, and "was also infested with roaches and rats, did not furnish inmates with adequate hot water or clean drinking water, and did not provide proper mental care" (Decker, 1997, pp. 1277–1278). An agreement was reached capping the population at 97 and improving overall conditions within the facility. Decker reported that, as of 1996, consent decrees and court orders affected prisons in 34 states and Washington, D.C. As these examples illustrate, they are powerful to the extent that they compel organizational changes that remedy conditions for a broad group of individuals beyond just the plaintiff in the particular case (Schwarzschild, 1984). In other words, current and future minority correctional officers in New York State and inmates within the U.S. Virgin Islands likely saw some benefit from the consent decrees without necessarily being part of the original lawsuit.

Two pieces of legislation passed by Congress within a two-year period during the mid-1990s significantly shaped the use of consent decrees as a means of promoting change within criminal justice organizations. The first, part of a sweeping crime bill enacted by Congress in 1994, expanded the range of possible plaintiffs in lawsuits targeting police organizations. Generally, court orders and consent decrees within the criminal justice system result from lawsuits filed by aggrieved citizens. For example, 1,359 suits were filed against law enforcement officers and departments between 1978 and 1990 under a section of the United States Code (42 U.S.C. § 1983) allowing individuals to seek damages for violations of civil rights such as false arrest, excessive use of force, and unlawful search and seizure (Kappeler, Kappeler, & Del Carmen, 1993; Ross & Parke, 2009). The new legislation (42 U.S.C. § 14141) empowered the U.S. Department of Justice's Civil Rights Division to take actions on its own to eliminate unlawful conduct by police departments in certain situations. According to the statute:

> It shall be unlawful for any governmental authority, or any agent thereof, or any person acting on behalf of a governmental authority, to engage in a pattern or practice of conduct by law enforcement officers or by officials or employees of any governmental agency with responsibility for the administration of juvenile justice or the incarceration of juveniles that deprives persons of rights, privileges, or immunities secured or protected by the Constitution or laws of the United States. (42 U.S.C. § 14141)

The legislation significantly expanded the process for remedying constitutional violations in policing by addressing recurring organizational problems (Walker, 2003). Between 1996 and 2005, the DOJ entered into agreements with 15 law enforcement agencies—including the Pittsburgh Police Department, discussed in this section's opening (Ross & Parke, 2009).[2] Although the actual content of consent decrees varies from organization to organization, common components include mandates related to training, handling citizen complaints, and the early detection of problem officers (Livingston, 1999).

If § 14141 expanded the possibilities for using consent decrees as a vehicle for organizational change in policing, the Prisoner Litigation Reform Act (PLRA) of 1995 greatly restricted their use in corrections. The law was designed to curtail the number of inmate lawsuits seemingly clogging up the federal district courts. Additionally, there was concern that the frequent use of consent decrees turned control over prisons and jails to the court system tasked with enforcing the decrees, contributing to judicial micromanagement (Decker, 1997; Schlanger, 2003). To reduce the number of frivolous lawsuits filed in the court system, various rules were enacted to dissuade inmates from wasting the court's time (e.g., requiring payment of filing fees, reducing good time credit for the filing of harassing lawsuits). More important for the purposes of the present discussion were the limits imposed on the use of consent decrees. While most consent decrees are entered without evidence or admission of wrongdoing, the PLRA forbids courts from accepting consent decrees without first finding a violation of a prisoner's constitutional rights, a provision that applied to consent decrees already in place (Belbot, 2004; Decker, 1997). Since consent decrees are usually agreed on to avoid litigation costs and unpredictable outcomes, most existing decrees lacked a violation finding. Consequently, some parties to existing consent decrees were able to successfully petition the court to terminate the agreements (Belbot, 2004; Smith & Nelson, 2002). The law also limits to two years those agreements that are reached in accordance with the law, preventing the prolonged court intervention evident in places such as Texas (Belbot, 2004; Decker, 1997). The net effect of the law has been a sharp decline in the number of inmate lawsuits in the federal courts, to the point where filing rates are nearly half what they were prior to the passage of PLRA (Schlanger, 2003; Smith & Nelson, 2002).

---

[2]The agreements included seven consent degrees and six memoranda of understanding, which are similar to but lack the court orders that back consent decrees (Ross & Parke, 2009).

Samuel Walker (2003) suggested that many consent decrees work to promote best practices in fields that are already in operation in other organizations and identified in the literature. Organizations tend to improve as a result. Useem and Piehl (2008) argued that court intervention likely improved prison management and prison conditions, contributing to overall prison order (e.g., fewer escapes, riots), even as overall institutional populations expanded. Nevertheless, such decrees and judicial orders are often criticized for a variety of reasons. First, the decrees and orders arguably strip control of an organization away from its leaders (see planned change) and place it in the hands of external bodies (e.g., the courts; Walker, 2003). Compliance is also incredibly costly; consent decrees will likely cost the Cincinnati and Los Angeles Police Departments $20 million and $30 million per year, respectively (Ross & Parke, 2009; Walker, 2003). Finally, they often intervene (micromanage) at levels considered absurd and well beyond what is necessary to correct organizational deficiencies, a problem that the PLRA was designed to correct. For example, Decker (1997) noted, "Consent decrees have regulated such issues as who can cut inmates' hair and what type of cleaning product can be used to wash the prison floors" (p. 1284). In spite of these criticisms, however, conflict, as evident by court intervention, was able to generate significant organizational change.

Life Cycle Change

The **life cycle motor** equates organizations to other forms of life. Just as humans pass through stages (e.g., infancy, adolescence, adulthood), all organizations pass sequentially through a series of stages (Van de Ven & Poole, 1995). Treating organizations in this fashion overcomes a substantial criticism levied at many organizational theories—the overwhelming tendency to study an organization at a single point in time without recognizing the dynamics and changes that occur over time (Kimberly, 1980). The pure life cycle theory views organizational changes as predetermined; "the goal and end point of the change process is defined from the start for a life cycle through a natural or logical developmental progression" (Poole & Van de Ven, 2004, p. 377). Additionally, organizations, like humans, will not ordinarily regress to an earlier stage of development (Cameron & Whetten, 1983). Unfortunately, there is no agreed-on set or number of stages. Scholars have identified at least 63 separate models (Aldrich & Ruef, 2006; Cameron & Whetten, 1983; Quinn & Cameron, 1983). A model developed by Downs (1964) included three stages to account for the life cycle of public organizations. When one is first formed, it works to carve out a unique function (e.g., police as experts in crime control), establish its worth (e.g., use crime statistics to show its significance to society), and secure resources. Without satisfying these goals that are merely designed to preserve the organization, it runs the risk of failure or termination, a phenomenon known as the liability of newness (Singh, House, & Tucker, 1986; Singh, Tucker, & House, 1986). Once the organization increases its prospects for survivability, it begins to expand and become more structurally complex. At the same time, it becomes more entrenched in its ways (Downs, 1964). Finally, the organization may enter a period of decline where demand for its services is diminishing. While Downs did not explicitly mention organizational death, recall from Section IV that public organizations are sometimes terminated. Consequently, scholars advise including death as a stage in the organizational life cycle (Whetten, 1987).

Critics of life cycle theories question their deterministic qualities. Do organizations change in a predetermined fashion across series of sequential stages (Whetten, 1987)? In addition, organizations tend to stall within a singular stage and may never experience organizational death (Demers, 2007). King (2009b) addressed these concerns by applying a modified life cycle perspective to the study of police organizations, recognizing that agencies may transition through only some of the stages and may actually revert to prior stages over time. These stages, then, are events across an organization's **life course**, rather than sequential steps in its life cycle. He proposed six stages for police organizations, though the stages are arguably applicable for all organizations: birth, early founding effects, growth, decline, crises, and death. During the *birth* stage, new departments are formed, new task forces are created, or new businesses enter the marketplace. While King acknowledged the historical accounts detailing the formation of early police departments in places such as London, Boston, and New York City, he was particularly interested in agencies that emerged more recently. Are the reasons explaining the birth of early police departments (e.g., crime, concern about dangerous classes) still viable explanations for the creation of departments today? The second stage addresses *early founding effects*; during the period following organizational birth, a variety of factors "imprint organizations with persistent, long-standing routines, structures, and behaviors" (King, 2009b, p. 222). Older correctional facilities are more likely to be surrounded by high walls and structured to include lengthy corridors on each side, both products of the trends in prison architecture at the time. Newer facilities are increasingly designed using a direct supervision model where correctional officers are located within housing units. Indeed, the American Jail Association (2012) explicitly endorses such a model "in planning, designing, constructing, and managing jails" (p. 14). Accounting for the adoption or rejection of organizational reforms is likely dependent on these early founding effects.

During the *growth* stage, organizations expand in size (e.g., number of officers) and become more structurally complex (see Section II; King, 2009b). Whetten (1987) explained this growth, in part, by stating, "As organizations successfully satisfy needs for their services, this success fosters growth" (p. 340). Alternatively, some organizations experience a period of *decline*. In recent years, police departments in East St. Louis (IL), Newark (NJ), and Camden (NJ), among others, saw substantial cuts in budgets and overall force strength as a result of deteriorating economic conditions. Due to budget constraints, the governor of Illinois ordered the closure of three halfway houses, two juvenile detention centers, and two state prisons, including the state's lone supermax facility. The point is that organizational growth is not necessarily sustained over the life course; periods of decline are also sufficient to produce change. King's fifth stage, *crisis*, is often the time where organizational changes are generated as individuals try to cope with or solve various problems (e.g., riots, union strife, police corruption). Sherman (1983), describing the importance of crises, stated:

> It may be that critical events produce an unfreezing of previous patterns of organizational behavior, a period in which anything new could happen, in which the organization is unusually sensitive to new directions. If the "right" administrative policies are adopted following critical events . . . then "significant" planned organizational changes may well be possible. (p. 99)

For example, Sherman wrote that the New York City Police Department modified its firearms policy in the early 1970s following a number of crises: the Knapp Commission's report on widespread police corruption in the city and the fatal shooting of an 11-year-old male fleeing from the police (and subsequent riot). The crises allowed the department to impose greater restrictions on the use of firearms (formalization) with only minimal opposition.

Finally, as discussed in Section IV, some organizations experience termination or *death*, the final stage in the organizational life course. Common causes of disbanding in police organizations include budgetary challenges, corruption, or poor relationships between police departments and city governments (King, 2009b).

Overall, the life cycle/life course perspective offers a framework for understanding organizational change over time, an important dimension absent from the other three change motors. Given that available evidence has questioned the hard predictions offered by a life cycle model (see, for example, Aldrich & Ruef, 2006), King's (2009b) modified life course perspective—a less rigid, less deterministic approach—is general enough to apply to most organizational types.

Evolution

The **evolutionary motor** explains change as occurring through a process of variation-selection-retention (Baum, 1999; Van de Ven & Poole, 1995). Organizations within a given population—a group of organizations that share a common purpose (loosely analogous to an industry)—exhibit variations in their structures and activities (Hannan & Freeman, 1977). For example, the companies that compete to run private correctional facilities vary in their size, services provided, administrative structures, and other organizational characteristics. Since states operate their own correctional facilities, the resources available for private prisons are necessarily finite, leading to competition through bidding and contracting processes. Just as the strongest species are going to survive in nature, the fittest organizations are going to survive in society. As Baum (1999) explained, "Some variations prove more beneficial than others in acquiring resources in a competitive environment and are thus selected positively" (p. 72). State correctional leaders may prefer certain prison models, facility design features, or structural arrangements. Companies that can meet these needs are more likely to be awarded contracts, while others face two choices: die out (terminate) or model the successful variations (Baum, 1999).[3] In this way, certain organizational forms are retained and "one organizational form comes to dominate because more such organizations arise and fewer fail than is the case for some alternative form" (Hannan & Carroll, 1995, p. 23). Even if organizations change to adopt successful variations, there is no guarantee that they will do so quickly enough. Hannan and Freeman (1984) argue that "the worst of all possible worlds is to change structure continually only to find each time upon reorganization that the environment has already shifted to some new configuration that demands yet a different structure" (p. 151). Consequently, organizations, particularly as they get older and larger, experience structural inertia that actually limits their ability to undertake substantial organizational changes. They tend to resist changing the major elements of the organization (e.g., its mission) in favor of reliability (Baum, 1999; Hannan & Freeman, 1984).

Maguire and King (2007) used the evolutionary perspective to explain changes in the overall policing industry over the past decade. First, the overall number of agencies is declining as departments battle for scarce government resources (e.g., funding, legitimacy). Large police departments are more successful in securing these resources, putting strains on smaller agencies. Some of these agencies eventually disband, merge, or contract with proximate large departments. Older police departments also tend to be more vertically complex in their structures, perhaps suggesting some type of evolutionary effect over time necessary to increase survivability. From an evolutionary perspective, if resources are plentiful, organizations have little incentive to change and survivability prospects are high. Organizations are more likely to suffer termination or change during periods of competition.

---

[3]One evolutionary theory, population ecology, does not generally afford as much attention to managerial ability to adapt. Instead, it is the environment that selects the fittest organizational form; some organizations experience death, and new ones emerge with the form intact. Simply stated, individual organizations are unable to adapt; population changes are observed over time (Demers, 2007). Other evolutionary theories, however, suggest that managers can adapt through modeling and imitation (see Baum, 1999; Lewin, Weigelt, & Emery, 2004).

Implications of Motors

The motors—planned change, conflictive change, life cycle, and evolution—are situated across two dimensions according to the mode of change and the number of organizations involved in the process (see Figure 12.1). It is worth noting that they differ in how they envision the change process. According to the life cycle and evolution motors, change follows a relatively predictable path that produces largely incremental adjustments or evolutionary changes within the organization (a prescribed mode of change). Planned and conflictive change motors suggest that the change process is apt to be more unpredictable and more likely to result in revolutionary, discontinuous, or second-order changes to the organization (constructive mode of change; Van de Ven & Poole, 1995). Major organizational transformations such as the shift to community policing, the wholesale change of control structures in Texas prisons, or the incorporation of therapeutic jurisprudence principles are most likely to be born out of planned change or conflict. Incremental changes, while often part of planned or conflictive motors, generally follow organizational evolution or stages in the life cycle. The typology also separates the motors according to the number of organizations implicated within the theory. Both evolution and conflictive motors require a multiorganization perspective; that is, the change process is based on the relationships between two or more organizations. Evolution is based on competition within a population of organizations, whereas conflictive change is based on differences in ideas about organizational forms. In contrast, by applying the planned change or life cycle motors, we can study change within a single organization (Van de Ven & Poole, 1995; Van de Ven & Sun, 2011).

Figure 12.1 Four Motors/Theories of Organizational Change

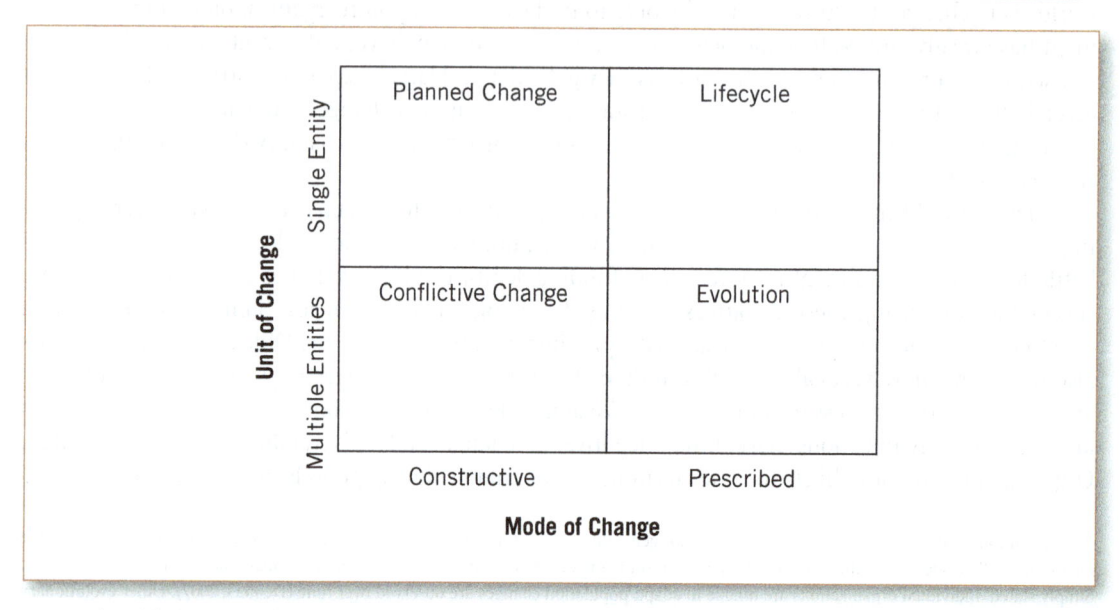

	Constructive	Prescribed
Single Entity	Planned Change	Lifecycle
Multiple Entities	Conflictive Change	Evolution

Unit of Change / Mode of Change

Source: Adapted from Van de Ven and Poole (1995).

Impediments to Organizational Change

Regardless of the mechanism for change, it is a common maxim that changes will be resisted within organizations (Dent & Goldberg, 1999). Lewin (1951) illustrated this tendency using what he referred to as force field analysis. The framework suggests that there are forces that promote change (driving forces) and forces that resist change (restraining forces). If the restraining forces are powerful or the driving forces (e.g., defined need for change, rewards) weak, fully implementing any change, planned or otherwise, will be a struggle. While the reasons for resistance vary (see Table 12.1), Connor and Lake (1988) place them into three categories: barriers to understanding, barriers to acceptance, and barriers to action. Misunderstandings about the organizational changes, including the need for or consequences of reforms, are common barriers to successful implementation. For example, when police departments implemented data collection systems to track field and motor vehicle stops, officers expressed concerns about, among other things, how the data were going to be used (Ramirez, McDevitt, & Farrell, 2000). Some wondered whether they could be disciplined or labeled as racist based on the outcomes. Officers did not know what to expect from the changes until management fully communicated intentions. Misunderstandings are also based on incompatible or inconsistent reward systems within organizations. Prosecutors' offices are likely to face difficulties adopting community prosecution strategies where desired outcomes include crime reduction, fear reduction, and improved quality of life if prosecutors continue to be evaluated on the basis of felony convictions (Coles, 2000). Changes expect one type of behavior, but actual performance measures reward another. Even if an organization's members understand the need, content, and consequences of change, they may still resist due to lack of acceptance. If a department of corrections opens direct supervision facilities that place officers within pods (living spaces and common areas for a group of inmates), officers may develop anxiety or feel threats to their safety, leading to resistance. Employees may feel threats to their status, power, or job security. Such is the case when organizational changes result in what have been referred to as "two-track" reforms (Coles, 2000). It is not uncommon for changes such as community policing and community prosecution to be implemented only in part of an organization rather than agency-wide. This creates two tracks where jealousies, tensions, and other problems can emerge. Finally, certain factors simply prevent workers from acting and implementing organizational changes. Research on expectancy theory from Section VIII indicated that individuals must have the capabilities to perform. They must also overcome habits and old ways of doing things.

Resistance is not insurmountable, and attempts to address the challenges can take many forms. In essence, these strategies attempt to weaken the restraining forces and enhance the driving forces that are part of the force field analysis. For example, the organization can more effectively communicate the purpose and content of the change, educate and train organizational members, and socialize them into new practices (Porter, Lawler, & Hackman, 1975). In one police department, the purpose of traffic-stop data collection was conveyed to personnel as an attempt to improve the professionalism of the department. In another, a training program was instituted to explain the purpose of data collection (Ramirez et al., 2000). Organizations can also modify reward systems to alter preferences, reduce uncertainty, and communicate expectations. Porter and colleagues (1975) also recommend structural adjustments to facilitate understanding, acceptance, and action. Craig (2004), for example, points out that decision making in correctional institutions often results in "managerial edicts" (p. 109). As such, line-level members are more likely to view the decisions with skepticism, distrust, or uncertainty. Involving a wider range of employees within the decision-making process (decentralization) aids in overcoming resistance. Boss (1979) further described an innovative use of organizational redesign to resolve strife

Table 12.1 Common Reasons for Resisting Organizational Change

Barriers to Understanding	Barriers to Acceptance	Barriers to Action
Insufficient comunication of need for, content of, or consequences emerging from change	Self-interest; concerned about personal rather than organizational needs	Poor training; lack of skills or abilities to execute change
Uncertainty about what to expect post-change	Lack of trust in motives of change agents	Inertia
Ignorance about need for or content of change	Threats to job security or physical/emotional safety	Inability to overcome prior ways of doing work; habit
Failure to reward or inconsistent rewarding of new behaviors	Loss of power under new organizational arrangements	Inhibition
Short-term thinking	Anxiety	Structural impediments
	Preference for status quo	
	Prior negative experiences with organizational change	

Source: Adapted from Connor & Lake (1988), Eccles (1994), Judson (1991), O'Toole (1995).

within a sheriff's department during the early 1970s. Many of the managers (e.g., district commanders, undersheriffs) expressed dissatisfaction with their responsibilities and their access to the sheriff. The sheriff allowed the command staff to request new positions and so indicate their preferences for assignments, effectively establishing an entirely new organizational chart. Given the level of input, the changes were instituted and ultimately communicated to the remaining employees with little resistance. As Judson (1991) noted, sometimes overcoming resistance requires one or more of a variety of specific managerial techniques: compulsion, persuasion, bargaining, rewarding, assuring, and/or discussing.

As this section demonstrated, criminal justice organizations frequently change, both of their own volition and due to conflict. Even though many changes are relatively minor (evolutionary), they amount to more significant changes over the long term as the result of incremental adjustments. In other situations, however, change is drastic and abrupt (revolutionary). Regardless of the type of change, evolutionary or revolutionary, significant attention must be paid to both unfreezing and freezing to ensure that resistance does not reverse or stifle the changes.

KEY TERMS

conflictive change motor
consent decrees
evolutionary motor
learning organization
life course
life cycle motor
limited or bounded rationality
motors
planned change motor
satisficing

DISCUSSION QUESTIONS

1. Van de Ven and Poole (1995) argue that changes can occur as a byproduct of two or more change motors. For example, a planned change on the part of a prison's leadership may be altered due to conflict with the correctional officers' union. Both the planned and conflictive change motors, in this case, prove relevant in understanding the precise form of change that emerged. Describe an example, real or hypothetical, that illustrates the convergence of two or more change motors contributing to organizational change.

2. In your opinion, should the court system be engaging in judicial policymaking by ordering organizational changes, or should such changes be solely the prerogative of organizational leadership?

3. As the section shows, organizational changes often breed individual resistance. Did you ever work in an organization that attempted to change one or more features of the work (e.g., structure, actual tasks, etc.)? If so, did you or other members of the organization express any resistance to the changes? Did the types of resistance mirror the forms frequently described in the organizational change literature?

WEB RESOURCES

U.S. Department of Justice special litigation cases (including cases related to justice agencies):
http://www.justice.gov/crt/about/spl/

Ruiz v. Estelle (documents from University of Texas at Austin, Tarlton Law Library):
http://tarlton.law.utexas.edu/exhibits/ww_justice/ruiz_v_estelle.html

Vera Institute of Justice:
http://www.vera.org/

Reading 25

Greg Berman and Aubrey Fox provide an account of the resiliency of the D.A.R.E. program, a school-based drug-prevention program many readers have likely experienced, in spite of considerable evidence that it fails to meet its core objective—reducing drug use among youth. D.A.R.E. is widely implemented across the United States and internationally, and more than 15,000 police officers serve as instructors within schools. While some districts and departments abandoned D.A.R.E. as an increasing amount of evidence questioned its efficacy, others retained the program, citing a variety of reasons. Even in school districts where D.A.R.E. remained, organizers were familiar with the criticisms and negative findings. Nevertheless, some saw their local implementation of D.A.R.E. as more effective than the modal program; cited secondary benefits, including improved police–youth relationships; or believed in the importance of D.A.R.E. as a part of a comprehensive drug-prevention strategy. Even the national D.A.R.E. organization modified the program to address some of the concerns. The example demonstrates that research alone is unlikely to shape policy; a variety of other local and extra-local considerations influence decision makers.

Lessons From the Battle Over D.A.R.E.

The Complicated Relationship Between Research and Practice

Greg Berman and Aubrey Fox

Introduction

Since its inception in Los Angeles in 1983, Drug Abuse Resistance Education (D.A.R.E.) has become one of the most well-known and widespread crime prevention programs in the country. D.A.R.E.'s model is relatively straightforward. Police officers are trained to lead educational sessions in local schools that are designed to help students resist peer pressure and live drug-free lives. The program's reach is nothing short of remarkable: D.A.R.E. has been responsible for training hundreds of thousands of police officers and educating millions of children.[1] The program has spread to 43 different countries. In recognition of this, every year for the last 18 years, four consecutive presidents have set aside a day in April as "National D.A.R.E. Day."

Alongside this impressive track record, however, there exists a counter-narrative. This story is written not by the administrators of D.A.R.E. but by scholars who have studied the program. To date, there have been more than 30 evaluations of the program that have documented negligible long-term impacts on teen drug use.[2] One intensive, six-year study even found that the program increased drug use among suburban teens by a small amount.[3] These less-than-inspiring results have received widespread press coverage, including numerous newspaper articles and a February 21, 1997 segment on the NBC newsmagazine show Dateline.

Source: Berman, G., & Fox, A. (2009). *Lessons from the battle over D.A.R.E.: The complicated relationship between research and practice.* New York: Center for Court Innovation.

Despite these setbacks, D.A.R.E. is alive and well, taught in about 75 percent of school districts across the country.[4] Over 15,000 police officers participate as D.A.R.E instructors, providing educational sessions about drugs and drug abuse largely targeted at 5th and 6th graders.[5]

To its critics, D.A.R.E. is a cautionary tale of how criminal justice programs can live on despite evidence of failure. To its defenders, D.A.R.E. is a case study of resilience in the face of adversity. This paper is an effort to examine the D.A.R.E. story. In particular, this essay seeks to unpack the complicated relationship between research and practice by examining a case where practitioners and researchers clashed and how it was resolved.

As this paper details, the D.A.R.E. story is more complicated than it appears at first glance. In fact, a strong case can be made that many of the local communities that have chosen to retain D.A.R.E. in the face of scholarly criticism had good reasons for doing so. For many policymakers, the only question that matters when it comes to crime prevention is a simple one: does this program work or not? As the D.A.R.E. story indicates, the reality is almost always more complicated than this. D.A.R.E. is a case study not in black and white verdicts but in shades of grey.

A Brief History of D.A.R.E.

In 1983, Glenn Levant was a commander in the Los Angeles Police Department when then-police Chief Darryl Gates hit on the idea of sending police officers into classrooms to educate young people about drugs. It was a time when the "war on drugs" was just starting in earnest. It was also the era of Nancy Reagan's well-publicized campaign to "Just Say No" to drugs. In this environment, the new program proved to be an immediate hit, and other schools began asking Gates for help in implementing the program. To raise money to pay for expenses, in 1984 Levant helped organize the Los Angeles Police Crime Prevention Advisory Council which evolved into D.A.R.E. California, which became D.A.R.E. America a few years later when it landed a $140,000 grant from the United States Department of Justice. The stage was set for the phenomenal growth of D.A.R.E.

At the same time, the Department of Justice also agreed to provide funding to the Research Triangle Institute to conduct a national study of D.A.R.E. Preliminary results from the study, which were released in 1993, did not show a reduction in drug abuse among participants.[6] D.A.R.E. publicly criticized the report. This would be the pattern for the better part of a decade, with negative research findings leading to public dissent from D.A.R.E. administrators.[7]

The controversy reached a fever pitch in 1998 with the release of an evaluation by University of Illinois at Chicago Professor Dennis P. Rosenbaum, which tracked 1,798 urban, suburban, and rural 6th graders who had participated in the D.A.R.E. program. The research confirmed earlier findings that program benefits such as educating young people about drugs, improving attitudes about the police, and giving young people the confidence to resist illegal drug use wore off within one or two years. What really got the attention of the press, however, was the finding that D.A.R.E. was associated with an increased level of drug use (3 to 5 percentage points) among suburban youth.[8]

According to Rosenbaum, D.A.R.E. America made a concentrated effort to shape how the report's findings were covered in the national press. "Behind the scenes, they had used high-powered lawyers to sue or threaten to sue people who criticized the D.A.R.E. program, arguing that reporters, producers, and researchers were making false statements," writes Rosenbaum. "Reputations and careers were ruined."[9]

With the benefit of hindsight, D.A.R.E. administrators now admit that the relationship with the research community grew hostile. "Glenn [Levant, the head of D.A.R.E. America at the time] was very vocal in his utter disdain for most of the researchers," recalled Jim McGiveney, a D.A.R.E. America Regional Director. McGiveney's take is that Levant, who had helped grow D.A.R.E. from humble origins, took the criticism personally. "I can understand why Glenn was so defensive," McGiveney said, "because D.A.R.E. was his baby."[10]

Levant couldn't stop the tide. Seattle Police Chief Norm Stamper decided to drop the program in 1996, calling it an "enormous failure." His decision attracted local and national media attention.[11] Even more ominously for D.A.R.E., the criticism was reaching Congress. "You'd walk into a congressman's office, and they'd meet you at the door with printouts of studies saying that D.A.R.E. didn't work," said D.A.R.E.'s McGiveney. "That was very tough to overcome."[12] In 1998, the House Appropriations subcommittee on Commerce, Justice, State, and Judiciary took the unusual step of calling for D.A.R.E. America to revise its curriculum.

At D.A.R.E.'s request, the U.S. Departments of Justice and Education intervened in May 1998. Several federal government officials (including Assistant Attorney General Laurie Robinson, Deputy Assistant Attorney General Reginald Robinson, and Bill Modzeleik, the head of the Department of Education's Safe and Drug-Free Schools Program) convened a meeting between a small group of researchers and D.A.R.E. America administrators.[13] According to several attendees, it was a tense meeting, but in the end D.A.R.E. America demonstrated that it was willing to make peace with the research community.

This made an impression on the Robert Wood Johnson Foundation, which was interested in making an investment in youth drug prevention initiatives. Although the foundation was aware of the critical research about D.A.R.E., they also noted some of the organization's achievements—achievements that were often overlooked in the controversy over D.A.R.E.'s long-term impacts. Most notably, the organization had built an impressive infrastructure. Through state and regional chapters, D.A.R.E. was training hundreds of new police officers every year. It was "one of the best training systems we had seen," according to the foundation's vice president, Nancy Kaufmann.[14] Also, with programs in over 70 percent of school districts across the country, D.A.R.E. America had an unmatched national network. Rather than trying to replace D.A.R.E. with something else, the executives at Robert Wood Johnson thought it made sense to re-tool it.[15]

In 1999, Robert Wood Johnson agreed to commit $14 million to D.A.R.E. over a five-year period.

Rather than invest directly in D.A.R.E., Robert Wood Johnson made the decision to have its funds administered by Zili Sloboda at the University of Akron. Working with Sloboda, D.A.R.E. agreed to a few changes to its model. First, D.A.R.E. would focus on an older cohort of students: many researchers believed it was important to supplement the educational services provided to 5th and 6th graders with a "booster shot" delivered to students a few years later. Second, D.A.R.E. agreed to revise its curriculum to make it less didactic and more participatory. Instead of lectures, the police officers involved would attempt to engage young people in a conversation about the consequences of illegal drugs.

Evaluating D.A.R.E.

Also with support from the Robert Wood Johnson Foundation, Harvard University professor Carol Weiss, an expert on how research informs government policy, decided to investigate the D.A.R.E. phenomenon. She dedicated a team of graduate students to the project, sending them out to school districts across the country to find out what effect, if any, the controversy about D.A.R.E. had had on the field.[16]

Weiss' operating assumption was that local communities had continued to stay involved with D.A.R.E. out of ignorance: "I initially thought it was because practitioners were not paying attention," she said.[17] To test this assumption, Weiss and her team selected 16 local school districts in four states—Colorado, Massachusetts, Kentucky, and Illinois—where large-scale evaluations of D.A.R.E. had already been completed, on the theory that it would make it more likely that school officials and other local decision makers had heard about the research findings on D.A.R.E. The districts were divided into two groups. Eight were using D.A.R.E. at the time the study began in 2001 and eight were not.

The team quickly learned that far from ignoring the evidence about D.A.R.E., individuals in the school districts were well aware of it. "When we got into the field, we found out they were paying attention," remarked Weiss.[18] While few had read the academic research first-hand, almost without exception they had seen or read something about the negative research findings. Some had even cut out stories about D.A.R.E. from newspapers, which they shared with the interviewers. As a result, they were very familiar with the broad outlines of the critique of D.A.R.E. Damage had been done: six communities had discontinued D.A.R.E. only a few years before the study started.

In each case, negative research findings played a role in the decision to drop D.A.R.E. In Gardner, Illinois,[19] the school district dropped the program in 1998 after the district's health coordinator saw a critical magazine article about D.A.R.E. that her husband had saved for her. In Marlboro, Kentucky, the city manager and a local police lieutenant jointly decided to discontinue D.A.R.E. after reading stories in the newspaper that confirmed their personal beliefs that the program was ineffective. In Orchard Grove, Massachusetts, a local gadfly used negative evaluation findings to convince the town's governing board to end the program over the objections of the school superintendent, a strong D.A.R.E. supporter.[20]

As these examples show, D.A.R.E. did not survive its battle with researchers unscathed. The negative research findings clearly damaged the program's reputation. Still, many communities in Weiss's study kept D.A.R.E. despite the research findings. In some cases, this decision was influenced by lobbying by D.A.R.E. officials. But it would be inaccurate to say that 75 percent of school districts in the United States simply caved to D.A.R.E. In attempting to understand why D.A.R.E. remained popular, Weiss and her team found that local decision makers were not blithely ignoring or dismissing the research. Rather, many gave relatively sophisticated reasons for retaining D.A.R.E. One reason commonly cited was that local officials were realistic about what D.A.R.E. could do to combat illegal drug use. To cite one example, a school board member in Massachusetts told interviewers that she thought it was "silly" to expect that D.A.R.E. alone would lower rates of drug use among young people.

Local officials also thought scholars had erred by focusing almost exclusively on the program's "official" goal of reducing drug use. Instead, they cited a number of secondary reasons to support the program, starting with the positive relationships built between police officers, students, and educators. As one Massachusetts school superintendent put it, "If you ask the question . . . 'Does it reduce the illegal use of drugs and alcohol?' apparently D.A.R.E. can't demonstrate that for various reasons. If you ask, 'Does it help kids understand their community better? Does it produce favorable relationships between police and kids?' all of the survey results . . . [are] positive." After helping a student with a difficult family situation, one police officer in Kentucky remarked that his interaction was almost impossible to capture in a study. "[It's] not something that you put on a bar graph or a pie chart or anything like that," he said.[21]

Weiss's research team uncovered several examples of ancillary benefits of D.A.R.E. For example, D.A.R.E. officers at one Colorado high school helped reassure students that it was safe to re-enter their school after the shootings at nearby Columbine High School. The benefits appeared to flow in both directions: a number of police officers interviewed said that participating in D.A.R.E. helped improve their understanding of young people because they had a chance to interact with them personally. And police chiefs valued the relationships they had built with school officials. "One of the most important benefits and by-products is the relationship we have now with the school department," said one Massachusetts police chief. "It couldn't be better . . . it really couldn't be better. If I need anything, I just have to pick up the phone."[22]

Finally, many of the school officials interviewed said that they believed their D.A.R.E. program was simply better than others and thus qualified as an exception to the rule. On the one hand, it's possible that these local officials were merely displaying examples of the so-called "Lake Wobegon" effect, named for Garrison Keillor's satirical observation that in his fictitious hometown, "all the women are strong, all the men are good-looking, and all the children are above average."[23] Yet, as researchers often point out, while research can help provide probabilities about whether a given program works or not, it does not foreclose the possibility that a particular version can be effective.

According to Weiss, communities continued on with D.A.R.E. in the face of negative research findings out of a combination of "rationality and rationalization." As she and her collaborators Sarah Birkeland and Erin Murphy-Graham conclude in their paper, "Good reasons for ignoring good evaluation," local officials were far from ignorant pawns in the hands of the D.A.R.E. America propaganda campaign. "Their decisions to continue implementing [D.A.R.E.]," they write, "are based in an assessment of the pros and cons, rather than simple ignorance."[24]

Responding to the Research

Local jurisdictions were not the only ones figuring out how to respond to the research about D.A.R.E. At the national headquarters of D.A.R.E. America in the early 2000s, administrators were actively working to re-think the organization's mission and methods. At the heart of this effort was the Robert Wood Johnson-funded project to construct and test a new D.A.R.E. curriculum.

This effort was led by Zili Sloboda at the University of Akron. Sloboda had formerly worked at the National Institute on Drug Abuse and was well known within the drug prevention community. With the help of an educational expert, Sloboda set about overhauling the D.A.R.E. curriculum. Working with consultants, she created a 17-week program, "Take Back Your Life," that focused on a smaller set of topics and allowed for more back and forth conversation between 7th and 9th grade students and D.A.R.E. instructors. "Kids learn better when they get a chance to ask questions and learn on their own terms," Sloboda said. "That takes a lot of patience." For example, in one session, students were told which parts of the brain are responsible for different types of behavior, then shown images of the brain after alcohol is consumed. "The kids love to figure out why people slur their words when they are drinking," said Sloboda. "They come up with the conclusions themselves."[25]

Based in part on Sloboda's research, in 2000, every D.A.R.E. instructor across the country was re-trained, with the goal of re-casting D.A.R.E. as an educational program that taught participants about how to make better decisions about a range of issues, including drug use. The plan was to test the new curriculum with more than 9,000 students in Detroit, Houston, Los Angeles, New Orleans, Newark, and St. Louis. Follow-up D.A.R.E. education would be given to students two years later when they reached the 9th grade, and the results would be compared to control groups in each city.[26]

D.A.R.E. America eagerly publicized Sloboda's efforts as a sign that the organization was open to change. For example, Glenn Levant told *The New York Times* in 2001, "There's quite a bit we can do to make it better and we realize it." Levant added "I'm not saying it was effective, but it was state of the art when we launched it. Now it's time for science to improve upon what we're doing."[27] The banner headline on D.A.R.E. America's website said it all: "It's a New D.A.R.E."

Early results, released in late 2002, were encouraging: students who participated in the new Take Back Your Life curriculum showed small but statistically significant improvements in terms of their attitudes towards drugs and their drug refusal skills. "It shows us that the program is doing what it intended to do, and in a very significant way," Sloboda told a reporter from Associated Press.[28] Of course, the key question was whether the results would hold true over the long haul, or if the benefits of D.A.R.E. would dissipate over time as they had in previous studies.

Unfortunately for Sloboda and D.A.R.E., events outside of their control complicated the ambitious research project. Hurricane Katrina presented enormous obstacles: many of the students who fled New Orleans moved to Houston, creating problems halfway through the research process. Even more critically, Sloboda realized that her control group had been, in effect, contaminated. Under ideal circumstances, the control group would receive no drug prevention education at all, which would allow for a better test of the effectiveness of D.A.R.E. However, the reality was that most students get some kind of drug prevention education these days. "That is good news for our kids," said Sloboda, "but a big challenge to researchers."[29] For their part, D.A.R.E. critics like Dennis Rosenbaum believe that these are not valid excuses, particularly given the study's large sample size (six cities and 14,000 students) and the reality that all drug prevention research faces the same challenge of potential control group contamination.

Although final results have not yet been published, in all likelihood, Sloboda's study will not settle the debate about D.A.R.E. After seven years and considerable expense, officials at D.A.R.E. America have limited expectations of what the research will tell them. "I'm not sure anyone is ready to rigorously test any substance abuse curriculum in a real world environment," said D.A.R.E. America Executive Director Frank Pegueros, noting the problems experienced by Sloboda. "Zili found out that the complexities of large scale research are such that it takes on a life of its own and you lose control of it."[30]

Despite these difficulties, Pegueros said that D.A.R.E. America has learned a number of important lessons in recent years. The most important change for the program involves the teaching style of its instructors. According to Pegueros, D.A.R.E. America has worked hard to encourage police officers to be less didactic in the classroom. "We found initially that some D.A.R.E. instructors had some difficulty," Pegueros said. "Their perception was that they were losing control, which is not a situation that many law enforcement officials are comfortable being in." After five years, however, the situation has changed, and Pegueros is encouraged by survey research indicating that students in Sloboda's experimental group reported satisfaction with the performance of police officers who taught the course. "I think we were ahead of the curve on this one," Pegueros said.[31]

In recent years, D.A.R.E. America has demonstrated its continuing willingness to re-think its approach to substance abuse prevention. For example, in 2007, D.A.R.E. America reached an agreement with the Pennsylvania State University to use "keepin' it REAL" as its new middle school curriculum.[32]

Deciding What Works

It would be comforting to imagine a world in which failure was clearly and decisively identified by scholars. If more than 30 studies have reported a consistent finding—that D.A.R.E. has no long-term impact on youth drug use—isn't the appropriate response to, in the words of Dennis Rosenbaum, "Just Say No to D.A.R.E."?[33] The persistence of programs like D.A.R.E. has led some scholars to question why the public and government officials continue to support programs that have been shown to be ineffective.[34]

Yet as Weiss's study shows, the D.A.R.E. story is more complicated than it first appears. Far from being ignorant of the research, local decision makers weighed the evidence about D.A.R.E. in deciding whether to keep the program or not. In many communities, the result was that D.A.R.E. was discontinued. In others, D.A.R.E. was retained. In some places, the decision to keep D.A.R.E. was politically motivated. In others, educators and elected officials valued the ancillary benefits of D.A.R.E., such as improved relationships with the police. These hard-to-measure qualitative benefits are the most likely explanation for why D.A.R.E. remains in place in 75 percent of school districts across the country.[35]

Ultimately, there is no single objective standard for determining whether a program works or not. This seems particularly true for D.A.R.E. While noting that local jurisdictions have articulated a number of reasons for keeping D.A.R.E., Dennis Rosenbaum flatly rules them out on the grounds that D.A.R.E. America had already committed itself to achieving a single goal. "While I appreciate these 'voices,'" he writes, "D.A.R.E. was marketed and sold exclusively for its drug prevention benefits, not for other possible outcomes."[36]

The oft-critical scholarship on D.A.R.E. has made an enormous contribution to the field, forcing D.A.R.E. America to make midcourse corrections to their program and injecting a healthy dose of skepticism into the youth drug prevention debate. But scholars like Rosenbaum have expressed disappointment that the research has not led to the wholesale abandonment of D.A.R.E.

The limited impact of D.A.R.E. research should not come as a surprise, as it conforms to the basic pattern observed in "knowledge utilization" studies of the last 30 years. As Carol Weiss and others have shown, evaluation research rarely has a direct effect on policymakers.[37] While research can at times help challenge conventional wisdom, more often than not it is used to justify preconceived beliefs and decisions. "If practitioners are in favor of some action and they find an evaluation doesn't show positive effects, they tend to disregard it or make up excuses," said Weiss. "On the other hand, if they're against the program or the policy, and the study shows it wasn't effective, they are apt to champion the findings."[38] Another factor limiting the influence of research is that good evaluations can take years to complete, which is much longer than policymakers typically have to make a decision. When research does influence policy, it tends to do so in an indirect way—what Weiss calls "knowledge creep."[39]

At the end of the day, the D.A.R.E. story is a lesson in the importance of modest expectations. It can be argued that D.A.R.E. was saved by the realism of many local officials who understood that a complex problem like youth substance abuse doesn't lend itself to solving through a series of lectures by police officers, no matter how impassioned or well-trained. The message of modest expectations is also appropriate for researchers, for whom the D.A.R.E. story provides ample evidence of the limits of their impacts on policymakers.

The D.A.R.E. story also demonstrates the importance of maintaining a dynamic balance among the key stakeholders involved in criminal justice policy—not just academics and criminal justice officials, but the public, the media, and politicians. While each group has something to contribute, tipping the balance too far in any direction can lead to trouble. As Carl Weiss says, "Evaluation is not a substitute for judgment."[40]

Conclusion

There have been dozens of articles written about D.A.R.E that tell a similar story: how D.A.R.E. America has been able to convince educators and the public into supporting the program over the objections of researchers.[41] A closer looks reveals that in the case of D.A.R.E. many local practitioners were able to sift through the competing claims of researchers and D.A.R.E. America and make more-or-less reasoned judgments about whether to keep D.A.R.E. In general, local officials reached their own conclusions about what made the most sense for their jurisdictions. In some places, this has meant that D.A.R.E. is still a vital, active presence; in others, this has meant that D.A.R.E. has been scrapped in favor of other programs.

While the fight over D.A.R.E. is mostly over, the controversy exposed a gap between researchers and practitioners that continues to this day. Some degree of conflict between these worlds is probably inevitable. Social scientists and criminal justice officials have different value systems and divergent world views—they are separated by training, location, professional rewards, and even the vocabulary they use.[42]

Despite the obstacles, criminal justice researchers and practitioners find themselves in a co-dependent relationship. Many practitioners are desperate for a more reflective approach to criminal justice that uses both qualitative and quantitative data to identify problems and assess solutions. Similarly, many researchers are eager to have their work taken more seriously and to have a broader impact on policy decisions.

The D.A.R.E. story offers a number of important lessons about the research-practice divide, including the challenges of implementing rigorous experimental studies, of assessing all of the potential impacts of a multifaceted program, and of creating an honest and civil dialogue between researchers and an evaluated program.

This last lesson is perhaps the most important. The conflict between D.A.R.E. administrators and researchers reached a fever pitch because so much was at stake for the participants: D.A.R.E. felt it was fighting for its very life and the researchers felt they were fighting for their professional integrity.[43] But it didn't have to be this way. If the culture of criminal justice policymaking in this country were different, the D.A.R.E. story might have unfolded with much less acrimony.

Is it possible to create a culture that values both reflection and results? That supports research but understands its limitations? That sets high expectations for practitioners but acknowledges the intransigent nature of many of the problems they are trying to solve? That understands that it is impossible to have trial without error? These are just a few of the questions raised by the D.A.R.E. case study that are worthy of exploration in the days ahead by those who seek to create a dynamic and positive relationship between criminal justice research and practice.

Notes

1. For an overview of D.A.R.E. results, see http://www.dare.com/home/about_dare.asp.

2. For a short introduction to the D.A.R.E. research, see Dennis P. Rosenbaum, "Just Say No to D.A.R.E.," *Criminology & Public Policy*, Vol. 6, No. 4, 815-824 (2007).

3. Dennis P. Rosenbaum and Gordon S. Hanson. "Assessing the Effects of School-Based Drug Education: A Six-Year Mutli-Level Analysis of Project D.A.R.E.," *Journal of Research in Crime and Delinquency*, Vol. 35, No. 4, 381–412 (1998).

4. See http://www.dare.com/home/about_dare.asp.

5. Author phone interview with D.A.R.E. America Executive Director Frank Pegueros, June 26, 2008.

6. S. T. Ennett, N. S. Tobler, C. L. Ringwalt and R. L. Flewelling, "How effective is drug abuse resistance education? A meta-analysis of Project DARE outcome evaluations," *American Journal of Public Health*, Vol. 84, Issue 9 1394-1401 (1994).

7. Patrick Boyle, "A D.A.R.E.ing Rescue: How an intervention by critics and federal officials brought the youth antidrug program into rehab," *Youth Today*, April 2001.

8. Dennis P. Rosenbaum and Gordon S. Hanson. "Assessing the Effects of School-Based Drug Education: A Six Year Mutli-Level Analysis of Project D.A.R.E.," *Journal of Research in Crime and Delinquency*, Vol. 35, No. 4, 381–412 (1998).

9. Dennis P. Rosenbaum, "Just Say No to D.A.R.E.," *Criminology & Public Policy*, Vol. 6, No. 4, 815-824 (2007).

10. Author phone interview with D.A.R.E. America Regional Director Jim McGiveney, June 23, 2008.

11. Paul Shukovsy, "Stamper Wants to Cut D.A.R.E., 17 Positions," *Seattle Post-Intelligencer*, 6/17/1996. Stamper also criticized D.A.R.E. in an interview with the PBS newsmagazine show "NewsHour with Jim Lehrer" on April 25, 1997.

12. D.A.R.E. America points to studies by Dennis Gorman and Carol Weiss in arguing that the D.A.R.E. program has been held to a higher standard than other youth drug prevention programs. For example, as Gorman has written, "what differentiates D.A.R.E. from many of the programs on evidence-based lists might not be the actual intervention but rather the manner in which data analysis is conducted, reported, and interpreted." Dennis M. Gorman and J. Charles Huber, Jr., "The Social Construction of 'Evidence-Based' Drug Prevention Programs: A Reanalysis of Data from the Drug Abuse Resistance Education (DARE) Program," *Evaluation Review*, Vol. 33, No. 4, 394-414 (2009). Also see "The Fairy Godmother—and Her Warts: Making the Dream of Evidence-Based Policy Come True," *American Journal of Evaluation*, Vol. 29 No. 1 29-47 (2008). Author phone interview with Jim McGiveney, July 14, 2008.

13. Patrick Boyle, "A D.A.R.E.ing Rescue: How an intervention by critics and federal officials brought the youth antidrug program into rehab," *Youth Today*, April 2001.

14. *Ibid.*

15. *Ibid.*

16. Much of the following section of this report is taken from Sarah Birkeland, Erin Murphy-Graham, and Carol Weiss, "Good reasons for ignoring good evaluation: The case of the drug abuse resistance education (D.A.R.E.) program," *Evaluation and Program Planning* 28, 247-256 (2005) and Carol Weiss, Erin Murphy-Graham, and Sarah Birkeland, "An Alternate Route to Policy Influence: How Evaluations Affect D.A.R.E." *American Journal of Evaluation*, Vol. 26 No. 1, 12-30.

17. Author phone interview with Harvard University Professor Carol Weiss, June 27, 2008.

18. *Ibid.*

19. The school districts that participated in the study were given fictional names.

20. Another important factor for local communities that dropped D.A.R.E. was the federal government's decision to omit it from its list of "effective" or "promising" approaches to youth drug prevention. The list was released in a preliminary document in 1998 and then embedded in federal legislation passed in 2002, over D.A.R.E. America's vigorous objections. Although this provision did not explicitly prohibit school districts from using D.A.R.E., in practice many local officials interpreted it as doing so. Sarah Birkeland, Erin Murphy-Graham, and Carol Weiss, "Good reasons for ignoring good evaluation: The case of the drug abuse resistance education (D.A.R.E.) program," *Evaluation and Program Planning* 28, 247-256 (2005).

21. *Ibid.*

22. *Ibid.*

23. Garrison Keillor, *Lake Wobegon Days*, Penguin, 1990.

24. Sarah Birkeland, Erin Murphy-Graham, and Carol Weiss, "Good reasons for ignoring good evaluation: The case of the drug abuse resistance education (D.A.R.E.) program," *Evaluation and Program Planning* 28, 247-256 (2005).

25. Author phone interview with University of Akron professor Zili Sloboda, June 23, 2008.

26. "Study Highlights Value of D.A.R.E. Network," Press Release, Carnavale Associates LLC. Available at http://www.carnevaleassociates.com/newD.A.R.E/21st%20Century%20School%20House%20Jan%2006.pdf.

27. Kate Zernike, "Anti drug Program Says It Will Adopt a New Strategy," *The New York Times*, February 1, 2001.

28. "Schools D.A.R.E. to get real," *Associated Press*, October 29, 2002.

29. Author phone interview with Zili Sloboda, June 23, 2008.

30. Author phone interview with Frank Pegueros, June 26, 2008.

31. *Ibid.*

32. The curriculum is listed on the Substance Abuse and Mental Health Services Administration's national registry of evidenced-based programs and practices. See: http://www.nrepp.samhsa.gov/programfulldetails.asp?PROGRAM_ID=119.

33. This issue is not confined to D.A.R.E. For example, in an influential review conducted in 1997 of the effectiveness of criminal justice programs in reducing recidivism, University of Maryland Professor Lawrence W. Sherman and his colleagues found more failures (23) than successes (15). While some of the ineffective programs named in the report like correctional boot camps have declined in popularity in the last decade, other pr ograms like D.A.R.E. and gun buyback initiatives are thriving. Lawrence W. Sherman, Denise Gottfredson, Doris MacKenzie, John Eck, Peter Reuter, and Shawn Bushway, "Preventing Crime: What Works, What Doesn't, What's Promising," A Report to the United States Congress, National Institute of Justice.

34. Dennis P. Rosenbaum, "Just Say No to D.A.R.E.," *Criminology & Public Policy*, Vol. 6, No. 4, p. 815-824 (2007).

35. Sarah Birkeland, Erin Murphy-Graham, and Carol Weiss, "Good reasons for ignoring good evaluation: The case of the drug abuse resistance education (D.A.R.E.) program," *Evaluation and Program Planning* 28, 247-256 (2005).

36. Dennis P. Rosenbaum, "Just Say No to D.A.R.E.," *Criminology & Public Policy*, Vol. 6, No. 4, p. 815-824 (2007).

37. Carol Weiss, Erin Murphy-Graham, Anthony Petrosino, and Allison G. Gandhi, "The Fairy Godmother—and Her Warts: Making the Dream of Evidence-Based Policy Come True," *American Journal of Evaluation*, Vol. 29 No. 1, 29-47 (2008).

38. Author phone interview with Carol Weiss, June 27, 2008.

39. Carol Weiss, "Knowledge Creep and Decision Accretion," *Science Communication*, Vol. 1, No. 3, 381-404 (1980).

40. "An EEPA Interview with Carol M. Weiss," Educational Evolution and Policy Analysis, Vol. 2, No. 5 p. 75—79 (1980).

41. Author phone interview with Carol Weiss, June 27, 2008.

42. For an overview of these issues, see Aubrey Fox, "Bridging the Gap: Researchers, Practitioners, and the Future of Drug Courts," Center for Court Innovation, 2004, available at http://www.courtinnovation.org/_uploads/documents/bridgingthegap.pdf.

43. Dennis P. Rosenbaum, "Just Say No to D.A.R.E.," *Criminology & Public Policy*, Vol. 6, No. 4, p. 815-824 (2007).

DISCUSSION QUESTIONS

1. D.A.R.E. proponents, including school administers, touted the program's secondary benefits, such as stronger relationships between students and law enforcement officers. In your opinion, does success in achieving secondary benefits, or what Berman and Fox refer to as ancillary benefits (p. 7), warrant the investment in D.A.R.E. if sufficient evidence pointing to drug-prevention benefits is lacking?

2. Consider your studies of the criminal justice system. Are there other policies or practices that persist today in spite of research questioning their effectiveness? If so, what additional "value" comes from maintaining these practices?

3. Scholars often publish the results of evaluation research findings in peer-reviewed journal articles. How might this communication format serve as an impediment when attempting to translate research into practice? What features of journal articles increase the likelihood that research findings will be overlooked or deliberately ignored by policymakers or practitioners? Draw on your own experiences consuming scholarly research in this course and elsewhere.

READING

Reading 26

As we have seen throughout this text, decision making plays an important role in the operation of organizations, from the choice of structure to the responses to crises to the selection of change strategies. Daniel P. Mears and Sarah Bacon lament the lack of overall attention devoted to an assessment of the quality of decisions made by actors within the criminal justice system. As discussed in this section, decisions are made under conditions of bounded rationality, and sometimes the decisions are incorrect, producing unintended or undesirable consequences. The authors suggest that we can make sense of decision-making errors by drawing parallels to the medical field. The two fields share a number of important similarities: (1) Both focus on diagnoses of particular problems (disease, crime); (2) accurate treatment is critical, and the consequences of misdiagnoses are potentially dire (e.g., drug interactions, wrongful conviction); (3) individualized decision making is often difficult due to large caseloads; (4) there is an increasing emphasis on evidence-based practices (learning); and (5) accountability is expected but is often difficult in practice. Mears and Bacon present 13 decision-making errors drawn from the medical field and apply criminal justice examples to each. Given these potential errors, they offer recommendations for improving overall, system-wide decision making in criminal justice.

IMPROVING CRIMINAL JUSTICE THROUGH BETTER DECISION MAKING

Lessons From the Medical System

Daniel P. Mears and Sarah Bacon

Introduction

Criminal justice expenditures at local, state, and federal levels have increased dramatically in recent decades, rising over 440 percent, from just under $36 billion in 1982 to over $193 billion in 2004 (Hughes, 2006; Hughes & Perry, 2007). At the same time, calls for government accountability, and in particular, a greater reliance on the use of performance monitoring and evidence-based practices have increased (Behn, 2003; Campbell, 2003; Cullen, 2005; Hatry, 2007; Julnes, 2006; Perry, McDougall, & Farrington, 2006; Welsh & Harris, 2004). Yet, criminal justice system practices and policies, including decisions about how to sanction and treat offenders, frequently go unmonitored and lack scientific support (Farabee, 2005; Lipsey, Adams, Gottfredson, Pepper, & Weisburd, 2005; MacKenzie, 2006; Marion & Oliver, 2006; Sherman et al., 1997). Even when performance monitoring occurs, it rarely involves a systems-level perspective or an

---

Mears, D. P., & Bacon, S. (2009). Improving criminal justice through better decision making: Lessons from the medical system. *Journal of Criminal Justice, 37*(2), 142–154.

assessment of the quality of decision making within and throughout various stages of criminal justice processing (Bazemore, 2006; Forst, 2004; Logan, 1993; Walker, 1992, 1993). Instead, the most prominent policy evaluations typically have examined specific initiatives (Farabee, 2005; Rossi, Lipsey, & Freeman, 2004). Far less attention has been given to assessing how improved decision making in everyday practice can improve the overall operations of criminal justice.

These observations assume greater urgency when one considers the large-scale increases in the numbers of individuals affected by the criminal justice system and the impact of decisions about offenders on victims, families, communities, and the offenders themselves (Travis & Visher, 2005). Today, over 650,000 prisoners are released each year, stemming from a dramatic escalation in the use of incarceration over the past twenty-five years (Petersilia, 2003; Travis, 2005). Released prisoners are not the sole source of growth in correctional populations, however. Between 1980 and 2005, the number of individuals under local, state, or federal correctional control increased from 1.8 million to over 7 million (Glaze & Bonczar, 2006, p. 2). A substantial contributor to this growth has been an increase in the number of individuals on probation and parole—as of 2005, 4.1 million individuals were on probation, 780,000 were on parole, 740,000 were in jail, and 1.4 million were in prison (Glaze & Bonczar, 2006, p. 2). Not surprisingly, justice system personnel, including police, court, and corrections officers, have increased, almost doubling between 1982 and 2003, from 1.2 to 2.3 million (Hughes, 2006). In addition, according to the U.S. Bureau of Justice Statistics, "cases of all kinds (criminal, civil, domestic, juvenile, and traffic) filed in the nearly 16,000 general and limited jurisdiction State courts went from about 86 million to 100 million [from 1987 to 2003]" (Hughes, 2006, p. 7).

Collectively, such statistics point not only to marked growth in all aspects of the criminal justice system, but also to a corresponding implication. Namely, more than at any time in U.S. history, an increasingly large number of critical decisions must be made on a daily basis by law enforcement officers, court personnel, probation and parole officers, and jail and prison employees about how best to fight crime and handle large case loads of individuals. These decisions influence such dimensions as: how scarce resources are expended; the types of crimes addressed; the communities and populations who are served; whether and how justice is achieved; how, if at all, victims are included in processing decisions; who is arrested, detained, sentenced, and incarcerated; who receives treatment; and which policies and programs will be supported. In short, decision making increasingly stands at the heart of everyday practice and ultimately determines the effectiveness of the system as a whole (Walker, 1992).

Even so, a critical problem remains—there has been no systematic or unifying attempt to document the quality of decisions throughout the criminal justice system, and there has been limited research on the range of decision-making errors that undermine appropriate and effective decision making. Consider, for example, the fact that most research on law enforcement focuses on arrest, not how officers treat people, even though "how the police treat people generally, and how the treat minorities in particular, appears to have a more profound impact on citizens' attitudes about the police and their willingness to cooperate than do police decisions to stop or arrest them" (Forst, 2004, p. 103). Studies of this issue would require examining how police are supposed to treat individuals, the judgment calls they make on a case-by-case basis, and the reasons why they fail to follow stated protocols or make effective decisions. Information from such studies could be used by policymakers and officials to hold the police accountable, to identify ways to improve officers' decision making, and, ultimately, to improve citizens' willingness to cooperate with the police. At present, however, few jurisdictions systematically collect the data necessary to monitor such decision making, or therefore, to make improvements in the quality of officers' everyday decisions.

To be certain, some studies on decision making by criminal justice system actors, and in particular the discretionary decisions made by law enforcement officers, prosecutors, and judges, exist. Yet, the bulk of this literature focuses primarily on the "problem of discretion" (Walker, 1993, p. 4) and how efforts to control or minimize discretion can have unintended effects, including the displacement of discretion from one part of the system to another, as has occurred under many sentencing guideline efforts (Miethe, 1987). By and large, this literature does not define what constitutes an appropriate or effective decision by any given criminal justice system actor and it typically focuses on a limited set of actors (e.g., law enforcement officers and prosecutors). Such oversights are notable because the success of any organization, program, or policy rests on the shoulders of those charged with implementing core activities and services (Rossi et al., 2004). Ultimately, effective implementation requires that these individuals make appropriate and effective decisions—that is, that they follow established rules, policies, or guidelines, and where discretion is required, that they are guided by evidence-based practices, or at a minimum, not by inaccurate stereotypes or assumptions.

Performance monitoring efforts can sometimes lead to a focus on the quality of decision making by criminal justice system actors. More typically, however, they treat decision making as a black box and instead focus on whether various activities that should be undertaken actually are (Gaes, Camp, Nelson, & Saylor, 2004; Hatry, 2007; Mears, 2008). Put differently, performance monitoring—an empirically-based approach to monitoring program and policy implementation and associated outcomes—tends to ignore decision making. It certainly does not preclude such a focus; it simply does not in any direct way call attention to it.

A focus on evidence-based practices—that is, programs, policies, and activities shown empirically to be effective in achieving particular outcomes (Cullen, 2005; Farabee, 2005)—also does not directly lead to a focus on decision making. Rather, it leads to an emphasis on identifying and adopting effective approaches to improving outcomes. As with performance monitoring, one is not precluded from examining decision making, but neither is one led to a systematic analysis of the quality of decision making by diverse actors and how their decisions influence a range of outcomes.

In sum, while recent efforts to place performance monitoring and evidence-based practice at the forefront of criminal justice policy are laudable, they fail to capitalize on a critical area in which improvements throughout the criminal justice system might be made—namely, the quality of decision making made by diverse system actors. This article argues that a systematic, empirical focus on decision making constitutes a critical supplement to performance monitoring and evidence-based practices, which are necessary but not sufficient tools for increasing the efficiency and effectiveness of the system. In addition, a focus on decision making offers a unique lens through which to identify those domains along which performance monitoring efforts could be most usefully directed. This issue is especially important given that monitoring can be costly, time-consuming, and unhelpful if focused on dimensions of performance that are not relevant (Logan, 1993; Rossi et al., 2004).

Sometimes insights can be gained about a phenomenon by looking away from it or by viewing it through a nontraditional perspective, the equivalent of employing a new paradigm by which to revisit topics of traditional interest (Kuhn, 1970). This article suggests that looking at parallels between decision making in the medical establishment and the criminal justice system can generate original insights, while also reinforcing some existing views about how to improve criminal justice practice. The focus of medicine is, of course, fundamentally different from that of criminal justice. Physicians seek to prevent and cure disease, whereas criminal justice practitioners and policymakers seek to prevent crime while achieving, through various approaches to sanctioning, the elusive goal of "justice." Nonetheless, important parallels exist, not least of which is the fact that medical and criminal justice systems struggle to process large numbers of cases while also providing the best decisions appropriate to individual cases.

Building off of these observations, this article examines a range of "cognitive errors" that undermine physicians' diagnoses and treatments, and then identifies parallels to and lessons for criminal justice. The analysis here highlights that systems-level factors are likely to contribute not only to specific errors but also to an accumulation of errors, many of which may amplify one another. In addition, it points to the utility both of applying performance monitoring to the entire criminal justice system, as compared with the traditional practice of single-stage performance monitoring, and of focusing particular attention on critical decision-making points throughout the system and how decisions made by policymakers, officials, and practitioners could be improved.

Other benefits exist as well. Applying a decision-making framework to criminal justice system operations can help in identifying how and why some patterns, such as disproportionate minority confinement, exist. It can contribute to understanding why one category of decision-making errors—errors of justice (e.g., the conviction of an innocent person)—arises (Forst, 2004). In addition, and not least, it highlights an important gap in current attempts by criminal justice systems to be more accountable, efficient, and effective (Gaes et al., 2004).

The article begins first by discussing parallels between the medical and criminal justice systems and why comparisons of the two are instructive. In so doing, it emphasizes that the focus is on decision making, not the application of a "medical model" (MacNamara, 1977) to criminal justice. The article then examines and illustrates specific decision-making errors and emphasizes the particular salience of system-level considerations to understanding the causes and impacts of such errors. Drawing on these discussions, the article explores at length their implications for criminal justice practice and policy, and in particular, the lessons for criminal justice policymakers, officials, practitioners, and researchers.

Parallels Between Medicine and Criminal Justice

At first blush, it is not necessarily evident that a focus on medicine—and in particular, the medical system's approach to diagnosis and treatment—has much to offer efforts to understand and improve criminal justice. That impression largely derives from the fact that medical practice targets a different problem. In reality, however, important parallels exist that are notable in their own right and also illustrate the centrality of decision making and systems to efficient and effective achievement of such societal goals as the production of more health and less crime.

First, in both medicine and criminal justice, diagnoses of various types constitute a central feature of everyday practice. Physicians attempt to diagnose whether certain diseases are present and then prescribe the appropriate treatment for the diagnosis. Similarly, policymakers must determine when crimes of various types constitute a sufficient problem to warrant special treatment, and criminal justice practitioners must develop sanctions and treatments for particular offenders or types of crimes. More generally, criminal justice practitioners must make a plethora of decisions on a daily basis, many of which are critical to the operations of the justice system even if they do not directly relate to accurate identification, sanctioning, and treatment of offenders. The police, for example, must routinely make decisions about how to respond to 911 calls and which crimes or calls receive more attention than others. Errors in judgment in such cases can, of course, have significant impacts for victims, offenders, communities, and more generally, the effective allocation of law enforcement efforts (Forst, 2004).

Second, the accuracy of diagnosis and treatment are paramount in both systems. In medicine, misdiagnosis can lead to mistreatment or no treatment, and given a correct diagnosis, mistreatment can lead to wasted resources and a failure to cure the disease. Notably, studies of medical diagnosis and treatment indicate that the "majority of errors are due to flaws in physician thinking" and that in situations where misdiagnoses caused "serious harm to patients," approximately "80 percent could be accounted for by a cascade of cognitive errors" (Groopman, 2007, p. 24). In criminal justice, misdiagnosis and mistreatment can have comparable impacts. For example, a failure to recognize the emergence of a gang problem can lead to a failure to implement strategies to combat the problem. In the event of accurate recognition of a gang problem, mistreatment—such as the imposition of strategies that do not actually address the specific causes of the problem—can needlessly expend scarce resources while failing to reduce it. When such a failure is visible to the public, the damage is compounded by the public's diminished faith in the competence and legitimacy of the criminal justice system. In short, in medicine and criminal justice, diagnostic and treatment errors, or more generally, cognitive errors that influence clinical decision making, are important because they lead to inefficiency and ineffectiveness, as well as, in the case of criminal justice, miscarriages of justice (Forst, 2004).

It should be emphasized that a focus on accurate diagnosis and treatment need not imply a "medical model" approach to criminal justice practice or crime reduction efforts. This model came into ascendance in corrections in the 1950s; the central view was that, essentially, offenders were "sick," that criminal behavior was symptomatic of their illness, and that accurate diagnosis and rehabilitative treatment could cure it (MacNamara, 1977, pp. 439–440). A variant of that approach arguably is embodied in the findings of recent meta-analyses, which show that effective offender-based programs must accurately take account of the specific criminogenic factors that give rise to criminal behavior for specific individuals (Cullen & Gendreau, 2000). Regardless, the goal here is not to evaluate the merits or pitfalls of such a model. Rather, this article seeks lessons from the medical system about ways in which problem-identification and problem-solving efforts in criminal justice might be improved. The "diagnosis" and "treatment" terminology simply provides a straight-forward terminology for capturing the idea that effective criminal justice operations, including efforts to prevent and reduce crime as well as to achieve justice, require effective decision making about a range of problems and solutions, whether the focus be on individuals, families, communities, or states.

Third, errors in judgment in criminal justice arguably are just as important as in medicine. The typical view is that accurate decisions are especially critical in medicine because they can involve life and death. Criminal justice decisions, however, ultimately involve such dimensions as justice and freedom and the lives of potential victims and communities where crime occurs. In short, the stakes may differ in kind but not necessarily in importance.

Fourth, individualized decision making in both medicine and criminal justice is considered the ideal, and yet is frequently precluded because of limited time, resources, and in no small part, the structure and administration of the two systems. This issue assumes particular importance for these systems because, in recent decades, each has had to confront dramatic increases in the numbers of cases they process (Forst, 2004; Groopman, 2007).

Fifth, medicine and criminal justice have been subject to calls for "evidence-based" practice, but both rely to a substantial degree on practices that lack an empirical basis. To illustrate, in obstetrics, an area of medicine the public might typically view as strongly evidence-based because it deals with life-and-death decision making, practice has not been consistently guided by research. Indeed, as Gawande (2007, p. 188) recently noted, "in a 1978 ranking of medical specialties according to their use of hard evidence from randomized clinical trials, obstetrics came in last." More generally, some assessments indicate that the vast bulk of medical treatment lacks a rigorous research foundation—for example, citing Millenson's (1997) discussion of a 1983 U.S. Office of Technology Assessment study, Sherman (2003, p. 7) noted, "that 85 percent of everyday medical treatments had never been scientifically tested." Similar critiques have been raised about many of the most prominent criminal justice policy initiatives that have emerged over the years (Farabee, 2005). Notably, for example, there is no body of experimental research that quantifies the precise relationship between incarceration and specific or general deterrence (Forst, 2004, p. 161). Equally notable is the fact that one of the most important goals of criminal justice—retribution—cannot be assessed through experiments (p. 166).

Sixth, in addition to calls for evidence-based practice, there have been calls for increased performance monitoring and accountability in medicine and criminal justice, yet systemwide measurement of actual practices and outcomes has been limited or inconsistent in both fields, though exceptions clearly exist. Consider a typical visit to a physician. Are all symptoms recorded? Is there any recording of possible differential diagnoses? Any documentation of whether the patient adhered to the treatment? Or, perhaps most importantly, any documentation of the outcome? In each instance, the answer typically is "no" (Gawande, 2007).[1] What about the critical issue of whether patients adhere to treatment protocols? Patients may not stick to treatment plans, and in such cases treatment success diminishes (p. 220). The issue, again, is that in medicine, as with the criminal justice system, systematic performance monitoring of relevant practices and outcomes is neither regular nor uniform (Bazemore, 2006; Behn, 2003; Gaes et al., 2004; Hatry, 2007; Logan, 1993). As but one example, federal and state governments enact numerous laws bearing on criminal justice policy or practice, but empirical examinations of the application and impact of these laws are rare.

Errors in Decision Making in the Medical System: Lessons for Criminal Justice Practice

This article's contention is that, as in medicine, monitoring and assessment of decision making in criminal justice can improve the system's efficiency and effectiveness.[2] Misdiagnosis of crime problems and their solutions, for example, can lead to investments in strategies that are not needed, may not work, and could be harmful. The main challenge lies in identifying which errors are most common and harmful or would improve the system most if corrected.

Table 1 reflects the distillation of a diverse range of errors in diagnostic decision making made by physicians, and as this article argues, by their criminal justice system counterparts—including policymakers, law enforcement, probation and correctional officers, judges, prosecutors, defenders, and more generally, practitioners. The discussion draws heavily on the errors identified in Groopman's (2007) recent review and investigation of the topic,[3] with a focus on those that may be especially common or salient. Below, the article discusses each of the errors, and in each instance, provide criminal justice examples to illustrate the utility of a decision-making error framework to improving system practices and policies.

Clinical Algorithm Error

This type of error arguably is most prevalent and most critical to diagnosis because it arises from the default mode of diagnosis used by physicians. For example, doctors typically are trained in the use of Bayesian analysis, an approach that may lead to misdiagnosis for atypical or unusual cases (Groopman, 2007, p. 5). Such errors are especially likely for problems and situations where there is little to no precedent or where little time exists to work systematically through such an analysis.[4] Consider, for example, that "studies show that while it usually takes twenty to thirty minutes in a didactic exercise for the senior doctor and students to arrive at a working diagnosis, an expert clinician typically forms a notion of what is wrong with the patient within twenty seconds" (p. 34). Indeed, "physicians begin to think of diagnoses from the first moment they meet a patient" (p. 35). To do so, they rely on "heuristics," or shortcuts. The use of heuristics occurs "largely without any conscious analysis," "draws most heavily on the doctor's visual appraisal of the patient," and "does not occur by a linear, step-by-step combining of cues" (p. 35). For these reasons, heuristics can be essential for accurate diagnosis, especially in emergency situations where there is little time for careful assessment to help make sense of a large amount of data, but they can also lead to misdiagnosis if the assumptions underlying them are incorrect or do not apply to a given case.[5]

The use of heuristics in criminal justice decision making, as in medicine, is essential for managing unwieldy case loads and large amounts of information.

Table 1 Types of Errors in Decision Making in Medical Practice

- *Clinical algorithm error.* Mode of diagnosis may lead to misdiagnosis for unusual cases. Two key types: Bayesian error may arise when there is insufficient time or information for a Bayesian analysis; heuristics error may arise when emphasis is placed on certain patterns over relevant ones.
- *Initial impression error.* Initial impressions or intuitions may be incorrect; a variant is confirmation bias error (a physician anchors on to a diagnosis and "cherry picks" supporting symptoms).
- *Availability error.* What is most available in a physician's mind may dictate diagnosis; a variant is "last bad experience" error (exploration of unlikely diagnoses to avoid more bad experiences).
- *Patient attribution error.* Preconceptions about patients and their attributes may cause misdiagnosis by leading to selective emphasis of symptoms and interpretations that fit with the preconceptions.
- *Disease prototype error.* Physicians may expect a disease to emerge only in certain "prototypical" cases, leading to misdiagnosis in atypical cases.
- *Satisfaction of search error.* Occurs when physicians stop searching for a diagnosis once they find one that seems to more or less fit the symptoms, even if the diagnosis is incorrect.
- *Inexperience or clinical intuition error.* Due to inexperience or limited clinical intuitiveness a physician may be unable to discern when a situation calls for a unique diagnosis.
- *Specialist error.* Given their narrow focus, specialists may misdiagnose "run-of-the-mill" cases.
- *Affective error.* Occurs when physicians prefer diagnoses more favorable than less appealing ones.
- *Inattention error.* Due to seeing high volumes of similar cases, physicians may make "easy" diagnoses, thus misdiagnosing cases where symptoms indicate that other diseases are present. Three key types: listening error may arise when physicians fail to listen carefully to patients; committed non-listening error may arise when physicians feel that they have exhausted all possible explanations or have accurately diagnosed an illness; reliance on technology error may arise when rote filling in of information reduces the discerning of connections necessary for making a correct diagnosis.
- *Action bias error.* Occurs when physicians feel compelled "toward action rather than inaction" and thus pursue any diagnosis, even a made-up one.
- *Framing (ripple effect) error.* Errors in initial diagnosis may cause ripple effects of misdiagnosis because care occurs within a system, and initial framing of cases may dictate subsequent diagnosis.
- *Unproven diagnosis and treatment error.* Certain diagnoses and treatments may lack much if any rigorous empirical support and yet be used. Two key types: common treatment error may arise when certain treatments are commonly used and yet lack a solid empirical (scientific) foundation; idiosyncratic treatment error may arise when physicians believe in idiosyncratic diagnoses and treatments. Such errors may stem from uncertainty error, which occurs when physicians disregard the amount of uncertainty concerning the evidence for a specific diagnosis or treatment.

Source: Adapted from Groopman (2007).

The potential for the greatest harm with their use occurs when they are based on incorrect assumptions or applied in nonemergency settings. The courtroom illustrates one such setting. Recent research has suggested that juries may associate a constellation of characteristics—race, age, gender, and social class—with criminality (Chiricos, Welch, & Gertz, 2004; Reiman, 2000). These constellations of individual characteristics become heuristics and may be used for the purpose of assigning guilt. Sentencing research, for example, has shown that specific subgroups, especially young, Black males, face more severe sanctioning after controlling for such legally relevant factors as the type and severity of offending and prior record (Steffensmeier, Ulmer, & Kramer, 1998). In these instances, heuristics may contribute not only to conviction of innocent individuals but also to the failure to convict guilty individuals as well as, more generally, to unfair sentencing practices (Forst, 2004; Paternoster, Brame, Bacon, & Ditchfield, 2004).

Just as with medicine, there arise occasions in criminal justice in which decision making demands the use of heuristics. For example, police on patrol routinely confront the challenge of devising an immediate course of action in the face of incomplete information. The critical question is whether they use appropriate or accurate heuristics and operate with an awareness of the limitations of them. Here, paralleling the courtroom example above, perhaps the most prominent example of a heuristic of questionable appropriateness and accuracy is racial profiling. As Warren, Devey, Smith, Zingraff, and Mason (2006, p. 715) recently observed, "racial categorization and the associated stereotypes of dangerousness and criminality may influence [police] determination of who seems suspicious or otherwise worthy of special attention." The basic problem, one that extends to other types of profiling (e.g., age, sex), lies in the fact that the stereotypes may have no empirical foundation in a given place or time.

Before proceeding, a note about theory bears mention. The traditional argument is that theories provide a foothold for sifting through the innumerable possibilities that might account for a particular phenomenon (Merton, 1968). A counter-argument, however, is that rigid adherence to particular theories blinds researchers or practitioners to other important explanations of the phenomenon (Mears & Stafford, 2002). In practice, practitioners likely tend in one direction or the other. Some practitioners may, for example, hew consistently toward a particular theory about crime or how certain types of cases can most effectively be handled, while others may be more agnostic and tend to "let the facts speak for themselves," following, for example, "gut instincts." This difference is problematic for everyday criminal justice practice because, to the extent a given theory or "gut instinct" is incorrect, it contributes to systematic decision-making mistakes and to inconsistency in how cases are processed.

Initial Impression Error

When physicians diagnose a patient based only on their initial impressions or intuitions, they may misdiagnose patients some unknown percentage of the time (Groopman, 2007, p. 9). A variant of this error is confirmation bias error, wherein the physician anchors on to a particular diagnosis and then "cherry picks" those symptoms that support it while downplaying, ignoring, or distorting the significance of other clinically relevant symptoms (p. 65). The bias results from focusing only on those symptoms or interpretations that "confirm" the initial diagnosis. This type of error is more likely to occur where little time exists for reflection, as occurs in emergency rooms (p. 75).

Initial impression error can occur at many points throughout the criminal justice system. As the racial profiling example conveys, it can occur when a police officer uses a heuristic (e.g., a stereotype about the characteristics of offenders) that predisposes him or her to having a particular type of first impression (e.g., young, Black males likely committed a given crime). In this situation, the heuristic dictates the initial impression, which in turn can reinforce to the officer the putative validity of the heuristic.

Consider the decision making at a much later stage in the criminal justice system—the initial meeting between a parole officer and a newly released parolee. This discussion typically involves a conversation directed by the supervising officer designed to fill in gaps in the case file material to determine the most appropriate reentry plan. Imagine such a conversation between the officer and a new parolee with a history of violence but no documented drug problem. The officer's initial impression may be that drug use is not an issue, especially if he or she assumes that any such issue would surface in case file materials. The parolee may be asked whether he has a drug problem and report some infrequent experimentation but no chronic or serious use of illegal drugs. Based on this exchange, the parole officer's initial impression is reinforced and he or she then may turn their attention to other criminogenic risk factors. Observe, however, that drug problems will not necessarily be documented and that even if drug screen (e.g., urine analysis) results were available, the parolee could have passed by chance (Peters et al., 2000; Wish, Rinehart, Hsu, & Artigiani, 2006).

Conversely, a scenario could emerge in which a newly released parolee celebrates his first night home drinking with friends. Upon reporting to the parole office the next day, the parole officer may smell alcohol and form an initial impression that this individual has a drinking problem. Subsequent supervision and treatment efforts may then be directed at keeping the parolee sober, perhaps at the expense of targeting other criminogenic needs that might, if addressed, be more likely to contribute to desistance. When parole boards or other release-granting authorities mandate substance abuse counseling for offenders with any drug-related conviction offenses, such decisions may become more likely.

First impressions can, in short, be highly consequential, especially when made by individuals whose impressions carry substantial weight. The focus on parole officers in the example above is illustrative. A recent study found, for example, that these "officers and not prosecutors play the most significant role in revocation decisions" (Rodriguez & Webb, 2007, p. 23). Given the large increase in probation and parole populations nationally (Travis, 2005), any decisions, including mistakes in judgment, made by community supervision officers can have substantial impacts on overall system operations and effectiveness.

Availability Error

Availability error occurs when "what is most available in your mind strongly colors your thinking about a new case that has some similarities [and leads] you to ignore important differences and come to an incorrect diagnosis" (Groopman, 2007, p. 188). The error results from "the tendency to judge the likelihood of an event by the ease with which relevant examples come to mind" (p. 64). In such cases, a physician is more likely to see a case as being like the ones that preceded it, thus imposing a diagnosis that may not be appropriate. A variant is "last bad experience" error in which, because of a problematic experience involving a recent patient, one that perhaps led to a lawsuit, a physician considers illnesses that are not likely, and in so doing, may miss the correct, if more mundane, diagnosis (p. 189).

Within criminal justice, availability error can emerge in different guises. Prosecutors, for example, who work in areas where drug crimes occur frequently, may tend to assume that every offender they see is a drug dealer or user and then prosecute cases accordingly. Prosecutors may differ, of course, in how they believe such cases should be prosecuted. Regardless, the mistake lies in assuming that a characteristic found in prior cases applies to a new case and in applying an approach to the case that is premised on the presence of that characteristic.

A different type of example is reflected in policy fads. Although new policies may be adopted for many reasons, when a policy is widely and suddenly adopted, one reason may be a type of availability error in which policymakers draw immediate implications from a study reported in the media. Sherman and Berk's (1984) randomized experiment on police response to domestic violence in Minneapolis is illustrative. The results of the study were widely publicized and supported the notion that arresting domestic violence perpetrators has a significant specific deterrent effect. Within six years, fifteen states adopted mandatory arrest laws (Sherman, Smith, Schmidt, & Rogan, 1992), even though the authors had clearly indicated that further research on mandatory arrest was needed. The problem, which surfaced in subsequent studies, was that later research produced equivocal results (Schmidt & Sherman, 1996). In this example, a widely available and discussed study may have disproportionately colored policymaker thinking about the appropriate way to address domestic violence, leading, on the one hand, to a special emphasis on mandatory arrest laws and to a failure to consider carefully the wider range of strategies for reducing domestic violence (Mears, 2003; Roberts, 2002).

An example of the variant—"last bad experience" error—is reflected in the so-called "Willie Horton" effect. Horton was a convicted felon, incarcerated for murder, who raped a woman while on furlough. Governor Michael Dukakis, who campaigned in the 1988 Presidential race, supported this program. His opponent ran political advertisements criticizing Governor Dukakis for his views, contributing in part to a political climate in which "get tough" views toward crime were seen as needed (Hurwitz & Peffley, 2005). Such cases may drive policymakers to focus on the "last bad case" and create laws that assume the widespread prevalence of such cases. This type of error is likely to be especially pernicious if coupled with action bias error, the tendency, as discussed below, to default to taking action rather than doing nothing.

Patient Attribution Error

When physicians work from incorrect preconceptions or stereotypes about patients, misdiagnosis may result from selectively emphasizing symptoms and interpretations that fit with the preconceptions (Groopman, 2007, pp. 43-44). This error arises as when, for example, physicians allow certain impressions—such as that a person is mentally disordered (p. 39), looks healthy (p. 43), has a drug problem (p. 44), or is homeless (p. 55)—to govern their diagnoses. In such cases, physicians' preconceptions may lead them to attribute certain symptoms to a diagnosis that they associate with people who they believe fit a particular profile (e.g., homeless people, drug addicts); at the same time, such preconceptions may lead them to overlook, ignore, or disvalue certain clinically relevant symptoms. A similar phenomenon, in which individuals generalize on the basis of stereotypes, has been explored more generally in psychology (Gladwell, 2005).

Attribution errors likely contribute to heuristics and initial impression errors in criminal justice. Regardless, one type of such error occurs in jury decision making. To illustrate, in her study of jurors, Visher (1987, pp. 13-14) found that "the defendant's educational level [affected jurors'] judgments of defendant guilt net of evidential factors," noting that the effect may have stemmed from "jurors' attributions about the defendant's character and his propensity for criminal activity." As with various courtroom actors, jurors clearly may operate from certain assumptions about what the characteristics of a given person indicate (e.g., they may assume that educated people do not commit crimes), which in turn colors their decision making.

Attribution error is most common when an individual fits a negative stereotype (Groopman, 2007, p. 44). To illustrate, a correctional intake officer may encounter an indigent, inarticulate prisoner with a history of drug abuse who seems to be experiencing delirium tremors, and assume that the prisoner is experiencing the effects of withdrawal. Such an interpretation may fit with their attribution of the individual as a drug addict. This assumption, however, may preclude consideration of other explanations—such as diabetes or dyskinesia—for the prisoner's behavior. Such decision-making mistakes, involving medical-related issues, may arise frequently in criminal justice, given the marked prevalence of mental and physical illnesses among correctional populations (Lurigio & Swartz, 2002; Mears, 2004; Travis, 2005).

Disease Prototype Error

Whereas patient attribution error stems from an initial assumption about an individual, this type of error stems from adhering too strongly to an assumed prototype about a given disease and then ascertaining whether the individual fits that prototype. That is, when physicians expect a disease to emerge only in certain cases—the "prototype" for the disease—they may "fail to consider possibilities that contradict the prototype and thus attribute the symptoms to the wrong cause" (Groopman, 2007, p. 44). The prototype may, for example, be that only certain populations get certain diseases, and so atypical cases (e.g., the rare time when someone unlikely to have a certain disease actually gets it) go misdiagnosed. It is the equivalent of failing to recognize that statistically significant risk factors reflect differential, not absolute, probabilities of an outcome occurring.

A focus on police resource allocation decisions highlights how prototype errors can arise in criminal justice practice. Consider drug interdiction efforts, which typically are directed toward "drug-ridden" communities where drug dealers and users are assumed to congregate. Such a focus is a logical result of problem analysis and "intelligence-led" policing

(Ratcliffe, 2003). A lack of enforcement in atypical neighborhoods, and the prototype error it represents, however, has significant implications not only for unchecked criminal activity but also for concerns about equal protection and treatment.

A different type of prototype error can be seen in what has been argued to be the criminal justice system's disproportionate emphasis on male offending (Bloom, Owen, & Covington, 2004). Despite the closing of the gender gap for violent offending (Heimer, 2000; Steffensmeier, Zhong, Ackerman, Schwartz, & Agha, 2006; U.S. Bureau of Justice Statistics, 1999), violence is still an overwhelmingly male phenomenon. Violent offending by females is thus still viewed as the atypical case. The failure, however, to consider the possibility of violent and aggressive females, who unquestionably exist (Baskin & Sommers, 1997; Heimer, 2000; Reisig, Holtfreter, & Morash, 2006), has important implications. Most notably, it can lead to a failure to consistently sanction violent offenders, regardless of sex, and to fail to apply sanctions and services most appropriate to violent female offenders.

Satisfaction of Search Error

Diagnostic errors may arise when doctors stop searching for a diagnosis once they find one that seems to more or less fit the symptoms (Groopman, 2007, p. 169). This error may be especially common in high-volume situations because there is minimal time to do more than apply a heuristic in both the generation and interpretation of data (p. 185).

In the criminal justice system, police typically face considerable pressure to solve cases quickly. After a call for service, police seek to identify suspects as soon as possible. In turn, this emphasis, especially in high-profile cases, can lead, on the one hand, to focusing primarily on identifying evidence supporting law enforcement's selection of suspects, and on the other hand, to neglecting consideration of other suspects. As Forst (2004, p. 70) has noted: "For high visibility unsolved cases, the pressure on the police to find a pool of candidate suspects, sometimes starting with police modus operandi (MO) files and vague offender descriptions, and deal aggressively with them can be especially high." Of course, case processing pressures also confront court, community supervision, and prison system personnel and can lead to analogous errors. Consider, for example, jury deliberations—jurors may seek to come to a speedy verdict so as to return more quickly to their everyday work responsibilities, and in the course of deliberating, give precedence to information that enables a rapid decision (see, generally, Casper, Benedict, & Perry, 1989; Devine, Clayton, Dunford, Seying, & Pryce, 2001).

A different type of satisfaction of search error can arise when criminal justice practitioners seek to expeditiously arrive at a sanctioning and treatment plan. Given substantial case loads, practitioners may prioritize the most conspicuous or seemingly obvious causal factor, such as drug use, that they believe contributes to the offender's behavior. In such cases, even though an offender's behavior likely arises from multiple factors, only one factor is apt to be given much attention. The emphasis on drugs is, in fact, illustrative. Drug courts have proliferated in recent decades (Nolan, 2003), and their very focus on drug use and addiction arguably creates a structured incentive to give greater attention to drug problems—whose causal relationship to criminal behavior remains subject to debate (White & Gorman, 2000)—than, say, employment, family, housing, or mental health problems. Most drug courts operate under a model that calls for comprehensive assessment and services, but in practice, in a context of large case loads and minimal resources, priority may be given primarily if not exclusively to drug treatment. There is, of course, no error if the drug use is the sole or primary cause of an offender's behavior.

Inexperience or Clinical Intuition Error

Misdiagnosis may result when a physician, whether due to inexperience or limited clinical intuition, is unable to discern when a case calls for a unique diagnosis, or when certain symptoms, whether in isolation or in the presence of others or unique conditions, indicate a unique case (Groopman, 2007, p. 20). Inexperience error is not particular to medicine, and indeed, it arguably is more pervasive and problematic in criminal justice because of the diverse types of needs among correctional populations, high rates of practitioner turnover, underresourcing of programs and services, and substantial correctional population growth (Lynch & Sabol, 2001; Petersilia, 2003; Travis, 2005).

Staff turnover in a context of dramatic increases in offenders under some form of correctional supervision almost necessarily leads to inexperience error.[6] Conover's (2000) account of his year working at Sing Sing prison in New York provides a colorful illustration of the repeated mistakes first-year officers, "new jacks," make—such as failing to appreciate the specific warning signs of a violent outburst from an inmate or of a riot—which in turn can lead to increased risk of harm to inmates and officers alike.

As with medical practice, criminal justice administrative structures and cultures can contribute to inexperience and clinical intuition errors. For example, a failure to train prison officers how to recognize signs of mental illness can result in officers interpreting certain behaviors as evidence of a propensity to be violent rather than, say, evidence of schizophrenia. More generally, large case loads and concerns about such issues as consistency can lead to an increased reliance on uniform methods of handling cases, methods that may work well in "average" but not atypical cases. Indeed, one of the more frequent complaints about mandatory sentencing guidelines, which typically have been enacted to reduce inconsistency in sentencing, is that they preclude consideration of unique dimensions of particular cases that bear on appropriate sentencing, service, and treatment decisions (Forer, 1994). Similar complaints have been leveled against systems that rely heavily on actuarially-based risk assessment instruments to the exclusion of clinical judgment (Cullen & Gendreau, 2000).

Specialist Error

Medical specialists may—because of their emphasis on narrow categories of diseases—accurately diagnose diseases for diseases that fall under their purview but may be prone to misdiagnose "run-of-the-mill cases." The reason, as Groopman (2007, p. 98) has noted, is that "people used to doing complicated things usually do complicated things in simple situations—for example, ordering tests or X-rays when waiting a few days might suffice—thus overtreating people with simple illnesses and overlooking the clues about other problems that might have brought the patient to the doctor."

Specialist error can occur in criminal justice as well. For example, specialists may "see" only the symptoms or problems related to their area of focus: drug treatment providers may "see" only drug problems, mental health providers may "see" only mental illness, and so on, when in fact other factors may contribute to an individual's offending patterns. As with satisfaction of search error, addressing one criminogenic factor will likely be ineffective if other factors are ignored (Cullen & Gendreau, 2000; MacKenzie, 2006). That is true not only at the individual level but at a systems level. To illustrate, consider the possibility that gang and prison management experts may, in some cases, be prone to see more of a problem than exists. "Get tough" responses to immigrant crime have, for example, been spurred in no small part by law enforcement attention to immigrant gangs. The presence, though, of immigrant gangs, or even an influx of such gangs, does not mean that immigrants, legal or illegal, are increasingly committing crime or that increased immigration causes increased crime (Butcher & Piehl, 1998; Freilich & Newman, 2007; Mears, 2001).

One related consequence of specialist error is overdiagnosis and mistreatment. One positive drug screen may, for example, lead a drug treatment provider to immediately recommend increased supervision and substance abuse counseling. A dysthymic period affects most everyone at some point, but to a mental health counselor it may resemble symptoms antecedent to major depression or disordered behavior, and accordingly, lead the counselor to recommend treatment. In both cases, the "proactive" response may be appropriate "on average" but nonetheless be inappropriate in a large number of cases.

Affective Error

This type of error may arise when physicians prefer diagnoses that are more favorable than "the less appealing alternatives" (Groopman, 2007, p. 47). Put differently, physicians, like many people, are subject to a tendency to let hope and optimism dictate their judgment—"[physicians] lull themselves into thinking that what we wish for will occur when we get the first inkling, however fragmentary, that our wish may come true. In short, [physicians] value too highly information that fulfills [their] desires" (p. 47).

As with the other types of errors, examples of this type of error can be found in criminal justice. Consider court-appointed defense attorneys, who frequently receive limited compensation for their work with indigent defendants. In such cases, some attorneys may fail to exercise due diligence in defending their client and do so in part based on a hope that an outcome that they feel is certain will not in fact occur. Such errors may be especially likely in situations where pressure to quickly plea bargain cases allows limited time or support for exploring a full range of legal strategies. Like doctors, defense attorneys also may be influenced by their attachments to defendants, and allow such attachments to affect the legal strategies they pursue.

Different types of affective errors may arise in criminal justice. For example, prosecutors may pursue charges that they feel are not necessarily the appropriate ones but that they believe will sit better with the public. In addition, with some crimes, such as rape, systematic mislabeling, or vague labeling, of the offense may happen out of a desire to protect victims (e.g., a rape may be classified as an "aggravated assault"). Such labeling, however, may lead to misclassification by the criminal justice system.

Inattention Error

Physicians may become prone to making "easy" diagnoses, in turn misdiagnosing cases where clinically relevant symptoms actually indicate that different diseases are present (Groopman, 2007, p. 77). At least three types of inattention error exist, each of which in part stems from pressures in high case load settings to diagnose and treat cases quickly. The first is listening error, wherein physicians fail to listen carefully to patients, or to elicit and respond thoughtfully to clinically relevant information from patients (p. 17). The second, a variant, is committed non-listening error, wherein physicians cease listening to a patient, especially when they feel that all possible explanations have been exhausted, that they have actually accurately diagnosed an illness, or simply do not like the patient (pp. 25,125).[7] The error lies in the fact that, in such situations, physicians may fail to hear a relevant clinical symptom or have not actually exhausted all possibilities. It is more likely in situations where physicians are unaware of their limitations, too strongly assume that their diagnoses are correct, that it is not possible to diagnose a problem, or lack the experience or knowledge to diagnose an illness, the latter being an especially acute problem if the physician does not recognize his or her limitations (p. 125).[8] The third type arises from reliance on technology, such as rote filling in information on templates, which may lead to misdiagnosis through a reduced likelihood of discerning or intuiting connections from clinically relevant information that would lead to a correct diagnosis (Groopman, 2007, p. 99). Under these circumstances, "the doctor's mind is set on filling in the blanks on the template," and thus "is less likely to engage in open ended questioning, and may be deterred from focusing on data that do not fit on the template" (p. 99).

Such errors are likely in criminal justice, where individualized sanctioning and treatment frequently are promoted, but where large case loads largely preclude such individualized and careful attention. Consider, for example, that "85 percent of all U.S. parolees are supervised on regular caseloads, averaging 66 cases to one parole officer, in which they are seen (face to face) less than twice per month" (Petersilia, 2003, p. 84). Large case loads would, on the face of it, appear to preclude officers from providing more than superficial monitoring or assessment of parolee behavior. In addition, excessive case loads might well contribute to institutionalize officer inattention and related errors, leading officers to fail to identify when a particular individual may be especially prone to recidivate.

Risk assessments increasingly are called for and used in criminal justice settings, and their major advantage is that they can create more objective assessments about individual offenders (Cullen & Gendreau, 2000). Such approaches, however, also may lead to situations in which risk assessors miss what might otherwise be obvious problems for a given offender. For example, a constellation of risk factors might be due to a problematic family situation (Agnew, 2005), yet the risk assessment might not draw attention to that fact because of the emphasis on counting a range of specific factors to create an overall risk score.

Action bias Error

When doctors feel compelled "toward action rather than inaction" and thus pursue any diagnosis—out of overconfidence or "when a physician is desperate and gives in to the urge to 'do something'"—they may misdiagnose patients (Groopman, 2007, p. 169). Physicians also may feel compelled to provide any diagnosis, or indeed, simply to make one up, rather than acknowledge that they do not know what illness a patient has (p. 160).

Policymakers appear to be especially prone to action bias, which results in ever-increasing numbers of new policies, few of which ever are evaluated and many of which not only are poorly implemented, but likely are ineffective. For example, in the wake of the murders of Polly Klaas in California and Meghan Kanka in New Jersey—both perpetrated by released offenders—the public pressured state legislatures to abolish parole (Petersilia, 1999). By 1999, fourteen states abolished parole release, and many more increased restrictions on release decisions. Although abolishing parole was a politically palatable response to public fear, many have argued that it led to an unnecessary and ineffective correctional practice that ultimately endangered rather than ensured public safety (Burke, 1995; Kuziemko, 2006; Petersilia, 1999).

Action bias error also occurs at the practitioner level. Criminal justice practitioners are required, by policy, practice, or specific rules, to automatically take action in certain cases. For example, if a parolee is even a few minutes late for their check-in, a parole officer might be required to document the fact that the parolee was late and to apply some type of sanction. Although such steps may make sense in some cases, it likely is unnecessary in many others.

Similarly, courtroom actors are subject to action bias error. Prosecutors may feel compelled to obtain more convictions and to do so quickly. In so doing, they give priority to their role as adversaries—acting in opposition to defense lawyers—rather than their role as fact finders. As noted by Forst (2004, p. 118): "Prosecutors err . . . when they play the role of adversary aiming for a high conviction rate rather than fact finder in pretrial disclosure proceedings." Finally, defendants accused of particularly heinous crimes may be subject to action bias error on the part of juries, who may feel a moral obligation to hold someone accountable (Hoiberg & Stires, 1973).

Framing (Ripple Effect) Error

A diagnosis may be incorrect, and because it "frames" the description of the patient, may have ripple effects by predetermining not only the initial but also all subsequent selection and interpretation of clinically relevant information (Groopman, 2007, pp. 3, 22). Incorrect framing of a case may lead subsequent physicians to think about the patient only through one frame and ignore other possible diagnoses (p. 22).

In criminal justice, some individuals may, from an early age, be cast as "offenders," and then the label follows them. "Sex offender," for example, conjures images of individuals who are sick psychopaths who never change and commit terrible acts. Yet, a wide range of offenses fits within that broad category. In addition, under many laws, initial labels have long-term repercussions. Regardless of the specific sex offense, for example, a "sex offender" will typically be subject to mandatory sentences and be required to have their address and personal information included on sex registries (Sample & Bray, 2003). Similarly, preconceptions about what causes a particular individual to offend (e.g., mental illness) may lead to long-term treatments and interventions, including supervision plans, that bear little relation to the true cause (e.g., low self-control) of the person's offending.

Framing error can operate at the systematic level as well. Farrington, Jolliffe, Loeber, Stouthamer-Loeber, and Kalb (2001) have highlighted the possibility in their focus on which individuals garner police attention, and by research on how probation officer reports and detention decisions influence conviction and sentencing decisions (Bridges & Steen, 1998; Sampson & Lauritsen, 1997). In the Farrington et al. (2001) study, the authors argued that parents' criminality might engender police and court bias in responding to the behavior of the parents' children. Put differently, the children of known criminal parents may be more likely to arouse police suspicion and interference, and their behavior may then be addressed more punitively by the courts. A large literature reveals an analogous framing error effect by place—residents in some areas may be given more intense police scrutiny, leading to disproportionately more arrests relative to areas with similar levels of offending (Ratcliffe, 2003).

Unproven Diagnosis and Treatment Error

Certain diagnoses and treatments may lack much if any rigorous empirical support and yet be used (Groopman, 2007, pp. 135, 206, 217).[9] Two variants exist. First, common diagnosis and treatment error occurs when certain diagnoses and treatments are commonly used and yet lack a solid empirical foundation (Groopman, 2007, p. 135). In pediatric cardiology, for example, much of daily practice consists of making up solutions "on the fly" (p. 135). Over time, physicians may come to believe certain treatments are the only and best ones, and thus fail to consider other potentially better interventions (pp. 137-140). This error also emerges when certain treatments are viewed as appropriate for all cases, even when no disease is present or when different approaches might be indicated. To illustrate, post-menopausal women frequently are encouraged to take estrogen even when there is no disease present—the goal is to prevent onset of heart disease and stroke—or when such treatment may not be appropriate for them (p. 218). Second, idiosyncratic diagnosis and treatment error occurs when physicians come to believe in certain diagnoses and the effectiveness of specific treatments even though both the diagnoses and treatments are unproven (pp. 206, 217). Pharmaceutical companies, for example, pressure physicians to write prescriptions for certain drugs even where use of the drug may be unwarranted and where the effectiveness, as well as the relative effectiveness of the drugs (as compared with other drugs), may be unknown or based on only a handful of studies (p. 206).[10]

Unproven treatment error appears highly prevalent in criminal justice, reflected in part in crime policy fads, such as the increased use of drug courts (Nolan, 2003) and supermax prisons (Mears & Watson, 2006). There also are trends in common treatment from one decade to the next—as noted above, parole once was popular and increasingly is less so (Travis, 2005). Examples of programs and policies that have been enacted without formal testing or evaluation are ubiquitous in criminal justice, and indeed, in many social policy arenas (Mears, 2007). Policies designed around the idea of selective incapacitation are illustrative. Beginning with the long-standing and well-replicated observation that a small group of chronic offenders is responsible for a large portion of all crime (Wolfgang, Figlio, & Sellin, 1972), the logical policy application was to identify and incapacitate that group of offenders in hopes of achieving substantial reductions in crime. The consequences of such policies, however, have been far from a realization of the original intent (Shichor, 1997) and have been undermined in no small part by the limited accuracy of many risk prediction instruments (Hart, Michie, & Cooke, 2007).

Unproven treatment error is also evident in attempts to transplant effective practices and policies from one implementation site to another, without sufficient consideration of how context influences effectiveness (Bardach, 2004; Heckman & Smith, 1995). To illustrate, in her discussion of the Greater Newark Safer Cities Initiative, which proved successful in reducing violent in Newark, New Jersey, McGloin (2005) emphasized the importance of a thorough, context-specific problem analysis, and noted that the effectiveness of the "pulling levers" strategy, central to the Initiative, stemmed from the three years of collaboration, regular meetings with all stakeholders, spatial mapping, and network analysis of Newark data.

In sum, many of the cognitive errors that lead to poor decision making in medicine have analogues in criminal justice decision making. Other types of errors exist that do not appear to have obvious parallels to criminal justice.[11] Ultimately, as is discussed below, what is needed is not only an index of errors that occur at various stages of the criminal justice system, but also identification of those that may be unique to any given stage.

Implications for Criminal Justice Policy, Practice, and Research

A systematic and comprehensive focus on decision-making errors provides a platform for improving the efficiency and effectiveness of the criminal justice system, especially if coupled with current performance monitoring efforts and a commitment to evidence-based practice. To this end, a number of implications arise from a focus on decision making. These implications provide a road map for policymakers, officials, practitioners, and researchers to take steps toward making improved decision making and monitoring a central feature of the criminal justice system, changes that in turn can increase the effectiveness of this system.

First, for any benefits to arise, research on the various types of decision-making errors is paramount. In particular, studies should be undertaken that assess the prevalence of different types of decision-making errors throughout all stages of the criminal justice system (e.g., enactment of criminal law by legislators, assignment of law enforcement to particular areas, arrest, detention, sentencing, incarceration, supervision, and treatment) and among all practitioner groups (e.g., judges, prosecutors, probation, parole, and correctional officers).[12] A systems-oriented perspective is critical to such research because it highlights the fact that some errors may be more prevalent at certain stages, and that errors at any given stage may contribute to those at other stages. For example, action bias errors may be more common among prosecutors than among probation officers, and framing errors that take place at the prosecution stage may continue to exert an effect on decision making at the reentry stage.

Research on the various types of decision-making errors should be coupled with research on which types of errors are most consequential. Such research is essential because it is neither feasible nor necessary to monitor the system for virtually all errors (Forst, 2004, p. 6) and because reducing some errors may have greater impacts. Specialist error, for example, may be particularly problematic among policymakers. Their narrow, and indeed almost exclusive, focus on creating laws to address exigent societal problems may lead them to develop extreme responses to "run-of-the-mill" problems. Given that such errors can have profound ripple effects throughout the criminal justice system, they merit especially close monitoring. In identifying the most prevalent and consequential errors, it is, at the same time, important to identify the causes of such errors to be able to reduce or eliminate them.

Second, efforts to improve decision making should be guided by a focus on systemic rather than "silver bullet" solutions, especially given that many errors result from the structure, culture, and interconnectedness of different parts of the criminal justice system. The appeal of "silver bullet" solutions lies, of course, in their simplicity. In commenting on the state of medical practice, Gawande (2007, p. 21) has written: "We always hope for the easy fix: the one simple change that will erase a problem in a stroke. But few things in life work this way. Instead, success requires making a hundred small steps go right—one after the other, no slipups, no goofs, everyone pitching in." His comments were directed to medical practice but apply equally well to the criminal justice system (Marx, 1995). In both medicine and criminal justice, for example, the sheer volume of cases alone dictates that certain types of errors will occur (Groopman, 2007, p. 86; see also Gawande, 2007). When physician case loads expand, they necessarily have less time to spend with each patient. They therefore must increasingly rely on a limited set of heuristics, thus increasing the likelihood that heuristic errors will occur (Groopman, 2007, p. 178). A similar process can be expected to unfold in criminal justice, especially in corrections, where populations have greatly increased (Forst, 2004; Travis, 2005).

Other systemic factors may increase decision-making errors. Physicians, for example, occupy a status role in which nurses and other practitioners may be reluctant to challenge them, use language that frequently may create a barrier between them and patients, and treat patients who, in general, lack the knowledge or wherewithal to challenge their decisions. Similarly, the adversarial nature of courtroom proceedings likely ensures that certain decision-making errors occur. For example, criminal court prosecutors focus on convicting criminals, and thus may be prone to availability and attribution errors—that is, because they see criminals on a daily basis, they may assume that most defendants in fact are guilty (availability error), and because they assume such guilt, they may tend to focus only on those facts that support the "diagnosis" of guilt (attribution error) (see, generally, Davis, 2007). More generally, research shows that work group culture varies from court to court, and that this culture influences decision making, including, not least, sanctioning and treatment determinations (Ulmer & Bradley, 2006).

A systems focus highlights the interconnectedness of the various components of the criminal justice system, and in particular, how multiple errors may occur at the same time, how one error may amplify the effects of another, and how an accumulation of errors may contribute to such decisions as whether someone is treated, incarcerated, or paroled. To illustrate, if a satisfaction of search error occurs early on by a probation officer, that assessment may color any written or orally transmitted descriptions of the offender, as might occur with a pre-sentence investigation report, in turn creating a framing error with ripple effects for sentencing and classification decisions (Forst, 2004, p. 174).

Third, and more concretely, a focus on decision making can contribute to more effective individualized processing, sanctioning, and treatment decisions, including efforts to customize prevention programs to the unique contexts of specific communities. In criminal justice, both the causes of and effective treatment for offending among specific individuals may vary, and so successful attempts to prevent and reduce offending among such individuals must proceed on a case-by-case basis. As meta-analyses indicate (e.g., Cullen & Gendreau, 2000), individualized sanctioning and treatment can lead, on average, to better outcomes (e.g., reduced recidivism). The critical task, then, lies with ensuring that practitioners responsible for making sanctioning and treatment decisions make appropriate and effective decisions about particular individuals.

In a similar vein, a focus on decision making can highlight the importance of individualizing crime prevention strategies for local communities. Epidemiological efforts must, if they are to be successful, take account of the unique conditions in communities (Rothman & Greenland, 1998). It is not necessarily the case that different treatments are needed, as may be the case with offenders, but rather that different strategies for distributing a treatment may be necessary because of the specific social conditions or cultural traditions in particular communities (Gawande, 2007; Mrazek & Haggerty, 1994). Similarly, crime prevention efforts are more likely to be effective when they involve, as with community policing programs, local citizen and police partnerships to identify the specific causes of crime in an area and how best to address them given the unique social and historical context of the area (Greene,

2000; McGloin, 2005). Such efforts may be more effective if coupled with systematic, empirical analysis, and the application of general knowledge about crime causation (Peak & Glensor, 2004; Ratcliffe, 2003). Here, again, the lessons from medicine point to the need to identify how decisions are made to allocate crime prevention resources, what assumptions underlie the decisions, and whether there is any flaw—a cognitive error, for example—affecting the decisions.

Fourth, an emphasis on decision making can highlight the importance of performance monitoring, and in turn, increase accountability by explicitly identifying individuals or groups responsible for specific decisions. For example, monitoring efforts frequently entail repeated measurement of various activities that a given agency or program is supposed to undertake. By focusing on activities rather than specific systems agents, however, organizations obscure who exactly is responsible for the activities. By contrast, by focusing on decision making as an organizing principle for performance monitoring, organizations must explicitly identify not only which decisions are important, but also who is responsible for making them.

Fifth, systematic efforts to monitor and assess decision making throughout the criminal justice system can draw attention to the fact that "evidence-based" programs need not be, and often cannot be, based on the "gold standard" of research—experiments. Instead, in many instances, recourse to other types of research is needed. Studies of "what works" are, of course, essential to identifying programs that can reduce recidivism (Farabee, 2005; Farrington & Welsh, 2007; MacKenzie, 2006; Sherman, 2003). Yet, much of what occurs in criminal justice cannot be studied through experiments. The same is true in medicine; for example, randomized clinical trials involving different birthing techniques are not conducted, nor would such research be ethical (Gawande, 2007). In addition, experiments frequently focus on unrealistic scenarios—the use of a particular intervention in isolation from other interventions, sufficient funding, resources, and staffing, and the like (Heckman & Smith, 1995). They also typically privilege individual-level focused interventions, given that experiments with communities involve too many challenges (Mrazek & Haggerty, 1994). In turn, excessive emphasis on experiments to the exclusion or diminishment of monitoring efforts can indirectly create the groundwork for a fundamental cognitive error among policymakers, practitioners, and researchers—namely, the notion that the causes of crime lie primarily with individuals rather than with social conditions.

Juxtaposed against such issues stands the fact that basic monitoring efforts of critical decisions can serve to identify areas where substantial improvements can be made to reduce recidivism, or more generally, to improve decision making (Walker, 1992). For example, many criminal justice systems use risk and needs assessment instruments to determine which individuals merit closer supervision, or say, drug treatment. To what extent, however, do practitioners use the resulting information? Also, how often do they use it appropriately? How often are decisions about detention and treatment based on subjective assessments rather than the use of objective, actuarial assessments? Given that the latter have been found to be more accurate (Cullen & Gendreau, 2000), any substantial discrepancy would point to a need for change, which in turn could result in improved supervision of offenders and potentially, in turn, reduced recidivism rates (Petersilia, 2003; Piehl & LoBuglio, 2005).

Finally, one way to encourage monitoring of decision-making errors throughout the criminal justice system, and performance monitoring more generally, is to charge state-run independent agencies with monitoring and assessing criminal justice system practices. The need for such an agency stems from at least two considerations: most criminal justice systems are not unified under one umbrella agency, and even when they are, monitoring efforts by criminal justice system researchers may be viewed as biased. By contrast, a legislatively established autonomous agency could be charged with providing ongoing assessments of criminal justice system decision making and activities. Full autonomy is not realistic, but close approximations, such as the now disbanded Texas Criminal Justice Policy Council, exist (see, generally, Blumstein, 1997; Cullen, 2005; Petersilia, 1991). The U.S. General Accountability Office represents another potential model to guide states in developing independent agencies charged with continuous, systematic assessment of criminal justice operations.

Conclusion

Despite calls for increased government accountability and the fact that performance monitoring can be critical to increasing the accountability, efficiency, and effectiveness of criminal justice systems, there remains much room for improvement (Gaes et al., 2004). There is, in particular, a need to focus on the quality of decision making made by actors throughout the criminal justice system. This focus on decision making as it occurs throughout the system is critical given that what occurs in one part of a system can influence another. Yet, at present, few states have independent agencies responsible for ensuring that all aspects of the criminal justice system are monitored, much less for monitoring decision making among diverse system actors.

The situation cannot be attributed to a decreasing need for accountability. To the contrary, the increases in correctional populations and expenditures, the broad-ranging harms that can result from recidivism, miscarriages of justice, and the impact of system inefficiencies and ineffectiveness on taxpayers, victims, offenders, families, and communities—these all point to the need for more, not less, accountability.

Against that background, this article highlights the centrality of decision making to efforts to promote accountability in the criminal justice system and to increase its efficiency and effectiveness. Although a large body of studies exist that sometimes examined specific decision points (Walker, 1993), such as police officer decisions to conduct traffic stops, to date no systematic foundation exists for organizing such studies or for identifying the types of decision-making errors that can undermine effective decision making.

As a corrective to the problem, this article argues that efforts to improve the efficiency and effectiveness of the criminal justice system can emerge by drawing lessons from other social policy arenas, the medical system in particular. Such a comparison highlights that decision making is a critical dimension throughout the medical and criminal justice systems—not just at a few select points where key personnel have the ability to exercise considerable discretion (Miethe, 1987; Walker, 1993)—and that an understanding of that fact requires recognizing the role of systems in affecting decision making. Larger case loads, for example, increase the likelihood that different types of "cognitive errors" occur, accumulating with or amplifying the effects of one another and potentially causing ripple effects that ultimately lead to inefficiencies and poor outcomes. To illustrate, an officer who inappropriately profiles a person—a prototype error—may lead to that person being arrested and even prosecuted and sentenced while the true offender remains untouched. In a high-volume urban district, prosecutors may feel pressure to process cases quickly and so be more likely to commit "satisfaction of search" errors, where they rapidly search for and find guilt and then cease questioning their judgment. The effects of such errors can be compounded in situations where public defenders, due to similar case load pressures, commit listening errors and so fail to adequately represent clients.

This article details a series of implications for policymakers and criminal justice officials, practitioners, and researchers. Here, these implications are summarized. First, not all decision making is necessarily plagued by errors or especially consequential. Thus, any effort to incorporate decision-making monitoring into a broader performance monitoring strategy requires that researchers first document which errors occur most frequently and appear likely to have the greatest impact. For example, policymakers, because their main role is to create policy, may be especially prone to commit action bias errors in which they feel compelled to implement any policy, regardless of the evidence for a problem or the effectiveness of the policy for the problem. Such errors would seem to merit close attention precisely because they can result in costly investments in strategies that not only consume considerable resources, but also impose demands on systems that already are overburdened.

Second, policymakers' and officials' efforts to improve decision making should be targeted toward the system as a whole, rather than isolated parts of it. Such an approach can help ensure that system-wide changes, if needed, can be identified. It also can serve as a reminder that "silver bullet" approaches to increasing the efficiency and effectiveness of the criminal justice system are unlikely to work.

Third, at the same time, policymakers, officials, and practitioners should focus on ways that decision making can be improved at many specific points throughout the criminal justice system. Here again, investing in systematic, empirical monitoring of decision making can provide a platform for making improvements in such dimensions as efforts to individualize sanctioning and treatment and to develop appropriate and effective community-level crime prevention efforts.

Fourth, a decision making-focused performance monitoring system should be used to establish who is accountable for specific activities and outcomes and to evaluate how well those who are accountable performed. From this perspective, it is not sufficient simply to establish whether, for example, specific activities were or were not performed. Separate from establishing such facts is the need to assess whether appropriate decisions were made and whether room for improvement—through better decision making—could be obtained.

Fifth, a decision-making monitoring system should be used by policymakers and criminal justice officials, practitioners, and researchers to identify areas where improvements can be made. Such an approach holds the promise of yielding significant increases in the efficiency and effectiveness of the criminal justice system, possibly more so than a sustained attempt to focus only on adopting evidence-based practices. Indeed, as the evaluation literature establishes, even the best programs and policies will fail if poorly implemented (Rossi et al., 2004), and if decision making is poor, then so, too will be the implementation of most programs and policies. More generally, poor decision making can contribute to misguided, and in turn, ineffective, practice.

Ultimately, accountability stems from identifying who is responsible for specific actions, monitoring those actions, determining when problems exist, and taking corrective steps. When the actions occur within a systems context, such efforts require that monitoring occur by an organization charged with assessing a given system. For this reason, the final, and central implication arising from the analysis here is the need for state level agencies that operate, to the extent possible, independently of the criminal justice system, legislatures, and the executive branch. The Texas Criminal Justice Policy Council and the U.S. Government Accountability Office illustrate two ways in which such agencies might be structured.

Much of what happens in criminal justice occurs within a "black box" (Mears, 2008). The almost inevitable result is that needless errors in judgment occur that impose substantial costs on individuals and society. In his recent Sutherland address, Nagin (2007) argued that "choice" should be moved to center stage in criminological research. His focus was on the need for greater research on the diverse factors that influence the choices—criminal behavior, in particular—individuals make. Extending that general argument to criminal justice system actors, this article submits that one way to illuminate the "black box" is to implement performance monitoring for documenting and assessing decision making throughout all parts of the justice system, including decision making by all of the diverse actors within it. In short, system-wide decision making should be moved to the center stage of accountability efforts in criminal justice.

✎ Notes

1. Gawande (2007, p. 207) has written about the problem, observing: "In recent years, there has been a proliferation of efforts to measure how various hospitals and doctors perform. No one has found the task easy. One difficulty has been figuring out what to measure." One notable federal monitoring effort, conducted between 1986 and 1992, focused on hospital death rates (pp. 207-208); however, "death rates are a poor metric for how doctors do . . . What one really wants to know is how we [doctors] perform in typical circumstances—some kind of score for the immediate results, perhaps, and also a measure of the processes involved. For patients with pneumonia, how often does my hospital get them the correct antibiotic, and on the whole how do they do? How do our results compare with those of other hospitals?" (p. 208).

2. Forst (2004) has investigated ways in which "errors of justice" arise (e.g., wrongful convictions) and how they can undermine the perceived legitimacy of the justice system. The focus of the present research was more broadly on cognitive decision-making errors, such as occur in medicine, that may influence the quantity and quality of decision making throughout all stages of the criminal justice system, and in turn, the system's efficiency and effectiveness.

3. In some cases, a type of error identified by Groopman (2007) was renamed to clarify distinctions among the different types examined here. The topic of clinical decision making has been increasingly investigated in medicine (Downie & Macnaughton, 2000; Mamede, Schmidt, & Rikers, 2007; Redelmeier, 2005; Sandhu, Carpenter, Freeman, Nabors, & Olson, 2006).

4. Under this clinical algorithm approach, diagnosis proceeds in linear manner, evaluating hypotheses one by one, and assigning statistical probabilities each step of the way (Groopman, 2007, p. 11). In reality, few doctors think this way, and even if they do, may assign incorrect probabilities or fail to think "outside the box" in situations where doing so might result in a more accurate diagnosis and thus treatment (p. 12). Such error is less likely when sufficient time exists to work systematically through various differential diagnoses, as occurs with "bedside rounds" during medical training. The problem, however, is that sufficient time rarely exists in day-to-day practice and that doctors typically make decisions on their own, not in groups (p. 34).

5. Such errors are likely given that doctors are not formally trained in the use of heuristics and their limitations (Groopman, 2007, p. 36). Put differently, many physicians lack well-developed and accurate pattern recognition skills and thus may make more mistakes (pp. 167, 196). They also may fail to recognize when an accurate diagnosis may require considering diagnoses beyond those suggested by the heuristics on which they are relying. One example—radiologists may review up to 25,000 cases annually (p. 178). In this field, "conclusions from first impressions, or 'gestalt,' are supposed to be the mark of good training, much as 'shooting from the hip' is prized among ER doctors" (p. 178). The approach can lead, however, to errors that, without a review process, go unchecked. The problem is acute when measurement error (e.g., taking X-rays of only part of what may be clinically relevant) and intraobserver variability (e.g., differences in how clinicians interpret the data) exist (pp. 179-181).

6. In theory, an endless supply of former correctional officers willing to return to the field of corrections might exist. That, however, does not appear to be the case.

7. Notably, Groopman (2007) asked physicians what they would do if they "perceived a negative attitude from their doctor"; they reported that they would "find another doctor" (p. 26). That view is of interest because it indicates that the "insider" perspective is that physicians who harbor a negative view of patients are unlikely to change their decision making algorithm.

8. This type of error can also be termed "yin-yang out" error—a patient may be "worked up the 'yin-yang'" and then be put "out" (i.e., dismissed)—the "failure to think of a new direction, because you assume all have been explored," is a "yin-yang out" mistake (Groopman, 2007, p. 72).

9. Such error may stem from uncertainty error, which occurs when physicians disregard the amount of uncertainty concerning the evidence for a specific diagnosis and its treatment, leading to misdiagnosis or arbitrary treatment, as occurs when the default treatment for a given illness at one hospital is different than that used at another (Groopman, 2007, p. 153).

10. Many examples exist, including the increased promotion of testosterone drugs to enhance sexual function (Groopman, 200, p. 206), such pain medicines as Vioxx (p. 213), and surgery for back pain (pp. 224-231). This problem is amplified by certain medical insurance industry practices, such as greater and more certain reimbursement for certain practices (p. 228).

11. Two examples illustrate the point. The first is rare illness retreat error. Here, misdiagnosis occurs when physicians retreat from exploring whether rare diagnoses fit particular cases even though a rare illness may actually be present (Groopman, 2007, p. 127). Modern medicine, as influenced by the health insurance industry, strongly shies away from performing exploratory tests to identify rare illnesses. That is, there is a bias against looking for "zebras" (i.e., rare illnesses) in a context where most of the time there are horses (i.e., run-of-the-mill illnesses) (p. 127). "In fact, some physicians are called to account for ordering too many tests because they may turn up only one correct diagnosis out of twenty-five, a hundred, or five hundred, and because the money would be better spent on something else. Unless, of course, that one zebra case turned out to be the bean counter's own child" (p. 127). "To add to that pressure, doctors who hunt zebras are often ridiculed by their peers for being obsessed with the esoteric while ignoring

the mainstream" (p. 127). In addition, physicians frequently will lack the "courage of their convictions" because of their minimal experience with "zebras" (p. 127). The second is phrasing error–how a physician "phrases his recommendations can powerfully sway a patient's choices" (Groopman, 2007, p. 242), leading patients to decisions that may not be in their best interests. For example, patients will more likely accept a recommendation when the treatment is stated in positive ways (e.g., you have a 30 percent chance of living) rather than negative ways (e.g., you have a 70 percent chance of dying) (p. 242). The error is not misdiagnosis but rather of consciously or unconsciously pushing patients to accept certain treatments over others. This error is manifest in other ways, as when physicians deliver information in a way that leads patients to trust overly in their assessment (p. 266).

12. In a similar vein, Forst (2004) has noted that one type of error of justice—inappropriate sanctions—can be caused by "officials in any of the three branches of government" (p. 173), including legislators, probation and parole officers, judges, governors, and presidents. By extension, attempts to reduce inappropriate sanctioning requires attention to all these groups.

References

Agnew, R. (2005). *Why do criminals offend? A general theory of crime and delinquency*. Los Angeles: Roxbury.

Bardach, E. (2004). Presidential address–the extrapolation problem: How can we learn from the experience of others? *Journal of Policy Analysis and Management, 23*, 205–220.

Baskin, D., & Sommers, I. (1997). *Casualties of community disorder: Women's careers in violent crime*. Philadelphia: Westview Press.

Bazemore, G. (2006). *Performance measures: Measuring what really matters in juvenile justice*. Alexandria, VA: American Prosecutors Research Institute.

Behn, R. D. (2003). Why measure performance? Different purposes require different measures. *Public Administration Review, 63*, 586–606.

Bloom, B., Owen, B., & Covington, S. (2004). Women offenders and the gendered effects of public policy. *Review of Policy Research, 21*, 31–48.

Blumstein, A. (1997). Interaction of criminological research and public policy. *Journal of Quantitative Criminology, 12*, 349–362.

Bridges, G. S., & Steen, S. (1998). Racial disparities in official assessments of juvenile offenders: Attributional stereotypes as mediating mechanisms. *American Sociological Review, 63*, 554–570.

Burke, P. B. (1995). *Abolishing parole: Why the emperor has no clothes*. Lexington, KY: American Probation and Parole Association.

Butcher, K. F., & Piehl, A. M. (1998). Cross-city evidence on the relationship between immigration and crime. *Journal of Policy Analysis and Management, 17*, 457–493.

Campbell, R. (2003). *Dollars and sentences: Legislators' views on prisons, punishment, and the budget crisis*. New York: Vera Institute of Justice.

Casper, J. D., Benedict, K., & Perry, J. L. (1989). Juror decisionmaking, attitudes, and the hindsight bias. *Law and Human Behavior, 13*, 291–310.

Chiricos, T., Welch, K., & Gertz, M. (2004). Racial typification of crime and support for punitive measures. *Criminology, 42*, 359–389.

Conover, T. (2000). *Newjack: Guarding Sing Sing*. New York: Random House.

Cullen, F. T. (2005). The twelve people who saved rehabilitation: How the science of criminology made a difference. *Criminology, 43*, 1–42.

Cullen, F. T., & Gendreau, P. (2000). Assessing correctional rehabilitation: Policy, practice, and prospects. In J. Horney (Ed.), *Policies, processes, and decisions of the criminal justice system* (pp. 109–175). Washington, DC: National Institute of Justice.

Davis, A. J. (2007). *Arbitrary justice: The power of the American prosecutor*. New York: Oxford University Press.

Devine, D. J., Clayton, L. D., Dunford, B. B., Seying, R., & Pryce, J. (2001). Jury decisionmaking: 45 years of empirical research on deliberating groups. *Psychology, Public Policy, and Law, 7*, 622–727.

Downie, R. S., & Macnaughton, J. (2000). *Clinical judgment: Evidence in practice*. New York: Oxford University Press.

Farabee, D. (2005). *Rethinking rehabilitation: Why can't we reform our criminals?* Washington, DC: AEI Press.

Farrington, D. P., Jolliffe, D., Loeber, R., Stouthamer-Loeber, M., & Kalb, L. M. (2001). The concentration of offenders in families, and family criminality in the prediction of boys' delinquency. *Journal of Adolescence, 24*, 579–596.

Farrington, D. P., & Welsh, B. C. (2007). *Saving children from a life of crime: Early risk factors and effective interventions*. New York: Oxford University Press.

Forer, L. (1994). *A rage to punish: The unintended consequences of mandatory sentencing*. New York: Norton.

Forst, B. (2004). *Errors of justice: Nature, sources, and remedies*. New York: Cambridge University Press.

Freilich, J. D., & Newman, G. R. (Eds.). (2007). *Crime and immigration*. Hampshire, UK: Ashgate.

Gaes, G. G., Camp, S. D., Nelson, J. B., & Saylor, W. G. (2004). *Measuring prison performance: Government privatization and accountability*. Lanham, MD: AltaMira Press.

Gawande, A. (2007). *Better: A surgeon's notes on performance*. New York: Metropolitan Books.

Gladwell, M. (2005). *Blink: The power of thinking without thinking*. New York: Back Bay Books.

Glaze, L. E., & Bonczar, T. P. (2006). *Probation and parole in the United States, 2005*. Washington, DC: U.S. Bureau of Justice Statistics.

Greene, J. R. (2000). Community policing in America: Changing the nature, structure, and function of the police. In J. Horney (Ed.), *Policies, processes, and decisions of the criminal justice system* (pp. 299–370). Washington, DC: National Institute of Justice.

Groopman, J. (2007). *How doctors think*. Boston: Houghton Mifflin.

Hart, S. D., Michie, C., & Cooke, D. J. (2007). Precision of actuarial risk assessment instruments: Evaluating the "margins of error" of group v. individual predictions of violence. *British Journal of Psychiatry, 49*, 60–65.

Hatry, H. P. (2007). *Performance measurement: Getting results* (2nd ed.). Washington, DC: Urban Institute.

Heckman, J. J., & Smith, J. A. (1995). Assessing the case for social experiments. *Journal of Economic Perspectives, 9*, 85–110.

Heimer, K. (2000). Changes in the gender gap in crime and women's economic marginalization. In G. LaFree (Ed.), *The nature of crime: Continuity and change* (pp. 427–483). Washington, DC: National Institute of Justice.

Hoiberg, B. C., & Stires, L. K. (1973). The effect of several types of pretrial publicity on the guilt attributions of simulated jurors. *Journal of Applied Social Psychology, 3*, 267–275.

Hughes, K. A. (2006). *Justice expenditure and employment in the United States, 2003*. Washington, DC: U.S. Bureau of Justice Statistics.

Hughes, K. A., & Perry, S. W. (2007). *Justice expenditure and employment extracts 2004, percent distribution of expenditure for the justice system by type of government, fiscal 2004* (CSV version) [Data file]. Retrieved from Bureau of Justice Statistics Web site: http://www.ojp.usdoj.gov/bjs/

Hurwitz, J., & Peffley, M. (2005). Playing the race card in the post-Willie Horton era: The impact of racialized code words on support for punitive crime policy. *Public Opinion Quarterly, 69*, 99–112.

Julnes, P. D. (2006). Performance measurement: An effective tool for government accountability? The debate goes on. *Evaluation, 12*, 219–235.

Kuhn, T. S. (1970). *The structure of scientific revolutions* (2nd ed.). Chicago: University of Chicago Press.

Kuziemko, I. (2006). *Going off parole: How the elimination of discretionary prison release affects the social cost of crime*. Retrieved July 5, 2007, from Harvard University Web site: http://www.people.fas.harvard.edu/~kuziemko/papers_files/paper_kuziemko_parole.pdf

Lipsey, M. W., Adams, J. L., Gottfredson, D. C., Pepper, J. V., & Weisburd, D. (Eds.). (2005). *Improving evaluation of anticrime programs*. Washington, DC: National Academies Press.

Logan, C. (1993). Criminal justice performance measures for prisons. In *Performance measures for the criminal justice system* (pp. 15–59). Washington, DC: U.S. Bureau of Justice Statistics.

Lurigio, A. J., & Swartz, J. A. (2002). Changing the contours of the criminal justice system to meet the needs of persons with serious mental illness. In J. Horney (Ed.), *Policies, processes, and decisions of the criminal justice system* (pp. 45–108). Washington, DC: National Institute of Justice.

Lynch, J. P., & Sabol, W. J. (2001). *Prisoner reentry in perspective*. Washington, DC: Urban Institute.

MacKenzie, D. L. (2006). *What works in corrections: Reducing the criminal activities of offenders and delinquents*. New York: Cambridge University Press.

MacNamara, D. E. J. (1977). The medical model in corrections: Requiescat in pace. *Criminology, 14*, 439–448.

Mamede, S., Schmidt, H. G., & Rikers, R. (2007). Diagnostic errors and reflective practice in medicine. *Journal of Evaluation in Clinical Practice, 13*, 138–145.

Marion, N. E., & Oliver, W. M. (2006). *The public policy of crime and criminal justice*. Upper Saddle River, NJ: Pearson.

Marx, G. T. (1995). The engineering of social control: The search for the silver bullet. In J. Hagan & R. Peterson (Eds.), *Crime and inequality* (pp. 225–246). Palo Alto, CA: Stanford University Press.

McGloin, J. M. (2005). *Street gangs and Interventions: innovative problem solving with network analysis*. Washington, DC: U.S. Department of Justice, Office of Community Oriented Policing Services.

Mears, D. P. (2001). The immigration-crime nexus: Toward an analytic framework for assessing and guiding theory, research, and policy. *Sociological Perspectives, 44*, 1–19.

Mears, D. P. (2003). Research and interventions to reduce domestic violence revictimization. *Trauma, Violence, and Abuse, 4*, 127–147.

Mears, D. P. (2004). Mental health needs and services in the criminal justice system. *Houston Journal of Health Law and Policy, 4*, 255–284.

Mears, D. P. (2007). Towards rational and evidence-based crime policy. *Journal of Criminal Justice, 35*, 667–682.

Mears, D. P. (2008). Accountability, efficiency, and effectiveness in corrections: Shining a light on the black box of prison systems. *Criminology and Public Policy, 7*, 143–152.

Mears, D. P., & Stafford, M. C. (2002). Central analytical issues in the generation of cumulative sociological knowledge. *Sociological Focus, 35*, 5–24.

Mears, D. P., & Watson, J. (2006). Towards a fair and balanced assessment of supermax prisons. *Justice Quarterly, 23*, 232–270.

Merton, R. K. (1968). *Social theory and social structure*. New York: The Free Press.

Miethe, T. (1987). Charging and plea bargaining under determinate sentencing: An investigation of the hydraulic displacement of discretion. *Journal of Criminal Law and Criminology, 78*, 155–176.

Millenson, M. (1997), *Demanding medical excellence: Doctors and accountability in the information age*. Chicago: University of Chicago Press.

Mrazek, P. J., & Haggerty, R. J. (Eds.). (1994). *Reducing risks for mental disorders: Frontiers for preventive intervention research*. Washington, DC: National Academy Press.

Nagin, D. S. (2007). Moving choice to center stage in criminological research and theory: The American Society of Criminology 2006 Sutherland address. *Criminology, 45*, 259–272.

Nolan, J. L. (2003). *Reinventing justice: The American drug court movement*. Princeton, NJ: Princeton University Press.

Paternoster, R., Brame, R., Bacon, S., & Ditchfield, A. (2004). Justice by geography and race: The administration of the death penalty in Maryland, 1978-1999. *Margins: Maryland's Law Journal on Race, Religion, Gender and Class, 4*, 1–97.

Peak, K. J., & Glensor, R. W. (2004). *Community policing and problem solving: Strategies and practices* (4th ed.). Englewood Cliffs, NJ: Prentice Hall.

Perry, A., McDougall, C., & Farrington, D. P. (Eds.). (2006). *Reducing crime: The effectiveness of criminal justice interventions.* Hoboken, NJ: Wiley.

Peters, R. H., Greenbaum, P. E., Steinberg, M. L., Carter, C. R., Ortiz, M. M., Fry, B. C., et al. (2000). Effectiveness of screening instruments in detecting substance use disorders among prisoners. *Journal of Substance Abuse Treatment, 18,* 349–358.

Petersilia, J. (1991). Policy relevance and the future of criminology. *Criminology, 29,* 1–16.

Petersilia, J. (1999). Parole and prisoner reentry in the United States. In M. H. Tonry &J. Petersilia (Eds.), *Prisons* (pp. 479–529). Chicago: University of Chicago Press.

Petersilia, J. (2003). *When prisoners come home: Parole and prisoner reentry.* New York: Oxford University Press.

Piehl, A. M., & LoBuglio, S. M. (2005). Does supervision matter? In J. Travis & C. Visher (Eds.), *Prisoner reentry and crime in America* (pp. 105–138). New York: Cambridge University Press.

Ratcliffe, J. H. (2003). *Intelligence-led policing.* Canberra: Australian Institute of Criminology.

Redelmeier, D. A. (2005). The cognitive psychology of missed diagnoses. *Annals of Internal Medicine, 142,* 115–120.

Reiman, J. H. (2000). *The rich get richer and the poor get prison.* Boston: Allyn and Bacon.

Reisig, M. D., Holtfreter, K., & Morash, M. (2006). Assessing recidivism risk across female pathways to crime. *Justice Quarterly, 23,* 384–405.

Roberts, A. R. (Ed.). (2002). *Handbook of domestic violence intervention strategies: Policies, programs, and legal remedies.* New York: Oxford University Press.

Rodriguez, N., & Webb, V. J. (2007). Probation violations, revocations, and imprisonment: The decisions of probation officers, prosecutors, and judges pre- and post-mandatory drug treatment. *Criminal Justice Policy Review, 18,* 3–30.

Rossi, P. H., Lipsey, M. W., & Freeman, H. E. (2004). *Evaluation: A systematic approach* (7th ed.). Thousand Oaks, CA: Sage.

Rothman, K. J., & Greenland, S. (1998). *Modern epidemiology.* New York: Lippincott.

Sample, L. L., & Bray, T. M. (2003). Are sex offenders dangerous? *Criminology and Public Policy, 3,* 59–82.

Sampson, R. J., & Lauritsen, J. L. (1997). Racial and ethnic disparities in crime and criminal justice in the United States. In M. Tonry (Ed.), *Crime and justice: Comparative and cross-national perspectives on ethnicity, crime, and immigration* (Vol. 21, pp. 311–374). Chicago: University of Chicago Press.

Sandhu, H., Carpenter, C., Freeman, K., Nabors, S. G., & Olson, A. (2006). Clinical decisionmaking: Opening the black box of cognitive reasoning. *Annals of Emergency Medicine, 48,* 713–719.

Schmidt, J. D., & Sherman, L. W. (1996). Does arrest deter domestic violence? In E. S. Buzawa & C.G. Buzawa (Eds.), *Do arrests and restraining orders work?* (pp. 43–53). Thousand Oaks, CA: Sage.

Sherman, L. W. (2003). Misleading evidence and evidence-led policy: Making social science more experimental. *The Annals, 589,* 6–19.

Sherman, L. W., & Berk, R. A. (1984). *The Minneapolis domestic violence experiment.* Washington, DC: Police Foundation.

Sherman, L. W., Gottfredson, D. C., MacKenzie, D. L., Eck, J., Reuter, P., & Bushway, S. (Eds.). (1997). *Preventing crime: What works, what doesn't, what's promising.* Washington, DC: Office of Justice Programs.

Sherman, L. W., Smith, D. A., Schmidt, J. D., & Rogan, D. P. (1992). Crime, punishment, and stake in conformity: Legal and informal control of domestic violence. *American Sociological Review, 57,* 680–690.

Shichor, D. (1997). Three strikes as a public policy: The convergence of the new penology and the McDonaldization of punishment. *Crime and Delinquency, 43,* 470–492.

Steffensmeier, D., Ulmer,J., & Kramer, J. (1998). The interaction of race, gender, and age in criminal sentencing: The punishment cost of being young, Black, and male. *Criminology, 36,* 763–798.

Steffensmeier, D., Zhong, H., Ackerman,J., Schwartz, J., & Agha, S. (2006). Gender gap trends for violent crimes, 1980 to 2003: A UCR-NCVS comparison. *Feminist Criminology, 1,* 72–98.

Travis, J. (2005). *But they all come back: Facing the challenges of prisoner reentry.* Washington, DC: Urban Institute Press.

Travis, J., & Visher, C. (Eds.). (2005). *Prisoner reentry and crime in America.* New York: Cambridge University Press.

Ulmer, J. T., & Bradley, M. S. (2006). Variation in trial penalties among serious violent offenders. *Criminology, 44,* 631–670.

U.S. Bureau of Justice Statistics. (1999). *Compendium of federal justice statistics.* Washington, DC: U.S. Department of Justice, Office of Justice Programs.

Visher, C. A. (1987). Jury decisionmaking: The importance of evidence. *Law and Human Behavior, 11,* 1–17.

Walker, S. E. (1992). The creation of the contemporary criminal justice paradigm: The American Bar Foundation survey of criminal justice, 1956-1969. *Justice Quarterly, 9,* 201–230.

Walker, S. E. (1993). *Taming the system: The control of discretion in criminal justice, 1950–1990.* New York: Oxford University Press.

Warren, P., Devey, D. T., Smith, W., Zingraff, M., & Mason, M. (2006). Driving while Black: Bias processes and racial disparity in police stops. *Criminology, 4,* 709–737.

Welsh, W. N., & Harris, P. W. (2004). *Criminal justice policy and planning* (2nd ed.). Dayton, OH: LexisNexis, Anderson.

White, H. R., & Gorman, D. M. (2000). Dynamics of the drug-crime relationship. In G. LaFree (Ed.), *The nature of crime: Continuity and change* (pp. 151–218). Washington, DC: National Institute of Justice.

Wish, E. D., Rinehart, C., Hsu, M., & Artigiani, E. (2006). *Using urine specimens from parolees/probationers to create a statewide drug monitoring system.* College Park: University of Maryland, Center for Substance Abuse Research.

Wolfgang, M. E., Figlio, R. M., & Sellin, T. (1972). *Delinquency in a birth cohort.* Chicago: University of Chicago Press.

DISCUSSION QUESTIONS

1. Reading 7 (see Section IV) described the police shooting of Amadou Diallo in New York City using a normal accidents theory framework. Briefly review the circumstances surrounding that incident. Are any of the decision-making errors applicable to the Diallo situation?

2. Is on-the-job experience enough to reduce the likelihood of committing each of the 13 errors in decision making? Explain. What other steps can an organization take to limit these problems?

3. Is it ever acceptable to use age, race, ethnicity, or gender as a basis for decision making in the criminal justice system (e.g., as part of a decision-making algorithm, initial impression, or patient attribution), even if it does not result in a decision-making error?

Glossary

achievement motive: A prominent motive (symbolized *n* achievement) addressed by scholar David McClelland where people desire to be successful and accomplish something. To develop a sense of achievement, a person with a high *n* achievement needs to establish challenging but reachable goals, take responsibility for his or her work, and receive feedback on job performance.

acute onset: The sudden appearance of a more substantial phase of burnout due to significant work events. In many cases, burnout gradually progresses from initial to more severe phases (see *chronic burnout*). With acute onset burnout, it rapidly appears due to critical events such as the death of a partner or working through a prison riot.

administrative breakdown: A cause of organizational deviance produced by the failure to implement or enforce administrative principles (e.g., unity of command, discipline). See *administrative management*.

administrative management: A classical school theory associated with Henri Fayol. The theory provided prescriptions for upper-level managers to efficiently and effectively plan, coordinate, and control work. Fayol's 14 principles included guidelines such as division of labor, unity of command, discipline, and authority.

affiliation motive: A prominent motive (symbolized *n* affiliation) addressed by scholar David McClelland where individuals desire to enter into interpersonal relationships where conflict and criticism are avoided.

anticipatory socialization: Part of the overall organizational socialization process, it includes learning and preparation that occur prior to assuming a new role in an organization. Anticipatory socialization shapes both occupational choice and organizational choice.

arbitration: A form of labor dispute resolution where a third party (arbitrator) makes actual decisions on the appropriate resolution, either on an overall contract or on an issue-by-issue basis. The arbitrator's decisions can be binding or nonbinding (advisory) on the parties.

autonomy: An element of the job characteristics model designed to increase an individual's feelings of responsibility for the work. Job tasks that afford workers the freedom to make decisions and work independently are considered autonomous since they allow employees to feel responsible for the work's successes and failures.

behavioral or style theories of leadership: A group of theories emerging from research conducted at the Ohio State University beginning in the 1940s; the focus was on what leaders did rather than the traits they possessed. Generally, two key dimensions of leader behavior dominate the literature: initiating structure and consideration.

blue flu: A type of job action where a large number of employees collectively take sick leave at the same time (mass sickouts), potentially disrupting the organization's operations. It is referred to as blue flu when performed by police personnel.

Boston Police Strike (1919): Significant event in the history of criminal justice unionization where more than 1,100 members of the Boston Police Department voted to strike and walked off the job. Officers had violated departmental regulations by affiliating with the American Federation of Labor, and key leaders were subsequently suspended, leading to the strike. The city succumbed to violence before the National Guard was called in; striking workers were dismissed. The strike's legacy included a period of limited union activity in criminal justice organizations.

bureaucracy: An organizational structure identified in the writings of Max Weber; characterized by a division of labor, hierarchy of authority, extensive formalization, merit selection and promotion, and impersonal relations.

burnout: A response to ongoing job stress that emerges when individuals are unable to adequately address the stressors they confront. Burnout is commonly associated with three characteristics: emotional exhaustion, depersonalization, and a diminished sense of accomplishment.

business organizations: Part of a method of classifying organizations by primary beneficiary. Business organizations operate to further the interests of ownership. For-profit companies typically fall into this category.

centralization: A dimension of organizational structure referring to the location in the organization where important decisions are made. If decisions are left in the hands of people at the top, the organization is centralized. If decision-making authority is pushed down to lower points in the organization, decentralization is evident.

charismatic power: Power based on the power holder's ability to inspire enthusiasm among followers.

chronic burnout: The gradual development of burnout from less visible, less pronounced forms to more significant forms characterized by high degrees of depersonalization and emotional exhaustion, and a diminished sense of personal accomplishment. Contrasts with *acute onset*.

closed systems: One of two major perspectives addressing the relevance of an organization's environment, it views organizations as largely immune to outside environmental influences. Contrasts with *open systems*.

coercive power: Power based on the capacity of the power holder to punish (or at least threaten to punish) those who fail to comply with directives. Compliance with demands allows the power recipient to avoid punishment.

collaborative advantage: When a collaboration allows an organization to produce outcomes superior to those possible if it had acted alone.

collective bargaining: The process whereby a union or other employee organization negotiates the terms and conditions of its work with representatives designated by the appropriate unit of government (e.g., state, county, local). Common issues subject to bargaining include economic benefits and working conditions.

collective socialization: A socialization tactic where a group of individuals transitioning together (e.g., entering an organization, moving up the hierarchy) are socialized in unison. Police and correctional officer recruits commonly train together in their respective academies. Contrasts with *individual socialization*.

commonwealth organizations: Part of a method of classifying organizations by primary beneficiary. Commonwealth organizations benefit society as a whole. Examples include the military, police departments, and prosecutors' offices.

complexity: The number of work divisions—horizontal, vertical, and spatial—within an organization. The more divisions, the more complex the organization.

complexity (normal accidents): A dimension of normal accidents theory capturing the degree of predictability in how the parts of a system operate. When system parts are complex—either serving many functions or interacting with many other parts—accidents become more likely. When system parts are linear, the parts operate in more predictable ways.

compliance observability: A characteristic of the work of many criminal justice employees that weakens the overall power of managers. Most criminal justice employees, including the police officer on the street, the prosecutor in the courtroom, and the treatment counselor in the office, work independently with little supervision. It is difficult for managers to know whether or not workers are complying with directives.

concentration: The distribution of employees across an organization's hierarchical levels. It is one indicator of vertical complexity (see also *segmentation*), often illustrated by the shape of a pyramid.

conflictive change motor: Views organizational change as the result of differences in ideas about key elements of the organization (e.g., structures, activities). If a new view comes to dominate, the organization may be transformed from its current state. For example, court orders might force organizations to dramatically alter their structures to ensure compliance with constitutional requirements.

consent decrees: Legal agreements negotiated between organizations and other parties (e.g., government) designed to remedy the conditions that give rise to disputes. Consent decrees typically require changes to organizational structures and practices, and the court monitors compliance with the order.

consideration: One of two key dimensions of behavioral or style theories of leadership (see also *initiating structure*). A considerate leader is concerned about relationships with followers and pays attention to their needs (e.g., satisfaction, stress).

content theories: A broad category of motivational theories linked by their focus on identifying either an exhaustive list of human needs producing motivation or the most salient needs driving behavior. Examples of content theories include need theory, motivator-hygiene theory, and achievement, affiliation, and power motives. Contrasts with *process theories*.

contingency theory: Theory developed in the 1960s suggesting that there is no single best way to organize. The best structure depends on (is contingent on) a variety of factors, including organization size and environmental conditions.

counterproduction: A problem associated with individual organizational action. One organization's activities adversely affect those of another. Collaboration is designed to prevent counterproduction.

coupling: A dimension of normal accidents theory, it is the degree of dependency or connectedness of system parts. When coupling is evident, there is no slack in the system to absorb the effects of other system parts, so accidents become more likely.

crisis management: Preparing for, responding to, and addressing the aftermath of organizational deviance.

crisis paralysis: The failure of an organization to implement an effective response in the midst of an emergency.

culture: A set of beliefs, values, and behavioral guides shared by an organization's members. Some organizations have a single culture, while others comprise many different cultures operating within different subpopulations (e.g., police subculture, management subculture).

decouple: Occurs when organizations separate institutionally prescribed practices from day-to-day activities. Decoupling allows the organization to maintain its regular workflow but also meet external demands.

disjunctive socialization: Socialization tactic drawing on individuals outside of the organization to provide training and education. A probation office, for example, might rely on outside consultants to offer a seminar for employees on a promising program. Contrasts with *serial socialization*.

distributive justice: A component of organizational justice, it addresses perceived equity or inequity of outcomes received by any individual or group in the workplace.

divergence: A problem associated with individual organizational action. Organizations pursue individual goals rather than common system goals. Resources are spread out rather than focused on a larger goal. Collaboration is intended to prevent divergence in goals.

divestiture socialization: Tactic whereby the organization removes certain characteristics of an individual before an organizational boundary is crossed. Police recruits learn discipline and strength and leave behind certain civilian qualities as part of the training academy. Contrasts with *investiture socialization*.

dues check off: Agreement where employing organizations automatically deduct union dues from employee paychecks and forward the money to the union. This enables the union to more readily collect dues from members.

effort–performance expectancy: A component of the expectancy theory of motivation (see also *valence* and *performance–outcome expectancy*). This component addresses whether a person believes he or she can perform at a given level; in other words, does he or she have the ability and/or opportunity to perform?

encounter: Part of the overall organizational socialization process, it occurs once the individual enters the organization. While disagreements exist as to how long the encounter stage lasts, it includes some of the worker's initial experiences (e.g., training).

engagement: Considered the opposite of burnout, an engaged worker exhibits high energy, involvement, and feelings of success rather than emotional exhaustion, depersonalization, and diminished sense of accomplishment.

environment: The elements external to the organization that influence and support it (e.g., other organizations, resource providers, larger societal changes). The environment generally consists of individuals, groups, organizations, and institutions outside of the boundaries of the focal organization.

equity theory: A process theory of motivation that argues that motivation and other work-related behaviors and attitudes are determined by the perceived fairness of exchanges in the workplace. Individuals compare their ratio of inputs (e.g., their education, skills, effort) to outputs (e.g., pay, job assignments) against those of other workers in a subjective process when determining fairness. If inequity is observed, motivation may suffer.

evolutionary motor: An explanation of organizational change occurring through a process of variation-selection-retention. Certain organizational structures and activities are going to be rewarded—the organization may receive external funding or effectively reduce crime—while others may prove insufficient. Successful organizational forms are retained, and other organizations may adopt them.

expectancy theory: A process theory of motivation wherein people are assumed to base behavioral decisions on a calculation. They must value the reward or outcome that follows any particular action (valence), they must believe that the outcomes are likely (performance–outcome expectancy), and they must have the opportunity and capability to engage in the behavior that produces the outcome (effort–performance expectancy). Motivation will suffer if any one or more of these three components break down.

expert power: Power based on the power holder's extensive knowledge in a specific field. Power recipient compliance is based on deference to this expertise.

fact finding: A form of labor dispute resolution whereby a neutral third party (fact finder) investigates disputed issues to discover the true facts relevant to each claim. For example, the fact finder might independently assess disputed budget figures to facilitate continued movement in the negotiations.

feedback: An element of the job characteristics model designed to enable a worker to learn about the outcomes of his or her efforts. According to the model, learning about successes and failures from the job itself (e.g., seeing a less disorderly neighborhood) is more important feedback than a commendation from a supervisor.

Fiedler's contingency theory of leadership: A theory developed by Fred Fiedler representing a major advancement in the study of leadership. Fiedler argued that the best style of leadership—task-oriented behavior or relationship-oriented behavior—was contingent on relationships with followers, the amount of power possessed by the leader, and the clarity of the task. Task-oriented behavior was appropriate when all contingencies were either favorable or unfavorable; relationship-oriented behavior was appropriate when the favorability of contingencies was mixed. Leadership style was measured using the least preferred coworker score.

fixed socialization: Occurs if organizations delineate the amount of time necessary to complete a boundary crossing or complete the socialization process. For example, a new police recruit must complete an average of 613 hours of academy training. Contrasts with *variable socialization*.

formal socialization: Occurs when individuals new to the organization, position, or rank are socialized apart from those already occupying those roles. Police officer recruits, for example, are separated from the actual work and experienced workers during the training stage. Contrasts with *informal socialization*.

formalization: The degree to which an organization and its members are guided by written rules and procedures intended to produce predictable behavior (more rules equals greater formalization).

functional differentiation: An indicator of horizontal complexity, it is the degree to which an organization's workers are grouped into identifiable units, departments, or divisions.

Hawthorne effect: Phenomenon observed during the course of the Hawthorne studies. Worker productivity increased because of the special attention and treatment they were given for participation in the study.

Hawthorne studies: Series of studies begun in 1924 that established the human relations school of management. The studies found that informal organization and worker needs influenced productivity as much as or more than formal organizational structures.

horizontal collaborations: A type of task force comprising regional or contiguous agencies.

horizontal complexity: The extent to which nonsupervisory tasks of the organization are subdivided into specific jobs and separate divisions.

human relations school: A major school of thought about organizations. Recognized the importance of the worker's needs and behaviors, as well as the informal organizational structure, in shaping the overall effectiveness of the organization.

individual socialization: A socialization tactic involving single individuals in a period of more personalized training. Individual socialization is observed when police officers work with field-training officers post-academy or sergeants are socialized into their new roles. Contrasts with *collective socialization*.

influence tactics: Strategies used by power holders to ensure goal accomplishment by others. Nine common influence tactics include rational persuasion, consultation, inspirational appeals, personal appeals, ingratiation, exchange, legitimate request, pressure, and coalition tactics.

informal socialization: A socialization tactic where newcomers are socialized alongside more experienced workers; there are no formal socialization programs or visible identifiers indicative of newcomer status. New prosecutors learn their roles through on-the-job training, working alongside veteran prosecutors. Contrasts with *formal socialization*.

information power: Power based on the power holder's control of information flows with an organization or access to information sought by others. Power recipient compliance is based on desire to receive this information from the power holder.

initiating structure: One of two key dimensions of behavioral or style theories of leadership (see also *consideration*). Leaders who initiate structure provide followers with direction on accomplishing the work (e.g., how to complete work, deadlines).

institutional theory: Contemporary theory of organization suggesting that organizational structures and practices are a product of expectations of what organizations should do, irrespective of efficiency and effectiveness concerns.

instrumental rationality: The organizational focus on identifying and implementing the most effective means for reaching organizational goals.

interactional justice: A component of organizational justice, it addresses the interpersonal conduct of the individuals who make decisions. Individuals assess fairness based on how they are treated (respect and information provided), independent of assessments of fairness regarding outcomes or procedures.

investiture socialization: Socialization strategy that recognizes the value of what individuals bring to the organization in terms of values, knowledge, and attitudes. Prosecutors and public defenders, for example, bring their law school backgrounds to their jobs; this legal training is embraced. Contrasts with *divestiture socialization*.

isomorphism: The tendency of organizations to resemble one another as a result of coercive, mimetic, and normative processes. The environment supports only a limited number of structural options, so organizations tend to take similar forms.

job characteristics model: A model of job design produced by Hackman and Oldham in the 1970s. The model suggests that internal motivation is produced when people believe that their work is meaningful, experience responsibility, and receive knowledge of results. Enhancing skill variety, task identity, and task significance can increase feelings of meaningfulness; affording autonomy can provide a sense of responsibility; and giving feedback can improve overall knowledge of results.

job design: A method of matching workers to tasks and manipulating the nature of the work (e.g., changing the level of responsibilities, providing additional feedback) to facilitate feedback. Hackman and Oldham produced a widely known job design model known as the job characteristics model.

learning organization: A type of organization capable of adjusting goals and structures as new knowledge becomes available. Learning organizations establish mechanisms that allow them to acquire and interpret knowledge, disseminate information throughout the organization, and establish an organizational memory.

least preferred coworker score: A measure of leadership style developed by Fred Fiedler as part of his contingency theory of leadership. Respondents are asked to think about a coworker with whom they have difficulty working and rate that individual on a variety of items. If the coworker is described in favorable terms, the respondent is viewed as manifesting relationship-oriented behavior. If the coworker is described in unfavorable terms, the respondent is viewed as relying on task-oriented behavior.

legitimate power: Power based on the power holder's right to make demands and secure compliance, usually derived from his or her position or rank.

life course: A modified perspective on the life cycle motor of organizational change. As organizations progress throughout the life course, they pass through stages, though not in any predetermined fashion, and may actually revert to earlier stages.

life cycle motor: A theory of organizational change that argues that organizations pass through a series of predetermined stages (e.g., birth, growth, decline). Changes represent the progression through the life cycle.

limited or bounded rationality: A description of the planned change process. Organizational leaders are often unable to make optimum decisions because they lack full and complete information on all alternatives. Instead, they make decisions based on what information is available; their actions are based on limited or bounded rationality, not irrationality.

mediation: A form of labor dispute resolution where an impartial third party (the mediator) participates in the negotiations. The mediator's role is to encourage communication and suggest avenues for dispute resolution.

metamorphosis: The final stage of the organizational socialization process. Metamorphosis represents the individual's transition to a full-fledged organizational member.

mission distortion: Occurs when agencies shed their own traditional responsibilities and assume those more consistent with their partnering agencies.

motivator–hygiene theory: A content theory of motivation developed through empirical research by Frederick Herzberg and his colleagues in the 1950s. The theory classifies needs into two independent categories. Hygiene factors, generally matters related to the work context (e.g., quality of supervision, workplace policies), contributed to dissatisfaction but did not necessarily lead to motivation. Motivators represented intrinsic factors that drove employees, such as challenging work, achievement, and responsibility.

motors: Theories of organizational change that describe the mechanisms through which changes are produced. The four major change motors include planned change, conflictive change, evolutionary change, and life cycle motors.

mutual benefit organizations: Part of a method of classifying organizations by primary beneficiary. Mutual benefit organizations are designed to benefit the membership at large; examples include unions and professional associations.

need theory: A content theory of motivation associated with the work of Abraham Maslow in the 1940s and 1950s. The theory suggests that human needs can be ordered into five categories from lowest to highest: physiological, safety, belonging, esteem, and self-actualization. Individuals are motivated by the lowest unfulfilled need.

normal accidents: Theory used to describe the likelihood of organizational deviance when systems are complex and system parts tightly coupled. See *complexity (normal accidents)* and *coupling*.

occupational differentiation: The degree to which the work of an organization is broken down into smaller parts and individuals are assigned to handle only their part. Also known as role specialization, it is an indicator of horizontal complexity.

omission: A problem associated with individual organizational action. Certain tasks are ignored, as no one organization takes responsibility for their completion. Collaboration is designed to prevent omission.

open systems: One of two major perspectives addressing the relevance of an organization's environment. It views external influences as important in shaping organizational structures and activities. Contrasts with *closed systems*.

organization: A collective of individuals or groups who work together on a relatively consistent basis to realize common goals by dividing up and coordinating the work.

organizational behavior: Field of study that focuses on the individuals and groups within an organization. The primary interest is in how the larger organizational context shapes worker/group behavior and attitudes. Topics include motivation, leadership, power, socialization, and occupational stress.

organizational deviance: A disaster, mistake, accident, or some other incident that does not fit the organization's goals or expectations of performance, generally producing a negative outcome. Examples include a wrongful conviction, prison riot, or shooting of a bystander.

organizational justice: A process theory of motivation extending equity theory arguments. It is concerned with fairness in the workplace in three areas: distributive justice, procedural justice, and interactional justice.

organizational socialization: Process whereby a worker learns the necessary skills, appropriate values, and expected behaviors associated with a given job.

organizational structure: The division of work within an organization and the methods used to coordinate the parts. Structure generally includes two broad dimensions: complexity and control mechanisms.

organizational termination: The death or disbanding of an organization. Definitional challenges remain but may include situations where organizations cease to exist or are subsumed by other organizations.

organizational theory: Field of study that examines the organization itself as a unit or part of a larger group of relationships (e.g., an industry). Common topics include structure, organizational termination, and partnerships/collaborations.

output goals: A measure of task force performance based on the achievement of stated goals. Output goals are typically measured via arrest statistics.

path–goal theory: A contingency theory of leadership comprising a large number of propositions. The theory attempts to link the expectancy theory of motivation to leader behavior. The leader's role becomes helping satisfy the motivational needs of followers.

performance–outcome expectancy: One of three components of the expectancy theory of motivation (see also *valence* and *effort–performance expectancy*). Individuals gauge the likelihood that certain outcomes will follow their performance. If the outcomes are unlikely to occur, then motivation will suffer, even if the outcome's valence is high.

personal power: Power bases derived from personal qualities, independent of one's position in the organization. Personal power bases include expert, referent, and charismatic power. Contrasts with *position power*.

personalized power motive: A manifestation of the power motive where the primary goal of securing power and influence is to demonstrate superiority over others. Contrasts with *socialized power motive*.

planned change motor: A process linked to goal achievement where organizations recognize the need for adjustment and implement organizational changes as opposed to reacting to unplanned crises or events.

position power: Power bases derived from one's location in the organization's structure. Position power bases include legitimate, resource, reward, coercive, and information power. Contrasts with *personal power*.

power: A social phenomenon where one person has the ability to control or obtain compliance from another. In many situations, power has reciprocal qualities where the power flows in both directions in a relationship.

power motive: A prominent motive (symbolized n power) addressed by scholar David McClelland. Individuals are motivated by the desire to exert control and influence. Some use this power to demonstrate superiority over others (personalized power motive), while others use it to benefit the organization as a whole (socialized power motive).

prescriptive: A category of organizational theories that offer principles or propositions detailing the ideal organizational structure. Theories within the classical and human relations schools are considered prescriptive.

primary appraisal: An individual's evaluation of whether stressors are of the magnitude to produce strain.

primary interventions: Efforts to reduce occupational stress by reducing or modifying the intensity of stressors within the organization. Common strategies include clarifying roles, adjusting workloads, and altering organizational structures.

procedural justice: A component of organizational justice, it is focused on the perceived fairness of the procedures used to make decisions on rewards, punishments, and dispute resolution.

process goals: A measure of task force performance related to the internal functioning of the collaboration. These processes are presumed to contribute to output goals. Examples include improved cooperation and communication between participating organizations.

process theories: A broad category of motivational theories concerned with how needs are translated into actual behavior. Rather than assume that unfulfilled needs will automatically lead to action, these theories focus on factors such as rewards (e.g., expectancy theory) and fairness in the workplace (e.g., equity theory). Contrasts with *content theories*.

qualitative overload: A task-related stressor that occurs when workplace demands exceed the time available to complete the work (e.g., a probation officer does not have enough time to supervise a large caseload of clients).

quantitative overload: A task-related stressor that occurs when an individual lacks the skills or knowledge to perform a given task.

random socialization: Socialization tactic where there is only a single stage to complete or the sequence of stages is ill defined. Prospective sergeants often lack paths to prepare them for the first-line supervision role; there are no specifically defined steps to follow prior to assuming the new position. Contrasts with *sequential socialization*.

readiness: The key contingency in situational leadership theory (previously described as follower maturity). Job readiness refers to an individual's ability to perform a task, including experience, training, and education. Psychological readiness addresses follower motivation and willingness to perform a task.

referent power: Power based on the power recipient's admiration or respect for, or desire to associate with, the power holder.

repetition: A problem associated with individual organizational action. Organizations duplicate the efforts of another. Collaboration is supposed to prevent repetition.

resource dependence theory: A contemporary organizational theory stating that organizations adopt structures and practices supported by providers of critical resources (e.g., money). The level of external control increases as resources become more important or scarcer.

resource power: Power based on the power holder's control of much-needed resources within the organization. If a person can acquire resources (e.g., grant funds, contraband), he or she develops a resource power base.

reward power: Power based on the power holder's ability to distribute intrinsic and extrinsic rewards. Power recipients comply if they want to receive valued rewards (e.g., extra privileges).

role ambiguity: A role-related stressor caused by the lack of clear or definite expectations about the work to be performed. For example, a police officer may be tasked with engaging in community policing but may experience strain if he lacks an understanding of what community policing requires.

role conflict: A role-related stressor caused by the presence of two or more workplace demands that are in opposition to each other. For example, a probation officer is often asked to serve both law enforcer and social worker roles.

routine occupational stressors: Stressors (demands producing strain) encountered on a regular basis within the workplace. Examples of routine occupational stressors include inadequate compensation, role conflict, and poor work relationships. Contrasts with *traumatic stressors*.

satisficing: A type of organizational decision making where outcomes are assumed to be sufficient and satisfactory rather than optimum. Limited or bounded rationality often precludes the search for optimum outcomes.

scientific management: Associated with the early 20th century writings of Frederick Taylor, who advocated the use of empirical research to identify the best methods for performing work tasks. The goal of scientific management is to reduce inefficiency and increase productivity in the workplace.

secondary appraisal: An individual's assessment of the availability of coping mechanisms in the event that strain is experienced.

secondary interventions: Efforts to reduce occupational stress by addressing the ways individuals respond to stressors. Organizations have implemented a variety of wellness programs designed to alter the primary appraisal process, hoping to prevent stressors from becoming strains.

segmentation: The number of layers in the chain of command of an organization (e.g., count of rank levels) from top to bottom. One indicator of vertical complexity (see also *concentration*), often illustrated by the height of a pyramid.

sequential socialization: Process where individuals must complete predetermined and ordered stages to be considered fully prepared for their new role. Deputy sheriffs must generally work in the jail before moving on to the law enforcement role. Contrasts with *random socialization*.

serial socialization: Socialization tactic where members already in a given role socialize those preparing to make the transition. For example, an experienced prosecutor may be tasked with mentoring new attorneys in the office. Contrasts with *disjunctive socialization*.

service organizations: Part of a method of classifying organizations by primary beneficiary. Service organizations operate to benefit specific clients who receive services from the organization. Examples include drug treatment facilities and public defenders' offices.

situational leadership theory: A contingency theory of leadership that argues that the most appropriate style of leadership depends on the psychological and job readiness of followers. The four styles of leadership behavior—telling, selling, participating, and delegating—are linked to the subordinate's understanding of and willingness to perform the work.

skill variety: An element of the job characteristics model designed to increase an individual's sense that his or her work is meaningful. Skill variety occurs when workers are tasked with a number of different activities requiring a diverse range of skills and abilities.

slowdown: A type of job action sometimes observed during times of labor conflict. Workers only minimally perform their responsibilities (e.g., not writing traffic tickets).

socialized power motive: A manifestation of the power motive where the desire for power is coupled with self-restraint, allowing the power to be used for the good of the organization as a whole rather than for personal benefit. Contrasts with *personalized power motive*.

span of control: The number of subordinates working under the direction of each supervisor. Narrow spans of control refer to situations where fewer workers are under a single supervisor's control. Wider spans are evident when a supervisor oversees more workers.

spatial complexity: The degree to which the organization's parts are distributed geographically. Common spatial divisions include beats, judicial districts, and field offices.

stalking horse: A practice where probation or parole officers serve as surrogates for the police, satisfying a law enforcement request rather than their own job responsibilities. For example, a probation officer may conduct a search at the request of a local police officer.

strains: Part of the process model of occupational stress, strains represent the individual's reactions—psychological, physical, and behavioral—to actual or threatened stressors. Examples include sleeplessness, hypertension, and aggression.

street-level bureaucrats: Frontline public-sector workers (e.g., police officer, social worker) who possess considerable discretion but work with limited resources. The fact that discretion is exercised suggests that policy is, for all intents and purposes, a product of the decision making of street-level workers rather than policymakers.

stress: The overall process wherein stressors (causes) produce strain (outcomes) in individuals.

stressors: Part of the process model of occupational stress, these are the demands (e.g., factors intrinsic to the job, role problems, relationships at work, career development issues, structural factors, work–home interface) that contribute to strain.

structural secrecy: A contributor to organizational deviance produced by the limited information sharing inherent in a structurally complex (horizontally, vertically, spatially) organization. The structural divisions preclude fully rational decision making.

supplemental pay: Forms of compensation beyond base salary. Types of supplemental pay include bonuses for longevity, shift differentials (e.g., working nights or weekends), hazardous duty, merit, and education.

surveillance: A necessary condition for the success of coercive and reward power bases. The promise of rewards and threat of punishments are ineffective unless the power holder is able to monitor power recipient behavior. Rewards and punishments cannot be meted out unless compliance (or lack of compliance) is observed.

synergy: The combination of expertise, historical knowledge, perspectives, skills, and human, material, and financial resources generated through collaboration.

task identity: An element of the job characteristics model designed to increase an individual's sense that his or her work is meaningful. Task identity is the extent to which a job involves the completion of an entire task from beginning to end rather than only a piece of a task.

task significance: An element of the job characteristics model designed to increase an individual's sense that his or her work is meaningful. Task significance is based on the degree of impact the job has over the lives of others. As the impact increases, task significance increases.

tertiary interventions: Efforts to address occupational stress targeting negative strain outcomes (e.g., aggression, absenteeism, health problems) once they appear; includes programs such as counseling, therapy, and medical care intended to address the symptoms of strain.

Theory X: A view of human nature associated with the writings of Douglas McGregor, it takes the position that individuals are uninterested in work, lack ambition, and prefer not to exercise personal initiative. They need to be coerced and controlled into working. Contrasts with *Theory Y*.

Theory Y: A view of human nature associated with the writings of Douglas McGregor, it assumes that individuals can reap satisfaction from work, especially when committed to the organization's goals. Workers want to use skills and their own judgment; excessive coercion and control are unnecessary. Contrasts with *Theory X*.

trait theory: A theory of leadership that dominated thinking until the 1940s. Researchers were interested in identifying individual traits and characteristics that distinguished leaders from nonleaders and effective leaders from ineffective leaders. A large number of traits were subsequently identified through research but generally fell into four categories: personality, skills and ability, social factors, and physical characteristics.

transactional leadership: A type of leadership based on an exchange between leader and follower where both parties satisfy their immediate interests. For example, a police chief can highlight the rewards officers will receive if they perform as expected. The chief obtains desired behavior from officers, and officers receive rewards from the chief.

transformational leadership: A type of leadership based on the notion of inspiring followers to move beyond self-interests to achieve and help the organization flourish.

traumatic stressors: Stressors (demands producing strain) considered relatively rare critical incidents. Examples of traumatic stressors include police-involved shootings and notifying individuals about deaths of family members. Contrasts with *routine occupational stressors*.

unit determination: The process through which the composition of a collective bargaining unit is established. The resulting body is recognized as the authorized bargaining unit for purposes of collective bargaining negotiations (i.e., who is covered by an agreed-on contract).

valence: One of three components of expectancy theory (see also *performance–outcome expectancy* and *effort–performance expectancy*). Valence refers to the importance of a particular outcome to any one person. If an outcome is not important, it is unlikely that a person will engage in the behavior that produces the outcome.

variable socialization: Occurs when the length of time to complete the socialization process or transition is unknown. Variable socialization is common when the number of people interested in crossing a boundary (e.g., applicants awaiting promotion) exceeds the number of positions. In such a case, individuals may wait indefinitely for opportunities for promotion. Contrasts with *fixed socialization*.

vertical collaborations: A type of task force comprising agencies representing different levels of government, including local, county, state, and federal organizations.

vertical complexity: The hierarchical division of work within an organization. Related to power, authority, and supervision.

workplace bullying: A workplace stressor associated with repeated aggression (e.g., workplace humiliation, impossible deadlines) directed at an individual. It is usually related to some difference in power between the bully and the victim (e.g., rank differences), thereby leading to challenges for the victim in trying to address the problem.

References

Aaron, J. D. K. (2000). Stress and coping in police officers. *Police Quarterly, 3*(4), 438–450.

Adam, C., Bauer, M. W., Knill, C., & Studinger, P. (2007). The termination of public organizations: Theoretical perspectives to revitalize a promising research area. *Public Organization Review, 7,* 221–236.

Adams, J. S. (1963). Towards an understanding of inequity. *Journal of Abnormal and Social Psychology, 67*(5), 422–436.

Agreement between the Department of Corrections, State of Missouri and the Missouri Corrections Officers Association (MOCOA). (2007–2012). Retrieved from http://oa.mo.gov/pers/documents/MOCOAAgreement020107t008312012.pdf

Alaska Intertribal Council v. State of Alaska, 110 P.3d 947 (Sup. Ct. Alaska 2005).

Aldrich, H. E., & Pfeffer, J. (1976). Environments of organizations. *Annual Review of Sociology, 2,* 79–105.

Aldrich, H. E., & Ruef, M. (2006). *Organizations evolving* (2nd ed.). Los Angeles: Sage.

Allen, J. M., & Sawhney, R. (2010). *Administration and management in criminal justice: A service quality approach.* Los Angeles: Sage.

Almgody, G., Bala, M., & Rivkind, A. (2007). The approach to suicide bombing attacks: Changing concepts. *European Journal of Trauma and Emergency Surgery, 33*(6), 641–647.

Alpert, G. P., Dunham, R. G., & Stroshine, M. S. (2006). *Policing: Continuity and change.* Long Grove, IL: Waveland Press.

Alpert, G. P., & MacDonald, J. M. (2001). Police use of force: An analysis of organizational characteristics. *Justice Quarterly, 18*(2), 393–409.

Amabile, T. M. (1993). Motivational synergy: Toward new conceptualizations of intrinsic and extrinsic motivation in the workplace. *Human Resource Management Review, 3*(3), 185–201.

Amendola, K. L., Weisburd, D., Hamilton, E. E., Jones, G., & Slipka, M. (2011). *The impact of shift length in policing on performance, health, quality of life, sleep, fatigue, and extra-duty employment: Executive summary.* Retrieved from https://www.ncjrs.gov/pdffiles1/nij/grants/237331.pdf

American Jail Association. (2012). *Resolutions of the American Jail Association.* Hagerstown, MD: Author.

Anderson, G. S., Litzenberger, R., & Plecas, D. (2002). Physical evidence of police officer stress. *Policing: An International Journal of Police Strategies and Management, 25*(2), 399–420.

Andreescu, V., & Vito, G. F. (2010). An exploratory study on ideal leadership behaviour: The opinions of American police managers. *International Journal of Police Science and Management, 12*(4), 567–583.

Angell, J. E. (1971). Toward an alternative to the classic police organizational arrangements: A democratic model. *Criminology, 9*(2–3), 185–206.

Anheier, H. K. (1999). *When things go wrong: Organizational failures and breakdowns.* Thousand Oaks, CA: Sage.

Anshel, M. H. (2000). A conceptual model and implications for coping with stressful events in police work. *Criminal Justice and Behavior, 27*(3), 375–400.

Armstrong, G. S. (2012). Factors to consider for optimal span of control in community supervision evidence-based practice environments. *Criminal Justice Policy Review, 23*(4), 427–446.

Armstrong, G. S., & Griffin, M. L. (2004). Does the job matter? Comparing correlates of stress among treatment and correctional staff in prisons. *Journal of Criminal Justice, 32*(6), 577–592.

Armstrong, J. H., & Frykberg, E. R. (2007). Lessons from the response to the Virginia Tech shootings. *Disaster Medicine and Public Health Preparedness, 1*(Suppl. S1), S7–S8.

Ashford, S., & Nurmohamed, S. (2012). From past to present and into the future: A hitchhiker's guide to the socialization literature. In C. R. Wanberg (Ed.), *The Oxford handbook of organizational socialization* (pp. 8–24). New York: Oxford University Press.

Austin, J., Clark, J., Hardyman, P., & Henry, D. A. (2000). *Three strikes and you're out: The implementation and impact of strike laws.* Washington, DC: U.S. Department of Justice, National Institute of Justice.

Babb, J., & Ammons, R. (1996). BOP inmate transport: A high reliability organization. *Corrections Today, 58*(4), 108–110.

Baird, S., & Jenkins, S. R. (2003). Vicarious traumatization, secondary traumatic stress, and burnout in sexual assault and domestic violence agency staff. *Violence and Victims, 18*(1), 71–86.

Bardach, E. (1996). Turf barriers to interagency collaboration. In D. F. Kettl & H. B. Milward (Eds.), *The state of public management* (pp. 168–192). Baltimore, MD: Johns Hopkins University Press.

Barnett, W. P., & Carroll, G. R. (1995). Modeling internal organizational change. *Annual Review of Sociology, 21,* 217–236.

Baro, A. L., & Burlingame, D. (1999). Law enforcement and higher education: Is there an impasse? *Journal of Criminal Justice Education, 10*(1), 57–73.

Bass, B. M. (1985a). *Leadership and performance beyond expectations.* New York: Free Press.

Bass, B. M. (1985b). Leadership: Good, better, best. *Organizational Dynamics, 13*(3), 26–40.

Bass, B. M. (1990a). *Bass & Stogdill's handbook of leadership: Theory, research, and managerial application* (3rd ed.). New York: Free Press.

Bass, B. M. (1990b). From transactional to transformational leadership: Learning to share the vision. *Organizational Dynamics, 18*(3), 19–31.

Bass, B. M. (1999). Two decades of research and development in transformational leadership. *European Journal of Work and Organizational Psychology, 8*(1), 9–32.

Bass, B. M., & Riggio, R. E. (2006). *Transformational leadership* (2nd ed.). Mahwah, NJ: Lawrence Erlbaum.

Baum, J. A. C. (1999). Organizational ecology. In S. R. Clegg & C. Hardy (Eds.), *Studying organization: Theory and method* (pp. 71–108). Thousand Oaks, CA: Sage.

Bayley, D. H. (1994). *Police for the future.* New York: Oxford University Press.

Bayley, D. H., & Shearing, C. D. (2001). *The new structure of policing: Description, conceptualization, and research agenda.* Washington, DC: U.S. Department of Justice, National Institute of Justice.

Beehr, T. A., & O'Hara, K. (1987). Methodological designs for evaluation of occupational stress intervention. In V. S. Kasl & C. L. Cooper (Eds.), *Stress and health: Issues in research methodology* (pp. 79–112). New York: Wiley.

Behn, R. D. (2008). Designing PerformanceStat: Or what are the key strategic choices that a jurisdiction or agency must make when adapting the Compstat/Citistat class of performance strategies? *Public Performance & Management Review, 32*(2), 206–235.

Belbot, B. (2004). Report on the Prison Litigation Reform Act: What have the courts decided so far? *Prison Journal, 84*(3), 290–316.

Bell, G. D. (1967). Determinants of span of control. *American Journal of Sociology, 73*(1), 100–109.

Bennett, R. R. (1984). Becoming blue: A longitudinal study of police recruit occupational socialization. *Journal of Police Science & Administration, 12*(1), 47–58.

Benson, J. K. (1977). Organizations: A dialectical view. *Administrative Science Quarterly, 22*(1), 1–21.

Benson, J. S., & Decker, S. H. (2010). The organizational structure of international drug smuggling. *Journal of Criminal Justice, 38*(2), 130–138.

Berman, G., & Feinblatt, J. (2001). Problem-solving courts: A brief primer. *Law & Policy, 23*(2), 125–140.

Berman, G., & Fox, A. (2009). *Lessons from the battle over D.A.R.E.: The complicated relationship between research and practice.* New York: Center for Court Innovation.

Bies, R. J. (2001). Interactional (in)justice: The sacred and the profane. In J. Greenberg & R. Cropanzano (Eds.), *Advances in organizational justice* (pp. 89–118). Stanford, CA: Stanford University Press.

Bies, R. J., & Moag, J. S. (1986). Interactional justice: Communication criteria of fairness. In R. J. Lewicki, B. H. Sheppard, & M. H. Bazerman (Eds.), *Research on negotiations in organizations* (Vol. 1, pp. 43–55). Greenwich, CT: JAI Press.

Bittner, E. (1990). Florence Nightingale in pursuit of Willie Sutton: A theory of the police. In E. Bittner (Ed.), *Aspects of police work* (pp. 233–268). Boston: Northeastern University Press.

Blake, R. R., & Mouton, J. S. (1964). *The managerial grid: Key orientations for achieving production through people.* Houston, TX: Gulf.

Blake, R. R., & Mouton, J. S. (1978). *The new managerial grid.* Houston, TX: Gulf.

Blau, P. M. (1970). A formal theory of differentiation in organizations. *American Sociological Review, 35*(2), 201–218.

Blau, P. M., & Schoenherr, R. A. (1971). *The structure of organizations.* New York: Basic Books.

Blau, P. M., & Scott, W. R. (2003). *Formal organizations: A comparative approach.* Stanford, CA: Stanford University Press. (Original work published 1962)

Bluestein, G. (2011, October 26). State budget cuts clog criminal justice system. *Wall Street Journal.* Retrieved from http://online.wsj.com/article/AP2911fb9c56e845e98145441192b3a5aa.html

Blumberg, A. S. (1967). The practice of law as a confidence game. *Law and Society Review, 1,* 15–39.

Bohm, R. (2006). "McJustice": On the McDonaldization of criminal justice. *Justice Quarterly, 23*(1), 127–146.

Bohte, J., & Meier, K. J. (2001). Structure and the performance of public organizations: Task difficulty and span of control. *Public Organization Review, 1*(3), 341–354.

Boin, A. (2001). *Crafting public institutions: Leadership in two prison systems.* Boulder, CO: Lynne Rienner.

Boin, A., & Hart, L. G. (2003). Public leadership in times of crisis: Mission impossible? *Public Administration Review, 63*(5), 544–553.

Boin, R. A., & Van Duin, M. J. (1995). Prison riots as organizational failures: A managerial perspective. *Prison Journal, 75*(3), 357–379.

Boland, B. (2001). *Community prosecution in Washington, D.C.: The U.S. Attorney's Fifth District pilot project.* Washington, DC: U.S. Department of Justice, National Institute of Justice.

Boss, R. W. (1979). It doesn't matter if you win or lose, unless you're losing: Organizational change in a law enforcement agency. *Journal of Applied Behavioral Science, 15*(2), 198–220.

Bouza, A. V. (1985). Police unions: Paper tigers or roaring lions? In W. A. Geller (Ed.), *Police leadership in America: Crisis and opportunity* (pp. 241–280). New York: Praeger.

Bozeman, B. (1987). *All organizations are public: Bridging public and private organizational theories.* San Francisco: Jossey-Bass.

Bozeman, B., & Bretschneider, S. (1994). The "publicness puzzle" in organization theory: A test of alternative explanations of differences between public and private organizations. *Journal of Public Administration Research and Theory, 4*(2), 197–224.

Bradley, H. B. (1969). Community-based treatment for young adult offenders. *Crime & Delinquency, 15*(3), 359–370.

Braga, A. A. (2008). Pulling levers focused deterrence strategies and the prevention of gun homicide. *Journal of Criminal Justice, 36*(4), 332–343.

Braga, A. A., Hureau, D., & Winship, C. (2008). Losing faith? Police, black churches, and the resurgence of youth violence in Boston. *Ohio State Journal of Criminal Law, 6,* 141–172.

Braga, A. A., Kennedy, D. M., Piehl, A. M., & Waring, E. J. (2000). *The Boston Gun Project: Impact evaluation findings.* Washington, DC: U.S. Department of Justice, National Institute of Justice.

Braga, A. A., Kennedy, D. M., Waring, E. J., & Piehl, A. M. (2001). Problem-oriented policing, deterrence, and youth violence: An evaluation of Boston's Operation Ceasefire. *Journal of Research in Crime and Delinquency, 38*(3), 195–225.

Braga, A. A., McDevitt, J., & Pierce, G. L. (2006). Understanding and preventing gang violence: Problem analysis and response development in Lowell, Massachusetts. *Police Quarterly, 9*(1), 20–46.

Braga, A. A., & Weisburd, D. L. (2012). The effects of "pulling levers" focused deterrence strategies on crime. *Campbell Systematic Reviews, 6,* 1–90.

Braga, A. A., & Winship, C. (2006). Partnership, accountability, and innovation: Clarifying Boston's experience with pulling levers. In D. Weisburd & A. A. Braga (Eds.), *Police innovation: Contrasting perspectives* (pp. 171–187). New York: Cambridge University Press.

Brass, D. J., & Burkhardt, M. E. (1993). Potential power and power use: An investigation of structure and behavior. *Academy of Management Journal, 36*(3), 441–470.

Bratton, W., & Knobler, P. (1998). *Turnaround: How America's top cop reversed the crime epidemic.* New York: Random House.

Brewer, T. W., Jefferis, E., Butcher, F., & Wiles, T. D. (2007). A case study of the Northern Ohio Violent Fugitive Task Force. *Criminal Justice Policy Review, 18*(2), 200–220.

Brief, A. P., Aldag, R. J., Russell, C. J., & Rude, D. E. (1981). Leader behavior in a police organization revisited. *Human Relations, 34*(12), 1037–1051.

Briggs, C. S., Sundt, J. L., & Castellano, T. C. (2003). The effect of supermaximum security prisons on aggregate levels of institutional violence. *Criminology, 41*(4), 1341–1376.

Brockner, J., & Wiesenfeld, B. M. (1996). An integrative framework for explaining reactions to decisions: Interactive effects of outcomes and procedures. *Psychological Bulletin, 120*(2), 189–208.

Bromley, M. L. (1992). Campus and community crime rate comparisons: A statewide study. *Journal of Security Administration, 15*(2), 49–64.

Brown, L. P., & Wycoff, M. A. (1987). Policing Houston: Reducing fear and improving service. *Crime & Delinquency, 33*(1), 71–89.

Brown, M. K. (1988). *Working the street: Police discretion and the dilemmas of reform.* New York: Russell Sage Foundation.

Bryman, A. (1999). Leadership in organizations. In S. R. Clegg, C. Hardy, & W. R. Nord (Eds.), *Managing organizations: Current issues* (pp. 26–42). Thousand Oaks, CA: Sage.

Brzezinski, M. (2004). Red alert. *Mother Jones.* Retrieved from http://www.motherjones.com/politics/2004/09/red-alert

Buckley, L. B., McGinnis, J. J., & Petrunik, M. G. (1992). Police perceptions of education as an entitlement to promotion: An equity theory perspective. *American Journal of Police, 12*(2), 77–100.

Buhler, M. L. (1999). The fugitive task force: An alternative organizational model. *FBI Law Enforcement Bulletin, 68*(4), 1.

Bullock, R. J., & Batten, D. (1985). It's just a phase we're going through: A review and synthesis of OD phase analysis. *Group & Organization Management, 10*(4), 383–412.

Bureau of Justice Assistance. (1996). *A report to the attorney general: Multijurisdictional task forces use of overtime and related issues, FY1994.* Washington, DC: U.S. Department of Justice, Bureau of Justice Assistance.

Bureau of Justice Statistics. (2007). Law enforcement management and administrative statistics (LEMAS), 2007. Retrieved from http://www.icpsr.umich.edu/icpsrweb/NACJD/studies/31161

Bureau of Justice Statistics. (2010). Local level reported crime. *Uniform Crime Reporting Statistics.* Retrieved from http://www.bjs.gov/ucrdata/Search/Crime/Local/LocalCrime.cfm

Bureau of Labor Statistics. (2011, January 21). Union members, 2010 [Press release]. Retrieved from http://www.bls.gov/news.release/pdf/union2.pdf

Burke, R. J. (1989). Toward a phase model of burnout: Some conceptual and methodological concerns. *Group & Organization Management, 14*(1), 23–32.

Burke, R. J., & Deszca, E. (1986). Correlates of psychological burnout phases among police officers. *Human Relations, 39*(6), 487–501.

Burke, W. W. (2002). *Organizational change: Theory and practice.* Thousand Oaks, CA: Sage.

Burnes, B. (2004). Kurt Lewin and the planned approach to change: A re-appraisal. *Journal of Management Studies, 41*(6), 977–1002.

Burnett, R., & Appleton, C. (2004). Joined-up services to tackle youth crime: A case-study in England. *British Journal of Criminology, 44*(1), 34–54.

Burns, J. M. (1978). *Leadership.* New York: Harper & Row.

Burns, T., & Stalker, G. M. (1961). *The management of innovation.* New York: Oxford University Press.

Burruss, G. W., Giblin, M. J., & Schafer, J. A. (2010). Threatened globally, acting locally: Modeling law enforcement homeland security practices. *Justice Quarterly, 27*(1), 77–101.

Burruss, G. W., Schafer, J. A., Giblin, M. J., & Haynes, M. R. (2012). *Homeland security in small law enforcement jurisdictions: Preparedness, efficacy, and proximity to big-city peers* (No. 239466). Washington, DC: U.S. Department of Justice, National Institute of Justice.

Cameron, K. S., & Whetten, D. A. (1983). Models of the organizational life cycle: Applications to higher education. *Review of Higher Education, 6*(4), 269–299.

Campbell, I., & Kodz, J. (2011). *What makes great police leadership? Rapid evidence assessment.* London: National Policing Improvement Agency.

Carlson, P. M. (1999). The organization of the institution. In P. M. Carlson & J. S. Garrett (Eds.), *Prison and jail administration: Practice and theory* (pp. 25–31). Gaithersburg, MD: Aspen.

Carter, D. L., & Carter, J. G. (2009). The intelligence fusion process for state, local, and tribal law enforcement. *Criminal Justice and Behavior, 36*(12), 1323–1339.

Carter, D. L., & Sapp, A. D. (1992). A comparative analysis of clauses in police collective bargaining agreements as indicators of change in labor relations. *American Journal of Police, 12*(2), 17–46.

Cartwright, S., & Cooper, C. L. (1997). *Managing workplace stress.* Thousand Oaks, CA: Sage.

Chao, G. T., O'Leary-Kelly, A. M., Wolf, S., Klein, H. J., & Gardner, P. D. (1994). Organizational socialization: Its content and consequences. *Journal of Applied Psychology, 79*(5), 730–743.

Chaos in Charm City. (1974, July 22). *Time.* Retrieved from http://www.time.com/time/magazine/article/0,9171,942930,00.html

Chapin, M., Brannen, S. J., Singer, M. I., & Walker, M. (2008). Training police leadership to recognize and address operational stress. *Police Quarterly, 11*(3), 338–352.

Chappell, A. T., & Lanza-Kaduce, L. (2010). Police academy socialization: Understanding the lessons learned in a paramilitary-bureaucratic organization. *Journal of Contemporary Ethnography, 39*(2), 187–214.

Cheek, F. E., & Miller, M. D. S. (1983). The experience of stress for correction officers: A double-bind theory of correctional stress. *Journal of Criminal Justice, 11*(2), 105–120.

Chemers, M. M. (1997). *An integrative theory of leadership.* Mahwah, NJ: Lawrence Erlbaum.

Chen, R. K. (2004). State incarceration of federal prisoners after September 11: Whose jail is it anyway? *Brooklyn Law Review, 69,* 1335–1367.

Chermak, S., & McGarrell, E. (2004). Problem-solving approaches to homicide: An evaluation of the Indianapolis Violence Reduction Partnership. *Criminal Justice Policy Review, 15*(2), 161–192.

Child, J. (1972). Organization structure and strategies of control: A replication of the Aston study. *Administrative Science Quarterly, 17*(2), 163–177.

Church, R. L., & Robertson, N. (1999). How state police agencies are addressing the issue of wellness. *Policing: An International Journal of Police Strategies and Management, 22*(3), 304–312.

Church, T. W. (1985). Examining local legal culture. *American Bar Foundation Research Journal, 10*(3), 449–518.

Cimini, M. H. (1998, Fall). 1982–97 state and local government work stoppages and their legal background. *Compensation and Working Conditions,* 32–39.

City without cops. (1969, October 17). *Time.* Retrieved from http://www.time.com/time/magazine/article/0,9171,840236,00.html

Clarity, J. F. (1972, April 3). State strike ends as workers win raise and bonus. *New York Times,* p. 1.

Clark, G. (1969, November 16). What happens when the police strike? *New York Times Sunday Magazine,* 45.

Clarke, L., & Short, J. F. (1993). Social organization and risk: Some current controversies. *Annual Review of Sociology, 19,* 375–399.

Clynch, E. J., & Neubauer, D. W. (1981). Trial courts as organizations. *Law and Policy Quarterly, 3*(1), 69–94.

Cohen, A. R., & Bradford, D. L. (1989). Influence without authority: The use of alliances, reciprocity, and exchange to accomplish work. *Organizational Dynamics, 17*(3), 5–17.

Cohen-Charash, Y., & Spector, P. E. (2001). The role of justice in organizations: A meta-analysis. *Organizational Behavior and Human Decision Processes, 86*(2), 278–321.

Colbridge, T. D. (2003). Probationers, parolees, and the Fourth Amendment. *FBI Law Enforcement Bulletin, 72*(7), 22–31.

Coles, C. M. (2000). *Community prosecution, problem solving, and public accountability: The evolving strategy of the American prosecutor* (Working Paper No. 00-02-04). Cambridge, MA: Harvard University, John F. Kennedy School of Government.

Colquitt, J. A., Conlon, D. E., Wesson, M. J., Porter, C. O. L. H., & Ng, K. Y. (2001). Justice at the millennium: A meta-analytic review of 25 years of organizational justice research. *Journal of Applied Psychology, 86*(3), 425–445.

Colvin, H. M., & Taylor, R. M. (2012). *Building a resilient workforce: Opportunities for the Department of Homeland Security: Workshop summary.* Washington, DC: National Academies Press.

Colvin, M. (1982). The 1980 New Mexico prison riot. *Social Problems, 29*(5), 449–463.

Comeau, P. R. (1971). Labor unions for prison inmates: An analysis of a recent proposal for the organization of inmate labor. *Buffalo Law Review, 21,* 963–985.

Connor, P. E., & Lake, L. K. (1988). *Managing organizational change.* New York: Praeger.

Conser, J. A. (1979). Motivational theory applied to law enforcement agencies. *Journal of Police Science and Administration, 7*(3), 285–291.

Conti, N. (2009). A visigoth system: Shame, honor, and police socialization. *Journal of Contemporary Ethnography, 38*(3), 409–432.

Cooper, C. L., Dewe, P. J., & O'Driscoll, M. P. (2001). *Organizational stress: A review and critique of theory, research, and applications.* Thousand Oaks, CA: Sage.

Corbett, R. P. (1998). Probation blue? The promise (and perils) of probation-police partnerships. *Corrections Management Quarterly, 2*(3), 31–39.

Cordes, C. L., & Dougherty, T. W. (1993). A review and an integration of research on job burnout. *Academy of Management Review, 18*(4), 621–656.

Cordner, G. W. (2000). Community policing: Elements and effects. In G. P. Alpert & A. R. Piquero (Eds.), *Community policing: Contemporary readings* (2nd ed., pp. 45–62). Prospect Heights, IL: Waveland Press.

Cornelius, L., & Dively, C. (2008). Leading into tomorrow: Developing leaders for the challenges ahead. *Corrections Today, 70*(4), 66–69.

Corsaro, N., Brunson, R. K., Gau, J. M., & Oldham, C. (2011). *The Peoria pulling levers drug market intervention: A review of program process, changes in perception, and crime impact.* Chicago: Illinois Criminal Justice Information Authority.

Corsaro, N., Brunson, R. K., & McGarrell, E. F. (in press). Problem-oriented policing and open-air drug markets: Examining the Rockford pulling levers deterrence strategy. *Crime & Delinquency.* doi:10.1177/0011128709345955

Corsaro, N., & McGarrell, E. F. (2009). Testing a promising homicide reduction strategy: Re-assessing the impact of the Indianapolis "pulling levers" intervention. *Journal of Experimental Criminology, 5*(1), 63–82.

Cowie, H., Naylor, P., Rivers, I., Smith, P. K., & Pereira, B. (2002). Measuring workplace bullying. *Aggression and Violent Behavior, 7*(1), 33–51.

Craig, S. C. (2004). Rehabilitation versus control: An organizational theory of prison management. *Prison Journal, 84*(Suppl. 4), 92–114.

Crank, J. P., & Caldero, M. (1991). The production of occupational stress in medium-sized police agencies: A survey of line officers in eight municipal departments. *Journal of Criminal Justice, 19*(4), 339–349.

Crank, J. P., & Giacomazzi, A. (2009). A sheriff's office as a learning organization. *Police Quarterly, 12*(4), 351–369.

Crank, J. P., & Langworthy, R. (1992). An institutional perspective of policing. *Journal of Criminal Law and Criminology, 83*(2), 338–363.

Critchley, T. A. (1967). *A history of police in England and Wales 1900–1966.* London: Constable.

Crouch, B. M., & Marquart, J. W. (1989). *An appeal to justice: Litigated reform of Texas prisons.* Austin: University of Texas Press.

Cummings, L. L. (1978). Toward organizational behavior. *Academy of Management Review, 3*(1), 90–98.

Cummings, L. L., & Berger, C. J. (1976). Organization structure: How does it influence attitudes and performance? *Organizational Dynamics, 5*(2), 34–49.

Cummings, T. G., & Cooper, C. L. (1979). A cybernetic framework for studying occupational stress. *Human Relations, 32*(5), 395–418.

Dabney, D. A., Copes, H., Tewksbury, R., & Hawk-Tourtelot, S. R. (2011, November 21). A qualitative assessment of stress perceptions among members of a homicide unit. *Justice Quarterly.* doi:10.1080/07418825.2011.633542

Daft, R. L. (2010a). *Management* (9th ed.). Mason, OH: South-Western.

Daft, R. L. (2010b). *Organization theory and design* (10th ed.). Mason, OH: South-Western Cengage Learning.

Dahl, R. (1957). The concept of power. *Behavioral Science, 2*, 201–215.

Dalton, D. R., Todor, W. D., Spendolini, M. J., Fielding, G. J., & Porter, L. W. (1980). Organization structure and performance: A critical review. *Academy of Management Review, 5*(1), 49–64.

Daly, K. (1987). Structure and practice of familial-based justice in a criminal court. *Law & Society Review, 21*(2), 267–290.

Damanpour, F. (1996). Organizational complexity and innovation: Developing and testing multiple contingency models. *Management Science, 42*(5), 693–716.

Daniels, M. R. (1997). *Terminating public programs: An American political paradox.* Armonk, NY: M. E. Sharpe.

Davies, G. K. (2008). Connecting the dots: Lessons from the Virginia Tech shootings. *Change: The Magazine of Higher Learning,* 8–15.

Davis, R. C., Henderson, N. J., & Ortiz, C. W. (2005). *Can federal intervention bring lasting improvement in local policing? The Pittsburgh consent decree.* New York: Vera Institute of Justice.

Day, D. V. (2001). Leadership development: A review in context. *Leadership Quarterly, 11*(4), 581–613.

Decker, D. (1997). Consent decrees and the Prison Litigation Reform Act of 1995: Usurping judicial power or quelling judicial micromanagement. *Wisconsin Law Review,* 1275–1321.

Decker, S. H., Katz, C. M., & Webb, V. J. (2008). Understanding the black box of gang organization: Implications for involvement in violent crime, drug sales, and violent victimization. *Crime Delinquency, 54*(1), 153–172.

DeFrances, C. J. (2002). *Prosecutors in state courts, 2001.* Washington, DC: U.S. Department of Justice, Bureau of Justice Statistics.

Dejong, C., Mastrofski, S., & Parks, R. (2001). Patrol officers and problem solving: An application of expectancy theory. *Justice Quarterly, 18*, 31–61.

Delaney, J., & Feuille, P. (1988). Police interest arbitration: Awards and issues. In D. Lewin, P. Feuille, T. A. Kochan, & J. T. Delaney (Eds.), *Public sector labor relations: Analysis and readings* (pp. 386–398). Lexington, MA: Lexington Books.

Deluga, R. J., & Souza, J. (1991). The effects of transformational and transactional leadership styles on the influencing behaviour of subordinate police officers. *Journal of Occupational Psychology, 64*(1), 49–55.

Demers, C. (2007). *Organizational change theories: A synthesis.* Los Angeles: Sage.

Denison, D. R. (1996). What is the difference between organizational culture and organizational climate? A native's point of view on a decade of paradigm wars. *Academy of Management Review, 21*(3), 619–654.

Densten, I. L. (1999). Senior Australian law enforcement leadership under examination. *Policing: An International Journal of Police Strategies and Management, 22*(1), 45–57.

Dent, E. B., & Goldberg, S. G. (1999). Challenging "resistance to change." *Journal of Applied Behavioral Science, 35*(1), 25–41.

Department of Public Safety, Alaska State Troopers. (2013). About VPSO Program. Retrieved from http://dps.alaska.gov/ast/vpso/about.aspx

Deutsch, M. (1975). Equity, equality, and need: What determines which value will be used as the basis of distributive justice? *Journal of Social Issues, 31*(3), 137–149.

Dewe, P. (1991). Primary appraisal, secondary appraisal and coping: Their role in stressful work encounters. *Journal of Occupational Psychology, 64*(4), 331–351.

Dias, C. F., & Vaughn, M. S. (2006). Bureaucracy, managerial disorganization, and administrative breakdown in criminal justice agencies. *Journal of Criminal Justice, 34*, 543–555.

DiIulio, J. J. (1990). Managing a barbed-wire bureaucracy: The impossible job of corrections commissioner. In E. C. Hargrove & J. C. Glidewell (Eds.), *Impossible jobs in management* (pp. 49–71). Lawrence: University Press of Kansas.

DiMaggio, P. J., & Powell, W. W. (1983). The iron cage revisited: Institutional isomorphism and collective rationality in organizational fields. *American Sociological Review, 48*(2), 147–160.

Dixon, J. (1995). The organizational context of criminal sentencing. *American Journal of Sociology, 100*(5), 1157–1198.

Doerner, W. M., & Doerner, W. G. (2010). Collective bargaining and job benefits: The case of Florida deputy sheriffs. *Police Quarterly, 35*(4), 367–386.

Donaldson, L. (1995). *American anti-management theories of organization: A critique of paradigm proliferation.* New York: Cambridge University Press.

Donaldson, L. (2001). *The contingency theory of organizations.* Thousand Oaks, CA: Sage.

Dowler, K. (2005). Job satisfaction, burnout, and perception of unfair treatment: The relationship between race and police work. *Police Quarterly, 8*(4), 476–489.

Downs, A. (1964). *Inside bureaucracy.* Santa Monica, CA: RAND.

Duffee, D. E., & Allan, E. (2007). Criminal justice, criminology, and criminal justice theory. In D. E. Duffee & E. R. Maguire (Eds.), *Criminal justice theory: Explaining the nature and behavior of criminal justice* (pp. 1–22). New York: Routledge.

Dugan, L., & Gibbs, C. (2009). The role of organizational structure in the control of corporate crime and terrorism. In S. S. Simpson & D. Weisburd (Eds.), *The criminology of white-collar crime* (pp. 111–128). New York: Springer.

Dunford, F. W., Huizinga, D., & Elliott, D. S. (1990). The role of arrest in domestic assault: The Omaha police experiment. *Criminology, 28*(2), 183–206.

Dunworth, T., Haynes, P., & Saiger, A. J. (1997). *National assessment of the Byrne Formula Grant Program.* Washington, DC: U.S. Department of Justice, National Institute of Justice.

Eccles, T. (1994). *Succeeding with change: Implementing action-driven strategies.* New York: McGraw-Hill.

Eisenberg, D. (2003). Evaluating the effectiveness of policies related to drunk driving. *Journal of Policy Analysis and Management, 22*(2), 249–274.

Eisenstein, J., Flemming, R. B., & Nardulli, P. F. (1988). *The contours of justice: Communities and their courts.* Boston: Little, Brown.

Eisenstein, J., & Jacob, H. (1991). *Felony justice: An organizational analysis of criminal courts.* New York: University Press of America.

Elliott, C. (2011, October 26). New tax on air travel makes some see red. *Seattle Times.* Retrieved from http://seattletimes.nwsource.com/html/travel/2016616462_webtroubleshooter26.html

Emans, B. J. M., Munduate, L., Klaver, E., & Van de Vliert, E. (2003). Constructive consequences of leaders' forcing influence styles, *Applied Psychology, 52*(1), 36–54.

Emerson, R. M. (1962). Power-dependence relations. *American Sociological Review, 27*(1), 31–41.

Emmelman, D. S. (1996). Trial by plea bargain: Case settlement as a product of recursive decision making. *Law & Society Review, 30*(2), 335–360.

Engel, R. S. (2000). The effects of supervisory styles on patrol officer behavior. *Police Quarterly, 3*(3), 262–293.

Engel, R. S. (2002). Patrol officer supervision in the community policing era. *Journal of Criminal Justice, 30*(1), 51–64.

Erez, E., & Tontodonato, P. (1990). The effect of victim participation in sentencing on sentence outcome. *Criminology, 28*(3), 451–474.

Etzion, D. (1984). Moderating effect of social support on the stress–burnout relationship. *Journal of Applied Psychology, 69*(4), 615–622.

Etzioni, A. (1964). *Modern organizations.* Englewood Cliffs, NJ: Prentice Hall.

Evan, W. M. (1963). Indices of the hierarchical structure of industrial organizations. *Management Science, 9*(3), 468–477.

Evans, M. G. (1996). R. J. House's 'a path-goal theory of leader effectiveness.' *Leadership Quarterly, 7*(3), 305.

Fagan, J., & Davies, G. (2000). Street stops and broken windows: Terry, race and disorder in New York City. *Fordham Urban Law Journal, 28,* 457–504.

Falcione, R. L., & Wilson, C. E. (1988). Socialization processes in organizations. In G. M. Goldhaber & G. A. Barnett (Eds.), *Handbook of organizational communication* (pp. 151–169). Norwood, NJ: Ablex.

Falcone, D. N., & Wells, L. E. (1995). The county sheriff as a distinctive policing modality. *American Journal of Police, 14*(3–4), 123–124.

Farber, H. S. (2005). *Union membership in the United States: The divergence between the public and private sectors.* Princeton, NJ: Princeton University.

Farkas, M. A., & Manning, P. K. (1997). The occupational culture of corrections and police officers. *Journal of Crime and Justice, 20*(2), 51–68.

Farmer, S. J., Beehr, T. A., & Love, K. G. (2003). Becoming an undercover police officer: A note on fairness perceptions, behavior, and attitudes. *Journal of Organizational Behavior, 24*(4), 373–387.

Fayol, H. (1949). *General and industrial management* (C. Storrs, Trans.). London: Sir Isaac Pitman and Sons.

Federal Bureau of Investigation. (2001). *Safe street violent crime initiative report, fiscal year 2000.* Washington, DC: U.S. Department of Justice, Federal Bureau of Investigation.

Federal Bureau of Investigation. (n.d.). *Protecting America from terrorist attack: Our joint terrorism task forces.* Retrieved from http://www.fbi.gov/about-us/investigate/terrorism/terrorism_jttfs

Federal Bureau of Prisons. (n.d.). Prison types and general information. Retrieved from http://www.bop.gov/locations/institutions/index.jsp

Feeley, M. M., & Rubin, E. L. (1998). *Judicial policy making and the modern state: How the courts reformed America's prisons.* New York: Cambridge University Press.

Feeley, M. M., & Sarat, A. D. (1980). *The policy dilemma: Federal crime policy and the Law Enforcement Assistance Administration.* Minneapolis: University of Minnesota Press.

Feldman, D. C. (1976). A contingency theory of socialization. *Administrative Science Quarterly, 21*(3), 433–452.

Feldman, D. C. (1981). The multiple socialization of organization members. *Academy of Management Review, 6*(2), 309–318.

Fergus, M. A. (2004, March 7). Josiah Sutton: One year later. *Houston Chronicle.* Retrieved from http://www.chron.com/life/article/Josiah-Sutton-One-Year-Later-1976295.php

Fiedler, F. E. (1965). Engineer the job to fit the manager. *Harvard Business Review, 43*(5), 115–122.

Fiedler, F. E. (1967). *A theory of leadership effectiveness.* New York: McGraw-Hill.

Fine, J. (Director), & Marabella, M. (Writer/Director/Executive Producer). (2005). *Grounded on 9/11* [Television broadcast]. New York: A&E Television Networks.

Finn, P. (2000). *Addressing correctional officer stress: Programs and strategies.* Washington, DC: U.S. Department of Justice, National Institute of Justice.

Finn, P., & Kuck, S. (2003). *Addressing probation and parole officer stress.* Washington, DC: U.S. Department of Justice, National Institute of Justice.

Finney, M. (1997). Scale economies and police department consolidation: Evidence from Los Angeles. *Contemporary Economic Policy, 15*(1), 121–127.

Fogelson, R. M. (1977). *Big-city police.* Cambridge, MA: Harvard University Press.

Ford, R. E. (2003). Saying one thing, meaning another: The role of parables in police training. *Police Quarterly, 6*(1), 84–110.

Fox, C., & Harding, D. J. (2005). School shootings as organizational deviance. *Sociology of Education, 78*(1), 69–97.

Fox, J. A., & Hellman, D. A. (1985). Location and other correlates of campus crime. *Journal of Criminal Justice, 13*(5), 429–444.

Franklin, B. A. (1974, July 15). Striking Baltimore police told to work or lose jobs. *New York Times,* pp. A1, A12.

French, J. R. P., & Raven, B. (1959). The bases of social power. In D. Cartwright (Ed.), *Studies in social power* (pp. 150–167). Ann Arbor: Research Center for Group Dynamics, Institute for Social Research, University of Michigan.

Freudenberger, H. J. (1974). Staff burn-out. *Journal of Social Issues, 30*(1), 159–165.

Freudenberger, H. J. (1975). The staff burn-out syndrome in alternative institutions. *Psychotherapy: Theory, Research & Practice, 12*(1), 73–82.

Frumkin, P., & Reingold, D. (2004). *Evaluation research and institutional pressures: Challenges in public-nonprofit contracting* (No. 23). Cambridge, MA: Harvard University, Hauser Center for Nonprofit Organizations.

Fuoco, M. A. (2006, January 9). Police chief McNeilly's tenure saw wrenching changes. *Pittsburgh Post-Gazette.* Retrieved from http://www.post-gazette.com/stories/local/neighborhoods-city/police-chief-mcneillys-tenure-saw-wrenching-changes-416443/

Fyfe, J. J. (1987). Police shooting: Environment and license. In J. E. Scott & T. Hirschi (Eds.), *Controversial issues in crime and justice* (pp. 79–94). Beverly Hills, CA: Sage.

Fyfe, J. J. (1988). Police use of deadly force: Research and reform. *Justice Quarterly, 5*(2), 165–205.

Gaines, L. K., Falkenberg, S., & Gambino, J. A. (1993). Police physical agility testing: An historical and legal analysis. *American Journal of Police, 12,* 47–66.

Gaines, L. K., Van Tubergen, N., & Paiva, M. A. (1984). Police officer perceptions of promotion as a source of motivation. *Journal of Criminal Justice, 12,* 265–275.

Gajduschek, G. (2003). Bureaucracy: Is it efficient? Is it not? Is that the question? Uncertainty reduction: an ignored element of bureaucratic rationality. *Administration Society, 34*(6), 700–723.

Gardner, J. W. (2000). The nature of leadership. In M. Fullan (Ed.), *Jossey-Bass reader on educational leadership* (pp. 3–12). San Francisco: Jossey-Bass.

Garrett, T. M. (2001). The Waco, Texas, ATF raid and Challenger launch decision: Management, judgment, and the knowledge analytic. *American Review of Public Administration, 31,* 66–86.

Garrett, T. M. (2004). Whither Challenger, wither Columbia. *American Review of Public Administration, 34*(4), 389–402.

Geller, W. A. (1997). Suppose we were really serious about police departments becoming "learning organizations"? *National Institute of Justice Journal,* (234), 2–8.

Gershon, R. R. M., Barocas, B., Canton, A. N., Li, X., & Vlahov, D. (2009). Mental, physical, and behavioral outcomes associated with perceived work stress in police officers. *Criminal Justice and Behavior, 36*(3), 275–289.

Giblin, M. J. (2002). Using police officers to enhance the supervision of juvenile probationers: An evaluation of the Anchorage CAN program. *Crime and Delinquency, 48*(1), 116–137.

Giblin, M. J. (2006). Structural elaboration and institutional isomorphism: The case of crime analysis units. *Policing: An International Journal of Police Strategies and Management, 29*(4), 643–664.

Giblin, M. J., Schafer, J. A., & Burruss, G. W. (2009). Homeland security in the heartland: Risk, preparedness, and organizational capacity. *Criminal Justice Policy Review, 20*(3), 274–289.

Gilmore, T., & McCann, J. E. (1982). Designing effective transitions for new correctional leaders. *Review of Policy Research, 2*(2), 253–261.

Gladwell, M. (2000). *The tipping point: How little things can make a big difference.* New York: Little, Brown.

Glueck, S., & Glueck, E. (1929). Predictability in the administration of criminal justice. *Harvard Law Review, 42,* 297–329.

Goldberg, J. (2008, November). The things he carried. *Atlantic Monthly,* 100–104.

Goldstein, H. (1979). Improving policing: A problem-oriented approach. *Crime & Delinquency, 25*(2), 236–258.

Goldstone, J. A., & Useem, B. (1999). Prison riots as microrevolutions: An extension of state-centered theories of revolution. *American Journal of Sociology, 104*(4), 985–1029.

Golembiewski, R. T., Boudreau, R. A., Sun, B.-C., & Luo, H. (1998). Estimates of burnout in public agencies: Worldwide, how many employees have which degrees of burnout, and with what consequences? *Public Administration Review, 58*(1), 59–65.

Golembiewski, R. T., & Kim, B.-S. (1990). Burnout in police work: Stressors, strain, and the phase model. *Police Studies: International Review of Police Development, 13,* 74–80.

Golembiewski, R. T., Munzenrider, R., & Carter, D. (1983). Phases of progressive burnout and their work site covariants: Critical issues in OD research and praxis. *Journal of Applied Behavioral Science, 19*(4), 461–481.

Golembiewski, R. T., Scherb, K., & Boudreau, R. A. (1993). Burnout in cross-national settings: Generic and model-specific perspectives. In W. B. Schaufeli, C. Maslach, & T. Marek (Eds.), *Professional burnout: Recent developments in theory and research* (pp. 217–236). Washington, DC: Taylor & Francis.

Goodman, B. (2008, June 10). Plan to cut back public defenders stirs worry in Georgia. *New York Times.* Retrieved from http://www.nytimes.com/2008/06/10/us/10defenders.html

Goodpaster, G. (1987). On the theory of American adversary criminal trial. *Journal of Criminal Law and Criminology, 78*(1), 118–154.

Gortner, H. F., Nichols, K. L., & Ball, C. (2007). *Organization theory.* Belmont, CA: Wadsworth.

Gottfredson, M. R., & Gottfredson, D. M. (1988). *Decision making in criminal justice: Toward the rational exercise of discretion* (2nd ed.). New York: Plenum.

Gover, A. R., Brank, E. M., & MacDonald, J. M. (2007). A specialized domestic violence court in South Carolina: An example of procedural justice for victims and defendants. *Violence Against Women, 13*(6), 603–626.

Governors Highway Safety Association. (2011). *Drunk driving laws.* Washington, DC: Author. Retrieved from http://www.ghsa.org/html/stateinfo/laws/impaired_laws.html

Graeff, C. L. (1983). The situational leadership theory: A critical view. *Academy of Management Review, 8*(2), 285–291.

Gray, B. (1985). Conditions facilitating interorganizational collaboration. *Human Relations, 38*(10), 911–936.

Greenberg, J. (1987). A taxonomy of organizational justice theories. *Academy of Management Review, 12*(1), 9–22.

Greenberg, J. (1990). Employee theft as a reaction to underpayment inequity: The hidden cost of pay cuts. *Journal of Applied Psychology, 75*(5), 561–568.

Greene, J. A. (1999). Zero tolerance: A case study of police policies and practices in New York City. *Crime & Delinquency, 45*(2), 171–187.

Greene, J. R. (1998). Evaluating planned change strategies in modern law enforcement: Implementing community based policing. In J.-P. Brodeur (Ed.), *How to recognize good policing: Problems and issues* (pp. 141–160). Thousand Oaks, CA: Sage.

Greene, J. R., Bergman, W. T., & McLaughlin, E. J. (1994). Implementing community policing: Cultural and structural change in police organizations. In D. P. Rosenbaum (Ed.), *The challenge of community policing: Testing the promises* (pp. 92–109). Thousand Oaks, CA: Sage.

Greenhouse, S. (2004, June 30). Democrats fear Boston police union may picket during party convention. *New York Times,* p. A16.

Griffin, M. L., Armstrong, G. S., & Hepburn, J. R. (2005). Correctional officers' perceptions of equitable treatment in the masculinized prison environment. *Criminal Justice Review, 30*(2), 189–206.

Griffin, M. L., Hogan, N. L., & Lambert, E. G. (2012). Doing "people work" in the prison setting: An examination of the job characteristics model and correctional staff burnout. *Criminal Justice and Behavior, 39*(9), 1131–1147.

Grimes, W. (2005, June 15). Calculating the incalculable in the aftermath of Sept. 11. *New York Times*. Retrieved from http://www.nytimes.com/2005/06/15/books/15grim.html

Grinc, R. M. (1994). "Angels in marble": Problems in stimulating community involvement in community policing. *Crime and Delinquency, 40*(3), 437–468.

Gross, S. R., Jacoby, K., Matheson, D. J., & Montgomery, N. (2005). Exonerations in the United States 1989 through 2003. *Journal of Criminal Law & Criminology, 95*, 523–560.

Guerra, S. (1995). The myth of dual sovereignty: Multijurisdictional drug law enforcement and double jeopardy. *North Carolina Law Review, 73*, 1159–1210.

Guillén, M. F. (1994). *Models of management: Work, authority, and organization in comparative perspective*. Chicago: University of Chicago Press.

Gulick, L. (1937). Notes on the theory of organization. In L. Gulick & L. Urwick, J. D. (Eds.), *Papers on the science of administration* (pp. 1–46). New York: Institute of Public Administration.

Gutterman, M. (2002). "Failure to communicate": The reel prison experience. *SMU Law Review, 55*, 1515–1560.

Haarr, R. N. (1997). Patterns of interaction in a police patrol bureau: Race and gender barriers to integration. *Justice Quarterly, 14*(1), 53–85.

Haarr, R. N. (2001). The making of a community policing officer: The impact of basic training and occupational socialization on police recruits. *Police Quarterly, 4*(4), 402–433.

Hackman, J. R., & Oldham, G. R. (1980). *Work redesign*. Reading, MA: Addison-Wesley.

Hackman, J. R., Oldham, G., Janson, R., & Purdy, K. (1975). A new strategy for job enrichment. *California Management Review, 17*(4), 57–71.

Hage, J., Aiken, M., & Marrett, C. B. (1971). Organization structure and communications. *American Sociological Review, 36*, 860–871.

Hall, R. H. (1999). *Organizations: Structures, processes, and outcomes* (7th ed.). Upper Saddle River, NJ: Prentice Hall.

Hall, R. H., Johnson, N. J., & Haas, J. E. (1967). Organizational size, complexity, and formalization. *American Sociological Review, 32*(6), 903–912.

Hannan, M. T., & Carroll, G. R. (1995). An introduction to organizational ecology. In G. R. Carroll & M. T. Hannan (Eds.), *Organizations in industry: Strategy, structure, and selection* (pp. 17–31). New York: Oxford University Press.

Hannan, M. T., & Freeman, J. (1977). The population ecology of organizations. *American Journal of Sociology, 82*(5), 929–964.

Hannan, M. T., & Freeman, J. (1984). Structural inertia and organizational change. *American Sociological Review, 49*(2), 149–164.

Harcourt, B. E., & Ludwig, J. (2006). Broken windows: New evidence from New York City and a five-city social experiment. *University of Chicago Law Review, 73*, 271–1513.

Harish, A. (2011, February 18). New Haven police officers call in sick. *Yale Daily News*. Retrieved from http://www.yaledailynews.com/news/2011/feb/18/new-haven-police-officers-call-sick/

Harris, D. A. (1999). *Driving while black: Racial profiling on our nation's highways*. Retrieved from http://www.aclu.org/racialjustice/racialprofiling/15912pub19990607.html

Haueter, J. A., Macan, T. H., & Winter, J. (2003). Measurement of newcomer socialization: Construct validation of a multidimensional scale. *Journal of Vocational Behavior, 63*, 20–39.

Hayeslip, D. W., & Russell-Einhorn, M. L. (2002). *Evaluation of multijurisdictional task forces project: Phase 1 final report*. Cambridge, MA: Abt Associates.

Haynie, S. L. (1992). Leadership and consensus on the U.S. Supreme Court. *Journal of Politics, 54*(4), 1158–1169.

He, N., Zhao, J., & Archbold, C. A. (2002). Gender and police stress: The convergent and divergent impact of work environment, work-family conflict, and stress coping mechanisms of female and male police officers. *Policing: An International Journal of Police Strategies and Management, 25*(4), 687–708.

Hellriegel, D., & Slocum, J. W. (2004). *Organizational behavior* (10th ed.). Cincinnati, OH: South-Western.

Hemphill, J. K., & Coons, A. E. (1957). Development of the leader behavior description questionnaire. In R. M. Stogdill & A. E. Coons (Eds.), *Leader behavior: Its description and measurement* (pp. 6–38). Columbus: Ohio State University, Bureau of Business Research.

Henderson, H., Wells, W., Maguire, E. R., & Gray, J. (2010). Evaluating the measurement properties of procedural justice in a correctional setting. *Criminal Justice and Behavior, 37*(4), 384–399.

Hendrick, H. W. (1997). Organizational design and macroergonomics. In G. Salvendy (Ed.), *Handbook of human factors and ergonomics* (2nd ed., pp. 594–636). New York: Wiley.

Hepburn, J. R. (1985). The exercise of power in coercive organizations: A study of prison guards. *Criminology, 23*(1), 145–164.

Herbert, S. (1998). Police subculture reconsidered. *Criminology, 36*, 343–369.

Herbert, S. (2007). The "Battle in Seattle" revisited: Or, seven views of a protest-zoning state. *Political Geography, 26*(5), 601–619.

Herman, S. N. (2005). Collapsing spheres: Joint terrorism task forces, federalism, and the war on terror. *Willamette Law Review, 41*, 941–970.

Hersey, P., & Blanchard, K. H. (1969). Life cycle theory of leadership. *Training and Development Journal, 23*, 216–224.

Hersey, P., & Blanchard, K. H. (1974). So you want to know your leadership style? *Training and Development Journal, 28*(2), 22–37.

Hersey, P., Blanchard, K. H., & Johnson, D. E. (1996). *Management of organizational behavior: Utilizing human resources* (7th ed.). Englewood Cliffs, NJ: Prentice Hall.

Herzberg, F., Mausner, B., & Snyderman, B. B. (1959). *The motivation to work*. New York: John Wiley.

Heumann, M. (1977). *Plea bargaining: The experiences of prosecutors, judges, and defense attorneys*. Chicago: University of Chicago Press.

Hickman, M. J., Fricas, J., Strom, K. J., & Pope, M. W. (2011). Mapping police stress. *Police Quarterly, 14*(3), 227–250.

Hicks, A. M. (2008). Role fusion: The occupational socialization of prison chaplains. *Symbolic Interaction, 31*(4), 400–421.

Hiller, M. L., Knight, K., Leukefeld, C., & Simpson, D. D. (2002). Motivation as a predictor of therapeutic engagement in mandated residential substance abuse treatment. *Criminal Justice and Behavior, 29*(1), 56–75.

Himmelman, A. (2001). On coalitions and the transformation of power relations: Collaborative betterment and collaborative empowerment. *American Journal of Community Psychology, 29*(2), 277–284.

Hinings, B., & Greenwood, R. (1988). The normative prescription of organizations. In L. G. Zucker (Ed.), *Institutional patterns and organizations* (pp. 53–70). Cambridge, MA: Ballinger.

Hirschel, J. D., Hutchinson, I. W., & Dean, C. W. (1992). The failure of arrest to deter spouse abuse. *Journal of Research in Crime and Delinquency, 29*(1), 7–33.

Hoffman, B. (2008). The myth of grass-roots terrorism: Why Osama bin Laden still matters. *Foreign Affairs, 87,* 133–138.

Hogan, J., Bennell, C., & Taylor, A. (2011). The challenges of moving into middle management: Responses from police officers. *Journal of Police and Criminal Psychology, 26*(2), 100–111.

Holgate, A. M., & Clegg, I. J. (1991). The path to probation officer burnout: New dogs, old tricks. *Journal of Criminal Justice, 19*(4), 325–337.

Horowitz, M. A. (1994). *Collective bargaining in the public sector.* New York: Lexington Books.

House, R. J. (1971). A path goal theory of leader effectiveness. *Administrative Science Quarterly, 16*(3), 321–339.

House, R. J. (1996). Path-goal theory of leadership: Lessons, legacy, and a reformulated theory. *Leadership Quarterly, 7,* 323–352.

House, R. J., & Podsakoff, P. M. (1994). Leadership effectiveness: Past perspectives and future directions for research. In J. Greenberg (Ed.), *Organizational behavior: The state of the science* (pp. 45–82). Hillsdale, NJ: Lawrence Erlbaum.

Howard, A. (2007). Best practices in leader selection. In J. A. Conger & R. E. Riggio (Eds.), *The practice of leadership: Developing the next generation of leaders* (pp. 11–40). San Francisco: Jossey-Bass.

Hsu, C., Marsh, R. M., & Mannari, H. (1983). An examination of the determinants of organizational structure. *American Journal of Sociology, 88*(5), 975–996.

Huber, G. P. (1991). Organizational learning: The contributing processes and the literatures. *Organization Science, 2*(1), 88–115.

Hudson, B., Hardy, B., Henwood, M., & Wistow, G. (1999). In pursuit of inter-agency collaboration in the public sector: What is the contribution of theory and research? *Public Management, 1*(2), 235–260.

Huff, C. R. (1974). Unionization behind the walls. *Criminology, 12*(2), 175–194.

Hummel, R. P. (2006). The triumph of numbers. *Administration & Society, 38*(1), 58–78.

Hunt, J. (1984). The development of rapport through the negotiation of gender in field work among police. *Human Organization, 43*(4), 283–296.

Hunt, J. (1985). Police accounts of normal force. *Journal of Contemporary Ethnography, 13*(4), 315–341.

Huxham, C. (1993). Pursuing collaborative advantage. *Journal of the Operational Research Society, 44*(6), 599–611.

Huxham, C. (2003). Theorizing collaboration practice. *Public Management Review, 5*(3), 401–423.

Huxham, C., & Macdonald, D. (1992). Introducing collaborative advantage: Achieving inter-organizational effectiveness through meta-strategy. *Management Decision, 30*(3).

Ichniowski, C., Freeman, R. B., & Lauer, H. (1989). Collective bargaining laws, threat effects, and the determination of police compensation. *Journal of Labor Economics, 7*(2), 191–209.

Illinois Campus Security Task Force. (2008, April 15). *State of Illinois Campus Security Task Force report to the governor.* Retrieved from http://www.illinois.gov/ready/SiteCollectionDocuments/CSTF_Report_PartI.pdf

Ivković, S. K. (2009). Rotten apples, rotten branches, and rotten orchards. *Criminology & Public Policy, 8*(4), 777–785.

Izzett, R. R. (1981). Equity theory, discretionary sentencing, and attitudes toward the legal system. *Journal of Social Psychology, 115*(2), 207.

Jablin, F. M. (2001). Organizational entry, assimilation, and disengagement/exit. In F. M. Jablin & L. L. Putnam (Eds.), *The new handbook of organizational communication* (pp. 732–819). Thousand Oaks, CA: Sage.

Jackson, S. E., Schwab, R. L., & Schuler, R. S. (1986). Toward an understanding of the burnout phenomenon. *Journal of Applied Psychology, 71*(4), 630–640.

Jacobs, J. B., & Grear, M. P. (1977). Drop outs and rejects: An analysis of the prison guard's revolving door. *Criminal Justice Review, 2*(2), 57–70.

Jacobs, J. B., & Olitsky, E. (2004). Leadership and correctional reform. *Pace Law Review, 24,* 477–496.

Jacoby, J. E. (2002). The endurance of failing correctional institutions: A worst case study. *Prison Journal, 82*(2), 168–188.

Jaffee, D. (2001). *Organization theory: Tension and change.* Boston: McGraw-Hill.

Jago, A. G. (1982). Leadership: Perspectives in theory and research. *Management Science, 28*(3), 315–336.

Jannetta, J., & Lachman, P. (2011). *Promoting partnerships between police and community supervision agencies: How coordination can reduce crime and improve public safety.* Washington, DC: Office of Community Oriented Policing Services.

Jefferis, E. S., Frank, J., Smith, B. W., Novak, K. J., & Travis, L. F. (1998). An examination of the productivity and perceived effectiveness of drug task forces. *Police Quarterly, 1*(3), 85–107.

Jenne, D. L., & Kersting, R. C. (1998). Gender, power, and reciprocity in the correctional setting. *Prison Journal, 78*(2), 166–185.

Jerin, R. A., Moriarty, L. J., & Gibson, M. A. (1995). Victim service or self service: An analysis of prosecution based victim-witness assistance programs and providers. *Criminal Justice Policy Review, 7*(2), 142–154.

Jermier, J. M., & Berkes, L. J. (1979). Leader behavior in a police command bureaucracy: A closer look at the quasi military model. *Administrative Science Quarterly, 24*(1), 1–23.

Johnson, K. (1991, September 23). Three killed in New Haven during a sickout by police. *New York Times.* Retrieved from http://www.nytimes.com/1991/09/23/nyregion/three-killed-in-new-haven-during-a-sickout-by-police.html

Johnson, R. R. (2009). Explaining police officer drug activity through expectancy theory. *Policing: An International Journal of Police Strategies and Management, 32*(1), 6–20.

Johnson, R. R. (2010). Making domestic violence arrests: A test of expectancy theory. *Policing: An International Journal of Police Strategies and Management, 33*(3), 531–547.

Jones, G. R. (1986). Socialization tactics, self-efficacy, and newcomers' adjustments to organizations. *Academy of Management Journal, 29*(2), 262–279.

Jones, M. A., & Sigler, R. T. (2002). Law enforcement partnership in community corrections: An evaluation of juvenile offender curfew checks. *Journal of Criminal Justice, 30*(3), 245–256.

Jones v. North Carolina Prisoners' Labor Union, 433 U.S. 119 (1977).

Judge, T. A., & Piccolo, R. F. (2004). Transformational and transactional leadership: A meta-analytic test of their relative validity. *Journal of Applied Psychology, 89*(5), 755–768.

Judson, A. S. (1991). *Changing behavior in organizations: Minimizing resistance to change.* Cambridge, MA: Blackwell Business.

Jurik, N. C. (1985a). Individual and organizational determinants of correctional officer attitudes toward inmates. *Criminology, 23*(3), 523–540.

Jurik, N. C. (1985b). An officer and a lady: Organizational barriers to women working as correctional officers in men's prisons. *Social Problems, 32*(4), 375–388.

Jurik, N. C., Halemba, G. J., Musheno, M. C., & Boyle, B. V. (1987). Educational attainment, job satisfaction, and the professionalization of correctional officers. *Work and Occupations, 14*(1), 106–125.

Juris, H. A., & Feuille, P. (1973). *Police unionism: Power and impact in public-sector bargaining.* Lexington, MA: Lexington Books.

Kadleck, C. (2003). Police employee organizations. *Policing: An International Journal of Police Strategies and Management, 26*(2), 341–351.

Kadleck, C., & Travis, L. (2008). *Police department and police officer association leaders' perceptions of community policing: Describing the nature and extent of agreement.* Washington, DC: U.S. Department of Justice, National Institute of Justice.

Kahn, R. L., & Byosiere, P. (1992). Stress in organizations. In M. D. Dunnette & L. M. Hough (Eds.), *Handbook of industrial and organizational psychology* (2nd ed., Vol. 3, pp. 571–650). Palo Alto, CA: Consulting Psychologists Press.

Kaminski, R. J. (1993). Police minority recruitment: Predicting who will say yes to an offer for a job as a cop. *Journal of Criminal Justice, 21*, 395–409.

Kappeler, V. E., Kappeler, S. F., & Del Carmen, R. V. (1993). A content analysis of police civil liability cases: Decisions of the Federal District Courts, 1978–1990. *Journal of Criminal Justice, 21*, 325–337.

Karmen, A. (2000). *New York murder mystery: The true story behind the crime crash of the 1990s.* New York: New York University Press.

Katz, C. M. (2001). The establishment of a police gang unit: An examination of organizational and environmental factors. *Criminology, 39*(1), 37–73.

Katz, C. M., Maguire, E. R., & Roncek, D. W. (2002). The creation of specialized police gang units: A macro-level analysis of contingency, social threat, and resource dependency explanations. *Policing: An International Journal of Police Strategies and Management, 25*(3), 472–506.

Katz, D., & Kahn, R. L. (1966). *The social psychology of organizations.* New York: Wiley.

Kaufman, H. (1976). *Are government organizations immortal?* Washington, DC: Brookings Institution.

Kaufmann, H., & Seidman, D. (1970). The morphology of organizations. *Administrative Science Quarterly, 15*(4), 439–451.

Kelling, G. L., & Bratton, W. J. (1993). *Implementing community policing: The administrative problem.* Washington, DC: U.S. Department of Justice, National Institute of Justice.

Kelling, G. L., & Bratton, W. J. (1998). Declining crime rates: Insiders' views of the New York City story. *Journal of Criminal Law and Criminology, 88*(4), 1217–1231.

Kennedy, D. M. (1996). Pulling levers: Chronic offenders, high-crime settings, and a theory of prevention. *Valparaiso University Law Review, 31*, 449–484.

Kennedy, D. M. (2006). Old wine in new bottles: Policing and the lessons of pulling levers. In D. Weisburd & A. A. Braga (Eds.), *Police innovation: Contrasting perspectives* (pp. 155–170). New York: Cambridge University Press.

Kennedy, D. M. (2007, February 15). *Making communities safer: Youth violence and gang interventions that work.* Retrieved September 20, 2012, from http://judiciary.house.gov/hearings/February2007/021507 kennedy.pdf?ID=736

Kennedy, D. M., & Braga, A. A. (1998). Homicide in Minneapolis. *Homicide Studies, 2*(3), 263–290.

Kenney, D. J., & Alpert, G. P. (1997). A national survey of pursuits and the use of police force: Data from law enforcement agencies. *Journal of Criminal Justice, 25*(4), 315–323.

Kessler, R. (2010). *In the President's Secret Service: Behind the scenes with agents in the line of fire and the presidents they protect.* New York: Three Rivers Press.

Kidd, R. F., & Utne, M. K. (1978). Reactions to inequity: A prospective on the role of attributions. *Law and Human Behavior, 2*(4), 301–312.

Kim, B., Gerber, J., & Beto, D. R. (2010). Listening to law enforcement officers: The promises and problems of police-adult probation partnerships. *Journal of Criminal Justice, 38*(4), 625–632.

Kim, W. C., & Mauborgne, R. (2003). Tipping point leadership. *Harvard Business Review, 81*(4), 60–69.

Kimberly, J. R. (1980). The life cycle analogy and the study of organizations: Introduction. In J. R. Kimberly & R. H. Miles (Eds.), *The organizational life cycle: Issues in the creation, transformation, and decline of organizations* (pp. 1–17). San Francisco: Jossey-Bass.

King, M. S. (2008). Problem-solving court judging, therapeutic jurisprudence and transformational leadership. *Journal of Judicial Administration, 17*(3), 155–177.

King, W. R. (in press). Organizational failure and the disbanding of local police agencies. *Crime and Delinquency.* doi:10.1177/001112 8709344675

King, W. R. (2003). Bending granite revisited: The command structure of American police organizations. *Policing: An International Journal of Police Strategies and Management, 26*(2), 208–230.

King, W. R. (2005). Toward a better understanding of the hierarchical nature of police organizations: Conception and measurement. *Journal of Criminal Justice, 33*(1), 97–109.

King, W. R. (2009a). Police officer misconduct as normal accidents. *Criminology & Public Policy, 8*(4), 771–776.

King, W. R. (2009b). Toward a life-course perspective of police organizations. *Journal of Research in Crime and Delinquency, 46*(2), 213–244.

Kipnis, D., Schmidt, S. M., & Wilkinson, I. (1980). Intraorganizational influence tactics: Explorations in getting one's way. *Journal of Applied Psychology, 65*(4), 440–452.

Kirchhoff, S. M. (2010). *Economic impacts of prison growth* (No. R41177). Washington, DC: Congressional Research Service.

Kirkpatrick, S. A., & Locke, E. A. (1991). Leadership: Do traits matter? *The Executive, 5*(2), 48–60.

Klinger, D. (2005). *Social theory and the street cop: The case of deadly force*. Washington, DC: Police Foundation.

Klinger, D. A. (1997). Negotiating order in patrol work: An ecological theory of police response to deviance. *Criminology, 35*(2), 277–306.

Klockars, C. B. (1985). *The idea of police*. Beverly Hills, CA: Sage.

Koppl, R. (2005). How to improve forensic science. *European Journal of Law and Economics, 20*(3), 255–286.

Kotter, J. P. (1990a). *A force for change: How leadership differs from management*. New York: Free Press.

Kotter, J. P. (1990b). What leaders really do. *Harvard Business Review, 68*(3), 103–111.

Kramer, M. W. (2010). *Organizational socialization: Joining and leaving organizations*. Malden, MA: Polity Press.

Krause, K. C. (2003). Putting the Transportation Security Administration in historical context. *Journal of Air Law and Commerce, 68*, 233–251.

Kuhnert, K. W., & Lewis, P. (1987). Transactional and transformational leadership: A constructive/developmental analysis. *Academy of Management Review, 12*(4), 648–657.

Kuykendall, J. L. (1977). Police leadership: An analysis of executive styles. *Criminal Justice Review, 2*, 89–101.

Kuykendall, J., & Roberg, R. R. (1988). Police manager's perceptions of employee types: A conceptual model. *Journal of Criminal Justice, 16*(2), 131–137.

Kuykendall, J., & Unsinger, P. C. (1982). The leadership styles of police managers. *Journal of Criminal Justice, 10*(4), 311–321.

Lambert, E. (2003). The impact of organizational justice on correctional staff. *Journal of Criminal Justice, 31*(2), 155–168.

Lambert, E. G., Hogan, N. L., Dial, K. C., Jiang, S., & Khondaker, M. I. (2012). Is the job burning me out? An exploratory test of the job characteristics model on the emotional burnout of prison staff. *Prison Journal, 92*(1), 3–23.

Lambert, E. G., & Paoline, E. A. (2008). The influence of individual, job, and organizational characteristics on correctional staff job stress, job satisfaction, and organizational commitment. *Criminal Justice Review, 33*(4), 541–564.

Lambert, E. G., Paoline, E. A., & Hogan, N. L. (2006). The impact of centralization and formalization on correctional staff job satisfaction and organizational commitment: An exploratory study. *Criminal Justice Studies, 19*(1), 23–44.

Landsberger, H. A. (1958). *Hawthorne revisited*. Ithaca, NY: Cornell University Press.

Langford, L. (2004). *Preventing violence and promoting safety in higher education settings: Overview of a comprehensive approach*. Newton, MA: Higher Education Center for Alcohol and Other Drug Abuse and Violence Prevention.

Langworthy, R. H. (1986). *The structure of police organizations*. New York: Praeger.

LaPorte, T. R., & Consolini, P. M. (1991). Working in practice but not in theory: Theoretical challenges of "high-reliability organizations." *Journal of Public Administration Research and Theory, 1*(1), 19–48.

Lasker, R. D., Weiss, E. S., & Miller, R. (2001). Partnership synergy: A practical framework for studying and strengthening the collaborative advantage. *Milbank Quarterly, 79*(2), 179–205.

Latham, G. P. (2007). *Work motivation: History, theory, research, and practice*. Thousand Oaks, CA: Sage.

Lawler, E. E. (1969). Job design and employee motivation. *Personnel Psychology, 22*(4), 426–435.

Lawler, E. E. (1973). *Motivation in work organizations*. Monterey, CA: Brooks/Cole.

Lawler, E. E., & Porter, L. W. (1967). The effect of performance on job satisfaction. *Industrial Relations, 7*(1), 20–28.

Lawrence, P. R., & Lorsch, J. W. (1967). *Organizations and environment: Managing differentiation and integration*. Boston: Harvard Business School Press.

Lazarus, R. S., & Folkman, S. F. (1984). *Stress, appraisal, and coping*. New York: Springer.

Leavitt, M. O., Spellings, M., & Gonzales, A. R. (2007, June 13). *Report to the president on issues raised by the Virginia Tech tragedy*. Retrieved from http://www.justice.gov/opa/pr/2007/June/vt_report_061307.pdf

Lee, R. T., & Ashforth, B. E. (1990). On the meaning of Maslach's three dimensions of burnout. *Journal of Applied Psychology, 75*(6), 743–747.

Lee, R. T., & Ashforth, B. E. (1996). A meta-analytic examination of the correlates of the three dimensions of job burnout. *Journal of Applied Psychology, 81*(2), 123–133.

Leiter, M. P., & Maslach, C. (1988). The impact of interpersonal environment on burnout and organizational commitment. *Journal of Organizational Behavior, 9*(4), 297–308.

Leiter, M. P., & Maslach, C. (1999). Six areas of worklife: A model of the organizational context of burnout. *Journal of Health and Human Services, 21*, 472–489.

Leo, R. A. (1996). Inside the interrogation room. *Journal of Criminal Law and Criminology, 86*(2), 266–303.

Lester, R. E. (1987). Organizational culture, uncertainty reduction, and the socialization of new organizational members. In S. Thomas (Ed.), *Culture and communication: Methodology, behavior, artifacts, and institutions* (pp. 105–113). Norwood, NJ: Ablex.

Leung, R. (2009). *DNA testing. Foolproof?* Retrieved from http://www.cbsnews.com/stories/2003/05/27/60II/main555723.shtml

Leventhal, G. S. (1980). What should be done with equity theory? In K. J. Gergen, M. S. Greenberg, & R. H. Willis (Eds.), *Social exchange: Advances in theory and research* (pp. 27–55). New York: Plenum.

Levy, A., & Merry, U. (1986). *Organizational transformation: Approaches, strategies, and theories*. New York: Praeger.

Lewin, A. Y., Weigelt, C. B., & Emery, J. D. (2004). Adaption and selection in strategy and change: Perspectives on strategic change in organizations. In M. S. Poole & A. H. Van de Ven (Eds.), *Handbook of organizational change and innovation* (pp. 108–160). New York: Oxford University Press.

Lewin, D., Feuille, P., Kochan, T. A., & Delaney, J. T. (Eds.). (1988). *Public sector labor relations: Analysis and readings*. Lexington, MA: Lexington Books.

Lewin, K. (1951). *Field theory in social science* (D. Cartwright, Ed.). New York: Harper & Row.

Lewis, D. E. (2002). The politics of agency termination: Confronting the myth of agency immortality. *Journal of Politics, 64*(1), 89–107.

Liberman, A. M., Best, S. R., Metzler, T. J., Fagan, J. A., Weiss, D. S., & Marmar, C. R. (2002). Routine occupational stress and psychological distress in police. *Policing: An International Journal of Police Strategies and Management, 25*(2), 421–441.

Lin, Y., & Beyerlein, M. M. (2006). Communities of practice: A critical perspective on collaboration. In M. M. Beyerlein, S. T. Beyerlein, & F. A. Kennedy (Eds.), *Innovation through collaboration* (pp. 53–80). Amsterdam: JAI Press.

Lind, E. A., & Tyler, T. R. (1988). *The social psychology of procedural justice*. New York: Plenum.

Lipshitz, R., Friedman, V. J., & Popper, M. (2007). *Demystifying organizational learning*. Thousand Oaks, CA: Sage.

Lipsky, M. (1980). *Street-level bureaucracy: Dilemmas of the individual in public services*. New York: Russell Sage Foundation.

Livingston, D. (1999). Police reform and the Department of Justice: An essay on accountability. *Buffalo Law Review, 2*, 817–859.

Logan, C. H. (1993). Criminal justice performance measures for prisons. In J. J. DiIulio, G. P. Alpert, M. H. Moore, G. F. Cole, J. Petersilia, C. H. Logan, et al. (Eds.), *Performance measures for the criminal justice system* (pp. 19–60). Washington, DC: U.S. Department of Justice, Bureau of Justice Statistics.

Long, N., Shouksmith, G., Voges, K., & Roache, S. (1986). Stress in prison staff: An occupational study. *Criminology, 24*(2), 331–345.

Lord, R. G., De Vader, C. L., & Alliger, G. M. (1986). A meta-analysis of the relation between personality traits and leadership perceptions: An application of validity generalization procedures. *Journal of Applied Psychology, 71*(3), 402–410.

Louis, M. R. (1980). Surprise and sense making: What newcomers experience in entering unfamiliar organizational settings. *Administrative Science Quarterly, 25*(2), 226–251.

Lovell, J. (2007, December 9). Left-hand-turn elimination. *New York Times Magazine*. Retrieved from http://www.nytimes.com/2007/12/09/magazine/09left-handturn.html

Lovell, R. (1988). Research utilization in complex organizations: A case study in corrections. *Justice Quarterly, 5*(2), 257–280.

Lucas, J. W., & Baxter, A. R. (2012). Power, influence, and diversity in organizations. *Annals of the American Academy of Political and Social Science, 639*(1), 49–70.

Lum, C., Kennedy, L. W., & Sherley, A. J. (2006). The effectiveness of counter-terrorism strategies. *Campbell Systematic Reviews, 2*, 1–49.

Lum, C., Koper, C. S., & Telep, C. W. (2011). The evidence-based policing matrix. *Journal of Experimental Criminology, 7*(1), 3–26.

Lundman, R. J. (1980). *Police and policing: An introduction*. New York: Holt, Rinehart, & Winston.

Lynch, D. R. (1997). The nature of occupational stress among public defenders. *Justice System Journal, 19*(1), 17–35.

MacKenzie, D. L. (2000). Evidence-based corrections: Identifying what works. *Crime & Delinquency, 46*(4), 457–471.

Maguire, E. R. (2003). *Organizational structure in American police agencies: Context, complexity, and control*. Albany: SUNY Press.

Maguire, E. R., & King, W. R. (2007). The changing landscape of American police organizations. In J. A. Schafer (Ed.), *Policing 2020: Exploring the future of crime, communities, and policing* (pp. 337–371). Washington, DC: U.S. Department of Justice, Federal Bureau of Investigation.

Maguire, E. R., Shin, Y., Zhao, J. S., & Hassell, K. D. (2003). Structural change in large police agencies during the 1990s. *Policing: An International Journal of Police Strategies and Management, 26*(2), 251–275.

Maguire, E. R., & Uchida, C. D. (2000). Measurement and explanation in the comparative study of American police organizations. In D. E. Duffee (Ed.), *Measurement and analysis of crime and justice* (pp. 491–558). Washington, DC: U.S. Department of Justice National Institute of Justice.

Maguire, K. (Ed.). (2013). *Sourcebook of criminal justice statistics*. Hindelang Criminal Justice Center, University at Albany. Retrieved from http://www.albany.edu/sourcebook/

Maier, N. R. F. (1955). *Psychology in industry*. Boston: Houghton Mifflin.

Makarios, M. D., & Maahs, J. (2012). Is private time quality time? A national private-public comparison of prison quality. *Prison Journal, 92*(3), 336–357.

March, J. G. (1981). Footnotes to organizational change. *Administrative Science Quarterly, 26*, 563–577.

March, J. G. (1994). *A primer on decision making: How decisions happen*. New York: Free Press.

March, J. G., & Simon, H. A. (1958). *Organizations*. New York: John Wiley.

Marquart, J. W. (1986). Prison guards and the use of physical coercion as a mechanism of prisoner control. *Criminology, 24*(2), 347–366.

Marquart, J. W., & Crouch, B. M. (1985). Judicial reform and prisoner control: The impact of Ruiz v. Estelle on a Texas penitentiary. *Law & Society Review, 19*(4), 557–586.

Martin, J. (1992). *Cultures in organizations: Three perspectives*. New York: Oxford University Press.

Martin, J. L., Lichtenstein, B., Jenkot, R. B., & Forde, D. R. (2012). "They can take us over any time they want": Correctional officers' responses to prison crowding. *Prison Journal, 92*(1), 88–105.

Martin, S. E. (1980). *Breaking and entering: Policewomen on patrol*. Berkeley: University of California Press.

Maslach, C. (1998). A multidimensional theory of burnout. In C. L. Cooper (Ed.), *Theories of organizational stress* (pp. 68–85). Oxford, UK: Oxford University Press.

Maslach, C., & Jackson, S. E. (1981). The measurement of experienced burnout. *Journal of Organizational Behavior, 2*(2), 99–113.

Maslach, C., & Schaufeli, W. B. (1993). Historical and conceptual development of burnout. In W. B. Schaufeli, C. Maslach, & T. Marek (Eds.), *Professional burnout: Recent developments in theory and research* (pp. 1–18). Washington, DC: Taylor & Francis.

Maslach, C., Schaufeli, W. B., & Leiter, M. P. (2001). Job burnout. *Annual Review of Psychology, 52*(1), 397–422.

Maslow, A. H. (1943). A theory of human motivation. *Psychological Review, 50*(4), 370–396.

Maslow, A. H. (1954). *Motivation and personality*. New York: Harper.

Masse, T., & Krouse, W. (2003). *The FBI: Past, present, and future* (No. RL32095). Washington, DC: Congressional Research Service.

Mastrofski, S. D. (2001). The romance of police leadership. In E. J. Waring & D. Weisburd (Eds.), *Crime and social organization* (Vol. 10, pp. 153–195). New Brunswick, NJ: Transaction.

Mastrofski, S. D., Ritti, R. R., & Snipes, J. B. (1994). Expectancy theory and police productivity in DUI enforcement. *Law & Society Review, 28*(1), 113–148.

Matthews, C., Monk-Turner, E., & Sumter, M. (2010). Promotional opportunities: How women in corrections perceive their chances for advancement at work. *Gender Issues, 27*(1–2), 53–66.

Maurer, D. C. (2012). *Department of Homeland Security: Preliminary observations on DHS's efforts to improve employee morale*. Washington, DC: Government Accountability Office.

Mawby, R. C., & Worrall, A. (2004). "Polibation" revisited: Policing, probation and prolific offender projects. *International Journal of Police Science and Management, 6*(2), 63–73.

McCall, M. W., & Hollenbeck, G. P. (2007). Getting leader development right: Competence not competencies. In J. A. Conger & R. E. Riggio (Eds.), *The practice of leadership: Developing the next generation of leaders* (pp. 87–106). San Francisco: Jossey-Bass.

McCleary, R. (1992). *Dangerous men: The sociology of parole* (2nd ed.). New York: Harrow & Heston.

McClelland, D. C. (1961). *The achieving society*. Princeton, NJ: D. Van Nostrand.

McClelland, D. C. (1962). Business drive and national achievement. *Harvard Business Review, 40*(4), 99–112.

McClelland, D. C. (1965). Toward a theory of motive acquisition. *American Psychologist, 20*(5), 321–333.

McClelland, D. C. (1985). *Human motivation*. Glenview, IL: Scott, Foresman.

McClelland, D. C., & Burnham, D. H. (1976). Power is the great motivator. *Harvard Business Review, 54*(2), 100–110.

McGarrell, E. F., & Schlegel, K. (1993). The implementation of federally funded multijurisdictional drug task forces: Organizational structure and interagency relationships. *Journal of Criminal Justice, 21*(3), 231–244.

McGregor, D. (1960). *The human side of enterprise*. New York: McGraw-Hill.

McIntyre, L. J. (1987). *The public defender: The practice of law in the shadows of repute*. Chicago: University of Chicago Press.

McKendall, M. A., & Wagner, J. A. (1997). Motive, opportunity, choice, and corporate illegality. *Organization Science, 8*(6), 624–647.

McNamara, J. H. (1967). Uncertainties in police work: The relevance of police recruits' backgrounds and training. In D. J. Bordua (Ed.), *The police: Six sociological essays* (207–215). New York: John Wiley.

Mears, D. P., & Bacon, S. (2009). Improving criminal justice through better decision making: Lessons from the medical system. *Journal of Criminal Justice, 37*(2), 142–154.

Mears, D. P., & Watson, J. (2006). Towards a fair and balanced assessment of supermax prisons. *Justice Quarterly, 23*(2), 232–270.

Mechanic, D. (1962). Sources of power of lower participants in complex organizations. *Administrative Science Quarterly, 7*(3), 349–364.

Mehay, S. L. (1979). Intergovernmental contracting for municipal police services: An empirical analysis. *Land Economics, 55*(1), 59–72.

Merton, R. K. (1936). The unanticipated consequences of purposive social action. *American Sociological Review, 1*(6), 894–904.

Meyer, J. C. (1976). Discontinuity in the delivery of public service: Analyzing the police strike. *Human Relations, 29*(6), 545–557.

Meyer, J. W., & Rowan, B. (1977). Institutionalized organizations: Formal structure as myth and ceremony. *American Journal of Sociology, 83*(2), 340–363.

Meyer, M. W. (1968). Expertness and the span of control. *American Sociological Review, 33*(6), 944–951.

Meyer, M. W., & Zucker, L. G. (1989). *Permanently failing organizations*. Newbury Park, CA: Sage.

Mignerey, J. T., Rubin, R. B., & Gorden, W. I. (1995). Organizational entry: An investigation of newcomer communication behavior and uncertainty. *Communication Research, 22*(1), 54–85.

Miller, A. H. (2001). The Los Angeles riots: A study in crisis paralysis. *Journal of Contingencies and Crisis Management, 9*(4), 189–199.

Mills, J. H., Dye, K., & Mills, A. J. (2009). *Understanding organizational change*. London: Routledge.

Mintzberg, H. (1979). *The structuring of organizations: A synthesis of the research*. Englewood Cliffs, NJ: Prentice Hall.

Mintzberg, H. (1983). *Power in and around organizations*. Englewood Cliffs, NJ: Prentice Hall.

Monkkonen, E. H. (1992). History of urban police. In M. Tonry (Ed.), *Crime and justice: A review of research* (Vol. 15, pp. 547–580). Chicago: University of Chicago Press. Retrieved from http://www.jstor.org/stable/1147625

Monk-Turner, E., O'Leary, D., & Sumter, M. (2010). Factors shaping police retention: Does Herzberg's theory of satisfaction hold? *Police Journal, 83*(2), 164–180.

Mooney, T. (2000, September 16). ACI guards approve new 3-year pact with state. *Providence Journal-Bulletin*, p. 1A.

Moore, M. H. (2006). Improving police through expertise, experience, and experiments. In D. Weisburd & A. A. Braga (Eds.), *Police innovation: Contrasting perspectives* (pp. 322–338). New York: Cambridge University Press.

Morgan, G. (2006). *Images of organization*. Thousand Oaks, CA: Sage.

Morgan, R. D., Van Haveren, R. A., & Pearson, C. A. (2002). Correctional officer burnout: Further analyses. *Criminal Justice and Behavior, 29*(2), 144–160.

Morris, R. G., & Worrall, J. L. (in press). Prison architecture and inmate misconduct: A multilevel assessment. *Crime & Delinquency*. doi:10.1177/0011128710386204

Morrison, E. W. (1993). Newcomer information seeking: Exploring types, modes, sources, and outcomes. *Academy of Management Journal, 36*(3), 557–589.

Moskos, P. (2008). *Cop in the hood: My year policing Baltimore's Eastern District*. Princeton, NJ: Princeton University Press.

Muir, W. K. J. (1977). *Police: Streetcorner politicians*. Chicago: University of Chicago Press.

Mullen, K. L. (1996). *The computerization of law enforcement: A diffusion of innovation study*. Unpublished doctoral dissertation, State University of New York, Albany.

Murphy, D., & Lutze, F. (2009). Police-probation partnerships: Professional identity and the sharing of coercive power. *Journal of Criminal Justice, 37*(1), 65–76.

Murphy, D., & Worrall, J. L. (2007). The threat of mission distortion in police-probation partnerships. *Policing: An International Journal of Police Strategies and Management, 30*(1), 132–149.

Murphy, S. A. (2008). The role of emotions and transformational leadership on police culture: An autoethnographic account. *International Journal of Police Science and Management, 10*(2), 165–178.

Murphy, S. A., & Drodge, E. N. (2004). The four I's of police leadership: A case study heuristic. *International Journal of Police Science and Management, 6*(1), 1–15.

Murton, T. (1971). Inmate self-government. *University of San Francisco Law Review, 6,* 87–102.

Nadler, D. A., & Lawler, E. E. (1977). Motivation: A diagnostic approach. In J. R. Hackman, E. E. Lawler, & L. W. Porter (Eds.), *Perspectives on behavior in organizations* (pp. 26–38). New York: McGraw-Hill.

Nadler, D. A., & Tushman, M. L. (1995). Types of organizational change: From incremental improvement to discontinuous transformation. In D. A. Nadler, R. B. Shaw, & A. E. Walton (Eds.), *Discontinuous change: Leading organizational transformation* (pp. 15–34). San Francisco: Jossey-Bass.

National Commission on Terrorist Attacks Upon the United States. (2004). *The 9/11 commission report.* Retrieved from http://www.9-11commission.gov/report/911Report.pdf

National summit on campus public safety. (2004). Washington, DC: U.S. Department of Justice, Office of Community Oriented Policing Services.

Nealey, S. M., & Fiedler, F. E. (1968). Leadership functions of middle managers. *Psychological Bulletin, 70*(5), 313–329.

Neher, A. (1991). Maslow's theory of motivation: A critique. *Journal of Humanistic Psychology, 31,* 89–112.

Neubauer, D. W., & Fradella, H. F. (2011). *America's courts and the criminal justice system* (10th ed.). Belmont, CA: Wadsworth.

Neveu, J. (2007). Jailed resources: Conservation of resources theory as applied to burnout among prison guards. *Journal of Organizational Behavior, 28*(1), 21–42.

Newton, T. J. (1989). Occupational stress and coping with stress: A critique. *Human Relations, 42*(5), 441–461.

Northouse, P. G. (2007). *Leadership: Theory and practice* (4th ed.). Thousand Oaks, CA: Sage.

Nugent, M. E., Johnson, J. L., Bartholomew, B., & Bromirski, D. (2005). *Local prosecutors' response to terrorism.* Alexandria, VA: American Prosecutors Research Institute.

Nutt, P. C. (1999). Surprising but true: Half the decisions in organizations fail. *Academy of Management Executive, 13*(4), 75–90.

O'Brien, K. M. (1994). The impact of union political activities on public-sector pay, employment, and budgets. *Industrial Relations, 33*(3), 322–345.

O'Hara, P. (2005). *Why law enforcement organizations fail: Mapping the organizational fault lines in policing.* Durham, NC: Carolina Academic Press.

Ohio Department of Rehabilitation and Correction. (2013). Ohio Department of Rehabilitation and Correction: Corrections Training Academy. Retrieved from http://www.drc.ohio.gov/web/cta.htm

Oliver, W. M. (2000). The third generation of community policing: Moving through innovation, diffusion, and institutionalization. *Police Quarterly, 3*(4), 367–388.

Oliver, W. M. (2006). The fourth era of policing: Homeland security. *International Review of Law, Computers, and Technology, 20*(1–2), 49–62.

Olson, C. A. (1986). Strikes, strike penalties, and arbitration in six states. *Industrial and Labor Relations Review, 39*(4), 539–551.

O'Neill, C. (2004). Legislating under the influence: Are federal highway incentives enough to induce state legislatures to pass a 0.08 blood alcohol concentration standard? *Seton Hall Legislative Journal, 28,* 415–438.

Ostberg, C. L., Wetstein, M. E., & Ducat, C. R. (2004). Leaders, followers, and outsiders: Task and social leadership on the Canadian Supreme Court in the early 'nineties. *Polity, 36*(3), 505–528.

Ostroff, C., & Kozlowski, S. W. J. (1992). Organizational socialization as a learning process: The role of information acquisition. *Personnel Psychology, 45*(4), 849–874.

Ostrom, E., Parks, R. B., & Whitaker, G. P. (1973). Do we really want to consolidate urban police forces? A reappraisal of some old assertions. *Public Administration Review, 33*(5), 423–432.

O'Toole, J. (1995). *Leading change: Overcoming the ideology of comfort and the tyranny of custom.* San Francisco: Jossey-Bass.

Owen, S. S. (2006). Occupational stress among correctional supervisors. *Prison Journal, 86*(2), 164–181.

Pachon, H. P., & Lovrich, N. P. (1977). The consolidation of urban public services: A focus on the police. *Public Administration Review, 37*(1), 38–47.

Page, J. (2011a). Prison officer unions and the perpetuation of the penal status quo. *Criminology & Public Policy, 10*(3), 735–770.

Page, J. (2011b). *The toughest beat: Politics, punishment, and the prison officers union in California.* New York: Oxford University Press.

Paoline, E. A. (2003). Taking stock: Toward a richer understanding of police culture. *Journal of Criminal Justice, 31*(3), 199–214.

Papachristos, A. V., Meares, T. L., & Fagan, J. (2007). Attention felons: Evaluating project safe neighborhoods in Chicago. *Journal of Empirical Legal Studies, 4*(2), 223–272.

Parent, D., & Snyder, B. (1999). *Police-corrections partnerships.* Washington, DC: U.S. Department of Justice, National Institute of Justice.

Parks, R. B., Mastrofski, S. D., Dejong, C., & Gray, M. K. (1999). How officers spend their time with the community. *Justice Quarterly, 16*(3), 483–518.

Paternoster, R. (1987). The deterrent effect of the perceived certainty and severity of punishment: A review of the evidence and issues. *Justice Quarterly, 4*(2), 173–217.

Paternoster, R., Brame, R., Bachman, R., & Sherman, L. W. (1997). Do fair procedures matter? The effect of procedural justice on spouse assault. *Law & Society Review, 31*(1), 163–204.

Pearson, N. M. (1945). Fayolism as the necessary complement of Taylorism. *American Political Science Review, 39*(1), 68–80.

Pelfrey, W. V. (2000). Precipitating factors of paradigmatic shift in policing: The origin of the community policing era. In G. P. Alpert & A. R. Piquero (Eds.), *Community policing: Contemporary readings* (2nd ed., pp. 79–92). Prospect Heights, IL: Waveland Press.

Perlmutter, E. (1971, January 17). Parity key issue. *New York Times,* pp. 1, 64.

Perrine, A. (2001). The First Amendment versus the World Trade Organization: Emergency powers and the Battle in Seattle. *Washington Law Review, 76,* 635–668.

Perrow, C. (1986). *Complex organizations: A critical essay* (3rd ed.). New York: McGraw-Hill.

Perrow, C. (1999). *Normal accidents: Living with high-risk technologies.* Princeton, NJ: Princeton University Press.

Perrow, C. (2007). *The next catastrophe: Reducing our vulnerabilities to natural, industrial, and terrorist disasters.* Princeton, NJ: Princeton University Press.

Petersilia, J. (2008). California's correctional paradox of excess and deprivation. In M. Tonry (Ed.), *Crime and justice* (Vol. 37, pp. 207–278). Chicago: University of Chicago Press.

Pfeffer, J., & Salancik, G. R. (1978). *The external control of organizations: A resource dependence perspective.* New York: Harper & Row.

Pfuhl, E. H. (1983). Police strikes and conventional crime. *Criminology, 21*(4), 489–504.

Phillips, P. W. (1999). De facto police consolidation: The multi-jurisdictional task force. *Police Forum, 9*(3), 1–5.

Phillips, P. W., & Orvis, G. P. (1999). Intergovernmental relations and the crime task force: A case study of the East Texas Violent Crime Task Force and its implications. *Police Quarterly, 2*(4), 438–461.

Picarelli, J. T. (2009). The future of terrorism. *National Institute of Justice Journal,* (264), 26–30.

Pines, A. M. (1993). Burnout. In L. Goldberger & S. Breznitz (Eds.), *Handbook of stress: Theoretical and clinical aspects* (2nd. ed., pp. 386–402). New York: Free Press.

Piskulich, J. P. (1992). *Collective bargaining in state and local government.* New York: Praeger.

Podsakoff, P. M., & Schriescheim, C. A. (1985). Field studies of French and Raven's bases of power: Critique, reanalysis, and suggestions for future research. *Psychological Bulletin, 97*(3), 387–411.

Poole, E. D., & Pogrebin, M. R. (1988). Deputy sheriffs as jail guards: A study of correctional policy orientations and career phases. *Criminal Justice and Behavior, 15*(2), 190–209.

Poole, M. S., & Van de Ven, A. H. (2004). Theories of organizational change and innovation processes. In M. S. Poole & A. H. Van de Ven (Eds.), *Handbook of organizational change and innovation* (pp. 374–397). New York: Oxford University Press.

Porter, L. W., & Lawler, E. E. (1965). Properties of organization structure in relation to job attitudes and job behavior. *Psychological Bulletin, 64*(1), 23–51.

Porter, L. W., Lawler, E. E., & Hackman, J. R. (1975). *Behavior in organizations.* New York: McGraw-Hill.

Powers, K. J., & Thompson, F. (1994). Managing coprovision: Using expectancy theory to overcome the free-rider problem. *Journal of Public Administration Research and Theory, 4*(2), 179–196.

President's Commission on Law Enforcement and the Administration of Justice. (1968). *The challenge of crime in a free society.* New York: E. P. Dutton.

Priest, D., & Arkin, W. M. (2010, July 19). A hidden world, growing beyond control. *Washington Post.* Retrieved from http://projects.washingtonpost.com/top-secret-america/articles/a-hidden-world-growing-beyond-control/print/

Prison union leaders curb strike talk at Pearsall facility. (2009, February 11). *Lubbock Avalanche-Journal.* Retrieved from http://lubbockonline.com/stories/021109/sta_386768393.shtml

Project Safe Neighborhoods. (2013). *Media.* Retrieved from http://www.psnchicago.org/Media.html

Prottas, J. M. (1978). The power of the street-level bureaucrat in public service bureaucracies. *Urban Affairs Review, 13*(3), 285–312.

Pugh, D. S., & Hickson, D. J. (2007). *Writers on organizations* (6th ed.). Thousand Oaks, CA: Sage.

Pugh, D. S., Hickson, D. J., Hinings, C. R., Macdonald, K. M., Turner, C., & Lupton, T. (1963). A conceptual scheme for organizational analysis. *Administrative Science Quarterly, 8*(3), 289–315.

Putchinski, L. J. (2007). *Union influence and police expenditures.* New York: LFB Scholarly Publishing.

Pynes, J. E., & Corley, B. (2006). Collective bargaining and deputy sheriffs in Florida: An unusual history. *Public Personnel Management, 35*(4), 299–309.

Quick, J. D., Quick, J. C., & Nelson, D. L. (1998). The theory of preventive stress management in organizations. In C. L. Cooper (Ed.), *Theories of organizational stress* (pp. 246–268). Oxford, UK: Oxford University Press.

Quinn, R. E., & Cameron, K. (1983). Organizational life cycles and shifting criteria of effectiveness: Some preliminary evidence. *Management Science, 29*(1), 33.

Rainey, H. G. (1983). Public agencies and private firms: Incentive structures, goals, and individual roles. *Administration Society, 15*(2), 207–242.

Rainey, H. G. (2009). *Understanding and managing public organizations* (4th ed.). San Francisco: Jossey-Bass.

Rainey, H. G., Backoff, R. W., & Levine, C. H. (1976). Comparing public and private organizations. *Public Administration Review, 36*(2), 233–244.

Rainguet, F. W., & Dodge, M. (2001). The problems of police chiefs: An examination of the issues in tenure and turnover. *Police Quarterly, 4*(3), 268–288.

Rainville, G., & Nugent, M. E. (2002). Community prosecution tenets and practices: The relative mix of "community" and "prosecution." *American Journal of Criminal Justice, 26*(2), 149–164.

Ramanujam, R., & Goodman, P. S. (2003). Latent errors and adverse organizational consequences: A conceptualization. *Journal of Organizational Behavior, 24*(7), 815–836.

Ramirez, D., McDevitt, J., & Farrell, A. (2000). *A resource guide on racial profiling data collection systems: Promising practices and lessons learned.* Washington, DC: U.S. Department of Justice, Bureau of Justice Assistance.

Rankin, B. (2010, April 6). Georgia's public defender system may go back under county control. *Atlanta Journal-Constitution.* Retrieved from http://www.ajc.com/news/news/local-govt-politics/georgias public-defender-system-may-go-back-under-/nQdyR/

Raven, B. H. (1993). The bases of power: Origins and recent developments. *Journal of Social Issues, 49*(4), 227–251.

Raven, B. H., Schwarzwald, J., & Koslowsky, M. (1998). Conceptualizing and measuring a power/interaction model of interpersonal influence. *Journal of Applied Social Psychology, 28*(4), 307–332.

Rayner, C., & Hoel, H. (1997). A summary review of literature relating to workplace bullying. *Journal of Community & Applied Social Psychology, 7*(3), 181–191.

Reaves, B. A. (2009). *State and local law enforcement training academies, 2006.* Washington, DC: U.S. Department of Justice, Bureau of Justice Statistics.

Reaves, B. A. (2010). *Local police departments, 2007.* Washington, DC: U.S. Department of Justice, Bureau of Justice Statistics.

Regoli, R., Poole, E., & Schrink, J. (1979). Occupational socialization and career development: A look at cynicism among correctional institution workers. *Human Organization, 38*(2), 183–187.

Reisig, M. D. (1998). Rates of disorder in higher-custody state prisons: A comparative analysis of managerial practices. *Crime and Delinquency, 44*(2), 229–244.

Reiss, A. J. (1992). Police organization in the twentieth century. In M. Tonry & N. Morris (Eds.), *Modern policing* (pp. 51–97). Chicago: University of Chicago Press.

Reuss-Ianni, E. (1983). *Two cultures of policing: Street cops and management cops.* New Brunswick, NJ: Transaction.

Rice, R. W. (1978). Construct validity of the least preferred co-worker score. *Psychological Bulletin, 85*(6), 1199–1237.

Richman, D. C. (2001). "Project Exile" and the allocation of federal law enforcement authority. *Arizona Law Review, 43*(2), 369–411.

Richmond, T. (2003, February 7). Union agrees to end prison guard sick-out. *Chippewa Herald.* Retrieved from http://chippewa.com/article_5d25e12d-d2b7–5f16–9cb7–83fa50930b5b.html

Ridgeway, G., Lim, N., Gifford, B., Koper, C., Matthies, C., Hajiamiri, S., et al. (2008). *Strategies for improving officer recruitment in the San Diego Police Department.* Santa Monica, CA: RAND.

Rijpma, J. A. (1997). Complexity, tight–coupling and reliability: Connecting normal accidents theory and high reliability theory. *Journal of Contingencies and Crisis Management, 5*(1), 15–23.

Rison, R. H., & Wittenberg, P. M. (1994). Disaster theory: Avoiding crisis in a prison environment. *Federal Probation, 58*(3), 45–50.

Robbins, S. P., & Judge, T. A. (2008). *Essentials of organizational behavior* (9th ed.). Upper Saddle River, NJ: Pearson.

Roberg, R. R. (1979). *Police management and organizational behavior: A contingency approach.* St. Paul, MN: West.

Roberg, R. R., & Krichhoff, J. J. (1985). Applying strategic management methods to law enforcement: Two case studies. *American Journal of Police, 4,* 133.

Roberg, R. R., & Kuykendall, J. (1990). *Police organization and management: Behavior, theory, and processes.* Pacific Grove, CA: Brooks/Cole.

Roberts, K. H., Bea, R., & Bartles, D. L. (2001). Must accidents happen? Lessons from high-reliability organizations. *Academy of Management Executive, 15*(3), 70–79.

Roethlisberger, F. J., & Dickson, W. J. (1949). *Management and the worker.* Cambridge, MA: Harvard University Press.

Rojek, J., & Smith, M. R. (2007). Law enforcement lessons learned from Hurricane Katrina. *Review of Policy Research, 24*(6), 589–608.

Rollins, J. (2008). *Fusion centers: Issues and options for Congress* (No. RL34070). Washington, DC: Congressional Research Service.

Rosecrance, J. (1988). Maintaining the myth of individualized justice: Probation presentence reports. *Justice Quarterly, 5*(2), 235–256.

Rosenbaum, D. P. (2007). Just say no to DARE. *Criminology & Public Policy, 6*(4), 815–824.

Rosenfeld, R. (2002). Why criminologists should study terrorism. *The Criminologist, 27*(6), 1–4.

Ross, D. L., & Parke, P. A. (2009). Policing by consent decree: An analysis of 42 U.S.C. § 14141 and the new model for police accountability. *Police Practice and Research, 10*(3), 199–208.

Sadd, S., & Grinc, R. M. (1993). *Issues in community policing: An evaluation of eight innovative neighborhood-oriented policing projects.* New York: Vera Institute of Justice.

Sageman, M., & Hoffman, B. (2008). Does Osama still call the shots? Debating the containment of al Qaeda's leadership. *Foreign Affairs, 87,* 163–166.

Saks, A. M., & Ashforth, B. E. (1997). Organizational socialization: Making sense of the past and present as a prologue for the future. *Journal of Vocational Behavior, 51*(2), 234–279.

Saks, A. M., & Gruman, J. A. (2012). Getting newcomers on board: A review of socialization practices and introduction to socialization resources theory. In C. R. Wanberg (Ed.), *The Oxford handbook of organizational socialization* (pp. 27–55). New York: Oxford University Press.

Salancik, G. R. (1981). The effectiveness of ineffective social service systems. In H. D. Stein (Ed.), *Organization and the human services* (pp. 142–150). Philadelphia: Temple University Press.

Samnani, A.-K., & Singh, P. (2012). 20 years of workplace bullying research: A review of the antecedents and consequences of bullying in the workplace. *Aggression and Violent Behavior, 17*(6), 581–589.

Scarborough, K. E., Van Tubergen, G. N., Gaines, L. K., & Whitlow, S. S. (1999). An examination of police officers' motivation to participate in the promotional process. *Police Quarterly, 2*(3), 302–320.

Schafer, J. A. (2010a). Effective leaders and leadership in policing: Traits, assessment, development, and expansion. *Policing: An International Journal of Police Strategies and Management, 33*(4), 644–663.

Schafer, J. A. (2010b). The ineffective police leader: Acts of commission and omission. *Journal of Criminal Justice, 38*(4), 737–746.

Schafer, J. A., Heiple, E., Giblin, M. J., & Burruss, G. W. (2010). Critical incident preparedness and response on post-secondary campuses. *Journal of Criminal Justice, 38*(3), 311–317.

Schaufeli, W., & Enzmann, D. (1998). *The burnout companion to study and practice: A critical analysis.* London: Taylor & Francis.

Schaufeli, W. B., & Buunk, B. P. (2004). Burnout: An overview of 25 years of research and theorizing. In M. J. Schabracq, J. A. M. Winnubst, & C. L. Cooper (Eds.), *The handbook of work and health psychology* (pp. 383–425). Chichester, UK: John Wiley.

Schaufeli, W. B., Enzmann, D., & Girault, N. (1993). Measurement of burnout: A review. In W. B. Schaufeli, C. Maslach, & T. Marek (Eds.), *Professional burnout: Recent developments in theory and research* (pp. 199–215). Washington, DC: Taylor & Francis.

Schein, E. H. (2005). Defining organizational culture. In J. M. Shafritz, J. S. Ott, & Y. S. Jang (Eds.), *Classics of organization theory* (6th ed., pp. 360–367). Belmont, CA: Wadsworth.

Schlanger, M. (2003). Inmate litigation. *Harvard Law Review, 116*(6), 1555–1706.

Schlegel, K., & McGarrell, E. F. (1991). An examination of arrest practices in regions served by multijurisdictional drug task forces. *Crime & Delinquency, 37*(3), 408–426.

Schmidt, J. D., & Sherman, L. W. (1993). Does arrest deter domestic violence? *American Behavioral Scientist, 36*(5), 601–609.

Schultz, M., & Withrow, B. L. (2004). Racial profiling and organizational change. *Criminal Justice Policy Review, 15*(4), 462–485.

Schwartz, J. (2012, July 24). New Orleans police, mired in scandal, accept plan for overhaul. *New York Times*. Retrieved from http://www.nytimes.com/2012/07/25/us/plan-to-reform-new-orleans-police-department.html?pagewanted=all&_r=0

Schwarzschild, M. (1984). Public law by private bargain: Title VII consent decrees and the fairness of negotiated institutional reform. *Duke Law Journal*, (5), 887–936.

Schwarzwald, J., Koslowsky, M., & Agassi, V. (2001). Captain's leadership type and police officers' compliance to power bases. *European Journal of Work and Organizational Psychology, 10*(3), 273–290.

Sciolino, E., & Schmitt, E. (2008, June 8). A not very private feud over terrorism. *New York Times*, p. WK 1.

Scott, W. G. (1961). Organization theory: An overview and an appraisal. *Journal of the Academy of Management, 4*(1), 7–26.

Scott, W. R. (1998). *Organizations: Rational, natural, and open systems*. Upper Saddle River, NJ: Prentice Hall.

Scott, W. R., & Davis, G. F. (2007). *Organizations and organizing: Rational, natural, and open system perspectives*. Upper Saddle River, NJ: Pearson.

Seattle Police Department. (2000). *Seattle Police Department after action report*. Seattle, WA: Author.

Selzer, M. (2003). Federalization of airport security workers: A study of the practical impact of the Aviation and Transportation Security Act from a labor law perspective. *University of Pennsylvania Journal of Labor and Employment Law, 5*(2), 363–381.

Shartle, C. L. (1957). Introduction. In R. M. Stogdill & A. E. Coons (Eds.), *Leader behavior: Its description and measurement* (pp. 1–5). Columbus: Ohio State University, Bureau of Business Research.

Shelby, R. A., Stoddart, R. M., & Taylor, K. L. (2001). Factors contributing to levels of burnout among sex offender treatment providers. *Journal of Interpersonal Violence, 16*(11), 1205–1217.

Sherman, L. (1983). Reducing police gun use: Critical events, administrative policy, and organizational change. In M. Punch (Ed.), *Control in the police organization* (pp. 98–125). Cambridge: MIT Press.

Sherman, L. W. (1992). *Policing domestic violence: Experiments and dilemmas*. New York: Free Press.

Sherman, L. W. (1998). *Evidence-based policing*. Washington, DC: Police Foundation.

Sherman, L. W., & Berk, R. A. (1984). The specific deterrent effects of arrest for domestic assault. *American Sociological Review, 49*, 261–272.

Sherman, L. W., & Eck, J. E. (2002). Policing for crime prevention. In L. W. Sherman, D. P. Farrington, B. C. Welsh, & D. L. MacKenzie (Eds.), *Evidence-based crime prevention* (pp. 295–329). New York: Routledge.

Sherwood, C. W. (2000). Job design, community policing, and higher education: A tale of two cities. *Police Quarterly, 3*(2), 191–212.

Shimabukuro, J. O., & Mayer, G. (2010). *The Public Safety Employer-Employee Cooperation Act* (CRS Report for Congress No. R40738). Washington, DC: Congressional Research Service.

Silverman, D. (1968). Formal organizations or industrial sociology: Towards a social action analysis of organizations. *Sociology, 2*, 221–238.

Silverman, E. B. (1999). *NYPD battles crime: Innovative strategies in policing*. Boston: Northeastern University Press.

Silvestri, M. (2007). "Doing" police leadership: Enter the "new smart macho." *Policing and Society, 17*(1), 38–58.

Simmons, C., Cochran, J., & Blount, W. (1997). The effects of job-related stress and job satisfaction on probation officers' inclinations to quit. *American Journal of Criminal Justice, 21*(2), 213–229.

Simon, H. A. (1946). The proverbs of administration. *Public Administration Review, 6*(1), 53–67.

Singh, J. V., House, R. J., & Tucker, D. J. (1986). Organizational change and organizational mortality. *Administrative Science Quarterly, 31*(4), 587–611.

Singh, J. V., Tucker, D. J., & House, R. J. (1986). Organizational legitimacy and the liability of newness. *Administrative Science Quarterly, 31*(2), 171–193.

Sirene, W. H. (1985). Management: Labor's most effective organizer. In J. J. Fyfe (Ed.), *Police management today: Issues and case studies* (pp. 162–170). Washington, DC: International City Management Association.

Skogan, W., & Frydl, K. (Eds.). (2004). *Fairness and effectiveness in policing: The evidence*. Washington, DC: National Academies Press.

Skogan, W. G., & Hartnett, S. M. (1997). *Community policing, Chicago style*. New York: Oxford University Press.

Slater, J. (1997). Public workers: Labor and the Boston police strike of 1919. *Labor History, 38*(1), 7–27.

Smith, B. D., & Sapp, A. D. (1985). Fringe benefits: The hidden costs of unionization and collective bargaining in corrections. *Journal of Police and Criminal Psychology, 1*(2), 32–39.

Smith, B. W., Novak, K. J., Frank, J., & Travis, L. F. (2000). Multijurisdictional drug task forces: An analysis of impacts. *Journal of Criminal Justice, 28*(6), 543–556.

Smith, C. E., & Nelson, C. E. (2002). Perceptions of the consequences of the Prison Litigation Reform Act: A comparison of state attorneys general and federal district judges. *Justice System Journal, 23*, 295–316.

Smith, H. P., Applegate, B. K., Sitren, A. H., & Springer, N. F. (2009). The limits of individual control? Perceived officer power and probationer compliance. *Journal of Criminal Justice, 37*(3), 241–247.

Smith, P. A., Themessl-Huber, M., Akbar, T., Richards, D., & Freeman, R. (2011). What motivates dentists to work in prisons? A qualitative exploration. *British Dental Journal, 211*, 1–6.

Southerland, M. D., & Potter, G. W. (1993). Applying organization theory to organized crime. *Journal of Contemporary Criminal Justice, 9*(3), 251–267.

Southerland, M. D., & Reuss-Ianni, E. (1992). Leadership and management. In G. W. Cordner & D. C. Hale (Eds.), *What works in policing? Operations and administration examined* (pp. 157–178). Highland Heights, KY: Academy of Criminal Justice Sciences/Anderson.

Sparrow, M. K. (2011). *Governing science*. Cambridge, MA: Harvard Kennedy School, Program in Criminal Justice Policy in Management.

Spelman, W., & Brown, D. K. (1984). *Calling the police: Citizen reporting of serious crime*. Washington, DC: U.S. Department of Justice, National Institute of Justice.

Starbuck, W. H., & Farjoun, M. (Eds.). (2005). *Organization at the limit: Lessons from the Columbia disaster*. Malden, MA: Blackwell.

Steers, R. M., Mowday, R. T., & Shapiro, D. L. (2004). The future of work motivation theory. *Academy of Management Review, 29*(3), 379–387.

Stein, M. (2005). Urban bombing: A trauma surgeon's perspective. *Scandinavian Journal of Surgery, 94*(4), 286–292.

Stephan, J. J. (2008). *Census of state and federal correctional facilities, 2005.* Washington, DC: U.S. Department of Justice, Bureau of Justice Statistics.

Stewart, D. M. (2011). Collaboration between federal and local law enforcement. *Police Quarterly, 14*(4), 407–430.

Stichman, A. J. (2002). *The sources and impact of inmate perceptions of correctional officers' bases of power.* Unpublished doctoral dissertation, University of Cincinnati. Retrieved from http://cech.uc.edu/content/dam/cech/programs/criminaljustice/docs/phd_dissertations/2002/Stichman.pdf

Stinchcomb, J. B. (2004). Searching for stress in all the wrong places: Combating chronic organizational stressors in policing. *Police Practice and Research: An International Journal, 5*(3), 259–277.

Stogdill, R. M. (1948). Personal factors associated with leadership: A survey of the literature. *Journal of Psychology, 25,* 35–71.

Stohr, M. K., & Collins, P. A. (2009). *Criminal justice management: Theory and practice in justice-centered organizations.* New York: Oxford University Press.

Stohr, M. K., Lovrich, N. P., Menke, B. A., & Zupan, L. L. (1994). Staff management in correctional institutions: Comparing DiIulio's "control model" and "employee investment model" outcomes in five jails. *Justice Quarterly, 11,* 471–497.

Stojkovic, S. (1984). Social bases of power and control mechanisms among prisoners in a prison organization. *Justice Quarterly, 1*(4), 511–528.

Stojkovic, S. (1986). Social bases of power and control mechanisms among correctional administrators in a prison organization. *Journal of Criminal Justice, 14*(2), 157–166.

Stojkovic, S., Kalinich, D., & Klofas, J. (2012). *Criminal justice organizations: administration and management* (Vol. 5). Belmont, CA: Wadsworth.

Sudnow, D. (1965). Normal crimes: Sociological features of the penal code in a public defender office. *Social Problems, 12*(3), 255–276.

Swidler, A. (1986). Culture in action: Symbols and strategies. *American Sociological Review, 51*(2), 273–286.

Sykes, G. M. (1958). *The society of captives: A study of a maximum security prison.* Princeton, NJ: Princeton University Press.

Tannenbaum, R., & Schmidt, W. H. (1973). How to choose a leadership pattern. *Harvard Business Review, 51*(3), 162–180.

Taxman, F. S. (2008). No illusions: Offender and organizational change in Maryland's Proactive Community Supervision efforts. *Criminology & Public Policy, 7*(2), 275–302.

Taxman, F. S., Cropsey, K. L., Melnick, G., & Perdoni, M. L. (2008). COD services in community correctional settings: An examination of organizational factors that affect service delivery. *Behavioral Sciences & the Law, 26*(4), 435–455.

Taylor, F. W. (1913). *The principles of scientific management.* New York: Harper & Brothers.

Thompson, C. (2005, October 16). Meet the life hackers. *New York Times Magazine.* Retrieved from http://www.nytimes.com/2005/10/16/magazine/16guru.html

Thompson, W. C. (2008). Beyond bad apples: Analyzing the role of forensic science in wrongful convictions. *Southwestern University Law Review, 37,* 1027–1050.

Tifft, L. L. (1978). Control systems, social bases of power and power exercise in police organizations. In P. K. Manning & J. Van Maanen (Eds.), *Policing: A view from the street* (pp. 90–105). Santa Monica, CA: Goodyear.

Tillyer, M. S., Engel, R. S., & Lovins, B. (in press). Beyond Boston: Applying theory to understand and address sustainability issues in focused deterrence initiatives for violence reduction. *Crime & Delinquency.* doi:10.1177/0011128710382343

Tillyer, R., Engel, R. S., & Cherkauskas, J. C. (2010). Best practices in vehicle stop data collection and analysis. *Policing: An International Journal of Police Strategies and Management, 33*(1), 69–92.

Tompkins, J. R. (2005). *Organization theory and public management.* Belmont, CA: Wadsworth.

Torbet, P. M. (1996). *Juvenile probation: The workhorse of the juvenile justice system.* Washington, DC: U.S. Department of Justice, Office of Juvenile Justice and Delinquency Prevention.

Tosi, H. L., Rizzo, J. R., & Carroll, S. J. (1986). *Managing organizational behavior.* Cambridge, MA: Ballinger.

Traub, L. M. (1977). Jones v. North Carolina Prisoners' Labor Union: A threat to unionization in prisons. *New England Journal on Prison Law, 4,* 157–171.

Trottier, T., Van Wart, M., & Wang, X. (2008). Examining the nature and significance of leadership in government organizations. *Public Administration Review, 68*(2), 319–333.

Tyler, T. R. (1988). What is procedural justice? Criteria used by citizens to assess the fairness of legal procedures. *Law & Society Review, 22*(1), 103–135.

Uchida, A. (2010, June 11). Why are Galveston cops writing fewer tickets? *ABC13.com.* Retrieved from http://abclocal.go.com/ktrk/story?section=news/local&id=7483859

Ulmer, J. T. (1995). The organization and consequences of social pasts in criminal courts. *Sociological Quarterly, 36*(3), 587–605.

U.S. Census Bureau. (2012). Business enterprise: Establishments, employees, payroll. In *The 2012 statistical abstract: The national data book.* Retrieved January 28, 2013, from http://www.census.gov/compendia/statab/cats/business_enterprise/establishments_employees_payroll.html

U.S. General Accounting Office. (1993). *War on drugs: Federal assistance to state and local drug enforcement.* Washington, DC: Author.

Useem, B., & Kimball, P. (1989). *States of siege: U.S. prison riots, 1971–1986.* New York: Oxford University Press.

Useem, B., & Piehl, A. M. (2008). *Prison state: The challenge of mass incarceration.* New York: Cambridge University Press.

Van de Ven, A. H. (1976). On the nature, formation, and maintenance of relations among organizations. *Academy of Management Review, 1*(4), 24–36.

Van de Ven, A. H., & Poole, M. S. (1995). Explaining development and change in organizations. *Academy of Management Review, 20*(3), 510–540.

Van de Ven, A. H., & Sun, K. (2011). Breakdowns in implementing models of organization change. *Academy of Management Perspectives, 25*(3), 58–74.

Van Maanen, J. (1973). Observations on the making of policemen. *Human Organization, 32*(4), 407–418.

Van Maanen, J. (1978). People processing: Strategies of organizational socialization. *Organizational Dynamics, 7*(1), 18–36.

Van Maanen, J. (1984). Making rank: Becoming an American police sergeant. *Urban Life, 13*(2-3), 155-176.

Van Maanen, J., & Schein, E. H. (1979). Toward a theory of organizational socialization. In B. M. Straw (Ed.), *Research in organizational behavior* (Vol. 1, pp. 209-264). Greenwich, CT: JAI Press.

VanLaerhoven, S., & Anderson, G. (2009). The science and careers of CSI. In M. Byers & V. M. Johnson (Eds.), *The CSI effect* (pp. 29-60). Lanham, MD: Lexington Books.

Vaughan, D. (1996). *The Challenger launch decision: Risky technology, culture, and deviance at NASA*. Chicago: University of Chicago Press.

Vaughan, D. (1998). Rational choice, situated action, and the social control of organizations. *Law & Society Review, 32*(1), 23-61.

Vaughan, D. (1999). The dark side of organizations: Mistake, misconduct, and disaster. *Annual Review of Sociology, 25*, 271-305.

Vaughn, M. S. (1996). Prison civil liability for inmate-against-inmate assault and breakdown/disorganization theory. *Journal of Criminal Justice, 24*(2), 139-152.

Veatch, K. C. (2008). *The effect of collective bargaining on the use of innovative police policy*. Jacksonville: University of North Florida.

Vinzant, J. C., & Crothers, L. (1998). *Street-level leadership: Discretion and legitimacy in front-line public service*. Washington, DC: Georgetown University Press.

Virginia Tech Review Panel. (2007). *Mass shootings at Virginia Tech, April 16, 2007: Report of the review panel*. Retrieved from http://www.governor.virginia.gov/tempcontent/techPanelReport-docs/FullReport.pdf

Vroom, V. H. (1964). *Work and motivation*. New York: John Wiley.

Vroom, V. H. (2005). On the origins of expectancy theory. In K. G. Smith & M. A. Hitt (Eds.), *Great minds in management: The process of theory development* (pp. 239-258). Oxford, UK: Oxford University Press.

Vuorensyrjä, M., & Mälkiä, M. (2011). Nonlinearity of the effects of police stressors on police officer burnout. *Policing: An International Journal of Police Strategies and Management, 34*(3), 382-402.

Wahba, M. A., & Bridwell, L. G. (1976). Maslow reconsidered: A review of research on the need hierarchy theory. *Organizational Behavior and Human Performance, 15*, 212-240.

Walker, S. (1993). Does anyone remember team policing? Lessons of the team policing experience for community policing. *American Journal of Police, 12*(1), 33-55.

Walker, S. (2003). The new paradigm of police accountability: The U.S. Justice Department pattern or practice suits in context. *Saint Louis University Public Law Review, 22*, 3-52.

Walker, S. (2008). The neglect of police unions: Exploring one of the most important areas of American policing. *Police Practice & Research, 9*(2), 95-112.

Walker, S., & Bumphus, V. W. (1992). The effectiveness of civilian review: Observations on recent trends and new issues regarding the civilian review of the police. *American Journal of Police, 11*, 1-26.

Walsh, W. F. (2001). Compstat: An analysis of an emerging managerial paradigm. *Policing: An International Journal of Police Strategies and Management, 24*(3), 347-362.

Walster, E., Walster, G. W., & Berscheid, E. (1978). *Equity: Theory and Research*. Boston: Allyn & Bacon.

Wanous, J. P. (1977). Organizational entry: Newcomers moving from outside to inside. *Psychological Bulletin, 84*(4), 601-618.

Waters, J. A., & Ussery, W. (2007). Police stress: History, contributing factors, symptoms, and interventions. *Policing: An International Journal of Police Strategies and Management, 30*(2), 169-188.

Weber, M. (1946). *From Max Weber: Essays in sociology* (H. H. Gerth & C. W. Mills, Trans.). New York: Oxford University Press.

Weick, K. E. (2007). *Managing the unexpected: Resilient performance in the age of uncertainty* (2nd ed.). San Francisco: Wiley.

Weick, K. E., & Quinn, R. E. (1999). Organizational change and development. *Annual Review of Psychology, 50*(1), 361-386.

Weick, K. E., Sutcliffe, K. M., & Obstfeld, D. (2008). Organizing for high reliability: Processes of collective mindfulness. In A. Boin (Ed.), *Crisis management* (Vol. III, pp. 31-66). Thousand Oaks, CA: Sage.

Weiner, B. (1992). *Human motivation: Metaphors, theories, and research*. Thousand Oaks, CA: Sage.

Weisburd, D., & Braga, A. A. (Eds.). (2006). *Police innovation: Contrasting perspectives*. New York: Cambridge University Press.

Weisburd, D., Mastrofski, S. D., McNally, A. M., Greenspan, R., & Willis, J. J. (2003). Reforming to preserve: Compstat and strategic problem solving in American policing. *Criminology & Public Policy, 2*(3), 421-456.

Weisburd, D., & Neyroud, P. (2011). *Police science: Toward a new paradigm*. Cambridge, MA: Harvard Kennedy School, Program in Criminal Justice Policy in Management.

Weiss, A. (1998). *Informal information sharing among police agencies*. Washington, DC: U.S. Department of Justice, National Institute of Justice.

Weiss, C. H., Murphy-Graham, E., & Birkeland, S. (2005). An alternate route to policy influence: How evaluations affect D.A.R.E. *American Journal of Evaluation, 26*(1), 12-30.

Weiss, J. A. (1987). Pathways to cooperation among public agencies. *Journal of Policy Analysis and Management, 7*(1), 94-117.

Wellington, H. H., & Winter, R. K. (1988). The limits of collective bargaining in public employment. In D. Lewin, P. Feuille, T. A. Kochan, & J. T. Delaney (Eds.), *Public sector labor relations: Analysis and readings* (pp. 37-46). Lexington, MA: Lexington Books.

Wener, R. (2006). Effectiveness of the direct supervision system of correctional design and management. *Criminal Justice and Behavior, 33*(3), 392-410.

Wenzel, S. L., Longshore, D., Turner, S., & Ridgely, M. S. (2001). Drug courts: A bridge between criminal justice and health services. *Journal of Criminal Justice, 29*(3), 241-253

West, H. C., Sabol, W. J., & Greenman, S. J. (2010). *Prisoners in 2009*. Washington, DC: U.S. Department of Justice, Bureau of Justice Statistics.

Westley, W. A. (1970). *Violence and the police: A sociological study of law, custom, and morality*. Cambridge: MIT Press.

Whetstone, T. S. (2001). Copping out: Why police officers decline to participate in the sergeant's promotional process. *American Journal of Criminal Justice, 25*(2), 147-159.

Whetten, D. A. (1987). Organizational growth and decline processes. *Annual Review of Sociology, 13*, 335-358.

White, M. D., Cooper, J. A., Saunders, J., & Raganella, A. J. (2010). Motivations for becoming a police officer: Re-assessing officer attitudes and job satisfaction after six years on the street. *Journal of Criminal Justice, 38*(4), 520–530.

Whitehead, J. T. (1986). Job burnout and job satisfaction among probation managers. *Journal of Criminal Justice, 14*(1), 25–35.

Whitehead, J. T., & Lindquist, C. A. (1986). Correctional officer job burnout: A path model. *Journal of Research in Crime and Delinquency, 23*(1), 23–42.

Widenor, M. (1991). A small city police strike: Klamath Falls, Oregon, 1973. *Journal of Collective Negotiations, 20*(3), 175–191.

Williams, D. A., Smith, V. E., Manning, R., & Fuller, T. (1978, August 28). The siege of Memphis. *Newsweek,* 24.

Williams, E. J. (2003). Structuring in community policing: Institutionalizing innovative change. *Police Practice and Research, 4*(2), 119–129.

Williams, P. (2002). The competent boundary spanner. *Public Administration, 80*(1), 103–124.

Willis, J. J., Mastrofski, S. D., & Weisburd, D. (2004). Compstat and bureaucracy: A case study of challenges and opportunities for change. *Justice Quarterly, 21,* 463–496.

Willis, J. J., Mastrofski, S. D., & Weisburd, D. (2007). Making sense of COMPSTAT: A theory-based analysis of organizational change in three police departments. *Law & Society Review, 41*(1), 147–188.

Wilson, J. M., Rostker, B. D., & Fan, C.-C. (2010). *Recruiting and retaining America's finest: Evidence-based lessons for police workforce planning.* Santa Monica, CA: RAND.

Wilson, S., Zhao, J., Ren, L., & Briggs, S. (2006). The influence of collective bargaining on large police agency salaries: 1990–2000. *American Journal of Criminal Justice, 31*(1), 19–34.

Wohlers, E. T. (1978). One strike and you may be out: The legal realities of the hardball game of fire fighter and police strikes. *Idaho Law Review, 15,* 39–63.

Wolfe, S. E., & Piquero, A. R. (2011). Organizational justice and police misconduct. *Criminal Justice and Behavior, 38*(4), 332–353.

Won-Jae, L., Koenigsberg, M. R., Davidson, C., & Beto, D. R. (2010). A pilot survey linking personality, leadership style, and leadership success among probation directors in the U.S. *Federal Probation, 74*(3), 34–42.

Wood, D. (2000). *Turnover among Alaska village public safety officers: An examination of the factors associated with attrition.* Anchorage: University of Alaska Anchorage, Justice Center.

Wood, D. (2001, January). Police turnover in isolated communities: The Alaska experience. *National Institute of Justice Journal, 246,* 16–23.

Wood, D. J., & Gray, B. (1991). Toward a comprehensive theory of collaboration. *Journal of Applied Behavioral Science, 27*(2), 139–162.

Wood, D. S. (2002). Explanations of employment turnover among Alaska Village Public Safety Officers. *Journal of Criminal Justice, 30*(3), 197–215.

Worrall, J. L., & Gaines, L. K. (2006). The effect of police-probation partnerships on juvenile arrests. *Journal of Criminal Justice, 34*(6), 579–589.

Worrall, J. L., Schram, P., Hays, E., & Newman, M. (2004). An analysis of the relationship between probation caseloads and property crime rates in California counties. *Journal of Criminal Justice, 32*(3), 231–241.

Worrall, J. L., & Zhao, J. (2003). The role of the COPS Office in community policing. *Policing: An International Journal of Police Strategies and Management, 26*(1), 64–87.

Wright, K. N. (1994). *Effective prison leadership.* Binghamton, NY: William Neil.

Wrightsman, L. S. (1999). *Judicial decision making: Is psychology relevant?* New York: Kluwer Academic/Plenum.

Wynne, J. M. (1978a). *Prison employee unionism: The impact on correctional administration and programs.* Washington, DC: U.S. Department of Justice, National Institute of Law Enforcement and Criminal Justice.

Wynne, J. M. (1978b). Unions and bargaining among employees of state prisons. *Monthly Labor Review, 101*(3), 10–16.

Yukl, G. (1994). *Leadership in organizations* (3rd ed.). Englewood Cliffs, NJ: Prentice Hall.

Yukl, G., & Falbe, C. M. (1991). Importance of different power sources in downward and lateral relations. *Journal of Applied Psychology, 76*(3), 416–423.

Yukl, G., Guinan, P. J., & Soitolano, D. (1995). Influence tactics used for different objectives with subordinates, peers, and superiors. *Group & Organization Management, 20*(3), 272–296.

Zegart, A. B. (2007). *Spying blind: The CIA, FBI, and the origins of 9/11.* Princeton, NJ: Princeton University Press.

Zhao, J., He, N., & Lovrich, N. (2002). Predicting five dimensions of police officer stress: Looking more deeply into organizational settings for sources of police stress. *Police Quarterly, 5*(1), 43–62.

Zhao, J., & Lovrich, N. (1997). Collective bargaining and the police: The consequences for supplemental compensation policies in large agencies. *Policing: An International Journal of Police Strategies and Management, 20,* 508–518.

Zhao, J., Thurman, Q. C., & Lovrich, N. P. (1995). Community-oriented policing across the U.S.: Facilitators and impediment to implementation. *American Journal of Police, 14*(1), 11–28.

Zimmer, L., & Jacobs, J. B. (1981). Challenging the Taylor Law: Prison guards on strike. *Industrial and Labor Relations Review, 34*(4), 531–544.

Zimmerling, R. (2005). *Influence and power: Variations on a messy theme.* Dordrecht, Netherlands: Springer.

Index

Aaron, J. D. K., 393
Abkar, T., 332
Abu Ghraib prison, 148, 149
Accidents. *See* Normal accident theory (NAT); Organizational deviance
Accountability, 153–154, 181, 243, 559
Achievement motive (*n* achievement), 323, 324
　See also Achievement/power/affiliation theory
Achievement/power/affiliation theory, 318, 323
　achievement motive/*n* achievement individuals and, 323, 324
　affiliation motive/*n* affiliation individuals and, 323–324
　extrinsic/intrinsic motivators and, 318–319, 319 (table)
　occupational choice in policing and, 324–325
　personalized power motive and, 324
　power motive/*n* power and, 324–325
　socialized power motive and, 324
　See also Content theories; Motivation
Acute onset burnout, 388
Adam, C., 140
Adams, J. S., 325, 350
Adler, P. S., 39, 46
Administrative breakdown, 132–133
　See also Administrative breakdown/managerial disorganization in bureaucracies study article; Organizational deviance
Administrative breakdown/managerial disorganization in bureaucracies study article, 145–147
　accountability dysfunction, subculture of misconduct and, 153–154
　authority hierarchy, dysfunction in, 151–152, 153
　breakdown/disorganization theory and, 146
　bureaucratic agencies, theoretical legitimacy of, 147
　coercive force, constitutional limits on, 150
　command/control principles and, 152–153
　communication deficiencies and, 149, 154–156
　coordination/efficiency problems and, 149
　decision making goals and, 149
　decision-making process, environmental factor assessment and, 154
　division of labor, job training/specialization and, 149–150
　dysfunctional organizational systems and, 146–147
　formalization, principle of definition and, 154–155
　front-line supervision, organizational dysfunction and, 153
　goals/objectives of organizations, clarity in, 148–149, 155
　management efficacy and, 145, 148–149, 150
　mechanistic/formalistic organizations and, 146
　methods, elements of organizations and, 147–156
　operational success, essential elements for, 146
　organizational failure, manager contribution to, 146, 147
　procedure-goal-objective relationship and, 149
　resource allocation decisions and, 149
　role conflict, authority hierarchy changes and, 149
　summary/conclusion and, 156–157
　top management-subordinate incongruity and, 149
　traditional organizational elements, deviation from, 146
　See also Administrative breakdown; Organizational deviance; Readings
Administrative management, 87
　criminal justice organizations and, 88–89
　criticisms of principles and, 89
　deviation from principles, ramifications of, 89
　principles of, 87–88
　specialized workforce and, 89
　unity-of-command principle and, 89
　upper-level management and, 87
　See also Administrative breakdown/managerial disorganization in bureaucracies study article; Classical theories
Affiliation motive (*n* affiliation), 323–324
　See also Achievement/power/affiliation theory

Affirmative action policies, 253
Agnew, R., 358
Aiken, M., 45
Airport security, 2–3
Alaska Intertribal Council v. State of Alaska (2005), 379
Alaska State Troopers, 378–379
   job-related stressors and, 379
   Village Public Safety Officers and, 379
   See also Occupational stress
Allen, J. M., 8
Alpert, G. P., 26, 289, 298, 327, 521, 529
al Qaeda, 22, 25, 31, 93
Altruism, 176
Alwin, D., 115
Amabile, T. M., 319
Amaranto, E., 397
Amendola, K. L., 382
American Civil Liberties Union (ACLU), 192, 200
American Correctional Association (ACA), 54
American Federation of Labor (AFL), 225, 226
American Federation of Labor/Congress of Industrial Organizations (AFL/CIO), 226, 251, 263, 267
American Federation of State, County, and Municipal Employees (AFSCME), 260, 261
American Jail Association, 544
American Medical Association Council on Scientific Affairs, 207
American Probation and Parole Association (APPA), 50, 52
American Psychiatric Association (APA), 341
Anderson, G. S., 279, 381
Angell, J. E., 335
Anticipatory socialization, 278, 279–280, 288, 310
Antidrug task forces, 179–180
Anti-Terrorism Information Exchange, 197
Antiterrorism task forces, 2
Applegate, B. K., 487, 506
Appleton, C., 177
Arbitration process, 232–233
Archbold, C. A., 384
Arizona Counter Terrorism Information Center (ACTIC), 178
Arkansas Crime Information Center, 178
Arkin, W. M., 2
Armacost, B. E., 352
Armstrong, G. S., 50
Aronson, D. C., 309
Ashforth, B. E., 276
Association of Black Correctional Workers, 253
Attica prison riots, 137, 138
Authority hierarchy, 17, 19–20, 19 (figure), 151–152, 153
Autonomy, 335, 365, 367, 373, 374, 385, 390, 391

Babbie, E., 304, 521, 522
Bachman, R., 208, 328
Baird, S., 379
Baltimore Police Department, 91, 236, 237, 390, 392, 409, 482
Bardach, E., 177
Bargaining rights. *See* Collective bargaining
Barker, T., 240
Barnard, T., 424
Barnett, W. P., 535
Barocas, B., 392
Bartholomew, B., 2
Bartles, D. L., 138
Barton, S., 36
Bass, B. M., 433, 439, 444, 445
Batten, D., 537, 538
Battle in Seattle, 137
Bauer, L., 102, 106
Bauer, M. W., 140
Baum, J. A. C., 545
Bayley, D. H., 12, 240
Bea, R., 138
Beehr, T. A., 328, 394
Behavioral/style theories of leadership, 433
   achievement-oriented style and, 443
   authority-obedience style and, 434
   conceptualization of leadership and, 433
   consideration dimension and, 433
   country club management style and, 434
   courtroom leadership, behavioral dimensions of, 434–435
   dimensions of leadership and, 433–435
   directive style and, 442–443
   impoverished management style and, 434
   initiating structure dimension and, 433
   Leader Behavior Description Questionnaire and, 433
   Managerial Grid dimensions and, 434
   middle-of-the-road style and, 434
   participative style and, 443
   path-goal theory and, 442–443
   relationship/task-orientated behavior measures and, 434–435
   supportive style and, 443
   team management style and, 434
   See also Fiedler's contingency theory of leadership; Leadership; Organizational behavior; Organizational culture; Organizational socialization; Power; Trait theory
Bell, C., 416
Benjamin, G. A., 417
Benson, J. K., 540
Berg, B. L., 289
Bergman, W. T., 537

Berk, R. A., 163, 567
Berkes, L. J., 443, 452
Berkson, L., 37
Berman, G., 550
Bernard, C. I., 151
Berry, S. M., 108
Berscheid, E., 326
Bethlehem Steel Company time-motion studies, 83
Beyerlein, M. M., 175
Bianchi, M., 52
Birkeland, S., 539, 554
Bittner, E., 482
Blackburn, J., 40
Blacksburg (VA) Police Department, 175, 177
Black swan stories, 290, 296
Blake, R. R., 434
Blanchard, K. H., 439, 440
Blau, P. M., 8, 12, 17, 21, 85
Blomberg, T. G., 106
Blood alcohol concentration (BAC), 94, 95
Blue flu/mass sickouts, 237
Blum, T., 40
Blumberg, A. S., 416
Boeckmann, R., 257
Bohm, R. M., 99, 106, 109
Boin, R. A., 137, 138
Boland, B., 24
Bonczar, T. P., 560
Bordenkircher v. Hayes (1978), 105
Borys, B., 39, 46
Boss, R. W., 547
Boston Police Strike (1919), 225–226, 235
Boston Regional Intelligence Center (BRIC), 178
Bouchard, M., 78
Boudreau, R. A., 388, 389
Bounded rationality. *See* Limited/bounded rationality
Bouza, A. V., 240
Bowman, C. G., 209
Boyle, B. V., 280
Bozeman, B., 39, 46
BP Gulf Coast oil spill disaster, 326
Bradford, D. L., 487
Bradley, H. B., 386
Brady v. United States (1970), 101
Brame, R., 208, 328
Branch Davidian compound raid, 135, 148, 155–156
Brank, E. M., 206
Bratton, W. J., 19, 429, 430
Breakdown/disorganization theory, 146
   See also Administrative breakdown; Organizational deviance

Breener, J. M., 339
Bridwell, L. G., 319, 320
Briggs, S., 230
Bright, S. B., 108
Broken windows argument, 163
Bromirski, D., 2
Brown, J., 252, 266, 267
Brown, L. P., 24
Brown, M. K., 488, 489
Bruce, W., 40
Buerger, M. E., 290
Building tenders (BTs), 480–481, 484
Bullock, R. J., 537, 538
Bullying. *See* Workplace bullying
Bumphus, V. W., 540
Bureaucracy, 85
   bureaucratic organizations, characteristics of, 85–86
   classical vs. behavioral perspectives on, 36–37
   closed-system perspective and, 87
   division of labor and, 85
   dysfunction/inefficiency and, 87
   efficiency and, 100
   formalization and, 85, 154–155
   hierarchy/vertical complexity and, 85
   impersonal organizational governance and, 86
   merit-based recruitment/promotion and, 86
   role ambiguity and, 45
   span of control issues and, 152–153
   streamlined organizational functioning and, 86
   street-level bureaucrats and:
   worker compliance, rational-legal principles and, 85, 86
   See also Administrative breakdown/managerial disorganization in bureaucracies study article; Classical theories; McJustice/McDonaldization of criminal justice study article
Bureau of Alcohol, Tobacco, Firearms, and Explosives (ATF), 23, 135, 191, 199
Bureau of Justice Assistance (BJA), 179, 180
Bureau of Justice Statistics (BJS), 207, 230, 429, 560, 569
Bureau of Labor Statistics (BLS), 229, 298
Burke, R. J., 289, 388, 389
Burke, T. W., 398
Burke, W. W., 536
Burnett, C., 108
Burnett, R., 177
Burnham, D. H., 323, 324
Burnout phenomenon, 386
   acute onset of, 388
   autonomy/control and, 390, 391

burnout components, interrelationships among, 388–389
chronic burnout, 388
community of workers and, 391
consequences of, 392
correlates of, 389–391
definition of, 386–387
depersonalization/detachment and, 388, 389
diminished sense of accomplishment and, 388, 389
emotional exhaustion and, 388, 389
engagement and, 387, 390
fairness/procedural justice and, 391
interventions for, 392–394
job/role characteristics and, 389–390
Maslach Burnout Inventory instrument and, 387–388
organizational policies/practices and, 390
phase model of, 388–389, 389 (table)
primary interventions for, 392–393, 394
secondary interventions for, 393
tertiary interventions for, 393
theoretical framework for, 390–391
value conflict and, 391
worker-workplace mismatch framework and, 391
work overload and, 391
 See also Occupational stress; Qualitative assessment of stress perceptions/homicide units study article; Sex offender treatment providers/burnout factors study article
Burns, J. M., 444, 445
Burruss, G. W., 97, 177
Burt, R. S., 67
Bush, T., 149
Business organizations, 12
 See also Organizational change; Organizational structures
Buunk, B. P., 386, 387
Byosiere, P., 380, 392
Byrne assistance program, 179–180

Caldero, M. A., 350
California Coalition of Law Enforcement Associations, 253
California Correctional Peace Officers Association (CCPOA), 12, 224–225, 226, 228, 229, 232, 249, 266, 267, 268
 See also Prison officer unions/perpetuated penal status quo study article
California District Attorneys Association, 253, 257, 258
California Fair Political Practices Commission, 258
Californians United for Public Safety (CUPS), 255, 257
Californians United for Public Safety-Independent Expenditure Committee (CUPS-IEC), 255
California Police Chiefs Association, 253, 258
California probation system, 115, 125
California State Sheriffs Association, 253
Camp, C. G., 106
Camp, G. M., 106
Camp, S., 38, 39, 40
Campus safety policies, 174–175
Canton, A. N., 392
Capital punishment costs, 106–107
Carlson, N., 152, 153
Carroll, G. R., 535, 545
Carroll, L., 151
Carroll, S. J., 491
Carter, D. L., 190, 228, 240, 368, 388, 389
Carter, J. G., 190
Carter, R. M., 103, 114, 124
Cartwright, S., 382, 385
Catellano, C., 397
Center for Juvenile and Criminal Justice, 253
Centers for Disease Control and Prevention (CDC), 207
Central Intelligence Agency (CIA):
 inflexibility in, 22, 93
 information sharing, problems with, 16, 25
Centralization dimension, 27
 accountability and, 27, 28
 central/single decision maker and, 27
 Compstat strategy and, 27–28
 decentralized criminal organization structure and, 31
 individual workers, motivation/satisfaction and, 28
 maximum centralization and, 27
 measurement of, 27
 minimum centralization/decentralization and, 27, 28
 uniformity and, 27
 See also Centralization/formalization impact study article; Formalization dimension; Organizational control; Span of control
Centralization/formalization impact study article, 35
 bureaucracy, classical vs. behavioral perspectives on, 36–37
 centralization literature and, 37–39
 centralization measures and, 41, 42 (table)
 discussion/conclusion and, 44–46
 formalization literature and, 39–40
 formalization measures and, 41, 42 (table)
 job satisfaction measures and, 41, 42 (table), 43
 job satisfaction/organizational commitment and, 35–36
 literature review for, 37–40
 measures and, 41–43, 42–43 (table)
 methods and, 41
 organizational commitment measures, 42–43 (table), 43
 research questions in, 40–41
 results and, 43–44
 See also Organizational structures; Readings
Chains of command, 17, 19–20, 19 (figure), 151–152
Challenger disaster, 134, 135

Change. *See* Crisis management; Downsizing-oriented prison reform; Organizational change; Transformational leadership
Change to Win Coalition, 251
Chao, G. T., 277
Chappell, A. T., 277, 355
Charismatic power, 485, 491
Cheek, F. E., 383, 392, 393
Chemers, M. M., 437
Chemical weapons, 194
Chermak, S., 175
Cherniss, C., 416, 417
Chesney-Lind, M., 519
Chicago Policy Department, 23
Chicago School of social ecology, 163
Chicano Correctional Workers Association, 253
Christopher Commission report, 148, 151
Chronic burnout, 388
Chubb, J. E., 148
Church, R. L., 393
Cincinnati Initiative to Reduce Violence, 188
Ciulla, J. B., 463, 464
Civil rights violations legislation, 542
Classical theories, 36, 37, 82, 335
    administrative management and, 87–89
    bureaucracy and, 85–87
    instrumental rationality and, 82
    prescriptive theories and, 82
    scientific management and, 83–85
    Theory X and, 90–91
    See also Human relations theory; Organizational theory
Clear, T. R., 250, 524
Clegg, I. J., 392
Closed systems approach, 7, 8
    bureaucracy and, 87, 154
    classical/human relations theories and, 92
Cloward, R. A., 507
Code-of-silence attitudes, 349, 350, 354–355, 356, 358, 359
Coercive isomorphism, 97
Coercive power, 150, 324, 484, 486, 487, 491
Cohen, A. R., 487
Cohen, L., 164
Cohen-Charash, Y., 351
Colbridge, T. D., 185
Cole, G. F., 524
Coleman v. Wilson (1995), 267
Collaboration, 175
    See also Criminal justice collaborations; Interagency collaboration
Collaborative advantage, 175, 176–177
Collective bargaining, 226
    arbitration process and, 232–233

conflicts of interest and, 229
content of agreements and, 227–228
coverage of agreements and, 228–229
dues check off agreement and, 228, 242
economic benefits of, 229–231, 230 (table)
fact finding process and, 232
justice agencies and, 227
labor relations, improvements in, 238–239
mass sickouts/blue flu and, 237
mediation agreements and, 232
merit pay provisions and, 326–327
multiple-year contracts and, 227
negative effects, potential for, 231–232
post-and-bid job assignment process and, 228
prevalence of, 226
public-sector employees and, 227, 231–232, 241
slowdowns and, 237–238
strike actions, stages in, 233–234
strike options, differences among, 233
supplemental pay and, 230–231, 230 (table)
unit determination process and, 228–229
See also Labor; Labor unions; Police employee organizations study article
Collective socialization, 280
Colorado Information Analysis Center (CIAC), 178
Commonwealth organizations, 12
Communication:
    administrative breakdown/managerial disorganization and, 147, 154–156
    distortion in, 20
    formalization in bureaucratic organizations and, 45, 154–155
    ineffective leadership, communication deficiencies and, 460–461
    information sharing problems and, 16, 24–25
    spatial complexity and, 24–25
Community corrections officers (CCOs), 184, 185
Community-oriented policing (COP), 21, 22, 30, 95, 109, 163, 296, 332, 535–536
Community policing/job design and education level factors study article, 364
    autonomy/control, preference for, 368
    community policing, effect of, 374
    community policing, job redesign initiatives and, 367
    crime analysis data, mobile technology and, 373
    data collection instrument and, 370
    departments studied, characteristics of, 368–369
    discussion and, 371–375
    findings and, 370–371, 370 (table)
    higher education, effects of, 367–368, 375
    hypotheses, testing of, 369–370
    Job Diagnostic Survey and, 370
    job enrichment, intrinsic motivation and, 365

job enrichment/job characteristics approaches and, 365–367, 371–374, 372 (table)
  management implications and, 375
  methods and, 368–370
  natural work units, formation of, 366–367, 373
  participant pool and, 368–370
  police training, significant changes in, 369
  prevention programs, at-risk community members and, 369
  procedure and, 370
  work alienation/self-estrangement and, 368
  work redesign implementation and, 366–367
  See also Community-oriented policing (COP); Motivation; Readings
Community prosecution, 24, 87
Community supervision. *See* Span of control in evidence-based community supervision study article
Complexity. *See* Normal accident theory (NAT); Organizational complexity; Organizational structures
Compliance observability and, 490
Compstat strategy, 27–28, 97, 104, 109, 539
Concealment principle, 162, 165, 167
Concentration of hierarchies, 17, 19
Confessore, N., 262
Conflictive change motor, 540–543, 546, 546 (figure)
Congress of Industrial Organizations (CIO). *See* American Federation of Labor/Congress of Industrial Organizations (AFL/CIO)
Connectedness. *See* Coupling
Connor, P. E., 547, 548
Conover, T., 260, 570
Consent decrees, 535, 541–543
Conser, J. A., 321
Consideration leadership dimension, 433
Content theories, 318
  achievement/affiliation/power theory and, 323–325
  extrinsic/intrinsic motivators and, 318–319, 319 (table)
  motivator-hygiene theory and, 321–323
  need theory and, 319–321
  See also Motivation; Process theories
Conti, N., 281, 284
Contingency theories, 92, 435
  components of, 92
  criminal justice field and, 93
  criticisms of, 93–94
  evidence-based practice and, 94
  organizational inflexibility and, 93
  path-goal theory and, 442–443
  structural-adaptation-to-regain-fit model and, 92–93
  See also Fiedler's contingency theory of leadership; Open systems theories

Contingent reward, 444, 445
Control. *See* Organizational control; Span of control
Cook, C. R., 45
Coons, A. E., 430
Cooper, C. L., 380, 381, 382, 385, 392
Cooper, T. W., 151
Coordinated Agency Network (CAN) program, 184
COP-2-COP hotline, 393
Copes, H., 388, 395
Coping mechanisms. *See* Occupational stress
Corbett, R. P., 183
Cordes, C. L., 389
Cordner, G. W., 148
Correctional Service Corps, 474
Corrections. *See* Centralization/formalization impact study article; Court system; Criminal justice collaborations; Criminal justice system; Incarceration; Interagency collaboration; Prison officer unions/perpetuated penal status quo study article
Corrections Corporation of America, 12
Corrigan, P. W., 424
Counterproduction problem, 176
Counter Terrorism Intelligence Center (CTIC), 178
County Intelligence Center, 178
Coupling dimension, 135–136, 166, 167
Courtroom workgroups:
  goals of, 9–10
  plea bargaining, law in action and, 91
  See also Court system; Criminal justice system
Court system:
  bail schedules and, 84
  bureaucratized functioning of, 86, 87
  community prosecution and, 24, 87
  defense attorneys, ineffectual behavior of, 108
  determinate sentencing and, 103, 104, 107
  exculpatory evidence, withholding of, 108
  indeterminate sentencing and, 103, 125, 252
  inmate lawsuits, filing of, 540–541, 542, 543
  mandatory minimum sentences and, 103
  perjury, tainted testimony and, 108
  plea bargaining and, 91, 100–102, 105
  probation presentence reports and, 96, 97, 114–126
  problem-solving courts and, 205–206, 444, 445, 536
  prosecutor's office, organizational structure of, 17, 18 (figure), 335
  scientific management and, 84
  sentencing guidelines and, 84, 86, 102–103, 104
  soft on crime allegations and, 103
  spatial organizational complexity and, 23, 24
  therapeutic jurisprudence and, 536

three strikes law and, 105
truth-in-sentencing statutes and, 103
victim impact statements and, 96, 97
victim-witness programs and, 10
See also Courtroom workgroups; Criminal justice system; Domestic violence court/procedural justice study article; Incarceration; Occupational stress/public defenders study article
Covey, S., 41
Cowie, H., 384
Craig, S. C., 547
Crank, J. P., 292, 295, 296, 297, 298, 350
Cressey, D., 65, 68, 78
Crime Gun Centers, 191
Crime industry monopoly, 154
Crime Victims Bureau (CVB), 253
Crime Victims United of California (CVUC), 253, 255, 268
Criminal Domestic Violence Court (CDVC), 209–212, 211 (figure)
See also Domestic violence court/procedural justice study article
Criminal Intelligence Coordinating Council, 202
Criminal justice agency failure. *See* Organizational deviance; Organizational termination
Criminal justice collaborations, 179
 accountability issues and, 181
 Byrne assistance program and, 179–180
 community corrections officers and, 184
 deterrence theory, crime reduction effects and, 185–186
 double jeopardy protections and, 181
 federalism principles and, 181–182
 federal-state task forces and, 181
 fugitive apprehension/violent crime activity task forces and, 180, 182
 gang affiliations, intelligence sharing and, 182
 horizontal collaborations and, 179
 illegal drug trafficking, antidrug task forces and, 179–180
 joint-terrorism task forces and, 180, 181–182
 law enforcement task forces and, 179–182
 mission distortion, potential for, 185
 multijurisdictional task forces and, 179–181
 mutually beneficial power enhancement and, 184–185
 networks of capacity and, 188
 Operation Night Light and, 183
 output goals and, 180–181
 policbation officer role and, 185
 police-community corrections partnerships and, 183–185
 police-corrections partnerships and, 182–185, 183 (table)
 process goals of task forces and, 180, 181
 pulling levers/focused deterrence strategies framework and, 186–188

 scalar chain/unity-of-command principles and, 181
 span of control issues and, 184–185
 stalking horse role and, 185
 vertical collaborations and, 179, 181
 See also Criminal justice system; Domestic violence court/procedural justice study article; Intelligence fusion process article; Interagency collaboration
Criminal justice system, 1–2
 capital trials/capital punishment, costs of, 106–107
 contingency theory and, 93
 continuity of operations and, 11
 courtroom workgroups, goals of, 9–10
 crime control leverage, spatial complexity issue and, 24
 crime control model and, 100–101
 crime-related intelligence, sharing of, 24–25
 customers of, 8
 Department of Homeland Security and, 3–4, 4 (table)
 drunk-driving prevention and, 94–95
 firearms violators, targeting of, 24
 fiscal policies, cost effectiveness issues and, 105–106
 formalization, limitations of, 27
 homeland security responsibilities and, 2–3
 human relations theory and, 91
 mid-management personnel, surplus of, 19
 9/11 terrorist attacks, influence of, 2
 planning agencies in, 95–96
 privatization trend and, 12, 13
 rank structure/chain of command and, 17
 service delivery, indirect payment for, 8
 spatial complexity, location-specific strategies and, 23–24
 team policing and, 20
 vertical complexity in, 17, 19–20, 19 (figure)
 See also Centralization/formalization impact study article; Court system; Criminal justice collaborations; Criminal organizations; Incarceration; International drug smuggling organizational structure study article; McJustice/McDonaldization of criminal justice study article; Medical system lessons/criminal justice decision making study article; Police organizations
Criminal organizations, 30
 decentralized structure, law enforcement challenge of, 31
 horizontal complexity and, 31
 member socialization/indoctrination, unwritten rules and, 31
 operating rules within, 30–31
 terrorist organizations, structures of, 31
 white-collar crime and, 31
 See also Criminal justice collaborations; International drug smuggling organizational structure study article; Organizational structures; War on Drugs

Crisis management, 137–138
   administrative breakdown, crisis management plans and, 147, 156
   crisis negotiators and, 167–168
   crisis paralysis and, 137
   narrow span of control and, 152
   See also Normal accident theory (NAT); Organizational deviance
Crisis paralysis, 137
Critical Incidents Scale (CIS), 521
Cropsey, K. L., 445
Crotty, N. M., 260
Crouch, B. M., 480, 519, 521, 529
Crozier, M., 153
Cruel/unusual punishment, 103
Culture. *See* Organizational culture
Cummings, L. L., 5
Cummings, T. G., 380, 381
Cunniff, M. A., 51, 62
Cushman, R. C., 52

D.A.R.E. America, 551, 555, 556
D.A.R.E. lessons/research-practice relationship study article, 550–551
   ancillary positive benefits and, 553
   conclusion/summary and, 556–557
   curriculum development initiatives and, 554, 555
   D.A.R.E. phenomenon, evaluation of, 552–554
   drug prevention research, responses to, 554–557
   history of D.A.R.E. program, 550–552
   instructor re-training initiative and, 554, 555
   Just Say No to Drugs campaign and, 551
   keepin' it REAL curriculum and, 555
   Lake Wobegon effect and, 553
   midcourse programming corrections and, 554, 555
   modest/realistic expectations and, 553, 556
   negative research findings, program persistence and, 551, 552–554, 555
   organization mission/methods, re-thinking of, 554–555
   program evaluation research/policy decisions, knowledge creep and, 556
   program failure, program termination and, 551–552, 553, 555
   researcher-practitioner co-dependence and, 556
   state/regional infrastructure and, 552
   Take Back Your Life curriculum and, 554
   trial-and-error approach, value of, 557
   See also Organizational change; Readings
Dabney, D. A., 388, 395
Daft, R. L., 333
Dahl, R., 481, 482

Dallas County Judicial Treatment Center (DCJTC), 340–342
Dalton, D. R., 26, 27
Daly, K., 519
Damanpour, F., 22
Darling, E., 417
Davis, G., 232, 259, 267
Davis, G. F., 3, 5, 6, 82, 88, 92
Davis, R. C., 209
Day, D. V., 447
Deadly force policies, 26, 103, 136, 165, 355, 361, 544
   See also Deadly force/social theory and street cops study article; Use-of-force policies
Deadly force/social theory and street cops study article, 161–163
   barricaded suspect scenario, 167–168
   concealment principle and, 162, 165, 167, 170, 171
   deterrence theory and, 163
   Diallo killing scenario and, 168–170
   Kray standoff scenario and, 170–171
   lethal confrontations, police involvement in, 162–163, 165
   normal accident theory, deadly force and, 166–172
   officer-involved shootings, low-frequency event of, 164–165
   officer-involved shootings, public concern about, 161–162
   preventable shooting scenarios, 168–171
   robbery call/unavoidable shooting scenario and, 168
   SARA policing model and, 163, 164
   social reality of deadly force, understanding of, 162
   social theory, guidance function of, 161, 163
   social theory, police work/public understanding and, 163–164
   sociology-of-risk framework, socially-determined mistakes and, 164
   suicide-by-cop and, 165–166
   summary/conclusion and, 171–172
   suspect refusing surrender/dialogue scenario, unavoidable shooting and, 168
   SWAT teams/crisis negotiators and, 167–168
   tactical knowledge, principle of, 162–163, 165–166, 166 (figure)
   unavoidable shooting scenarios and, 168
   zero-tolerance policing and, 163–164
   See also Organizational deviance; Readings
Death Penalty Information Center, 108
Decentralization, 27, 67
Decker, D., 541, 543
Decker, S. H., 30
DeCotiis, T. A., 40, 240
Decoupling dimension, 97
Defects of total power study article, 493
   authority rights, absence of, 497
   bureaucratic custodial structures and, 493–494
   coercive power, monopoly on, 494, 498

corruption of rulers, unexercised power and, 500–503
custodial regime, mass commands/regulations and, 497–498
custodial staff personnel, workplace inadequacies and, 503–504
Gebietsver-band social system and, 498
infinite power, terror vs. government and, 494
inmate population, centers of opposition in, 494
legitimate control/no duty to conform, incomplete subjugation and, 498, 499
myth of custodial dominance and, 496–497, 498, 502–503
reciprocal power relations and, 501–502
reward/punishment system, inadequacies in, 499–500
systems of norms/laws, curbs on capricious action and, 494
use of force, inefficient control mechanism of, 498–499, 500
See also Power; Readings
Defense-of-life doctrine, 165
Delaware Information Analysis Center, 178
del Carmen, R. V., 151
De Leon, G., 341
Demers, C., 545
Deming, w. E., 39
Dennis, G., 38
Dentsen, I. L., 445
Department of Homeland Security (DHS), 3–4, 4 (table), 5, 142
 all-hazards focus mandate and, 193–194
 Fusion Capability Planning Tool and, 195
 information/intelligence activities, fusion center integration into, 193–194
 Intelligence and Analysis Directorate and, 196, 199
 intelligence fusion centers and, 177, 178 (figure), 190, 191–192
 National Preparedness Guidelines and, 195
 surveillance-industrial complex and, 200
 See also Homeland security responsibilities; Terrorism
Department of Justice (DOJ), 192, 195, 202, 534, 535, 542
Dependency. See Coupling dimension
Deszca, E., 388, 389
Determinate sentencing, 103, 104, 107
Deterrence theory, 163, 185–186
 See also Pulling levers/focused deterrence strategies
Devey, D. T., 566
Deviance. See Organizational deviance; Organizational termination
Dewe, P. J., 380, 385, 392
Diagnostic and Statistical Manual of Mental Disorders (DSM-IV), 341
Diallo, A., 168–170
Dias, C. F., 89, 132, 145
Dickson, W. J., 90
Diederiks, J., 45
Dienes, T., 309
DiIulio, J. J., 38, 146, 152, 153, 154, 157, 446

Dillman, D. A., 243
Disjunctive socialization, 284
Dispute resolution. See Labor unions
Distributive justice, 326–327
Divergence problem, 176
Divestiture socialization, 284
Division of labor. See Bureaucracy; Horizontal organizational complexity; Organizational complexity; Vertical organizational complexity
DNA technology, 108, 129, 130, 136
Doerner, W. G., 230, 231
Doerner, W. M., 230, 231
Domestic violence cases, 163, 172, 206–207, 332, 490
Domestic violence court/procedural justice study article, 206
 case adjudication, participation of court representatives and, 211
 court process, general impressions of, 213–215
 criminal domestic violence investigators and, 210
 data collection instruments and, 212–213
 discussion/conclusion and, 219–220
 domestic violence courts, development of, 207
 domestic violence problem, scope of, 206–207
 fairness/justice/respect, perceptions of, 217–219
 intervention strategy, case processing and, 210–212, 211 (figure)
 intimate partner homicide and, 207
 Lexington County Criminal Domestic Violence Court, 209–212
 mandatory arrest policies and, 207
 multiagency collaborative approach and, 210
 no-contact order and, 210–211
 pretrial intervention programs, participation in, 211–212, 215
 procedural justice, overview of, 208–209
 reoffending rates and, 206, 209
 research procedure and, 212–213
 results, 213–219
 subsequent victimizations, reporting of, 209
 victim advocates, involvement of, 212
 voice effect, court process and, 208, 215–217, 220
 See also Court system; Interagency collaboration; Readings
Donald, L., 66
Donaldson, L., 92, 93
Doris Tate Crime Victims Bureau (CVB), 253
Dorn, S., 194
Double jeopardy protections, 181
Dougherty, T. W., 389
Dowler, K., 390
Downs, A., 543
Downsizing-oriented prison reform, 249, 250, 259, 260–263
Draft, R. L., 45
Driving under the influence (DUI), 94–95, 331–332

Drug Abuse Resistance Education (D.A.R.E.) program, 94, 96, 369, 550–552
    See also D.A.R.E. America; D.A.R.E. lessons/research-practice relationship study article
Drug Abuse Treatment Outcome Studies (DATOS), 339, 343
Drug arrest behavior, 332
Drug courts, 205
Drug distribution networks. *See* Criminal organizations; International drug smuggling organizational structure study article; War on Drugs
Drug Enforcement Administration (DEA), 23, 97, 191, 199
Drug Policy Alliance, 258
Drunk-driving prevention, 94–95
Dues check off agreement, 228, 242
Dugan, L., 31
Dukakis, M., 567
Dunbar, R. L. M., 368
Dunham, R. G., 327
Durose, M. R., 101
Dwyer, J., 108
Dye, K., 535
Dyer, L., 375
Dysfunction. *See* Organizational deviance; Power

Eccles, T., 548
Edmunds, S. B., 424
Effort-performance expectancy, 330, 332
    See also Expectancy theory
Eighth Amendment, 103
Eisenstein, J., 9
Electronic information systems, 197
Electronic Privacy Information Center, 192, 202
Ellerby, L., 424, 427
El Paso Intelligence Center, 191
Eltzeroth, R. L., 240
Emans, B. J. M., 487
Emerson, R. M., 481, 482
Emery, J. D., 545
Employee Assistance Program (EAP), 40
Encounter phase, 278
Engagement, 387, 390
Engel, R. S., 188, 434
Environmental factors, 6–7, 7 (figure)
    closed systems and, 7, 8
    open systems and, 7–8
    See also Organizational structures; Organizations
Enzmann, D., 386
Equity theory, 318, 325
    disaster compensation distribution and, 326
    distress, perceived inequity and, 326
    distributive justice and, 326–327, 350

    gender-based inequities and, 326
    inequity, negative job attitudes and, 325, 326
    inequity, subjective evaluation of, 325–326
    interactional justice and, 328
    merit principle, role of, 325
    procedural justice and, 327–328
    reciprocated exchange, fairness of, 325
    See also Expectancy theory; Motivation; Organizational justice; Organizational justice/police misconduct study article; Process theories
Erikson, R., 291, 297
Etzioni, A., 5, 507
Evan, W. M., 17
Evidence-based practice (EBP), 49, 84, 94, 539, 559
    See also Medical system lessons/criminal justice decision making study article; Scientific management; Span of control in evidence-based community supervision study article
Evolutionary change motor, 545, 546, 546 (figure)
Evolutionary/continuous change, 536, 546
Expectancy theory, 318, 329
    community policing implementation and, 332
    components of, 329–331
    criminal justice employee behaviors, explanations of, 331–333
    effort-performance expectancy and, 330, 332
    individual perceptions, role of, 329
    motivational forces on individuals and, 330–331
    path-goal theory and, 442–443
    performance-outcome expectancy and, 330, 332
    valence and, 329, 330
    workplace/nonworkplace behaviors, explanations for, 332
    See also Equity theory; Motivation; Process theories
Expert power, 485–486, 487, 491
Extrinsic motivators, 318, 319, 319 (table)

Fact finding process, 232
Fagan, J., 187, 188
Failure in organizations. *See* D.A.R.E. lessons/research-practice relationship study article; Organizational deviance; Organizational termination
Fairness:
    burnout and, 391
    distributive justice and, 326–327
    domestic violence court and, 217–219
    interactional justice and, 328
    outcome variance, perceptions of fairness and, 328–329
    power recipient compliance and, 487
    procedural justice and, 208–209, 327–328
    See also Equity theory; Expectancy theory; Occupational stress; Organizational justice; Organizational justice/police misconduct study article; Process theories

Falbe, C. M., 490
Falcone, R. L., 276, 278
Falcone, D. N., 21
Farmer, S. J., 328
Farrenkopf, T., 423, 424
Farrington, D. P., 573
Farview State Hospital (PA), 132–133, 140
Fayol, H., 53, 87, 88, 89, 132, 146, 147, 157, 181
Federal Bureau of Investigation (FBI), 15
    Branch Dividian raid and, 135, 148, 155–156
    field office structure, problems with, 15–16, 23
    Hostage Rescue Team and, 156
    information/intelligence activities, fusion center integration into, 193–194
    information sharing and, 16, 24
    intelligence fusion centers, assistance for, 192
    Middle Eastern individuals, interviewing of, 181
    spatial complexity challenges in, 23, 134
    Special Agent in Charge and, 156
    task force coordination by, 180
Federal Bureau of Investigation National Academy (NA), 453–454
Federal Bureau of Prisons (BOP), 24, 29, 139, 152–153, 447, 471, 541
Federal Emergency Management Agency (FEMA), 51, 195
Federalism principles, 181–182
Feedback, 56, 57, 58, 60, 61
    administrative breakdown, external feedback mechanisms and, 147
    burnout, correlate of, 390
    job characteristics model and, 335, 373
    See also Job characteristics model
Feeley, M. M., 95, 151
Feinberg, K., 326
Felon-a-Day campaign, 256 (figure), 257
Felson, M., 65, 164
Feuille, P., 236, 242
Fiedler, F. E., 435, 436, 437
Fiedler's contingency theory of leadership, 435
    contingencies-leadership style, relationship between, 437–438, 437 (figure)
    criminal justice setting, U.S. Supreme Court justices and, 438
    effective leadership style, factors in, 436–437
    leader position power and, 437, 438
    leadership style-worker performance relationship and, 436, 437, 438
    least preferred coworker score and, 435–436, 436–437 (figures), 437
    relationship-oriented leadership and, 435
    task-oriented leadership and, 435
    task structure and, 436–437
    time ordering of relevant concepts and, 438
    See also Leadership

Fielding, G. J., 26, 27
Finlay, W., 40
Finn, P., 383, 393
Finney, M., 143
Fischer, B., 262
Fixed socialization, 282–283, 283 (table)
Flaherty, D., 350
Flat organizations, 17, 20
Fleeing-felon doctrine, 26, 136, 165, 355, 361, 544
Florida Department of Law Enforcement, 195
Florida Fusion Center, 195
Florida Highway Patrol, 195
Fogelson, R. M., 27, 86, 228
Folger, R., 208
Folkman, S. F., 380
Fondacaro, M. R., 208
Force policy. *See* Deadly force policies; Deadly force/social theory and street cops study article
Ford, R. E., 287
Formalization dimension, 25–27
    appropriate behavior, codification of, 26–27
    assessment of, 26
    bureaucratic organizations and, 85
    cross-agency variations in, 26
    documentation requirements and, 26
    excessive formalization and, 27, 46
    job descriptions/role standardization and, 25–26
    organizational inflexibility and, 27
    police response guidelines and, 25, 26
    role ambiguity/role conflict and, 45
    See also Centralization dimension; Centralization/formalization impact study article; Organizational control; Span of control
Formal socialization, 281
For-profit companies. *See* Business organizations
Forst, B., 108, 109, 560, 563, 569, 572, 574, 575
Fossum, J., 375
Fourth Amendment rights, 103, 534
Fox, A., 550
Fox, C., 131, 134, 136
Frank, J., 181
Frank, L., 179, 180
Frase, R. S., 107
Fraternal Order of Police (FOP), 243
Freeman, J., 545
Freeman, R., 332
French, W., 416, 482, 484, 485, 508
Freudenberger, H. J., 386
Fricas, J., 381
Frieberg, A., 257
Frumkin, P., 96

Fry, B., 36
Frydl, K., 2
Fugitive Apprehension Program (MN), 182
Functional differentiation, 20, 21, 22
Functional management, 83
Fusion Capability Planning Tool, 195
Fyfe, J. J., 26, 162, 163, 166

Gagnon v. Scarpelli (1973), 104
Gaines, L. K., 182, 183
Gambling. *See* Criminal organizations
Gangs. *See* Criminal justice collaborations; Criminal organizations; International drug smuggling organizational structure study article
Gardner, P. D., 277
Garland, D., 257
Garrett, T. M., 134, 135
Gawande, A., 563, 564, 574
Gebietsver-band social system, 498
Gender gap in violent offending, 569
Gender/power/reciprocity in corrections study article, 518–519
　authority, gender and, 530–531
　caring ethic and, 519, 520
　conclusions/implications and, 531–532
　Critical Incidents Scale and, 521
　exchange relationships and, 524–528
　feminist-centric perspectives and, 519
　institutional role in supervision and, 519
　inventive role in supervision and, 519–520
　literature review and, 519–521
　methods/sample and, 521–522, 523 (table)
　occupational role/female sex-role norms, conflict between, 519
　qualitative interviews/discussion and, 524–531
　quantitative results analysis and, 522–524, 524–525 (tables)
　reciprocity, gender differences and, 520, 521
　selective enforcement and, 528–530
　supervision styles and, 519–521
　See also Power; Women officers in men's prisons/organizational barriers study article
Gender roles. *See* Equity theory; Gender/power/reciprocity in corrections study article; Organizational socialization; Women officers in men's prisons/organizational barriers study article
Generalized workers, 21, 22
Geneva Convention protocols, 149
Geographic distribution. *See* Spatial organizational complexity
Georgia Information Sharing and Analysis Center (GISAC), 178, 193
Georgia Public Defender Standards Council (GPDSC), 141
German, M., 192

Gershon, R. R. M., 392
Giacomazzi, A., 350
Gibbons, S. G., 510, 515
Gibbs, C., 31
Giblin, M. J., 95, 97, 137, 177, 184
Gibson, M. A., 10
Giguère, C., 78
Gilman, E., 38, 39, 40
Gilmore, T., 446
Giuliani, R., 429
Glaze, L. E., 560
Global Intelligence Working Group, 192, 195, 197, 201
Glueck, E., 84
Glueck, S., 84
Gmel, G., 354
Goldberg, J., 2, 3
Goldstein, H., 87, 240
Golembiewski, R. T., 388, 389
Goodman, B., 141
Goodstein, L., 107
Gottschalk, M., 248, 250
Government Accountability Office (GAO), 192, 577, 578
Governor's Commission on Capital Punishment, 106, 110
Governors Highway Safety Association, 95
Gray, B., 176, 177
Grear, M. P., 281
Greenberg, J., 325, 327, 328
Greene, J., 260
Greene, J. R., 535, 537
Greenfield, L. A., 423
Greenspan, R., 28, 109, 391
Greenwood, R., 96
Griffin, G. R., 368
Grinc, R. M., 332
Griset, P. L., 103, 107
Groopman, J., 562, 564, 565, 566, 567, 568, 569, 570, 571, 572, 575
Gross, S. R., 108
Grover, A. R., 206
Gruman, J. A., 280
Guerra, S., 181
Guinan, P. J., 488
Gulick, L., 87
Gutterman, M., 279
Guyot, D., 240

Haarr, R. N., 278, 279
Haas, J. E., 17, 23
Hackman, J. R., 6, 7, 8, 10, 333, 334, 335, 364, 366, 371, 373, 374, 375, 547

Hagan, J., 114, 115
Hage, J., 45
Halemba, G. J., 280
Hall, R. H., 6, 16, 17, 23
Hamilton, E. E., 382
Hamilton, I., 51
Hannan, M. T., 545
Harding, D. J., 131, 134, 136
Harris, D. A., 97
Harris, K., 265, 266
Hattrup, G. P., 52
Hawk-Tourtelot, S. R., 388, 395
Hawthorne effect, 90
Hawthorne studies, 89–90
Haynes, M. R., 177
Hays, S., 37
He, N., 384, 385
Hellriegel, D., 487
Hemphill, J. K., 430
Heneman, H., 375
Henry, V. E., 398
Hepburn, J. R., 38, 107, 486, 487, 509, 515
Herbert, S., 321
Herman, S. N., 181
Hersey, P., 439, 440
Herzberg, F., 319, 321, 322, 329, 365
Heumann, M., 276, 277, 281, 283, 416
Hewitt, J., 115
Hickman, L. J., 209
Hickman, M. J., 381
Hickson, D. J., 25, 86
Hierarchy. *See* Bureaucracy; International drug smuggling organizational structure study article; Vertical organizational complexity
High Intensity Drug Trafficking Area (HIDTA) intelligence centers and, 191
Highland Park (MI) Police Department, 141
High-reliability organizations (HROs), 138–140, 139 (figure)
Hiller, M. L., 338
Himmelman, A., 177
Hinings, B., 96
Hinings, C. R., 25
Hoel, H., 384
Hoffman, B., 31
Hogan, N. L., 35, 36
Hogarth, J., 114
Holgate, A. M., 392
Hollenback, G. P., 446
Holzman, C., 424
Homeland Security Advisory Council, 194

Homeland Security Grant Program, 195
Homeland Security Information Exchange, 197, 200
Homeland security responsibilities, 2
    airport security and, 2–3
    Federal Bureau of Investigation field offices and, 15–16
    federalism principles and, 181
    intelligence industry and, 2
    preparedness, enhancement of, 97
    See also Criminal justice system; Department of Homeland Security (DHS); Terrorism
Homicide work. *See* Qualitative assessment of stress perceptions/homicide units study article
Horizontal collaborations, 179
Horizontal organizational complexity, 20
    challenges in, 22
    criminal organizations and, 31
    expertise/deep knowledge foundation and, 22
    flat vs. tall organizations and, 17, 20
    functional differentiation and, 21, 22
    generalized workers and, 21, 22
    innovation and, 22
    occupational differentiation/role specialization and, 20–21, 22
    pyramidal width and, 19
    size of organizations and, 21
    specialized workers and, 21, 22
    See also Organizational complexity; Spatial organizational complexity; Vertical organizational complexity
Hostage Rescue Team (HRT), 156
House, R. J., 431, 442
Houston Police Department, 24, 130
Huber, G. P., 538
Hudson v. McMillian (1992), 148, 150
Hughes, E. C., 115
Hughes, K. A., 560
Huling, T., 264
Hull, R., 452
Human relations theory, 36, 37, 89, 146
    criminal justice settings and, 91–92
    criticisms of, 92
    Hawthorne effect and, 90
    Hawthorne studies and, 89–90
    humanized workplaces, greater productivity and, 92
    human relations school of organizations and, 89
    informal structures and, 89, 90, 91
    interpersonal factors and, 92
    structural implications of, 91–92
    Theory Y and, 91
    work activities, influence of human nature on, 90
    worker needs/behavior, recognition of, 89, 92
    See also Classical theories; Organizational theory; Theory X

Hummel, R. P., 134
Humphrey, J. A., 108
Hunt, J., 274
Hurricane Katrina disaster, 137, 138, 554
Huxham, C., 175, 176

Illinois Statewide Terrorism Intelligence Center (STIC), 178
Incarceration:
    abusive/unconstitutional prisons and, 148, 149
    building tenders and, 480–481, 484
    consensual model facilities and, 93
    contingency theory and, 93
    control-oriented facilities and, 93
    downsizing-oriented prison reforms and, 249, 250, 259, 260–263
    economic decline, public punitiveness and, 248–249
    federal prosecution, tougher sentencing guidelines and, 24
    gang affiliations in correctional facilities and, 182
    Geneva Convention protocols and, 149
    good time credits and, 258, 268
    human relations theory and, 91
    inmate lawsuits, filing of, 540–541, 542, 543
    jailer, formalized responsibilities of, 25–26
    mass imprisonment and, 248–249, 250–251, 252
    minimum security facilities and, 30
    overcrowding, early release provisions and, 267, 268
    prison architecture/structures and, 335–336
    prison construction/expansion and, 106
    prison guard strike and, 234, 235, 238
    prison inmate unions and, 226
    prison performance measures and, 10, 93
    privatization trend and, 12, 13
    punitive segregation practice and, 252
    rehabilitation initiatives, 258–259
    responsibility model facilities and, 93
    snitching, information power and, 486
    spatial organizational complexity and, 23
    specialized prison workers and, 21
    staff-to-inmate ratio, span of control and, 29–30
    supermax prisons and, 16, 29, 544, 573
    Three Strikes law and, 105, 224, 225, 254
    tough-on-crime measures, ballot initiative process and, 254–259
    See also Centralization/formalization impact study article; Court system; Criminal justice system; Defects of total power study article; Leadership and correctional reform study article; Organizational deviance; Parole; Prison officer unions/perpetuated penal status quo study article; Probation; Women officers in men's prisons/organizational barriers study article
Indeterminate sentencing, 103, 125, 252
Indiana Intelligence Fusion Center (IIFC), 178
Indianapolis Violence Reduction Partnership, 188
Indianapolis Metropolitan Police Department, 140, 143
Individual control/perceived officer power and probationer compliance study article, 506
    bases of power and, 508–510, 512–514, 513 (table)
    coercive institutions, power and, 507–508
    dependent variable, operationalization of, 511
    discussion/conclusion and, 514–516
    findings and, 512–514
    independent variables, operationalization of, 511–512
    limitations of current study and, 514–515
    literature review and, 507–511
    methods and, 511–512
    null findings and, 515, 516
    officer-client relationship, probation situation and, 506–507
    organizational-level power and, 516
    power bases in corrections, previous studies of, 509–510
    power bases in probation settings, current study and, 510–511
    sampling/data collection and, 511
    See also Power; Readings
Individualized justice myth/probation presentence reports study article, 114
    California probation system and, 115
    deal cases and, 119
    designation, official court reports and, 116
    diversion cases and, 119
    extralegal information, presentence interviews and, 120–122, 124
    findings of, 117–123
    heavy-duty designation and, 119
    interview questions in, 116–117
    joint cases and, 119–120
    lightweight designation and, 118–119
    methods in, 116–117
    presentence investigation process and, 115–116, 120–122, 124–126
    presentence reports, filing process for, 122–123
    probation cases and, 120, 121–122
    probation officers, autonomy of, 124–125
    probation recommendations, judicial outcomes and, 114–115
    probation with jail time cases and, 120, 121
    summary/conclusions of, 123–126
    typing process, presentence reports and, 116, 117–120, 124
    See also Organizational theory; Readings
Individual socialization, 280–281
Ineffective police leadership study article, 449–450
    acts of commission/omission and, 451, 459, 461, 462, 464
    adaptation, failure in, 458
    capriciousness characteristic and, 458–459
    closed-mindedness characteristic and, 457–458
    communication deficiencies and, 460–461

dark side of leadership and, 450, 464
data collection/methods and, 453–454
discussion and, 462–465
effectiveness, characteristics of, 450–451, 462
ego-centeredness/arrogance characteristics and, 457
emergence of ineffective leaders/leadership practices and, 452
failure to act/decide and, 460
findings and, 454–462, 455 (table)
future research, recommendations for, 464–465
honesty/integrity, lack of, 461–462
individual problems and, 462–463
ineffective leaders, characteristics of, 455–456, 463–464
interpersonal skills, deficiencies in, 461
leadership-as-positive-action orientation and, 450, 463–464
leadership problems and, 463–464
literature review and, 450–452
micromanagement practice and, 449, 456, 458, 463
occupational problems and, 463
Peter principle and, 452
policing environment, significance of ineffectiveness in, 451
politically-motivated leadership and, 459
problematic/sub-standard performance and, 464
research objective and, 452–453
self-focused over others, careerism and, 456–457
street cop-supervisor gap and, 452
work ethic deficiencies and, 459
See also Leadership; Readings
Infinite power. *See* Defects of total power study article
Influence tactics, 487–489, 488 (table)
Informal socialization, 281, 288
Informational justice, 328
Information power, 485, 486, 489
Information Sharing Environment Implementation Plan, 195, 201–202
Initiating structure leadership dimension, 433
Innocence Project (Cardoza School of Law), 108
Innovation, 22, 30
Institutional theory, 96
    decoupling prescribed practices from daily operations and, 97
    institutional myths, symbolic programs/procedures and, 96, 97
    isomorphism, processes in, 97
    organizational worth, demonstration of, 96
    See also Open systems theories
Instrumental rationality, 82, 104, 539
Intelligence and Analysis Directorate (DHS), 196, 199
Intelligence community, 2, 4, 93, 192
Intelligence fusion centers, 177, 178 (figure), 190, 193–195
Intelligence fusion process article, 190
    access to intelligence and, 192
    all-hazards focus, fusion center responsibilities and, 193–194, 196, 197

baseline capabilities for fusion centers and, 195–196
civil rights concerns, personal information and, 192, 200, 201
collateral issues, emergence of, 199–202
counterterrorism information-sharing and, 191–192, 193, 195, 196
current intelligence capacity/models, reorientation of, 198–199
data integration mechanism, holistic development trend and, 193
electronic information systems and, 197
federal support for fusion centers and, 192–193
Fusion Capability Planning Tool and, 195
fusion center concept, law enforcement resistance to, 200
fusion center concept, refining of, 193–194, 196–197
fusion center effectiveness, evaluation of, 202–203
fusion centers, development of, 190, 191–193
fusion process, description of, 190–191, 196–198
High Intensity Drug Trafficking Area intelligence centers and, 191
human resource issues and, 199
Information Sharing Environment Implementation Plan and, 195, 201–202
local police, domestic intelligence agent role and, 192
National Criminal Intelligence Sharing Plan and, 195, 198
National Preparedness Guidelines and, 195
National Strategy for Information Sharing and, 196
personnel recruitment/retention and, 192
private sector role, surveillance-industrial complex and, 199–200
proactive threat identification/prevention and, 196
Program Manager for the Information Sharing Environment and, 192, 193, 195, 201, 202
regional intelligence centers and, 191
right to know/need to know standards and, 200
stovepipe of information problem, information dissemination and, 198, 199
structural issues, fusion center models and, 194–195
summary/conclusion and, 203
training/technical assistance and, 193
transjurisdictional complex criminality and, 196
two-way information sharing and, 197
See also Criminal justice collaborations; Interagency collaboration; Readings
Intelligence Reform and Terrorism Prevention Act of 2004, 196
Interactional justice, 328
    informational justice and, 328
    interpersonal justice and, 328
    See also Equity theory; Organizational justice; Organizational justice/police misconduct study article
Interagency collaboration, 174
    altruism motivation and, 176

campus public safety agencies and, 174–175
collaboration, definition of, 175
collaborative advantage and, 175, 176–177
counterproduction problem and, 176
divergence problem and, 176
impediments to collaboration and, 177
individual agency action, risks associated with, 176
intelligence fusion centers and, 177, 178 (figure)
joined-up services/partnerships and, 175
large agency-small agency collaborations and, 177
limited mass-casualty incidents and, 175
modern societal problems, common properties of, 175–176
mutual-aid agreements/joint trainings and, 175, 177
omission problem and, 176
power within collaborations and, 177
rational self-interest motivation and, 176
repetition problem and, 176
synergy and, 177
turf battles and, 177
See also Criminal justice collaborations; Domestic violence court/procedural justice study article; Intelligence fusion process article
International Association of Chiefs of Police (IACP), 12, 242, 243
International drug smuggling organizational structure study article, 64–65
ad hoc organizational structure and, 67, 69–70, 73–74
analysis of organizational structures, 73–77
conclusion and, 77–79
co-offending groups, characteristics of, 66–68
gangs and, 66–67
group context of offending and, 65–66
hierarchy-decentralization perspectives and, 66–67
hierarchy of authority and, 68, 69, 73–77
indirect communication, network security and, 69, 75
individual study participants, characteristics of, 71, 72–73 (table)
methods and, 71
organizational adaptability/flexibility and, 67–68, 69–70, 75–76
organizational literature review and, 68–71
ram raiders and, 66
recruitment/promotion systems and, 70–71, 76–77
rules/procedures, statement of, 69, 74–75
social network framework and, 67–68, 70
specialization, coordinated activities and, 67, 70, 76
teamwork vs. co-acting and, 66
See also Criminal organizations; Organizational structures; Readings
Interpersonal justice, 328
Intrinsic motivators, 319, 319 (table), 333–334

Investiture socialization, 284
Iowa Community Based Correctional System, 50
Isomorphism, 97
 coercive isomorphism and, 97
 mimetic pressures and, 97
 normative processes and, 97
 See also Institutional theory
Ivković, S. K., 130, 349, 350

Jackson, K. E., 424
Jackson, S. E., 386, 387
Jackson, S. L., 208
Jacob, H., 9
Jacobs, J. B., 234, 235, 236, 260, 281, 446, 468, 518
Jacobson, M., 250, 260, 264
Jacoby, J. E., 132, 140
Jago, A. G., 431
Jannetta, J., 182, 183
Janson, R., 334
Jefferis, E. S., 179, 180
Jenkins, S. R., 379
Jenne, D. L., 518, 521, 522, 531
Jerin, R. A., 10
Jermier, J. M., 40, 443, 452
Job characteristics model, 333–334, 334 (figure)
 autonomy and, 335, 365, 367, 373, 374
 feedback and, 335, 373
 internal motivation, facilitation of, 335
 internal motivation, factors in, 333–334
 job enrichment strategy, evaluation of, 365
 knowledge of results and, 333–334, 335
 meaningfulness, experience of, 333
 prison architecture/structures and, 335–336
 responsibility, experience of, 333
 skill variety and, 335, 366, 373
 task identity and, 334, 335, 366, 373
 task significance and, 334–335, 374
 vertically loaded job tasks and, 335, 367
 work redesign implementation and, 366–367
 See also Community policing/job design and education level factors study article; Job design
Job design, 333
 internal motivation, facilitation of, 335
 internal motivation, factors in, 333–334
 job enlargement, skill variety and, 335, 365
 job enrichment and, 365–367
 job tasks, characteristics of, 334–335, 334 (figure)
 n achievement individuals and, 323
 natural work units, formation of, 366–367, 373
 prison architecture/structures and, 335–336

specialized workers, demotivation and, 335
vertically loaded job tasks and, 335
See also Community policing/job design and education level factors study article; Job characteristics model
Job Diagnostic Survey, 370
Job satisfaction, 5, 20, 28, 352, 491
measures of, 41, 42 (table), 43
organizational commitment and, 35–36
See also Centralization/formalization impact study article
Joe, G. W., 339, 341
Johnson, B. R., 194
Johnson, D. E., 439, 440
Johnson, J. L., 2
Johnson, N. J., 17, 23
Johnson, R. R., 332
Johnson v. Johnson (2004), 148, 150
Johnston, K. B., 147
Joint Regional Intelligence Center (JRIC), 178
Joint-terrorism task forces (JTTFs), 180, 181–182
Joliffe, D., 573
Jones, G. R., 284, 285, 382
Jones v. North Carolina Prisoners' Labor Union (1977), 226
Judge, T. A., 17, 29, 30, 483
Judson, A. S., 548
Junction City Police Department gang study, 81, 82
Jurik, N. C., 37, 280, 302
Juris, H. A., 242
Justice. *See* Court system; Criminal justice system; Equity theory; Organizational justice; Police organizations; Procedural justice
Justice for Homicide Victims, 255
Just Say No to Drugs campaign, 551

Kadleck, C., 228, 231, 237, 240
Kahn, R. L., 380, 392
Kalb, L. M., 573
Kalleberg, A. L., 37, 45
Kaminski, R. J., 279
Kansas Threat Integration Center (KATIC), 178
Kant, I., 463
Kanter, R. M., 303, 306, 308
Kappeler, V., 289, 298
Karmen, A., 429, 430
Katz, C. M., 30, 81, 95
Kaufman, H., 140, 141, 142
Kaufmann, N., 552
Keepin' it REAL curriculum, 555
Keillor, G., 553
Keinan, G., 259
Kellerman, B., 450

Kelling, G. L., 19, 163, 243, 430
Kellner, D., 110
Kennedy, D. M., 187, 188
Kennedy, R. F., 179
Kentucky Intelligence Fusion Center, 178
Kercher, G., 521
Kersting, R. C., 518, 522, 531
Kessler, R., 282
Kets de Vries, M. F. R., 464
Kevartarini, W. Y., 424
Kim, B. -S., 388
Kimball, P., 157
Kinetic power, 482
King, M. S., 444, 445
King, R., 89, 133, 148, 153, 264
King, W. R., 17, 19, 28, 138, 140, 141, 142, 543, 544, 545
Kingsnorth, R., 114
Kirkpatrick, S. A., 324
Kittle, N. G., 416
Klamath Falls Police Department strike, 234
Klaver, E., 487
Klein, H. J., 277
Kleiner, B. H., 52
Kliesment, R. B., 243
Klinger, D., 161, 331
Klockars, C. B., 8, 350
Knapp Commission report, 349, 357
Knepper, P., 38
Knight, K., 338
Knill, C., 140
Knobler, P., 429
Knowledge conflict, 133–135
Knowledge utilization studies, 556
Kobasa, S., 417
Kochan, T. A., 236, 240
Konovsky, M. A., 208
Koslowsky, M., 484
Kotter, J. P., 431
Kozlowski, S. W. J., 277
Krakowski, A., 417
Kramer, M. W., 279
Kray, S., 170–171
Krebs, V. E., 69
Kuck, S., 383
Kunen, J., 416
Kuykendall, J. L., 434, 441, 442

Labor:
arbitration and, 232–233
blue flu mass sickout and, 237

concentration of employees and, 17, 19
dues check off agreement and, 228, 242
mediation and, 232
monetary compensation, worker productivity/motivation and, 231
occupational differentiation and, 20–21
scientific management, worker dissatisfaction with, 84–85
street-level bureaucrats and, 489–490
supplemental pay and, 230–231, 230 (table)
vertical organizational structures and, 20
See also Boston Police Strike (1919); Collective bargaining; Hawthorne effect; Human relations theory; Job characteristics model; Job satisfaction; Labor unions; Occupational stress; Organizational behavior; Organizational commitment; Organizational socialization; Span of control

Labor unions:
across-the-board pay increases and, 327
Boston police strike and, 225–226
criminal justice, historic unionism in, 225–226
dues check off agreement and, 228, 242
labor relations, improvements in, 238–239
labor relations legislation, 237
mass sickouts/blue flu and, 237
mutual benefit organizations of, 225
political activities, resource flow effects and, 232
prison inmate unions and, 226
public-sector employees and, 225, 226, 227
right-to-work states and, 251
slowdowns and, 237–238
strike actions, stages in, 233–234
strike options, differences among, 233
See also American Federation of Labor (AFL); American Federation of Labor/Congress of Industrial Organizations (AFL/CIO); Boston Police Strike (1919); California Correctional Peace Officers Association (CCPOA); Collective bargaining; Labor; Police employee organizations study article; Prison officer unions/perpetuated penal status quo study article

Lachman, P., 182, 183
Lackawana Six, 180
LaFree, G., 105
Laissez-faire leadership, 445
Lake, L. K., 547, 548
Lake Wobegon effect, 553
Lakewood (CO) Police Department, 140
Lambert, E. G., 35, 36
Langan, P. A., 101
Langford, L., 174
Langworthy, R. H., 21, 30

Lanza-Kaduce, L., 277
Lasker, R. D., 177
Law Enforcement Assistance Administration, 95
Law Enforcement Management and Administrative Statistics (LEMAS), 26, 243
Law Enforcement Online, 197, 200
Lawler, E. E., 6, 7, 8, 10, 319, 329, 330, 331, 547
Lazarus, R. S., 380
Leach, M. N., 255
Leader Behavior Description Questionnaire (LBDQ), 433, 434
Leader Effectiveness and Adaptability Description (LEAD) survey, 440, 441
Leadership, 429–430, 483–484
behavioral/leadership styles theories and, 433–435
consideration dimension of, 433
criminal justice/courtroom leadership and, 434–435
definition of, 430–431
dimensions of, 433–435
influence tactics and, 487–489, 488 (table)
initiating structure dimension of, 433
laissez-faire leadership, 445
leadership development initiatives and, 433, 446–447, 471–472
long-term organizational change and, 431
management functions and, 431, 434
micromanagement practice and, 449, 456, 458, 463, 542
on-the-job behaviors and, 433
organizational commitment, shared decision-making and, 435
path-goal theory and, 442–443
position power and, 437, 438
theoretical frameworks for, 431–446
trait theory and, 431–433, 432 (table)
transactional leadership, 444
transformational leadership, 443–446
See also Behavioral/style theories of leadership; Fiedler's contingency theory of leadership; Ineffective police leadership study article; Organizational behavior; Organizational change; Organizational culture; Organizational socialization; Power; Situational leadership theory; Trait theory
Leadership Adaptability and Style Inventory (LASI), 440, 441, 442
Leadership and correctional reform study article, 468
correctional leadership, crucial importance of, 468–470
Correctional Service Corps, establishment of, 474
corrections reform, development/implementation of, 470
cross-agency cooperative programs and, 473
effective leadership, characteristics of, 469–470
human infrastructure requirements, corrections system and, 470, 472–474
investing in leadership training and, 472–474
lateral recruitment, advantages of, 470

mid/upper management, college courses in, 473–474
personal/leadership development and, 471–472
promotions, transition leadership programs and, 473
recruitment challenge and, 470–471, 474
retention of personnel and, 471
sabbaticals, human capital development and, 473
state directors of correction, turnover of, 471
subordinates, empowerment of, 470
summary/conclusion and, 474
systematic leadership development programs and, 471–472
university-prison partnerships and, 473–474
See also Leadership; Readings
Learning organizations, 58, 60, 538–539
See also Organizational change; Organizational structures
Least preferred coworker score, 435–436, 436–437 (figures), 437
See also Fiedler's contingency theory of leadership
Legitimate power, 483, 484, 486, 491
Leiter, M. P., 386, 387, 390, 391
Lessons Learned Information Sharing, 196, 200
Leukefeld, C., 338
Levant, G., 551, 554
Leventhal, G. S., 208, 326, 327, 328
Levi, M., 242
Levy, A., 536
Lewin, A. Y., 545
Lewin, D., 236
Lewin, K., 535, 537, 547
Lewis, D. E., 140, 142
Li, X., 392
Life course perspective, 544–545
Life cycle change motor, 543–545, 546, 546 (figure)
Life cycle theory, 543
 determinism and, 543, 545
 liability of newness phenomenon and, 543
 life course perspective and, 543, 544
 police organizations, modified life cycle perspective and, 543–544, 545
See also Organizational change; Situational leadership theory
Limited/bounded rationality, 53
Lin, Y., 175
Lincoln, J., 37
Lind, E. A., 351
Lindquist, C. A., 38, 390
Lipsky, M., 94, 96, 489, 530
Little Hoover Commission (LHC), 250
Litzenberger, R., 381
Locke, E. A., 38, 324
Loeber, R., 573
Logan, C. H., 10
Lombardo, L. X., 38, 529, 530, 531

London Metropolitan Police, 8
Longshore, D., 176
Los Angeles Joint Regional Intelligence Center, 191
Los Angeles Police Crime Prevention Advisory Council, 551
Los Angeles Police Department (LAPD):
 authority hierarchy in, 151
 centralized risk management system and, 151
 Christopher Commission report and, 148, 151
 consent decrees, compliance costs and, 543
 crisis paralysis and, 137, 148, 153
 D.A.R.E. program and, 550–552
 executive leadership in, 460
 Los Angeles riots and, 89, 133, 137, 148, 152
 needs theory concepts and, 321
 Rampart corruption incident and, 148, 151
 Terrorism Liaison Officers and, 197
 vertical organizational complexity and, 17, 19 (figure)
Louisiana State Analytical and Fusion Exchange (LASAFE), 178
Love, K. G., 328
Lovell, R., 539
Lovins, B., 188
Lovrich, N. P., 38, 230, 336, 385
Lucken, K., 106
Luescher, J., 208
Lukes, S., 508
Lundman, R. J., 288
Luo, H., 389
Lupton, T., 25
Lutze, F., 185
Lyon, P., 109

Macdonald, D., 176
MacDonald, J. M., 26, 206
Macdonald, K. M., 25
MacLellan, T., 201
MacNamara, D. E. J., 563
Maddox, C., 242
Maguire, E. R., 17, 23, 26, 95, 142, 545
Maine Information and Analysis Center (MIAC), 178
Malach-Pines, A., 259
Management by exception, 444, 445
Management By Walking Around (MBWA), 149
Managerial disorganization. *See* Administrative breakdown/managerial disorganization in bureaucracies study article
Managerial Grid leadership dimensions, 434, 440
Mandated substance abuse treatment. *See* Substance abuse treatment/motivation-engagement relationship study article
Mandatory minimum sentences, 103, 104
March, J. G., 538

Marijuana possession, 258
Marion County (IN) Sheriff Department, 140, 143
Marquart, J. W., 91, 276, 480, 507, 529, 530
Marsden, P. V., 45
Marsy's Law of 2008/Proposition 9, 267–268
Martin, J., 40, 277
Martin, S. E., 279, 303, 385, 519, 521
Maryland Coordination and Analysis Center (MCAC), 178
Maryland's Proactive Community Supervision (PCS) program, 539
Maslach, C., 386, 387, 389, 390, 391, 424
Maslach Burnout Inventory (MBI) instrument, 387–388, 422, 425
Maslow, A., 319, 320, 321, 322, 329, 365
Mason, M., 566
Massachusetts Commonwealth Fusion Center, 178, 194
Mass-casualty incidents, 175
Masse, T., 193, 194
Mass incarceration, 248–249, 250–251, 252
Mass sickouts/blue flu, 237
Mastrofski, S. D., 28, 91, 109, 240, 331, 391
Mathews, C., 257
Matthews, J., 257
Matza, D., 289
Mauer, M., 260, 264
Maurer, D. C., 3, 4
Mausner, B., 319, 321, 322, 365
Mawby, R. C., 185
Maxfield, M. G., 521
Mayo, E., 146
Mays, G. L., 39
McCall, M. W., 446
McCann, J. E., 446
McCleary, R., 117, 516
McClelland, D. C., 319, 323, 324, 329
McCoy, L., 253
McGarrell, E. F., 175, 180
McGill, M. E., 368
McGloin, J. M., 574
McGregor, D., 90, 91, 365
McIntyre, L. J., 416
McJustice/McDonaldization of criminal justice study article, 99–100
    calculability, costs of administering justice and, 102
    capital trials/capital punishment, costs of, 106–107
    Compstat strategy, military model of policing and, 109
    control, rules/structures and, 103–104, 105, 107–109
    criminal justice officials, mistakes/miscarriages of justice and, 107–109
    dehumanized/mechanized workforce and, 105
    determinate sentencing, problems with, 107
    DNA technology, suspect exclusion and, 108

    fiscal policies, criminal justice cost effectiveness and, 105–106
    habitual-offender statutes and, 105
    innocent people, wrongful convictions/police killing of, 108–109
    iron cage of McDonaldized society and, 109
    irrationality of rationality and, 100, 104–109, 110
    military model of policing and, 109
    plea bargaining, irrationality of, 105
    plea bargaining, speedy case closure and, 100–102
    political enterprise of McJustice and, 110
    predictability, reduced sentencing/parole discretion and, 102–103
    rational/bureaucratic institutions and, 100
    responses to McDonaldization trend and, 109–110
    rubber cage of McDonaldized world and, 109
    systemic alternatives, impossibility of, 109–110
    technology, crime data/performance evaluation and, 104, 108, 109
    velvet cage of McDonaldized world and, 109
    See also Organizational theory; Readings
McKendall, M. A., 31
McLaughlin, E. J., 537
McManus, K., 62
McNally, A. M., 28, 109, 391
McNulty, E., 288, 289, 297
McPeak, A., 417
McShane, M. D., 35
Meaningfulness. *See* Job characteristics model; Motivation
Meares, T. L., 187, 188
Mechanic, D., 481, 482
Mediation, 232
Medical system lessons/criminal justice decision making study article, 559
    accountability issues and, 559, 564, 576, 577
    action bias error and, 572
    affective error and, 571
    availability error and, 567–568
    clinical algorithm error and, 564–566
    conclusion and, 577–578
    criminal justice decision process and, 560–561, 577
    criminal justice research/practice/policy, implications for, 574–578
    criminal justice system, marked growth/complexity in, 560, 577
    decision errors, research on, 574
    decision quality, whole-system improvements in, 561–562
    diagnosis, central feature of, 562
    diagnosis/treatment, accuracy in, 562–563
    disease prototype error and, 568–569
    evidence-based practice and, 559–560, 561, 563, 576
    framing/ripple effect error and, 572–573
    inattention error and, 571–572
    individual decision effectiveness, focus on, 575–576

Index   **631**

individualized decision making, ideal of, 563
inexperience/clinical intuition error and, 569–570
initial impression error and, 566–567
insight, systems comparison and, 561
judgment, errors in, 562, 563
last bad experience error, Willie Horton effect and, 567–568
medical decision errors, criminal justice applications and, 564–574, 565 (table)
medical model approach and, 563
medicine/criminal justice, parallels between, 562–564, 577
patient attribution error and, 568
performance monitoring and, 559–560, 561, 564, 576–577
satisfaction of search error and, 569
specialist error and, 570–571
systemic solutions, focus on, 574–575
unproven diagnosis/treatment error and, 573–574
See also Organizational change; Readings
Melaney, J. T., 236
Mello, M., 108
Melnick, G., 445
Menke, B. A., 336
Merit pay provisions, 326–327
Merit principle, 325
Merry, U., 536
Metamorphosis phase, 278–279
Metro Conflict Defender Office (GA), 141
Meyer, J. C., 233, 234, 235, 236
Meyer, J. W., 96
Meyer, M. W., 140
Michigan Intelligence Operations Center, 195
Michigan State Police, 195
Micromanagement practice, 449, 456, 458, 463, 542
Miles, S., 110
Military prisons, 148, 149
Millenson, M., 563
Miller, A. H., 137
Miller, M. D. S., 383, 392, 393
Miller, R., 177
Mills, A. I., 535
Mills, J. H., 535
Mimetic pressures, 97
Minneapolis Domestic Violence Experiment study, 84, 567
Minnesota Department of Corrections/Advanced Leadership Development Program, 447
Minnesota Joint Analysis Center, 191
Minorities in Law Enforcement political action committee (MILE PAC), 253
Mintzberg, H., 10, 147, 481, 482
Misconduct. See Organizational justice/police misconduct study article
Mission distortion, 185

Missouri Department of Corrections agreement, 228
Mitchell, R., 397
Moe, T. M., 148
Mollen Commission report, 147–148, 349, 357
Monke, B., 38
Monkkonen, E. H., 225
Monk-Turner, E., 322, 323
Montana All Threat Intelligence Center, 194
Mooney, T., 228, 231
Moore, M. H., 109, 150
Morgan, G., 90
Morgan, K. D., 512
Morgan, R. D., 390
Moriarty, L. J., 10
Morrison, E. W., 276
Morrissey v. Brewer (1972), 103–104
Morselli, C., 67, 70, 78
Moskos, P., 91, 483
Motivation, 317–318
    achievement motive, 323
    affiliation motive, 323–324
    effort-performance expectancy and, 330, 332
    extrinsic motivators and, 318, 319, 319 (table)
    intrinsic motivators and, 319, 319 (table), 333–334
    monetary compensation, worker productivity/motivation and, 231
    path-goal theory and, 442–443
    personalized power motive, 324
    power motives, 323, 324–325
    rewards/needs and, 318–319, 320
    self-interest motivation, 176
    socialized power motive, 324
    specialized workers, demotivation and, 335
    transtheoretical model and, 339
    vertical structures, opportunities in, 20
    See also Content theories; Equity theory; Expectancy theory; Job characteristics model; Job design; Motivator-hygiene theory; Need theory; Organizational justice; Organizational justice/police misconduct study article; Power; Process theories; Substance abuse treatment/motivation-engagement relationship study article
Motivation interviewing (MI), 57
Motivator-hygiene theory, 318, 321
    extrinsic/intrinsic motivators and, 318–319, 319 (table)
    job enrichment and, 365
    negative work attitudes, extrinsic factors and, 322
    positive work attitudes, intrinsic factors and, 321–322
    two-factor nature of, 322–323
    See also Content theories; Motivation
Motors of change. See Organizational change
Mottaz, C., 368

Moussaoui, Z., 16
Mouton, J. S., 434
Mowday, R. T., 318, 319, 320
Muir, W. K. J., 482
Mullen, K. L., 93
Multijurisdictional task forces (MJTFs), 179–181
Munduate, L., 487
Munzenrider, R., 388, 389
Murphy, D., 185
Murphy-Graham, E., 539, 554
Murrah, A., 114
Murton, T., 91
Musheno, M. C., 37, 280, 309
Mutual benefit organizations, 12

n achievement. *See* Achievement motive (*n* achievement)
Nadler, D. A., 329, 330, 331, 536
n affiliation. *See* Affiliation motive (*n* affiliation)
Nagin, D. S., 578
Nass, C. I., 151
National Association of Police Organizations, 243
National Center for State Courts, 207
National Commission on Terrorist Attacks Upon the United States, 193
National Crime Information Center (NCIC), 210
National Criminal Intelligence Sharing Plan (NCISP), 195, 198, 200, 201, 202
National Governors Association, 201
National Guard, 199, 201, 225, 233, 235, 494
National Infrastructure Advisory Council, 199
National Institute of Corrections (NIC), 50, 472, 473
National Institute of Justice (NIJ), 207, 304, 340, 354
National Institute on Drug Abuse, 554
National Preparedness Guidelines, 195
National Research Council (NRC), 2, 451
National Strategy for Information Sharing, 196
National Summit on Campus Public Safety, 175
Natural disasters, 194
Natural work units, 366–367, 373
Naylor, P., 384
Need theory, 318, 319
　basic/deficiency needs and, 320, 321
　belonging need and, 320, 321
　criminal justice-specific criticisms of, 320–321
　esteem need and, 320
　extrinsic/intrinsic motivators and, 318–319, 319 (table)
　hierarchy of needs and, 320, 321, 322
　higher-order/growth needs and, 320, 321
　physiological needs and, 319, 320, 321
　safety needs and, 320, 321
　self-actualization need and, 320, 321
　See also Content theories; Motivation

Need to know information-sharing standard, 200
Neher, A., 320, 321
Nenneman, M., 195
Neubauer, D., 119
Neufeld, P., 108
Neveu, J., 390
New Jersey Regional Operations Intelligence Center, 194
New Jersey State Prison, 493, 494–504
New Mexico prison riot, 132, 137, 138, 148
New Orleans Police Department strike, 235
New York City Police Department (NYPD):
　Compstat strategy and, 27–28, 97, 104, 109, 539
　corruption incident, Mollen Commission report and, 147–148
　Diallo killing scenario and, 168–170
　murder/violent crime, turnaround efforts and, 429–430
　Operation Nexus and, 197
　spatial organizational complexity and, 23
New York Department of Correctional Services, 261, 262
New York Department of Corrections, 260, 264
New York Police Department Intelligence Division (NYPD-INTELS), 178
New York State Correctional Officers & Police Benevolent Association (NYSCOPBA), 260–263, 266
　See also Prison officer unions/perpetuated penal status quo study article
New York State Intelligence Center, 194
Nicholas, H. T. III, 255
Nightlight (CA), 183
The 9/11 Commission Report, 15–16
9/11 terrorist attacks, 2–3, 16, 142, 181, 191, 193, 200, 201, 326
Noble-cause beliefs, 349, 350, 354–355, 356, 358, 359
Nonviolent Offender Rehabilitation Act (NORA) of 2008/Proposition 5, 258–259, 266
Normal accident theory (NAT), 135
　complex systems and, 136, 166, 167, 168
　coupling dimension and, 135–136, 166, 167, 168
　deadly force incidents and, 166–172
　Diallo killing scenario and, 169–170
　Kray standoff scenario and, 170–171
　linear systems and, 136
　multiple failures, interaction of, 136, 139
　See also Crisis management; Deadly force/social theory and street cops study article; Organizational deviance
Normative processes in isomorphism, 97
North Carolina Regional Analysis Center, 178
North Dakota Homeland Security Fusion Center, 178
Northern California Regional Intelligence Center, 191
Northern CA Regional Terrorism Threat Assessment Center (RTTAC), 178
Northern Illinois University shootings, 174

Northouse, P. G., 430, 431, 433, 436, 437, 442, 446
Novak, K. J., 179, 180, 181
Nugent, M. E., 2
NVivo software, 400

Occupational differentiation, 20–21
  challenges with, 22
  generalized workers and, 21
  measurement of, 21
  size of organizations and, 21
  specialized workers and, 21
  See also Horizontal organizational complexity
Occupational stress, 378–379
  anticipatory stress response and, 381–382
  career-based issues and, 385
  consequences of, 392
  coping mechanisms and, 381
  criminal justice workers, major stressors for, 381–385, 382 (figure)
  definition of, 379–381
  home-work interface, spillover effect and, 385
  individual evaluation of stressors and, 381
  individual role ambiguity/role conflict and, 383
  inherent-to-the-job factors and, 381–383
  interpersonal work relationships and, 384
  organizational factors in, 385
  place-based stressors and, 381–382
  primary appraisal and, 381
  primary interventions for, 392–393, 394
  qualitative overload situations and, 383
  quantitative overload situations and, 383
  role ambiguity and, 383
  role conflict and, 383
  routine occupational stressors and, 380
  scheduling/shift arrangements and, 382–383
  secondary appraisal and, 381
  secondary interventions for, 393
  stimulus-response connections, process model of, 380–381
  strains and, 380
  stressors and, 380
  tertiary interventions for, 393
  traumatic stressors and, 380
  uncertainty and, 276
  work overload conditions and, 383
  workplace bullying and, 384
  See also Burnout phenomenon; Occupational stress/public defenders study article; Qualitative assessment of stress perceptions/homicide units study article
Occupational stress/public defenders study article, 414–415
  assigned counsel programs and, 414
  discussion/implications and, 419–421
  docket reform and, 421
  judges, working relationship with, 420
  methods and, 417–418
  objective role conflict and, 416–417
  personal competence, concern with, 416
  previous qualitative studies and, 414, 415–417
  previous quantitative studies and, 414–415, 417
  questionnaire development and, 417
  response rates and, 418
  results and, 418–419, 419 (table)
  role insufficiency and, 416
  scale development and, 417–418
  stress, definition of, 415
  subjective role conflict and, 416
  subjects, characteristics of, 418
  work overload and, 415–416, 420–421
  See also Occupational stress; Readings
O'Driscoll, M. P., 380, 385, 392
Office of Community-Oriented Policing Services, 95
Office of National Drug Control Policy, 191
Ogletree, C., 415, 416
O'Hara, K., 394
O'Hara, P., 131
Oldham, G. R., 333, 334, 335, 364, 366, 371, 373, 374, 375
O'Leary, D., 322, 323
O'Leary-Kelly, A. M., 277
Olitsky, E., 446, 468
Oliver, W. M., 95
O'Loughlin, M. G., 154
Omission problem, 176
Ontario Police College, 388–389, 389 (table)
Open systems, 7–8
Open systems theories, 92
  contingency theory and, 92–94
  external environmental factors and, 92
  institutional theory and, 96–98
  resource dependence theory and, 94–96
  See also Organizational theory
Operation Ceasefire (MA), 188
Operation Night Light (MA), 183
Oregon Terrorism Intelligence Threat Assessment Network, 194
Organizational behavior, 5
  job satisfaction and, 5
  repetition problem and, 176
  resource dependence theory and, 94–96
  segmentation and, 17
  structural secrecy and, 133–135
  See also Interagency collaboration; Organizational change; Organizational control; Organizational culture; Organizational deviance; Organizational structures; Organizations; Process theories

Organizational change, 534–535
　catalyst for, 535
　citizen complaints and, 535
　community policing reforms and, 535–536
　conceptual use of research and, 539
　conflictive change motor and, 540–543
　consent decrees and, 535, 541–543
　decline, change impetus and, 544
　definition of, 535
　evolutionary change motor and, 545
　evolutionary/incremental/continuous change and, 536, 546
　failed decisions and, 538
　fusion process, description of, 190–191
　impediments to change and, 547–548, 548 (table)
　inmate lawsuits, filing of, 540–541
　instrumental use of research and, 539
　leadership, function of, 431
　learning organizations, evidence-based practices and, 538–539
　life course perspective and, 543–544
　life cycle change motor and, 543–545
　motors of, 537–546, 546 (figure)
　multiorganization perspective and, 546, 546 (figure)
　organizational memory, role of, 539
　organizational termination and, 543, 544
　planned change motor and, 537–540
　revolutionary/episodic/discontinuous change and, 536, 546
　satisficing and, 538
　single entities and, 546, 546 (figure)
　symbolic/political use of research and, 539
　two-track reforms and, 547
　unfreeze-move-freeze model of, 535, 537
　variation-selection-retention process and, 545
　See also Crisis management; Crisis paralysis; D.A.R.E. lessons/research-practice relationship study article; Learning organizations; Medical system lessons/criminal justice decision making study article; Occupational stress; Organizational culture; Organizational socialization; Organizational structures
Organizational commitment, 36, 42–43 (table), 43
Organizational Commitment Questionnaire (OCQ), 43
Organizational complexity, 17, 18 (figure)
　concentration of hierarchies and, 17, 19
　coupling dimension and, 135–136
　hierarchical dimension of, 17
　horizontal complexity and, 20–22
　job tasks, division/differentiation of, 17
　multiple dimensions of, 16
　rational coordination and, 10–11
　scalar chain, chains of command and, 17
　segmentation of hierarchies and, 17
　size of organizations and, 21
　spatial complexity and, 23–25
　structural secrecy and, 133–135
　vertical complexity and, 17, 19–20, 19 (figure)
　See also Organizational behavior; Organizational control; Organizational structures; Span of control in evidence-based community supervision study article
Organizational control, 25
　centralization and, 27–28
　formalization and, 25–27
　span of control and, 28–30, 29 (figure)
　See also Centralization/formalization impact study article; Organizational complexity
Organizational culture, 277–278
　social control function of, 353
　See also Organizational change; Organizational justice; Organizational socialization; Organizational structures; Organizations
Organizational deviance, 131, 143–144
　ad hoc disaster responses and, 137
　administrative breakdown and, 132–133
　case example of, 129–131
　complex systems and, 136
　coupling dimension and, 135–136
　crisis management skill and, 137–138
　crisis paralysis and, 137
　definition/description of, 131–132
　high-reliability organizations and, 138–140, 139 (figure)
　linear systems and, 136
　multiple failures, interaction of, 136, 139
　normal accidents/inevitable problems and, 135–136
　prevention of, 138–140
　structural secrecy, knowledge conflict and, 133–135
　See also Administrative breakdown/managerial disorganization in bureaucracies study article; Deadly force/social theory and street cops study article; Organizational termination
Organizational justice, 327
　distributive justice, 326–327
　informational justice and, 328
　interactional justice, 328
　interpersonal justice and, 328
　procedural justice, 208–209, 327–328
　voice effect and, 208, 215–217, 220
　See also Equity theory; Occupational stress; Organizational justice/police misconduct study article; Strain
Organizational justice/police misconduct study article, 347–348
　analysis process and, 356
　citizen complaints prediction and, 356, 358–359
　code-of-silence attitudes and, 349–350, 354–355, 356, 358, 359

control variables and, 355–356
departmental disciplinary charges and, 357
dependent variables and, 354, 359
deviant peer association vignettes, 360–361
discussion/summary and, 357–360
distributive justice/equity theory models and, 350–351, 352
independent variables and, 354–356, 359
individual-level correlates of misconduct and, 349, 350, 352
interactional justice perspective and, 351
internal affairs department investigations and, 357, 358–359
method and, 353–356
Minor Deviant Peers scale, 355, 356
noble-cause beliefs and, 349, 350, 354–355, 356, 358, 359
organizational-injustice perceptions, retaliatory behavior and, 352–353, 358
organizational justice/fairness, analyses of, 350–351, 354
organizational justice framework and, 350–351, 352, 359–360
organizational-level correlates of misconduct and, 348, 350, 351–353
organizations/human behavior, social psychological relationship between, 348
participant pool and, 353–354
police misconduct research literature and, 348–353
procedural justice perspective and, 351, 352
results and, 356–357
Serious Deviant Peers scale, 356
similar response pattern imputation and, 354
unjust/unfair organizations, employee deviance and, 348, 351–352, 353, 358
See also Motivation; Organizational justice; Readings
Organizational socialization, 274, 275
anticipatory socialization and, 278, 279–280
boundary negotiation, newcomers/rookies and, 275–276, 278, 280
classification of socialization strategies and, 284–285, 285 (figure)
collective socialization and, 280
content of socialization and, 277–279
disjunctive socialization and, 284
divestiture socialization and, 284
encounter phase and, 278
fixed socialization and, 282–283, 283 (table)
force levels, definition of, 274–275
formal socialization and, 281
gender, role of, 279, 284
individual socialization and, 280–281
informal socialization and, 281
information-seeking strategies and, 276–277
investiture socialization and, 284
metamorphosis phase and, 278–279

organizational culture, elements of, 277–278
organizational information, learning of, 277–278
random socialization and, 282
role expectations/job-related values, formation of, 278
sequential socialization and, 282
serial socialization and, 283–284
strategies for socialization and, 280–285
subcultures, workgroup subpopulations and, 278
task requirements/performance proficiency, learning about, 277
uncertainty reduction goal and, 276–277
variable socialization and, 283
See also Parables in police training study article; Women officers in men's prisons/organizational barriers study article
Organizational structures, 16
centralization dimension and, 27–28
closed systems and, 7, 8
concentration of hierarchies, 17, 19
coupling and, 135–136
decoupling and, 97
dimensions of, 10, 11 (figure), 16
environmental factors and, 6–8, 7 (figure)
formalization and, 25–27
functional differentiation and, 20, 21, 22
hierarchical dimension of, 17
horizontal organizational complexity and, 17, 19, 20–22
institutional theory and, 96–97
isomorphism and, 97
job tasks, division/differentiation of, 17
open systems and, 7–8
prescriptive theories and, 82, 92
purposes of, 16
resource dependence theory and, 94–96
segmentation and, 17
spatial complexity and, 23–25
vertical organizational complexity and, 17, 19–20, 19 (figure)
See also Business organizations; Contingency theories; Criminal organizations; Organizational change; Organizational complexity; Organizational culture; Organizational socialization; Organizational theory; Organizations; Service organizations
Organizational termination, 140, 543, 544
contingency factors, inability to adapt and, 142–143
definition/description of, 140–141
dysfunctional habits/practices and, 142–143
institutional theory, external constituent demands and, 143
lost services, replacement of, 143–144
organizational boundaries, uninterrupted maintenance of, 140
public organizations, resilience/decline of, 141–143

susceptibility to, 142–143
symbolic programs/procedures and, 143
See also Organizational deviance
Organizational theory, 5, 81–82
  administrative management and, 87–89
  bureaucracy and, 85–87
  classical theories and, 82–89
  contingency theory and, 92–94
  human relations theory and, 89–92
  institutional theory and, 96–98
  instrumental rationality and, 82
  life cycle theory and, 543
  open systems theories and, 92–98
  prescriptive theories and, 82
  principle of definition and, 154–155
  resource dependence theory and, 94–96
  scientific management and, 83–85
  significance of, 82
  See also Individualized justice myth/probation presentence reports study article; McJustice/McDonaldization of criminal justice study article; Organizational complexity; Organizational structure
Organizations, 5
  beneficiaries of, 12
  business organizations and, 12
  closed systems approach and, 7, 8
  commonwealth organizations and, 12
  components of, 6
  conflicting goals, reconciliation of, 10
  customer focus of, 8
  definitions of, 5–6
  durability, continuity of operations and, 11
  environmental factors in, 6, 7–8, 7 (figure)
  formal organizations and, 10–11
  funding/resources for, 12, 13
  job tasks of, 17
  membership in, 7–8
  mutual benefit organizations and, 12
  open systems approach and, 7–8
  personnel in, 6–8, 9
  public vs. private organizations and, 11–13
  purposes/goals of, 8–10
  rational coordination and, 10–11
  service organizations and, 12
  structures of, 10–11, 11 (figure)
  studying of, 3–5
  typology of, 12–13
  units of organization in, 6, 7 (figure)
  See also Criminal justice system; Organizational complexity; Organizational structures; Organizational theory

Orvis, G. P., 179
Ostroff, C., 277
O'Toole, J., 548
Output goals, 180–181
Owens, S. D., 102, 106
Ownership interests. *See* Business organizations

Packer, H., 100, 101, 105
Page, J., 226, 228, 248, 252, 253, 254, 255, 260, 267, 268
Pandey, S., 39, 46
Paoline, E. A. III, 35, 278
Papachristos, A. V., 187, 188
Parables in police training study article, 287
  anticipatory socialization, values/attitudes transfer and, 288
  attitudes/value shifts, factors in, 289–290
  black swan stories, rookie cynicism/defensiveness and, 290, 296
  citizen tales, officer disrespect for citizens and, 293–294
  classification of war stories and, 291, 291 (table), 295, 295 (table)
  commonsense knowledge, generation/transmission of, 288–289
  community policing values and, 296
  cynicism theme and, 295, 297
  danger/uncertainty, warnings about, 292–293, 297–298
  discussion and, 296–299
  epic/heroic stories, romanticized media recounting and, 289
  ethical perspective, endorsement of, 296
  force-in-the-line-of-duty stories and, 295
  formal academy curriculum, undermining of, 290
  informal socialization, training experiences and, 288, 289–290
  interactive world, social recipe transmission and, 289, 299
  latent content analysis of war stories, 295–296, 295 (table)
  manifest content analysis of war stories, 291–295, 291 (table)
  method and, 290–291
  peer pressure/group norming and, 289
  police administrative bureaucracy stories and, 294
  police culture, persistent behavior patterns and, 287–288, 296–297, 298
  police solidarity stories and, 295, 297, 298
  prejudicial parables, attitude reinforcement and, 294–295, 297
  rookies, positive values/work ethic and, 288
  scenario-based training and, 298, 299
  street/police skills, transmission of, 291–292
  subcultural messaging, shifts in, 298–299
  summary/conclusion and, 299–300
  vague/open-ended stories, imprecise guidelines and, 296
  war stories, behavioral socialization process and, 288–289, 290
  See also Organizational socialization; Readings
Parent, D., 182, 184
Parker, M., 109

Parole:
    discretionary power of, 516
    plans of action, adjustment of, 30
    predictability, reduced parole discretion and, 102–103
    recidivism risk and, 249
    revocation guidelines for, 104
    searches, latitude with, 185
    visitations, documentation of, 26
    See also Incarceration; Probation; Span of control in evidence-based community supervision study article
Paternoster, R., 185, 208, 328
Path-goal theory, 442–443
Pearson, C. A., 390
Pearson, N. M., 87
Peer relationships, 89, 91, 289, 321
Pegueros, F., 555
Penitentiary of New Mexico, 132, 137, 138
Pennsylvania Criminal Intelligence Center (PACIC), 178
Perdoni, M. L., 445
Pereira, B., 384
Performance-outcome expectancy, 330, 332
    See also Expectancy theory
Perkins, P. J., 108
Perrow, C., 3, 90, 135, 166, 167, 169, 305
Personalized power motive, 324
Personal power, 485, 491
Peter, L. J., 452
Peter principle, 452
Petersilia, J., 225, 249, 252, 572
Petit, K., 78
Pfeffer, J., 94
Pfuhl, E. H., 235
Philadelphia Police Department (PPD), 354
    community policing, adoption of, 538
    decentralized management approach and, 538
    MOVE bombing and, 537
    planned change process and, 537–538
    See also Organizational justice/police misconduct study article
Philadelphia Police Department Special Investigations Bureau, 10, 11 (figure)
Philipsen, H., 45
Phillips, P. W., 179, 181
Phoenix Regional Police Training Academy, 277
Piehl, A. M., 543
Pines, A. M., 386, 387
Piquero, A. R., 238, 347, 353, 355
Piskulich, J. P., 232
Pittsburgh Police Department, 534, 535, 542
Planned change motor, 537–540, 546, 546 (figure)

Plata v. Davis/Schwarzenegger (2003), 267
Plea bargaining, 91, 100–102
    crime victims interests and, 105
    habitual-offender statutes and, 105
    irrationality of, 105
    probation recommendation, supplanting of, 115
    speedy case closure and, 100–102
    three strikes law and, 105
Plecas, D., 381
Podsakoff, P. M., 40, 431, 491
Pogrebin, M. R., 46, 519, 531
Police employee organizations study article, 240
    accountability issues and, 243
    collective bargaining, regional differences in, 241
    data sources in, 243
    discussion/conclusions and, 244–246
    dues check off agreement and, 242
    elected leadership and, 242
    findings/descriptive analysis and, 243–244, 244–245 (table)
    fraternal/benevolent associations and, 241
    literature review for, 241–243
    locally based organizations and, 241–242
    methods in, 243
    organizational characteristics and, 241, 243–244, 244–245 (table)
    police labor relations issues and, 242–243
    research problem statement and, 240–241
    See also Collective bargaining; Labor unions; Readings
Police organizations:
    bureaucratized policing, reforms toward, 86
    community-oriented policing and, 21, 22, 30, 95, 109, 163, 296, 332
    community police officers and, 21, 22
    Compstat strategy and, 27–28, 97, 104, 109
    consolidation and, 143
    control issues, rules/regulations and, 103–104
    crime-related intelligence, sharing of, 24–25
    customers of, 8
    deadly force policies and, 26, 103, 136, 161–172, 353, 361, 544
    documentation requirements and, 26
    drunk-driving prevention and, 94–95
    establishment of, 8–9
    formalization and, 25, 26
    horizontal complexity, occupational differentiation and, 21
    human relations theory and, 91
    illicit organizations, structures of, 16
    innovative solutions and, 30
    military model of policing and, 109
    occupational differentiation, measurement of, 21
    problem-oriented policing and, 30, 109, 163

random preventive patrol and, 96
rapid response to 911 calls and, 96
recruitment, factors in, 7–8, 9
SARA policing model and, 163, 164
scalar chain, chains of command and, 17
scientific management, mandatory arrest policies and, 84
security jobs, moonlighting in, 12, 238
span of control, narrowing of, 30
spatial complexity, station houses/precincts and, 23
specialization and, 143
street cops vs. management cops and, 151
team policing, 20
turf battles and, 22, 104
understaffing, computer technology and, 93
use-of-force policy and, 26, 234, 534
vertical complexity, chains of command and, 17, 19–20, 19 (figure)
zero-tolerance policing, 163–164
See also Criminal justice collaborations; Criminal justice system; Criminal organizations; Deadly force/social theory and street cops study article; Intelligence fusion process article; McJustice/McDonaldization of criminal justice study article; Organizational complexity; Organizational justice/police misconduct study article; Organizational structures
Pollock, J. M., 519, 520, 529
Poole, E. D., 46, 519, 531
Poole, M. S., 537, 540, 543, 546
Pope, M. W., 381
Porter, L. W., 6, 7, 8, 10, 26, 27, 319, 547
Portland Seven, 180
Position power, 437, 438, 485, 486, 491
Post-and-bid job assignment process, 228
Poulin, J., 38
Power, 480
    authority/legitimate power and, 483
    bases of power, 484–487, 490–491
    building tenders and, 480–481, 484
    charismatic power, 485, 491
    classification of, 484–485
    coercive power, 150, 324, 484, 486, 487, 491
    compliance observability and, 490
    criminal justice applications and, 485–487
    definitions of, 481–483
    effectiveness of, 489–491
    employee behavior, contingent nature of, 490
    expert power, 485–486, 487, 491
    incentive systems, weaknesses in, 490
    influence tactics and, 487–489, 488 (table)
    information power, 485, 486, 489
    kinetic power and, 482
    leadership vs. power, differences between, 483–484
    legitimate power, 483, 484, 486, 491
    personalized power motive and, 324
    personal power, 485, 491
    position power, 437, 438, 485, 486, 491
    power/influence/compliance relationship and, 482, 483 (figure)
    power recipient compliance and, 486–487, 491
    reciprocal power relations and, 482–483, 487–489
    referent power, 484–485, 486, 487, 491
    resource power, 481, 485
    reward power, 484, 485, 486, 487
    social desirability bias and, 487
    socialized power motive and, 324
    social power, 484, 486, 487
    street-level bureaucrats, weakened managerial power and, 489–490
    surveillance and, 491
    unilateral/bilateral power flows and, 481, 482
    workplace bullying and, 384
    See also Behavioral/style theories of leadership; Defects of total power study article; Fiedler's contingency theory of leadership; Gender/power/reciprocity in corrections study article; Individual control/perceived officer power and probationer compliance study article; Leadership; Power motive (<I>n power); Resource dependence theory; Workplace bullying
Power motive (<I>n power), 323, 324–325
    personalized power motive and, 324
    socialized power motive and, 324
    See also Achievement/power/affiliation theory
Pranana, W., 424
Precursor crimes, 2
PRELIS software, 354
Prescriptive theories, 82, 92
President's Commission on Law Enforcement and the Administration of Justice (1967), 367, 540
Priest, D., 2
Primary appraisal, 381
Primary interventions, 392–393, 394
Prisoner Litigation Reform Act (PLRA) of 1995, 541, 542, 543
Prison officer unions/perpetuated penal status quo study article, 248
    affirmative action policies and, 253
    code of silence, rogue officers and, 252–253
    collateral consequences of mass incarceration and, 250–251
    crime victims' rights groups and, 253, 254, 255, 263, 268
    dominant narrative, challenging of, 265–266
    downsizing-oriented prison reforms and, 249, 250, 259, 260–263

economic decline, public punitiveness and, 248–249
employment opportunity commitment, maintenance of, 263–264
Felon-a-Day campaign, anti-Prop 66 effort and, 256 (figure), 257
impoverished communities, concentrated incarceration in, 250
mass incarceration trend and, 248–249, 250–251, 252
mutually beneficial alliances, establishment of, 263
Nonviolent Offender Rehabilitation Act/Proposition 5 and, 258–259
penal policy, prison officer union power and, 249, 250–251, 252, 258–259, 260–263
political tacticians, framing penal policies and, 255, 257
power bloc, development of, 251–254, 251 (figure)
prison reform, prospects for, 249, 250–251
public-sector unions, political nature of, 252–253, 262–263
punitive segregation orientation and, 252, 255, 265
right-to-work states and, 251
scapegoating unions and, 268–269
Three Strikes law/Proposition 66 and, 254–258, 255 (table), 256 (figure), 259
tough-on-crime measures, ballot initiative process and, 254–259, 263
union stonewalling tactic, personalized assertion of, 266–268
See also California Correctional Peace Officers Association (CCPOA); Incarceration; Labor unions; Leadership and correctional reform study article; Women officers in men's prisons/organizational barriers study article

Private organizations, 11–13
Privatization trend, 12, 13
Proactive Community Supervision (PCS) program (MD), 539
Probation:
designations, official court reports and, 116
intensive supervision programs, benefits of, 29
juvenile probationers, supervision of, 183, 184
Operation Night Light and, 183
plans of action, adjustment of, 30
policing tasks, probation officer role and, 185
probation officer power, perceptions of, 487
probation officer role and, 115, 116, 487
probation presentence reports and, 96, 97, 114–126
probation recommendation, judicial outcome and, 114–115
recidivism risk and, 249
revocation guidelines for, 104, 508–509
searches, latitude with, 185
See also Incarceration; Individual control/perceived officer power and probationer compliance study article; Individualized justice myth/probation presentence reports study article; Parole; Span of control in evidence-based community supervision study article

Problem-oriented policing, 30, 109, 163
Problem-solving courts, 205–206, 444, 445
therapeutic jurisprudence and, 536
See also Domestic violence court/procedural justice study article; Drug courts
Procedural justice, 208–209, 327
burnout and, 391
practices of, domestic violence cases and, 208–209
procedural justice factors and, 208, 327–328
voice effect and, 208, 215–217, 220
See also Domestic violence court/procedural justice study article; Equity theory; Organizational justice; Organizational justice/police misconduct study article
Process goals of task forces, 180, 181
Process theories, 318, 325
equity theory, organizational justice and, 325–329
expectancy theory, workplace motivation and, 329–333
See also Content theories; Equity theory; Motivation
Professionalization, 37, 305
Program Manager for the Information Sharing Environment (PM-ISE), 192, 193, 195, 201, 202
Project Safe Neighborhoods, 187
Project Sea Hawk, 178
Proposition 5/Nonviolent Offender Rehabilitation Act (NORA) of 2008, 258–259, 266
Proposition 9/Marsy's Law of 2008, 267–268
Proposition 66/Three Strikes and Child Protection Act of 2004, 254–258, 255 (table), 256 (figure), 259, 266
Prottas, J. M., 490
Prus, R., 116, 118
Public organizations, 11–13, 141
performance improvement, failure in, 142–143
resilience of, 141–142
termination, susceptibility to, 142–143
Pugh, D. S., 25, 86
Pulling levers/focused deterrence strategies, 186–188
Purdy, K., 334
Putchinski, L. J., 233

Qualitative assessment of stress perceptions/homicide units study article, 395
adjudication demands and, 404, 407
administrative pressure and, 405
community stakeholders and, 408
crime scene duties and, 400–402
discussion and, 408–412
events/occupational stressors and, 400–404
external demands and, 406–408
future research, recommendations for, 411–412
gender, role of, 397

homicide work, inherent job stressors and, 398–399, 409–410
inductive ethnographic methods and, 396, 399, 408
inductive vs. deductive approaches and, 395–396
media demands and, 407–408
methods and, 399–400
middle range theory on police stress and, 409–410
organizational stressors and, 404–408, 409
paperwork demands and, 403–404
research, limitations of, 397–398, 410–411
stress, sources of, 396–397, 409–410
time pressures and, 402–403
unit culture and, 406
See also Burnout phenomenon; Occupational stress; Readings
Qualitative overload situations, 383
Quantitative overload situations, 383

Racial profiling, 97
Rainey, H., 39, 89
Rampart corruption incident, 148, 151
Ram raiders, 66
Randall, F., 240
Random socialization, 282
Rank structure, 17, 19–20, 19 (figure), 151
Rationality:
    instrumental rationality, 82, 104, 539
    irrationality of, 100, 104–109
    limited/bounded rationality and, 53
    satisficing and, 538
    self-interest motivation and, 176
    structural secrecy and, 133–135
    See also Bureaucracy
Raven, B. H., 481, 482, 484, 485, 508
Rayner, C., 384
Readiness for treatment models, 339–340
Readiness of followers, 440–441
Readings:
    administrative breakdown/managerial disorganization in bureaucracies, 145–160
    centralization/formalization impact, 35–49
    community policing/job design and education level factors, 364–376
    D.A.R.E. lessons/research-practice relationship, 550–557
    deadly force/social theory and street cops, 161–173
    defects of total power, 493–505
    domestic violence court/procedural justice, 206–222
    individual control/perceived officer power and probationer compliance, 506–517
    individualized justice myth/probation presentence reports, 114–126

ineffective police leadership, 449–467
intelligence fusion process, 190–205
international drug smuggling organizational structure, 64–80
leadership and correctional reform, 468–479
McJustice/McDonaldization of criminal justice, 99–113
medical system lessons/criminal justice decision making, 559–582
occupational stress/public defenders, 414–428
organizational justice/police misconduct, 347–364
parables in police training, 287–301
police employee organizations, 240–247
prison officer unions/perpetuated penal status quo, 248–271
qualitative assessment of stress perceptions/homicide units, 395–413
sex offender treatment providers/burnout factors, 423–428
span of control in evidence-based community supervision, 49–64
substance abuse treatment/motivation-engagement relationship, 338–346
women officers in men's prisons/organizational barriers, 302–315
See also Research articles
Reaves, B. A., 30, 243, 282, 283
Recidivism risk, 135, 249, 340
Reciprocal power relations, 482–483, 487–489
Reckless, W. C., 123
Redfield, R., 300
Redmond Police Department, 184
Reed, P., 39
Referent power, 484–485, 486, 487, 491
Regional Information Sharing System, 197, 200
Regional Intelligence and Operations Center (RIOC), 178
Regional Terrorism Threat Assessment Center (RTTAC), 178
Reingold, D., 96
Reisig, M. D., 93
Reiss, A. J., Jr., 65
Ren, L., 230
Repetition problem, 176
Research articles:
    criminal justice policy, implications for, 34
    hypothesis of, 33
    literature review section and, 33
    methodology and, 33
    persuasiveness, assessment of, 34
    qualitative/quantitative study, determination of, 33–34
    results, summary/presentation of, 34
    subject knowledge, strengthening of, 34
    target audience for, 34
    thesis in, 33
    See also Readings

Research Triangle Institute, 551
Resilience of public organizations, 141–143
Resource dependence theory, 94
    asymmetrical power relationships and, 94
    criminal justice settings and, 94–95
    external control, issues in, 95–96
    interdependence, scarce/critical resources and, 94
    organizational decisions, constraints on, 94
    resource dependence, example of, 94–95
    See also Open systems theories
Resource power, 481, 485
Reuss-Ianni, E., 278
Reuter, P. H., 78
Revolutionary/discontinuous change, 536, 546
Reward power, 484, 485, 486, 487, 491
    vertical structures, advancement opportunities and, 20
    See also Content theories; Motivation; Power
Rhode Island Brotherhood of Correctional Officers, 233
Rhode Island prisoners' union, 152
Richards, D., 332
Ridgely, M. S., 176
Riggio, R. E., 445
Right to know information-sharing standard, 200
Right-to-work states, 251
Rinehart, J. A., 109
Risk/mistake tradition, 164
Rison, R. H., 131
Ritti, R. R., 91, 331
Ritzer, G., 99, 100, 102, 103, 104, 105, 109, 110
Rivers, I., 384
Rizzo, J. R., 491
Rizzo, L., 114
Robbins, S. P., 17, 29, 30, 483
Roberg, R. R., 6, 441, 442
Robert Wood Johnson Foundation, 552, 554
Roberts, K. H., 138
Robertson, N., 393
Rockland County Intelligence Center (NY), 191
Rodriguez, N., 567
Roethlisberger, F. J., 90
Rojek, J., 137
Role ambiguity, 45, 383, 389
Role conflict, 45, 149, 383, 389
    objective role conflict, 416–417
    subjective role conflict, 416, 417
Role insufficiency, 416, 417
Role overload, 417
Role specialization, 20–21
Rollins, J., 178, 193, 194
Roman, P., 40

Roncek, D. W., 95
Rosecrance, J. D., 114, 510, 515
Rosenbaum, D. P., 367, 551, 555
Rousseau, D. M., 40
Routine activities theory, 164
Routine occupational stressors, 380
Rowan, B., 96
Rowan-Szal, G. A., 339
Rowe, D., 261
Ruiz v. Estelle (1980), 540, 541
Rules. *See* Formalization; Organizational control

Sageman, M., 31
Saks, A. M., 276, 280
Salancik, G. R., 94
Salerno, H., 255
Sales, B., 417
Salyor, W. G., 38, 39, 40
San Diego Police Department, 324
Sapp, A. D., 228, 368
SARA (scan/analyze/respond/assess) policing model, 163, 164, 277
Sarat, A. D., 95
Satisficing, 538
Sawhney, R., 8
Scalar chain principle, 17, 181
Scarborough, K. E., 148
Schafer, J. A., 97, 177, 432, 433, 446, 449
Schaufeli, W. B., 386, 387, 391
Scheck, B., 108
Schein, E. H., 280, 281, 284, 353
Scherb, K., 388
Schiray, M., 67
Schlanger, M., 540
Schlegel, K., 180
Schoenherr, R. A., 21
School shootings, 134, 174, 175
Schriesheim, C. A., 491
Schwab, D., 375
Schwarzenegger, A., 255, 257, 266, 267
Schwarzschild, M., 541
Schwarzwald, J., 484
Schweiger, D., 38
Scientific management, 83–85, 365
    criminal justice decision process and, 84
    criminal justice practices, standardization of, 84
    delivery route mapping, cost savings and, 84
    evidence-based policing/corrections policies and, 84
    functional management and, 83
    job analyses, task-based physical agility tests and, 84

management role, definition of, 83–84
specialization, expertise/efficiencies and, 83
time-motion studies and, 83
worker dissatisfaction with, 84–85
work flow interruptions, workplace productivity and, 84
See also Classical theories
Scott, P. G., 39, 46
Scott, W. R., 3, 5, 6, 8, 12, 82, 85, 88, 92
Search/seizure prohibitions, 103
Seattle Police Department:
   crisis response, coordination problems with, 137
   D.A.R.E. program, termination of, 551–552
   post-crisis response assessment and, 138
   WTO protests, poor preparation for, 137
Sechrest, D., 52
Secondary appraisal, 381
Secondary interventions, 393
Segmentation of hierarchies, 17
Selye, H., 415
Senese, J. D., 155
Sentencing guidelines, 84, 86, 102–103
September 11, 2001. *See* 9/11 terrorist attacks; Terrorism
Sequential socialization, 282
Serial socialization, 283–284
Service organizations, 12
Sewell, J. D., 398, 399, 400, 408, 409, 411
Sex offender treatment providers/burnout factors study article, 423–425
   burnout, components of, 424
   client characteristics, provider burnout and, 426–427
   discussion and, 426–428
   facility type/subscale scores, regression analyses of, 426
   gender of providers, burnout levels and, 427
   inpatient/prison providers and, 427
   Maslach Burnout Inventory instrument and, 425
   method and, 425
   provider characteristics/subscale scores, bivariate analyses between, 426
   research literature on, 423–424
   results and, 425–426
   staff training/supports, development of, 427–428
   subjects and, 425
   subscale scores/subscale norms, comparison of, 425–426
   See also Burnout phenomenon; Readings
Sexual assault, 150
Shapiro, B., 253
Shapiro, D. L., 318, 319, 320
Shearing, C. D., 12, 297
Sheehan, R., 148
Shein, E. H., 280

Shelby, R. A., 423
Sherman, L. W., 163, 208, 288, 328, 544, 563, 567
Sherwood, C. W., 364
Shilton, M. K., 51, 62
Shover, N., 123
Similar response pattern imputation (SRPI), 354
Simon, D., 409
Simon, H. A., 89, 538
Simon, J., 248, 266
Simon, J. D., 531
Simon, R. J., 531
Simpson, D. D., 338, 339, 341
Simpson, S. S., 209
Sing Sing Prison, 570
Sirene, W. H., 243
Sitren, A. H., 487, 506
Situational leadership theory, 146, 439
   adapted leader behaviors and, 440
   criticisms of, 442
   delegating leadership style and, 439–440
   leader behavior-follower maturity relationship and, 439–440, 439 (table)
   Leader Effectiveness and Adaptability Description survey and, 440, 441, 442
   participating leadership style and, 439
   police employee characteristics, leadership style and, 441–442, 441 (table)
   readiness of followers and, 440–441
   selling leadership style and, 439
   task behavior, definition of, 439
   telling leadership style and, 439
   See also Leadership
Skill variety, 335, 366, 373
Skogan, W. G., 2, 367
Skolnick, J. H., 287, 349, 350
Slater, J., 233
Slipka, M., 382
Sloboda, Z., 552, 554, 555
Slocum, J. W., 487
Slowdowns, 237–238
Smart Partners Program (WA), 184
Smith, B. W., 179, 180, 181
Smith, H. P., 487, 506
Smith, M. R., 137
Smith, P. A., 332
Smith, S., 109
Smith, W., 566
Snipes, J. B., 91, 331
Snyder, B., 182, 184
Snyderman, B. B., 319, 321, 322, 365

Social control, 307, 311, 347, 353
Social desirability bias, 487
Socialization. *See* Organizational socialization
Socialized power motive, 324
Social network framework, 67–68, 70
Social power, 484
Social theory:
   broken windows argument and, 163
   crime/justice arena and, 161
   deterrence theory, 163
   domestic violence, pro-arrest policies and, 163, 172
   goals/procedures, development of, 161
   normal accident theory, deadly force and, 166–172
   police work/public understanding and, 163–164
   routine activities theory, 164
   SARA policing model and, 163, 164
   sociology-of-risk framework and, 164
   zero-tolerance policing and, 163–164
   See also Deadly force/social theory and street cops study article
Sociology-of-risk framework, 164
Soft on crime allegation, 103
Soitolano, D., 488
Soros, G., 258
Sourcebook of Criminal Justice Statistics, 102
Souryal, S. S., 152
South Carolina domestic violence. *See* Domestic violence court/procedural justice study article
South Carolina Intelligence Fusion Center (SCIEX), 178
Span of control, 20, 28, 152–153
   appropriate span, organizational task completion and, 28–29, 30
   complex/unpredictable situations, narrow span of control and, 29–30
   definition of, 152
   narrow spans of control, costs of, 30
   police-community corrections partnerships and, 184
   staff to inmate ratio and, 29–30
   subordinate-supervisor ratio and, 28
   vertical organizational complexity and, 28–29, 29 (figure)
   See also Centralization dimension; Formalization dimension; Organizational control; Span of control in evidence-based community supervision study article
Span of control in evidence-based community supervision study article, 49–51
   appropriate span of control, theoretical factors and, 52–53
   conclusions and, 62–63
   discussion and, 61–62
   method and, 53–55
   participants and, 53–54

probation jurisdictions, span of control ratios in, 51–52, 53–54 (tables)
probation officers/supervisors, dynamic roles of, 60
probation supervisor role, evidence-based practice and, 55–56, 60
procedure and, 54–55
results and, 55–60
span of control, definition of, 51
staff capabilities/workforce skill levels and, 58–60
task complexity issues and, 57–58, 60
theoretical span of control factors, evidence-based probation/parole practice and, 56–57
time investment issues and, 56–57
See also Organizational complexity; Readings
Spatial organizational complexity, 23
   access to services and, 24
   communication/coordination challenges in, 23, 24–25
   community prosecution and, 24
   crime-related intelligence and, 24–25
   federal judiciary, spatial divisions in, 23
   firearms violators, targeting of, 24
   local concerns, location-specific strategies and, 23–24
   measurement of, 23
   prison populations, distribution of, 23
   state/local level and, 23–24
   See also Horizontal organizational complexity; Organizational complexity; Vertical organizational complexity
Special Agent in Charge (SAC), 156
Specialized workers, 21, 22, 67, 83, 143, 335
Spector, P. E., 36, 351
Spendolini, M. J., 26, 27
Springer, N. F., 487, 506
St. Louis Police Relief Association, 225
Stalking horse role, 185
Stanley, J., 192
State Terrorism Threat Assessment Center (STTAC), 178
Steers, R. M., 318, 319, 320
Steinberg, J., 397
Stephan, J. J., 260
Stephens, D. W., 368
Stevens, E., 45
Stichman, A. J., 487, 509, 510, 514, 515
Stillman, R. J., 145
Stinchcomb, J. B., 392, 393
Stoddart, R. M., 423
Stohr, M. K., 38, 336
Stojkovic, S., 509, 515
Storytelling. *See* Parables in police training study article
Stouthamer-Loeber, M., 573

Strain, 380
  uncertainty and, 276
  unfairness, perceptions of, 358
  See also Burnout phenomenon; Occupational stress
Strategic Analysis and Information Center, 178
Stratten, J., 116
Strauss, L., 450
Street-level bureaucrats, 489–490
Stressors, 380
  See also Burnout phenomenon; Occupational stress; Strains
Strikes, 233
  crime/disorder, risk of, 235
  generation stage and, 234
  illegal strikes, 237–238
  labor relations, improvements in, 238–239
  National Guard, role of, 233, 234, 235
  perpetuation stage and, 234–235
  prison guard strike, 234, 235, 238
  public-sector employees and, 236–237
  resolution stage and, 236–237
  strike actions, stages in, 233–234
  strike options, differences among, 233
  See also Boston Police Strike (1919); Collective bargaining; Labor unions
Strom, K. J., 381
Stroshine, M. S., 327
Structural-adaptation-to-regain-fit (SARFIT) model, 92–93
Structural secrecy, 133–135
Studer, R., 289, 298
Studinger, P., 140
Styles of leadership. See Behavioral/style theories of leadership; Leadership
Substance abuse treatment/motivation-engagement relationship study article, 338
  bivariate analyses and, 342
  corrections-based programs, motivation/postrelease outcomes and, 339–340
  criminality/criminal history and, 341
  Desire for Help scale, 342
  discussion/summary and, 342–345
  Drug Abuse Treatment Outcome Studies and, 339, 343
  drug problem classification and, 341
  length of treatment stay and, 339
  measures and, 341–342
  methods and, 342
  multivariate analyses and, 342
  Personal Involvement Scale and, 341, 342
  Personal Progress scores and, 342
  Psychological Safety scale and, 342
  readiness for treatment models and, 339–340, 342
  recidivism risk and, 340
  results and, 342
  retention/engagement, motivation as predictor of, 338–339
  sample population and, 340–341
  sociodemographic information and, 341
  substance users, cognitive stages of change and, 339
  Texas Christian University motivation model and, 339
  Texas Christian University treatment process model and, 343–344, 344 (figure)
  therapeutic engagement scales, results from, 341–342
  transtheoretical motivation model and, 339
  treatment engagement, cognitive indicators of, 339
  Treatment Motivation Assessment scores and, 340, 341, 342, 344
  treatment practitioners, recommendations for, 344–345
  Treatment Readiness scale, 342
  See also Motivation; Readings
Suicide-by-cop, 165–166
Suicide prevention, 153
Summers, T., 40
Sumter, M., 322, 323
Sun, B. -C., 389
Supermax prisons, 16, 29, 544, 573
Supervision:
  authority hierarchy and, 151–152
  bureaucratic organizations and, 85, 86
  centralization and, 27–28
  documentation requirements and, 26
  formalization and, 25–27, 45
  functional management and, 83
  management by walking around and, 149
  rank and file personnel and, 19
  span on control and, 28–30, 29 (figure)
  supervision from above and, 19–20
  unity-of-command principle and, 89
  vertical organizational structures and, 19–20
  See also Centralization/formalization impact study article; Organizational control; Span of control in evidence-based community supervision study article
Supplemental pay, 230–231, 230 (table)
Surveillance, 491
Surveillance-industrial complex, 200
SWAT teams, 167–168, 170–171, 486
Swidler, A., 278
Sykes, G. M., 491, 493, 507, 520, 525, 531
Synergy, 177

Taft-Hartley Act of 1947, 237
Taggart, W. A., 39
Take Back Your Life curriculum, 554

Tall organizations, 17, 20
Task forces. *See* Criminal justice collaborations
Task identity, 334, 335, 366, 373
Task significance, 334–335, 374
Task structure, 436–437
Taxman, F. S., 445, 539
Taylor, B. G., 209
Taylor, F., 83, 84, 87, 145, 146, 365
Taylor, K. L., 423
Taylor, S., 109
Team policing, 20
Teamsters, 252
Technological rationality, 104
Tennes*See* Regional Information Center, 178
Tennessee v. Garner (1985), 103
Tenth Amendment, 181
Termination. *See* Organizational deviance; Organizational termination
Terrorism:
    Abu Ghraib prison and, 148, 149
    airport security and, 2–3
    airspace security, grounding of aircraft and, 27
    antiterrorist task forces and, 2
    centralized vs. decentralized leadership in, 31
    counterterrorism efforts and, 2, 31, 93
    Department of Homeland Security and, 3–4, 4 (table), 5
    Federal Bureau of Investigation field office structure and, 15–16, 24
    inflexible organizational response to, 22, 24, 93
    information sharing, problems with, 16, 24–25
    intelligence fusion centers and, 177, 178 (figure)
    intelligence industry and, 2, 93
    joint-terrorism task forces and, 180, 181–182
    organizational structures, enforcement strategies and, 16
    precursor crimes, prosecution of, 2
    suspects, detention of, 2
    terrorist organizations, structure of, 31
    Transportation Security Administration and, 2–3
    unlawful enemy combatant status and, 149
    War on Terror and, 257
    See also Criminal justice system; Criminal organizations; Homeland security responsibilities; Intelligence fusion process article; 9/11 terrorist attacks
Terrorism Early Warning (TEW) Group, 197
Terrorism Fusion Center (TITAN), 178
Tertiary interventions, 393
Tewksbury, R., 388, 395
Texas Christian University motivation model, 339
Texas Christian University treatment process model, 343–344, 344 (figure)

Texas Criminal Justice Policy Council, 577, 578
Texas Department of Corrections (TDC), 149, 150
Texas Security Alert and Analysis Center (TSAAC), 178
Themessl-Huber, M., 332
Theory X, 90–91
Theory Y, 91
Thibault, J., 208
Thompson, W. C., 130, 139
Three Mile Island nuclear disaster, 135
Three Strikes and Child Protection Act of 2004/Proposition 66, 254–258, 255 (table), 256 (figure), 259, 266
Three strikes law, 105, 224, 225, 254
Tifft, L. L., 485, 486
Tillyer, M. S., 188
Tobin, T. J., 37
Todor, W. D., 26, 27
Tokenism problem, 306, 397
Tompkins, J. R., 83, 84
Tonry, M., 103, 107
Tosi, H. L., 491
Total power. *See* Defects of total power study article
Tough-on-crime measures, 106, 232, 250, 254–259, 263, 265
Trait theory, 431–433, 432 (table)
Transactional leadership, 444
    contingent reward and, 444, 445
    effective leadership practices and, 445
    management by exception and, 444, 445
    problem-solving court judges and, 444
    See also Leadership; Transformational leadership
Transformational leadership, 443–444
    charisma/idealized influence and, 444
    criminal justice system environment and, 445–446
    criticisms of, 446
    dimensions of, 444–445
    effective leadership practices and, 445–446
    gender, role of, 445
    individualized consideration behaviors and, 444–445
    inspirational motivation and, 444
    intellectual stimulation and, 445
    problem-solving court judges and, 445
    See also Leadership; Transactional leadership
Transportation Security Administration (TSA), 2–3, 142
Traumatic stressors, 380
Travis, L. F., 179, 180, 181, 231, 237
Treatment Motivation Assessment scores, 340, 341, 342, 344
    See also Substance abuse treatment/motivation-engagement relationship study article
Tribal law enforcement. *See* Intelligence fusion process article
Truth-in-sentencing provision, 103, 224
Tudor, W. D., 40

Turf battles, 22, 104, 177
Turner, C., 25
Turner, S., 176
Tushman, M. L., 536
Two-way information sharing, 197
Tyler, E. R., 351
Tyler, T. R., 208, 257

U.S. Marshals Service, 23
U.S.S. *Cole* bombing, 25
Uncertainty, 276–277, 289, 292–293
Unfreeze-move-freeze model, 535, 537
Unions. *See* Collective bargaining; Labor unions
Unit determination process, 228–229
United Parcel Service (UPS) delivery routes, 84
Unity-of-command principle, 89, 152–153, 181
Unlimited power. *See* Defects of total power study article
Unsinger, P. C., 441, 442
Uphoff, R. J., 415
Useem, B., 157, 543
Use-of-force policies, 26, 234, 534
   See also Deadly force policies
Ussery, W., 392, 393
Utah Criminal Intelligence Center, 178

Valence, 329, 330
   See also Expectancy theory
Van de Ven, A. H., 177, 537, 540, 543, 546
Van de Vliert, E., 487
Van Duin, M. J., 137, 138
Van Haversen, R. A., 390
VanLaerhoven, S., 279
Van Maanen, J., 276, 280, 281, 282, 283, 284, 288, 289
Van Patten, I. T., 398
Variable socialization, 283
Variation-selection-retention process, 545
Vaughan, D., 131, 133, 134, 135
Vaughn, M. S., 89, 132, 145, 151
Veatch, K. C., 231
Vermont Fusion Center, 178
Vertical collaborations, 179, 181
Vertical organizational complexity, 17
   communication distortion and, 20
   concentration of hierarchies and, 17, 19
   direct service, rank and file personnel and, 19–20
   mid-management ranks, personnel concentration in, 19
   opportunities for advancement and, 20
   organizational growth, additional units/divisions and, 20
   policy formation/supervisory responsibilities, 19–20
   pyramidal representation of, 17, 19, 19 (figure)
   scalar chain, chains of command and, 17
   segmentation of hierarchies and, 17
   span on control and, 28–29
   supervision from above and, 19–20
   tall vs. flat organizations and, 17, 20
   team policing, demise of, 20
   worker satisfaction/motivation and, 20
   See also Horizontal organizational complexity; Organizational complexity; Organizational structures; Spatial organizational complexity
Victim organizations, 253–254, 255, 263, 268
Village Public Safety Officers (VPSOs), 379
Violence Against Women Act (VAWA) of 1994, 209
Violence Policy Center, 207
Violent Crime Control and Law Enforcement Act of 1994, 95, 534
Virginia Fusion Center, 178
Virginia Tech University shootings, 174, 175, 177, 326
Visher, C. A., 568
Vlahov, D., 392
Voice effect, 208, 215–217, 220
von Mises, L., 153
Vroom, V. H., 318, 330

Wagner, J. A., 31
Wahba, M. A., 319, 320
Walker, L., 208
Walker, S. E., 115, 229, 240, 540, 543, 561
Walsh, A., 125
Walsh, W. F., 539
Walster, E., 326
Walster, G. W., 326
Walton, R. E., 39
wa Mwachofi, N., 109, 110
War on Drugs, 5, 106, 179–180, 258, 551
War on Terror, 257
Warr, M., 65, 78
Warren, P., 566
Washington Department of Corrections Regional Community Corrections office, 184
Washington Joint Analytical Center (WAJAC), 178
Washington Metropolitan Police Department, 24
Washington State Prison Anti-Gang Program, 182
Waters, J. A., 392, 393
Watts, D. J., 69
Weapons of mass destruction (WMD), 194
Webb, V. J., 30, 567
Weber, M., 36, 85, 86, 87, 99, 100, 145, 146, 147, 149, 151, 155, 157, 493, 497, 508

Weber v. Lincoln County (2004), 153
Weick, K. E., 138, 139
Weigelt, C. B., 545
Weiner, B., 318
Weisberg, R., 249
Weisburd, D., 28, 109, 382, 391
Weiss, A., 175
Weiss, C. H., 539, 552, 553, 554, 555, 556
Weiss, E. S., 177
Weiss, J. A., 177
Wellington, H. H., 238
Wells, L. E., 21
Wenzel, S. L., 176
Westervelt, S. D., 108
West Virginia Joint Information Center, 178
Whetstone, T. S., 317, 318
Whetten, D. A., 544
White-collar crime, 31
Whitehead, J. T., 38, 385, 390
Whitley v. Albers (1986), 150
Wholers, E. T., 233
Wice, P. B., 415
Wichita Police Department, 17, 19 (figure)
Wilkins, L. T., 114
Wilkinson, D. L., 367
Williams, F. P., 35
Williams, L. J., 40
Williams, P., 67, 68, 73, 175
Willie Horton effect, 567–568
Willis, J. J., 28, 109, 391
Wilson, A., 66
Wilson, C. E., 276, 279
Wilson, J. Q., 163
Wilson, P., 255
Wilson, S., 230
Winter, R. K., 238
Wittenberg, P. M., 131
Wohlers, E. T., 233
Wolf, S., 277
Wolfe, S. E., 238, 347
Women officers in men's prisons/organizational barriers study article, 302
   advancement opportunities, organizational problems and, 308, 310–314
   conflicting/ambiguous organizational directives and, 306–307
   duty assignments and, 311–313
   extra-organizational conditions, expanding prison populations and, 307–308
   female correctional officers, additional organizational barriers for, 305–309
   female workers, entry into corrections and, 304–305
   informal organizational structure, old-guard hostilities and, 308–309, 311–313
   method/setting and, 304
   organizational parity problem and, 302–303
   organizational structures, women's occupational role performance and, 303, 309
   performance evaluations, universalistic criteria and, 313–314
   pre-employment experience/on-the-job training and, 310–311
   reform-oriented policies, inadequate implementation of, 309
   service philosophy, resistance to, 307, 308
   social control vs. inmate rehabilitation and, 307–308
   staff-to-inmate ratio, dangerous levels of, 308
   status quo occupational culture and, 308–309
   stereotypes, biased attitudes and, 305–306, 307, 311–313, 314
   summary/conclusion and, 314–315
   tokenism problem and, 306
   See also Gender/power/reciprocity in corrections study article; Organizational socialization; Readings
Women Peace Officers Association of California, 253
Wood, D. J., 176, 177
Wood, D. S., 379
Worden, R. E., 240, 368
Workplace bullying, 384, 392
World Trade Organization (WTO), 137, 138
Worrall, A., 185
Worrall, J. L., 95, 182, 183
Wright, K. N., 38, 39, 40, 435
Wrightsman, L. S., 438
Wycoff, M. A., 24, 367
Wynne, J. M., 229
Wynyard, R., 110

Yates, J., 415
Yeh, S., 367
Yukl, G., 483, 485, 488, 490

Zaitch, D., 67, 70
Zegart, A. B., 15, 16, 24, 25, 131, 136
Zeidler, F. P., 243
Zero-tolerance policing, 163–164
Zhao, J., 95, 230, 384, 385
Zimmer, L. E., 234, 235, 236, 519, 520, 528, 530
Zingraff, M., 566
Zucker, L. G., 140
Zupan, L. L., 38, 336, 520

About the Author

Matthew J. Giblin is an associate professor and undergraduate program director in the Department of Criminology and Criminal Justice at Southern Illinois University Carbondale. He earned his doctorate in criminal justice from Indiana University in 2004. His primary research interest involves applying organizational theories to the study of criminal justice agencies. Specifically, he and his colleagues have tested contingency, resource dependence, and institutional theory explanations of police homeland-security preparedness, community policing implementation, and crime analysis unit adoption.